Ana D. thompson
fr. Cate S
16 August 1999

# HERBACEOUS PERENNIAL PLANTS

# HERBACEOUS PERENNIAL PLANTS

## A Treatise on their Identification, Culture, and Garden Attributes

Second Edition

## Allan M. Armitage

University of Georgia

Published by:

*S*tipes *P*ublishing, L.L.C.
10-12 Chester Street
Champaign, Illinois 61820

**Library of Congress Cataloging in Publication Data**

Armitage, Allan M.
 Herbaceous Perennial Plants
 A Treatise on their Identification, Culture and Garden Attributes
 Second Edition

Summary: A reference guide to the identification and culture of over 3500 herbaceous
  perennial plant species, varieties and cultivars. Includes bibliography, common
  name and scientific indexes.

   1. Plant Identification. 2. Plant Culture. 3. Plant Propagation. 4. Encyclopedia of
   Specific Identification and Cultural Requirements of Herbaceous Perennial Plants.


ISBN 0-87563-723-X

Copyright © 1989, 1997 by Allan M. Armitage

*Illustrations by Bonnie L. Dirr:* pages xx–xxiv, 7, 10, 12, 13, 15, 25, 28, 51, 57, 75, 80, 82, 85,
   90, 103, 104, 107, 112, 122, 137, 141, 144, 145, 152, 155, 158, 163, 164, 169, 187, 194, 200, 241,
   252, 253, 264, 270, 271, 272, 287, 294, 312, 350, 356, 372, 382, 399, 411, 413, 435, 441, 454,
   459, 464, 469, 470, 471, 493, 497, 498, 502, 505, 508, 520, 524, 530, 550, 552, 564, 579, 582,
   595, 599, 602, 604, 625, 635, 639, 670, 675, 692, 701, 713, 724, 728, 732, 737, 778, 812, 813,
   814, 815, 827, 830, 838, 841, 861, 869, 873, 894, 895, 904, 906, 919, 950, 951, 980, 985 (leaf),
   987, 997, 1003, 1008, 1015, 1019, 1043, 1052, 1057, 1062, 1066, 1070, 1071, 1074, 1088, 1089

*Illustrations by David Sandrock:* pages 31, 35, 41, 44, 58, 72, 92, 94, 117, 118, 119, 128, 130,
   134, 173, 185, 191, 198, 202, 217, 223, 236, 248, 278, 292, 315, 325, 329, 339, 357, 361, 393,
   404, 429, 440, 495, 512, 517, 529, 534, 560, 574, 601, 616, 623, 668, 680, 687, 698, 702, 754,
   755, 765, 772, 774, 775, 791, 795, 805, 832, 848, 879, 883, 898, 900, 909, 911, 922, 924, 939,
   965, 978, 985 (flower), 988, 1013, 1025, 1026, 1027, 1038, 1047, 1050

*Cover photograph by:* Allan M. Armitage

*Cover photo:* The lovely garden of Mrs. Robert Segrest in Athens, Georgia, in which
      *Hosta* 'Frances Williams', foxgloves, peonies and Japanese Maple provide
      color and tranquility.

## Dedication

This book is dedicated to my wife, Susan, and my children, Laura, Heather, and Jonathan. If my garden was even one-tenth as wonderful as my family, it would put all others to shame. Thank you for everything.

# Acknowledgements

This book would still be a distant dream if not for the following people. This edition is no different.

Dr. Michael Dirr, whose vast knowledge of plant materials, keen sense of the obvious, and editing skills were invaluable. His time, enthusiasm and support are gratefully appreciated. Mike's belief in the book never faltered, and his friendship is cherished.

Judy Marriott Laushman, who proofread countless times, collected flowers, spent hours in the library doing research, and whose sense of humor kept things in perspective. Her encouragement, advice and love of the work is reflected in every page. Without her, this book would not have been completed.

Stephanie Shelton, who proofread the second edition until her eyes were red and blurry. Her eagle eyes and incisive comments have made the text much easier to read.

Bonnie Dirr and David Sandrock, for the excellent line drawings which bring life to the endless ocean of words.

Laura Ann Segrest, for passing on to me so much of her knowledge of Southern plants and gardens.

Sharon Illingsworth, for her insight into gardening in Canada.

Sandy MacKenzie, for sharing her holiday with a computer.

# Some Thoughts of the Author

## On The Meaning of Gardening:

When gardeners are asked to describe reasons for gardening, three words emerge time and again; Therapeutic, Creative and Exciting. Such words are more often associated with sporting events than gardening; however, therapy, creativity, and excitement are an integral part of gardening.

Therapeutic because of the feeling that all is well with the world when our hands are in Mother Earth. Therapeutic because when a seed is sown, a cutting rooted, or seedling planted, we have accomplished something important.

Creative because artistry is an inescapable part of gardening. A swath of *Astilbe* brightens the shade, a grouping of cool-leaved *Artemisia* brings calm to its neighbors and a half dozen forget-me-nots sing of spring. Each grouping creates vistas of beauty. We do not require a degree in landscape architecture to create such beauty, all we need is the simple love of gardening.

Exciting is a word seldom attributed to gardening. But is it not exciting to watch a garden change with time? To watch *Asarum*, wild ginger, bull through the soil in early spring, anticipate the popping of the buds of balloon flower, and the magic of the reemergence of resurrection flower, is truly exciting.

## On a Garden:

A garden is a melding of different plants, including trees, shrubs, and herbaceous species. A garden lacks grandeur and grace without the architecture and framework provided by stately trees. A single specimen, such as a Cedar-of-Lebanon, can define an entire garden. Like a snow-capped mountain in the distance, it is never out of sight or out of mind. Shrubs are indispensable for screening, massing, form and texture. From *abelia* to *zenobia*, they provide the glue which bonds the trees and herbaceous plants together. Broad sweeps of annuals such as geraniums, celosia and marigolds provide interest through the gardening season and, like magnets, draw the eye to their carpet of color. Herbaceous perennials add a unique charm and flavor to any garden.

There are few times when perennials do not add interest and change. From barren winter ground, through frenzied activity in the spring, until flower buds are visible, perennials are always changing. Finally, the flowers can wait no longer, and islands of color blaze like flares in the night. Many have foliage more colorful than flowers, fruits that compete with holly, and fall colors as dramatic as sugar maples. To the connoisseur and amateur, there is nothing more colorful and interesting than a well-conceived perennial border. However, all great borders have backdrops of hedges or tree canopies and annuals to fill in occasional gaps. Perennials are an important part of the garden but are just that, a part of the garden. Perennials or a perennial border should be woven into a garden, rather than being the garden. A well-conceived garden is much more beautiful than the sum of the beauty of the individual parts.

What does gardening mean to people? Perhaps a couple of quotes from the past and the future are appropriate. The first is attributed to the great plant hunter and plantsman, Ernest Henry Wilson, who wrote it just three years before his death in 1930. The quote was tracked down by one of my excellent former students, Mr. Kevin Redecker.

"There are no happier folk than plant-lovers and none more generous than those who garden. There is a delightful freemasonry about them; they mingle on a common plane, share freely their knowledge and with advice help one over the stepping stones that lead to success. It is truthfully said that a congenial companion doubles the pleasures and halves the discomforts of travel and so it is with the brotherhood who love plants." E. H. Wilson, Plant Hunting, v.1, 1927.

A second quote comes from another one of my former students, who wrote an essay on the why people embrace perennials in their gardens. Those who believe our students aren't among the finest in the world need to come and visit my classes.

"Americans, as a rule, live with a certain sense of urgency. Perhaps this is the price we pay for living in such a young country. Why waste time with some fickle plant which will only flower for a few short moments each year when there are countless annuals just begging to bloom all summer long? The commitment perennials require represents the driving force behind gardening as a whole. When someone kills a window box of petunias, there is no love lost. Odds are that a quick trip to K-Mart will have the window box blooming again in short order. Let there be no doubt about the glorious beauty of a well-planted annual garden. But, for all their show and eagerness-to-please, annuals provoke no anticipation. To be among an established garden teaches one why we have gardens at all; gardens are our refuge from the irritations of everyday life, a place of peace and serenity and provide the hope and anticipation of good things to come." Ken James, Student, 1995.

## On a Gardener:

Gardening is hard work! Low maintenance does not mean no maintenance. "No maintenance" gardening does not exist, although lower maintenance is possible with proper plant selection. I travel and talk with gardeners of all ages all the time. There are elderly gardeners, there are many tired gardeners, but I've seldom met old gardeners. I guide tours through some of the slickest, hilliest, and forbidding garden terrain, and, if physically possible, the "oldsters" will be elbowing me out of the way to be sure they see it all. To many, plants and gardens are the elixirs and rewards of advancing age, and, while I know many elderly gardeners, the majority are young at heart. Gardening simply does not allow one to be mentally old, because there are too many hopes and dreams yet to be realized.

The one absolute of gardeners is faith. Regardless of how bad past gardens have been, every gardener believes that next year's will be better. It is easy to age when there is nothing to believe in, nothing to hope for; gardeners, however, simply refuse to grow up. As Thomas Jefferson so eloquently stated, "Though an old man, I am but a young gardener."

## On North and South:

Many of the same species are cultivated in Montreal, Canada, and Athens, Georgia, areas stereotyped as far north and deep south, respectively. I have gardened in both areas as well as East Lansing, Michigan and traveled with open eyes throughout the United States, Canada, Australia, New Zealand, and Europe. Certain species thrive in one area but perform poorly in another. Obvious climatic differences exist among areas in the United States, and even subtle differences within a garden influence plant performance. No absolute demarcation exists where North ends and South begins, but in this book the South incorporates zones 7-10 of the United States Department of Agriculture hardiness zone map. Zone 7 (minimum 0°-10° F) ranges as far north as Rhode Island, into Virginia, and cuts across Tennessee, Arkansas, central Oklahoma, central Texas, southern New Mexico and into Arizona and California. Many climatic factors interact with the plants ability to thrive or languish in a given zone, and hardiness ratings must be treated cautiously (see thoughts on hardiness ratings). In general, summers are hotter and more humid, winters milder (although frosts are not uncommon), and less accumulation of snow occurs in the South.

Several differences are obvious between plants of the same species grown in northern and southern locales. In the South, plants flower earlier, are taller and may have weaker stems due to the accumulated heat. Tall forms tend to collapse without support, and dwarf selections are usually more effective in the southern garden. Fertilizer need not be applied as generously in the South as in the North, particularly on tall cultivars, as additional growth is not the goal. Lanky, leggy growth occurs at the expense of flower production if too much nitrogen is applied. This happens regardless of latitude but is more prominent in the South. The lack of snow is a major detriment to overwintering perennials in the South. Snow provides insulation from the cold, and plants tucked beneath the snowy eiderdown survive cold winters well. Where rain replaces snow (as in the South), the major survival problem is inadequate drainage. This is particularly true on heavy clay where cold winter rains result in soggy, water-logged soils, and roots, crowns, and bulbs are literally immersed in free standing water. Rot organisms proliferate and plants disappear, not because of lack of cold hardiness but because they rotted in the ground. Addition of bark, peat moss or other materials which aid drainage alleviate root rot problems. Summer temperatures and humidity in the South are also detriments to perenniality. Plants not adapted to the South often perform poorly because of high night temperatures. Plants use oxygen and release carbon dioxide (similar to humans) in the process of respiration. Heat significantly affects the rate of plant respiration. In general, for every 16° F rise in temperature, respiration doubles. When night temperatures remain above 70° F, the process of respiration continues unabated and competes more aggressively for the carbohydrates produced during the day by photosynthesis. The result is lack of stored carbohydrates, inhibition of chlorophyll synthesis, and lack of secondary cell wall formation. The end result is reduced vigor, weak stunted plants and small foliage. Species not capable of acclimatizing cannot store the reserves necessary to survive the winter. In many cases, death is due not to lack of winter hardiness, but lack of summer tolerance. Many problems may be minimized with fall planting, thereby allowing plants time to build starch reserves and develop an extensive root system prior to the onset of winter. Fall planting is more critical in the South than the North for most temperate plant species.

Upon reading all the problems associated with gardening in the South, one would believe that I think southern gardening is more difficult than northern gardening; I do. However, that is not to say that a garden anywhere cannot be the most wonderful thing in the world. Regardless of where one gardens, two things become self-evident: The first is that soil preparation is half the battle. The second has to do with the plants one selects. Choosing plants that are adapted to the site and climate makes more sense than constantly trying to grow plants which are doomed to failure within a year or two. This is not to say that we shouldn't experiment with plant selection; half the fun of gardening is to try plants which "are not supposed to grow here". A quick read of good catalogs quickly shows that there is no end to species and cultivars to try, without trying to overwinter a plant native to the tropics.

One of the objectives of the research program at the Department of Horticulture, University of Georgia is to evaluate perennial species for summer hardiness. Much of that information has been used to determine hardiness zone ratings.

### On Hardiness Ratings:

United States Department of Agriculture (USDA) hardiness zones have been used by growers and gardeners for many years. Zones provide guidelines to provide a measure of the plant's ability to survive cold temperatures. To be sure, they are imperfect, but they are the best we have at present to objectively evaluate geographical limits of adaptability. Hardiness maps (see page xxv) are based on minimum winter temperatures and must be interpreted cautiously. Many factors affect plant growth other than average minimum temperatures. For example, zone 7 in Athens, Georgia is a different world from zone 7 in central California. Although minimum temperatures may be similar, summer temperatures during the night, humidity and rainfall are quite different. Valleys and mountains in the same hardiness zone are different climatically, and plants which survive in higher elevations may perish when they descend 500 feet. Microclimates exist even in a small garden, and plants which performed poorly in one location often perk up when moved to a more sheltered environment.

Heat tolerance is more difficult to evaluate than cold tolerance. Plants respond to cold by dying, to heat by languishing. However, heat tolerance or summer hardiness ratings are equally important in predicting plant performance. European garden literature is a rich source of information, but descriptions must be taken with a grain of salt. Similarly, descriptions of plant habit in the North and West may not mirror performance in the South or East. This is primarily due to differences in summer hardiness. In this text, I have attempted to provide summer hardiness ratings for all species based on experimentation, observation, existing literature, and discussions with gardeners. The southern hardiness range listed is one in which the species performs well, if other factors such as shade/sun, drainage, etc. are provided. Plants may survive south of that rating, but performance is significantly reduced. The ratings should not be considered gospel but hopefully add to the body of horticultural knowledge. Plants do not read, and testing species where they are not supposed to grow often provides pleasant surprises.

### On Garden Design:

Design is an important aspect of gardening. Great garden designers are born, not made, and nurtured through observation and experience. Principles of design abound and even I try to adhere to the basics. Most importantly, the design should be pleasing to the owner and not planned with others in mind. Select one or two dominant colors which appeal and use colors which compliment, rather than distract from each other. The aim of color is to tie plants together and then wed the planting to the site. One of the reasons for the popularity of gray and silver foliage, as well as white flowers, is their ability to tie the planting together. I am the first to admit that I am a poor designer. I garden with a palette of mixed colors. To me, the most important part of design is that the plants perform well in the site. I can be found with a trowel in one hand and a potted plant in the other, searching for any empty ground in which to place it. Good performance is defined by persistent, fresh foliage, vigorous growth, and copious effective flower production. Selection on the basis of plant performance is more important than selection based on the color wheel. To totally ignore design, however, is to relegate a garden to a collection of plants.

Water should be included in every garden. The presence of water, be it a birdbath, fountain, pond, or stream does more to soften and define a garden than all other features combined. I am always learning about garden design and someday will discourse competently on hues, shapes, feelings, and combinations. Until then, however, I will enjoy the eclectic combination of plant material around my garden pond.

### On Plant Nomenclature:

Plant names are no different than any other names; some are long and complicated, others are short and sweet. A scientific name defines a single species only, but a common name may describe a dozen or more. A valid scientific name is valid throughout the world, regardless of language or politics. The science of nomenclature is practiced by taxonomists who attempt to bring order out of chaos. Because one of their goals is to validate current scientific names and replace incorrect ones, scientific names are constantly being changed. Two main problems occur when taxonomist meets gardener. The first occurs when a new scientific name replaces one of long standing. According to some authorities, *Chrysanthemum morifolium* is now *Dendranthema grandiflorum*; *Vinca rosea* is *Catharanthus roseus*; *Helleborus corsicus* has become *H. argutifolius*; and *Euphorbia polychroma* is *E. epithymoides*. At times, it seems like a change in nomenclature is accomplished just to keep someone busy; however, if the new name is agreed on by taxonomic authorities, it should also be accepted by horticulturists and gardeners. This brings up the second problem. Taxonomists don't always agree on valid nomenclature. Names accepted by one authority aren't necessarily accepted by other equally respected authorities due to valid differences of opinion and methodology. That leaves everyone else in a muddle. Originally, Hortus III was used as the authority for scientific names in this text. However, Hortus III was published in 1976, and many changes have occurred since then. Several other respected texts (see Bailey, *Manual of Cultivated Plants*; The New Royal Horticultural Society, *Dictionary of Gardening*; Thomas, *Perennial Garden Plants*; Wyman, *Encyclopedia of Gardening*) and recent monographs were consulted to sort out nomenclature.

Plants are listed by genus, species, variety and cultivar. A genus is a closely-related group of plants consisting of one or more species. Species within a genus have more characteristics in common with each other than they do with species in other genera. Often genera are closely related, and differences are difficult to discern. Although *Silene* and *Delphinium* are obviously different, *Silene*, *Agrostemma* and *Lychnis* may be confused. The genus name begins with an upper case letter and is underlined or written in italics. A species is difficult to define but may be thought of as a type of plant distinct from other types by identifiable features. The unique characteristics are reproducible from generation to generation through seed. A species name begins with a lower case letter and is underlined or written in italics.

Often individual plants may be slightly different from other members of the species, and the definable characteristic is reproduced each generation. This group of plants is known as a variety and has enough similarities with others to be in the same species but is sufficiently different to be grouped as a separate variety. Often varieties are geographically distinct and have their own range. Varieties breed relatively true from seed, passing on their definable differences from parent to offspring. Varieties are preceded with "var." and underlined or written in italics. For example, *Muscari comosum* var. *monstrosum* infers that a group of plants of *Muscari comosum* differs in some way to be placed in var. *monstrosum*.

A cultivar refers to a cultivated variety and may be the result of hybridization, random mutation, or plant selection. For our purposes, cultivar differs from variety in that the definable factors that make a cultivar unique are not passed on from generation to generation by seed. Cultivars are propagated vegetatively by tissue culture, cuttings, grafting or divisions (although seed firms maintain homozygous lines so seed-propagated cultivars may be offered). Cultivars begin with upper case letters and are surrounded with single quotation marks. For example, *Lychnis coronaria*

'Abbotswood Rose' has lighter pink flowers than the species. Seeds produced by plants of 'Abbotswood Rose' do not produce similar plants. The distinction between variety and cultivar is lost, however, when varieties are given cultivar names. For example, var. *alba* is a common variant of many species and usually refers to the presence of white flowers. If those plants are given a cultivar name such as 'White Knight' or 'Snow White', it is impossible to know if plants are reproducible sexually or asexually. Unfortunately, in horticultural and gardening circles, the terms cultivar and variety are used interchangeably. Hybrids are common, and characteristics from each parent may be found in the offspring. Interspecific hybrids are designated by a multiplication sign (×) and are usually only reproducible vegetatively. For example, *Polygonatum* × *hybridum* is a hybrid between *P. multiflorum* and *P. biflorum* and is reproduced by division of the rootstock. Intergeneric hybrids occasionally occur and are designated by an uppercase multiplication sign (X) before the name. X *Heucherella alba* is a hybrid between *Heuchera brizoides* and *Tiarella wherryi*. The X is not sounded.

I have attempted to sort out the nomenclature where possible. There is still a long way to go. Comments from readers are welcome.

### On Common Names:

I like common names. Names like cardinal flower, naked ladies, pussytoes, and blackberry lily are far more "user friendly" than *Lobelia cardinalis*, *Lycoris squamigera*, *Antennaria dioica*, and *Belamcamda chinensis*. They also bring with them part of the history of discovery and use of the species. Lily-of-the-valley tells me more about the plant I am about to buy than *Convallaria majalis*, while lungwort describes the philosophy of naming plants much better than *Pulmonaria officinalis*. Common names may describe the flower, such as pincushion flower (*Scabiosa*); leaves, spotted geranium, (*Geranium maculatum*); origin, Persian buttercup (*Ranunculus asiaticus*); medicinal properties, self-heal (*Prunella vulgaris*); or the discoverer, Stokes aster (*Stokesia*). Unfortunatly, the same common name may be used for more than one species, or a single species may be known by several common names, depending on area of the country. Although scientific names may be considered correct or incorrect, few efforts to standardize common names have been attempted. One such attempt was Standardized Plant Names, 1942, to which I referred wherever possible. Many species and hybrids, however, were not assigned common names in that text. Other reference books and serious gardeners were consulted, and a common name has been included for most species. Other names may be equally appropriate. Assistance from readers to provide appropriate missing common names is appreciated.

### On Pronunciation:

Most people like to pronounce names with some degree of confidence. Scientific names are intimidating, and often people will not say them for fear of sounding ignorant. Pronunciation is something about which one feels confident only with continued use. If scientific names are seldom part of one's gardening vocabulary, proper pronunciation will always be difficult. Pronunciation is also subjective. It does not matter if *paniculata* is pronounced (pa-nik-ew-lah' ta) or (pa-nik-ew-lay' ta). I prefer to pronounce *Stokesia* as (stoks' ee-a), in recognition of Dr. John Stokes, for whom the genus was named. However (stow-keys' ee-a) is commonly used and equally correct. The lesson here: Get the syllables in the right order, then fire away. Don't worry about sounding silly; it is only the garden snob who continually tries to correct you. And who needs snobs in a garden? I have provided pronunciation guides for most genera and specific epithets, principally based on *Dictionary of Plant Names* (Coombes, 1985), to help get the syllables in the right order. Other references are available which use different formats. I find pronunciation guides useful, but they are simply guides.

# How to Use this Book

Generic entries are provided with a pronunciation guide, common name and family. Each specific epithet (the species term) has a pronunciation guide, common name, and average height and width of mature flowering plants. The height and width are guides to help with placement in the garden. Climate, soils, rainfall, irrigation practices and fertility will influence these guidelines. The next line provides season of flowering (based on zones 5–7), flower color, origin and hardiness range.

| Genus | Pronunciation | Common name | Family |
| --- | --- | --- | --- |
| ↓ | ↓ | ↓ | ↓ |
| *Baptisia* | (bap-tiz-i-a) | Wild Indigo | Fabaceae |

| Species | Pronunciation | Common name | Avg height/spread |
| --- | --- | --- | --- |
| ↓ | ↓ | ↓ | ↓ |
| *-australis* | (ow-strah-lis) | Blue Wild Indigo | 3–4'/4' |

| Spring | Indigo Blue | Eastern United States | Zones 3–9 |
| --- | --- | --- | --- |
| ↑ | ↑ | ↑ | ↑ |
| Flowering season | Flower color | Origin | Hardiness range |

A quick reference table is provided for genera with three or more cultivated species and easily identifiable differences among them may be located. Descriptions for each species, known cultivars and varieties are listed. Not every cultivar or variety has found its way into the book, but ideally most of the presently available selections are present. Related species are described briefly. In general, related species are not as available to the gardening public but have worthy garden characteristics.

A quick key to separate species in the genus is provided for genera with two or more species in the reference tables. I have tried to refrain from including too much botanical "jargon"; however, in some cases technical terms were necessary. The keys are based on observation and available literature. In some cases, they are precise and well done. In others, such as *Hosta*, where many more hybrids exist than species, the key can be considered a rough guide only. In general, cultivars and varieties are not included in the keys. A small glossary of technical terms is provided in the back of the book.

Additional reading is listed if the reading is specific to that genus. Most citations may be located in university or public libraries. Additional general reading is also listed in the bibliography.

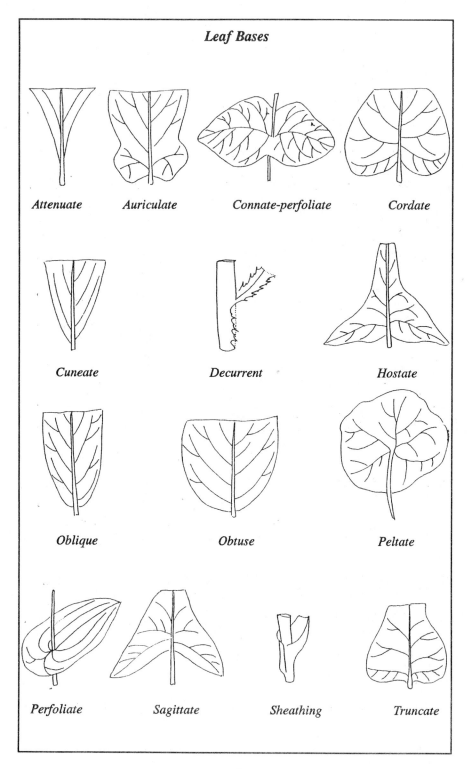

## Leaf Bases

Attenuate    Auriculate    Connate-perfoliate    Cordate

Cuneate    Decurrent    Hostate

Oblique    Obtuse    Peltate

Perfoliate    Sagittate    Sheathing    Truncate

# Leaf Shapes

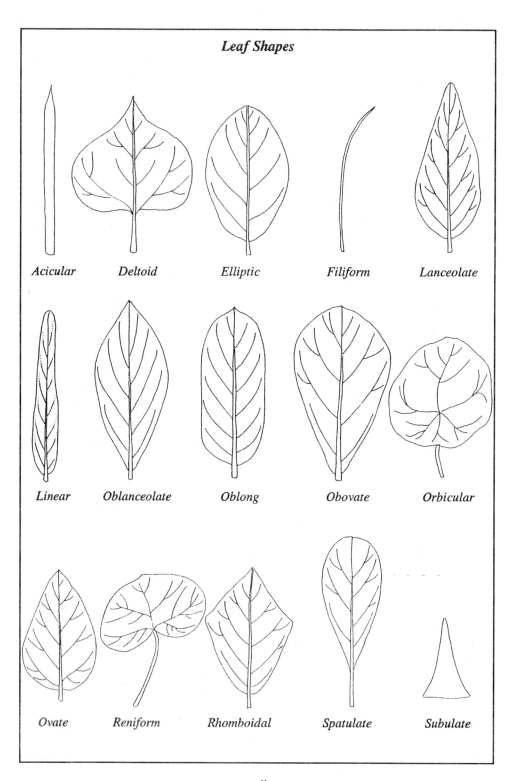

Acicular Deltoid Elliptic Filiform Lanceolate

Linear Oblanceolate Oblong Obovate Orbicular

Ovate Reniform Rhomboidal Spatulate Subulate

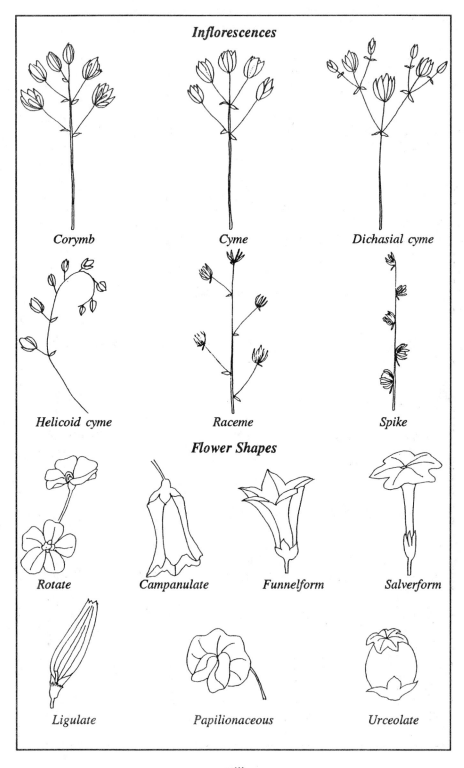

**Inflorescences**

Corymb

Cyme

Dichasial cyme

Helicoid cyme

Raceme

Spike

**Flower Shapes**

Rotate

Campanulate

Funnelform

Salverform

Ligulate

Papilionaceous

Urceolate

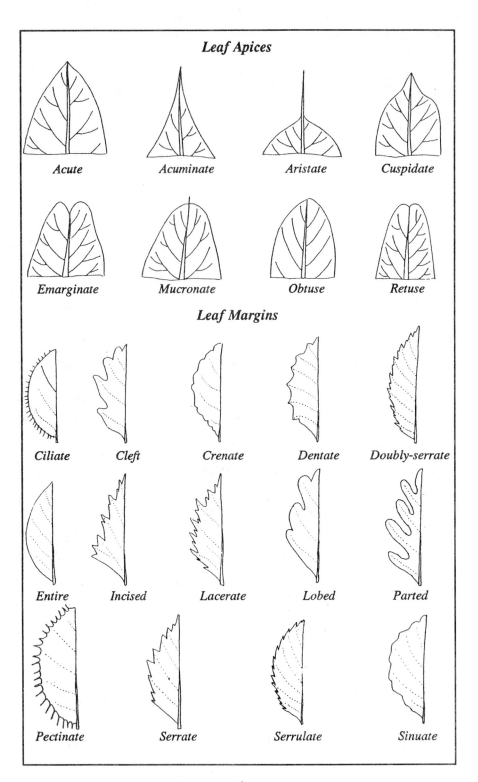

## Leaf Apices

*Acute*    *Acuminate*    *Aristate*    *Cuspidate*

*Emarginate*    *Mucronate*    *Obtuse*    *Retuse*

## Leaf Margins

*Ciliate*    *Cleft*    *Crenate*    *Dentate*    *Doubly-serrate*

*Entire*    *Incised*    *Lacerate*    *Lobed*    *Parted*

*Pectinate*    *Serrate*    *Serrulate*    *Sinuate*

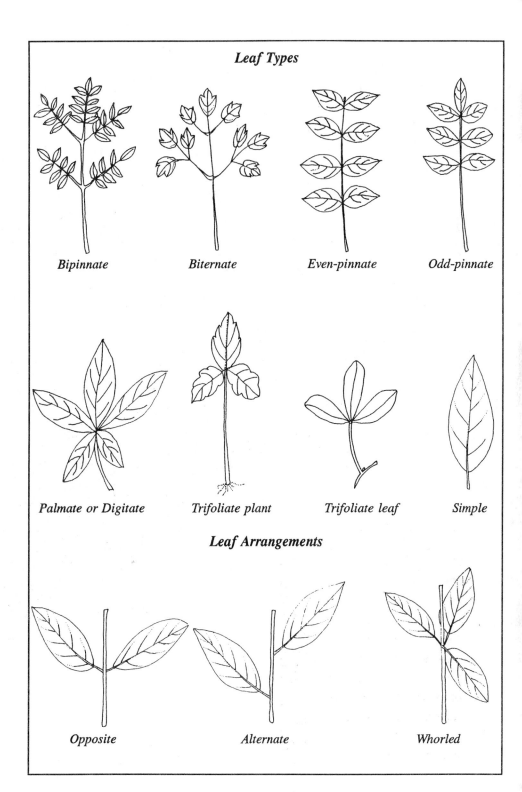

## Leaf Types

Bipinnate  Biternate  Even-pinnate  Odd-pinnate

Palmate or Digitate  Trifoliate plant  Trifoliate leaf  Simple

## Leaf Arrangements

Opposite  Alternate  Whorled

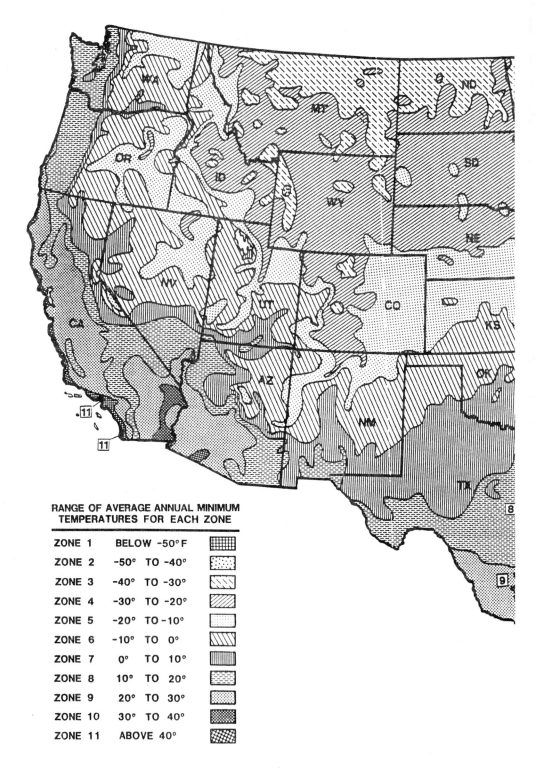

RANGE OF AVERAGE ANNUAL MINIMUM
TEMPERATURES FOR EACH ZONE

| | | |
|---|---|---|
| ZONE 1 | BELOW -50°F | |
| ZONE 2 | -50° TO -40° | |
| ZONE 3 | -40° TO -30° | |
| ZONE 4 | -30° TO -20° | |
| ZONE 5 | -20° TO -10° | |
| ZONE 6 | -10° TO 0° | |
| ZONE 7 | 0° TO 10° | |
| ZONE 8 | 10° TO 20° | |
| ZONE 9 | 20° TO 30° | |
| ZONE 10 | 30° TO 40° | |
| ZONE 11 | ABOVE 40° | |

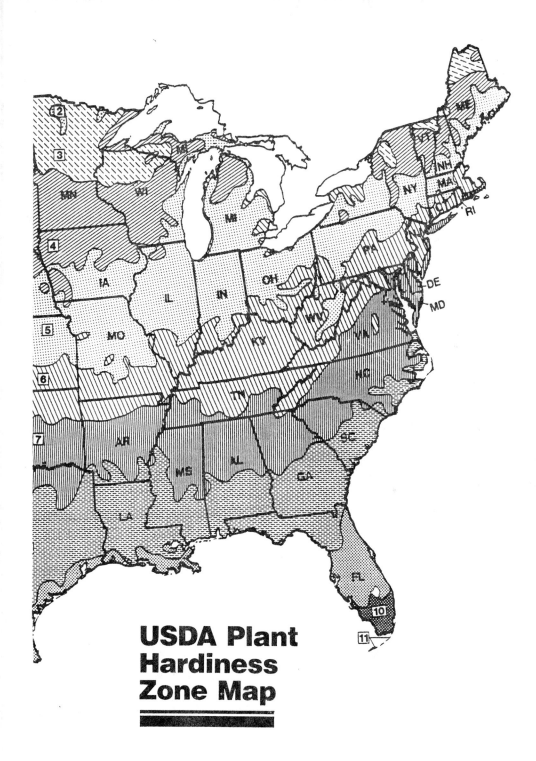

# USDA Plant Hardiness Zone Map

# A

*Acaena* (a-sane' a)               New Zealand Bur               Rosaceae

Of the 100 species in this genus, we are lucky to see one or two in this country. As the common name suggests, many species are native to New Zealand, including its namesake, *A. novae-zealandiae*. Other common names for this plant are much more alliterative and perhaps any plant with names like Pirri-Pirri Bur, Bidgee-Widgee and Biddy Biddy are worth the price of purchase alone. The excellent plantings one sees in New Zealand and throughout the British Isles have not made the transition to North America particularly well. Being native to New Zealand generally equates to sure and rapid death for eastern and northern gardeners, but a good chance of success for West Coasters. Plants are hardy to about 10° F (zones 7–8) and prefer low humidity and excellent drainage. Nevertheless, where conditions are favorable, the dense, 2–3″ tall mat-forming plants make attractive ground covers and are highly sought after. Some gardeners find them a little too aggressive (some lucky gardeners call them thugs), taking over significant areas of the rock garden or small border. All species prefer full sun, although *A. microphylla* and *A. inermis* are more shade tolerant  than others. They are grown primarily for their pea-green to steel-blue, pinnate-serrated foliage and colorful, bur-like fruit (achenes). Most leaves are about 2″ long, but *A. myriophylla* has 6–8″ long green leaves with 15–17 leaflets. The burs are held at the end of 6–9″ flower stems. The flowers of all species, which consist entirely of sepals, are carried in tight, round heads followed by spherical burs, which are often spiny and brightly colored relative to the foliage.

The more of these I see, the more I would like to see some selection work done to enhance their tolerance to "real" weather. The vigor of *A. fissistipula* crossed with blue foliage forms would provide some potentially tough, handsome offspring. Many other combinations await the Burbreeder.

Propagation is usually by division, but cuttings and seed are also used.

1

*-anserinifolia* (an-sir-in-i-fo' lee-a)  Goose-Leaf Bur  2–4"/10"
   Spring  Rose  New Zealand  Zones 7b–9

This species bears dull green hairy leaves, which are paler green beneath, and bronze or red fruit. Five to eight pairs of leaflets are tinged with pink and the combination is handsome indeed. The species is seldom offered, but 'Blue Haze' ('Pewter') has marvelous finely cut blue-green foliage with red burs and 'Bronze' has bronze foliage and amber burs. These cultivars are sometimes listed under *A. magellanica*.

### Related species:
*A. buchananii* is occasionally offered by specialist nurseries and bears light gray-green, 3" long leaves followed by amber burs. The leaflets, which occur in 3–6 pairs, are about 1" long and have soft silky margins on the underside.

*A. microphylla* has small, slightly silky, bronze-green leaves and handsome crimson burs which remain attractive throughout the summer. Absolutely fabulous as a ground cover. May be a little more cold hardy than *A. buchananii*. Plants are more tolerant of poorly drained soils than other species and can be one of the most aggressive.

## *Acantholimon* (a-kanth-o-lee' mon)  Prickly Thrift  Plumbaginaceae

This large group of plants (about 120 species) occurs predominantly in rocky, high altitude habitats and have a loyal, if small, following among gardeners. They are becoming a little better known in the north where rock gardens and well-drained areas are common. Plants are evergreen and grow in dense clumps of short, prickly 3-angled narrow leaves. To tell it like it is, plants actually resemble green hedgehogs stuck in the middle of a garden. They are slow-growing and bear long-lasting sprays of small flowers. It is difficult to find *Acantholimon* in the trade and gardeners are forced to raise plants from seeds or softwood cuttings from other enthusiasts; however, species such as *A. glumaceaum*, with bright rosy pink flowers, and *A. venustum* (*A. olivieri*), with whitish pink flowers well above the mat, are becoming a little better known. Rooting near the base of the plant is encouraged by spreading sand around the base.

All species need gritty soils but may be grown on dry stone wall, gravel beds or sunny slopes with stony soils. Areas of high rainfall are not a problem as long as drainage is impeccable. Full sun and cool nights are necessary. An excellent collection resides in the alpine garden at the Denver Botanical Garden.

## *Acanthus* (a-kanth' us)  Bear's Breeches  Acanthaceae

The genus contains approximately 30 species of which three or four are particularly ornamental, providing foliage of great beauty and statuesque flowers. The basal leaves are simple, opposite, and often have soft, thorny margins. The flowers are held in long, erect spikes and each flower is subtended by a showy, spiny, leaf-like bract. The spikes are lovely, albeit somewhat unnerving, but the ornamental value of the genus resides in the handsome foliage. Once established, *Acanthus* is almost indestructible and will colonize an area with its invasive roots. If one tires of bear's breeches and wishes to remove same, it is next to impossible not to leave some root pieces behind, which, like amoebae, will regenerate and recolonize their old homesite.

I have always wondered where the name bear's breeches came from, for the combination of the two words makes no sense at all, and it is difficult to imagine what a pair of bear's breeches is even supposed to look like. Nowhere could I find an explanation, therefore I felt much better when I learned that the eminent British horticulturist, Graham Stuart Thomas, was equally stumped. He contacted Professor William Stearn who shed some possible light on the subject. Professor Stearn believed that the term resulted from a confusion of the medieval latin description *branca ursina*, meaning bear's claw. The upper part of the hooded flower, upon proper squinting, could be said to resemble a bear's claw. But the breeches, where did they come from? Madame Audrey Serreau, a gardener from Pultiers, France, believes that additional confusion between two latin words resulted in the "breeches." The word *branca*, which means claw, was confused with the old Gaulish word *braca*, which later became "braies" and finally breeches. Is this clear yet? Such explanations may be confusing in themselves, however, as Madame Serreau stated, "Isn't it fascinating to reflect upon such word changes, bringing, as they do across the centuries, echos of long-silenced voices?"

*Acanthus* is a popular genus throughout the country, although most authors state that it is insufficiently hardy for much of the North. Those authors need to see the wonderful plantings of *Acanthus* in Gardenview Horticultural Park, the fine horticultural gardens of Henry Ross, located in Strongsville, OH (near Cleveland, zone 6). Persistent, long lived and certainly cold hardy.

The leaves are hardier than the flowers and foliage may survive in particularly cold winters, but plants may not always flower. Plants do well in full sun or partial shade and are relatively drought resistant. Poor drainage is synonymous with poor performance and death. The foliage is occasionally evergreen in the South; however, in severe winters, it becomes tattered and torn. In the North, plants are deciduous.

The most effective means of propagation is by 2–3″ long root cuttings taken in the spring. Insert them vertically in a well-drained medium and keep moist and warm. Shoots appear in 3–5 weeks. In the garden, a roto-tiller does wonders for multiplication. Plants may also be divided in early spring but adequate moisture is necessary to insure establishment. Fresh seed germinates in about 3 weeks if kept moist and warm (70–75° F).

Quick Reference to Acanthus Species

|  | Height (in.) | Leaves spiny | Leaf color |
|---|---|---|---|
| A. balcanicus | 30–48 | No | Dark green |
| A. dioscoridis | 12–24 | Yes | Gray green |
| A. mollis | 30–48 | No | Dark green |
| A. spinosus | 36–48 | Yes | Dark green |

| -balcanicus (bal-kan' i-cus) | Balkan Bear's Breeches | 30–48"/36" |
|---|---|---|
| Late Spring     Purple | Serbia, Romania, Greece | Zones 7–9 |

Sold under the names of *A. hungaricus* and *A. longifolius*, plants are similar in habit and flower to *A. mollis*. The dull green leaves are lobed with wide gaps between the lobes (the gap is referred to as a sinus). The sinuses are connected to each other with a flange of leaf parallel to the midrib. The sinuses are deep and the lobes are narrowed at the base, characteristics which distinguish it from *A. mollis*. The flower stems rise an additional 3–4' and bear numerous white and purple flowers in mid- to late summer. The bracts surrounding the flowers have 5–7 veins and are very sharp. The foliage is more winter hardy than the flowers and in particularly cold winters the leaves may emerge in the spring, but no flowers appear.

Plants perform well in most gardens; they are better in southeastern gardens than *A. mollis*.

| -mollis (mol' lis) | Common Bear's Breeches | 30–48"/36" |
|---|---|---|
| Late Spring     Purple | Southern Europe | Zones 7–9 |

In the fifth century B.C., one of the species of *Acanthus* was immortalized in the design of the sculptured leaves on Greek Corinthian columns. Some historians believe the design to be based on this species, others believe it is based on the foliage of *A. spinosus*. The lustrous green, 8–12" wide foliage is lobed but not as deeply as *A. balcanicus*. Although small, soft spines are borne at the end of the lobes, the foliage does not feel at all spiny. The flowers are similar to those of *A. balcanicus*.

The plants, having a spread of up to 3', are best used as specimens or in groups of 3 to 5 plants. I have grown a number of species in the heat of north Georgia (zone 7b) and this one has flowered poorly. The magnificent plantings seen in southern California have never quite been duplicated in the Southeast.

### Cultivars:

Var. *latifolius* is most common although less free-flowering than the species. Plants bear 3–4' tall stalks of mauve pink flowers and glossy green arching leaves which are sometimes scarcely dissected. Plants appear to be more robust and cold tolerant than the species. 'Oakleaf' has large, deep green, oak-shaped leaves.

*-spinosus* (spine-o' sus)　　　Spiny Bear's Breeches　　36–48"/36"
　　Late Spring　　　Mauve　　Southern Europe　　　　Zones 6–10

The main difference between this species and the previous is the presence of spiny leaf margins which look a good deal more lethal than they really are. The 10" diameter leaves are lanceolate and more deeply divided than those of *A. mollis*. The flowers are similar except that 3–4 veins occur on the purplish bracts rather than 5–7 found in common bear's breeches. If late freezes occur, *A. mollis* is killed to the ground while this species is little affected. The flowers are produced consistently each year and the leaves remain fresh all season. Plants also tolerate warm, humid summers better than the previous species—a definite advantage for southern gardeners.

## Cultivars:

'Lady Moore' is an interesting plant occasionally seen in the British Isles but seldom in the United States. The foliage is creamy white in the spring, greening up as the weather warms up. Named for the wife of Sir Frederick Moore, keeper of the Botanic Garden at Glasnevin, Dublin.

Var. *spinosissimus* is a man-eater and should only be grown by masochists or those who can command someone else to do the pruning, training and actual gardening of such vicious plants. The leaf spines are white and the divisions are much narrower and more sharply cut than those of the species. I have enough trouble with belligerent people, why tolerate belligerent plants?

Significant variation exists among plants called *spinosissimus*, and they are actually a group of plants rather than a single variety. Some of the hybrids between *A. mollis* and *A. spinosus* are placed with this group.

## Related Species:

*A. caroli-alexandri* (syn. *A. syriacus*) bears lanceolate, thistle-like leaves. Plants grow about 18" tall and bear white or rose-colored flowers.

*A. dioscoridis* is only 1–2' tall and has rosy pink bracts. The leaves are sessile (no petiole), gray-green, and are usually, but not always, spiny. Good drainage is essential. Being native to mountainous areas of Asia Minor, it is likely hardy in zones 6–9, although insufficient plants have been evaluated to provide confident hardiness ratings. Var. *perringii* (*A. perringii*) has pink flowers.

## Quick Key to Acanthus Species

　　A. Leaves spiny or apparently so . . . . . . . . . . . . . *A. spinosus*
　　AA. Leaves without sharp spines
　　　　B. Leaves dull green, deeply lobed,
　　　　　　lobes narrowed at the base . . . . . . . . . . . . *A. balcanicus*
　　　　BB. Leaves lustrous green, not as deeply lobed,
　　　　　　lobes not narrowed at the base . . . . . . . . . . . . *A. mollis*

**Additional Reading:**

Rix, Marilyn. 1980. The genus *Acanthus L.*, an introduction to the hardy species. *The Plantsman* 2(3):132–140.
Thomas, G. S. 1994. Classic beauty. *The Garden* 119(9):404–405.

## *Achillea* (a-kil-lee′ a)      Yarrow      Asteraceae

Although there are approximately 100 species, less than a dozen are truly ornamental. They range in height from 4″ (*A. nana*) to 4′ tall (*A. filipendulina*) with flowers of almost every hue. Leaves of all species are alternate and, with the exception of *A. ageratum*, sweet yarrow and *A. ptarmica*, sneezewort, the foliage is deeply divided into a fine fern-like appearance. In several species, the foliage has a heavy spicy odor and a gray-green tint. The outer ray flowers are pistillate (female only) and may be yellow, white, or pink, while the inner disc flowers are bisexual (male and female together) and usually yellow. The flower heads (inflorescences) are flat compound corymbs.

Some species of yarrow are, at times, considered weeds, particularly those which multiply rapidly from invasive rhizomes. This characteristic, however, is only true for one or two species and most others behave themselves and stay at home. Unless otherwise noted, all species should be grown in full sun and well-drained soils. They tolerate poor, slightly acid soils (if well-drained), although *A. clavennae* prefers limey soils to do well. Many of the upright forms will grow too tall and lanky if fertilized or grown in rich soil. The flowers of most species make excellent fresh or dried specimens, but the pollen must be visible before the flowers are cut or vase life will be significantly reduced.

Quick Reference to Achillea Species

|  | Height (ft.) | Flower color | Foliage color |
|---|---|---|---|
| *A.* × 'Coronation Gold' | 2–3 | Yellow | Gray-green |
| *A. filipendulina* | 3–5 | Yellow | Green |
| *A. grandifolia* | 2–3 | White | Gray-green |
| *A. millefolium* | 1–2 | Pink, red | Green |
| *A.* × 'Moonshine' | 1–2 | Sulphur | Gray-green |
| *A. ptarmica* | 1–2 | White | Green |
| *A. tomentosa* | ½–1 | Yellow | Gray-green |

**-× 'Coronation Gold'**      Coronation Gold Yarrow      2–4′/3′
     Late Spring      Yellow      Hybrid Origin      Zones 3–9

This hybrid was first offered in 1953 by Miss Pole of Lye End Nursery in southern England to commemorate the coronation of Elizabeth II. An amateur hybridizer, she crossed *A. filipendulina* with *A. clypeolata*, a small yellow-flowered species, to raise the best upright golden yellow yarrow available today. Unfortunately, it is sometimes incorrectly listed as a cultivar of *A. filipendulina*. The plant is shorter than *A. filipendulina*, better branched, and does not require staking. It requires less maintenance and should be the plant of choice for landscapers. The inflorescences are 3–4″ across and look like shiny golden plates. Flowering begins in late May in north Georgia, June in the Northeast, and continues for 8–12 weeks. The foliage is gray-green and has a strong aromatic smell. It tolerates a wide range of climates and soils and is grown in gardens from Manitoba to Florida.

'Coronation Gold' is popular as a cut flower throughout the world. It is interesting to note the differences in stem and flower size between northern and southern climates. In North Georgia, over 50 flowering stems per plant are produced, while the same plants growing in Holland yield fewer than 15 stems but each one is 1½–2 times longer with larger flowers.

Propagate by terminal cuttings in spring or early summer or by spring or fall division every 3–4 years. Seed purchased as 'Coronation Gold' will likely be *A. filipendulina* or one of its cultivars.

| *-filipendulina* (fi-li-pen-dew′ lye-na) | Fern-Leaf Yarrow | 3–5′/3′ |
|---|---|---|
| Summer | Yellow | Caucasus | Zones 3–8 |

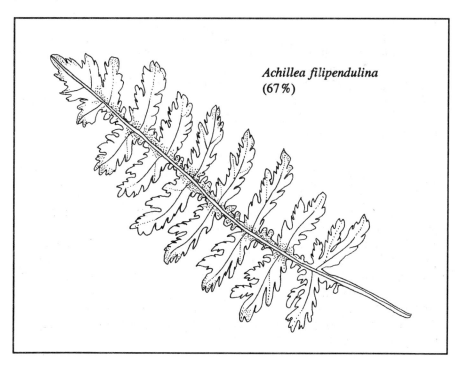

*Achillea filipendulina*
(67%)

The foliage is deeply cut and feathery but bears little of the gray-green tint that is so appealing in *A.* × 'Coronation Gold'. In general, foliage is greener, flowers are larger and plants are taller than those of *A.* 'Coronation Gold'. This is a handsome plant but when grown in rich soils or when over-fertilized, it usually requires staking, a job most smart people view with disdain. The flat yellow flower heads are 3-4″ across and make excellent cut flowers. Provide full sun. Yellow-flowered yarrows combine well with pink phlox, purple-foliaged plants, blue delphiniums and red hot pokers.

Plants may be propagated by spring division, terminal cuttings in early summer, or by seed. Seed sown in a mixture of 1:1 peat:vermiculite and placed at 70-72° F in a humid area germinate within 21 days. The cultivars mentioned are available from seed.

### Cultivars:

'Altgold' stands about 2′ tall and bears deep yellow flowers in late spring and again in early fall. An interesting rebloomer.

'Cloth of Gold' bears large, pure yellow flowers and grows 3-4′ tall.

'Gold Plate' has deep yellow flowers on stems up to 5′ tall.

'Parker's Variety' bears golden yellow flowers on 3-4′ tall stems. All produce large numbers of flowers and have better stem strength than the species but may require support in areas with hot, humid summers.

### Related Species:

*A.* × 'Flowers of Sulphur' ('Schwefeblute') is a slow-spreading hybrid of *A. filipendulina* and *A. ptarmica*. The best sulphur-colored flowers in the genus on 2′ tall plants.

*A.* × 'Schwellenburg' is likely a hybrid with *A. filipendulina* and a yet to be determined species. The golden flowers sit atop silvery, ferny foliage and stand about 2′ tall. Plants do not appear to be particularly vigorous or tolerant of adverse weather.

| | | | |
|---|---|---|---|
| *-grandifolia* (grand-i-fo′ lee′-a) | White Yarrow | | 2-4′/2′ |
| Summer | White | South Balkans | Zones 5-8 |

I first admired this terrific plant in England where it filled the bill for a good, upright, white-flowered yarrow. I looked forward to sowing the seeds I had collected when I returned home. The 9″ long leaves are gray-green, lacy and deeply cut, while the flowers are held on strong stems in a 3-4″ diameter flat inflorescence. It is a far better white than found in any cultivars of common yarrow, *A. millefolium*, and should be offered in the United States by some enterprising nurserymen. I hope someone does it soon as my seeds did not survive the rigors of being dry cleaned with my jacket.

Once established, plants are commonly propagated by seed or division similar to *A. filipendulina*.

**Related Species:**

*A. clavennae* grows 2–3′ tall and bears up to 25 small white flowers in the inflorescence. Plants form handsome clumps of silky gray foliage. Prefers limey soils. Hardy in zones 5–8.

*A. sibirica* is highly variable but should be much better known. Its leathery pinnatifid leaves are sessile, more compact and quite handsome compared with other yarrows. The ray flowers are yellow and the discs are brown. The cultivar 'Kamschaticum' has pastel pink flowers. 'Kiku-San' is about 18″ tall with creamy white ray flowers and brown centers. It has been an exceptional performer in our Georgia trial garden.

| *-millefolium* (mil-lee-fo′ lee-um) | Common Yarrow | 1–2′/5′ |
|---|---|---|
| Summer     White to Cerise Red | Europe | Zones 3–9 |

Common yarrow is "common" because of its ability to spread rapidly and take over any ground available. Often seeded as a wild flower on roadsides, the ferny foliage and off-white flowers fill in median stripes and combine well with other roadside plants such as bachelor's buttons and poppies. In Europe, it is often discarded as a troublesome weed not to be included on the grounds of any self-respecting gardener. Yet the same people will find fresh and dried flowers of common yarrow in florist shops where they are widely used in colorful bouquets. This species was cultivated in Europe before 1440, used as a remedy for toothache, and mixed in ale in place of hops to increase the inebriating quality of that drink. It was thought to have a magical quality similar to our "apple a day keeps the doctor away," and was said to grow in churchyards as a reproach to the dead, "who need never have come there if they had taken their yarrow broth faithfully every day while living." The main use, however, was that of a herb to heal wounds. The genus was named after Achilles, who is said to have used *A. millefolium* to staunch the wounds of his soldiers. Soldier's Woundweed and Carpenter's Weed are other old English names. And everyone thought this was just a common old flower!

The habit is mat-like and the dark green foliage is deeply cut. In early summer, the flower stalks rise about 2′ and are quite strong where night temperatures consistently stay below 70° F. Where night temperatures are too warm, the stems do not acquire enough carbohydrates to "fatten up" and may topple. Plants fill in rapidly and those placed 4′ apart produce an unbroken mat in 2 years. If planted 2′ apart, they fill in by the end of the first year. An interesting experiment using yarrow as a lawn was carried out at El Alisal, the water-conserving demonstration house in Los Angeles. Two thousand square feet of yarrow lawn was installed to demonstrate that it could

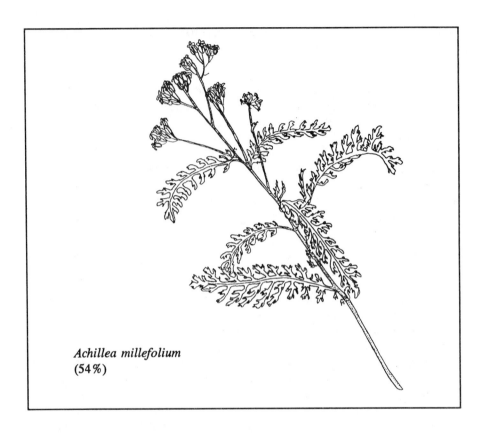

*Achillea millefolium*
(54%)

be a water-wise substitute for turf. While not sufficiently tough for football games and children with dogs, it was, however, effective as a mowed lawn and saved significant water (see Connelly, 1992).

A few cultivars are offered from seed but the seed companies have a long way to go before gardeners or commercial people use the seed of some cultivars. With the exception of 'Summer Pastels', seed is notoriously variable. It is not uncommon that 'Rose Beauty' will have 4 or 5 different colors. In our studies, 'Cerise Queen' seed yielded at least 6 colors, five of them poor. It is just as easy to divide good specimens to retain the desired colors.

**Cultivars:**

Many of the following may also be hybrids.

'Borealis' bears dense clusters of rose-pink flowers.

'Cerise Queen' is one of the best of the cerise-red flowered cultivars and performs well throughout the country. It grows about 18″ tall and provides bright drifts of color.

'Citronella' bears butter yellow flowers on a erect habit.

'Creamy' bears large heads of creamy yellow flowers. Plants fill in quickly.

'Credo' is a tall (3–4') cultivar with light yellow flowers which tend to fade to creamy white. Good for cut flowers.

'Debutante' is a mixture of plants, bearing rose to creamy white flowers. 'Pink Debutante' is an excellent selection.

'Fire King' and 'Fire Beauty' have dark red flowers; there is little difference between them.

'Fireland', bred in Germany, opens red then fades to pink and finally to a tawny gold. The plants grow about 3' tall but the stems are reasonably stout.

'Jambo' bears medium yellow flowers on 15–18" tall stems.

'Kelwayi' bears magenta-red flowers on 18" stems.

'Lilac Beauty' produces lilac flowers on strong upright stems.

'Lilac Queen' has flat heads of pastel lilac flowers and is offered occasionally by mail order nurseries.

'Lusaka' has white flowers and is a vigorous grower.

'Martina' has large, flat yellow flower heads on 2–2½' tall stems. The foliage is ferny and green.

'Maskarade' bears interesting pale yellow flower heads with red flecks along the edges as they mature. Quite a different look.

'Nakuru' produces purple and white bicolor flowers.

'Orange Queen' has unusual orange-gold flowers. Plants are about 30" tall and about 18" wide.

'Paprika' produces red and yellow flowers on a flattened inflorescence. One of the most handsome cultivars available.

'Pink Island Form' is about 2' tall and produces pastel pink flowers.

'Ortel's Rose' was introduced by Goodness Grows Nursery in Lexington, GA and blooms heavily with rosy pink and white flowers. A terrific selection for Southern gardeners.

'Red Beauty' bears 2' tall cerise-red flowers in mid summer.

'Rose Beauty' has rather nondescript rose-pink flowers on 2' tall stems.

'Sawa Sawa' bears lavender-purple flowers on 20" stems.

'Schneetaler' ('Snowtaler') is a hybrid with pure white flowers. Plants are good for cut flowers and may rebloom if cut back hard after the initial bloom.

'Snow Sport' is a vigorous grower with dark green foliage and dozens of clean white flowers on 18" tall stems.

'Summer Pastels' is a seed-propagated hybrid which includes numerous pastel colors (pink, rose, lavender, salmon to orange) on 2' tall plants. Plants flower the first year from seed. The yellow hues are particularly good.

'Weser River Sandstone' ('Weserandstein') has deep rose-pink flowers on 2–3' tall plants.

'White Beauty' produces creamy white flowers.

**Related Hybrids:**

Galaxy hybrids have been available for about a decade and are exciting hybrids of *A.* × 'Taygetea' and *A. millefolium*. The foliage is similar to that of *A. millefolium*, but the flower heads are larger and the stems much stronger. The only problem I have seen is the tendency of the flowers to fade, particularly when temperatures are above 80° F. In our trials, 'Beacon' and 'Great Expectations' faded less than others. In the Northeast, little fading is seen. This is an excellent group of plants and do well in most gardens in North America. All are easily propagated by division.

'Appleblossom' ('Apfelblute') is a vigorous 3' tall plant with peach to lilac-pink flowers.

'Great Expectations' ('Hope', 'Hoffnung') produces primrose yellow flowers on 2' high stems.

'Heidi' produces pastel pink flowers on 20″ stems in the spring and reblooms a little later in the summer.

'Salmon Beauty' ('Lachsschonheit') bears large heads of salmon flowers on 3' tall stems.

'The Beacon' ('Fanal') stands 2–3' tall and bears rich red flowers with yellow centers. It is the best cultivar I have seen.

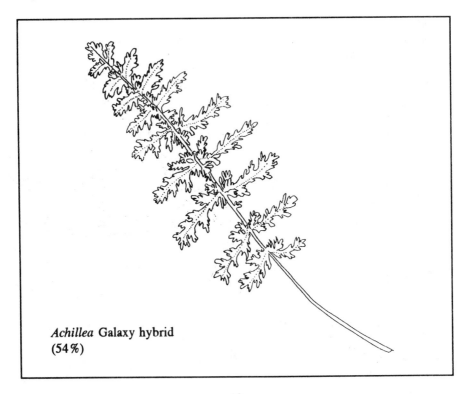

*Achillea* Galaxy hybrid
(54%)

**-× 'Moonshine'**        Moonshine Yarrow        1–2′/1′
   Summer    Lemon Yellow    Hybrid Origin        Zones 3–7

This hybrid, between *A. clypeolata* and *A.* × 'Taygetea', was introduced in the 1950's by Alan Bloom of Bressingham Gardens in Diss, England. In the garden, 'Moonshine' is similar to *A.* × 'Coronation Gold' except in size and shade of flower color. The inflorescences are flat-topped, dense, deep lemon-yellow and 2–3″ in diameter, while the gray-green foliage is filigreed. It is one of the most popular yarrows in American landscapes and is often recommended because of habit and interesting flower color. While a handsome plant, 'Moonshine' tends to become twiggy, loses some of its foliage and dies out after 2–3 years in the garden.

The flowers appear in early June (late June in New England) and continue until September. However, it is much more perennial in the North than in the South. In the Southeast where summer days are frequently punctuated by late afternoon rains and high humidity, *A.* × 'Moonshine' tends to "melt out." This is not surprising considering that one of its parents, *A.* × 'Taygetea', is also susceptible to many foliar diseases. 'Moonshine' does best in the Southeast during summers with little rainfall. Spraying for diseases such as *Botrytis* and

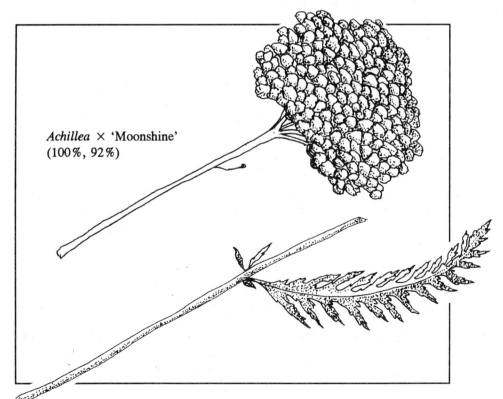

*Achillea* × 'Moonshine'
(100%, 92%)

various root rot organisms such as *Pythium* is helpful and should be practiced in July and August. One of the finest landscape architects in the city of Atlanta simply treats the plant as an annual, enjoys the early summer beauty and removes plants as they decline in late summer. Regardless of the region of the country in which it is grown, excellent drainage is necessary to ensure longevity more than 2 years. This was one of the finest hybrid yarrows to be developed in many years and, if sited properly and grown well, can still be a popular plant for commercial landscapers and gardeners.

Propagate by division any time during the growing season.

### Related Species:

*A.* × 'Anthea' was introduced by Alan Bloom by crossing 'Moonshine' with *A. clypeolata* because of some of the problems inherent in 'Moonshine' and bears flowers which are more sulphur-yellow than 'Moonshine'. Plants are more erect and the foliage is soft and silver-gray. In our trials at Georgia, the flower heads were about 3″ across but tended to fade to creamy yellow as they mature. At the same time, secondary flowers emerged freely. Flower heads should be deadheaded to extend flowering. A terrific introduction named after Mr. Bloom's daughter.

*A.* × 'Alabaster', a new hybrid from Germany, bears flat heads of pale yellow flowers on stiff 30″ tall gray-green foliage.

*A.* × 'Taygetea' is a plant that plantspeople talk about because of the many hybrids it has spawned, but it is seldom seen in American gardens. Likely a hybrid between *A. millefolium* and *A. clypeolata,* the pale yellow flowers are borne on 18″ tall stems adorned with silver-gray leaves. It is susceptible to a number of foliar diseases and is much better in the North than in the South, where humidity and warm temperatures tend to make the plant decline. However, it is an important parent of the Galaxy hybrids and *A.* × 'Moonshine'.

| *-ptarmica* (tar′ mah-ca) | | Sneezewort | 1–2′/1′ |
|---|---|---|---|
| Early Summer | White | Europe | Zones 2–9 |

I can think of few other common names in the plant kingdom as ugly as sneezewort. Hearing the name for the first time certainly doesn't endear this species to anyone. The common name is derived from the fact that "the floures make one neese exceedingly." In Victorian England, the leaves and roots were also dried and reduced to powder and used as an inexpensive substitute for snuff.

The species differs from most yarrows due to the lack of dissected leaves. The sessile foliage is finely toothed and fern-like, and linear to lance-shaped. The species itself is of little ornamental value but a number of good cultivars are available. The cut flowers are occasionally used as a substitute for baby's breath and also dry well. It is an aggressive plant and will spread considerably in good soils. Susceptible to powdery mildew in wet soils and shady conditions.

*Achillea ptarmica*
(69%)

Propagate by division in the spring.

**Cultivars:**

'Angels' Breath' bears many ½" wide, clean, white flowers on 15-18" tall plants. Good filler for bouquets.

'Ballerina' is a relatively new cultivar with clean, white flowers. Good as a dried cut flower.

'Globe' has small button-like blossoms on 12-18" tall stems.

'The Pearl' ('Boule de Neige', 'Schneeball') is the most popular cultivar and bears a profusion of double white flowers on 2' high stems. The flowers are cream colored, but in warm climates plants sprawl and are weedy looking. All double-flowered cultivars produce some single flowers as well. Up to 30% single flowers may be produced depending on weather and cultivar.

'Perry's White' is taller (up to 30"), with flowers similar to the species but opening about a week earlier.

**Related Species:**

*A. declorens* 'W.B. Child' bears single, creamy white flowers similar to sneezewort. If not for the difference in leaf shape, one would be challenged to tell the difference by looking only at the flowers. The plants, however, have dissected, deep green leaves whereas those of sneezewort are almost entire. Some authorities believe this to be a cultivar of *A. ageratum*, sweet Nancy, and some nurseries offer it as such.

*A.* × *jaborneggii* is a hybrid between *A. clavennae* and the alpine species *A. erbo-rota* ssp. *moschata*. Clean, white flowers over deeply cut clumps of gray-green foliage occur in late spring. Plants are only about 4–6″ tall and most suitable for the rock garden.

*A.* × *kellereri* also bears creamy white flowers but with soft yellow centers on 6–8″ tall plants. The plant is a hybrid between *A. clypeolata* and *A. ageratifolia*, Greek yarrow, which has small white daisies and silver foliage. The resulting hybrid has wonderful fern-like gray leaves which are as pretty as the flowers.

*A.* × *wilcezkii* is a low growing white-flowered hybrid between *A. ageratifolia* and *A. lingulata*. The plants form mats under conditions of good drainage and sunshine. Particularly useful for the rock garden.

| | | | |
|---|---|---|---|
| *-tomentosa* (tow-men-tos' a) | | Woolly Yarrow | 6–12″/18″ |
| Early Summer | Yellow | Europe | Zones 3–7 |

The common name provides an excellent description of the deeply-cut, light-green foliage which is covered with long hairs, providing a truly woolly appearance. Good drainage is essential and the rock garden is a particularly suitable location; however, plants also make good subjects for the front of the border. It is most handsome in the spring when the hairy new growth begins to clamber over rocks and invades small niches. Many sulphur-yellow flowers, similar to, but smaller than those of *A.* × 'Moonshine', are produced in June (May in the south) and continue for 3–5 weeks.

Unfortunately, plants are intolerant of hot, humid conditions and cannot be recommended for areas south of zone 6. Although they will survive in zone 7, plants perform well only through early summer and decline by mid to late July, unlikely to be seen again the next year. This is not a species for southern landscapes unless frequent fungicide applications are made. I grow it in zone 7 as an annual because I enjoy the woolly texture enough to replace it each spring. Not everyone is as tolerant.

Most cultivars are usually propagated by division, but the species and var. *aurea* may also be seed-propagated.

**Cultivars:**

Var. *nana* ('Nana') has golden yellow flowers on 3–6″ tall stems. Sometimes sold as 'Little Beauty'.

16

'Maynard's Gold' produces bright yellow flowers on 10–12″ stems. Some authorities believe var. *aurea* and 'Maynard's Gold' to be one and the same. They are probably correct.

'Moonlight' is taller than the species (up to 18″) but otherwise is not particularly different.

**Related Species:**

*A. chrysocoma*, Grecian yarrow, is similar to *A. tomentosa* but the leaves are more hairy, appear to be coated with white fur and the golden yellow flowers are a little wider. 'Grandiflora' has larger flowers.

*A.* × *lewisii*, a hybrid between *A. clavennae* and *A. clypeolata*, bears woody stems and soft silver-green foliage. The leaves are not as hairy as *A. tomentosa* and a little taller. 'King Edward' bears primrose yellow flowers on 4–10″ stems. Both species are better in the North than South and require excellent drainage.

Quick Key to Achillea Species

```
A. Flowers yellow
   B. Leaves gray-green
      C. Flowers bright yellow,
         plants 2–3′ tall . . . . . . . . . .   A. × 'Coronation Gold'
      CC. Flowers sulphur yellow,
         plants 1–2′ tall . . . . . . . . . . . . . .   A. × 'Moonshine'
   BB. Leaves green, little gray
       color apparent
      C. Plants 3–5′ tall . . . . . . . . . . . . . . .   A. filipendulina
      CC. Plants 3–6″ tall . . . . . . . . . . . . . . . .   A. tomentosa
AA. Flowers pink, red, or white
   B. Leaves deeply cut
      C. Leaves gray-green, plants 2–3′ tall,
         upright habit, flowers white . . . . . . . . . .   A. grandifolia
      CC. Leaves dark green, plants 1–2′ tall,
          mat-like habit, flowers usually pink
          or red, occasionally white . . . . . . . . . . .   A. millefolium
   BB. Leaves not divided, linear-lanceolate . . . . . . . .   A. ptarmica
```

**Additional Reading:**

Armitage, A.M. 1991. Yarrows. *Fine Gardening* 19:46–49.

Bender, S. 1992. Yarrow: living sunshine from the garden. *Southern Living*, June:60.

Connelly, K. 1991. A yarrow lawn. *Pacific Horticulture* 52(3):28–30.

Hawke, R.G. 1995. A performance report of cultivated yarrows (*Achillea*). *Perennial Plants* (J. of the Perennial Plant Assoc) 3(3):10–17.

## *Aconitum* (ak-ko-ny' tum)　　　Monkshood　　　Ranunculaceae

*Aconitum* has a number of common names, one of which is monkshood, so called because of the enlarged sepal which resembles a hood, under which the rest of the floral parts are hidden. Roots were used as poison bait for wolves, thus accounting for another popular common name, wolfsbane. All aconitums have poisonous roots, leaves, and stems; warnings concerning their poisonous properties have been sounded since the late 1500's. In A New Herbal, William Turner writes, "Let oure Londiners which of late have receyved this blewe wolfes bayne . . . take hede that poyson of the rote of this herbe one daye do not more harme than the freshness of the flower hath done pleasure in seven yeres, let them not saye but they are warned." It may even have been used to rid oneself of an unwanted husband or wife, but "it was considered rather a vulgar poison and was not employed by persons of high rank, who probably thought Socrates' hemlock more distinguished." The turnip-shaped tuberous roots, however, are the most toxic and should not be planted near root crops such as potatoes or horseradish in case of accidental harvesting. Roots have even been confused with those of celery, while, incredibly, some people ate leaves thinking they were parsley! I would think you would have to be drunk or something to get them mixed up. Perhaps one should plant species such as *A. septentrionale* which has quite fibrous roots. The "poison" yielded by *A. napellus* is the drug aconite, which has been used worldwide as a local analgesic in liniments and as a heart sedative.

Regardless of the morbid properties, aconitums are excellent garden plants. The flowers are arranged in terminal racemes or panicles and open in summer to early fall. Flowers of the more common species occur in various shades of blue; however, several species such as *A. lycoctonum* ssp. *neapolitanum* (syn. *A. lamarckii*), *A. lycoctonum* ssp. *lycoctonum* (syn. *A. barbatum*), ssp. *vulparia* (syn. *A. vulparia*) and *A. orientale* have sulphur-yellow flowers, while rose colored flowers occur in *A. pyramidale*. The leaves are alternate, dark green and usually palmately divided. The leaves superficially resemble those of *Delphinium* but the flowers of the two genera are distinctly different. Among other things, flowers of *Aconitum* only have two petals whereas those of *Delphinium* have four.

Aconitums should be planted in full sun but will tolerate afternoon shade, particularly when planted near the southern boundary of their range (zone 6). They also tolerate moist soils but abhor swampy conditions. Aconitum must have cool nights to flourish, which is why it languishes in southern regions of the country. If summer night temperatures do not regularly fall below 70° F, they should not be planted. A couple of native species, *A. uncinatum* and *A. reclinatum* extend as far south as North Carolina but are always found at higher elevations. One of the few disappointments I have had in gardening in the South is the absence of the stately spires of *Aconitum*. It did well in southern Ontario (zone 4), but, try as I may, I cannot grow monkshood well in north Georgia (zone 7b).

Most species are at least 3′ tall and look out of place in the front of the garden; however, *A. septentrionale* 'Ivorine', a 2–3′ tall plant with ivory colored blossoms in early summer, may be planted in the foreground. A few species, such as the Asian *A. volubile* and the eastern United States natives, *A. uncinatum* and *A. reclinatum*, are ramblers and can be trained to run through shrubs. Flowering time for most of the monkshoods is late summer and fall; however, the 6′ stately dark-purple spires of *A. henryi* open with the summer phlox and daylilies. Aconitum produces good cut flowers but care should be taken not to get any sap from the cut stem on open wounds.

Plant the tuberous roots in the fall to establish the root system before the first hard frost. Set the crowns just below the soil surface about 12–18″ apart. Do not disturb established plants as they do not transplant well. Plan where you would like them to be for the next 10 years for that is where they should stay.

Seed propagation is particularly difficult because the seed develops a deep dormancy upon ripening. Sow seed as soon as collected from the plant. Germination of old seed will occur but very slowly (12–18 months is not uncommon). Seed-grown plants take 2–3 years to flower. To propagate vegetatively, the brittle tuberous roots can be separated in late fall or very early spring.

## Quick Reference to Aconitum Species

|  | Height (ft.) | Flower color | Leaves divided all the way to base |
|---|---|---|---|
| *A.* × *cammarum* | 3–4 | Various | Yes |
| *A. carmichaelii* | 2–3 | Dark blue | No |
| *A. lamarckii* | 3–4 | Yellow | Yes |
| *A. napellus* | 3–4 | Dark blue | Yes |

| -× *cammarum* (kam-mar′ um) | | Bicolor Monkshood | 3–4′/2′ |
|---|---|---|---|
| Summer | Various | Hybrid | Zones 3–7 |

(Syn. *A. bicolor*, *A. napellus* 'Bicolor', *A. ottonianum*)

A group of hybrids between *A. variegatum* and *A. napellus*, with variable growth habit depending on the dominant parent in a particular cultivar. The inflorescences are often branched and the "helmet" is often strongly arched forward. The leaves are 2–4″ long and divided into 5–7 segments.

### Cultivars:

'Bicolor' is 3–4′ tall and has blue and white flowers loosely borne on wide branching panicles derived from *A. variegatum*.

19

'Blue Sceptre' has erect 2–3' stems terminating in dense inflorescences of blue and white flowers. Flowering stems are not as branched as in 'Bicolor'.

'Bressingham Spire' is 2½–3' tall with violet blue flowers in dense, upright panicles, suggesting the influence of *A. napellus*. Lateral flowers develop after the terminal flower begins to open. This cultivar is particularly valuable because staking is not required. The latter two cultivars resulted from seedlings from crosses between 'Newry Blue' and the bicolored *A. × cammarum* by Alan Bloom.

'Newry Blue', raised by Mr. Tom Smith of Daisy Hill Nursery in Newry, Northern Ireland, is 4–5' tall with navy blue flowers and has the same upright flowering habit as 'Bressingham Spire'.

**Related Species:**

*A. henryi* has leaves divided into 3 segments and bears indigo blue flowers. 'Spark's Variety', a 4–5' tall, dark blue cultivar, is similar to 'Bicolor' in flowering habit. Both cultivars may require staking, particularly if grown in too much shade.

| -*carmichaelii* (kar-my-keel' lee-eye) | Azure Monkshood | 2–3'/3' |
|---|---|---|
| Late Summer     Dark Blue | Central China | Zones 3–7 |

(Syn. *A. fischeri*)

The leaves are thicker and more leathery than those of *A. × cammarum* and not as deeply dissected. The leaves are cut about two-thirds of the way to the midrib into 3–5 lobes. It is a sturdy plant which seldom needs staking and has dark blue flowers in late summer and early fall. Afternoon shade and sufficient moisture are necessary for plants to be at their best. When planting, large amounts of organic matter should be incorporated in the planting hole. This species flowers about 2 weeks later than *A. × cammarum* and is often referred to as the fall flowering aconitum. The flowers are deep purple within and lighten to pale mauve on the outside. A planting incorporating Japanese anemones, late monkshoods, and autumn sedums, such as 'Autumn Joy', is truly breathtaking.

**Cultivars:**

'Arendsii' (syn. *A. × arendsii*) is a hybrid between *A. carmichaelii* and its var. *wilsonii*. Raised by Georg Arend's of Arend's Nursery in Ronsdorf, Germany, it is now available in the United States and definitely deserves to be used more. Plants bear large helmets of intense blue in September and October and stand 3–4' tall. The stems are sturdy enough to be self-supporting and, everything considered, is the best late flowering aconitum in cultivation.

'Barker's Variety' has deep blue flowers and comes true from seed.

'Kelmscott Variety' has lavender blue flowers and is similar in habit to 'Barkers Variety'. Both cultivars were raised by Mr. Barker of Kelmscott, near

Ipswich, England. They grow to a height of 6' under ideal conditions. Var. *wilsonii* is up to 6' tall with 12" long loose panicles of deep blue flowers.

**Related Species:**

*A. septentrionale* 'Ivorine' was raised by Alan Bloom in the early 1950's and is finally finding its way over to this country. It is a terrific compact, early flowered plant. The creamy white flowers are held in short spikes. Becoming more popular as plants become more available. If you can grow *Aconitum*, try this one.

| *-lamarckii* (la-mark-ee' eye) | | Yellow Wolfsbane | 3-4'/2' |
|---|---|---|---|
| Late Summer | Yellow | Southern Europe | Zones 3-6 |

(Syn. *A. lycoctonum* ssp. *neapolitanum, A. pyrenaicum*)

It is nice to see some yellow flowers in a genus so seemingly populated with blues and purples. The light green leaves consist of 5-7 deeply divided lobes arranged up the 4' long stalk. The plants are laden with large yellow terminal racemes of flowers in late summer and early fall, and stems may topple on other plants when in flower. This is not altogether bad as a little touch of aconite can do wonders to some old tired plants in the fall.

**Related Species:**

*A. reclinatum*, trailing wolfsbane, is native to Virginia and Georgia and bears white to yellow flowers on weak reclining stems. It looks best falling over and through other plants in the garden. Stems grow 6-8' long.

| *-napellus* (na-pel' lus) | | Common Monkshood | 3-4'/1' |
|---|---|---|---|
| Late Summer | Dark Blue | Europe | Zones 3-6 |

Common monkshood has been in the trade for many years and easiest to locate in catalogs and garden centers. The leaves are divided to the base and divided again into linear or lance-like segments. The flowers are in spike-like terminal racemes. The popularity of *A. napellus* has declined with the introduction of newer garden cultivars but it is still an outstanding plant. Although plants are toxic, the ground-up leaves have been used as an external treatment for rheumatism and neuralgia and internally to relieve fevers.

**Cultivars:**

'Album' bears white flowers on erect 3-4' tall stems.

'Carneum' is a pink-flowered form that is sometimes offered as 'Roseum' or 'Rubellum'. The pink color adds a new dimension to *Aconitum*, but plants must be grown where night temperatures are consistently cool or flowers fade to a washed out white. Spectacular where happy.

## Quick Key to Aconitum Species

A. Flowers cream colored to yellow . . . . . . . . . . *A. lamarckii*
AA. Flowers not yellow, generally blue, violet or purple
   B. Plants usually greater than 5' tall . . *A. carmichaelii* var. *wilsonii*
   BB. Plants usually less than 5' tall
      C. Leaves dissected all the way to base
         D. Inflorescence dense, not usually
           branched, flowers single color
           E. Plants approximately 3' tall . . . . . *A.* × *cammarum*
                                 'Bressingham Spire'
           EE. Plants approximately 4–5' tall . . . . . . . . *A. napellus*
         DD. Inflorescence usually branched,
           flowers bicolored . . . . . . . *A.* × *cammarum* 'Bicolor'
      CC. Leaves dissected but not all
        the way to base . . . . . . . . . . . . . . . . . *A. carmichaelii*

**Additional Reading:**

Cohen, S. 1994. Perennials for a brilliant finale. *Fine Gardening* 40:30–33.
Gilbert, Susan. 1985. Monkshood. *Horticulture* 63(9):50–53.
Lovejoy, Ann. 1992. Monkshoods and wolfsbanes. *Horticulture* 70(6):36–40.
Mussel, H. 1986. A study of the cultivars of *Aconitum napellus* and *A. variegatum* complex according to the characteristics for destination of the inferior taxa. *Acta Horticulturae* 182:89–93.

*Acorus* (aye' cor-us)          Sweet Flag          Araceae

    Looking at this fine genus, one would guess that they are closer to the grass or iris family than to the Jack-in-the-Pulpit family. The flowers are rather inconspicuous and plants are mainly grown for their handsome grass-like foliage. They are naturalized in shallow water by lakes and slow rivers, therefore excellent for wet areas or bog gardens. While wet conditions are important, they may also be grown in well-irrigated garden conditions. Terrific plants that have earned a spot in the American garden.

## Quick Reference to Acorus Species

|  | Height (ft.) | Foliage highly fragrant |
|---|---|---|
| *A. calamus* | 2–4 | Yes |
| *A. gramineus* | ½–1 | No |

*-calamus* (kal' a-mus)    Sweet Flag          2–3'/2'
   Spring        Foliage     Asia, SE United States     Zones 4–8

    The foliage, which resembles a large flag iris, releases a pleasing cinnamon scent when crushed or broken. One of the first air fresheners, sweet flag leaves were strewn around rooms to counteract the smells of cooking or garbage. An aromatic group of chemicals known as Oil of Calamus are extracted from the foliage and rhizomes and is still available. Leaves also contain a chemical, asarone, which was also used for a flavoring ingredient but is no longer used.

The leaves may be 4' tall, but most forms are about 2–2½'. The flowers are minute and greenish, on a 2–3" long spadix without the ornamental spathe seen in most members of this family. Full sun is preferred but partial shade is tolerated.

Propagate by division when plants become crowded.

### Cultivars:
'Variegatus' is the most popular cultivated form and bears long narrow leaves with clean lines of creamy white bands. Terrific by or in the pond.

| *-gramineus* (gram-in' ee-us) | Dwarf Sweet Flag | 6–12"/12" |
|---|---|---|
| Spring     Foliage | Eastern Asia | Zones 5–8 |

The differences between this species and the previous include smaller stature, pendulous sedge-like leaves and a greater choice of cultivars. The foliage is not as aromatic as *A. calamus*, but the greater choices of leaf color and stature provide worthy plants for the garden. Plants perform well in partial shade to full sun where they form a wide clump, often being used as a slow growing ground cover. The flowers are small and the spadix is enveloped in a 2–3" long spathe, but without doubt, the flowers are secondary to the foliage. The species is not always available, but many of the selections are terrific.

### Cultivars:
'Licorice' is a recent introduction from the US Arboretum and is one of the plants that has to be abused to be enjoyed. Rub up against the foliage or dig a few roots and the anise scent will be quite obvious. From the outside, it is similar to the species.

'Masamune' is a dwarf form (6–8") with creamy variegation on the narrow leaves.

'Minimus' is only 3" tall with dark green leaves. 'Minimus Aureus' is a golden form of this dwarf cultivar, which is a sock-knocker offer, particularly when combined with some of the purple heucheras.

'Oborozuki' is a robust grower with green leaves and yellow variegation. Plants grow 10–12" tall.

'Ogon' has been the most popular cultivar and for good reason. The fan-like leaves appear golden yellow because of the chartreuse and cream variegations on the evergreen foliage. Plants are 8–10" tall.

'Tanimanoyuki' can't be pronounced but can be enjoyed. The green leaves are brushed with yellow along the blades.

'Pusillus Nanus' bears fan-shaped fronds of 2–4' tall, dark green foliage. Hard to find much difference between this and 'Minimus'.

'Variegatus' grows about 12″ tall and bears narrow leaves nicely striped with cream.

'Yodonoyuki' has variegated, pale green leaves. Growing about 12″ tall, the foliage is slightly more muted than 'Ogon'.

<u>Quick Key to Acorus Species</u>

    A. Leaves iris-like with a distinct midrib,
      plants usually over 2′ tall . . . . . . . . . . . . . . . . . *A. calamus*
    AA. Leaves sedge-like without a distinct midrib,
      plants usually less than 2′ tall . . . . . . . . . . . *A. gramineus*

*Actaea* (ak-tee′-a)          Baneberry          Ranunculaceae

The three common species of *Actaea* are grown for their compound leaves and colorful berries. Unfortunately, the berries and roots are poisonous, which accounts for the common name, baneberry. It is reported that eating only 6 berries can produce severe symptoms. For this reason, plants should not be grown where children and pets play. Baneberries are woodland species and do well in shady locations, particularly in moist, humus rich soil. The white flowers appear early in the spring in terminal racemes and give way to ¼″ long oval berries in late summer and early fall. The leaves are alternate and 2–3 times ternately compound.

Seed should be sown when fresh, as old seed is much more difficult to germinate uniformly. In sowing this and other genera of Ranunculaceae, place the moist seed tray at about 70° F for 3 weeks, then transfer to freezing conditions (28–30° F) for about 5 weeks. After the cold treatment, remove the tray from the freezer and place at 40–50° F until germination occurs. All this is more easily accomplished by sowing in the fall, allowing snow cover or mulch to maintain slightly freezing temperatures, followed by cool spring temperatures to satisfy the requirements. A more rapid means of propagation is by root division in the spring.

<u>Quick Reference to Actaea Species</u>

|  | Height (ft.) | Flower stalks thickened | Color of berries |
| --- | --- | --- | --- |
| *A. alba* | 2–4 | Yes | White |
| *A. rubra* | 2–4 | No | Red |
| *A. spicata* | 2–4 | No | Black |

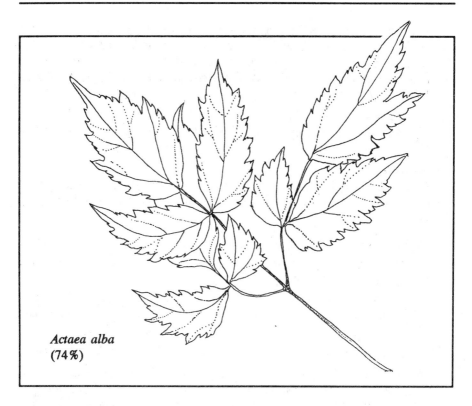

*Actaea alba*
(74%)

*-alba* (al' ba)           White Baneberry, Doll's Eye      2-4'/3'
   Late Spring    White    Eastern North America       Zones 3-7a
(Syn. *A. pachypoda*)

The ternately compound leaves are similar to those of *Astilbe*. The fringed flowers are borne in 2-4" long terminal racemes on green flower stalks well above the foliage. The flower stalks (pedicels) become thicker and turn a pinkish red as the white berries develop. Although the fruit of *A. alba* and *A. rubra* usually are different colors, there is a red-fruited form of *A. alba*, making the shape of the pedicel the best means of distinguishing the two species. This is a handsome plant for the shady area of a woodland setting or border. The deep green leaves appear fresh well into the late summer, and the berries provide interest into late fall. Abundant moisture is required in areas of hot summers. I coaxed mine along in the Armitage garden for a few years, but it kicked its legs up and finally succumbed.

*-rubra* (rew' bra)           Red Baneberry          2-4'/3'
   Spring       White    North America         Zones 3-7a

The flowers appear about a week earlier, are larger and not as fringed as those of the previous species. The ¼" long red berries are borne on slender green pedicels which turn red as they mature. The berries are particularly poisonous, and roots are violent purgatives, irritants, and emetics. The leaves are usually more hairy than those of *A. alba*, but, except for the color of fruit and shape of pedicels, few differences exist. Plants require the same growing conditions as *A. alba*.

**Cultivars:**
'Neglecta' is a white berried form with slender stalks. Plants are also a little taller.

**Related Species:**
*A. spicata*, also known as *A. nigra*, black baneberry, is similar to *A. rubra* but has jet black berries (also very poisonous) carried on short, black slender pedicels.

Quick Key to Actaea Species

A. Pedicels swollen, fruit usually white . . . . . . . . . . . . *A. alba*
AA. Pedicels slender, fruit usually not white
     B. Fruit usually red . . . . . . . . . . . . . . . . . . . . . *A. rubra*
     BB. Fruit usually black . . . . . . . . . . . . . . . . . . . *A. spicata*

## *Adenophora* (a-den-off' or-a)     Ladybells     Campanulaceae

The ladybells are often confused with members of *Campanula* but are unique in having a thick, disc-like structure at the base of the style of the flower. If you really don't relish the thought of tearing apart flowers to find such mundane organs, it is helpful to know that *Adenophora* has numerous branched, slender stems and nodding, bell-shaped, lilac-blue flowers. The leaves are alternate and sessile or have very short petioles. Plants prefer a rich, well-drained soil in full sun or partial shade. In Montreal, I regarded *Adenophora* as an innocuous weedy member of gardens. Although better behaved in Georgia, I still have trouble getting excited about it. More tolerant of heat than many of the campanulas, it may be included in the southern garden where other members of the Campanulaceae must be excluded. There are about 50 species, and, although the most available members are *A. confusa* and *A. lilifolia* (often incorrectly listed as *A. liliifolia*), occasionally species such as *A. pereskiifolia* and *A. bulleyana* may be offered.

Quick Reference to Adenophora Species

|  | Height (in.) | Leaf arrangement | Flower color |
|---|---|---|---|
| *A. confusa* | 24–30 | Alternate | Blue, lilac |
| *A. lilifolia* | 18–24 | Alternate | Blue, lilac |
| *A. pereskiifolia* | 24–30 | Whorled | Blue, purple |

| *-confusa* (con-fuse' a) | | Common Ladybells | 2–2½'/2' |
|---|---|---|---|
| Late Spring | Blue | China | Zones 3–7 |
| (Syn. *A. farreri*) | | | |

This 2–2½' tall species bears ¾" long, nodding, bell-shaped, deep blue flowers in late spring. The leaf bases are 2–3" wide and tapered. The flowers have entire petals, open in late May to early June and continue for about 3–4 weeks. Seed is fine and should be mixed with sand or talcum powder to insure even distribution. Press seed in gently, do not cover. Keep seed tray at 70–75° F soil temperature and moist at all times. Germination takes 2–3 weeks. The roots are deep, fleshy and therefore difficult to divide or move without significant damage.

**Related Species:**

*A. stricta* is only beginning to be produced by overseas nurseries and will take a while to find its way to America, but it looks like a most handsome plant. Seed of *A. stricta* var. *sessilifolia* was brought to England by Roy Lancaster of Hampshire, England from northwest Sichuan, China. Nodding, blue, bell-shaped flowers are produced on a branching raceme over kidney-shaped, basal leaves. The lower leaves are stalked while the upper ones are sessile. It was originally identified as *A. aurita*, and plants may appear in catalogs that way.

*A. triphylla* is a charming, 12–20" tall plant which flowers in late summer and fall. Long exserted styles protrude from the blue to violet flowers. The leaves are whorled, usually four per whorl. Native to China, hardy to zones 4–7.

| *-lilifolia* (lily-foe' lee-a) | | Lilyleaf Ladybells | 1½–2'/1½' |
|---|---|---|---|
| Late Spring | Pale Blue | Europe | Zones 3–7 |

This species resembles *A. confusa* but is not as tall, and the flowers are paler blue or creamy white. The style of the flowers is obviously exserted (projects from the petals), whereas the style of the former is only slightly so. The petals are finely serrated, and the leaves are narrower (approximately 1" wide). This species tolerates heat better than *A. confusa* and is a good plant for southern gardeners.

**Related Species:**

*A. bulleyana* is native to western China and differs from the above species by having glossy green, ovate leaves with single serrations. The leaves are wider than the above species, all but the uppermost being about 1" wide. The pale blue flowers are often borne in threes. Handsome but uncommon.

*A. pereskiifolia* bears purple bell flowers on 2–2½' tall stems. The whorled leaves are pointed and slightly hairy. Excellent plants for heat and humidity.

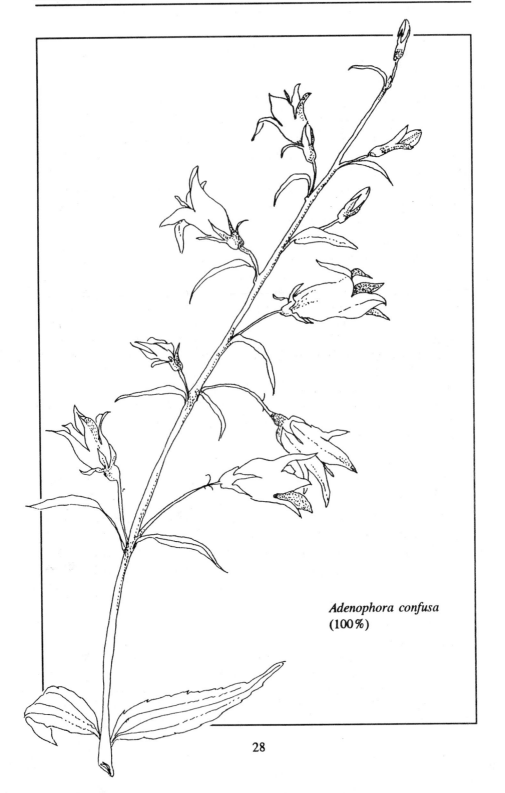

*Adenophora confusa*
(100%)

## Quick Key to Adenophora Species

    A. Leaves whorled . . . . . . . . . . . . . . . . . . . *A. pereskiifolia*
AA. Leaves alternate
      B. Style of flower much exserted,
          calyx lobes finely serrated . . . . . . . . . . . . . . *A. lilifolia*
      BB. Style of flower slightly exserted,
          calyx lobes entire . . . . . . . . . . . . . . . . . . . *A. confusa*

**Additional Reading:**

Bailey, L.H. 1953. *The Garden of Bellflowers*. The Macmillan Co., NY. 155 p. This classic book provides information about the many genera known as bellflowers, including *Adenophora*.

Lancaster, R. 1993. *Adenophora stricta* var. *sessilifolia*. *The Garden* 118(9):418–419.

## *Adiantum* (add-ee' an-tum)      Maidenhair Fern      Adiantaceae

The maidenhairs provide some of the most handsome ferns in the garden. The stems are usually dark purple to black, and the blades are arranged in fan-like segments. Of the 200 or so species, only two or three are offered to gardeners, but a few additional species are sufficiently cold tolerant to be used, if spores or plants are available. The northern maidenhair, *A. pedatum*, is the most cold hardy while the delta maidenhair, *A. raddianum*, and southern maidenhair, *A. capillus-veneris*, are best grown south of zone 7. Trailing or walking maidenhair, *A. caudatum*, is native to the tropics but its long pendulous fronds and attractively lobed segments make a handsome summer fern.

The maidenhairs do not perform as well in deep shade as other species. An area with bright filtered light and good air circulation is made for maidenhairs. Well-drained alkaline soils are best and may be provided with the addition of marble chips or dolomitic lime.

Plants are relatively easy to produce from spores. Sand and peat moss at a pH of about 6.5–8.5 is satisfactory.

## Quick Reference to Adiantum Species

| | Height (in.) | Foliage arranged in horseshoe shape on stem |
| --- | --- | --- |
| *A. capillus-veneris* | 12–18 | No |
| *A. pedatum* | 12–20 | Yes |

*-capillus-veneris* (ca-pill' us ven-er'is)   Southern Maidenhair   12–18"/12"
   Spring     Light Green Foliage         Europe, Tropics        Zones 7–10

Southern maidenhair fern is widely distributed from semi-tropical to tropical areas and often grown as a greenhouse plant. Although plants are difficult to grow in temperate areas due to lack of cold tolerance and susceptibility to disease, they are showstoppers where they are happy. I remember the row of southern maidenhairs at the Southern Living headquarters in Birmingham, AL, and the bright light and sheltered location made these plants glisten. The petioles are dark brown to black, and the lacy, delicate foliage is light green, particularly when young. Steve Bender at Southern Living recommends southern maidenhair combined with white caladiums and nipponlily, *Rohdea japonica* as an outstanding combination. Bright light is essential for good growth, and, if overgrown with other plants, they tend to develop dark spots on the fronds and decline. Good air movement and basic pH are recommended.

### Cultivars:
'Fimbriatum' has segments cut into deeply-cut, finger-like lobes.
'Imbricatum' is smaller with cascading fronds.

### Related Species:
*A. hispidulum*, rosy maidenhair, has possibilities for gardeners in the southern part of the country and as far north as zone 7. It is variable in form but generally has dark glossy green, horseshoe-shaped ferns and adaptable to a wide range of soil conditions. The new growth is rosy pink, and, in the spring, well-grown plants are outstanding. Harsh winters may damage the fronds and impede the new growth; some mulching to protect from winter winds may be useful.

*-pedatum* (pe-day' tum)        Northern Maidenhair Fern    12–20"/12"
   Spring     Mid-Green        North America, East Asia        Zones 3–8

Everyone loves this native fern and is one of the most sought after and popular ferns in temperate gardens. The northern maidenhair fern provides a graceful and lacy feel in the shaded garden and quickly spreads in moist, bright areas. They thrive in cold areas and are difficult south of zone 7. The foliage is forked and consists of 8–20 segments held in a horseshoe-like arrangement. The black, shiny stems are among the most handsome in the plant kingdom.
   Plants perform well in areas of bright filtered light and good air circulation.

### Cultivars:
Many forms have been selected or developed, but few are any better than the species.

Var. *aleuticum* is native to as far north as Alaska and is particularly cold hardy.
   The branches are pendulous and weeping; the fronds are deeply cut.

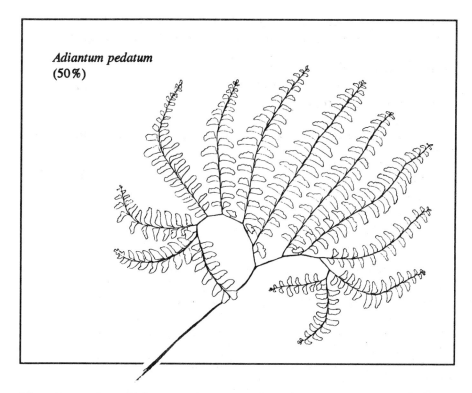

*Adiantum pedatum*
(50%)

'Eco Aurora-borealis' comes from Eco Gardens in Decateur, GA and has
fronds consisting of ruffled, overlapping segments.
'Japonicum' has pinkish bronze new fronds.
'Miss Sharples' produces larger leaflets and has a noticeable chartreuse color.
'Montanum' is much more compact and dense than the species.

### Related Species:

*Adiantum raddianum*, Delta Maidenhair Fern, grows 1-2' tall and is
native to central and South America and only hardy in zones 8-10. Probably
the most common maidenhair in the world, it is little seen in this country
because of its lack of cold tolerance. It is renowned for its variability, with
over 60 cultivars named by fern growers. Plants grow naturally in rocky
area and bluffs and generally prefer neutral to alkaline soils. In my garden
in Athens, GA (zone 7b), plants overwinter only in mild winters and
struggle to make decent colonies. The segments are lobed, narrowly
triangular and are borne on handsome black stems. Dozens of cultivars have
been developed or selected, but few are commonly available. However, fern
organizations may supply spores or plantlets for fern fanciers.

'Bridal Veil' has drooping fronds with small teardrop segments. 'Elegans'
bears lobed, wedge-shaped segments. One of the easiest to raise. 'Variegatum'

31

produces upright fronds with segments flecked with white. Spores gathered from the strongest variegated fronds tend to produce variegated sporelings.

## Quick Key to Adiantum Species

    A. Fronds arranged in horseshoe or circular pattern . . . *A. pedatum*

   AA. Fronds not arranged in horseshoe
       pattern, hanging vertically, each
       segment distinctly wedge-shaped . . . . . . . *A. capillus-veneris*

**Additional Reading:**

Bender, Steve. 1992. A masterful mixture of leaves. *Southern Living Magazine* 27(12):54.

*Adlumia* (add-loom-ee' a)       Allegheny Vine,       Fumariaceae
                              Climbing Fumitory

This climbing biennial vine is represented by *A. fungosa*, native to the northeastern United States, thus its common names, Mountain Fringe and Allegheny Vine. The delicate, light green foliage is thrice pinnate and fern-like. Plants use the petioles of new leaves to clamber and scramble over shrubs and bushes or may be trained up arbors. The pale pink and whitish flowers are similar to those of bleeding heart plant, *Dicentra*, and are formed in hanging clusters at the axils. Plants are hardy to zone 3 and may be grown as far south as zone 7.

Plants are low and bushy the first year and then, after winter, climb as fast as helium balloons released from the football stadium. Growing 10–12' tall in a few weeks, it is one of those plants that one should plant and then get out of the way. Provide some afternoon shade for best performance. This is never going to be a mainstream garden plant, but is fun and easy to grow.

Propagate from seed; seed will self sow in areas where plants are happy.

*Adonis* (a-don' is)           Adonis           Ranunculaceae

Supposedly a favorite flower of the god Adonis, who, upon his death, was changed into this flower by the goddess Aphrodite. There are about 20 species, but only *A. amurensis* and *A. vernalis* are perennial throughout most of the country. The leaves are alternate, dissected and light green. The plants are erect but normally do not exceed 18" in height and are most effective as rock garden plants or in the front of a small border. They must be planted in masses, as one or two plants do not provide enough "flower power." Although said to perform better at a basic pH, they don't seem particularly fussy about soil as long as it is well drained. An area that receives some afternoon shade should be chosen in the South, although full sun below zone 5 is satisfactory. They are relished by slugs, and spring application of slug preventative reduces damage.

Approximately 6 weeks of temperatures below 40° F is necessary for the rhizomes to break dormancy in the spring. Both species go dormant by midsummer. Plant late-emerging perennials such as *Platycodon* or *Gladiolus* or summer annuals to cover the vacant area.

If fresh seed is sown in the spring, and if seedlings are grown in a cold frame through the summer and transplanted to the garden in the fall, plants will flower in the spring. Seed is notoriously difficult to germinate if not fresh, and even if collected from garden plants, seeds may need more than 1 year to germinate. Division is the most rapid means of multiplication, and it may be accomplished in late spring after the foliage dies down.

Quick Reference to Adonis Species

|  | Height (in.) | No. of leaves | Flower color | Flowering time |
|---|---|---|---|---|
| *A. amurensis* | 9–12 | Few | Yellow | Early Spring |
| *A. vernalis* | 12–15 | Many | Yellow | Late Spring |

| *-amurensis* (am-ew-ren' sis) | | Amur Adonis | 9–12″/12″ |
|---|---|---|---|
| Early Spring | Yellow | Japan, Manchuria | Zones 4–7 |

This species flowers as early as February in southern gardens and progressively later further north. The stems are branched, each stem branch bearing triangular, 3–6″ long leaves which are cut into 3 sections to the base. Each section in turn is divided into linear segments. At the base of each petiole are leafy stipules. The 2″ wide flowers are usually buttercup-yellow but may occasionally be white, rose, or have red stripes. Each flower has 20–50 petals slightly longer than the sepals and appears just before the leaves fully emerge.

The leaves are deep red and unfurled as the flowers begin to open. If the weather remains cool when flowers open, they persist for up to 6 weeks, less if hot weather comes along. The golden flowers contrast well with the reticulated iris (*I. reticulata*), crocus, and other spring flowering bulbs.

Propagation is best accomplished by division in late spring or early summer.

### Cultivars:

'Flore-plena' is a commonly grown double cultivar and is much showier than the species.

'Fukuju Kai' has fully open, sulphur yellow flowers and is the earliest to bloom. Other cultivars having copper, orange, pink, and white flowers have been developed by Japanese nurserymen but have not been widely distributed.

*-vernalis* (ver-nah' lis)     Spring Adonis, Pheasant's Eye     12–15"/12"
  Spring      Yellow      Europe                                 Zones 4–7

This species is more winter hardy (zone 3 with protection) than the former and flowers 3–6 weeks later. It differs from the previous species by having unbranched stems, and the many stem leaves are sessile (no petioles) and 1–2" long. The flowers have fewer petals than *A. amurensis* (10–15), are slightly toothed, and about 2½" wide. They open flat as a dinner plate, as if knowing their time in the sun was fleeting, to be enjoyed while they can. Plants do not go completely dormant as do *A. amurensis*.

Propagation is more difficult than *A. amurensis* and may take several years to recover from the disturbance of dividing.

**Related Species:**

*A. apennina* is similar to *A. vernalis* but has larger flowers (up to 3"), and the lower leaves are rounded and sheathlike.

Quick Key to Adonis Species

    A. Stem leaves few, petioled, stem
       branched, petals 20–50 . . . . . . . . . . . . . . . . . *A. amurensis*
    AA. Stem leaves many, sessile,
       stem not branched, petals 10–15 . . . . . . . . . . . . *A. vernalis*

*Aegopodium* (aye-go-pow' dee-um)   Goutweed, Bishop's Weed   Apiaceae

About 6 species have been described in this genus, all of which grow by creeping rhizomes and can be incredibly invasive. The foliage occurs in threes, and the flowers are usually white or yellow. The only species commonly seen in cultivation is *A. podagraria*, bishop's weed.

*-podagraria* (pod-a-grair' ee-a)   Bishop's Weed          6–9"/spreading
  Late Spring        White      Europe, Western Asia       Zones 2–8

Some people politely call this plant "fast growing and one which fills in well." However, it is invasive and jumps and frolics through the garden. This in no way diminishes its value, for if areas require some greenery or soil must be conserved, this plant is perfect. The leaves are produced in two groups of three (biternate), and creamy white flowers are produced in late spring and summer. In Montreal, this plant was everywhere; in Michigan, it was not much different. However, in the southeastern United States, plants are somewhat better behaved. It is still invasive but requires a few more minutes to take over. Plants are tolerant of nearly all soils, prefer partially shaded areas and do not reproduce as well in full sun. Plants

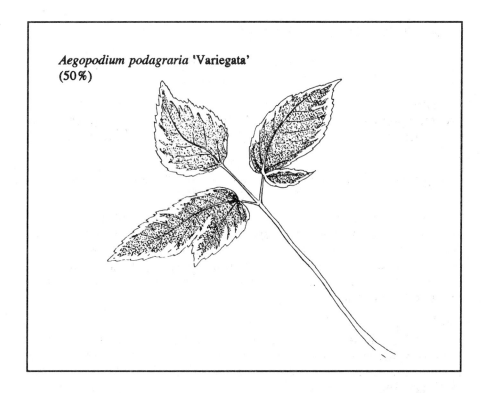

*Aegopodium podagraria* 'Variegata'
(50%)

multiply with creeping rhizomes and move quicker with cooler soil temperatures. This plant also looks good in nursery pots; therefore, it is a favorite of nurserypeople who sell weeds in a pot. Creativity is alive in America.

## Cultivars:

'Variegata' is more common than the species and much more ornamental. The green leaves bear creamy white margins but plants are only a little less invasive. The leaves, however, are clean and bright, and, if this genus must be used, the variegated form is far more handsome. I yank it up from my garden and stick it in the woods to brighten them up, and it still does well.

## *Aethionema* (ieth-ee-o-nee' ma)          Stonecress          Brassicaceae

*Aethionema* has been slow to be embraced in the United States and Canada; one reason is that it is considered an alpine plant only. Plants do poorly in warm climates, although they can be fall planted for spring enjoyment. After flowering, they may decline. In northern areas, *Aethionema* is underused. Some handsome species and cultivars are available, and, given sharp drainage, they are easily grown. All flowers consist of 4 petals and 4 sepals.

35

## Quick Reference to Aethionema Species

|  | Height (in.) | Flower color | Foliage color |
|---|---|---|---|
| *A. armeneum* | 6–9 | Pink | Light green |
| *A. grandiflorum* | 12–20 | Rose-red | Blue-green |
| *A. iberideum* | 6–9 | White | Blue-green |

| *-armeneum* (ar-meen' e-um) | Turkish Stonecress | 8–12″/12″ |
|---|---|---|
| Spring    Pink-White | Turkey, Caucasus | Zones 5–7 |

This is a very variable species with narrow, linear, light green to gray-green leaves and whitish pink flowers held in tightly clustered racemes. They dislike moist clay soils and shade and are best on sunny, well-drained slopes or raised beds. Plants respond well to slightly alkaline soils. It is difficult to find the species, but a couple of handsome cultivars can usually be located in the trade.

### Cultivars:
'Warley Rose' is the most popular stonecress and carries brilliant, dark pink flowers densely borne over 6–8″ tall mats of gray-green foliage. Introduced in the early 1920's by the eccentric Mrs. Wilmot of Warley House, England.
'Warley Ruber' has dark maroon flowers.

### Related Species:
*A. oppositifolium* is only 1–2″ tall but makes handsome mats of pink-lilac flowers. Perfect for the rock garden, this woody-based plant creeps from rock to rock.

| *-grandiflorum* (gran-di-flo' rum) | Persian Stonecress | 12–20″/15″ |
|---|---|---|
| Spring    Rose-Pink | Western Asia | Zones 5–7 |

(Syn. *A. pulchellum*)

Plants produce dozens of flowers in crowded, upright, terminal racemes which are showy for many weeks. The rose-colored flowers bear petals about 4 times as long as the sepals. The blue-green leaves are needle-like, and the base of the plant becomes woody.

### Related Species:
*A. cordifolium* is similar to *A. grandiflorum* but is smaller in almost every way. The foliage has a blue-green hue. Plants grow to 8″, and the flowers are only about ⅓″ long. Native to Lebanon.

**-iberideum** (i-be-ri′ dee-um)    Iberis Stonecress    6-9″/12″
   Spring        White       Eastern Mediterranean    Zones 5-7

The white flowers are similar to those of *Iberis*, thus its common name. Gray-green, silvery mats of leaves carry many small, fragrant flowers less than 1″ long in a terminal raceme. Plants require excellent drainage and are best used as rock garden plants or in raised beds. The diminutive height and free flowering nature of this plant make it highly sought after by alpine enthusiasts. In warm humid climates, it melts like an ice cream cone.

Quick Key to Aethionema Species

   A. Flowers white . . . . . . . . . . . . . . . . . . . . . . *A. iberideum*
  AA. Flowers not white
     B. Plants usually greater than 12″ tall . . . . . . . *A. grandiflorum*
   BB. Plants usually less than 12″ tall . . . . . . . . . . *A. armeneum*

## *Agapanthus* (ag-a-pan′ thus)    African Lily    Alliaceae

Agapanthus is a rhizomatous plant with fleshy roots and elongated, leathery leaves. Most species have strap-shaped, glossy, dark green 2-3′ long leaves. The flowers are carried in a rounded umbel on a thick scape and appear in late summer. In favorable climates, plants are extremely tough and durable. In areas of Britain, southern Europe and throughout Australia and New Zealand, "Aggies" are common and long lasting, being used as edgings, roadway dividers and hedging. It appears that broad-leaved forms are less winter hardy than narrow-leaved forms. Although species such as *A. praecox* (formerly *A. umbellatus*) and *A. campanulatus* are fully hardy in areas of California and Florida, the hardiest and most available forms of Agapanthus are the hybrids, particularly the popular 'Headbourne Hybrids'. In north Georgia (zone 7b), it is difficult to overwinter *Agapanthus*, yet there are areas as far north as zone 5, where winter temperatures may reach −10° F, where they overwinter. Moderation of temperatures by a lake effect, sandy well-drained soils, and snow cover help create this unusual situation. For the majority of gardeners in this country, *Agapanthus* should be treated as potted plants for deck, porch or around a garden pool to be brought into a frost-free area during the winter.

Allow the crowns to dry out over the rest period and begin adding water as spring approaches. The crowns should be set approximately 2″ below ground level, watered well and left undisturbed. During the growing season, plants require copious amounts of water and must not be allowed to dry out.

**Cultivars:**

Many beautiful garden forms and hybrids have been developed, and a few are gaining popularity. Some cultivars are particularly good for cut flowers.

'Albus' ('Albidus') bears creamy white flowers on 2-3′ tall plants.

'Alice Gloucester' has purple flower buds and stems and bears large, warm white flowers in mid to late summer.

'Blue Giant' bears rich blue trumpets on plants which may reach 3½' tall.

'Blue Moon', raised by Eric Smith of Hillier's Nursery, has densely-packed, pale blue flowers on 2-2½' tall stems.

'Blue Triumphator' is 2-3' tall and produces clean blue flowers.

'Bressingham Blue' grows about 3' tall and produces deep amethyst-blue flowers. 'Bressingham Bounty', with slightly broader leaves and large, rich blue flowers, has recently been introduced (1992). 'Bressingham White' is a vigorous plant with clean, white flowers. All arose from initial seedlings raised in 1967 at Blooms of Bressingham, Diss, England.

'Cayle's Lilac' which came from New Zealand bears soft lilac flowers on 15-18" tall plants with broad leaves.

'Cobalt Blue', selected by Beth Chatto of Elmstead Market, England, bears cobalt blue flowers on 2' tall plants.

'Elaine' was a wild hybrid found among seedlings at the Los Angeles State and County Arboretum. Plants bear large, dense umbels of dark violet-blue flowers. Flower stalks are up to 4' long.

'Ellamae', also selected by the Los Angeles State and County Arboretum, appears to be a cross from *A. orientalis* 'Praecox' and *A. inapertus*. Very vigorous, plants produce dozens of violet flowers on long stalks. The availability of the latter two clones will be limited until sufficient numbers can be built up through tissue culture.

'Getty White' is a hybrid with dense heads of creamy white flowers. Vigorous and handsome.

'Headborne Hybrids' arose during the 1950's and 60's from Mr. Lewis Palmer of Headbourne Worthy near Winchester, England. As a mix, they have 2-3" long, deep violet to pale blue flowers. Mr. Palmer was a leader in the breeding of Agapanthus, and many of his original crosses were used in the continued improvement of this genus, including many of the single-colored hybrid clones available today.

'Isis' bears large inflorescences (6" across) of deep blue flowers.

'Kingston Blue' is about 2' tall and produces blue-black flower buds which open to dark royal blue flowers in early summer.

'Liliput' has 8-12" long leaves, grows only 12-18" tall and produces small pendulous dark blue flowers. Terrific for containers but slow to divide.

'Loch Hope' is one of the finest blue agapanthus in cultivation today. It is late flowering and produces flowers of the deepest violet atop 4-5' tall stems. In many of the older blue selections, the flowers faded to an unsightly reddish purple. This is not the case with this hybrid, as the flowers maintain their deep color until they fall from the plant.

'Peter Pan' is a dwarf (about 12" tall) cultivar with narrow foliage and handsome sky blue flowers. Excellent in containers.

'Profusion' grows to 3' in height and bears many light to dark blue flowers. The variability in flower color produces a striped effect when in flower.

'Snow Drops' is a dwarf form with white flowers. Introduced from New Zealand.

'Snowy Owl' is an excellent clone with creamy white flowers on 3' high stems.

'Streamline' arose from Auckland Botanical Garden, is about 18" tall and produces blue flowers.

'Tinkerbell' is a short (10–12" tall) plant with variegated foliage consisting of light green leaves with narrow, clean white edges. The foliage is truly beautiful, but plants seldom flower. As beautiful as the foliage is, it simply looks like a variegated liriope if the blue flowers don't appear. Beautiful when placed in sunny, moist area.

'White Christmas' is about 2' tall when not in flower, but the white spires of flowers reach nearly 5' in height.

**Related Species:**

*A. inapertus* bears long, narrow, blue-green foliage on 2–3' tall plants. I have always admired the plants in the British Isles but have not seen many in this country. The tubular flowers are dark blue, erect at first, then becoming pendulous. Sometimes the var. *pendulus* can be found where the flowers droop all the time. A white form, 'Alba', also occurs.

**Additional Reading:**

Higginbotham, J.S. 1990. New plants for 1990. *American Nurseryman* 171(2):40–47.

## *Agastache* (a-gah' sta-kee)          Anise Hyssop          Lamiaceae

A genus consisting of approximately 20 species, mostly native to southwest United States and Mexico, often smelling of licorice or other child-like fragrances. Plants produce many spikes of flowers in red, orange and red although yellow flowers are occasionally seen (*A. nepatoides*). A few species such as Mexican Hyssop, *A. mexicana*, and Orange-flowered Hyssop, *A. coccinea*, are hardy only to zone 7 or 8, but others like *A. barberi* and Rock Anise Hyssop, *A. rupestris*, are cold hardy to zone 5 or 6. Many species are native to the United States and a good deal of hybridization has taken place, resulting in some excellent garden plants. All species do well in full sun and slightly alkaline well-drained soils.

Quick Reference to Agastache Species

|                 | Height (in.) | Flower color  |
| --------------- | ------------ | ------------- |
| *A. cana*       | 12–36        | Rose-pink     |
| *A. foeniculum* | 20–30        | Purple        |
| *A. rugosa*     | 24–30        | Violet-rose   |
| *A. rupestris*  | 36–48        | Orange-salmon |

*-cana* (can' a)                    Mosquito Plant                 1–3'/2'
   Late Spring          Pink, Rose        Southwest United States        Zones 6–9

The blue-green foliage and pink-rose tubular flowers on many branched stems make this an excellent plant to try in the garden. The color of the flowers are difficult to describe, as people call them deep rose, off-pink, near scarlet and various combinations thereof. The upright racemes consist of 6–12 flowers held in each whorl. The whorls are loosely arranged on 12–18″ flowering stems. The foliage is fragrant but not nearly as much as *A. rupestris*. Full sun and well-drained soils are essential.

Propagate from seed at 72° F and high humidity.

*-foeniculum* (foe-nick' ew-lum)        Anise Hyssop           20–30″/30″
   Summer              Purple            North America          Zones 6–9

Growing tall, bearing many flower stems which are easily dried, anise hyssop is a favorite for cut flower producers and gardeners alike. The flowers are tightly arranged in long dense racemes. The flowers range from lavender to purple and the foliage is distinctly anise-like. They perform well in full sun but get tall and lanky if grown in too much shade. Easily propagated by seed.

**Cultivars:**

'Alba' ('Alabaster') is a common, creamy white form of the species.
'Licorice Blue' and 'Licorice White' bear lavender-blue and off-white
   flowers respectively.

*-rugosa* (rew-go' sum)                 Anise Hyssop            24–30″/2'
   Summer           Violet-Rose        China, Japan            Zones 5–8

This oriental native is offered by a number of nurseries because of enhanced cold tolerance. The branching flower stems carry violet-rose whorled flowers on 2–3' tall plants over fragrant foliage. The leaves are 2–3″ long and 2″ wide with serrated margins and are pubescent chiefly along the veins on the underneath. Not as ornamental as other species but a good performer.

**Cultivars:**

'Alba' is a white-flowered form of the species.

*-rupestris* (rew-pes' tris)          Rock Anise Hyssop          3–4'/3'
   Summer        Salmon-Orange      Southwest United States       Zones 5–8

The striking, rosy-orange, verticillate flowers and gray-green foliage provide a lovely wildflower to add color to the garden. One of the hardiest of the native hyssops, it has been used to incorporate cold tolerance to a number of hybrids. The flower color is unusual, and flowering persists for at least 8 weeks. The best part of these plants is the fragrance of the foliage. People keep coming

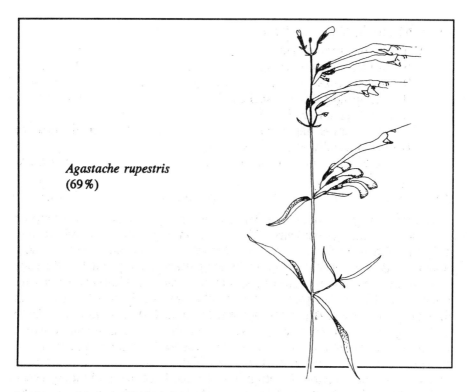

*Agastache rupestris*
(69%)

back to get their sniff, then bring their friends to get theirs. I call it the licorice plant, and plants transport me to the old-fashioned candy store.

Full sun and well-drained soils are necessary.

**Hybrids:**
'Apricot Sunrise' is a cross between *A. coccinea* and *A. auriantica*, hybridized by Richard Dufresne of North Carolina, and bears many 1½" golden orange tubular flowers.

'Firebird', also from Richard Dufresne, is a hybrid of *A. coccinea* and *A. rupestris* and bears many orange-salmon flowers on 3' tall plants. Plants are fuller than either of the parents and are cold hardy to zone 6. Terrific plant for hummingbirds.

'Fragrant Delight' produces pale blue flowers on 3' tall stems. The foliage is particularly fragrant.

'Pink Panther' (*A. coccinea* × *A. mexicana*) grows 3–4' tall and produces many 1½" long, tubular, rose-pink flowers held in long racemes, starting in mid summer.

'Tutti Frutti' (*A. barberi* × *A. mexicana*) has tubular, pink flowers from mid summer to frost. The foliage, to some noses, smells like tutti frutti. What does tutti frutti smell like, anyway?

Quick Key to Agastache Species
  A. Plants much branched
    B. Flowers salmon-orange ................. *A. rupestris*
    BB. Flowers rose ......................... *A. cana*
  AA. Plants upright, little branched
    B. Plants usually 2–3' tall,
      lower leaves finely hairy ............. *A. foeniculum*
    BB. Plants usually 4' tall, lower
      leaves hairy along veins only .......... *A. rugosa*

## *Ajuga* (a-jew' gah)       Bugle Weed       Lamiaceae

Approximately 40 species are known; however, only three have become available to American gardeners. They grow in any reasonably well-drained soil, and, although tolerant of full sun, growth is more rapid in partial shade. *Ajuga reptans* can become a persistent weed particularly if planted on the edge of a lawn, but other slower growing species are available. Flowers of *Ajuga* are usually violet-blue, but pink- and white-flowered cultivars have also been developed. All have square stems, opposite leaves and whorled flowers. A large drift of *Ajuga* in full bloom is spectacular, but the foliage is the main reason for its popularity. In the South, crown rot (caused by *Sclerotium rossii*) can be a problem, particularly with *A. reptans*. Entire plantings may die or large patches develop infection. Planting in well-ventilated areas, dividing every 2–3 years, and application of fungicides help reduce this problem. If the affected leaves are cut away and disposed of when temperatures cool down, plants often recover without lasting damage.

Seed should be sown in late summer for fall planting or in November for spring planting. Cultivars will not come true-to-type from seed, but cuttings and divisions may be used. Division may be accomplished any time the ground is workable. Tissue culture techniques have also been developed.

Quick Reference to Ajuga Species

|  | Height (in.) | Stoloniferous | Stems (erect or prostrate) |
|---|---|---|---|
| *A. genevensis* | 6–12 | No | Erect |
| *A. pyramidalis* | 6–9 | No | Erect |
| *A. reptans* | 4–12 | Yes | Prostrate |

**-genevensis** (gen-e-ven' sis)      Geneva Bugle Weed      6–12"/9"
    Summer       Various       Europe       Zones 4–9

This upright species is becoming more popular because it spreads less vigorously than *A. reptans* but grows faster than *A. pyramidalis*. If constant moisture is provided, it tolerates more sun than *A. pyramidalis* or *A. reptans*. The dark green basal leaves are coarsely toothed, hairy, and about 3″ long. The upper leaves are 1–3″ long, sessile and only slightly serrated. The 2″ tall flower spikes are usually blue but may be pink or white. Although most *Ajuga* grow in zone 3, this species should receive winter protection in zone 4.

**Cultivars:**
'Alba' bears creamy white flowers.
'Pink Beauty' is 4–5″ tall with light pink flowers in May and June.
'Robusta' is more vigorous and produces larger flowers and bigger foliage.
    Flowers are lavender-blue.
'Rosea' has rosy-pink flowers but is otherwise identical to the species.
'Tottenham' is the best cultivar, bearing dense spikes of lilac-pink flowers.
'Variegata' has dark green leaves, mottled creamy white.

**Related Species:**
    *A.* × 'Brockbankii' (*A. genevensis* × *A. pyramidalis*) is a smaller, more vigorous form of the species with deep blue flowers and shorter stolons.

| | | |
|---|---|---|
| *-pyramidalis* (pi-ra-mid-ah′ lis) | Upright Bugle Weed | 6–9″/9″ |
| Late Spring      Blue | Europe | Zones 3–9 |
| (Syn. *A. alpina*) | | |

This good-looking plant incorporates the fine flowers and dark foliage of *A. reptans* without the spreading habit. The basal rosette is slightly toothed and hairy. The stems are hairy, and the 4–6″ long flower spikes consist of large purple bracts which appear to press against the blue flowers. The leaves subtending the flowers are 2–4 times as long as the violet-blue flowers. Although the plant does not spread as rapidly as *A. reptans*, it does produce short stolons late in the season in response to short days.

**Cultivars:**
'Alba' produces crinkled, oval leaves and white flowers.
'Metallica-crispa' ('Crispa') has deep blue flowers and brownish red, crinkly foliage with a metallic luster. It is an outstanding garden plant. Also listed as 'Metallica-crispa Purpurea' and 'Min Crispa Red'.

**Related Species:**
    *A. australis* is native to eastern Australia and is a 3–4″ tall mat former. The thick, dark green, pubescent (hairy) leaves are aromatic when crushed, and the light blue flowers rise to about 8″ in height. Probably effective in zones 6–9. Underused and well worth trying.

**-reptans** (rep' tanz)     Common Bugle Weed     4–12"/24"
    Late Spring     Violet     Europe     Zones 3–9

Much of the breeding and selection in this genus has been accomplished with *A. reptans*, and remarkable advances in foliage color have resulted. Regardless of cultivar, *A. reptans* is stoloniferous and can spread rapidly. This characteristic makes this species an excellent ground cover, and a large clump in flower is a spectacular sight. Plant where its invasive qualities are welcome, such as on a bank or under the dappled shade of trees. Do not plant it as an edging to the lawn or the insidious disease of "buglelawn" will occur. One of the symptoms includes the appearance of small islands of green foliage that soon form a large archipelago in an ocean of lawn. Weapons to destroy these islands include shovels, sprayers, or, as my neighbour Rick Lafleur did, simply expanding the flower bed to create a bugleweed garden. His lawn became smaller every year. The best prevention is proper planning; plan to keep the *Ajuga* away from all grassy areas. If all else fails, remember that the ingestion of leaves of *A. reptans* is a mild narcotic. After trying some of the leaves, buglelawn will not seem as serious.

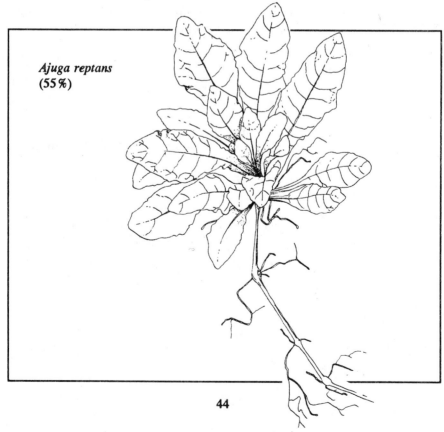

*Ajuga reptans*
(55%)

**Cultivars:**

*Selections for flower color or size.*

'Alba' has creamy white flowers.

'Pink Elf' is a dwarf cultivar with clear pink flowers.

'Pink Spire' is a fine green-leaved cultivar bearing 7" long, pink-flower spikes.

'Pink Surprise' has bronze-green leaves which are more narrow than many others and purplish pink flowers. Introduced by Terra Nova Nursery, Tigard, OR.

'Purple Torch' bears tall torches of 12" lavender-pink flowers with glossy green foliage.

'Rosea' produces rose flowers.

*Selections for leaf color, all have blue to violet flowers.* Some may be hybrids with other species.

'Arboretum Giant' comes from Tony Avent of Plant Delights Nursery in Raleigh, NC. The long, narrow, green leaves are outlined in deep purple.

'Atropurpurea' ('Purpurea') has dark bronzy-purple leaves which color best in full sun. It is an excellent landscape plant to provide drifts of bronze.

'Braunherz' ('Bronze Heart') bears glossy, wine-red leafs and deep blue flowers. Very eye-catching.

'Bronze Beauty' produces metallic bronze foliage with bright blue flowers. Very popular, very handsome selection.

'Burgundy Glow' has foliage with shades of white, pink, rose and green. In the fall, the older leaves turn a deep bronze, and the young leaves have a rosy hue. The combination is interesting if your eyes can stand the clashing hues.

'Catlin's Giant' has tall (up to 8" long) spikes of blue flowers and bronze-green foliage. Continues to produce fine foliage even after flowering and fills in rapidly.

'Cristata' is probably one of the ugliest little plants available today. The leaves are crinkled and distorted, and the whole plant looks like crumpled spinach. To each his own. May go under 'Ripple Leaf'.

'Gaiety' has bronze purple leaves and lilac flowers.

'Gray Lady' produces classy gray-green foliage and blue flowers. Growth is relatively slow, but clumps are most handsome.

'Jungle Beauty', originally introduced by Alan Bush of the late Holbrook Farms in North Carolina, bears dark purple leaves outlined with a soft red border. A similar form known as 'Jungle Beauty Improved', selected by Beth Chatto in East Anglia, England, seems to have larger leaves and more persistent purple color. Both are good selections.

'Multicolor' (syn. 'Rainbow', 'Tricolor') is similar to, but more vigorous than 'Burgundy Glow', and the foliage colors are deeper. Sometimes comments concerning leaf colors are best left to the gardener. This is one of those times.

'Pink Silver' produces bronze leaves with a touch of pink.

'Purple Brocade' is 6-8″ tall, with deep purple brocaded leaves. A slow grower, but handsome.

'Royalty' resulted as a sport of 'Gaiety'. It has some of the darkest purple flowers (almost black) with scalloped edges. Terrific cultivar.

'Silver Beauty' has grey-green leaves edged with silver-white and is particularly handsome.

'Silver Carpet' produces leaves which are uniformly silver-gray but with green margins. Plants are about 6″ tall.

## Quick Key to Ajuga Species

   A. Plant stoloniferous, stems prostrate, hairless . . . . . *A. reptans*
   AA. Plant not stoloniferous, stems upright, with long hairs
      B. Leaves coarsely toothed . . . . . . . . . . . . . . *A. genevensis*
      BB. Leaves slightly or not toothed . . . . . . . . . . *A. pyramidalis*

**Additional Reading:**

Weathers, L.A. 1992. Grow a colorful carpet of *Ajuga. Southern Living Magazine* May:54.

*Alcea* (al-see′ a)             Hollyhock             Malvaceae

Approximately 60 species of biennial and short-lived perennial species are found, and some of them are exceptionally popular. Hollyhocks, *A. rosea*, have been gracing gardens for centuries and are presently undergoing a renaissance in the United States. All species are found in sunny, well-drained habitats and provide exceptional color for short periods of time. Although hollyhock is the best known member, one or two other species provide additional interest as well. Flowers are generally large and appear singly or in racemes, and the stems are usually hairy. All can be grown from seed and require little more than sun and good air circulation.

The genus is part of the family Malvaceae, which contain similar genera, such as *Lavatera, Malva* and *Sidalcea*. Whenever my friend, Michael Dirr, and I come across a flowering hollyhock-like plant, he always asks me how to distinguish the difference between those look-alike genera. They are closely related and appear very similar, particularly to my leaden brain. Upon a close inspection, *Alcea* differs from other genera by having 6-9 bracts immediately beneath the sepals which completely envelop the emerging bud. The bracts are joined rather than separate as in the genus *Malva*. I'm not sure anyone other than Michael

46

really wants to know such things, but for those who do, I have provided a basic chart to help distinguish these genera.

|  | Bracts below sepals | Flower arrangement |
|---|---|---|
| *Alcea* | 6–9, joined | Solitary, raceme |
| *Lavatera* | 3, joined, connate-pointed | Raceme |
| *Malva* | 3, narrow, distinct | Solitary, clusters |
| *Sidalcea* | Usually none | Raceme, spike |

| *-rosea* (rose-ee′ a) | | Hollyhock | 4–8′/2′ |
|---|---|---|---|
| Spring, Early Summer | Mixed Colors | Turkey, Asia | Zones 3–7 |

My mother knew very little about gardening, other than the lawn-mower was a good way to keep her sons out of trouble. But how she loved her hollyhocks. They grew with their backs up the stucco wall of our garage, held up with ugly white strings which extended from rusty nails on either side. Like tape measures across a boxer's chest, these strings were often more visible than the plants. But every year, they would come back from roots or seeds and provide a riot of color along a otherwise drab path. By mid summer, the leaves were eaten up by rust, but by that time, hollyhocks gave way to other activities and, thus ignored, disappeared once again.

She would be pleased to see the renaissance in hollyhocks today. The old red, single flowers are still around, but so are many other colors and forms, including double flowers 5″ across. Plants are generally 3–6′ tall, but 8′ monsters are not rare. They are unbranched, thus are rather pole-like, and the stems are hairy to the point of being bristly. The leaves have 3, 5 or 7 lobes, and the flowers occur in terminal racemes, made up of 3–10 flowers. The 6–9 bracts beneath the flowers are joined together and turn brown as the flowers mature. Today's cultivars are also less susceptible to the nemesis of hollyhock, hollyhock rust. Caused by a fungus, *Puccinia malvacearum*, orange-brown pustules occur on the undersides of the leaves and stems. If my mother had known that the spores overwintered on those blistered, ignored leaves by the garage, she would have removed them. Actually, she would have told her sons to do it, and we would have probably taken the trusty Lawn Boy to them. Fungal sprays are available, but removing any affected leaves or trying different cultivars is equally effective and more satisfying.

Propagate by planting seeds directly in the prepared soil immediately after the last frost date or in containers about two weeks before that time. If sowing in containers, place the container at 72–75° F and cover the moist soil with plastic until the seedlings emerge. Do not germinate the seeds too early or plants will be weak and stretched before the transplant date.

## Cultivars:

*Single flowers:*

'Barnyard Pink-red' is offered by an enterprising nursery who claim seeds were collected from an old barnyard in Vermont. They are single, tall and old fashioned. I bet they collected them by our stucco garage.

'Indian Spring' is available in white, yellow, rose and pink. Plants are 7–8' tall.

'Nigra' has some of the deepest purple flowers of any cultivar. Plants attain about 6' in height.

'Simplex' is a mixture of colors on 4–5' tall stems.

*Double, semi-double flowers:*

'Chaters Double Hybrids' occur in a range of colors. Each double flower resembles a ruffled peony. Plants with single colors may be purchased, including 'Chaters Pink', 'Chaters Scarlet', 'Chaters Violet', 'Chaters White' and 'Chaters Yellow'.

'Nigrita' has dark, almost purple-red, double flowers.

'Pinafore' is more branched and compact than other cultivars and bears semi-double flowers in numerous colors. Plants are 3–4' tall.

'Powder Puffs' grow 6–8' tall and produce 4" wide, fully double flowers in white, yellow, rose and red.

## Related Species:

*A. ficifolia*, Antwerp hollyhock, is similar to *A. rosea*. The leaves are 7-lobed, irregularly toothed and resemble fig leaves. Flowers are mostly pale yellow (occasionally copper or orange), and the robust plants grow about 6' tall. Native to Siberia, exceptionally cold hardy.

*A. rugosa*, Russian hollyhock, is becoming more popular due to its classical form and less problem with hollyhock rust. The large, single flowers are pale yellow, and the leaves are deeply 5-lobed. The 5–6' tall stems are hairy all over.

## Related Genus:

*Althaea*, also known as hollyhock, is often confused with *Alcea*, for obvious reasons. Most of the ornamental hollyhocks belong to *Alcea*. The flowers of *Althaea* are smaller, seldom exceeding 1½" wide and usually rose, rose-pink or occasionally white. While not as flashy as *Alcea*, they are useful for naturalistic plantings. Approximately 12 species are known; the 3–5' tall *A. officinalis*, which has small rose, pink or white flowers, is best known. The roots of this species were the original source of marshmallows.

*Alchemilla* (al-kem-ill′ a)  Lady's Mantle  Rosaceae

The genus received its name because of its popularity with alchemists of old and was reputed to have many healing powers. Today we know it as a wonderful, low-growing, shade-tolerant plant with sprays of small yellow flowers in the spring. Some 300 species are known, most of which are palmately lobed and excellent garden plants. The foliage is light green, pubescent and soft to the touch, particularly on the underside. The apetalous (no petals) flowers are only about ¼″ wide and range from green to yellow. Although many species have been described, only two or three are easily located through catalogs or retail centers in the United States and Canada.

All species of *Alchemilla* require partial shade and consistent soil moisture to thrive. Plants will be stunted if planted in full sun or allowed to dry out. Cool climates are preferable, but they do quite well as far south as zone 7a, providing there is ample shade and moisture. I have grown lady's mantle in Athens, Georgia (zone 7b), and it is lovely to those who have never seen large drifts grown under favorable conditions; however, the luxuriant growth taken for granted further north is seldom attained.

Fresh seed germinates readily, but purchased or old seed should be given a cold treatment similar to *Actaea. Alchemilla* self-sows readily, which helps increase the planting size. Plants should be divided in early spring prior to flowering.

<u>Quick Reference to Alchemilla Species</u>

|  | Height (in.) | Lobes cut more than half way | Hairiness on leaves |
|---|---|---|---|
| *A. alpina* | 6–8 | Yes | Lower surface |
| *A. ellenbeckii* | 3–6 | Yes | Both surfaces |
| *A. erythropoda* | 6–9 | No | Both surfaces |
| *A. glaucescens* | 9–12 | No | Both surfaces |
| *A. mollis* | 20–24 | No | Both surfaces |

-*alpina* (al-pine′ a)  Mountain Lady's Mantle  6–8″/12″
  Spring  Green  Europe  Zones 3–7

This species is not used enough in the United States, and, although the flowers are not outstanding, the silver edges of the deeply cut, 2″ wide foliage and the low neat habit make this a wonderful garden plant. The 5-lobed leaves have small, sharp teeth at the end of each lobe and are hairy

49

on the lower surface only, being rather naked above. Self-seeding is common, and, if this becomes a problem, the seed heads should be removed prior to maturity. This is more important in the North than in the South. It is native to mountainous areas and as far north as Greenland. Cold hardiness is not a problem in most of the northern states and Canada, but they are not as heat tolerant as *A. mollis*.

**Related Species:**

*A. conjuncta* is a closely related but more robust species, growing 12–18″ tall. Leaves generally have 7 deep cut lobes but without the sharp teeth found in *A. alpina*. Often sold as *A. alpina*.

*A. sericea* is similar to *A. alpina* but has more conspicuous teeth and irregular teeth in the upper half of the leaves. The upper surface of the leaves have small hairs, whereas those of *A. alpina* are smooth.

| | | | |
|---|---|---|---|
| *-ellenbeckii* (el-len-beck-ee′ eye) | Carpet Lady's Mantle | 3–6″/12″ | |
| Spring | Yellow-Green | East Africa | Zones 5–7 |

This shade-loving little plant deserves more use in American gardens. The diminutive height and the spreading nature make this a charming ground cover for a shady nook. The 1″ wide leaves are deeply 5-lobed, and the plant spreads by rooting at the nodes. The yellow-green flowers are not as freely produced as on the larger species but are handsome nevertheless. Plants are not as cold hardy as others but should be fine to zone 5 with some protection.

Plants are best propagated vegetatively by division.

**Related Species:**

*A. abysinnica*, Abysinnian lady's mantle, is similar in spreading habit but differs in having larger (2″ across) 7-lobed leaves. Also native to East African mountains. Little is known about hardiness.

*A. faeroensis* var. *pumila* is another tiny plant, only growing 2–3″ tall. Terrific for rock gardens but can easily get gobbled up by larger plants.

| | | | |
|---|---|---|---|
| *-erythropoda* (e-rith-ro-po′ da) | Red-Stemmed Lady's Mantle | 6–9″/12″ | |
| Spring | Yellow-Green | Turkey, Russia | Zones 3–7 |

Similar to other medium size species but with small, scalloped gray or blue-green leaves and dense hairs on the petioles (leaf stalks). These diminutive plants often develop a red color on the stems when they are grown in partially sunny location. The lobes of this species look like they were cut across their width with pinking shears (called truncate in botanical circles), whereas the lobes of similar species are rounded.

**Related Species:**

*A. caucasica*, Caucasus lady's mantle, is indistinguishable from *A. erythropoda*, mainly differing in the way in which the hairs are arranged on the flowering stems.

***-glaucescens*** (glock' es-sends)    Hairy Lady's Mantle    9–12"/18"
   Spring, Summer    Yellow-Green    Europe    Zones 3–7
(Syn. *A. pubescens*)

This small plant is densely hairy throughout and bears circular leaves with 7–9 shallowly cut rounded lobes. The kidney-shaped foliage may be slightly blue-green (glaucous) but not always. Dense clusters of yellow-green flowers are produced in late spring and into summer. Similar to *A. erythropoda*.

***-mollis*** (mol' lis)    Lady's Mantle    20–24"/24"
   Spring    Yellowish    Asia Minor    Zones 4–7

The common lady's mantle is a splendid ground cover and will grow in almost any moist, shady area except a bog. The dense pubescence gives the

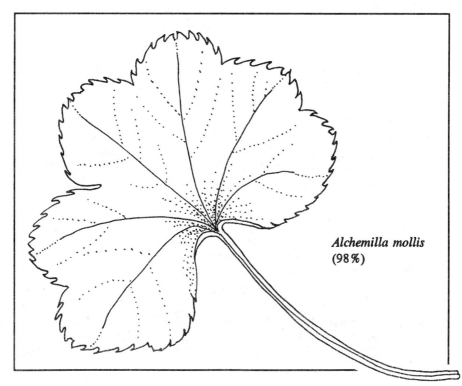

*Alchemilla mollis*
(98%)

foliage a soft velvet feel, and the yellow-green starry flowers which are held above the foliage make long-lasting cut flowers. When grown side by side, the flowers are obviously the most showy of any of the commonly seen *Alchemilla* species. The leaves, which are among the largest in the genus, have 9–11 shallow lobes and are particularly pretty after a soft rain when the captured droplets glisten in the sun. This species is too large for the rock garden but can be used successfully to edge a path or border. The densely hairy leaves create a problem in areas such as the Southeast, where thundershowers punctuate hot summer afternoons. The water trapped in the leaves and crown does not dry out during the night and provides excellent breeding grounds for a number of foliar diseases. Use of a fungicide during wet, rainy periods partially alleviates the problem.

### Cultivars:
'Auslese' is offered by a few nurseries but differs little from the species. Perhaps the flowers are more chartreuse.

'Robusta' is more robust and simply larger in every way than the species. However, since most of the *A. mollis* in cultivation is propagated from seed, there may be little difference from a vigorous seedling and this cultivar.

'Senior' is shorter than the species, growing only about 12″ tall.

'Thriller' has large pleated leaves with many chartreuse, foamy flowers.

### Related Species:
*A. vulgaris*, common lady's mantle, is similar to *A. mollis* but is less pubescent and has much smaller, greener flowers. The foliage is also more deeply lobed. Most of the plants of *A. vulgaris* sold in the United States are often *A. mollis*.

*A. xanthochlora* is a relatively large growing plant like *A. mollis*, growing 15–20″ tall. The plant differs in that the leaves are almost hairless on the upper surface and are more kidney shaped compared to the circular leaves of *A. mollis*. Good garden plants with chartreuse, airy flowers.

Quick Key to Alchemilla Species

    A. Low growing, mat forming, rooting at nodes . . .   *A. ellenbeckii*
    AA. Plants of varied habit, not normally rooting at nodes
      B. Leaves deeply incised, cut at least half way to base . .*A. alpina*
      BB. Leaves generally lobed, usually not half way to base
        C. Plants robust, more than 12″ tall, 9–11 lobes  . .  *A. mollis*
        CC. Plants smaller, usually no more than 12″ tall, 7–9 lobes
          D. Nodes rounded . . . . . . . . . . . . . . . . *A. glaucescens*
          DD. Nodes not rounded, cut across their width . .*A. erythropoda*

**Additional Reading:**

Reed, Christopher. 1987. Lady's mantle: refined company for many plants. *Horticulture* 65(1):16.

Swan, G.A. and Walters, S.M. 1988. *Alchemilla gracilis* Opiz, a species new to the British flora. *Watsonia* 17:133–138.

Walters, Max. 1991. Alchemilla update. *The Garden* 116(2):62–63.

## *Allium*     Ornamental Onion     Alliaceae

I have always enjoyed growing ornamental onions. They allow me to converse with vegetable gardeners without feelings of guilt. While they don't garnish my hamburgers, they surely embellish my garden. The genus contains approximately 500 species including onions (*A. cepa*), garlic (*A. sativum*), and chives (*A. schoenoprasum*). Although ornamental forms of chives such as the rosy-pink 'Forescate' and the dwarf 'Schnittlauch' have been selected, few consumers know anything but these tasty but breathy vegetables. All species are bulbous or rhizomatous and are characterized by the presence of a superior ovary, cymose umbels of small flowers and the emission of an onion or garlic smell when crushed. The flowers consist of many petal-like flower parts called tepals. Scientists in several locations have tried to eliminate the odor from alliums, particularly the culinary species, but I, for one, hope they have little success. An allium without odor is like a book without a cover. The odor occurs only when plants are broken or crushed and is not given off spontaneously. In fact, the flowers of some members have a mild fragrance of violets.

*Allium* used to be part of the family Liliaceae because of the superior ovary, but some taxonomists argued that the presence of the umbellate inflorescence should place *Allium* in the Amaryllidaceae. Others yet argued that a separate family, Alliaceae, should be created for all genera with a superior ovary and an umbellate inflorescence. Such is the present situation. Other genera now included under Alliaceae are *Agapanthus*, *Brodiaea*, and *Triteleia*.

The number of species has always been in question. When Carl Linnaeus (1707–1778) wrote *Species Plantarum* in 1753, he distinguished 30 species of *Allium*. Many additional species were described since Linnaeus and continue to be discovered today. There is no modern monograph of *Allium*; the last work which embraced all the known species was produced by Eduard von Regel (1815–1892) in 1875 and included 256 species. Other botanists have placed the number at 325 (1925), 400 (1976) and 700 (1987). The last word comes from William Stearn who took the major accounts of the genus, subtracted species listed in other accounts and added those not covered in any. Stearn concludes that the genus *Allium* comprises about 750 known species and is the largest genus of petaloid monocotyledons. Finally, for us gardeners, Dilys Davies wrote an eminently readable book on ornamental alliums in 1992 (see Additional Reading).

The ornamental alliums range in size from the 2–3″ high plants of *A. circinatum* to the 4′ tall scapes of *A. giganteum*. Although many alliums bear lilac-blue flowers, some species send up umbels of white (*A. neapolitanum*), pink (*A. acuminatum*), mauve (*A. validum*), yellow (*A. moly*), greenish (*A. obliquum*) or interesting multicolors (the very un-allium looking *A. siculum* var. *dioscoridis*). Most species bear 3–8 linear leaves (except *A. karataviense*) which die back before or soon after flowering. The seed heads are persistent in many species and extend the ornamental value of plants well into summer.

In general, the planting depth of the bulb is approximately 3 times the diameter. Bulbs should be fall planted in full sun and in well-drained areas. As lovely as many of these species are, they are poor plants if not combined with other perennials or annuals. Because the foliage dies during or immediately after flowering, many gaps in the garden eventually exist. Planting in ground covers such as *Vinca* or *Pachysandra* or having other plants growing around them camouflage the empty spaces. An area devoted strictly to alliums (or any genera of bulbs) is a collection, not a garden, and should be avoided like the plague.

Quick Reference to Allium Species

|  | Height (in.) | Flower color | Fragrant flowers | Flowering time |
|---|---|---|---|---|
| *A. acuminatum* | 8–12 | Pink | No | Early Summer |
| *A. aflatunense* | 24–36 | Lilac | No | Late Spring |
| *A. caeruleum* | 12–24 | Blue | No | Late Spring |
| *A. christophii* | 12–24 | Violet | No | Summer |
| *A. giganteum* | 36–60 | Lilac | No | Late Spring |
| *A. karataviense* | 6–12 | Lilac | No | Late Spring |
| *A. moly* | 12–15 | Yellow | No | Early Spring |
| *A. narcissiflorum* | 6–12 | Pink-rose | No | Spring |
| *A. neapolitanum* | 8–12 | White | Yes | Early Spring |
| *A. nigrum* | 24–36 | White | No | Early Spring |
| *A. oreophilum* | 8–12 | Violet | Yes | Early Summer |
| *A. schubertii* | 18–24 | Pink | No | Spring |
| *A. senescens* | 6–12 | Lilac-pink | Yes | Summer |
| *A. sphaerocephalum* | 18–36 | Lilac | No | Late Spring |
| *A. thunbergii* | 18–24 | Violet | Yes | Fall |
| *A. triquetrum* | 8–15 | White | No | Summer |

*-acuminatum* (a-cum-in-aye' tum)    Tapertip Onion    8–12"/12"
  Early Summer    Rose-Pink    Western North America    Zones 4–7
(Syn. *A. murrayanum*)

Two or four narrow, channelled leaves emerge from a round bulb, above which an 8" scape holds erect, star-shaped flowers with pointed segments. Many ½" long flowers form a loose umbel approximately 2" wide. The 10–30 flowers range from deep rose to lilac-pink and bloom for about 2 weeks starting the end of May. Leaves are usually withered by flowering time. Plants do best in dry areas, and in hot, rainy, climates such as the Southeast, do not often persist more than a year. Plant in a well-drained sunny location. Flowers dry well when cut from the garden, retaining color when placed in a warm, dry room.

It is a pretty plant when used in colonies of at least a dozen bulbs. Bulbils which form at the base of the bulbs result in a slow spreading colony.

*-aflatunense* (a-fla-tun-en' se)    Persian Onion    2–3'/2'
  Late Spring    Lilac    China    Zones 4–8

This is one of the taller alliums and produces fine 4" diameter spherical umbels of star-shaped flowers atop 3' tall scapes. The lilac to violet flowers have yellow anthers and tend to twist and reflex with age. Often thought of as a smaller version of *A. giganteum*, it lacks the majesty and grandeur of the latter. The bulbs, however, are available at one-third the cost and allow the gardener to plant this species with abandon. The 6–8 basal, strap-shaped basal leaves are up to 4" wide and disappear soon after the flower appears.

This is one of the few species in the genus truly at home among other plants in the border. Plants do well in any sunny, well-drained location; however, they are susceptible to root rot organisms prevalent in heavy soils. I have seen wonderful plantings in Philadelphia gardens and as far north as Cleveland. Results in the South have been variable. Some years it is outstanding, other years, disappointing. This may be due to the fact that a number of impostors are sold under the banner of *A. aflatunense*. The flowers are excellent cut and persist nearly 2 weeks.

Seed should be sown in moist seed trays and placed at about 70° F for 2–4 weeks, then placed at 30–40° F for an additional 4–6 weeks. After the cold treatment, bring the tray to 50–60° F until germination occurs. Keep moist at all times. Plants self-sow on the West coast and occasionally in the Northeast.

Cultivars:

'Purple Sensation' has deeper violet flowers and are more uniform than the species. A little more expensive, but more handsome.

**Hybrids:**

Hybrids of *A. macleanii* and *A. aflatunense* were developed by F. Bijl van Duyvenbode of J. Bijl Nurseries in Holland. Leaves decline quickly and flowers are sterile, therefore persisting on the plant for a long time. More expensive but well worth it.

'Gladiator' is 3–4' tall with large lilac-purple flowers.

'Lucy Ball' is a sport of 'Gladiator' with dark violet flowers. Stands about 4' tall.

'Rien Poortvliet' bears great lilac flowers on 3–4' tall stems.

| | | | |
|---|---|---|---|
| *-caeruleum* (ce-rue' lee-um) | | Blue Globe Onion | 12–24"/18" |
| Late Spring | Blue | Russia | Zones 2–7 |
| (Syn. *A. azureum*) | | | |

The deep blue flowers are held very tightly in a 1–2" diameter umbel. The leaves are 3-sided and 6–12" long. The cup-shaped flowers, which open in late May in zone 7 and about 2 weeks later in zone 3, persist for about 2 weeks. Unfortunately, it is difficult to establish in most American gardens, as it comes from the steppes and deserts of Central Asia and requires hot, dry conditions to flourish. Similar to many other allium flowers, this is also an excellent cut flower. Plants may be divided easily to provide good sized clumps. Occasionally bulbils are formed within the inflorescence (particularly on var. *bulbiliferum*) and may be used for propagation. Seed should be treated as with *A. aflatunense*.

**Related Species:**

*A. cyaneum* is a rhizomatous onion, native to western China, and a terrific summer bloomer. The dark blue to purple star-shaped nodding flowers are borne over grassy foliage on 6–9" tall scapes.

*A. sikkimense* has bell-shaped pendant, deep blue to purple flowers. A summer bloomer, likely hardy in zones 6–8.

*A. cernuum*, wild nodding onion, is native to the northeastern United States and bears nodding umbels of lilac-pink flowers in sun or light shade. Plants are about 18" tall but can be quite variable. Leaves persist into the late summer. Bulbs are carried on a short rhizome and are easy to grow. Plants provide a wonderful early summer show when placed in groups of 3–6. If self-sowing is a problem, flowers should be deadheaded immediately after flowering.

| | | | |
|---|---|---|---|
| *-christophii* (kris-tof' ee-eye) | | Downy Onion, Star of Persia | 15–24"/24" |
| Summer | Violet | Turkey, Afghanistan | Zones 4–8 |
| (Syn. *A. albo-pilosum*) | | | |

Although short in stature, this is one of the largest flowering species in cultivation. Up to 100 metallic violet, star-shaped flowers are carried on a

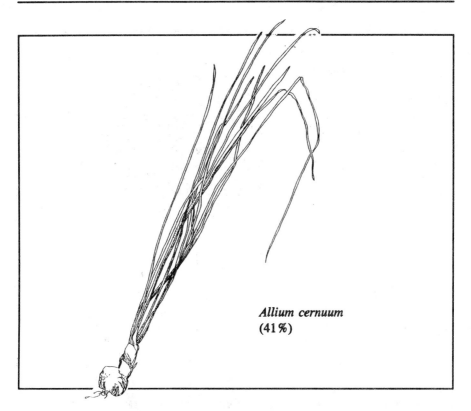

*Allium cernuum*
(41%)

spherical umbel often 10–12″ in diameter. The stems and the margins of the 2–7 strap-shaped leaves are covered with white hairs which are responsible for the common name. The leaves die before the flowers have completely opened.

When in flower, there is no more eye-catching member of the genus. It is also one of the best alliums for long-lasting dried flowers, literally looking good for years. A sunny, well-drained area at the front of the border is necessary for best performance.

Propagate by seed similar to *A. aflatunense*.

**Hybrids:**

'Globemaster', a hybrid between *A. christophii* and *A. macleanii*, is without doubt, the best ornamental onion I have ever tried. The robust plants stand about 2½′ tall on strong, self-supporting stems. The stems must be strong because the deep lavender flowers are held in 4–6″ wide globular heads. The flowers continue to open over many weeks, the newer ones "replacing" the older ones. While other members of the genus have come and gone in the Armitage garden, 'Globemaster' still shines. The seed heads remain ornamental well into the summer. It was originally bred as a cut flower in Holland by van Duyvenbode, and, as more gardeners discover it, perhaps the expensive price will decrease.

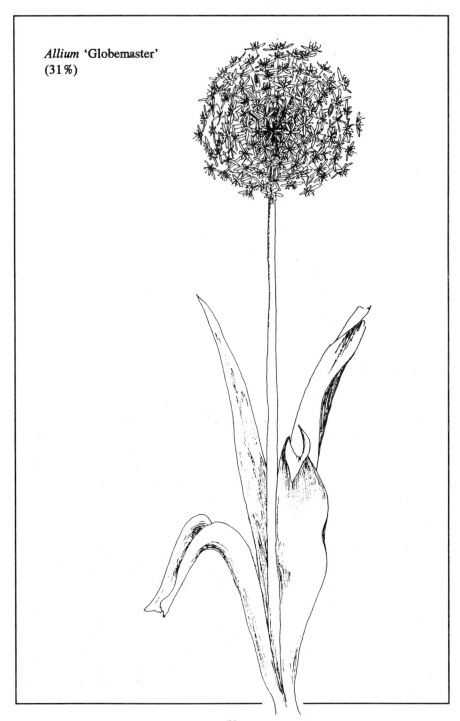

*Allium* 'Globemaster'
(31%)

| *-giganteum* (gi-gan' tee-um) | | Giant Onion | 3–5'/2' |
|---|---|---|---|
| Late Spring | Lilac | Central Asia | Zones 4–8 |

This is, as the name implies, the giant of this genus. The bulb itself is 2–3" in diameter and resembles a large, misshapen ball. The discovery of this species, like many other plant species, makes for fascinating reading. Eastern European politics, a newspaper reporter and a Victorian society artist were instrumental in bringing this species to western gardens (see Dadd, 1987).

In early spring, 6 to 9 broad (5–8" wide) gray-green leaves emerge as a rosette, followed by a thick, strong scape carrying the many lilac flowers. By the time the scape is 6–12" long, the leaves lie on the ground. Three to four weeks are required for the scape to grow to a final height of 4', but the wait is justified. There are over 100 individual flowers, each ½" long, which are held closely together in a dense, 4" diameter rounded umbel.

Plant in groups of three, more if you can afford the pricey bulbs, in full sun and well-drained soils. It is an excellent late spring and summer flower for the back of the border, and, because the leaves disappear soon after flowering, there is no "dead time" waiting for the leaves to wither as with tulips and daffodils. Plantings as far south as zone 8 have been excellent, and, if mulch is applied, the bulbs appear to be cold tolerant to zone 4. In zone 7, flowering occurs in mid May but not until early June in Michigan (zone 4). As a cut flower, it is outstanding and has gained much popularity with florists and designers.

Propagation is accomplished by separating the two portions of the bulb which tend to split after 2 years.

### Related Species:

*A. rosenbachianum* is another tall species, easily growing 4' tall and producing 4" wide spherical umbels of many star-shaped, deep lavender flowers in the spring. 'Album' is a creamy white form growing about 3½' tall. The foliage disappears quickly, leaving the long, naked flower stem with its cargo of flowers and later seed heads. I grow mine through a large *Baptisia pendula*, so that after the flowers of the *Baptisia* are finished, the globes of the onion continue.

*A. stipitatum* is similar, bearing 3–4' tall scapes topped with globular, fragrant, lilac flowers. It differs in that the tepals (petals) reflex downward and wither after flowering, while those of *A. giganteum* are persistent. The leaves are narrower, about 1–1½" wide. This is also a highly useful species.

The above two species differ from *A. giganteum* in that their tepals become twisted and reflexed, but whose umbels remain well formed as they dry and produce large quantities of seed. *A. giganteum* has tepals which remain unreflexed; the umbel falls apart by late summer and seldom produces much seed.

**-*karataviense*** (ka-ra-tah-vee-en′ se)      Turkistan Onion          6–12″/15″
   Late Spring     Silver-Gray     Turkey, Afghanistan   Zones 4–8

This unique species is grown for the foliage as much as for the flowers. The thick, gray-green leaves (usually 2) are up to 4″ wide and mottled purple, particularly underneath and near the base. The leaves may be more ornamental than the flower, which is a rather washed-out silver-lilac. The dense umbels are 6–8″ across and compete with those of *A. christophii* for the largest in the genus. The plant is particularly suited to open, windy locations because of the strong, thick, 6″ tall scape which carries the flowers. The leaves and seed capsules persist well after the flower has abscised and remain handsome until mid June.

Seed propagated plants (accomplished as with *A. aflatunense*) require about 3 years to flower.

**-*moly*** (mah′ lee)                  Lily Leek, Golden Onion      12–15″/12″
   Late Spring     Yellow    Southern Europe        Zones 3–9

Even before the time of Homer, the lily leek was endowed with magical properties. Reference to the "Moly" can be found in the Odyssey, in which Ulysses walked unharmed under its protection. It has been looked upon as a good luck charm for many years, and this combination of magic and beauty makes the plant difficult not to include in the garden. The two flat, lance-like leaves are blue-green and up to 2″ wide and 8–12″ long. The small, ½″ star-shaped flowers are held in a 2″ wide open umbel and are a lovely shade of golden yellow. A dozen bulbs planted in a sunny, well-drained area quickly increase to form a golden vista in late spring and early summer.

Propagate by bulb offsets or seed. Seed-propagated plants will flower in one year.

**Cultivars:**

'Jeannine' is a marked improvement on the species. She grows 12–18″ tall but is compact with bright yellow flowers in early summer.

**Related Species:**

*A. obliquum* has unique lemon-yellow flowers which are much less strident than some of the other yellows found in the early summer garden.

**-*narcissiflorum*** (nar-ciss-i-flo′ rum)  Narcissus Onion            6–12″/9″
   Summer        Pink    Northern Italy, Portugal   Zones 5–8

A wonderful dwarf species best suited for rock garden or cozy, partially shaded nook in the garden. In bud, the plants looks like a small jonquil but soon open to erect clusters of bright pink, bell-shaped flowers. The 3–5 blue-green leaves are persistent through the season. This species and a few others (*A. thunbergii, A. tanguticum*) have their small bulbs clustered together on a small rhizome.

**Related Species:**

*A. insurbricum* also bears pink, bell-shaped flowers and is often confused with *A. narcissiflorum*. Plants differ by having green leaves and flowers that are pendulous both in bud and in flower. *A. insurbricum* tolerates wetter conditions than *A. narcissiflorum*.

*-neapolitanum* (nee-ah-pol-i-tay′ num)     Naples Onion          6–12″/12″
   Early Spring              White             Southern Europe     Zones 7–9

Two to three linear leaves, about ½–¾″ wide and keeled, are held in a basal rosette resembling daffodil foliage. The scape carries a loose, many-flowered umbel (2½″ across) of starry, white flowers with rosy stamens. The individual flowers are about ¾″ in diameter and are among the most fragrant in the genus. It is one of the earliest to flower, opening the end of April and persisting for about 4 weeks. It is not reliably hardy in zone 7, but if heavily mulched, will overwinter. Mulch should also be applied further south to reduce temperature fluctuations in the soil. Plant about 5″ deep in a sheltered corner of the garden, preferably at the foot of a low, south-facing wall.

The fragrance of the flowers has made this a popular cut flower, as well as an excellent species for greenhouse pot plant production. Cover 4–5 bulbs with an inch of soil in a 5″ diameter pot and place at 45° F for 8–10 weeks. Bring to a warm area and enjoy the flowers.

**Cultivars:**

Var. *grandiflorum* has 3″ diameter umbels consisting of white flowers with a dark eye. Plants are more vigorous than the species. It is used for forcing in pots, cut flower production, and is more ornamental than the species.

**Related Species:**

*A. ramosum*, fragrant flowered garlic, bears many bell-shaped, white flowers with a dark red stripe in 2″ wide umbels. The foliage is narrow and persists until the flowers are produced in late summer or fall.

*A. tuberosum*, garlic chives, has creamy white flowers and narrow chive-like leaves. It is similar to *A. ramosum* but differs by having star-shaped flowers with a faint green or brown stripe. Introduced from southeast Asia, it has become an aggressive weed in many parts of the country.

*-nigrum* (nye' grum)      Black Onion      2–3'/8"
    Spring     White      Southern Europe, North Italy      Zones 5–8
(Syn. *A. multibulbosum*)

Bulbs produce 3–6 basal leaves in early spring and then send a long, straight flower stem up to 3' tall. The many star-shaped white flowers are borne in a round 4–6" wide umbel. Sometimes bulbils may form in the inflorescence. The ovary of each flower is dark green to black and appears to give the flowers a black center (thus the name *nigrum*). The flowers appear relatively late in the spring, and the seed heads remain highly ornamental for 3–4 additional weeks.

*-oreophilum* (o-ray-o' fi-lum)      Mountain Onion      4–12"/9"
    Early Summer     Rose      Turkey, Afghanistan      Zones 3–8
(Syn. *A. ostrowskianum*)

This is an excellent species for the patio planter or front of the garden. The 2–3 linear leaves are flat, bluish green, and somewhat limp. The star to bell-shaped flowers are held in a 2" diameter, many-flowered umbel. They have a mild, pleasant fragrance, but the onion smell is particularly noticeable when the leaves and stem are crushed. The flowers become thin and papery as they age and persist for many weeks, while the foliage usually is withered by flowering time or remains for a week or so after flowering. Plant in a sunny, well-drained area.

### Cultivars:
'Zwanenberg' has carmine-pink flowers which are a little brighter than those of the species.

*-schubertii* (shoo-ber' tea-eye) Tumbleweed Onion      18–24"/12"
    Spring     Pink      Mediterranean, Central Asia      Zones 5–9

This onion defies description; suffice it to say that the flowers look like the hair on Don King's head (or for my more mature readers, Phyllis Diller's hairdo). I try vainly to teach this species to my students, and, while the slides help, seeing the real thing up close and personal makes instant alliophiles. The ½" wide, pink, starry flowers are first produced on short flower stalks (pedicels) like a normal onion but then proceed to form additional infertile flowers on pedicels longer than the first ones. The effect reminds one of the chemistry experiment with the static machine where peoples' hair stands on end.

As gruesome as the above description sounds, it really is a lovely garden plant. The 4–8 blue-green leaves are produced early in the spring and deteriorate after flowering has finished. The stems are compact and stout and require no help to support their floral and seed display. The floral fireworks leave behind the same exploding seed head, ornamental long after the pink of the flowers has faded into some dim memory. The seed heads may be dried for winter decoration; however, if left to their own devices, they eventually fall off and become garden tumbleweeds, rolling around with each gust of wind. The main reasons why fewer of these bulbs are found in American gardens are the expense and relative lack of cold hardiness. Plants should be well mulched in zone 5. How else can you bring Don and Phyllis in your garden and not have to listen to them?

| *-senescens* (sen-es' ens) | German Garlic | 6-12"/6" |
|---|---|---|
| Summer      Lilac-Pink | Europe, Northern Asia | Zones 4-7 |

The cup-shaped flowers are clustered on a 1-2" wide umbel in late spring to mid summer. The 4-9 basal green leaves are flat and somewhat grass-like. The plants are best for rock gardens or an area where the small plants will not get lost or overgrown. They tolerate full sun, but a little afternoon shade is appreciated. The species itself is nothing to write home about; however, the variety sold as *glaucum* is popular and rather dramatic. The flowers are debatably more pink than in the species, but the foliage is blue-green and twisted. Some authorities have named this variant *A. spirale* and is known as the Circle Onion. They are not dramatic like 'Globemaster' but garner plenty of comments.

**Cultivars:**
'Roseum' has pink flowers and, if twisted leaves are not terribly important, is the best choice of the species.

| *-sphaerocephalum* (sfay-roe-sef' a-lum) | Drumstick Chives | 18-36/15" |
|---|---|---|
| Late Spring      Purple | Europe | Zones 4-8 |

This is one of the finest alliums for cut flowers and use in the border. The 3-5 hollow, semi-cylindrical leaves resemble inflated chive leaves. The oval to round, 2" diameter flower heads consist of 50-100 flowers. Each flower bud is green and, with maturity, flowers turn purple, giving the inflorescence a two-tone effect. Flowers open in mid-June and persist for 2-3 weeks. The stamens are longer than the tepals and provide an airy feel to the flower heads. It is excellent in hot climates and performs well in zone 8. The flowers are persistent on the plant and, as a cut flower, last up to 10 days in water. I cannot understand why this species has been so overlooked and underused in American gardens.

Plant multiple bulbs 6" apart and 6" deep in a sunny exposure. One or two plants are not effective, and a grouping is essential. Bulblets may be separated after 2-3 years, and seed may be treated similar to *A. aflatunense.*

| *-thunbergii* (thun-berg-ee' eye) | | Japanese Onion | 18–24"/10" |
|---|---|---|---|
| Fall | Violet | Japan | Zones 5–8 |

I first saw this onion with my friend, Galen Gates, of the Chicago Botanical Garden. On that cool, fall day, other plants were bedding down, but the shiny, grass-like, green leaves and purple flowers of this onion were outstanding. He shared a few bulbs with me, and they were equally good in my garden in Athens. The tufts of leaves persist throughout the season, and, in September to November, the starry violet flowers are fresh and inviting. The stamens and style are elongated and appear to dramatically increase the size of the umbel. The only available form I know of is 'Ozawa', which grows about 9–12" tall. Full sun is necessary for best performance.

### Related Species:
*A. amabile* flowers in late summer and fall and, like *A. thunbergii*, produces slender bulbs clustered on a rhizome and persistent grassy leaves. The funnel-shaped, nodding flowers are magenta to deep pink, and plants are 5–6" tall. Similar to *A. mairei*, which technically differs by having erect, paler pink flowers. However, some taxonomists argue that they are simply variations within the same species. Good garden plants regardless, probably hardy in zones 6–8.

*A. tanguticum* also produces narrow, persistent foliage, although the lavender flowers are produced in mid summer rather than fall. Native to western China, they appear to be hardy to zone 5 (4 with protection). I saw some stunning dark lavender plants in the Cleveland area, which turned out to be one of the cultivars, 'Summer Beauty'. Another handsome cultivar is 'Blue Skies', which is much lighter in color. Mature plants stand about 15" tall. They appear to be happier in the North than the South, where they produce many more leaves and far fewer flowers.

*A. virgunuculae* produces stems with 2–12 pink, star-shaped flowers in October and November. The grassy leaves look good all season. A small grouping makes a lovely setting.

| *-triquetrum* (tri-kwee' trum) | | Three Cornered Onion | 8–15"/12" |
|---|---|---|---|
| Summer | White | Western Europe | Zones 5–9 |

This is easily recognizable by the three-sided scape which supports a 2½" diameter inflorescence of six to eight ½" long pendulous, white flowers, borne primarily on one side of the inflorescence. Each bell-shaped flower has a central stripe of green, and the stigma is deeply 3-parted, another characteristic useful in separating the three cornered onion from others. The flowers are fragrant, but not nearly as sweet as those of *A. neapolitanum*. The foliage consists of three to four 1" wide, keeled leaves. It is common in hedgerows in England and New Zealand.

Plant bulbs in well-drained soils in full sun. Seeds germinate readily and can create a weed problem the following spring if growing conditions are conducive. The seeds are dispersed by ants, and ants can travel a long way! Many gardeners remove the flowers as soon as flowers have wilted.

Propagate by the many bulblets formed after the first year or by seeds treated similarly to those of *A. aflatunense*.

**Cultivars:**

Var. *pendulinum* has larger flowers borne on all sides of the umbel. It is more useful as a cut flower than the species.

**Related Species:**

*A. carniatum*, keeled garlic, has about 30 cup-shaped, purple flowers in the pendulous umbels. The inflorescences usually include bulbils. Variety *pulchellum* has rosy lilac flowers and lacks bulbils.

*A. ursinum*, ramsoms, is about 10″ tall and bears 15–20 white flowers in flat 2″ diameter umbels in late spring. The strongly onion-scented plants consist of 2–3 elliptical leaves with long petioles. Plants are more tolerant of shade than most alliums.

Quick Key to Allium Species

      A. Flowering plants usually taller than 2′
        B. Leaves half-rounded, hollow, upright . . . *A. sphaerocephalum*
        BB. Leaves flat or keeled, not half-round or hollow
          C. Leaves less than 3″ wide, plants 2–3′ tall
            D. Flowers lilac to purple . . . . . . . . . . . *A. aflatunense*
            DD. Flowers white . . . . . . . . . . . . . . . . . . . *A. nigrum*
          CC. Leaves more than 3″ wide, gray-green,
            plants 3–5′ tall . . . . . . . . . . . . . . . . . . . . *A. giganteum*
    AA. Flowering plants usually less than 2′ tall
        B. Flowers lilac, blue, or violet
          C. Flowers lilac or blue
            D. Flowers lilac or violet
              E. Flowers lilac, leaves flat, mottled purple,
                2–4″ wide, spring flowering . . . . . . . *A. karataviense*
              EE. Flowers violet, leaves grassy,
                fall flowering . . . . . . . . . . . . . . . . . *A. thunbergii*
            DD. Flowers blue, leaves triangular,
              not mottled, ½–¾″ wide . . . . . . . . . . *A. caeruleum*
        BB. Flowers yellow, white, or pink
          C. Flowers white
            D. Flowers star-shaped, upright,
              scape round . . . . . . . . . . . . . . . . . *A. neapolitanum*

DD. Flowers bell-shaped, nodding, scape
    three-sided .................. *A. triquetrum*
CC. Flowers yellow, pink
    D. Flowers yellow, plants 12–15″ tall ....... **A. moly**
    DD. Flowers pink
        E. Plants more than 12″ tall,
           flowers borne on unequal pedicels .... *A. schubertii*
        EE. Plants less than 12″ tall
           F. Flower segments sharply pointed,
             recurved at tips ............ *A. acuminatum*
           FF. Flower segments not pointed
             G. Stamens of flowers exserted ..... *A. senescens*
             GG. Stamens included
                H. Pendulous in bud,
                  flowers erect .......... *A. narcissiflorum*
                HH. Buds erect,
                  flowers erect .......... *A. oreophilum*

**Additional Reading:**

Bilj van Duyvenbode, J. 1990. Breeding ornamental onions. *The Plantsman* 12(3):152–156.

Buffler, C.R. 1992. Plants. A new giant allium. *Fine Gardening* 27:72–77.

Dadd, Richard. 1987. The discovery and introduction of *Allium giganteum*. *Kew Magazine* 4(2):91–96.

Davies, Dilys. 1992. Alliums. Timber Press, Portland, OR.

Gates, Galen. 1992. *Allium thunbergii. The Public Garden* 7(1):38.

Harper, P. 1976. The ornamental onion. *Horticulture* 54(8):19–22.

Mathew, B. 1993. *Allium schubertii. The Garden* 118(9):399.

Moore, Harold E. Jr. 1954. The cultivated alliums. *Baileya* 2(3):103–113.

Moore, Harold E. Jr. 1954. The cultivated alliums II. *Baileya* 2(4):117–123.

Moore, Harold E. Jr. 1955. The cultivated alliums III. *Baileya* 3(3):137–149.

Moore, Harold E. Jr. 1955. The cultivated alliums IV. *Baileya* 3(3):157–167.

Stearn, William T. 1992. How many species of *Allium* are known? *Kew Magazine* 9(4):180–182.

## *Alstroemeria* (ahl-strurm-e′ ree-a)    Peruvian Lily    Alstroemeriaceae

Approximately 50 species are known, all native to South America, and generally grow from tubers and produce alternate leaves and wonderfully interesting flowers. The Peruvian lilies have become extremely popular as cut flowers, produced in fields and greenhouses in California, Holland, Columbia, Israel and other cut-flower producing regions. Generally cut-flower production involves hybrids of *A. ligtu* and *A. aurea*, but most of these are poor garden plants in all but a few areas of the country. In areas on the West Coast, the bright orange-yellow flowers of *A. aurea* brighten gardens and, once established, can roam about at will. *A. aurantiaca* is another wonderful golden-orange flowered species but seldom survives extremes of heat and cold common to most areas of the United States. 'Lutea' is particularly handsome.

Gardeners in the South and Southeast are not without a member of this interesting genus. The parrot lily, *A. psittacina*, otherwise known as *A. pulchella*, is hardy to at least zone 7 (plants have survived winter temperatures of 7° F in the Armitage garden) and even hardy in Boston. In the Southeast, plants can become a bit of a nuisance once established in the garden. Low growing in spring, the basal foliage gives rise to 3' tall flowering stems. Two to three flowers are produced in the terminal umbel and are an odd mix of green and wine red, spotted or streaked with maroon. Sounds rather weird, but weirdly delightful. Flowers begin in early June and continue for 4–5 weeks. Like all members of the genus, they are excellent cut flowers, albeit a rather difficult color to place with anything else. That's why bud vases are sold. *A. psittacina* tolerates partial shade; however, too much shade results in leafy, poor flowering plants. Easy to divide, these are the ultimate pass-along plants.

**Additional Reading:**

Smith, Peter. 1994. Lily of the incas. *The Garden* 119(10):464–468.

## *Alyssum* (a-lis' um)　　　　　Madwort　　　　　Brassicaceae

The name comes from *a* (without) and *lyssa* (rage), alluding to the plants reputation of allaying anger, perhaps rabies. The large genus consists of over 150 species, usually small in stature and with yellow flowers. Many are native to alpine and northerly areas (*A. repens*, *A. tortuosum*) and perform poorly in hot, wet summer climates. These are outstanding for rocky crevices or rock garden areas. Taxonomists moved the most popular old alyssum, *A. saxatile*, to the genus *Aurinia* and it may be found under *Aurinia saxatilis*.

A number of fine species are occasionally offered, and seed may also be found through specialty organizations. *A. montanum*, mountain madwort, is about an 8" tall ground cover, with finely cut foliage and masses of bright yellow, spring flowers. 'Mountain Gold' is a more compact, floriferous cultivar. Hardy in zones 2–7. *A. wulfenianum* is also prostrate, about 8" tall, and bears light yellow flowers in early spring. *A. argenteum*, silver madwort, produces handsome gray foliage. All require excellent drainage and do best in full sun. Most do poorly in the South, although if planted in the fall, they are wonderfully bright in the spring but decline as the heat of summer arrives.

## *Amianthium* (am-ee-an-the′ um)        Fly-Poison        Liliaceae

Who said fly traps have to come in a spray can or sticky strips? All parts of this plant are poisonous, although the folklore about poisoning flies is a bit of a mystery. Only one species occurs in this genus, *A. muscaetoxicum*, and plants not only have a rich folk lore but also are very handsome in the woodland garden. Plants occur from small bulbs, and, when the bulbs are mixed with honey or syrup, an excellent fly poison results. Plants are native from Pennsylvania and New York, south to Florida and west to Arkansas. Cattle have been known to be poisoned from eating plants, thus common names like Fall-poison and Stagger Grass have also been attached to these plants. Such morbidity makes for good stories, but plants are also quite ornamental. The plants, when allowed to grow in large groups, produce long racemes of clean, white flowers which brighten the woodland landscape. The basal leaves are usually more than a foot long but only about an inch wide. They flower in May in the South and in June further north. A wonderful population may be seen at the Atlanta History Center in the terrific native garden tended with great care by Sue Vrooman.

## *Amorphophallus* (a-mor-fo-fal′ lus)        Snake Palm        Araceae

That plants of this genus belong in a garden is a given, that they belong in yours or mine may be debatable. Belonging to the family Araceae puts them in the same company as caladiums, calla lilies and jack-in-the-pulpits with their unmistakable spathe and spadix arrangement of flowers. They are denizens of leafy, moldy places in moist, shaded habitats and are grown for their compound foliage, often marbled stems and dramatic, if evil-smelling, inflorescences. Flowers of this group of plants have memorable effluviums, often assailing the nostrils with a mine field of odor. Sir Joseph Hooker described the odor of *A. titanum* as a "mixture of rotting fish and burnt sugar, which turns your stomach over and makes your eyes run." Perhaps that is why its common name is corpse flower! Knowing my fondness for such weird plants, Tony Avent of Plants Delight Nursery in Raleigh, North Carolina brought me a tuber of *A. rivieri*, known as devil's tongue. I placed it in heavy shade and a reasonably moist area, and, every June, long after most plants have risen and are growing well, *Amorphophallus* gives a big yawn, stretches, and breaks through the soil. Seeing that purple-mottled stem rise like a phoenix and watching the foliage unfurl can keep me occupied for days. Generally a single leaf emerges and branches repeatedly, the two branches of each division basically equal. The name for this kind of leaf shape is dichotomous, as if anyone cares. Regardless of my ineptness at describing it, the leaves really are handsome. Plants have not yet produced flowers in the Armitage garden; however, it is approaching its fifth birthday, and flowering may soon occur. As for now, it is probably just as well, as my neighbors, let alone Susan, would likely not be impressed. The scent of this species was described by a visitor at a flower show when "we detected the scent of pure rot. Following our noses, we came across two huge, liver colored inflorescences atop 5' stalks which arose from naked corms the size of pumpkins." Other similar genera such as *Dracontium* and *Sauromatum* are occasionally presented to the gardener, which offer weirdness of habit, foul odor, and curious, often disparaging, comments. Who could ask for more? Some of the more obvious differences between them follow.

|  | *Amorphophallus rivieri* | *Dracontium vulgaris* | *Sauromatum venosum* |
| --- | --- | --- | --- |
| Spathe color | Dark purple | Dark purple | Dull violet with yellow |
| Spathe shape | 3–4' wide | 1' long, 6" wide, arching | 2' long, pointed, flattened back |
| Spadix | Purple | Purple | 3' long, skinny, erect |
| Leaf number | Usually one | Several | One |
| Leaf shape | Dichotomous | Sickle-shaped | Sickle-shaped |

A selection of *Amorphophallus rivieri*, long known as 'Konjac', may be offered simply as *A. konjac*. While its garden attributes may be debated, its importance as a food crop is well known in Indonesia, southeast Asia, India and the Pacific. In many regions, the corms are important standbys when the rice crop fails. In Japan, a traditional food made from the corm is known as konnyaku, but industrial uses for the carbohydrates (mannose, starches) in the dark-skinned corm have also been discovered. Gelling properties for convenience foods and dietary supplements for weight loss are being investigated.

A number of species have long intrigued gardeners looking for weird plants, and a few are starting to become available, slowly but surely. *A. bulbifer*, the Voodoo lily, has 30–36" tall mottled stems and palmate lobed foliage. The leaves form small cormlets in late summer, which may be removed for new plants. The spadix is green with a tinge of pink and appears in the spring before the foliage. Hardy in zones 7–10. Sometimes a black-stemmed form is offered, which is probably *A. koratensis*. Like having a rare 2' tall black bamboo. Beautiful and absolutely gives everyone pause. The most famous is the above mentioned *A. titanum*, giant voodoo lily, which in its native Indonesian environment has flowers up to 15' tall, followed by mottled stems and foliage equally tall. You have reached la-la land when you see such things.

Most species are winter hardy to zone 7 (*A. rivieri* to zone 6), but, if you are fortunate to find one, you have ornamental value, food value, dietary value and nasal exercise all in one. Have fun.

**Additional Reading:**

Brown, Demi. 1988. Aroids, plants of the *Arum* family. Timber Press, Portland, OR. A delightful book about all the members of this fascinating family. The beauty and function of these plants are discussed in detail.

*Amsonia* (am-sown' ee-ah)         Blue Star Flower         Apocynaceae

This North American genus contains some fine low-maintenance, resilient species for the garden. Light blue, star-shaped flowers are held in terminal panicles above the alternate leaves. There are approximately twenty species in the genus, although only 3 or 4 are available to the gardener. Amsonias provide early blue flowers, disease and insect resistance, and fall color. The fruits (follicles) are long and narrow; in some species they are erect, while others bear spreading or pendant fruit. Certainly one of my favorite plants is blue star flower, *A. tabernaemontana*; however, the Arkansas amsonia, *A. hubrectii* and the downy amsonia, *A. ciliata*, are also excellent garden plants.

Quick Reference to Amsonia Species

|                      | Young leaves obviously hairy | Approx. width of leaves | Flower color |
| -------------------- | ---------------------------- | ----------------------- | ------------ |
| *A. ciliata*         | Yes                          | 1½"                     | Blue         |
| *A. hubrectii*       | No                           | ¾ "                     | Light blue   |
| *A. tabernaemontana* | No                           | 2"                      | Blue         |

-*ciliata* (sill-e' a-ta)         Downy Amsonia                         1–3'/3'
    Spring      Sky Blue      Southeastern United States         Zones 6–10
(Syn. *A. angustifolia*)

An excellent plant for many gardens; the hairy foliage, which emerges in early spring, remains healthy all season. With maturity, the linear to linear-lanceolate, dark-green leaves lose much of their silkiness. However, if the plant is cut back after flowering, the new growth returns as feathery as before. The leaves are crowded toward the upper end of the stems and the margins slightly curled back toward the underside of the leaves (called revolute). The starry flowers are sky blue and persist for 3–4 weeks. Species of *Amsonia* are some of the few herbaceous species which provide fall color in the garden. The foliage turns a lovely golden yellow and lasts until frost.

Plant in full sun or light, dappled shade and provide sufficient moisture to survive dry periods. No serious pests occur, but the stems may need cutting back at least once during the season to keep them from falling over, particularly if planted in a shady area.

Seed, division, and terminal cuttings taken during the spring are all viable means of propagation. Store the seed at about 40° F for 4–6 weeks because untreated seed germinates irregularly. Chipping or cutting away a small piece of one end of the seed and soaking overnight in water also results in better germination. Division is not necessary for 8–10 years but is a quick way to increase a planting. Cut through the crown in early spring or fall so that each division consists of at least one growing point. Terminal cuttings from lateral branches collected in May and treated with a rooting hormone (one labeled for herbaceous plants) root faster and more uniformly.

*-hubrectii* (ew-breckt-ee′ eye)   Arkansas Amsonia                          2–3′/3′
   Spring      Pale Blue     South Central United States   Zones 6–9

Not as well known as blue star flower, but equally handsome. The foliage is feathery, like *A. ciliata*, but leaves are a little wider and longer. The flowers are lighter blue than blue star flower and are almost white as temperatures warm up in spring. The early flowers are easily visible, but the foliage tends to cover the later opening flowers. The narrow foliage (less than 1″ wide) makes a marvelous display throughout the season, and the golden-yellow spectacle in the fall is second to none among herbaceous plants.

Plants have been difficult to locate in the past, but the garden attributes have been recognized by more nursery people, and plants are much more available. Well worth growing.

*-tabernaemontana* (tay-ber-nay-mon-tah′ na)   Blue Star Flower   1–3′/3′
   Spring      Sky Blue     Eastern United States    Zones 3–9
(Syn. *Tabernaemontana amsonia*)

This differs from the others in that the leaves are wider, more evenly spaced along the stem, and are not hairy as they emerge. It is native from Pennsylvania to South Carolina and as far west as Kansas, and can be found along roadsides or in sunny fields. This species is more cold hardy than the previous and much more common. The lovely blue hues of the flowers and the fall color of the foliage are similar in both species. Blue star flower is always on my list of "no-brainers." Plant and get out of the way.

Plants have alternate willow-like leaves and many ½–¾″ pale blue, star flowers clustered in loose, terminal inflorescences in spring to early summer. They are particularly lovely in the early spring as they break through the ground and rapidly extend to their mature stature. If grown in full sun, pruning is not necessary; however, if grown in shade, plants may be pruned to maintain shape or supported. In my shaded garden, I grow plants through a circular support frame to keep plants from toppling. Deep, moist soils and partial shade are ideal.

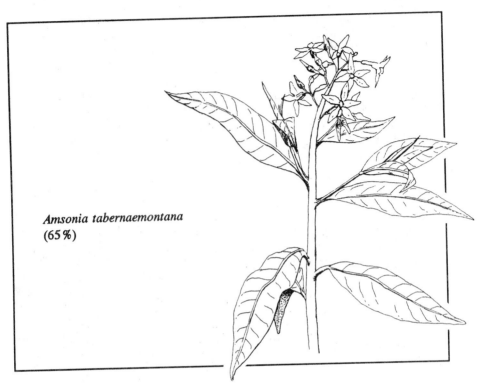

*Amsonia tabernaemontana*
(65%)

## Cultivars:

Var. *montana* is a dwarfer version of the species. Some taxonomists have split it into *A. montana*. Exceptionally good plant, small enough to even find a place in the rock garden.

Var. *salicifolia* (sometimes listed as *A. salicifolia*) has leaves 5–10 times longer than they are wide and is less erect than the species. The flowers have a white throat and a small beard within. Native to the southeastern United States. Propagation is similar to *A. ciliata*.

## Related Species:

*A. illustris* is native to the central United States and resembles *A. tabernaemontana*, bearing similar foliage and flowers. Plants differ by having thicker, leathery leaves and pendant fruit. Cold hardiness to about zone 5.

*A. ludoviciana*, Louisiana blue-star flower, is native to southern Louisiana only and is distinguished by the white wool on the undersides of the leaves. Handsome even without flowers.

*A. orientalis* superficially resembles *A. tabernaemontana* but is native to southern Europe. With close inspection, one can see short hairs along the margin and midribs of the leaves, whereas the leaves of *A. tabernaemontana* are smooth (glabrous). Plants do appear to be as cold hardy.

*Rhayza orientalis* is so similar to *A. orientalis* that it is considered a synonym. The late spring and summer flowers range from bright blue to violet. Plants are native to Greece and Turkey.

Quick Key to Amsonia Species:

A. Leaves narrow, feathery
    B. Plants hairy, particularly when young,
        leaves crowded on stem, margins curled back . . . . *A. ciliata*
    BB. Plants not obviously hairy,
        margins not curled back . . . . . . . . . . . . . . . . *A. hubrectii*
AA. Leaves ovate to lanceolate, shiny . . . . . . . *A. tabernaemontana*

**Additional Reading:**

Arrington, N. 1993. Bluestar. *Horticulture* 71(5):96.
Anon. 1995. *Amsonia* and *Rhazya*. *Perennial Plants* (J. of the Perennial Plant Assoc.) 3(3):31–36.
Taloumis, George. 1985. Amsonia. *Horticulture* 63(8):30–31.

## *Anacyclus* (an-a-psyc' lus)    Mt. Atlas Daisy    Asteraceae

Of the approximately 9 species of annual and perennial species, only the Mt. Atlas daisy, *A. pyrethrum* var. *depressus* (*A. depressus*), is easily available to North American gardeners. Plants produce fine basal foliage, forming ferny mats with a lovely gray-green cast. Plants grow 4–6″ tall and bear 1–1½″ wide single, white daisies with yellow centers and purple to red backs. Being native to the Mediterranean, excellent drainage is a necessity, at least in the East, and plants are more persistent in sunny, dry rock gardens or embedded in rock walls than in the border. Our plants at Georgia were wonderful the first year but succumbed to the winter wetness. Hardy from zone 5 to 7.
    Propagate by division or seed.

**Cultivars:**

'Silberkissen' is even more compact than the above and bears gray foliage with silver hairs and pink-tinged, white daisies.

## *Anagallis* (an-a-gah' lis)    Pimpernel    Primulaceae

The genus is best known for common pimpernel, *A. arvensis*, a European field weed with scarlet or white flowers throughout Europe. A number of variants occur, but plants are seldom seen in North American gardens. A fine species which is occasionally offered is *A. monellii*, blue pimpernel, with upright to lax, 2′ tall branching stems. The 1–2″ long leaves are sessile and often whorled. The 5-petalled blue flowers are usually reddish beneath and are carried on 2″ pedicels in the upper leaf axils.

Although difficult to find, plants are worth a try, particularly in areas of sunny, dry conditions. They perform better on the west coast than in the east, where summer and winter moisture can do them in. Place in well-drained areas and treat like rock garden plants.

**Cultivars:**
'Phillipii' bears deeper blue flowers.

## *Anaphalis* (an-naff' al-iss)  Pearly Everlasting  Asteraceae

*Anaphalis* produces masses of small, white flowers in August and September, usually with a brownish yellow center, but the foliage is special throughout the growing season. The gray-white leaves create a cooling effect in the border and tone down the bright reds and oranges of plants beside them. They are particularly useful in areas which are too wet for other gray-green plants such as *Artemisia* and *Perovskia*. Plants in the genus are especially tough and withstand significant abuse. Although rich soil is not a prerequisite, it should be grown in evenly moist areas because the foliage looks shabby under dry conditions. They are also at home in the naturalized or wild flower garden in full sun to partial shade.

The leaves are alternate, entire, and sessile. The flower heads are small and crowded like small pearls at the ends of the branches. They can be cut and dried to make excellent "everlastings."

Seed sown in late summer will produce flowering plants the next year, but division is the most rapid means of propagation. Plants should be divided every 3–4 years.

Quick Reference to Anaphalis Species:

|  | Height (in.) | Underside of leaves woolly | Flower color |
|---|---|---|---|
| *A. margaritacea* | 24–36 | Yes | White |
| *A. triplinervis* | 12–24 | Yes | White |

*-margaritacea* (mar-ga-ri-tay' see-a)  Pearly Everlasting  24–36"/24"
  Late Summer  White  North America, Northeast Asia  Zones 4–7

The 2–4" long, gray-green, lanceolate leaves have a white, woolly pubescence on their undersides, and the margins are rolled in. The rounded flower heads consist of dozens of ¼–½" diameter flowers which cover the plants like a carpet of snow. The common name refers to the long-lasting dried flowers. Under evenly moist conditions, plants can grow up to 3' tall and equally wide. This is a plant which takes a few years to appreciate, but, once its potential is expressed, gardeners cherish it for the late flowering and gray foliage.

**Cultivars:**

Var. *cinnamomea* (syn. *A. cinnamomea*) is the most common form available. The 1″ long leaves are 3-nerved and bear a lovely cinnamon hue on the undersides. Hardy in zones 4–7. It is interesting to note that most of the tall-growing *Anaphalis* offered by American nurserymen is var. *cinnamomea*, native to India, while the majority of everlastings in English gardens is our native *A. margaritacea*.

Var. *yedoensis* (syn. *A. yedoensis*) produces about 2 inch long, 1-nerved, hairy leaves. Native to Japan and likely a little more cold hardy.

| | | | |
|---|---|---|---|
| *-triplinervis* (tri-plee-ner′ vis) | Three-Veined Everlasting | | 12–24″/12″ |
| Late Summer | White | Himalayas | Zones 3–8 |

This makes an excellent plant for the front of the garden and the dense, white, woolly pubescent leaves contrast and soften other green-leaved species. The stems have a more or less zigzag or wavy form (flexuous), which is especially evident if a few leaves are removed. The flowers, which open in July, are long lasting and continue until frost. The leaves are usually 3-veined; the veins are easily visible on the underside.

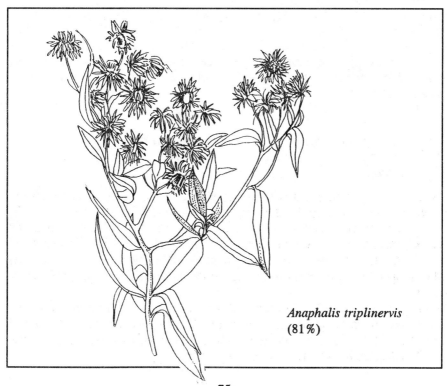

*Anaphalis triplinervis*
(81%)

75

**Cultivars:**

'Summer Snow' ('Sommerschnee') has clear white flowers over tufts of silvery gray foliage. The flowers are a "cleaner" white than those of the species.

**Related Species:**

*A. nubigena* (syn. *A. nepalensis* var. *monocephala*) is similar but only 6–9″ tall.

<u>Quick Key to Anaphalis Species</u>

    A. Plant 24–36″, stems straight . . . . . . . . . . . . *A. margaritacea*
    AA. Plant 12–24″, stems flexuous . . . . . . . . . . . . . . *A. triplinervis*

*Anchusa* (an-koo′ sa)          Alkanet          Boraginaceae

There are about 30 species, but few are suitable for the garden. All are biennials or short-lived perennials (living for 2–3 years) and provide flowers in the blue range, a color often difficult to find in the spring and summer garden. Members of *Anchusa* are characterized by the presence of alternate leaves, hairy stems, and flowers arranged together in the shape of a scorpion's tail (scorpioid cyme). *A. capensis* is approximately 1–2′ tall and is best treated as a biennial or an annual. Another fine species is *A. caespitosa*, which grows only 3–5″ tall and bears bright blue flowers. Plants require excellent drainage for best performance. The most popular and tolerant species is *A. azurea*, available in a number of stately cultivars.

*-azurea* (a-zewr-ree′ a)          Italian Alkanet        3–5′/2′
    Late Spring          Blue          Caucasus          Zones 3–8
(Syn. *A. italica*)

This tall-growing, coarsely hairy species is a beautiful background specimen for the late spring garden. The entire 4–8″ long leaves are sessile or attached to the stem by the clasping base. The bright blue flowers are ½–¾″ across and persist for about 4 weeks. It performs best in deep soil in full sun. In the South, plants may reach 4′ in height and require support. Plants may become invasive in rich soils and too lanky if fertilizer is applied.

    Propagation is mainly by root cuttings. Take ½–¾″ diameter cuttings, 2–3″ long, in early spring, place horizontally in moist, loose, well-drained soil at 65–75° F (also see *Anemone*). If seed is used, sow 1–2″ deep, place at 70–75° F and cover to maintain high humidity.

**Cultivars:**

Various selections were made between 1900 and 1931, and some of these are still popular today.

'Feltham Pride' has deep blue flowers and grows about 3' tall.

'Dropmore' was selected in 1905, and the deep blue flowers are still in demand. It reaches a height of 4' and is one of the more commonly offered cultivars.

'Little John' is a compact version of the species (1½' tall), with dark blue flowers and a compact habit.

'Loddon Royalist' is about 3' in height and has lovely gentian-blue flowers.

'Morning Glory' bears gentian-blue flowers on 4' tall plants.

'Opal' was raised in 1906 and has azure blue flowers. This and 'Dropmore' are untidy in habit and occupy a great deal of garden space.

'Royal Blue' is similar to 'Loddon Royalist' but has a deeper blue color.


*Androsace* (an-dros' a-kee)          Rock Jasmine          Primulaceae

This relatively unknown group of plants are more or less xerophytic, low-growing alpines which require excellent drainage. They are grown for their open, flat-faced flowers with a marked eye, borne over tight rosettes of leaves. In general, they prefer light, sandy soils, low nutrient status, and good air movement. Most of the 100 or so species perform well in full sun, although *A. geraniifolia* is best in partial shade. Low altitude species such as *A. sempervivoides*, *A. carnea*, and *A. sarmentosa* are most tolerant of American gardens, and, while no species relishes the hot humid summers so common to the eastern United States, *A. sarmentosa*, *A. carnea*, *A. lactea* and *A. lanuginsona* are a little more forgiving. *Androsace* is most popular with gardeners on the west coast and plain states, where temperatures are cool and/or rainfall is limited.

A few species are offered by national mail order nurseries, as well as a few retail garden centers. *A. carnea* is a 4" tall tufted ground cover with white or pink flowers. The subspecies, *brigantica*, is larger, more robust and bears white flowers. Hybrids between *A. carnea* and *A. pyrenaica* are occasionally available. *A. sarmentosa* is offered by most nurseries who sell plants of this genus. Plants produce hairy, silver rosettes in early spring, later becoming less hairy. Plants are spread by stolons to make a small patch and bear pink flowers with tiny, yellow eyes. Plants grow about 6" tall. The variety *chumbyi* is more dwarf (about 3") and bears deeper pink flowers. *A. villosa* is densely tufted with rosettes that look like little cushions and usually bears lots of shaggy hairs on the leaves. Flowers are pink to white. The variety *jacquemontii* bears pink flowers.

*Anemone* (a-nem' o-nee)          Windflower          Ranunculaceae

*Anemone* is a diverse genus of approximately 100 species including fibrous- and tuberous-rooted species. They are enjoyed as greenhouse potted plants, florist cut flowers and garden plants. One can find anemones blooming in spring, summer and fall, and most will grow in ordinary garden soil. In 1629, John Parkinson wrote in Paradisi that "the sight of them doth enforce an earnest longing desire in the minde of anyone to be a possessour of some of them at the least, for . . . is of it selfe alone almost sufficient to furnish a garden with their flowers for almost halfe the yeare. . . ." Most species have compound leaves and apetalous (no petals) flowers consisting of showy sepals. Three main groups of *Anemone* occur, based on their rootstalks and growth habit.

| Rootstalk | Flowering time | Examples |
|---|---|---|
| Fibrous | Late Summer, Autumn | *A. hupehensis, A.* × *hybrida, A. tomentosa, A. vitifolia* |
| Tuber, rhizomes | Spring | *A. blanda, A. canadensis, A.* × *lesseri, A. nemorosa, A. sylvestris* |
| Tuberous-rooted | Spring, Early Summer | *A. coronaria, A.* × *fulgens, A. pavonina* |

Confusion reigns about those ubiquitous Japanese anemones, which refer to a complex of closely related plants, none of which originated in Japan. It makes more sense to call them autumn-flowering anemones. They include *A. vitifolia, A. tomentosa, A. hupehensis, A.* × *hybrida* and are vigorous growers.

The tuberous types (*A. blanda, A. coronaria*) are best planted in mid to late October, approximately 3" deep. All species appreciate shelter from the afternoon sun and do poorly if allowed to dry out. The early spring-flowering, tuberous species are usually dormant by the time the hot sun of summer arrives.

Propagation by seed is possible, but, for most, division is the quickest and surest method of multiplication. For tuberous/rhizomatous species, the tubers may be lifted in early June and divided. Ripe seed should be rubbed in dry sand to remove the cottony down adhering to the seed. The autumn-flowering forms are easily increased by division in the fall. Root cuttings of the fibrous forms are extensively used to propagate those species.

Quick Reference to Anemone Species

|  | Height (in.) | # of sepals | Flower color | Flowering time |
|---|---|---|---|---|
| *A. blanda* | 6–8 | 9–14 | Blue | Early spring |
| *A. canadensis* | 12–24 | 4–5 | White | Spring |
| *A. coronaria* | 7–15 | 6–20 | Various | Early spring |
| *A.* × *hybrida* | 30–48 | 6–11 | White, pink | Fall |
| *A.* × *lesseri* | 15–18 | 5–8 | Rosy red | Early summer |
| *A. magellanica* | 6–8 | 5–10 | White | Early spring |
| *A. nemorosa* | 6–8 | 5–9 | White | Spring |
| *A. sylvestris* | 10–18 | 5–8 | White | Spring |
| *A. tomentosa* | 18–36 | 5–7 | White, pink | Fall |

| *-blanda* (blan' da) | | Grecian Windflower | 6–8″/8″ |
|---|---|---|---|
| Early Spring | Sky Blue | Greece | Zones 4–7 |

The Grecian windflower is one of the earliest harbingers of spring. The small stature makes plants most suitable for naturalizing or filling in small areas of the garden. The oval tuber produces deeply cut foliage resulting in a fern-like appearance. Although the flowers of the species are dark blue, cultivars are available in sky blue, white, pink or purplish red. The narrow sepals are about ½″ long and the flowers nearly 2″ across. The flowers last but 2 weeks and give rise to hairy seed heads known as achenes. These fruiting bodies persist 3–4 weeks but are not particularly attractive and should be removed. The tubers should be planted 1–3″ apart in dappled shade and soil amended with organic matter. In the South (south of zone 6), plants do not spread as rapidly as in the North, nor are they as long-lived. One to two years is necessary to establish the tubers, especially if they are dried out when purchased. Once established, however, plants will self-sow (if you are not silly enough to remove the achemes), and the seedlings will flower the second year. Provide winter protection in zone 4 with leaves or pine boughs.

**Cultivars:**

'Charmer' produces deep rose flowers.

'Blue Star' has dark blue flowers about 2–2½″ in diameter.

'Bridesmaid' and 'White Splendor' both bear flowers of pure white. There is little difference between them.

'Pink Star' and 'Rosea' have differing shades of purple. The former has larger flowers than the latter.

'Radar' is one of the finest cultivars and has large, mauve flowers with white centers.

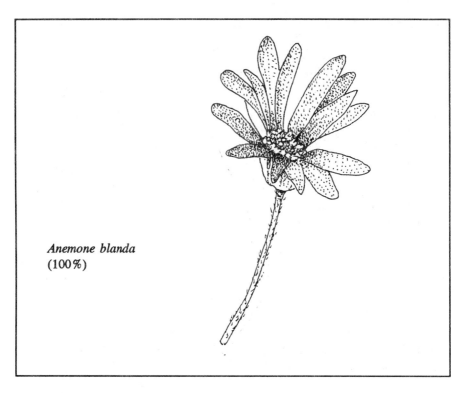

*Anemone blanda*
(100%)

'Violet Star' bears violet flowers with white centers.

'White Splendour' has lovely, single, creamy white flowers.

### Related Species:

*A. altaica* is native to northern areas of Russia and the arctic and, therefore, particularly cold hardy. Plants are about 8″ tall and bear single, white flowers with blue or purple veins in the spring.

*A. apennina*, Apennine windflower, is similar but not as cold hardy. Plants have larger leaves and bright blue flowers with yellow stamens.


*-canadensis* (kan-a-den′ sis)     Meadow Anemone     12–24″/Spreader
    Spring     White     Northern United States, Canada     Zones 3–7
(Syn. *A. pennsylvanica*)

The common name is particularly appropriate because the species will spread and fill an entire meadow. That it is invasive is probably its only flaw, and, if placed in a difficult corner or other area where it can run, it will reign supreme in the spring and into early summer. The light green leaves are 5–7 parted and broader than long. They are hairy beneath, and the leaf segments are toothed. Each clear white flower is almost 2″ across and consists of 4–5 sepals.

Plants do best in partial shade but tolerate full sun. It is native to low-lying areas and thus requires moist conditions to become established. As long as its exuberant habit can be enjoyed, this is an excellent plant for those who think they can't grow anything.

Propagate by division any time from May to September.

**Related Species:**

*A. narcissiflora*, native to the mountains of Europe and Japan, grows about 12–18″ tall over deeply divided foliage. Plants bear 2–6 white to cream-colored flowers per umbel in the spring. Each flower is about 1″ wide. Does well in zones 4–7a.

| *-coronaria* (ko-ro-nah′ ree-a) | | Poppy Anemone | 7–10″/8″ |
|---|---|---|---|
| Early Spring | Various | Mediterranean | Zones 6–9 |

Gardeners seldom see the actual species any more, for it has been replaced with more colorful hybrids. All *A. coronaria* strains have finely-divided foliage and rounded sepals in various colors. Regardless of the pedigree, they make lovely spring garden plants, as well as good cut flowers. They may be planted in the North (zone 6) as late as October and in the South in November for early spring flowering. Further north than zone 6, pot the tuber at the beginning of March and plant outside after threat of frost, and flowers will emerge in late May and early June. Research in Georgia (zone 7b) has shown that planting as late as December does not affect the number of flowers (4–5 flowers/plant). The flowering season was also extended a few weeks with late planting. However, plantings in January, February, and March resulted in few flowers of questionable quality. This was probably because insufficient cold was accumulated by the tubers. This research also indicates that corms are best treated as annuals, dug up and discarded after flowering. Flower production declines, and tubers decline after 2 years in the ground. Tubers of *A. blanda* and *A. coronaria* are relatively inexpensive, and can be replaced at a nominal cost.

**Cultivars:**

'Cleopatra' was recently introduced as a cut flower mix. A mix of flower colors are held on tall stems. Difficult for the gardener to find.

'De Caen' hybrids were developed early in the 18th century around the Caen and Bayeux districts of northern France and became known as the De Caen anemones. The flowers are single, saucer shaped and available as 'Florist Mix' or as separate colors. 'The Bride', white; 'Mr. Fokker', violet-blue; and 'Sylphide', violet rose are only a few of the cultivars which were developed within the De Caen series.

'Hollandia' (syn. 'His Excellency') has scarlet sepals with white bases surrounding a black center.

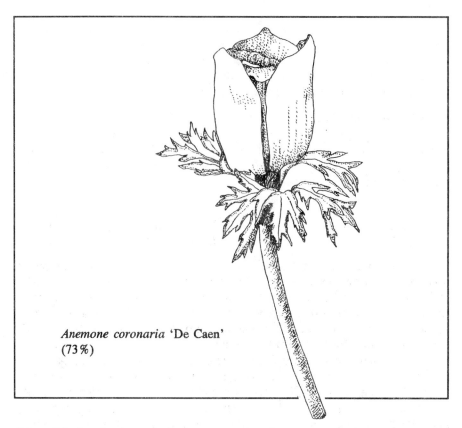

*Anemone coronaria* 'De Caen'
(73%)

'Mona Lisa' series is a relatively new strain of poppy anemone which is much preferable to the 'De Caen' series. Separate colors, as well as a mixture, have been developed. The flowers are larger, the stems are 1½–2 times longer, and the vase life of the cut flowers is longer. They are presently available for greenhouse forcing but should soon be available to the general public.

'St. Brigid' series has semi-double flowers and is available as a mixture or in separate colors. 'Lord Lieutenant', purple blue; 'Mt. Everest', white; 'The Admiral', blue; and 'The Governor', crimson scarlet are available in this series.

'St Piran' were developed in Cornwall, England and bear long stems of single and semi-double flowers. They are only available in a mix.

### Related Species:

*A. pavonina* is native to southern Europe, mainly around the Mediterranean, and also arises from tubers. Plants grow about 9–12" tall and bear solitary, 2–3" wide flowers. The flowers, consisting of 7–9 segments, are often scarlet; however, pink, purple and violet colors occur.

-× *hybrida* (hi-bred' a)   Hybrid Anemone, Japanese Anemone   2½–3'/2'
Fall         White, Pink          Hybrid Origin            Zones 5–7

The nomenclature of *Anemone* is rather confused, but nowhere is it as befuddled as with Japanese anemone and the various hybrids. Probably most plants sold as *A. japonica* are masquerading under that name and are actually hybrids which are wonderful garden plants and provide much needed color in late summer and early fall gardens. They perform best in well-drained soils and partial shade. They are often slow to establish but are free flowering after the second year and can soon take over. In the South, plant early in the fall to allow root establishment or early in the spring. Planting in mid summer is possible, but often plants don't establish well. Plants do not do well south of zone 7a.

Propagation by division in the spring can be accomplished, but root cuttings are most effective. Take thick sections of root approximately 3–4" long from lifted plants and place vertically in a moist well-drained medium. Cover the tops of the root sections with a thin layer of sand or vermiculite and place in a cold frame or unheated greenhouse. This method of propagation should be accomplished when the plants are dormant in the winter.

### Cultivars:

There are some absolutely wonderful hybrids available, and, although my preferences in anemones reside with the single forms, there are many cultivars also available with semi-double or double flowers. The only defect with many of the cultivars is that they are 4–5' tall and often need some support to look their best.

'Alba' bears single, clear white, 2–3" diameter flowers and stands 3' tall. This
   is often listed in catalogs but is probably the same as 'Honorine Jobert'.
'Alice' has semi-double, light pink flowers and is 2–2½' tall.
'Elegantissima' grows 3–4' tall and bears double rosy sepals. A tetraploid
   plant, it is very vigorous.
'Honorine Jobert' was a sport of the pink-flowered *A. × hybrida*, discovered
   in the garden of M. Jobert in Verdun, France in 1858. It has graced European gardens since the beginning of the American Civil War and is still the
   most popular and highly sought after white anemone today. It is 3–4' tall,
   and the clean white sepals contrast beautifully with the yellow stamens in the
   center. The flowers are only 2–3" across, not as large as some of the newer
   clones, but the plant is floriferous and worthy of a place in the garden.
'Kriemhilde' is one of the finest semi-double, pink-flowering cultivars available
   today with 10–15 broad, overlapping sepals. Introduced in 1909.
'Lady Gilmore' is a recent introduction with 2–3" wide, semi-double,
   rosy-pink flowers. The outside of the flower is darker than the inside, a
   trait found in many pink cultivars.

'Luise Uhink' was bred by the German nurseryman, Wilhelm Pfitzer, but is little known in this country. This is unfortunate as it has 3–4" diameter, semi-double, white flowers on 4' tall stems and is a prolific flowerer.

'Margarete' has semi-double to double, deep pink flowers and is about 2–3' tall. Sterile flowers.

'Max Vogel' is one of the most impressive pink flowering anemones I have observed. It stands about 4' tall and carries dozens of single, 3–4" wide, clean pink flowers. Not as cold hardy as many other cultivars.

'Montrose' ('Monterosa'), introduced in 1899, bears semi-double to double, deep rose, sterile flowers on 3' tall stems. Flowers consist of about 40 slightly twisted, narrow sepals.

'Pamina' has semi-double, lavender to rose flowers in late summer and fall.

'Queen Charlotte' ('Konigin Charlotte') bears lovely pink, semi-double flowers, which measure 3" across. The tips of the sepals have a ragged appearance. It grows about 3' tall and was also bred by Pfitzer in Germany.

'Richard Ahrens' produces pink-lilac, single to semi-double flowers, which fade to almost white.

'Whirlwind' is 4–5' tall and has 4" wide, semi-double, pure white flowers consisting of 20–30 narrow, flattened sepals.

'White Giant' grows to 4' tall and produces large, semi-double flowers.

**Related Species:**

*A. hupehensis* has 5–7 rosy mauve sepals, grows 2–2½' tall and flowers a week or so earlier than *A.* × *hybrida*. It is generally shorter than *A.* × *hybrida* and may produce flowers which lack fertile pollen. Originally, plants with 10–20 narrow sepals were found in 1695 in Japan and finally sent to England in 1844 by Robert Fortune, where it was called *A. japonica*. Its proper name has finally been established as *A. hupehensis* var. *japonica* and has never again been found in the wild except where it has escaped from cultivation.

A number of available cultivars should probably be listed under *A. hupehensis* rather than *A.* × *hybrida*. Some of the better known include: 'Bressingham Glow' which produces deep rose-pink, semi-double flowers. Recently introduced but becoming widely available; 'Hadspen Abundance', with pink-rose, single flowers with dark and light pink petals and prominent, golden-yellow stamens on 3' tall plants. From Hadspen House, England; 'Prince Henry' ('Prinz Heinrich') has deep rose, semi-double flowers and is smaller than most of the hybrids but still stands nearly 3' tall. 'Praecox', an early-flowering form with single, dark pink flowers; 'September Charm' which produces single, rose-pink flowers that are darker on the outside than inside; and 'Splendens', with purple to pink flowers. Average garden height of most cultivars is 2–3'.

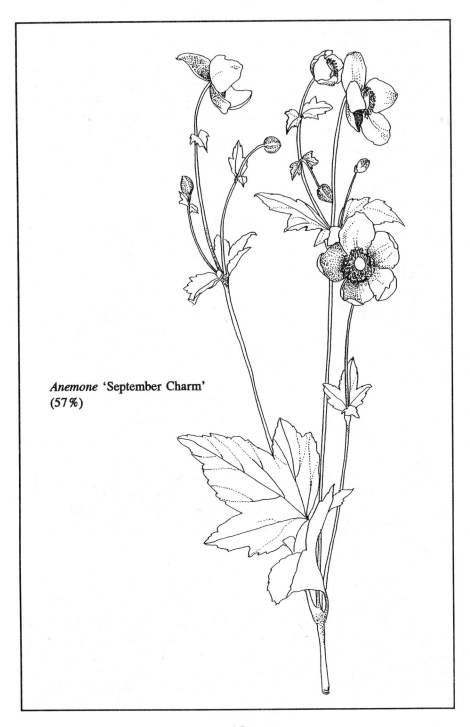

*Anemone* 'September Charm'
(57%)

-× *lesseri* (les' sa-ree)                                                    15-18"/12"
Early Summer          Rose-Red          Hybrid          Zones 5-7

This hybrid between *A. multifida* and *A. sylvestris* bears 5" wide palmately-divided leaves. The 1½-2" diameter flowers are in shades of red to rose, an unusual color for low-growing anemones. Plants are slow growing and make compact clumps. It is best for the front of the border and, like other species, should have afternoon shade. The plants are relatively heat tolerant and perform well in the South. However, they are short lived and seldom persist for more than 2 years.

Propagate by division or root cuttings.

**Related Species:**

*A. multifida* is a fine native species which is finally being offered to growers by bright nursery people. Plants form 8-12" high mounds of light green, delicately cut foliage, with 2-3 long-stalked, yellowish flowers in early spring. Flowers may also be clear red or tinged with blue or purple. The styles are red or pink, and silky seed heads add additional interest after flowering. Some handsome colonies occur in the alpine area of the Denver Botanical Garden. Native from Alaska to Quebec and Saskatchawan and south to California and Colorado. The cultivar 'Major' is better than the species due to the larger, creamy yellow flowers. 'Magellanica' is taller, growing 18-24" in height. Plants perform well in zones 3-6, as well as in the Northwest.

-*magellanica* (ma-jel' lan-i-ca)          Magellan Anemone          6-8"/6"
Early Spring          White          Chile          Zones 2-7

The main claim to fame of this low-growing, garden species is that it is one of the most cold tolerant species of this genus, allowing gardeners from Alaska to North Carolina to enjoy it. The hairy leaves are much divided, and plants are covered with numerous 1" creamy-white flowers on 12" long scapes. The seed heads (achenes) are densely hairy. Culture is not difficult in rich soil in sun or light shade.

-*nemorosa* (nem-o-ro' sa)          Wood Anemone          6-8"/8"
Early Spring          White          Europe          Zones 4-8

The foliage is three times divided into deeply-toothed, linear segments. The flowers are about 1½" wide and often tinged rose on the margins. Plants are single-stemmed with leaves borne halfway up the stem, terminating in a solitary flower. It has a worm-like rhizome which branches extensively. Wood anemones are widely distributed in Europe, being absent only in the more southerly Mediterranean areas, and it should not be surprising that plants are extremely variable in size, color, and even structure of the flowers. There are usually 5-8 sepals, but forms with reduced sepals and others with 50 or more are known. The common flower color is white, but a number of clones have blue or pink flowers, and a yellow-flowered variant has also been described. *A. nemorosa* performs best in slightly acid soil (pH 5.5-6.5) containing liberal amounts of peat or leaf mold and in dappled to deep shade. Plant in fall only.

## Cultivars:

Many cultivars and varieties have been described, but unfortunately, few are available to the general gardener.

*Blue flowers:*

Var. *allenii* is about 1' tall and has large (2" diameter), deep lavender-blue flowers. The reverse is streaked with purplish red dots of varying intensity.

'Blue Beauty' is the tallest of the blue forms, growing 15-18" in height and bears perfect sky blue, cup-shaped blooms. It is the best blue form of the species.

'Bowle's Mauve' has lavender-blue flowers.

Var. *caerulea* is about 6" tall with sky blue ¾" wide flowers. The flower reverse is paler blue. Perhaps all the blue forms should be lumped under this category, as there is little difference between them.

'Robinsoniana' has 1½" diameter bright lavender-blue flowers. It grows 12-14" tall and is one of the oldest varieties still offered by perennial growers. Probably discovered by William Robinson in Oxford Botanical Garden, having "been sent there by a lady in Ireland."

*Pink flowers:*

Var. *rosea* is 10-14" tall and carries nodding 1" wide, light rose flowers with a paler reverse. It is slow to increase vegetatively, and seed production is poor.

*White flowers:*

'Flore Plena' ('Alba Plena') stands 10" tall and has semi-double to double flowers. It is an excellent garden plant.

Var. *grandiflora* has the largest flowers, sometimes attaining 3" in diameter. It is vigorous and grows 20" tall in rich soil.

'Lychette' is one of the best white-flowered cultivars and bears large, 2" diameter flowers which are pure white above and beneath. There are green blushes around the bases of the 6-8 sepals. I have seen plants grow up to 20" tall, but they are normally 10-12" in height.

'Lady Doneraile' is similar to 'Lychette' but only 8-10" tall.

'Vestal' has pure white sepals surrounding a center filled with broad stamen filaments (petaloid stamens). Closely resembles 'Flore Plena', but the flowers are larger, and petaloid segments are more regular. They are different, but in commerce I am not sure what is being sold out there.

**Related Species:**

*A. quinquifolia,* American wood anemone, was initially considered to be a variety of *A. nemorosa* (*A. n.* var. *quinquifolia*). It is native from Quebec to north Georgia and common in moist, rich woodlands. The white flowers are ¾–1″ across and appear in spring. This is a lovely addition to the shaded woodland garden.

*A.* × *lipsiensis* (syn. *A.* × *semanii*) is a pale yellow-flowered hybrid between *A. nemorosa* and *A. ranunculoides.* The flowers, held above finely-cut, bronze foliage, can be quite variable. A woodland location is preferable.

| *-sylvestris* (sil-ves′ tris) | | Snowdrop Anemone | 10–18″/12″ |
|---|---|---|---|
| Spring | White | Europe | Zones 4–7 |

One of the prettiest spring anemones, it combines light green, 3–5 parted leaves with fragrant 1½–2″ diameter, dainty, white flowers. The 5-sepaled flowers are slightly nodding when fully open and are solitary on the flower stalk. The lovely flowers give way to interesting white, woolly fruit. *A. sylvestris* requires light soil and a partially shaded area for best performance. The major drawback is that it runs freely, particularly in loose soils, and can overrun less aggressive plants. Plantlets, however, are not difficult to remove, and gardening friends will be more than happy to accept a few. It is at home from Athens, GA to Denver and Montreal. Cold weather is to its liking, and it is more aggressive in northern climates than in the South.

**Cultivars:**

'Compacta' is offered by a few nurseries and is a more dwarf, compact form of the species. I have never found the species to be particularly large or in need of compaction, but such is the benefit of diversity.

Var. *macrantha* has larger and more abundant flowers.

'Flore Pleno' is a double-flowered, white cultivar but is not nearly as pretty as the species.

**Related Species:**

*A. leveillei* has kidney-shaped, basal leaves which are divided into three sessile lobes, each divided deeply. The 1–2″ wide, white flowers are stained pink on the outside. Hardy to about zone 6.

*A. rivularis* is native to India and China and grows up to 3' tall in zones 5–7. The white flowers are stained blue throughout and are borne in 3–5 flowered umbels in late spring and summer. It is a terrific plant, particularly suited to semi-shaded ponds and water features.

*A. rupicola* is another white-flowered species with blue or pink staining on the sepals but is only about 6–9" tall. The basal leaves are three parted and strongly lobed, while the solitary flowers are up to 2–3" across. Hardy in zones 4–7.

*A. virginiana*, thimbleweed, is a native woodland species with greenish white to white, 1" wide flowers. The early spring flowers usually occur in 3's and consist of 5 sepals. Plants grow about 2' tall and are particularly suited to the woodland garden. Thimbleweed is hardy in zones 3–7.

| *-tomentosa* (toe-men-toe' sa) | Grapeleaf Anemone | 18–36"/18" |
|---|---|---|
| Fall          White | Nepal | Zones 5–8 |

(Syn. *A. vitifolia*)

As with many of the fall-flowering anemones, confusion as to the true identity of *A. tomentosa* runs rampant, being sold for many years as *A. vitifolia*. *A. tomentosa* has more tomentose stems and lower leaf surfaces than *A. vitifolia*. When a separate species, *A. tomentosa* never had pink flowers, one of the reasons why *A. vitifolia* was listed separately, but they are now simply thought to be different species or variants of a single species. Regardless of the name under which it is purchased, it is an exceptional plant, one in which I include in my "no-brainer" list of plants. The leaves are lobed rather than divided, as in the forms of *A.* × *hybrida*. One of the best characteristics is the clumping habit. The foliage is outstanding, remaining healthy and dark green from spring to frost, an exceptionally valuable trait. Similar to *A. sylvestris*, the plants are stoloniferous, and dozens of new plantlets emerge in the spring. In the spring, I curse as I remove intruders from the garden, but I always leave a few clumps, knowing the pleasure I will derive throughout the gardening season.

The single, whitish to pale pink flowers have 5–8 sepals and are one of the earliest fall-flowering anemones. Three to five flowers are held on strong scapes 1½–2' above the foliage. Flowering begins in early August; plants are at their best in August and September and continue to flower sporadically into October. Full sun to partial shade.

**Cultivars:**

'Robustissima' produces mauve-pink flowers held well above the foliage. The leaves are gray-green underneath. It is more winter-hardy than the species and can be grown in zone 4. Robust, to the point of thuggery, in the shade. Much better behaved in full sun.

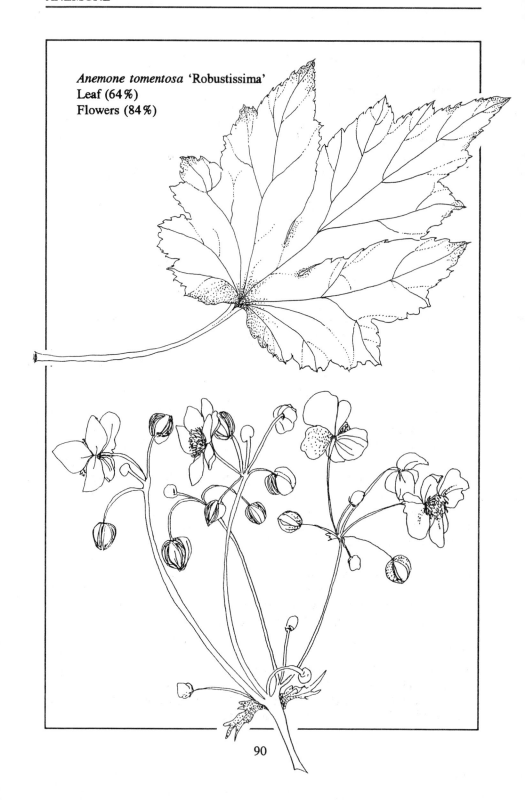

*Anemone tomentosa* 'Robustissima'
Leaf (64%)
Flowers (84%)

Quick Key to Anemone Species

    A. Flowering stems bearing solitary flower
        B. Leaves on flower stem sessile . . . . . . . . . . . *A. coronaria*
        BB. Leaves on flower stem petioled
            C. Fruit woolly . . . . . . . . . . . . . . . . . . . . . *A. sylvestris*
            CC. Fruit not woolly, usually smooth
                D. Sepals 9-14 . . . . . . . . . . . . . . . . . . . . . *A. blanda*
                DD. Sepals usually 5-9
                    E. Flowers usually white, sometimes blue . . *A. nemorosa*
                    EE. Flowers usually red . . . . . . . . . . . . . *A.* × *lesseri*
    AA. Flowering stems branched, bearing 3-5 flowers
        B. Plants 6-8", spring flowering . . . . . . . . . . *A. magellanica*
        BB. Plants taller, summer or fall flowering
            C. Flowers 1-1½" across, flowers early summer . *A. canadensis*
            CC. Flowers 2-3" across, flowers late summer and fall
                D. Leaves 5-lobed, not divided into 3 leaflets . . . *A. tomentosa*
                DD. Leaves not lobed, divided into 3-5 leaflets . *A.* × *hybrida*

**Additional Reading:**

Chatto, Beth. 1986. Japanese Anemone. *Horticulture* 64(10):18–19.

Leslie, A. 1993. *Anemone nemorosa*. *The Garden* 118(12):554–556.

Lovejoy, A. 1994. Woodland wildflowers. *Horticulture* 72(3):38–41.

McKendrick M. 1990. Autumn flowering anemones. *The Plantsman* 12(3): 140–157.

Toubol, Ulrich. 1985. Clonal variation in *Anemone nemorosa*. *The Plantsman* 3(3):167–174.

*Anemonella* (a-nem-o-nell' a)          Rue-Anemone        Ranunculaceae
(Syn. *Thalictrum thalictroides*)

A wonderful diminutive woodland plants native to a large slice of North America, from southwest Maine to northern Florida, and west from Minnesota to Oklahoma. The genus is represented by *A. thalictroides* only. Flowers in the East tend to be white but have more pink in them as the plants extend west. In the Armitage garden, plants compete with the roots of a large, mature oak without complaint. In woodland gardens throughout the eastern United States, rue-anemone is a welcome and familiar sight in early spring. Plants grow about 8-10" tall and bear foliage similar to anemone, except much daintier and finer. They are blue-green, basal and 1-2 ternate, each terminal leaflet being 3-toothed at the apex. The ½" wide flowers are arranged in 2-5 flowered umbels and consist of 5-10 petal-like sepals and numerous stamens. There are no petals.

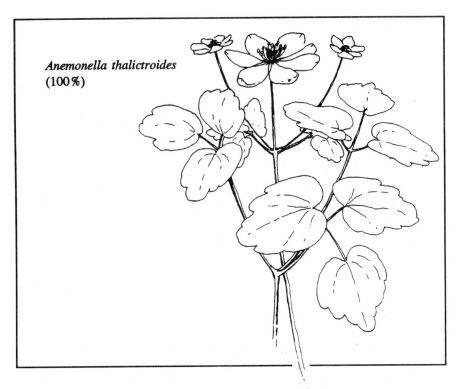

*Anemonella thalictroides*
(100%)

They love to be grouped in partially shaded areas with moisture-retentive soils. If they dry out, they look ratty early. With the exception of slugs, few diseases or insects bother them. Plants are hardy in zones 4–8.

Propagate by seed or division of well-developed clumps.

**Cultivars:**

'Cameo' is a name given to a light pink-flowered, double form. They are very similar to 'Schoaf's Double Pink' and differ by having flowers which are off-white to light pink.

'Eco Pink' from Don Jacobs of Eco Gardens in Decatur, GA has single, pink flowers.

'Eco Starry Night' has unique pointed sepals and bronzy foliage. Quite different.

'Eco Atlas Double' bears white pompon, double flowers.

Var. *favilliana* is a handsome, double white form. Flowers persist much longer than the species, but plants are slow to increase. Difficult to locate.

'Jade Feather' produces double flowers with pink and greenish sepals.

'Rosea' bears single, light pink flowers.

'Schoaf's Double Pink' bears double, rose-pink flowers. It was the result of a chance sighting by Mr. Oscar Schoaf in a graveyard in Owatonna, MN.

While Mr. Schoaf brought the plants into cultivation in his garden, it was Mrs. Louise Koehler of Bixby, MN who sent plants to friends and nurseries and brought the plant out of obscurity. Propagated only by division, plants are slow to increase and difficult to locate, but they are worth the hunt. They are stunning in Garden in the Woods, Framingham, MA.

**Additional Reading:**

Blecken, A.D. 1991. Rue anemone. *Horticulture* 69(2):72.

Foster, H.L and Foster, L.L. 1990. Many of the fine writings of H. Linc Foster and Laura Louise Foster, the late rock garden gurus of this country, were compiled in *Cuttings from a Rock Garden*, Atlantic Monthly Press. The essay on this species is particularly enlightening.

## *Anemonopsis* (a-nem-o-nop′ sis)    False Anemone    Ranunculaceae

As I stared at this plant in a shady Cleveland garden, I knew the foliage looked like an anemone, but I couldn't for the life of me place the flowers. All I could say to my inquisitor about this most handsome plant was that it looked like an anemone. It turned out to be a pretty good guess when one considers that the name *Anemonopsis* is translated "resembles anemone." Only one species, *A. macrophylla*, native to Japan, has been described, and it is occasionally offered by specialty nurseries. The 1″ wide, waxy, lavender-pink flowers are held in loose racemes well above the glossy green basal leaves. The pendulous flowers are particularly lovely if plants are planted on a bank where the flowers can be viewed from beneath. Partially shaded, moist conditions serve plants well. A terrific garden plant, they likely perform well in zones 4–7a. Propagate from seed or division.

## *Angelica* (an-gel′ i-ca)    Angelica    Apiaceae

Plants are better known for their angelic medicinal properties (from which the generic name comes) than as an ornamental garden plant. The 50 or so species are found in the northern United States and Canada to Japan and Europe. In general, they are tall and stout, and at home in semi-shaded, moist areas. The leaves are in 3's (ternate) to pinnate, and the petioles are usually sheathed around the stem. The garden forms available are impressive but often short-lived.

Quick reference to Angelica species

|                  | Height (ft.) | Flower color |
| ---------------- | ------------ | ------------ |
| *A. archangelica* | 5–6          | Creamy white |
| *A. gigas*        | 3–5          | Purple       |

| *-archangelica* (ark-an-gel′ i-ka) | | Wild Parsnip | 5-6′/4′ |
|---|---|---|---|
| Early Summer | Creamy White | Europe, Asia | Zones 5-7 |

Say the name *Angelica archangelica* a few times, and it begins to take on poetic qualities of its own. The specific name came from the Archangel Raphael. The plant has been cultivated for generations in Asia and Europe for its confectionery properties and as a vegetable. The stems and petioles may be crystallized for candying, and the young shoots are prepared similar to asparagus or cooked with rhubarb, to reduce the tartness. However, let not your taste for rhubarb (or lack of it) limit the use of this plant! As a cultivated plant, it lends a stateliness of its own to the garden. The large, flat, creamy white to greenish compound umbels are handsome enough, but the resulting seed heads can be absolutely majestic. These large plants can take over an area and will reseed if allowed to do so. Plants are monocarpic, meaning they die after seeding. Some gardeners have found that removing the flowers before they go to seed increases the chance of perennialization. Seedlings require 2 years to flower.

| *-gigas* (gee′ gas) | | Purple Parsnip | 3-5′/4′ |
|---|---|---|---|
| Late Summer, Fall | Purple | Japan, Korea, China | Zones 5-7 |

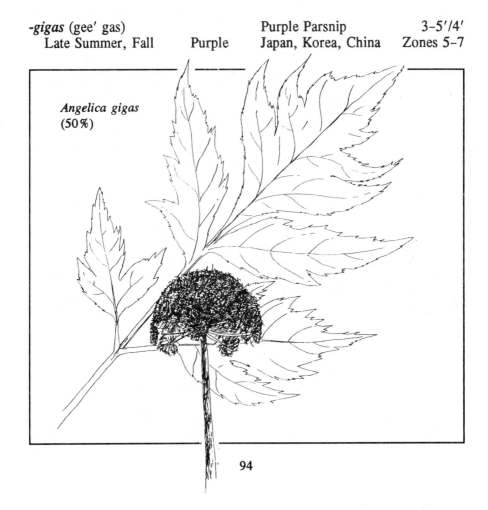

*Angelica gigas*
(50%)

94

Introduced to this country from Korea by Barry Yinger, this large, coarse plant never fails to draw attention when in flower. The light green leaves are attached to the thick stems with inflated, purple sheaths. The flowers are deep purple, in umbels 3-4″ across. Similar to the above species, the drying seed heads are also magical. Although tolerant of shade, if placed in too heavy shade, the dark flowers get lost. Plants love moisture and will be stunted in dry summers. Only recently finding its way into American nurseries, this is an exciting biennial plant for the late summer and fall garden. Plants will self-sow in favorable conditions and may be considered a "perennial biennial." Seed-grown plants generally require 2 years before flowering. In the shaded Armitage garden, plants were magnificent in June into July, although the seed heads never developed as well as I would have liked. The quality of the seed heads increases with sunny areas, cool night temperatures and low humidity.

Quick Key to Angelica Species

    A. Petioles purple-tinged, flowers deep purple . . . . . . . . *A. gigas*
    AA. Petioles not purple-tinged, flowers
        creamy white to greenish white . . . . . . . . . . *A. archangelica*

## *Antennaria* (an-ten-ar′ i-a)         Pussytoes         Asteraceae

About 15 species are used in gardens, primarily because of the carpeting, gray foliage. The flowers are dioecious, meaning that male and female occur on separate plants. The actual flowers are non-descript (like pussy-toes) but are surrounded by dry, chaffy scales which provide the color. However, the gray foliage is the most valuable garden asset. Plants tolerate poor, infertile soils and hot, dry locations. They are best suited for the front of the garden or rock garden. Pussytoes are gaining a steady following due to their toughness, neatness and silvery foliage. Some of the more common forms are native to Europe; however, a number of good species call North America home. *A. neglecta* var. *gaspensia* is one of the neatest, bearing small, silvery leaves on 2-3″ tall ground-hugging mats over which rise silvery-white flowers. *A. parvifolia*, Contock pussytoes, native to southwest Canada and the western United States, is also an excellent rock garden plant.

| *-dioica* (die-o-i′ ka) | | Common Pussytoes | 4-10″/18″ |
|---|---|---|---|
| Early Summer | White | Europe | Zones 4-7 |

Plants send up crowded corymbs of light green flowers with pinkish tips which resemble the toes of your favorite pussycat. The spatulate, basal leaves are about 1″ long and gray-green (some call them silver). The foliage becomes less gray-green as the season progresses and may be almost green by midsummer. The stoloniferous plants fill in rapidly and are occasionally used as an herbaceous lawn by more creative gardeners. If not used as a ground cover, they should be divided every 2 years. Plants are tolerant of poor soil, and good drainage is necessary to reduce root rot.

Propagate by division in the spring or by seed. The seeds are very small and should be mixed with fine sand to insure even distribution in the seed tray. Provide temperatures of about 72–75° F and maintain consistent soil moisture. Transfer seedlings to 60° F conditions for subsequent growth.

### Cultivars:

Var. *hyperborea* (var. *tomentosa*) produces wide, densely hairy leaves.

Var. *minima* is only about 1″ tall and forms a dense carpet. Best for containers or sunny rock gardens.

Var. *minima rubra* is similar to the above but bears rosy-red flowers.

'Nyewood' is a more compact and slower-growing form than the species. The cherry-red flowers cover the tight silver-gray leaves in late spring to early summer. About 3″ tall.

Var. *rubra* has rosy-red flowers and is 8–10″ tall.

### Related Species:

*A. plantaginifolia*, Ladies' Tobacco, is an interesting, if not dramatic, native species. The basal, rather smooth leaves, have 3–7 conspicuous veins, resembling those of plantain, and slowly form a colony of gray-green rosettes. From these basal rosettes arise the white-tan, tight flower heads on 8–12″ tall stems. Useful in zones 3–7.

*A. rosea* (*A. dioica* 'Rosea'), rose pussytoes, is the most common offering and produces rose-pink flowers on 8″ tall plants. The leaves are a little thinner than those of *A. dioica*. The fluffy, rose-pink flowers rise well above the permanently gray-green foliage in late spring and early summer. Native to the mountains of western North America.

*A. rupicola* is native to the northeastern United States and forms 2–3″ tall, loose mats of gray-green foliage which turn beet red in the fall.

## *Anthemis* (an' them-is)          Golden Marguerite          Asteraceae

Of the 80 species in the genus, only a few are worth growing and fewer yet are available in the United States. All have strongly-scented, alternately-arranged foliage which is divided 2–3 times. Flowers of some species are white (*A. cupaniana, A. nobilis*), but most have yellow or orange flowers borne singly on long stems. All need full sun and well-drained soils for best results. Most tolerate relatively poor soils and, in fact, become too leggy if fertilized heavily. The genus is most suitable for northern climates, and, while *A. tinctoria* prospers during spring and early summer in southern gardens, it usually collapses into a messy heap, making it rather useless south of zone 7.

Propagation is easy by division and is necessary within 2–3 years for all species listed. Seeds germinate readily and are available for some cultivars of *A. tinctoria*.

Quick Reference to Anthemis Species

|  | Height (in.) | Foliage color | Flower color |
|---|---|---|---|
| *A. cupaniana* | 6–9 | Gray-green | White |
| *A. marschalliana* | 12–18 | Silver-green | Yellow |
| *A. tinctoria* | 24–36 | Green | Yellow |

**-*cupaniana*** (kew-pan-ee-ah′ na)                               8–12″/36″
    Early Summer            White            Italy            Zones 5–7
(Syn. *A. cretica* var. *cupaniana*, *A. punctata* var. *cupaniana*)

Although this handsome low-grower is offered as *A. cupaniana*, taxonomists are fighting to include it as a variety of one or another species. Since I am not sure into which species it will tumble, I took the cowardly route and retained its older, popular name. Regardless, plants form sprawling, gray-green mats which remind me of lacy artemisia, and which provide wonderful contrasts to other plants in the garden. They are most useful as edging, placed strategically at the front of the border, or as an indispensable rock garden addition. The 1–2″ diameter white daisies consist of 20–25 rays around yellow centers and are borne on 10–12″ flower stems. The flowers are nothing to write home about, but the contrast with the ferny, aromatic leaves is terrific. This species remains relatively compact compared with others. Good drainage helps prevent plants dying during cool, rainy winters. If plants are not in flower and you are not sure if you are looking at *Anthemis* or *Artemisia*, simply smell the foliage. The characteristic artemisia-scent is totally lacking.

**Related Species:**

*A. cretica* ssp. *carpatica* forms 6″ tall cushions of gray-green, hairy foliage and white daisy flowers. 'Snow Carpet' seems to be the same as the above but is a much better name. Hardy from zone 3–7.

97

*-marschalliana* (mar-shal-ee-ah' na)     Marshall Chamomile   12–15″/24″
   Early Summer        Yellow        Caucasus              Zones 5–7
(Syn. *A. biebersteiniana*)

Plants are dressed in finely-divided, silvery foliage, atop which are borne 1–2″ diameter golden yellow daisy flowers. The pinnately-segmented foliage has long hairs and is silky to the touch. If spent flowers are removed immediately, flowering will continue throughout the summer. This is a better species for the South than *A. tinctoria*. Excellent drainage is necessary; full sun is best, but some afternoon shade is tolerated.

*-tinctoria* (tink-to' ree-a)          Golden Marguerite          2–3′/2′
   Summer          Yellow        Europe                 Zones 3–7

This is the most common *Anthemis* available and, with proper culture, is a magnificent plant in the northern United States and Canada. The 3″ long-toothed leaves are parsley-like and somewhat downy beneath. The stem is not round but angled, and the 1½″ diameter flowers are single, yellow and plentiful but rather short-lived.

If grown in rich soil, plants attain 3′ in height and require staking. Cut back the plant severely after flowering to encourage basal growth, and divide every 2 years. Sharon Illingsworth of Thunder Bay, Ontario, Canada, takes cuttings from overwintered young shoots in early spring and roots them in vermiculite covered with plastic bags. Roots are formed within 14 days, and good-sized plants for transplanting result by early June.

### Cultivars:

*A. tinctoria* and *A. sancti-johannis* (a similar species with deep orange-yellow flowers) have hybridized freely, and some of the listed cultivars may be hybrids between them.

'Alba' is very un-alba-ish, bearing pale cream-colored flowers over dark green, finely-divided leaves.

'E. C. Buxton' is a superb 2–2½′ tall cultivar which bears off-white daisies with lemon yellow centers. Probably still the best of the *Anthemis* cultivars.

'Grallagh Glory' ('Beauty of Grallagh') has bright gold flowers atop 3′ tall stems.

'Grallagh Gold' bears pale yellow to yellow-orange flowers and usually grows 2–2½′ tall. It has superseded 'Perry's Gold', an older, taller, golden yellow form.

'Kelway's Variety' ('Kelwayi') has become very popular recently. Plants bear a profusion of bright yellow flowers.

'Moonlight' bears handsome, light yellow blossoms with a deeper yellow center.

'St. Johannes' has bright orange flowers. The three previous cultivars are more compact than the species, but even more dwarf cultivars would still be most welcome.

'Tetworth' is a welcome addition to this plant group. A hybrid between *A. tinctoria* and *A. cupaniana*, plants bear the gray foliage and small stature of the latter but the profusion of flowers of the former. The semi-double, white daisies are produced in early summer on 10–18" tall plants.

'Wargrave' bears masses of pale yellow daisy flowers and deep green, ferny foliage.

**Related Species:**

*A. triumfetti* is similar to *A. tinctoria* but carries many white flowers with yellow centers. Plants grow 18–24" tall. Likely only hardy to zone 6 or 7.

Quick Key to Anthemis Species

    A. Plants 6–18" tall, flowers white or yellow
      B. Flowers yellow, foliage silky,
         usually taller than 12" . . . . . . . . . . . . . . *A. marschalliana*
      BB. Flowers white, foliage glabrous,
         usually less than 12" tall . . . . . . . . . . . . . . *A. cupaniana*
    AA. Plants 2–3', flowers yellow to orange . . . . . . . . . *A. tinctoria*

## *Anthericum* (an-ther' i-cum)                  Liliaceae

About 50 species of this little-used genus are known, but two are cultivated with some success in North America. Plants emerge from rhizomes, and flowering occurs in late spring and summer. All species are native to southern Europe, Turkey or Africa. Not easy to locate but well worth a spot in the garden.

Quick Reference to Anthericum species

|  | Flower color | Flower stem branched | Height (in.) |
|---|---|---|---|
| *A. liliago* | White | No | 24–30 |
| *A. ramosum* | White | Yes | 15–24 |

| *-liliago* (lil-ee' a-go) | | St. Bernard's Lily | 24–30"/12" |
|---|---|---|---|
| White | Summer | Southern Europe | Zones 4–7 |

Native to alpine meadows, where it bears racemes of small, starry, white flowers with upwardly curled styles and yellow stamens. Arranged in groups of at least three, the 3–4' tall plants catch the eye in the late spring or summer garden. Full sun and well-drained soils are necessary. Plants do not perform well in the south.

**Cultivars:**
'Major' is taller (3') and bears flattened, pure white flowers.

| *-ramosum* (ray mo' sum) | | | 15–24"/12" |
|---|---|---|---|
| White | Summer | Southern Europe | Zones 4–8 |

Native to lower valleys than *A. liliago*, this species is a little more heat tolerant and a better choice for hot summers. The gray-green, upright foliage combines with many white flowers on a branched inflorescence. The flowers have yellow stamens and straight styles. Full sun and well-drained soils help make this plant successful in the garden.

Quick Key to Anthericum Species

    A. Flowers occur on unbranched racemes,
        style of flower curved upwards . . . . . . . . . . . . . . . *A. liliago*
    AA. Flowers on branched scapes,
        style of flower straight . . . . . . . . . . . . . . . . . . . *A. ramosum*

## *Aquilegia* (ack-wi-lee' gee-a)      Columbine      Ranunculaceae

A garden without columbine is simply incomplete. The genus consists of approximately 65 species, and, if all were available, they would probably all be outstanding garden plants. The flowers, which may be nodding or upright, consist of 5 petals with a short, broad tube in front (petal tube) and backward projecting spurs. The spurs were thought to resemble the claws of an eagle—the Latin translation being *aquila*, thus the genus name. The 5 sepals are often the same color as the petals but may be different in some species and hybrids. The leaves are held in groups of 3 leaflets (ternate), and in some species they are bi- or even triternate. The leaves are always attached to the stem by long petioles. All columbines are spring or early summer flowering and prefer a rich soil in light to moderate shade with plenty of moisture. Many species are short-lived, particularly if drainage is poor, and should not be counted on for more than 3 years. After flowering, the seed is held in erect, long, narrow follicles which are ornamental for several weeks.

Species vary considerably, ranging from 3' tall species to miniatures, and vary in color from white to blue and purple to pink. In fact, for those gardeners who can't control their columbine habit, there is even a green-flowered species, *A. viridiflora*, which no one will like but you. The white-flowered *A. fragrans* is even sweetly fragrant. Several columbines reseed freely, particularly *A. canadensis* and *A. vulgaris*, but the hybrid cultivars do not come true from seed. Natural hybridization occurs among species, so they should be planted in separate areas of the garden if one does not want illegitimate seedlings among the parents. However, many of the chance offspring are handsome in their own right and may be very vigorous. Some of the hybrids ('McKana', 'Biedermeier', 'Mrs. Scott Elliot') are not nearly as stately as many of the species; however, they often satisfy the needs of the "bigger is better" gardeners.

Propagation of the species is not difficult from seed, and most seeds respond to a cold treatment. Sow the seed in a well-drained medium and place in the cold (a refrigerator will do) for about 6 weeks. Many of the named cultivars of both the hybrids and the species may be purchased from seed.

Quick Reference to Aquilegia Species

|  | Flower color (sepals/petals) | Spurs Straight, Hooked, Curved | Spur length (in.) | Flower Nodding or Upright |
|---|---|---|---|---|
| A. alpina | Blue/blue (white) | C | ¾–1 | N |
| A. caerulea | Blue/white | S | 1–2 | U |
| A. canadensis | Yellow/red | C | ½–1 | N |
| A. chrysantha | Yellow/pale yellow | H | 2–2½ | U |
| A. flabellata | White/white | C, H | ¾–1 | N |
| A. × hybrida | Various | S | 2–6 | U |
| A. longissima | Yellow/pale yellow | S | 4–6 | U |
| A. vulgaris | Blue/blue | H | ½–¾ | N |

| -alpina (al-pine' a) | | Alpine Columbine | 1–3'/2' |
|---|---|---|---|
| Spring | Blue | Switzerland | Zones 3–8 |

This species belies its name, as some of the most vigorous and stately plants in my Georgia garden are *A. alpina*. All columbines appear to be taller in the South when compared with the same plants in the North, and this columbine is usually only 1–1½' in northern areas but is 2½–3' in the South. The gray-green foliage is deeply divided into linear lobes. The basal leaves are 2-ternate, and the stem is hairy, particularly near the top. The abundant, nodding flowers have short-curved or slightly-hooked spurs, flared 2" wide sepals, and are usually blue throughout, although the petal tube may sometimes be white. This is, without question, one of the finest species available for the garden.

Propagation from seed is easy, and although a cold treatment is beneficial, it is not necessary.

## Cultivars:

Var. *alba* is a white form whose flowers contrast well with the dark green foliage. It grows a little shorter than the species.

Var. *superba* is larger than the species but otherwise similar.

## Related Species:

*A. einseliana* is another alpine species with nodding, blue-violet flowers and short (½") straight spurs. Plants are smaller than *A. alpina* and usually grow 9–12" tall.

*A.* × 'Hensol Harebell' is a hybrid between *A. alpina* and *A. vulgaris* and has deep blue flowers which continue well into summer. The branched flower stems produce an open, airy effect and persisted about 2 years in the Armitage garden. After that, various unrecognizable offspring took over.

*A. pyrenaica*, native to the Pyrennees in northern Spain, bears nodding, violet-blue flowers with straight or slightly curved spurs. They are suitable for small areas or rock gardens due to their 8–12" height.

| *-caerulea* (ce-ru′ lee-a) | Rocky Mountain Columbine | 1–2′/2′ |
|---|---|---|
| Spring     Blue/White | Rocky Mountains | Zones 3–8 |

This long-spurred, blue and white-flowered species really isn't much different than many of the hybrids of the same color, but to encounter a grove of these flowers in the spring mountain meadows is close to a religious experience. The state flower of Colorado bears large (2–3" across), upright, facing flowers which have been an important parent in the evolution of long-spurred hybrids. The spurs are straight or outward curving and are often tipped with green. Although not as vigorous as many of the other species or hybrids, it is longer lasting, 4–5 years in the garden not being uncommon. Propagation is similar to *A. alpina*.

## Cultivars:

Some catalogs provide an impressive list of cultivars, but most belong with the hybrids (*A. caerulea* is only one of the parents).

'Crimson Star' is the best known cultivar in this species but likely harbors additional parentage. However, plants grow 2½′ tall with crisp crimson sepals and white petals.

'Mrs. Nicholls' has 3" wide Cambridge blue outer petals and whitish blue inner petals. It is an old cultivar and, unfortunately, difficult to find.

Var. *ochroleuca* (syn. 'Albiflora') has creamy white flowers but is otherwise similar to the species.

'Red Hobbit' is an *A. caerulea* hybrid, having been selected from 'Crimson Star'. Rose-red flowers are produced on a compact, 12–15" tall plants.

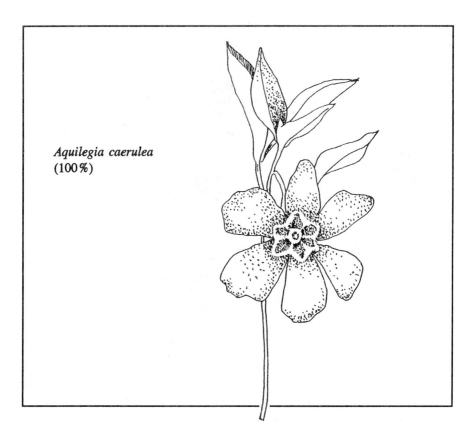

*Aquilegia caerulea*
(100%)

## Related Species:

*A.* × *helenae* ('Helenae') is a hybrid between *A. caerulea* and *A. flabellata*. It has the blue and white flowers of *A. caerulea* and the short ½" long spurs of *A. flabellata*.

*A. laramiensis* is also native to the Rocky Mountains and bears small, white flowers which barely surpass the foliage. Plants grow 6-9" tall and are best for well-drained rock garden sites.

-*canadensis* (kan-a-den' sis)    Canadian Columbine    2-3'/1'
   Early Spring   Yellow/Red   Eastern United States, Canada   Zones 3-8

This is one of my all-time favorite spring-flowering plants. To be sure, they are not as spectacular as many of the hybrids but have a certain grace and elegance that puts them in a class of their own. Native to much of eastern North America, it is found in moist, shady areas. Plants look best in clumps of three or more and reseed to double the area within 2-3 years.

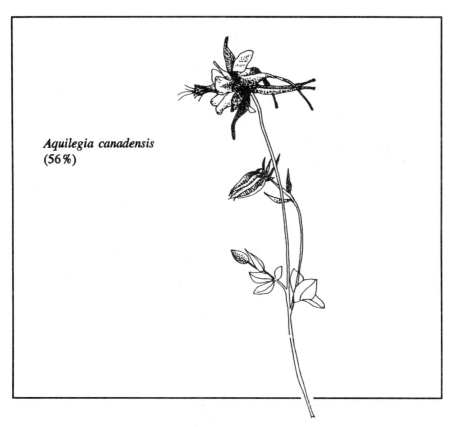

*Aquilegia canadensis*
(56%)

The 1½" long nodding flowers appear in early spring and remain in bloom for approximately 6 weeks. The short spurs are slightly curved but do not have the obvious hook seen in *A. vulgaris* or *A. flabellata*. In the Armitage garden, plants range from light pink/yellow to blood red/yellow. In climates with cooler nights, the sepals are decidedly redder. It has somewhat evergreen foliage in southern climates, and new growth begins as soon as temperatures rise above 40° F. Due to its vigor, it is one of the few columbines that can be placed at the back of the bed or used to hide a distracting object such as an electrical box or fire hydrant (although my dog is not fooled and has not yet learned the meaning of respect).

Propagation by seed is easy. Do not be surprised to find plants emerging quite a distance from the initial planting. If fresh seeds are needed, wait until the seeds loosen and turn jet black. One of the favorite projects in my Perennials class at Georgia is to place each student beside a plant in my garden just after the seeds have ripened in their cozy follicles. The assignment is to gather the seeds and fling them around the garden, leaving a legacy for the student and increasing my pleasure next spring. Everyone gets a grade of A. Plants flower the second year from seed. Thinning the area by transplanting young plants rejuvenates the clump as well as increases numbers.

This species also shows a relative disdain for that voracious enemy of columbine—the leaf miner! Based on observations over the years, there is little doubt that, when grown side by side, *A. canadensis* is less susceptible to leaf miner damage than many other species and certainly much more so than the hybrids. Leaf miners will mine this species also and eventually cause significant disfiguration, but not as rapidly as with others.

**Cultivars:**

'Corbett' was selected by Richard Simon of Bluemont Nursery near the town of Corbett, Maryland. Plants grow 8-10″ tall and bear pale yellow flowers. Unfortunately, I have little success in establishing this plant in the south and am still puzzled by its relative lack of vigor in the heat.

**Related Species:**

*A. atrata* is a handsome 2-3′ tall columbine with 1-2″ wide, nodding, purple-violet flowers. This is similar to another dark-flowered form, *A. nigresens*. Hardy to about zone 4.

*A. formosa*, Formosa columbine, is native to the western United States and quite similar to *A. canadensis*. Plants are taller and have sepals longer than the spurs. Even grown side by side, this species and *A. canadensis* are difficult to separate. The var. *truncata* is sometimes offered as *A. eximia* and differs from the species in having much reduced petals. The formosa group is of little use in Eastern gardens.

| *-chrysantha* (kris-anth′ a) | Golden Columbine | 2-4′/1′ |
|---|---|---|
| Spring          Yellow | New Mexico, Arizona | Zones 4-8 |

Probably one of the most spectacular columbines when in flower, particularly when planted against a blue-flowered background. My students pointed out that my plants would probably be a little easier to see if they were not planted in the middle of late yellow daffodils. I have to find that darn color wheel. The flowers are 2-3″ across, and the petals are a deeper yellow than the sepals. The 3″ long spurs spread away from the flower. This is a tall, loose grower which has been used as one of the parents of the long-spurred hybrids. If provided with sufficient moisture, no staking should be necessary.

**Cultivars:**

'Alba-plena' has very pale yellow (almost white) flowers which are occasionally tinged with pink and about 1¾″ across.

Var. *hinckleyana*, Hinckley's columbine, is native to Texas and is more compact than the species. Seems to be more persistent.

Var. *jaeschkanii* and *nana* are dwarf varieties (1½′ tall), the former bearing yellow flowers and red spurs, while the latter is the same color as the species.

'Silver Queen' has 3″ diameter white flowers.

'Yellow Queen' bears 2–3″ wide lemon-yellow flowers. Looks terrific combined with blue or gray-foliaged plants.

**Related Species:**

*A. buergeriana* is related in that it bears nodding flowers of dull yellow petals and purple sepals on 1–2′ tall plants. The straight short spurs are dull purple.

*A. oxysepala* is more closely related to *A. buergeriana* than *A. chrysantha*, and grows 2–3′ tall with interesting claret sepals and yellow petals. The spurs are strongly hooked. Native to Siberia, the plants have not enjoyed great success in the Armitage garden, but I have seen excellent plants in the Northeast and Midwest.

| *-flabellata* (flay-bel-lah′ ta) | | Fan Columbine | 8–18″/1′ |
|---|---|---|---|
| Spring | Blue | Japan | Zones 3–9 |

The leaves are unique in that they are thicker and bluer than most species, and the round leaf segments are fan-shaped and often overlap. The overlapping leaf segments and the bluish tinge to the leaves make this one of the easiest species for my students to identify and separate from the other dozen columbines I throw at them. Plants have been described as "squat or short and fat;" however, the term compact is kinder and more accurate. It is an excellent plant for the front of the garden or the rockery. The species bears lilac to blue flowers, and the spurs are curved to hooked. The terminal flower opens first, followed by those in the lower axils.

Propagate from seed.

**Cultivars:**

'Alba' is the most common form of the species offered by nurseries. The creamy white, nodding flowers are often tinged pink. 'Nana Alba' ('Pumila Alba') is a dwarf form.

'Mini-Star' is a dwarf 6–8″ tall cultivar with blue sepals and white petals. One of the best selections for the rock garden.

Var. *nana* is similar in habit and flower to the above cultivar. They appear to be a different name for the same thing.

'Kurilensis' (var. *pumila* 'Kurilensis') is only 4″ tall with blue or blue and white flowers.

**Related Species:**

*A. bertolonii*, alpine rock columbine, is only 4–9″ tall and bears rich blue-violet flowers. This is a wonderful dwarf columbine for the front of the border or rock garden.

*A. glandulosa* (syn. *A. transsilvanica*), Siberian columbine, is almost identical to *A. flabellata*, having fan-like, bluish foliage and nodding, blue flowers. If one looks closely, the pistils of this species are pubescent, while the pistils are smooth in the fan columbine. The spur is strongly hooked in this species, while it is curved in *A. flabellata*. The var. *jucunda* has white petals and is similar to *A. flabellata* 'Alba'.

-× *hybrida* (hy-brid′ a)          Hybrid Columbine          18″–3′/1′
Spring          Various          Hybrids          Zones 3–9

The hybrids are particularly popular and with good reason. The flowers are large, upright, and in a wide range of colors. There are two generally accepted divisions in this group: long-spurred and short-spurred hybrids. Crosses involving *A. canadensis*, *A. chrysantha*, *A. caerulea*, and *A. formosa* became known as the long-spurred hybrids and are most popular.

The recent upsurge in passion for hybrid columbines began with the McKana hybrids, an All America bronze medal winner in 1955, which

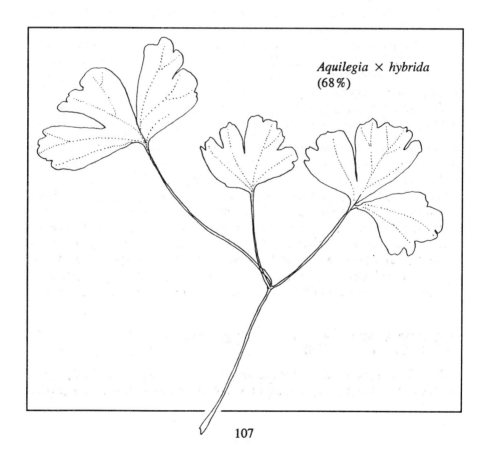

*Aquilegia* × *hybrida*
(68%)

brought large flowers and pastel shades to the gardener. McKana hybrids superseded 'Mrs. Scott Elliott', another excellent strain. The breeding of hybrids continues at a furious pace, and many excellent cultivars are available today.

## Cultivars:

'Biedermeier' is a 9–12″ compact blue and white cultivar, but other colors are also available in the mix. Often referred to as nosegay columbine.

'Dragonfly' consists of a mix of colors on 18–24″ tall plants.

'Fairyland Mix' is a dwarf group of plants with short-spurred, upright, facing flowers in various colors.

'McKana Hybrids' are a series of columbines which have stayed the test of time. Large, long-spurred flowers, which occur in many colors, are borne over 18–24″ tall plants.

'Musik' is a series of seed-propagated columbines probably as good as the 'Song Birds'. They are available in many colors, although yellow is the best. They are free-flowering and relatively compact.

'Song Bird', also known as the 'Dynasty' series, is the work of the late Charles Weddle, one of this country's finest plant breeders. The plants are 2–3′ tall and come in vibrant colors which are truly impressive. Some of those available include 'Blue Bird', light blue and white; 'Blue Jay', deep blue and white; 'Cardinal', rich violet and white; 'Dove', nodding, small, blue and white flowers; Robin; pale pink and white.

'Spring Song' consists of 3′ tall plants with spurs up to 3″ long. The flowers are available in mixed colors, and some are nearly double.

'Windswept' has short-spurred, deep blue flowers on a 12–15″ tall plant.

Many of the older long-spurred hybrids were crossed with *A. vulgaris* to yield the short-spurred hybrids. These are more popular in Europe than in the United States, are smaller in stature and bear smaller flowers.

Some hybrids are available from seed, but self-sown seed will not necessarily resemble the parent. Leaf miner can be a serious pest and is more disruptive to the hybrids than to many of the species. If leaf miner becomes very invasive, the easiest control is to simply cut the plants down to the ground after flowering and destroy the leaves. New growth will soon appear. An all purpose insecticide may be applied in early spring as a preventative measure, but they are not effective once the damage is evident.

| *-longissima* (long-gis′ si-ma) | | Longspur Columbine | 2–3′/2′ |
|---|---|---|---|
| Early Summer | Yellow | Southern United States | Zones 4–8 |

The obvious attributes of this species are the very long (4″), slender spurs on pale yellow flowers. A grouping of 5–6 plants makes an impressive display.

Unfortunately, though vigorous, it is a short-lived perennial, seldom persisting for more than 2 years.

**Cultivars:**

'Longissima Hybrids' resulted from crosses among some of the long-spurred hybrids and *A. longissima* and contains different colors.

'Maxistar' is the most common cultivar available and has larger but similar flowers.

| | | | |
|---|---|---|---|
| *-vulgaris* (vul-gah' ris) | | Granny's Bonnet | 1½–2'/1' |
| Spring, Early Summer | Blue | Europe | Zones 3–8 |

So much natural interbreeding among *A. vulgaris* and other species has occurred that it is becoming more and more difficult to find the true *A. vulgaris*. There is a great deal of variability, but in general the flowers are blue or violet, with short incurved spurs which end in small knobs. It does not possess the classic statuesque form of *A. alpina*, the sparkle of *A. canadensis*, or the airiness of *A. longissima*. However, it is a durable performer and persists well in most gardens. Although I am surely in the minority, I believe that some of the ugliest flowers in the plant kingdom are the doubles and near triple cultivars of *A. vulgaris*.

**Cultivars:**

'Adelaide Addison' bears double purple and white flowers. For some reason, this is sometimes listed as 'Nora's Sister'.

Var. *alba* is a good single, white-flowered form.

'Cap de Rossitiere' was given to me by Charles Cresson of Swarthmore, PA, and its wonderful small pink and white, dahlia-like flowers have become a favorite in the University gardens. Plants grow 2–3' tall, and flowers are persistent.

'Clematatiflora', stormy columbine, bears lovely light pink to burgundy, spurless flowers. The flat, nodding flowers are carried on 2' tall, branching stems.

'Double Rubies' ('Burgundy Double') produces deep maroon, double flowers on 3' tall plants. Flowers are very persistent. I have seen a similar plant listed as 'Ruby Port'.

'Mellow Yellow' has golden yellow foliage with white or pale blue flowers in the spring. Plants are about 20" tall.

Var. *nivea* has single, white flowers and pale gray foliage. It is vigorous, often attaining 3' in height. Var. *nivea* is sometimes referred to as Munstead White Columbine, in reference to Gertrude Jekyll's fondness for the plant.

'Nora Barlow' is a most interesting and unusual cultivar. Flowers are fully double and look more like small dahlias than columbines. The sepals are reddish pink with white margins, and plants grow 2–2½' tall. Nora was the granddaughter of Charles Darwin, and I can't help thinking of turtles when I look at Nora. Association comes in strange forms.

'Trevor Bath', introduced by Canyon Creek Nursery in Oroville, CA, carries short-spurred, semi-double flowers with white petals and rose-red spurs and sepals.

'Variegata' (syn. *A. vervaeneana* 'Variegata') or 'Woodside Garden' has foliage marbled with yellow or gold. Plants are handsome in the spring but tend to fade as temperatures rise. Flowers are usually blue but may be white or purple.

**Related Species:**

*A. viridiflora*, green columbine, has nodding, bicolored flowers with chocolate petals and yellow-green sepals over blue-green foliage. Growing less than 1' tall, it is at first an interesting then a quite forgetable plant for the garden.

Quick Key to Aquilegia Species

    A. Spurs small, generally less than 1" long
      B. Flower red and yellow, spurs
        straight or slightly curved . . . . . . . . . . . . . *A. canadensis*
      BB. Flower not red and yellow, spurs hooked
        C. Leaves divided into 3 rounded
          and fan-shaped leaflets . . . . . . . . . . . . . . *A. flabellata*
        CC. Leaves deeply divided, leaflets linear
          to somewhat rounded
          D. 2–3 flowers to a leafy stem,
            leaflets more linear . . . . . . . . . . . . . . . . . *A. alpina*
          DD. Many flowers to stem, leaflets
            more or less rounded . . . . . . . . . . . . . . . *A. vulgaris*
    AA. Spurs longer than 1"
      B. Flower usually blue and white,
        spurs 1–2" long . . . . . . . . . . . . . . . . . . . . . . *A. caerulea*
      BB. Flower usually yellow, spurs longer
        C. Spurs 2–3" long, sepals much
          longer than petals . . . . . . . . . . . . . . . . . *A. chrysantha*
        CC. Spurs 4–6" long, sepals slightly
          longer than petals . . . . . . . . . . . . . . . . . *A. longissima*

**Additional Reading:**

Armitage, A.M. 1993. Columbines. *Fine Gardening* 31: 58–61.

Dewolf, Gordon. 1984. Columbine. *Horticulture* 62(6):12–13.

Hermes, A.R. 1993. Consider the columbines. *Horticulture* 71(3):24–28.

Van Horn, K.S. 1994. Remembering columbines. *National Gardening* 17(3):50–53.

*Arabis* (ar′ a-bis)                    Rock-Cress                    Brassicaceae

About 120 species are distributed over the northern hemisphere, and most are alpine species. All produce basal rosettes and then send up stems which produce racemes of rose, purple or white flowers. Species are difficult to separate unless one looks closely at the stem leaves and flowers. The cultivated species are effective for the front of the garden or rock walls and are all less than 12″ tall. The principal species in the trade is *A. caucasica* (*A. albida*), wall rock-cress, but others also have garden value. *A. alpina* has smaller rosettes than *A. caucasica*, is less hairy, and more compact (especially var. *compacta*). *A. blepharophylla* (a native of California) has rose-purple flowers but is more tender and needs winter protection in parts of the country. *A. procurrens* grows to 9″ tall, has entire evergreen leaves, and larger white flowers. *A. soyeri* is about 10″ high with white flowers, while *A. sturii* is only 2–3″ tall with glossy leaves and relatively large white flowers. A compact, white-flowering species with a large following in the United States is *A. ferdinandi-coburgi*. The species has gray-green foliage, but the variegated form ('Variegata') is most eye-catching in early spring.

The majority of species are cool climate plants and perform far better in the North than in the South. In hot weather, the centers tend to "melt out," and the stems become long and spindly. I have been moderately successful with *A. procurrens*, *A. albida* and *A. sturii* in Georgia, but none spread vigorously during the summer. All species should be planted in full sun, preferably in areas where drainage is excellent. Cut back after flowering if plants start to look a little dog-eared.

All are easily propagated by division, cuttings, or seed.

Quick Reference to Arabis Species

|  | Height (in.) | Flower color | Stem leaves sessile |
|---|---|---|---|
| *A. blepharophylla* | 4–8 | Rose, pink | Yes |
| *A. caucasica* | 8–15 | White | Yes |
| *A. ferdinandi-coburgi* | 4–6 | White | No |

| *-blepharophylla* (ble-fa-ro-fil′ a) | Fringed Rock-Cress | 4–8″/12″ |
|---|---|---|
| Early Spring        Rose-Purple | California | Zones 5–7 |

This tufted, rock garden plant generally consists of rosettes of 1–3″ long, entire to toothed leaves. The flower stems bear sessile, oblong leaves and terminate in short, dense racemes of carmine-red flowers. The petals are about ½″ long, and the flowers are slightly fragrant.

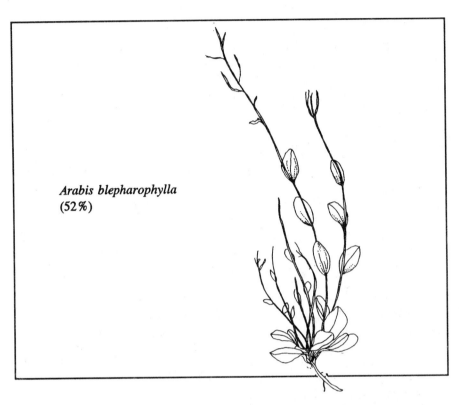

*Arabis blepharophylla*
(52%)

## Cultivars:
'Alba' bears white flowers.
'Spring Charm' ('Fruhlingszauber') is the best cultivar of this species, bearing fragrant rose-pink flowers on compact plants.

*-caucasica* (caw-caz' i-ca)   Wall Rock-Cress  8–15″/18″
 Early Spring   White   Mediterranean  Zones 4–7
(Syn. *A. albida*)

The plant forms a loose mat, and the hairy, succulent foliage is particularly effective climbing over rocks or cascading down walls. The numerous, white flowers are held in a loose raceme in early spring. Plants should be cut back severely after flowering, or by midsummer branches will be nude except for the terminal leaves. The subsequent year's performance is also enhanced by late spring pruning. In the North, plants make a wonderful spring show and form large clumps which need division every 2–3 years. In north Georgia, flowers are present by the end of February and persist until the end of April. Plant in the fall in the South for enjoyment the following spring (similar to a pansy), as plants tend to decline in the summer heat south of zone 7.

## Cultivars:

'Bakkely' is a compact (4–6") plant with single, white flowers.

'Corfe Castle', discovered at Corfe Castle in England, is a handsome 6–8" tall plant with deep magenta flowers.

Var. *flore-plena* is an excellent plant because the double, white flowers are mostly sterile, and little seed is produced. The lack of seed production results in more persistent flowers.

'Gilian Sharman' is a difficult-to-locate form with gold-edged leaves and white flowers.

'Pink Pearl' has deep pink flowers on mat-forming plants.

'Snowball' ('Schneeball') bears white flowers over 4–6" tall plants.

'Snow Cap' is a large, white-flowered cultivar more ornamental than the species.

'Sulphurea' bears sulphur-yellow flowers. Plants are not as floriferous, but the flower color is unique.

'Variegata' has yellow-white stripes on the leaves. It is an interesting variety, but the leaf color detracts from the flowers and the plant is altogether too busy.

## Related Species:

*A.* × *arendsii* resulted from the natural hybridization of *A. aubrietiodes* and *A. caucasica* and includes a few excellent selections. 'Compinkie' has handsome, pink flowers; 'Rosabella' produces rose-colored flowers which become paler as temperatures rise in the spring; 'Rubin' bears wine-colored flowers.

*-ferdinandi-coburgi* (fer-di-nahn' dye ko-burg' ee-eye)      4–6"/10"
                              Ferdinand's Rock-Cress

| Early Spring | White | Bulgaria | Zones 4–7 |

Named after King Ferdinand of Bulgaria, plants provide carpets of white flowers over narrow-oblong leaves with long petioles. Like other members of the genus, plants require excellent drainage and cutting back in the summer. The species itself is seldom offered by nurseries; however, variegated forms are quite common. All bear white flowers.

## Cultivars:

'Limedrop' bears deep green leaves with a lime-green center. Plants grow 4" tall.

'Old Gold' produces shiny leaves which are variegated with gold.

'Variegata' is the most valuable cultivar and bears handsome leaves splashed and edged with clean white.

**Related Species:**

*A. procurrens* is a stoloniferous cultivar which is similar to *A. ferdinandi-coburgi* but has shiny, ovate leaves rather than narrow leaves. Appears to be more heat tolerant than other species. 'Glacier' has dark green leaves and white flowers.

*A. sturii* is one of my favorite rock garden plants. It has small (<2" long) dark green, lustrous leaves arranged in compact mounds. Plants produce many small (½"), clean white flowers in early spring. The clean leaves, the white flowers and the compact growth habit make this a wonderful species. It is occasionally offered by nurseries but may, in fact, be sold as *A. procurrens*. 'Glacier' is very similar and a good choice if *A. sturii* cannot be located.

Quick Key to Arabis Species

   A. Flowers rose to purple . . . . . . . . . . . . . . . *A. blepharophylla*
   AA. Flowers white
      B. Stems not over 6" tall . . . . . . . . . . . *A. ferdinandi-coburgi*
      BB. Stems usually 8–12" tall . . . . . . . . . . . . . *A. caucasica*

## *Arachnoides* (a-rack-noi' deez)      Shield Fern      Dryopteridaceae

The shield ferns are some of the most outstanding plants for the shaded garden, difficult to locate and terribly underused. Those useful for American gardeners are native to China, Japan and Korea and probably not hardy much south of zone 7. I have seen outstanding stands of *A. standishii*, the upside-down fern, in the wonderful garden of Mr. Charles Cresson in Swarthmore, PA. This fern forms a handsome rosette of thin, bright green, narrow fronds whose black sori are visible from above, hence the common name. A far more coarse relative is spiny leather fern, *A. aristata*, whose glossy, dark green fronds are almost prickly to the touch. The most colorful species, however, is *A. simplicior* 'Variegata', variegated shield fern, which I think is one of the "sleeping" gems of the shady palette. The leathery fronds are notable for the prominent yellowish bands on each side of the glossy-green midribs; the color does not fade in hot summers, and the plant is evergreen to about 10° F. In the Armitage garden, plants ducked underground when temperatures fell to about 5° F, but emerged unscathed in early spring. Everyone stops to admire the clump, and this handsome variegated species should be much more widely planted. Certainly, it is a winner for gardeners in zones 7–10, who have been desperate for additional ferns for a long time. It may be marginally hardy in zone 6, with protection.

Plant in partial shade and provide lots of water, particularly in early spring. Variegated shield fern is more tolerant of drying out than the upside-down fern.

## *Arisaema* (a-ris-aye′ ma)　　　　　Jack-in-the-Pulpit　　　Araceae

Some of the wildest, weirdest, most handsome and therefore most highly sought after plants are found in the genus. With over 150 species of mostly tuberous species, there is something for everyone. *Arisaema* is widely distributed, occurring from Tanzania (7°S) to Mexico, through eastern North America and all the way north to about 51°N latitude. Leaves are almost always palmately compound, and generally only one or two mottled stems are produced from the tuber. The flowers consist of a bewildering array of spathes and spadices, which provide some of the most unusual architectural arrangement of flowers in the plant kingdom. *Arisaema* is also unique in its ability of individual plants to change gender. Plants of some species start out bearing male flowers only on the spadix and spontaneously change to female (and vice versa) the next year.

Plants are woodland in nature and perform best in cool, moist areas with plenty of organic matter. Nearly all species go dormant in the summer after flowering and fruiting is complete. Some of the most interesting species are native to Korea and Japan and may grow to 3′ in height (*A. angustatum*) and bear distinctive, large flowers. Unfortunately, the biggest problem for the gardener is finding nurseries who propagate sufficient species of *Arisaema*, well-known or not. The demand definitely exists among American gardeners, and it is simply the supply that keeps many of the species from becoming more common. Without doubt, this problem is being slowly resolved as more plantspeople, such as Don Jacobs from Eco Gardens in Decateur, GA, Dan Hinkley from Heronswood Nursery in Washington and Barry Yinger, find and propagate new species for the clamoring public.

Plant approximately 3–4″ deep and allow to remain undisturbed unless propagation is necessary. Propagation is generally accomplished by lifting tubers and separating young tubers. However, try to control yourself and don't disturb unless necessary.

### Quick Guide to Arisaema Species

|  | Spathe | Spadix | Height (in.) |
|---|---|---|---|
| *A. candidissimum* | Pale pink and white | Yellow-green | 15–18 |
| *A. dracontium* | Green | Green | 18–30 |
| *A. ringens* | Striped green and white | Yellow-white | 10–20 |
| *A. sikokianum* | Striped purple | White | 18–25 |
| *A. triphyllum* | Greenish, mottled purple | Green, brownish | 12–30 |

***-candidissimum*** (kan-di-dis′ si-mum)  White Jack  15–18″/15″
   Late Spring    Pink and White Spathe    Western China    Zones 7–9

I first saw a group of these plants in the garden of Mrs. Helen Dillon in Dublin, Ireland and quickly became a convert to the White Jack. The solitary leaf consists of 3 leaflets and generally emerges with or just after the flower. It is late to emerge (mid-May in most areas) and is therefore less susceptible to late frosts. The loveliest part of the plant is the white spathe, which is suffused with delicate pink. The spathe is only slightly hooded; therefore, the pink can be seen inside as well. The spadix is yellow-green and slightly fragrant.

I have since planted this in the Armitage garden and seen it used as a summer plant in the garden of Wayne Winteroud and Joe Eck in southern Vermont. In the North, plants are overwintered in a cold greenhouse and brought out again for summer bloom.

Plant in groups of a half dozen in a slightly shaded area rich in organic matter.

***-dracontium*** (dra-kon′ tee-um)  Green Dragon  18–30″/20″
   Spring    Green    Eastern North America    Zones 4–8

Extending as far north as Maine and south to northern Florida, green dragon is a frequent, if not common, woodland inhabitant. Although plants are distinctive, their complete green color also makes them easy to walk by without being noticed. However, those who stop a moment are quickly bending down to study this most interesting species. The single leaf consists of 7–15 oblong leaflets arranged in a horseshoe shape, underneath which the green spathe may be found. The narrow spathe is only about 2–3″ long, but the spadix looks like licorice which has been pulled to form a 10–12″ long string-like tail.

Plants flower in mid- to late spring and are best placed in a shady area where they can be viewed along a path or walkway. To be honest, plants are more interesting than they are handsome, but the oblong tubers are inexpensive and easy to locate, and what's the matter with interesting, anyway?

### Related Species:

*A. tortuosum*, whipcord Jack, is also of great interest in that the long, S-shaped, spadix sticks out from the enveloping spathe like the tongue of a tired bulldog. These shade tolerant plants grow 24–36″ tall and are useful in zones 7–10.

***-ringens*** (rin′ gens)  Cobra Jack  10–20″/20″
   Early Spring    Striped Green and White    Japan    Zones 5–7

A most wonderful species, the tubers produce two leaves, each composed of three leaflets and an incurved contorted spathe which looks like a striped

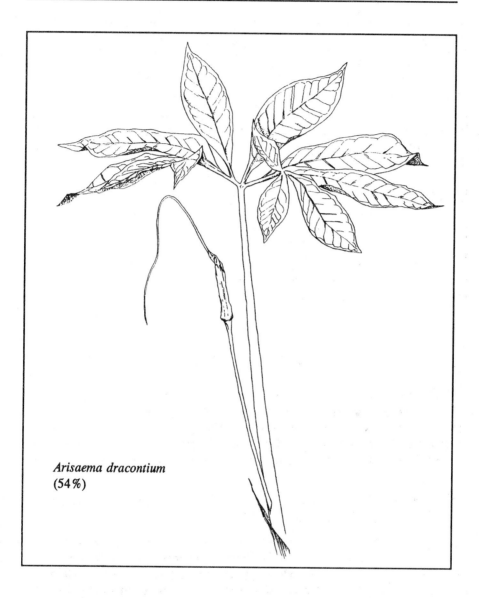

*Arisaema dracontium*
(54%)

helmet. The hood of the spathe is deep chocolate color, while the white to yellow spadix is almost entirely enclosed. Plants are robust and produce some of the largest spathes relative to the overall size of the plant in this genus.

Plants are best suited to groups of six or more and tolerate wetter conditions than other species. Partial shade and soils with sufficient organic matter are essential for best performance.

117

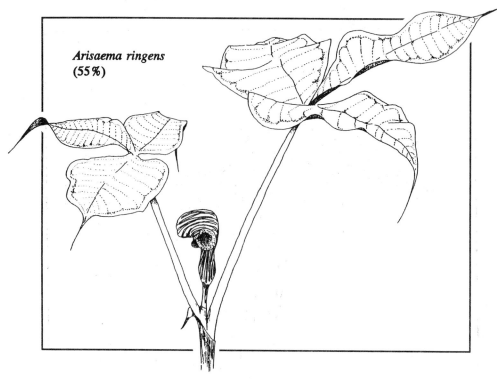

*Arisaema ringens*
(55%)

## Related Species:

*A. consanguineum*, purple jack, grows about 3' tall and has a single leaf cut into 11–20 leaflets with long, narrow tips. The many leaflets have given rise to its other common name, palm tree jack. The spathe is deep purple within, while the green spadix has an elongated tail. Likely hardy in zones 5–8.

| *-sikokianum* (si-koke-ee' aye-num) | | Gaudy Jack | 18–25"/20" |
|---|---|---|---|
| Early Spring | Striped Purple and White | Japan | Zones 5–7 |

If I had to pick but one Jack for my garden, it would come to a vote between this species and *A. candidissimum*, but this one would win. The two leaves consist of five leaflets in the lower, three in the upper and emerge about the same time as the flower. The beauty of this plant lies in the contrast of the purple spathe and the elegant white spadix. The spathe forms a funnel-shaped tube ending in a long, narrow projection. Inside the spathe nests the lovely, pestle-shaped spadix, easily visible in early spring. The only drawback to this plant, other than cost and availability, is that it emerges very early in the spring and has been clubbed to death by late frosts on more than one occasion in the Armitage garden. I use peat moss and baskets to cover the plants in the spring if a frost is forecast, but I have

*Arisaema sikokianum*
(46%)

lost my share. The later emergence of *A. candidissimum* is one of the reasons why it is gaining in popularity, particularly with southern gardeners.

Plants with silver markings on the leaves are also being selected, for foliar interest even when plants are not in flower. I hesitate to give cultivar status ('Variegata'?); however, if a variegated form is offered, this is what it is.

### Related Species:

*A. speciosum*, big-leaf jack, is native to southwestern China and has only recently been introduced. The 2' tall plants have three, one-foot long leaflets and bear a blackish purple spathe and a long, white spadix. Plants are hardy to zone 7 but may make it to zone 6.

*A. takedae*, fancy-stalk jack, grows about 3' tall, with a purple-splotched stem and a purple spathe. A beautiful plant in its own right, it has also become a parent. Hybrids between this species and *A. sikokianum* have been developed by Don Jacobs, and they are absolutely lovely. The 2' tall plants with a purple spathe and whitish spadix are intermediate between the parents. Outstanding in the Armitage garden.

| | | |
|---|---|---|
| *-triphyllum* (tri-fil' lum) | Jack-in-the-Pulpit | 12–30"/25" |
| Spring Green, Mottled Purple | Eastern North America | Zones 4–8 |

By far the most common species in the genus, it is nevertheless a most satisfying plant for the woodland garden. Plants are found from southern Canada to Louisiana and Texas; therefore variability is not surprising. And variable it is! I have seen plants a mere 12" tall with 3-leaflet leaves and other giants which easily attain 3' in height and bear large, 5-leaflet leaves. The color of the spathe also varies from deep purple to green with a few purple stripes. I am sure there is a taxonomist who could split out at least three botanical varieties from the populations commonly found in eastern North America.

The entire plant, including the tuber, contains numerous microscopic bundles of needle-like crystals of calcium oxalate. If one is crazy enough to bite into one, one bite will be enough. The crystals pierce the tender tissues of the mouth, tongue and throat. These are not at all like the potato chip ads that bet you can't eat just one! The best soothers are cool liquids and antihistamines. Despite these irritants, the dormant tubers were cooked by native Indians to produce a fine flour similar to arrowroot. They were peeled, mashed and washed through sieves to obtain a fine starch solution which was dried, boiled or roasted and then ground to flour. The tubers were known as Indian Turnip, and that common name still is used today.

Plants bear two leaves and emerge from early spring to early summer. The spathe may be striped with green or purple or possess a handsome deep purple hue. The green to brown spadix is generally exserted (sticks out) from the spathe. New tubers are formed in abundance, and a source of small, dormant tubers is not difficult to locate. Plant in groups of a dozen or more.

Quick Key to Arisaema Species

    A. Plants produce a single leaf
        B. Leaves generally consist of 3 leaflets  . . . . *A. candidissimum*
      BB. Leaves consist of 7–15 leaflets  . . . . . . . . . *A. dracontium*
    AA. Plants produce 2–3 leaves, seldom 1
        B. Spathe obviously hooded, spadix whitish yellow  . . *A. ringens*
      BB. Spathe open, spadix white or greenish brown
          C. Spadix white, ending in swollen tip . . . . . . *A. sikokianum*
        CC. Spadix greenish brown, cylindrical . . . . . . . *A. triphyllum*

## *Arisarum* (a-ris-ar' um)  Mouse Plant  Araceae

An interesting group of 3 species from the Mediterranean and SW Europe, which are grown for the fun of growing rather than their beauty. The most common species is *A. proboscideum*, mouse plant, whose mouse tail-like tips of the long spadix dangle in the air in early spring, then finally are covered by the dark green, rounded foliage. The leaves make a pleasant mound but then poof, they want to go dormant in early summer. They are slow growers, but if you like tails of mice, then it is indeed fascinating. Partial shade, moisture and humus-rich soil are necessary for success. Likely hardy to about zone 7 (zone 6 with protection).

## *Armeria* (ar-meer' ee-a)  Thrift Sea  Plumbaginaceae

*Armeria* consists of approximately 80 species, several suitable for edging, the rockery or front of the garden. Flowers appear in solitary, dense, globe-shaped heads high above the foliage on leafless stems. They are great garden plants and also useful for cut flowers. Plants perform best in sunny locations but benefit from afternoon shade, particularly in the South. Plants are tough as nails and can be found in rock-hard clay, upon which pedestrians trample, as well as poor, sandy soils near any coast. The foliage is tufted, similar to tufts of grass, and flowers occur in dense heads. Few obvious differences exist between many of the species, and horticultural classifications are principally based on stature and size of leaves.

Propagation is by division and seed. Seeds placed under warm (70–75° F), moist conditions germinate in 14–21 days.

Quick Reference to Armeria Species

|  | Height (in.) | Leaves > 1" wide | Flower color |
|---|---|---|---|
| *A. alliacea* | 12–18 | Yes | White-Pink |
| *A. juniperifolia* | 2–4 | No | Lilac |
| *A. maritima* | 6–12 | No | Various |

**-*alliacea*** (al-lee-ah' say-a)  Plantain Thrift  12–18"/12"
Summer  Whitish Pink  Central and Southern Europe  Zones 4–9
(Syn. *A. plantaginea*)

The white to pink flower head is approximately ¾" across and more oblong than the rounded flower shape of *A. maritima*. The flowers are more white than pink but are particularly handsome. The leaves are much wider

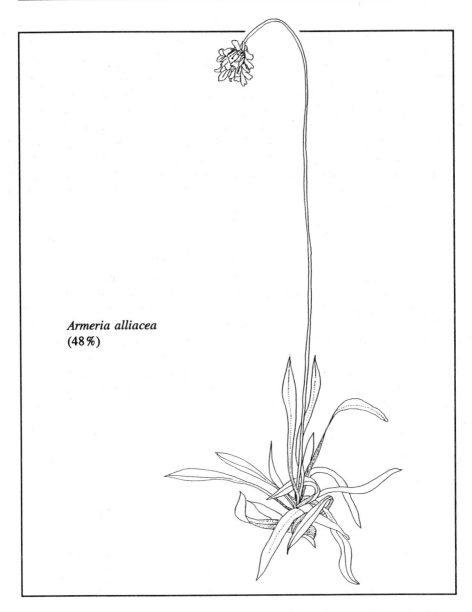

*Armeria alliacea*
(48%)

(1–2″ across) than the previous species, resembling those of plantain. They are mostly erect and have 3–7 veins running lengthwise.

## Cultivars:

Formosa hybrids (*A. alliacea* × *A. leucocephala* 'Corsica') form cushions of green and bear deep pink to white flowers.

Var. *leucantha* is a white-flowered form.

**Related Species:**

*A. pseudoarmeria* (syn. *A. cephalotes*), pinkball thrift, is similar and has large, 1–2" diameter, white to rose flower heads. When well grown, the flowers look like those of chives. The foliage can appear limp and flaccid and in constant need of water when conditions are unfavorable.

| | | | |
|---|---|---|---|
| *-juniperifolia* (jew-ni-pe-ri-fo′ lee-a) | | Pyrenees Thrift | 2–4"/6" |
| Summer | Lilac | Spain | Zones 4–8 |

(Syn. *A. caespitosa*)

This low-growing plant is occasionally offered by rock garden plant specialists but deserves greater use. It is densely tufted with peculiar linear, 3-angled leaves seldom longer than ¾". The small, pale lilac flower heads are only about ⅜" across and held on 1" scapes. Place in a sunny location and well-drained soil.

**Cultivars:**

'Alba' produces a dense canopy of creamy white flowers.
'Beechwood' is a compact-growing plant with short, compact, deep pink flowers.
'Beven's Variety' is a real gem. The tiny, green compact hummocks bear short, almost stemless, pink flowers.
'Rubra' bears rosy-red flowers.

| | | | |
|---|---|---|---|
| *-maritima* (ma-ri′ ti-ma) | | Common Thrift | 6–12"/10" |
| Summer | Pink | Europe | Zones 4–8 |

This diverse species contains over 20 botanical varieties. Common thrift has pink, mauve-red, lilac, or white flowers, depending on the variety or cultivar. The specific epithet is derived from the species' salt tolerance, and plants may be found growing on coastlines where few others can survive the saline conditions. As the common name implies, it is the most common species of the genus and has undergone extensive selection. The 1–1½" diameter flower head, which consists of many tiny flowers attached to the central flower dome, persists for about 3 weeks in the North, a week less in the South. The plant forms a tuft of narrow, 4–8" long linear leaves, each of which has one vein running lengthwise. It is relatively easy to grow; however, in the South, it should be shaded from the afternoon sun.

*Armeria maritima* is also grown as a flowering potted plant. Approximately 12 weeks are required from seed to produce a flowering plant under greenhouse conditions. No cold treatment is necessary to induce flowering.

Seeds sown under high humidity and warm conditions produce seedlings ready to transplant in 3–4 weeks. They can be overwintered in a cool greenhouse or outside and flower in the spring. Division is risky; more plants are damaged than reproduced.

## Cultivars:

'Alba' is about 5″ tall with a creamy white flower, unusual in this species. It is handsome in the garden, but, unfortunately, the white flowers discolor faster than colored flowers and decline more rapidly in heavy rains or winds.

'Bees Ruby' is one of the most spectacular of the plantain thrifts. The intense, bright cerise flowers are carried on smooth 18″ stems. This is probably a hybrid of *A. alliacea* × *A. maritima*.

'Bloodstone' produces a 9″ tall stem of intense blood-red flowers, some of the largest in the group. This also may be an *A. alliacea* × *A. maritima* hybrid.

'Dusseldorf Pride' ('Dusseldorfer Stolz') grows 6–8″ tall and carries large, wine-red flower heads. It is gaining a large following in this country.

'La Pampa' bears deep pink flowers over 6–9″ tall plants.

'Laucheana' produces 20–40 leaves, resulting in a highly-tufted rosette. It is about 6″ tall and has outstanding, deep rose-pink flowers.

'Merlin' is only 6–9″ tall with pastel-pink flowers.

'Ornament' is an excellent hybrid with evergreen foliage and large, white and rose flowers.

'Robusta' is the most vigorous form I have seen. It grows 12–15″ tall and produces 3″ wide pink flower heads.

'Rosa Stolz' produces low mounds of grassy foliage and pink, rounded flowers on short, sturdy stems.

'Ruby Glow' is 8–10″ tall with ruby-colored flowers similar to 'Dusseldorf Pride'. It can get rather washed out in the South.

'Splendens' is 8–10″ tall and bears intense red flowers. This is one of the most ornamental cultivars.

'Victor Reiter' is a clump former, only about 6″ tall, with narrow leaves (< ¼″ wide) and many pink flowers.

'Vindictive' is a compact, free-flowering cultivar growing 6″ tall and bearing bright rosy-red flowers.

## Related Species:

*A. girardii* (syn. *A. juncea, A. setacea*) bears many pink flowers on 3–4″ tall stems over tufts of grass-like foliage. A good choice for the front of the garden.

Quick Key for Armeria Species

    A. Leaves over 1″ wide, lance-shaped,
       usually fewer than 10 . . . . . . . . . . . . . . . . . . . . . *A. alliacea*
   AA. Leaves less than ¾″ wide, linear, usually more than 10
      B. Plants 6–12″ tall . . . . . . . . . . . . . . . . . . . . . *A. maritima*
     BB. Plants 2–6″ tall . . . . . . . . . . . . . . . . . . . . . *A. juniperifolia*

## *Arnica* (ar′ ni-ca)          Arnica          Asteraceae

The genus consists of about 30 species, all similar in appearance to each other and confused with the leopard's banes and inulas. *Arnica* differs from similar genera, such as *Doronicum* and *Inula*, by having opposite stem leaves rather than alternate. A good number of species are native to the Northwest and the Rocky Mountains, and a couple are useful for the rock garden in areas with cool summer nights. They are relatively difficult to locate, but two species, *A. montana* (mountain arnica) and *A. chamissonis*, are sometimes available. Both have deep yellow flowers on upright stems and flower in late spring and early summer. *A. montana* bears light green, basal leaves and is easily the most popular in European gardens, while *A. chamissonis* bears lustrous, deep green foliage and a lighter yellow flower. The former is native throughout Europe, while the latter is native from Alaska to the mountains of New Mexico.

## *Artemisia* (are-ti-meez′ ee-a)          Wormwood          Asteraceae

This large genus (about 200 species) has an ancient and curious history, the aromatic properties having attracted herbalists for many hundreds of years. The common name resulted from the fact that many species were recommended to expel worms from the intestinal tract by herbalists such as Dioscorides and Pliny the Roman. The chemical, santonin, derived from some of the Asiatic species, is still used for treatment of intestinal worms. Mugwort, *A. vulgaris*, was widely used to flavor beer prior to the introduction of hops, while hypochondriasis, gout, scurvy, kidney stones, and liver problems all received the medical attention of *Artemisia* prior to the 19th century.

The genus contains 4–5′ tall plants which become woody with age, as well as mat-formers which never grow over 18″ tall. Some of the famous members of this noble genus are tarragon, *A. dracunuculus*; the symbol of the Old West—the tumbling sagebrush, *A. tridentata*; and the cause of much heartache and headache, absinthe, *A. absinthium*. All species except *A. lactiflora* are characterized by having small, alternate leaves and inconspicuous, often dioecious flowers (male and female flowers on separate plants). The leaves on many species are finely divided and highly aromatic when crushed. Smelling crushed leaves is one of the best ways to determine the difference between plants of this genus and gray-leaved plants of closely related genera such as *Anthemis* and *Senecio*. Fragrance of the foliage is now being analyzed in laboratories as a means to separate cultivars within a species. For example, in the *A. arborescens* group of plants, 'Powis Castle' and other similar selections, 'Faith Raven' and 'Brass Band', had similar fragrance "finger-prints." The major component was identified as thujone. Other plants in the same species had different fingerprints, often exhibiting little thujone. Fragrance fingerprinting may be the only way to tell some of these cultivars

125

apart or find out that they are all the same, but happen to have 3 or 4 different names. Some species like to hide behind the fragrance of other herbs. *A. chamaemelifolia*, chamomile wormwood, is a terrific little mat former which has a distinctive chamomile smell when leaves are bruised.

Many species are from arid regions, particularly suitable for dry, sunny areas, and make few soil demands. In the South, however, where summers are humid and hot, many of the mat-forming species tend to open their centers and fall apart. Some species, such as the lovely *A. splendens*, are very sensitive to wet soils and must be grown in loose, rocky areas. One of the finest foliage plants for warm, dry areas is *S. palmeri* (*Artemisia palmeri*), native to southern California. The shrubby forms are more useful, as they can be rejuvenated from time to time with hard pruning. This gives the pruner a wonderful sense of power and teaches the prunee to behave. Prune woody forms, such as 'Powis Castle', in the spring, not the fall. Most of the ornamental species have silvery-green foliage and are used as a foil for harsh colors in the garden, providing a cool note in hot, sunny weather. Applying fertilizer, particularly nitrogen, causes more harm than good to most species, and tall, spindly growth results. Except for *A. lactiflora*, plants are best grown lean and dry.

The method of propagation differs for herbaceous and shrubby species. In general, herbaceous species are divided in the fall or early spring. Cuttings with a small piece of stem attached may also be taken in late summer and placed in a clean bed consisting of a 3:1 ratio of perlite and peat. With the shrubby species, take 3–4" long, semi-hardwood cuttings in late summer or fall and place in a cold frame in a similar medium. A rooting hormone is beneficial. Roots should be present in 3–4 weeks. Artemisia may be propagated under intermittent mist, but cuttings rot quickly, so plantlets must be removed as soon as roots form.

A number of silver foliage plants are similar to *Artemisia*, including *Achillea*, *Senecio* and *Seriphidium*. The foliage of *Artemisia* is usually palmately-divided or finely-dissected and aromatic, whereas the foliage of *Seriphidium* is generally simple and non-aromatic.

Quick Reference to Artemisia Species

|  | Height (in.) | Woody | Silver foliage |
|---|---|---|---|
| *A. abrotanum* | 36–48 | Yes | No |
| *A. absinthium* | 24–36 | Yes | Yes |
| *A. lactiflora* | 48–72 | No | No |
| *A. ludoviciana* | 24–48 | No | Yes |
| *A. schmidtiana* 'Nana' | 6–12 | Yes | Yes |
| *A. stelleriana* | 15–24 | Yes | Yes |

| *-abrotanum* (a-broe' tan-um) | | Southernwood | 3–4'/18" |
|---|---|---|---|
| Summer | Gray Foliage | Southern Europe | Zones 5–8 |

This species has light green (sometimes with some silver-green), finely-divided, intensely fragrant foliage. Under good cultural conditions, plants grow 4' tall. The pinnately-divided foliage is softly hairy at first and becomes less so later in the season. Some people like to plant it near a garden bench or a path, so that the foliage can be brushed against to take advantage of the fragrance. Prune back hard in spring and early summer if necessary, otherwise plants will look weedy by midsummer. Flowers are yellowish white but rather inconspicuous.

### Related Species:

*A. pontica*, Roman wormwood, is also very fragrant and bears finely-divided, light green foliage, somewhat resembling the leaves of common yarrow. Plants grow up to 2' tall but can be pruned to stay low to the ground. It is a handsome plant; however, they can reseed where comfortable and have been cursed as thug-esque as often as they have been lauded as garden-esque. 'Old Warrior' is shorter (18") and more silver than the species.

| *-absinthium* (ab-sin' thee-um) | | Wormwood, Absinthe | 2–3'/2' |
|---|---|---|---|
| Late Summer | Gray Foliage | Europe | Zones 3–9 |

Many of the artemesias have been used as herbal remedies and as local curatives for various ailments. *A. absinthium* was used to cure stomach aches and intestinal worms. Perhaps it is best known, however, as an important ingredient in the preparation of absinthe, a dry, bitter, popular spirit containing 68% alcohol. Scientists subsequently discovered that *A. absinthium* contains thujone, which, if ingested repeatedly, caused a disorder known as absinthism. Effects of absinthism included delirium, hallucinations, and permanent mental illness. First made by Pernod in 1797, production was banned in Switzerland, then France, but continued to be manufactured in Spain until 1939. The effects of absinthe were graphically displayed by the French painter, Degas, in his famous painting, "Absinthe." Absinthe may still be purchased today but is an imitation and contains no parts of the absinthe plant. Tea was also made from this plant, and, as L.H. Bailey stated in 1944, "Wormwood tea is an odorous memory with every person who was reared in the country."

This woody artemisia has deciduous, finely-divided, silvery-gray foliage. The 2–5" long leaves are more silvery than the previous species but not as fragrant. The flowers are tiny, gray and carried on long-branched panicles. Plant in a dry, well-drained location in full sun.

### Cultivars:

'Lambrook Silver', selected at East Lambrook Manor, the garden of Margery Fish, is about 2½' tall and more gray-green than the type. If necessary, cut back heavily in the summer to discourage floppiness. This is one of the best artemisias for the North and the gray, finely-divided foliage provides an effective break for green-leaved plants in the garden. 'Lambrook Giant' is a taller form and occasionally offered.

'Silver Frost' bears finely-cut, silver-green foliage and grows 15–18″ tall.

### Related Species:

*A. frigida*, Mountain fringe, native to the Plains States, bears deeply-cut, silver foliage with woody stems and yellow tufts of flowers. Plants grow 8–12″ tall and are useful for the front of the garden. 'Laramie' is a compact selection (8–10″ tall) from Rice Creek Gardens in Minneapolis, MN.

*A.* × 'Powis Castle' took the gardening world by storm when it was introduced and is still one of the finest plants in cultivation. Two stories as to its origin may be found. Graham Stuart Thomas suggested that it was a hybrid of *A. arborescens* and *A. absinthium* raised by Mr. J. Hancock at Powis Castle in Wales. However, according to Dr. J.D. Twibell, Mr. Hancock obtained the material as a cutting from a gardener in Yorkshire, England and was already propagating and distributing the plant when he moved to Powis in 1972. Regardless of its origins, it is an outstanding

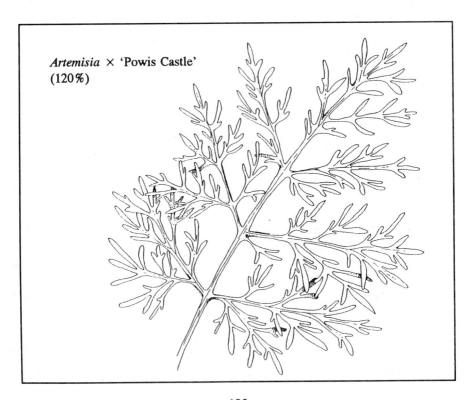

*Artemisia* × 'Powis Castle'
(120%)

filigreed silver artemisia. It blends relative hardiness with beauty and combines with many plants to perfection. Plants are sterile, or occasionally throw out a small flower, and are uniform. They are reliably cold hardy to zone 6 and heat tolerant to zone 8. This is one of the finest artemesias I have seen. Prune in spring or summer, not fall.

*A.* × 'Huntington' ('Huntington Gardens') is likely a hybrid with *A. absinthium* in its bloodlines. Plants become woody at the base and grow about 18″ tall, but can reach 4′. The handsome silver foliage is deeply cut and soft to the touch. As with other taxa of wormwood, wet soils are sure death. However, plants appear to be relatively heat-tolerant. Hardy in zones 5–7.

| *-lactiflora* (lak-ti-flo′ ra) | | White Mugwort | 4–6′/4′ |
|---|---|---|---|
| Late Summer | Cream | China, India | Zones 3–8 |

This is the oddball of the group, having green foliage, conspicuous flowers, and growing best in moist areas. The 8–9″ long leaves are pinnately-compound, each leaflet is about 3″ long, coarsely-lobed and toothed, and the green rosette is evergreen in milder zones. Under suitable growing conditions, it easily attains 6′ and requires staking. The magnificent cream-white flowers are borne in large, 1–2′ long, plume-like panicles and persist well into the fall. This is an ideal background plant whose late season flowers provide a nice change from the daisies which are so abundant at that time. It is also useful to cut for dried flowers. Plants do best in sunny locations in soils which do not dry out (unlike other species).

Propagate by division every 3–4 years.

### Cultivars:

'Guizho', recently selected by Bloom's of Bressingham, bears dark green (close to black) foliage and stems. Sprays of creamy white flowers are formed above the foliage in early summer. A handsome plant.

'Variegata' has green and gray leaves with white flowers. Propagation is exacting, and plants are particularly difficult to locate.

| *-ludoviciana* (loo-do-vik-ee′ aye-na) | | White Sage | 2–4′/2′ |
|---|---|---|---|
| Late Summer | Gray Foliage | North America | Zones 4–9 |

This deciduous, non-woody species provides compact growth and good silver foliage color. It differs from most of the other gray-leaved species in having entire, rather than dissected, leaves. The 2–4″ long leaves are white-woolly beneath and almost hairless above. The stems are white and branched towards the top. The gray flowers are produced in late summer on narrow, branched, compound panicles. The roots can run rampantly underground and quickly result in large clumps. This is an excellent species

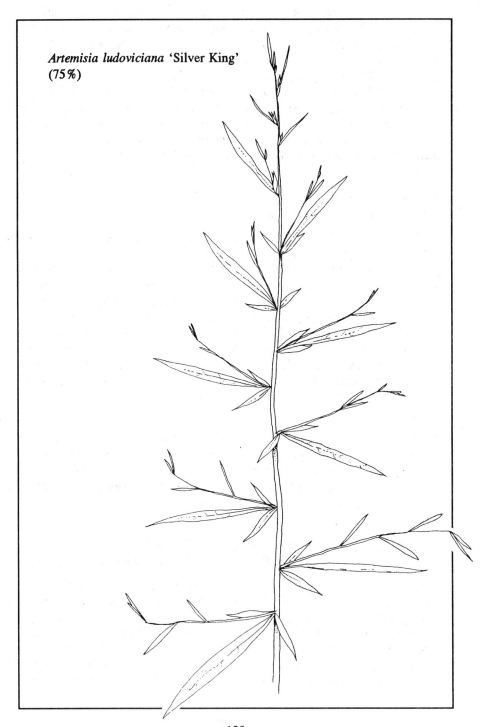

*Artemisia ludoviciana* 'Silver King'
(75%)

for southern gardens, as it tolerates warm temperatures, is less prone to disease, and grows back quickly after pruning.

Propagate by division in late summer or fall and cuttings in late spring and summer.

**Cultivars:**

'Latiloba' has wide (3″ across), gray-green leaves with 3–5 lobes near the ends. It stands 12–24″ high and makes an effective ground cover. It is not as heat tolerant as the species.

'Silver King' is an excellent cultivar and is more compact than the species, hardy to zone 3 and offers excellent deep silver foliage. The flower plumes sport red fall color not found in the species. Very invasive where comfortable.

'Silver Queen' produces sparse, female flowers and wide, silvery leaves with deeply-cut, jagged margins. 'Silver Queen' is a little shorter, but with slightly larger leaves, than 'Silver King'.

'Valerie Finnis' stands only 15–18″ tall and produces handsome silver, entire leaves. Unlike the previous two cultivars, she is non-invasive. I have not yet been impressed with her performance in the South, as plants tend to lose lower leaves in warm weather. Years with heavy summer rains are also destructive. However, if placed in well-drained soils, plants can be handsome.

**Related Species:**

*A. purshiana*, pursh sagebrush, is similar to 'Silver King' but only 2–3′ tall, with narrower, less divided, almost entire, leaves. It also flowers about a week earlier and more profusely. This is listed as a synonym of *A. ludoviciana* by some authorities or a selection of *A. ludoviciana* by others.

| *-schmidtiana* (shmit-ee′ aye-na) | Silvermound Artemisia | 15–24″/18″ |
|---|---|---|
| Summer  Silver Foliage | Japan | Zones 3–8 |

The species is about 2′ tall but seldom seen in gardens. It is represented by the dwarf form 'Nana' and usually sold as 'Silver Mound'. The finely-cut, silver foliage grows in a silky cushion which completely covers the small, drooping, yellow flowers. The handsome mounding habit has resulted in this plant being immensely popular in the North. The mounded shape is retained most of the season in the Northeast and Canada, but, unfortunately, it "melts out" in hot summers and is disappointing south of zone 6. Melt out also occurs in the Midwest, only later. The center of the plant opens, and any semblance of a mound is lost, making it a particularly poor choice for southern gardens. It is rather woody at the base, and cuttings consisting of the leaf, petiole and a piece of the stem should be taken in the summer.

### Related Species:

*A. rupestris* is a finely-cut sub-shrub growing to about 18″ tall. Cold hardy to zone 4, plants are tough and easy to grow in well-drained soils.

'Silverado' is offered by a few nurserypeople as a non-melting substitute for 'Silver Mound'. Similar foliage but not quite as "moundy."

| *-stelleriana* (stel-la-ree-ah′ na) | Beach Wormwood | 15–24″/30″ |
|---|---|---|
| Summer    Silver Foliage | NE Asia, United States | Zones 4–8 |

Plants are known as old lad and perennial dusty miller, as well as beach wormwood, and are cold hardy to zone 4. They are highly tolerant of salt air and saline water but intolerant of poorly-drained soils. The white, silky leaves are densely hairy, lobed and divided. Many ¼″ wide, yellow flowers are borne in a narrow panicle.

### Cultivars:

'Mori's Form' ('Broughton Silver') is a compact, low-growing, silvery plant recently introduced from Japan. A handsome selection for rock gardens or raised beds.

'Silver Bouquet', recently released from the University of British Columbia, is a low-growing, mat former with excellent silver foliage.

'Silver Brocade' is a good low-growing (6–12″), gray-leaf form which is becoming a standard for low-growing artemisias. Its prostrate and compact habit sets it apart from other cultivars. Excellent drainage is necessary. Plants have a tough time in the Southeast, but if planted in containers, it is terrific. Introduced by the University of British Columbia Botanical Garden.

### Quick Key to Artemisia Species

    A. Leaves green or nearly so
      B. Leaves coarsely-divided, slightly aromatic,
          plants 4′ or taller, flowers showy . . . . . . . . . . *A. lactiflora*
      BB. Leaves finely-divided, fragrant,
          plants 3–4′ tall, flowers not showy . . . . . . . . *A. abrotanum*
    AA. Leaves silvery, pubescent
      B. Leaves entire, or lobed at ends, not divided . . *A. ludoviciana*
      BB. Leaves divided
        C. Leaves coarsely-divided into lobes
          D. Plants 2–3′ tall, pubescence silky . . . . . . *A. absinthium*
          DD. Plants 18–24″ tall, pubescence woolly . . . *A. stelleriana*
        CC. Leaves finely-divided,
          plants 6–12″ tall . . . . . . . . . . . *A. schmidtiana* 'Nana'

**Additional Reading:**

Mitchell, Irene. 1978. The plant and painting that shocked Paris. *Horticulture* 56(4):32–37.

Nicholls, W. 1993. Plants, a perennial dusty miller. *Fine Gardening* 34:22, 24.

Sheldon, Elisabeth. 1987. Shades of gray. *Horticulture* 65(12):37–43.

Twibell, J.D. 1992. Plant identification from vapor analysis. A short study of *Artemisia arborescens* varieties. *The Plantsman* 14(3):184–190.

Twibell, J.D. 1993. *Artemisia* 'Faith Raven'. In: Letters to the Editor, *The Plantsman* 15(4):255–258.

## *Arum* (ar' um)       Arum       Araceae

Approximately twenty species belong to this genus, and all are characterized by a spadix consisting of unisexual flowers; the females at the base, the males above them with sterile flowers between. The spathe is the showy part and envelops the spadix in the spring. Plants emanate from tubers; the shoots generally arise from the top of the tuber, and the roots are produced from the base of the shoots. More and more woodland species are being offered to gardeners for use in shady, moist areas. Some of the most handsome foliage to be found on any garden plant belongs to *A. italicum* 'Pictum'. Recently, a new taxonomic classification of this genus was completed by Peter Boyce of Kew, trying to clarify the similarities and differences between species.

| | | |
|---|---|---|
| *-italicum* (ee-ta' li-kum) | Italian Arum | 12–20"/18" |
| Spring    Creamy White | Southern Europe | Zones 6–9 |

*Arum italicum* is a woodland species native to Italy, the Mediterranean and south to the Canary Islands. The habit is unusual to most gardeners in that new foliage appears late in the fall (November in the Armitage garden) and remains green over winter. The leaves are followed by creamy yellow spathes in spring which look like Jack-in-the-Pulpit (*Arisaema triphyllum*) flowers. They are easy to distinguish from Jack-in-the-pulpits because arum has simple leaves, while "Jacks" have compound leaves. The flowers disappear in summer and are replaced with strong columns of bright orange-red berries as ornamental as any part of the plant. The berries are more common in northern gardens than in southern gardens, probably because the soil temperatures are too warm for exuberant fruit development in the South. Although most at home in the woodland garden, plants are particularly handsome at the front of any shade area. The 12" long, hastate (like an arrowhead) leaves are at their best in late fall and winter. For this reason, it is an exceptional plant for the winter garden. Combined with the winter foliage of *Bergenia* or *Heuchera*, and the architectural forms of ornamental grasses such as *Miscanthus*, the garden

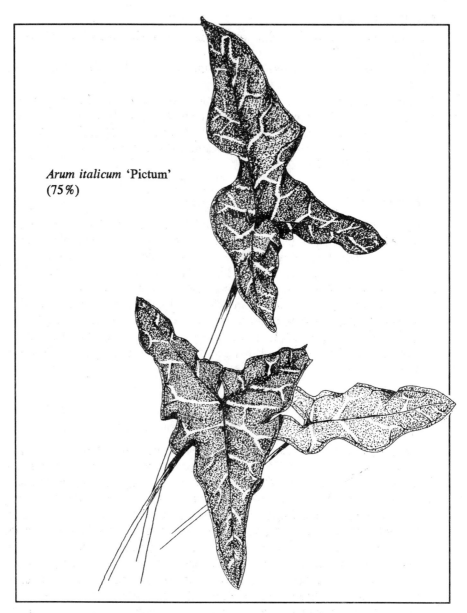

*Arum italicum* 'Pictum'
(75%)

may be enjoyed 12 months of the year. Similar to *Arisaema*, plants contain calcium oxalate; don't eat them.

Propagate the species and cultivars by division after leaves appear in fall. Seed of the species must be stratified (provided with cool, moist conditions) in the fall and left until spring, at which time some germination may occur. Seed often requires a year to germinate.

**Cultivars:**

'Eco Italian' is similar, but the foliage is much lighter in color, with more white than the species.

'Marmoratum' has broad, gray-green leaves marbled with splotches of yellow-green. The leaves are larger than those of the more common 'Pictum', and the yellow-green spathe is purple at the base. Unfortunately, it is difficult to find in the trade. This may be because the name is used interchangeably with 'Pictum', and the distinction between the two has almost disappeared.

'Pictum' is the best form of this species and has dark-green leaves which are narrowly spear-shaped and conspicuously blotched with gray and cream. It grows approximately 18″ tall, spreads by tuberous roots, and is an excellent ground cover. In the fall, shiny, clustered spikes of bright orange berries brighten the landscape.

'White Winter' is probably the most ornamental form I have seen. I found it at Avon Bulbs in southern England, the excellent nursery of Chris Ireland-Jones. The leaves are heavily mottled with silvery lines.

**Related Species:**

*A. dioscoridis* is extremely variable but generally has large, triangular leaves and purple-spotted spathes with a dark spadix within. Flowers are rather malodorous, smelling of dung and carrion. Bet you can't wait to find this one. Plants are winter hardy only to zone 7 or 8.

*A. maculatum*, Lords and Ladies or Cuckoo-plant, bears glossy green leaves, often with black spots and creamy yellow spathes. They differ from *A. italicum* by having a violet-yellow or violet-flushed spadix, compared to the creamy-yellow spadix of *A. italicum*. Orange-red berries are produced in late summer and fall.

**Additional Reading:**

Boyce, P. 1989. A new classification of *Arum* with keys to the infrageneric taxa. *Kew Bulletin* 44(3):383–395.

## *Aruncus* (ah-run′ kus)          Goat's Beard          Rosaceae

Only two or three species occur, and each possesses excellent qualities for the garden. Male and female flowers occur on different plants (dioecious) and are carried in tall, showy panicles (compound inflorescences). The light green foliage is bipinnately compound. A little afternoon shade is useful, and moisture is necessary for best growth and flowering in southern areas of its range (zones 5–7), although plants perform best in full sun further north. Consistent moisture is important regardless of locale; the leaf margins of plants grown in dry areas will turn brown and crispy.

Propagate by division (see section under *A. dioicus*) in the spring or by seed collected fresh and place in a warm (70–75° F), humid area. Germination will occur in 2–3 weeks. If seed is old, place at 40° F for about 4 weeks prior to putting them in the warmth.

**-dioicus** (die-o-eye′ kus)          Goat's Beard                                    4–6′/6′
     Late Spring   Creamy White   Europe, Asia, North America     Zones 3–7
(Syn. *A. sylvester, Spiraea aruncus*)

This is a spectacular plant when given sufficient moisture, dappled shade, and plenty of room. The flowers of *Aruncus* are either male or female, but the two sexes are rather unisexual in appearance and difficult to tell apart from a distance. The 2–3′ long, light green leaves are bi- to tri-pinnately compound, and each lanceolate leaflet is sharply doubly-serrated. Plants are similar to some of the tall, white forms of *Astilbe*. Three ways may be used to separate *Aruncus* from *Astilbe biternata* and *A.* × *arendsii* cultivars, such as 'Prof. van der Wielen'. In general:

1. Leaves of *Aruncus* are doubly-serrated; leaves of *Astilbe* are usually singly-serrated,

2. There are always 10 stamens in *Astilbe* flowers; there are either 20 (male) or 0 (female) stamens in *Aruncus* (they are small and difficult to count, but nobody will laugh), and

3. In each fruit (follicle), *Aruncus* has two to four seeds; *Astilbe* has many seeds.

In the northern states, plants are far more tolerant of afternoon sun than in the South. I have tried to grow goat's beard in Athens, Georgia (zone 7b) for many years and have not succeeded. It is either too hot or I can't provide sufficient moisture, or both. However, I have seen fine specimens in Raleigh, North Carolina (zone 7a). Because of these experiences, I don't recommend its use south of zone 7a (although it will survive a little further south).

Where well-grown, large, plume-like panicles of small (⅛″), creamy flowers appear in late spring and provide a magnificent sight. I read that males are more sought after than females because the plumes are supposedly fuller. I have stared at clumps of goat's beard for hours, trying to determine the garden differences between male and female plants. As I stuck my head through foliage, flowers and fruit, the conclusion was painfully obvious—the gender makes little difference. One can argue that the male plumes are more feathery and upright than the drooping seed-ladened females, but unless you are a chauvinist of some kind, it does not matter. Plants form large clumps in rich soils, but unfortunately many of today's smaller gardens cannot afford the space.

In my earlier edition of this book, I casually mentioned that one could divide plants if additional plants were desired. A letter arrived a few months

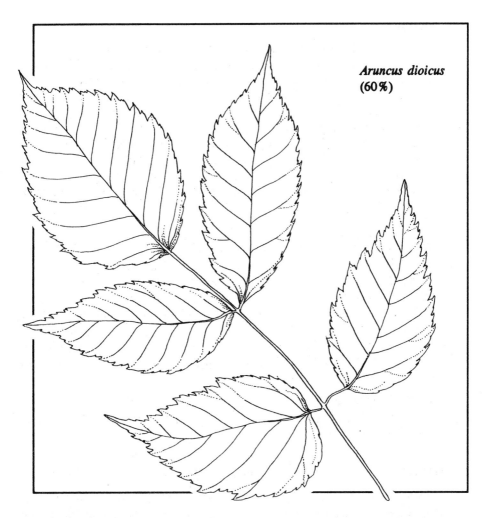

*Aruncus dioicus*
(60%)

later showing me the error of my ways. Perhaps back hoeing should be the method of choice. *"I would like to know what kind of mischievous smile you had when you wrote . . . that Aruncus is propagated . . . by division . . . Let me briefly tell you my experience with a 6–7 year old clump. It took: 1 pick (which broke), three shovels (one of which broke), an ax and two people (in your next book, you might suggest that a husband/wife team not attempt this project together). Then it went through pruners (dumb on my part) to loopers (still quite dumb), to a pruning saw (we're getting smarter), to a big hand saw, with serious consideration on getting out the chain saw. At one point there was discussion on laying it on its side, varnishing it, and making end tables out of it. Anyway, it was an experience to remember."* Robyn Duback, Robyn's Nest Nursery, Vancouver, Washington.

## Cultivars:

Var. *astilboides* is a smaller version (18-24") of the species, and, although difficult to find in the American trade, it is worth the hunt. The leaves are more deeply serrated and the inflorescence less compound.

'Glasnevin', from the wonderful Irish Botanical Gardens, bears deeper green, fuller leaves and is dwarfer than the species. Apparently, it is also more tolerant of dry soils.

'Kneiffii' is only 3' tall, with foliage deeply cut into threadlike segments. This foliage is wonderfully handsome, but the flowers are not as dramatic.

'Zweiweltenkind' ('Child of Two Worlds') is a shorter, more airy, form with pendulous, white flowers. This cultivar is thought to be a form of *A. sinensis*.

## Related Species:

*A. aethusifolius*, native to Korea, is a wonderful addition to the perennial trade and a true miniature. It attains a mature height of 8-12", has deeply-cut, dark green leaves and a panicle of creamy white flowers. Plants tolerate partial shade and are most at home in the rock garden or the front of the border. I saw a magnificent hybrid between this species and *A. dioicus* at Bluemont Nursery in Maryland, the excellent establishment of Richard Simon. The plant had fine white flowers and its habit was intermediate between the two.

## Additional Reading:

Frett, J. 1993. Perennials with panache. *American Nurseryman* 177(3):24-29.
Haywood, Gordon. 1994. Goatsbeard. *Horticulture* 72(6):88.

## *Asarum* (a-sar' um)          Wild Ginger          Aristolochiaceae

*Asarum* contains about 70 species, most of which are native to north temperate areas. The common name comes from the ginger-like smell that arises from the roots when bruised or cut. The plant which provides true ginger, however, is *Zingiber officinale*. Wild ginger spreads by rhizomes, produces 1 or 2 leaves and is generally less than 1' tall. Many of the best species are native to North America, but some of the far-eastern species are starting to become available. These include some species with outstanding foliage textures and variegations. *A. splendens* is an outstanding Chinese species with large, dark green leaves mottled with silver throughout. It has remained evergreen in the Armitage garden to 10° F. *A. kumagianum* (my favorite) and *A. magnificum*, one of the biggest species (12-15" tall), were recently introduced from Japan by the Arnold Arboretum. A good deal of study and collection has occurred in this genus, and Japanese species continue to be described. Recently, two additional Japanese species, *A. fudsinoi* and *A. minamitanianum*, were described from plants at Kew Gardens. Many of these species will never be common garden plants, but, with the possible aid of tissue culture, they may be available on a limited scale in the future.

All species prefer woodland conditions of slightly acid soils, heavy shade, constant moisture and good drainage. In the wild, plants generally occur in the dappled shade of deciduous forests. In the garden, they are used mainly as shade-tolerant ground covers whose glossy green leaves, often mottled with white or yellow, are amazingly eye-catching for such diminutive plants. The urn-shaped flowers consist of sepals only and are borne underneath the foliage. The "little brown jugs" are wonderfully handsome but are seldom seen by the uninitiated. The sepals usually end in turned back lobes, referred to as the calyx lobes and are exciting in their own right. Some taxonomists have split this genus into 2 main sections, placing evergreen species in the genus *Hexastylis* and the deciduous species in *Asarum*. I have retained all species under *Asarum*.

Species may be propagated by seed, although the most foolproof method is division in spring or early fall.

### Quick Key to Asarum Species

|  | Foliage<br>evergreen/deciduous | Leaves<br>pubescent |
| --- | --- | --- |
| *A. arifolium* | Evergreen | Not pubescent |
| *A. canadense* | Deciduous | Highly pubescent |
| *A. europaeum* | Evergreen | Highly pubescent |
| *A. shuttleworthii* | Evergreen | Not pubescent |

| *-arifolium* (ar-i-foe-lee' um) | Arrow-Leaf Ginger | 6–8″/12″ |
| --- | --- | --- |
| Spring      Dull Brown | Southeastern United States | Zones 4–8 |

Some of the larger gingers are found in this species. The evergreen leaves are up to 8″ long and 10″ across and usually visibly mottled. They are triangular to arrow-shaped (deltoid to sagittate) and smooth throughout. A great deal of variability occurs, resulting in some plants having different degrees of leaf mottling, which shows up more in the spring than in the summer. The leaves and roots also smell terrific when crushed. In late spring, flask-shaped, brown flowers with prominent spreading lobes are formed, although significant variability also occurs with the flowers. A reliable, excellent native ginger.

**Related Species:**

*A. heterophyllum* generally bears round, green leaves and urn-shaped flowers. Dr. Richard Lighty pointed out a clump of marvelously variegated *A. heterophyllum* in the woodland at Mt. Cuba estate in Delaware. Seeing that beautiful form simply re-enforced the fact that all species of this genus are highly variable, and that green and mottled forms will occur in most of them. Plants are native to the eastern United States.

| *-canadense* (can-a den' see) | Canadian Ginger | 4–8″/10″ |
|---|---|---|
| Spring      Dull Brown | Canada, United States | Zones 3–7 |

A deciduous ginger, two soft-green, kidney-shaped, downy leaves emerge early in the spring about the same time as the flowers. Canadian gingers tend to ramble a good bit, and, given cool, moist areas, plants form a large colony within a few years. The 1″ wide flowers are very hairy, greenish on the outside and brown within. The three-flared, pointed flower lobes look like they have been peeled back to allow a few ground-hugging bugs to do their pollinating.

**Cultivars:**

'Eco Choice' and 'Eco Red Giant' are more dense and larger than the species, respectively.

**Related Species:**

*A. virginianum* (syn. *Hexastylis virginianum*) is native to Virginia and the Carolinas and has evergreen, heart-shaped, 2–3″ long, dark green leaves, often with white spots on the upper side. *A. minor* grows 3–5″ tall and has widely-spreading calyx lobes about ½″ wide. The heart-shaped evergreen leaves may be solid green or prominently mottled. It is often considered a subspecies of *A. virginianum*.

| *-europaeum* (eur-o' pay-um) | European Wild Ginger | 6–8″/8″ |
|---|---|---|
| Spring      Dull Brown | Europe | Zones 4–7 |

This is an excellent ground cover for the woodland garden. The 2–3″ wide, kidney-shaped leaves are leathery, glossy dark green, and evergreen in most areas. The leaves are hairy, particularly on the veins on the upper surface. The small, dull brown flowers are hairy and bear three-pointed lobes about half as long as the flower. I think the foliage is some of the most handsome in the genus, but the flowers are not the most memorable. Being hidden from flying insects, they are pollinated by ground-hugging insects. This is one of the hardiest species and easiest to establish in the North; I have seen this stuff taking over pathways and shade gardens of my gardening friends in Long Island. I feel like Santa Claus when I visit the garden of Suzie Bales in Long Island, going home with a sack of ginger on my back. Unfortunately, plants don't tolerate high temperatures associated with southern summers as well, but they still work to zone 8. Moist, shady conditions are needed for best performance.

**Related Species:**

*A. caudatum* has slightly hairy, rounded, evergreen leaves and densely hairy petioles when young. The reddish brown flowers are most fascinating, due to the long twisted tails ("cauda") on the lobes. Native to Washington, eastward to western Montana, and south to northeastern Oregon. A white-flowered form, forma *alba*, is an interesting plant, although the flowers are well-hidden by the foliage.

*-shuttleworthii* (shut-tle-worth-ee′ eye)     Shuttleworth Ginger     4–9″/8″
    Spring          Brown          Southeastern United States          Zones 5–8

Also known as *Hexastylis shuttleworthii*, plants bear beautiful, mottled evergreen, heart-shaped to rounded foliage. The 1–2″ long, urn-shaped

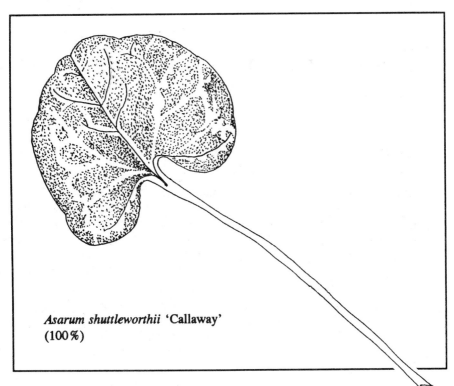

*Asarum shuttleworthii* 'Callaway'
(100%)

flowers are pale brown to red with broad calyx lobes. Plants are not as winter hardy but are more heat tolerant than either of the previous species. It is native from Virginia to Alabama and Georgia.

## Cultivars:

'Callaway', selected from Callaway Gardens in Pine Mountain, Georgia is more compact, growing only about 6″ tall and having wonderfully mottled foliage. Probably a selection of *A. shuttleworthii* var. *harperi*. This is one of the finest mat formers but also one of the slowest growers. In the Armitage garden, it has taken about 8 years to form a clump 18″ square, but oh what a clump it is!

'Eco Medallion' has a silver hue on the foliage with a compact growth habit.

## Related Species:

*A. hartwegii*, Sierra wild ginger, is a western representative, native to Oregon and California. The green leaves have conspicuous silver veining, and the outstanding mottling has earned the common name of cyclamen-leafed wild ginger. 'Silver Heart' has a silver streak through the midsection of the green leaf. Terrific plants, but excellent drainage is a must.

## Additional Reading:

Boyce, Peter. 1992. Two Japanese species of *Asarum. Kew Magazine* 9(2):67–75.

Kohler, Gary. 1989. The magnificent ginger. *Arnoldia* 49(3):41–43.

Scott, B. 1988. Wild ginger. *American Horticulturist* 67(4):11–14.

Yinger, B.R. 1983. A horticultural monograph of the genus *Asarum*. M.S. (Hort.) Thesis. University of Delaware.

Yinger, B. R. 1991. Asarum. *Bull. of the Amer. Rock Garden Soc.* 51(2):82–91.

*Asclepias* (as-klee′ pe-as)          Silkweed, Milkweed          Asclepidaceae

It may be argued that *A. tuberosa*, butterfly weed, is the only species worthy of inclusion in the formal garden, but numerous plants in this genus are highly ornamental. *A. curassavica*, blood flower, is as ornamental as any species but is considered an annual in most of the country. *A. lanceolata*, red milkweed, is found as far north as New Jersey and bears handsome, orange-red flowers on 3–4′ tall stems. Numerous native species are handsome in their own right; however, few have found their way into any other than meadow gardens. An exception is the new-found popularity of swamp milkweed, *A. incarnata*, which I remember cursing as a "weeder" on a farm in southern Quebec. Anyone who has farmed and tried to rid the fields of the other great pest, common milkweed, *A. syriaca*, knows how tenacious members of this genus can be. However, to be fair, some highly creative people have found that other creative people will actually pay a pretty good dollar for the inflated pods of the common milkweed to be used as dried ornaments. Rather than growing it for the pods, collect them from roadside weeds or from the fields of your friendly neighborhood farmer. He will be most appreciative. Members of this genus have milky sap (although butterfly weed is much less obvious than others), inflated seed pods (follicles), and silky seeds. All species are highly coveted by aphids. A horde of ladybugs or a strong stream of water will help keep them under control.

Quick Reference to Asclepias Species:

|              | Flower color | Leaf arrangement   |
|--------------|--------------|--------------------|
| *A. incarnata* | Rose-pink    | Opposite           |
| *A. tuberosa*  | Orange       | Alternate (spiral) |

| *-incarnata* (in-kar-nay′ ta) | | Swamp Milkweed | 3–4′/2′ |
|---|---|---|---|
| Spring | Rose-Pink | North America | Zones 3–7 |

Swamp milkweed has opposite, 3–6″ long leaves and clusters of rosy-pink flowers (occasionally white) atop 3–4′ tall plants in late spring and summer. The flowers have a faint vanilla scent and are real come-ons for many butterflies. The sap of this species is milkier than in butterfly weed, thus complicating cutting for flowers. Performance is best under moist soils, but well-drained sites are also tolerated.

### Cultivars:

'Cinderella' has been selected for the larger, rosy-pink flowers and more compact flower heads.

'Ice Ballet' is a really fine selection with persistent white flowers on 3–5′ stems. When butterflies hover, which they will, the contrast is fabulous.

| *-tuberosa* (tew-be-ro′ sa) | | Butterfly Weed | 2–3′/2′ |
|---|---|---|---|
| Spring | Orange | Eastern North America | Zones 4–9 |

The orange flowers of butterfly weed are so vibrant that they seem to jump out at you. There is a good deal of variation in flower color, and I've seen plants ranging from pure yellow to dark red at the edge of woods in north Georgia. Mature plants do not transplant well, thus removing plants from the wild should not be attempted. The 4–4½″ long leaves are more or less alternate to spiral up the stiff stems and are spaced very closely together. The stems are topped by umbels of many small flowers in spring and continue to bloom at least 6 weeks in the garden. Cut flowers have

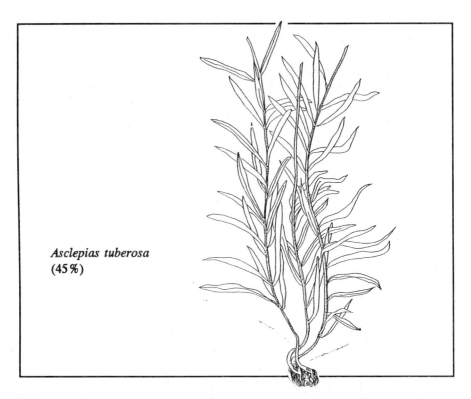

*Asclepias tuberosa*
(45%)

a good vase life if immediately placed in warm water, then transferred to the refrigerator for 12 hours. Some gardeners flame the base of the stem to reduce the flow of sap; flowers will not decline if flaming is not accomplished. Cutting the flowers also results in additional flowering three to four weeks later.

Flowers allowed to remain on the plant give way to narrow, 3-6" long, ornamental follicles which provide an additional dimension to the plant. They should be removed before they split because the seeds dehisce at that point, and ornamental soon gives way to messy. Butterfly weed is slow to emerge in the spring, and patience is a must.

Some research on forcing the flowers in the greenhouse may be of interest. Essentially, *A. tuberosa* requires short nights (i.e., long days) in order to flower. Growers use a 60W incandescent light bulb from 11:00PM to 2:00AM each night to "trick" them into thinking the nights are short. Under the long nights of winter, plants just sit there and decline.

Seed germination is highly variable, and results as low as 5% to as high as 90% have been reported. If fresh seed is collected, cleaned, and sown immediately, 50-80% germination will result. Old seed or seed that is purchased germinate more uniformly if seeds are sown in a well-aerated soil

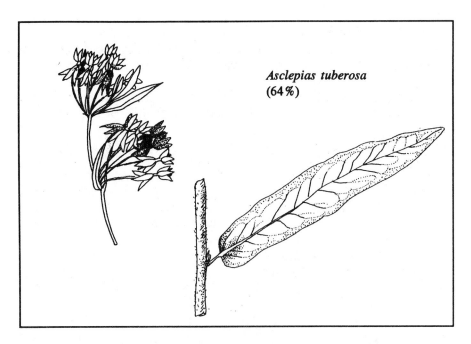

Asclepias tuberosa
(64%)

mix, watered in well, covered with plastic, and placed in the refrigerator or other cool place for about six weeks. A good deal of variation in flower color results in seed-sown material. Root cuttings can be used to increase colored forms which have merit (See *Anemone*).

**Cultivars:**

'Gay Butterflies' is a mix of yellow, orange and red-flowered forms. Plants are generally 2–3' tall.

'Hello Yellow' bears vibrant yellow flowers atop 24–30" plants. A show-stopper.

**Related Species:**

*A. verticilatta*, horsetail milkweed, has narrow, sessile-whorled leaves and small, creamy white flowers along the length of the unbranched stems. Flowers occur from June to September. Native to open areas of Massachusetts, southern Ontario west to the Canadian Praires and south through Texas, Mexico and Florida. Handsome and tough.

Quick Key to Asclepias Species:

 A. Leaves opposite, flowers rosy-pink, 3–4' tall . . . . *A. incarnata*
AA. Leaves alternate, flowers orange,
 plants usually less than 3' tall . . . . . . . . . . . . . *A. tuberosa*

145

**Additional Reading:**

Albrecht, M.L and J.T. Lehmann. 1991. Daylength, cold storage and production method influence growth and flowering of *Asclepias tuberosa*. *HortScience* 26(2):120–121.

Borland, Jim. 1987. Clues to butterfly milkweed germination emerge from a literature search. *American Nurseryman* 165(3):91–92, 94–96.

## *Asphodeline* (a-sfod-e-lee′ nee)      Jacob's Rod      Liliaceae

Eighteen to twenty species occur in the Mediterranean area and north to Austria. The leafy, unbranched stems arise from rhizomes and produce many-flowered, conical inflorescences. All species were at one time part of *Asphodelus*, but in 1830 this genus was created. They are most easily distinguished from *Asphodelus* by having erect and leafy stems. Stems of plants of *Asphodelus* are generally leafless and branched. Plants perform best in full sun and can be spectacular in late spring and early summer. Of the numerous species found in the wild, only King's Spear, *Asphodeline lutea*, is readily available.

| *-lutea* (loo-tee′ a) | | King's Spear | 3–4′/2′ |
| --- | --- | --- | --- |
| Late Spring/Early Summer | Yellow | Mediterranean | Zones 5–8 |

This is the true Asphodel of the ancients, connected in Greek mythology with the dead and the underground. It was planted on graves and associated with Persephone, the Goddess of agriculture and fertility, who was kidnapped by Hades, God of the dead. In this gruesome story, Persephone appears crowned with a garland of asphodels. It was suggested that the grayish foliage and the yellow flowers intimated the gloom of the underworld and the pallor of death. Sounds pretty awful, doesn't it?

It really is a fine plant, regardless of what the mythologists did to it. The deep green leaves are grass-like with paler veins and are found all the way to the inflorescence. Each of the many star-like, fragrant flowers are about 1″ long and open from bottom to top on a 6–18″ long raceme. I have seen this plant looking outstanding in cool summer climates but seldom has it reached its potential in the harsher summers of the South and central plains. In the heat, the open flowers decline rapidly, while the top flowers are still waiting to open. The stems are rather ugly and should be interplanted among other plants so the flowers can be the focal point.

**Cultivars:**

A double form, var. *flore-pleno*, has been described but is very difficult to locate.

**Related Species:**

*A. liburnica* has soft yellow flowers, but the racemes are more lax, and plants grow only 1-2' tall. The primrose color makes this a fine plant for the garden. The foliage only extends about halfway up the stem, and flowers open a little later than those of *A. lutea*. Native to southern Europe, plants perform well in zones 4-7, as well as on the west coast.

*A. taurica* is 1-2' tall and bears lovely, white flowers. Sometimes confused with *Asphodelus albus*; however, the leafy stem and more diminutive stature of *A. taurica* should help to keep them separate.

## *Aster* (as' tur)                    Aster                    Asteraceae

This large genus consists of species native to North and South America, Europe, Africa and Asia. While many remain weed-like, horticultural improvements have greatly enhanced the garden value of asters in recent years. Numerous species are native to the United States and have common names such as New York Aster and New England Aster. Perhaps it is this familiarity with our roadside asters that have held back the popularity of the named cultivars in this country. Although many useful species are native to the U.S., credit for much of the improvement must be given to English and German nurserymen. Many selections were raised in the late 1890's, and new ones continue to be introduced every year. Asters are also raised in greenhouses and fields as commercial cut flowers and are becoming an important item in the flower designer's palette. The most important species for cut flowers are *A. ericoides* and *A. novi-belgii*.

The leaves are alternate, and the daisy flowers are borne either singly on the flower stem or in multiple-flowered panicles or corymbs. Some species of the genus *Aster* are very similar to some *Erigeron* species, particularly our native forms. In general, *Erigeron* mostly flowers in the spring and summer and have bracts beneath the flower in a single circle all about the same length. *Aster* generally flower in summer and fall, and the bracts underneath the flowers occur in two rings of different sizes.

Species and their cultivars range in height from 6" (*A. alpinus*) to the giant 8' *A. simplex*; however, so much hybridization has occurred in cultivation that proper identification is highly questionable. If you don't know what species you are looking at, don't worry about it, it is probably a hybrid of some kind. A great deal of breeding work has been accomplished with *A. novi-belgii*, and cultivars and hybrids of that species alone are now available in heights from 6" to 6'. Flower color of most species is white or in the blue-purple range (although many pink cultivars have been selected). Yellow does or does not occur in aster, depending on whether you follow the taxonomic lumpers or splitters. Goldilocks is the common name of the 18" tall, fall-flowering *A. linosyris*; however, the taxonomic splitters have renamed this plant as *Linocyris vulgaris*. Speaking of taxonomists, some authorities have even split a number of well-known asters to a separate genus. Based on chromosomal number, the wand-shaped inflorescences, the presence of rhizomes, and characteristic basal leaves, some common plants such as New England aster and Heath aster now belong to the genus *Lasallea*. Splitting off some of the species into *Lasallea* occurred in 1980 but has yet to be embraced by botanists and has been totally ignored by horticulturists (including myself).

Division is the easiest means of propagation. The outside portions of the clumps should be split and replanted in early spring or fall. The centers of stronger-growing species become bare within 1–2 years, and, if not divided every few years, plants will degenerate and lose their ornamental usefulness (an exception to this *A. amellus*, which should be left undisturbed for 2–3 years). Terminal cuttings of most species can also be rooted. Collect 1–2″ long cuttings with 2–3 leaves in the spring or early summer and insert in a clean mixture of sand and perlite, and rooting will occur within 2–3 weeks. This is the best and sometimes the only method to clean up prized plants which suffer from aster wilt caused by *Verticillium vilmorinii*. Since the fungus resides in the rootstock, terminal cuttings of new growth may result in clean plants. *A. novi-belgii* types are most susceptible, while *A. novae-angliae* is least affected. The other major problem of New England and New York asters is powdery mildew (*Erysiphe cichoracearum*). Some cultivars are more susceptible than others, but fungicides should be applied to all cultivars starting around July 1 to reduce infection. Rust can also be troublesome with many species of asters. Maintain good air circulation, cut out stems if the plants are too dense, and stay away from highly susceptible cultivars.

Asters are useful for fall flowering, but some flower in the summer and may reflower in the fall if spent blossoms are removed immediately. Tall varieties need staking and should be avoided if one is an anti-staker. This is still a major drawback to asters, particularly the New England and New York types. Regardless of where they are grown, most cultivars must have support or they look shabby. Staking can be reduced and even eliminated in many medium size cultivars if plants are grown in full sun and pinched back once or twice in spring and early summer. This is a good practice for all tall flowering plants and results in more compact, dense plants. Pinch back 4–6″ of growth from each growing point but do not do it later than June 15 in the North and July 1 in the South, or you may remove the developing flowers. A sharp pair of hedge trimmers does the job in the Armitage garden.

Plants which are sold under the name of China aster are *Callistephus chinensis*. These are beautiful plants but are annuals and not to be confused with the perennial asters.

Quick Reference to Aster Species

| | Height (ft.) | Flowers single or in clusters | Flowering time |
|---|---|---|---|
| *A. alpinus* | ½–¾ | Single | Early Summer |
| *A. amellus* | 2–2½ | Single, Cluster | Summer |
| *A. carolinianus* | 7–12 | Single | Late Fall |
| *A. cordifolius* | 4–6 | Cluster | Early Fall |
| *A. divaricatus* | 1–2 | Cluster | Summer |
| *A. ericoides* | 3–4 | Cluster | Late Summer |
| *A. × frikartii* | 2–3 | Cluster | Summer |
| *A. lateriflorus* | 2–3 | Cluster | Fall |
| *A. novae-angliae* | 4–6 | Cluster | Fall |
| *A. novi-belgii* | 1–6 | Cluster | Fall |
| *A. sedifolius* | 2–3 | Cluster | Fall |
| *A. tataricus* | 3–6 | Cluster | Late Fall |
| *A. thomsonii* | 1–3 | Cluster | Early Fall |
| *A. tongolensis* | 1–2 | Single | Early Summer |

| | | | |
|---|---|---|---|
| *-alpinus* (al-pine′ us) | | Alpine Aster | 6–9″/1′ |
| Early Summer | Purple | Europe | Zones 4–7 |

This is an excellent front-of-the-garden plant for cooler areas of the country. It is a variable plant bearing solitary, 1–2″ diameter, purple flowers consisting of 20–40 ray flowers with yellow centers. The foliage is entire and gray-green in the spring but loses the gray color in the heat of the summer, particularly in the South. It is not tolerant of hot, humid climates and thus is not a particularly long-lasting species, 3–4 years being an average life span. Terrific plant for the West and Plains states.

Seed germinates readily when placed in moist, warm (70–75° F) conditions.

**Cultivars:**
'Abendschein' bears handsome, pink flowers on 2′ tall plants.
Var. *albus* has white flowers but is a rather spindly grower.
'Beechwood' is seldom offered but has flowers of clear blue with yellow centers.
'Dark Beauty' ('Dunkel Schone') has dark blue, almost purple flowers in early summer.
'Goliath' is so-called because of the 2–2½″ diameter, light blue flowers. It is taller than the species and grows to 15″.
'Happy End' offers soft pink flowers, gray foliage in the spring, and a compact habit.
'Wargrave Variety' ('Wargrave Park') has pale pink flowers tinged with purple, which, unfortunately, tend to fade in bright sun.

## Related Species:

*A. diplostephoides*, native to southeastern Tibet and western China, bears narrow, reflexed, lavender ray flowers with dusty lavender to reddish orange disk flowers. Plants are about 2' tall and flower in late spring and early summer.

| *-amellus* (a-mel' lus) | | Italian Aster | 2–2½'/2' |
|---|---|---|---|
| Summer | Purple | Italy | Zones 5–7 |

Plants have pubescent stems and leaves, giving a rough appearance and feel. The leaves are entire, sessile and about 5" long. The large, 2–2½" diameter, purple flowers consist of 20–30 narrow petals with orange-yellow centers. They are borne singly or in dense corymbs in early fall and bloom continuously to frost. The species itself, however, is seldom seen, and improvements have been made to reduce height, increase color range, and reduce floppiness. Most of the new cultivars are 1–2' tall and do not need staking unless overfertilized or if temperatures become exceptionally high. It is a particularly fine species for zones 5 and 6 and is good, but not as spectacular, in the heat and humidity of zones 7 and 8. *A. amellus* is one of the parents of the hybrid *A.* × *frikartii*.

## Cultivars:

'Blue King' bears large, violet-blue flowers on 2' tall stems.

'Joseph Lakin' has flat heads of blue flowers, 18" to 2' tall.

'King George' is an exceptionally fine selection, offering deep purple flowers on 2–3' tall stems. It is floriferous and requires no support.

'Nocturne' is often cited as a pink-flowered form but appears to be more bluish purple than pink. Although not as floriferous as 'King George', it is nevertheless a good selection.

'Peach Blossom' has violet-pink flowers.

'Pink Zenith' and 'Lady Hindlip' bear pink flowers with yellow centers on 2–3' tall stems. The former is darker pink and shorter (2') than the latter.

'Rudolph Goethe' was selected in 1914 and is still popular today. It bears violet flowers on 2–3' tall stems.

'Sonia' is probably the best pink-flowered form and produces many 2" diameter, rich pink flowers with yellow centers on plants 1–2' tall.

'Violet Queen' ('Veilchenkonigin') produces many deep violet-blue flowers with yellow eyes. This plant is probably as close to the species in color as any cultivar.

## Related Species:

*A.* × *alpellus* is a cross between *A. alpinus* and *A. amellus*. Plants are 12–15" tall and bear blue ray flowers around orange centers. It is sometimes offered as 'Triumph'.

*A. sibiricus*, Siberian aster, are well-branched plants producing violet flowers with yellow disks in the early fall. A handsome plant.

---

**-carolinianus** (car-o-lyn-ee-ane' us) Climbing Aster      7–12'/4'
  Fall            Pink           Southeastern United States    Zones 6–9
(Syn. *Lasallea caroliniana*)

If you are fortunate enough to live in mild areas of the country, you might want to give this aster a try. Its common name is a bit deceptive because plants don't climb by themselves but consist of long, lanky, arching stems. The plant is actually a big, messy shrub, but, if you train it on a trellis or run it through bamboo stakes, it is really rather impressive. Not a clematis, but then how many clematis flower in October?

This is a terrific rollicking plant but takes up a good deal of space. Growing up to 12' in length, each arching stem produces dozens of 1–2" wide, pink to purple flowers with yellow centers along their lengths. Best to grow in full sun, but a little shade is tolerated.

Propagate from divisions or terminal cuttings. Plants may be grown further north if a few cuttings are taken indoors before frost.

---

**-cordifolius** (kord-i-foe-lee' us)     Heart-Leaf Aster        4–6'/2'
  Summer       Pale Blue       Eastern North America     Zones 3–8

Plants generally are highly branched with many small flowers, each generally less than 1" wide. Ten to twenty narrow ray flowers, ranging in color from dark blue to off-white, surround a yellow center. Although a good deal of variability occurs, plants usually bear smooth stems and thin, hairy leaves. The thin, sharply-toothed leaves provide the plant with common names such as Bee Weed and Bee Tongue. Although plants often look bedraggled in the wild, cultivation tends to make them stand up straight and put their shoulders back. The lower leaves are heart-shaped (cordate), and the upper leaves are ovate to lanceolate. The small flowers lend themselves to cut flowers, particularly as fillers with larger flowers in arrangements. The species itself is offered, but numerous cultivars have also been selected. Plants grow well in both the North and the South, but leaf spotting becomes a bigger problem in the humidity of the South.

**Cultivars:**
'Elegans' bears many white flowers and is one of the best selections.
'Ideal' is 4–6' tall with many violet-blue flowers. In the cut flower trials at the University of Georgia, plants are vigorous and yield dozens of flower heads. Unfortunately, without fungicide applications, leaves tend to develop black spots in the summer.

'Photograph' produces lilac flowers in arching sprays rather than upright inflorescences.

**Related Species:**

*A. oblongifolius* is a handsome garden plant which grows in dry prairies and rocky bluffs from Pennsylvania to Wisconsin and south to North Carolina and Texas. The large daisy flowers are purple with yellow centers. The stiff, hairy plants grow 2–3′ tall in the garden; the rather open plants seen in the field become more dense and full. 'Raydon's Favorite' came from Holbrook Farm in North Carolina, and the early fall, blue-purple flowers were a pleasant surprise in the Armitage garden. The foliage also has a nice hint of mint. Plants need full sun and well-drained soils.

| | | | |
|---|---|---|---|
| *-divaricatus* (di-var-i-cah′ tus) | White Wood Aster | 1–2′/3′ |
| Summer | White | North America | Zones 4–8 |
| (Syn. *A. corymbosus*) | | | |

This spreading aster is native from Maine to Georgia but is seen far more in European gardens than in this country. It bears many thin, nearly black,

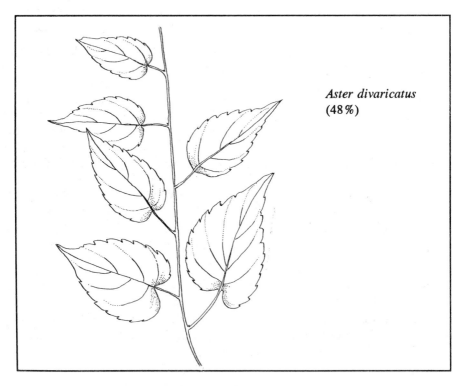

*Aster divaricatus*
(48%)

cascading branches, at the end of which are corymbs of small (¾ ″ diameter), star-like, white flowers with yellow centers. The blossoms may be small, but they are so plentiful that the plant is covered with clouds of flowers from mid-August through September in the South and as late as October in the North. The leaves are about 3″ long, heart-shaped, and coarsely-toothed.

This is one of the few asters which tolerate shade. Plants may be used at the edge of woodlands or placed at the front of the border to grow through other plants. However, while shade is tolerated, more flowers and fewer foliar diseases occur in areas of morning sun and good air movement. Flowers are particularly pretty running in and among bergenias, a combination made popular by Gertrude Jekyll, the Grand Dame of English gardening. If, like me, you are not a big bergenia fan, allow the plants to ramble over hostas. In hot summers, it tends to be leggy in the Midwest and further south. I cut my plants back to about 12″ in early June.

Division, terminal cuttings taken in the spring, or seed sown in the spring or fall are appropriate methods of propagation.

**Related Species:**

*A. ptarmicoides*, upland aster, bears many white flowers in the summer on low-growing plants. The foliage is erect, up to 6″ long and less than ½″ wide. Likely hardy from zones 3–8.

| *-ericoides* (e-ri-koi- deez) | Heath Aster | 3–4′/2′ |
|---|---|---|
| Summer, Fall   White | United States, Mexico | Zones 5–8 |

(Syn. *A. pringlei, Lasallea ericoides*)

Another roadside weed, but one which can become a fine garden plant and an economically important crop. The many needle-like, sessile leaves are very narrow and stiff and seldom more than 1″ long (like *Erica*, heath). The leaves are generally paler green than many other aster species. The white flowers consist of 15–25 ray flowers, each only about ¾″ wide, giving each flower a starry appearance. One of its old names was *A. multiflorus* (many-flowered), a much more descriptive name for this plant. The bracts beneath the flowers end in broad, conspicuous green tips and a minute spine. Useless information, unless one wants to try to identify various species in this frustrating genus.

The small but numerous flowers (literally hundreds of flowers are produced) have resulted in cultivars used as a commercial cut flower from South America to Holland and United States. They are most used as fillers (like baby's breath) and harvested by the acre in fields and greenhouses. Most available cultivars were selected mainly for cut flower production but are useful for garden plants as well.

153

## Cultivars:

'Blue Star' bears hundreds of star-shaped, dark blue flowers on 3' tall stems.

'Blue Wonder' has blue flowers with a tinge of pink.

'Erlkonig' produces light lavender flowers on 30–36" tall plants.

'Esther' has white flowers with a tinge of pink and is similar in growth habit to 'Monte Cassino', but only about 18–24" tall.

'Monte Cassino' is not particularly well known to gardeners, but it is the most popular cultivar for cut flower producers. It bears many stems with clusters of small, white flowers on 24–30" stems.

'Pink Cloud' produces clouds of starry, light pink flowers on 3' tall plants.

'Ringdove' was selected for its multitude of ½" wide, lilac-rose flowers.

'White Wonder' is similar in growth habit to 'Blue Wonder' but has creamy white flowers.

## Related Species:

*A. linariifolius*, savory-leaved aster, is 1–2' tall with 1" entire, linear, stiff, sessile leaves. The many 1" wide flowers are porcelain-blue to violet.

*A. pilosus* is considered a weed by most people who drive by it on the side of the road. However, with little trouble, plants will become much less sprawling and covered with white flowers in late fall. The leaves are almost needle-like and similar to those of *A. ericoides*. I have seen wonderful garden specimens at the Mercer Botanic Garden in Houston, TX.

*A. vimineus*, native to Kansas and Oklahoma, also bears stiff, narrow leaves but has a twiggy, dense appearance. The leaves are slightly gray-green, and many off-white flowers are held on slightly arching branches. 'Lovely' bears lovely lilac-pink flowers in late summer and early fall. Not well-known and deserving of far more use.

| | | | |
|---|---|---|---|
| -× *frikartii* (fri-kart' ee-eye) | | Frikart's Aster | 2–3'/3' |
| Summer | Lavender | Hybrid | Zones 5–8 |

*A.* × *frikartii* was raised in Switzerland around 1920 and is the result of crossing *A. amellus* × *A. thomsonii*. The large flowers of *A. amellus* combined with the long flowering season of *A. thomsonii*, provide one of the most popular but overrated asters today. Interestingly, it is a little taller than either parent. The dark green, pubescent foliage is mildew resistant and remains disease-free throughout the season. The 2–3" diameter, lavender-blue flowers start in late June in the South, late July further north and continue for about 8 weeks. Plants should be placed in full sun and fertilized sparingly.

## Cultivars:

Four selections were named from the original hybrid, but 'Eiger' and 'Jungfrau' are seldom seen in the United States. 'Monch' and 'Wonder of

Aster × frikartii 'Monch'
(92%)

Staffa', however, are easily obtained. 'Monch' is reputed by many garden authorities to be the best *A. × frikartii* clone. It bears lavender-blue flowers and stands 2½–3' tall with a 3' spread. Plants differ from 'Wonder of Staffa', in being less prone to falling and having darker blue flowers.

'Wonder of Staffa' supposedly has lighter blue flowers than 'Monch', but the differences between these cultivars have been overstated. It is a challenge, to say the least, to distinguish between the flowers of each cultivar even when placed side by side. 'Wonder of Staffa' may be slightly taller (although I have seen little difference) than 'Monch' and in warm climates might require more support. Perhaps differences in cultivars have been obscured over the years as the demand continued to rise. It is possible that some material has been seed-propagated to keep up with demand or that stock blocks have been mixed up on occasion. Nevertheless, both cultivars are useful garden plants and well worth a little, but not too much space in any garden.

Seeds of Frikart's aster are available, but the resultant flowers occur in many different shades of lavender and blue.

155

**Related Species:**

*A.* × 'Flora's Delight' was bred by Alan Bloom of Bloom's of Bressingham, using *A. thomsonii* 'Nana' and *A. amellus* 'Sonia' in the hope of widening the color range offered by Frikart. Named after his wife, 'Flora's Delight' is a little shorter than the Frikart hybrids and produces daisies of lilac-blue. Plants require well-drained soils and full sun.

*A. spectabilis* looks similar to Frikart's aster but grows only 1–2' tall and flowers much later. Plants are covered with showy, violet-blue flowers on many branched stems. Native from Massachusetts to North Carolina, plants are way underused.

| | | |
|---|---|---|
| *-lateriflorus* (lat-er-i-flor' us) | Calico Aster | 2–3'/3' |
| Late Summer, Fall    White | North America | Zones 5–7 |

One description of this species reads "many branched stems with narrow, lanceolate, dark green leaves and small, bristly, white flowers." Hardly makes you want to run out and buy a dozen. The species itself stands about 3' tall, and flowers are often borne along one side (*lateri-*) of the stem in late summer and early fall. The tiny-toothed leaves turn a nice coppery hue in the fall. If no improvements had occurred, it is doubtful that plants would have made their way into many gardens. However, a number of cultivars have gained this species many fans. Plants need well-drained soils and full sun. Native to the Plains states, they struggle south of zone 7a.

**Cultivars:**
'Coombe Fishacre' has dark green leaves with small, pink ray flowers and dark centers. Not as horizontal as the favorite, var. *horizontalis*.
Var. *horizontalis* ('Horizontalis') is a marvelous plant when grown in full sun and well-drained soils. Dark green leaves on horizontal branched stems make this bush-like aster quite unique. Add the white flowers with reddish centers, also borne on one side of those stems, and one has a wonderful garden plant. It may be used as a shrublike mass or even as a low-growing hedge. Flowers in mid-fall.
'Prince' is as good as, if not better than, 'Horizontalis'. Plants are about 3' tall, have the same small, white flowers but also have handsome, deep purple foliage. The foliage and flowers make an excellent contrast. In hot summers and in shady areas, the purple color turns green. Much better in climates with relatively cool nights and lower humidity.

**Related Species:**

*A. azureus* is also one of our native asters, also naturally occurring in the Plains states. Plants grow 2–3' tall and bear deep blue to violet flowers. Sometimes called the Sky Blue Aster.

*-novae-angliae* (no'vay-ang' glee-aye)   New England Aster         4–6'/4'
   Late Summer        Violet-Purple       Eastern United States    Zones 4–8
(Syn. *Lasallea novae-angliae*)

This common wild flower is one of the largest and prettiest in the genus but is seldom seen, having been superseded by improved cultivars. The entire, 4–5" long leaves are numerous and very hairy. This species and a few others similar to it may be separated from many others by looking at the base of the leaves. The two basal lobes of the leaves clasp the stem, poking out on either side. The flowers are 1½–2" across and consist of 40–50 ray flowers surrounding a yellow center. The flowers are excellent for cutting and last longer in water than those of *A. novi-belgii*, New York aster. My colleague, Chris Hussey, found out the hard way that harvesting the hairy stems of New England asters can cause a serious skin rash on hands and arms. Chris recommends gloves and a long-sleeved shirt when tackling these fellows.

## Cultivars:

'Alma Potschke' ('Andenken an Alma Potschke') is an excellent 3–4' tall, bright rose selection. The flowers are 1–2" across and have slightly-curled petals. It is more compact (but still requires support) than other selections and less prone to topple.

'Barr's Pink' has 1½" wide, bright rose-pink, semi-double flowers on 4' tall stems. 'Barr's Blue' and 'Barr's Violet' are similar in habit with blue and violet flowers respectively.

'Fanny's Aster' is covered with blue flowers and grows up to 4' tall. She flowers in late fall and is spectacular with fall sunflowers. An absolutely terrific aster, particularly in the South. Introduced by Nancy Goodwin, nursery lady and plantsperson extraordinaire after her friend, Fanny.

'Harrington's Pink' was developed by Mr. Millard Harrington of Williamsburg, Iowa, and is one of the most popular asters today. This 3–5' tall plant bears large (1½" diameter), salmon-pink flowers in September through October.

'Hella Lacy', named for the wife of garden writer Allen Lacy, is 3–4' tall and covered with 2" wide, violet-blue daisies in the fall. Quite big and lanky in the heat.

'Honeysong Pink' bears pink flowers with bright yellow centers. Plants are strong growers on 3' tall stems. A favorite of Mr. Bud Heist of Heistaway Gardens in Conyers, GA. In the South, people know that if Bud endorses a plant, it is a winner.

'Lye End Beauty' has lovely cerise flowers but grows 4–5' tall and must be supported.

'Lyon's White' produces dozens of clean white flowers on 4–5' tall plants in late September (October in the South).

'Martha' has silvery-pink flowers growing 3–4' tall and may be a cross between 'Hella Lacy' and 'Alma Potschke'. Selected by Allen Lacey.

'Mt. Everest' is 3' tall with good, clear white flowers.

'Purple Dome' is a terrific introduction from Mt. Cuba Gardens in Delaware. Late flowering on compact 18–24" stature, the plants maintain a mounded habit even while supporting hundreds of deep blue flowers. Under high humidity environments, leaf and stem disease can become a major problem in mid-July and August. In Atlanta, plants do well most years, but the heat and humidity takes its toll in a cumulative manner. Regardless, this is a fine aster for the front of the sunny garden.

'Rosa Sieger' has large, salmon-rose flowers on 4' tall plants. Very eye-catching.

'Rose Serenade' is about 30" tall and bears soft pink flowers in early fall.

'September Ruby' has 1" diameter, deep ruby-red flowers on 3–5' high stems. If planted in rich soils or overfertilized, heights up to 5' are not uncommon for this cultivar. Although classified as a late bloomer,

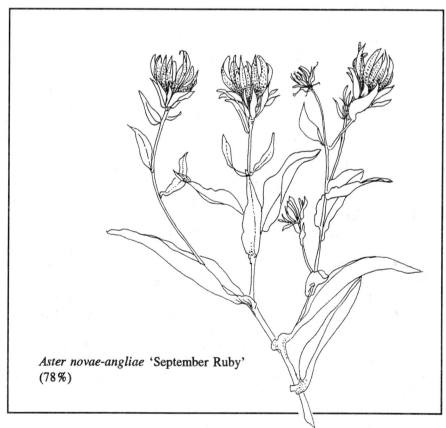

*Aster novae-angliae* 'September Ruby'
(78%)

flowering begins in late May in north Georgia and continues through late June. If the flowers are removed, it blooms again in September. Flowering is 3-4 weeks later in the Northeast but seldom do flowers peak in the fall. This is true with many so-called fall-flowering asters.
'Treasure' is 4-6' tall with light purple to violet flowers.
'Wedding Lace' is 3-4' tall with clean white flowers in early fall.

### Related Species:

*A. grandiflorus*, great aster, is one of the latest asters to flower and bears some of the largest (up to 1½″ wide) flowers. They are violet-blue and held on 2-3' tall plants. Native from Virginia to Florida and hardy in zones 5-9.

*A. puniceus*, swamp aster, can produce thick, treelike stems up to 6' tall, although a great deal of variability occurs in the wild. Plants are most at home in damp, swampy conditions and look particularly ragged in dry soils. The stems and leaves are generally quite hairy, and the leaves clasp the stem in the same manner as New England aster. Flowers are usually light blue, not the phoenician purple that the Latin name suggests.

*-novi-belgii* (no' vee-bel-gee' eye) New York Aster, Michaelmas Daisy 1-6'/3'
Late Summer      Violet      Eastern United States      Zones 4-8

There are literally hundreds of cultivars of this wonderful roadside weed. The specific epithet, *novi-belgii*, arose when the state of New York was once known as New Belgium. The history of breeding of Michaelmas daisies is a who's-who of Horticulture, including the Honorary Vickary Gibbs, Ernest Ballard, A.H. Harrison, Barrs of Taplow and Alan Bloom, all of whom threw their talents into the aster fray. The smooth or nearly glabrous leaves differentiate them from New England asters. The leaves clasp the stem similar to New England asters, but flowers normally have only 15-25 ray flowers. The flowers are not as good for cutting as the New England asters but provide excellent color in the late summer and fall garden. They are called Michaelmas daisies because they bloom around September 29, St. Michael's Day, in the British Isles.

Somewhere along the production line, many cultivars have been placed under the name *A.* × *dumosus*. This was likely the result of European growers listing plants under this name and American growers following suit. The species, *A. dumosus*, is a bushy, rather short, plant (1-3') native to fields and meadows from Florida to Texas, and north to Maine, Ontario and Illinois. It seems that any cultivar under 15″ tall has summarily been pushed into *A.* × *dumosus*. I can find no taxonomic evidence for the name change, so I will maintain the listing of short cultivars under *A. novi-belgii*.

It is likely that all the cultivars I list under "dwarf cultivars" are listed in some catalogs under *A.* × *dumosus.*

Propagate all cultivars by division or by terminal cuttings.

### Cultivars:

*Dwarf cultivars* (less than 15″ tall). (*A.* × *dumosus*). Many of the dwarf cultivars are excellent for the front of the garden and, best of all, require no staking. Dozens more are available than these listed, but how many can we use?

'Alert' produces double, crimson-red flowers on 10–12″ plants.

'Alice Haslem' was raised in the 1950's by Mr. A. H. Harrison of Gayborder Nurseries, in Derbyshire England. She has wonderful, double, rosy-pink flowers.

'Audrey' bears 1″ wide, lilac flowers on 12″ tall plants.

'Buxton's Blue' is only 4–6″ tall but produces many small, dark blue flowers.

'Heinz Richard' forms compact 12″ mounds of foliage covered with semi-double, salmon-pink flowers in late summer and early fall.

'Jenny' ('Jenny Margaret Rose') from the Gayborder Nursery in Derby-shire, England bears lovely red flowers on 12–15″ tall stems. Many Michaelmas daisies bear the Gayborder name, and all are in the short to medium height range.

'Kassel' has semi-double, carmine-rose flowers in early fall.

'Kristina' bears white daisy flowers on 18″ tall plants.

'Lady-in-Blue' is about 12″ tall with blue flowers in the fall.

'Little Pink Beauty' is one of my favorites, becoming covered in semi-double, pink flowers in the fall. There is a complementary 'Little Blue Beauty' lurking about in catalogs as well.

'Nesthakchen' sounds like a sneeze but bears rather striking, compact, pinkish red flowers on 12–18″ tall plants. More mildew resistant than most others.

'Newton Pink' is another good pink, bearing semi-double flowers, on 12–15″ tall plants.

'Niobe' produces single white flowers with yellow eyes on 6–10″ tall plants.

'Peter Harrison' is a handsome gentleman offering pink flowers in September and October on his trim 15–18″ frame. From the Gayborder Nursery.

'Pink Bouquet' is about 12″ tall with soft pink, daisy-like flowers in late summer and fall.

'Prof. Kippenburg' is 9–12″ tall and carries lavender-blue, semi-double flowers. This excellent cultivar has withstood the test of time.

'Rosenwitchel' was introduced in 1971 in Germany but has only been here for a few years. Plants are about 15–18″ tall and are covered with lavender-pink flowers.

'Snow Cushion' ('Schneekissen') is a late bloomer (late September-October) with white flowers on 6-8″ tall plants.

'Snowsprite' has semi-double, white flowers with a yellow center. It grows to 15″ tall.

'Violet Carpet' bears rich violet daisy flowers, forming 8″ tall carpets.

'Wood's Dwarfs' are wonderful 8-12″ tall plants with purple-blue ('Wood's Purple') and pink ('Wood's Pink') flowers. In the Armitage garden, they begin flowering around mid-September and persist for 4-6 weeks.

*Medium cultivars* (less than 4′). Many require staking, especially those with large flowers.

'Ada Ballard' has double, lavender-blue flowers atop 3′ tall stems.

'Arctic' bears double, white flowers.

'Beechwood Rival' produces wine-red flowers on 3′ tall stems. At least five cultivars carry the Beechwood name, a popular series of cultivars, all with rather large flowers and about 3′ tall.

'Bonningdale Blue' and 'Bonningdale White' grow nearly 3′ tall and produce 1-2″ wide, blue and white, semi-double to double flowers in September and October.

'Crimson Brocade' is about 3′ tall and produces crimson-red flowers in late fall.

'Eventide' produces 2″ wide, semi-double, violet-blue flowers on 3-4′ high plants.

'Ernest Ballard' has reddish pink, semi-double flowers up to 3″ wide. Many of the medium size cultivars are the result of the work of Mr. Ernest Ballard of Colwall, Malvern, England, who stands as a leader in the breeding of Michaelmas daisies. One of his traits was breeding large (1-2″ diameter) flowers on 2½-3′ tall plants. Most Ballard family members have at least one cultivar as their namesake.

'Patricia Ballard' has semi-double, rose-pink flowers.

'Priory Blush' is at least 4′ tall with double, white flowers tinged with a little pink. Very handsome but needs some judicious early summer pruning.

'Royal Ruby' and 'Royal Velvet' are 20-30″ tall and produce semi-double, red and violet-purple flowers, respectively. Both raised by Alan Bloom of Bressingham Nursery.

'The Bishop' ('The Archbishop') bears deep red flowers on 2-3′ tall plants.

'Winston Churchill' would be proud of the handsome red daisy flowers on 2-3′ tall stems. They were fantastic in our cut flower trials at Georgia.

*Tall cultivars* (over 4′). I recommend none for the South and hesitate to recommend them at all. They are too tall for most gardens, require extensive support, and can become invasive. All could use some pruning in the summer, but if grown well, they are show stoppers. They are exceptional in flower and can be grown as long as they are pinched at least once in the spring or early summer and then supported.

'Cardinal' has deep rosy-red flowers surrounding a yellow center.

'Climax' is a 5' tall giant with outstanding large (2–3" across), light blue flowers in early fall. This was raised over 80 years ago and is one of the few old-time Michaelmas daisies still in cultivation.

'Fellowship' bears large, clear, semi-double, pink flowers on 4–5' tall stems.

'Mount Everest' has large (2–3"), semi-double, white flowers in September and October.

'White Ladies' is 5–6' tall, with clear white flowers and an orange-yellow center.

### Related Species:

*A. laevis*, smooth aster, combines dozens of blue ray flowers with yellow centers, dark stems and slightly blue-green, smooth foliage on 3' tall plants. Although a fairly common roadside plant, a little tending can make a handsome, eye-catching garden plant. 'Bluebird' bears 1" wide, violet-blue flowers and arching stems with handsome blue-green foliage. Plants were introduced by Richard Lighty of Mt. Cuba Center in Greenville, DE.

*A. × versicolor*, bicolor aster, resulted from a cross between *A. laevis* and *A. novi-belgii*. Plants grow 3' tall with ray flowers which open blue or white and change to purple.

| | | | |
|---|---|---|---|
| *-sedifolius* (say-di-fo' lee-us) | | Rhone Aster | 2–3'/3' |
| Fall | Lilac | Southern Europe | Zones 4–7 |
| (Syn. *A. acris*) | | | |

This relatively unknown aster has rough, hairy, linear, entire leaves and many stems resulting in a bushy habit of growth. Each stem terminates in a corymb of 30–40 small (1–1¼" across), starry blossoms. The individual flowers are not particularly ornamental, but the plants are literally covered in a sea of lavender-blue. The ray flowers are widely spaced around the yellow center. Plants should be grown in full sun and they tolerate most soils, assuming drainage is adequate.

Division is the surest and easiest means of propagation, but seed sown and placed at 70–75° F under constant moisture germinates readily.

### Cultivars:

'Nanus' is the most common form, the species is seldom seen anymore. It is 18"–2' tall, and the flowers are only slightly smaller (1") than those of the species.

**-tataricus** (ta-tar' ri-cus)          Tatarian Daisy          3-6'/3'
   Late Fall          Blue          Siberia          Zones 4-8

Only one of the reasons for the popularity of this tall aster is that plants rarely require stalking. Although it will reach heights of 6' or more, seldom does growth exceed 3-4' the first year. Plants resemble swiss chard in the spring and summer, but, in early fall, the flower stalks begin to emerge from the leafy mass. The erect stems are covered with straight, bristly hairs (hispid), and the entire, lanceolate leaves are large (the basal leaves are up to 6" wide and 2' long) and sessile. The flower stems branch near the top, resulting in many 1" wide, blue to purple ray flowers with yellow centers. One of the best features of this aster is its late flowering. Although many asters flower until frost, they often look tired and worn out. This species does not start flowering until late September or early October, so it still looks fresh in November. Tough to beat as a late-flowering garden plant. Plants will make large colonies within a few years, and division not only allows for more plants but keeps the garden from becoming one big chard patch. Full sun is a must.

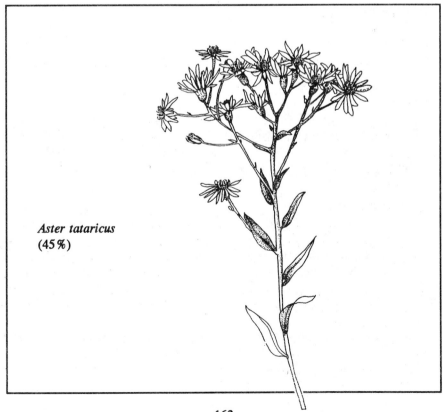

*Aster tataricus*
(45%)

163

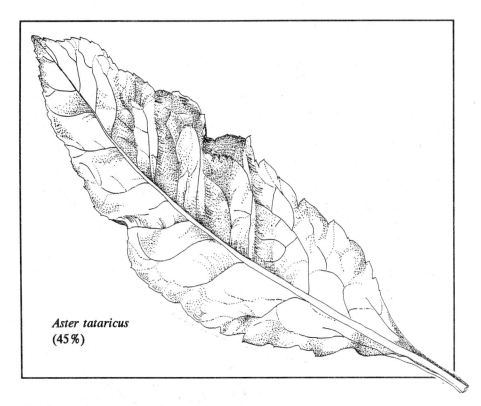

**Aster tataricus**
**(45%)**

## Cultivars:

'Jin-Dai' was found by Rick Darke and Skip March of Longwood Gardens and the National Arboretum, respectively, at the Jin-Dai Botanical Garden near Tokyo. It is probably a better selection for most gardens in that it is only 3–5′ tall. It may flower a little earlier than the species.

## Related Species:

*A. macrophyllus*, bigleaf aster, native to the eastern United States, is about 4′ tall and flowers in August and September. It produces 8–10″ long, serrated, heart-shaped (cordate), basal leaves with long petioles. The uppermost leaves become less cordate and are sessile at the top. The 1″ diameter, pale blue to violet flowers are held in a rounded, many-flowered corymb. A white-flowered form ('Alba') is also known. It does not flower as late as *A. tataricus*.

*A. umbellatus* is found from Newfoundland to Georgia and bears umbel-like heads of small, white flowers with yellow centers on 4–5′ tall, stoloniferous plants. Very fine, but large. Plants perk up significantly when given a little garden care.

| *-thomsonii* (tom-son′ ee-eye) | | Thompson's Aster | 1–3′/2′ |
|---|---|---|---|
| Late Summer | Lilac | Western Himalayas | Zones 4–8 |

The leaves are coarsely-toothed, and the 1–2″ diameter lilac flowers are borne on long, slender flower stems. One of the outstanding characteristics is its long blooming period and, as one of the parents of *A.* × *frikartii*, this trait was passed on to that hybrid.

### Cultivars:

'Nanus' is only 12–18″ tall and is essentially the only form of *A. thomsonii* represented in gardens. It resembles a dwarf *A.* × *frikartii*. The 1–3″ long, pointed leaves are gray-green, and the starry, blue flowers are about 1–1½″ in diameter. This is an excellent plant for the front of the garden where late color is desired. One of the favorite species of aster lovers.

| *-tongolensis* (ton-go-len′ sis) | | East Indies Aster | 1–2′/1′ |
|---|---|---|---|
| Early Summer | Violet | Western China | Zones 5–8 |
| (Syn. *A. subcoeruleus*) | | | |

Rosettes of dark green, hairy leaves and solitary, 2″ diameter, violet-blue flowers with bright orange centers are characteristics of this aster. The strong stems carry the flowers well, and no support is necessary. Plants are stoloniferous, and significant clumps can form under suitable conditions. Unfortunately, this summer-flowering aster is not long-lived and survives only 2–3 years in the South, perhaps a little longer in zone 5.

Divide after flowering to keep plants vigorous.

### Cultivars:

'Berggarten' has 2–3″ diameter, violet-blue flowers with an orange-yellow eye. Flowers appear in June.

'Wartburg Star' bears 1½″ diameter, lavender-blue flowers with orange centers. The best of the cultivars offered.

### Related Species:

*A. yunnanensis*, Yunnan aster, is native to western China. Plants are not stoloniferous and have a habit similar to *A. alpinus*. They are 9–12″ tall, and bear pale blue to mauve flowers with yellow centers. 'Napsbury' has lovely blue flowers with orange centers.

### Quick Key to Aster Species

    A. Plants climbing, shrubby . . . . . . . . . . . . . . *A. carolinianus*
  AA. Plants not climbing
      B. Flowers usually solitary on flower stem

C. Plant 6–9″, stem leaves lanceolate . . . . . . . . . *A. alpinus*
CC. Plant taller than 1′
    D. Leaves coarsely hairy,
        leaves and stem rough . . . . . . . . . . . . . *A. amellus*
    DD. Leaves often pubescent,
        but not rough . . . . . . . . . . . . . . . . *A. tongolensis*
BB. Flowers numerous on flower stem
  C. Leaves entire
    D. Ray flowers white
      E. Leaves 3–4″ long . . . . . . . . . . . . . *A. lateriflorus*
      EE. Leaves needle-like,
        usually less than ½″ long . . . . . . . . . *A. ericoides*
    DD. Ray flowers blue or lilac
      E. Over 10 flowers per stem . . . . . . . . . *A. sedifolius*
      EE. Less than 5 (sometimes only 1)
        flower per stem . . . . . . . . . . . . . . . . *A. amellus*
CC. Leaves toothed
    D. Leaves, particularly on base of flower
    stems, mostly heart-shaped
      E. Plants less than 2′ tall,
        stems purple to black . . . . . . . . . . . *A. divaricatus*
      EE. Plants taller than 2′, stems green . . . . . *A. cordifolius*
    DD. Leaves not usually heart-shaped
      E. Base of upper stem leaves clasping stem
        F. Leaves pubescent or rough . . . . . *A. novae-angliae*
        FF. Leaves smooth or nearly so . . . . . . . *A. novi-belgii*
      EE. Base of stem leaves petioled, not clasping
        F. Plant dwarf (at least garden
          cultivar), 1–1½′ tall . . . . . . *A. thomsonii* 'Nanus'
        FF. Plant taller than 2′
          G. Basal leaves up to 2′ long,
            plants over 4′ tall . . . . . . . . . . . *A. tataricus*
          GG. Basal leaves less than 2′ long,
            plants generally 2′ tall . . . . . . . *A.* × *frikartii*

## Additional Reading:

Seals, J.L. 1992. Perennial asters, stars of the flower garden. *Fine Gardening* 27:26–30.

Semple, J.C. and L. Brouillet, 1980. A synopsis of American asters: the subgenera, sections and subsections of Aster and Lasallea. *American Journal of Botany* 67(7):1010–1026.

Winterrowd, W. 1991. American asters, late-blooming stars of the perennial border. *Horticulture* 69(8):28–32.

## *Asteromoea* see *Kalimeris*

## *Astilbe* (as-til' bee)     False Spirea     Saxifragaceae

Astilbes have enjoyed immense popularity for many years and are excellent plants for shady, moist conditions. If grown in areas to their liking, they are plants of incomparable beauty. The individual flowers are small and without much merit, but the plume-like inflorescence ranges from 6″ to 2′ tall and is very striking. It is easy to confuse the white species, *A. biternata*, and hybrid cultivars such as 'Prof van de Wielen' with goatsbeard, *Aruncus dioicus*. See *Aruncus* for hints to tell them apart. There are about 25 species of *Astilbe*, some of which are less than 1′ tall and useful for the front of the garden or rockeries, while others are over 4′ in height and better suited for the back of the border. None require staking, and all are long lasting under average garden conditions. The mid to deep green foliage is 2 or 3 times divided into groups of three and is often copper colored when young (particularly red-flowered hybrids). The biggest enemy of *Astilbe* is dryness, but ample moisture and rich soil result in a rewarding planting. If the soil dries out, the foliage develops brown margins, and whole leaves may wither and die prematurely. Plants are particularly effective grouped around the edge of ponds or other water features in the garden.

Astilbes can also be used as potted plants forced into flower in the greenhouse. Plant the crowns in 6″ pots in late summer and allow them to establish good root and foliage systems during the fall. Place them in a cold frame or bury under straw mulch so they receive approximately 3 months of sub-40° F temperatures. At that time, bring the pots inside, water and fertilize as foliage and flowers appear. Astilbes also make excellent cut flowers if harvested when half open.

Propagate from divisions in spring or fall. Some of the species may be raised from seed, but the hybrids must be propagated vegetatively. Seed should be sown in moist sand-peat mixture and placed at 70–75° F for 2 weeks, followed by 40° F for 4 weeks.

Quick Reference to Astilbe Species

|  | Height (in.) | Flowering season | Flower color |
|---|---|---|---|
| *A.* × *arendsii* | 24–48 | Late Spring | Various |
| *A. biternata* | 36–60 | Spring | White |
| *A. chinensis* | 8–15 | Summer | Red-pink |
| *A. chinensis* var. *taquetii* | 24–48 | Late Summer | Lilac |
| *A.* × *rosea* | 24–36 | Summer | Salmon, pink |
| *A. simplicifolia* | 12–18 | Summer | Pink, white |

| -× *arendsii* (ah-rendz′ ee-ie) | | Hybrid Astilbe | 2-4′/2′ |
|---|---|---|---|
| Late Spring | Various | Hybrid Origin | Zones 4-8 |

Over 95% of the astilbes sold in this country probably belong to this group of hybrids. Not enough can be said about the accomplishments of Georg Arends (1862–1952) of Ronsdorf, West Germany, who studied and hybridized such genera as *Bergenia, Sedum, Phlox* and *Campanula*. His passion, however, was *Astilbe*. One of his first introductions (1903), using *A. chinensis* and *A. japonica*, was a light pink cultivar called 'Peach Blossom', still enjoyed by gardeners today (this has since been reclassified as *A. × rosea* to designate hybrids of *A. chinensis* and *A. japonica* parentage only). Additional clones arose from crosses among other species, including *A. grandis, A. thunbergii, A. davidii*, and *A. astilboides*. In 1933, a major breakthrough came with the appearance of a bronze leaf, red-flowered cultivar later named 'Fanal'. He continued crossing combination after combination and between 1902 and 1952 introduced over 74 cultivars, many of which are available in American nurseries still. Astilbes also caught the attention of other nurseries such as the Lemoine Nursery in Nancy, France and Bressingham Gardens in Diss, England. Over fifty cultivars may be found today, ranging from those with copper to dark green foliage, flower colors from clear white to blood red, and flowering times of early June to mid-August.

**Cultivars:**

It is impossible to name all cultivars within the confines of this book, but the following list includes some personal favorites as well as other popular varieties. Many cultivars have been reclassified under *A. × hybrida, A. × japonica, A. × rosea* and *A. × thunbergii*, but differences from the garden point of view are inconsequential. All cultivars may be divided in early spring.

*White flowers:*

'Avalanche' is about 2′ tall, with wide, arching inflorescences.
'Bergkristall' is offered by a few nurseries, although nobody can pronounce the name. Plants, however, bear handsome white plumes on 3′ tall plants.
'Bridal Veil' ('Brautschlier') is approximately 2½′ tall with white-pink flowers.
'Bumalda' produces rosy-white plumes and grows about 2′ tall.
'Deutschland' bears dense flower spikes on 2′ tall plants.
'Diamond' ('Diamont') has fairly clean white flowers on 2-3′ tall plants.
'Ellie' bears large, white flowers on thick, mid- to dark green foliage. Showier than most whites.
'Gladstone' ('W.E. Gladstone') produces 18-24″ tall plants with creamy white inflorescences.
'Irrlicht' has rosy-white flowers over dark green foliage. It grows 2-2½′ tall.

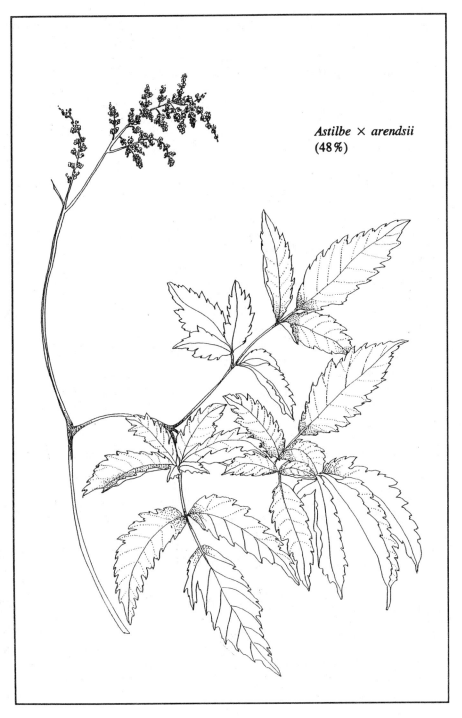

*Astilbe* × *arendsii*
(48%)

'Professor van der Wielen' has loose flower spikes on 3' high plants. A terrific plant which can also substitute for goatsbeard. A hybrid of *A. thunbergii*.

'Queen of Holland' bears white flowers tinged with pink and bronze foliage.

'Snowdrift' is a sport of 'Irrlicht' and produces clear white flowers over 2½' tall stems.

'Washington' bears glossy green leaves and white flowers on 2–3' tall plants.

'White Gloria' ('Weisse Gloria') is an early-flowering cultivar about 2' tall. The tight flowers are not as graceful as some of the more airy-flowered forms, but they flower well and without complaint.

*Pink to salmon flowers:*

'Anita Pfeifer', bred in 1930 by the Arends nursery, produces bright salmon-rose flowers on 24–30″ plants.

'Betsy Cuperus' is one of the oldest cultivars, bred in 1917, and is occasionally offered today. Long sprays of blush pink flowers are held on 3' tall plants. A hybrid of *A. thunbergii*.

'Bressingham Beauty' has arching plumes of clear pink flowers on 3½' tall plants.

'Catherine Deneuve' is almost as beautiful as its namesake. Fluffy rose-pink flowers top 24–30″ tall plants.

'Cattleya' bears orchid-pink, long-blooming flowers on 3' high plants. A cultivar that performs well all over the country.

'Elizabeth Bloom' has dark green foliage with handsome pink flowers.

'Erica' is about 3' tall and has large, open panicles of clear pink flowers.

'Europa' is an early-flowering cultivar bearing pale pink flowers over 2' tall plants.

'Gloria' flowers in mid-summer with rosy-lavender flowers on 30″ tall plants.

'Grete Pungel' is at least 3' tall, has pink flowers and blooms in early to mid-summer. An Arends introduction dating back to 1924.

'Irene' has lovely light pink flowers on 2' tall plants.

'Mainz' produces handsome lavender-pink flowers with dark green foliage.

'Ostrich Plume' ('Straussenfeder') bears many bright pink, arching spikes over 3' tall plants. A cultivar of *A.* × *thunbergii*.

'Rheinland' is popular and has early, clear pink flowers on 2' tall plants.

'Sheila Haxton', a new introduction from Bloom's Nursery, has *A. chinensis* 'Pumila' in its parentage. The flowers are deep pink and a little over 2' tall.

*Red to magenta flowers:*

'America' bears lilac-rosy flowers on open plumes. Old-fashioned but tough.

'Etna' has dark red plumes with dark green foliage on 2' tall plants.

'Fanal', first offered in 1933, is still one of the most popular astilbes offered. It is small (2' in height), early to flower, and produces blood red blooms above dark bronze leaves.

'Federsee' adapts well to dry conditions. Plants produce 2' long panicles of carmine-rose flowers.

'Fire' ('Feuer') produces eye-catching, fiery-red flowers on 30" plants.

'Gertrud Brix' is also carmine-red, and plants are only 2' tall.

'Glow' is only 1–1½' tall with intense red flowers.

'Granet' is about 2' tall and bears carmine red blooms.

'Jo Ophorst' has late-flowering, stiff magenta spikes on 3' tall plants.

'Lilli Goos', raised in 1930, is still a handsome red to pink, late-flowering cultivar. About 30" tall with dark green foliage.

'Mars' is an early violet-flowering cultivar growing about 2' tall.

'Montgomery' is a terrific scarlet-red flowering plant 2–3' tall.

'Obergartner Jurgens' was bred in 1954 from *A. japonica* parentage. The dark green foliage is outstanding and contrasts well with the rosy-red flowers.

'Red Charm' has a good deal of *A. thunbergii* in its pedigree, accounting for its robust size (3–4' tall) and arching, red flower plumes. Close to true red as any cultivar I've seen.

'Red Light' ('Rotlicht') has intense red flowers and exceptionally handsome, shiny green foliage.

'Red Sentinel', an early-flowering cultivar, produces red flowers on 3' tall plants.

'Spartan' bears dark red flowers on 2–3' tall, deep green plants.

'Spinell' bears salmon-red flowers atop 3' tall stems.

'Vesuvius' has early, bright salmon flowers on 2' tall plants.

| *-biternata* (bye-ter-nay' ta) | American Astilbe | 3–5'/3' |
|---|---|---|
| Spring          White | Southeastern United States | Zones 4–8 |

Talk about an uncut diamond, this relatively unknown native is just waiting to be discovered. Plants grow at least 3' tall, and 5' plants are not uncommon in moist, organic soils. The serrated foliage is biternate (blade divided into 3 segments, which are again divided into 3 segments) and is slightly hairy. The yellowish white flowers are held in large, drooping panicles which, while they can't compete with the shocking reds and carmines of some of the cultivars, lend a wonderful classical feel to the garden. Compared with the hybrids, it is most similar to 'Professor van der Wielen', which can be substituted if *A. biternata* cannot be located. Partial shade, rich soil and ample moisture are necessary for best performance. It also closely resembles *Aruncus dioicus*, goat's beard (see *Aruncus*).

It can be propagated from seed, division or root cuttings. One of the most successful propagations occurred inadvertently when we tilled our University garden in the fall. The next spring a half dozen plants emerged, the result of our tiller cutting the roots of dormant plants. Not recommended but effective.

*-chinensis* (chin-en′ sis)  Chinese Astilbe  1½–2′/2′
  Summer  Rosy-White  China  Zones 4–8

The species is seldom seen in gardens and was once almost totally represented by the dwarf variety *pumila*. Recently, renewed interest in this tough
species has resulted in a number of new cultivars for American gardeners.
The dark green, ternate foliage is rounded at the base of the hairy segments
and is occasionally doubly-serrated. A group of plants makes an excellent
ground cover for a moist, shaded area. The flowers are held in a branched,
rather narrow, panicle, and while the species itself is rosy-white, most of
the cultivars are rose to purple. Plants are doubly handsome due to the
deeply incised, bronze-green foliage. Although garden performance is far
better in moist soils, it is one of the more drought-tolerant astilbes.

**Cultivars:**
'Finale' grows about 18″ tall and bears handsome spikes of light pink flowers.
'Intermezzo' has salmon-pink flowers on 24–30″ tall plants.
'Pumila' (var. *pumila*) is the most common form offered. Plants bear dense,
  branched inflorescences of lavender-purple. It is obvious that not all
  material labelled as var. *pumila* has been propagated vegetatively or
  originated from the same parent stock block. I have seen this variety as
  an 8″ ground cover and also as a 2–2½′ border subject. Some of the
  variations can be attributed to climate and presence of soil moisture
  (plants will be taller and more vigorous in constantly moist soils than in
  those that dry out); however, even in the same climatic zones and in
  relatively similar moisture regimes, variation in height is considerable.
'Purple Glory' stands about 2′ tall with tight purple inflorescences.
'Serenade' bears rosy-pink flowers a little later than other cultivars on
  15–18″ plants.
'Spatsommer' is very late and produces bright rose flowers on 2′ plants.
'Veronica Klose' grows 2′ tall with many purple-rose flowers.
'Visions' has more upright flowers than others in the species and deep
  bronze-green foliage. The flowers are pink-purple. In the Armitage
  garden, it is outstanding.

Var. *taquetii* has always been known and sold as *A. taquetii* (ta-get′ ee-eye)
but has recently been reclassified as a variate of *A. chinensis*. This variety is
most commonly represented in gardens by the very vigorous and late-flowering
'Superba', but a number of other cultivars have been offered. Compact
columnar panicles up to 5′ tall extend the flowering season of *Astilbe* into late
summer and occasionally early fall. In north Georgia, flowering ceases in mid-
to late June, whereas those of *A.* × *arendsii* hybrids finish 2–4 weeks earlier.
Further north, flowering may continue into late August and early September.
The flower stems are far more hairy, and the flowers are more dense than those
of the *A.* × *arendsii* hybrids and make excellent cut flowers, persisting over a

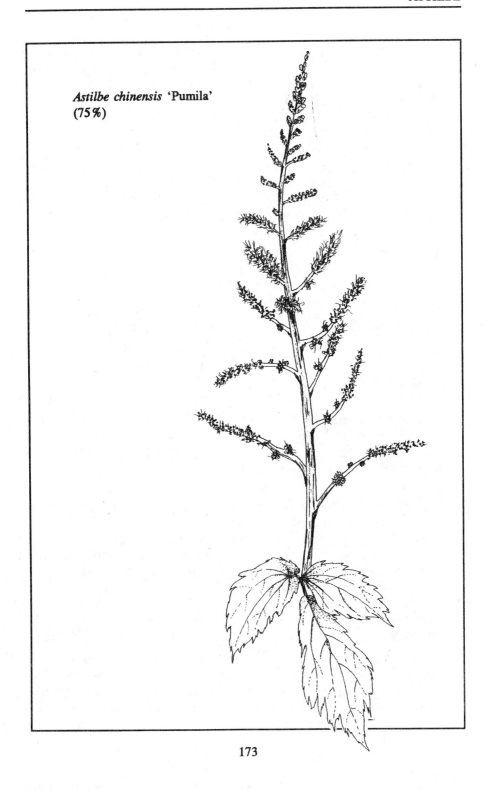

*Astilbe chinensis* 'Pumila'
(75%)

week in water. The seed heads retain the majesty of the flower spires and persist throughout the winter. Many cultivars (and hybrids) of this variety have recently appeared. They will still often be found under *A. taquetii* in most catalogs.

'Pink' produces flowers which are more pink than they are purple, the common color of this variety. The pink is still not a true pink but is a little less harsh than the common forms.

'Purple Candles' bears purple-red flowers on 3' tall plants.

'Purple Lance' ('Purpurlanze') is large (4–4½' tall) with big, purple-red blooms appearing in late summer. The flower plumes are longer and considerably narrower than others. In cool summers, even the flower stems will be red.

'Superba' is the most common form, bearing tall, narrow stalks of lavender-purple flowers.

### Related Species:

*A.* × *crispa* has been in horticultural literature since 1924; however, compared to other hybrids, it is relatively unknown. The 12–15″ tall hybrid, also raised by the Arends nursery, forms a mat of dark green, fern-like foliage which turns bronze in the fall. The flowers of the species are creamy white, but flowers of 'Liliput' are salmon-pink. 'Perkeo' is the most available cultivar in the United States and bears dark pink flower spikes and grows 8–10″ tall.

| -× *rosea* (ros' ee-a) | | Rose Astilbe | 2–3'/2' |
|---|---|---|---|
| Summer | Pink | Hybrid | Zones 4–8 |

The result of crossing *A. chinensis* and *A. japonica*, a 3' tall, white-flowered species, this hybrid has the habit of *A. japonica* and the flower color of *A. chinensis*. The original hybrid is seldom seen in gardens, having been superseded by various selections.

### Cultivars:

'Peach Blossom' is 3–4' tall and produces salmon-pink blooms clustered in large, racemose panicles.

'Queen Alexandra' is a deeper pink but otherwise similar to 'Peach Blossom'. These cultivars are both excellent for damp places and intolerant of drought conditions. They were some of the first hybrids (1903) raised by Georg Arends.

| -*simplicifolia* (sim-pli-si-fo' lee-a) | | Star Astilbe | 1–1½'/2' |
|---|---|---|---|
| Summer | White | Japan | Zones 4–8 |

This dwarf species has undergone considerable selection and hybridization, having caught the attention of Arends in 1911. The 3″ leaves are either simple (not compound) or a single group of three (ternate leaves). Hybridization has resulted in more compound leaves than simple leaves and has made identification more difficult. The leaves are nearly always more glossy green than other hybrids or species and are good looking even without flowers or fruit. Plants form compact mounds of mid-green, glossy, deeply-cut foliage which give rise to white, starlike flowers in airy, open panicles in June and July in the South and July and August in the North. The seed heads are nearly as ornamental as the flowers and provide an additional few months of useful garden effect.

## Cultivars:

Most cultivars are likely hybrids between *A. simplicifolia* and other species, but resemble *A. simplicifolia*. They are slower to establish than the *A.* × *arendsii* hybrids and require about 3 years to reach mature size.

Var. *alba* has white flowers which are "cleaner" than those of the species.
'Aphrodite' is one of the larger cultivars in this species, growing 15–20″ tall, and bears upright, salmon-red flowers over dark green leaves. The upright, rather than arching, plumes set this plant apart from the others.
'Atro-rosea' has 18–20″ tall, bright rose-salmon plumes.
'Bronze Elegance' produces rose-pink blooms in August over bronze foliage. Very handsome.
'Carnea' grows about 15″ tall and bears deep salmon flowers in late summer.
'Dunkellachs', raised in 1940, has recently appeared in the United States. A little taller than other cultivars, plants grow about 2′ tall and produce large trusses of salmon flowers over deep bronze foliage.
'Hennie Graafland' grows about 16″ tall and produces rosy flowers over shiny, dark green leaves. Flowers in July and remains handsome for 4–6 weeks.
'Inshriach Pink' produces 10″ tall, pink spikes over bronze-green, crinkled foliage. Raised by the nurseryman Jack Drake of Inshriach Nursery in Aviemore, Scotland.
'Sprite', raised by Alan Bloom, is the most popular cultivar and was the 1994 Perennial Plant of the Year awarded by the Perennial Plant Association. It has airy, shell-pink blooms over bronze foliage and grows 12–18″ tall. The rust-colored seed heads are particularly outstanding.
'William Buchanan' is one of the most dwarf cultivars. Growing only about 6–10″ tall, pale pink flowers are formed over dense, curly foliage.

## Related Species:

*A. glaberrima* only grows about 3–5″ tall. The leaves are bronze, and the flowers are purple. It is generally offered as 'Saxatilis'.

Quick Key to Astilbe Species

    A. Leaves simple or in 1 group of 3 (1 ternate)  . . . *A. simplicifolia*
    AA. Leaves compound in 2–4 groups of 3 (2–4 ternate)
        B. Stems of inflorescence densely woolly
           C. Height 6–24″, dense, upright
           panicles, rose-purple . . . . . . . . . . . . . . . *A. chinensis*

CC. Height 3–5′, dense, upright
panicles, lilace, late summer
to fall flowering . . . . . . . . . . . *A. chinensis* var. *taquetii*
BB. Stems of inflorescence not densely woolly
C. Height 2–3′, flowers in various colors . . . . . *A.* × *arendsii*
CC. Height 2–4′, airy panicles, usually pink,
late spring to summer flowering . . . . . . . . . *A.* × *rosea*

**Additional Reading:**

Lacy, Allen. 1987. The ascent of astilbes. *Horticulture* 164(6):44–49. This
provides an excellent account of Arends and his love of Astilbes.

## *Astilboides* (a-stil-boy′ deez)                          Saxifragaceae

This genus is the result of a taxonomic split from the genus *Rodgersia*,
and in this case, the split seems to make sense. Only one species is recognized, *A. tabularis* (syn. *Rodgersia tabularis*). Leaves are not compound as
in *Rodgersia* but are large, circular and slightly lobed. They are peltate,
meaning that the petiole attaches to the middle of the leaf, and may be 3′
across. The leaves resemble those of *Peltiphyllum peltatum*, while the
flowers resemble those of a large astilbe. The inflorescence is made up of
long plumes of creamy white flowers which extend well above the foliage. Both
sepals and petals are found on the flowers, whereas those of *Rodgersia* are
apetalous. Plants grow at least 3′ tall and equally wide. These are not small
plants for the small garden. Although hardy in zones 5–7, plants are not
easy to establish, and moist, cool conditions are necessary for success. A
wonderful plant where well-grown, sure to elicit all sorts of comments.

## *Astrantia* (a-stran′ tee-a)          Masterwort          Apiaceae

This interesting genus encompasses about 10 species, although none are
common in American gardens. Plants are useful for moist, shady areas and
benefit from copious amounts of organic matter. The white to pink flowers
are surrounded by a "collar" of bracts which produce a starlike effect. The
flower head is a compound umbel and consists of both sterile and fertile
flowers. The sterile flowers have long flower stalks (pedicels), and the
fertile flowers are short-stalked. They persist for 10–14 days as a cut flower
and are produced commercially as such in the Netherlands, California and
parts of the Midwest. Night temperatures are too warm to grow *Astrantia*
much further south than Tennessee unless at higher altitudes. Cool night
temperatures, partial shade, and consistent soil moisture are necessary for
best performance. *Astrantia major*, the most common garden species, is
well known in flower gardens in Europe, particularly the British Isles, and
is now finding its way over here. It is about time!

*Astrantia* is easily increased by division of the black roots in autumn or early spring. It also spreads by runners just below the surface and reseeds itself where it is comfortable.

Quick Reference to Astrantia Species:

|  | Height (ft.) | Flower color |
|---|---|---|
| *A. major* | 2–3 | Greenish white to white with tinge of pink |
| *A. maxima* | 2–3 | Rose-pink |

| *-major* (may′ jor) | | Great Masterwort | 2–3′/1½′ |
|---|---|---|---|
| Late Spring | Greenish White | Europe | Zones 5–7 |

The 2–3″ diameter flowers are greenish white with a collar of green bracts and borne in a many-flowered umbel. The basal leaves have a petiole, 3–7 deeply-cut lobes and are toothed, while the leaves on the flower stem have widely expanded petioles which clasp directly to the stem and are seldom toothed. The bracts are often tinged purple, which give the effect of pink flowers. Plants spread rapidly under good growing conditions and form a formidable clump. A tremendous amount of variation occurs within the species, due to the large amount of seed and the propensity to shift colors. White, rose, and pink flowers can all occur in the same planting over a few years. I've noticed that some enterprising nurserypeople have taken advantage of this natural occurrence and offer a range of colors under the name Rainbow. The rainbow will only get more colorful if planted where they can multiply.

Plant in semi-shaded, moist areas. They are at their best in cool, moist, shaded areas.

**Cultivars:**

'Alba' bears white flowers. In the shaded area, flowers light up the area more than the species.

Ssp. *involucrata* includes a number of cultivars with an extra long collar of pink bracts. One of the most impressive cultivars is 'Margery Fish', better known as 'Shaggy', a most apt description of the flowers. The true cultivar should be vegetatively reproduced from cuttings, although some seedlings with long bracts will occur.

'Lars' is a new selection with improved vigor and dark red flowers.

'Moira Reid' is a most interesting plant with large, pink flowers and salmon-peach collars.

'Rosea' bears rose-colored flowers with deeply-incised leaves.

'Rose Symphony' ('Rosensymphonie') is a wonderfully handsome plant with rosy pink flowers with a silver collar of bracts. Plants are about 2′ tall.

'Sunningdale Variegated' is lovely in the spring when the margins of the light green leaves are splashed with yellow and cream. The variegation fades in summer. This is an elegant plant.

## Related Species:

*A. carniolica*, lesser masterwort, is similar but smaller (6–12″ tall) than *A. major*. The purple flowers of 'Rubra' contrast well with the greenish bracts surrounding them. Some taxonomic authorities lump this species with *A. major*. I will leave it separate for now.

| | | |
|---|---|---|
| *-maxima* (mahk′ si-ma) | Large Masterwort | 2–3′/2′ |
| Late Spring      Rose-Pink | Southern Europe | Zones 5–7 |
| (Syn. *A. helleborifolia*) | | |

I really like this species, and it is good to see its availability increasing in this country. The flowers are larger and much more rose-pink than white, as in *A. major*. The foliage are often 3-parted, although some 5-parted leaves may occur. The basal leaves are petioled; however, the upper leaves are usually sessile and appear wrapped around the stems.

The plants are not as vigorous or self-sowing as *A. major*, but the flowers are eye-catching in a subtle way.

## Cultivars:

'Alba' is a white-flowered form but quite difficult to locate.

### Quick Key to Astrantia Species

    A. Basal leaves 3-parted, flowers pink . . . . . . . . . . . . *A. maxima*
    AA. Basal leaves usually 5–7 parted, flowers
       greenish white, flushed with rose or pink . . . . . . . . *A. major*

## *Athyrium* (a-thi′ ree-um)      Lady Fern      Dryopteraceae

Approximately 68 species of *Athyrium* have been listed by one fern expert or another, but only three or four are found in American gardens. Some of the most common and handsome, hardy ferns are to be found in the genus. *Athyrium* is widespread in temperate and tropical regions, and bears sori (fruit dots) which are generally curved and the indusium, a thin layer of cells surrounding the sorus, is attached only on one side. Most have a delicate texture and thrive in moist, humid conditions. All species die down over the winter. Ferns in this genus are some of the most reliable, colorful and easiest ones to grow.

| | Amount of color on fronds | Habit |
|---|---|---|
| *A. felix-femina* | None | Upright, 2–3′ |
| *A. nipponicum* | Highly | Spreading, 1–2′ |

*-felix-femina* (fi' liks fem' mi-na)     Lady Fern                    2–3'/2'
                                          Northern Hemisphere     Zones 4–8

Valued for ease of cultivation, this graceful fern is one of the most satisfying for new fern gardeners. Although the frond shape can be highly variable, they are often up to 3' tall, 1' wide and generally stand up on their own. The vigorous flush of new growth in the spring is wonderful. Shady to semi-shady conditions in loamy humus-rich soils are recommended.

## Cultivars:

Dozens of cultivars have been selected, ranging from dwarf forms ('Congestum'), bunched fronds ('Corymbiferum'), crested like a celosia ('Cristatum', 'Glomeratum'), slender pinnae ('Setigerum'), balled up pinnae ('Frizelliae') and long, terminal, narrow crest ('Victoriae'). The majority are interesting at best, many are ugly enough to induce nausea, and none can compete with the classic beauty of the species itself.

## Related Species:

*A. asplenoides*, southern lady fern, grows 2–3' tall and spreads more aggressively than its northern cousin. Native to southern and eastern United States. Likely a subspecies (*A. felix-femina* var. *asplenoides*) and not a true species.

*A. distentifolium* (syn. *A. alpestre*), alpine lady fern, has light green, finely-textured fronds. Native to the alpine areas of North America and Eurasia, plants are extremely cold hardy, not so heat hardy.

*-nipponicum* (nip-pon-i' cum)     Japanese Painted Fern          1–2'/2'
                                   East Asia                      Zones 3–8

(Syn. *A. goeringianum*)

The Japanese painted fern is native to China, Korea and Japan and has handsome green fronds. Although a reliable and useful plant, it is usually offered as its colorful variant, var. *pictum* ('Pictum'). The fronds, a soft metallic gray suffused with reddish or bluish hues, are among the most colorful foliage available to gardeners. The color is maintained in the old fronds, and the emerging shades of the new ones paint a pleasant contrast. Plants tolerate deep shade but display their best color when they receive some direct sunlight, preferably in the morning. Ferns will be of bragging quality when provided with a humusy soil and sufficient water. A great deal of variability occurs.

## Cultivars:

'Ursala's Red' has more red in the fronds than the normal species. Selected by Ursala Herz in South Carolina.

**Related Species:**

*A. otophorum*, painted fern, is a taller, more subtle, colored fern. Fronds are dark green with a reddish to purplish stem (stipe) and midrib (rachis). Not quite as hardy as Japanese painted fern but almost as handsome. Provide some direct sun and humus-rich soil.

## *Aubrieta* (o-bree' sha)          Rock Cress          Brassicaceae

The genus consists of about a dozen species and a large number of cultivars. Some of the available garden forms are cultivars of *A. deltoidea*, although most are hybrids, listed as *A.* × *cultorum*, of obscure origin but probably with *A. deltoidea* and *A. gracilis* in the parentage. *Aubrieta* is closely related to *Arabis*, also commonly known as rock cress. The differences are not obvious, and with the introduction of many cultivars, it is more difficult for the uninitiated to tell them apart. In general, *Aubrieta* is more compact with smaller foliage having 1-2 teeth on each side of the blade. The flowers are larger and have a cylindrical calyx (sepals) below the petals about half as long as the petals. Flowers of *Aubrieta* are lilac to red color with a few blue forms, while flowers of *Arabis* are usually white or pink. A summary follows.

|  | Habit | Petal length | Flower color | Foliage toothed | Sepals tubular |
|---|---|---|---|---|---|
| *Aubrieta* | More compact | ¾ " | Lilac, red | Yes | Yes |
| *Arabis* | Less compact | ½ " | White, pink | No | No |

Both genera have alternate, silver-green, pubescent, evergreen foliage. *Aubrieta* is not tolerant of warm nights, often declining in warm climates, and should be treated similar to *Arabis*. Many of the cultivars can be propagated by seed, and those not available from seed may be propagated by terminal cuttings or division.

*-deltoidea* (del-toi' dee-a)          Rock Cress                    6-8"/2'
  Spring                    Lilac          Sicily to Asia Minor          Zones 4-7

The species and hybrids (*A.* × *cultorum*) perform best where sunny conditions and well-drained soils are present. So much interbreeding occurs within varieties that a great deal of variability occurs. The foliage is somewhat wedge-shaped with large teeth. The ¾ " long, red to lilac flowers are clustered in racemes that emerge from the leaf axils. They are best grown cascading over rocks or walls where water will not collect. After the plants flower in the spring, the stems continue to grow and become leggy by midsummer. Some of the hybrids are more compact, but in general, they are best cut back to 6-8" to allow new growth to emerge. Otherwise stems will be naked in the middle with a few leaves on the end. This is especially true in the South where plants will not survive if allowed to deteriorate. Plants tend to lose vitality and may deteriorate badly after a few years unless new plants are purchased.

Seed is available for many cultivars and germinates in about 2 weeks under moist, warm (70–75° F) conditions. Division, however, is the easiest means of propagation. Stem cuttings may also be taken from new growth in the spring or after cutting back in late spring or early summer.

## Cultivars:

'Aurea' has golden-green foliage and blue to violet flowers.

'Aurea Variegata' ('Golden King') has green leaves with yellow variegation. It is otherwise similar to 'Aurea'.

'Barker's Double' has double, purple-blue flowers.

'Bengal Hybrids' are seed-propagated forms with a mixture of lavender, purple and rose flowers on 6–8″ tall plants.

'Bressingham Pink', introduced in 1953, are relatively vigorous and bear double, pink flowers.

'Bressingham Red' produce double, red flowers.

'Campbellii' has double, rose-purple flowers.

'Carnival' is very free-flowering and produces hummocks of purple-violet flowers.

'Cascade Hybrids' provide flowers in shades of purple, red and lavender.

'Dr. Mules' is similar to 'Carnival' but a little less floriferous.

'Graeca Superba' has large leaves and light blue flowers.

'Greencourt Purple' has semi-double to double, lavender-purple flowers.

'Gurgedyke' also has maroon-purple flowers. Free-flowing and compact.

'J.S. Baker' bears bluish flowers with a white eye.

'Leichtlinii' has handsome, bright red flowers on 4″ tall plants.

'Parkinsii' produces lavender blooms with a white eye.

'Rosea Splendens' has bright rose flowers which do not fade with age.

'Purity', introduced in 1997, has excellent pure white flowers. One of the few good whites in the species.

'Purple Gem' bears deep purple flowers over 6″ tall plants.

'Red Carpet' produces 6″ tall plants which form a mat of red-rose flowers.

'Royal Blue' has dark blue flowers.

'Royal Red' bears flowers in shades of red and magenta.

'Silberrand' produces handsome, wedge-shaped leaves with a sharp band of creamy white around the margins. Blue flowers appear in early spring.

'Whitewall Gem' produces 6″ mats of deep blue flowers.

'Vindictive' has large (up to 1″ wide), rosy-red flowers.

'Variegata' has yellow-edged foliage in a tight clump. Lavender-blue flowers are a bonus.

*Aurinia* (ow-rin′ ee-a)　　　　　Basket-of-Gold　　　　　Brassicaceae

There is general agreement among taxonomists that this plant should be called *Aurinia* rather than the old name of *Alyssum*, although from the gardener's point of view, it matters not at all. Of the approximately seven species, *A. saxatilis* is the most popular because of the intense yellow, early spring flowers. I grew this species with ease in East Lansing, Michigan and Guelph, Ontario but had little success in north Georgia. In the South, if planted in early fall, performance is beautiful the first spring, but plants gradually melt out during the summer. Planting under the shade of summer-flowering perennials may help it return in subsequent years, but it should be replanted each fall for best form and color.

*-saxatilis* (saks-ah′ ti-lis)　　　　Basket-of-Gold　　　　　12″/18″
　　Spring　　　　　Yellow　　　　Eastern Europe　　　　　Zones 3–7
(Syn. *Alyssum saxatile*)

When *Aurinia* is in flower, the canary-yellow flowers can be seen shimmering across the length of a football field. It requires full sun and excellent drainage and should be cut back after flowering. The foliage is gray-green and spreads into clumps very rapidly. The yellow flowers combine beautifully with purple flowers of *Verbena* 'Homestead Purple' or *Phlox divaricata* 'Louisiana'. It is a classic rock garden and wall plant.

Seed germinates in 2–3 weeks in moist, warm (70–75° F) conditions. Seeds are available for the species and a few cultivars, but division in the fall is the easiest method of propagation. Cuttings may also be taken in the spring or fall.

**Cultivars:**

'Citrina' ('Sulphurea') has lemon-gold flowers and grows 12–15″ tall.

'Compacta' is similar to 'Gold Ball' but more compact.

'Dudley Neville Variegated' has apricot-salmon flowers over leaves with cream-colored margins. Interesting if you like the color combination.

'Flore' ('Flore-plena') has double flowers but is generally less vigorous than the singles.

'Gold Ball' ('Goldkugel') starts to flower in early to mid-April in the South and about 2 weeks later further north. Plants have a globose habit and grow about 8″ tall.

'Golden Queen' is certainly not much different than 'Gold Ball'. The plants grow into a 9–12′ mound with light yellow flowers.

'Sunny Border Apricot', raised by the fine nursery, Sunny Border of Kensington, CT, has apricot-colored flowers. Very handsome.

'Tom Thumb' is only 3–6″ tall but vigorous.

# B

*Baptisia* (bap-tiz' I-a)  False Indigo  Fabaceae

The genus contains about 35 species and comes from the Greek word bapto, meaning "to dip," referring to the flower extract once used as a substitute for indigo. *B. australis* was often used for blue dyes, while *B. tinctoria* was a source of yellow dye in the southern United States. *Baptisia* is one of the most rewarding and historically fascinating genera available to gardeners. Native to large areas of the United States, plants afford exceptional garden performance and a mini-lesson in early American history. The common name refers to its use as a substitute, albeit not a great substitute, for the true indigo, *Indigofera*, of the West Indies. When *Indigofera* was in short supply, the English government contracted with farmers in Georgia and South Carolina in the mid 1700's to "farm" false blue indigo, *B. australis*, to increase the supply of the dye. The farming of *Baptisia* was one of the first recorded examples of agricultural subsidies. The process used to extract the dye was very cumbersome and time consuming. A report in *The Georgia State Gazette* on May 10, 1788 provided directions "For the Cultivation and Manufacture of Indigo" by "an Indigo Planter." What with planting, cutting, beating, draining and pressing, the process was doomed to a short life. Today, *Baptisia* provides gardeners with a living example of Americana and, more importantly, with reliable, beautiful garden plants.

The genus is in the midst of taxonomic reshuffling, and it is difficult to have confidence in the specific names being offered. For example, some people would like to see all white forms grouped into *B. albescens*, while others wish to place plants with minor differences in separate species. The genus provides white flowers in *B. alba*, white wild indigo, and *B. leucantha*, prairie wild indigo, cream-colored flowers in *B. bracteata*, cream wild indigo, yellow flowers (*B. megacarpa*, stream side wild indigo,

183

*B. tinctoria*, yellow wild indigo) and blue flowers (*B. australis*, blue wild indigo, *B. minor*, lesser wild indigo). *Baptisia* produces racemes of pea-like flowers over alternate, gray-green, usually 3-parted compound leaves. One of the ways to separate similar species is the presence or absence of the small, leaf-like structures (stipules) at the base of each leaf. They are not always obvious, but, with a little effort, they can usually be found. Several studies of *Baptisia* have shown that significant natural breeding takes place, and interspecific hybrids are common in nature.

Plants tolerate warm temperatures and require full sun for best performance, although the white forms tolerate partial shade. All grow best in deep, rich soils but are tolerant of poor soils. I think these plants are some of the most trouble free and marvelous plants for American gardeners; however, I also hear those who have had problems. It appears that voles love the roots of *Baptisia* as much as gardeners do and can cause no end of frustration.

Quick Reference to Baptisia Species

|  | Height (ft.) | Flower color | Flowering time |
|---|---|---|---|
| *B. alba* | 2–3 | White | Late Spring |
| *B. bracteata* | 2–3 | Creamy white | Spring |
| *B. australis* | 3–4 | Blue | Spring |
| *B. tinctoria* | 2–4 | Yellow | Early Summer |

| *-alba* (al' ba) | | White Wild Indigo | 2–3'/3' |
|---|---|---|---|
| Late Spring | White | Southeastern United States | Zones 5–8 |

This is one of my favorite plants for the garden. The plant's popularity began in southern gardens and has made its way north in the last few years. When plants first emerge in the spring, they resemble dark shoots of asparagus. The new shoots often have a handsome black-purple tint which remains throughout most of the season. It grows best in full sun but tolerates partial shade better than the blue forms. The 12–20" long racemes of ½" long, white flowers last 3–4 weeks. The flowers are occasionally blotched purple and are not as dense as those of *B. australis*. The plants are smooth but often covered with a thin whitish or bluish bloom. The leaves are divided into 3 segments, each widest near the rounded end. Stipules are minute, and most are soon lost. The foliage of *Baptisia* can look ragged and diseased during the fall, particularly in the south. The foliage of this species tends to remain attractive even into the fall. The upright seed pods are cylindrical, yellow-brown, and persistent. This is a stunning specimen for the smaller garden where an easy-to-grow, long-lived plant is desired. It looks good with almost everything.

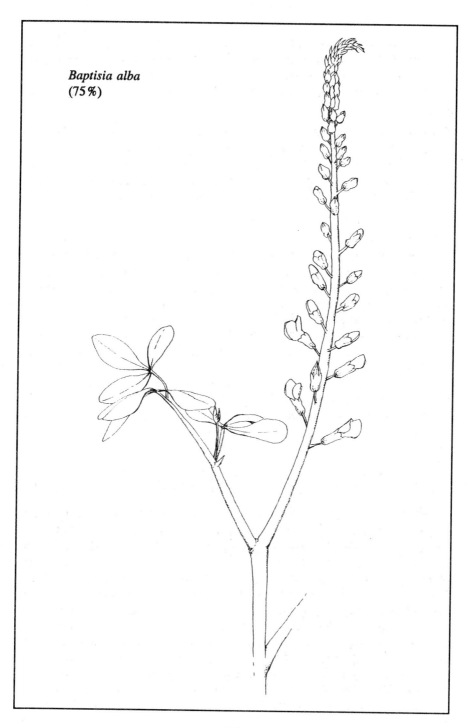

*Baptisia alba*
(75%)

Propagation by seed is slower and more difficult than *B. australis*, and a scarification treatment is beneficial. Division of the roots may be accomplished in early spring or fall. Care must be taken to make a clean cut of the roots with a sharp knife and provide abundant water upon transplanting.

### Cultivars:

'Pendula' has usually been offered as a separate species (*B. pendula*), but I am pleased to see that some authorities are now treating it as a cultivar. The only difference I can see is that the upright racemes give way to pendulous seed pods in late spring. The plant habit may also be more pendulous than *B. alba* and not as tall (2–3′ tall). An equally stunning plant.

### Related Species:

*B. bracteata* (syn. *B. leucophaea*) is a more spreading plant with soft pubescence throughout (sometimes called *B. villosa*). A distinctive feature is the large stipules (⅘″ to 1⅗″) which persist longer than the other white-flowered forms. Flowers are loosely clustered and range from white to creamy white to soft yellow. The 8–10″ long racemes slope downward, and the fruit are somewhat pendulous. Full sun is necessary.

*B. lactea* (syn. *B. leucantha*), prairie false indigo, is a western representative of the species, occurring naturally from Ohio to Nebraska and south to Texas. Upright white racemes occur in late spring atop blue-green foliage. The minute, pointed stipules fall off prematurely. The main difference between this and *B. alba* is the bloated fruit (2″ × 1½″), compared to the more cylindrical fruit (1½″ × 1″) of *B. alba*. What is being sold as white baptisia is anyone's guess.

| -*australis* (ow-strah′ lis) | False Blue Indigo | 3-4′/4′ |
|---|---|---|
| Spring    Indigo Blue | Eastern United States | Zones 3–8 |

This is the most cold hardy species and performs well over a wider range of environments than others. In the early spring, it is one of the first plants to emerge, and the gray-green leaves quickly fill out into a substantial sized bush. The 10–12″ long, flowering stalks arise in the spring, carrying 1″ long, indigo-blue, pea-like flowers which last for about 4 weeks. Although the flowers are violet-blue, there is much variation when plants are raised from seed. Flowers will vary from light to deep indigo blue, the latter much preferable to the former. The flowers were once used for indigo (see introduction to *Baptisia*) but are now simply viewed as good garden plants. Two to 2½″ long brown to black pods appear in early summer and remain until the plant dies back in the fall. The pods become dry by midsummer, and the seeds inside rattle around and should be collected at this time. Arrangers find these pods attractive and use them as dried ornaments in the house. In my

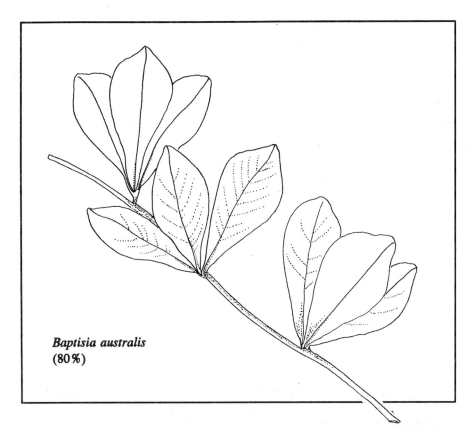

*Baptisia australis*
(80%)

partially shaded garden, I must support my plants; if grown in full sun, however, no staking is required. The plant spreads by rhizomes and consumes considerable garden space. It does not require dividing from the plant's point of view, but division every 4–5 years may be beneficial to ease overcrowding.

The flower looks a little like lupine flowers, but the leaves and habit are distinct. Some people also confuse it with *Thermopsis* which has dark green rather than blue-green leaves and yellow flowers. Although *B. australis* is cold hardy to zone 3, the leaves turn black with the first hard frost.

The key to successful seed propagation is to harvest the seed as they turn black and sow when fresh. Seed propagation is less erratic when seeds are given a scarification treatment. Piercing or scraping the seeds with sandpaper or other abrasive substance is helpful, but not essential. This allows moisture and oxygen to penetrate the seed coat. Acid scarification is used commercially but should be performed only by trained individuals. Once the seeds have been treated, place them in a peat-vermiculite mix in a moist, warm environment. Germination of over 90% occurred regardless of acid and mechanical scarification, cold and hot water soaking or cold stratification. (See article by Dirr in Additional Reading.) A cold treatment (40° F) is also useful and can be accomplished in a cold frame or in a refrigerator or incubator. The fleshy roots may also be divided between October and March.

### Related Species:

*B. minor*, lesser wild indigo, is essentially the same as *B. australis* except half the size. Equally beautiful, equally tough but smaller in every way. This is often offered as a cultivar of *B. australis* (*B. a.* 'Minor').

*B.* 'Purple Smoke', a natural cross between *B. australis* and *B. alba*, has smoky blue flowers on 3–4' plants. Recently released through North Carolina Botanical Garden and Niche Nursery in Chapel Hill, NC. Terrific potential.

| *-tinctoria* (tink-tor-ee′ a) | | Yellow Wild Indigo | 2–4′/1′ |
|---|---|---|---|
| Early Summer | Yellow | Eastern United States | Zones 5–8 |

This species has not been widely embraced as a formal garden plant but is excellent in a meadow garden or sunny informal area. The lower leaves have petioles, but the upper leaves are nearly sessile (with very short petiole). The 4–20 terminal flowers are less than an inch long and held in arching, 4–5″ racemes. There is also considerable variation within the species, and flowers range from clear yellow to cream-colored. Full sun is necessary.

### Related Species:

*B. perfoliata*, Georgia wild indigo, and *B. arachnifera*, hairy wild indigo, an endangered species in Georgia, have yellow flowers and simple, perfoliate leaves (the stem passes through the leaf) rather than compound leaves. Interesting but hardly garden-worthy.

*B. sphaerocarpa*, native to Arkansas and Oklahoma, has light yellow flowers and handsome blue-green foliage. The upper leaves may be simple or have two leaflets, rather than three. A marvelous plant, to be tried if plants or seed are available.

Quick Key to Baptisia Species

    A. Leaves simple, perfoliate . . . . . . . . . . . . . . . . *B. perfoliata*
    AA. Leaves compound, leaf stalk present
        B. Flowers blue, white
            C. Flowers blue, pods inflated . . . . . . . . . . . . *B. australis*
            CC. Flowers white, pods cylindrical . . . . . . . . . . . . *B. alba*
        BB. Flowers yellow . . . . . . . . . . . . . . . . . . . . . . *B. tinctoria*

### Additional Reading:

Bush, A. 1987. *Baptisia*, true or false? or Bush's best bet on baptisias. *Perennial Plant Assoc. Newsletter* 10:8–10.

Dirr, Michael A. 1987. *Baptisia australis. American Nurseryman* 165(5):166.

Frett, J. 1993. Perennials with panache. *American Nurseryman* 177(3):24–29.

Isely, D. 1981. Leguminosae of the United States. III The subfamily Papilionoidae; Tribes Sophoreae, Podalyrieae, Loteae. *Memoirs of the New York Botanical Garden* 25(3):1–89.

Isely, D. 1986. Notes about *Psoralea* sensu auct. *Amorpha, Baptisia, Sesbania,* and *Chamaecrista* (Leguminosae) in the southeastern United States. *SIDA* 11(4):429–440.

Midgley, J. 1993. *Baptisia australis. Native Notes* 5(1):2–5.

## *Barbarea* (bar-bar-ee′ a)   St. Barbara's Herb, Bittercress   Brassicaceae

Of the 12 species of this mustard relative, most are grown as leafy salad greens. One of our introduced weeds from Europe is bittercress or wintercress, *B. vulgaris,* which has become naturalized all over North America. However, it is this weed that also possesses some ornamental value in its double-flowered and variegated forms. Plants are biennial, occasionally perennial, but reseed themselves with abandon. Generally the yellow flowers are formed early in the spring, and plants soon decline in most areas of the country. They may be discarded after seed has formed.

No sane gardener would introduce the species to their garden; however, the double-flowered form 'Flore-pleno' is a little more handsome. The best form is 'Variegata' with yellow splashes on the green foliage. The variegation is most obvious in the winter or early spring, and flowering and seeding are less prolific than on the green-leafed species. This was one of the many ornamental "weeds" in Janette Waltmath's fabulous Portland garden that she allowed me to abscond with. They have been in the Horticulture gardens for a few years and have been nearly as aggressive in Georgia as in Oregon. However, if you grow this plant, in any form, you take your chances.

All forms prefer full sun or partial shade and well-drained soils. Plants perform well in zones 5–8.

## *Begonia* (beg-on′ ee-a)                     Begonia                     Begoniaceae

Residents of the province of Quebec can take some pride in knowing that the name of this great genus commemorates Michael Begon, a governor of that province-to-be in the mid 1670's and a great supporter of botany. Although *Begonia* is an unusually large genus, with approximately 900 species at last count, only one or two species can be embraced as perennials in the United States. Nevertheless, it was suggested by my friend and excellent gardener and begonite, Janet Welsh of Huntington Valley, PA, that hardy begonias must be included in this treatise. I do so poorly but with pleasure. Hardy begonias tolerate shade and prefer moist, but not wet, conditions.

| *-grandis* (gran' dis) | | Hardy Begonia | 15–24"/12" |
|---|---|---|---|
| Summer | Pink | Southeast Asia | Zones 6–9 |

This is a true perennial species, which has been reported hardy to −15° F if heavily mulched and 5° F when unprotected. Plants are handsome for the large, heart-shaped leaves, which are green above and red beneath. The red veins on the underside of the leaves are particularly lovely, and the foliage contrasts beautifully with ferns and annual caladiums. Sprays of slightly fragrant, pale pink flowers are produced in early summer and continue until frost.

Plants are tuberous and are propagated by bulblets, although they often reseed themselves as well.

**Cultivars:**

'Alba' bears white flowers and green foliage, lacking the red pigment found in the species. Brightens up the shade.

**Related Species:**

*B. sinensis*, introduced by We-Du nursery in North Carolina, is similar but smaller (10–12") than *B. grandis*. Flowers are light pink, and leaves are consistently green throughout.

## *Belamcanda* (bel-am-kan' da)          Blackberry Lily          Iridaceae

There are only two species of blackberry lily, the most common being *B. chinensis*. They are tolerant of almost all environments, and they bear colorful flowers and even better seed pods.

| *-chinensis* (chin' en-sis) | Blackberry Lily, Leopard Flower | | 3–4'/2' |
|---|---|---|---|
| Summer | Orange, Red-Spotted | China | Zones 5–10 |

In early to midsummer, stems bear loosely-arranged clusters of 3–12 orange flowers, each peppered with gaudy red spots from which one of the common names, leopard flower, is derived. The flowers are about 2" across, the petals and sepals barely distinguishable from each other. The 6 segments are narrow at the base and are, unfortunately, very fleeting. The pear-shaped seed pods, however, are persistent and contain the shining, black, round seeds for which the blackberry lily is named. In the fall the black seeds line up like kernels of corn inside the open pod and are an attractive part of the autumn garden. The stoloniferous roots give rise to about six sword-like, clustered leaves that resemble those of *Gladiolus*. Plant in full sun in a well-drained soil and mulch heavily above zone 5. Iris borer can be a problem but removal of dying or decaying leaves will greatly reduce the damage. I have seen dwarf

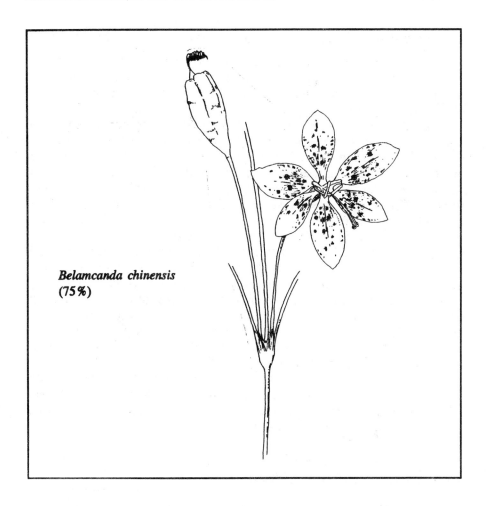

*Belamcanda chinensis*
(75%)

forms at Longwood Garden, but plants raised from that seed grew almost as tall as the species in my Georgia garden.

Seeds germinate within 3 weeks if provided with moist, warm conditions. Rootstocks may be divided in early spring.

### Cultivars:

'Freckle Face' is a welcome addition to the species due to its shorter (12–15") stems. The flowers are similar but slightly paler.

### Related Species:

*B. flabellata* has handsome gray-green leaves and unspotted, yellow flowers on 2' tall plants. Plants are often sold as 'Hello Yello'. Terrific selection.

## *Bergenia* (ber-gen' i-a)       Bergenia, Pigsqueak       Saxifragaceae

The genus contains about eight glossy, leather-leaved species, most of which flower in early spring. If you rub the leaf between thumb and forefinger just right, it sounds just like a pig squeaking. Talent comes in many forms; learning pig squeaking is not to be taken lightly.

Plants tolerate full sun in the North but prefer afternoon shade in the South. They are evergreen, although the foliage is often damaged in harsh winters. When planted in groupings of 10 or 20, the cabbage-like leaves of bergenia can make an impressive sight. The flowers of most species are rose- to red-colored, but hybrids exist with pink and white flowers. The flower buds, however, are less cold hardy than the foliage and may abort during particularly cold winters. This should not deter one from using bergenia because the foliage is as attractive as the coarse flowers. They soften the hard lines of paving and brickwork and accentuate the curves of beds and borders. The large, shiny leaves are often used to provide greenery for florist bouquets since they persist for a long time after cutting. However, before we get too carried away in praise of pigsqueak, let us be honest. At times, plants look like a cold homeless drunk, whose leafy blanket is torn and nose is red. They are at their best in the northwest and southern California, but I have not seen a great many "English" plantings in the East.

To obtain best performance, place plants in moist shade and morning sun. They dislike heavy soils and standing water. Most of the cultivars offered today are hybrids and are far superior to many of the cultivars offered ten years ago. Bergenia can be propagated easily from seed or by division in early spring.

### Quick Reference to Bergenia Species

|  | Height (in.) | Flower color | Leaf shape | Flower season |
|---|---|---|---|---|
| *B. ciliata* | 12–18 | Pale pink | Heart | Early Spring |
| *B. cordifolia* | 12–18 | Rose-pink | Heart | Early Spring |
| *B. crassifolia* | 12–18 | Rose-pink | Oval | Early Spring |

**-*ciliata*** (sil-ee-ah' ta)       Fringed Bergenia       12–15"/12"
Early Spring      Pale Pink      Nepal, Kashmir      Zones 5–7

By far the most handsome in leaf of all the bergenias and quite likely the most difficult to locate. The large (up to 12" across), undulating, round leaves are pubescent on both sides and look altogether like a well-behaved

African violet. The leaves are deciduous, and the pale pink flowers are almost white, but flushed with rose, and appear as the new leaves unfurl. Flowers often darken with age. The plants are not as floriferous as other common species, but the plants are fabulous. Not as cold hardy and needing excellent drainage. Early frosts and late frosts will decimate the flowers and foliage, but the growth buds are reasonably hardy, and plants will come back. In its native habitat, the mountains of west Pakistan, south Kashmir and Nepal, plants are covered with a winter-long canopy of snow; therefore, a light mulching in the fall may be useful. Plants are hard to find but worth the effort.

Propagate the rhizomes into 1″ long pieces carrying roots and growth buds in late spring and fall.

**Cultivars:**

Var. *ligulata* is more common than the species. The leaves are similar in size and shape, but the upper surface is smooth and shiny, and the hairs are confined to a distinctive fringe along the margin. May be easier to locate, but plants are no more cold hardy than the species.

**Related Species:**

*B. × schmidtii*, a cross between *B. ciliata* var. *ligulata* and *B. crassifolia*, is a hardy evergreen cross, first described in 1868. The toothed leaves are bright green, and the clear pink flowers appear as the foliage appears. To avoid confusion with other bergenias, it is sometimes offered under the name 'Ernst Schmidt'.


-*cordifolia* (kor-di-fo′ lee-a)   Heart-Leaf Bergenia, Megasea   12–18″/12″
Early Spring        Rose-Pink        Siberia           Zones 4–8

This is the most common species available and a vigorous grower. The 10″ long, glossy, evergreen leaves are leathery, waxy and thick. They turn a deep burgundy with the advent of cold weather and, if not buried by snow, make an effective show in the winter. However, even in my north Georgia garden, the purple foliage becomes damaged and is not particularly attractive in the winter. The panicles consist of a dozen or so flowers but do not rise much higher than the foliage.

**Related Species:**

*B. purpurescens*, purple bergenia, is about 15″ tall and has larger (petals ¾–1″ wide), deep magenta flowers. The foliage is green with a red blush. One of the best features of this species is the new growth in the spring. The leaves are deep purple, shiny and much less messy from winter damage than any of the other species or selections.

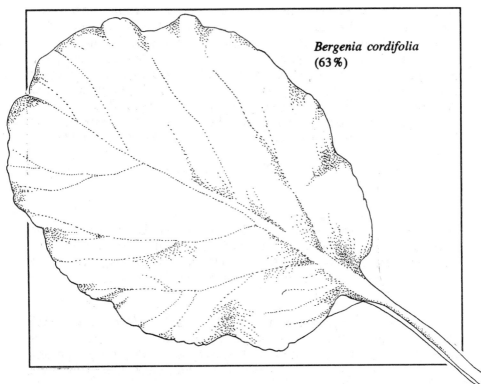

*Bergenia cordifolia*
(63%)

*B.* × *smithii* (syn. *B.* × *newryensis*) encompasses some of the more common garden cultivars. Plants of this hybrid arose from crosses between *B. cordifolia* and *B. purpurescens*.

| *-crassifolia* (kra-si-fo′ lee-a) | Leather Bergenia | 12–18″/12″ |
|---|---|---|
| Spring     Purple | Siberia | Zones 4–8 |

There are few differences between this species and *B. cordifolia*, and they serve the same garden function. The toothed, undulating leaves are obovate (like a hen's egg with the broad part above the middle) rather than heart-shaped. The flowers are held higher above the foliage than those of *B. cordifolia*, and the inflorescence is more branched. The leaf blade of *B. crassifolia* runs down along the petiole (decurrent) rather than being two obviously distinct parts of the leaf (i.e. petiole and blade), as with heart-leaf bergenia. Performance is better in the North than the South.

**Related Species:**

*B. omeiensis* is a new species recently found on Mt. Omei in Japan. The nodding, white flowers, which have handsome brown calyces, are some of the largest I have seen. Probably not hardy in most areas but should make an excellent breeding parent.

*B. stracheyi* is wonderful for the rock garden or small garden and is perfect for those who enjoy more diminutive garden plants. This is a small plant from Afghanistan and the western Himalayas with rounded leaves and clusters of rose-pink flowers. 'Alba' is a white-flowered form.

### Hybrid Cultivars of Bergenia:

If ever a genus had too many cultivars with too few differences, this is the one. To provide the best show, plant in groups of 10–20 plants in partial shade, in someone else's garden.

'Abendglut' (Evening Glow), raised by Arends nursery in Germany, is becoming more popular in this country. It is shorter and more prostrate than most other clones and richly colored in the winter.

'Admiral' has cherry-pink flowers over bronze-green leaves in the spring. Good bronze and crimson foliage during the winter.

'Autumn Red' is so named because of the vivid red foliage in the winter. Flowers are soft pink.

'Baby Doll' is about 12″ tall with soft pink flowers and small leaves.

'Bach' is one of a series of cultivars raised by Eric Smith of England and named after composers. This selection has light pink to cream flowers and dark green leaves.

'Ballawley' ('Delbees') is a massive plant with 8–12″ wide leaves. It makes a wonderful ground cover in areas where moisture is available. Plants are grown more for the foliage than the sprays of 2′ tall, magenta flowers, which are not freely produced.

'Bell Tower' ('Glockenturm') bears pinkish red flowers on 15″ tall plants.

'Beethoven' bears large clusters of white flowers surrounded by coral-red sepals. About 1′ tall.

'Brahms' bears creamy white flowers over long, light green foliage.

'Bressingham Bountiful' is vigorous with much-branched inflorescences of pink flowers.

'Bressingham Ruby' bears glossy, reddish purple leaves in cool weather, fading to dark green as the weather warms up. Flowers are bright pink.

'Bressingham Salmon' resulted from crossing 'Silberlicht' with some pink cultivars. It bears salmon-pink flowers.

'Bressingham White' also resulted from the same batch of seedlings that produced 'Bressingham Salmon'. Plants produce clean white blooms which are smaller than those of 'Silberlicht'.

'Distinction' has pink flowers on 1′ long, brownish red pedicels.

'Eco Pink Cherub' has pink flowers and compact, 3″ long leaves.

'Eric Smith', named after the excellent plant breeder of the United Kingdom, has some of the finest winter foliage, with polished bronze-tints on the upperside and carmine-red on the lower side.

'Morning Red' ('Morgenrot') is 8–12″ tall with carmine-red flowers.

'Perfecta' has rosy-red flowers held well above the foliage and has performed well in many regions of the country.

'Profusion' is an excellent pink hybrid. The last two cultivars were some of the original ones raised near the turn of the century by Mr. T. Smith of Northern Ireland. The rounded foliage is characteristic of their *B. cordifolia* parent.

'Pugsley's Purple' grows 2′ tall and is a late, purple-flowering hybrid.

'Purple King' ('Purpurkonig') bears rose-red flowers with a touch of salmon.

'Red Start' has good winter color and rose-purple inflorescences.

'Rotblum' has, as the name suggests, red flowers. The flowers are produced over deep green foliage.

'Silberlicht' (Silver Light), also raised by Arends, has pink-tinged, white flowers with red centers and shiny, dark green foliage. Both this and 'Abendglut' have *B. ciliata* in their pedigree.

'Snow Queen' ('Schneekonigin'), also from Germany, bears large, pale pink flowers, almost to the point of being white.

'Sunningdale', one of the better hybrids for winter color, is approximately 12″ tall with excellent foliage color all year. The coral-red flower stalks support rich carmine flower heads.

'Sunshade' has lilac-rose flowers and maroon foliage in the fall and spring.

'Sunshine' bears rose-red flowers which have a slightly darker center. Quite handsome.

'Winter's Tale' ('Wintermarchen') has small, narrow-pointed leaves and grows only about 1′ tall. Some leaves turn brilliant red in the winter, and deep rose flowers are formed in the spring.

### Quick Key to Bergenia Species

A. Leaves obviously hairy on both sides . . . . . . . . . . . *B. ciliata*
AA. Leaves shiny, not hairy
    B. Leaves cordate (heart-shaped), petioles
    long and thick . . . . . . . . . . . . . . . . . . . . . . . *B. cordifolia*
    BB. Leaves obovate, blades decurrent on petioles . . *B. crassifolia*

### Additional Reading:

Beckett, Kenneth A. 1983. *Bergenia. The Garden* 108(12):480–484.

DeWolf, Gordon. 1983. *Bergenia. Horticulture* 61(3):8–9.

Lancaster, R. 1994. *Bergenia ciliata. The Garden* 119(2):72–73.

Nicolay, K. 1990. Back to bergenia. *Horticulture* 68(3):24–29.

Yeo, Peter F. 1961. Two bergenia hybrids. *Baileya* 9:20–28.

Yeo, Peter F. 1962. *Bergenia* × *Smithii*, the correct name for *B. cordifolia* × *B. purpurescens. Baileya* 10:110–111.

*Bletilla* (ble-til′ la)          Bletilla          Orchidaceae

Few plants in the orchid family are suitable for the outdoor garden; *Bletilla* is one of them. These terrestrial orchids produce pseudobulbs useful for propagation while terminal flowers, consisting of similar sepals and petals, are produced on racemes. The bulbous roots should be planted no deeper than 2″ below the surface.

*-striata* (streye-ah′ ta)          Hyacinth Bletilla          8–12″/10″
  Spring        Purple          China          Zones 5–9
(Syn. *B. hyacinthina*)

Three- to six-pleated, papery leaves emerge early in the spring and look rather nondescript but later give rise to rosy-purple sprays of orchid-like flowers. Racemes consist of about 6–10 flowers, each measuring 1–1½″ across and persisting for 2–3 weeks.

Partial shade and well-enriched soil are ideal, allowing a single plant to enlarge into a fine garden clump in a few years. They are suited to growing in large containers on the patio or deck. This method is most useful for gardeners north of zone 5 who can bring the container in for the winter to be returned outside in the spring. It is too fine a species to ignore simply because winters are cold. I like the idea of having orchids in my garden, and *Bletilla* adds a touch of class to any deck or border planting.

The only problems I have seen result from late frosts. Leaves emerge so early that the ends often get nipped, resulting in tattered tips. Summer drought causes poor initiation of flowers, resulting in little or no flowering the following spring. Late frosts occasionally result in death of the flowers, although I have seen plants in Houston, TX knocked down hard by a late frost only to quickly rise again. Propagate by division of the pseudobulbs. They are tuber-like structures about ¾ ″ in diameter. Separate them from the mother plant in the fall or simply divide the clump with a sharp shovel.

## Cultivars:

'Alba' has creamy white flowers which contrast better with the dark green leaves than the purple flowers of the type.

'Albostriata' ('Variegata') is the most ornamental form and has white stripes along the length of each leaf. Purple flowers similar to the type are produced, and the foliage remains ornamental all season. Best growth occurs in a rich, cool, moist soil.

'Eco White Edge' has white margins around the leaves. From Eco Gardens in Decateur, GA.

A hybrid between *B. striata* and *B. formosa*, a low-growing, pink species has been developed by We-Du Nursery in Marion, NC. This $F_2$ hybrid is supposed to have pale pink flowers on vigorous plants.

*Bletilla striata* 'Alba'
(68%)

**Additional Reading:**

Anon. 1993. An early spring orchid to grow. *Hobby Greenhouse* 15(2):7.

*Boltonia* (bowl-tone' ee-a)          Boltonia          Asteraceae

Most species of Boltonia are native to the United States and easy to grow. They produce vast numbers of daisy-like, white or purple flowers in late summer. The leaves are alternate, lance-shaped, and sessile. Many species are too large and lanky to be considered for anything but the wild flower garden.

*-asteroides* (as-tur-oide' ees)     White Boltonia          5–6'/4'
Late Summer    White, Purple    Eastern North America    Zones 4–8

The 3–5" long, blue-green leaves are entire, broadly lanceolate and narrowed at both ends. The numerous ¾–1" wide flowers are held in large, billowy, terminal panicles. Although the species produces showy flowers, it is too large, floppy, and weedy for my liking and should not be grown in the "formal" garden. However, one of the finest garden plants is a selection of this "weed." Propagation is by division in the spring; a small shovel of basal rosettes yields dozens of offspring. Divide every 3–4 years. Seed of the species may be collected and will germinate readily. Seed of 'Snowbank' will not come true.

**Cultivars:**

Var. *latisquama*, violet boltonia, native from Missouri to Oklahoma, is similar to the species in habit but is about 4' tall and has larger, purple flowers. A dwarf form of this variety, 'Nana', is only 2–3' tall and requires no staking.

'Pink Beauty', found by the wonderful plantsperson, Edith Edelman, in a North Carolina garden, has been offered under various names, including *Boltonia rosea*. Plants are more open and lanky than 'Snowbank' and bear dozens of pale pink flowers in late summer and fall. Provided with sun and decent soil, they grow 5' tall and often require some support.

'Snowbank' is a cultivar of which I am most fond. It is about 3–4' tall and does not require staking when grown in full sun. In partial shade, however, plants will not be as compact and require support. The simple leaves are blue green, and the top half of the plant is blanketed by clear white daisies with yellow centers. In my garden, flowering begins in early August and continues well into September. Although plants perform best in deep, moist, organic soils, plants have tolerated two severe Georgia droughts with only occasional watering. 'Snowbank' associates well with other late summer and fall bloomers such as *Perovskia atriplicifolia, Sedum* × 'Autumn Joy', *Eupatorium purpureum* and *Lespedeza thunbergii*.

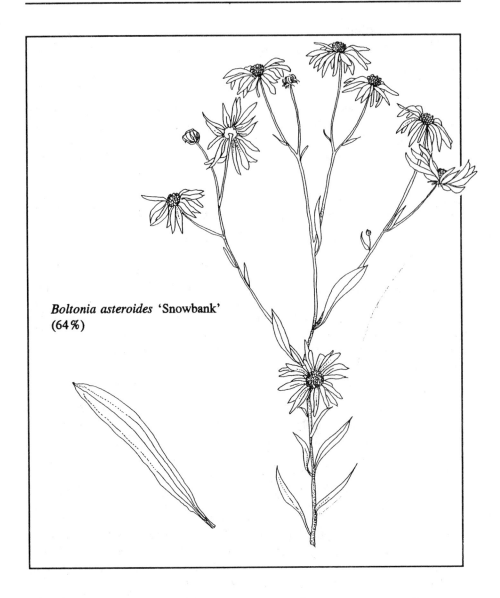

*Boltonia asteroides* 'Snowbank'
(64%)

## *Borago* (bor-rah' go)    Borage    Boraginaceae

Most species of borage are annuals, but the flowers are such a lovely shade of blue, it is worth the effort to include at least one species. Borage has long been used as a pot-herb, and young leaves were often (and still are) included in salads. Medicinal properties attributed to borage (mainly *B. officinalis*) include relief for stomach distress and a curative for local inflammation.

| *-laxiflora* (laks-i-flo′ ra) | | Borage | 1–2′/1′ |
|---|---|---|---|
| Early Summer | Blue | Corsica | Zones 6–9 |

Most appropriate for wall or rock gardens, this borage bears light blue, drooping flowers about ¾ ″ across, similar in shape to flowers of tomatoes (rotate). The loose racemes are produced in late spring and persist for approximately 4 weeks. The many stems are covered with short, backward-pointing bristles, and the 4–6″ long leaves are rough and coarsely hairy. Plants need deep mulching in the fall in most parts of the country.

Propagate by division in the spring, by seeds sown in the fall, or by 2–3″ long, terminal cuttings in summer.

**Additional Reading:**
Balf, K. 1993. Herbs, the forget-me-not family. *Gardens West* 7(2):13–15.

## *Boykinia* (boy-kin-ee′ a)  Brook Saxifrage  Saxifragaceae

About 9 species of this moisture-loving genus occur; plants are best suited to moist woodlands or shady rock gardens. Named after Dr. Samuel Boykin of Savannah, Georgia, most are native to the United States. The alternate, kidney-shaped leaves are held on long petioles, and flowers are held in lax panicles with the foliage.

Only two species are used to any degree in this country, but, with the discovery of our native flora, more of these interesting plants are being offered. *B. aconitifolia* is an eastern native, hardy in zones 6 to 8 and has rounded, lobed, basal leaves and white flowers in late spring. Plants are 10–15″ tall. *B. rotundifolia* is native to southern California, also has white flowers, but the lobed foliage is rounded with hairy stems. Plants are about 12″ tall and likely hardy only to zone 7.

## *Brunnera* (brunn′ er-a)  Brunnera  Boraginaceae

The genus contains three species, but only one is of ornamental interest. *Brunnera* is most at home in moist, shady areas and does particularly well along shaded stream banks or around shaded water features in the garden. After flowering in the spring, large, basal, heart-shaped leaves are produced. The flowers and inflorescence remind people of forget-me-nots (*Myosotis*), resulting in the other common name, false forget-me-not. The leaves are similar to Virginia bluebells, *Mertensia virginica*.

| *-macrophylla* (mak-ro-fil′ a) | | Heartleaf Brunnera | 12–18″/20″ |
|---|---|---|---|
| Spring | Light Blue | Caucasus | Zones 3–7 |
| (Syn. *Anchusa myosotidiflora*) | | | |

The azure blue flowers arise early from the soft, light green foliage and continue into early summer. Plants branch from the base, spread quickly and produce mounds of lovely, cool foliage. The basal leaves are much larger (up to 6" across) and held on longer petioles than those near the top, resulting in a light, airy effect in the landscape. The ¼" diameter flowers have a yellow center and are carried in a loose, 1–2" wide, panicled raceme.

In the South, partial shade and consistent moisture are necessary for vigorous growth. In the North, morning sun is welcome, but moisture must still be maintained. I have seen moist woodlands covered with these plants, and their quiet understated beauty is soothing to the soul. Some of the finest plantings of *Brunnera* I have seen in this country are in Gardenview Horticultural Park, the fine garden of Henry Ross in Strongsville, Ohio and at Old Westbury Gardens on Long Island, NY, where they romp about in the company of forget-me-nots and poppies.

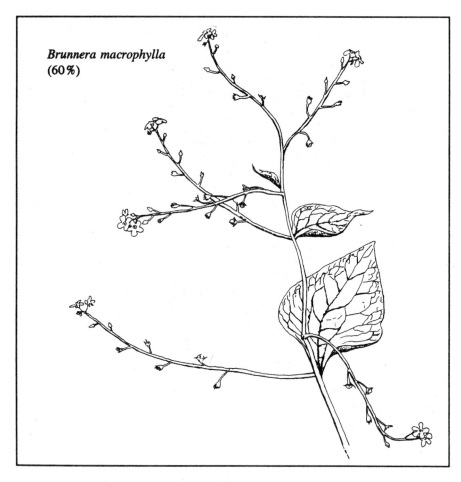

*Brunnera macrophylla*
(60%)

Propagate the species by seed sown in moist, warm (70–75° F) medium in late summer and transplant in the fall. Root cuttings (similar to *Anemone*) may also be used. Variegated forms are slow to increase but may be propagated by division. However, it is almost impossible to propagate them commercially to obtain large numbers. They do not come true from seeds, and root cuttings seldom survive as variegated forms. They will continue to be difficult to locate and relatively expensive. Tissue culture is the only way to obtain sufficient numbers for commercial production, and, as plants increase in numbers, they will become more available and less expensive.

### Cultivars:

'Hadspen Cream' produces light green leaves with irregular, creamy white borders. Somewhat more tolerant of sun and dryness than 'Variegata', but, if subjected to full afternoon sun, the leaf margins will turn brown. Strikingly beautiful where well-grown, miserable looking where abused.

'Langtrees' has dark green leaves with silver-white spots on the border. Sometimes called 'Aluminum Spot', it is more tolerant of dry conditions than other cultivars.

'Smith's Gold' has handsome yellow margins around light green leaves.

'Variegata', also known as 'Dawson's White', is characterized by large, clear white borders which may take up most of the leaf, together with lavender-blue flowers. It is intolerant of drought and prefers cool, moist, shady areas. It is a most handsome plant if grown well.

### Additional Reading:

Anon. 1993. Under-utilized herbaceous perennials for the northeast. *HortIdeas* 10(5):55.

## *Bulbinella* (bul-bi-nel' a)　　　　Bulbinella　　　　Liliaceae

Not a genus one can find without a great deal of searching, and it is perennial only on the West Coast and in warm winter areas. The most available and easiest of the 20 species to grow is *B. hookeri*, an 18–24" tall, yellow, bulbous plant. Native to New Zealand, plants may be raised in pots in cold areas of the country and brought in like caladiums and dahlias.

The individual flowers are less than 1" across; however, there may be more than 100 flowers on each raceme. The flowers at the base of the inflorescence open and finish first, the upper third is still in bud, while the middle one third is open. The flowers remind me of a not quite ripe cob of corn eaten at one end only. The foliage is narrow and in a basal tuft. Plants require copious amounts of organic matter and grow well in full sun. Mulch well in late frosts; plants can't handle much more than 28° F.

*Buphthalmum* (buf-thahl' mum)          Oxeye          Asteraceae

Although the genus features rather common yellow, dark-centered daisies, they have their moments in the sun. The name is derived from *bous*, ox and *opthalmos*, eye, in reference to the appearance of the disc of the flower head. I suppose I have not seen enough oxen eyes, but it doesn't look a great deal different than most other daisies. They are best in moist areas and tolerate poor soil. The large blossoms make reasonably good cut flowers. The foliage is alternate, dark green, and toothed. All species may be easily propagated by division in early spring or immediately after flowering. Seeds germinate in 14–21 days if placed in warm (70–75° F), moist conditions. Only one genus, *B. salicifolium*, is offered; the former *B. speciosum* has been reclassified as *Telekia speciosa*.

-*salicifolium* (sa-li-si-fo' lee-um)     Willowleaf Oxeye          1–2'/2'
     Late Summer          Yellow          Southeastern Europe     Zones 5–8

The alternate leaves are long and narrow like those of a weeping willow, usually toothed, and have white pubescence on the undersides. The terminal, solitary flower heads are about 2" wide. The stems are slender and, without support, tend to topple, particularly in rich soils. Fertilization should be discouraged, or foliage will be produced at the expense of flowers. Like most daisies, flowering continues for many weeks if spent flowers are removed.

**Cultivars:**

'Dora' grows 24–30" tall and bears 2" wide daisies. She has handsome dark purple stems which contrast well with the willowy leaves and yellow flowers.

'Sunwheel' is about 2' tall with golden yellow flowers from July to September.

# C

*Calamagrostis* (ka-la-ma-grost′ is)  Feather Reed Grass  Poaceae

Approximately 250 species of this genus occur; however, a couple of forms have been extensively used in gardens for the last 10 years. The plants are stoloniferous and thrive on permanently damp, fertile, even heavy soils. This is an understated genus, which, as Kim Hawkes of Niche Gardens in North Carolina states, "go quietly unnoticed until they bloom."

-× *acutiflora* (acute-i-floor′ a)  Feather Reed Grass  3–4′/3′
Summer  Hybrid  Zones 6–9

These tight, tufted, erect grasses are the result of hybridization between *A. arundinacea*, reed grass, and *C. epigejos*, rush grass, both natives of Europe and Asia. The foliage is lax, and the loose inflorescence is branched with flowers ranging from silvery-bronze to purple-brown. Full sun is best. Some terrific cultivars have been offered.

## Cultivars:

'Karl Foerster' ('Stricta') produces feathery, golden inflorescences on 4′ tall plants in early summer. Plants grow tightly together and may be grouped together for best effect. They make a marvelous vertical element in the garden.

'Overdam' has white stripes on the green foliage and 2–3′ tall, mounding plants. Golden plumes of flowers occur in mid to late summer.

## Related Species:

*C. arundinacea*, reed grass, is quietly spectacular in its own right. The tall clumps of green to blue-green grass bear handsome, airy plumes in late summer. The foliage looks like silvery wheat as late fall and winter occurs. I have seen particularly striking plants in containers around pools and ponds.

*C. bracytricha*, feather grass, is also known as *C. arundinacea* 'Bracy-tricha'. Handsome, blond inflorescences give rise to purple spikelets in the fall on 2–3' tall plants. Plant en masse.

### Additional Reading:

Cramer, H.L. 1994. Graceful grasses for small places. *Fine Gardening* 40:64–69.

## *Calamintha* (kal-a-min' tha)       Calamint       Lamiaceae

Some 7 species of these aromatic mints may be found, and a few of them make handsome low-growing garden plants if provided with full sun to partial shade and well-drained soils. They are often woody at the base, may be cut back heavily when overgrown, and provide some good ground covers for the rock garden or border. A number of species have been reclassified to other genera. *Calamintha acinos* is now *Acinos arvensis*, and *C. clinopodium* is *Clinopodium vulgare*, both of which are fine garden plants. The most popular species is *C. nepeta*. None of the calamints perform particularly well in warm, wet climates.

| *-nepeta* (nep-e' ta) | | Savory Calamint | 9–12"/12" |
|---|---|---|---|
| Early Summer | Lavender | Southern Europe | Zones 4–7 |

The small (less than 1" long), hairy leaves are strongly aromatic, and the whorled, light blue to pale lavender flowers are produced slightly above the 12" tall mats. Plants make good fillers and are terrific if one wants to attract bees to the garden. Cut back if plants become overgrown. They do well in the north-west, look fine in the northeast and upper midwest, but struggle anywhere in the south. Good drainage or raised beds are necessary for areas of hot, wet summers. Cut back hard after flowering in all but areas of the coolest summers.

### Cultivars:

'Alba' bears dozens of small, white flowers on plants about 1' tall.

Ssp. *nepeta* has more flowers per inflorescence and leaves about 1½" long.

'White Cloud', an introduction from Canyon Creek Nursery in Oroville, CA, bears many small, white flowers with oregano-scented foliage. Similar to 'Alba' but appears to be a little more floriferous. However, it is difficult to see a great deal of difference between them.

### Related Species:

*C. grandiflora*, large-flowered calamint, is also aromatic but bears ½' long, rosy-pink flowers in mid summer. Plants grow to about 18" tall. 'Variegata' ('Forncett Form') has creamy flecks on the leaves, bears pink flowers, and is usually a little shorter than the species.

*C. sylvatica*, common calamint, is similar to *C. nepeta* but may be distinguished by the paler green leaves and pale pink flowers with white spots.

## *Callirhoe* (ka-lee-ro' ee)　　　　Poppy Mallow　　　　Malvaceae

In his outstanding three volume work, *The Standard Cyclopedia of Horticulture*, L.H. Bailey wrote that "callirhoes are of easiest culture and deserving of a much greater popularity." That was written in 1944, and fifty years later callirhoes are still no more difficult to grow and have earned no greater respect. Why is this genus so difficult to find? Even the up-scale, mail order nurseries seldom offer it.

About 8 species have been described, and all bear alternate leaves, lobed or palmately-cut, and showy, cup-shaped, white to purple flowers. Most species are cold hardy to about 5° F and tolerate heat, although they prefer cool summers. They require full sun and well-drained soils. Plants are particularly effective growing over walls and raised beds. The main species seen in gardens is the purple-flowered *C. involucrata*, but *C. alcaeoides* has triangular, basal leaves and often produces white flowers; *C. digitata* grows 3–4' tall, has palmately-divided leaves and beautiful, long-stalked, rose-red, deeply-cleft petals. Occasionally the clustered poppy mallow, *C. triangulata*, with triangular, basal leaves and a cluster of red-purple flowers, is offered. All are native to the United States.

*Callirhoe* can be easily distinguished from other members of Malvaceae by the 5 sticky, thread-like style branches in the flower. The styles of other genera in Malvaceae are either more numerous or are tipped with round, sticky stigmas.

## *-involucrata* (in-vol-yew-krah' ta)　　Purple Poppy Mallow　　1–2'/2'
### Early Summer　　　　Purple　　　　Central United States　　Zones 4–7

The rough, hairy stems and palmately-divided leaves tend to grow horizontally, which result in a good deal of ground being covered. The leaves are covered with short, stiff hairs and are dark green with pale veins. The handsome, 2" wide, wine-colored, cup-shaped flowers are found throughout the plant but mainly on the terminals. Generally, flowers are entirely wine to magenta in color, but occasionally the bases of the flowers may be white. This is a terrific plant that starts flowering after the main flush of spring plants, beginning in June and often continuing until frost. Beneath the flower are 3 bracts that are similar to the sepals. Most other species of *Callirhoe* do not possess these bracts.

Plants are easy to grow from seed, and, if placed in well-drained soils in full sun, they provide a long show of eye-catching flowers. In some gardens, they self-sow prodigiously. They do poorly in wet conditions. If plants get too leggy, simply whack them back, if you have the heart for it.

**Additional Reading:**

Hayward, P. 1993. *Callirhoe involucrata. American Nurseryman* 178(3):98.

## *Caltha* (kal' tha)  Marsh Marigold  Ranunculaceae

About 10 species of these moisture-loving plants occur, and their garden value is beginning to be recognized. They all flourish in wet areas near running water but can succeed in rich, well-irrigated garden sites. The early spring flowers are white or yellow and made up entirely of sepals with numerous stamens. The leaves are alternate, usually basal, and have an entire to slightly-lobed margin.

| *-palustris* (pal-lus' tris) | Marsh Marigold | 1–2'/1' |
|---|---|---|
| Spring  Yellow | North America | Zones 5–7 |

Growing in shallow water or boggy ground, plants are less adaptable to common garden conditions than some of the other species. One- to two-inch wide, bright yellow flowers open over succulent, kidney-shaped leaves which tend to get smaller as they progress up the stem. Plants tend to make larger clumps, but var. *palustris* is more spreading and forms large colonies. Plants may grow to 2', but 12–15" is more common. Full sun is necessary for best performance.

Occasionally, plants can be confused with some species of buttercups, *Ranunculus*. Both groups of plants love it wet, are low growers, and have yellow flowers. *Caltha* have simple (not compound) leaves, and the flowers usually have 5 sepals and no petals. *Ranunculus* often have compound leaves (or at least divided) and have 5 sepals and 5 petals.

### Cultivars:

'Alba' produces white flowers but is much more difficult to obtain than the species. The white flowers make a splendid contrast to the green foliage. Expensive but striking.

'Flore plena' ('Multiplex') is an outstanding plant with double, yellow flowers.

'Tyermannii' is a more dwarf plant with dark stems and clear yellow flowers.

### Related Species:

*C. leptosepala* (syn. *C. biflora*), Western white marsh marigold, has basal leaves and no stem. The scape (flower stem) is slender and bears 2 marvelous white flowers with gold stamens. Native from California to Alaska.

## *Camassia* (ka-ma' see-a)  Quamash  Liliaceae

*Camassia* is a true bulb and was used extensively by the Indians of the Northwest as a food staple. Bitter wars were fought over possession of the Quamash grounds. All are native to North America, extending from the west coast to Georgia, yet are underused in gardens in this country. The foliage is long, lance-like and grassy, and flower stems are erect and may be up to 4' tall. The star-shaped flowers consist of 6 petal-like segments (called tepals), blue, purple, white, or cream-colored, and appear at about the same time as the late tulips. The genus is closely related to *Scilla* and *Ornithogalum*, but the veins on the tepals provide a handy clue to their identification. In *Camassia*, the tepals are distinctly veined; in *Scilla*, there is only one vein on the tepals; in *Ornithogalum*, the veins are very indistinct. They are inhabitants of rich meadows, wet in spring and dry in summer. Plants tolerate some shade but perform better in full sun. Plant in the fall approximately 3 times deeper than the diameter of the bulb and in groups of at least a dozen. Nothing looks worse than one lonely flowering bulb.

The foliage is not as persistent as that of daffodils, and bulbs may be planted in the formal garden. However, they do look rather scruffy after flowering, and some gardeners prefer to plant them in a slightly more out of the way area such as the naturalized garden, where enough can be planted to insure a good supply of cut flowers for indoors.

Bulb offsets are produced after several years, but natural production is very slow. Wounding the bulbs greatly enhances offset production and is practiced commercially. Seed propagation is not difficult if seed is fresh. Seeds germinate readily, but 3–4 years are required before plants flower.

Quick Reference to Camassia Species

|  | Height (ft.) | Number flowers open at once | Total flowers on stem |
|---|---|---|---|
| *C. cusickii* | 3–4 | Many | 30–100 |
| *C. leichtlinii* | 3–4 | 1–4 | 20–50 |
| *C. quamash* | 2–3 | Many | 10–40 |

| *-cusickii* (kew-sik′ ee-eye) | | Cusick Quamash | 3–4′/1′ |
|---|---|---|---|
| Early Summer | Blue | Oregon | Zones 3–8 |

The bulbs are large and can weigh up to half a pound! Numerous, slightly wavy leaves about 15″ long and 1½″ wide appear in a basal cluster. The lovely, pale blue, star-shaped flowers are approximately 1½″ across, and 30–100 flowers are held in long racemes on 3–4′ long scapes. Each narrow flower segment has 3–5 faint veins running its length. The flowers do not twist together as they wither.

This is the cold-hardiest species and grows as far north as zone 3 with suitable winter protection.

**Cultivars:**
'Zwanenburg' has large, deep blue flowers.

209

*-leichtlinii* (liekt-lin′ ee-eye)  Leichtlin Quamash  3–4′/1′
  Early Summer  Various  California to British Columbia  Zones 5–9

This is the best species of *Camassia* for the garden. The foliage is broader than in *C. quamash* but not as wide as in *C. cusickii*. Plants are strong and stout and seldom need support except in windy areas. The flowers are large (up to 1″ across) and may be white, cream, blue or purple. Each segment has 5–7 nerves. When the flowers wither, they twist around the capsule before falling away. This is one of the few characteristics which distinguishes this species from others, clearly pointing out how few differences exist among members of the genus.

### Cultivars:
'Atroviolacea' has single flowers of deep violet.
'Blue Danube' produces dark blue flowers.
'Electra' bears large flower heads of deep blue.
'Eve Price' is the finest cultivar I have seen and produces a magnificent clump of light blue spikes.
'Plena' bears creamy yellow, double flowers.
'Semi-plena' produces semi-double, creamy white to yellow flowers.

*-quamash* (kwah′ mash)  Common Quamash  2–3′/1′
  Early Summer  Various  Western North America  Zones 4–8
(Syn. *C. esculenta*)

The 12″ long leaves are linear and grass-like (about ½″ wide). The flowers are usually white or in various shades of violet with 3–5 nerves per segment. This is a particularly variable species, and the segments taking up the flowers may be closely or loosely spaced, often on the same raceme. It is distinguished by the irregular flowers which have 5 segments, more or less on one side, and the last one on the other. Each of the 10–30 flowers in the inflorescence are persistent but don't twist around as in the former species. The colors are not as deep as in *C. leichtlinii*.

### Cultivars:
'Flore-alba' is an attractive, semi-double, white-flowering cultivar.
'Orion' bears dense inflorescences with purple buds and dark blue flowers.
'San Juan' has even darker blue flowers than 'Orion'.

Quick Key to Camassia Species

  A. Leaves 1–1½″ wide, flowers blue,
    3–5 faint veins per segment . . . . . . . . . . . . . . . . . *C. cusickii*

AA. Leaves less than 1″ wide, flower color
   various, 3–7 nerves per segment
   B. Flowers all regular, few in bloom at once,
      withered segments twisted, soon deciduous  . . .  *C. leichtlinii*
   BB. Flowers irregular, many in bloom at once,
      withered segments not twisted, persistent . . . . . . *C. quamash*

## *Campanula* (kam-pahn′ ew-la)          Bellflower          Campanulaceae

This fascinating genus consists of approximately 250 species, many of which are useful for the garden. Campanulas can get into one's blood and bring out the collecting urges in many people. The great horticulturist, Liberty Hyde Bailey, took immense pleasure in his garden which "was fully inhabited by bellflowers, representing genera and species of *Campanula*, and related plants. . ." The British authority Alan Bloom stated that he had "furtively accumulated 109 species and varieties of campanula before the nurseryman in me took control." Shades of blue tend to dominate, but flowers are often tinted with lilac, lavender, violet and other hues. Species with white and pink flowers can also be found. They range in height from the low-growing, rockery species to 5′ tall monsters. The leaves are simple, usually alternate, and toothed. The basal leaves of the upright forms are often different in size and shape than the stem leaves. The genus includes annuals (*C. americana, C. ramosissima*), biennials (*C. medium*), and even food crops (*C. rapunculoides*), but most are long-lived, ornamental perennials. Although many wonderful species for the American garden occur, unfortunately most of the upright bellflowers do not perform particularly well in the South (*C. persicifolia* is one exception). This is certainly a generalization, and, at higher altitudes or in cooler microclimates in the South, experiences with other upright forms are more positive. Bellflowers do not appreciate night temperatures consistently above 70° F, although the dwarf forms are more forgiving than the erect species.

Propagation for all but double-flowered cultivars is easy by seed. Even most of the named cultivars come true from seed. Terminal stem cuttings, root cuttings, and divisions can be used when necessary. Most are sun-loving, but a few of the rock garden plants benefit from partial shade.

To quote L. H. Bailey once more is to understand some of the finer qualities of *Campanula*. "They are eminently plants for the garden-lover, for those persons who graciously accept cool nights and soft rains and dews, who respond to the milder sensations and derive sustaining satisfactions from gentle experiences. They are for those who love to grow plants for the joy of growing them. . ."

Quick Reference to Campanula Species

| | Height (in.) | Habit Erect, Low | Flower color | Flower shape | Flower Pendulous, Upright |
|---|---|---|---|---|---|
| C. alliariifolia | 18–36 | E | White | Bell | P |
| C. carpatica | 9–12 | L | Blue | Cup | U |
| C. cochlearifolia | 4–6 | L | Blue | Bell | P |
| C. garganica | 5–6 | L | Blue | Star | U |
| C. glomerata | 12–18 | E | Purple | Bell | U |
| C. lactiflora | 36–60 | E | Lilac | Bell | U |
| C. latifolia | 48–60 | E | Purple | Tubular | U |
| C. latiloba | 12–36 | E | Lilac | Saucer | U |
| C. persicifolia | 12–36 | E | Blue | Saucer | U |
| C. portenschlagiana | 4–6 | L | Blue | Bell | U |
| C. poscharskyana | 8–12 | L | Lilac | Bell | U |
| C. pyramidalis | 36–48 | E | Blue | Bell | U |
| C. rotundifolia | 6–12 | L | Purple | Bell | P |
| C. takesimana | 24–36 | E | Off-white | Tubular | P |

*-alliariifolia* (a-lee-ah-ree-i-fo′ lee-a) Spurred Bellflower     18–36″/24″
    Summer          White          Caucasus, Asia Minor     Zones 3–7
(Syn. *C. lamiifolia*)

This is one of the few white-flowered species, although white cultivars of other species are also available. The plant forms a clump of attractive, heart-shaped, basal leaves above which 2–3′ long flower stems arise. The lower leaves are larger and have longer petioles than leaves further up the stem. The nodding, white, 1–2″ long flowers appear in each leaf axil, and, as they open, the stems arch over, taking up more room than anticipated. The sepals are tan-colored and provide an attractive contrast with the white bells. Flowers are often borne on one side of the racemes only. Plants are rather short-lived (2–3 years) but reseed freely.

Being floppy, it may be cut back after flowering to keep in bounds. Plants are intolerant of summer heat and humidity and are poor choices for southern gardens. Full sun and well-drained soil are necessary for best growth. Fertilize lightly to restrict height.

Seed sown in summer or fall germinate well but irregularly. Place seed in moist medium and maintain high humidity and warmth (70–75° F).

**Cultivars:**

'Ivory Bells' is sometimes listed as a cultivar or used as a common name
    for the species. There is so little difference between the two, I believe it

is more accurately used as a common name. The name is certainly better than spurred bellflower.

'Flore-pleno' bears double flowers. Difficult to locate.

### Related Species:

*C. ochroleuca* resemble *C. alliariifolia,* but the lower leaves are deltoid rather than heart-shaped. The flowers, which range from white to very pale yellow, may be distinguished by the style which extends beyond the petals. A handsome, although similarly lanky, plant. Plants are likely hardy to zone 5.

| | | | |
|---|---|---|---|
| *-carpatica* (kar-pa' ti-ca) | Carpathian Harebell | 9–12"/12" |
| Summer | Bright Blue | Eastern Europe | Zones 3–7 |

One of the most popular bellflowers in this country, Carpathian harebell tolerates a wide range of conditions and spreads readily as long as adequate drainage is provided. The numerous bell-shaped flowers are solitary and up to 2" across. The leaves are triangular, toothed and dark green. Plants are excellent for the rock garden or front of the border and are covered with bloom in summer under good conditions. I have not found this species particularly outstanding in my north Georgia garden, but I haven't tried all available cultivars. I have been more successful in the South with some of the other smaller-flowered, low-growing species. All cultivars of *C. carpatica* prefer to have roots in cool soil; therefore, a summer mulch is useful, particularly in hot summers.

This is a relatively easy plant to force in the greenhouse. Plants can be cooled at temperatures around 40° F or can be frozen by leaving outdoors. If plants are provided with artificial long days (putting incandescent lights on to provide a "short night"), then plants will flower between 30 and 45 days later. Long days are a condition beneficial to the artificial flowering of many perennials.

Propagation of most cultivars is easiest by seed. Place the seed on top of medium and lightly cover with a thin layer of vermiculite. Keep the seed moist by covering with plastic and keep out of direct sun. Germination should occur within 3 weeks, and seedlings can be transplanted 2 weeks later. Plants should be divided every other year to maintain habit and vigor.

### Cultivars:

'Alba' has white flowers.

'Blue Clips' is an excellent compact, 6–9" tall plant bearing blue flowers up to 3" wide.

'Blue Moonlight' bears china blue cups on 6–9" tall mounds.

'Bressingham White' has 2–3" wide, clean white flowers.

'Chewton Joy' has interesting two-toned flowers over 10" tall plants. The petals are pale blue with much deeper blue margins.

213

'China Cup' and 'China Doll' are about 9″ tall and have azure blue flowers. Habits are similar.

'Jingle Bells' produces a mixture of white and blue flowers and grow 8–12″ tall.

'Kobalt Bell' ('Kobaltglocke') has intense cobalt-blue flowers on 6–8″ tall plants. Stunning color.

Var. *turbinata* has a more compact habit, growing 6–9″ tall and producing purplish blue flowers. A number of cultivars belong to this variety, but, unfortunately, few are offered in the United States. The most popular is 'Karl Foerster', mainly used as a forced greenhouse plant or hanging basket, which bears saucer-shaped flowers of deep blue. Other excellent cultivars include 'Isabel' with wide-spreading, deep violet flowers, 'Pallida' which bears blue flowers up to 1″ in diameter, and 'Snowsprite' with handsome white flowers on a 4″ tall frame.

'Wedgewood Blue' bears 2½″ diameter, violet-blue flowers over 6″ tall plants.

'Wedgewood White' is one of the most compact white-flowered cultivars.

'White Clips' is a fine plant and a little better than 'Wedgewood White'.

'White Star' is similar to 'Alba'. The flowers are a cleaner white, but plants are not as compact as 'Wedgewood White'. To be honest, it is almost impossible to tell the whites apart, and it is not much easier to separate the blues. If plants grow well in your area, you will likely enjoy them all.

**Related Species:**

*C. barbata*, bearded bellflower, bears 1″ long, lilac-blue, pendulous, bell-shaped flowers which have woolly hairs (bearded) within. In the summer, the rosettes of dark green leaves send up the strong, 12–18″ tall flower stems. So many flowers are produced that it has been said to "flower itself to death." A white form, 'Alba', is occasionally listed. Likely hardy in zones 5–7.

*C.* × *hendersonii* is a cross between *C. alliariifolia* and *C. carpatica*. Plants are about 18″ tall with pale lilac flower spikes.

-*cochlearifolia* (kok-lee-ah-ree-i-fo′ lee-a) Spiral Bellflower    4–6″/12″
    Summer          Blue-Violet        European Mountains   Zones 4–7
(Syn. *C. pusilla*)

A campanula with a virtually unpronounceable name, but easily grown in spite of the fact that nobody can say it. Another common name is Fairies' Thimbles, which attests to its diminutive habit and the creativity of gardeners to find a name for tongue-twisting plants. The mat-forming plants, suitable for the front of the garden or along pathways, produce ¾″ diameter, pendulous, sky-blue flowers on wiry stems. The lower leaves are heart-shaped and deeply serrate, while the upper leaves are more narrow, almost elliptical. Nothing more than good drainage and mid-afternoon shade is required for success.

Propagate by seed similar to *C. carpatica* or by division in spring or fall.

214

**Cultivars:**

'Alba' bears clear white flowers and is particularly vigorous.

'Bavaria Blue' and 'Bavaria White' are about 4″ tall, more compact than the species and bear dark blue and white flowers respectively.

'Blue Tit' produces bright blue flowers.

'Cambridge Blue' bears light blue flowers on 2-3″ tall plants. The latter two cultivars were bred by Alan Bloom in the 1930's.

'Elizabeth Oliver' is interesting in that she has very pale, double flowers.

'Miranda' is a vigorous grower which produces pale icy blue flowers.

'Patience Bell' bears large diameter, deep blue flowers on 6-9″ mounds of foliage.

**Related Species:**

*C. sarmatica*, Sarmatican bellflower, has nodding, pale blue, soft hairy flowers on one side of the flower stem. The 3-5″ long, arrow-shaped, basal leaves have long petioles, while the stem leaves are smaller and become sessile as they climb the stem. The 4-8″ long flowers are bearded within, and the lobes of the petals flare outward. Plants grow 1-2′ tall and bear clumps of hairy, gray-green leaves. Well worth trying.

*C. cashmeriana*, Kashmir bellflower, is only about 6″ tall but bears many pendulous, lilac-blue flowers over gray-green, soft, hairy leaves. Best for well-drained site and full sun.

| *-garganica* (gar-gah′ ni-ca) | Gargano Bellflower | 5-6″/12″ |
|---|---|---|
| Spring          Blue | Italy | Zones 5-7 |

This species was discovered in 1827 at the base of Mt. Garganica in Italy. Although treated by some authorities as a variant of *C. elatines* or *C. portenschlagiana*, it is usually offered as *C. garganica*. The basal leaves are ovate, while the stem leaves are heart-shaped. Both are grayish green with rounded teeth. Star-like, blue flowers with white eyes are produced in clusters in the leaf axils and persist for 2-3 weeks.

This is an aggressive species and needs to be divided often. Full sun is preferable, but partial shade is tolerated, particularly in the southern range of cultivation. It is a hardy rock garden plant which should be grown for the unique, non-campanulate flowers, prostrate habit, and gray-green leaves.

Propagate by seed (similar to *C. alliariifolia*), terminal cuttings or division in early spring or fall.

**Cultivars:**

'Alba' bears white flowers.

'Blue Diamond' produces icy blue flowers with a dark blue center.

'Dickson's Gold' ('Aurea') is unique for its golden foliage. The contrast between the foliage and the blue flowers is striking, although not particularly attractive. The plants need some protection to maintain the golden hue. Some afternoon shade in the south is essential.

'Glandore' bears dark blue flowers with a lighter blue center.

Var. *hirsuta* is a gray, downy-leaved form with lighter blue flowers and longer stems than the species.

Var. *hirsuta alba* has the same form as var. *hirsuta* but with white flowers.

'W.H. Paine' produces star-shaped flowers with a clean white center.

**Related Species:**

*C. elatines*, Adriatic bellflower, is similar but has heart-shaped basal leaves compared to the ovate leaves of *C. garganica*. The blue or white flowers are borne in a spike. A number of variants occur, including var. *fenestrellata* with a more upright habit and larger leaves. None are particularly good subjects for warm, humid conditions.

*C. pulla* is among the smallest species in the genus. This tufted, 3-4" tall species bears small, dark blue, nodding flowers. Often seen in rock gardens.

| | | | |
|---|---|---|---|
| *-glomerata* (glo-me-rah' ta) | Clustered Bellflower | | 12–18"/12" |
| Summer | Blue, Purple | Eurasia | Zones 3–8 |

The common name of this showy bellflower comes from the clustered arrangement of flowers atop the flowering stem. There may be as many as 15 flowers in a cluster (raceme) which persist for 2-3 weeks. Cut flower stems also last up to 2 weeks when placed in water. The ovate, toothed foliage is hairy above and below and varies in size. The stem leaves are 3-4" long, sessile or short-petioled and usually narrower and more pointed than the 5" long, basal leaves. Plants may be single-stemmed or branched.

Full sun in the North or partial shade in the South is recommended. Plantings in the State Botanical Garden of Georgia held up for approximately 3 years. Trialing in the Horticulture Gardens at the University of Georgia has shown that plants may be recommended for the Southeast as long as partial shade and water are present. For most aesthetic results, place in groups of at least 3 plants.

Propagate using 2-3" long, terminal cuttings in summer after flowering. Seed is available for many of the cultivars, as well as the species, and should be treated similar to *C. alliariifolia*.

**Cultivars:**

Var. *acaulis* is a dwarf, early-flowering, violet-blue form which is almost stemless and only 3-5" tall. Plants taller than 8" are not likely this variety. A white form (var. *acaulis alba*) is 8-12" tall.

'Caroline' bears starry shell-pink flowers with pink to mauve markings. Difficult to find, perhaps just as well.

'Crown of Snow' ('Schneekrone') is 18-24" tall and bears large, white flower clusters.

Var. *dahurica* (syn. *C. dahurica*, *C. speciosa*) has large, deep-violet flowers (clusters 3" across) and stands about 2-3' tall.

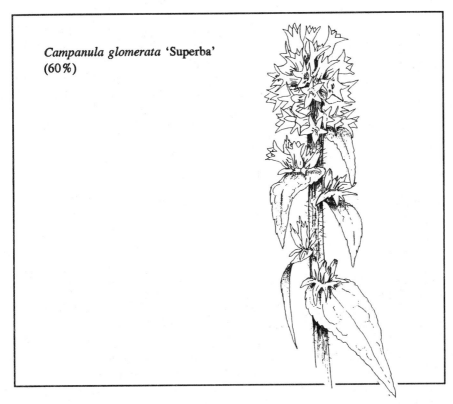

*Campanula glomerata* 'Superba'
(60%)

'Joan Elliott' sends up many flowering stems of deep violet-blue flowers and is 1½' tall. Probably the most floriferous of the group.

'Odessa' bears upright, facing clusters of deep purple flowers. Plants are 2-3' tall.

'Purple Pixie' is about 1½' high with lavender-blue flowers. Plants remain in a tight clump, displaying no spreading tendencies common in many other cultivars.

'Snow Cushion' ('Schneekissen') is a clean white form and grows 2' tall.

'Superba' has violet flowers and grows 2½' tall. It is vigorous and tolerates heat better than many other selections.

'Superba Alba' is a white form of the above cultivar.

'White Barn', introduced by Beth Chatto of England, has dense heads of violet-purple flowers on short, 12-15″ tall spikes. An excellent habit.

| *-lactiflora* (lak-ti-flor' a) | | Milky Bellflower | 3-5'/3' |
|---|---|---|---|
| Summer | Lavender-Blue | Caucasus | Zones 5-7 |

This tall bellflower has a bushy habit and sometimes reaches 5' under optimum conditions. The 3-5″ long, basal leaves are serrated and have short

217

petioles. They become smaller, more pointed and sessile as they ascend the stem. The 1–2″ long, bell-shaped flowers point upwards and are often milk-white (thus its common name) to pale blue. They are borne on 12–15″ long, leafy, terminal panicles on each axillary shoot. Hundreds of flowers can occur on well-grown plants, distinguishing them from other tall campanulas such as *C. latifolia* and *C. latiloba*. People often have trouble distinguishing some of the tall species apart; perhaps the following table will help.

| | Flowers | Flower attachment | Comments |
|---|---|---|---|
| *C. lactiflora* | Many | Pedicel | Many flowers, think "flora" |
| *C. latifolia* | Few | Pedicel | Few flowers comp. to *lactiflora* |
| *C. latiloba* | Few | Sessile | Spikes, like a delphinium |
| *C. persicifolia* | Many | Pedicel | Leaves narrow, not serrated |

Although milky bellflower is tolerant of full sun in northern climates, plants are more at home in partial shade and do not look out of place in a semi-shaded, wild flower garden. A consistent moisture level is necessary for vigorous growth. Well-drained soils are necessary, especially in the South. Plants do not transplant well and direct sowing (i.e. sowing seeds directly in the garden) helps them establish. In fact, once established, plants multiply rapidly due to the prolific, self-sowing tendency. This is particularly true in the Northwest. If a problem, flowers should be removed immediately after flowering. If plants are cut back immediately after flowering, a second flush of flowers occurs in the fall.

Propagate the species and varieties by seed or division; the cultivars by division. Treat the seeds similar to *C. alliariifolia*. All varieties exhibit a great deal of variation when raised from seed.

### Cultivars:

Var. *alba* is a 4–5′ tall, white-flowering variety.

Var. *coerulea* bears violet-blue flowers.

'Loddon Anna' is a strong, 4′ tall plant with soft, pale pink flowers. This is a lovely cultivar.

'Pouffe' is a dwarf cultivar raised by Alan Bloom. It stands only 10–18″ high and is covered with pale blue flowers for 4–5 weeks. Many of the taller cultivars are floppy; this is not.

'Prichard's Variety', bearing purple-blue flowers and growing 3–4′ tall, is the most common cultivar available.

Var. *rosea* has pink flowers.

'Superba' has large (1½–2″), dark violet-blue flowers and is more vigorous than the type.

'White Pouffe' is similar to 'Pouffe' but with white flowers.

**Related Species:**

*C. medium* (syn. *C. media*), Canterbury Bells or Cup and Saucer, are some of Grandmother's favorites; however, perhaps because they are biennials, plants are less available than "in the old days." The species, bearing single flowers up the 3' tall stem, is known as Canterbury Bells, while the double forms ('Calycanthema'), with white, rose or purple flowers, are known as Cup and Saucer plants. Plant one-year-old plants in the fall; flowers will occur next spring or early summer.

| *-latifolia* (lah-ti-fo' lee-a) | | Great Bellflower | 4–5'/3' |
|---|---|---|---|
| Early Summer | Purple-Blue | Europe | Zones 3–6 |

This erect perennial has a running rootstock which results in rapidly spreading clumps. The 5–6" long, basal leaves are held on a long, slightly-winged petiole but become smaller and virtually sessile as they ascend the stem. All are slender-pointed, double-toothed and hairy. The erect, bell-shaped flowers are about 2–3" long and held in a short, leafy, terminal raceme, as well as in the leaf axils. The old basal flowers turn down while the new ones are still opening.

Plants are not as showy but do make reasonably good garden specimens. Support is required to remain upright, and plants are best placed in the rear of informal settings. I have had no success in establishing plants, and I have seen few good stands south of zone 6. Where successful, seed capsules should be removed prior to maturity if new colonies are not wanted.

Propagate the species by seed or division in early spring. Seed normally germinates quickly but may first require 2–4 weeks of 40–50° F to assure a high germination percentage. Cultivars should be divided in early spring.

**Cultivars:**

'Alba' has white flowers but is otherwise similar to the species.

'Brantwood' is violet-colored and the best known cultivar of the species.

'Gloaming' has pale blue flowers and is particularly attractive. Propagated vegetatively only for best forms.

'Macrantha' has larger flowers but otherwise is similar to the species.

'Macrantha Alba' is a good white form, although not remarkably different from 'Alba'.

'White Ladies' bears clear white flowers. Propagated vegetatively only.

**Related Species:**

*C. americana*, tall bellflower, is native to moist, shady areas in eastern North America. Although not as showy as other upright forms, the spikes of 1" wide, pale blue flowers associate well with other shade-tolerant perennials. Unfortunately, plants are short-lived and often treated as biennials.

*C.* × 'Burghaltii' is a cross between *C. latifolia* and *C. punctata*. Plants bear pale mauve flowers which arise from amethyst-colored flower buds.

I find the long, pendulous flowers on the lanky stems messy at best, but, if room allows, it is worth a try.

*C. trachelium*, throatwort, has an angular stem and somewhat bristly stems and leaves. The blue or white, bell-shaped flowers are initially erect, then later droop in a loose raceme. Very hardy and dependable. 'Bernice' is about 2' tall with double, blue flowers.

| *-latiloba* (lat-ee-lobe' a) | | Delphinium Bellflower | 3–4'/3' |
|---|---|---|---|
| Blue, White | Summer | Europe | Zones 5–7 |

The proper name for this plant is *C. persicifolia* ssp. *sessiliflora*, which probably better describes the sessile flowers and similar leaves found in the peachleaf bellflower. However, *C. latiloba* is still used in the trade, and the name slips off your tongue so much better. Apologies to all the botanists, but *latiloba* it will stay at least until the next edition. I also made up the common name, delphinium bellflower, because the plants so remind me of a delphinium when I first look at the flower stalks. The flowers are large (2–3″ long), and numerous cultivars occur.

### Cultivars:

'Alba' is one of the best white-flowered plants I have seen. Clean, clear and handsome.

'Hidcote Amethyst' bears pale amethyst flowers with a faint median stripe of deeper blue.

'Highcliffe' bears deep violet-blue flowers.

'Percy Piper' is very similar to 'Highcliffe' but supposedly a little more dwarf.

| *-persicifolia* (per-sis-i-fo' lee-a) | | Peachleaf Bellflower | 1–3'/2' |
|---|---|---|---|
| Summer | Blue-Violet | Europe, North Africa, Asia | Zones 3–7 |

This popular European cut flower is becoming more familiar to American consumers and gardeners. The erect flowers are 1–1½″ long and broadly bell-shaped, almost resembling a saucer. Flowers occur in various shades of blue in open, terminal racemes. The evergreen, basal leaves are 4–8″ long, while the sessile stem leaves are 2–4″ long. All are narrow, leathery, and have rounded teeth or are wavy and certainly don't resemble peach leaves. Clumps increase in size by shoots arising from the base of the plant, and new colonies are formed everywhere through self-sowing. Flower color, plant habit and size are variable.

In zones 3–6, this is an excellent garden plant. Garden performance in the South has been mixed. In zone 7, plants perform fairly well and persist for 2–3 years; in zone 8, flower color is faded, and plants usually decline after 1 year.

Propagate by seed (similar to *C. alliariifolia*), division, or terminal cuttings.

**Cultivars:**

'Alba' has white flowers.

'Alba Coronata' bears semi-double, white flowers.

'Alba Flore-plena' has fully double, white flowers.

'Beechwood' bears pale, soft blue flowers.

'Bluebell' has single, blue flowers and grows 2–3' tall.

'Blue Gardenia' produces double, blue flowers. This may be the same (they look the same) as 'Coerulea Flore-plena' but certainly sounds better.

'Boule de Neige' bears large, double, white flowers.

'Chettle Charm' is a marvelous plant, producing creamy white flowers with light lavender margins.

'Coerulea Coronata' produces semi-double, purple-blue flowers.

'Coerulea Flore-plena' has double flowers of the same color.

'Grandiflora Alba' has larger (2" diameter) white flowers.

'Hampstead White' is a particularly handsome white form, bearing semi-double, hose-in-hose flowers.

'Moerheimii' bears double, white flowers and is quite similar to 'Alba Flore-plena' but is longer lived.

'Telham Beauty' is 3–4' tall with bell-shaped, pale china-blue flowers. A most attractive cultivar.

'Snowdrift' also has large, 2" diameter, white flowers.

**Related Species:**

*C. rhomboidalis* is an upright plant, growing about 2' tall with racemes of bell-shaped, lilac to blue flowers. The flowers are nearly 1" long and held almost horizontally. Seldom seen in North America but worth trying in zones 3–6.

*C. thrysoides* is the most unbellflower bellflower I have seen. They form a 2–3' tall plant with pale yellow flowers in a compressed, narrow, almost cylindrical, spike. It is a lot more interesting than ornamental, but, because it is so different, it has appeal to the crazy gardeners of the world. The variety *carniolica* has yellow-white flowers in an even narrower inflorescence. The main drawback to this species is its tendency to be monocarpic, meaning that it will die after setting fruit. Plants may self-sow where they are happy.

*-portenschlagiana* (por-ten-schlag-ee-ah' na)  Dalmatian Bellflower  4–6"/12"
    Spring               Blue-Purple          Southern Europe   Zones 4–8
(Syn. *C. muralis*)

This is a particularly effective plant for rock gardens, rock walls, or as potted plants. In the British Isles, it scampers over walls and transforms rockeries and walls into glorious seas of blue. I use it in my garden, and, although the performance does not compare to English standards, it makes an effective ground cover at the front of the bed. The 1–2″ long foliage is triangular and forms low-growing, dark green mats. The 1″ diameter, bell to cup-shaped flowers virtually cover the plant in late spring and early summer.

Although the flowers are smaller than those of *C. carpatica*, it is a better plant for the South. Plants persist for 3–4 years. They are not particularly fussy about growing conditions except drainage must be excellent.

Propagation of the species is easy from seeds or divisions; cultivars are easily divided. The seeds are extremely small and should not be covered. Water from the bottom so seeds will not be washed away. A four-week treatment at 35–40° F promotes germination.

### Cultivars:

'Alba' is a lovely white-flowered cultivar, otherwise similar to the species.
'Bavarica' is a named cultivar, but it looks so similar to the species that I cannot see any difference.
'Major' has larger flowers than the type.
'Resholt's Variety' bears the most vivid blue of the bunch. The best by far.

### Related Species:

*C.* × 'Birch Hybrid' resulted from a cross between *C. portenschlagiana* and *C. poscharskyana*, Serbian bellflower. Nodding, cup-shaped, purple-blue flowers smother the 6″ tall plants. Effective for walls and crevices.

| | | | |
|---|---|---|---|
| *-poscharskyana* (po-shar-skee-ah′ na) | | Serbian Bellflower | 8–12″/12″ |
| Spring | Blue-Lilac | Yugoslavia | Zones 3–7 |

The long 18″ stems are prostrate, resulting in excellent plants for dry walls, rockeries, or edgings of paths. The ½–1″ wide, star-shaped flowers have deeply-cut petals about 4 times as long as the flower tube. The easiest way to remember the difference between this unpronounceable species and the former unpronounceable one is the following. When you see a prostrate, blue campanula with small flowers growing in cracks or on walls, look at the flower shape. If the flowers are star-shaped, star rhymes with *schar* in *poscharskyana*. If they are not, then it is likely the Dalmatian bellflower. The 1½″ long leaves are rounded with wavy margins. This is a good species where a rapidly-spreading, low-growing plant is needed for a sunny area.

Propagate by seed (similar to *C. alliariifolia*) or division in early spring or fall.

### Cultivars:

'Blue Gown' has larger, blue flowers than the species.
'E.H. Frost' bears milky white flowers.
'Lilacina' produces lilac-pink flowers.
'Stella' has wide, star-shaped flowers of vivid violet-blue.

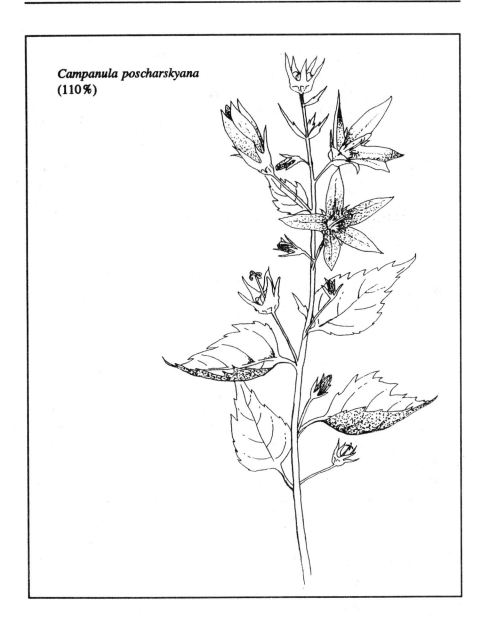

*Campanula poscharskyana*
(110%)

## Related Species:

'E.K. Toogood' is a hybrid of unknown origin but is a handsome garden plant. The heart-shaped, smooth leaves form 6–9″ tall mats on which blue, star-shaped flowers with paler centers are formed in spring and early summer. Probably hardy in zones 4–7.

*-pyramidalis* (pi-ra-mi-dah' lis)      Chimney Bellflower          3–4'/3'
   Summer       Blue, White      Southern Europe      Zones 3–6

This plant is grown as a biennial as it deteriorates badly after the second year. The 2" long, heart-shaped, basal leaves have 6–8" long petioles and dentate margins. Twelve- to fifteen-inch long, pyramidal, racemose panicles of bell-shaped, blue flowers arise from the axil of each stem leaf. More flowers open at the base of the flower stem than at the top, resulting in the pyramidal shape of the inflorescence.

Similar to most other upright species, chimney bellflower does not tolerate heat and humidity and struggles as far north as zone 6. Regardless of locale, stems are brittle, and the plant should be supported. This is a good species for growing in patio containers.

Propagation is similar to other species.

### Cultivars:
'Alba' is similar to the type but with clear white flowers.

'Aureo-variegata' has yellow, variegated foliage.

'Compacta' is a dwarf, 2–3' tall form. It is easier to manage in the garden and requires less room than the type but lacks the characteristic pyramidal shape.

### Related Species:
*C. × fergusonii* (*C. pyramidalis* × *C. carpatica*) has erect, 2' tall stems with carpatica-like, blue flowers. It is seldom seen in North American gardens.

*-rotundifolia* (ro-tund-i-fo' lee-a)      Harebell          6–12"/12"
   Summer       Blue-Violet      Northern Hemisphere      Zones 2–7

This species is circumboreal in distribution and is found in many regions of North America. It is known as the Bluebells of Scotland and well entrenched in song and verse in that country. Probably, the most cold tolerant of the available bellflowers. The 1" wide, basal leaves are rounded, thus "rotundifolia," but often disappear by the time flowering occurs. The 2–3" long stem leaves are linear and grass-like. Many flowering stems are formed, and several ½–1" wide, bell-shaped, nodding flowers are borne in each terminal raceme.

Performance is far better in mountain or northern climates, and plants are ideally suited to the northern United States and Canada. In other areas, they are much more sprawling and weed-like.

Propagate by seeds (similar to *C. alliariifolia*) or division.

### Cultivars:
'Alba' has creamy white flowers but is otherwise similar to the species.

'Flore-plena' has double, blue flowers that are more persistent than the species.

'Olympia' is a good, bright blue-flowered cultivar with 12" tall stems. In our gardens at the University of Georgia (zone 7b), this was pretty the first year, weedy the second, and dead the third.

'Purple Gem' bears rich purple bell flowers in early summer, and the rosette turns a handsome maroon in winter.

'Soldanelliflora' is a unique semi-double variety whose blue flowers are split to the base into about 25 divisions. It is most appropriate for the northern States and Canada.

**Related Species:**

C. divaricata, southern harebell, is native to the southern Appalachians from Maryland to Georgia. The many, small, pale blue flowers are pendulous and are borne in terminal panicles. Little known, but should be more used, particularly by southern gardeners.

| | | | |
|---|---|---|---|
| *-takesimana* (tak-ease-ee-mane' a) | | | 2–3'/3' |
| Summer | Creamy White | Korea | Zones 5–7 |

Relatively new to gardeners, the plants are beginning to enjoy some popularity. From a rosette of heart-shaped leaves, each measuring about 3–4" long, tubular, lilac-pink to off-white flowers are suspended from stems in mid to late summer. The flowers are usually spotted inside, which may be visible from the outside through the thin tissue. Plants can get large and gangly and require a lot of space. Well-drained soils and full sun are necessary.

**Related Species:**

C. punctata, spotted bellflower, bears pendulous, tubular flowers which are spotted or flecked with tiny purple spots. It is similar in habit to C. takesimana but smaller and better behaved. There are a number of color forms ranging from the white 'Alba' to 'Rosea' and the handsome 'Rubrifolia', with purplish flowers spotted with bright red. I am also really smitten with the cultivar 'Elizabeth'. Plants have light green foliage and arching stems carrying dozens of purplish pink bells. If sufficient numbers become available, she could be a winner. 'Cherry Bells', 'Kent Bells' and 'Wedding Bells', from Terra Nova Nursery in Tigard, OR, appear to be outstanding new selections. They have red, cobalt blue and white, bell-shaped flowers respectively. 'Wedding Bells' consist of hose-in-hose flowers (i.e., look like double flowers) on strong, upright stems.

Quick Key to Campanula Species

    A. Plants normally less than 1' tall
      B. Flowers pendulous
        C. Plants less than 6", stem leaves slightly
           toothed or absent, basal leaves ovate . . . . C. cochlearifolia
      CC. Plants greater than 6", stem leaves
           entire and linear, basal leaves
           kidney-shaped to rounded . . . . . . . . . . . C. rotundifolia

BB. Flowers upright or horizontal, not pendulous
   C. Flowers star-shaped
      D. Blue flowers small with white center,
         stem leaves round-toothed . . . . . . . . . . *C. garganica*
      DD. Blue flowers large, stem
         leaves sharply-toothed . . . . . . . . . *C. poscharskyana*
   CC. Flowers not star-shaped
      D. Flowers large (1½″ wide),
         broadly cup-shaped, solitary . . . . . . . . *C. carpatica*
      DD. Flowers smaller, bell-shaped,
         few to a stem . . . . . . . . . . . . . *C. portenschlagiana*
AA. Plants normally greater than 1′ tall
   B. Flowers white, nodding . . . . . . . . . . . . . . *C. alliariifolia*
   BB. Flowers not white (in species), upright
      C. Stem leaves linear to narrowly lance-shaped
         D. Flowers with pedicel . . . . . . . . . . . *C. persicifolia*
         DD. Flowers sessile . . . . . . . . . . . . . . . . . . *C. latiloba*
      CC. Stem leaves oval or rounded in shape
         D. Flowers in dense, clustered head . . . . . . *C. glomerata*
         DD. Flowers in spike-like or racemose inflorescences
            E. Flowers widely bell-shaped to
               saucer-shaped, inflorescence
               pyramidal in shape . . . . . . . . . . . . *C. pyramidalis*
            EE. Flowers narrowly bell-shaped to
               tubular, flowers in branched
               inflorescence or in leaf axils
               F. Flowering stems arching . . . . . . . *C. takesimana*
               FF. Flowering stems upright
                   G. Flowers bell-shaped,
                     carried in panicles . . . . . . . . . . . *C. lactiflora*
                   GG. Flowers much longer than wide,
                     carried singly in leaf axils . . . . . . *C. latifolia*

## Additional Reading:

*Books:*

Bailey, L.H. 1953. *The Garden of Bellflowers.* Macmillan Co. I strongly recommend this book for any would-be Campanulite. It is an excellent reference to the campanulas and other bellflowers (including *Adenophora, Platycodon,* and *Codonopsis*). Unfortunately, it is out of print and will have to be found in a good library or in a book store specializing in old garden books.

*Manuscripts:*

Kelley, J. 1992. Campanulas. *The Garden* 117(7):325–330.
McGary, J. 1993. Campanulas, blue bellflowers can ring in every garden. *Fine Gardening* 34:54–57.

Sheldon, E. 1988. Try campanulas for diversity. *American Horticulturist* 67(6):22–26, 32–35.

## *Canna* (kan′ na)  Canna Lily, Indian Shot  Cannaceae

Approximately 50 species occur in the genus, but finding a true species in the garden is well nigh impossible. The plants which adorn gardens today are known as *C.* × *generalis, C.* × *hybrida,* or just plain garden hybrids. They resulted from crosses among *C. glauca,* gray canna; *C. speciosa; C. iridifolia,* Peruvian canna; *C. warscewiczii;* and the native *C. flaccida,* southern marsh canna. Suffice it to say the nomenclature is rather confusing, and I prefer "garden hybrids." Nomenclature aside, many beautiful hybrids are available which outperform their parents 100 times over.

Cannas placed in rich, well-drained soil in full sun begin to flower in mid summer and continue well into the fall, depending on cultivar. In most of the country, the rootstocks must be lifted after frost has knocked down the leaves. Allow the roots to dry in a warm area for a few days and then store them in moist (not wet!) peat moss where temperatures will remain above 40° F. In zones 7–10, the plants may be overwintered in the ground but no damage will be done if rootstocks are lifted. In the spring, start the rhizomes indoors in pots about 4 weeks before the date of the last frost. Do not plant them too early as they are tender and may be killed by late frosts. Plant single colors en masse, 1′ apart, for maximum effect.

### Cultivars:

There are hundreds of cultivars with single- to multiple-colored flowers and green, dark bronze or purple foliage. Heights range from 1½′ to 7′. Canna specialists are continually releasing new cultivars.

A List of Some Reliable Hybrid Cultivars

|  | Height (ft.) | Leaf color | Flower color |
|---|---|---|---|
| 'Bengal Tiger' ('Pretoria') | 4 | Yellow, green | Orange |
| 'Black Knight' | 3 | Bronze | Dark red |
| 'Brandywine' | 5 | Green | Dark red |
| 'Conestoga' | 5 | Green | Lemon-yellow |
| 'Lucifer' | 3 | Green | Red and yellow |
| 'Orange Beauty' | 4 | Green | Orange |
| 'Pfitzer Chinese Coral' | 2½ | Green | Red |
| 'Pfitzer Crimson Beauty' | 2½ | Green | Crimson-red |
| 'Pink President' | 3 | Green | Pink |
| 'Richard Wallace' | 4 | Green | Yellow |
| 'Rosamunde Cole' | 3½ | Green | Red |
| 'The President' | 3 | Green | Red |
| 'Tropicana Rose' | 2 | Green | Rose |
| 'Wyoming' | 5 | Bronze | Orange |

Propagation of cultivars is accomplished by division of the rootstock. On the roots are many dormant buds, and at least one bud must be present to reproduce the plant. The strongest buds yield the strongest plants. Large clumps can be produced by using root pieces with multiple buds. Seed is available for a number of cultivars, and germination is easy if the seed is first soaked in water for 24 hours to soften the hard coat. The seeds are so hard that natives of the West Indies were said to have used them for shot, thus its other common name, Indian shot. Seeds germinate in 14 days, and plants may flower the first year.

## *Cardamine* (kar-dah' mi-nee)    Bittercress, Cardamine    Brassicaceae

The majority of the 100 species in this genus are natives of cool temperate climates, usually in areas of shade and moisture. Some are rather obnoxious weeds, such as our native hairy bittercress, *C. hirsuta*, but a few are excellent plants for the woodland garden. Recently, the genus *Dentaria*, to which the native toothwort, *D. diphylla*, belongs has been reassigned to the genus *Cardamine*. It seems to me that sufficient differences occurred in these genera to keep them separate, but the genus *Dentaria* ran headlong into the lawnmower of taxonomy and no longer exists. The genus is difficult to characterize, but many of the species have pinnately-divided foliage (*C. diphylla*), while others have round, undivided leaves (*C. bulbosa*). The flowers are usually white, occasionally pink, and are borne on racemes in early spring.

Some European species are grown, including meadow cress or cuckoo flower, *C. pratensis*. Plants have rosettes of finely-dissected, gray-green to glossy green foliage. The small, white to pale pink flowers are blushed with lilac and held on racemes approximately 15" tall. 'Edith' is unique in that she bears lovely double, rose-like, white flowers, which are pink in bud. Plants are more vigorous than the species. This may be a renaming of 'Flore-pleno', which is occasionally offered through specialist nurseries. Native to Europe but hardy in zones 5–7. *C. trifolia*, also native to Europe, has trifoliolate, dark green leaves with long petioles. The plants tend to creep along the ground and send up dozens of white flowers with yellow anthers in the spring. Good looking in moist, woodland gardens and shaded rockeries. The European species may often be found in the western part of the country, but a few of our natives are enjoying a bit of a renaissance in America.

One need not look to Europe for fine garden plants, as numerous natives make outstanding woodland additions. The smooth, rounded-leaf blades of the 10–12" tall *C. bulbosa*, spring cress, with its small (½" long), white spring flowers are worth growing in the woodland area. Native in wet places north to Quebec, south to Florida and west to South Dakota and

Texas. *C. laciniata*, pepper-root, has a similar native range and is characterized by having 3 leaves, each divided into 5 narrow segments and
terminal, white flowers. 'Eco Flamingo' has pink flowers.

The most common species to most gardeners is toothwort or crinkleroot,
*C. diphylla* (syn. *Dentaria diphylla*), easily distinguished from others by
having two leaves (*diphylla*) per stem, both of which are palmately-divided
(like a hand) into 3-toothed segments. The yellowish veins contrast nicely
with the light green leaves. White, 4-petaled flowers arise in April or May.
Native from Quebec and Minnesota, south to Georgia and Alabama. I
visited Don Jacobs at Eco Gardens and was truly impressed with 'Eco
Moonlight', a form with unusually large, creamy white flowers. A
wonderful addition to this little-cultivated plant. 'Eco Cut-leaf' is a smaller
form with deeply-cut leaves. Hardy in zones 3–7. All of the native species
are wonderful woodland plants, asking nothing but giving much.

*Cardiocrinum* (kar-dee-o-kry' num)          Giant Lily          Liliaceae

A genus of about 3 species, but only *C. giganteum* is ever seen or
offered. The flowers resemble true lilies, but the foliage is heart-shaped in
*Cardiocrinum* rather than linear in *Lilium*. Another major difference
between this genus and the true lilies is that plants die after flowering,
although offshoots continue.

Non-flowering shoots grow and die to the ground every year and may
take up to 5 years to flower. Flowering shoots can grow 10' tall and require
considerable room. The huge, heart-shaped, basal leaves give rise to the
leafy stem at the top of which large (6–12" long), white, fragrant trumpets
are formed. No written description can do justice to these remarkable
plants. Unfortunately, one generally has to travel considerable miles to find
such treasures. I have seen them in various gardens in the United Kingdom
but not yet been privy to their beauty in America. That the bulbs are
difficult to find, require ages to flower, are susceptible to voles, moles and
mice, cost a small fortune, die immediately after flowering, and are cold
hardy only to about 15° F, may explain their relative lack of abundance.
However, such minor details never stopped real gardeners. Go find, go
spend, and go enjoy.

Bulbs should be planted with the growing tips at the surface of the
organic soil in semi-shaded conditions. After flowering, remove the offsets
and redistribute about 3' apart. The offsets will reflower in about 5 years,
which is faster than the 7 years required from seed. Have fun!

**Additional Reading:**

Anderton, S. 1993. A bulb to look up to: Cardiocrinum—the giant Himalayan lily. *Gardens Illustrated* 2:116–117, 124.
Johnson, P. 1993. A tale of tall lilies. *New Zealand Gardener* 49(11):30–33.

*Carex* (kah' reks)                    Sedge                    Cyperaceae

Here are some wonderful plants that are laboring as "unknown little grasses" but are easy to grow, relatively available, and provide some marvelous foliage colors for the garden. Perhaps they are ignored because there are about 1000 species of these grass-like plants, many of which are absolutely indistinguishable without keys, magnifiers, and a touch of insanity. Plants are native to many areas of the world, including the United States, Japan, and New Zealand, often occurring in moist areas and swales, forming large areas of marsh land. The flowers may be inconspicuous, and plants are often grown for the foliage, but to say flowers of some species are not ornamental would be an injustice. The unisexual flowers (male and female flowers separate but on the same plant), however, are one of the ways to separate the genus from the closely-related genera *Cyperus* and *Scirpus*, which bear bisexual flowers.

They are frequently described under the section on grasses or sold as "grass look-alikes." The foliage is the most difficult means of telling them apart, but sedges differ from true grasses in a number of ways. In general:

1. The flowering stems of sedges are triangular, easily distinguished by rubbing between your fingers. When looking at sedges and grasses, I always think, "if stems are a wedge, it must be a sedge." My students raise their eyebrows too.

2. The flowering stems are solid and without nodes; in grasses they are usually hollow with nodes.

3. The flowers of sedges are either male or female; in grasses they are perfect (male and female parts on the same flower).

4. Ligules (appendage at junction of sheath and blade) of sedges are obsolete or absent; those of grasses are usually conspicuous.

Many of the species do well in normal garden conditions, and their diversity has led a number of nurseries to offer more of these plants every year. Some foliage is thin and grassy, such as *C. albula*, while others have wider leaves (*C. siderostica*). Plants have been selected for colored or variegated, mostly evergreen, foliage, which make handsome contrast to other low-growing garden species. Every year more species and selections pop up, and differences between them are tough to discern, unless one is a nursery person trying to sell them to you. Few problems occur when growing them in lightly-shaded and moist conditions. I cut back the previous year's foliage in the spring and allowed the new leaves to take over as quickly as possible.

Quick Reference to the Carex Species

|  | Leaf color | Leaf width | Height |
|---|---|---|---|
| *C. buchananii* | Red-brown | < ½" | 15–18" |
| *C. conica* | Green | ≈ 1" | 4–15" |
| *C. elata* | Green | ≈ 1" | 24–30" |
| *C. glauca* | Blue-green | < 1" | 6–10" |
| *C. morrowii* | Deep green | ≈ 1" | 12–18" |
| *C. muskingumensis* | Light green | < 1" | 18–30" |
| *C. siderostrica* | Green | 1–2" | 6–9" |

*-buchananii* (bew-kan-an-ee' eye)     Leatherleaf Sedge     15–18"/18"
                                        New Zealand           Zones 7–9

A terrific sedge for architectural features, the dense tufts of evergreen, very narrow leaves (about ⅟₁₆" wide) are coppery-red, bronze to light brown and look good with many golden and variegated plants. Flowers are inconspicuous. Plants perform well in the northwest but are finicky in most other areas. Beautiful where happy; unfortunately, not often happy. They are best planted in full sun to partial shade in moist soils. Propagate by seed or division.

**Related Species:**

*C. comans*, New Zealand Hair Sedge, is also native to New Zealand and forms long, very thin (less than ⅟₁₆" wide), lax, evergreen leaves. Looks like a long, 1960's head of hair. Foliage color ranges from light green to pale whitish green. Inconspicuous flowers are tucked into the foliage in the summer. Some cultivars offered include 'Bronze', whose brownish foliage gives the appearance of dry, dead plants throughout the season. I can kill plants myself without having to buy them. 'Frosty Curls' is similar to the species but has frosty-white leaves. Plants grow about 1' tall.

*-conica* (kon-i' ca)     Birdfoot Sedge          6–15"/10"
                          Japan, South Korea      Zones 5–8

The tufted plants bear 3-angled stems and flat, evergreen leaves around 1" long but up to 1½" wide. The purplish flowers consist of a terminal, male spike, below which are the small, erect, lateral, female flowers. Plants are quite variable in height, being shortest in areas of cool summer nights and tallest in the heat. A popular sedge for rock gardens and effective even between stepping stones.

**Cultivars:**

'Gold Fountains' is a hybrid form with narrow leaves bordered in gold stripes. Plants grow 12–18" tall.

'Marginata' bears leaves with silver margins.

'Variegata' ('Hime-Kan-suge') has variegated, white foliage. The most handsome and popular cultivar of the species.

| | | |
|---|---|---|
| *-elata* (ee-lay' ta) | Tufted Sedge | 2–3'/3' |
| | Northern Europe | Zones 5–8 |

This tufted sedge forms dense hummocks of light green-yellow, ½–1" wide leaves. Plants grow at the edge of ponds or streams but also perform well in consistently moist soils. They look terrible if allowed to dry out. Not as good for warm climates as for cool areas. The flowers are brownish and arch up and out of the foliage but are not particularly showy. The species is seldom found, but a couple of cultivars are well-known.

**Cultivars:**
'Aurea' has deeper yellow margins, sometimes sold as 'Bowles Golden'.
'Bowles Golden' is terrifically handsome and most available. The leaves are
    golden-yellow with thin, green margins. The yellow color fades as
    temperatures rise in the summer.
'Knightshaye's' is similar, not quite as big, but the foliage has no green
    margins.

| | | |
|---|---|---|
| *-glauca* (glau' ca) | Blue Sedge | 6–10"/10" |
| | Europe | Zones 5–8 |

(Syn. *C. flacca*)

A number of sedges have bluish foliage, and this slow grower is one with narrow leaves and a rhizomatous growth habit which makes it effective as a ground cover. Plants are stoloniferous, and decent colonies occur after 2–3 years. The foliage is bluer on the underside than on top but makes a good contrast with dark green leaves of neighboring plants. Prefers moisture but quite tolerant of drying out.

**Related Species:**
    *C. flaccosperma*, wide blue sedge, has wide (1"), blue-gray, evergreen foliage. The compact plants are about 18" tall. Moisture is needed for best performance.

| | | |
|---|---|---|
| *-morrowii* (mo-row-ee' eye) | Japanese Sedge | 12–18"/12" |
| | Japan | Zones 5–9 |

Compact tufts of plants occur under partial shade or sun. In the heavily-shaded Armitage garden, the dense growth keeps getting denser. Plants of the species grow about 15" tall; the stiff, evergreen leaves have margins rough to the touch and taper at the tip. Species are seldom seen, but some good cultivars are available.

**Cultivars:**
'Goldband' ('Aureovariegata') has a clean golden variegation around the margins of the green leaves. Plants produce rigid, semi-upright growth about 12″ tall. Similar to 'Variegata', but the gold margins provide a distinctive golden cast.
'Hime-kansuge' is relatively new to the United States, with dark green, stiff leaves with a clean white edge.
'Silk Tassel', also sold as 'Temnolepis', has looked terrific in the Armitage shade, producing long, lax, narrow leaves, resulting in a 6″ tall mophead. Narrow, white bands run down the length of the long leaves.
'Variegata' is the most popular of the cultivars of the genus, has silvery-white margins on 12″ tall plants. Similar in habit to 'Goldband'.

**Related Species:**
*C. oshimensis* 'Evergold' forms dense clumps with a pale yellowish or white center on the narrow, weeping leaves. The lush, arching foliage is used to advantage, spilling over rocky slopes or into pools. Very similar to 'Silk Tassel'. This is sometimes listed as a cultivar of *C. morrowii* or *C. hachioensis* as well as having numerous cultivar names in the last few years.

*-muskingumensis* (mus-king-u-men′ sis)     Palm Sedge     18–30″/18″
Eastern North America     Zones 5–8

One of the most distinct sedges, the crowded, willowy, green foliage forms atop the 1–2′ tall stems, resembling miniature palm trees. The "palm-like" form can be seen easier in mid-season than at the beginning of the year. The plants tend to flop, spill, and then slowly creep. They prefer a little shade, but full sun is tolerated, as long as moisture is present. Too much shade results in toppled plants.

**Cultivars:**
'Oehme', selected from the garden of the fine designer, Wolfgang Oehme, has a clear yellow border around the leaves. Similar in habit to the species but brighter in the summer.
'Wachtposten' ('Sentry') is similar but with handsome weeping foliage. More architecturally pleasing than the species.

**Related Species:**
*C. pendula*, drooping sedge, is tall (2–3′) and bears pendulous, 3′ leaves and drooping inflorescences. It is noted for its long, arching, flower spikes and vertically-hanging flowers. Needs moisture and semi-shaded conditions.

*-siderostrica* (sid-er-o-stric′ a)     Broad-Leaved Sedge     6–10″/9″
Zones 5–8

Plants form a slow-growing colony and produce some of the widest leaves (1–2″) in the genus. Plants are deciduous in all but the mildest climates. They grow well in semi-shaded, moist conditions. In cooler areas, the new growth is tinged pink as it emerges.

### Cultivars:

'Variegata' is the most popular cultivar due to the white stripes along the margins of the leaves.

### Related Species:

*C. plantaginea*, plantain sedge, also has wide (over 1″ wide), flattened, green leaves. The showy flowers are brownish black and emerge before the foliage matures in early spring.

Quick Key to Carex Species

A. Leaves wider than 1″
   B. Leaves deciduous, usually 6–10″ tall . . . . . . *C. siderostrica*
   BB. Leaves evergreen, usually more than 10″ tall . . . . *C. conica*
AA. Leaves less than 1″ wide
   B. Leaves usually brownish or purple . . . . . . . *C. buchananii*
   BB. Leaves usually green
      C. Usually more than 2′ tall
         D. Leaves crowded at top of stem,
           leaves less than 1″ wide . . . . . . . *C. muskingumensis*
         DD. Leaves not at top of stem,
           leaves approx. 1″ wide . . . . . . . . . . . . . *C. elata*
      CC. Usually less than 2′ tall
         D. Leaves with blue cast, at least
           on lower side, ¼ to ½″ wide . . . . . . . . . *C. glauca*
         DD. Leaves not blue, approx. ½ to 1″ wide . . . *C. morrowii*

### Additional Reading:

Anon. 1993. Switch grass and sedges. *Avant Gardener* 25(10):74–75.
Greenlee, J. 1993. Sedge lawns. *Plants and Gardens* 49(3):75–79.

### *Caryopteris* (ka-ree-op′ te-ris)       Bluebeard       Verbenaceae

Although this genus consists of woody species, plants lose leaves and may die back to ground in the winter, thus are often treated as herbaceous perennials. Violet-blue to lavender-blue flowers that almost encircle the stem appear in late summer and fall on the current season's growth. Excellent plants for the garden with few insect or disease problems. There are about 10 species from eastern Asia, of which two are valuable and overlooked garden plants.

Quick Reference to Caryopteris Species:

|  | Height (ft.) | Flowers whorled all the way around stem |
|---|---|---|
| *C.* × *clandonensis* | 3–5 | No |
| *C. incana* | 3–5 | Yes |

| -× *clandonensis* (klan-don-en' sis) | | Blue Mist | 3–4'/4' |
|---|---|---|---|
| Summer | Blue | Hybrid Origin | Zones 5–9 |

This hybrid, between *C. indica* and *C. mongholica*, was raised in West Clandon, England (thus its specific epithet), in 1930. The opposite leaves are narrow, up to 3½″ long, and the undersides are gray-white. They are usually entire but occasionally may be coarsely-toothed. Up to 20 flowers are held in a tight, 1–2″ diameter cyme, and two cymes are borne in each of the upper, 3–4 leaf axils. The inflorescences lean toward the outside of the plant, giving the appearance of the flowers being one-sided.

Full sun and well-drained soils result in maximum performance. Wet winters can cause significant dieback when plants releaf in the spring. The flowers are a welcome late summer relief from the many yellow daisies which flower at that time. They contrast well with those same yellows.

Propagate by terminal cuttings in spring or early summer.

**Cultivars:**

'Arthur Simmonds' was selected in the 1930's in the garden of the late Arthur Simmonds of West Clandon, Surrey, England. Plants are 2' tall and consist of dull green, 1–2″ long leaves and dark blue flowers.

'Azure' has light blue flowers on a 3' tall shrub.

'Blue Mist' has gray-green foliage and light blue flowers.

'Dark Knight' bears the darkest blue flowers of any other cultivars.

'Ferndown' has dark green foliage and dark blue flowers. Raised in Ferndown Nurseries, Dorset, England. As dark-flowered as 'Dark Knight', which look suspiciously alike.

'Heavenly Blue' is of American origin and has darker green leaves, deeper blue flowers, and is altogether a superior plant to *C.* × *clandonensis*. Seed propagation of this cultivar has resulted in much variation, making it more difficult to distinguish. 'Blue Mist' and 'Dark Knight' may have resulted as sports of 'Heavenly Blue'.

'Kew Blue' resulted from a seedling of 'Arthur Simmonds' and was raised in Kew Gardens. Flowers are a darker blue than 'Arthur Simmonds'.

'Longwood Blue' was selected at Longwood Gardens, Kennett Square, PA. Plants have silvery foliage, bear sky blue flowers in late summer, and grow 1½–2' tall.

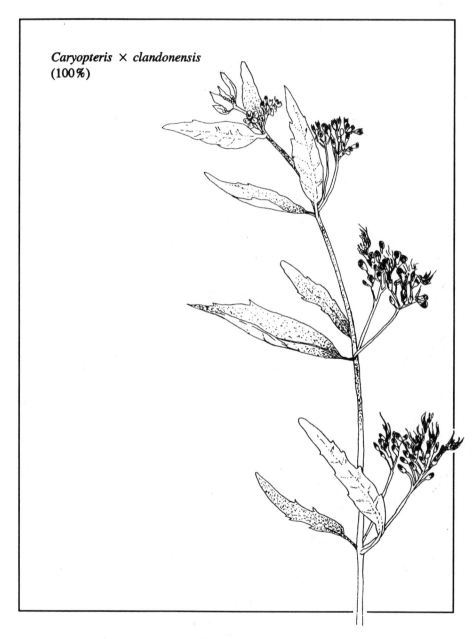

*Caryopteris* × *clandonensis*
(100%)

'Worcester Gold' is the easiest form to distinguish due to the yellow-gold foliage which contrasts with the blue flowers. Raised by St. Johns Nursery, Worcester, England. The foliage fades in climates with hot summers but looks wonderful in the spring and early summer.

**Related Species:**

*C. nepalensis* (syn. *C. divaricata*) bears many loose, blue-purple flowers on 4' tall plants. The large leaves are smelly, and, regardless of the claims of those who sell plants, they stink when crushed. Certainly an interesting plant.

| | | | |
|---|---|---|---|
| *-incana* (in-cah' na) | | Common Bluebeard | 3–5'/4' |
| Late Summer | Blue | China, Japan | Zones 8–10 |
| (Syn. *C. mastacanthus*) | | | |

There are few obvious differences in the foliage between this and the previous species. The leaves of this species are not quite as gray-green or as long (only 1–3") and linear, and are always coarsely-toothed. The flowers are violet-blue and held in cymes in the upper leaf axils. The main differences between this and the previous species are in the habit (more upright) and the flower arrangement. Each cyme has many more flowers than *C.* × *clandonensis*, and totally envelop the stem. It is much more ornamental, and the flowers are not one-sided as in the previous hybrid. Flowering begins in early August and persists for at least 8 weeks. We have experimented with this species in the cut flower trials at Georgia, and the flowers are excellent and long lasting.

Plants require full sun and well-drained soils. The main drawback is the relative lack of cold hardiness, and plants are not suitable north of zone 7b. Even in zone 7b, mulch should be applied around the base of the plant. The first hard frost kills back the top growth, and plants may be cut back to 18–24" any time thereafter.

Propagate by seed in warm, humid conditions. Two- to three-inch terminal cuttings of new growth also root readily.

Quick Key to Caryopteris Species

    A. Leaves 2–3½" long, flowers one-sided on stem,
        flowers bright blue, foliage gray-green . . . . *C.* × *clandonensis*
    AA. Leaves 1–3" long, flowers envelop stem,
         flowers violet-blue, foliage green . . . . . . . . . . . . *C. incana*

**Additional Reading:**

Pattison, G. 1989. *Caryopteris* × *clandonensis*. *The Plantsman* 11(1):16–19.

*Catananche* (kat-a-nan' ke)      Cupid's Dart      Asteraceae

The common name comes from the fact that the plants were once used by the ancient Greeks as an important ingredient in love potions, and its presence in bouquets is still used to symbolize love. Flowers are useful for fresh or dried cut flowers. Plants should be placed in full sun in well-drained soils. There are five species in the genus, but only one, *C. caerulea*, is grown to any extent.

*-caerulea* (se-ru' lee-a)          Blue Cupid's Dart          18–30"/12"
  Summer          Blue          Southwest Europe          Zones 4–7

The foliage is mostly basal and narrow, and usually entire or with a few small teeth. Each leaf is woolly pubescent on both sides, with 3 veins running the length. The 8–12" long leaves are silver-green, particularly when young, as are the flower buds. The blue, dandelion-like flowers are about 2" in diameter and borne singly on long, naked flower stems. The bracts beneath the flowers are arranged in many series, like shingles on a roof. Each ray flower is strap-shaped, while the disk flowers (the center) are darker blue. The yellow stamens provide a pleasing contrast. They perform poorly in southern gardens due to the warm temperatures and high humidity in the summer.

Some commercial growers force flowers on this plant in the greenhouse in early spring. To do so, long days (day lengths longer than 12 hours) are necessary for flower production.

Propagation of the species is not difficult from seed. If sown in March or April, plants will flower the first year. Barely cover the seed in the seed tray. Cultivars can be raised by root cuttings (see *Anemone* × *hybrida*) in the spring.

### Cultivars:

'Alba' is a white-flowered form which is not nearly as handsome as the type.
'Bi-color' may be the solution for those who can't decide between white- and blue-flowered cultivars. It has white petals with a dark center and is often used for dried, floral bouquets.
'Blue Giant' has dark blue flowers decorating a 2' tall, stout plant.
'Major' produces lavender-blue flowers and is nearly 3' tall.
'Perry's White' is similar to 'Alba' and may even be the same clone.

### Related Species:

*C. caespitosum* is a yellow-flowered form of the genus, growing about 12" tall with handsome blue-green foliage. I saw this growing in the Edinburgh Botanical Garden but have not been able to find any sources in North America. Interesting possibilities.

*Caulophyllum* (kaw-lo-fill' um)          Blue Cohosh          Berberidaceae

This little-known genus contains 2 species, one Asian and one North American. The later is the only one occasionally offered by nurserymen. They are plants for the lightly-shaded garden and thrive in moist conditions, doing poorly if allowed to dry out. They may be propagated by seed or division in the fall or spring.

*-thalictroides* (tha-lik' troi-deez)          Blue Cohosh          12–18"/12"
  Spring          Yellow-Green          Eastern North America          Zones 4–7

This woodland plant is native from southeastern Canada to Alabama and Mississippi. The thickened rootstock sends up fleshy, grayish green stems, with one to two many-divided (triternate) leaves. The leaf is 3-lobed at the base, with each lobe deeply cut into three, 1-4" long, narrow segments. The small, ½" long, yellow-green flowers occur before leaves mature. They are rather nondescript and are held in a loose panicle. The main reason for including this species in the shade garden, however, is the appearance of the blue, grape-like berries in late summer which stand erect above the foliage. The berries remain even after the foliage has withered and provide a rich, deep blue for the late fall landscape. These are outstanding in Garden in the Woods in Framingham, MA, and don't look half bad in the Armitage garden as well. However, they are not well adapted to heat and humidity.

## *Centaurea* (sen-tor′ ree-a)     Cornflower, Knapweed     Asteraceae

*Centaurea* contains approximately 500 species, and about a dozen are useful garden plants. A number of excellent annual species occur such as *C. cyanus* (bachelor's button), *C. americana* (purple basket flower), and *C. moschata* (sweet sultan). The latter two species produce excellent cut flowers. *C. cineraria* (dusty miller) is a popular gray-leaf bedding and edging plant. The cornflowers are a diverse group of plants, but all have overlapping scales immediately beneath the petals as one of the identifying characteristics of the genus. The leaves are alternate and may be once or twice divided.

All prefer full sun and good drainage. If placed in too much shade, plants become lanky and weedy. They are easily propagated from seed, and no particular problems with germination should be encountered if the seed is fresh. Many of the hardy species can also be propagated from divisions and should be divided every 2-3 years.

*Centaurea* is a genus awash in ancient Greek folklore. It is said to have healed Chiron the Centaur. This, in itself, may not seem reason enough to name a genus after such an event because, as we all know, most Centaurs were wild and lawless. Chiron, however, unlike most of his kind, was wise and just. He was a magnificent teacher and, having been healed by that innocuous cornflower, went on to teach many Greek heroes, including Achilles. Next time you see a bachelor's button, think of Chiron.

Quick Reference to Centaurea Species

|  | Height (in.) | Flower color | Flower diam. (in.) | Foliage color (top) |
|---|---|---|---|---|
| *C. dealbata* | 20–30 | Lavender | 2½–3 | Green |
| *C. hypoleuca* | 8–24 | Rose, pink | ½–2 | Gray-green |
| *C. macrocephala* | 36–48 | Yellow | 3–3½ | Green |
| *C. montana* | 18–24 | Blue | 1–2 | Green |
| *C. nigra* | 12–18 | Violet | 1–1½ | Green |
| *C. pulchra* | 24–36 | Pink | 3–3½ | Gray-green |

*-dealbata* (deel-bah' ta)      Persian Cornflower      20–30"/18"
Late Spring      Lavender      Asia Minor, Persia      Zones 3–7

The foliage is up to 2' long, coarsely cut into pinnate lobes, with long, whitish hairs on the underside. The deeply-fringed flower heads are solitary and carried atop a slender stem bearing small, sessile, entire leaves. The bracts at the base of the petals (involucre bracts) are deeply fringed like the flowers. The 2–3" diameter flowers appear in late spring in the South (early summer in the North) and continue for approximately 4 weeks. The warm days and nights in zones 7 and 8 tend to make them stretch and require staking. In zone 7b, plants melt out in the summer and decline within 3 years. They are better plants for the North, where their stems are thicker and less likely to fall over.

## Cultivars:
'Steenbergii' is more compact in plant habit and flowers longer than the species. The flowers have clear white centers, surrounded by deep rosy petals.

## Related Species:
*C. simplicicaulis* is shorter, growing only 9–15" tall. The deeply-segmented foliage has handsome whitish venation on the top and gray coloration on the underside of the leaves. The pink flowers occur in June and July. Full sun and good drainage are necessary. Hardy in zones 4–7.

*-hypoleuca* (high-po-loo' ka)      Knapweed      18–24"/18"
Summer      Rose-Purple, Pink      Armenia      Zones 4–7

There is little difference between this species and the previous, except that it is more compact and the leaves are grayer. The flowers are smaller (1 ½–2" diameter), although named cultivars may have flowers up to 4" across.

## Cultivars:
There has been some confusion concerning the parentage of 'John Coutts', an excellent lavender-colored centaurea. It was originally thought to be a cultivar of *C. dealbata* and is usually offered as such in catalogs. Further study by Graham Stuart Thomas, the noted British plantsman, switched it to *C. hypoleuca*, and some catalogs offer it in that manner. Other nurseries have decided that it really does not matter and offer it as *C.* 'John Coutts'. The bottom line to the gardener is that if you obtain 'John Coutts', you will have a pretty good garden performer.

*-macrocephala* (mak-ro-ceph' a-la)    Armenian Basket Flower    3–4'/2'
Summer      Yellow      Armenia      Zones 3–7

This is one of my favorite plants when grown in a favorable environment. The large, bright yellow flowers are 3–4" in diameter and excellent

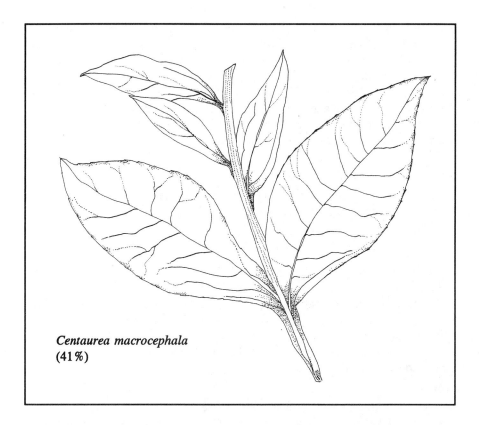

*Centaurea macrocephala*
(41%)

cut flowers. They last up to 10 days in water and are well established in upscale florists' shops. The coarse, 5-6″ long leaves are entire with wavy margins. The involucre bracts (see *C. dealbata*) are brown and papery and add to the coarse appearance of the flower. In Michigan (zone 5), it reaches 4′ tall with full yellow flowers and deep green leaves. On the other hand, in our trials in North Georgia (zone 7b), it struggles to reach 2′, and the flowers are small and persist but a short time.

| *-montana* (mon-tan′ nah) | | Mountain Bluet | 18–24″/12″ |
|---|---|---|---|
| Early Summer | Blue | Europe | Zones 3–8 |

In the North, this plant is a weed—a very pretty weed, but a weed nevertheless. I remember this plant taking over almost the entire garden in Montreal and the difficulty in removing it. Where we could keep it confined, it was lovely, but little did we suspect its travelling ways when we so innocently planted it. Even aware of its dark side, I still enjoy the bluets for their rich blue flower color and unique flower shape. It is a cool season species and does not have the same vigor in the South as in the North. Regardless of locale, it is stoloniferous and will be something of a rover. Plants perform best in high pH soils. The 2–2½" diameter flowers consist of long ray petal flowers around the margin and short disc flowers in the center. The outer ray flowers are tubular, and the ends are divided into 3–5 short segments. The normal color of the flowers is deep blue with a reddish center. Another lovely characteristic of this species is the black margin around each involucre bract (see *C. dealbata*). The bracts overlap like shingles and add to the value of the flower. The foliage is entire and silvery-white when young.

**Cultivars:**
'Alba' has white flowers.
'Grandiflora' has larger violet-blue flowers than the species.
'Rosea' ('Carnea') bears pink flowers.
'Violetta' produces amethyst flowers.

| *-nigra* (ni' gra) | | Hardhats | 1–1½'/1' |
|---|---|---|---|
| Summer | Violet | Europe | Zones 3–7 |

Having escaped from cultivation, plants can be found in fields throughout the eastern United States. The flowers and petioles are dark violet, and the solitary, ball-like flowers are responsible for the common name. This is a coarse, somewhat weedy species, but the violet color contrasts well with the whites and pale yellows of summer.

**Cultivars:**
'Rivularis' is similar to the species but more compact.
'Variegata' has leaves edged with creamy white and is most striking.

**Related Species:**
*C. kotschyana*, Kotschy's cornflower, grows 3' tall and bears deep purple to blood red flowers. Plant in full sun in well-drained soil.

| *-pulchra* (pul' kra) | | Pink Knapweed | 2–3'/2' |
|---|---|---|---|
| Summer | Rose-Pink | Kashmir | Zones 5–7 |

This species is seldom seen in the United States, a fact I cannot figure out. There is no reason why this handsome plant should not be as common as *C. macrocephala*. In Holland, I have seen fields of this plant grown for cut flower production, and in many countries of northern Europe it is an outstanding garden plant. In *Hardy Plants of Distinction* (1965), Alan Bloom states, "the real aristocrat amongst centaureas is surely *C. pulchra* 'Major'." What are we waiting for?

It is similar in habit to *C. macrocephala*, and, without the flower, the two may be confused. The pinnately-compound leaves are smooth and more gray-green than the former species. The flowers are large (3" in diameter), borne singly on stout stems, but differ from *C. macrocephala* in being pink and having almost white flower buds, compared to the tawny brown flower buds of the Armenian Basket Flower. It may be slightly less hardy than *C. macrocephala*, but limits of hardiness have not been established with certainty in North America.

**Cultivars:**
'Major' is larger and more vigorous than the type and is a better garden plant.

**Related Species:**
*C. pulcherrima*, pink bachelor button, bears large heads of rosy-pink flowers in late spring and early summer. Persistent flowerer and attractive to butterflies and goldfinches. Hardy in zones 3 to 7.

Quick Key to Centaurea Species

    A.  Leaves entire
        B.  Flowers blue or violet
            C.  Flowers blue, ray flowers on margins very
                 different than ray flowers near center  . . . . . . *C. montana*
            CC. Flowers violet, ray flowers similar . . . . . . . . . *C. nigra*
        BB. Flowers yellow or rose
            C.  Flowers yellow, foliage green
                 on both sides . . . . . . . . . . . . . . . . . . *C. macrocephala*
            CC. Flowers rose to pink, foliage gray-green  . . . . . *C. pulchra*
    AA. Leaves cut once or twice, not entire
        B.  Leaves smooth above, white, hairy beneath  . . . . *C. dealbata*
        BB. Leaves gray-green on both sides  . . . . . . . . . *C. hypoleuca*

*Centranthus* (ken-tran' thus)  Red Valerian, Jupiter's Beard  Valarianaceae

The genus consists of about a dozen species, but few are used in American gardens. They are all good border plants and grow in alkaline soils in full sun. The name comes from *kentron*, spur, and *anthos*, flower, as the corolla (the petals) is spurred at the base.

*-ruber* (rew' ber)                  Red Valerian           18–36"/24"
    Spring          Pink-Red         Europe                 Zones 5–8

This old-fashioned garden plant is the best of the genus. The sessile, opposite, blue-green leaves are about 4" long and sometimes toothed at the base, although more often entire. The individual flowers are only ½" long but numerous flowers occur on the terminal cymes in late spring and summer. Red valerian thrives on infertile, limey soils, and there are few stone walls this plant has met that it does not like.

The white cliffs of Dover, England take on a red hue in spring as the precariously perched plants flower profusely up and down the limestone cliffs. In fact, there are few nooks and crannies in northern Europe that this plant does not inhabit. In the United States, Salinas, California is the Dover of America, where *Centranthus* beautifies side streets and sidewalks. Wander through much of coastal California, and you will find this plant right at home. It may not be quite as nomadic as in England but is certainly no slouch where it is comfortable. In this country, particularly in the North and West, plants are equally aggressive, to the point that gardeners yank it out of the ground, stomp all over it, and toss it nonchalantly into the compost pile. In the South, plants are not nearly as tough. Insects and pests are non-existent, and little more than irrigation and sunshine are required. Cut flowers last about 1 week in water.

Propagation is easy by seed, and, in most seed batches, reds, whites, and sometimes rose-flowered plants will occur. Plants flower the first year from seed. Division in the spring or fall is necessary to maintain true colors.

### Cultivars:

Var. *albus* produces clean white flowers and is an excellent plant.
Var. *coccineus* has deep red flowers.
Var. *roseus* bears rose-colored flowers.

## *Cephalaria* (seff-al-ay′ ri-a)  Cephalaria  Dipsacaceae

Although consisting of over 60 large, coarse species, few are encountered in the United States. They are closely related to *Scabiosa* and bear opposite toothed or pinnate-like leaves and terminal white or yellow flowers. Of the many species identified, one is commonly available with 3 or 4 others occasionally found in the trade. *C. scabra* is about only 3′ tall and bears white flowers, and *C. radiata* is a little over 3′ tall with creamy white flowers. Double-flowered forms may also be found in selections of *C. uralensis*. I think all species are marvelous and should be used far more.

| | | | |
|---|---|---|---|
| *-gigantea* (gi-gan′ tee-a) | Tatarian Cephalaria | | 5–6′/4′ |
| Summer | Yellow | Caucausus | Zones 3–7 |
| (Syn. *C. tatarica*) | | | |

*C. gigantea* is a coarse, tall plant whose 7–8′ height can dominate the summer garden. Grown in full sun, plants may not need staking; however, if pinched early (not recommended), they may mature at 5–6′ and be 5′ wide. The striped stem produces dark green, pinnatifid leaves (leaves are deeply cleft in broad divisions almost to the midrib but without separating into distinct leaflets) with each division having toothed margins and hairy undersides. The primrose-yellow flowers produced at the end of the 2′ wiry stems are flattened and scabiosa-like (at one time this species was in the genus *Scabiosa*). The 2″ diameter flower heads are made up of many individual, 4-parted florets, and the marginal florets are enlarged and radiate outward. Flowering persists on and off throughout the summer.

Plants look best at the back of the garden where their coarseness may be reduced, but where their attributes may still be enjoyed. The flowers provide a lovely soft yellow not often found in gardens. Place in full sun and provide adequate moisture. If allowed to dry out, the leaf margins turn black, and the foliage quickly deteriorates. Plants decline in the fall and should be cut back after flowering.

Occasionally I get confused between this species and the very similar-flowered *Scabiosa ochroleuca*, cream scabious. Both bear primrose-yellow flowers, similar pinnatifid leaves, and flower at the same time. The most obvious difference is the much larger stature of *Cephalaria gigantea*, being triple or quadruple the height, and larger flowers. However, height and vigor are not particularly precise, and additional differences may be of interest. The flower heads of *S. ochroleuca* are seldom wider than 1½″. The leaves are coarser; each division of *C. gigantea* leaves is roughly toothed, while those of *S. ochroleuca* are finer and almost entire. Lastly, the most fundamental difference, although the least obvious, occurs under the flower heads. In all species of *Cephalaria*, the bracts immediately under the flower heads occur in many series (more than two), while in all *Scabiosa* species the bracts always occur in one or two series only.

Propagation by seed is easiest if seed is placed in sand at 40° F for approximately 6 weeks. After 6 weeks, sow seed and sand in peat:vermiculite mix under warm (70–75° F), humid conditions. Divisions may also be used, and plants need dividing every 2–3 years to maintain vigor. Plants will reseed where comfortable.

**Related Species:**

*C. alpina*, yellow cephalaria, is shorter and differs mainly in the marginal flowers, which are not as enlarged and about half the size. The plants are 3–4′ tall, and the stems are covered with fine, soft hairs, giving an appearance and feel of velvet. Sometimes plants offered as *C. alpina* are simply smaller variants of *C. gigantea*.

*Cerastium* (ser-ass′ ti-um)     Snow-in-Summer     Caryophyllaceae

The genus is sufficiently confusing that taxonomists cannot decide if there are 60 or 100 species; probably the number is somewhere between. The main species found in gardens, however, evoke emotions of love or hate from gardeners. When in flower, the plants literally look like shiny mounds of snow in summer. Perhaps because I watch *Cerastium* "melt out" in summer in the South, I appreciate it more than most. In England, it is rampageous and has been described as "A thug and a strangler . . .", and an "unpromising race of weeds . . ." by Alan Titchmarsh in *The Rock Gardeners Handbook*. Few areas in this country, other than the Pacific Northwest, enjoy the luxury of it being a weed. In any event, *Cerastium* provides several excellent species for the wall, rock garden, or borders along paths, and, if plants gets out of hand, simply "tear them up by the roots . . . or burn by the barrow-load" (Titchmarsh).

Ideally full sun is required in the North and partial shade in the South. Shear off the flowers after they fade to maintain plant vigor. The fact that it will grow in pure sand is a telling reminder that drainage should be excellent and feeding minimal. In the Horticulture Gardens at Georgia, the plants are wonderful until about the first of June, then rapidly decline to return the next spring.

Propagate by seed collected in summer, by divisions in spring or fall, or by softwood cuttings.

| *-tomentosum* (toe-men-toe' sum) | Snow-in-Summer | 6–8"/12" |
|---|---|---|
| Late Spring          White | Italy, Sicily | Zones 2–7 |

This is the most common species, and the silvery leaves and bright white flowers are a welcome sight in late spring and early summer. Plants do not tolerate heat well, and the centers decline where summers are hot and humid. The leaves are ½–¾" long, and the tips resemble the end of a spatula (spatulate). The petals are deeply divided, so there appear to be 10 petals instead of 5. It spreads by underground runners and quickly fills in an area or covers a wall. Plants look terrific around dwarf conifers.

This is a fine, tough plant for northern areas and often cursed by its own performance. Where it does well, people take it for granted and belittle its contributions to the spring garden. In the South, gardeners hold their breath in the summer, hoping that it will establish itself well enough to provide another show next spring. Unfortunately, they are often disappointed.

Sow seeds on the top of the peat:vermiculite mix but do not cover. Place the tray in warm (70–75° F), humid conditions. Germination occurs in 14–21 days, after which the seedlings should be placed at 55–65° F. Division may be accomplished anytime during the growing season.

### Cultivars:

'Columnae' and 'Silver Carpet', which may be the same, are more matted and compact than the type. 'Columnae' may be less aggressive.

'Yo-yo' has a compact growth habit (about 6" tall), silvery-gray leaves, and does not spread as rapidly as the species. With a name like that, it should be a hit.

### Related Species:

*C. alpinum*, alpine chickweed, forms silver-gray, 2–3" tall mats more or less densely covered with wavy, gray-white hairs. Hardy as far north as zone 2.

*C. biebersteinii*, taurus chickweed, is similar except that leaves are larger (1–1½" long, ⅕" wide) and not spatulate. The petals are deeply notched at the ends and about twice as long as the calyx. The foliage is silvery-gray because of the long, white hairs covering the plant. The minor differences between these two species and others have resulted in some authorities lumping them all together in a collective sense, and the two species are often placed in the "*C. tomentosum* group."

**Additional Reading:**
Kelaidis, P. A celebration of silver leaves. *Fine Gardening* 31:64–67.

## *Ceratostigma* (ser-at-o- stig' ma)          Leadwort          Plumbaginaceae

This genus of 7–8 species has alternate, rather bristly leaves. There are two excellent garden species, one commonly available, and one which deserves greater use in the American landscape, particularly in the South.

Quick Reference to Ceratostigma Species

|  | Height (in.) | Fall color |
| --- | --- | --- |
| *C. plumbaginoides* | 8–12 | Yes |
| *C. willmottianum* | 24–36 | No |

| *-plumbaginoides* (plum-bah-gi-noi' deez) | Leadwort | 8–12"/18" |
| --- | --- | --- |
| Late Summer          Blue | China | Zones 5–8 |

(Syn. *Plumbago larpentae*)

The 1–2" long, alternate leaves have short petioles and are borne on many branched, angular stems which die back to the ground in the fall. The deep gentian blue, ¾" diameter flowers are arranged in terminal heads and flower from late summer well into fall.

This is a terrific species, looking equally good in Athens, Georgia and Columbus, Ohio. They tolerate full sun, but afternoon shade results in more open plants which spread more freely. As a ground cover in sunny areas or as a plant to ramble over small rocks, it is difficult to beat. In the fall, the foliage turns bronzy-red, and, although plants won't compete with red maple or kochia for fall color, they are quite striking. Leaves emerge late in the spring, so patience is important. Plants in zone 5 should be mulched.

Leadwort is also a good subject for forcing into flower in the greenhouse. The use of artificial long days in the winter or spring causes flower initiation and development. Plants which are forced to flower in the spring will also flower in late summer if placed in the garden.

Propagate by cuttings, spring division or seed. Seed germinates more uniformly if placed in sand in a plastic bag and stratified for 4–6 weeks at 40° F. Root cuttings may also be used (See *Anemone*).

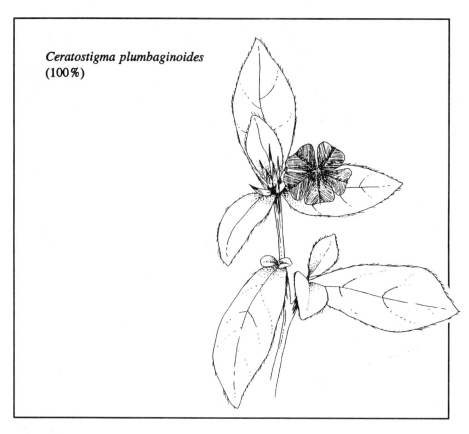

*Ceratostigma plumbaginoides*
(100%)

## Related Species:

*C. griffithii*, Griffith's leadwort, differs from the above in that the leaves have a red margin and are evergreen. A handsome plant with deep blue flowers. Probably hardy in zones 6 to 8.

*-willmottianum* (wil-mot-ee-a' num)      Chinese Leadwort        24–36"/2'
   Late Summer          Blue          Western China       Zones 8–9

This shrubby member may grow 5' tall, although 2–3' is more realistic. The 2" long, pointed leaves have coarse hairs on both sides and taper at the base, while the 5-lobed flowers, violet-blue with a rosy-red tube, persist for 6–8 weeks. The leaf buds are covered with short scales in this species but are naked in *C. plumbaginoides*.

This is a most interesting plant, being a subshrub similar to *Caryopteris* and *Perovskia*. The leaves are smaller than those of the previous species, yet the plant is twice as tall. The greatest drawback is the relative lack of cold hardiness but is a fine plant where it is hardy.

Propagation is similar to *C. plumbaginoides*.

Quick Key to Ceratostigma Species

   A. Plant low-growing, less than 18″, foliage
      turns red in the fall, buds without scales . . . . *C. plumbaginoides*
  AA. Plants greater than 18″ tall, foliage
      remains green in the fall, buds scaly . . . . . . *C. willmottianum*

## *Chamaelirium* (cam-aye-leer-e′ um)    Fairy Wand    Liliaceae

Only one species occurs, *C. luteum*, which extends from eastern Massachusetts to Ontario and Michigan, south to Florida, Mississippi, and Arkansas. All sorts of common names exist for this plant, but most make no sense at all. Names such as blazing star (neither star-like nor blazing), Devil's-bit or Devil's-bite (nothing devilish here) are also bandied about. The name *Chamaelirium* means "dwarf lily," but it is not lily-like, the specific epithet *luteum* means yellow, and the flowers are white. Plants do, however, resemble a wand, fairy's or otherwise.

The plants are about 2–3′ tall, although they can reach 4′ in height. The basal leaves are blunt and broadest at the tips, and the stem leaves are narrow and generally point upward. Plants arise from rhizomes, and bear cylindrical racemes of either male or female flowers (similar to *Aruncus*). Male flower stems are longer and more pendant than the shorter, upright, female flower stems. Plants are not well-known except to native plant enthusiasts, but it is terrific for shady, woodland conditions. Do not dig from the wild!

## *Chasmanthium* (chas-man-the′ um)    Northern Sea Oats    Poaceae
(Syn. *Uniola*)

Although about 6 species occur in the genus, only *C. latifolium*, northern sea oats, is grown for the garden. Plants produce many linear to narrow, lance-like leaves, followed by panicles of small, silvery flowers. The flowers, however, give way to groups of flattened spikelets, the most ornamental part of the plant. The pendulous spikelets occur in groups of 5 to 10 at the end of the flowering stems. They start green and turn a handsome bronze color as fall approaches. They may be picked when mature and are terrific in fresh or dried arrangements. They are at their best in late summer and fall. Hardy in zones 3–8.

Their main drawback is their tendency to reseed and travel underground with fervor. They can fill in large areas in a few years, but they look much better in large drifts than as single specimens anyway. It is so aggressive that many gardeners have eradicated it from their gardens. At the University, my students, fellow workers, and I took a poll when we planted *Chasmanthium* in a bed that was being taken over by *Oenothera speciosa*. Since both species are very invasive, a bloody brawl was anticipated. The betting was wild, while the plants went at it root to root and node to node. The outcome: come see the *Chasmanthium* bed when you visit; it isn't going anywhere.

Propagate by seed or dig a shovelful of plantlets from the base of the plants.

### *Cheiranthus* (cher-ranth' us)          Wallflower          Brassicaceae

Designed to brighten the spring garden, wallflowers explode into bright yellows and oranges, as well as pastel-muted shades, as soon as winter releases its grip. Another short-lived but colorful member of the mustard family (*Aethionema, Arabis, Aubrieta, Barbarea, Cardamine, Erysimum*), they are best used for bold winter foliage and early spring color in mild climates. In all areas, plants generally persist for no more than 3 years, and, in the South, they should be treated as annuals or biennials. In areas of cool summers, wallflowers bloom into early summer. There is very little difference between this genus and *Erysimum*, and many authorities have dismissed *Cheiranthus* entirely and lumped everything into *Erysimum*.

The subtle, morphological differences between the two genera are not particularly easy to distinguish, the differences mainly residing in the shape of the long, narrow fruit. In *Chieranthus*, the fruits are compressed, with the seeds usually being borne in 2 rows; in *Erysimum*, the fruit is circular in cross-section, with seeds being in one row only.

The most common species is *C. cheiri*, common wallflower, also known as *Erysimum cheiri*. *C. cheiri* has lanceolate, entire, 2–4" long leaves which are usually bunched beneath the flowers. The yellow to yellow-purple flowers consist of 4 rounded petals, are ¾–1" wide and wonderfully fragrant. The flowers turn into long, narrow fruit (siliques) which remain persistent until plants decline. The plant is a subshrub, and the stems become quite woody as the plant matures. This is the common wallflower seen in the British Isles and the West Coast. 'Harpur Crewe' is a double-flowered form with numerous pastel colors. Also see *Erysimum*.

*C. alpinum* (syn. *Erysimum alpinum, E. hieraciifolium*), alpine wallflower, is similar to the above but has wavy to toothed foliage and is more hairy. The flowers are yellow. I have been pleased with the perennial performance of the alpine wallflower in the Horticulture Gardens at Georgia, but it should still be treated as a short-lived plant at best.

Grow in full sun and very well-drained soils. They are tolerant of basic soils, and the addition of lime may extend their longevity. Fall planting is recommended.

### *Chelidonium* (chel-i-do' nee-um)    Greater Celandine    Papaveraceae

A pretty, although rather weedy, member of the poppy family. Only one species is known, *C. majus*, native to Europe and western Asia but naturalized all over the eastern United States. Stems and leaves exude an orange sap when bruised, which was once used as a cure for warts (wartweed or wortflower) but is really no more than a skin irritant. The leaves are alternate, usually deeply divided, the terminal leaflet 3-lobed. The ½–1″ wide, yellow, terminal flowers have 2 sepals, 4 petals, and about 20 stamens. Plants self-seed everywhere, but are terrific for shady, woodland areas. Best propagated from seeds; plants do not transplant well.

Some people confuse this plant with the native Celandine poppy, *Stylophorum diphyllum*. The flowers of the Celandine poppy are about 2″ wide and generally bear two-paired, pinnately-divided leaves on the stem, while the greater celandine has smaller flowers (about half the size of those of Celandine poppy), and generally the leaves are more deeply cut.

**Cultivars:**
'Flore Pleno' has double flowers and is more ornamental than the species.
'Grandiflora', sometimes known as 'Asiatica', has bigger flowers and is much more ornamental than the species.

**Additional Reading:**
Taylor, J. 1991. Offbeat Papaveraceae. *The Plantsman* 13(2):65–74.

## *Chelone* (chel-o′ nee)     Turtle-Head     Scrophulariaceae

The flowers of the 4 species in this genus are rather reptilian in appearance, and, if you squint your eyes and count to 10, you may see the resemblance to a turtle head. The sessile flowers are inflated and held in a terminal spike. The species are native to North America and prefer partial shade and rich, moist soil. They are particularly useful for shady areas and excellent plants for bog gardens and stream bank areas with acid soil. Pinching the shoot tips in the spring results in better performance in all species.

Quick Reference to Chelone Species

|            | Height (ft.) | Flower color |
|------------|--------------|--------------|
| *C. glabra*   | 2–3 | White |
| *C. lyonii*   | 2–3 | Rose-pink |
| *C. obliqua*  | 2–3 | Deep rose |

| *-glabra* (gla′ bra) | White Turtle-Head | 2–3′/2′ |
|---|---|---|
| Summer  White, tinged with Red | United States | Zones 3–7 |

(Syn. *C. obliqua* var. *alba*)

Native from Newfoundland to north Georgia and west to Minnesota, plants are making their way into gardens in increasing numbers. The opposite, dark green, lanceolate leaves have short petioles and are obscurely veined. The flowers are white with a red to rose tinge and borne in a dense, terminal spike for 3–4 weeks in late summer.

Plants do well in full sun and constantly moist areas but do poorly south of zone 7, although if moist conditions are provided, they tolerate heat much better. This species is handsome because of the contrast of flowers and foliage not seen in the other species.

Sow seed in moist peat:vermiculite and cover with ¼" of fine peat. Place the tray at 40° F for 6 weeks for best germination. Bring out to 60° F and maintain moisture. Seed germinates in 10–14 days and may be transplanted to larger containers in 4–6 weeks. Vegetative cuttings (4–6" long) may also be used in the spring and summer. Divisions are possible in early spring and fall.

*-lyonii* (lie-on′ ee-eye)    Pink Turtle-Head    2–3′/1½′
   Summer    Rose-Pink    Southeastern United States    Zones 3–7

The 3–7" long leaves are smooth, pointed, and evenly-toothed. They differ from the other species by being broadly ovate and long-petioled. The 1" long, rose-pink flowers have a yellow beard on the lip of the outermost

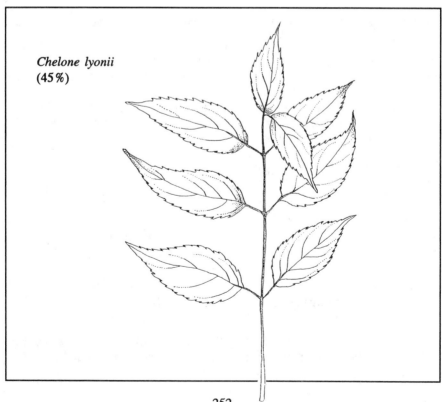

*Chelone lyonii*
(45%)

252

petals and are held in a dense, terminal spike. Flowers persist for about 4 weeks in the summer.

This is the most common turtlehead in North America but, similar to the previous species, is most suitable for cool climates. It should be planted in full sun, although afternoon shade is not detrimental in moist, rich soils. It tolerates basic soils better than the other species of *Chelone*. With sufficient moisture, large clumps develop within 3–4 years.

Propagate similar to *C. glabra*.

**-obliqua** (o-blee′ kwa)          Rose Turtle-Head          2–3′/2′
  Late Summer, Fall   Deep Rose   Southeastern United States   Zones 5–8

Plants have smooth, large (up to 8″ long), prominently-veined leaves which are shallowly toothed and broadly lanceolate. Some references claim that this is much shorter than *C. lyonii*, but I have seen little difference between them. The flowers are also similar to those of *C. lyonii* but are deeper rose.

While *C. lyonii* is native to the mountains of the Southeast, *C. obliqua* is native to wetlands and less cold hardy. Late flowering makes it a

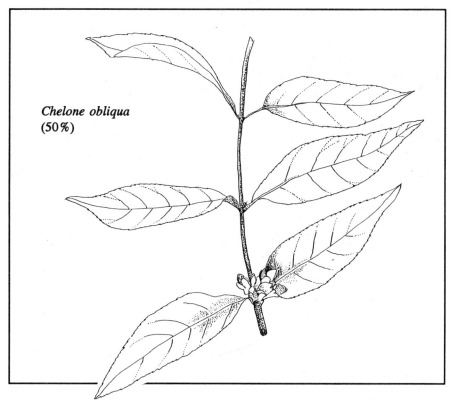

*Chelone obliqua*
(50%)

desirable addition to an area where moisture is plentiful. Plants make handsome companions to *Anaphalis, Aster, Anthemis* and *Sedum* in the fall garden. Its upright habit, rosy-red flowers, and handsome foliage make it a perfect companion for many plants. It is in its glory at the Royal Botanical Garden in Hamilton, Ontario, in September.

Propagate similar to *C. glabra.*

**Cultivars:**

'Alba' is a white-flowered form of the species.

'Bethelii' has many more flowers on each spike, and the deep rose color is more vibrant than the species.

Quick Key to Chelone Species

    A. Petioles very short, leaves lanceolate
      B. Flowers white, often tinged with pink . . . . . . . . . *C. glabra*
      BB. Flowers rose to deep rose . . . . . . . . . . . . . . . *C. obliqua*
    AA. Petioles long, leaves ovate . . . . . . . . . . . . . . . . . *C. lyonii*

## *Chiastophyllum* (ky-as' to-fy-lum)      Cotyledon      Crassulaceae

This is a monotypic genus, having only one species, *C. oppositifolium* (syn. *Cotyledon simplicifolia*). I first discovered this little gem in England a few years ago and was intrigued with this unique plant. From the 3 to 4 pairs of rounded, opposite, fleshy, basal leaves emerge upright inflorescences of dangling chains of pea-like, yellow flowers in spring and early summer.

The plant is most suited for draping over walls or in a rock garden and requires excellent drainage and afternoon shade. The species occurs in limestone outcroppings in its native habitat; therefore, garden soils should be well-limed. A grouping of 3 or 4 will definitely draw attention if well grown. Plants failed their test in the Horticulture Gardens in Athens (zone 7b) but are doing well further north. Milli Piccione gardens in Rochester, NY (zone 5), and she told me her clumps have been returning for at least 10 years. Although I have not seen many plants around the United States, I believe they are hardy in zones 4 to 6 (maybe 7a).

Propagate by division in the spring or late summer. Seed propagation requires that the tiny seeds be mixed with sand and then spread out on the seed flat uncovered. Place the seed flat at 60–70° F for 2–3 weeks, then transfer to 40° F for 4–6 weeks. After cooling, remove and germinate at 65–75° F. This is more easily accomplished by sowing in flats in the fall, placing outside in a cold frame, and waiting until spring after Mother Nature has done her job.

**Cultivars:**

'Goldtrop' is, as far as I can tell, almost identical to the species. Plants may be a little more compact, but I wouldn't pay extra for it.

## *Chimaphila* (chim-a-fil' a)          Pipsissewa          Pyrolaceae

A group of native woodland species which arise from rhizomes, they bear pink to white in the spring and unusually handsome leaves. Of the 6 species, two are common to eastern North America, one to the Northwest (*C. menziesii*) and one to eastern Asia (*C. japonica*). Probably the best known is spotted pipsissewa, *C. maculata*, which has widely-toothed, pointed, green leaves with a pale white stripe along the midrib of each leaf. The white, waxy, 1" wide, nodding flowers are fragrant and occur in early to midsummer. The plants spread well but are not aggressive. Useful for the woodland garden; however, don't expect to be overly impressed. Native to woods from southern New Hampshire to Georgia, west to Alabama and Michigan.

Another fine species is *C. umbellata*, prince's pine, native further north and west than the previous species. The leaves are sharply-toothed all around and broader and wider than spotted pipsissewa. The flowers are pale pink to white, also hanging from a leafless flower stem. The leaves of both species are refreshing when chewed, and those of *C. umbellata* have been used in making root beer. *Chimaphila* belongs to the rather non-descript shinleaf family (Pyrolaceae), derived from the early use of the leaves of the native plant, shinleaf (*Pyrola rotundifolia*), in making plasters for injured shins. No part of the human anatomy seems to have escaped the attention of the plant world, but shins?

## *Chionodoxa* (ky-on-o-dox' a)          Glory-of-the-Snow          Liliaceae

*Chionodoxa* contains a wonderful group of spring-flowering bulbs which, in their native habitats, bloom even through the snow. Flowering occurs in March–April when bulbs are planted approximately 3" deep in full sun or partial shade in the fall. *Chionodoxa* is often confused with *Scilla* (squills); however, the perianth (flower segments) pieces are obviously united at the base, whereas those of *Scilla* are not. Also, usually there are only 2 leaves, and they are thicker, stiffer, and darker green than those of *Scilla*.

### *-luciliae* (loo-sil' ee-aye)          Glory-of-the-Snow          4–6"/4"
Early Spring    Blue with White Eye          Asia Minor          Zones 4–8

This is the best species of the genus. The two linear leaves arise in the spring, followed by 3–6, wide open flowers on each flower stem. Each intense blue flower is about 1" wide with a large, white center. If the weather remains cool, flowers persist for 3–4 weeks. Warm weather accelerates flowering (as in all spring bulbs) and results in reduced flowering time.

Bulbs require good drainage, and, if planted on sides of hills or banks, they soon spread to make a spectacular display. They are also at home in the garden, but at least 50, preferably one hundred or more, should be planted together.

Propagation is by offsets, small bulbs which form around the older bulbs, just after flowering. Fresh seed should be sown in seed flats at 65–70° F. If seed dries out, cold, moist stratification (35–40° F) for 4–6 weeks provides more uniform germination.

### Cultivars:

'Alba' has white flowers on 6″ tall stems, and 'Rosea' has pink flowers on 8″ high stems. Other than flower color, they are similar, although not as pretty as the species.

Var. *gigantea* has large (2″ diameter), blue flowers, and var. *tmolusii* (mo-lose-ee-eye) produces late-flowering, blue and white flowers. These varieties have recently undergone some taxonomic hair splitting and are now considered distinct species.

'Pink Giant' is taller than the species and produces bright pink flowers. It is surprisingly attractive.

### Related Species:

*C. albescens* bears pale blue to whitish flowers which are only about ½″ in diameter, the smallest of the genus. Plants are often confused with *C. luciliae* 'Alba'.

*C. sardensis*, Sardenian glory-of-the-snow, has 6–8 sky blue flowers which have no white disc (or very diminutive) at the throat of the flower. Some gardeners find that the lack of white center intensifies the flower color; however, I feel the white of *C. luciliae* provides interest as well as beauty. It flowers about a week earlier than *C. luciliae*.

X *Chionoscilla allenii* is a natural intergeneric hybrid between *C. forbesii* and *Scilla bifolia* but is seldom offered in the trade. It is similar in habit to *Chionodoxa* but subject to the fungal diseases which attack *Scilla*.

### Additional Reading:

Anon. 1994. Growing: harbingers of spring. *Garden Design* 13(5):32–33.

## *Chrysanthemum* (kris-an-the′ mum)     Chrysanthemum     Asteraceae

The chrysanthemum is one of the oldest cultivated plants in existence. Chrysanthemums provide a common bond with the people of China who lived 500 years before the birth of Christ. As happens with plants in cultivation that long, breeding efforts have changed the natural form and size so that some species exist in habits (e.g., cascading forms, tree forms), colors, and flower shapes quite different from the species. This is particularly true for the decorative *C. × morifolium* (*Dendranthema × grandiflorum*). Although most people think of the fall-flowering "mum" as the only plant in the genus, over 100 species are recorded, including many useful garden plants. A number of common wild flowers such as ox-eye daisy, *C. leucanthemum* (*Leucanthemum vulgare*), and Nippon daisy, *C. nipponicum* (*Nipponanthemum nipponicum*), greenhouse flowers such as marguerite daisy, *C. frutescens* (*Argyranthemum frutescens*), and commercially-grown cut flowers like the pungent feverfew, *C. parthenium* (*Tanacetum parthenium*), are commonly cultivated. Species flower in summer and fall, and almost every color of flower but blue is available. Several miniatures such as *C. atlanticum* (*Pyrethropsis atlantica*), with lovely white daisy flowers, and *C. hosmariense* (*Pyrethropsis hosmariensis*) grow less than 1' tall, while underused annuals, including *C. carinatum*, rainbow daisy, and *C. segetum*, corn daisy, offer additional possibilities. The leaves of all species are alternate but may be divided, lobed, or entire.

The genus has recently undergone extensive taxonomic bludgeoning. Scientific study of the plant structure and the date in which the plants were originally named has resulted in the *Chrysanthemum* genus being plundered. The only species remaining in the genus are *C. carinatum. C. coronarium*, and *C. segetum*. All others have been placed in "new" genera. From the gardeners' point of view, all this rearrangement does not change anything about the plants themselves. It is important that the proper names are listed; however, gardeners will never give up the chrysanthemum name, regardless of what the taxonomists decide. The purge on the species of the genus is not yet finished, so let's not take any of this too seriously.

Chrysanthemums are best planted in full sun and need little more than adequate drainage to thrive.

## Quick Reference to Chrysanthemum Species

| | Height (ft.) | Flower color | Flower time | Leaf shape |
|---|---|---|---|---|
| *C. coccineum* | 1–2 | Various | Early summer | Finely-divided |
| *C. frutescens* | 1–3 | White | Summer | Divided |
| *C. × morifolium* | 1–3 | Various | Fall | Lobed |
| *C. nipponicum* | 1–3 | White | Late fall | Slightly-toothed |
| *C. pacificum* | 1–2 | Yellow | Late fall | Lobed |
| *C. parthenium* | 1–3 | White, yellow | Summer | Lobed, cut to midrib |
| *C. × rubellum* | 2–3 | Various | Fall | Lobed |
| *C. × superbum* | 2–2½ | White | Summer | Coarsely-toothed |

**-coccineum** (kok-sin' ee-um)     Pyrethrum, Painted Daisy     1–2'/1'
    Early Summer     Various     Western Asia     Zones 3–7
(Syn. *Tanacetum coccineum*)

This species is not only a fine garden plant in cool areas of the country, but also the source of pyrethrum, an insecticide widely used for control of fleas and lice. The finely-divided leaves are a vivid green; the lower ones are about 10″ long and attached to the stem by a long petiole, while the upper are sessile. Above the handsome foliage rise wiry stems supporting solitary, 2–3″ wide flowers. Most of the flowers are in shades of red or white with yellow centers and occur as singles or doubles.

Plants can be placed in full sun in the North but should be protected from afternoon sun in the South. Painted daisies do not tolerate heat particularly well and, unfortunately, are not good garden plants south of zone 7a. In fact, one of the common complaints of gardeners is that plants look beautiful the first year and decline rapidly the second. Another problem is that they often require support, but, with the advent of good dwarf cultivars, this problem will be largely overcome. Flowers last 2–4 weeks, but plants are not long-lived, requiring replanting or dividing every 2 years to maintain vigor. Some excellent dwarf cultivars are presently being introduced to this country which should result in many more painted daisies in American gardens.

Seed germinates readily in warm (70–75° F), humid conditions, or divisions may be taken in early spring or fall.

## Cultivars:

'Atrosanguineum' bears single, dark red flowers and is the darkest red of any the cultivars.

'Duro' produces bright purple-red flowers about 2–3′ tall. A good form for the cutting garden.

'Eileen May Robinson' has single, pink flowers.

'Evenglow' is one of the best selections, producing rich salmon-red, single flowers.

'James Kelway' produces single, dark red flowers.

'Pink Bouquet' produces double, pink flowers.

'Robinson's Hybrids' bear double flowers, available in mixed colors and in pink, rose, and crimson.

'Sensation' has double, red flowers.

| *-frutescens* (froo-tes′ enz) | Marguerite Daisy | 1–3′/3′ |
|---|---|---|
| Summer        White | Canary Islands | Zones 7–9 |
| (Syn. *Argyranthemum frutescens*) | | |

Particularly beautiful in ornamental containers, the fern-like, light green foliage makes beautiful accent points. The single, daisy, white flowers have yellow centers and are held on thin, wiry stems. The stems are woody at the base and grow into a significant bush. If the bottom foliage declines, the plants can look poor after a couple of years. Plants are mainly treated as annuals; however, they may be winter hardy in mild areas in the northwest and in zones 8 and 9 in the east.

Propagate by cuttings in late winter or spring.

**Cultivars:**
Some single and double hybrids have been developed.

'Jamaica Primrose' has wonderful primrose-yellow flowers.
'Mary Wooton' bears double, pink flowers.

-× *morifolium* (mo-ri-fo' lee-um)    Chrysanthemum    1–3'/3'
    Fall        Various        China, Japan    Zones 5–9
(Syn. *Dendranthema* × *grandiflorum*)

The fall-flowering mums are complex hybrids which have been derived over hundreds of years, using wild species in China and Japan. *C. indicum*, a handsome bright yellow, daisy-flowered species and *C. morifolium* are probably the parents of the thousands of cultivars available today. I remember seeing my first fall chrysanthemum show many years ago in rundown display greenhouses in Hamilton, Canada, and the colors, habits, and flower shapes were absolutely phenomenal. I have seen many such shows since, but, perhaps because it was my first visit to the "land of the mum," I have not seen any better. There are many shapes and sizes of flowers for outdoor culture as well, although not the diversity of forms capable of being grown under protection.

All fall mums flower in response to the length of the night. As fall approaches, the night length increases, and, when it reaches a certain number of hours (critical night length), the flowering response is triggered. The difference between late-flowering and early-flowering mums is simply the number of weeks of critical night length required to flower. Obviously it is important to purchase early-flowering cultivars in areas where frost comes early. In the North, florists' mums received as gifts may be planted outdoors, but these decorative forms usually require too many weeks of long nights before frost and often freeze before flowering. In the South, early- and late-flowering mums can be used. There is no relationship between quality of flower or plant and flowering time.

The importance of night length was made very obvious to me when I moved south and noticed chrysanthemums flowering in April. It took me a while to realize that in southern latitudes, long, spring nights occur when temperatures are warm enough for plant growth. In the North, plants do not respond to the long nights of early spring because they are still shivering in the ground. Although plants flower in the South in the spring, they make a poor display and should not be allowed to do so. Flowering stems should be pinched to encourage vegetative growth.

Plant mums in full sun and well-drained soil. They are heavy feeders but should be fertilized no more than 3 times a year. If fed too heavily, it is impossible to keep the height down. Except for dwarf cultivars, cut the plants back heavily once or twice (up to 3 times in the South) to keep plants compact and encourage flowers. Don't cut back later than August 1 in the North or August

15 in the South, or all the developing flowers will be removed. Aphids and spider mites are serious pests, and pesticides should be used when necessary.

All mums can be propagated by division in spring and fall. In fact, division once every 3 years is advisable. New plants may also be propagated by 2–4″ long, terminal cuttings taken from vegetative stems in spring and summer.

**Cultivars:**

The hundreds of cultivars of hardy mums are bred by a handful of flower breeders. They are bred for ease of production and self-branching. So many new cultivars are introduced and grown for the mass market outlets that it is difficult to find much difference between them. Plants are classified by flower shape.

Cushions: Double-flowered forms with compact growth, usually less than 20″ tall.

Daisies: Single, daisy-like flowers with yellow centers.

Decoratives: Taller forms with larger double or semi-double flowers than cushion mums.

Pompons: Very free-flowering plants with small, ball-shaped blooms, usually less than 18″ tall.

Buttons: Plants with small, double flowers (less than 1″ across), usually less than 18″ tall. 'Bronze Elegans' is a popular button form with late, bronze flowers on 3′ tall, bushy plants.

The 'Minn' series of hardy mums was developed at the University of Minnesota to provide cultivars which flower in the North before frost. 'Minn Yellow' and 'Minn Gold' are examples of this series.

**Related Species:**

Some relatively new hybrids (1937) referred to as Korean hybrids were developed by an American breeder, Mr. A. Cumming, and were the result of crossing an early-flowering cultivar with *C. coreanum*. They are variously-colored, well-branched, and go under names such as 'Venus' and 'Apollo', pale pink and dark red, respectively. Extremely floriferous in late fall. The following appear to have korean hybrid parentage, but I do not know how much. There may be some Nippon daisy in these as well.

*C.* × 'Mei-kyo' produces many small (2″ diameter), double, rose-colored flowers with yellow centers. They do not open until late October in my garden and continue until frost. It is hardy in zones 4–9.

*C.* × 'Ryan's Daisy' is a marvelous fall-flowering plant which bears dozens of single, rosy-pink daisies in September through November. The plant is likely winter hardy to about zone 6, but flowers appear so late that early frosts in the North may knock off developing flowers. Plants were found in the garden of Mr. Ryan Gainey, a fine garden designer in Atlanta.

*C.* × 'Single Apricot' is similar to Ryan's daisy in that they are both covered with flowers in late fall. I saw this one absolutely covered in soft, apricot flowers at Bluemount Nursery in Maryland in late October, and I went ga-ga. Richard Simon, the owner of Bluemount, took pity on me and I now have it in Georgia. Outstanding.

*-nipponicum* (nip-pon-i' cum)  Nippon Daisy, Montauk Daisy  1–3'/3'
  Late Fall  White  Japan  Zones 5–9
(Syn. *Nipponanthemum nipponicum*)

Plants are seldom used to advantage in American gardens; however, it is an excellent garden specimen. Plants produce shiny, succulent-like, dark green foliage which are covered with 2–3" diameter, white flowers with green centers. Flowers open in September or October and flower until frost. The bushy plants range from 3–5' tall. The common name Montauk daisy refers to its escape in the Montauk area of Long Island, NY, where it flowers happily in late fall in that area.

Grow in full sun and provide moist but well-drained soils. Plants may be pinched once in the spring to induce more bushy growth. This little-known plant, if provided with a little fertilizer and water, can be as rewarding as any chrysanthemum grown.

*-pacificum* (pa-si-fi' cum)  Silver and Gold  1–2'/2'
  Late Fall  Yellow  Japan  Zones 5–9
(Syn. *Ajania pacifica*)

Here is a plant which offers a little bit for everyone. The foliage is the most ornamental aspect throughout the spring and summer. Mounds of light green leaves are edged in well-defined, narrow bands of silver and make a useful, low-growing ground cover. Late in the season, dozens of flower buds give rise to bright golden-yellow, button-like flowers in October and November, providing some of the brightest color in the late fall garden. They are particularly handsome growing through gray leaf plants such as *Artemisia* 'Powis Castle' but also are wonderful container plants, which are often used as a substitute for fall mums. Because of the outstanding contrast between the bright flowers and the variegated foliage, garden centers offer them for sale both as spring and fall plantings.

Plants have been plagued with reports of poor winter hardiness, and seem to disappear for no apparent reason. However, this is as much a problem of poor drainage as cold temperatures. Provide excellent drainage and full sun. Plants should not be expected to give more than 3 years of good performance. Propagate by terminal cuttings in the spring or summer.

## Cultivars:

'Pink Ice', introduced in this country in 1994 by Tony Avent of Plant Delights Nursery, has light pink petals around a yellow center over 18″ tall plants. A wonderful introduction.

| *-parthenium* (par-then' ee-um) | Feverfew, Matricaria | 1–3'/2' |
|---|---|---|
| Late Summer    White, Yellow | Caucasus | Zones 5–7 |

(Syn. *Tanacetum parthenium*)

This excellent cut flower is highly branched and often covered with ¾″ diameter, button-like flowers. The pinnately-lobed foliage is strongly scented, which may explain why few insects bother it, and many people don't like it. Each leaf is 2–3″ long, slightly hairy, and toothed. This is one of those "old-fashioned" plants which is presently undergoing a renaissance as a cut flower and a bedding plant. In 1597, *Gerard's Herbal* described feverfew as very good for "them that are giddie in the head." Roman legend states that it saved the life of a man who fell from the Parthenon during its construction, thus accounting for the specific name *parthenium*. (I don't believe it either.) The foliage is also supposed to be very good fried with eggs. Please let me know.

Plants are not fussy as to soil but should be placed in full sun. The dwarf forms can be used as an edging, while the larger forms are excellent as border plants. In the South, dwarf forms tend to melt out, particularly if allowed to dry out, and cannot be recommended for that area of the country. Even when cut back, the new growth declines in the heat and humidity. However, when kept well-watered, an excellent crop has been produced in the flower trials at the University of Georgia.

Propagate similarly to *C. × morifolium*. Seed may also be used.

## Cultivars:

'Album' has single, white flowers on 2' stems.
'Aureum' has yellow foliage which turns green with the advent of flowers. It grows 8–12″ tall and is known as golden feather.
'Crispum' is a uniquely foul form with foliage curled like parsley.
'Flore Pleno' has white, double flowers on 2' stems.
'Golden Ball' is an 18″ tall, yellow, double-flowering cultivar.
'Rowallane' has dozens of tennis ball-shaped, white flower heads.
'Roya' bears white daisies atop 2' tall plants.
'Santana' is only 10–12″ tall with creamy white flowers. Plant's performance has been erratic in our garden (zone 7b), growing poorly in some years and well in others. It has done well in more northerly areas.
'Snowball' is 1–2' tall with white, double flowers.
'White Bobbles' is another of the double, white "fews". Originally grown in England in the 1920's and 1930's as a cut flower, it was simply

known as 'Stinker'. Now that it has reappeared, it was given a more civilized name by Alan Bloom.

-× *rubellum* (roo-bell' um)  Hybrid Red Chrysanthemum  2-3'/3'
 Late Summer  Various  Hybrid Origin    Zones 4–8
(Syn. *Dendranthema zawadskii* hybrids)

This free-flowering, little-known species is likely a hybrid, although the parentage is obscure. It is similar to *C. zawadskii,* Siberian daisy, and is considered to be a variant (var. *latilobum*) of that species by some authorities. The compact plants are much branched, and each leaf is deeply 5-lobed and about 4″ long. Plants are woody at the base, and the leaf segments are coarsely-toothed and quite hairy, particularly on the underside. The pink to rosy-red, single flowers are 2–3″ across and held singly or in a few-flowered inflorescence well above the foliage. The ray flowers, which are narrow and well separated from each other, surround a small, yellow center.

It flowers earlier than the hybrid fall mums and is not fussy about soil but should receive as much sun as possible. The flowers are fragrant and make pleasant additions to garden bouquets. Pinch once early to encourage compact, multiple stems.

Propagate by division or cuttings similar to *C.* × *morifolium.*

**Cultivars:**

'Clara Curtis' is the best and easiest to locate cultivar. It grows 18–24″ tall
 and is covered with 2–3″ diameter, deep pink, daisy flowers with raised,
 yellow centers.
'Duchess of Edinburgh' has muted red flowers on 2' tall plants.
'Mary Stoker' bears pale butter-yellow daisies which have a slight pink
 tinge throughout the ray flowers.
'Paul Boissier' is a good, early, light copper form.

**Related Species:**

 *C. weyrichii* (syn. *Dendranthema weyrichii*) is an 8–12″ tall, stoloni-ferous species. The 1–2″ wide, pink flowers are carried over palmately-parted, shiny green leaves. 'Pink Bomb' bears rosy-pink flowers, and 'White Bomb' has 2″ creamy white flowers on 12″ stems. Both flower in late fall. Should be used much more often. Perform well in zones 3–8.

-× *superbum* (soo-perb' um)  Shasta Daisy   2-2½'/2'
 Summer    White   Hybrid Origin  Zones 4–9
(Syn. *Leucanthemum* × *superbum*)

The Shasta daisy is one of the most popular daisies because of availability and ease of cultivation. It was hybridized in 1890 by the American plants-man, Luther Burbank, by crossing *C. lacustre,* Portuguese chrysanthemum, and

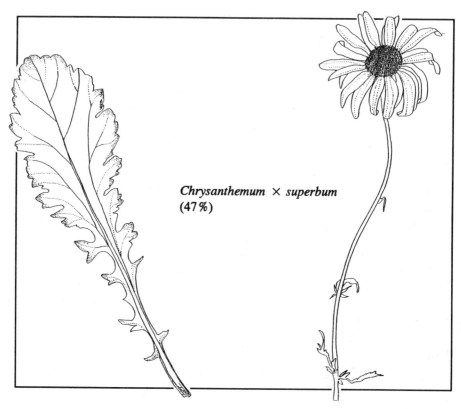

*Chrysanthemum* × *superbum*
(47%)

*C. maximum*, Pyrenees chrysanthemum, two similar daisy-flowering plants. Unlike other chrysanthemums, the leaves are coarsely-toothed, not deeply-lobed or divided. The lower leaves are up to 12″ long with short petioles, while the upper leaves become shorter as they ascend the stem and are sessile. All the foliage is dark green and toothed. The 2–3″ diameter, white flowers are borne singly, and cultivars are available in single and double forms.

Plant in full sun with good drainage, especially in areas where winter rain is common. It is a good plant for southern gardens; however, it is short-lived and usually declines after 2–3 years. Remove spent flowers before they go to seed. Deadheading may allow a second bloom on some of the more vigorous cultivars. Divide or replace any time.

All cultivars can be propagated by divisions in spring or fall, and many cultivars can be obtained from seed.

**Cultivars:**

*Singles:*

'Alaska' is one of the oldest and still one of the best cultivars. The pure white flowers have yellow centers and are 3″ in diameter and borne on 2–3′ tall stems. It is also cold hardy.

'Barbara Bush' was introduced in 1994 by Walters Garden of Zeeland, Michigan to honor the former first lady. Flowers are similar to 'T. Killin', but the foliage has creamy gold margins.

'Becky' is one of the best forms I have grown and is particularly good in the heat of the south. They stand upright, even after flowering and a hard rain, and flower for up to 8 weeks if the large, white flowers are deadheaded. Named for plantswoman Becky Stewart of Garden Designs in Decatur, GA.

'Everest' is similar to 'Alaska' but has 3–4" diameter flowers and is 3–4' tall.

'Little Miss Muffet' is only 8–12" tall with 2–3" wide, creamy white flowers and an orange center.

'Little Princess' bears large, white flowers with yellow centers.

'Majestic' has 3–4" diameter flowers with small, yellow centers borne on 3' tall plants.

'Polaris' is a magnificent 3' tall selection with 4–5" diameter, clean white flowers.

'Silver Princess' is a dwarf selection similar to 'Little Miss Muffet' and may be raised true from seed. These two cultivars can be used as bedding plants, as they flower about 12 weeks from sowing and remain in flower most of the season.

'Snowcap' is a compact, bushy, low-growing (15–18") plant which is very weather tolerant. Rainfall and high winds don't affect it as much as the taller cultivars. Raised by Alan Bloom of England.

'Snow Lady' is a seed-propagated dwarf (12–15" tall), shasta daisy with 2" wide, clean white flowers. Plants flower the first year from seed and won the prestigious All-America award in 1991.

'Starburst' is one of the more vigorous cultivars, growing to 4' tall. The white flowers are up to 4" wide.

'Switzerland' produces white flowers over a long period of time. Plants grow 2–3' tall and appear to be hardier than many other white-flowered forms.

'T. Killin' is an old-fashioned, cut flower form, with large, white flowers around a crested gold center. Plants grow about 30" tall.

'Tinkerbelle' is about 2½' tall with stiff stems and single, white daisies.

'White Knight' is also propagated from seed and bears white, single flowers on 18–24" tall plants. They are extremely floriferous but short-lived.

*Doubles:*

'Aglaia' has fringed petals which make the flower look like it has been attacked by caterpillars. Awful looking thing.

'Cobham Gold' has flowers which are creamy outside with a raised, yellow center.

'Esther Reed' flowers earlier than most cultivars and is only about 2' tall.

'Diener's Double' bears flowers with frilled petals on 2' tall stems.

'Marconi' is a popular cultivar with 3" diameter, clear white flowers on 3' tall stems.

'Mount Shasta' is 2' tall and has fully-double flowers surrounding a raised center.

'Sedgewick' is one of the most cold hardy double shastas, bearing large domes of white flowers.

'Wirral Pride' is 2–3' tall, and flowers are obviously raised in the center.

**Related Species:**

*C. uliginosum* (syn. *Leucanthemella serotina*), giant daisy, produces many two- to three-flowered clusters of 2–3" wide, white flowers with green centers in late summer and fall. The foliage is 3–4" long, coarsely-toothed and sharply-pointed. It is one of the tallest species growing 4–7' tall.

Quick Key to Chrysanthemum Species

   A. Leaves with thin, white to silver margins ...... *C. pacificum*
  AA. Leaves without variegation
     B. Leaves toothed, not distinctly lobed or divided
       C. Leaves thick and succulent, bluntly
         toothed towards apex .............. *C. nipponicum*
      CC. Leaves not thick or succulent, leaves
         toothed over half the margins ........ *C.* × *superbum*
    BB. Leaves lobed or divided, not distinctly toothed
      C. Leaves lobed but not deeply divided
        D. Leaves very hairy beneath,
          late summer flower .............. *C.* × *rubellum*
       DD. Leaves glaucous or slightly hairy
         E. Leaves glaucous, not hairy,
           usually fall flowering ......... *C.* × *morifolium*
        EE. Leaves slightly hairy, plant very
          aromatic, late summer-flowered ..... *C. parthenium*
      CC. Leaves deeply divided, not merely lobed
        D. Leaves doubly divided, producing
          multiple flower head, white or yellow ... *C. frutescens*
       DD. Leaves deeply divided, producing single
          flower heads, usually red or pink shades . *C. coccineum*

**Additional Reading:**

Anderson, N.O. 1987. Reclassification of the genus *Chrysanthemum*. *HortScience* 22(2):313.

*Associations:*

National Chrysanthemum Society Inc., 2612 Beverly Blvd., Roanoke, VA 24015. Publication: *The Chrysanthemum.*

*Chrysogonum* (kris-og' o-num)  Goldenstar, Green and Gold    Asteraceae

This genus is represented by one species, *C. virginianum*, a useful, shade-tolerant ground cover. Plants are "doers," although they are not terribly imaginative. They tolerate fairly heavy shade but also do fine in sunny, moist areas.

| *-virginianum* (vir-jin-ee-aye' num) | Green and Gold | 6–8"/12" |
|---|---|---|
| Early Spring          Yellow | Eastern United States | Zones 5–8 |

This is such a popular plant in many parts of the country that nurseries cannot keep up with demand. The 1–2" long, toothed leaves are triangular and dark green. The ends of the petals are slightly notched and the stamens are brown, nicely contrasting with the 1" diameter, bright yellow, daisy flowers.

Many catalogs state that plants bloom constantly all summer; however, they peak in spring, flower on and off in May and June, and usually come to a standstill in the heat of the summer. This is particularly so in zones 6 through 8, although flowers are more persistent in northern gardens. Plants should be placed in moist, well-drained soil and heavy shade, particularly at the southern end of their range. *Chrysogonum* may be grown in full sun only if soils are constantly moist. Although cold hardy to zone 5, an application of mulch in that zone may be prudent. The much respected R.H.S. Dictionary of Gardening states that *Chrysogonum* is "of no striking beauty," but I strongly disagree. While it is surely not endowed with eye-catching attributes, it most certainly deserves a place in the wild flower or moist shade garden. W.H. Pierce stated it best in his book, *North American Rock Plants* (1937), when he wrote, "I must admit I do not know why I am so fond of this little plant: it has neither splendour nor prodigality of blossom; it gives forth no intriguing perfume; it has neither airy grace nor stately form; . . . its habit is humble and lowly; just the same, to grow it is to love it."

Division is the surest means of propagation and should be accomplished in late spring every second year. Seed germinates within 3 weeks when sown in warm (70–75° F), moist conditions. Seedlings may also be found at the base of mature plantings and transferred to other areas of the garden.

**Cultivars:**

A couple of variations to the species and a few named cultivars have appeared; however, except for one of them, the difference between any of them is debatable. All bear 5-rayed, bright yellow flowers and make excellent ground covers.

Var. *australe* is similar to the species but has above-ground stolons and shorter stems. Plants spread more rapidly than *C. virginianum*, but the flowers appear to decline more rapidly. 'Mark Viette' is an example of this variation.

'Eco Laquered Spider', a recent introduction from Don Jacobs at Eco Gardens, has lacquered, gray-green foliage and long stolons. Plants grow at an amazingly rapid speed, growing on top of itself in its zeal to cover all available space. It is truly different from the others.

'Springbrook' is the most compact, only growing 4–8″ tall.

Var. *virginianum* has light green leaves, grows 4–8″ tall, and the flowers occur well above the foliage. It also appears to remain in flower for a longer period of time than var. *australe*. 'Alan Bush', named for the retired and greatly-missed owner of Holbrook Farm in North Carolina, is an example of this variety. 'Pierre', for Pierre Bennerup, is also a long-blooming form. Who is next?

### Additional Reading:

Anon. 1993. A carpet of green and gold. *Southern Living* 28(3):13.

Oliver, M. 1993. Ground covers for shade. *Fine Gardening* 20:54–57.

## *Chrysopsis* (kris-op′ sis)　　　　　Goldaster　　　　　Asteraceae

This genus contains about 10 native species; 2 or 3 are occasionally found in the flower garden. As gardeners experiment with more native genera, this one should definitely find a niche. All species have entire, alternate foliage and many golden-yellow flowers. There is so little difference between this genus and *Heterotheca* that plants are undoubtedly mixed up. See the latter genus for generic differences. The only species of importance in American gardens is the southeastern native, *C. mariana*, Maryland goldaster, which grows 1–3′ tall and bears many 1–1½″ wide, yellow flowers. Plants prefer sandy soils and good drainage and are exceedingly drought-tolerant.

### Related Species:

*C. falcata* (syn. *Pityopsis falcata*), sickleleaf goldaster, is only 5–12″ tall with linear leaves and small (less than 1″ across) flower heads. For those looking for small wild flowers, the plant has merit.

## *Cimicifuga* (sim-me-sif-fyou′ ga)　　　　Bugbane　　　　Ranunculaceae

This genus contains a number of native species which have become popular in recent years as more gardeners discover their timeless beauty. About eight species occur, and, of the 3 most available, 2 are native to North America. *Cimicifuga* is slender, tall, and prefers a moist, shady location and rich, acid soil similar to its native habitat at the edge of woods, where leaf mold is plentiful. The species of garden value have white flowers with minute petals, while the stamens provide much of the beauty. They are similar in habit to *Actaea*, but the flowers are much more densely arranged on longer inflorescences, and the fruits (berries in *Actaea*, follicles in *Cimicifuga*) are not ornamental. There are few obvious differences among Cimicifuga species, and close inspection is necessary to distinguish one from the other. All species have ternately-compound leaves, meaning that the leaves are divided into three segments, three times. All species but *C. japonica*, Japanese bugbane, have small leaves on the flower stems. The flowers are held in long racemes. For identification purposes, determine if the pistils are stalked, as in *C. americana*, or sessile, as in *C. racemosa*. Looking for stalked pistils is not my idea of fun, but it may help identify a wayward bugbane.

Plants of *Cimicifuga* provide a tall, airy foil and a balance between spiked and rounded plants. Fall-flowering, hybrid anemones such as 'Queen Charlotte' combine magnificently with the white, wiry bugbanes. Plants with variegated leaves show off bugbane's dark green foliage.

They often require 3–4 years before decent flowering occurs, and patience is necessary. Unfortunately for southern gardeners (zone 7b south), bugbanes are often disappointing. Unless they receive just the right micro-environment, they tend to be stunted and do not flower particularly well. Perhaps if plants were never seen growing in their prime in other gardens, people wouldn't be so picky. They are finally flowering in the Armitage garden, but I wouldn't put them in a southern landscape I was designing for someone else.

The common name, bugbane, is a translation from *cimex*, a bug, and *fugo*, to drive away. When Linnaeus named this plant in 1750, he knew that *C. foetida*, a species from Asia, was dried and ground up into powder and used to stuff pillows, mattresses, and cushions as a protection against biting insects. For retailers, however, this name does little to attract customers; perhaps we could call it White Spire plant or something a little less itchy.

Quick Reference to Cimicifuga Species

| | Height (ft.) | Flower time | Leaflet size (in.) | Inflorescence size (ft.) | Number of pistils |
|---|---|---|---|---|---|
| *C. americana* | 2–6 | Mid | 1–3 | 2–3 | 3–8 |
| *C. racemosa* | 6–8 | Early | 3–4 | 3–4 | 1–2 |
| *C. simplex* | 3–4 | Late | 1–2 | 2–3 | 2–3 |

| *-americana* (a-me-ri-kah′ na) | American Bugbane | 2–6′/3′ |
|---|---|---|
| Early Fall      White | Eastern United States | Zones 3–7 |

Although not as common in gardens as the other species, it is easier to cultivate. Native from New York to Pennsylvania and as far south as the mountains of Georgia, plants are adaptable to a wide range of conditions. The 1–3″ long, rounded leaflets have 3–5 toothed lobes and heart-shaped bases. The flower stalks are sometimes branched near their base, providing additional flowers as the season progresses. If you look closely at the

*Cimicifuga americana*
(48%)

flowers, the bracts at the base of the flower stalks (pedicels) are evident, a distinguishing characteristic of this species.

Propagation by seed is difficult, and best results are obtained with fresh seed. Even then, germination is erratic, and seedlings emerge over a long time. After collecting the seed, place in sand in the cold (35–40° F) for 6–8 weeks. Sow seed in a 1:1 mix of peat:vermiculite, and place in a warm (70–75° F), humid area. Plants can be divided, but this should not be done for at least 3 years after planting. They have a deep root system and do not divide well.

**Related Species:**

*C. japonica*, Japanese bugbane, is 3–4′ tall and bears long, branched racemes of white flowers. The foliage is similar to that of *C. americana*, except that it is all basal, and no leaves ascend the flower stems. Flowers later than *C. racemosa* but a little earlier than *C. ramosa*.

*C. acerina* has dark green, maple-like leaves with long, pointed lobes and purple stems. Plants are often classified as a variety of *C. japonica* (var. *acerina*). An outstanding species.

**-racemosa** (ray-ce-mo′ sa)  Snakeroot, Cohosh  6–8′/4′
 Late Summer  White  Eastern United States  Zones 3–7

This is the aristocrat of the genus, whose tall, white spires provide an unforgettable sight in the late summer garden. It is also the easiest to locate at nurseries and from mail order catalogs. The leaves are deeply cut, and

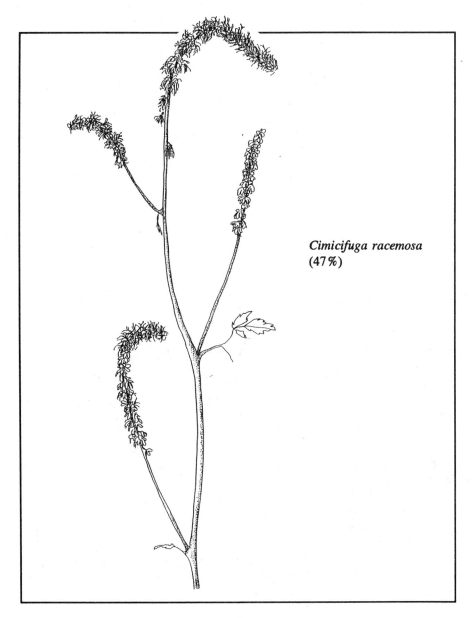

*Cimicifuga racemosa*
(47%)

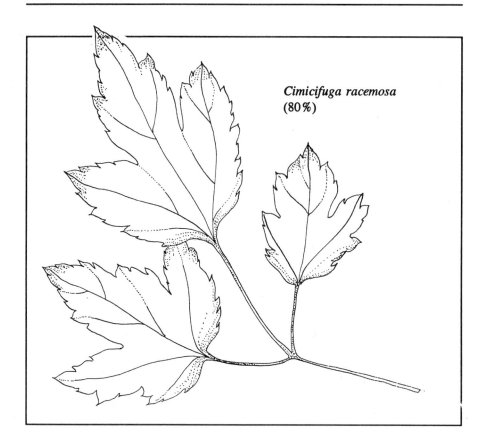

*Cimicifuga racemosa* (80%)

the 1-3" long leaflets are ovate and irregularly-toothed. The long racemes of creamy white flowers reach 2' in length and are often branched near the base of the terminal inflorescence. Flowers open in midsummer in zone 7 but not until late summer or early fall in zones 3 and 4. The 1-2 pistils of the flowers are sessile, that is, they have no pistil stem. This is not easy to distinguish, but it is one of the characteristics which make this species unique. The flowers persist for about 4 weeks, and the spent flower spires continue to be decorative for many more weeks. I can't think of a more beautiful planting than at Naumkeag Garden, designed by Fletcher Steele, in the Berkshires of Western Massachusetts. Plants have naturalized in the woodland setting and are absolutely stunning in mid-July.

There are fewer flower stalks produced on this species than others, but its graceful, yet wiry, form has made it popular in American gardens. They look terrific with many cultivars of *Phlox paniculata*. Plants need a constant supply of moisture, or leaf margins turn brown, and plants become stunted.

Propagate similar to *C. americana*.

**Cultivars:**

Var. *cordifolia* (syn. *C. cordifolia*) grows 4–5' tall. Leaves consist of 4–10" long leaflets, the base of the terminal leaflet being heart-shaped. Flowers are similar to those of the species.

**Related Species:**

*C. ramosa*, branched bugbane, is taller than *C. racemosa* and more ornamental. It grows 6–7' tall and produces many long, dense racemes of white flowers. 'Atropurpurea' is 4–6' tall and bears many flower spires over foliage which changes to purple flushed with green in full sun. This cultivar is relatively available in American gardening. 'Brunette' has deep bronze foliage and is only 3–4' tall. The foliage is truly bronze throughout the season. When I wrote my last edition, this cultivar was almost impossible to locate in the United States. Today it is much easier. These two selections are outstanding and highly recommended.

| *-simplex* (sim' plex) | | Kamchatka Bugbane | 3–4'/3' |
|---|---|---|---|
| Late Fall | White | Russia | Zones 3–7 |

Although Kamchatka bugbane does not have the majesty of the previous species, it has gained a significant following. The flower stalks are more arching than those of *C. racemosa*, and the secondary stalks are often taller than the terminal raceme. Flowers of this species are generally the last of the bugbanes to open, often taking a minor frost or two, a bonus for gardeners looking for late season color. Plants are more tolerant of basic soils than other species. They are also the best species for the south.

Propagate similar to *C. americana*.

**Cultivars:**

'Braunlaub' has purple foliage and is similar to some of the purple cultivars of *C. ramosa*.

'White Pearl' ('Armleuchter') has large (over 2' long), dense, white flower spikes. Flowers open in late October in the Armitage garden.

'Elstead Variety' has finely-cut, dark green foliage, over which purplish brown flower buds open to pure white flowers.

'Pritchard's Giant' is an immense cultivar, easily growing 4–5' tall. All cultivars are vast improvements on the species.

**Related Species:**

*C. dahurica* is native to China and Japan and hardy in zones 5 to 7. All leaflets are cordate (heart-shaped). Plants grow 5–6' tall and bear creamy white flowers in simple or compound racemes. Flowers, which occur in mid-summer, have a subtle fragrance.

## Quick Key to Cimicifuga Species

A. Height in flower 4' or less
   B. Number of pistils 3–8 . . . . . . . . . . . . . . . . *C. americana*
   BB. Number of pistils 2–3 . . . . . . . . . . . . . . . . . *C. simplex*
AA. Height in flower greater than 4', usually 6' or more . *C. racemosa*

**Additional Reading:**

Bloom, A. 1993. Brunette stands out from the crowd. *The Garden* 118(6):272.
Compton, J. 1992. Cimicifuga. *The Garden* 117(11):504–506.

## *Cirsium* (sir-see' um)          Plume Thistle          Asteraceae

Most cirsiums are undoubtedly noxious weeds, to be found only in maso-chists' gardens or where people want to keep others away. They are usually thorny and not at all user-friendly, but that does not deter the gardening spirit in some of us. Over 200 species exist, and one or two have found their way into garden gentrification and are handsome in a contradictory way. *C. japonicum* is most often used as an annual, and the red flowers are harvested and dried for bouquets. Occasionally fresh flowers are seen in roadside markets or florists, but they do not have enough flower power to be in great demand.

The most common perennial species is the purple-flowered *C. rivulare*, which does relatively well in gardens on the West Coast and midwest. Plants grow 3' tall and bear 2–5 flowered clusters of 1–2" wide, rounded globes. The spiny leaves are entire to slightly-pinnate and not fun to handle. Plants, however, are striking in the middle or as a backdrop to other flowers in the garden and provide some height in late spring and summer. Where content, they will self-sow with abandon. Removal of the flowers immediately upon their decline may be good housekeeping. The cultivar 'Atropurpureum' is sometimes offered with deeper purple flowers than the type.

## *Claytonia* (klay-ton-ee' a)          Spring Beauty          Portulacaceae

One of the earliest American botanists, John Clayton, was honored with the name of these woodland native species, which provide handsome flowers on unobtrusive plants. Plants occur from Newfoundland to Minnesota, and south from Georgia to Texas. The genus is characterized by 2-leaf stems, persistent sepals, and a raceme of white to pink, 5-petaled flowers with deeper veins.

## Quick Reference to Claytonia Species

|  | Height (in.) | Stem leaves | Flower color |
|---|---|---|---|
| *C. caroliniana* | 6–12 | Oblong | Pink |
| *C. virginiana* | 4–6 | Linear | White |

*-caroliniana* (car-o-lin-ee' ane-a)    Wide-Leaved Spring Beauty    4–9"/6"
  Pink            Spring          North America             Zones 4–7

Plants are less well-known than *C. virginiana* and characterized by weak, upright stems with oblong leaves and distinct petioles. About 2–10 pink flowers (sometimes white flowers with pink stripes) with deeper veins occur in late spring. Plants are less tolerant of humidity and heat than *C. virginiana*.

Propagate by terminal cutting or division immediately after flowering.

*-virginiana* (vir-gin-i' ca)    Narrow-Leaved Spring Beauty    4–6"/8"
  Spring   White to Pale Pink   North America            Zones 4–7

These ground-hugging plants (decumbent) consist of many 6–12" long stems arising from deep corms. The two opposite stem leaves are 3–6" long, about ½" wide without well-defined petioles. The 10–15 white flowers are generally tinged with pink and held in long racemes.

Propagate similar to *C. caroliniana*.

**Related Species:**

*C. lanceolata* is a western representative in the genus, which is similar to *C. virginiana* but flowers a little earlier. Plants have 1–2 stalked, basal leaves, but the stem leaves are sessile. The petals are whitish pink, although some variants may be yellow. Native from the Cascade Mountains to Wyoming and Colorado.

<u>Quick Key to Claytonia Species</u>

    A. Plants decumbent, stem leaves
       linear, less than ½" wide . . . . . . . . . . . . . . . *C. virginiana*
    AA. Plants weakly upright, stem leaves
       oblong, greater than ½" wide . . . . . . . . . . . *C. caroliniana*

*Clematis* (klem' a-tis)    Clematis    Ranunculaceae

Over 230 species of woody and herbaceous species have been described in this diverse genus. Certainly, the best known are the large-flowered vines, and there is no lack of exceptional hybrids and species for the garden. One of the most vigorous climbers, *C. vitalba*, Dutchman's beard, traveller's joy, is quickly strangling many of the forests of New Zealand. It has been designated a noxious weed, and eradication programs are being carried out. I grow clematis vines over every shrub in my garden, from 'Nellie Stevens' holly to *Fothergilla* 'Mt. Airy'. It is difficult to beat the hybrid vines for color and vigor, but numerous species and their cultivars are becoming more available to American gardeners. In the north, most hybrids are winter hardy to zone 5; a number of species such as *C. macropetela*, *C. orientalis*, and *C. maximowicziana* grow well to zone 4. In the south, most hybrids and species do well; however, I have had very difficult times with *C. orientalis* and *C. tangutica*. In the spring, they seem to grow a few feet a day, but in midsummer, they succumb to the infamous "clematis wilt." They die back to the ground, only to go through this frustrating cycle the next year. On the other hand, *C. montana* takes over the place. *C. cirrhosa*, the winter clematis, has some of the best glossy, green foliage and flowers in late winter, although in the South, the foliage looks poor in the summer. The best of the viners is the Texas clematis, *C. texensis*, with chalice flowers and long flowering time. The cultivar 'Duchess of Albany' scrambles through my sweetshrub and flowers from May to July.

The genus also includes some fine herbaceous, non-climbing species, and they shall be discussed in some detail in this book. Most people feel that the herbaceous species are not as showy as the climbers, but I would not be without the solitary clematis, *C. integrifolia*. The non-climbers can be handsome garden plants ranging from 1–3'. The leaves are opposite and may be lobed, entire, or divided.

The discovery of new species continues, one of the latest being *C. marmoraria*, a dioecious subshrub found in 1973 near Nelson, New Zealand and first described in 1987. It is the smallest known species in the genus, bearing white flowers and spreading slowly by rhizomes. Not yet available in the trade.

## Quick Reference to Non-Climbing Clematis Species

|  | Height (ft.) | Flower color | Number of leaflets |
|---|---|---|---|
| *C. heracleifolia* | 2–3 | Blue | 3–5 |
| *C. integrifolia* | 1½–2 | Blue | Entire |
| *C. recta* | 3–4 | White | 5–7 |

| *-heracleifolia* (he-ra-klee-i-fo' lee-a) | Tube Clematis | 2–3'/3' |
|---|---|---|
| Late Summer      Blue | China | Zones 3–7 |

This subshrub has compound foliage, each leaf divided into three, 3–6" long leaflets with sharply-pointed teeth. About 6–12 tubular, hyacinth-like, blue flowers are produced in short, axillary clusters. They have 4 reflexed sepals (there are no petals), and some flowers are male, while others are perfect (male and female parts present). The 1" long, fragrant flowers are produced in late summer and fall and followed by fluffy seedheads.

These are lovely plants but sprawl everywhere by late summer and fall. They are vigorous growers and should not be fertilized unless necessary. Interplant closely with plants of equal size or provide support such as twigs to keep them from falling over. They are a bit of a pain in the behind when they do. Plants prefer full sun and plenty of moisture.

Propagate by 2″ long, terminal cuttings in the spring and summer. Seeds may be cooled for 2–4 weeks at 40° F and then sown in a warm, humid area.

## Cultivars:
'Cote D'Azur' has lighter blue flowers but otherwise is similar to the type.

Var. *davidiana* has wider flowers and less reflexed sepals than the species. The flowers are violet-blue, and plants are 6–12″ taller than the type. The foliage is heavily scented when dried and may be used in potpourri.

'Wyevale' has darker blue flowers than the type, and the small flowers are lightly scented.

Var. *davidiana* is one of the parents of *C.* × *jouiniana*, a vigorous lavender-white, flowered sprawler.

## Related Species:
*C. stans*, japtube clematis, is similar but has ¾″ long, light blue flowers borne in terminal, as well as axillary clusters. It is less woody and must be supported. It is not as good a garden plant as *C. heracleifolia* or *C. integrifolia*.

| | | | |
|---|---|---|---|
| *-integrifolia* (in-teg-ri-fo′ lee-a) | | Solitary Clematis | 1½–3′/3′ |
| Summer | Blue | Southern Europe | Zones 3–7 |

The common name comes from the single, urn-shaped, nodding flowers borne at the ends of the stems. They are indigo-violet, 1–2″ long, with the sepals turned up at the ends. This species contains some of the most handsome plants for the herbaceous garden. This has to be one of the finest, most overlooked plants in American gardening. In the Armitage garden, it starts flowering in mid-May and continues on and off for 6–8 weeks. Further north, flowering occurs in late summer, about 1–2 weeks earlier than *C. heracleifolia*, followed by the appearance of ornamental, plumose seed heads. The Armitage planting is my favorite but I have seen wonderful specimens in late May in Asheville, NC; I also saw a wonderful planting, covered with spiral, translucent seed heads, on an early August trip to the superb Botanical Garden in Montreal. The 2–4″ long leaves are sessile and entire (not trifoliate as in most species). The whole plant is slightly hairy.

Plants do not sprawl as much as the previous species but should still be supported. I place twigs and old stems around the emerging plant (pea staking) and let the plant grow through and over this homemade support. Place in full sun, although partial shade is tolerated (shade causes fewer flowers and thinner stems). The best of the non-vining clematis.

Propagate similar to *C. heracleifolia*.

## Cultivars:
'Olgae' has lightly-scented, light blue flowers with long, recurved sepals.

*Clematis integrifolia*
(95%)

'Pastel Blue' and 'Pastel Pink' have powder blue and light pink flowers respectively.

'Rosea' bears rose-colored flowers.

'Tapestry' bears large, mauve to red flowers.

**Related Species:**

*C.* × *eriostemon* (*C. integrifolia* × *C. viticella*) is a sprawling, semi-woody shrub which is more vigorous than solitary clematis. Flowers are often borne in sets of three, and leaves generally consist of 7 leaflets.

'Bergeronii' is a vigorous grower with mauve, campanulate flowers, usually grouped in sets of threes. 'Hendersonii' has single, violet-blue flowers and is the most popular selection.

| *-recta* (rek' ta) | | Ground Clematis | 3-4'/3' |
|---|---|---|---|
| Summer | White | Southern Europe | Zones 3-7 |

This is different than either of the previous species, as it bears hundreds of fragrant, white-fringed flowers. They are borne in large, terminal and axillary panicles in summer and followed by silky fruits. The pinnately-compound leaves are divided into 5-9 entire leaflets, each pointed and 1-3″ long. Plants can be allowed to crawl along the ground or supported similar to other climbers. This species does not know whether to climb or crawl, but I have seen plants climbing through hollies and supported around pea staking at the back of the garden bed. At Longwood, it was supported and in full flower in late May and early June. Looks good no matter what it does.

Propagate similar to *C. heracleifolia.*

**Cultivars:**

'Flore-plena' has double flowers that persist longer than the type.

'Peveril' is more upright to about 3' tall and is quite floriferous.

'Purpurea' bears purple leaves which make a wonderful contrast to the creamy white flowers. Absolutely wonderful.

Quick Key to Clematis Species

    A. Leaves divided, not entire
        B. Leaflets 5-9, flowers white . . . . . . . . . . . . . . . *C. recta*
        BB. Leaflets 3, flowers blue . . . . . . . . . . . . . *C. heracleifolia*
    AA. Leaves entire, not divided . . . . . . . . . . . . . . *C. integrifolia*

**Additional Reading:**

Austin, Susan. 1988. The other clematis. *Horticulture* 66(7):41-47.

Evison, Raymond, J. 1979. *Making the Most of Clematis.* Floraprint Ltd, Nottingham, England. 78 pages.

Gray-Wilson, C. 1987. *Clematis marmoraria. Kew Magazine* 49(3): 116-119.

*Clerodendrum* (kle-ro-den' drum)     Glory Bower     Verbenaceae

Over 400 species of woody trees, shrubs, and vines occur with opposite or whorled leaves. However, nearly all are tropical plants, better suited for the greenhouse than the garden. The species may be divided into shrubby or vining forms; however, the only species to enjoy some popularity in American gardens is *C. trichotomum*, a large, vigorous plant cold hardy to about zone 7b.

*-trichotomum* (tri-ko' to-mum)     Harlequin Glory Bower     8–10'/10'
Summer          White          Eastern China, Japan     Zones 6–9

A crazy, big tree that sets records for the amount of growth per day, growing up to 10' tall and almost as wide in a single year. Plants often die back to the ground in severe winters and have survived as far north as New York City. The white, 5-petaled flowers are tubular at the base, starting in July, and crowded together in stalked cymes, 6–9" across. The reddish, leathery sepals are at the base of the flowers, and the ¼" diameter, bright blue, pea-like fruits (drupe) occur in late summer through the fall. The fruit are not particularly showy until they are right in front of your nose. The dark green leaves are opposite, simple, usually entire, and smell awful when bruised. Spreads by root suckers which can be divided and replanted.

Certainly not a plant for everyone, but a plant to look forward to if it is happy. One of the best specimens I have seen is at the State Botanical Garden of Georgia, where dark red calyces, clean white flowers, and bright blue fruits make one want to be ill or sing the National Anthem. Place plants in an area of full sun and well-drained soils.

Propagate by terminal cuttings in late spring.

**Related Species:**

*C. bungei* is a spreading, 3–6' tall shrub with opposite, pubescent, malodorous foliage and spiny stems. The handsome ¾" wide, rosy-red flowers, with a flower tube, are 3–4 times longer than the calyx. Plants are hardy to about zone 8 but may survive as far north as Philadelphia if the crown is protected.

*C. indicum*, Turk's turban, is native to Asia and bears glossy green leaves and long (4"), tubular, fragrant, white flowers very late in the season. In zone 7, it is hardy, but flowers seldom occur before a hard frost. They are more common further south. Plants are invasive, appearing like magic late in the season. I pinch mine to obtain more branched stems, but in general they are totally unsuitable for zones north of zone 8. However, they are certainly worth trying in zones 8–10.

*C. ugandense* bears handsome light blue flowers and dark green foliage. Plants grow to substantial subshrubs. Hardiness has not been clearly established but likely hardy in zones 8–10.

*Clintonia* (klin-tone-ee′ a)          Wood Lily          Liliaceae

The governor of New York State in the early nineteenth century had tremendous foresight and aggressively promoted the building of the Erie Canal. The canal, built between 1817 and 1825, connects the Hudson River to Lake Erie and made New York a major shipping port. The governor, whose name was DeWitt Clinton, was also a plant enthusiast and was honored with this marvelous genus. Five species are known, two native to the American west (*C. andrewsiana, C. uniflora*), one native to the Himalayas and Japan (*C. udensis*), and the two most common forms native to eastern North America (*C. borealis, C. umbellulata*).

Quick Reference to Clintonia Species

|  | Flower color | Flower number | Fruit color |
| --- | --- | --- | --- |
| *C. borealis* | Greenish yellow | 2–8 | Blue |
| *C. umbellulata* | White | 10–30 | Black |

*-borealis* (bore-ee′ al-is)          Bluebeard, Dogberry          9–15″/12″
   Spring     Greenish Yellow     Eastern North America     Zones 4–7

The flower stems generally arise from 2–5 (usually 3) obovate, thin, glossy green, basal leaves. The slightly-drooping, green-yellow flowers occur in umbels and consist of 6 spreading petals. The flowers are handsome but sparsely produced. The shining blue fruit are more familiar and account for the common names of bluebeard and dogberry.

Propagate by removing the seed from the fruit and germinating in cool conditions.

*-umbellulata* (um-bel-ewe-lah′ ta)     Speckled Wood-Lily     9–12″/12″
   Spring          White          Eastern North America     Zones 4–7

Although not as widely distributed as the previous species, it still may be found in mountains from New York to Ohio and south to Georgia and Tennessee. The white flowers are held in a 5- to 30-flowered umbel in early spring above light green, shiny, basal leaves. The flowers are often spotted with green and purple and are only about ⅛″ long. After flowering, blackberries are formed which provide food for birds and other small critters.

A most handsome woodland plant. Provide rich soils and partial shade. Propagate similar to *C. borealis*.

**Related Species:**

*C. andrewsiana*, native from middle California to southwestern Oregon, is far more colorful and striking than the previous species, bearing deep

281

rose-purple flowers on 2-3' tall stems. Five to six shiny, basal leaves are produced in the spring, and blue fruit occur after flowering. Worth trying, also cold hardy to about zone 7.

### Quick Key to Clintonia Species

    A. Flowers greenish yellow, 2-5 flowers per stem  ...  *C. borealis*
    AA. Flowers white, 5-30 flowers per stem ....... *C. umbellulata*

## *Codonopsis* (ko-don-op'sis)     Asia Bell     Campanulaceae

This little-used genus consists of about 40 species of herbaceous plants, often with twining stems, native to Central Asia, the Himalayas, and southeastward to Java. I never understood why this genus is ignored by gardeners and growers, as it is handsome, easy to grow, and fits well with other garden plants. Perhaps it is ignored because the bell-shaped flowers are nodding and require close inspection to appreciate, and because the foliage has a distinctly unpleasant odor. The genus name is from the greek *kodon*, bell, and *opis*, appearance, alluding to the shape of the corolla. The genus differs from the genus *Campanula* in subtle ways, mostly having to do with the ovary and fruit capsule. The ovary is inferior, and the fruit splits open from the side in *Campanula*. The ovary is superior, and the fruit splits open on the top in *Codonopsis*.

*-clematidea* (klem-a-tid' ee-a)    Asian Bell Flower    2-3'/2'
  Summer     Light Blue     Asia     Zones 5-7

The stems are erect when young but eventually begin to sprawl and twine. The ¾" long, lanceolate to ovate leaves are entire, lightly pubescent, and alternate or sub-opposite. The 1" wide, nodding, light blue, bell-shaped flowers have lovely orange centers which remain hidden from view unless you take the trouble to pick them up and look inside. The flowers are usually solitary at the ends of the many branches. The lobes of the calyx (sepals) are about half the length of the corolla (petals) and reflexed. Plants require a good deal of room because of their sprawling habit and are best planted on banks or other areas where the inside of the flowers can be admired. Otherwise they are not as interesting. Place them in full sun to moderate shade and provide plenty of moisture.

    Propagate by terminal cuttings or seed. Take 2" terminal cuttings of basal shoots emerging in spring and root in a peat:vermiculite mix. Seeds should be covered lightly and placed in a warm (70-75° F), humid atmosphere. Germination occurs within 2-3 weeks.

### Related Species:

    *C. cardiophylla* is similar to *C. clematidea*, but differs by having smaller flowers and more cordate leaves. The leaves also have narrow, white, slightly-thickened margins.

*C. ovata* is also often confused with *C. clematidea*. Plants are shorter (9–12″) and less sprawling. The calyx, which is less than ½ as long as the corolla, consists of spreading sepals. The sepals of *C. clematidea* are strongly reflexed back.

*C. lanceolata* is a twining species with 2–3″ long, pointed leaves with a very short petiole and flowers which are light blue and lilac outside and violet inside. Often confused with *C. ussuriensis*, which differs by having obtuse, smaller leaves (1–1½″ long). They are lumped together by some authorities.

**Additional Reading:**

Grey-Wilson, C. 1990. A survey of *Codonopsis* in cultivation. *The Plantsman* 12(2):64–99.

## *Colchicum* (kol-chi′ kum)          Autumn Crocus          Liliaceae

Approximately 45 species of plants occur, all of which arise from corms. The name comes from Colchis, a former country on the Black Sea, now part of the Georgian Republic, where the genus is plentiful. The common name comes from the flowering time and the resemblance of the flowers to crocus. Flowers in nearly all species occur in late summer or fall. The basal leaves usually arise in early spring and generally die down by early summer. The flowers are often solitary or in short-stalked clusters, with a tubular perianth and 6 stamens. In general, flower color is rose, pink, or white but can vary from purple to white (one species, *C. lutea* is yellow and blooms in the spring). *Colchicum* and *Crocus*, particularly the fall-flowering species, may be confused. Four major differences occur between the two:

1. *Crocus* has 3 stamens, *Colchicum* has six.
2. There are 3 distinct styles in *Colchicum*; in *Crocus*, there is just one, which is divided into 3 just below the tip.
3. The leaves of *Crocus* always have a whitish line down the center and are narrow; in *Colchicum* they are broad and never have a line down the center.
4. The corm of *Crocus* is symmetrical with the shoot on top; in *Colchicum* the corm is irregular, and the shoot is produced on the side.

In general, cultivation is easy; however, their reputation for beauty is overdone. Without foliage, the flowers often fall over and look like tired pink dogs. They are much more effective when planted through some low-growing ground covers such as dwarf artemisias, mossy saxifrage, sedums, or phlox, where they stand up much more effectively and are protected from splashing rain. I have had reasonable success when I planted some corms through low-growing, blue-leaved hostas, such as 'Blue Cadet' or 'Blue Wedgewood'. Blooms are short-lived, although some species produce numerous flowers in quick succession. Although flowers are beautiful, the corms are relatively expensive, particularly for the length of bloom time. On the other hand, they open at a time when many other flowers are declining in the garden.

Corms must be ordered to arrive and to plant in late summer or early fall, or they may bloom in the box. Plant the top of the corm 1–2" deep in areas well supplemented with organic matter, good drainage, and in partial shade to full sun. Do not disturb unless they are in need of division or if the flowering has declined in recent years. Slugs are a major nuisance as they love to attack the emerging flowers. Heavy late summer rainfall can also result in significant loss of corms, particularly where drainage is suspect.

Quick Reference to Colchicum Species

|  | Height (in.) | Flower color | Number of flowers |
|---|---|---|---|
| C. autumnale | 3–4 | Purple-pink | 1–4 |
| C. byzantinum | 2–3 | Lilac-purple | 12–20 |
| C. speciosum | 4–5 | Violet | 1–4 |

| *-autumnale* (ow-tum-nah' lee) | Autumn Crocus, Naked Boys | 4–6"/6" |
|---|---|---|
| Fall          Purple-Pink | Europe | Zones 4–7 |

This is the best known and most widely-distributed species. The flowers occur before the leaves and vary from purple to rose-colored to lilac. The perianth tube is 4–8" long and about 1–2' wide, and flowers are among the earliest to appear, often as early as late August or early September. The 5–8 narrow leaves may be up to 12" long where they are happy. My experiences have been similar to the comments above; I look forward to their arrival but am often disappointed by their lackluster performance.

Plant in partial shade to full sun; by the time the hot summer sun arrives, little remains of the plant. Well-drained soils are important as boggy soils contribute to corm rot. Probably the most cold hardy of the available species, tolerant to at least −5° F soil temperature.

**Cultivars:**
'Album' is a white-flowered form
'Pleniflorum' bears large, double flowers.
'Alboplenum' produces double, white flowers.

| *-byzantinum* (bi-zan-tee' num) | Byzantine Colchicum | 4–6"/6" |
|---|---|---|
| Fall          Lilac-Purple | Turkey | Zones 6–8 |

One of the best species, but not as well known as the more common ones. Plants bear up to 20 lilac flowers per corm, although 10–12 is more common in most American gardens. Flowers usually have a white center and appear in September and October, and the dark green, wide (up to 4″ across) leaves appear in late winter or early spring.

**Related Species:**

*C. cilicicum* is very similar and differs by having deeper lilac-colored flowers, with leaves appearing just after the flowers disappear.

| *-speciosum* (spe-cee-o′ sum) | | Showy Colchicum | 4–6″/6″ |
|---|---|---|---|
| Fall | Violet | Southern Turkey | Zones 5–7 |

Another species worth trying, it differs from others by having stronger colors, although a good deal of variability occurs. The species probably produces the largest flowers, usually 1–4 per corm. Flowers in September and October, with 4–5 leaves, each 3–4″ wide and up to 15″ long. The leaves are produced in the late winter and spring.

**Cultivars:**

'Album' is a fine white-flowered form, which some gardeners feel is the best white autumn "bulb."

'Maximum' has even larger flowers.

**Related Species:**

*C. giganteum*, giant colchicum, flowers a little later than *C. speciosum* and may be somewhat more robust. The flowers are more broadly funnel-shaped than campanulate, as in *C. speciosum*.

**Hybrids of Colchicum:**

A number of hybrids have been developed which incorporate *C. speciosum*, *C. giganteum*, and *C. bivonae* in their parentage.

'Autumn Queen' ('Princess Astrid') has purple flowers with a white center. Flowers have a crisscrossed pattern (tesselated) on the petals, a characteristic of *C. bivonae*.

'Lilac Wonder' has large, rosy-purple flowers with a long, narrow tube. The flowers soon flop over.

'The Giant' bears large, lilac-pink flowers, white in center with faint tessellation.

'Violet Queen' produces flowers which are dark purple throughout.

'Waterlily' is the best known double form. The deep rose-pink flowers resemble a waterlily and can be quite handsome. After a heavy rain, they can also look whipped and dog-eared.

Quick Key to Colchicum Species

    A. Number of flowers 1–4
        B. Leaves 3–4″ wide ................... *C. speciosum*
        BB. Leaves 1–2″ wide ................... *C. autumnale*
    AA. Number of flowers 12–20 ............... *C. byzantinum*

## *Conradina* (kon-rah-deen' a)     Cumberland Rosemary     Lamiaceae

Seven species of low-growing, shrubby plants, native to the southern United States occur. All are characterized by narrow leaves which are usually rolled under at the edges, and two-lipped flowers. Most are native to Florida; however, the best garden plant, *C. verticillata*, extends northward to the Cumberland mountains of Tennessee and Kentucky. The needle-like foliage resembles rosemary and has a strong herbal fragrance. The pink-lavender flowers are produced at or near the end of the procumbent stems. Plants are found growing in sandy soils, indicating the need for excellent drainage. They look wonderful growing over walls. These are not the easiest plants to grow; I have managed to kill my fair share; however, in well-drained soils and full sun to partial shade, they can be excellent. Hardy in zones 5–9. My friend, Willis Hardin, of Commerce, GA has been quite successful with the conradinas and plants them in a sandy, very well-drained area. He has a nice collection which benefit from the chance to get out of the normally wet clay.

A beautiful white-flowered form, 'Cumberland Snow', was found by Leo Collins of North Carolina and is available at selected nurseries. This species (and any varieties or cultivars) is a federally-protected species, and plants can only be purchased by nurseries with the appropriate propagation permit.

Another species with potential for southern gardeners is *C. canescens*, native to the pinelands of the gulf coast of Florida and Alabama. Plants can grow to 3' tall, have gray foliage, and have rosy-pink flowers. Native to sandy soils, excellent drainage is necessary. A compact form can occasionally be found.

## *Convallaria* (kon-val-air' ee-a)     Lily-of-the-Valley     Liliaceae

The only species in the genus, *C. majalis*, is native to most of the Northern Hemisphere. The creeping rootstock allows rapid spread under optimum conditions. In the North, it is often looked upon as a benevolent, fragrant, aggressive weed, but, as one travels further south, the creeping tendency is severely retarded, and plants do not fill in nearly as rapidly or as well. Growing up in Montreal, I loved and hated it with equal passion. Plants filled in everywhere, and dynamite was needed to dislodge them. However, nothing compared to the thick fragrance of the flowers in the spring. Living in Georgia, where it struggles to send up a few flowers in the spring, I have decided that I know of no finer weed. The 2–3 basal leaves are lanceolate-ovate and about 8″ long. The arching, one-sided racemes carry 5–8 drooping, white, wonderfully fragrant flowers which should be brought inside the house to be fully enjoyed. The plants are about 12″ tall in flower and thrive in zones 2–5, do well in zones 6 and 7a, and struggle in zones 7b and 8. Grow in semi-shade and consistently moist conditions. Plants should not be overlooked by those in

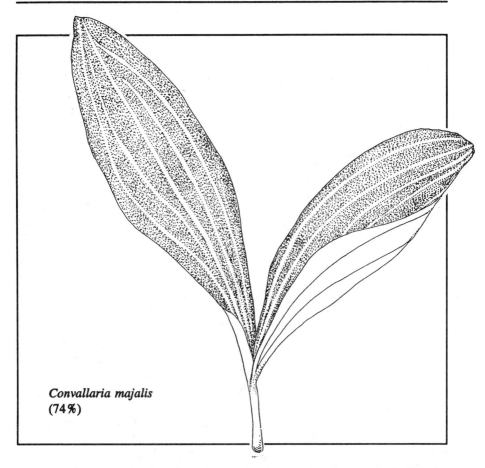

*Convallaria majalis*
(74%)

the commercial arena. Cut flowers are always sought after, and, during the wedding season, flowers are sold at an exorbitant price. Fathers with daughters should think about planting a large patch today and talking the bride and groom into a spring wedding. Also, plants may be forced relatively easily in the greenhouse for flower and pot plant use.

Propagate by division immediately after flowering.

### Cultivars:

'Fortin's Giant' ('Fortin's Variety') is 12–15″ tall and has larger flowers (¾″ long) than the species.

'Plena' has cream-colored, double flowers, larger and more persistent than the type.

'Prolificans' is a most unusual form of this handsome species. Plants bear tiny flowers congested in a tightly-branched inflorescence. They appear to be double but are occasionally malformed in appearance. Difficult to find but an interesting addition.

287

'Rosea' has handsome, light pink flowers but is otherwise similar to the species.

'Striata' ('Aureo-variegata', 'Lineata', 'Variegata') has green leaves with pale yellow stripes and white flowers. Very handsome.

*Convolvulus* (kon-vol' vew-lus)        Bindweed,        Convolvulaceae
                                        Morning Glory

Few of the 250 species are ever voluntarily planted in gardens, but the appearance of the strangling common bindweed, *C. arvense*, is certainly not uncommon. The fear of bindweed and the lack of cold hardiness in most ornamental species have limited their availability. Few species do well in eastern gardens, but their tolerance of hot, dry conditions allow species to perform well in the southwest and West Coast.

Three to four species are offered to the American gardener, but those on the west coast have the most chance of success. A handsome, weedy species, *C. althaeoides* (*C. elegantissima*), produces pink flowers with dark venation over trailing, silver-leaved stems. Cold hardy to zone 7 or 8 but can be quite invasive. *C. cneorum*, silver bush morning glory, is a 2–4' tall, shrubby plant whose white, pink-tinged flowers contrast well with silvery-gray foliage. Sun and absolutely well-drained soils are essential. If plants begin to look ratty, renew them by hard pruning when necessary. Hardy in zones 7–9, although they are not particularly tolerant of heat or humidity. *C. boisseri* is occasionally offered, and the compact form grows only 3" tall and 8" wide. White flowers are produced over cushions of silver rosettes. Best for the very well-drained rock garden in zones 7–8. *C. sabaticus* (*C. mauritanicus*) is a handsome, trailing, evergreen rambler with violet-blue flowers, often with a yellow center. Plants are well suited to climb over and around other plants or trail over walls. Good drainage and full sun, zones 7–10. 'Baby Moon' and 'Full Moon' are darker blue variants of the species. Excellent introductions.

For those of you who can only grow bindweed and have been frustrated with trying to untangle it from other plants and trying to pull it up without success, this tip may be helpful. Put posts (bamboo, tomato stakes) in the plantings in the spring and allow the bindweed to climb up the posts. Once they are above the good planting, paint some Round-Up or other systemic herbicide on the leaves. The plants will eventually die, and the planting will be forever thankful.

Propagate the good species by root cuttings or seed.

*Coptis* (kop' tis)                Goldthread                Ranunculaceae

The goldthreads, so named for the bright golden, slender, underground sto-lons, are terrific small plants for shady, moist places. Native to northern areas, they are seldom seen in the south because they do poorly in hot, humid conditions. The small, white flowers consist of 5–7 showy sepals and occur in early spring. The flowers are much like small white buttercups and held over shiny, dark green, fern-like, scalloped leaves. In the northwest or buried under some mulch, plants may remain evergreen throughout the winter. Three or four species are sometimes offered, often by rock garden specialists. *C. asplenifolia*, native to the northwest, has fine lacy foliage and greenish white flowers on 8–10″ tall plants. Grows well in zones 3–7. *C. laciniata*, native from Washington to California, is more robust with larger leaves and flowers but is not as cold tolerant, being hardy in zones 5–8. *C. trifolia*, native to the northeast, has handsome, shining, trifoliate leaves and similar white flowers. Hardy in zones 3–7.

Propagate by dividing the mats at any time.

## *Coreopsis* (ko-ree-op′ sis)  Tickseed  Asteraceae

Many of the 100 or more species are popular with gardeners today. They have opposite leaves, which may be entire or lobed, and yellow, daisy-like flowers. One of the characteristics of *Coreopsis* (and *Bidens*) is the presence of two distinct circles of bracts around each flower head. The outer bracts are generally green, like small leaves; the inner bracts are broader, thinner, and often yellowish. A number of fine annuals exist, particularly *C. tinctoria*, plains coreopsis, and many perennial wild flower species such as *C. tripteris*, Atlantic coreopsis, and the large-flowered, pretty *C. major*, trefoil coreopsis, brighten roadsides from Pennsylvania to Florida. *C. palmata*, stiff coreopsis, is another fine prairie species, growing about 18″ tall. Many of the perennial species were once known as *Leptosyne*, a name no longer used, and the annual species were called *Calliopsis*, which seedsmen and nurserymen persist in using, resulting in unnecessary confusion within the genus. The name *Coreopsis* translates "like a bug" and refers to the shape and color of the seeds. This is likely how the common name, tickseed, evolved. A number of genera are referred to as coneflowers, and general differences between them are mentioned under *Rudbeckia*.

*Coreopsis* should be planted in well-drained soil in full sun. All perennial members can be propagated by division, and several are easily raised from seed or terminal cuttings. Seeds germinate in 2–3 weeks if sown in a well-drained medium such as peat:perlite (1:1) in warm (70–75° F), moist conditions.

Quick Reference to Coreopsis Species

|  | Height (in.) | Flower time | Leaf shape |
| --- | --- | --- | --- |
| *C. auriculata* 'Nana' | 6–9 | Spring | Entire |
| *C. grandiflora* | 12–24 | Summer | Deeply cut |
| *C. lanceolata* | 12–24 | Summer | Moderately cut |
| *C. rosea* | 3–6 | Summer | Entire |
| *C. verticillata* | 18–36 | Summer | Thread-like segments |

-*auriculata* (ow-rik-ew-lah' ta)     Mouse Ear Coreopsis          1–2'/1'
   Spring         Yellow      Southern United States    Zones 4–9

The 1–2" diameter, solitary flowers, made up of about 8 yellow petals surrounding yellow disc flowers, are held well above the dark green, evergreen foliage. The rounded, pubescent leaves are 2–5" long and often have 1 or 2 small lobes at the base of the blade. It is stoloniferous but does not spread rampantly.

The species is easily propagated from division and can be divided every 2–3 years to maintain vigor. Plants may also be propagated from seed. Cover seeds lightly, and place seed tray in warm, humid area.

## Cultivars:

'Nana' is by far the best cultivar in the species and one of the best of the whole genus. There is nothing flashy, but flocks of bright yellow flowers are produced in April and May over foliage which remains in good condition all season if moisture is provided. If plants dry out, however, the foliage self-destructs. Like the species, it is stoloniferous but not invasive. This is a terrific plant for the front of the border or along a path. Flowers of the true 'Nana' are sterile, and the leaves are less than 1" long. Over time, some natural hybridization has occurred with cultivars of *C. grandiflora*. The resultant hybrid is taller than 'Nana', shorter-lived, not as stoloniferous, and the flowers are not sterile. Therefore, if plants are grown from seed, it is not 'Nana'. I am not sure what it is, and there may be nothing wrong with that hybrid, but it is not the true 'Nana'. 'Nana' may be propagated by cutting the stolons, inserting them vertically in a tray, and putting them under long days.
'Superba' has large (2–3" diameter), orange flowers with a maroon center and is good for cutting.

## Related Species:

*C. integrifolia*, Chipola River coreopsis, has entire leaves and grows 2–3' tall. Plants are native to northwest Florida and produce beautiful dark-eyed daisies in August and September. Hardiness is not well known, but probably zones 7b–9.

-*grandiflora* (gran-di-flo' ra)     Tickseed          1–2'/1'
   Summer     Yellow      Southern United States    Zones 4–9

This is the mainstay of many a summer garden. The lowermost leaves are simple, while the upper ones are often deeply 3–5-lobed. The flower heads are 1–2½" across and orange to yellow. It has a particularly long flowering season when handled properly, but, unfortunately, plants are short-lived, lasting 2–3 years in the South and up to 4 years in the North. In southern California, it never winterkills in milder climates and often self-sows.

Flowers on all species of *Coreopsis*, but particularly this one, must be deadheaded if plants are to flower to their potential. Flowering occurs late May to early August if spent flowers are removed, a tiring task but one well worth the fatigue. Don't get lazy and simply flick off the flower heads with your thumb, or all that will appear above the foliage is naked flower sticks. Not only will the potential of the plants be unfulfilled by the lack of deadheading, but the worn out flowers are excellent candidates for disease. Cultivars which come true from seed have been produced, and singles, semi-doubles, and doubles are now available.

Propagate by divisions in the spring or fall, or from seed treated similar to *C. auriculata*.

## Cultivars:

'Badengold' bears bright yellow flowers. An older cultivar but still popular.

'Domino' produces single, golden yellow flowers with dark centers. Plants are only about 1½' tall.

'Early Sunrise' was an All-America winner in 1989. Plants are easily raised from seed and bear semi-double, bright yellow, 2" wide flowers. Short-lived but excellent for a couple of years.

'Mayfield Giant' is an old cultivar with 2–3" diameter, gold-yellow flowers, grows 2–3' tall and useful for cut flowers.

'Ruby Throat' bears yellow flowers with a deep claret throat.

'Schnittgold' produces golden yellow flowers.

'Sunburst' is about 2' tall with large, semi-double, golden yellow flowers.

'Sunray' is an exceptional selection which bears 2" diameter, double flowers for 8–12 weeks on 2' plants.

'U.F.O.' is a single, yellow-flowered form from David Tristram of England. Compact (about 15" tall) and free-flowering.

## Related Species:

*C. tripteris*, tall coreopsis, grows 4–10' and bears dozens of dark-centered, single, yellow flowers. The flowers are slightly anise-scented. Very showy, but can get very big. Foliage has 3–5 narrow leaf segments. Native from southern Ontario to Wisconsin, south to Florida and Louisiana, and west to Kansas.

| *-lanceolata* (lan-cee-o' lah-ta) | Lanceleaf Coreopsis | 1–2'/2' |
|---|---|---|
| Late Spring    Yellow | Eastern United States | Zones 3–8 |

There is little difference between this and *C. grandiflora*, and some cultivars are hybrids between the two. Plants are rather variable, but the flowers are always borne singly and up to 2½" across. The stems are leafy, mainly toward the base of the plant, compared to *C. grandiflora* which is leafy throughout. The leaves are not as deeply cut as *C. grandiflora* and sometimes may be entire. It is a good garden performer, perhaps a little longer lived than *C. grandiflora* but not as floriferous. Comments concerning deadheading of *C. grandiflora* also pertain to this species.

Propagate similar to *C. auriculata*.

**Cultivars:**

'Baby Sun' provides excellent compact, 12–18″ tall plants with yellow-orange flowers.

'Brown Eyes' is an excellent long-lived cultivar with single, yellow flowers that have a maroon ring near the center. We grew plants for about 5 years in the Horticulture Garden at Georgia before we removed them.

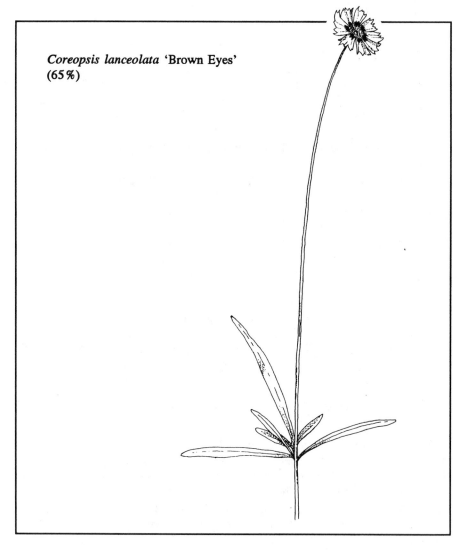

*Coreopsis lanceolata* 'Brown Eyes'
(65%)

'Goldfink' produces many 2" wide, single, yellow flowers with an orange center, yet only grows to about 9" in height. Plants are excellent for the front of the garden. Should be raised from cuttings or divisions.

'Sternthaler' is similar to 'Brown Eyes' and has gold flowers with a brown ring over 12–18" tall plants.

'Summer Sprite' is a recent development from Carroll Gardens of Westminster, MD. Plants produce single, yellow flowers with a mahogany-red ring around the center on 10–12" tall plants.

'Sundancer' is also bright yellow.

**Related Species:**

*C. palmata*, stiff coreopsis, is native to the American prairie and bears 7–8 rayed, yellow flowers on 2–3' tall plants. The leaves are sessile, but the lower half resembles a stalk, and the upper half is deeply cleft into 3 narrow lobes.

| *-rosea* (rose-ee' a) | | Pink Coreopsis | 9–15"/Spreader |
| --- | --- | --- | --- |
| Summer | Rose-Pink | Eastern United States | Zones 4–7 |

I have seen wonderful rosy-pink, spreading mounds in northern Ohio and lousy, spotty plants in the south. At their best, the thread-like leaves are covered with ¾" flowers, each with a yellow center. Plants are rhizomatous and rapidly form handsome, 8–10" tall ground covers which combine well with many taller plants. At its worst, it survives by sending up a few spindly stems and flowers, soon to be ripped out and put out of its misery. Those who enjoy the plant find that it comports well with *Echinacea* and *Rudbeckia*, where the rose and yellow of the *Coreopsis* are repeated in the flowers of the other two species. Best in cooler climates, but still useful as far south as zone 7. Plants offered in the trade are probably var. *nana*, since the species itself is approximately 2' tall. Plants are native from southwest Nova Scotia to Maryland. In 1993, the Dutch growers named this a plant of the year in Holland and called it 'American Dream'. Same as the species.

Place in full sun and provide excellent drainage. Planting on a sloping bank helps with the drainage and enhances the view of the flowers.

Propagate by division any time.

| *-verticillata* (ver-ti-si-lah' ta) | | Thread Leaf Coreopsis | 18"–3'/3' |
| --- | --- | --- | --- |
| Summer | Yellow | Eastern United States | Zones 5–9 |

The combination of new cultivars with brighter, better colors combined with drought tolerance, long flowering time, and long life put this species at the top of the list among *Coreopsis*. The sessile, 2–3" long leaves are palmately-divided into thread-like segments, and therefore there is little leaf area from which to lose water under times of drought. The 1½–2″ diameter, single flowers are borne in a few-flowered inflorescence (corymb) and held on slender stalks. Two or three plants grouped in a well-drained, sunny location grow into a sizable clump by the end of the summer. After the burst of summer flowering, cut off the flowers, and an autumn flush follows. I have not been as successful with the species in north Georgia as expected. Hordes of flower buds are produced which proceeded to blacken and rot. This has not been the case, however, with several cultivars.

Propagate similar to *C. auriculata.*

### Cultivars:

'Golden Showers' ('Grandiflora') is 18–24″ tall, produces 2–2½″ diameter, bright yellow flowers, and is larger in every way than the type.

'Moonbeam' is the most popular cultivar. Plants are 18–24″ tall and bear many soft, muted yellow flowers which never fail to catch the eye.

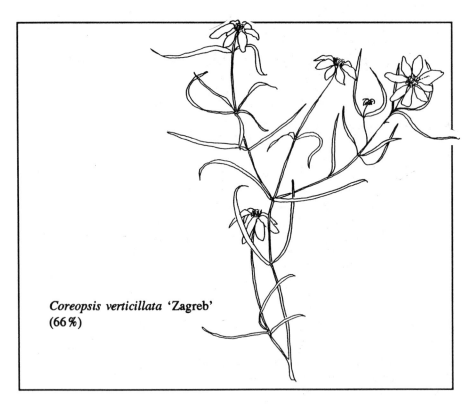

*Coreopsis verticillata* 'Zagreb'
(66%)

Flowers open continuously from late June to October and combine well with purple foliage of everything from *Setcrasea* 'Purple Heart' to *Pennisetum setaceum* 'Rubrum'. Plants have performed well throughout the country. Perennial Plant of the Year, 1992.

'Zagreb' has deeper yellow flowers than 'Moonbeam'. Compact upright plants are bushy and only 8–12″ tall in the North. In the South, 18″ tall plants are not uncommon. This is the toughest and best performing cultivar of this species.

**Related Species:**

*C. pulchra*, beautiful coreopsis, has similar foliage as *C. verticillata* and produces handsome yellow flowers, each with a red eye. Flowers in summer; hardy in zones 6–9. Requires excellent drainage for best performance. Native to Alabama.

<u>Quick Key to Coreopsis Species</u>

    A. Leaves divided or lobed, not entire
       B. Leaves finely divided, thread-like
          C. Plants generally at least
            2′ tall, flowers yellow . . . . . . . . . . . . . . . *C. verticillata*
          CC. Plants generally less than
            2′ tall, flowers rose-pink . . . . . . . . . . . . . . . *C. rosea*
      BB. Leaves divided into broad segments,
        not thread-like
          C. Leaves deeply divided into 3
            segments, plant leafy throughout . . . . . . . *C. grandiflora*
          CC. Leaves divided shallowly, sometimes
            entire, plant leafy mainly near base . . . . . . . *C. lanceolata*
    AA. Leaves entire
       B. Height 12–18″ . . . . . . . . . . . . . . . . . . . . . *C. auriculata*
      BB. Height 6–9″ . . . . . . . . . . . . . . . . . . *C. auriculata* 'Nana'

**Additional Reading:**

Anon. 1993. Plants in the spotlight. *Minnesota Horticulture* 121(7):4.

Brown, E. 1986. Some garden daisies and sunflowers. *Pacific Horticulture* 47(1):24–28.

Dean, M. 1993. The carefree flower of summer. *Flower and Garden* 37(3):32–33, 72.

Damann, M.P. 1993. Juvenility and light affects the flowering of *Coreopsis*. *Perennial Plants* 1(4):19.

Sawyers, C. 1990. *Coreopsis verticillata*. *Horticulture* 68(7):64.

Singer, C. Waves of gold. *Fine Gardening* 32:34–37.

## *Cornus* (kor' nus)  Bunchberry  Cornaceae

To include a species of this woody genus testifies to the incredible diversity of structure and form within a single group. Bunchberry, *C. canadensis*, is anything but woody, seldom attaining more than 6″ in height and disappearing in the fall. However, the dark green foliage and handsome, 2″ wide, white flowers which blanket the leaves make a spectacular show as a ground cover in the spring. The white of the flowers consists of 4–6 bracts subtending a very small, greenish flower. The 4–6 oval to obovate leaves are whorled on top of the stem and multiply thanks to an aggressive, creeping rootstalk. After flowering, red fruit, about ¼″ across, are formed and persist until eaten by wildlife. Plants are native in North America from Greenland to Alaska and south to Indiana, West Virginia and Colorado. Unfortunately for southern gardeners, plants abhor sustained warm weather, but, in semi-shaded, moist, cool areas, it is beautiful where allowed to naturalize. Growing up in Quebec, I took this plant for granted, but now that I live in north Georgia, never more. Probably the finest planting I have ever seen was at Kildrummy Castle in Scotland, where the white flowers floated on the light green leaves of a patch at least 400 ft² in area.

Acid soil, semi-shaded, and moist areas are necessary for best performance. Propagate by division in the early spring.

## *Cortaderia* (kor-ta-dare-ee' a)  Pampas Grass  Poaceae

Pampas grass consists of about 24 species of robust, tussock-forming perennials from South America, New Zealand, and New Guinea. Many species are highly ornamental and favored for the showy, feathery flowers and tough, thin foliage. Most species bear either male or female flowers, and, while the panicles of female flowers are more fluffy and often more showy, all flower plumes are eye-catching. The only species grown to any extent in this country is *C. selloana*, although occasionally one or two other species are offered by specialty growers.

| *-selloana* (sel-oh-ah' na) | Pampas Grass | 4–7′/4′ |
|---|---|---|
| Summer  Whitish | South America | Zones 6–9 |

This evergreen grass is the royalty of ornamental grasses. The ugliest, trash-strewn, treeless yard can be made almost inviting when the magnificent plumes proudly rise above the light green foliage. Plants are tough as nails; even the aforementioned yard cannot dull its vigor. I have seen pampas grass escape from gardens in the south and west of the United States and become weed-like along fields and roadways. But what a marvelous weed.

The leaves are ½–1″ wide and sharply edged, with the ability to snatch clothing and shred hands. The flowers are individually very small, but the panicles may be 1–2' long and 6–12" wide. Flower color varies from silver to creamy white, and cultivars also include pink forms. Flowers generally emerge in July and are handsome throughout the winter.

After a few years, plants make a dense, wide clump which must be maintained from one year to the next. Does old foliage have to be removed in early spring before new growth gets under way? Plants growing on the pampas of Argentina don't have any cowboys out there hacking away the old growth to make prettier plants. Plants do just fine without this intervention. Occasionally, fire does the same thing in wild plantings, but not removing the old growth every year does little to harm the plant. However, most people do housework on their pampas grass simply because they look better when cleaned up in the spring. Do not attack these plants without being fully armed! Leaves are lethal, even in the spring, and plants do not accept attacks to its person mildly. Use long-handled secateurs. Some people burn the old foliage in the spring, and, along with attendant air pollution, throwing a match into the plant results in an inferno, potentially dangerous to home, people, and other plants. Burning, however, seldom harms the plants if done before the new growth gets underway.

Propagate by division; a small pie-shaped wedge is sufficient to start a new clump. Use a large axe and be prepared to grunt.

**Cultivars:**
'Bertini' is more dwarf than the common dwarf form, 'Pumila'. Plants grow only 2–3' tall with handsome, female panicles.

'Carminea Rendatleri' is one of the most handsome forms when it looks good; disastrous at other times. The flowers are pinkish but unfortunately all too weak, frequently pushed down by the wind.

'Carnea' is a better plant than the former, bearing tougher, soft pink flowers.

'Gold Band' ('Aureo-lineata') has green foliage with bright yellow bands on each side. Slow growing but grows 4–6' tall.

'Marabout' is one of the most handsome cultivars, producing huge plumes of pure white flowers.

'Pumila' is a dwarf form of pampas grass. Creamy white flowers grow 3–4' above the foliage in August and remain handsome in the winter. A terrific choice for gardens of limited space. Probably the most floriferous of available cultivars.

'Rosea' is the pink pampas grass which looks good in clumps of 2 or 3. Rather washed out color.

'Silver Stripe' ('Albo-lineata') has thin, white margins on the leaves. A slow-growing but effective variegated foliage plant. Plants bear female flowers.

'Sun Stripe' bears leaves reverse of those of 'Gold Band', that is, yellow centers with green margins. Flowers tend to flop over more than those of other variegated forms.

'Sunningdale Silver' has robust, tall (6–9'), female plumes of silvery-white. Very vigorous and strong, rigid flower stems which withstand all but the fiercest storms.

'Violacea' produces violet panicles. Distinct coloring but almost impossible to locate.

**Related Species:**

*C. jubata*, purple pampas grass, generally bears thin, dark green foliage and loose, pinkish flowers. Plants grow 9–12' tall, and flowers may be pink, reddish, and even creamy yellow. Plants can be weedy, are less cold hardy then common pampas grass, and the flower stems are weak.

*C. richardii*, black pampas grass, is native to New Zealand and grows 6–10' tall, with showy, creamy white, outward-arching flower plumes. More tolerant of wet soil conditions.

## *Corydalis* (ko-ri' dal-is)          Corydalis          Fumariaceae

All 300 species produce 4-petaled, irregular flowers, and many have finely-divided, fern-like foliage. Although the genus is well represented throughout northern Europe, it is not particularly easy to find in the United States. Many species are ornamental, and while *C. lutea*, yellow corydalis, has always been easily available, others such as the blue corydalis, *C. flexuosa*, and ferny corydalis, *C. cheilanthifolia*, are quickly gaining popularity. Species range in size to the 4–6", yellow-flowered *C. thrysifolia*, native to the high mountains of the Himalayas, to the 3' tall, robust *C. nobilis*, native to central Asia. Most are yellow-flowered, but a good number also bear pink to purplish flowers such as *C. anthriscifolia*, *C. popovii*, a low grower from central Asia, and *C. solida* (syn. *C. bulbosa*), fumewort. *C. solida* includes a particularly good cultivar, 'George Baker', with rich terracotta-red flowers. The foliage of all species is handsome, and, for some, like *C. ophiocarpus*, the lacy, gray-green leaves are probably the best part. A tremendous potential exists in this genus, and it should not be long before half a dozen good species become available to the garden public. Good drainage, basic soils (pH > 6.5), and partial shade are useful for best performance.

<u>Quick Reference to Corydalis Species</u>

|  | Height (in.) | Rootstock | Flower color |
|---|---|---|---|
| C. cheilanthifolia | 9–12 | Stolons | Yellow |
| C. flexuosa | 12–15 | Stolons | Blue, purplish |
| C. lutea | 9–15 | Rhizome | Yellow |

**-*cheilanthifolia*** (chee-lanth-i-fo' lee-a)    Ferny Corydalis      9–12"/10"
   Spring                  Yellow                Central China        Zones 3–6

Growing in rock walls and well-drained crevices, this gray-leaved plant produces dozens of bright yellow flowers over a dense rosette. The 2–3 pinnate leaves are long and look more like the fern, *Cheilanthus*, than a corydalis. Plants are winter hardy to zone 4 or 5 but do not take well to warm, humid climates. They can distribute themselves with abandon by throwing out its seed everywhere. In the quarry garden at Longwood, these plants are cropping up like dandelions. At Branklyn Garden outside Perth, Scotland, I was astonished to see these spreading like weeds everywhere in early spring. The head gardener looked at them disdainfully as only one who must remove such obnoxious things can. As for me, I have tried three times in the Armitage garden but without success. This is such a favorite of mine that I am thinking of building a stone wall, if for no other reason than to grow these crazy plants.

Propagate by divisions after flowering or from seed.

**Related Species:**

*C. chaerophylla* has a taproot and produces many stems of bright yellow flowers. Plants produce distinctly triangular, biternate, basal leaves, and the stem leaves are sessile and 3-parted. Plants differ mainly from *C. cheilanthifolia* by having stems and growing up to 3' tall. A little easier to grow than ferny corydalis.

*C. nobilis* is native to central Asia and in mountainous areas in China. This early-flowering plant (late April in Denver) bears 18–24" tall, upright stems, terminating in a cluster of 20–30 yellow flowers with a dark spot in the inner petals. The weight of the flowers causes the stems to bend over slightly. Plants can be quite robust and grow 3' tall and equally wide under optimum conditions. Summer dormancy occurs in dry soils. Good drainage and sunny areas are necessary for best performance. Likely perform well in zones 3 to 6.

**-*flexuosa*** (flex-ewe-o' sa)        Blue Corydalis        12–15"/12"
   Spring           Blue              China                 Zones 5–8

Few plants have caused the excitement that the plants of blue corydalis have caused. The finely-divided, glaucous foliage is similar to *C. lutea*, but the deep blue to lavender-blue flowers seldom fail to catch the eye. In late spring or early summer, up to 10 thin, tubular, spurred flowers are held on 12" pedicels (flower stems). They were first collected by the French missionary naturalist Pere Armand David (of *Davidia* and *Buddleia davidii* fame) in 1865 Western China. They were "rediscovered" and brought back in 1989 from steep, shady slopes around 5000 ft. elevation in western Sichuan province. There native habitat helps to explain why they perform best in cooler climates and in areas of sharp drainage. Try them in containers if you are unable to find the right site. Where they do well, they are outstanding and persistent in flower.

As marvelous as these plants can be, the jury is still out on their worthiness in parts of this country. They are doing well in the northwest (as do most other *Corydalis* species), multiplying well at Longwood Gardens; they look good at Old Westbury Gardens in Long Island, NY and in the midwest but have not been proven themselves in the southeast. Performance is questionable in the northeast and lower midwest, although accounts of winter hardiness to 5° F have been reported. Plants tend to self-destruct after flowering, partly because they are summer dormant, dismaying many a gardener who first tries them. However, if drainage is reasonably good, plants return early the following spring. Most species of *Corydalis* perform better in more basic soils; therefore try adding a little lime to the soil.

Propagate by division or seed immediately after flowering.

### Cultivars:

Without doubt, it is difficult to tell the difference between any of these cultivars, as intensity of color is so tied to soil and temperature.

'Blue Panda' was discovered in 1986 and bears sky-blue flowers, particularly in cooler climates, on 9–12' tall plants. Like most of the other cultivars, the blue color is more intense in areas with cool nights and mornings. A chance seedling with more purple-blue flowers arose in Heronswood Nursery in Kingston, WA and is offered as 'Purple Panda'.

'Blue Dragon' has smokey-blue flowers on 10" tall plants.

'China Blue' has more smokey-blue flowers than the species. The foliage is brownish green in winter, and flowers fade to purple after blooming. This is the tallest cultivar.

'Pere David' has lavender to light blue flowers. Leaves distinctly blue-green.

'Purple Leaf' is the earliest to bloom and has purplish blue flowers and leaves with a purple blotch in the center. The leaves are purple, especially in late winter, with blood dark red markings at the base of the leaflets. The smallest and neatest clone.

### Related Species:

*C. cashmeriana* is native to the Himalayas and bears dark blue flowers on short (< 9" tall) plants. They are better used as an alpine plant for well-drained rock gardens. Perfectly hardy but require outstanding drainage and partial shade; cannot be allowed to dry out.

**-lutea** (loo' tee-a)          Yellow Corydalis          9–15"/18"
    Spring          Yellow          Europe          Zones 5–7

The 1–4" long leaves are blue-green on the top sides and 2–3 times pinnately compound, resulting in divided fern-like foliage. Many wiry stems push through the soil, terminating in small, golden yellow, spurred flowers. The flowers superficially resemble those of the fringed bleeding heart, *Dicentra eximia*.

Plants bask in shady, moist areas and are tolerant of soils with basic pH. This is a most ubiquitous plant in the British Isles, where it grows in cracks of walkways and fissures in walls and revels in areas scorned by more "uptown" plants. When one visits Portland and Seattle gardeners, and up to Vancouver and Victoria, one finds similar yellow pools of flowers everywhere. The rest of our North American climate is not as much to its liking, but yellow corydalis is still a useful addition in the shaded rock garden.

The species is well known for its self-sowing tendencies; however, purchased seed is notoriously difficult to germinate because it is not fresh. The best means of seed propagation is to collect fresh seed and sow immediately. All seed should be sown in a seed tray in 1:1 mixture of peat:vermiculite and placed in a warm (70–75° F) area for 6–8 weeks. After the warm treatment, place at near freezing conditions for an additional 6–8 weeks. Warm the trays slowly, and germination will occur, although erratically. Fortunately, nature takes care of these conditions. If seed flats are placed outdoors in late summer and allowed to overwinter under snow or other protection, germination will begin as the weather warms in the spring. Plants may also be divided in spring or fall.

**Related Species:**

*C. sempervirens*, rock harlequin, is a 2–4' tall biennial which naturalizes by reseeding. Flowers are pale pink to purple with yellow tips, and the fern-like foliage is gray-green. Plants are native from Newfoundland to Georgia and west to British Columbia. Plants can become a nuisance due to its reseeding tendency.

*C. ochroleuca*, white corydalis, resembles *C. lutea* but bears paler yellow flowers, often with green lips. The foliage is glaucous-blue on both sides rather than on the top sides only. Plants are native to southern and eastern Europe. Terrific in the Northwest, needs to be proven elsewhere. Tolerates sun but prefers moisture and shade. Grow similarly to *C. lutea*.

**Additional Reading:**

Elliot, J. 1993. Small and perfectly formed: adaptable, low-growing perennials that won't invade your space. *The Garden* 118(6):246–249.

Leslie, Alan. 1992. *Corydalis solida. The Garden* 117(7):334–336.

Ownbey, G.B. 1947. Monograph of the North American species of *Corydalis. Annals Missouri Bot. Garden* 34:187–259.

Rix, Martyn. 1993. *Corydalis flexuosa* from Western China. *The Plantsman* 15(3):129–130.

## *Cosmos* (kos' mos)  Cosmos  Asteraceae

Most gardeners think of *Cosmos* only as an annual, but there are a couple of marginal perennials lurking among the 26 species that make up this genus. To be accurate, the perennials are only cold hardy in the mildest areas in the South and the moderate climates of the coastal northwest. The best perennial species, arguably, is the elusive chocolate cosmos, *C. atrosanguineus*. Native to Mexico, it tolerates no more than 10° F (zone 8, zone 7 with lots of protection), but, perhaps because it is so difficult to establish, it is highly sought after. Plants grow from tuberous roots (like a dahlia) which can be dug in colder climates and overwintered in loose peat in moderate temperatures. The compound leaves are often lobed at the bases and attached to the stems by winged petioles. The velvety deep-crimson flowers, formed on 2–3' tall stems, smell to some noses like chocolate; mine seems uncooperative, and I often smell vanilla.

Propagate by seed. Sow seed at 70° F in moist, medium, and humid conditions. Germination occurs in 14–21 days.

## *Crambe* (kram' bay)  Crambe, Kale  Brassicaceae

The genus contains several exceptional cultivars with many small, 4-petaled flowers in large, branching inflorescences (racemes). The large foliage is variable and cabbage-like, and all the species require significant space in the garden.

Quick Reference to Crambe Species

|  | Height (ft.) | Flower color | Basal foliage |
|---|---|---|---|
| *C. cordifolia* | 4–7 | White | Thin, heart-shape |
| *C. maritima* | 2–3 | White | Thick, fleshy |

| *-cordifolia* (kord-i-foe-lee' a) | | Giant Kale | 4–7'/4' |
|---|---|---|---|
| Summer | White | North Caucasus | Zones 5–8 |

A 55-mph plant, which can be seen when in flower from cars, trains and bicycles. A perfect plant to hide the Demsey Dumpster or the trailer park. The basal leaves are heart-shape and more or less hairy, but, as the leaves ascend the stem, they become larger (2' across), thicker, and more variable in shape. They are great big cabbages when not in bloom but are stately in flower. Hundreds of small, white flowers are produced above the plants, giving the appearance of huge clouds of baby's breath.

These are not plants for the small garden and are best used as accent plants in open areas. They require full sun and well-drained soils for best performance. While they are quite happy in the zone 8 of the west coast and northwest, they are useless in the eastern zone 8, and not much better in zone 7.

Propagate by root cuttings of 3–4 year plants in early spring. Seed takes 2–3 years to flower.

**Related Species:**

*C. koktebelica* is seldom seen in this country, and I have only seen it in one or two gardens in the British Isles. It is similar to *C. cordifolia* but is a little shorter (3–4′) and bears white flowers with yellow sepals. The flowers are more stiffly held than those of giant kale.

| | | | |
|---|---|---|---|
| *-maritima* (ma-ri-ti′ ma) | | Sea Kale | 2–3′/3′ |
| Summer | White | Western Europe | Zones 5–8 |

This plant brings a few additional uses to the garden other than its questionable ornamental value. The emerging leaves were used as blanched vegetables and were particularly useful in coastal areas where salt spray and saline soils were common. The wavy, thick, bluish foliage is handsome in its own right, and, in the early summer, stiff sprays of creamy white flowers are carried above the leaves. The basal stems become woody at the end of the first year. In areas of cool nights, many of the flowers have a decided yellowish tint as well.

Plants need full sun and are tolerant of moist soils but not waterlogged conditions. Similar problems of heat tolerance occur with this species as with the former one. I have tried plants in my north Georgia garden, and, while they are decent the first year, they seldom persist much longer. However, they can be most ornamental in the midwest and lower northeast.

Propagate by root cuttings or seed.

Quick Key to Crambe Species

    A. Plants usually more than 4′ tall,
        basal leaves heart-shape . . . . . . . . . . . . . . . . . *C. cordifolia*
    AA. Plants usually less than 4′ tall, leaves
        wavy, thick, and blue-green . . . . . . . . . . . . . . *C. maritima*

*Crocosmia* (kro-caws′ me-a)      Crocosmia, Montbretia      Iridaceae

*Crocosmia* is becoming more popular as new cultivars and hybrids emerge. The sword-like leaves arise from a corm, and myriads of

303

one-sided, nodding flowers resembling small funnels are produced along the length of the arching flower stems. As well as being excellent in the garden, they are widely sought after as cut flowers and used commercially by florists in arrangements and bouquets.

About seven species occur, but many of the colors available today are interspecific hybrids, mainly with *C. paniculata* (formerly known as *Curtonus paniculatus* and *Antholyza paniculata*), and the additional vigor and colors continue to win converts.

Plant in full sun, in soil which does not water log. In the North, corms should be lifted in the fall and treated similar to gladioli. Plants are generally hardy from zones 6 to 8. Alan Bloom, who has bred many fine cultivars, states that the degree of cold hardiness depends on the corm size. The larger the corm, the more tolerant of cold. Plant the smaller corms about 3″ deep, the larger about 4″ deep. Plants can be propagated by division or by lifting and removing offsets from the corms. They become crowded after a few years, and flowering will be reduced if not divided after 2 or 3 years.

-× *crocosmiiflora* (kro-kos-mee-i-flo′ ra)  Crocosmia, Montbretia  2–3′/1′
Summer  Various  Hybrid  Zones 5–8

This hybrid occurred in the early 1880's when the French hybridizer Lemoine introduced a hybrid between *C. aurea*, a golden, large-flowered but tender species, and *C. pottsii*, a vivid red, hardy species. This was once listed as *Montbretia × crocosmiaeflora* by Lemoine and became known as *Montbretia*, a name which no longer has any botanical stature. Additional selections and hybridization in England resulted in free-flowering, brilliantly-colored plants. The nodding to erect flowers are borne on a zigzag rachis (the central axis of the inflorescence which bears the flowers) and persist for up to 4 weeks. They were included in our research on commercial cut flower production and produce 8–10 stems per plant for 2–3 years before requiring division.

Plant in full sun and well-drained soils. The corms should be planted in spring about 3″ deep and 6″ apart. Spider mites cause a great deal of damage to the foliage and discourage flowering. A number of chemicals are available, and, although I do not enjoy the idea of spraying, these plants are worth the trouble.

**Cultivars:**

The parentage of many of these cultivars is not known, and all are thought to be hybrids. Most cultivars have been bred in England. A few have filtered our way, and, with luck, more will make it across the pond.

'A. E. Amos' is brilliant orange-red but not particularly vigorous.

'Bressingham Beacon' produces many orange and yellow, bi-colored flower sprays on dark stems. Stunning.

'Bressingham Blaze' has intense orange-red flowers on 2–3′ tall plants.

'Citronella' (syn. 'Citrinum') has small, pretty, orange-yellow flowers above the light green foliage.

'Emberglow' produces burnt orange-red flowers atop 2–3′ tall plants.

'Emily McKenzie' is truly impressive. It was introduced in the mid-1950's, and I have yet to see a more vibrant cultivar. The large, orange flowers contrast beautifully with the crimson throat.

'George Davidson' is one of the granddaddies of the group, bred prior to 1902. Small, soft, yellow flowers are produced on 2′ tall plants.

'James Coey' has deep red flowers with yellow centers. Not as vigorous as some of the new cultivars.

'Jenny Bloom', named after Mr. Bloom's youngest daughter, is a vigorous selection with butter-yellow flowers on 2–3′ tall plants.

'Lucifer' is exceptional and covered with scarlet-red flowers in the summer. It has been grown in the United States for a number of years and has proven its garden value over and over.

'Meteore' bears red and yellow, bicolored flowers in mid-summer. About 2′ tall.

'Norwich Canary' is a late-flowered form with bright yellow flowers on 2′ tall plants.

'Solfatare', one of the oldest hybrids, was bred in the late 1800's by the French nursery, Lemoine. It is 2′ tall with apricot-yellow flowers and dark green leaves.

'Spitfire' is a cross between *C. masonorum* and *C.* × *crocosmiiflora* 'Jackanapes', a red and yellow, bicolored cultivar. It is a large plant with stunning orange-red flowers with a yellow throat.

'Walberton Yellow' has golden yellow, upward-facing flowers.

'Venus' is only 18–24″ tall and produces peach-yellow flowers on darkened stems.

'Vulcan' is also relatively short, compared to 'Lucifer', and bears scarlet-orange flowers.

**Related Species:**

*C. masonorum* has 3′ long flower stems, narrowly-lanceolate leaves, and bright orange-red, upright flowers, each measuring about 1½″ long. 'Firebird' was selected by Alan Bloom of Bloom's Nursery in England and has fiery orange-red flowers with a bright yellow throat and is eye-stopping in its brilliance. 'Rowallane Yellow' has apricot-yellow flowers and commemorates the garden at Rowallane, Northern Ireland. May require additional mulching.

**Additional Reading:**

Kostelijk, Pieter J. 1984. Crocosmia in gardens. *The Plantsman* 5(4):246–253.

## *Crocus* (kro' kus)          Crocus          Iridaceae

"All the world loves a crocus. There can be no two opinions about this," states Loiuse Beebe Wilder in her delightful book, *Adventures with Hardy Bulbs*. Most gardens boast a few plants in March and April, and, while these plants are surely exquisite gems to the gardener, they show but a fraction of the potential of the 75 species in the genus. *Crocus* may flower in September, October, November, February, March, and April. In some places, they can even be coaxed into bloom in December and January. Of course, not all are available to the gardener nor all of them as easy to grow as the common Dutch hybrids, but at least a third of them may be successfully grown in the United States. The common crocuses of gardens are the large-flowered hybrids of *C. aureus* and *C. vernus*, comprised of innumerable, spring-flowering cultivars, but fall-flowering species and cultivars of *C. chrysanthus* have their adamant admirers.

The genus also includes a plant of great historical interest—the saffron crocus, *C. sativus*. The bright orange-red stigmas of this plant were dried and made into "karcom" of the ancient Hebrews, and corms were widely cultivated by the ancient Greeks and Romans. Saffron took on medicinal and culinary uses, as well as being an important dye and perfume. It is still cultivated today in Spain, India, and a handful of other areas but is difficult to grow well in this country because of the need for a long dry period. Interesting enough, a fair amount of saffron is grown today in east Texas. It is estimated that it requires about 50,000 flowers to produce one pound of saffron. Any wonder it is so expensive! There are, however, many species more ornamental, and, except for the engaging stories you can tell your garden visitors, it probably is not worth the space.

The crocus corm is covered by scaly leaves from which arise leaf and flower buds, as well as buds which form the new corm from the old. The leaves are usually channeled and appear before the flowers, with bright yellow or red stigmas. Crocuses may be divided into two groups, the first consisting of late winter and early spring-flowering species, and the second being the autumn-flowerers (these are different from *Colchicum*, often referred to as the autumn crocus which has 6 stamens instead of the 3 found in *Crocus*). The first group should be planted from September to November, while the second must be planted no later than early September. Plant in full sun about 4" deep and close together, in groups of 25 or more. The spring-flowerers perform reasonably well in shady areas, particularly the early-flowering species, but are at their best in the sun. Fall-flowerers must soak up the sunshine. Corms require well-drained areas, and all are suitable for the rock garden.

Flowers of all crocus are short-lived, persisting for only 1–2 weeks, but what glorious weeks they are. Naturalized in grassy meadows, crocus are a beautiful sight when they are in bloom. I have seen marvelous drifts of crocus in March on sides of highways or along grassy verges and nearly always cause an accident as I slam on the brakes of the car. However, they should not be planted in lawns if the lawn is to be kept cut. Seldom is mowing finished for the year that the emerging buds of autumn-flowering species will not be injured, and mowing starts in the spring before the leaves of the spring-flowering types have yellowed.

Propagation of all crocus can be accomplished by lifting the corms, dividing them into various sizes, and replanting in a larger area. Most species can also be raised from seed. Unfortunately, many animals love the corms as much as gardeners love the flowers. Squirrels, chipmunks, rabbits, mice, and birds can be an awful nuisance, and desperate measures must sometimes be taken. As Ms. Wilder also concludes, "It is easy to see what a rabid state of mind the gentlest and most humane of persons may be brought by the destruction of his beloved Crocuses. The gun in a sure hand is the most unfailing weapon."

Many of the differences between species are found in the covering of the corm, the color of the anthers, and branching pattern of the styles. A good deal of careful study is necessary to discern the identity of unknown plants. Many species are not commonly found in home gardens, and botanical gardens are often worth a visit to appreciate the diversity of the genus, particularly those which flower in the fall.

## Quick Reference to Crocus Species

|                   | Flower color      | Flowering season |
| ----------------- | ----------------- | ---------------- |
| C. ancyrensis     | Yellow            | Spring           |
| C. biflorus       | White, light blue | Spring           |
| C. chrysanthus    | Various           | Spring           |
| C. kotschyanus    | Rose              | Fall             |
| C. speciosus      | Blue              | Fall             |
| C. tommasinianus  | Mauve             | Spring           |
| C. vernus         | Various           | Spring           |

| *-ancyrensis* (an-see-ren′ sis) | | Golden Bunch Crocus | 4–6″/6″ |
| ------------------------------- | ------- | ------------------- | ------- |
| Early Spring | Various | Turkey | Zones 3–8 |

One of the earliest of the spring-flowering crocus to bloom, plants bear 1″ long, ½″ broad flowers which are bright yellow inside and out. Occasionally the outer segments may be feathered with bronze. Normally, each corm produces 2–3 flowers and 3–4 narrow leaves which appear with the flowers.

## Cultivars:

'Golden Bunch' was said to be selected for its prolific flowering and may have up to 10 golden-yellow flowers per corm, 5 being average. However, in many cases, 'Golden Bunch' is nothing more than a fancy name for the species itself.

| *-biflorus* (bi-flo' rus) | | Scotch Crocus | 4–6"/6" |
|---|---|---|---|
| Early Spring | White, Blue | Italy to Iran | Zones 5–9 |

This reliable plant flowers as early as February and often bears two flowers at once, thus accounting for the specific name, *biflorus*. Although not native to Scotland, it has become naturalized there as an escapee from gardens. Typically the flowers are white with a yellow throat and have purple stippling on the outer petals. This combination gives the flowers a slight metallic sheen, resulting in its other common name, cloth-of-silver. Performance is better in dry summers than wet ones, and, like all crocus, full sun is preferable to shade.

## Cultivars:

'Adamii' bears flowers which are lilac inside and light brown outside with
  darker veining.
Var. *alexandri* produces flowers of pure white, with glossy purple outside
  but no yellow throat.
'Pusillus' has small flowers of white with an orange throat.
Var. *waldenii* has small, white flowers with a bluish base and is one of the
  best forms of the species. A grayish blue selection is sold as 'Fairy'.

| *-chrysanthus* (kris-anth' us) | | Golden Crocus | 4–6"/6" |
|---|---|---|---|
| Spring | Various | Greece, Asia Minor | Zones 4–7 |

One of the best known of the spring-flowering crocus species, plants are available in a wide range of colors. It flowers earlier than the hybrids and helps provide a longer flowering season when combined with them. The wild species is yellowish orange throughout and has a honey-like scent. A couple of features of the flowers distinguish the species from others, but neither are obvious without some squinting. The anthers are tipped in black (although some are more brown than black), and the styles are trilobed, as opposed to many-branched in other species. Plants bear more than one flower per corm and produce 3–6 narrow leaves.

I have tried many cultivars in my garden, and I can get excited about most of them. However, as wonderful as they are, most are not as long-lived as the Dutch hybrids, returning for 2–3 years before disappearing.

## Cultivars:

The following are but a few of the dozens of cultivars available. Refer to a reliable bulb catalog for additional selections.

'Advance' has blue-violet outer petals and lemon-yellow inner petals.

'Bluebird' is lavender-blue throughout with white tinges on the inside of all petals.

'Blue Pearl' has been one of my favorites, bearing flowers of a delicate blue which darken at the base.

'Cream Beauty' is light yellow with contrasting orange stamens. The base of the flowers are bronze-green. A lovely plant and a reliable performer.

'E.A. Bowles' was named after one of the authorities on this genus and has canary-yellow flowers with bronze veining towards the base.

'E.P. Bowles' is a little shorter than the former, but the petal markings are more pronounced. Flowers have a hint of purple.

'Elegance' bears handsome flowers of brown and gold.

'Gypsy Girl' has yellow flowers with brown stripes on the petals.

'Lady Killer' is lilac-white outside and violet-white inside.

'Moonlight' is one of the earliest to flower, unfolding deep yellow flowers as soon as the soil warms up in the least. In the Armitage garden flowers appear as early as January 15 in mild winters, February 1 not being uncommon.

'Snow White' bears white to yellow outer petals with a bluish purple veining at the base and white inner petals with a blotch of yellow.

'Zwanenberg Bronze' is yellow on the inside with an interesting bronze exterior.

**Related Species:**

*C. sieberi* has broad, dark green leaves and flowers with a tapering, rounded perianth tube. Flower color of the species itself is lavender-purple with a deep yellow throat. Cultivars sometimes offered are 'Bowle's White', with clean white petals and yellow anthers, 'Hurbert Edelsten', with pale flowers banded with purple and white, and 'Violet Queen', with stunning, iridescent violet flowers in the spring. Short-lived but memorable.

| | | |
|---|---|---|
| *-kotschyanus* (kot-shee-ah' nus) | Kotschy's Crocus | 4–6"/6" |
| Fall　　　　Rose-Lilac | Europe to Syria | Zones 5–8 |
| (Syn. *C. zonatus*) | | |

This fall-flowerer opens a little earlier than *C. speciosus*, and the rose-lilac, goblet-shaped flowers appear before the leaves. The flowers have a white or deep yellow throat and usually have two deep orange-yellow spots at the base of the flower segments. The anthers are creamy white compared with the orange anthers of Dutch crocus, *C. vernus*. Plants are often recommended for naturalization due to their vigor and ability to quickly multiply.

**Cultivars:**

'Albus', a white-flowered form, is sometimes available.

**Related Species:**

*C. laevigatus* is quite late to flower, opening in late fall to early winter, depending on climate. The leaves appear first, followed by flowers which vary from white to deep purple. The most common form available is 'Fontenayi', which has pale violet flowers strongly stripped deeper purple on the outside and yellow in the center. An excellent, relatively unknown crocus.

*-speciosus* (spe-see-o' sus)   Showy Crocus                                           4–6"/6"
   Fall        Light Blue        Southern Russia, Western Turkey    Zones 5–7

This is one of the easiest fall crocus to grow. The lavender-blue petals and the large, much divided, orange-scarlet stigma make the flowers particularly attractive. The outside of the segments is painted with 3 main purple veins. It is one of the earliest fall crocus and emerges while the foliage is very short. The 3–4 leaves are broad, dark green, and grow 15" long after flowering.

As beautiful as these plants are, I have had little success relative to the tales of the bulb catalogs. The first year, they flower "picture perfect," but, perhaps because temperatures are still warm in north Georgia in late September and early October, they persist for less than a week. The other problem is that the flowers tend to stretch if placed in any shade, resulting in a long-eared, floppy puppy look. Obviously, full sun (rock garden is terrific) and well-drained soils are recommended. In cooler climates, plants are better behaved.

It seeds freely and also increases by offsets. When first planted, locate them in a permanent place as corms do not like to be disturbed.

**Cultivars:**

Var. *aitchisonii* has 1½" broad, pale lavender flowers.

Var. *albus* has flowers of white.

'Cassiope' flowers about 1 week after the species and has rich blue petals.

'Conqueror' has clear, deep blue flowers.

'Oxonian' has large, dark blue flowers.

'Pollux' has large, violet-blue outer segments and is silvery-blue on the inside.

**Related Species:**

*C. goulimyi*, native to southern Greece, produces star-shaped, pale to deep lavender flowers with a white throat and pale yellow anthers. Flowers emerge with or slightly before the leaves in October and November. Corms increase rapidly by offsets. An excellent fall-flowering crocus.

**-tommasinianus** (tom-a-see-nee-ah' nus)    Tommasini's Crocus    4–6"/6"
Early Spring    Lavender-Blue    Western Yugoslavia    Zones 5–9

Plants increase rapidly by self-sowing, and this is one of the better species to naturalize for large drifts and masses. Three to five leaves are present when the flowers appear, each leaf growing about 10" long. The flowers are lavender to silvery-blue outside, and, when warmed by the sun, they unfurl to boast a soft amethyst center. It flowers very early and is excellent to naturalize with hellebores or snowdrops, *Galanthus*. Winterthur House and Gardens in Delaware bear spectacular drifts of these crocus in early spring.

### Cultivars:

'Albus' produces milky white flowers but is otherwise similar to the species.
'Barr's Purple' has flowers of soft lilac-mauve.
'Ruby Giant' produces large blooms of deep ruby-purple. Outstanding.
'Whitewell Purple' bears flowers of deep reddish mauve which contrast
    beautifully with the yellow stigmas.

### Related Species:

*C. gargaricus* has some of the brightest orange flowers in the genus. With orange-yellow sepals, yellow anthers and orange style, it is a March to April stoplight in the garden.

**-vernus** (ver' nus)                Dutch Crocus                4–6"/6"
Spring        Various        Europe                    Zones 3–8
(Syn. *C. albiflorus*)

Plants are widely distributed in alpine regions from the Pyrenees to the Carpathian Mountains. The 3–4 narrow leaves usually have a white line running their length and eventually grow 12–14" long. *C. vernus* has given rise to the many dutch hybrids available today, all of which are more vigorous and generally larger-flowered than those of the species. Occasionally, varieties of the true species are offered and well worth trying if space is unlimited.

### Cultivars:

Var. *albiflorus* bears small, white flowers.
Var. *leucorhynchus* has pale lavender flowers with white tips on the outside.
Var. *leucostigma* has blue flowers with cream-colored stigmas.
'Obovatus' has feathered, purple veins on the outer segments, giving it an
    interesting appearance.

### Dutch hybrids:

The Dutch hybrids have been selected for size and color and include other parentages such as *C. aureus* and/or *C. tommasinianus*, as well as

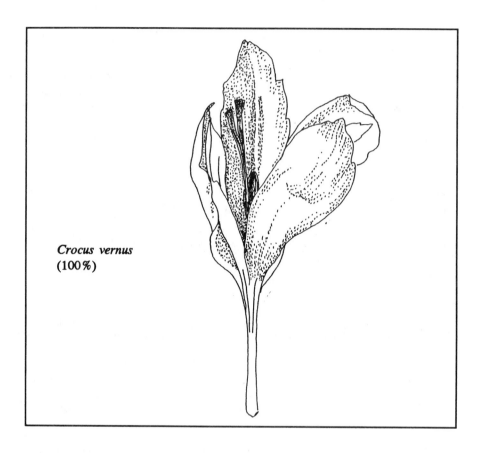

*Crocus vernus*
(100%)

*C. vernus.* Flowers are 2-4″ long, 1-3″ wide, and the color range is extensive. All are as useful in containers as they are in the garden.

**Cultivars:**

There are numerous hybrids which should be perused at leisure from fall catalogs. Some I am familiar with include:

'Enchantress' has lovely, pale blue flowers.

'Flower Record' bears many dark purple flowers. Probably a little more long-lived than 'Queen of the Blues'.

'Jeanne d'Arc' is a clean white-flowered form which has performed well in many gardens.

'Peter Pan' has large, white flowers.

'Pickwick' ('Mr. Pickwick') has lilac flowers with dark blue stripes on the outside. It is the most popular of the striped cultivars.

'Queen of the Blues' has large, deep violet flowers with yellow stamens.

'Rememberence' has purple flowers with a dark blue flower tube. This cultivar is often forced in dish or bowl gardens for Valentine's Day.

'Yellow Mammoth' is an apt name for this very popular, large-flowered, bright yellow selection. Although commonly offered as a typical Dutch hybrid, it is likely a hybrid of the yellow crocus, *C. flavus*.

<u>Quick Key to Crocus Species</u> (not including cultivars)

```
A. Fall flowering
   B. Flowers lilac to deep blue,
         style much dissected, anthers yellow . . . . . . . . C. speciosus
  BB. Flowers rose to lilac, style slightly
         divided near top, anthers white  . . . . . . . . . C. kotschyanus
AA. Spring flowering
   B. Style divided or entire, not trilobed
      C. Style divided, flowers slender with
         pointed segments, leaves blunt,
         not tapering at end . . . . . . . . . . . . . C. tommasinianus
     CC. Style entire, flowers broad with rounded
         segments, leaves tapering at ends . . . . . . . . . C. vernus
  BB. Style trilobed
      C. Flowers yellow inside and out . . . . . . . . . C. ancyrensis
     CC. Flowers not yellow (except cultivars),
         anthers yellow
         D. Anthers tipped black or dark brown  . . . C. chrysanthus
        DD. Anthers not tipped black or dark brown . . . . C. biflorus
```

**Additional Reading:**

Davidson, Roy. 1984. Crocus days. *Pacific Horticulture* 45(2):24–28.

Mackaness, F.P. 1991. Crocuses in a November garden. *Pacific Horticulture* 52(3):35–38.

Mathew, B. and A. Edwards. 1996. Autumn-flowering crocus. *The Garden* 12(7):403–405.

Rees, A.R. 1988. Saffron—an expensive plant product. *The Plantsman* 9(4):210–217.

## *Cyclamen* (cyke' la-men)  Hardy Cyclamen  Primulaceae

Most people are familiar with the greenhouse cyclamen, *C. persicum*, which make wonderful house plants and are reasonably useful garden plants if placed outside in early spring. However, there is a wealth of other useful species in this genus. Approximately 19 species are known, and a half dozen are used in semi-shaded gardens for winter and early spring color. All arise from large, flattened corms and often have heart-shaped leaves and mottled foliage. The distinctive fragrant flowers have reflexed petals borne on slender stalks.

The genus is centered in the Mediterranean basin, with species in all countries except Spain, Morocco, Syria, and Egypt. Most are native to rocky terrain in semi-arid locations, and excellent drainage is necessary for best performance and longevity. Without rapt attention to drainage, success in the garden is unlikely. Some authors claim that 5 species are hardy in zone 5 (possibly 4), although I would not want to bet my house on their cold tolerance. Certainly many can be grown south of zone 6. One of our best growers of this genus is Nancy Goodwin, whose former nursery, Montrose Gardens, in Hillsboro, NC, was the best source of information and hardy plant material. She separates the many species into fall, winter, spring, and summer bloomers according to the following table.

| Fall | Winter | Spring | Summer |
|------|--------|--------|--------|
| C. africanum | C. coum | C. balearicum | C. purpurescens |
| C. cilicium | C. libanoticum | C. creticum | |
| C. graecum | C. parviflorum | C. pseudibericum | |
| C. hederifolium | C. trochopteranthum | | |
| C. intaminatum | | | |
| C. mirabile | | | |

The most cold hardy include *C. coum*, *C. hederifolium*, and *C. trochopteranthum*, followed by *C. cilicium*, *C. intaminatum*, and *C. purpurescens*. *C. hederifolium* tolerates cold temperatures to about 0° F (zone 7), as does *C. coum* and *C. purpurescens* if soil is particularly well-drained. If snow cover occurs regularly, then these species can tolerate temperatures as low as −20° F (zone 5) for short periods of time. All cyclamen, except *C. purpurescens*, are summer dormant and can rot if drainage is poor and summer rains are excessive. I generally add some organic matter and small gravel to the soil when I first place the tubers. I place, not plant, the tubers almost on top of the soil, having barely scraped out a small crater. Once the plants become established, they will find their own comfort depth. In the heavy clay in north Georgia, about the only things covering the tubers are the oak leaves which fall each year. Even then, I lose my fair share. Some people are fortunate enough to have critters carry seed about the garden, but I have not yet found such friendly fellows. Most of the critters at my place scratch, dig, eat, or smother; few have caught on to the carry bit. Although many species can be found with sufficient persistence, the easiest to locate and most hardy species is *C. hederifolium*.

Propagation is usually by seed. Soak newly-collected seed for 24 hours then sow in moist, medium temperatures of 60–65° F. Keep seeds in the dark until germination occurs. Germination occurs within 4 weeks; if not placed in darkness, seeds can take up to a year to germinate. After germination, place in the light and wait until small corms form at the base before transplanting. There was, and still is to some degree, a huge trade in tubers dug from the wild. You are doing the world a favor by buying only nursery-produced tubers. Please check before you buy, or, better yet, buy the seed and produce your own. Two to three years is needed to reach flowering size.

*-hederifolium* (he-de-ri-fo' lee-um)     Hardy Cyclamen          4–6"/12"
    Fall          Pink, White     Southern Europe        Zones 5–7
(Syn. *C. neapolitanum*)

There are few garden scenes as delightful as a bed of pink and white, hardy cyclamen gracing the base of a mature tree in a fall garden. One of the finest examples I have seen is at Snowshill Manor in the Cotswolds of England, although the scenes at Montrose Garden are their equal. The pointed flower buds arise in the fall before the foliage and open into glorious stands of warm pink and white. The ivy-shaped leaves are up to 4–6" long but more beautiful than any ivy. They are gray-green and have attractive patterns of purple marbling. The foliage persists all winter before going dormant in late spring. The leaves vary from deep green to those with silver sheen. In the Armitage garden, the leaves begin emerging in October

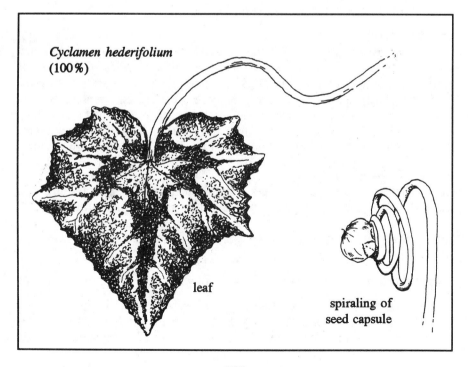

*Cyclamen hederifolium*
(100%)

leaf

spiraling of
seed capsule

and fill in to a wonderful clump by mid-November; flowering occurs from October to December. In the North, flowering occurs in early spring. The foliage continues into April, and plants are totally dormant by the first of June. Reseeding results in all sorts of wonderful foliage patterns.

Cyclamen should be planted in partial shade and out of afternoon sun in a soil amended with lime. They do not tolerate deep planting, particularly in areas of hot summers. Plant them so the top of the corms are only about ½" below the surface. Since they are dormant in summer, water should not be applied where cyclamen are resting, or corm rot may occur. Annuals such as begonias, which do not wilt readily, are excellent for overplanting. Once planted, cyclamen need not be moved.

In the garden, plants multiply by seed or cormels. Dense plantings are the result of liberal formation of cormels, which may be removed in the fall after flowering has occurred. It is also interesting to watch how Mother Nature makes sure seeds are shed. As the flowers fall off, the flower stem bearing the seeds begins to twist and coil until the seed capsule is brought close to the ground. At that point, the seeds are released, ensuring they fall near the original planting. The spiralling of the peduncle is responsible for the genus name, after the greek *kyklos*, meaning circular.

### Cultivars:

'Album' has white flowers. This variety is often interplanted with the pink species and makes a beautiful combination.

### Related Species:

*C. coum* are a little more difficult to establish but almost as cold tolerant as *C. hederifolium*. The flowers, which occur after *C. hederifolium*, are a vivid magenta to white, the leaves glossy green, and plants are more dwarf than other hardy species. Flowering occurs in late fall and winter.

*C. pseudibericum* is cold hardy to zone 8 but more difficult to find. It is considered by many the most beautiful of all cyclamen. The flowers open with *Anenome blanda*. The rosy-red flowers that have a faint fragrance of violets.

### Additional Reading:

Grey-Wilson, C. 1991. Cyclamen-a reappraisal. *The Plantsman* 13(1):1–20.
Kelly, J. 1993. Cyclamen, in all their infinite variety. *The Garden* 118(1): 15–21.
Shreet, S.A. 1991. Growing hardy cyclamen. *Fine Gardening* 21:31–33.

## *Cymbalaria* (sim ba-lah′ ree-a)      Kenilworth Ivy      Scropulariaceae

Approximately 10 species of short-lived, creeping and vining plants are known, but they are not seen nearly as much in the United States as they are in Europe. A few species are occasionally offered, growable in zones

6/7–10, but none do well in hot, humid areas. All can be rampant, aggressive growers in cool summers and moderate winters but can also provide a cool delight to the summer morning. *C. aequitriloba* hugs rocks, thrives in cracks and crevices of old walls, and bears hundreds of tiny, lavender-pink, snapdragon-like flowers in late spring through the summer.

*C. hepaticifolia*, cold hardy to zone 7, uses its stoloniferous habit to creep and climb on walls and over rocks. Growing to about 2″ tall, the species bears small, violet-blue flowers. A white-flowered form, 'Alba' is even more handsome.

The most common species is *C. muralis*, the true Kenilworth ivy, also known as coliseum ivy, pennywort, and ivy-leaved toad flax. The shallowly-lobed leaves are kidney-shaped (reniform) to semi-circular, and roots form at each node. Like English ivy, *Hedera*, the tenacious roots can find any moisture in walls or bark of trees and secure itself. Covering walls or any cool, shady crevices with small, scalloped foliage and lilac-blue flowers, they make pleasant backgrounds to old gardens. Provide areas of ample moisture for best performance. Plants are naturalized throughout southwest and central Europe.

'Alba' is a white-flowered form whose flowers make a terrific contrast to the light green foliage. A more compact form, var. *compacta* or var. *nana*, may also be used. 'Maxima' has larger flowers, but plants should be selected for the foliage, rather than the flowers.

Propagate by rooting the stems at any node.

## *Cynara* (si-nah′ ra)　　　　Cardoon　　　　Asteraceae

The genus is probably best known for the globe artichoke, *C. scolymus*, a vegetable best known for the stares of disbelief by people expected to eat the thing. However, every now and then, gardeners want a plant for its architectural value, and cardoon, *C. cardunculus*, is such a plant. Why else would anyone put a 6′ tall seriously prickly plant with mundane, lavender-purple flowers in their garden? The architectural part comes from the robust stature and deeply-cut, handsome foliage, gray-green above and white, hairy below. They are at their architectural best from spring to mid-summer, then depending on the severity of the summer, can look like an old, tired field thistle. People love them for their size and the contrast with other green-leaved plants growing with them. Plants are native to the Mediterranean area and can be used as a short-lived perennial in zones 6–10, and as an annual elsewhere.

Provide full sun and well-drained soils.

## *Cynoglossum* (sy-no-gloss′ um)　　Hound's Tongue　　Boraginaceae

The 55 species have hairy stems and alternate, long-stalked, basal leaves which were said to resemble the tongue of a dog; hence the common name. Plants are valued for the intense blue of the flowers but also may exhibit a

317

range of colors from flower bud to flower death. The flowers are less than 1″ across and held in coiled inflorescences called scorpioid cymes. This genus differs from *Borago* (borage) by having tubular flowers which evolve into small nutlets covered with prickles.

None of the perennial species is easy to locate, but *C. nervosum*, with dark blue flowers, and *C. virginianum*, with lighter blue flowers, are useful garden plants. The Chinese forget-me-not, *C. amabile*, is a 1–2′ tall biennial and has lovely, funnel-shaped flowers of blue, pink, or white. 'Firmament' is more compact and bears particularly ornamental, intense blue flowers.

It is difficult to tell the difference between some genera in the family Boraginaceae, and people ask me how to distinguish the genus *Cynoglossum* from *Lithodora*, particularly *L. diffusa*. Separation of the genera in the family Boraginaceae is based on the flowers being rounded (*Borago*) or tubular (all others). The fruit is the easiest way to tell the difference between the two genera; the fruit of *Cynoglossum* is covered with prickles, and the fruit of *Lithodora* is smooth. Another distinction is that the flowers in many genera have small bracts (such as *Brunnera*, *Myosotis* and *Lithodora*). *Cynoglossum* does not have bracts at the base of the flowers. It takes a good deal of study the first few times but then is a little easier.

| *-nervosum* (ner-vo′ sum) | | Hairy Hound's Tongue | 2–2½′/2′ |
| --- | --- | --- | --- |
| Spring | Blue | Himalayas | Zones 4–7 |

The leaves and stems are quite rough due to the presence of short, stiff hairs. The 6–8″ long, basal leaves are narrowly-lanceolate, entire, and petioled, while the upper leaves are more oblong and sessile. Branching sprays of intensely blue, forget-me-not-like flowers are produced in the upper axils, as well as on the terminal shoot. The ½″ long flowers first appear in a rounded head which uncoils to a 6–9″ long, erect inflorescence. Flowers persist for about 4 weeks.

Plants require abundant water and do not tolerate dryness. They may be planted in full sun in the northern part of their range, but afternoon shade should be provided in zones 7 and 8. Rich soils are beneficial, but heavy doses of fertilizer cause plants to grow tall and weak. Growing plants well in humid areas is difficult because the hairy leaves trap water and the high temperatures and humidity result in foliar disease.

Propagate from seed or divisions in fall or spring. Seed requires no special treatment other than sowing in a warm (70–75° F), humid environment.

**Related Species:**

*C. grande*, Pacific hound's tongue, native to western North America, is occasionally seen in gardens in the West but seldom in the East. Plants are 1–2′ tall with bright blue flowers and oval, hairy leaves.

*C. virginianum*, wild comfrey, is native to open woodlands from Connecticut to Missouri and south to Texas and Florida. This little known plant, with a basal rosette of soft, hairy leaves and ½" wide, pale blue spring flowers, is terrific for shade gardens. Plants return year after year and are unperturbed by drought or flood. Much easier to grow, if not quite as colorful, for gardeners in the South or those with warm summers.

## *Cyrtomium* (cer-tom-ee′ um)          Holly Fern          Dryopteridaceae

Holly ferns are often seen in floral decorations and dish gardens and of the 20 or so species, 2 or 3 are candidates for the shaded, moist garden. They are prized for the evergreen, shiny, once-pinnate fronds which contrast well with other plants. I think some of the finest plantings occur at the Cloisters Resort on Sea Island, Georgia. Shining in the landscape, they act as lustrous green fillers in the landscape, as well as bringing out the colors in the annuals nearby.

The Japanese holly fern, *C. falcatum*, with its glossy, leathery fronds which are curved sideways, resembling a scythe or sickle (falcate), is the most common. The margins are entire or slightly wavy (undulate). They are excellent in zones 8–10 but can be devastated by winter winds and abnormally cold temperatures. They have survived winter temperatures of about 0° F with no snow cover in the Armitage garden (zone 7b), but the fronds were badly desiccated and brown on the margins. The next summer was a slow one indeed. 'Rochfordianum' is a popular cultivar which differs by having coarsely-toothed or lobed margins.

The most cold hardy of the group is *C. fortunei*, native to Japan, and cold hardy to zone 6 (5 with adequate protection). It differs from *C. falcatum* by having more pairs of pinnae or segments—12–26 pairs in *C. fortunei*, 3–11 pairs in *C. falcatum*, and narrower and longer, more drawn out segments. This is, arguably, the best choice of the holly ferns for most outdoor situations.

Another handsome fern in this little-used group is large-leaved holly fern, *C. macrophyllum*, performing well in zones 8–10. The plants are not as full as the others mentioned, having only 2–8 pairs of entire or slightly-toothed pinnae on each frond. Each pair, however, is larger, and the terminal segment is usually 3-lobed.

Site all species in light to heavy shade, and water well in the spring and early summer. If fronds get badly damaged over the winter, trim back in the spring and fertilize with a slow-release fertilizer.

319

# D

*Dactylorhiza* (dak-til-o-rise′ a)    Marsh Orchid    Orchidaceae

There is no overwhelming or even sensible reason to include this genus in a book for American gardeners; however, like the alluring *Meconopsis*, its beauty combined with its degree of difficulty brings out the obstinance in many gardeners. They are stately, terrestrial orchids which, if they can be established, are quite trouble-free. The main problem is that they nearly always die, but other than that, they are terrific. Most species are almost unavailable to gardeners in this country, and all require moist, but not wet, conditions and temperate temperatures. *Dactylorhiza* is one of the most eye-catching garden orchids, and while they may be successfully grown in the northwest and areas of the northeast, seldom will they look as good as they do in the British Isles or wherever else you fell in love with them. After saying all that, I know that some readers will be growing this stuff everywhere. My friend, Don Jacobs of Eco Gardens, contends that a number of them are reasonably easy given proper conditions for growing. If you are successful, ignore the previous remarks and spread the word.

Approximately 30 species are known, all of which arise from finger-like tubers. Most are native to Europe, Asia, and North Africa, although *D. aristata* is also found in North America. The pink to deep purple flowers consist of lipped flowers (like snapdragons) and are spurred (like columbine). The most common species, *D. elata*, robust marsh orchid, is 1–2′ tall and bears pink to maroon flowers. *D. foliosa* also produces unspotted, light green foliage with stately, purple flowers. *D. maculata*, spotted marsh orchid, is similar to the above but has spotted foliage.

The tubers persist for one year, and new tubers are produced on the fingers of the old ones. Do not disturb unless necessary. Provide areas rich in compost with high water-holding capacity. Afternoon shade is helpful. Beautiful plants, but don't buy a dozen until you first try one or two.

## *Dahlia* (dah′ lia)    Dahlia    Asteraceae

Although approximately twenty species occur, it is mainly the hybrids that grace gardens today. Dahlias originate from Central and South America and have a long history of cultivation. Dahlias were probably an important crop to the Aztecs, being used as animal feed and in the treatment of urinary disorders. The Aztec word for dahlia was *cocoxochitl*, meaning water pipes, and their use as a urinary treatment was based on the Doctrine of Signatures (see *Pulmonaria*). The long stems of the tree dahlia (*D. imperialis*) were also used to transport water from mountain springs to villages. The modern garden dahlia is thought to be derived from three Mexican species: *D. pinnata*, Aztec dahlia, with double, purple flowers; *D. coccinea*, fire dahlia, with single, red flowers; and *D. rosea*, old garden dahlia, with single, pink flowers. Dahlias have a natural tendency to hybridize, and breeders in the 19th century took full advantage, deriving new hybrids from chance seedlings. Throughout Europe and the United States, the passion for dahlias in the 1840's matched the tulip mania of the 17th century in intensity and prices realized.

Since its introduction to Europe in the early 1800's, thousands of cultivars have been raised, particularly in France, England, Germany, Holland, and United States, resulting in approximately 20,000 cultivars listed in the International Register of Dahlia Names, first started in 1966. These efforts have resulted in plants ranging from 1–8′ tall, with flowers up to 12″ across. Plants may bear huge, spider-like flowers or tiny, pompom-like balls. One of the more recent trends in dahlias is the use of seed-propagated dwarfs for bedding plants. They can be raised true from seed, allowing greenhouse operators to offer them far more inexpensively than before.

There are so many shapes, colors, and sizes of flowers that they have been arranged into different groups by the International Registration Authority and used by the American Dahlia Society. The groups are based on the morphology of the head and flowers. Briefly, the groups listed in the table on the next page have been registered, and several cultivars are provided. To obtain a listing and definition of various classifications and additional appropriate cultivars for each, consult the American Dahlia Society (listing at end of *Dahlia*).

Regardless of the seemingly infinite hybrids, occasionally one can find a few species offered for those who love a combination of beauty and history. I had the pleasure of seeing the 12′ tall tree dahlias, *D. imperialis*, when I lived in New Zealand a few years ago. Dozens of pink flowers occurred in the fall and my, how beautiful the sight. In this country, they are likely frost-tolerant to lower zone 7; however, they are not particularly happy with high humidity and heat. In the northwest, they are marginal in that an early frost may cut down the flowers before they open, but well worth trying. Another tree species which flowers over a much longer period of time is *D. tenuicaulis*, with single, lavender flowers on 6′ tall plants. Both are woody when mature.

| Group | Name | Description | Cultivars |
|-------|------|-------------|-----------|
| 1 | Single | Open-centered blooms with one or two outer rows of ray flowers surrounding a disc. Common in bedding plant forms. | Bambino, Coltness Gem, Liliput, Reddy, most bedding plant cultivars. |
| 2 | Anemone | One or more rows of ray flowers surrounding a dense group of upward-pointing, tubular florets. | Bridesmaid, Comet, Fabel, Honey, Scarlet Comet. |
| 3 | Collarette | Open-centered, surrounded by an inner ring of short florets (the collar) and one or two outer rows of usually flattened ray flowers. | Alstergruzz, Bride's Bouquet, Esther, La Cierva. |
| 4 | Waterlily | Fully double blooms, with broad ray flowers which are flat or slightly incurved. The overall effect is a flat or shallow bloom, as in a waterlily. | Bluesette, Gerrie Hoek, le Castel, Peace Pact, Pearl of Heemstede, Twiggy. |
| 5 | Decorative | Blooms fully doubled, with no central disc, with broad, flat or slightly inwardly rolled ray flowers. The tips of the ray flowers may also be cut (fimbricated). | Arabian Night, Aspen, Autumn Fairy, Duet, Extase, Ellen Houston, Garden Wonder, Hamari Gold, Rosella, Snow Country, Suzette, Twilight Time. |
| 6 | Ball | Ball-shaped or globose, often slightly flattened at the top. The ray flowers are blunt or rounded at the tips. | Bonny Blue, Golden Torch, Opal, Safe Shot, Wootton Cupid. |
| 7 | Pompon | Similar to Ball types, but more globose in shape. Flower heads are not flattened but almost circular. | Black Diamond, Charmant, Moor Place, Golden Scepter, Hallmark, Snowflake. |
| 8 | Cactus | Fully double blooms showing no central disc. The ray flowers are long and narrow and tightly rolled (revolute) for over half the length. Subdivided into those with long, straight rays and those in which the ray flowers curve upward. | Apache, Banker, Bonnie Esprit, Fluffy Ruffles, Icicle, Klankstad Kerkrade, My Love, Promise, Sonia. |
| 9 | Semi-cactus | Fully double blooms, with slightly pointed ray flowers which are broader at the base than at the tips. Revolute for less than half their length and either straight or curving. | Jura, Munchen, Pianella, Red Marjorette, Red Pigmy. |
| 10 | Miscella-neous | A group of relatively small, variable classes. Examples include Orchid-flowered, Peony-flowered, Star-flowered, etc. | Akita, Fascination, Giraffe. |

Dahlias have tender, tuberous roots, normally lifted at first frost. Although they can be left in the ground in zones 7(7b)–10 (assuming good winter drainage), some gardeners report that lifting the roots even in those zones results in better performance the following year. After lifting, soak the roots in a fungicide, such as benomyl, and store in a cool area in moist, but not wet, peat moss or sand. Inspect them occasionally over the winter for rot and moisture.

Propagation is accomplished by separating the tubers at planting time. At least one bud or eye must be present on the separated piece of tuber; otherwise no growth will occur. Use a sharp knife for separation of the tubers. Dipping the knife in rubbing alcohol or peroxide before each cut reduces the spread of disease organisms. Cuttings from the base of the plant can also be used as propagation material. Take 1–1½" long terminal growth from the basal shoots, apply rooting hormone (such as Rootone which is available at most nurseries), and root in a warm, humid area. If cuttings are taken early in the season, plants should flower the first year.

Dahlias are certainly not low maintenance plants in most areas of the country. Many require support to prevent flopping and are prone to mosaic, stunt, and ring spot viruses, as well as fungal and bacterial problems. Insects feast on them, the worst being aphids and spider mites. However, many people would not have a garden without dahlias and are willing to spend the time necessary to show off their brilliance, because brilliant they are when properly grown.

I have been fortunate to see two of the loveliest plantings anywhere in the Western world. One of these was in Vancouver, British Columbia when my colleagues and I visited Queen Elizabeth Park. Brilliant beds of decorative-, spider-, and anemone-flowered dahlias shimmered in the late afternoon light, and we marvelled at their uniformity and color range. On my return to Georgia, I looked at the gaps in my garden where I had yanked out my 4' tall, lanky, spider mite-infested plants and again pondered the fact that certain species of plants simply are more content in some climates than others. The beauty of the Vancouver planting was challenged by the dahlia garden at Anglesey Abbey near Cambridge, England, where a great semicircular swath of 3–5' tall plants boasted magnificent flowers of every shape and color. Each photograph I took was to be the last, but each new plant found me exclaiming and firing away with my Canon. I finally pulled myself from that glorious Garden of Eden, very proud of the self-discipline I demonstrated. Running out of film and the onset of darkness also helped.

In the South, dahlias need to be sprayed every other week for spider mites, something I am not willing to do. I must admit that for me, dahlias are not worth the problems involved trying to raise them well. I no longer grow dahlias in my southern garden, but now I have a great excuse to get to Vancouver and England again.

**Additional Reading:**

McClintock, E. 1993. Dahlias in cultivation. *Pacific Horticulture* 54(3): 51–53.

Pavord, Anna. 1995. The irrepressible dahlia. *The Garden* 120(2):68–71.

Sorensen, P.D. 1969. Revision of the genus *Dahlia* (Compositae, Helianthae, Coreopsidinae). *Rhodora* 71:309–416.

**Associations:**

American Dahlia Society, 2044 Great Falls St., Falls Church, VA 22043. Publication: *Bulletin of the American Dahlia Society.*

*Darmera* (dar-mer' a)          Umbrella Plant          Saxifragaceae

A single, water-loving species, *D. peltata*, is grown, which used to be known as *Peltiphyllum peltatum*. The species is large and aggressive and definitely not a plant for the small backyard garden. Sometimes known as the "poor man's gunnera."

| *-peltata* (pel-tay' ta) | Umbrella Plant, Indian Rhubarb | 3–5'/6' |
|---|---|---|
| Spring          Pink | California, Oregon | Zones 5–7 |

(Syn. *Peltiphyllum peltatum*)

The peltate leaves (the petiole is attached to the leaf inside the margin, usually near the middle) are 6–18" across, have 6–10 sharply-cut lobes, and are much paler beneath than above. The leaf petioles arise directly from the rhizome and are cylindrical and hairy. Plants are best suited for shaded stream banks, beside ponds, or any watery environment where the roots may be constantly cool and moist. The flowers are small, about ½" across, pink to white and are borne in tall (3') terminal cymes, providing a bergenia-like appearance. They appear on bristly stems before the leaves appear but remain attractive long after the plant has leafed out. Plants do well as far south as zone 7 (occasionally zone 8) if constant moisture is provided. The thick, matted roots make plants most effective as stabilizers for muddy or marshy banks.

This species is often confused with *Peltoboykinia tellimoides* (syn. *Boykinia tellimoides, Saxifraga tellimoides*), also a relatively large, coarse, water plant. *D. peltata* is taller and has larger leaves with more lobes. However, the flowers of *P. tellimoides* occur with the leaves in early summer and are white, much larger, and somewhat campanulate. To be sure, the number of stamens may be counted. They both have 10; however, those of *P. tellimoides* are arranged in two groups of five, while those of *D. peltata* are separate. See the section on *Peltoboykinia* for differences between some of the large-leaved water plants.

Propagate by division with a pick axe or back hoe in the summer or fall.

**Cultivars:**

'Nana' is a dwarf (12–18″ tall) plant which I have not seen in this country. This may allow some smaller water gardens the luxury of including this species.

## *Delosperma* (del-o-sperm′ a)     Ice Plant     Aizoaceae

The hardy ice plants are mostly native to the hot-dry climates of South and East Africa and form mats of succulent foliage and bright, daisy-like flowers. They are terrific plants for hot sunny locations where soils are well-drained. There are approximately 150 species in this variable genus; however, only two are commonly available in the United States.

The main difference between *D. cooperi*, purple hardy ice plant, and the more popular *D. nubigenum*, orange-yellow hardy ice plant, is pretty obvious from the common names. Both are native to South Africa, need full sun, and do best on banks or in rock gardens. Flowering starts in mid-spring and persists for 4–6 weeks, after which light green, succulent foliage remains as a handsome reminder of the bright flowers. The fluorescent, purple-red flowers of *D. cooperi* are almost 2″ wide and plants are about 6″ tall, while the orange-yellow flowers of *D. nubigenum* are a little less than 1″ wide on 2–3″ tall matted plants. The other main difference is that *D. nubigenum* is more cold

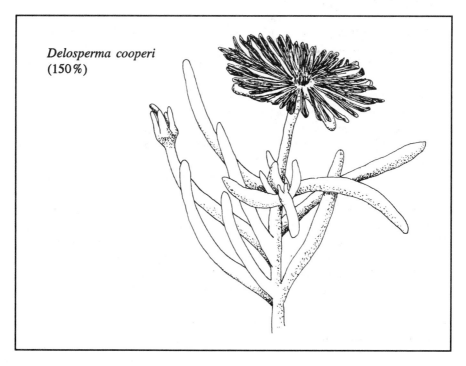

*Delosperma cooperi*
(150%)

tolerant, performing as far north as zone 5, while planting *D. cooperi* north of zone 7 is risky. I have seen only one cultivar offered, that of *D. n.* 'Basutoland', perhaps being more yellow than the species.

The other species which has joined the establishment is the 2–4" tall, white-flowered *D. macei*. A persistent bloomer, even after the first couple of frosts. Plants should become more available as gardeners discover their versatility. Excellent drainage is a must. *Delosperma* offers colorful, useful plants for the sunny garden. As additional species become more available, more plants will be used.

**Additional Reading:**

Kelaidis, P. 1994. Ice plant, a hardy flowering ground cover. *Fine Gardening* 38:20.

*Delphinium* (del-fin' ee-um)          Delphinium          Ranunculaceae

Delphiniums seen in today's gardens usually are hybrids whose development began in the late 1800's, although over 300 species of annuals, biennials, and perennials occur. *Delphinium* is closely related to *Aconitum*, differing in having a spurred, rather than a hooded, sepal and four, rather than two, petals. Similar to *Aconitum*, *Delphinium* prefers more northern latitudes and are not good perennials in the South. The leaves are palmately lobed, or divided, and plants range from the bright blue 9" (*D. tatsienense*) to 6' tall (*D. elatum*). Although blue is the dominant color in the genus, red (*D. nudicaule*) and yellow (*D. zalil*) flowers occur.

Larkspur is the common name for annuals of this genus, but taxonomic changes have placed the two common annual species in the genus *Consolida*. The common larkspur, *C. ambiqua*, and the candle larkspur, *C. regalis*, are often listed as *D. ajacis* and *D. consolida*, respectively. Is it any wonder why so many people prefer common names?

In most areas of the country, delphiniums are short-lived perennials and often lose vigor after 2–3 years. Many excellent cultivars can be raised from seed, and new plants should be grown for replacement each year. In the South, plants are placed outside in fall or early winter to flower in early spring. After flowering, they are pulled and replaced. A well-drained soil with a basic pH (adding lime to the soil helps provide this condition) and full sun are preferable. They are heavy feeders, and the use of well-rotted compost or manure, in combination with granular fertilizer such as 5-10-5 or 8-8-8, results in stronger, more vigorous plants. The two common hybrids of delphinium are the *elatum* and *belladonna* types; both have hollow and brittle stems, which if not staked, can be ravaged by rain and wind. Removing spent flower stems as soon as possible allows formation of secondary blooms in the fall.

Numerous native species may be seen in the higher elevations of several central and southern states and in the Rocky Mountain area. On each and every visit to the Smoky Mountains of North Carolina, the Armitage Pinto screeches to a halt whenever *D. exaltatum* is spotted. As my family peels themselves off the back of seats and the windshield, I jump out to admire the 6' tall spires of blue or occasionally white flowers. The segments of the leaves are wide and shallowly cut. Plants are native from Pennsylvania to Ohio and south to North Carolina and Alabama. Smaller species include the greenish white *D. virescens* and the 4' tall, deep blue or purple flowers of the Carolina delphinium, *D. carolinianum*. The Carolina delphinium is the most heat-tolerant species, extending to the sand hills of Florida. In the central and western states, there are dozens of species from the creamy yellow *D. xantholeucum* of the Wenat- chee Mountains to the variable blue flowers of *D. geyeri* of the western plains. It is unfortunate that so few nurseries raise these wonderful native plants, but perhaps it is best that they are admired from a distance.

Propagation can be accomplished, albeit with difficulty, by seed. Germination is most successful if seed is collected fresh and sown as soon as possible. If this is not possible, store the seeds in the refrigerator (35–40° F) for 4–6 weeks. Germination should occur in 14–21 days. Another more reliable method of propagation is basal cuttings in the spring. Take 3–4" long terminals of new shoots arising from the base of the plants. The base of the cutting should be solid (i.e., not hollow) and white. They can be rooted in partial shade in sand or sand/peat mix in 3–4 weeks.

The major pest is slugs, which find delphinium shoots particularly hearty, while crown rot is a severe disease in poorly-drained soils or where plants have been planted too deeply. Powdery mildew and various leaf blights can also be serious problems in all delphiniums.

Quick Reference to Delphinium Hybrids

| | Height (ft.) | Single/double flowers | Branched or single flower spike |
|---|---|---|---|
| *D.* × *belladonna* | 3–4 | Single | Branched |
| *D.* × *elatum* | 4–8 | Single, double | Single |

| | | | |
|---|---|---|---|
| -× *belladonna* (bell-ah' don-a) | | Belladonna Delphinium | 3–4'/3' |
| Summer | Blue Shades | Hybrid | Zones 3–7 |

The belladonna hybrids resulted from crosses between forms of *D. elatum* and *D. grandiflorum*, a 2' tall, blue-flowered species. Most cultivars are shorter and more branched than *D.* × *elatum* cultivars. Instead of a central flower stem followed by smaller branches, as in *D.* × *elatum*, many flower stems of belladonnas occur at the same time, although the central stem still dominates. Flowering occurs from midsummer to fall. Most cultivars have single, cup-shaped flowers which are often sterile.

## Cultivars:

'Bonita' has gentian-blue flowers.
'Bellamosa' produces deep blue flowers on 4' tall plants.
'Casa Blanca' has pure white blossoms.
'Clivenden Beauty' bears sky blue flowers and grows 3' tall.
'Lamartine' has deep violet flowers on 4' high stems.
'Moerheimii' has white flowers but is not as vigorous as 'Casa Blanca'.
'Pennant' is a seed-propagated strain with blue, lavender, creamy white, and rose flowers.
'Volkerfrieden' ('World Peace') is a fabulous selection with deep blue flowers. This is an unusually good cut flower form.
'Wendy' bears gentian-blue flowers on 12–15" tall plants.

## Additional Species:

*D. grandiflorum* is gaining a following in this country, even though it is a short-lived plant. The few flowers in the lax inflorescence may be violet, blue, or white. 'Azureum' is a light blue dwarf form, and 'Blue Mirror' has dark blue flowers on 3' tall stems. 'Blue Butterfly' is an excellent 3' tall plant with deep blue flowers in loose spikes.

| -× *elatum* (ay-lay' tum) | | Hybrid Bee Delphinium | 4–8'/3' |
|---|---|---|---|
| Summer | Various | Hybrid | Zones 2–7 |

These hybrids likely resulted from crosses between *D. elatum*, *D. exaltatum*, and *D. formosum*, and although early records were lost, *D. elatum* was surely one of the parents. Hybridization and selection by nurseries in England, Germany, and America resulted in groups of plants referred to as strains or series. Within these groups are plants with different flower colors, but similar in habit and culture. They include the Blackmore and Langdon strains, Pacific Hybrid series (also known as the Round Table series), Wrexham strain, New Century hybrids, and others with equally imaginative names. All are characterized by having large, flat flowers on a central flower raceme.

Additional flowering spikes arise from the base, especially if the first inflorescence is removed immediately after flowering. These are the aristocrats of the garden, and in cool climates, such as in the Pacific Northwest and the Northeast, plants will last up to 5 years, performing better each year. In the Midwest and Central Plain states, 2–3 years of enjoyment is not uncommon.

## Cultivars:

For simplicity's sake, cultivars are arranged by height. The following are but a small fraction of those available.

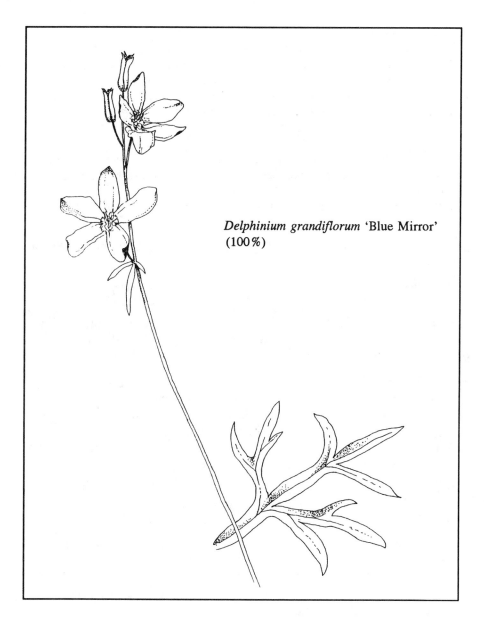

*Delphinium grandiflorum* 'Blue Mirror'
(100%)

## Tall (greater than 4'):

### *Pacific Hybrids*:

It has been stated by several experts that the original strains of Pacific Hybrids have been lost, and a great deal of variability is now common place. However, they are still very common.

'Alice Artindale' has bright blue, double flowers on dense racemes.

'Astolat' has lavender-pink flowers with a black center.

'Black Knight' is the darkest of the series, bearing dark purple, almost black, flowers.

'Blue Bird' has clear blue flowers with a white center.

'Cameliard' is 6' tall, with lavender-blue flowers.

'Galahad' has magnificent white flowers and is one of the latest of the series to flower.

'Guinevere' bears lavender flowers with a tinge of pink and a white bee. The contrast in color sometimes gives the impression of a bicolor.

'Lanceolot' has lavender flowers with a white eye.

'King Arthur' is a most impressive 3-5' tall, dark blue-flowering selection.

'Summer Skies' is light blue with a white center.

All the Pacific hybrids are usually raised from seed; therefore, variation in color is common.

*Mid-Century Hybrids*:

This relatively new strain bears flowers of pink ('Rose Future'), white ('Ivory Towers'), light blue ('Moody Blues'), and dark blue ('Ultra Violet'). They are 4-5' tall, have stronger stems than other tall delphiniums, and are more resistant to mildew.

*Giant Imperial Series:*

'Blue Spires', 'Blue Bell', and 'Rosalind' belong to this series. They are often listed as perennials but are mainly derived from annual larkspur, *C. regalis*. Due to the short-lived nature of delphiniums in most parts of the country, there is often little difference in longevity between these and the hybrid types.

*Independents:*

Many delphiniums have been bred as independent cultivars, not closely allied to a particular strain or series, and because of this, they are often more difficult to locate.

'Betty Hayes' has pale blue flowers with a white eye.

'Canada' is sky-blue with a black eye.

'Cressida' bears pale blue flowers with a white eye but is taller and more vigorous than 'Betty Hayes'.

'Jack Tar' is very late flowering and has large, rich, dark blue flowers.

'Xenia Field' produces beautiful pale lavender flowers with a creamy white center.

Small (2½-3½' tall):

These require less staking and are most impressive in groups of 3-5 plants.

*Connecticut Yankee Series:*

Similar to the belladonna types, cultivars are more heavily branched than many of the previous selections. 'Blue Fountains' is one of my favorites because of its reliability as far south as zone 7b. Flowers are produced in various shades of blue, white, and mauve.

'Baby Doll' has pale mauve flowers with a yellow-white eye.

*Magic Fountains Strain:*

Plants occur in lilac, white, white with a dark center, dark blue, sky blue, and pink. Generally they grow about 2½-3' tall.

**Additional Reading:**

Dodge, Michael H. 1984. Delphiniums: perennial blue bloods. *Horticulture* 62(1):27-31.

Honour, M. 1994. Propagating delphiniums. *The Garden* 119(4):154-155.

Rathbone, L. 1994. Growing great English delphiniums. *Fine Gardening* 39:46-49.

*Associations:*

The Delphinium Society, 11 Long Grove, Seer Green, Beaconsfield, Buckinghamshire, HP9 EYN, England. Publication: *Delphiniums*.

## *Dentaria* see *Cardamine*.

## *Deschampsia* (des-camp-see' a)　　　Hairgrass　　　Poaceae

Hairgrass consists of approximately 50 species of grasses, including annuals and perennials. Plants are generally native to woods, meadows, and plains. They are best grown in moist fertile soils, tolerate some shade, and are quite drought tolerant. Plants are tufted, and leaves are generally narrow and inrolled, looking like tufts of long, thin hair. There are probably no other grasses that look quite so delicate in flower and may be the most ethereal of our available grasses. The most common species are *D. caespitosa*, tufted hairgrass, and *D. flexuosa*, crinkled hairgrass, both native to North America and most other continents. Flowers are handsome on the plant and also popular as dried flowers for arrangements. One or two unusual forms may occasionally be found, such as *D. caespitosa* 'Vivipara' ('Fairy's Joke'), which produces small plantlets on the diminutive flowers at the ends of the stems.

| *-caespitosa* (ces-pi-tose' a) | Tufted Hairgrass | 2-3'/3' |
|---|---|---|
| Spring　Bronze to Cream | North America, Eurasia | Zones 4-8 |

Tufted hairgrass produces handsomely-pleated leaves which are less than ½" wide and often flattened or occasionally inrolled. Plants may be used in zones 4 to 8, but they do not perform as well under hot, humid conditions. In most of the country, plants will be winter dormant, but where winters are mild, leaves turn bronzy yellow and remain evergreen. Hundreds of flowers arch upward and outward in loose, airy panicles in such numbers as to almost obscure the foliage. It is one of the earliest grasses to flower, and its tolerance of shade makes it a handsome addition to ferns and hostas. Moisture is more important for good performance than the amount of shade or sun. Consistent moisture is necessary, and plants will tolerate significant shade if moisture is available. Deep shade, however, results in poor flowering.

**Cultivars:**

'Bronzeschleier' ('Bronze Veil') is more heat tolerant than other forms. Plants grow 2–3' tall and bear bronze-yellow panicles.

'Holciformis', Pacific hairgrass, is only 1–2' tall and suitable as a ground cover in northern and western gardens. Plants produce bright green foliage and dense, narrow panicles, very much unlike previous forms.

'Goldschleier' ('Gold Veil') bears large plumes of silvery flowers in late summer and early fall on 1–3' tall plants.

'Tardiflora' is a late-flowering selection, bearing flowers in early fall on 2–3' tall plants.

| | | |
|---|---|---|
| *-flexuosa* (flex-ewe-o' sa) | Crinkled Hairgrass | 1–2'/2' |
| Summer  Purple-Tinged | North America, Eurasia | Zones 4–7 |

An excellent small, cool-season grass with narrow, wiry leaves and nodding, purple-tinged flowers in June and July. The panicles are slightly twisted, thus accounting for the botanical name. These fine-textured plants are useful as small accents in moist, partially-shaded gardens and best planted in groups of at least three. Crinkled hairgrass grows well in zones 8 and 9 of the west coast, but does poorly in similar zone numbers in the south. They do not tolerate high heat and humidity.

**Cultivars:**

'Aurea' is only about 18" tall with particularly golden foliage in early spring. The color fades with the approaching of summer.

Quick Key to Deschampsia Species

    A. Plants generally less than 2' tall,
       leaf blades flexuous . . . . . . . . . . . . . . . . . . . . . . . *D. flexuosa*
    AA. Plants generally taller than 2',
       leaves not flexuous . . . . . . . . . . . . . . . . . . . . . *D. caespitosa*

## *Dianthus* (dye-an' thus)  Pinks, Carnations  Caryophyllaceae

To recreate Grandmother's garden, one need not go further than this genus for an excellent start. Pinks have been in gardens as long as there have been gardens. Most garden species are low growing and suitable for rockeries and border edging. Natural and planned hybridization of the 300 species have occurred for at least two centuries, so that today the parentage of many of the pinks is somewhat cloudy, even muddy. However, garden interest in this genus has always been steady, and some of the oldest hybrids are still available to gardeners today. Considerable selection of annual pinks (*D. chinensis*) has occurred for the greenhouse trade, but wonderful breakthroughs in the breeding of this and Sweet William, *D. barbatus*, have produced exceptional hybrids. In many parts of the country, these hybrid pinks are hardy and overwinter; they are seen in combination with pansies and violas in fall and winter landscapes. The modern day carnations used for corsages and cut flowers are selections of *D. caryophyllus* and require greenhouse conditions to grow properly.

Perennial species may be hardy from zone 2 to zone 10, so there is no excuse for not having some *Dianthus* in the garden. Unfortunately, many are short-lived, and propagation every 2–3 years is required to keep plants vigorous and attractive. All should be provided with full sun, excellent drainage, and slightly-alkaline soils.

Propagation of many species is relatively easy from seed, but taking terminal cuttings is the most foolproof method for all of the garden species.

Quick Reference to Dianthus Species

| | Foliage color, gray or green | Height (in.) | Flowers solitary, in 2's or clusters | Flower color |
|---|---|---|---|---|
| *D.* × *allwoodii* | Gray | 12–20 | 2's | Various |
| *D. alpinus* | Green | 3–6 | Solitary | Pink |
| *D. barbatus* | Green | 10–18 | Clusters | Various |
| *D. deltoides* | Green | 6–12 | 2's | Red |
| *D. gratianopolitanus* | Gray | 9–12 | Solitary | Pink |
| *D. knappii* | Green | 15–24 | Clusters | Yellow |
| *D. plumarius* | Gray | 18–24 | 2's | Various |

-× *allwoodii* (awl-wud' ee-eye) Allwood Pinks, Modern Pinks 12–20"/12"
  Summer  Various  Hybrid  Zones 4–8

This hybrid was raised in the 1920's by the English nurseryman Montague Allwood, who crossed a garden pink (*D. plumarius* hybrid) with a carnation type, *D. caryophyllus*. Plants are highly variable, but in general, the foliage is

333

gray-green and usually bears two flowers per stem. Plants flower for up to eight weeks, have a more compact habit than the plumarius types (which see), and are more vigorous, requiring division every 2–3 years. Many fine cultivars have been raised, and although it is difficult to be sure of their parentage, a large number have been assembled under this hybrid group. All have some fragrance, some very strong and spicy, others less so. The degree of fragrance is dependent on the amount of *D. plumarius* parentage remaining. A few single-flowered forms are available, but most are double. Most can be cut back if they become lanky. Some have been raised specifically for exhibition and are known as show or imperial pinks.

Propagate by division in spring or fall or take 1–2″ long, terminal cuttings immediately after flowering. Root in a warm, humid area.

### Cultivars and Hybrids:

Border Selections (10–18″ tall):

'Alba' has clear white flowers on 10–15″ tall stems.

'Annabelle' bears handsome pink, double flowers.

'Aqua' grows 10–12″ tall with clear white, double, fragrant flowers.

'Baby Treasure' is a free-flowering plant and produces fragrant, shell-pink flowers with a scarlet eye.

'Becky Robinson' bears double, pink, rosy flowers over tufts of blue-green foliage.

'Constance' is a silver-pink form with red flecks on the petals.

'Danielle' (sometimes 'Danielle-Marie'), a recent sport of 'Helen', is a vigorous 10–12″ high plant bearing deep salmon flowers most of the summer.

'Doris' is one of the most popular cultivars and has wonderfully fragrant salmon-pink flowers with a deep pink eye. 'Doris' underwent a number of mutations resulting in two sports, 'Laura' and 'Doreen', both with orange-pink flowers.

'Helen' has fragrant, deep pink with salmon flowers. The color is a little deeper than 'Doris' and free blooming.

'Horatio' has double pink flowers with a handsome red eye. Grows to approximately 6″ tall.

'Ian' is a long-blooming plant bearing rich scarlet flowers, but it is not quite as cold hardy as many other cultivars (zone 5).

'Laced Romeo' has deep red flowers fringed with creamy white.

'Loveliness' was bred by Montague Allwood prior to 1926, and consists of flowers whose frilly lacy-cut petals are in shades of pink and rose. Highly fragrant. They are appearing in this country as 'Rainbow Loveliness Mix'.

'Mrs. Sinkins' is still one of my favorites whenever I happen to see it. Bred in 1868, she is one of the oldest, but seen less and less as new cultivars arise. Plants are about 15″ tall and bear wonderfully fragrant double white flowers (with a tinge of pink) and gray-green foliage.

'Rachel' has spicy, fragrant, double, pink flowers over dense blue-green foliage. Grows 10–15″ tall.

'Robin' is one of the brightest of the garden pinks, having bright coral-red flowers.

'Susan' is pink with a crimson center.

'Thomas' has deep red flowers over blue-green foliage.

Miniatures (3–6″ tall):

The miniatures can be used to advantage in rock crevices and as fillers in the rockery, and are finally becoming easier to locate in the trade.

'Alpinus' is the result of crossing *D.* × *allwoodii* with other dwarf species. It bears single, fragrant flowers and is exceptionally free blooming. Flowers are produced in a mixture of colors ranging from light pink to red and an occasional bicolor. Plants are also more cold hardy (zone 3) than the others.

'Dainty Maid' has single, bright purple flowers with a red eye.

'Elizabeth' bears pink flowers with a small crimson eye.

'Essex Witch' is one of the most popular cultivars with flowers in a range of pink hues, as well as whites and salmons.

'Evangeline' has double, rose-pink flowers.

'Fay' has bright purple flowers on 6″ tall stems.

'Frosty Fire', an excellent selection from Canada, is only about 6″ tall with double, brilliant red flowers and blue-green foliage.

'Little Bobby' ('Bobby'), named by John Donofrio of Carroll Gardens over 50 years ago, has cerise-colored, single flowers. The foliage is blue, and the height is about 6″ tall.

'Mars' bears double, rounded, deep pink flowers and grows 3–6″ tall.

'Wink' has lovely clear white flowers on 4″ high stems.

| *-alpinus* (al-pine′ us) | | Alpine Pink | 3–6″/1′ |
|---|---|---|---|
| Late Spring | Pink | Austrian Alps | Zones 3–7 |

The grass-green leaves are about 1″ long and ⅓″ wide with a prominent midrib. The leaves are entire and plants form a loose, matted clump which multiplies to cover large areas. The 1½″ diameter flowers are large relative to the plant, and literally hide the foliage for 4–6 weeks. The 5 petals are fringed, and the scentless flowers usually have a white central disc.

This is a garden gem if soils are well drained, somewhat alkaline, and summers are not consistently often above 85° F. It is an excellent rock garden or edging plant in moderate summers. Plant in moderate shade and minimize full afternoon sun. In the Armitage garden (zone 7b) it was spectacular until the end of July, whereupon it gave up, pooped out, and was not seen again. This is not uncommon in the southeastern states, and cuttings and/or divisions need to be taken each year.

Propagate vegetatively similar to *D.* × *allwoodii*. Seed germinates within 3 weeks if placed in warm (70–75° F), humid conditions.

**Cultivars:**
'Albus' has white petals with small purplish spots.

| *-barbatus* (bar-bah' tus) | | Sweet William | 10–18"/1' |
|---|---|---|---|
| Late Spring | Various | Eastern Europe | Zones 3–8 |

A little English history helps to undercover the origin of the intriguing common name. Sweet William is so named for that most likable fellow, William, Duke of Cumberland, who brutally crushed a number of rebellions, the most famous being the Jacobite Rebellion led by Bonnie Prince Charlie. Sweet is hardly an appropriate description for William's activities. English history stories aside, Sweet William is as well known in Edmonton, Alberta as it is in Athens, Georgia. Since many of the cultivars are seed propagated, there is a great deal of variation even within cultivars. Although classified as a biennial, it self sows so prolifically that it is always a guest in the garden. The 2–3" long lanceolate leaves are short-petioled and have a prominent midrib. The unscented flowers have toothed or fringed petals, often with a distinct eye of either a darker or different color than the petals. Although many of the species of *Dianthus* have only 1–2 flowers per stem, Sweet Williams have a characteristic flat topped cluster of flowers (cymes).

In the southern states, plants act as true perennials, particularly if flowers are removed before seed is produced. Plants are not long-lived and decline if not divided every 2–3 years.

Lime should be added to the garden yearly to provide a basic soil. They are sun lovers like the rest of the genus, although in the South, partial shade is tolerated. It makes a desirable cut flower, having an excellent shelf life in water. More and more Sweet Williams are appearing in bouquets and on dining room tables as modern day florists learn of their excellent properties.

Division is the surest means to maintain true colors, but terminal cuttings or starting plants from seed is not uncommon. Germination takes 7–14 days when seeds are placed in warm (70–75° F), humid conditions.

**Cultivars:**

'Blood Red' has one of the darkest red flower colors in the species and grows to 15" tall.

'Double Tall Mix' is a descriptive name for this group of 15–18" tall plants suitable for cut flowers.

'Harlequin' bears semi-double to double, pink and white flowers.

'Homeland' and 'Nigracans' are both deep red-flowered cultivars.

'Indian Carpet' is about 10″ tall and comes in various colors. A dwarf form ('Dwarf Indian Carpet') is a selection of shorter (6–8″ tall) plants. There is little difference between the two.

'Messenger Mix' is similar to 'Indian Carpet' but is about 15–24″ tall and one of the earliest cultivars to flower. Useful for cut flowers because of the strong stems.

'Midget Mix' and 'Double Midget Mix' are mixes of semi-double and double flowering 4–6″ tall plants.

'Newport Pink' bears deep pink flowers and is 10–12″ tall. Beautiful.

'Pink Beauty' has soft salmon-pink flowers on 15″ tall plants.

'Roundabout Mix' is another seed-propagated mix of low growers with bicolor flowers of white and pink or rose.

'Scarlet Beauty' bears flowers of rich scarlet.

### Related Species:

'Sweet Wivelsfield' is a hybrid between *D. plumarius* and *D. barbatus*. It is approximately 18″ tall with single or double flowers, and has a pleasant scent (from *D. plumarius*). Seed is available and, although not well known in United States, the ease of propagation may stimulate gardeners to try it.

| *-deltoides* (del-toi′ deez) | | Maiden Pinks | 6–12″/24″ |
|---|---|---|---|
| Summer | Red, Rose | Europe | Zones 3–8 |

This species forms loose mats and is an excellent ground cover when planted in full sun or partial shade. Two types of stems are found: the 8–12″ long flowering stems which are usually branched at the base as well as near the top, and non-bearing stems which are prostrate and 4–6″ long. The grass-like green leaves are narrow (less than ½″ wide), and 3–6″ long. They often have a rosy purple flush, especially at cooler times of the year. The ¾″ wide, solitary flowers usually bear a V-shaped pattern in the throat. They are purple to rose colored and borne at the end of the branched stems. Flowers persist for 8–10 weeks and can totally cover the foliage. Shearing the plants after flowering promotes more vigorous growth and additional flowers in the summer.

Plants spread rapidly under conditions of good drainage and moderately rich, alkaline soil. The species is as good as many of the named cultivars, particularly in the South, where some of the larger-flowered cultivars melt out in the summer. Sifting a layer of sand:soil mix on the centers of the planting helps alleviate the problem.

Propagation is not difficult from seed or cuttings. Remove 2″ long side shoots after flowering with a bit of the main stem attached and place in warm, humid conditions. Seed should be treated as with *D. alpinus*.

## Cultivars:

'Albus' has clear white flowers.

'Bright Eyes' bears white flowers with handsome red centers, about 3–6" tall.

'Brilliant', 'Coccineus' and 'Fanal' have scarlet-red flowers.

'Flashing Light' bears deep ruby-red flowers.

'Garland' produces pure pink flowers on 4–6" tall plants.

'Inshriach Dazzler' is 4–6" tall with chrome-red flowers. Some Allwoodii parentage can be seen in this cultivar.

'Nelli' grows flat along the ground and bear many flowers, each one dark red with a deeper red circle.

'Red Maiden' has reddish purple flowers which totally cover the 6" tall plants. Terrific performer in the heat.

'Rosea' bears flowers in various shades of pink.

'Samos' produces intensely red flowers over 4" tall plants.

'Vampire' and 'Wisley Variety' have carmine-red flowers with dark green foliage.

'Zing Rose' has large deep red flowers. While it is magnificent in flower, it is not as well adapted to hot, humid summers as the type.

*-gratianopolitanus* (grah-tee-ah-no-po-li-tay' nus)  Cheddar Pinks  9–12"/12"
Spring                    Rose, Pink                    Europe          Zones 3–8
(Syn. *D. caesius*)

This is a fragrant but highly variable species. The common name refers to the Cheddar Gorge in Southwest England, one of the native habitats of this plant. This is also the location of the Cheddar Caves, well known for their delightful cheese. When my colleague, Dr. Michael Dirr, and I visited there, it seems we ate far more cheese than we saw native pinks. Man cannot live by pinks alone!

The gray-green entire foliage is narrowly lanceolate (less than ⅛" wide) and forms compact tussocks. The 1" diameter flowers are carried singly or in twos and are usually rose, pink, or any shade between. If the flowers are not allowed to produce seed, flowering will continue from spring to late summer. In the Horticulture gardens at Georgia, plants are in full flower from late March to mid May. There is a great deal of variation within seed-propagated plants, but their fragrance and ease of culture make this species one of the best in the genus. In the South, this is an almost indestructible species.

Propagate by seed or terminal cuttings. Treat similar to *D. alpinus*.

## Cultivars:

So much natural interbreeding occurs that one can never be sure of absolute pedigree. However, most of the following have a reasonable percentage of Cheddar pinks within.

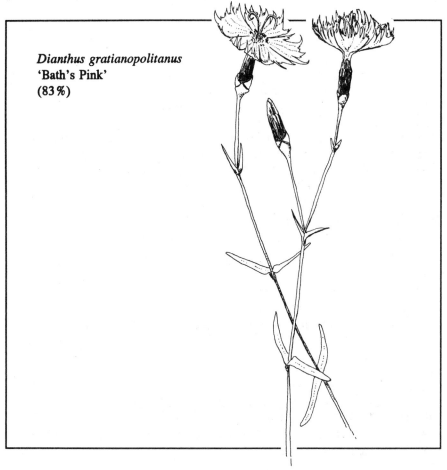

*Dianthus gratianopolitanus*
'Bath's Pink'
(83%)

'Bath's Pink' is one of the finest soft pink cultivars available. The flowers are
   fringed, 1″ across, and plants are particularly floriferous. They are tough,
   easy to grow, and handsome. The gray-green foliage is also attractive when
   not in flower. Plants were originally found by Jane Bath, one of America's
   Grand Dames of the garden world, of Stone Mountain, GA.
'Dottie' ('Pretty Dottie'), raised by Mr. Jim Fleming of Nebraska, is a
   hybrid between 'Spotty' and 'Snow Flurries'. The flowers are white with
   a maroon eye, and borne on a 6–9″ tall plant.
'Firewitch' ('Feuerhexe') has handsome deep blue foliage and single magenta
   flowers. The plants flower in the spring and then again during the summer.
'Flore-plena' has double, pink flowers which are interesting if not particu-
   larly ornamental.
'Grandiflorus' has 1½″ diameter rose-pink flowers.
'Karlik' is covered with wonderfully fragrant, deep pink fringed flowers.

'La Bourbrille' ('La Bourboule') has clear, single, pink flowers over mounds of silver-green foliage.

'Petite' produces an interesting, tiny 4″ tall tussock of gray-green leaves over which appear small pink flowers. For those looking for a truly dwarf dianthus, this is a good choice.

'Pink Feather' has pink flowers with feathery petals.

'Splendens' has deep red flowers.

'Spotty' ('Spotti') is an interesting red and white bicolor. This lovely cultivar from Jim Fleming (see 'Dottie') is well worth trying.

'Tiny Rubies' is a double flowered, deep pink form, which is rapidly becoming more popular in American gardens.

| *-knappii* (nahp-ee′ eye) | | Hairy Garden Pink | 15–24″/15″ |
|---|---|---|---|
| Summer | Pale Yellow | Central Europe | Zones 3–7 |

I remember first reading about this species in a catalog which stated that it was "very rare and uncommon, the only yellow-flowered species of pinks." The way this advertisement ran on, the plant was so rare that if I didn't purchase it, I would seriously add to its chances for extinction.

The truth is, that although *D. knappii* is the only yellow-flowered dianthus in cultivation, it is anything but rare. Plants are easy to grow from seeds (which are plentiful), short lived, reseed themselves everywhere, have no fragrance, and their washed out yellow flowers are dismally unexciting.

The 2–3″ long, hairy, gray-green leaves are less than ¼″ wide and carried on 4-sided upright stems. Eight to ten flowers are clustered in an inflorescence that persists for 4–6 weeks. It grows better and has brighter flower colors in the North than in the South, but it dies after one or two years, regardless.

Propagate similarly to other species.

| *-plumarius* (ploo-mah′ ree- us) | | Cottage Pinks, Grass Pinks | 18–24″/12″ |
|---|---|---|---|
| Early Summer | Various | Eastern Europe | Zones 3–8 |

The wild *D. plumarius* species is seldom seen but closely resembles *D. gratianopolitanus*, differing by having petals which are more deeply cut, and generally flowers in groups of two, seldom solitary as in the latter species. The foliage is gray-green and grass-like, and plants can be very vigorous. Beautiful in its own right, the species is also valuable because it is the dominant parent of the garden pinks, so popular in today's gardens.

The garden pinks are also known as old fashioned pinks. They are usually listed separately from the Allwood types, known as modern pinks, previously discussed under *D. × allwoodii*. The garden pinks grow more slowly than the Allwoods and need to be divided every 2–3 years. Since the nomenclature is so mixed up and so many terms have come into use, some people put the allwoods and plumarius types in the same grab bag. However, in trying to maintain some semblance of scientific decorum, I believe the following cultivars have a good deal of *D. plumarius* in their bloodlines.

### Cultivars (Garden and Cottage Pinks):

'C.T. Musgrave' ('Musgrave's White') bears marvelously fragrant, white flowers with a green eye, and is one of the few singles.

'Dad's Favorite' is a double bicolor of white with red fringes on the petals. Very old-fashioned, selected in the early 18th century.

'Excelsior' has carmine colored flowers with a darker eye.

'Inchmery' has pale pink flowers on a 8–10" tall compact plant. Nicely fragrant.

'White Ladies' produces clean white, strongly scented flowers.

'Spring Beauty' produces fragrant flowers in shades of pink over gray foliage.

### Other Hybrids:

Many other fine hybrids are offered which are difficult to place under one species or another. I list but a few.

'Baby Blanket', an introduction from Jackson and Perkins of Medville, OR, has blue-green leaves and 1" wide pink flowers with a white eye. Very handsome, only about 8" tall.

'Duchess of Westminster' is an old cultivar with a strong clove fragrance. The petals are believed to provide unlimited energy to the partaker (or is it partyer?).

'Itsaul White' produces all white, double flowers. Also marketed as 'Vanilla'.

'Lady Granville' bears white flowers with raspberry markings and a red center. An old cultivar, but wonderfully fragrant.

'Little Boy Blue' also has lovely blue foliage. The single white flowers have pink centers.

'Miss' series are tall plants designed for cut flowers. The seed-propagated series includes 'Miss Biwako' (rosy red), 'Miss Kobe' (magenta), and 'Miss Kyoto' (pink flowers).

'Mountain Mist' is another blue-green foliaged plant, but with many single pink flowers on 10" stems. I think this is the next great dianthus, with foliage which looks good in the winter (in the South) and summer and covered with pink flowers in the spring. Does not flower well south of zone 8.

'Oakington' grows about 4" tall, spreads well, and bears semi-double to double warm pink flowers. Raised by Alan Bloom in the 1930's and named for the site of the original Bloom nursery.

'Painted Lady' is a mat former (8–10" tall) with single light pink flowers splotched with red.

'Peppermint Patty' came from Rice Creek Nursery in Minneapolis, and has fragrant, double, pink flowers over blue-green foliage. Grows about 12' tall.

'Pheasant's Eye' bears white semi-double flowers with reddish centers. Noteworthy not only because of the pleasant 12" tall plants, but because it is one of the oldest cultivars still available, being selected in 1671.

'Pike's Pink' has double pink flowers only about 4" tall. Spreads to 1" across.
'Randy's Pink', introduced by Randy Kucera, is similar to 'Mountain Mist'
with bluish leaves and pink flowers.

## Quick Key to Dianthus Species

A. Plants with 1–2 flowers per flower stem
  B. Foliage gray-green
    C. Flowers usually 1 per stem, petals less
      than ½ cut . . . . . . . . . . . . . . . . . . . *D. gratianopolitanus*
    CC. Flowers usually 2 per stem, petals deeply cut . . *D. plumarius*
  BB. Foliage green
    C. Leaves grass-like, shorter than internodes,
      flowers 2 per stem . . . . . . . . . . . . . . . . . . . *D. deltoides*
    CC. Leaves longer than internodes,
      flowers 1 per stem . . . . . . . . . . . . . . . . . . . *D. alpinus*
AA. Plants whose flowers are in clusters
  B. Flowers yellow . . . . . . . . . . . . . . . . . . . . . . . *D. knappii*
  BB. Flowers not yellow . . . . . . . . . . . . . . . . . . . . . *D. barbatus*

**Additional Reading:**

McDonald, N. 1994. Perennial pinks scent the summer garden. *Fine Gardening*
38:58–61.

*Diascia* (die-ash-kee' a)          Diascia, Twinspur          Scrophulariaceae

Over 150 years have passed since the genus was first mentioned in
botanical journals and the 50 species of annuals and perennials have been
wallowing in obscurity ever since. Today, however, *Diascia* is one of the
up and coming perennials in gardens in America and Europe. The genus
name comes from *di* and *askos*, referring to the two sacs or pouches found
on *D. bergiana*, the type species. The position of the pouches is marked
with two translucent yellow patches, known as windows. Plants are usually
no taller than 18" and decumbent (lying on the ground, but with the ends
ascending), making them excellent for the front of the garden, hanging
baskets, or patio containers. Flowers are pink, salmon, or rose-colored,
held in terminal racemes, and usually, but not always, have two small
downward projecting spurs. All diascias prefer excellent drainage and full
sun in the North to partial shade in the South.

Diascias have only recently been available in the United States; therefore,
while the interest in diascias is high, the information on their performance is
limited. Many species are native to the summer-dry Cape region of South
Africa, and cold tolerance is questionable north of zone 7. To make matters
worse, while they tolerate hot and humid summers, they will go into summer

blahs if the heat and humidity persist for too long. A few inhabit moister areas of the Drackensburg region, and these tend to be more perennial. Deadhead to keep plants in flower for as long as possible, and cut back hard after flowering. As a perennial, some species may be another "good on the West Coast only" plant but should become much more popular as annuals throughout the country.

Species of *Diascia* are self-incompatible. Even in the wild, a plant needs to receive pollen from a separate clone of the same species before pollination will take place. Also, pollination in the wild is generally accomplished by a specially evolved species of bee whose forelegs have evolved approximately three times their normal length to reach into the spurs to extract the plant's nectar. Therefore, as I hope is becoming more obvious, most commercial propagation is accomplished by terminal or node cuttings, and some spread by stolons which may be divided when necessary.

The species are handsome but are not particularly eye-catching, and remained relatively unknown until the late 1980's and early 1990's when interest in the genus resulted in numerous cultivars and hybrids. In particular, Mr. Hector Harrison of Appleby, South Humberside, England, overcame the natural incompatibility of the species and raised many of the hybrids which have rekindled interest in the genus.

Quick Reference to Diascia Species:

|  | Flower color | Sprawler | Height (in.) |
|---|---|---|---|
| *D. barberae* | Rose | Yes | 10–12 |
| *D. rigescens* | Rose-pink | No | 12–24 |
| *D. vigilis* | Pale pink | Yes | 9–12 |

| *-barberae* (bar-ber-ee′ aye) | | Barber's Twinspur | 10–12″/12″ |
|---|---|---|---|
| Spring, Summer | Rose | South Africa | Zones 8–9 |

Plants, which are somewhat weedy-looking but handsome in flower, bear mats of small ovate-lanceolate leaves which cover the ground in late spring and early summer. The rose to salmon flowers have 2 patches of dark glands on either side and two ¼″ long spurs. Native to marshy grounds in the Drackensburg area.

Plants are among the least cold hardy and should be used as an annual throughout most of the country.

**Cultivars:**

'Ruby Field' is a hybrid between *D. barberae* and *D. cordifolia* and is probably the most popular form offered. It is more richly colored and floriferous than the species, but somewhat overrated. In the Armitage garden, it flowered heavily in the spring and early summer but quickly succumbed to the onslaught of heat and humidity in July. Plants resulted from a cross made by Mr. John Kelly of Abbotsbury, Dorset, England, and named for the wife of Paul Field of Lincolnshire.

**Related Species:**

*D. cordata* is very similar to *D. barberae* and plants sold as *D. cordata* are probably the latter. If anyone really wants to know, they differ in that the calyx segments of *D. barberae* are thin and slightly hairy whereas those of *D. cordata* are always glabrous (smooth). Talk about splitting hairs.

| *-rigescens* (ri-ges′ cens) | | Rigid Twinspur | 1–2′/2′ |
|---|---|---|---|
| Spring, Summer | Rose-Pink | South Africa | Zones 7–9 |

This is the most robust and impressive species, bearing 6–8″ long racemes densely packed with 2-spurred rosy pink flowers. *D. rigescens* has considerable natural range, roaming from southern Natal to the mountains of the eastern Cape. They are distinct from other species by having sessile leaves which are sharply serrated. The foliage takes on a beige tint with age. Like all diascias, they require good drainage and are terrific in raised beds, especially if planted at eye-level. One of the finest "eye-level" plantings I have seen was at Savill Gardens in Great Windsor Park outside London, England. Unfortunately, I have not been so impressed in the United States.

Plants are as cold tolerant as any species. They are propagated by node cuttings (take a piece of the stem with a solid node at the base) because new stems are hollow.

**Cultivars:**

'Forge Cottage' is 1–2′ tall with copper-pink flowers in long racemes. The foliage is speckled yellow when young.

**Related Species:**

*D. integerrima* is native to rocky areas and is tolerant of dry conditions. It is distinct in having numerous wiry but rigid decumbent (laying over) stems from the crown. The foliage is blue-green and tufted in appearance, resulting in plants about 18″ tall. The rose-pink flowers occur over most of the season.

| *-vigilis* (vig-ill′ is) | | | 9–12″/2′ |
|---|---|---|---|
| Spring, Summer | Light Pink | South Africa | Zones 7–9 |

This is one of the longest bloomers in the species, with small pale pink flowers on long wiry stems. A vigorous stoloniferous species which is easy to propagate from divisions. The light green foliage contrasts well with the flowers. The epithet comes from *vigil*, The Sentinel, the hugh volcanic rock on the northern end of the amphitheater wall that towers over Royal Natal park.

## Related Species:

*D. fetcaniensis* is quite distinct as the entire plant is covered in glandular tipped hairs, making it feel moist when touched. They are similar to *D. vigilis*, but the salmon-rose flowers are cup-shaped, unlike the open slightly flat flowers of *D. vigilis*. Plants are extremely floriferous and are fairly decent garden subjects. *D. fetcaniensis* is one of the most cold hardy species.

## Related Hybrids:

A number of exciting hybrids have arisen from Mr. Harrison's breeding program, as well as from a number of English and Australian nurseries.

'Dark Eyes' grows 8–10″ tall with pink flowers with eyes of purple-pink.

'Fiona' is a handsome apricot upright selection.

'Hopley's Apricot' and 'Blackthorn's Apricot', named after the two nurseries who found them, are likely the results of sports of 'Ruby Field'. 'Blackthorn's Apricot' was one of the finest performers in our Horticulture Gardens at University of Georgia.

'Joyce's Choice', named for Mrs. Harrison, has salmon-apricot flowers on 12″ tall plants. A hybrid of 'Salmon Supreme' × 'Hopley's Apricot'. The same cross yielded 'Stella' (pink flowers) and 'Lady Valerie' (smaller flowers with a salmon tint).

'Jack Elliot' bears large pink flowers on 12–15″ tall plants.

'Jacqueline's Joy', with large, bright purplish pink flowers, is a low spreading plant about 12″ tall. A hybrid between 'Lilac Belle' and 'Hopley's Apricot'.

'Langthorn's Lavender' has dozens of lilac colored flowers on upright 12″ tall stems. A hybrid of *D. lilacina*, a small-flowered sprawling plant with lilac-pink flowers.

'Lilac Belle' resulted from a cross between 'Ruby Field' and *D. lilacina*, a small flowered but vigorous species. The small lilac-pink flowers are held in long racemes. Most handsome.

'Lilac Mist' used 'Lilac Belle' and *D. rigescens* as its parents, resulting in 12–18″ tall plants which spread 3–4′ wide. The silver-lilac flowers age almost to white as they mature, providing a two-tone effect.

'Pink Spot' is about 10″ tall with purple-pink flowers. A hybrid between two forms of *D. vigilis*.

'Rupert Lambert' has rosy red flowers on upright stems, and is similar, but larger and better in all respects, to 'Ruby Field'.

'Salmon Supreme' arose from the hybridization of 'Ruby Field' and *D. stachyoides*, a rose-pink species, and bears beautiful salmon-pink flowers. One of the best for flowing out of containers or for baskets.

'Strawberry Sundae' and 'Raspberry Sunday' recently arose from Mal Morgan's efforts at Glenfield Nursery, New South Wales, Australia. Heat tolerant, well branched and floriferous. Terrific.

'Twinkle' ('Lilac Belle' × 'Ruby Field') has lilac-rose flowers.
'Wendy' ('Lilac Belle' × 'Hopley's Hybrid') bears large rich dark pink flowers on 12″ spreading plants.

## Quick Key to Diascia Species

A. Plants stoloniferous, loose racemes less than 3″ long
    B. Flowers rose-pink, leave bases slightly rounded . . *D. barberae*
    BB. Flowers light pink, leave bases more acute . . . . . . *D. vigilis*
AA. Stems mainly arise from central crown, dense
    racemes longer than 3″, leaves sessile . . . . . . . . *D. rigescens*

**Additional Reading:**

Benham, Steve. 1987. *Diascia*—A survey of the species in cultivation. *The Plantsman* 9(1):1–17.
Garbut, Simon. 1994. The up-and-coming *Diascia*. *The Garden* 119(1):18–21.
Kelly, John. 1987. *Diascia* 'Ruby Field' In: Letter to the Editor. *The Plantsman* 9(2):128.
Lord, Tony. 1996. Diascia on trial. *The Garden* 121(4):192–194.
Rader, J. Elliot's variety Diascia: *Diascia vigilis*. *Grower Talks* 57(4):21.

*Dicentra* (dy-sen′ tra)        Bleeding Heart        Fumariaceae

One of the most popular plants for the shaded garden year after year is the bleeding heart. The common name comes from the heart-shaped flowers whose inner petals protrude from the outer petals giving the appearance of a bleeding heart (rather a morbid name for such a lovely flower). The genus includes other colorful members such as Dutchman's breeches (*D. cucullaria*), golden ear-drops (*D. chrysantha*), and squirrel corn (*D. canadensis*). In the garden, common bleeding heart, *D. spectabilis* is the most popular, but the virtues of fringed bleeding heart, *D. eximia*, and Pacific bleeding heart, *D. formosa*, have elevated them to mainstream garden plants as well.

Plants of common bleeding heart were first introduced to England from Japan in the 1840's by one of the great plant explorers, Robert Fortune. About 15 species of *Dicentra* occur, characterized by deeply cut, compound leaves and flowers in racemes. All prefer rich moist soil in a shaded location. Propagation is accomplished by taking 3–4″ long root cuttings (see *Anemone*) in the summer or fall, division in the fall, or by sowing seed in late summer. Seed should be placed at 60–65° F for 2–4 weeks, 40° F for 4–6 weeks, and finally warmed slowly to 65° F until seed germinates. If placed in a seed flat in the fall and put outside under mulch or snow, nature will take care of these requirements. Sometimes fresh seed may germinate well without any special treatment but if stored for more than two weeks, the above program should be followed.

Quick Reference to Dicentra Species

|  | Height (in.) | Flower color | Dormant in summer | Inflorescence branched |
|---|---|---|---|---|
| *D. cucullaria* | 6–12 | Creamy white | No | No |
| *D. eximia* | 9–18 | Rose-pink | No | Yes |
| *D. scandens* | 36–60 | Yellow | No | No |
| *D. spectabilis* | 18–24 | Rose-pink | Yes | No |

| | | | |
|---|---|---|---|
| *-cucullaria* (kuk-ew-lah′ ree-a) | Dutchman's Breeches | 6–12″/12″ |
| Spring    Creamy White | Eastern United States | Zones 3–7 |

A well known native plant, found in sunny forest floors from Nova Scotia to Georgia, and west to Missouri. Plants arise from a loose cluster of whitish tubers, each eye giving rise to gray-green dissected leaves. The short tapering spurs stick upward, looking like a pair of upside-down breeches.

Plants are marvelous additions to the shady woodland garden, and while they certainly are not show stoppers, they add quiet charm all their own. Place in a shaded moist area. If plants dry out, they may go dormant in the summer.

Propagate by breaking apart the tuber after flowering. Do not allow to dry out.

| | | | |
|---|---|---|---|
| *-eximia* (eks-ee′ mee′ a) | Fringed Bleeding Heart | 9–18″/18″ |
| Spring    Rose-Pink | Eastern United States | Zones 3–9 |

The fringed bleeding heart is native to forest floors from Georgia all the way up to northern New York. It is stemless—foliage and flowers arise directly from the scaly rootstock. The leaves are deeply cut, fern-like, and usually gray-green in cultivation. The inner petals of the 1″ long rosy pink heart-shaped flowers protrude from the outer petals and are easily visible. Flowers are carried on long branched racemes (an elongated inflorescence with stalked flowers) resulting in a more floriferous species than common bleeding heart when optimal growing conditions are provided.

**Cultivars:**
'Alba' has lovely milky-white flowers over light green foliage.

**Related Species:**
*D. formosa*, Pacific bleeding heart, is the western form of fringed bleeding heart and similar to the above. The main difference is that the inner petals barely protrude from the outer petals. Native from British Columbia to central California, it is more drought tolerant but less resistant to hot, wet summer weather than *D. eximia*. 'Alba' has white flowers over

blue-green foliage. 'Ruby Mar' bears some of the reddish flowers over glaucous bluish foliage.

### Related Hybrids:

Considerable confusion exists as to the parentage of most of the garden cultivars. The debate is centered on whether the cultivars are selections of *D. eximia*, *D. formosa*, or hybrids. All may be divided after about 3 years.

'Adrian Bloom' was a chance seedling from 'Bountiful' and produces ruby-red flowers on blue-green foliage.

'Bacchanal' has some of the deepest wine-colored flowers of these hybrids. The persistent flowers arch over the darkly pigmented foliage.

'Boothman's Variety' is a magnificent soft pink-flowered form with blue-green foliage.

'Bountiful' has soft rosy-red flowers and finely cut foliage.

'Langtrees' bears dozens of white flowers over blue-green deeply cut foliage. One of the best whites.

'Luxuriant' is almost certainly a hybrid between the two species and bears cherry-red flowers over 15″ tall blue-green foliage. An exceptional cultivar.

'Margery Fish' is a relatively new introduction from England. She has white flowers and some of the bluest foliage I have seen.

'Pearl Drops', selected in 1977, is similar to the other white flowering forms with blue-green foliage. Flowers are slightly tinged pink. Very similar, if not the same as, 'Langtrees'.

'Silversmith' has white flowers flushed with pink, and is quite different from other cultivars.

'Snowdrift' has pure white flowers without the pink tinge of 'Silversmith'. Lovely deeply divided foliage.

'Snowflakes' is really handsome. A low-growing clump former, discovered by Joyce Fussey in Goathland, Yorkshire, plants have beautiful finely-cut light green foliage and creamy white flowers.

'Stuart Boothman' is similar to 'Boothman's Variety', but the specimens I have seen have redder flowers and more glaucous foliage.

'Sweetheart' appears to be a cultivar of *D. formosa*. Plants bear snow white flowers on 12″ stems.

'Zestful' grows about 18″ tall and has large deep rose flowers over blue-green foliage.

| *-scandens* (scan-dens) | Climbing Bleeding Heart | 7–8'/3' |
| Summer    Yellow | Himalayas | Zones 6–8 |

Looking for a handsome vine to flower in the summer but want something other than a clematis? This seldom seen plant always excites gardeners and makes them salivate on the spot. Generally, it is best to check pockets after people have seen this one. The light green vines have thin tendrils at the end of the divided foliage which allows them to climb over and around by themselves. While the foliage is handsome, it is the beautiful butter-yellow lockets which seize the attention of visitors. They are held in loose racemes of 2–14 flowers and occur in late spring and throughout the summer.

Although they should be planted in partial shade, they require less shade than common bleeding hearts. Too much shade results in few flowers. Provide consistent moisture and some support to allow the plants to climb. This is a vine which one needs to be close to in order to appreciate. It is not a "55-mph plant" like the clematis. The only drawback I have seen is that the tips of the individual flowers turn brown as they age, distracting from the new flowers just emerging.

Propagate from terminal cuttings; little seed is produced.

### Cultivars:

'Athens Yellow' is similar to the species but the flowers are brighter yellow. Selected by the author and named after Athens, Georgia.

| | | | |
|---|---|---|---|
| *-spectabilis* (spek-tah' bi-lis) | Common Bleeding Heart | | 18–36"/18" |
| Spring | Rose-Pink | Japan | Zones 2–8 |

Common bleeding heart is difficult to beat when grown in partial shade and provided with adequate water. The leaflets are the largest of *Dicentra* species and the flowers, made up of white inner petals extending from rosy outer petals, look like they have been hung out to dry on the arching flower stems. It is a great joy to watch the foliage emerge in the spring and then the flowers, which follow soon after. If well watered, the foliage is attractive until early summer in the South and into the fall in the North. However, if rainfall is light or plants dry out, the foliage yellows and disappears by mid June. This is one of the differences between this species and *D. eximia*, which does not go dormant.

Bleeding hearts can easily be forced in greenhouses or cool conservatories. Plants should be dug early in the spring when dormant, potted and brought into a cool greenhouse (55° F) for forcing. With the addition of heat and water, leaves appear in 10–14 days followed by open flowers four weeks later. It is one of the fastest species to force and is particularly appreciated on St. Valentine's Day.

The dormant rhizome is divided after flowering or 3–4" long root cuttings are taken in March and inserted in a cold frame in clean soil. Pot up or line out when young leave are well developed and plant in the garden in the fall.

### Cultivars:

'Alba' is the ever-present white form which is very impressive, but not as vigorous as the type.

'Pantaloons' is pure white and is a more vigorous selection of 'Alba'.

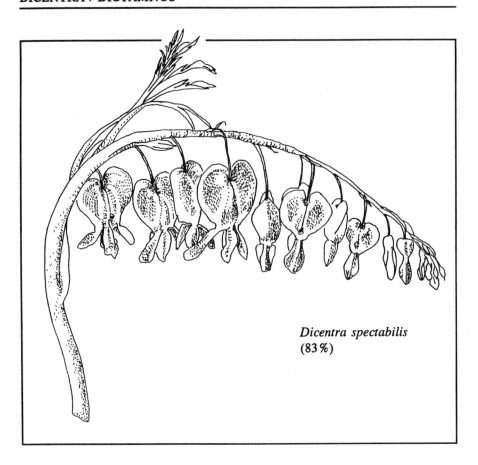

*Dicentra spectabilis*
(83%)

## Quick Key to Dicentra Species

A. Plant a vine, flowers yellow . . . . . . . . . . . . . . . . . *D. scandens*
AA. Plant not a vine
    B. Racemes simple
        C. Flowers rosy-red, rootstocks
           without tubers . . . . . . . . . . . . . . . . . . . . . . *D. spectabilis*
        CC. Flowers white, rootstocks with tubers . . . . . . . *D. cucullaria*
    BB. Racemes compound . . . . . . . . . . . . . . . . . . . . . . . *D. eximia*

## *Dictamnus* (dick-tam' nus)        Gas Plant        Rutaceae

The genus contains only a few species but the main garden species is so outstanding that it makes up for lack of members. Gas plants are rich in volatile oils, which supposedly can be lit on a still, warm evening. I have gone through many a match, but have yet to see even a tiny spark.

I have recently been told that it is the roots that emit this flammable stuff, but I have no intention of yanking up any plants to test them. It is easy, however, to rub the leaves and smell the lemon fragrance present in the foliage. Regardless of what is rubbed or ignited, this is an exquisite plant when established. The alternate leaves are glossy green and the plants are long lived. Two-year-old plants are usually purchased and require at least two more years to look their best.

| *-albus* (al' bus) | | Gas Plant | 3–4'/3' |
|---|---|---|---|
| Early Summer | White | Europe, Asia | Zones 3–7 |
| (Syn. *D. fraxinella*) | | | |

The alternate pinnate leaves are divided into 9–11 finely toothed leaflets about 2" long, each covered with translucent dots. The 1" long white or purple flowers have long exerted stamens and are held in a extended terminal raceme. Although plants can grow 4' tall, the bases of the stems are woody and support is unnecessary.

Plants should be placed in a well-drained, sunny location and left undisturbed. Over a number of years, large clumps bearing magnificent displays of flowers develop. Unfortunately this plant is not comfortable in all parts of the country, and cool nights are necessary for best performance. I tried a number of plants in the Horticulture Gardens at Georgia, and although they hung on for a number of years, they never came close to reaching the proportions of which they are capable. While the plant is one of my favorites, I cannot recommend it for southern gardens. However, fine specimens can be found in the gardens of the Biltmore House in Asheville, NC, pointing out the value of cool nights to the performance of this plant.

Propagation is time-consuming with *Dictamnus*. They are difficult to divide and the resulting injury may considerably damage the parent plant. Root cuttings have been used successfully (see *Anemone*), but the donor plant must be disturbed to harvest the roots. Although feasible commercially, it is not a good idea for the home gardener. The most common method is to gather the seeds in late summer (do this before they are ejected all over the garden) and plant them in a container and place outdoors. Keep the seed container moist. Do not expect germination until the following spring, at which time some seedlings should emerge. Do not throw away the seed flat as seedlings will continue to emerge for an additional 12 months. This is one of the species which has been the subject of a good deal of seed research, and as yet we have been unable to force the seeds to hurry along any faster than Mother Nature.

**Cultivars:**

'Purpureus' has flowers of soft mauve-purple with darker veins on the petals. It is most attractive and quite common.

**Additional Reading:**

Anon. 1993. Plant in the spotlight; *Dictamnus albus*: Minnesota. *Horticulture* 121(3):26.

## *Dierama* (dee-e-rah' ma)  Wandflower  Iridaceae

A genus of 44 species, native to South Africa, 3 or 4 of which are beginning to find their way into American gardens. The cold hardiness has yet to be firmly established, but it is doubtful that plants would be perennial north of zone 7b, and the heat and humidity tolerance is completely unknown.

Plants arise from corms which are renewed each year. The leaves are linear to grass-like, and the pendulous funnel-shaped flowers are held in long arching narrow flower stems. The shape of the long inflorescences with its suspended small flowers resulted in the other common name, Angel's fishing rod.

*D. pulcherrimum* is one of the prettiest species, bearing 3–4' long narrow (½" wide) arching leaves and many pink to red bell-shaped flowers on the terminal and lateral flower stems. 'Album' is a beautiful white-flowered selection. I have seen a number of other cultivars in botanical gardens but seldom in commerce. The development of *Dierama* occurred in two general phases. The first was the selection of color variants of *D. pulcherrimum* and *D. pendulum* and marketed mostly under names of birds. They included 'Falcon' (wine-purple), 'Blackbird' (violet flowers), 'Kingfisher' (pale pink), and 'Windhover' (lilac rose). The second phase involved crosses with dwarf forms (probably *D. dracomontanum*) and *D. pulcherrimum*, and resulted in intermediate hybrids often bearing Shakespearian names such as 'Puck' (rose-pink), 'Oberon' (peony-purple), and 'Iris' (violet).

Other types of wand flowers are occasionally offered, such as the soft pink-flowered *D. cooperi*, 'Titania' (light pink), the brick red flowers of *D. dracomontanum*, and its more diminutive cousin, var. *pumilum*. Unfortunately, plants may produce foliage but do not always flower. Many an experimental gardener has thrown plants away out of frustration and impatience. Don't spend the entire savings account on these plants quite yet, but trying one or two may provide a pleasant surprise.

**Additional Reading:**

Hilliard, O.M. and Burtt, B.L. 1990. *Dierama*: a neglected genus of Iridaceae. *The Plantsman* 12(2):106–112.

## *Digitalis* (dij-i-tah' lis)  Foxglove  Scrophulariaceae

If one surveyed flower gardens for foxglove, one would probably assume that only a single species, *D. purpurea*, existed in the genus. There are, however, over 20 species, and a half dozen deserve a place in the shaded garden. The common foxglove is a biennial but others are true perennials, and although not as spectacular, are fine garden plants nevertheless. The flowers are borne in tall racemes whose spike-like colorful spires dominate the garden. The leaves of all foxgloves occur in rosettes as well as alternately up the stem. Soil requirements are minimal but, plants perform well in soils rich in organic matter. They should be planted in partial shade and not be allowed to dry out.

The name *digitalis* means finger-like and they were called finger flowers because "they are like unto the fingers of a glove, the ends cut off" (Parkinson, Paradisi).

## Quick Reference to Digitalis Species

|  | Height (ft.) | Flower color |
|---|---|---|
| *D. ferruginea* | 4–5 | Rusty red |
| *D. grandiflora* | 2–3 | Yellow |
| *D. lutea* | 2–3 | Yellow |
| *D.* × *mertonensis* | 3–4 | Rose |
| *D. purpurea* | 4–5 | Purple, white |

| *-ferruginea* (fe-roo-gin′ ee-a) | | Rusty Foxglove | 4–5′/1½′ |
|---|---|---|---|
| Early Summer | Brown-Red | Southern Europe | Zones 4–7 |

This biennial has leafy spikes that arise from a rosette of lance-shaped mid-green leaves. The brownish red pendant flowers are borne on 2–3′ long racemes. The lower lip of the flower is considerably longer than the other lobe.

Place in areas of partial shade where plants will not dry out. I have had little success with this species in north Georgia, but I have seen it in flower further north. They were outstanding in the beautiful gardens on the Campus of Smith College in Massachusetts.

Propagate the species by seed similar to *D. grandiflora* in the spring or fall. A minimum of 2 years is necessary to flower.

### Cultivars:

'Gigantea' has large yellowish brown flowers and grows 4–5′ tall.
'Krik-Island' bears pure yellow flowers on 3–5′ tall plants.

### Related Species:

*D. parviflora*, native to northern Spain, bears 2½ to 3′ tall unbranched stems with cylindrical racemes of densely-packed, small, reddish brown flowers. Flowers appear in late spring and early summer. A true perennial.

***-grandiflora*** (gran-di-flo′ ra)          Yellow Foxglove          2–3′/1½′
   Summer          Yellow          Europe          Zones 3–8
(Syn. *D. ambigua*)

This perennial species is one of the toughest and best performers in the genus. Plants are made up of hairy, toothed, dark green, sessile leaves. The 2″ long pendant flowers are yellowish on the outside and netted with brown on the inside, and fit comfortably into almost any setting. The common name refers to the large flowers whose size helps separate this species from the small yellow flowers of *D. lutea*. The more I see this plant, the more I am taken with its understated charm and its tough disposition.

Seed germinates rapidly under warm conditions (70–75° F) and high humidity.

### Cultivars:
'Temple Bells' is shorter and bears smaller (1″ long) flowers than the species. Plants will bloom first year from seed.

### Related Species:
*D. lanata*, Grecian foxglove, has 1″ long pale flowers held in an erect dense raceme. The flowers are almost white with purplish netting within. It differs from the above species by being somewhat shorter (1–2′ tall) and by having the lower lip of the flower longer than the other flower segments. Flowers are not nearly as yellow as *D. grandiflora*. It is more or less perennial, and although not particularly showy, is a fine species.

***-lutea*** (loo-tee′ a)          Straw Foxglove          2–3′/1′
   Summer          Yellow          Europe          Zones 3–7

The 4–6″ long serrated glossy leaves are oblong to lanceolate. The ¾″ creamy yellow, nodding flowers are borne on one-sided branched racemes. The flowers are tiny relative to those of *D. grandiflora*, and the upper surface of the leaves and flower stems are smooth.

Plants tolerate some shade but prefer moist, sunny areas. They are not as heat tolerant as *D. grandiflora*, and are not as often seen in the south.

### Cultivars:
Var. *australis*, the smaller-flowered Italian form, is often used in place of the species. There is little difference in garden appearance or performance between the variety and the type. Propagate similar to *D. grandiflora*.

### Related Species:
*D. obscura*, native to Spain and northwest Africa, is 16–20″ tall with entire, linear leaves and nodding, beige-yellow flowers with red veins within. Plants have a shrubby appearance, and the narrow smooth leaves

have resulted in the name willow foxglove. Plants perform best in sunny conditions. Likely useful in zones 5–7.

| -× *mertonensis* (mer-ton-en' sis) | | Strawberry Foxglove | 3–4'/2' |
|---|---|---|---|
| Summer | Rose | Hybrid | Zones 3–8 |

This hybrid was raised at the John Innes Horticultural Institute in 1925, in Merton, England, by crossing *D. purpurea* and *D. grandiflora*. The offspring is tetraploid (twice the number of chromosomes of either parent) and the 6–8" long leaves and 2½" long flowers are bigger than those of either parent. It inherited the perenniality from *D. grandiflora*; however, the bienniality of *D. purpurea* results in plants which generally persist for 2–3 years only.

This is an excellent plant for a number of reasons. It is one of the few spike-like flowers in a rose-colored shade, and unlike many other species in the genus, the foliage always looks fresh. Even when not in flower, the large, mid-green, velvety leaves catch the eyes of the passers-by. In flower, the tall spires of coppery-rose flowers are interesting as well as ornamental. This species received a Gold Medal Award for excellence from the University of Georgia Horticultural Gardens in 1987.

Seed propagation is not difficult (see *D. grandiflora*). Dividing plants is difficult but can be attempted every two years to maintain vigor.

| -*purpurea* (pur-pewr' ree-a) | | Common Foxglove | 4–5'/3' |
|---|---|---|---|
| Spring | Purple, White | Europe | Zones 4–8 |

This old-fashioned plant is still the most stately of the foxgloves, and when in flower, cannot be rivaled. The are native to the British Isles and seldom does a summer day go by when visitors to England or Ireland fail to comment on the beauty of "that old English weed" in fence rows and the wood's edge. They make the lofty views on the Ring of Kerry even more beautiful but are equally handsome in large decorative urns. One of the finest displays I have seen was some potted foxgloves at Longwood Gardens in Kennett Square, Pennsylvania. Plants had been raised in greenhouses and moved to the containers when the flowers were at their peak. The 5' tall displays beckoned to the crowds passing by and those who stopped to admire them knew they were privileged to have visited that day.

The wrinkled, somewhat downy, oblong leaves form a large rosette the first year followed by many flowering stems the next spring. The basal leaves have long petioles and the smaller stem leaves become sessile as they ascend the stem. The 2–3" long pendulous flowers are usually lavender with large purple and white spots inside and held on a long one-sided raceme.

Plants require a good deal of water to "strut their stuff" and should be placed in a moist, semi-shaded area. Flowering begins in early spring and persists for about 4 weeks, after which the spent flower stalks should be removed. Unless sprayed with fungicides, the foliage becomes ragged by late summer. Since plants are biennials and will likely not survive the winter, they should be replaced with annuals after flowering. I leave mine in the garden long enough to release seed for next year's plantlets.

The species is the source of the powerful drug digitalin, used for heart diseases, but there is no way to know exactly when the value of the plant as a cardiac medicine was employed. The first mention occurred in 1640 in Parkinson's herbal and was introduced into *London Pharmacopoeia* in 1650, but its use by native people probably went back many hundreds of years. It

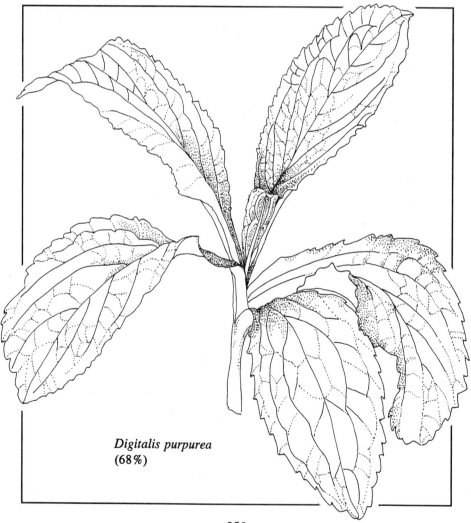

*Digitalis purpurea*
(68%)

*Digitalis purpurea*
(20%)

received its earliest scientific attention in 1776 when Dr. Withering, a British physician, published a clinical report on its usefulness in 1785. Prior to that, all sorts of fabulous medicinal properties were attributed to these plants. In the 13th century, leaves were used to treat "scrofulous complaints" and this is thought to be the origin of the family name to which it belongs.

Propagate from seed in the spring or fall. Allow 2 years for flowering except 'Foxy'.

**Cultivars:**

'Alba' is a white form of the species and is particularly pretty when naturalized at the edge of woods.

'Campanulata' has large bell-shaped flowers near the top of the raceme.

'Emerson' is a particularly good strain of white foxglove selected by Marc Richardson of Goodness Grows Nursery in Lexington, GA. Plants stand about 4' tall and bear strong stems.

'Excelsior Hybrids' produce their flowers around the entire flower stalk and are held more upright than those of the species. The 2–3" flowers are almost held horizontally, allowing an easier view of the handsome markings. Plants grow 5–7' tall.

'Foxy' is similar but is only about 2½' tall and has more side shoots. Flowers are produced the first year from seed. A breakthrough in foxgloves, 'Foxy' flowers the first year from seed. An All-America silver winner in 1966.

'Giant Shirley Hybrids' (bred by the Reverend Wilks, see Shirley poppies) are similar to the type but are 4–5' tall, with the potential of reaching 8 to 9' in height. The large bell-shaped flowers are densely packed and usually mottled in shades of pink.

'Sutton's Apricot' bear large flowers in shades of apricot and salmon. Very handsome.

## Quick Key to Digitalis Species

A. Middle lobe of flower longer than other lobes
  B. Plants 4–5' tall, flowers brownish red  . . . . . . . . *D. ferruginea*
  BB. Plants 2–3' tall, flowers yellowish . . . . . . . . . . . . . . *D. lanata*
AA. Middle lobe of flower shorter or hardly longer than others
  B. Flowers yellowish
    C. Leaves sessile, flowers over 1" long,
    netted with brown  . . . . . . . . . . . . . . . . . *D. grandiflora*
    CC. Leaves petioled, flowers around ½" long,
    not particularly netted . . . . . . . . . . . . . . . . . . . *D. lutea*
  BB. Flowers red, purple, white; not yellow
    C. Flowers 2–2½" long, strawberry colored,
    leaves smooth above and hairy beneath  . . . *D.* × *mertonensis*
    CC. Flowers 1½–2" long, usually purple
    or white, spotted within, leaves wrinkled
    above and less hairy beneath . . . . . . . . . . . . . *D. purpurea*

**Additional Reading:**
Hermes, A.R. 1994. A fancy for foxgloves. *Horticulture* 72(5):50–55.
Sawyer. R. 1993. Old-fashioned foxgloves. *Country Living* 16(8):21–22, 42.
Weathers, L.A. 1993. Stately spires. *Southern Living* 28(3):60–61, 64.

## *Diphylleia* (die-fell-ee' a)      Umbrella-Leaf      Berberidaceae

*D. cymosa* is one of a number of eastern wildflowers which can so easily enhance the woodland or shade garden. Native to woods by mountain streams from Virginia to Georgia, plants require cool nights and consistent moisture to do well in a "civilized" garden. A large peltate leaf, roundish in outline but with jagged margins, arises from a thick, knotty, jointed rhizome. The flowering stem also arises from the rhizome bearing two similar but smaller alternate leaves and a small inflorescence of about 10 white flowers. Blue berries are formed after flowering. The rhizome spreads reasonably rapidly and many leaf/flower stem pairs may occur on the same plant. Plants are strikingly handsome where comfortable.

They do not transplant well from the wild, nor do they grow well in areas where night temperatures do not consistently fall below 70° F, nor where soils dry out. Hardiness is probably from zones 4–7.

*D. grayi* is native to Japan, with smaller leaves which are not as deeply divided and bearing fewer flowers. Almost never available in this country.

## *Dipsacus* (dip-sa' cus)          Teasel          Dipsacaceae

Some people claim I am getting desperate for plant material if I include this 5–6' tall prickly biennial weed alongside other stately perennials. The main species, *D. sativus* (*D. fullonum*), is native to the Old World, from Asia to Europe, but has escaped to become a common roadside inhabitant in the northeastern and central states. Desperate though I may be, gardeners looking for a rugged coarse architectural feature also find that teasels provide terrific interest in summer and winter. The elongated flower heads carry dozens of small lilac flowers guarded by sharp bracts. This plant is not, in every respect, for the faint of heart, nor for those without heavy gloves. The stem, the leaves, and the flowers can puncture all but the most calloused hands.

Their main usefulness comes from their longevity as a dried flower, which can create attention in the house for many years. The ripe flower heads, or teasels, were also used extensively for raising the nap (teasing) of woolen cloth and earned the plant the common name of Fuller's Teasel. Plants were raised in the 1930's and 40's in central New York for this purpose. Their use in wool mills in the eastern and middle states accounted for their escaping to this country.

*D. laciniatus* is occasionally offered by specialists and worth a try. Flower shape is similar to *D. sativus*, but the bases of the stem leaves form "cups" to hold water and are of considerable interest after a rain. The flowers are whitish pink and not as prickly as *D. sativus*.

## *Disporum* (die' spor-um)     Fairy Bells, Mandarin     Liliaceae

Some of the more handsome shade-loving woodland species reside in this genus but nursery grown plants have only recently become available.

Approximately 15 species are known, native to eastern Asia, the Himalayas, and North America. *Disporum* differs from similar woodland genera such as *Uvularia* (bellwort) and *Polygonatum* (Solomon's seal) by having white, whitish green, or yellow flowers borne singly, or in a few-flowered umbel at the end of the stems. The flowers of *Uvularia* (yellow) and *Polygonatum* (white) usually appear at the axils of the leaves. The fruit of *Disporum* is a red berry, in *Uvularia* it is a three lobed pod, and in *Polygonatum*, a dark blue to black berry.

Only 2 or 3 species are reasonably easy to find, and these will likely be available from mail order sources which specialize in unusual or native plants. *D. smithii* is native to cool, moist areas of evergreen and redwood forests in the northwest United States and Canada. Shrub-like in habit, the many branched stems form a 2 to 2½' tall clump in 2–3 years. The nodding, narrow, creamy white bells usually occur in groups of 3–6 in early spring, then yield to orange berries in late spring and early summer. Probably hardy in zones 5 to 7 in the east, zone 8 in the west. Other handsome western species (although almost impossible to find commercially), include the bushy white-flowered *D. trachycarpum* and *D. hookeri* with creamy white flowers and scarlet berries.

An attractive native eastern species is common yellow mandarin, *D. lanuginosum*, growing from New York to Georgia in cool, moist areas. The terminal flowers are yellow-green, approximately 1″ long and the tepals (petals and sepals together) flare outward. Flowering occurs in late spring and early summer, after which brilliant orange-red fruit may be formed. The spotted mandarin, *D. maculatum*, has whitish to pale yellow flowers with purple spots. The stamens are longer then the tepals and project from the mouth of the flowers.

From China comes the purple-flowered bells of *D. cantoniense*, canton fairy bells. Growing about 3′ tall, they are hardy to about zone 6. Although probably politically incorrect, my favorite species is the Japanese native, *D. sessile*. Perhaps I am more disposed towards it because it grows so well in the Armitage garden. The leaves are sessile, and essentially clasp the stem. Plants are upright and vary in height from about 9″ to close to 2′. The creamy white hanging flowers give way to berries later in the summer. Two outstanding forms can be found. 'Variegata' has handsome green and white striped leaves. They are generally shorter (9–15″ tall) than the species but certainly brighten up the shade. Easy to grow and very perennial (zones 4–8), they also tend to roam, not necessarily appearing next spring where you thought they should be. The showiest of all is var. *flavum*, sometimes listed as *D. flavum*. The bright yellow flowers unroll with the leaves and pop open within days of the plant emerging. Plants are robust and 18–24″ tall. An outstanding woodland plant, but also tolerant of morning sun.

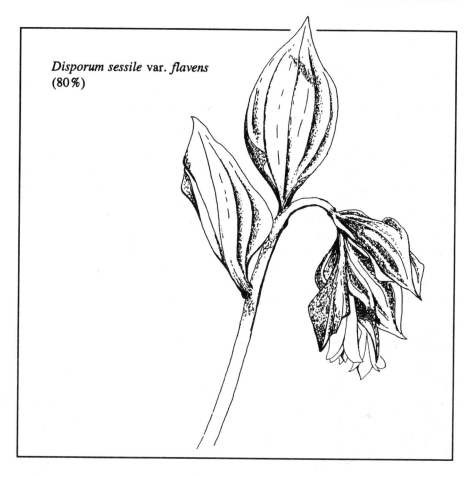

*Disporum sessile* var. *flavens*
(80%)

## *Dodecatheon* (do-dek-a-thee' on)     Shooting Star     Primulaceae

Grown for its elegantly reflexed flowers and "shooting" stamens, the approximately 14 species may be found from damp grasslands to prairie flatlands and mountain meadows. Species differ in the amount of reflexing of the petals, but all have shuttlecock-like flowers and basal rosettes of leaves. All species flower in spring or early summer and are summer dormant. Most are native to the central and western states of America, and a couple are native to the eastern United States. Plants prefer excellent drainage, protection from the afternoon sun, and moist but not wet soil.

Not commonly offered but well worth the effort are *D. jeffreyi*, Sierra shooting star, and *D. pulchellum*, both native to the Cascade and Rocky Mountain states. The former is one of the larger species (up to 2' tall), bearing large leaves and many reddish purple flowers with purple stamens. The flowering stems are slightly sticky to the touch. *D. pulchellum* is more

361

difficult to establish and extremely variable. The range encompasses northern California to Alaska. The flared flowers are pink to rosy-purple. Plants have escaped to the east and may be found in woodland and moist areas. Selections have resulted in a white-flowered form, 'Album', and a carmine-red form, 'Redwings'. Another extremely handsome but more difficult species of the western states is the white-flowered *D. dentatum*, with toothed or wavy margins on the leaves and 10–14″ tall flower stems.

Certainly the best known and easiest to grow for most gardeners, east and west, is the common shooting star, *D. meadia*. The tuft of smooth, narrow leaves, often reddish at the base, gives rise to a 6–12″ leafless flower stem. The flower head is an umbel of 3–7 lilac to pink blossoms whose petals are sharply bent back. Stamens are usually yellow. Flower color ranges from light to dark pink, but white flowers ('Alba') are also very handsome. Plants are found in open woods and meadows from Pennsylvania to Wisconsin, and south to Georgia and Texas.

For all species, provide some protection from the afternoon sun and plant in consistently moist, but not wet, conditions. Allow to grow through other plants in order to cover the area after summer dormancy occurs.

### *Doronicum* (do-ron′ i- kum)       Leopard's Bane       Asteraceae

Leopard's bane consists of approximately 35 species with bright yellow daisy flowers and alternate leaves. They range in height from the 12″ hybrids of *D. orientale* to 3′ tall *D. carpetanum*, and flower in the spring. A number of species, such as *D. pardalianches* and *D. plantagineum*, are useful for meadow planting and naturalize in dappled shade and moist woodland conditions. I have seen large meadows of *D. plantagineum* interspersed with forget-me-nots and coltsfoot in Europe, a particular outstanding planting being at Leith Hall in Scotland. In this country, they are not used as often because of the warm summers in much of the country. In fact, under warm conditions, a number of species go dormant in the summer and must be overplanted with annuals. They are not fussy as to soil type, thrive in full sun or partial shade, and may be propagated by seed or division. Few leopard's banes do well under warm conditions, where night temperatures do not consistently fall below 70° F. High humidity is also a curse. All species make excellent cut flowers.

Quick Reference to Doronicum Species

|               | Height (ft.) | Flower color |
| ------------- | ------------ | ------------ |
| *D. carpetanum* | 2–3        | Yellow       |
| *D. orientale*  | 1–2        | Yellow       |

*-carpetanum* (kar-pe-tane′ um)     Spanish Leopard's Bane     2-3′/2′
    Spring        Yellow        Spain        Zones 4–7

A tall coarse species suitable only in larger gardens with bright yellow flowers to wake up the spring garden. The 6–8″ long, heart-shaped leaves are entire and carried on long petioles. Plants are stoloniferous, and the tuber-like rhizomes spread rapidly into large clumps. The 2–3 flowers per stem are 1–2″ across and open a little later than other *Doronicum* species. The numerous ray flowers are thin and the button-like disks are dark yellow. Cut flowers are excellent fresh or dried.

Plants can be divided in spring. Excellent plants for moist soils and full sun to partially shady conditions. Seed germinates within 3 weeks if placed in warm (70–75° F), humid conditions.

**Related Species:**

*D. plantagineum*, also native to southern Europe, is a tall (2–4′) plant with spreading rhizomes to form extensive colonies. The basal leaves are ovate to elliptical with a clasping stem. The 1–2″ wide daisy yellow flowers are similar to other species, but these large colonizing plants can be quite impressive. Plants tend to fall apart after flowering. 'Excelsum' (also known as 'Harpur Crewe') has branched stems with many large flowers with yellow centers.

*-orientale* (ore-ee-en-tal′ ee)     Caucasian Leopard's Bane     1-2′/1′
    Spring        Yellow        Europe, Asia        Zones 4–7
(Syn. *C. caucasicum*)

This is the most common species in American gardens. Plants send up bright yellow daisy flowers over bright green clump-like foliage. The leaves are kidney to heart-shaped and deeply toothed but in warm climates, plants go dormant resulting in gaps in the garden. Plants spread slowly by fleshy underground rhizomes and can form wide patches with many flowering stems. The flowers are solitary and the bright splash of color can be a spectacular addition to the spring garden. This is not a particularly good subject in the South as it tends to look limp unless given a good deal of water. Plants are not long lived even in the Midwest due to warm summer temperatures and humidity. Its summer dormancy is of great survival value but other plants must be used to cover the bare ground.

Propagate similar to *D. carpetanum*.

**Related Species:**

*D. macrophyllum* is a handsome large-leaved species from Iran. Growing about 3′ tall, plants bear terminal clusters of 1′ wide daisy yellow flowers. Less hardy than other species, probably useful in zones 6–8.

**Hybrids:**

Hybrids of *D. orientale* are often more vigorous and better garden subjects. Plants generally have less tendency toward summer dormancy.

'Finesse' has semi-double, yellow-orange flowers on 15–18" tall stems. A good plant for the front of the garden.

'Magnificum' grows 2–2½' tall with 1–2" diameter flowers in early spring. The foliage is dark green and heart-shaped. An excellent hybrid.

'Miss Mason' is the most common form, being a hybrid of *D. orientale* and *D. austriacum*, a dwarf species with canary-yellow spring flowers. Plants are 1–2' tall and bear single daisies in May and June.

'Spring Beauty' ('Fruhlingspracht') has large double flowers on 12" tall stems. Although a fine hybrid, the double flowers can look particularly bad in warm wet summers, causing a friend to describe it as "Botyrtis on a stem." Another double-flowered hybrid ('Spring Bouquet') is also offered, but I have not noticed any significant difference between the two.

Quick Key to Doronicum Species

    A. Tall plants, over 2' tall,
       roots tuberous . . . . . . . . . . . . . . . . . . . . . . *D. carpetanum*
    AA. Shorter plants, generally less
       than 2' tall, roots fibrous . . . . . . . . . . . . . . . . *D. orientale*

## *Dracocephalum* (dra-ko-cef' a-lum)     Dragonhead     Lamiaceae

The common name refers to the shape of the hooded sage-blue flowers. This little known genus consists of over 40 species, most of which are native to Asia. The foliage is opposite and entire, or sometimes dentate (sharp indentations), and many species are pleasantly aromatic. The flowers are held in loose whorls and may be axillary or terminal. The four stamens distinguish it from salvias, and the lack of a crest or fold on the sepals distinguish the genus from *Scuttelaria*.

Plant in full sun and well-drained soils, often compatible with sunny rock gardens. A number of lovely plants have been moved out of this genus, including *D. virginicum*, (now *Physostegia virginiana*), and *D. sibericum*, (presently *Nepeta sibirica*), leaving a few rather unexciting salvia-like plants.

*D. ruyschianum* has many blue to violet 1" long flowers on 18–24" tall plants. A much more handsome form is the white-flowered 'Alba'. Tolerates partial shade and drought conditions. Hardy in zones 3–7.

*D. nutans* is only about 12" tall with 1–2" long serrated foliage and bright blue flowers in open whorls. Useful for rock gardens in full sun.

*D. grandiflorum* has larger flowers in more compact whorls which look like short spikes. Flowers are an intense blue with a conspicuous hood over each flower. Native to Siberia, hardy in zones 3–7.

Plants may be propagated from seed or terminal cuttings.

## *Dracunculus* (dra-kun' kew-lus)          Dragon Arum          Araceae

Another plant which once again demonstrates that gardeners' great passion for the bizarre can even overcome the senses, at least the sense of smell. Most who approach *D. vulgaris* in flower ends up holding their nose and gasping for breath. About 3 species occur, and each vie for the most obnoxious smell. Related to other malodorous genera (see *Amorphophallus* and *Sauromatum*), this tuberous plant produces a spotted stem and sickle-shaped leaves, divided into about 10 finger-like, white-streaked leaflets, resembling a dragon's claw. The wavy spathe is about 1' wide and purple throughout. The long narrow spadix is also deep purple and erect, extending well beyond the spathe. In the Armitage garden, I planted mine next to the old bird bath, and while in flower, nary a single bird alighted. This continued for about a month as one flower gave way to the next. After flowering, green berries may be formed which become orange-red as they mature. The foliage is similar to *Arisaema dracontium*, dragon-root, but differs in having purple flowers instead of green.

Place tubers in well-drained soils in partial to heavy shade. They are slow to emerge in areas where they overwinter, often not arising until late spring or early summer. Two to three years are needed for flowering. In most of the country, treat tubers like a dahlia, digging each fall and replanting in the spring. Cold hardiness can surprise gardeners. Plants sometimes return as far north as Philadelphia, but are usually marginally hardy north of zone 7. Remove the offsets from the tubers every 2–3 years to keep the plants vigorous. Seeds collected from the ripened fruit may also be propagated.

### Additional Reading:

Loewer, P. 1993. The devil's tongue and sinfully different plants. *Carolina Gardener* 5(4):21–22.

## *Dryas* (dree' as)          Mountain Avens          Rosaceae

A group of plants native to arctic areas of North America, found on rocky ledges, sea cliffs, and sand dunes. Such a nativity points out the need for cool nights and good drainage when transferring them to a garden. The 3 species bear evergreen leaves which superficially resemble oak leaves. The genus name comes from the greek *dryas* referring to the wood nymphs to whom the oak was sacred. Plants are 6" to 2' tall and are actually small shrubs (shrublets) with white to yellow flowers. One of the most ornamental aspects of the genus are the feathery seed heads, similar to those of *Pulsatilla*. They are terrific for planters, containers, and rock gardens.

The showiest species is *D. octopetala*, which consist of dull green leaves above which are white-hairy below. Plants grow 9–12" tall in open gardens, but are shorter in containers where plants or roots are restricted. If sited well, plants can form dense mats and have been recommended as an alternative to grassy areas. The white 8- to 10-petaled flowers are erect, and flower over a long period of time in late spring and early summer. The flowers also have many golden stamens typically bearing one flower per flower stem. The seed heads are formed by persistent styles (part of the female pistil) which elongate to about 1″ long after flowering. As the seeds ripen, they begin to turn brown. A number of forms, such as the diminutive var. *minor* and var. *lanata*, have grayish hairs on the top surface of the leaves. *D. drummondii* is smaller than *D. octopetala* and has nodding yellow flowers, and longer feathery styles. The upper surface of the leaves are slightly tanned and covered with long silky hairs, pressed close to the leaf surface. It seems more difficult to establish than *D. octopetala*. A hybrid between the two species is greatly sought after because of the increased vigor. *D.* × *suendermannii* bears nodding white flowers and grows about 12″ tall. Everything is a little larger than either of the species.

None of the species is particularly easy to propagate or establish. Seeds may be collected as soon as the seed heads turn brown and may germinate in 2 weeks, or may germinate in 2 years. Seedlings tend to produce only one root and are notoriously difficult to transplant. If you are patient, additional side roots will form and transplanting will be easier. Cuttings, with some new growth and a heel of old growth, may be taken in summer and rooted in shady, moist but well-drained medium. Divisions from a naturally layered plantlet may be cut off the mother plant, but allow it to root in a rooting area before planting to the garden. All are recommended from zones 2–6.

## *Dryopteris*  Wood Ferns  Polypodiaceae

The wood ferns are a diverse group ranging from evergreen to deciduous forms, and are adaptable over a wide range of growing areas. The name comes from *drys* (oak) and *pteris* (fern), an early indication of the abundance of this genus in oak forests. There are believed to be over 1200 species, one of the largest genera in the plant kingdom. Such a community of ferns naturally produces many hybrids as well as natural crosses between species, and their hybrids result in all sorts of shapes and sizes. Given such incredible diversity, we ought to be able to find one or two that do well in our gardens. Many gardeners will attest to the toughness and adaptability of this group of ferns, although several species of *Athyrium* and *Arachnoides* may be more colorful.

Plants of *Dryopteris* are usually medium sized woodland ferns, often evergreen, with their sterile and fertile fronds the same shape and size. The leaflets or subleaflets are generally deeply cut or toothed. The indusia (structures which cover the spores) are usually kidney-shaped, whereas those of other genera are rounded, star-shaped, or elongated.

Plants of marginal woodfern, *D. marginalis*, are marvelous, leathery ever-green ferns, which along with Christmas fern, *Polystichum acrostichoides*, make islands of green through the snowy landscape in the winter. The fiddleheads are covered with a golden-brown "fur" and the numerous leaf stalks are similarly shaggy. The top of the fronds have a subtle blue-green cast, while beneath they are light green. The sori are found around the margins (*marginalis*) on the bottom of the fertile fronds. Native to Nova Scotia to the mountains of Georgia, plants are best in northern zones.

A fern similar to the marginal woodfern is the male fern, *D. felix-mas*, which is native to Europe and northern North America. The main differ-ences are the lack of the blue cast, they are shorter and stouter, and the sori are nearer to the midvein than to the margin. This has been one of the best performers in the Armitage garden, always looking fresh and green. Should probably be used more in this country. Numerous forms of male fern are offered to gardeners, from the handsome narrow-leaved 'Barnseii' to the vigorous robust 'Undulata Robusta' to the mutilated 'Linearis Polydactylon', which is about as grotesque as the name. Both the marginal woodfern and the male fern are tolerant of relatively dry conditions, although consistent moisture is helpful. Another fine native fern is the narrow buckler fern, *D. carthusiana* (*D. spinulosa*), a northern fern from Alaska to Virginia with opposite leaflets and light green fronds. Needs moisture and cool nights to succeed.

If largeness is a requirement in the shaded woodland, then Goldie's fern, *D. goldiana*, should surely be considered. Growing to 4' tall and 12–15' wide, this magnificent fern vies for attention with other large ferns such as some of the forms of *Matteuccia* and *Osmunda*. The large backward tilting fronds are abruptly pointed at the tips, wider in the middle than at either end, and are a golden green color. The leaflets are cut almost to the midrib and the rootstalks are long and scaly. Native from New Brunswick to North Carolina and Tennessee.

Southern gardeners may have trouble establishing some of the more northern species; however, *D. ludovichiana*, southern shield fern, has glossy, bold, evergreen foliage and is one of the best choices for hot summers. Native west from Texas to Florida and north to North Carolina. Performs well in zones 6–10. Another southern fern that is occasionally offered is the log fern, *D. celsa*, with 2–3' long fronds which gradually taper at the tip. Plants perform well in semi-shady areas and soils rich in organic matter. Moist but not wet areas are best. Native along the Gulf Coast from Louisiana and up the east coast to New York.

One of the finest evergreen ferns which is widely available from many producers is the Autumn fern, *D. erythrosora*. Plants are found in China, Korea, and Japan and do well in zones 5–9. The best characteristic is the coppery-red color of the new fronds which contrast pleasantly with the older green fronds. The back of the fronds are densely speckled with red sori. One of the easiest ferns to establish, providing a picturesque fern for shade and partially sunny areas. Another excellent Asian species is Wallich's fern, *D. wallichiana*, notable for its strong flush of new growth in the spring and leathery green foliage. It is a widespread and diverse species and does well in shady areas and organic soils. Neither autumn fern nor Wallich's fern like wet feet.

For wet areas, the best species is probably the crested shield fern, *D. cristata*. The fronds are leathery and have the same bluish tinge found with *D. marginalis*. The leaflets are curiously arranged like a ladder, widely spaced and almost horizontal to the stem. They don't do well in warm areas, and do poorly regardless of location if roots are not kept consistently wet.

There are numerous other species in the genus which make good subjects for the woodland garden. Differences between them are found in their adaptability, heat and cold tolerance, and shape and hue of the fronds. Many can be propagated from division, and spores may be purchased from specialist societies.

### Additional Reading:

Lancaster, R. 1992. *Dryopteris wallichiana. The Garden* 117(9):414–415.
Lovejoy, A. 1993. Ferns for the border. *Horticulture* 71(9):29–32, 80.

# E

*Echinacea* (ek-in-ay′ see-a)     Purple Coneflower     Asteraceae

A very popular genus of 8–9 species of tough, coarse plants native to the eastern and central United States. Because the base of the flower is rather prickly, Konrad Moench of Germany named the genus in the late 1700's after the Greek word for hedgehog, *echinos*. *Echinacea* is closely related to *Rudbeckia*, a genus of yellow and orange coneflowers and was originally included therein. The dark green leaves are alternate, simple, and tend to clasp the stem. Roots are thick and black, and the purple flower petals are usually slightly reflexed. A number of fine cultivars of *E. purpurea* have been developed which have enhanced the range of colors and plant habit. All species are drought and heat tolerant, require full sun, and attract hordes of butterflies.

Many people have accepted *Echinacea*, particularly *E. angustifolia*, as a bona-fide health supplement. From a vitamin C supplement to combating colds and flu, the coneflower has become a bit of a medical celebrity. The chemistry, pharmacology, and clinical applications of *Echinacea* have been the subject of over 350 scientific studies. Tests have shown that tissue regeneration, anti-inflammatory and immuno-stimulatory properties have been enhanced with *Echinacea* supplements. Continued interest in the plant's ability to help in the treatment of cancer, AIDS, and other debilitating diseases continue. The cultivation of these plants for their medicinal use, rather than their ornamental use, is becoming much more widespread. Susan has begun to give me *Echinacea* pills, so they must be good. *Echinacea* is one of many plants in the "coneflower" group, and general differences between them can be found under *Rudbeckia*.

Propagate by division and seed. The seed of the various species is easy to germinate. Sow fresh seed at 70° F under humid conditions.

Quick Guide to Echinacea Species

|  | Height (ft.) | Flower color |
|---|---|---|
| *E. pallida* | 3–4 | Creamy white |
| *E. paradoxa* | 2–3 | Purple, white |
| *E. purpurea* | 2–3 | Purple, white |

| *-pallida* (pal' li-da) | Pale Coneflower | 3–4'/2' |
|---|---|---|
| Summer      Pale Purple | Southcentral United States | Zones 4–8 |

This most interesting wild flower is well worth trying in the herbaceous border. The dark green, hairy, 3–5" long leaves have 3–5 parallel veins. The lower leaves have long petioles while the upper are sessile. The leaves may not be terribly exciting, but the 3–4" diameter flowers, consisting of dark central cones surrounded by 8–10 narrow strap-like, drooping petals (ray flowers), tend to catch the eye and make the flowers more interesting than beautiful. Plants were commonly used by native Americans of the central plains to treat the pain of burns, snakebites, and stings.

Placed in full sun, plants attain 3–4'; however, if grown in partial shade, 5' tall, weak-stemmed plants result. Pinching in late spring induces branching and makes support unnecessary. The species tolerates poor soil and additional fertilization need not be applied. Plants are not long lived, and 2–3 years is all that should be expected without division, especially in warmer zones. Plants are generally found in dry open places from Illinois to Minnesota and Montana, south to Texas and Georgia.

Propagate by seed or by division every 2–3 years. Seed germinates in 2–4 weeks if placed in warm (70–75° F), humid conditions. Cover the seed very lightly as darkness inhibits germination.

### Related Species:

*E. angustifolia*, narrow-leaf purple coneflower, is the western representative of this species. Plants are 1–3' tall and have narrow, entire, 4–6" long leaves. They are as tough as any species but do not perform quite as well in the East as *E. purpurea*. Otherwise, they are similar in habit and appearance.

| *-paradoxa* (par-a-dox' a) | Yellow Coneflower | 2–3'/2' |
|---|---|---|
| Summer      Pale Yellow | Ozark Mountains | Zones 4–7 |

An interesting if not terribly vigorous plant. The flowers of the true species are rose to white, but the eastern variety, native to southeastern Oklahoma, has yellowish ray flowers. The yellow-purple (a paradox) coneflower is proving to have great interest and may become a popular plant if enough nurseries offer it.

| *-purpurea* (pur-pewr′ ree-a) | | Purple Coneflower | 2–3′/2′ |
|---|---|---|---|
| Summer | Purple | Central United States | Zones 3–8 |

In order to truly appreciate the glory and grandeur of this common species, you need only visit the Great Plains garden at the Holden Arboretum outside Cleveland, OH or native prairie gardens in the eastern and central United States. Growing alongside its natural natives such as *Liatris, Filipendula,* and *Silphium,* the incredible beauty of the prairies as our ancestors saw them is awe-inspiring. Although purple coneflower has been a common garden plant for many years, it is still one of the finest species for today's garden. The 4–8″ long, dark green leaves are coarse, serrated, and have short, stiff hairs. The 3–4″ diameter flowers consist of a brown central cone with bronze tint, surrounded by broad, rose to purple petals. These droop slightly, although not as much as those of the previous species. Plants are tough and handle summer heat well, performing as well in zone 8 as in zone 4. They do best in full sun and do not benefit by additional fertility, particularly if in partial shade. Plants begin to flower in midsummer, make a grand display about two weeks later, and continue sporadically until frost. The flower is also useful as a cut flower. Many flower arrangers remove the petals and use the naked cone in bouquets and arrangements. It makes a fascinating and long-lasting specimen.

## Cultivars:

'Abendsonne' has lighter, more cerise-pink flowers than the species.

'Alba' has creamy white petals surrounding a greenish disc.

'Bressingham Hybrids' are a seed strain arising from seed of 'Robert Bloom'. Plants vary slightly from light rose to red and are good garden performers.

'Bravado' has 4–5″ wide rosy red flowers with excellent horizontal ray flowers.

'Bright Star' is a rose-colored, free-flowering cultivar which has performed well throughout the country. Plants are seed-propagated and significant variability occurs.

'Dwarf Star' is a little shorter than 'Bright Star', but otherwise hardly different. Seldom offered, but a good plant.

'Magnus' is also rosy colored with petals that don't droop as much as those of the species.

'Overton' is a seed-propagated form with rosy pink, drooping ray flowers.

'Robert Bloom' bears 4–5″ diameter purple-rose flowers, upright petals, on 3′ tall stems.

'The King' is 4–5′ tall with 4–5″ diameter rose-red flowers. Its height is a disadvantage in today's smaller gardens and it has been superseded by more compact cultivars such as 'Bright Star' and 'Robert Bloom.'

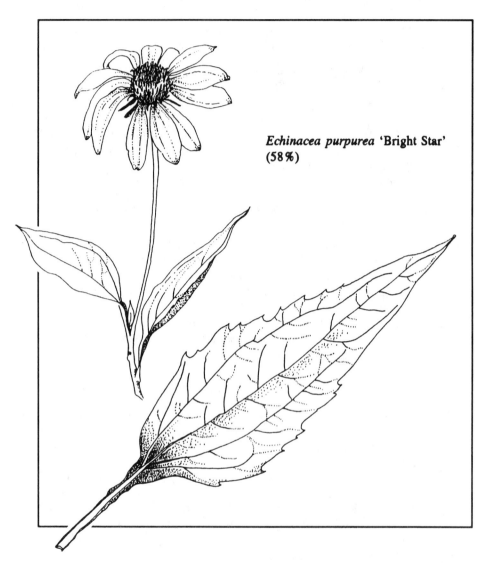

*Echinacea purpurea* 'Bright Star'
(58%)

'White Lustre' differs from 'White Swan' by having a little more bronze-orange center and more horizontal ray flowers. Plants are more uniform because they are often vegetatively propagated.

'White Swan' is a seed-propagated white form with drooping ray flowers.

**Related Species:**

*E. laevigata*, smooth coneflower, has leaves up to 3″ long but differ from common purple coneflower by being smooth, rather than hairy, on the upper sides.

*E. tennesseensis*, Tennessee coneflower, is a southeastern native, and on the Federal Endangered Species List. A small number of nurseries now offer nursery propagated plants to the gardener. The foliage is linear and plants grow 1½–2' tall. Dark mauve flowers with upturned ray flowers and greenish pink centers open from early June until August. In the garden, its lack of vigor compared with other plants often results in being overrun after a year or two.

Quick Key to Echinacea Species

A. Ray flowers rose to purple
    B. Ray flowers strap-like, pale purple
        to off-white, leaves entire ............... *E. pallida*
    BB. Ray flowers broad, purple, rose
        colored, leaves coarsely toothed ........... *E. purpurea*
AA. Ray flowers yellowish .................. *E. paradoxa*

**Additional Reading:**

Anon. 1993. *Echinacea angustifolia. Wildflower Notes* 10(3):4.
Bauer, R. and H. Wagner. 1991. *Echinacea* species as a potential immuno-stimulatory drugs. *Economic Med. Plant Research* 5:253–321.
Downey, James. 1996. The future's medicine today.
    http://www.herbsinfo.com/pages/echin.htm
Foster, Steven. 1985. *Echinaceas*, the purple coneflowers. *Horticulture* 63(8):14–16.

## *Echinops* (ek′ in-ops)          Globe Thistle          Asteraceae

About 120 species of globe thistle are known, but only one or two are common to gardens in North America. In species such as *E. nivens* and *E. spinosissimus*, both with leaves that are white on the undersides, the foliage is almost lethal to the touch. However, the foliage of the cultivated species, mainly *E. ritro*, appears more prickly than it really is. The flowers are surrounded by bristly bracts and are not particularly gardener-friendly. The leaves are alternate and often have white hairs beneath. The individual flowers are small but are bunched together in a steely blue, globe-like inflorescence. All species should be planted in full sun in well-drained soil.

| *-ritro* (rit′ ro) | | Globe Thistle | 2–4'/3' |
|---|---|---|---|
| Summer | Blue | Europe, Western Asia | Zones 3–7 |

This is probably the best of the globe thistles, although considerable confusion exists as to the true identity of many of the plants sold as *E. ritro*. The 6–8″ long leaves have deep wavy margins. The upper surface is smooth, while the underside is gray-green and hairy. The stems branch near the top and numerous 1–2″ diameter, globose, dark blue flowers are formed in early summer (mid-June to mid-August in zone 7, about 1 week later in zone 6). The flowers are a beekeeper's delight as they are particularly attractive to bumblebees and nocturnal moths.

I have grown *Echinops* in southern Ontario, Michigan, and Georgia, and found it to be a reliable plant. The cooler nights in the North, however, result in deeper blue flowers compared with plants in the South. Dry, poor soil is quite suitable for all species. Globe thistle produces 4–10 flowers per branched stem, which can be used fresh or as long lasting dried flowers. If placed in a dry, warm environment, flowers dry without loss of color. They are becoming more popular with florists and flower designers every year.

Propagate by seed, divisions, or root cuttings. Seeds germinate within 3 weeks if planted in peat-vermiculite and placed at 70–75° F and under high humidity. Division should not be attempted until plants are at least 3 years old. At that time, basal plantlets are visible. Approximately 2–3″ long pieces of roots may be cut in the spring. Treat root cuttings similar to those of *Anemone*.

### Cultivars:

'Blue Cloud' is seldom seen but has 2″ diameter flowers of soft blue shades.

'Blue Glow' has flowers of deeper blue than the species.

'Taplow Blue' is the most popular cultivar and bears 2″ wide, steel-blue flowers.

'Taplow Purple' is bluish purple but not as attractive as 'Taplow Blue'.

'Veitchii's Blue' has darker steel blue flowers than 'Taplow Blue' and is very popular in European gardens. The darker flower color also makes it the best choice for Southern gardens.

### Related Species:

*E. bannaticus* is almost identical to *E. ritro* but is native to southeastern Europe and Czechoslovakia. The stems may be unbranched (branched in *E. ritro*), the upper sides of the leaves are more hairy, and the foliage in general is more deeply divided. From the garden standpoint, I can see no difference. 'Blue Globe' ('Blue Ball') is about 3′ tall with dark blue flowers.

*E. exaltatus*, Russian globe thistle, is the tallest of the globe thistles and can grow to 8′. The stems are unbranched and the leaves are more spiny than the previous species. The flowers are silvery white and flower later than those of *E. ritro*. Native from eastern Europe to western Russia.

*E. ruthenicus* was, until recently, classified as a subspecies of *E. ritro*. It differs by having deeply divided basal leaves, whose segments are quite narrow, giving the plant the appearance of a cutleaf form of globe thistle. It was also once known as var. *tenuifolius*, meaning cutleaf. The undersides of the leaves are generally whiter and plants are shorter than those of *E. ritro*. A very handsome garden form, but not as cold hardy.

## *Echium* (e′ kee-um)  Viper's Bugloss  Boraginaceae

Only a few fortunate gardeners in North America, mainly in southern California, can be successful with the perennial forms of these incredible rocket-like plants. Most of the 40 species are native to Europe and the Canary Islands, and one or two of the short forms, such as *E. plantagineum* and *E. vulgare*, are becoming popular as annual or biennial garden fillers. 'Blue Bedder' and 'Dwarf Hybrids' are two bright selections of bedding type forms of the blue to pink-flowered *E. vulgare*.

A few of the more massive, impressive species appear like large, slanted rockets whose missiles of blue flower spikes look ready to launch. Between 6 and 10′ tall, plants bear hundreds of terminal blue or white flowers. Many are biennials, producing large, basal rosettes of smooth leaves the first year, then after the winter, sending up their tall spikes of flowers. Once they flower, they make seeds and die. The 6–8′ tall hybrids of *E. pininana* and *E. wildpretii* (*E. bourgaeanum*) are said to be cold hardy to around 15° F, although no hybrids or species enjoy hot or humid summer conditions. *E. pininana*, and the imposing *E. simplex*, Pride of Tenerife, are tall and unbranched, and are short lived perennials or biennials. *E. candicans* and *E. creticum* are also biennials but a few are perennial (*E. lusitanicum*). I first came across these noble plants in Ireland, and each time I see them, I marvel at the diversity of plant life on this great planet.

While no one should run out and import plants of Viper's Bugloss, they are easy to propagate from seed. Sow seeds in a warm, humid area and overwinter seedlings in a cool greenhouse. If planted out in the spring, after the last frost, flowering often occurs in the summer. Place in full sun in relatively poor soil, fertile soils result in leafy plants. Most attractive to bees and butterflies.

## *Endymion* see *Hyacinthoides*

## *Eomecon* (ee-om e′ con)  Snow Poppy  Papaveraceae

A genus of just one species, *E. chionantha*, the snow poppy has understated beauty when young, but can become a major nuisance as the years pass by. The leathery leaves, emerging from the rootstalk, have wavy margins and 3–4 main whitish veins. The sap is orange. The 1–2″ wide, white flowers arise in early to mid spring with centers of yellow stamens. Flowering is usually sparse.

The nuisance part of this plant results from the travelling tendencies of the vigorous creeping rhizomes, creating large mats of snow poppies where there were few before. This is obviously a major benefit only if a ground cover is preferred.

Plants are native to eastern China, and cold tolerant to about −5° F; I do not know their heat tolerance limit. They require cool moist conditions but can tolerate more sun providing the roots are constantly moist. They look miserable under drought conditions.

## *Epilobium* (e-pi-lo' bee-um)         Willowherb         Onagraceae

Over 200 species of *Epilobium* occur, and new additions, such as the inclusion of *Zauschneria* (which see), keeps it expanding. They are mainly native to western North America but also may be found in many temperate areas of the world. *E. glabellum*, for example, has attractive rose-violet flowers with yellow stamens and is native to New Zealand. Although the genus is large and plants are found over wide areas, plants are seldom found or used east of the Rocky Mountains. Many of the garden-worthy species bear handsome flowers in late summer to fall but all can be invasive. The most prolific and spreading species is *E. angustifolium*, rosebay willowherb, also called fireweed, so named because of its ability to colonize waste ground after a fire. Willowherb spreads by long white stolons and air-borne seeds, which can carry a tremendous distance. Both *E. angustifolium* and *E. hirsutum*, affectionately known as codlins and cream, make massive stands where conditions are to their liking.

Nearly all the species have pink to rose flowers, with occasional white varieties or cultivars available. The easiest species to distinguish is *E. luteum* with its yellow flowers, while the most common by far is *E. angustifolium*. The flowers of all species consist of 4 sepals and 4 petals, as well as 4 short and 4 long stamens and are typically held in racemes above the foliage. The seed pods are long slender rods and look like flower stalks of the spent flowers.

*-angustifolium* (an-gust-i-fo' lee-um) Rosebay Willowherb, Fireweed 4–9'/4'
     Summer         Rose, Purple         Western North America         Zones 3–7

Its common name was particularly appropriate in England, during and after the London Blitzes, when fireweed quickly colonized burnt out areas, not only in London but throughout devastated areas in England. That it is capable of such behavior should also make gardeners cautious about its use in any formal setting. Gardeners who enjoy the beauty of a mass of these plants (and they are beautiful) allow them to "do their thing" for a year or two, then religiously remove the flowers before seed is produced. On the West Coast, plants are every bit as rambunctious as in Europe, but they are a little better behaved in the northern plain states and in Canada. They do poorly in the South and are probably not worth the effort.

The reflexed, irregular shaped (zygomorphic) 4-petaled flowers, which may be rosy, purple or lavender, are held in many-flowered racemes. The stigma is 4-lobed and protrudes from the flowers on the long style. The alternate leaves are 4–8″ long and less than ½″ wide (much like a weeping willow leaf). The attractive seed heads are silky and translucent, but if you see them, you will likely be seeing a lot more plants next spring.

They also spread by stolons to make handsome colonies. Full sun is preferred but a little shade may be tolerated. Soil is not particularly important. It will grow almost anywhere where climate is reasonably cool.

Propagate by division or seed.

### Cultivars:

'Album' is a beautiful white-flowered form with green sepals. Seeds produce mainly white plants, with some rose.

'Isobel' has pale pink flowers and crimson sepals.

### Related Species:

*E. dodonaei* is only 1–2′ tall and is a multi-stemmed plant with reddish stolons. The linear leaves are only about 1″ long and the deep rose-purple flowers, with a slightly protruding style, are held in loose inflorescences. Native to central and western Europe and Asia. Probably hardy in zones 6–7 (8 on the west Coast).

*E. fleischeri* resembles *E. dodonaei*, but has a much longer style and less deeply colored flowers. Native to the European Alps, cold hardy to zone 5.

## *Epimedium* (ep-ee-mee′ dee-um)　　　Barrenwort　　　Berberidaceae

A genus whose time has come with plenty of attributes and very few faults. Whenever I speak to audiences about perennials, enthusiasm about this genus is always high. A few years ago, the genus could have been regarded as a relatively small one with perhaps 20–22 species. The classic work on the genus was the monograph "Epimedium and Vancouveria" published by Dr. W.T. Stern in 1938, in which he recognized 21 species. However, in the last 15 years, with increased access to China, the number has almost doubled, with new species and cultivars being regularly introduced (see additional reading) and more species surely to be found. In general, epimediums occur naturally in light woodlands and light shade; good drainage and a humus-rich soil are ideal in cultivation.

Once established, most species make magnificent ground covers, and a number of them are evergreen. Plants do best in soils which have been amended with copious amounts of organic matter, such as peat moss and manure. They compete well with roots of trees and tolerate heavy shade, growing in barren areas where many other species perish. Somewhere along the lecturing circuit, some speaker must have shouted that the genus enjoyed dry, shaded conditions, and if one had those conditions (which everyone does) they should run out and plunk in barrenwort. He or she must have been good, because everyone believed him. The fact is that epimediums tolerate such conditions better than many others, but they grow a whole lot better in light shade with even moisture. It is unfair to judge the performance of a genus based on the worst condition found in the garden. Have a heart, plant an epimedium where you plant hostas.

Although slow to establish, *Epimedium* forms wonderful clumps of compound foliage (leaves in 2 groups of three), and columbine-like flowers. Flowers consist of four petals and eight sepals. The sepals are arranged in two groups—outer and inner. The outer sepals are usually small, early deciduous and hardly noticeable, while the colored inner four look more like petals. These sepals may be spurred (like columbine) or hooded, giving rise to common names like Bishop's Hat or Bishop's Mitre. In the spring the leaves are often tinged pink or red, and in the fall they usually turn yellow, red, or bronze. A combination of *Epimedium* and *Narcissus* 'April Tears' is outstanding. If the foliage is clipped low to the ground very early in spring, the flowers can be better appreciated. Otherwise they may be lost in the old leaves. New foliage will soon reappear. All plants are excellent ground covers and persist for many years if provided the proper environment, although the hardiness of new species has yet to be well established.

Propagate by division in late spring, after flowering has been completed, or summer. They are easy to divide and move at any time.

Quick Guide to Epimedium Species

|  | Height (in.) | Flower color | Flowers with conspicuous spurs |
|---|---|---|---|
| *E. acuminatum* | 12–15 | Pinkish | Yes |
| *E. alpinum* | 6–9 | Dull red | Yes |
| *E. grandiflorum* | 8–15 | Pale pink | Yes |
| *E. perralderianum* | 10–12 | Yellow | No |
| *E. pinnatum* | 8–12 | Yellow | No |
| *E.* × *rubrum* | 8–12 | Bright red | No |
| *E.* × *youngianum* | 6–8 | White | No |

**-acuminatum** (a-kew-mi-nah′ ta)  Pointed Barrenwort  12–15″/15″
 Spring  Pinkish  China  Zones 5–8

Plants were originally discovered in 1858 by the French Missionary Perny, and a number of forms have come into cultivation since the early 1980's. The form most recognized was collected in 1981 by Roy Lancaster on Mt. Omei in China, and should appear in American catalogs more and more as stock is built up. The large dark green leaves (lime-green in the spring) are long and pointed at the tips (acuminate) and hairy along the margins. The outer sepals are creamy or pale pink, while the larger spurred inner parts are pink, rose, or purple. Protect from strong winds and provide a shaded, cool spot.

**Related Species:**

*E.* × 'Kaguyahime' is a hybrid between *E. acuminatum* and *E. dolchostemon*, a Japanese species, and has recently been introduced to cultivation. The evergreen foliage is flushed bronze in cool weather and the 18–20" tall flower stems carry pink/purple flowers.

| *-alpinum* (al-pine' um) | Alpine Barrenwort | 6–9"/12" |
|---|---|---|
| Spring    Dull Red | South and Central Europe | Zones 4–7 |

The leaves are arranged in two groups of three, and the 2–3" long leaflets are pointed at the end. There are 12–20 small flowers in a loose raceme above the foliage in April and May. The outer sepals are grayish with specks of red and the inner sepals are dark crimson, while the petals are yellowish and slipper-shaped. This is an excellent ground cover, particularly in the northern end of the range. The species has served well as a parent of numerous hybrids such as *E.* × *warleyense, E.* × *rubrum,* and *E.* × *cantabrigense.*

**Cultivars:**

'Rubrum' has brighter red inner sepals and yellower petals than the type. It is vigorous and multiples rapidly.

**Related Species:**

*E.* × *cantabrigense,* a hybrid with *E. alpinum* and *E. pubigerum,* a species with glossy leaves and creamy white yellowish flowers, has become popular. Plants arose in St. John's College in Cambridge, England and consist of 1–2' tall mounds of evergreen 9-leaflet leaves. Hardy to zone 4.

*E.* × *warleyense* arose in the early 1900s in Warley Place, Essex, England, the garden of Miss Wilmott (see *Eryngium giganteum*). The hybrid, a result of natural pollination of *E. alpinum* × *E. pinnatum* ssp. *colchicum,* has dull green leaves and eye-catching flowers of coppery-red inner sepals and yellow petals. I have not found it to be particularly vigorous.

| *-grandiflorum* (grand-i-flo' rum) | Longspur Barrenwort | 8–15"/15" |
|---|---|---|
| Spring    Pale Pink | Japan | Zones 5–8 |
| (Syn. *E. macranthum*) | | |

This is one of the larger-flowered species in the genus, and one of the better performers in the eclectic Armitage garden. The 1' long leaves are ovate, and the margins of the 2–3" long bright green leaflets are spiny-toothed. The young spring foliage is beige-brown, greening up in early summer. Outer sepals are white, inner ones pale yellow, and the petals are rose or violet colored with a conspicuous ½" long spur. About a dozen ¾–1½" diameter flowers are arranged in a tight raceme. Plants are intolerant of alkaline soils.

### Cultivars:
'Album' has creamy white flowers.

Var. *higonse* makes orderly compact mounds of more deeply cut leaves and clean white flowers.

'Rose Queen' is an excellent cultivar with crimson leaves. The flowers are among the more visible in the genus and are rose-pink with long white tipped spurs. They are larger but borne in smaller numbers than the species. There is a bit of controversy concerning this cultivar. According to epimedium expert Robbie White of Blackthorn Nursery, England, the real 'Rose Queen' has deep rose to crimson flowers without white or just a little white on the tips of the spurs, while the lighter colored form ('Rose Queen') is something else. They are all terrific, but the darker form without white spurs is probably the true 'Rose Queen'.

Ssp. *koreanum* produces handsome, long-spurred, creamy yellow flowers, but they are often sparsely produced and hidden by the foliage. Plants bear large leaves; the young ones are bronze in the spring.

'Lilafee' bears lavender-violet flowers.

'Nanum' is only about 4–6" tall with chocolate brown margins on the leaves. Creamy flowers occur in spring.

'White Queen' is similar to 'Rose Queen' but with silvery-white flowers.

'Violaceum' has large murky violet flowers. The new foliage has bronze veins.

### Related Species:
*E. leptorrhizum*, native to Sichuan, is a low growing species with leathery evergreen leaves and large rose-red flowers. Plants spread rapidly.

| *-perralderianum* (pe-ral-de-ree-ah' num) | | | 10–12"/12" |
|---|---|---|---|
| Spring | Yellow | Algeria | Zones 5–8 |

Each evergreen leaf consists of 3 spiny-edged shiny leaflets, each about 3" long, usually light green when young and later tinted red-brown. The unbranched inflorescence consists of 20–25 yellow flowers. This species is similar to *E. pinnatum*, but not as good a garden plant. The small brownish spur is hardly noticeable.

### Related Species:
*E.* × *perralchicum* 'Frohnleiten', selected in Germany, grows 4–8" tall and is one of the most robust forms available. Plants are natural hybrids between *E. perralderianum* and *E. pinnatum* ssp. *colchicum*. The evergreen, spiny leaves have a reddish tint, both when young and in the winter. They

have exceptional yellow flowers (sometimes with red centers) held on leaflets stems. The cultivar 'Wisley' also resulted from the same parentage and is similar to 'Frohnleiten'. A fabulous plant, on the Armitage top-five list of epimediums for the garden.

*-pinnatum* (pin-nay' tum)                                              8–12"/12"
   Late Spring      Yellow      Northern Iran      Zones 5–8

Plants were collected by Roy Lancaster in 1979 and the species, particularly ssp. *colchicum*, has been quickly embraced in cultivation. The leaves are composed of 5 or more leaflets and the whole plant is hairy, particularly when young. The bright citrus-yellow flowers have very small petals and short brownish spurs, and are arranged in a loose inflorescence of 12–30 flowers. This species has no stem leaves; all the leaves arise directly from the root.

## Cultivars:
Ssp. *colchicum* is the most common form of the species. Leaves are sparsely toothed and smooth on the margins. Plants have larger flowers and are more free flowering than the type.

## Related Species:
*E. × versicolor*, bicolor barrenwort, a cross between *E. grandiflorum* and *E. pinnatum* ssp. *colchicum*, usually has 9 leaflets, which are conspicuously red mottled when young. The leaflets turn green in early summer. The sepals are light rose, the petals yellow, and the spur has a red tinge. 'Sulphureum' is a popular, excellent clone with soft yellow to dark yellow flowers. Plants are evergreen in all but the hardest winters. The 5–11 leaflets give rise to a leafy flowering stem bearing pale yellow sepals and bright yellow petals. This has been one of the toughest epimediums in the shady, dry conditions under the oak trees in the Armitage garden. 'Neosulphureum' is similar but has 3–9 leaflets, brownish when young, and slightly shorter spurs. All cultivars flower earlier than most other barrenworts. 'Versicolor' ('Cupreum') is similar in leaf, but more likely to be deciduous. Flowers are much brighter, ranging from orangish to rosy-yellow.

*-× rubrum* (rew' brum)      Red Barrenwort      8–12"/12"
   Spring      Red      Hybrid      Zones 5–8

A hybrid between *E. alpinum* and *E. grandiflorum*, with the robustness of the latter and the height of the former. Each of the 15–20 flowers are up to 1" across and clustered in a loose inflorescence held slightly above the many leaflets. The heart-shaped leaflets are particularly pretty in the spring and fall when tinged red. The foliage remains tinged red in cool summers but changes to green in warm summers. The long thin rhizomes are adaptable to many soils and result in one of the fastest growing ground covers. The inner sepals are crimson red and the petals are pale yellow or tinted red. Probably the best species for a ground cover.

-× *youngianum* (yun-gee-aye' num)    Young's Barrenwort    6–8"/8"
   Spring            White          Japan               Zones 5–8

This hybrid resulted from crossing *E. diphyllum* and *E. grandiflorum*, and is one of the easiest to establish. The leaves, which are not evergreen, arise from the base of the plant and are usually divided into nine ovate pointed leaflets. The leaflets are sharply serrated, marked with red upon emergence in the spring, and turn a deep shade of crimson in the fall. Plants form small clumps of leaves with 2–6 small leaflets. The 3–8 pendulous flowers are about ¾" across and light pinkish white. Flowers are essentially spurless. Plants require more humus-rich soils than many others and are relatively slow growing. The species itself is seldom offered, being superseded by the cultivars.

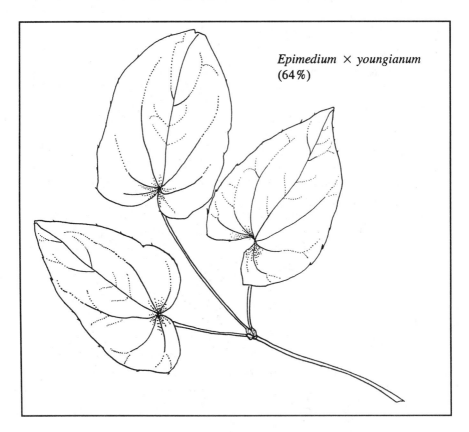

*Epimedium × youngianum*
(64%)

## Cultivars:

'Niveum' is the most common cultivar and bears lovely small white flowers. Similar to a form called 'Milky Way' and may be the same thing.

'Roseum' has rose to pinkish lilac flowers.

'Merlin' arose from a chance seedling in a garden in Dorset county, England. Plants are similar and flowers are a dusky purple.

'Yenomoto Form' bears larger rounder white flowers with more exaggerated spurs than 'Niveum'.

## Related Species:

*E.* × *setosum* is a low-growing hybrid, supposedly between *E. diphyllum* and *E. sempervirens*, two species from Japan. The leaves are lime green in the spring and green up in the summer. Small, starry white flowers occur in early spring.

*E. stellulatum* 'Wudang Star' was also collected by Roy Lancaster in central China. The foliage is evergreen, the leaf veins turning dark red in winter. The 15–18″ tall inflorescence carries 20–40 flowers with spreading white inner sepals and brownish orange petals.

Quick Key to Epimedium Species

A. Flowers yellow
   B. Flower stems leafless, basal
     leaves consist of 3 leaflets . . . . . . . . . . . . . . *E. pinnatum*
   BB. Flower stems with leaves, leaves
     made up of 5–11 leaflets . . . . . . . . . . . *E. perralderianum*
AA. Flowers not yellow
   B. Flowers with conspicuous spurs, nearly
     as long or longer than inner sepals
     C. Flowers large, 1–2″ across
       D. Leaflets very pointed at the tip,
         leaflets at least 4″ long . . . . . . . . . . *E. acuminatum*
       DD. Leaflets not highly pointed at tips,
         leaflets usually less than 4″ long . . . . *E. grandiflorum*
     CC. Flowers smaller, up to 1″ across . . . . . . . . *E. alpinum*
   BB. Flowers with very small spurs,
     much shorter than inner sepals
     C. Flowers bright red . . . . . . . . . . . . . . . . . *E.* × *rubrum*
     CC. Flowers usually white
       with tinges of pink . . . . . . . . . . . . . *E.* × *youngianum*

## Additional Reading:

Lancaster, Roy. 1984. Recent plant introductions. *The Garden* 109(6):244–247.
Lancaster, Roy. 1995. *Epimedium stellulatum* 'Wudang Star'. *The Garden* 120(3):134–135.

Lovejoy, Ann. 1994. Epimediums. *Horticulture* 72(4):42–46.

Stearn, William T. 1979. A new hybrid epimedium (*E. × cantabrigense*). *The Plantsman* 1(3):187–190.

Stearn, W.T. 1993. New large flowered Chinese species of *Epimedium (E. latisepalum)*. *Kew Magazine* 10(4):178–184.

van de Laar, H.J. 1994. Epimediums. *Perennial Plants (J. of the Perennial Plant Assoc.)* 2(1):8–12.

Weaver, R.E. 1987. In praise of Epimediums. *Perennial Plant Newsletter* XI:5–7.

White, Robin. 1996. Epimedium: dawning of a new era. *The Garden* 121(4):208–214.

## *Eranthis* (er-anth′ is)          Winter Aconite          Ranunculaceae

The seven species comprising the genus bear solitary bright yellow flowers in late winter and early spring. The petals are modified into small nectaries and the showy part of the flower consists of sepals only. The winter aconites have short stems, and are best massed under deciduous trees or along river banks where they can be naturalized. Where they are happy, pastures of aconites produce a riot of yellow in early- to mid-March followed by the fine fern-like foliage. Flowers do not show up well when planted in grass.

Tubers do better in alkaline soils, but will increase if left undisturbed in almost any soil, as they seed prolifically. Plant tubers about 2″ deep in late summer or early autumn. Propagation is most successful by lifting the tubers after they have been undisturbed for 2–3 years and breaking them into smaller pieces. The pieces may not flower the first winter, but will the next. Plants raised from seed require 3–4 years to flower.

### *-hyemalis* (hye-e-mah′ lis)          Winter Aconite          4–6″/4″
Winter, Early Spring          Yellow          Western Europe          Zones 3–7

The 3–5 lobed, palmately-cut foliage is carried on long petioles and is very attractive. The solitary, 1–2″ diameter flowers are made up of 6 sepals and appear before the leaves. Beneath each flower is a large leaf-like, collar-shaped bract which appears to support each blossom. One of the best reasons for having these ephemeral plants in the northern garden is their ability to flower through the snow in early spring. How can you leave them out of the garden? The late great gardener H. Lincoln Foster certainly couldn't. He described them as they "thrust their shining yellow cups through . . . the snow that overlay them, and they were spread in a profligate scattering of doubloons, as though flung across a white damask table cloth, each golden coin surrounded by a ruff of deep green leaves."

The tubers are ridiculously inexpensive, so there is little excuse not to plant in masses of 50 or more. Plant immediately upon purchase. Within a few years those 50 bulbs will form a golden carpet to welcome the onset of spring. They are particularly beautiful meandering down a slope or naturalized in a wild flower setting. They do not spread as rapidly in zone 7 as in zone 4, but are still effective. If less than successful in the garden, use them in containers where drainage is much better. If possible, purchase green-started seedlings in early spring to insure establishment. I have great disappointments with dried out tubers never emerging.

### Cultivars:
'Glory' has large lemon-yellow flowers.

### Related Species:
*E. cilicica* is similar to *E. hyemalis* but flowers earlier and is more robust. The leaves are tinged bronze on emergence, and the flowers are bright yellow.

*E.* × *tubergenii* is a hybrid of *E. hyemalis* and *E. cilicica*. It has 2–2½" wide flowers which, because they are sterile, persist longer than those of *E. hyemalis*. 'Guinea Gold' has leaves tinged with bronze and deep yellow, fragrant flowers. It is the most handsome form of all but, unfortunately, not easy to locate in the trade.

### Additional Reading:
Anon. 1994. Growing: Little drops of sun. *Garden Design* 13(5):28.
Lawrence, George H. M. 1960. *Eranthis hyemalis* and *Eranthis* × *tubergenii*. *Baileya* 8:18–19.

## *Eremurus* (air-uh-mure′ us)          Foxtail Lily          Liliaceae

Foxtail lilies are native to the drier regions of western and central Asia, occurring in areas with long, hot summers and fall-spring rains. All species are similar in a few basic characteristics. Their compact rhizome has a central bud, and long, fleshy roots radiate from all sides. The strap-shaped leaves, which are usually keeled, appear in early spring and generally die back before the flowers have matured. There are often hundreds of small, individual flowers borne on unbranched racemes. Few plants are as impressive as a foxtail lily in flower. The most stately species may be *E. robustus*, which bear 8–10′ tall, spike-like inflorescences of peach-colored flowers. *E. stenophyllus* (*E. bungei*), on the other hand, is only 2–3′ tall with bright yellow flowers, but is equally lovely. Of the fifty species, many of which have been hybridized, only a handful are widely available in the United States.

The genus belongs to the same group of plants as *Asphodelus* (they were originally thought to be a "really handsome, hardy, asphodelaceous plant"), the red hot poker (*Kniphofia*), aloes, and yuccas. All the leaves arise from the thick, fibrous root and disappear shortly after flowering. In their natural habitat, many species grow in steppe vegetation, often on mountain slopes. They need a thoroughly drained, rich soil and will not do well in heavy clays. To grow them successfully, dig a hole which easily accommodates even the long, fleshy, tentacle roots. Place some grit or sharp draining material (clay pieces, etc.) in the bottom of the hole and put the tuber on top. Fill in gently so as not to damage the roots. Mulch the plants as soon as the leaves emerge in the spring because spring frosts are deadly. Plant the crowns about 6″ deep as soon as they are received, for they must not be allowed to dry out. Choose a site in full sun out of prevailing winds. Although they are not the easiest plants to grow, they are well worth the effort.

| | | | |
|---|---|---|---|
| -× *shelford* (shell′ ford) | Shelford Foxtail Lily | 4–8′/3′ |
| Summer    Various | Hybrid | Zones 5–7 |
| (Syn. *E.* × *isabellinus*) | | |

The Shelford hybrids were raised by Sir Michael Foster in Great Shelford, Cambridge, England and have stood the test of time. Plants are variable and 3–4′ long racemes in shades of yellow, pink, white, and copper are produced in summer. These free-flowering hybrids are the result of crossing *E. stenophyllus*, a short species with bright yellow flowers, and *E. olgae*, a medium to tall, white-flowered species, and are sometimes listed as *E.* × *isabellinus*.

The spider-like roots should be spread out carefully in early spring or fall in planting holes 6–8″ deep and 18″ apart. Do not bury the crown more than 1–2″ below the surface as it may rot if rains occur before the plants are well established. Plants do well in full sun and well-drained soils, and generally look best against a green background, such as a hedge of Leyland cypress. Protection from high winds is essential if plants are to look their best. The flowers open from bottom to top and remain in flower for 2–3 weeks. The leaves decline after flowering, and foliage and flowers self destruct by late summer. Plant annuals or perennials which flop over, such as *Boltonia asteroides* or *Clematis heracleifolia*, to hide the foliage and fill in the gap when the leaves go dormant.

Propagate by division after 3–4 years. When the leaves have died back, carefully lift the crowns and gently separate into individual plants. Plants grown from seed will take 4–6 years to flower.

### Cultivars:
'Isobel' has pink-orange flowers on 5–6′ plants.
'Moonlight' bears pale yellow flowers.
'Rosalind' displays bright pink flowers and is 5–6′ tall.
'White Beauty' has clear white blossoms.

**Related Species:**

*E. elwesii*, Elwes foxtail lily, is similar to *E. robustus* in height and may be a hybrid between *E. himalaicus*, a 3' tall, white-flowered species, and *E. robustus*, but the parentage has not been verified. The flowers are fragrant and soft pink. 'Albus' is a white-flowered form.

Ruiter hybrids were raised by N.C. Ruiter between 1950 and 1980. They included single colors such as 'Cleopatra' (orange with red midribs on the flowers), 'Copperboy' (yellow), 'Oase' (pale pink), 'Obelisk' (white-tinged green), 'Odessa' (yellowish green), 'Romance' (salmon-pink), and 'Sahara' (coral-pink). Today they may be found as mixed Ruiter hybrids.

*E. stenophyllus* (syn. *E. bungei*) is a dwarf member of the genus, growing 2–3' tall. The yellow flowers turn burnt orange as they mature, providing a two-toned effect. It requires less maintenance because little support is required. 'Magnificus' bears large, bright yellow flowers on a 3' flower stalk.

**Additional Reading:**

Mathew, B. 1996. Tails of the desert. *The Garden* 121(6):322–326.


*Erianthus* (er-ee-anth' us)              Plume Grass              Poaceae

Over 20 species occur, native to tropical and temperate areas. They are adaptable to many areas of the garden, reliable in moist areas and well-drained sandy sites. In general, plants of *Erianthus* are large, erect, tufted, perennial grasses with flat leaf blades and dense, silky panicles of flowers in late summer and fall. Most are warm-season grasses, and have handsome, if not overwhelming, fall color.

The most common form is the massive 10–12' tall ravenna grass, *E. ravennae*, native to southern Europe. The gray-green leaves are about 1" wide and 3–4' long. The 4–5' wide clumps make dramatic specimens for the large landscape, useful for screens, highways, and golf courses. Plants perform best in moist areas, but they don't require bogs to be at their best. They are simply too large for many small landscapes, and flowers can break off in heavy winds. The fall color can be orange, tan, and purple, and the tan winter foliar costume is outstanding where sufficient room is allowed. Plants perform well in zones 6–9. *E. giganteus*, sugarcane plume grass, equally large and wide, is also used as a large backdrop for screening or specimen plants. Not as cold hardy or as tough as ravenna grass.

Another useful species includes a southeastern native, *E. contortus*, bent awn plume grass, which is about 2' tall in leaf and up to 4' tall in flower. The red fall color is one of the most handsome aspects of this species. Probably hardy in zones 7–10.

Numerous cultivars of *Erianthus*, for different foliage color, better fall hues and more compact forms, are said to be just around the corner.

## *Erigeron* (e -rij′ er-on)    Fleabane    Asteraceae

Many of the 200 species are native to North America. Although only 2-3 species are useful for the garden, many cultivars have been named and much hybridization and selection have taken place. They are attractive for many weeks in the summer, make good cut flowers, and are not fussy as to soil. Unfortunately this genus, like other roadside flowers, is often ignored by gardeners because it is considered a common weed. While many of the species are of little value to the garden, some of the selections are indeed worthy. All species and selections require full sun, and the taller forms should be deadheaded to provide a second flush of flowers. The taller, showier cultivars (generally forms and hybrids of *E. speciosus*) are not particularly good plants for the south. Unfortunately, a number of viruses affect *Erigeron* and require constant rejuvenation. Stock plants of some of the vegetatively propagated forms are obviously riddled with viruses.

Flowers of fleabane suggest native asters and are easily confused. If interested in telling them apart, it helps to get eyeball to eyeball with them and count a few of the flower parts. In general, flowers of *Erigeron* open earlier, have two or more series of ray flowers, and the bracts under the flowers are in 1-2 series (usually one). In *Aster*, flowers usually open later (often late summer and fall), the ray flowers occur in only 1-2 series, and the bracts occur in more than two series. Not much to go on, but the best we can do given the many similarities. The common name suggests its usefulness in repelling fleas; however, I have seen no modern mention of this. If it worked, every neighbor's dog, not to mention a few neighbors, would be dipped in fleabane stew.

Propagation is not difficult by seed, division, or cuttings. Sow the seed when collected or sow purchased seed in late fall. Seed should be covered very thinly, and placed at 70-75° F in a humid atmosphere. Seeds germinate in 10-14 days. Divide the plants in the fall every 2-3 years. Two inch long terminal shoot cuttings may be taken any time, but preferably before flower buds have formed.

### Quick Reference to Erigeron Species

|  | Height (in.) | Flower color |
|---|---|---|
| *E. aurantiacus* | 9–12 | Orange |
| *E. philadelphicus* | 18–30 | Pale lavender |
| *E. pulchellus* | 18–24 | Rose-purple |
| *E. speciosus* | 20–30 | Purple |

**-aurantiacus** (ow-ran-tee' ah-cus)   Orange Fleabane   9–12"/1'
  Summer        Orange        Turkestan      Zones 4–7

While most of the fleabanes are rose, violet, or purple, this species has bright scarlet-orange 1–2" diameter flowers atop 9–12" tall plants. The foliage is somewhat velvety and the leaves appear twisted at first glance. The basal leaves are 3–4" long and shaped like a spatula (spatulate) while the upper leaves are ovate and sessile. The solitary flowers have a small green center and open for 6–8 weeks in early summer. Plants tolerate partial shade, particularly in the South. A unique color, but a short-lived plant.

Propagates readily from seed.

**Cultivars:**

Var. *sulphureus* bears lovely pale yellow flowers and looks particularly nice in the rockery or the front of the border.

**Related Species:**

*E. aureus*, gold fleabane, is native to mountainous areas of western North America. It has solitary ½–¾" diameter yellow-orange flowers and is only 3–6" tall.

*E. scopulinum* is also tiny, only growing about 4" tall. The white flowers are equally small, but it stands out well in a rock garden. Cold hardy to zone 5, heat tolerant to zone 7, given excellent drainage.


**-philadelphicus** (fil-a-del-fi' cus)   Common Fleabane   18–30"/18"
  Early Summer   Whitish Pink   North America   Zones 3–8

Actually, this is a weed, but a fairly handsome weed. Probably no one striving for the neat garden look would include it, but it certainly grows and flowers well. The species extends from New Brunswick to British Columbia, and south from Texas to Florida. The narrow basal leaves are toothed or scalloped, and the stem leaves have lobes at their bases which extend to either side of the stem.

The flowers are among the smallest in the genus, but many of them open over a long period of time. They consist of very numerous rays which can vary from white to pinkish. Good for the "wild" flower look.

Propagate by division or seed.

**Related Species:**

*E. karvinskianus* (kar-vin-skee-ah' nus) is also known as *E. mucronatus*, but mostly not known at all. The flowers are small (less than 1" across) and can be incredibly plentiful. They range from pink to whitish pink. Native to Mexico, plants are not cold hardy much below 10° F; however, plants reseed themselves quite well. 'Blutenmeer' is a 4–6" tall selection with flowers which open white and fade through pink and lilac colors.

*-pulchellus* (pul-chel' lus)  Poor Robin's Plantain  18–24"/2'
 Early Summer  Rosy-Purple  East, Central USA  Zones 3–7
(Syn. *E. bellidifolius*)

This is one of the few stoloniferous fleabanes in cultivation. The 2–6" long, hairy, toothed basal leaves are tufted and attached to the slender stem with a short petiole. The stem leaves are usually sessile and entire. The solitary 1" diameter flowers consist of about 60 ray florets and are lavender with yellow centers. Although this can be one of the showiest fleabanes, they lose all semblance of tidiness when given too much fertilizer or rich soils. The poorer the soil, the better. This is a fair garden species, at best.

### Related Species:

*E. glaucus*, beach fleabane, native to western North America, is about 6–12" tall but with a somewhat sprawling habit. Numerous lilac to violet ray flowers occur in summer. A white form ('Albus') and a rosy form ('Roseus') are both handsome and 'Arthur Menzies' sports attractive pink flowers on compact plants. However, the best cultivar is 'Elstead Pink', with good bright pink flowers. This fine cultivar was raised by Ernest Ladham's nursery at Elstead, Surrey, England. Best in areas with cool summer nights.

*-speciosus* (spiece-ee-o' sus)  Daisy Fleabane  20–30/24"
 Summer  Purple  Western United States  Zones 2–7

This is the most common fleabane, although the species itself is seldom seen in gardens. The lanceolate stem leaves clasp the stem, and the 3–6" long basal leaves have winged petioles. The numerous flowers usually consist of over 100 ray florets. Each flower is 1–2" across and occurs in clustered corymbs held well above the foliage. Plants are upright and well branched.

Plants should be grown in full sun and moist soil. Native to western United States, they do poorly further south than zone 6, although occasionally worthy specimens are found in zones 7 and 8. Plants may be cut back after flowering to reduce weediness and rejuvenate the foliage.

### Cultivars:

Many cultivars are available, and while they are usually listed under *E. speciosus*, they are more likely hybrids which include some genetic infusion from *E. speciosus*, *E. s.* var. *macranthus*, *E. alpinus*, *E. aurantiacus*, and/or *E. glaucus*. In most of the hybrids listed, the first two appear to be the dominant parents. The following cultivars are showy, but those taller than 24" need support.

'Adria' has many narrow, lavender-blue ray flowers with pale yellow centers, growing about 2' tall. Flowers early in May.

'Azure Beauty' is one of a series which includes 'Azure Blue' and 'Azure Fairy'. These are usually propagated from seed resulting in a great deal of variation. 'Azure Fairy' and 'Azure Beauty' appear to be the same cultivar but sold under different names by different companies. They have semi-double lavender-blue flowers on 30″ tall stems.

'Azure Blue' is similar to the above but has lighter blue flowers.

'Black Sea' ('Schwarzes Meer') is about 2′ tall with deep violet ray flowers around a prominent yellow center.

'Darkest of All' ('Dunkelste Aller') is a much planted cultivar with violet-blue flowers on 2′ tall stems.

'Dimity' is only 10–12″ tall and produces orange tinted flower buds which open to light pink flowers with orange centers. Dwarfness is an asset as no support is necessary. All of the "ity" cultivars were raised by Alan Bloom in the 1950s but only about a half dozen of the thirteen cultivars are still in cultivation.

'Foerster's Leibling' ('Foerster's Darling') is a wonderful double pink form, only 18″ tall, and needs little staking.

'Gaiety' is about 2′ tall with bright pink flowers comprised of narrow ray segments.

'Loveliness' is one of the most handsome cultivars because of the very narrow foliage and semi-double pink flowers.

Var. *macranthus* is similar to the type but has ovate rather than lanceolate leaves and slightly larger flowers.

'Pink Jewel' was selected from 'Rose Jewel' and has a variety of pink shades.

'Prosperity' has large almost double lavender-blue flowers with yellow centers on 18″ tall plants.

'Quakeress' and 'White Quakeress' ('Alba') appear to be hybrids between *E. speciosus* and *E. s.* var. *macranthus*. The former has light mauve-pink flowers, while the latter has off-white blooms. Both grow 18–24″ tall.

'Rose Jewel' has lilac-rose flowers and can grow 30″ tall.

'Rose Triumph' bears semi-double, rose-pink blossoms on 24″ tall plants.

'Rosenballet' has lavender-rose flowers on about 2′ tall plants.

'Sincerity' does well in the northeast and is relatively tall (30″) with mauve-blue flowers.

'Strahlenmeer' ('Shining Sea') has pink flowers with fine narrow ray segments. About 2′ tall.

'Unity' is a about 20″ tall with bright pink narrow ray flowers.

## Related Species:

*E. grandiflorus* is native to the Rocky Mountains and bears large flowers with numerous lavender ray flowers. One of the better *Erigeron* for cut flowers.

## Quick Key to Erigeron Species

  A. Flowers orange-yellow, plant 9–12″ tall ...... *E. aurantiacus*
AA. Flowers white, violet, or purple, plant 18–30″ tall
    B. Flowers large, more than 1″ across ......... *E. speciosus*
  BB. Flowers small, less than 1″ across
      C. Plants produce stolons, leaves
        coarsely toothed above the middle ....... *E. pulchellus*
     CC. Plants with offsets, seldom by
        stolons, leaves usually entire ........ *E. philadelphicus*

## *Eriophyllum* (e-ree-o-fill′ um)    Woolly Sunflower    Asteraceae

About 12 species of this little known genus occur, but only one, *E. lanatum*, is easily available through American nurseries. The beautiful silver, hairy leaves are borne on tumbling woody stems which form large, silvery-gray mats. In general, they are only useful when pouring over retaining walls or in gritty, excellently drained areas. However, when they smile upon you, you are aglow in hundreds of small yellow daisies which match the sunshine ray for ray. Native to the west coast, some of the Oregonians have taken to calling it Oregon Sunshine. Perhaps a little overdone, but plants can be lovely.

They are best grown in areas of cool nights and low humidity, which deletes about two thirds of the country. Probably only cold hardy to about zone 6, which leaves about 500 lucky gardeners who get all that Oregon sunshine.

## *Erodium* (e-ro-dee′ um)    Heron's Bill, Erodium    Geraniaceae

Heron's bill is occasionally recognized as a weed in many areas, most likely the escaped old world species, *E. cicutarium*, known as filaree. Of the 50–60 species, only two or three have gained much popularity in gardens. To the naked eye, the flowers are similar to those of hardy geraniums and plants are often initially confused. If one feels destructive, one can see that the flowers differ because those of *Erodium* have 5 stamens instead of the 10 in *Geranium*. The leaves, however, are the easiest way to discriminate between the two genera. The leaves of *Erodium* are usually in a rosette and they are pinnately lobed or compound and wavy around the margins. Those of hardy geraniums are usually entire, palmate and not in a rosette. The fruit is similar in both genera, having the long beak of a crane or heron.

## Quick Reference to Erodium Species

| | Height (in.) | Flower color | Garden use |
|---|---|---|---|
| *E. manescavii* | 15–24 | Purple | Border |
| *E. reichardii* | 4–6 | Rose-pink | Rock garden |

**-manescavii** (man-es-kav' ee-eye)      Manescau Erodium      15–24"/18"
   Spring          Purple          France          Zones 3–7

Plants are native to the Pyrenees, mainly in France, and is one of the bigger species in the genus. Plants are about 18" tall and the basal 6–8" long leaves are pinnatisect (deeply lobed) to pinnately compound. The strongly rosy-purple flowers are about 2" across and occur in 5–20 flower umbels in early June through September. Useful for any well-drained garden and is useful for the flower garden or containers. Plants perform better in cooler climates than warm, and are most useful in zones 3–6.

### Related Species:

*E. castellanum* is a similarly large plant with compound leaves and pinkish red flowers. Most impressive, for an erodium.

*E. leucanthemum* is a small rock garden candidate of the genus. Growing only 6–9" tall, it nevertheless bears handsome 1" clean white flowers.

**-reichardii** (ree-chard-ee' eye)      Rock Geranium      4–6"/12"
   Spring          Whitish         Balearic Islands    Zones 3–7

*Erodium reichardii* 'Roseum'
(75%)

*E. reichardii*, forever sold as *E. chamaedryoides*, is a handsome (dare I say cute) plant for the rock garden or other well-drained areas calling for a 3–4″ tall filigree-leaved plant. The flowers, which are borne singly, are white with rosy veins. Excellent drainage is absolutely necessary, particularly in warmer, more humid areas. Terrific eye-catching plants where they are comfortable.

**Cultivars:**

'Album' has white flowers.

'Plenum' produces double pink blossoms.

'Roseum' is the most common form and bears pink-rose flowers with deeper rose veins. 'Bishop's Form' bears rose-pink flowers and is likely the same thing.

**Related Species:**

*E. chrysanthum* is a diminutive, tufted, 6″ tall plant with silvery hairy leaves and yellow flowers. Native to Greece, plants don't do well unless very well-drained and dry sites are provided. Plants are also of interest because they are diocious, meaning that male and female flowers occur on different plants. A pink flowered form has become recently available. Hardy in zone 6–9.

*E. guttatum* grows about 6″ tall on short woody stems and produces pale pink to white flowers. Two of the petals have deep purple blotches.

Quick Key to Erodium Species:

    A. Plants generally taller than 12″, flowers occur
       in many-flowered inflorescences . . . . . . . . . . . *E. manescavii*
    AA. Plants less than 12″ tall, flowers borne singly . . . *E. reichardii*

*Eryngium* (e-rinj-ee′ um)        Sea Holly        Apiaceae

Of the 100 or so species, only two or three are used in North America. This is a shame because some of the species in commerce are not particularly ornamental compared with some that are not available. The roots of the European sea holly, *E. maritimum*, were reported to have been given to "old and aged people that are consumed and withered with age, and which want natural moisture" and also "amended the defects of nature in the yonger" (Gerard). This species, from which the common name arose, is still available from specialist nurseries and thrives in coastal gardens where sandy soils are common. It may sometimes be found naturalized on the east coast.

Sea hollies tolerate poor, dry soil conditions, including high salt levels, although they also prosper in normal garden soil. They are native to coastal areas, particularly the Mediterranean, although *E. yuccifolium*, rattlesnake master, is native to the eastern United States. The rigid, spiny leaves are often long and narrow in American species, superficially resembling bromeliads. In European species, leaves are frequently rounded or lobed, and often have attractive contrasting white veins. The leaves are more or less sheathed at the base and are usually lobed or deeply cut with spiny margins.

This genus differs from other members of the Apiaceae (formally Umbelliferae) in not having flowers in umbels. The individual flowers are small but are held in dense oblong or roundish heads, which turn bright blue under cool temperatures, as do the supporting bracts and upper stems. The bracts (known as an involucre) range in shades of silver-blue to almost purple and look like the flared collar of an English Beefeater. They are often the most ornamental part of the inflorescence. The terminal flower colors first but persists long enough that the lateral flowers start to color while the terminals still look fresh. The sea hollies are usually thought of as large plants, and while *E. agavifolium* and *E. pandanifolium* can be up to 6' and 10' tall respectively, *E. varifolium* is only about 18" tall. Most of the common species are 2-3' tall.

Spinyness varies greatly among species, but flat sea holly, *E. planum*, is probably the least offensive, while the dense barbs on the flowers and foliage of *E. spinalba* and *E. tricuspidatum* do not beckon friendship.

Full sun is preferable because plants will be more open and not as intensely colored in partial shade. In areas of warm nights, the catalog-blue color never really occurs, because the intensity of color is dependent on the persistence of cool nights. Many plantlets are produced at the base of the mother plant. Separating the plantlets is the easiest method of propagation. Buying seed is usually a waste of money because the seed goes into dormancy rather quickly and 1-2 years may be required for germination. A 55% germination rate was obtained with seeds of *E. planum* collected fresh and sown within two weeks, but germination plummeted to 5% or less after 3 months. I do not know if this is true of all species but suspect it is a problem with many.

Quick Reference to Eryngium Species

|  | Height (ft.) | Shape of basal leaves |
|---|---|---|
| *E. alpinum* | 1-2 | Heart-shaped |
| *E. amethystinum* | 1-1½ | Pinnately divided |
| *E. bourgatii* | 1-2 | Palmate, 3-5 parted |
| *E. giganteum* | 4-6 | Heart-shaped |
| *E. planum* | 2-3 | Heart-shaped |
| *E. varifolium* | 1-2 | Rounded |
| *E. yuccifolium* | 2-4 | Strap-like |

-*alpinum* (al-pine' um)      Alpine Sea Holly      1-2'/2'
     Summer      Blue      Europe      Zones 4-7

The slightly toothed basal leaves are heart shaped, while the upper leaves are 3-lobed or palmately divided. The flower head is oblong, like a pineapple, and one of the bluest of the sea hollies. The upper part of the stem also turns a dark blue. Twelve to 18 finely divided, rather soft involucre bracts prominently extend from the flower head and give this species its marvelous ornamental value. The flower and associated involucre look like exploding fireworks. The involucre of immature flowers are almost white, then become bluer with age. For flower power, this is the best species.

Plant in full sun and well-drained soil. It is a popular cut flower and lasts for at least 2 weeks in water. If the terminal flowers are cut, the side branches reach flowering maturity earlier.

**Cultivars:**

'Amethyst' is 2½–3' tall with metallic light blue bracts and serrated foliage.

'Blue Star' has been popular because it has been one of the few cultivars available from seed, even though half the seed may never come up. Plants grow 2–3' tall and bear large lavender-blue involucres.

'Opal' is 2' tall and bears more silvery-blue flowers than 'Amethyst'.

'Slieve Donart', named for the fine Irish nursery, has handsome light blue bracts around dark blue flowers.

'Superbum' has large dark blue flowers on 2–3' tall stems.

**Related Species:**

Some magnificent hybrids with *E. alpinum* have been produced, but may be difficult to locate in the United States.

*E.* × *oliverianum* is a 3' tall hybrid which is likely the result of crosses between *E. giganteum*, *E. alpinum*, and *E. planum*. It bears pale blue, 1½" long flower heads and stiff involucre bracts. The foliage is deeply cut, often with white veins, adding to the ornamental value of the hybrid.

*E.* × *zabelii* is a magnificent hybrid and is probably a cross between *E. alpinum* × *E. bourgatii*. It grows 1½' tall and has 1–2" long flower heads with 10–12 long rigid lavender-blue bracts. 'Donard Blue' produces extra large flowers on 2' tall plants, 'Spring Hills' has long lavender bracts and is quite special, and 'Jewel' and 'Violetta' bear light and dark blue involucres respectively. Fortunately, this wonderful hybrid has become much more available in this country.

*-amethystinum* (a-me-thist-eye' num)   Amethyst Sea Holly   1–1½'/2'
Summer   Blue   Europe   Zones 2–8

This is one of the most cold hardy species and one of the most common in North America. The basal leaves are pinnately parted and differ from those of most of the other common species. The stems branch near the top, and bear many small (½–¾" long) flowers. The 7–8 involucre bracts are much longer than the flower heads and sharply pointed. The color is a steely blue and the flower stem is also deeply colored, adding a good deal of interest to the garden. Its cold hardiness allows plants to be used where others can not be grown successfully.

**-*bourgatii*** (bour-gat' ee-aye)     Mediterranean Sea Holly     1–2'/2'
    Summer        Blue-Green     Pyrenees        Zones 5–7

An excellent compact plant, this underused species has palmately cut foliage resembling a hand with 3–5 fingers. The dense, coarse foliage has conspicuous silver-white veins and is grayer than most species. Leaves are entire or with 1–2 pairs of spiny teeth. The flowers are ovoid and subtended by 12–18, silver, lance-like, spiny involucal bracts which are much longer than the flower head. The ¾ " long flowers are silver-blue to blue-green and borne on wiry stems which, associate well with the silvery venation of the foliage. This is a good garden plant, although a little too spiny for my liking, and quite useful in the main garden.

**-*giganteum*** (gi-gan' tee-um)     Miss Wilmot's Ghost     3–6'/4'
    Summer        Blue        Caucasus        Zones 4–7

For those gardeners who want a large-flowered, rather large plant, get out your shovels. The oval 3–4" long flowers are subtended by 8 or 9 rigid, long toothed, silvery white involucal bracts. The spineless basal leaves are deeply heart-shaped and entire. The leaves are pale green in color and consort well with other plants. The silvery flowers and pale green color give the plants a rather ghost-like appearance. They are biennial and flower in the spring to early summer of the second year.

Ellen Wilmot was beautiful, enormously wealthy, and not one to trouble much about the sensibilities of others. At her peak in the early 1900's, she would walk around the gardens of friends, neighbors, or nurseries, and surreptitiously scatter the seed of plants which she felt were unjustifiably missing. One her favorite additives was *E. giganteum*, and the conclusion of her forays was a great deal of head-scratching by those she visited, wondering where all those ghostly plants came from. The charming result was that plants became known as Miss Wilmot's Ghost. In my garden, all I ever have visit is The Chickweed Ghost. This can be a most lovely plant but looks rather menacing. Provide sufficient room and protect from winds. I have been unsuccessful in establishing Ellen's plant in the Armitage garden, but it seems to do just fine further north.

Seeds germinate easily where plants are happy, and may pop up here and there. To reduce the size of this plant, use it in containers where root restriction will control overall growth.

**Related Species:**
    *E.* × *tripartitum* is a 3½–4' tall hybrid of unknown origin. Plants bear massive numbers of metallic blue flowers. The basal leaves are 3 lobed and

coarsely toothed and nearly all the leaves have a gray venation color. The 6–9 involucre bracts are twice as long as the base of the flowers. Probably hardy in zones 5–8.

| *-planum* (plane' um) | | Flat Sea Holly | 2–3'/3' |
|---|---|---|---|
| Summer | Blue | Eastern Europe | Zones 5–8 |

The silver-blue flower heads are small (½–¾"), oval, and numerous. The 6–8 involucal bracts are about the same size or slightly longer than the flower head. The scalloped basal leaves are heart-shaped and not spiny. This is not as ornamental as *E. alpinum* and less ornamental than most of the species listed. However, it does well under conditions of heat and humidity and is an excellent long lasting cut or dried flower.

Interestingly, it is a more popular export flower in some countries than *E. alpinum*. The small flower heads ship well and more stems may be placed in each shipping box.

### Cultivars:

'Blue Cap' ('Blaukappe') bears deep blue flowers on 2' tall plants.

'Blue Diamond' is a dwarf form selected for the deep blue flowers. Not a great deal different than the next form.

'Blue Dwarf' ('Blauerzwerg') is similar to the species but grows 15–18" high.

'Blue Ribbon' has larger flowers, almost appearing to be double. Plants grow about 2' tall.

'Silver Stone' has creamy white flowers and stands 3–4' tall.

| *-varifolium* (var-ee' fol-ee-um) | | Moroccan Sea Holly | 1–2'/2' |
|---|---|---|---|
| Summer | Silver-Blue | Morocco | Zones 5–8 |

Another unused, rather unknown species, this is a delightful garden plant. It is one of the few evergreen members of the genus and is also unusual in that the leaves are as striking as the flowers. The small, rounded, spiny leaves have conspicuous white veins and appear variegated. The round flower heads are small but showy with narrow involucres of white-blue bracts. The small size allows it to be used in areas where some of the other species may be too large.

### Related Species:

*E. serbicum* looks more dangerous than it is, bearing soft spines on the palmately cut dark basal green leaves. The spines get tougher as the leaves move up the stem. The flowers are blue but there are only 5–7 very narrow silvery white bracts beneath.

*Eryngium planum*
(81%)

**-yuccifolium** (yuk-i-fo-lee' um)          Rattlesnake Master          3–4'/3'
   Summer          Creamy Chartreuse          United States          Zones 5–9

There are numerous native sea hollies in this country, but this is the only one which has enjoyed any semblance of popularity. Native from New Jersey to Minnesota, and south to Texas and Florida, plants relish a wide range of habitats. Plants grow up to 6' tall but 3–4' is more common. The stiff, narrow leaves with their unbranched parallel veins led to the yucca-like species name. Along the margins are widely spaced bristle. The creamy white flower heads are button-like, and the bracts are insignificant. All in all, they don't provide a great deal of color. They are fun to grow more for the habit and yucca-like foliage than the flowers. The common name comes from the belief that plants could cure rattlesnake bites or even drive them away. Fat chance.

Propagate from seed.

**Related Species:**

*E. agavifolium* has foliage which resembles that of the common agave, and similar to, but much spinier than *E. yuccifolium*. Although the flowers are a little bluer, they won't keep the rattlesnakes away from the posy patch. A few other similar species which can be confusing are *E. bromeliifolium*, which is taller than *E. agavifolium* and, of course, resembles a bromeliad, and *E. serra*, whose bright green vases of sword-like foliage also resembles an agave. These plants have a definite identity crisis.

*E. proteiflorum* is another species which is deeply envious of other forms of plant life. The flowers really do look like proteas, mainly because the flower head is brownish, while the 15–30 stiff bracts are white to light blue. The spiny foliage is deeply cut. Native to Mexico, performs in zones 7–9.

Quick Key to Eryngium Species

   A. Leaf veins parallel . . . . . . . . . . . . . . . . . . . *E. yuccifolium*
  AA. Leaf veins branched
      B. Basal leaves heart-shaped or rounded, not deeply cut
        C. Leaves conspicuously white-veined,
          plants 1–2' tall . . . . . . . . . . . . . . . . . . *E. varifolium*
       CC. Leaves not white-veined, plants 2–6' tall
          D. Plants 5–6' tall, biennial in nature . . . . . . *E. giganteum*
         DD. Plants 2–3' tall, perennial in nature
            E. Flower heads small (½–1"), involucal bracts
               as long or slightly longer than flower head . . *E. planum*
            EE. Flower heads large (1–1½"), involucal
               bracts much longer than flower head . . . . *E. alpinum*
     BB. Basal leaves deeply lobed or divided
        C. Leaves palmately 3–5 parted . . . . . . . . . . . *E. bourgatii*
       CC. Leaves pinnately parted . . . . . . . . . . . . *E. amethystinum*

**Additional Reading:**
Lloyd, C. 1994. Enigmatic eryngiums. *The Garden* 119(8):376–379.

## *Erysimum* (e-ri′ si-mum)    Wallflower    Brassicaceae

All the plants commonly grown as wallflowers, which were previously encountered under the genera *Cheiranthus* and *Erysimum*, have now been lumped under this one genus (also see *Cheiranthus*). This is a good thing because I never could tell the difference between the two. I can't even tell the differences between various species of the old *Erysimum*, let along the new expanded one. In the old breakdown, differences were found in insignificant parts of the flower and within the seed. *Erysimum* has no nectary glands at the base of the stamens, the fruit (silique) is not as flat, and seeds within the fruit are in a single row compared with two rows in the compressed fruit of *Cheiranthus*. In general, plants of *Cheiranthus* bore orange-yellow flowers, but as more of the *Erysimum* species were introduced, it soon became obvious that flower color could not be used to discriminate between the two genera. A small victory for the lumpers in the taxonomic world.

All flowers have four petals and are arranged in a raceme. There are six stamens, but four are longer than the other two. The fruit is a silique (long, narrow, splitting open longitudinally).

Wallflowers are common in the British Isles, Europe, and New Zealand; however, with the exception of a few annuals and one or two short-lived perennials, they have not enjoyed the same popularity in American gardens. This may because of the rather short-lived nature of most species, and their need for well-drained soils and neutral to slightly basic soil. They should be placed in full sun in the North and partial shade in the South. All should be cut back hard after flowering and should not be expected to persist longer than 3 years. Good drainage is a must and many species do much better in alkaline soils rather than acidic ones. In the South, fall plantings result in the best spring performance.

Propagate by seed, division, or cuttings.

Quick Reference to Erysimum Species

|  | Height (in.) | Flower color |
| --- | --- | --- |
| *E.* × *allionii* | 12–24 | Orange-yellow |
| *E. helveticum* | 2–4 | Yellow |
| *E. kotschyanum* | 3–6 | Yellow |
| *E. linifolium* | 12–15 | Purple |

-× **allionii** (al-lee-own-ee' eye)    Siberian Wallflower    12–24"/12"
  Spring      Orange-Yellow       Garden Origin       Zones 4–7

A hybrid of unknown parentage, which forms tufts of foliage and dozens of bright orange flowers with a strong spicy fragrance. The 2–3" long leaves are narrow and coarsely toothed. Plants are best grown as biennials, although they may prove longer lived in cooler climates. They are similar to the more common *E. cheiri*, the common wallflower, but are longer lived, more cold tolerant, and flower a little later.

### Related Species:

*E. cheiri*, common wallflower, is native in southern Europe but has undergone many developments in breeding to develop the "English" wallflowers. Flower color ranges from white to pale yellow through browns and purples. They are generally low growers but some tall forms have been developed for cut flower use. They are less cold tolerant (zone 6 or 7) and are best used as an annual or biennial. (See *Cheiranthus*)

### Hybrids:

Most of the following cultivars are seed-propagated and likely hybrids of various wallflowers, including *E. cheiri*, *E. bicolor*, and *E. sempervirens*. Treat as biennials although some may also perform either as annuals; occasionally as perennials.

'Aunt May' is only about 6" tall, bearing rose-lavender flowers.
'Aurora' has apricot, bronze, orange, and mauve flowers.
'Bredon' is a well-known hybrid with reddish buds and golden-yellow flowers. About 8" tall.
'Butterscotch' has orange flowers.
'Constant Cheer' grows about 15" tall and bears dull rose to amber flowers in late spring. Flowers start brownish orange before turning amber. Long flowering.
'Covent Garden' bears fragrant, deep magenta flowers.
'Golden Bedder' produces dozens on golden flower heads on 9–12" tall plants. This has been an excellent perennial in the Georgia Horticultural Gardens.
'Golden Gem' produces deep yellow flowers on 9–12" tall plants.
'Harper Crewe' is a double-flowered form of *E. cheiri*. One of the oldest wallflowers still in commerce, selected in the 17th century. Very fragrant, often listed as *E.* × *kewensis*.
'Jubilee Gold' has gold flowers over 6" bushy plants. Similar to 'Bredon' but with toothed leaves. One of the shortest forms.
'Plant World Gold' and 'Plant World Lemon' are recent introductions from Ray Brown of Plant World Nursery in Devon, England. They are compact with two-tone flowers. The latter is more subtle than the former.
'Scarlet Bedder' have rich red flowers.

'Turkish Bazaar' bear very fragrant yellow to gold flowers on 6" stems in the spring.

'Wenlock Beauty' produces yellow flowers with a bronze tint.

'Yellow Bird' is about 12" tall with yellow-gold flowers.

'Variegatus' has leaves variegated with cream.

| *-helveticum* (hel-vet-i' kum) | Tufted Wallflower | 2–4"/6" |
|---|---|---|
| Spring          Yellow | Alps | Zones 4–7 |

(Syn. *E. pumilum*)

This little-known species bears many pale yellow, fragrant flowers on tufted compact plants. The basal leaves are narrow, gray-green and somewhat toothed. This is more perennial than most of the other species and should be planted in limy soil in full sun.

Propagate similar to *E. kotschyanum*; however, non-flowering stems may be used for cuttings any time from emergence to midsummer.

**Related Species:**

*E. pulchellum* forms tufts of green foliage, the stems branching at the base. The stem leaves are sessile and the bright golden-yellow flowers are most handsome. More perennial than many others. 'Auranticum' bears flowers which are mauve and yellow.

| *-kotschyanum* (kot-shy-aye' num) | Kotschy Erysimum | 3–6"/12" |
|---|---|---|
| Spring          Yellow | Asia Minor | Zones 6–8 |

This excellent rock garden plant grows in compact tufts and is covered with bright yellow flowers in the spring. The ½" long basal leaves are narrow and finely toothed. The ½" long flowers are carried in crowded racemes and are not only pretty, but also pleasantly fragrant. They grow well in full sun in cracks and crevices in walls and rock gardens. Plants perform well as far south as zone 8 if planted in the fall; however, summer heat and humidity result in decline and plants seldom recover.

Seed sown in a warm (70–75° F) environment begin to germinate within two weeks. Germination is erratic, however, and seedlings may continue to appear over a 4–6 week period. Two inch long terminal cuttings may be taken immediately after flowering or in the fall.

**Cultivars:**

'Orange Flame' is about 6" tall and produces orange-yellow flowers in the spring. Not much different from the species other than its name.

**Related Species:**

*E. hieraciifolium* (syn. *E. alpinum*), alpine wallflower, has woody stems and bright yellow flowers on 9–12" tall plants. I was impressed by the brightness of these plants at Tony Avent's terrific nursery, Plant Delights, in Raleigh, NC.

*-linifolium* (line-i-fo' lee-um)          Flax Wallflower          12–15″/12″
   Spring          Purple          Spain          Zones 5–8

One of the larger species, it can be used as an edging specimen but is equally at home cascading from rock walls. The narrow leaves are gray-green, entire, and evergreen if winters are not too severe. The ¾″ long flowers are held in a dense raceme well above the foliage and the purple color is particularly brilliant in the early spring. The stems are woody and as plants age, they become like little shrubs.

Although plants are not long-lived (2–3 years), I consider them "no-brainers" for southern gardens and excellent early planted species for all gardeners.

Propagate similar to *E. kotschyanum*.

**Cultivars:**

'Bowles' Mauve' is named for one of the greatest English amateur gardeners, Edward Augustus Bowles, and is probably the best known of the many plants that bear his name. Plants have longer flower heads and are clearer purple than the type. In the Armitage garden (zone 7b), the leaves are evergreen and the flower buds appear in the winter, culminating in brilliant purple flowers in late winter and early spring.

'Variegatum' has white-variegated foliage and lilac flowers. A particularly handsome form.

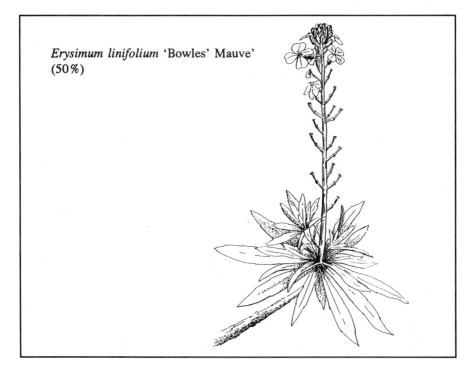

*Erysimum linifolium* 'Bowles' Mauve'
(50%)

**Related Species:**

*E. purpureum*, purple wallflower, is difficult to tell from *E. linifolium*. Generally, they are shorter (about 12″ tall) with smaller leaves. However, they have the same handsome gray-green foliage and purple to violet flowers held in long racemes. Not as cold hardy as 'Bowles' Mauve'.

Quick Key to Erysimum Species

    A. Flowers yellow or orange-yellow
      B. Plants very dwarf, 2–4″ tall . . . . . . . . . . . . *E. helveticum*
     BB. Plants taller, 6–15″ tall
        C. Flowers large, orange-yellow, 4–6″ tall . . *E. kotschyanum*
       CC. Flowers large, bright orange, 12–24″ tall . . . *E. × allionii*
   AA. Flowers mauve, not yellow or orange . . . . . . . . *E. linifolium*

## *Erythronium* (e-rith-roan′ ee-um)       Trout Lily       Liliaceae

Trout lilies consist of approximately 25 species, most of which are handsome in flower and foliage. Plants arise from small pointed fleshy corms and are tolerant of severe weather conditions. They are usually used in woodland or wild flower areas, and are particularly suitable for naturalizing in shade or near streams where moisture is constantly available. Some of the species are very cold hardy and most, but not all, have mottled leaves. The name *Erythronium* came from the Greek *erythos*, red, a reference to the leaf mottling. In general, the plant bears 2 leaves, one narrower than the other, although up to 4 leaves may sometimes be formed. The nodding flowers are borne singly or in twos or threes and the anthers protrude well away from the reflexed petals. The fruit which is formed in early summer, is a green capsule. The American species usually have yellow or white flowers, while European species are red or purple.

Many common names have been applied to species in the genus. The first species to be named had long, white, shiny tuberous roots resembling canine teeth and was called denscaninus, or dog-tooth violet. The term violet was used at the time for many small purple-flowered plants. That particular species is now known as *E. dens-canis*, a native of central Europe. The mottled leaves have given rise to the common names of trout lily, fawn lily, and adder's tongue.

Quick Guide to Erythronium Species

|  | Height (in.) | Flower color | Mottled leaves |
|---|---|---|---|
| *E. albidum* | 6–12 | White | Yes |
| *E. americanum* | 6–9 | Yellow | Yes |
| *E. dens-canis* | 4–6 | Purple | Yes |
| *E. grandiflorum* | 12–24 | Yellow | No |
| *E. revolutum* | 10–16 | Varied | Yes |

*-albidum* (al' bi-dum)  White Trout Lily  6–12″/9″
Late Spring  White  Eastern North America  Zones 4–8

One of the latest species to flower, the 1½″ long drooping blossoms are a lovely clear white, with a tinge of yellow at the base. The elliptical 4–6″ long leaves are occasionally mottled with silver-green, but under heavy shade, little mottling is apparent. This species recently came into commercial propagation and is more available than previously. Plant in light shade and provide adequate soil moisture. One of the few species to have stoloniferous roots, significant colonies are formed, albeit slowly, within 3–5 years.

Propagation by seed is slow and frustrating, particularly if not fresh. Keep seed warm (70–75° F) and moist for 2–4 weeks, cool seed to 30–35° F for 4–6 weeks and then raise temperatures again to 75° F. This sequence may be done naturally through the cycles of fall, winter, and spring. Place the seed flats outside in the fall in an area which will not fall below 25° F, such as a cold frame. A covering of snow will do the same thing. Seedlings appear in the spring as temperatures rise. Three to four years are required to obtain flowering plants from seed. Offsets may also be taken from mature plants. Offsets require 2 years to produce flowering plants.

*-americanum* (a-me-ri-kay' num)  American Trout Lily  6–9″/9″
Late Spring  Yellow  Eastern North America  Zones 3–8

This common trout lily is found in damp woodlands and pastures from Nova Scotia to Florida. Two dark, glossy green, 3–8″ long leaves mottled with brown and purple markings appear in early spring. The 1–2″ wide, nodding, pale yellow flowers are occasionally tinged with purple and are borne singly, opening about the same time as *E. albidum*. The anthers, sometimes a means of distinguishing species from each other, are usually yellow to brownish. Additional studies found that plants are tetraploids with 48 chromosomes rather than the usual 24 found in most other species.

It is also known as common trout lily, fawn lily, and yellow adder's tongue because of the leaf markings. Partial shade and adequate soil moisture must be provided. More nursery-propagated plants are becoming available, hopefully reducing the number of plants being wrenched from the wild. Each bulb produces abundant stolons and plants multiply readily.

Propagate similar to *E. albidum*.

### Related Species:

*E. umbilicatum* is similar to *E. americanum*, bearing yellow flowers and mottled leaves. It differs morphologically due to the absence of a tooth-like structure at the base of the petals found in *E. americanum*. Bulbs do not produce as many stolons and are less likely to fill in as rapidly.

***-dens-canis*** (dens-kay' nus)  Dog Tooth Violet  4-6"/6"
Spring  Purple  Central Europe  Zones 2-7

This is the most common species in Europe and has been cultivated since 1598. This short, early-flowering species has a more limited southern range than the American trout lily, but is more winter hardy. The 4-6" long lanceolate leaves are variable but often heavily splotched with dull crimson, through which rise the solitary 2" long flowers. The tepals (petals and sepals look alike) of the nodding rose-purple flowers are narrow with sharply reflexed tips and purple stamens. Flower color ranges from pink to deep purple, but all flowers have a ring of red-purple markings around the base. Many cultivars have been selected over the years, although they are seldom seen outside botanical gardens.

Propagate similar to *E. albidum*. Cultivars must be vegetatively propagated.

**Cultivars:**

'Charmer' has white flowers mottled with crimson on 8-12" tall plants.

'Lilac Wonder' has large muted lilac flowers with a small brown spot at the base of each segment.

'Pink Perfection' is early flowering, and has clear pink flowers larger than the species.

'Purple King' is a particularly eye-catching cultivar. Mauve flowers are edged with white and centers are marked with dark brown spots.

'Snowflake' has pure white flowers.

'White Splendour' has white flowers larger than the species.

***-grandiflorum*** (grand-i-flo' rum)  Lambstongue Trout Lily  12-24"/18"
Spring  Yellow  Western United States  Zones 5-8

Plants are native to the Cascade Range of northwestern California and Oregon and north into Washington, and one of the more difficult species to establish. This early-flowering species has large golden yellow star-shaped flowers with dark red or maroon anthers. They may be up to 2" long and held in 2-6 flowered racemes. The 4-8" long elliptical leaves are dark green and unmottled. The size of the flowers is arresting and the lack of leaf mottling seems to make the flowers even brighter. Plants are less tolerant to warm, humid climates than many others.

**Cultivars:**

'Albiflorum' has white flowers tinged with green.

Var. *candidum* has greenish to creamy white flowers with white anthers and a yellow interior.

'Parviflorum' has cream-colored anthers instead of the normal crimson color.

**Related Species:**

*E. tuolumnense* is also native to California and produces 4-8 golden-yellow flowers above unmottled yellow-green foliage. Flowers are up to 3"

407

wide and persist for about 2 weeks. Similar to *E. grandiflorum*, but has yellow rather than red anthers.

| | | |
|---|---|---|
| *-revolutum* (re-ve-loo' tum) | Mahogany Trout Lily | 10–16"/10" |
| Spring    Rose-Pink | Western North America | Zones 5–8 |

A favorite, particularly among West Coast gardeners, the mahogany trout lily or coast fawn lily is well adapted to western gardens and reseeds itself vigorously to quickly establish large colonies. The 6–8" long, deep green leaves are mottled with brown and white, and sport crinkled margins. The one or two rose-pink flowers, 3" across and up to 1¾" long, have yellow bands inside the flower and yellow anthers. Although the species is worthy of a place in the garden, several cultivars are much more common than the species.

**Cultivars:**

'Branklyn Form' is a sterile form found in Branklyn Garden in Perth, Scotland. It has not been named or released, but greatly admired by everyone who sees it in March and April.

'Pink Beauty' has reflexed petals of clear pink.

'Rose Beauty' bears rose-pink flowers.

'White Beauty' has creamy white flowers with crimson-brown centers but the petals are less reflexed.

**Related Hybrids:**

'Kondo' has 3–5 large sulphur-yellow flowers shaded brown at the center. Anthers are also yellow.

'Pagoda' has leaves slightly marbled with bronze and pale yellow flowers. This has been growing successfully in the Armitage garden for many years. Each year, the clump gets better but unfortunately, plants have not spread. These excellent hybrids are the result of crosses between *E. revolutum* and *E. tuolumnense*.

Quick Key to Erythronium Species

    A. Flowers yellow
      B. Flowers borne singly, less than 2" across  . . . *E. americanum*
    BB. Flowers borne in groups, larger than 2"
        C. Foliage mottled
          D. Flowers sulphur yellow,
            leaves lightly mottled . . . . . . . . . . . . . *E.* × *kondo*
         DD. Flowers pale yellow, leaves bronze . . . . . *E.* × *pagoda*
      CC. Foliage not mottled . . . . . . . . . . . . . . *E. grandiflorum*
  AA. Flowers not yellow
      B. Flowers white, leaves mottled silver-green . . . . . *E. albidum*
    BB. Flowers purple to pink

C. Flowers solitary, less than 2″ across,
leaves mottled crimson . . . . . . . . . . . . . *E. dens-canis*
CC. Flowers usually in 2's or 3's, larger than 2″
across, leaves mottled white and brown . . . . *E. revolutum*

**Additional Reading:**

Gessert, K.R. 1990. Western fawn lilies. *Horticulture* 68(5):104.

Mathew, B. 1992. A taxonomic and horticultural review of *Erythronium* L. (Liliaceae). *Bot. J. of the Linnean Soc.* 109:453–471.

Parks, C.R. and J.W. Hardin. 1963. Yellow erythroniums of the eastern United States. *Brittonia* 15:245–259.

*Eupatorium* (yew-pa-tor′ ium)     Boneset, Joe-Pye Weed     Asteraceae

A half dozen of the 600 species are common wild flowers in the eastern half of the country and excellent garden plants as well. Easily grown in moist well-drained soils and full sun or partial shade, the larger species reach 7′ in height and may require support. One of our roadside plants, *E. capillifolium*, dog fennel, starts to flower in late September and covers itself in small white flowers throughout the fall. This is a wonderful plant in the wild flower garden, but I respect its toughness even more as I see it smothering cars in junk yards. There should be a law that for every car junked, half a dozen dog fennels should be planted.

*E. hyssopifolium*, also a native with white flowers, is excellent for dry, sandy sites. This native has narrow leaves which occur in whorls up the 4′ tall stems. A more compact selection has been named 'Bubba' by Tony Avent of Plant Delights Nursery. Ol Bubba only grows about 3′ tall. Both *E. capillifolium* and *E. hyssopifolium* are terribly underused, and should at least be found in the wild flower garden. All the Joe-pye weeds are effective because of their late summer and fall flowering and architectural beauty.

Quick Reference to Eupatorium Species

|  | Height (ft.) | Flower color |
| --- | --- | --- |
| *E. cannabinum* | 4–5 | Mauve |
| *E. coelestinum* | 2–3 | Blue |
| *E. purpureum* | 4–7 | Purple |
| *E. rugosum* | 3–5 | White |

| *-cannabinum* (kan-a-been′ um) | Hemp Agrimony | 4–5′/4′ |
| --- | --- | --- |
| Late Summer     Mauve | Europe | Zones 5–8 |

The 5″ long leaves are palmately 3 to 5-lobed and resemble those of *Cannabis,* or so I am told. They are soft, opposite and more or less sessile.

Not seen much in this country, perhaps because of the plethora of useful native species, it nevertheless is a handsome addition to the late-flowering garden. Plants make large clumps, but grow more slowly than many of the native forms. The flat-topped inflorescence consists of many small mauve-pink flowers and like all of the eupatoriums, they are much visited by butterflies and moths.

**Cultivars:**

'Album' is a white-flowered form.

'Flore Pleno' is the best selection in the species with sterile, fully double flowers which persist for weeks on end.

*-coelestinum* (sow-les-teen' um)     Hardy Ageratum          2-3'/36"
    Late Summer          Blue     Eastern United States     Zones 6-10
(Syn. *Conoclinium coelestinum*)

The 2-3" long leaves of hardy ageratum are opposite, triangular, and coarsely toothed. The flower heads consist of up to seventy, ½" wide flowers clustered in dense racemes or corymbs, very similar to the annual *Ageratum*, for which they are named. In fact, at first glance they almost identical. The rhizomatous nature is the best clue to their difference, and plants of *Ageratum* smell when crushed. Because plants steal around by rhizomes, they may become a nuisance and can look rather weedy. Cut them back once or twice during the summer to force additional lateral shoots. With ample water and a sunny location, an outstanding fall show develops. Supporting the plants is helpful to avoid the weedy look, but they flop regardless of supporting technique. Numerous azure blue flowers celebrate the fall season in the garden and they should be welcomed. Often, they have been relegated to the edge of woods or in waste ground; however, they can be quite handsome especially if combined with *Aster tataricus*, *Sedum* × 'Autumn Joy', and other fall bloomers.

Divide plants in the spring every 2-4 years. Seed may require 4-6 weeks of cold moist treatment (35-40° F) if germination does not occur within 3 weeks. Cuttings may also be rooted.

**Cultivars:**

'Album' has white flowers, but is otherwise similar to the species. I saw some wonderful stands at Huntsville Botanical Garden resembling dusky shadows at the edge of the woods.

'Cori' is a selection with clearer blue flowers than the species.

'Wayside Variety' is a little shorter than the species and flowers heavily. I have trialed in the Horticulture Gardens and am impressed with its shorter, less weedy stature.

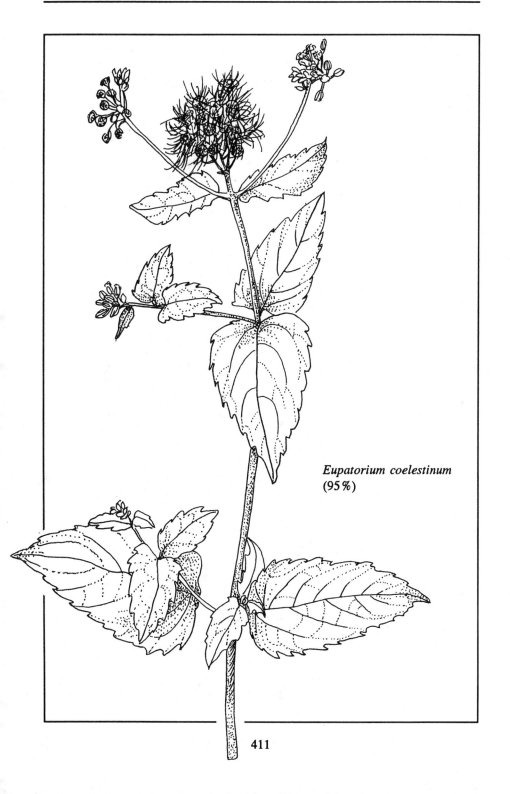

*Eupatorium coelestinum*
(95%)

| *-purpureum* (pur-pewr′ ree-um) | Joe Pye Weed | 4–7′/3′ |
|---|---|---|
| Fall | Purple | Eastern North America | Zones 4–8 |

Although this wild flower occurs from Quebec to southern Maine, to the mountains of north Georgia and as far west as Texas, one must search high and low for its presence in American gardens. On the other hand, it is one of the architectural building blocks of British gardens. People with whom I have travelled overseas in the fall always wonder why our native plant is so well used and cherished there and so scorned and ignored here. Perhaps knowing we can find it on meadows and hills everywhere provides some skewed justification not to use it in our cultivated areas. Plants are tolerant of cold winters, being common throughout the Laurentian mountains and Eastern Townships which encompass Montreal, Quebec on the north and southeast respectively. Joe Pye is said to be an Indian who used these plants to cure typhoid fever. However, the common name, Joe Pye weed, does nothing to enamor it to gardeners. Perhaps Joe Pye plant would be a little better.

The foliage is whorled, generally 3–5 leaves to a whorl, each 8–12″ leaf coarsely serrated and pointed. The leaves have a distinctive vanilla scent when crushed. The stems are hollow, green with purple nodes, and usually not mottled with purple. About 5–7 small purple flowers make up one of the flower heads, but 5–9 flower heads are packed together to make an impressive 12–18″ diameter compound inflorescence.

Plants require abundant water and full sun to be at their best. In shady locations, they become excessively tall. This is a large plant and is not for everyone's small urban garden. However, it should not be relegated to the back pasture. Unfortunately, Joe Pye weed does not tolerate the constant high summer temperatures in my Georgia garden. It is a cool season species and is a better plant for areas where night temperatures remain below 70° F.

Propagate similar to *E. coelestinum*. The divisions have long fibrous roots and a sharp spade is useful when separating the plantlets.

### Cultivars:

Var. *album* is an uncommon, white-flowered form.
'Big Umbrella' grows 7′ tall and 2–3′ wide. Selected by Ernst Pagels of Germany, plant has dark stems and broad flowering heads.

### Related Species:

*E. fistulosum*, hollow Joe Pye weed, differs by having 4–7 whorled leaves attached to the hollow stems. The flower heads consist of 5–8 flowers. Plants grow to 7′ in height. A white-flowered form, 'Album' is occasionally offered under a couple of names. The white form is sold as 'Battered Bride', but I agree with Alan Bush in backing the common name 'Joe Pye's Bride'. Family values, please. The cultivar, 'Gateway', is sometimes included here.

*E. maculatum*, spotted Joe Pye weed, is also known simply as Joe Pye weed. Plants are similar in height and form but have purple speckled and mottled stems rather than green stems as in *E. purpureum*. The flower heads consist of 9–15 flowers compared with 5–7 in *E. purpureum*. It is more cold hardy than *E. purpureum*, extending as far north as zone 3. 'Atropupureum' is a magnificent plant, eye-catching from a distance and impressive close up. It bears purple flowers, leaves, petioles, and upper stems. This is the architectural and color highlight of the fall garden. 'Gateway' is similar but more compact and shorter (although still 5′ tall) than the species.

**-*rugosum*** (roo-go′ sum)      White Snakeroot      3–5′/4′
    Late Summer      White      Eastern North America      Zones 3–7
(Syn. *E. ageratoides*)

This is seldom seen in cultivated gardens but makes an attractive and unusual display if conditions are favorable. The 5–7″ long pointed leaves

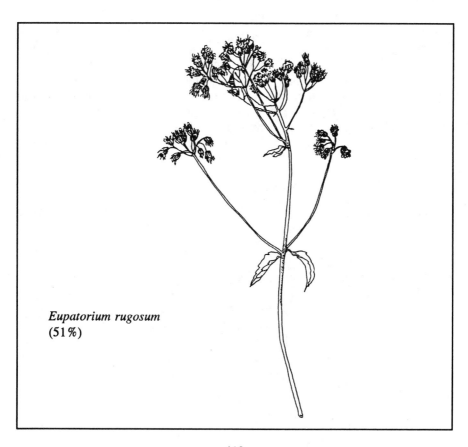

*Eupatorium rugosum*
(51%)

are opposite, ovate, and sharply toothed. The veins on the underside are often slightly hairy. Mature plants are covered with 3-4″ diameter white inflorescences, consisting of 12-24, ¼″ wide flowers arranged in dense corymbs. The flowers are long lasting, persisting well into the fall.

Plants look particularly good at the end of a flower bed where the whole plant may be appreciated, rather than just one side if viewed only from the front. Full sun and well-drained soils are prerequisites for success as well as cool night temperatures. Plants are more shade tolerant than most species of *Eupatorium* and can be used in areas with a few hours of afternoon shade. This is not a good plant south of zone 7 because warm nights result in loss of vigor. Plants should be cut to the ground after flowering.

Propagate similar to *E. coelestinum*.

### Cultivars:

'Braunlaub' has handsome bronze to purple foliage which contrast well with the white flowers.

### Related Species:

*E. lindleyanum*, native to China, is 2-3′ tall and smothered with small creamy white flowers in late summer. The lance-like foliage is whorled and irregularly toothed.

*E. perfoliatum*, common boneset, bears stems which appear to grow through the middle of the narrow, leathery leaves. The flowers are creamy white and open on 4-6′ high stems in late summer. An excellent overlooked native plant. Plant extracts were said to have tonic, cathartic and emetic effects; however, how it would set bones I do not know.

*E. triplinerve*, also smothered in white flowers, has cordate, scalloped leaves and grows 5-6′ tall.

### Quick Key to Eupatorium Species

| | |
|---|---|
| A. Foliage perfoliate | *E. perfoliatum* |
| AA. Foliage not perfoliate | |
|     B. Leaves whorled, flowers purple to pink | |
|         C. Stems mostly green | *E. purpureum* |
|         CC. Stems obviously mottled | *E. maculatum* |
|     BB. Foliage opposite | |
|         C. Flowers blue, height 2-3′ | *E. coelestinum* |
|         CC. Flowers white or mauve, height 3-5′ | |
|             D. Leaves deeply lobed, flowers mauve | *E. cannabinum* |
|             DD. Leaves not lobed, flowers white | *E. rugosum* |

### Additional Reading:

Leslie, A.C. 1993. *Eupatorium coelestinum. The Garden* 118(4):158-160.
Midgley, J. *Eupatorium fistulosum. Native Notes* 5(2):2-5.

## *Euphorbia* (yew-for' bee-a)  Spurge  Euphorbiaceae

Named for Euphorbius, a Greek physician to King Juba II of Mauretania, 1st century AD, who used the latex for medicinal purposes. This large genus contains approximately 2000 species, yet the best known is the greenhouse poinsettia, *E. pulcherrima,* a deciduous shrub reaching heights of 15' in its native habitat. A number of attractive annual species such as *E. heterophylla,* painted spurge, and the white-flowered *E. marginata,* snow-on-the-mountain, make wonderful conversation pieces. Only about 8 or 10 perennials are available and even these are sometimes difficult to find.

None of the species has petals or sepals and the "flowers" are actually highly colored bracts. The true flowers are reduced in the male to a single stamen and in the female to a long stalked ovary. Fused together, they are called a cyathium. Most bracts are yellow but those of *E. corollata,* flowering spurge, are white and petal-like, while *E. griffithii* has orange to red bracts. Another characteristic common to all species is the presence of milky sap, which in some species is poisonous and acrid, especially if it comes into contact with open cuts.

Propagate the herbaceous species by terminal cuttings in midsummer, by division, or by seed.

Quick Reference to Euphorbia Species

|  | Height (in.) | Bract color | Flowering time |
|---|---|---|---|
| *E. amygdaloides* | 12–20 | Yellow | Late Spring |
| *E. characias* | 30–60 | Green-Yellow | Spring |
| *E. corollata* | 12–24 | White | Spring |
| *E. cyparissias* | 12–15 | Yellow | Spring |
| *E. dulcis* | 12–15 | Yellow | Spring |
| *E. epithymoides* | 18–24 | Yellow | Early Spring |
| *E. griffithii* | 24–36 | Red | Summer |
| *E. myrsinites* | 6–9 | Yellow | Spring |
| *E. wallichii* | 24–30 | Yellow | Early Summer |

*-amygdaloides* (a-mig-dal-oi' deez)  Wood Spurge  12–20″/15″
  Late Spring  Yellow  Europe  Zones 5–7

Plants are native from Ireland to Portugal and Algeria, and to woodlands and grassy banks of Turkey and the Caucasus. They prefer moist soils and cool climates. The stems have tufted spoon-shaped (oblanceolate) leaves and the habit is more or less upright. The plant is distinguishable from many others in having purple stems with greenish yellow bracts.

415

Plants do well in full sun or partial shade but are best at higher elevations and where humidity is relatively low. They are susceptible to mildew in warm, wet areas.

## Cultivars:

'Purpurea' ('Rubra') is the most handsome form, bearing deep red stems and bronze foliage, especially when young. Plants come true from seed.

Var. *robbiae* (syn. *E. robbiae*), Robb's spurge, has green-yellow bracts and green foliage. It differs by being rhizomatous, thus making a useful evergreen ground cover by filling in rapidly. The wide spoon-shaped foliage is evergreen and plants are about 2' tall. Plants tolerate dry shade and blend well with a wide assortment of plant material.

'Variegata' has yellow-edged leaves but its reputation is one of being weak and difficult.

| | | | |
|---|---|---|---|
| *-characias* (ka-ra' kee-as) | Mediterranean Spurge | | 3–5'/3' |
| Early Spring    Yellow | Mediterranean | | Zones 6–8 |

Probably one of the most common spurges in European gardens, Americans have also discovered some of its charm along with its persistent nature. The green thick stems are woody at the base and somewhat purplish and the 4–6″ long linear leaves are arranged spirally along its length. Plants can look bare at the base but leaves become more closely spaced near the top. Dozens of green-yellow flowers with purple glands are held in a large inflorescence above the foliage.

Plants look terrific in foliage in the winter and in early spring flower, and except for their size, tend to retreat in the background in the summer. In the south, these are exceptionally handsome plants in the border, but persist no more than 2 years. After flowering, they mysteriously decline, going soft and mussy for no apparent reason. This is also the case a little further north, but seems to happen faster in the south. Fortunately, seedlings appear with regularity and may be moved around the garden. For some gardeners, they have taken on a weed-like status, particularly if all the seedlings are allowed to remain. Beware.

They are full sun plants and will be a little weaker if given too much shade.

## Cultivars:

'Blue Hills' has somewhat blue-green leaves and larger yellow flowers than the species.

'Ember Queen' is a recent introduction with clean green and white variegation on the leaves. It is also sold as 'Variegata'.

Ssp. *wulfenii* is shorter (2–3' tall) and bears similar flowers to the species, although the glands are a little more purple. This is the most common form in gardens and includes a number of interesting cultivars. 'Burrow Silver' is a fine, although slow growing, plant with yellow and green variegated foliage and creamy yellow flowers and golden centers. 'Humpty Dumpty' is shorter (about 2' tall) and more compact with large flower heads and dark red glands. 'Lambrook Yellow', arising from Lambrook Garden in England, bears impressive large green-yellow flowers. 'Lambrook Gold' has golden yellow flowers with blue-green foliage. Both are exceptional.

**Related Species:**

*E. × martinii* is a natural hybrid between *E. amygdaloides* and *E. characias*. They are very similar, but significantly more dwarf, than *E. characias*. The flower heads are not as elongated and the glands are redder than *E. characias*. A good garden plant, more easily used, but similar in longevity to *E. characias*. In the Armitage garden, it was a race to the death between *E. characias* and *E. × martinii*. It was a tie, they succumbed within two weeks of each other. But they surely were wonderful in their youth.

'Jade Dragon' is Dan Heim's cross between *E. characias* ssp. *wulfenii* and *E. amygdaloides* 'Rubra'. The foliage is purple as it emerges and turns green as it matures. The yellow flowers are held in wide inflorescences over compact plants. 'John Tomlinson' resulted from a backcross from *E. characias* to ssp. *wulfenii*. The plants appear robust and the bright yellow, spherical flower heads are very showy.


| *-corollata* (kor-o' lat-a) | | Wild Spurge | 1–3'/2' |
|---|---|---|---|
| Summer | White | Central United States | Zones 5–8 |

One of the few garden-useful native euphorbs, wild spurge is a long flowering species with white bracts at the tip of the radiating branches. Plants are native to the prairies and in dry open woodlands from southeastern South Dakota to southeastern Nebraska, Kansas, and Oklahoma. The star-shaped "flowers" are excellent for cutting and are sometimes known as false baby's breath. Plants bloom from summer to early fall and the foliage turns glossy wine-red at that time.

Full sun and relatively rich soil are needed for best performance.


| *-cyparissias* (sigh-pa-ris' ee-as) | | Cypress Spurge | 1–2'/2' |
|---|---|---|---|
| Spring | Yellow | Europe | Zones 6–8 |

Looking like a dwarf cypress or tiny spruce tree, plants are easily distinguished from most other garden euphorbias. They are stoloniferous and will run if provided with full sun and rich soil. The willowy leaves are blue-green and compact throughout the stem. An old fashioned plant and most handsome where happy. Be forewarned, however, plants can become a nuisance because of their running roots and can be a terrible reseeder as well. They have become naturalized in some western and southern states.

Good drainage is essential, plants grow well in sandy soils or rocky areas.

**Cultivars:**
'Baby' is a dwarf form, only about 1' tall.
'Bush Boy' bears feather-like branches, almost soft to the touch.
'Orange Man' has bright yellow flowers which turn orange in the spring.
'Tall Boy' is over 2' tall.

*-dulcis* (dull' chiss)                                                 12–18"/15"
  Spring             Yellow            Europe              Zones 5–7

The species itself has 1–2" long, succulent, oblong leaves which occasionally have a tinge of purple. The flowers are yellowish green. The plants are handsome enough, but would not have seen the light of popularity if not for the purple-leaved cultivar 'Chameleon'. This increasingly popular form grows in a tight mound, which is a different shape compared to most of the other species. In full sun, the small leaves are deep purple on the outside, but quite green if you look in the interior. In shade, the plants open up and are far less purple. Plants do well in cool climates, but do not perform "according to the picture books" in warm, humid summers. Destined to become a popular plant, mainly because of the interesting foliage color which contrasts well with other plants in the garden.

**Related Hybrids:**
'Excalibur' has purple foliage in the spring which turn green in the summer. Plants are about 3' tall, 2' wide, and bear yellow flowers in late spring.

*-epithymoides* (e-pi-thi-moi' deez)      Cushion Spurge      12–18"/18"
  Early Spring        Yellow       Europe             Zones 4–7
(Syn. *E. polychroma*)

A dazzling plant in early spring, the pale green leaves give way to shiny yellow bracts which light up the early spring garden. When in flower, the clump-forming plants look like yellow cushions. The 2" long, oblong, alternate leaves remain attractive throughout the year if planted in the right conditions, and produce some red fall color.

Cushion spurge tolerates full sun in zones 4 and 5, but even there, protection from afternoon sun is beneficial. Shade is essential in the South. I have grown it in north Georgia in full sun and partial shade—those in full sun performed poorly, while plants in afternoon shade prospered, spread, and lived up to expectations. The habit, however, becomes a little leggy and the clump opens up as the heat of a southern summer progresses. This is especially true after 2–3 years in the garden, at which time it should be repropagated.

Seed germinates irregularly but no special problems are encountered if placed in a warm, humid area. Plants may be carefully divided after 2–3 years. Care must be taken to provide adequate roots on each of the divisions. Two-to 4″ long terminal cuttings may be rooted after flowering is completed. Remove all vestiges of bracts and flowers, insert cutting in equal parts sand:vermiculite, and place in a warm (70–75° F), humid area.

The proper botanical name of this species is constantly in doubt. *E. polychroma*, named by an Austrian, Anton Josef Kerner in 1875, was superseded by *E. epithymoides*, given by Linnaeus, in 1770. Normally the first name takes precedence, and thus *E. epithymoides* should be the correct name. However, that name had been given to another species. Because of this confusion, cushion spurge will be listed by both names for many years to come; choose the one you like and stay with it.

**Cultivars:**

'Emerald Jade' is smaller than the species and has brighter fall color.
'Midas' bears brighter yellow flowers.
'Major' is more compact than the species, resulting in tighter mounds of growth. Flowers are also bright yellow.
'Pilosa Major' was selected for its larger flower heads.
'Purpurea' has purple-suffused foliage which makes a handsome contrast with the yellow foliage.
'Sonnegold' is vigorous with bright yellow flowers.

**Related Species:**

*E. palustris*, grows 2½–3′ tall and bears bright yellow-green bracts from late spring through July. They are vigorous growers which form large clumps from woody rootstocks. The foliage is long and narrow and numerous side branches occur. Plants are tolerant of wet soils and can grow in shallow water. Native throughout Europe, sometimes escaping in the southeast, they perform well in zones 5–7, zone 8 if placed in moist conditions in afternoon shade. Cut back after flowering.

| *-griffithii* (gri-fith′ ee-eye) | Griffith's Spurge | 24–36″/24″ |
|---|---|---|
| Summer          Orange-Red | Himalayas | Zones 5–7 |

I have been very excited about the future of this species ever since it become available in the United States. The mounding habit of the plants is similar to, but much larger than, *E. epithymoides*. The unique characteristic is the many brick-red bracts held above the lance-like mid-green leaves with pale pink midribs. After flowering and when the bracts fade, an attractive herbaceous shrub remains. I have seen good looking colonies in the northeast and far west but, unfortunately, I have had no luck in growing plants in the South. Summers with high heat and humidity result in plants that languish, begging to be put out of their misery.

Partial shade is best, although full sun can be tolerated in the North. As with other species of this genus, it must not be allowed to dry out.

## Cultivars:

'Dixter' arose from the garden of Christopher Lloyd at Great Dixter, Northiam, England, and has red flushed foliage and orange bracts. Flowers are oranger and stems are redder than 'Fireglow'.

'Fern Cottage' bears red stems and red margins on the leaves. Plants are more compact than 'Fireglow'.

'Fireglow' is most common and is similar to the species, but has flame-orange bracts, red midveins, and orange-brown stems. It is particularly attractive in combination with yellow-flowering plants such as Coreopsis.

## Related Species:

*E. seguieriana* bears bracts which are fire engine red, certainly redder than 'Fireglow'. The plant is woody at the base and has light green linear to oblong stem leaves. Plants grow at least 3' tall. The species is native to central and western Europe, east to Siberia, and may possibly be cold hardy to zone 5.

*E. sikkimensis*, native to Nepal, is one of the most handsome species in the garden. Plants grow to 3' in height and form significant colonies. The young shoots are bright red and as the plants mature, turn a duller purple-red color. The leaves have white midribs which results in a notable brightening in the garden. The bright yellow flower heads are large and showy and easily seen from a distance. Flowers are formed in late spring and summer.

*E. schillingii*, Schilling's spurge, also has large bright yellow bracts, but is taller and later to flower than the previous species. Native to the Himilayas, plants are likely hardy in zones 5-7.

| *-myrsinites* (mur-sin-ee′ teez) | | Myrtle Euphorbia | 6-9″/12″ |
|---|---|---|---|
| Spring | Yellow | Southern Europe | Zones 5-9 |

This evergreen trailing plant produces many gray-green sessile leaves in tight spirals along the prostrate stems. The 2-4″ wide flowers, which occur in early spring, are made up of sulphur-yellow bracts at the end of each 8-10″ long stem. The foliage color is an excellent contrast to the bracts. Plants tolerate heat well and have proven excellent for the Southeast. These can get away from even the most patient gardener, filling pathways and byways with little euphobettes. Be tough.

Propagate by seed and cuttings similar to *E. epithymoides*.

| *-wallichii* (wall-ich′ ee-eye) | | Wallich Spurge | 24-30″/18″ |
|---|---|---|---|
| Early Summer | Yellow | Himalayas | Zones 6-9 |
| (Syn. *E. longifolia*) | | | |

The 4-6″ diameter yellow-green bracts occur in groups of three and encircle the small flowers. Combined with the large eye-catching bracts are lanceolate dark-green leaves with clear white midribs. Although tolerant of full sun, plants do best with some afternoon shade and abundant water. Given these conditions, plants will remain attractive all season.

Seed may require a cold treatment (35–40° F) for 4–6 weeks prior to placing in a warm area for germination. Propagate by cuttings similar to *E. epithymoides*.

**Related Species:**

*E. lathyris*, caper or gopher spurge, is an unusual looking spurge, with pointed white-midribbed leaves and small greenish bracts. Each solitary flower gives rise to a capsule which superficially looks like a caper (the unopened bud of a caper bush, used in cooking), thus its common name. It has reseeded in the Armitage garden and pokes its way through the baptisias. Not a bad combination. In my curiosity about capers, I read Susan's cook book which specifically told me not to confuse them with fruit of the caper spurge, which are poisonous. Good thing! Plants are biennial but can grow 2–3' tall. They reseed everywhere and are thought to repel moles, voles, and gophers from the garden. Whether they do is debatable, but gardeners looking for any remedy to these burrowing rodents tend to leave nothing to chance.

Quick Key to Euphorbia Species

    A. Bracts yellow
        B. Plants generally taller than 18″
            C. Plants taller than 30″ . . . . . . . . . . . . . . . . *E. characias*
            CC. Plants shorter than 30″
                D. Midribs of leaves white, plant
                    habit upright, bracts large . . . . . . . . . . . *E. wallichii*
                DD. Midribs not conspicuously white,
                    habit domed, bracts small . . . . . . . . *E. epithymoides*
        BB. Plants usually less than 18″ tall
            C. Stems often purplish
                D. Stem leaves oblong, with short petioles . . . . . *E. dulcis*
                DD. Stem leaves oblanceolate, sessile . . . . *E. amygdaloides*
            CC. Stems green, not purple
                D. Leaves linear, less
                    than 2″ long, habit upright . . . . . . . . . *E. cyparissias*
                DD. Leaves obovate, arranged in
                    close spirals around stem . . . . . . . . . . *E. myrsinites*
    AA. Flowers not yellow
        B. Bracts orange to reddish . . . . . . . . . . . . . . . *E. griffithii*
        BB. Bracts white . . . . . . . . . . . . . . . . . . . . . *E. corollata*

**Additional Reading:**

Anon. 1993. Elegant hardy euphorbias. *Avant Gardener* 25(6):46.
Anon. 1994. Growing. *Garden Design* 13(3):26–27.

Rodriguez, A. 1993. A survey of succulent euphorbias. *The Plantsman* 14(4):204–233.

Turner, Roger. 1983. A review of spurges for the garden. *The Plantsman* 5(3):129–161.

## *Euryops* (ew-ree′ ops)  Euryops  Asteraceae

The genus consists of about 100 species of mostly tender, woody shrubs or herbaceous plants, but only one or two are occasionally seen in gardens. Much of the recent interest in the most popular species, *E. pectinatus*, has come from the many gardeners who travel to the British Isles. They discover plants at Sissinghurst, Powys Castle, Kew, or Wisley and see how wonderful this subshrub can be when provided with good growing conditions. The deep green deeply divided foliage makes an outstanding contrast with the bright yellow daisy flowers. Plants grow 3–4′ tall and are about 3′ across. They are best displayed in containers where drainage is well controlled.

Unfortunately, few places in this country show off euryops as well as such gardens in the British Isles. Except for gardeners on the west coast and in zones 8–10, plants are not sufficiently cold tolerant to be considered a perennial. While they certainly have no trouble surviving hot summers, flowering is poor in the hot summer months. Plants flower longer in the north, and look good in the spring and fall in the south. The foliage is probably the best feature of the plant, so if flowering is sparse, one need not despair. However, do as the Brits do and plant them in large containers in full sun or in an area with afternoon shade.

Another possible choice for containers or well drained areas of the garden is a low growing species, *E. acraeus*, likely hardy to zone 7. It is about half the height of the previous species and tends to be more spreading. Flowers are bright yellow, and plants may be trimmed back after flowering.

### Additional Reading:

Sperry, N. 1993. Tropical storm Texas. *Neil Sperry's Garden* 7(7):26–28.

# F

## *Festuca* (fes-too' ca)　　　　　　Fescue　　　　　　Poaceae

Almost all turf mixtures have at least some fescue grass in their composition; however, many gardeners are unaware of the potential beauty of some of the members in this large (over 300 species) genus. They prefer full sun and well-drained soils, although, as can be expected in a genus this large, exceptions occur. *F. gigantea*, giant fescue, is more tolerant of shade, while *F. vivipiaria* prefers moist conditions and does well at the edge of lakes or streams. Some of the most ornamental garden forms are character-ized by their blue foliage (*F. amethystina*, *F. cinerea*) although *F. tenuifolia*, fine-leaved fescue, has beautiful green, narrow foliage. The diminutive size and need for good drainage of many of the cultivars suggest that they are best suited for containers or rock gardens.

In general, the leaves are flattened and the flowers are held in narrow panicles. Most of the ornamental forms are relatively short (less than 2' tall) although *F. californica*, California fescue, and *F. gigantea*, can easily reach 3'. Fescues are poor grasses for southern gardens but perform well in cool climates where winters are not too severe and summers are moderate.

A great deal of confusion exists as to the proper names of some of the garden species, and the same plants are likely sold under two or three different names. But what else is new? The same is true for many other species and cultivars as well. Certainly the most popular group of fescues are the blue-foliage forms, sold as cultivars of *F. glauca*, *F. ovina* and *F. cinerea*. Botanically there are few enough differences between them, and horticulturally even fewer. They are all short (6–18" tall) clump formers which perform well in cool seasons. Heat is an anethma to all the blue-leaf grasses, resulting in summer dormancy or even death, particularly if rainfall is plentiful. From the garden perspective, find a well-drained sunny location, plant a grouping of about four to six plants, and plan on replanting every 2–3 years.

The oldest selection is probably *F. cinerea*, better known as *F. ovina* 'Glauca', which has been propagated from seed for many years. Thus, foliage ranges from deep blue to a washed out gray-blue color. Recently, numerous cultivars have been selected and propagated vegetatively to maintain the subtle differences between them. While good old Ovina Glauca is handsome, nearly all the new material is an improvement. Having arisen from European nurseries, they often carry several names.

Propagate the species by seed; cultivars by division.

**Blue leaved cultivars and hybrids:**

'April Gruen' ('April Green') grows about 8–12″ tall with olive-green foliage and handsome flowers. Likely a cultivar of *F. amethestina*.

'Azurit' has blue-gray foliage and is taller than most, growing to about 18″ in height.

'Blaufink' ('Blue Finch') bears fine textured dull blue leaves.

'Blausilber' ('Blue Silver') is a handsome, fine textured form with silvery blue leaves. A planting at Longwood Gardens was particularly effective.

'Daeumling' ('Tom Thumb') only grows 4–6″ tall. The blue foliage may fade to green as the season progresses.

'Elijah Blue' is my favorite, bearing soft blue leaves and growing 12″ tall. Even in flower, this is a handsome form. I saw this at the home of Dennis Mareb of Windy Hill Farm in late July, and it was outstanding.

'Fruehlingsblau' ('Spring Blue') has narrow intense blue foliage and grows 8–10″ tall.

'Harz' bears medium textured olive green foliage, sometimes tinted plum at the tips in the summer.

'Meerblau' ('Sea Blue') is more blue-green than many others. Medium textured, strong grower.

'Platinat' ('Platinum') has blue leaves with a tint of green. Grows 8–12″ tall.

'Seeigel' ('Sea Urchin') produces fine silvery blue leaves.

'Silberreiher' ('Silver Egret', 'Silver Heron') bears silvery blue foliage on 6–12″ tall plants.

'Soehrenwald' has olive-green leaves.

'Solling' is blue-gray, grows about 10″ tall, and was selected for its lack of flowering.

'Superba' is a fine-textured form of *F. amethystina*, with weeping blue-green foliage and ornamental pink flowers in the spring.

## *Filipendula* (fil-i-pen′ dew-la)     Meadowsweet     Rosaceae

This genus of nine or ten species was originally part of the genus *Spiraea* and is still frequently referred to as false spirea. Plants have alternate, pinnately or palmately lobed foliage and panicles of many small white or pink flowers. The genus name comes from *filum*, thread, and *pendulus*, hanging, and alludes to the root tubers hanging on the fibrous roots of *F. hexapetala* (now *F. vulgaris*), the species after which the genus is named. Most species are found in moist areas in nature and should be grown where high moisture levels can be maintained. The exception to this is *F. vulgaris,* which is more drought tolerant than the others.

Plant in alkaline soil (pH 7.0–7.5) in full sun to partial shade. Flowers appear in early summer. Propagate by division in fall, or by seed.

Quick Guide to Filipendula Species

|  | Height (ft.) | Flower color |
|---|---|---|
| *F. palmata* | 3–4 | Pink |
| *F. rubra* | 6–8 | Pink |
| *F. ulmaria* | 3–6 | White |
| *F. vulgaris* | 2–3 | White |

| **-palmata** (pahl-may' ta) | Siberian Meadowsweet | 3–4'/3' |
|---|---|---|
| Summer          Pink | Siberia | Zones 3–7 |
| (Syn. *Spiraea palmata*) | | |

The 4–8″ wide coarse leaves are palmately divided into 3–5 sections. The leaves are white and hairy beneath. A multitude of 6″ wide flattened heads (corymbose panicles) of pale pink flowers rise above the foliage in June, and turn white as they mature. Although the flowers only persist for 2–3 weeks, they make a wonderful show. In north Georgia, flowering begins at the end of May, and about 2 weeks later in zone 6.

This is an excellent garden species which lends a bold texture to the garden, remaining attractive all season if moisture is constant. However, if allowed to dry out, the margins of the leaves turn brown, and if continued, the leaves shrivel up and fall off. Copious amounts of compost or other moisture-retaining material incorporated in the garden is beneficial. I have grown this for years and have always been rewarded with its graceful habit and excellent performance. Plants are very persistent, returning for at least 10 years.

The two drawbacks of this plant are that it must be grown in full sun for best performance, and that it is highly attractive to Japanese beetles.

Propagate by fall division or by seed. Seed germinates within 3 weeks when lightly covered with soil, and placed in warm temperature (70–75° F) and high humidity, although germination is erratic.

**Cultivars:**

'Alba' has cleaner, whiter flowers.

'Elegans' ('Elegantissima') is a excellent performer and is more compact than the type. It has whitish flowers with red stamens, giving the appearance of rose-colored flowers. This is also listed as a cultivar of *F. purpurea.*

'Digitata Nana' ('Nana') is similar to the species but only 8–10″ tall.
'Rosea' bears pink flowers.
'Rubra' produces darker, redder flowers than the species.

### Related Species:

*F. purpurea*, Japanese meadowsweet, has much deeper pink flowers and crimson stems and is spectacular in flower. Probably the most beautiful species in the genus. Each leaf consists of 5–7 serrated, long pointed segments. A little-known white form, 'Alba', is also occasionally offered.

| | | |
|---|---|---|
| *-rubra* (rew′ bra) | Queen-of-the-Prairie | 6–8′/4′ |
| Summer    Pink | Central, Eastern United States | Zones 3–7 |

This native, found from Pennsylvania to Iowa to Georgia, is large and impressive and perhaps the common name is the result of its ability to support itself even in high winds. The size of this most imposing species somewhat limits it to larger gardens. The foliage consists of pinnately divided leaflets; the large 5–8″ long terminal leaflet has 7–9 small lobes and the laterals have 3–5. The lateral leaflets, however, are absent on the upper stem leaves. The pink to peach flowers are arranged in a 6–9″ wide congested panicle with exerted, very conspicuous stamens. This is a classic accent plant.

Propagate similar to *F. palmata*.

### Cultivars:

'Albicans' ('Magnificam Alba') has white cotton candy flowers and is a
little shorter than the type. Flowers open earlier than the species.
'Venusta' ('Venusta Magnifica', sometimes offered as *F. venusta*), is the
most available cultivar and has deep pink to carmine flowers. This is a
55-mph plant, easily seen from a speedy vehicle.

### Related Species:

*F. kamtschatica* is even more vigorous and taller than our native "Queen." The large 12″ wide leaves are dark green and sharply toothed. The white to pale pink flowers occur in large inflorescences at the top of the plants in late summer and early fall. Native to Japan, Manchuria, and Kamchatica, and likely hardy to at least zone 4.

| | | |
|---|---|---|
| *-ulmaria* (ul-mah′ ree-a) Meadowsweet, Queen-of-the-Meadow | | 3–6′/3′ |
| Summer    White    Asia, Europe | | Zones 3–7 |

This large, stout species is midway in size between *F. vulgaris* and *F. rubra*. The leaves consist of large 7–11 toothed leaflets. The leaflets are whitish and hairy beneath. The creamy white flowers are carried above the foliage in a branched, flat 4–6″ wide inflorescence similar to *F. vulgaris*.

Divide similar to *F. palmata*. Seed, however, should be placed in a seed flat at room temperature for about 2 weeks, then cooled for 4–6 weeks at 40° F. After the cool treatment, place at 70–75° F under high humidity.

## Cultivars:

'Aurea' is the best cultivar and is grown for the foliage rather than the flowers. The flowers are rather insignificant but the foliage is a lovely golden yellow. The flowers should be removed as they start to develop to encourage foliage vigor. Discourage the growth of seedlings as they will be green-leaved. The foliage holds up better in cooler climates. About 3' tall.

'Flore Pleno' is also superior to the species. The flowers are double, more showy, and more persistent.

'Variegata' ('Aureo-Variegata') has a central yellow stripe in the foliage, providing contrasting variegated foliage.


| | | | |
|---|---|---|---|
| *-vulgaris* (vul-gah' ris) | | Dropwort | 2–3'/2' |
| Summer | White | Europe | Zones 3–7 |

(Syn. *F. hexapetala*)

The 4–10" long shiny mid-green leaves are pinnately divided into many 1" long leaflets resulting in a somewhat fern-like appearance. The creamy white flowers are borne in many 4–6" diameter branched, flattened inflorescences and are often tinged with pink. I have seen an effective use of the small double form as an effective edging to stone paths. The rootstock is tuberous, allowing an almost ground cover-like habit.

Plants prefer constant moisture but tolerate dry soils. Plant in full sun to partial shade.

Propagate similar to *F. palmata*.

## Cultivars:

'Flore Pleno' is a double-flowered form, usually 1–2' tall and more ornamental than the species.

'Grandiflora' bears larger flowers.

'Rosea' has light pink flowers and is particularly handsome.

### Quick Key to Filipendula Species

    A. Leaflets numerous, small, all nearly alike . . . . . . . *F. vulgaris*
    AA. Leaflets few, terminal the largest
        B. Lateral leaflets 3–5 lobed, flowers usually pink or peach
            C. Leaves hairy beneath, plants usually 3–4' tall . *F. palmata*
            CC. Leaves smooth beneath, plants usually 6–8' tall . . *F. rubra*
        BB. Lateral leaflets few or none, not lobed,
            flowers usually white . . . . . . . . . . . . . . . . . . *F. ulmaria*

## *Foeniculum* (fee-nik′ ew-lum)     Fennel     Apiaceae

A plant for everyone's garden; one which satisfies the environmentalist, the ornamentalist, and the herbalist within us. Two forms of fennel are grown for seasoning and salads. *F. vulgare* var. *azoricum*, is known as Florence fennel or finocchio, and the swollen base of this annual is harvested and served fresh in salads or cooked as a vegetable. Common fennel, *F. vulgare*, native to southern Europe, is offered everywhere and provides light, airy, finely cut foliage and the fragrance of anise. The leaves may be harvested throughout the summer, and, freshly chopped, imparts a unique flavor to the evening salad. Young shoots may also be peeled, chopped, and tossed in. The seeds may also be used, further imparting an anise flavor to bread or salads.

As an ornament in the garden, the cultivar 'Purpurescens', also sold as 'Rubrum', is particularly attractive, providing purple-flushed foliage which earns the plant a garden place regardless of its culinary value. The leaves make a great foil for the light green or variegated foliage of neighboring plants. The other reason some people like to have this plant around is that it is the preferred host for the Swallow-tail butterfly. While I like to watch these beautiful creatures flit about my fennel as much as the next person, I really have not reached the stage of environmental altruism where I enjoy watching the resulting caterpillars voraciously devouring the plant. I suppose the caterpillars are pretty enough, but I am happy to knock them off and give them to my environmental friend with a wildflower (read weeds) meadow. Since then, I gave him the plants as well. Now I enjoy the butterflies while he admires the caterpillars. Works for me. The yellow-green flowers occur in summer in a compound umbel and are quite useful as cut flowers. Fennel has something for everyone and has made the transition from the herb garden to the main garden relatively painlessly. Performs as a perennial in zones 6–9.

Propagate from seed or by dividing established plants.

## *Fragaria* (fra-gah′ ree-a)     Strawberry     Rosaceae

Small fruits and vegetables have become common denizens of the ornamental garden. Purple fennel, asparagus fern, purple sweet potato vine, ornamental kale and highbush blueberries are but a few. The strawberry has been hanging around the fringes of ornamental horticulture for some time. The compact habit of the sweet tasting alpine strawberry, *F. vesca* 'Semperflorens', and its variegated form, 'Variegata', lend themselves well to edging. A few cultivars such as 'Alpine Yellow' are grown for the ornamental yellow fruit. The common cultivated strawberry, *F.* × *ananassa* also has a creamy variegated form, 'Variegata', to add excitement to the potager.

*Fragaria* 'Pink Panda'
(90%)

Add to this list the pink strawberry, 'Pink Panda', which has become a much sought after container plant and ground cover. Bred by Blooms of Bressingham, this hybrid resulted from the marriage of *Potentilla palustris* and an unnamed strawberry. Plants are terrific ground covers, filling large areas in a single growing season, while producing handsome pink flowers in early spring and throughout the rest of the season until frost knocks it down. The also make fine plants for windowboxes or hanging baskets. Occasionally, but not in great numbers, small strawberry fruit are produced, but they will never take the place of the real thing on anyone's breakfast cereal. A fine breakthrough in ornamental ground covers, useful in full sun to partial shade with adequate drainage.

## *Francoa* (frang-ko′ a)     Francoa          Saxifragaceae

A beautiful member of the saxifrage family (*Astilbe, Heuchera*) seldom seen in American gardens. None of the five species are easy garden plants

429

they tolerate a wide range of climates. The most dependable of the species is *F. sonchifolia,* which may be hardy to about 15° F (zone 8). Due to its lack of heat and humidity tolerance, it is more suitable to western zone 8 rather than southern zone 8. However, since plants can't read, it is worth a try for gardeners willing to take a chance. The basal hairy evergreen foliage is shallowly divided and dense. Above the leaves arises a raceme of closely spaced pink flowers with darker splotches on each of the four petals. Below the terminal inflorescence are smaller branches of flowers which open after the terminal. Altogether a handsome and interesting plant.

The other species which may be found once in a while are the white-flowered *F. ramosa* and the shell pink *F. appendiculata.* While they are fine garden plants where sited well, neither is as densely flowered nor as cold tolerant as *F. sonchifolia.*

They may be treated as biennials by starting seed in the spring or early summer, growing on, and then placing in cold frames or other protected winter area. Plant out in early spring and enjoy.

## *Fritillaria* (fri-ti-lah′ ree-a)          Fritillary          Liliaceae

The genus takes the name from *fritillas*, a chess-board or dice-box, because the flowers of many species are checkered on the outside. Over 80 species are known but only a small number are available or useful. All species have unbranched leafy stems, with leaves arranged in whorls or in pairs. The flowers on all but the Crown Imperial are arranged up the stem. When I gardened in Montreal, the guinea hen flower, *F. meleagris*, was everywhere in the spring and people constantly commented on its unusual appearance. The crown jewel of the species, however, is the crown imperial, *F. imperialis*, which when grown well, is truly impressive. I have visited the tulip fields of Holland in spring and it is always an enlightening and spectacular time. However, to see a field of crown imperials is a sight never to be forgotten. Numerous little-known species are offered to collectors and a few are seeing the light of the garden world. *F. pallidiflora*, a handsome pale yellow form, is one example; however, the more exotic forms, such as *F. michailovskyi* and *F. uva-vulpis* with yellow and purple flowers, have a ways to go before they become common in this country.

They require full sun and well-drained soil. The fleshy bulbs must be handled carefully and planted 4–6″ deep as soon as received in the fall. If you order bulbs in the mail, call to be sure that the shipper protects them from drying out. If allowed to dry out, it is unlikely that many of the bulbs will emerge in the spring. Propagation from offsets is not difficult. Bulbs should be lifted and offsets potted and grown until ready to replace in the garden. The offsets will bloom in about 12–18 months. Scales may also be used (see *Lilium*), however the number of scales taken from each bulb must be limited so as not to reduce the vigor of the parent bulb. Fresh seeds require about 4 years to reach flowering size.

Quick Guide to Fritillaria Species:

|  | Height (in.) | Flower mottled |
|---|---|---|
| *F. imperialis* | 30–36 | No |
| *F. meleagris* | 12–15 | Yes |
| *F. persica* | 24–36 | No |

| *-imperialis* (im-pe-ree-ah' lis) | Crown Imperial | 2½–3'/1' |
|---|---|---|
| Spring    Orange, Yellow | Turkey, Iran | Zones 5–7 |

When the crown imperial is planted in groups of a dozen or more, there are few bulbous species that compare. The alternate, lanceolate leaves are 4–6″ long, dark green and have a skunk-like odor when crushed (as do the flowers). On a calm evening, one does not linger by the fritillaries. The foliage persists into midsummer but is difficult to hide when senescence begins. The numerous 2–3″ long flowers hang down beneath a crown or whorl of leaves which protect the flowers from nature's elements. The stigma protrudes from the flowers like the clapper in a church bell. Large nectar drops reside inside the flowers which defy all laws of gravity by refusing to fall. Gerard compared each drop to a "pearl of the Orient."

Plant in full sun or afternoon shade. The bulbs may not perform well the first year, patience is often rewarded the second. Bulbs may be divided after 3–4 years.

**Cultivars:**

'Aurora' has orange-scarlet flowers.
'Lutea' bears lemon-yellow flowers.
'Lutea Maxima' has flowers which are even larger than the type.
'Orange Brilliant' produces clear orange flowers.
'Rubra' has red flowers.

| *-meleagris* (mel-ee-ah' gris) | Guinea Hen Flower | 12–15″/12″ |
|---|---|---|
| Spring    Pale Mauve | Western Europe | Zones 3–7 |

This is much more winter hardy but not nearly as magnificent as the previous species. The 1–2″ long solitary, drooping, checkered flowers are borne on 12–15″ stems and are mauve, marked with squares of dark purple "like the board at which men do play at chesse" (Gerard). It is also known as the snake's head daffodil, because before it opens, the broad budded flower resembles the head of a snake. The 3–6″ long foliage is narrow, alternate, and dark green, but not as persistent as *F. imperialis*. Bulbs may be divided in 2–3 years. Plants are highly tolerant of alkaline soil and may be naturalized in grass or in banks.

**Cultivars:**

Bulbs are usually offered in an awful assortment of mixed colors, but occasionally single colors are available.

'Alba' has creamy white flowers and is much more visible than the dark camouflage colors of the species. It has no markings but is an excellent cultivar.
'Aphrodite' is also white, but with larger flowers than 'Alba'.
'Artemis' bears purple checkered flowers with hints of green.
'Charon' probably has the darkest flowers of the species.
'Saturnus' bears bright violet flowers with a reddish cast.

**Related Species:**

*F. biflora*, mission bells, is native to the southwest United States. Plants have basal glossy green leaves with 1–6 (usually 2) nodding purple flowers tinged with green on each flower stem. 'Martha Roderick' has brownish red and white flowers. Likely hardy to zone 7.

*F. pallidiflora* has four to eight 1–2″ wide pale yellow flowers on 2′ tall stems with bluish green leaves. Not as eye-catching as crown imperials but much more pleasant than *F. meleagris*. I first saw them in Rob Proctor's splendid garden in Denver and have since seen their popularity rise. They open at the same time as other fritillarias. Hardy to zone 4.

| *-persica* (per′ si-ka) | | Persian Fritillary | 24–36″/12″ |
|---|---|---|---|
| Spring | Purple | Asia | Zones 5–8 |

Native to Cypress, southern Turkey, and Iran, plants are hardy in about zone 5 to 8. They are tall (up to 3′) and have gray-green alternate, sometimes twisted, stem leaves. Approximately 15–20 musky purple pendant flowers open up along the long raceme with a leafy bract at the base of each flower. They open wide to reveal a hint of green within.

They may be grown in light shade and moist, but not wet soils.

**Cultivars:**

'Adiyaman' is taller than the species and has dull maroon flowers.

## Related Species:

*F. assyriaca*, native to Turkey, is about 12–15″ tall with many greenish white flowers. Flower color may be variable, and occasionally some have a maroon tinge.

## Quick Key to Fritillaria Species

    A. Flowers topped with a crown of leaves . . . . . . . . *F. imperialis*
   AA. Flowers not topped with a crown of leaves
      B. Plant less than 18″ tall, flowers at
         the top of the stems . . . . . . . . . . . . . . . . . *F. meleagris*
     BB. Plant taller than 18″ tall, flowers occur
         up the flowering stem . . . . . . . . . . . . . . . . . *F. persica*

## Additional Reading:

Chatto, B. 1993. Ring out the bells. *Gardens Illustrated* 1:76–85.

Noltie, H. 1992. *Fritillaria delavayi. Kew Magazine* 9(2):51–54.

Wallis, B. 1993. Alpine anthology. Not rare but endangered. *Quarterly Bulletin of the Alpine Garden Society* 61(2):141–142.

Skelton, Gill. 1996. Fritillarias at Wisley. *The Garden* 121(4):202–204.

# G

*Gaillardia* (gay-lard′ ee-a)          Blanket Flower          Asteraceae

The blanket flower is still one of the most popular herbaceous plants in gardens today. They are valued for their mid-summer flowers in a range of predominantly hot colors, from deep yellows to rich burgundy. The reasons for their popularity are ease of culture, weather tolerance, and extremely long blooming season. Of the approximately 30 species, only two, *G. aristata* and *G. pinnatifida*, the western blanket flower, are available as perennials. A good deal of work has been done with the hybrids, expanding the range of colors and habits. Plants of *Gaillardia* need full sun, well-drained soil, and occasional removal of spent flowers.

-× *grandiflora* (grand-i-flo′ ra)     Blanket Flower          2–3′/2′
Summer          Red, Yellow          Hybrid          Zones 2–9

This hybrid is a cross between *G. aristata*, a 2–3′ tall perennial, and *G. pulchella*, a 2′ tall annual species. Although blanket flowers are often listed under *G. aristata*, that species is seldom seen in gardens today. The resulting tetraploid hybrid is vigorous and easy to grow. The 4–6″ long leaves are alternate, coarsely toothed, and gray-green. The 3–4″ diameter solitary flower heads are yellow with various amounts of maroon at the base of the petals. The center is often burgundy and the many colors result in a somewhat garish flower of many colors.

One of the decided disadvantages of the above-mentioned cross is that with the addition of genes from the annual species, the hybrid is shorter-lived than *G. aristata*. In the Horticulture Gardens at the University of Georgia, plants of *G. aristata* and *G.* × *grandiflora* 'Goblin' were planted side by side. Although 'Goblin' is a better garden plant from the point of view of habit and flowering time, it disappeared after 3 years, while *G. aristata* continued

434

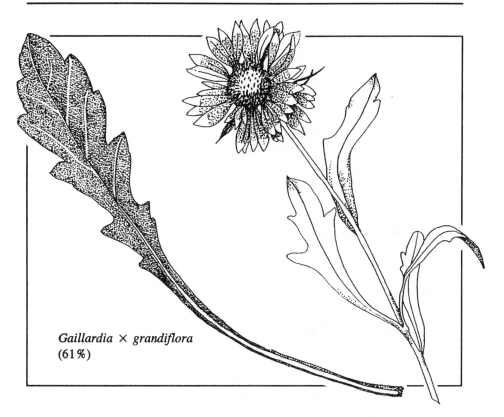

*Gaillardia* × *grandiflora*
(61%)

to prosper. Longevity may not be an important selection criterion, but this example points out the fact that desirable characteristics are often lost in breeding in order to gain other qualities. On the other hand, the genes of *G. pulchella* and other annual species have given the hybrid the distinction of having one of the longest flowering periods and most extensive environmental ranges of any perennial.

All but 'Baby Cole', 'Mandarin', and 'Goblin' may be propagated from seed, resulting in a good deal of variation. Germination is rapid under warm, humid conditions and seedlings should be ready to place in the garden within 8 weeks after sowing. Flowering occurs the first year from seed.

### Cultivars:

'Baby Cole' is an excellent dwarf (6–8″) selection with 2–3″ diameter yellow, red-banded ray flowers.

'Bremen' has coppery-scarlet flowers on 2–3′ tall stems.

'Burgundy' bears rich wine-red flowers and grows 2–3′ tall.

'Chloe' has yellow flowers on 2′ tall plants.

'Dazzler' produces blooms with crimson red tips and yellow centers.

'Goblin' ('Kobold') is another dwarf selection with 4" diameter flowers wearing red petals with yellow edges. It grows only 9–12" tall, but is rather variable in height and flower color. This is still the best cultivar out there.

'Golden Goblin' ('Goldkobold') bears pale yellow flowers on sturdy frames.

'Lollipop' series is a double-flowered, multi-colored group whose extra petals and many colors result in particularly loathsome plants.

'Mandarin' comes from Blooms of Bressinghams and is taller than 'Goblin', but more compact than the species.

'Monarch Strain' ('Portula hybrids') is a seed-propagated color mix.

'Summer Fire' ('Sommerfreude') is a dwarf form with yellow flowers and red zonations.

'Tokajer' ('Tokay Wine') is a old cultivar (1945) with bright rusty-orange flowers on 2–3' tall plants.

**Related Species:**

*G. aristata* is a fine flowering plant, but is much more variable than the hybrid. It grows to 3', often requiring support. Unlike the hybrids, plants raised from seed seldom flower the first year.

*G. pinnatifida* is a good performer but cold hardiness is marginal, maybe to zone 7. Plants are 1–2' tall and produce 2–2½" wide yellow flowers with burnt orange to red raised centers.

**Additional Reading:**

Stoutamire, Warren P. 1960. The history of cultivated gaillardias. *Baileya* 8:13–17.

## *Galactites* (gal-ac-tee' tees)                                     Asteraceae

Winter hardy only south of zone 7, the garden plant *G. tomentosa* is seldom seen in American gardens. However, these are eye-catching and skin-catching specimens. The 2' tall plants stand out in the landscape due to the gray-green, spiny, pinnately-cut foliage with milky-white veins. The underside of the spiny leaves are hairy (tomentose). The genus name comes from the greek *gala*, milk, alluding to the leaf veins. While the main garden value is the foliage, the small pink daisy flowers which occur in the summer contrast well with the rest of the plant.

Place in a sunny well-drained location, perhaps useful to place in pots which can be brought in to a protected area during the winter.

## *Galanthus* (ga-lanth' us)              Snowdrop              Amaryllidaceae

Snowdrops never fail to provide pleasure in late winter and early spring as they pop out of the ground, sometimes even before the snow has disappeared, and are known as pierce neige ("snow piercing") in

France. They are intolerant of heat and persist longer in the northern parts of the country than in the South, but are still a worthwhile addition to the southern garden (at least to zone 7), where they flower in February. A mix of various *Galanthus* species provides flowers from January to April, gladdening hearts at the dreariest time of year. I was fortunate enough to visit Scotland in March with my good friend and well-known woody expert, Michael Dirr. Overlooking drifts of snowdrops naturalized around clear streams and through woodlands rendered both of us speechless. That the impact of these tiny plants was immense was proven by the continuous clicking of the great tree-man's camera. It makes one want to go out and purchase bulbs in the thousands, or move to Scotland.

In all species the buds are solitary and erect, but the flowers nod on short, wiry stems. They have 3 outer and 3 shorter inner petals held above strap-like leaves. Bulbs should be planted in drifts of 25 or more, otherwise they make no impression. The spring landscape comes alive when snowdrops are combined with hellebores and winter aconites.

Plant about 3" deep in well-drained soil, in full sun to partial shade. In southern parts of the country, the combination of heavy soils and cold winter rains result in the loss of many bulbs. Where conditions are favorable, however, multiplication is rapid. Clumps may be lifted immediately after flowering, separated carefully into sections of 3–4 bulbs, and replanted as soon as possible.

Snowdrops are sometimes confused with snowflakes, *Leucojum*, another spring-flowering relative. The flower segments of snowflakes are all equal in size, plants are usually taller, and they bear 2–3 flowers on each stem.

Quick Reference to Galanthus Species

|  | Height (in.) | Leaf width |
| --- | --- | --- |
| *G. elwesii* | 8–10 | >1" |
| *G. nivalis* | 4–8 | ½" |

| *-elwesii* (el-wez' ee-eye) | Giant Snowdrop | 9–12"/6" |
| --- | --- | --- |
| Spring          White | Asia Minor | Zones 4–7 |

The outer segments of the flowers are usually about an inch long, but can be up to 2" long, and 1¼" wide. The inner segments have green blotches at the base (point of attachment) and the tip. The two gray-green, strap-like leaves are about 1¼" wide, 4" long, and deeply channelled. Everything about this plant is larger than the more common *G. nivalis*. Plants flower about one week later than *G. nivalis*.

**Cultivars:**

'Giant Form' is just that, although "giant" is perhaps being a little opportune.

Var. *globosus* has broad outer segments resulting in flowers up to 1″ wide.

**Related Species:**

*G. ikariae*, Nikarian snowdrop, is similar but has flared outer segments and broad recurved shiny green, rather than gray-green leaves. The green leaves contrast beautifully with the white flowers. The inner segments are green only at the apices. This is one of the most handsome of all the species.

| *-nivalis* (ni-vaal′ is) | | Common Snowdrops | 6–9″/12″ |
|---|---|---|---|
| Early Spring | White | Northern Europe | Zones 3–7 |

One of the earliest species to flower, plants may open as early as January in its southern range and push through the snow by March at the northern end. The foliage consists of 2 narrow (usually no wider than ½″) strap-like leaves above which the 1″ long and ½″ wide flowers are borne. They are pure white except for a green crescent at the apex of the inner segments. Bulbs multiply rapidly, but must be planted in large numbers to fulfill their potential. This species naturalizes better than others and can create large drifts in moist, cool climates.

**Cultivars:**

'Angustifolius' is a dwarf form with single white flowers.

'Atkinsii' is a vigorous form, growing 9″ tall and bearing many 1″ wide flowers.

'Cilicicus', Cilician snowdrop, is likely a sub-species (ssp. *cilicicus*). Flowers are earlier than *G. nivalis* and the leaves are narrower, particularly at the base.

'Flore Pleno' has 1″ wide double flowers, although the doubleness is only noticeable when the flowers are turned up. They are interesting and quite ornamental.

'Ophelia' bears large double flowers filled with green-tipped segments.

'Lutescens' has inner segments marked with yellow rather than green.

'Sam Arnott' is vigorous, nicely scented, and has large flowers.

'Scharlokii' has long bracteoles which resemble droopy ears. The outer segments are tinged green.

'Viridapicis' differs by having a green patch on both the inner and outer petals.

**Related Species:**

*G. reginae-olgae*, native to Greece, differs from *G. nivalis* by having dark green leaves with a gray stripe along the center. It differs from other species by flowering in the fall before the leaves appear, rather than in the winter or early spring.

Quick Key to Galanthus Species

 A. Leaves up to 1¼" wide, flowers to
  2" long, inner segments blotched
  green at base and apex . . . . . . . . . . . . . . . . . . . . *G. elwesii*
 AA. Leaves up to ½" wide, flowers to
  1" long, inner segments blotched
  green at tips only . . . . . . . . . . . . . . . . . . . . . . . *G. nivalis*

**Additional Reading:**

Anon. 1995. Growing: With snowdrops hope blooms eternal. *Garden Design* 13(6):32.
Yeo, Peter F. 1975. The hybrid origin of some cultivated snowdrops (Galanthus-Amaryllidaceae). *Baileya* 19:157–162.

## *Galax* (gay' lax)     Galax, Wandflower     Diaspensiaceae

Only one species of this American plant occurs, *G. urceolata* (formerly *G. aphylla*), and is native to the eastern mountains of Virginia through North Carolina and extending into Georgia. The circular leathery leaves persist for weeks after cut from the plant and are highly sought after for flower arrangements throughout the world. Tremendous numbers of leaves are harvested from native populations and exported to Europe and Asia. The evergreen foliage is tufted at the base and dull green throughout the summer. In the early spring and late fall and winter, the leaves turn bronze—even burgundy—especially in the sun. The tiny white flowers are held in a spike-like raceme on a long leafless scape in spring.

Plants are wonderful in woodland and shady gardens, mainly for their foliage; however, the flowers are also handsome. When not in flower, plants are 6–9" tall but extend to 18" in bloom. Hardy from zones 5–8. They may be propagated by careful division, or from seed.

## *Galega* (gal-ee' ga)     Goat's Rue     Fabaceae

Of the 6–8 species, only *G. officinalis* and *G. orientalis* have proven garden value. Plants were once grown for forage, and were prized for feeding to goats to increase milk flow. This was so common that the genus was named after the Greek word *gala*, meaning milk. They have pea-like flowers which are sometimes confused with those of *Baptisia*. Plants are useful for the back of the garden and bear odd-pinnate foliage and pea-shaped flowers of purplish blue or white. Under highly favorable conditions they can become aggressive, and in some countries, common goat's rue has become so abundant that it is considered a noxious weed and is under siege of eradication.

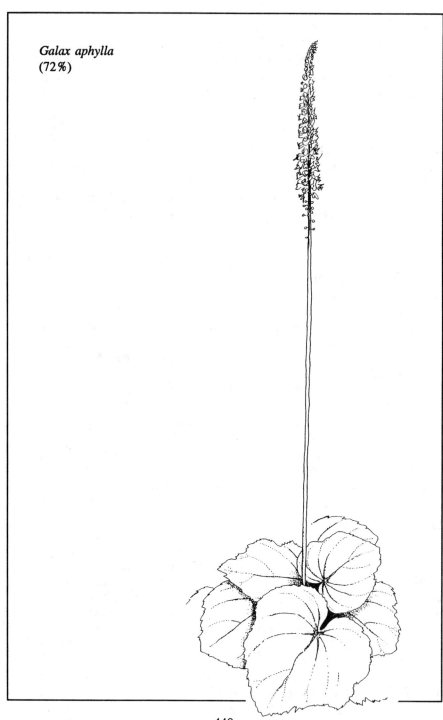

*Galax aphylla*
(72%)

## Quick Reference to Galega

|              | Height (in.) | Number of leaflets | Flower color     |
| ------------ | ------------ | ------------------ | ---------------- |
| *G. officinalis* | 3–4      | 4–8 pairs          | White, lavender  |
| *G. orientalis*  | 3–4      | 6–12 pairs         | Blue-violet      |

**-officinalis** (o-fi-chi-nah' lis)   Common Goat's Rue                3-4'/3'
  Late Spring   Blue, White   Southern Europe, Asia Minor   Zones 3–7
(Syn. *G. bicolor*)

The 1–2' long, pinnately compound leaves consist of 9–16 entire leaflets held on short petiolules (stalk of leaflet). At each leaf node is a lanceolate stipule, about ½" long. The pale blue, lilac, blue-pink to white, 1–1½" long flowers are held in long, many-flowered racemes pointing upward like

*Galega officinalis*
(56%)

many-colored candles. Bicolor flowers also occur in members of the Hartlandii group, which were originally thought to be a hybrid between *G. officinalis* and *G. bicolor*. Since those two species are now felt to be synonymous, the Hartlands are simply cultivars of this species.

The species is tolerant of poor soils, and if over fertilized, grows too tall and lanky and requires support. Plant in full sun in any well-drained soil. Cut back after the flowers are finished as plants are not particularly attractive after flowering, a problem common to many members of the pea family.

*Galega* is seldom used in this country, although I am not sure of the reason. It is tolerant of cool conditions, but does not adapt well to the heat and humidity in the South.

Propagate by division every 3–5 years. Seed germinates well in cool or warm conditions.

**Cultivars:**
'Alba' is an excellent form which bears showy white flowers.
'Her Majesty' has clear white and mauve-pink flowers.
'Lady Wilson' bears lilac-blue flowers.

| *-orientalis* (o-ree-en-tah′ lis) | Oriental Goat's Rue | 3–4′/3′ |
| --- | --- | --- |
| Late Spring    Violet-Blue | Caucasus | Zones 3–7 |

Similar to the previous species except having larger, more numerous leaflets which are slightly more tapered at the ends and with wider stipules. The violet-blue to lavender flowers are held well above the foliage, resulting in handsome, if somewhat aggressive, plants for the garden.

Propagate as with *G. officinalis*.

Quick Key to Galega Species

    A. Leaflets 9–17, leaflets oblong, elliptical
       or lanceolate, stipules broadly lanceolate . . . . . . . *G. officinalis*
    AA. Leaflets 13–25, leaflets ovate-orbicular,
        stipules broadly ovate . . . . . . . . . . . . . . . . . *G. orientalis*

*Galium* (gay-lee′ um)　　　Sweet Woodruff, Bedstraw　　　Rubiaceae

Most of the 400 species are weeds and have little place in the garden. The genus name comes from *gala*, meaning milk, because of the former use of *G. verum*, yellow bedstraw, in curdling milk for cheese manufacture. The only popular and easily available species is *G. odoratum*, sweet woodruff, a useful and popular ground cover.

**-odoratum** (o-dor-ah′ tum)     Sweet Woodruff     4–9″/12″
    Spring     White     Europe     Zones 4–7
(Syn. *Asperula odorata*)

The 1½″ long, ½″ wide, sessile leaves are borne in whorls of 6–8 at each node along the length of the square stems. The roots are slender and creeping, making the plants particularly effective ground covers. The white fragrant flowers are only ⅛–¼″ long and held in loosely branched cymes. When in flower in the spring, plants look like newly fallen snow.

The whole plant smells like new-mown hay when crushed or dried, thus one of its common names, bedstraw. It is also known as Ladies' Bedstraw, because it was thought to be part of the plants in the hay on which the Mother of Christ rested. They are an ingredient for potpourri and sachets and are used traditionally as a moth deterrent. It has also been used to flavor everything from wine and brandy to sorbets and fruit salads.

In the garden, plants tolerate partial shade in the North and require shade in the South. To grow rapidly and cover large areas, a consistent supply of water is necessary. It is particularly pretty in the dappled shade of *Gleditsia* or beneath high canopy trees. However, it can also become a noxious weed.

Propagate by division in the spring or fall, or by seed.

## *Galtonia* (gawl-tone′ ee-a)     Summer Hyacinth     Liliaceae

A group of three species of bulbous plants native to South Africa that are closely related to the garden hyacinth. They are all ornamental. However, *G. candicans* is the only one sufficiently winter hardy to be used in large areas of the country.

**-candicans** (kan′ di-kanz)     Summer Hyacinth     2–4′/3′
    Summer     White     South Africa     Zones 6–9

The strap-shaped leaves are 2–3′ long, 2″ wide, and have conspicuous midribs. A leafless scape arises from the basal leaves carrying a loose raceme of 20–30 dangling, bell-shaped flowers on 1–2½″ long pedicels. The 1½″ long flowers are slightly scented and clear white.

Plants should be grown in full sun and watered and fertilized copiously. If planted in a proper site, staking is not necessary. However, if grown in excessive shade or in lean soil, scapes will not be strong enough to support the heavy flowers. Plant bulbs in early spring about 6″ deep in groups of a dozen or more for the best show. Cut back foliage when leaves start to decline because plants tend to look weedy. Bulbs need to be lifted, similar to gladioli, north of zone 6, although bulbs in zone 5 may overwinter if well protected.

Propagate by lifting bulbs in spring and removing small offsets, which flower after two years. Sow the small seeds in well-drained soil under warm (70–75° F), humid conditions. Approximately 3 years is necessary for flowering plants from seed.

### Related Species:

*G. princeps* has broad gray-green foliage and bears greenish white flowers 1–2 weeks earlier than *G. candicans*. Hardy in zones 8–10.

*G. viridiflora* bears many (15–20) pale green flowers on 2' tall plants. They were handsome in the Georgia gardens but flowers persisted only for about 1 week.

## *Gaura* (gaw' ra)　　　　　Gaura　　　　　Onagraceae

The genus is a relative newcomer to the American garden scene, although most species are native to North America. There are about 20 species of annuals, perennials and biennials, but only one is widely available. Plants of *G. lindheimeri* have proven well suited to many areas of the country, and highly useful for the warmer regions of the country.

| *-lindheimeri* (lind-hay' mer-eye) | | White Gaura | 3–4'/3' |
| --- | --- | --- | --- |
| Summer | White | Louisiana, Texas | Zones 5–8 |

Plants are being used extensively throughout the country, and have been long popular in the South as they tolerate heat and humidity well, although some problems with leginess and lack of flowering have occurred. In areas of consistently cool summer nights, flowering occurs throughout the season on reddish stems. The 1–3" long, lanceolate leaves are alternate and sessile. The flowers are carried on a loose open panicle well above the foliage. The 1" long white flowers are rose-tinged and open up the spike much like a gladiolus, but only a few are open at any one time. As they age, the white gives way to pale rose. Plants prefer a rich, well-drained soil in full sun to partial shade.

If spent flower spikes are removed, flowering continues from late spring to fall. Although not the most showy plant in the landscape, gaura is one of the most durable. Plants grow 3' tall and flower prolifically throughout the summer and into the fall. If and when breeders produce a fuller inflorescence and brighter flowers, this plant will be used far more extensively. As further testimony to its adaptability, Elizabeth Crenota Clark states that gaura "is tough as a boot, delicate as a butterfly . . ." in Texas and is also highly valued by Mr. Jack Hobbs of the Auckland Botanical Garden in New Zealand.

Seed germinates within 14–21 days when sown in a warm, humid area. Division may be accomplished after 2–3 years.

## Cultivars:

'Corrie's Gold' is a variegated form with creamy and gold markings on the foliage. The flowers are similar to the species. The plant arose as a chance seedling in the garden of Beth Chatto near Colchester, England and was named for the daughter of one of her employees.

'Siskiyou Pink' is a new selection from Siskiyou Gardens in Washington. The flowers are deeper pink and a welcome departure from the normal white flowers.

'Swirling Butterflies' is a dwarfer form of the species and highly recommended.

## Additional Reading:

Anonymous, 1959. *Gaura lindheimeri*. Engelmann and Gray. *Baileya* 7:62.

Clark, Elizabeth Cernota, 1990. *Gaura*. *Horticulture* 68(6):80.

Farmer, Jenkins, 1993. *Gaura lindheimeri*. *American Nurseryman* 177(4):170.

## *Gentiana* (gen-tee′ ah-na)          Gentian          Gentianaceae

Gentians are some of the most handsome, highly sought-after plants for the cool season garden. Every gardener I have ever met lusts after gentians, although only a few of the more than 300 species are successfully employed in gardens east of the Rocky Mountains and south of zone 5. They are widespread across cool temperate and alpine zones of the world, and most thrive only in regions with cool summers. Gentians are found in a wide range of habitats and soil types and display a corresponding diversity of habit, size and cultural requirements. Because of the diversity, it is difficult to generalize about gentian culture. The great majority of gentians, however, are alpines, needing full light, lots of water, excellent drainage, and cool nights. Colors range from common deep blues, to which the genus has given its name, to yellows (*G. lutea*), whites (*G. alba*), and scarlet and gold (*G. scarlatina*). While numerous species are native to North America (including the wonderful fringed gentian, *G. crinita,* or more properly, *Gentianopsis crinita*), they are not the easiest plants to propagate and therefore not always easily available.

Some mail order nurseries offer an extensive collection of gentians, and since plants can't read, it may be worth planting a few types in the fall or early spring. For midwestern and eastern gardeners with marginal "gentian conditions," probably *G. acaulis*, *G. andrewsii*, and *G. puberulenta* are good places to start. Southern gardeners should not spend too much of their children's inheritance on gentians; however, *G. saponaria*, *G. septemfida* and *G. asclepiadea* may be useful. Tall gentians are suitable for borders and landscape planting and include *G. lutea, G. andrewsii, G. asclepiadea, G. saponaria,* and *G. septemfida*. Low growing forms generally have sessile flowers and are suitable for rock gardens, and include *G. acaulis* and *G. dahurica*.

## Quick Reference to Gentiana Species

|  | Flower color | Height (in.) | Flowering time |
|---|---|---|---|
| *G. acaulis* | Azure blue | 4–6 | Spring |
| *G. andrewsii* | Dark blue | 16–30 | Early fall |
| *G. asclepiadea* | Blue-purple | 20–30 | Late summer |
| *G. cruciata* | Blue | 8–12 | Summer |
| *G. dahurica* | Deep blue | 6–12 | Summer |
| *G. lutea* | Yellow | 48–72 | Summer |
| *G. makinoi* | Pale blue | 18–24 | Late summer |

| *-acaulis* (a-kaw' lis) | | Stemless Gentian | 4–6″/8″ |
|---|---|---|---|
| Spring | Azure Blue | South, Central Europe | Zones 3–6 |

One of the more common gentians in European gardens, plants produce a dark green rosette of many 1″ long, lance-like leaves. The term *acaulis* means "without stem," and the flowers appear to emerge from the rosette itself. The lack of a stem results in short plants with relatively large (2″) solitary, terminal flowers. The azure to dark blue flowers consist of a long tube ending with 5 lobes, sometimes flared back (recurved). The flower tube is usually spotted green within.

A very handsome species, but one which requires exceptional drainage, cool nights, and lime-free soils. Avoid constant sun; 4–5 hours a day seems to be sufficient.

Propagate by placing seed on light porous sandy mix and place under 55–65° F and high moisture. Seeds should not be covered as they require light to germinate. Best success occurs with newly ripened seed; if they are old, they descend into a deep dormancy which results in slow and erratic germination. Many seeds are set, but they lose vitality quickly. If seed must be stored, store in an airtight container, with a desiccant, in the refrigerator.

### Cultivars:
'Alba' is a white-flowered form.

'Belvedere' is more vigorous, forming larger clumps in less time. Flowers are deep blue.

'Rannock' is even shorter than the species, growing only about 2″ tall. The deep blue flowers are stripped green and white within.

'Trotter's Variety' flowers in the spring and fall.

### Related Species:
*G. sino-ornata* is also a prostrate gentian, only about 4″ tall, with basal leaves forming loose rosettes. The stems root at the nodes. Plants bear large (2″ long), tubular, azure blue flowers with bands of deep purple-blue in the fall. Very handsome; numerous cultivars have been developed.

*-andrewsii* (an-drooz-ee' eye)　　　Bottle Gentian　　　16–30"/2'
　Fall　　　　　Deep Blue　　　North America　　　Zones 3–7

One of our prettiest but lesser known natives, plants occur as far north as Quebec, west to Saskatchewan, into Nebraska, south to Arkansas and Georgia. The opposite leaves occur all the way up the 1½' tall plant. The deep blue flowers occur in groups of 2–5 sessile flowers which are terminal or in the upper one or two leaf axils. This species is one of the easiest to recognize, at least in flower, because the flowers never open. Their frustrating habit of expanding but never opening have lent the common name of bottle gentian and closed gentian to these plants.

Not quite as finicky as some of the alpine forms; nevertheless, good drainage and cool nights are necessary for success.

Propagate by seed similar to *G. acaulis*, or by 1–2" long cuttings.

**Cultivars:**

'Albiflora' has white flowers.
'Creamy' has creamy white flowers.

**Related Species:**

*G. flavida*, cream gentian, is a midwest native with creamy white flowers that retain the bottle-like refusal to open. Requiring little moisture and tolerant of limey soils, it is a little-known plant that is worth a try if it can be located.

*G. saponaria*, soapwort gentian, is similar to the above species in that the flowers don't open. The leaves are arranged in pairs or whorls of four. Native from New York to Florida and Minnesota to Texas. Flowers occur in the fall, bringing the rather non-descript plants into the limelight. Hardy in zones 5–8.


*-asclepiadea* (a-sklay-pee-ah' dee-a)　　Willow Gentian　　20–30"/18"
　Late Summer　　　Blue-Purple　　　Europe　　　Zones 3–7

The plants bear arching stems with 2–3" long, bright green, willow-like, 3–5 veined leaves. The blue-purple, narrow, sessile flowers occur in axillary clusters of 2–3 flowers. The flowers are variable, but most are purple-spotted within the tube and often striped white at the throat.

**Cultivars:**

'Alba' has white flowers.
'Knightshayes' is smaller and bears bluer flowers (less purple) with white
　throats.
'Phyllis' is a vigorous selection with pale blue flowers.

**Related Species:**

*G. septemfida* may be somewhat prostrate or erect to 6–12" tall. The leafy stems bear clustered, light blue, bell-shaped flowers in summer. There

447

are many color variants within this species, one of which is sold as var. *lagodechiana* with deeper blue flowers on more or less prostrate stems.

| *-cruciata* (cruc-ee-ah′ ta) | | | 8–12″/12″ |
|---|---|---|---|
| Summer | Blue | Eastern Europe | Zones 3–7 |

As one catalog states, "if you kill every gentian you touch, this one is safe even with you." This may help in raising confidence in growing gentians, but it is not one of the showier forms. In late summer, the small (< ½″) dark blue flowers are formed in terminal and axillary clusters in the nodes of the 3–4″ long and 1–2″ wide stem leaves.

Plants are tolerant of some shade and more tolerant of drought than many other species. A good gentian to start with.

| *-dahurica* (da-her-i′ ca) | | | 6–12″/12″ |
|---|---|---|---|
| Summer | Deep Blue | China | Zones 4–7 |

Flowering in mid- to late summer, the intense blue flowers are showy but not exceptional. They are held at the end of the 12″ stems as well as in the nodes of the leaves. The long narrow leaves are basal and held on the stem. The flowers are only about 1″ long and are often slightly spotted with white.

One of the easiest gentians to grow, although not without some problems.

**Related Species:**

*G. kurroo* is about 8″ tall with branched stems emerging form basal rosettes. Plants bear 1–2″ long, solitary, deep blue flowers with white and green spots at the end of the stems. Flowering occurs in late summer or fall.

| *-lutea* (loo′ tee-a) | | Yellow Gentian | 4–6′/2′ |
|---|---|---|---|
| Summer | Yellow | Europe | Zones 3–6 |

At first glance, this robust perennial looks nothing like a gentian, especially when not in flower. The broad basal leaves are 10–12″ long and strongly ribbed. The stems rise with vigor above the rosette and carry paired, narrow, sessile leaves. The nodes of the upper 5–7 stem leaves carry 3–10 bright yellow flowers which can be seen from miles away.

Yellow gentian is native to the Alps and Pyrenees Mountains at elevations of 3000 to 6000 feet and is most at home in areas where nights and days are cool. Plants must be at least 2 years old and maybe 3 or more before they will flower. This is a problem in most American gardens because plants are not as vigorous in our diverse climates as they are in their native habitats or in mild gardens found in the British Isles, and may not persist long enough to reach their flowering potential, although my optimism was elevated when I saw some handsome specimens in the Denver Botanical Garden.

The bitter yellow-brown root of this plant has been used as a medicine and is the plant for which the genus was named.

Propagate by seed in the fall and plant out in spring.

| *-makinoi* (mack-in' oy) | | | 18–24"/18" |
|---|---|---|---|
| Late Summer | Light Blue | Japan | Zones 3–7 |

Plants are erect, tall and very useful for cut flowers. The pale blue spotted flowers are clustered at the top of the plant and in the last few nodes. The 2–3" long lanceolate leaves are paired and have 3–5 veins.

Propagate by seed.

### Cultivars:
'Royal Blue' has deeper blue flowers than the species.

### Related Species:
*G. triflora* has deep blue to purple-blue flowers banded white on the outside. The flowers occur near the top of the upright 1–2' tall stems in late summer and fall. They never open very wide, even in full sun.

Quick Key to Gentiana Species

    A. Plants generally greater than 1' tall
      B. Flowers blue or purple
        C. Stems obviously arching, flowers occurring
          at axils along entire length of stem . . . . . . *G. asclepiadea*
        CC. Stems mainly erect, flowers terminal
          or in upper axils only
          D. Flowers never opening, closed at mouth . . *G. andrewsii*
          DD. Flowers open normally . . . . . . . . . . . . . *G. makinoi*
      BB. Flowers not blue or purple, but yellow . . . . . . . . . *G. lutea*
    AA. Plants generally less than 1' tall
      B. Plants stemless, less than 8" tall,
        flowers 2" long . . . . . . . . . . . . . . . . . . . . . . . *G. acaulis*
      BB. Plants with stems, greater than 8" tall,
        flowers less than 2" long
        C. Stems arising from basal rosette,
          flowers less than 1' long, campanulate . . . . . . *G. cruciata*
        CC. Multi-stemmed, flowers greater
          than 1" long, funnelform . . . . . . . . . . . . . *G. dahurica*

### Additional Reading:
Capettini, B. 1994. Native americans: Bottle gentian. *Horticulture* 72(3):88.

Kelly, John. 1992. Gentians. *The Garden* 117(10):465–469.

Parks, J.B. 1994. Last word: the pleasures of seeing. *Fine Gardening* 35:90.

*Geranium* (jer-aye' nee-um)   Cranesbill, Hardy Geranium   Geraniaceae

This wonderfully diverse genus consisting of well over 250 species, is known as cranesbill because of the beak-like fruit. Plants are often referred to as hardy geraniums to separate them from the annual geraniums which belong to the genus *Pelargonium*. Hardy geraniums have been woefully underused in American gardens, but a minor renaissance is occurring. As more people travel to fine gardens throughout the world, particularly those of the British Isles, they discover the beauty and variety of these fine plants. Fortunately, additional species are becoming available in North America and the good, the bad, and the ugly are being separated. Alas, we cannot expect equal performance from all species on this continent as in England, but there are many well worth including in the garden. A number of native species such as *G. maculatum*, spotted cranesbill, and *G. robertianum*, herb robert, are common. In fact, spotted cranesbill is an effective garden plant in the southern half of the country, outperforming many of its more sophisticated relatives. A niche may be found in every garden for at least one species as their diversity is extraordinary. A few species such as *G. renardii* appear to have narrow growing ranges, but most are far more adaptable.

Plants typically grow from basal rosettes of palmately lobed or dissected leaves. The flowering stems bear alternate or opposite stem leaves. The flowers have 5 equal and usually overlapping petals, and 10 stamens. In teaching my students how to distinguish geraniums from other genera, I suggest looking for palmate leaves, 5-petalled flowers, and cranesbill fruit. If all three characteristics are present, it is a geranium. The seeds are often explosively expelled from the fruit and the method of seed expulsion helps distinguish between similar species. The more species and cultivars I learn, the fewer I seem to know. As soon as I learn one, another two appear to surface. If you have a problem telling geraniums apart, you are not alone.

In general, most species prefer moist soils and full sun to partial shade, although some are tolerant of heavy shade. In the southern limits of their range, late afternoon shade should be provided. Propagation is by division in spring or fall, terminal cuttings in the spring or after flowering, or by seed.

Hardiness (cold and heat tolerance) is always an issue with all genera grown in the United States, and as expected from so diverse a genus, a great variation in adaptability occurs. Those native to Europe, such as *G. pratense*, often withstand cold better than heat, while those native to Madeira, such as the giant and incredibly beautiful *G. palmatum* and *G. maderense*, may tolerate deep southern climes, but are best grown in areas with a Mediterranean climate or in the greenhouse. Species native to New Zealand, such as *G. traversii* and its dark form 'Nigrasens', are difficult to establish almost anywhere. While sounding somewhat depressing, that still leaves another 250 or so species to experiment with.

Most species should be divided every 2–4 years; however, some have deep taproots making division difficult. Most of these may be raised by root cuttings (see *Anemone* for details), stem cuttings, or seed. Seed generally requires a ripening period before germination. If seed is collected from garden plants, store it for 2–4 weeks at room temperature prior to sowing in a warm (70–75° F), humid area. Some seed may require a cold treatment of 3–5 weeks, but this is not usually necessary.

In the time between the first edition and this revision, most of the species and/or cultivars I originally described have become widely available in this country. Much research and sorting out has yet to be done to find species which work as well in North America as in the British Isles, but we are getting there.

Quick Reference to Geranium Species

| | Height (in.) | Flower color |
|---|---|---|
| G. × *cantabrigiense* | 6–8 | Rose, pink |
| G. *cinereum* | 6–12 | Red, pink |
| G. *clarkei* | 15–20 | Purplish violet |
| G. *dalmaticum* | 4–8 | Pink |
| G. *endressii* | 15–18 | Pink |
| G. *himalayense* | 10–15 | Lilac, purple veins |
| G. *macrorrhizum* | 15–18 | Magenta |
| G. × *magnificum* | 18–24 | Blue |
| G. *phaeum* | 18–24 | Dark purple |
| G. *platypetalum* | 18–24 | Purple |
| G. *pratense* | 30–36 | Purple |
| G. *procurrens* | 6–9 | Magenta, black center |
| G. *psilostemon* | 24–48 | Magenta, black center |
| G. *sanguineum* | 9–12 | Magenta |
| G. *sylvaticum* | 30–36 | Violet blue |

-× *cantabrigiense* (can-tab-rig-ee′ en-se)  Cambridge Geranium  6–8″/8″
Spring, Summer  Rose, Pink  Hybrid  Zones 5–7

In 1974, Dr. Helen Kiefer of Cambridge University made a number of reciprocal crosses between *G. macrorrhizum* and *G. dalmaticum*. With *G. macrorrhizum* as the female parent, she successfully raised a seedling which was planted in the University gardens. The color of the petals was purple-violet, and the light green leaves grew into a weed-proof carpet. The flowers persisted for a long time because little seed was produced. The species name was coined by Dr. Peter Yeo in 1985 and commemorates the city of Cambridge, England. A number of excellent cultivars have arisen from this cross.

451

## Cultivars:

'Biokovo' is best known, bearing white flowers tinged with pink on 6–8″ tall plants. The calyces (sepals) are redder than the petals making a handsome contrast, and flowers are much easier on the eyes than the original hybrid. Plants have runners which extend further, and hence do not make as dense a carpet. Plants were found in the Biokovo mountains of the Dalmatica region of the present day Croatia.

'Biokovo Karmina' ('Karmina') has deeper, almost raspberry, red flowers. The more I see this, the more I like it.

'Cambridge' is offered by a number of nurseries and bears purple-violet flowers. It is likely the original Cambridge clone from the initial cross.

| *-cinereum* (si-ner′ ee-um) | Grayleaf Cranesbill | 6–12″/12″ |
|---|---|---|
| Spring        Red, Pink | Pyrenees | Zones 5–7 |

The cultivars of this species are some of the most colorful in the genus. The leaves consist of 5–7 wedge-shaped lobes divided almost to the base. Each division is 3-lobed for about one-third the length. The pale purplish pink flowers have dark veins and are 1″ wide. The plant is essentially stemless and its small stature dictates its placement at the front of the garden or in a well-drained rock garden. One of the most demanding as to siting, plants do poorly north of zone 5 or south of zone 7, although I have seen plants thriving in zone 8 Portland gardens. The cultivar 'Ballerina' did wonderfully well in the Horticulture Gardens (zone 7b) in the spring, but struggled for life during the summer. This is unfortunate as there are some stunning forms available. When provided with cool nights and well-drained soil, it can be a knockout.

Much variation within the species occurs and confusion exists in the classification. Two major varieties have been named, although differences require a taxonomist's eye. Var. *cinereum* differs from var. *subcaulescens* in that the latter has darker leaves, magenta colored petals, and blackish stamens and stigmas. Natural hybridization occurs readily, thus making separation even more difficult. From the garden and gardener standpoint, the parentage or history of the garden forms is unimportant if the plants perform well.

Propagate by divisions, stem cuttings, or by seed.

## Cultivars:

'Album' (of var. *cinereum*) has completely white flowers.

'Ballerina' (*G. cinereum* var. *cinereum* × var. *subcaulescens*), raised by Bloom's Nursery in England, has received numerous awards. Plants stand only 4–6″ tall and bear 2″ diameter lilac-pink flowers with a dark center and purple veining on the petals. Flowers are largely sterile which accounts for the long blooming time.

'Giuseppii' belongs to var. *subcaulescens*. It has deep magenta flowers with a dark spot in the center.

'Lawrence Flatman' is similar to 'Ballerina', but is more vigorous and has a deeper venation on the flowers. This was also raised by Alan Bloom and named for a valued employee of the firm.

'Splendens' (of var. *subcaulescens*) is 5-6" tall and covered with vibrant deep red flowers with dark centers. It appears to me to be one of the least vigorous of the species.

### Related Species:
*G. argenteum*, silverleaf geranium, is similar to the above species, but the leaves are densely covered with a silvery-gray pubescence. The notched flowers appear singly and are light pink with netted veins. Drainage is most essential and plants need be grown in rocks or raised containers.

### Related Hybrids:
*G. × lindavicum*, a hybrid between *G. cinereum* and *G. argenteum*, has deeply lobed leaves with white or pink densely net-veined flowers. 'Apple Blossom', also known as 'Jenny Bloom', has clear light pink flowers with silvery veins. The leaves are silvery gray. Plants only stand 4-6" tall. 'Alanah' ('Purpureum') has less silver hue to the foliage and bright crimson flowers.

| | | | |
|---|---|---|---|
| *-clarkei* (clar-key′ eye) | Clarke's Geranium | 15-20"/18" |
| Spring   Violet, White | Nepal | Zones 5-7 |

(Syn. *G. pratense* 'Kashmir Purple' and 'Kashmir White')

This species was separated in 1985 from *G. pratense* (which see) by Dr. Peter Yeo of Cambridge University. Plants are lower growing, leaves are much more deeply cut, more basal leaves are formed, and a more open inflorescence is produced than plants of *G. pratense*.

The 4-6" wide basal leaves are deeply divided into 7 divisions, each division deeply pinnately lobed. The ½-¾" diameter flowers are upward facing (as are the seed capsules) and purplish violet or white with dark veins. Plants are completely covered with flowers in late spring and summer and are among the prettiest geraniums I have seen.

Propagate by division in spring or fall.

### Cultivars:
'Kashmir Purple' bears deep blue flowers and comes relatively true from seed.

'Kashmir White' (syn. *G. rectum* 'Album') has clear white 2" wide flowers with pale lilac-pink veins. Can be totally covered in white when happily sited. When raised from seed, some plants will be purple flowered.

| | | | |
|---|---|---|---|
| *-dalmaticum* (dal-mat′ i-cum) | Dalmatian Cranesbill | 4-8"/6" |
| Late Spring   Pink | Balkan Peninsula | Zones 4-7 |

This low grower has trailing stems and spreads rapidly by rhizomes without being invasive. The smooth foliage is up to 2" wide and deeply

453

*Geranium clarkei* 'Kashmir White'
(48%)

divided. Each of the 5–7 divisions is 3-lobed for about ¼ its length. The light pink, 1″ diameter flowers have entire petals (i.e., not notched) and are usually borne 3 to a flower stem. The foliage has red to orange fall color and persists well into the winter.

Place in full sun in well-drained soil. Plants tolerate partial shade but will be taller and not as floriferous.

Propagate by division of the rhizome or from seed.

### Cultivars:
'Album' is a lovely white-flowered form, but not quite as vigorous as the type.

### Related Species:
*G. donianum* is related only in the fact that it is also a low growing species which lends itself to well-drained sunny spots in the garden. The flowers are reddish purple or magenta, and the plant grows about 12″ tall. Native to the Himalayas, plants are difficult to find and difficult to establish. The deeply divided leaves are carried on a compact plant, and flowers occur in late spring.

*-endressii* (en-dres' ee-eye)     Endress's Geranium        15–18"/18"
Summer          Pink          Pyrenees                  Zones 4–7

This vigorous species bears light pink 1" diameter flowers above 3–5" wide shiny green leaves. Leaves are deeply 5 times divided, each division having 3 lobes cut about halfway down. Plants flower from early summer through the fall in northern gardens, but due to the heat, stop flowering in mid-June in the South. In the North plant in full sun, but provide afternoon shade in the South. Good drainage is essential to plant survival. This species is a terrific plant in itself, but is also an important parent in a number of very useful hybrids.

Propagate by division every 2–3 years. Seeds of the species germinate within 3 weeks if placed in warm (70–75° F), humid atmosphere.

## Cultivars:

'Wargrave Pink' has superseded the species and is the most popular cultivar. It is a vigorous clone with salmon-pink flowers held well above the foliage. The petals are more distinctly notched than those of the species. Excellent plant for North or South.

## Related Species:

*G. nodosum* has the habit of *G. endressii*, but with glossy green leaves and saw-toothed edges on the leaf divisions. The lilac flowers have an obvious purple venation pattern. Does well in relatively deep shade. Works well in zones 5–7.

## Related Hybrids:

*G. × oxonianum* arose as a natural hybrid between *G. endressii* and *G. versicolor*, and bears pink funnel-shaped flowers with darker veins. Such hybrids seem to occur with impunity when these two species are planted close to each other, and a number of fine cultivars have been named. Plants are generally taller than either parent and have larger flowers. Full sun and well-drained soils are best for good performance. This species name, adopted by Yeo in 1985, commemorates the city of Oxford, England. Many cultivars have been named, all of which should be propagated by division.

'Armitageae' is a mediocre plant with a terrific name. Never having seen this plant anywhere, I have grave doubts whether real plants even exist, but with such a classic name it should be included in all garden books. I understand that flowers are a deep rosy-pink and plants look very similar in habit to *G. endressii*. Named for the garden of a Miss Armitage in Dadnor Garden, Herefordshire, England. Must be a great garden.

'A.T. Johnson' was named for the Welsh horticulturist, Arthur Johnson, and is supposed to be dwarfer than *G. endressii* and have silver-pink flowers. However, plants I have seen are very similar to the cultivar

'Rose Clair', also raised by A.T. Johnson, which has salmon-pink flowers. The true 'A.T. Johnson' may be lost to commerce.

'Claridge Druce', named after its discoverer, is vigorous with hairy grayish green foliage and lovely purple-pink flowers with dark veins. The foliage is vigorous, but after the plant flowers, can look terrible. Foliar diseases such as rust often disfigure the plants. Cut back hard after flowering and the fresh growth will help to renew your interest in this hybrid. Unfortunately, significant variation occurs and 'Claridge Druce' includes any plants have the approximate characteristics given above.

'Lady Moore' has lighter pink flowers than 'Wargrave Pink' and may be a cultivar of *G. endressii*.

'Phoebe Noble' was raised in Ms. Noble's garden in Victoria, British Columbia. Plants bear dark pink flowers.

'Rebecca Moss', introduced by Heronswood Nursery in Kingston, Washington, has light silver-pink flowers and is unique in having little or no conspicuous veining.

'Rose Clair' bears rose-salmon flowers with a hint of veining. Almost indistinguishable from 'A.T. Johnson' in habit and foliage.

'Sherwood' has light pink flowers consisting of narrow petals.

'Southcombe Star' bears flowers with many narrow bluish pink petals, often providing the appearance of double flowers. The habit is more spreading than many other selections.

'Thurstonianum' has purple flowers, occasionally semi-double, consisting of narrow, strap-shaped petals. It is more interesting than pretty. Quite variable, differing in the intensity of flower color and the amount of leaf blotching.

'Wageningen', named for the Dutch research station of the same name, has coral colored petals and compact growth.

'Walters Gift', another Heronswood selection, differs by having strongly bronze-zoned foliage. Flowers are similar to 'Claridge Druce'.

'Winscombe' is a little smaller than 'Wargrave Pink' and is distinguished by a greater change of petal color during the flowering time, from white to a moderately deep pink. The petals are slightly notched and veined. Found in the village of Winscombe, Somerset, England by the fine gardener and writer, Margery Fish.

*G.* × *riversleaianum* is a hybrid between *G. endressii* and *G. traversii*, a little-used geranium native to New Zealand. Flowers are pink to magenta and plants grow approximately 12″ tall. Two good cultivars have become available in the United States from the many progeny which have undoubtedly occurred. It is likely that these hybrids are less cold tolerant than *G. endressii* due to the New Zealand presence of one of the parents. Propagate by division.

'Mavis Simpson' has deeply indented leaves with broad lobes. The 1′ wide light pink flowers with dark purple veins tend to fade with age. The centers of the flowers are creamy white. Plants grow about 18″ tall. Named for a staff member at Kew Gardens.

'Russell Pritchard' is a well-known cultivar with 1½″ diameter magenta flowers and dull gray-green, lobed foliage. The flower color is much more intense than either parent, leading to speculation that this may be a hybrid between *G. sanguineum* and *G. endressii*.

| *-himalayense* (hi-mah-lay-en′ se) | Lilac Geranium | 10–15″/15″ |
|---|---|---|
| Summer    Lilac | Northern Asia | Zones 4–7 |

(Syn. *G. grandiflorum, G. meeboldii*)

Plants are large enough for the border but since they tend to sprawl, are better placed near pathways where their unruly growth can be used to informal advantage. The 3–6″ diameter leaves are deeply cut into 7 divisions, each division 3-lobed at the apex. The petioles are up to 6″ long, resulting in a sprawling habit. In the fall, the foliage turns bright orange and red before disappearing. The 1½–2″ diameter, violet-blue flowers have a warm reddish center and are the largest of any species of geranium. They are saucer shaped with prominent red-purple veins and flowering continues for 4–6 weeks. Plant in full sun in well-drained soil and do not allow to dry out.

Propagate by division every 2–3 years or from seed.

### Cultivars:

'Birch Double' (syn. 'Plenum') has ½″ diameter, washed-out, double, lavender flowers. It is less vigorous and less attractive than the species. The flowers, however, are sterile and persist much longer than the singles.

'Gravetye' (syn. 'Alpinum') bears 2″ wide bright blue flowers with reddish centers and dark veins. It is shorter (about 12″ tall) and less unruly than the species. This cultivar is a knockout.

'Irish Blue', found in Ireland in 1947 by the noted horticulturist, Graham Thomas, bears large pale blue flowers with a large purplish center area. The petals are slightly notched at the ends.

### Related Species:

*G.* × 'Johnson's Blue' is an excellent hybrid between *G. himalayense* and *G. pratense* and appeared in English gardens around 1950 from seed of *G. pratense* sent by A.T. Johnson from Holland. Seed set is minimal so flowering continues for a long time. Every gardener who comes back from the British Isles must have this plant in their garden, only to be disappointed. In the North and West, plants do well in the summer but don't always return, particularly after a cold winter. In the south, the heat results in long lanky stems with few flowers and slow frustration.

The parents are rather different in growth habit, and this hybrid is intermediate between them in leaf characteristics. At 15–18″ tall, it is taller than

457

*G. himalayense* but not as big as a well-grown *G. pratense*. The 1½–2″ diameter, clear blue, unnotched flowers are similar in color to those of *G. himalayense*, but without the reddish center.

| *-macrorrhizum* (mak-ro-rise′ um) | | Bigroot Geranium | 15–18″/15″ |
| --- | --- | --- | --- |
| Spring | Magenta | Southern Europe | Zones 3–8 |

One of the earliest geranium species in cultivation, plants of *G. macrorrhizum* were cultivated for their oil (Oil of Geranium) as early as 1576. When surrounded by dozens of geranium species, it is nice to know that at least one is easily distinguished from the rest. Crushing a leaf provides the unmistakable medicinal smell of *G. macrorrhizum*. The 6–8″ wide leaves have 7 divisions, cut two-thirds the way down, each division shallowly lobed. The 1″ diameter, purplish magenta flowers have entire petals and dark red calyces (the sepals) inflated like tiny balloons. They are held on a slightly hairy peduncle. The plant has thick, fleshy, rhizomatous roots and spreads well in areas of full sun to partial shade. The vigorous root system allows it to compete during drought when others falter, and thus is an excellent species as a ground cover. Plants are reasonably heat tolerant, performing well in zone 7 in partial shade. This is one of the easiest geraniums to grow.

Propagate by dividing the thick rootstock using the rosette bearing stems as cuttings, or by seed. Seed should not be covered before placing it in a warm, humid area.

### Cultivars:
'Album' bears white petals with pink calyces and is a lovely garden plant.

'Beven's Variety' is 8–10″ tall with 1″ wide flowers consisting of deep red sepals and magenta petals.

'Czakor' has a low habit, growing at most 15″ tall. The rosy sepals contrast with the magenta petals.

'Pindus' from Heronswood Nursery appears to be a dwarf form of 'Czakor'.

'Ingwersen's Variety', named after the noted English horticulturist, Walter Ingwersen, has pale pink flowers with slightly glossier leaves than the type. It is the finest cultivar for the garden.

'Spressart' originated in Germany and is already mixed up in the trade. Although white and pale pink flowering forms are sold under this name, the original name refers to plants with dark pink to rose-colored petals.

'Variegatum' has leaves irregularly variegated with cream, with typical flowers of the species.

### Related Species:
*G. thunbergii* is related only in that plants make an effective ground cover, particularly in the South. It is, however, a terrible weed. Plants consist of light green, hairy leaves on sprawling stems and dozens of ½″ diameter white to pink flowers which appear in late summer. Not recommended for the garden.

-× *magnificum* (mag-nif′ i-cum)     Showy Geranium     18–24″/24″
    Summer          Dark Blue          Hybrid             Zones 3–8

This sterile hybrid resulted from *G. ibericum* × *G. platypetalum* and bears hairy foliage with 5–7 deeply cut divisions. The peduncles are 4–5″ long, and the 1½″ diameter, deep violet-blue flowers are held erect and upright. Plants are quite similar to *G. ibericum* and are distinguished by their more vigorous growth and sterility. Plants are large and tend to flop over in rain and wind. They can be cut back after flowering to produce a new set of leaves; however, flowering will not occur again. Plants are more vigorous than either of the parents. Grow in full sun to partial shade in well-drained soil. There apparently are a number of clones here and there in botanic gardens, but I am not aware of any accepted cultivar names for the various clones.

Propagate by divisions every 2–3 years.

**Related Species:**

*G. ibericum*, Caucasus geranium, is similar to and a parent of the hybrid. Plants differ by having the divisions cut about three-quarters of the way

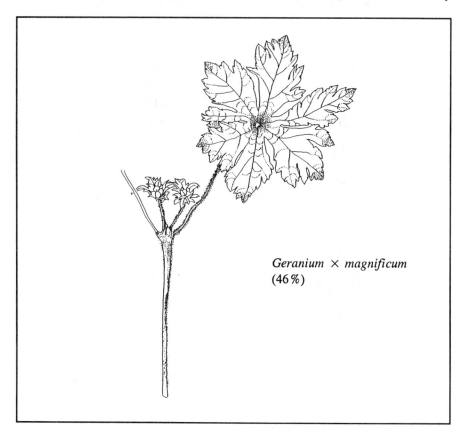

*Geranium* × *magnificum*
(46%)

down the leaf, and flowers are fertile. Caucasus geranium is also more drought tolerant, but a little less vigorous than the hybrid.

*-phaeum* (fie' um)                                    Mourning Widow         18–24"/18"
    Early Summer        Dark Maroon        Europe                        Zones 5–7

This distinct species produces very dark, almost black, nodding flowers which suggest "a widow in mourning." The petals, which are about as long as broad, are slightly reflexed resulting in the pistil and stamens being totally exserted. The flowers look like a can-can girl raising her purple skirt. The erect stems bear 5–7 deeply divided leaves, each division having small purple spots at their bases. The thick rhizomes allow plants to tolerate some drought, although they perform best under moist conditions. Plants are native to damp meadows and shady roadsides, and can be grown in shady, moist areas of the garden. This is not a plant which will knock you over with color, but I tend to agree with Walter Ingwersen's comments in 1946, who stated that plants "will appeal to those who have an eye for unusual and quiet charm." Little success has occurred in establishing plants in zone 8, and likely zone 7 is the southern limit.

**Cultivars:**
'Album' has white or faintly blushed petals.
'Lily Lovell' bears flowers of a deep mauve, but not as dark as the species. The leaves are lighter green and produce a handsome contrast with the mauve flowers. Plants flower a little earlier and are larger than the species.
Var. *lividum* has paler flowers occasionally streaked with lilac spots. They are more colorful and easier on the eyes. Within this variety is a tall, large flowered form called 'Majus'.
Var. *phaeum* probably bears the darkest flowers of the group, producing purple-black nodding flowers with white star-shaped centers.
'Variegatum' has leaves with irregular yellow margins, and often with purple blotches. Unusual and most difficult to locate.

**Related Species:**
*G. aristatum* is similar to *G. phaeum* but not as upright. The flowers are white to lilac-pink and the reflexed petals have lovely lilac veins. The leaves are also more pubescent.
*G. × monacense* is a hybrid between *G. phaeum* and *G. reflexum*, with characteristics intermediate between the two. The hybrid was first described in Germany and commemorates the city of Munich. Leaves may be blotched or not.
*G. reflexum* is also similar, but the flowers are not as dark purple and are smaller. The petals, which are twice as long as broad, are the most reflexed of any species. The immature fruits are downwardly inclined in this species, but upwardly inclined in *G. phaeum*.

***-platypetalum*** (pla-ti-pet-ah′ lum)   Broad-Petaled Geranium   18–24″/18″
   Late Spring    Deep Violet    Caucasus             Zones 3–7

The sticky flower stalks carry deep violet, 1″ diameter flowers with reddish veins. The 4–6″ wide rounded leaves have 7–9 divisions, each cut about halfway into the leaf. Partial shade, particularly in the South, is preferable to full sun. All parts of the plant are noticeably hairy. Although not as showy as one of its children, *G.* × *magnificum*, it is heat tolerant and makes a good show in the garden. The foliage persists all season and does not require cutting back as do most other species.

Propagate by divisions or seed.

### Related Species:
*G. renardii* is a beautiful but temperamental species not seen often enough in American gardens. The 5–7 divisions of the dull gray-green foliage are shallowly lobed and the flowers are unmistakable. Each 1″ diameter white flower is vividly marked with violet feathered veins and well worth trying. Excellent drainage and a sheltered location are required. Good garden performance can be expected in zones 5 and 6, and western zone 8.

***-pratense*** (prah′ ten′ see)    Meadow Cranesbill    24–36″/24″
   Late Spring    Purple        Northern Europe    Zones 5–7

Meadow cranesbill is widely distributed in the Old World and therefore quite variable. The 3–6″ wide leaves are deeply cut into 7–9 divisions, each of which is deeply serrated. The 1½″ diameter flowers have reddish, sometimes translucent, veins on the dark blue petals. This is one of the tallest and most vigorous of the cranesbills, and plants often need support to remain upright. One of the problems with this species is its enthusiasm for seed production, often resulting in rapid and messy shedding of flowers. When grown in zone 7, they tend to look weedy and foliage must be cut back after flowering. This species tolerates limey soils better than many others, naturally occurring on calcareous soils in Europe. Plant in full sun and provide plenty of moisture.

Propagate by division or seed.

### Cultivars:
'Galactic' is over 2′ tall, with flat topped inflorescences of white flowers with translucent veins. The petals overlap and are sometimes slightly notched. A number of white forms have been sold as 'Album' and 'Albiflorum'. They are all about the same.

'Mrs. Kendall Clarke' has pale blue flowers with rosy-white venation. A really handsome clone. The cultivar was first described in 1946 and there appear to be more than one form in commerce. It is definitely pale blue suffused with rose veins, but the same name has mistakenly been given darker forms as well.

'Plenum Album', 'Plenum Caeruleum', and 'Plenum Violaceum' have 1″
  diameter, small double flowers of white, pale blue, and purple, respectively. They persist longer than the single flower types because they do
  not shed as rapidly.
'Silver Queen' is 3′ tall and bears 1–2″ diameter silvery-blue flowers.
'Striatum' ('Bicolor') has white petals spotted with varying amounts and
  intensities of violet-blue.

| -*procurrens* (pro-cure′ ens) | | Trailing Geranium | 6–9″/3′ |
|---|---|---|---|
| Summer | Magenta | Himalayas | Zone 5–7 |

Plants bear 1″ diameter flowers of blindingly-rich magenta, with black
centers in the summer. The petals do not overlap and the flowers are not as
handsome as those of *G. psilostemon*. Essentially, plants are ground covers
which can ramble and scramble through and about other plants. The red
stems trail for long distances like strawberry runners and root at the nodes,
making them effective ground cover plants for a sunny area. They are
effective, but harsh of flower and foliage.

**Related Species:**
  'Dilys' is a cross between *G. sanguineum* and *G. procurrens* with late
purple flowers on prostrate stems.
  *G. malvaeflorum* is a tuberous plant and is similar to the above only in that
they both act as ground covers. Native to Northwest Africa, plants are only
cold tolerant to zone 7; however, they are wonderfully heat tolerant. This is
because the tubers are deep rooted and plants go summer dormant after
flowering. The mauve to violet flowers are about 1″ wide and are produced in
early- to mid-spring. In mild winters, the foliage arises in winter, in harsher
winters, foliage may not arise until early spring. A good plant for everyone,
but a particularly good one for Southern gardeners to try.

| -*psilostemon* (sye-lo′ ste-mon) | Armenian Geranium | 24–48″/36″ |
|---|---|---|
| Summer  Magenta with black center | Armenia | Zones 5–7 |
| (Syn. *G. armenum*) | | |

The first time I saw this plant was at Sissinghurst Castle and Garden,
Kent, England. I observed and studied well over a thousand plant species
that trip, but the stateliness and beauty of this one was unforgettable. The
6–8″ wide, heart-shaped, basal, evergreen foliage is cut nearly four-fifths
of the length into 5–7 sections, while the stem leaves are triangular. The
1½–2″ diameter, bright magenta flowers have a conspicuous black spot in
the middle. It is a color one either hates or loves.
  This is not a small plant; heights of 3–4′ are not uncommon and the
stems need support. Plants should be placed in broken shade and in rich

moist soil to perform their best. They look better planted against a dark background where their luminous flowers will stand out even more. At the time of the writing of the first edition, plants were almost non-existent in the United States. I grew some plants in the Armitage garden (zone 7b), and they stood only 2' tall after 4 years. As the shade of the oaks grew, I finally replaced them with other plants more adaptable to the changing conditions. Today, plants are much more available than five years ago. In general, plants in the East will disappoint if compared to those in the British Isles, but so what? They are handsome if sited well and deserve a greater following in this country.

Propagate by division of the root stalk or by seed.

### Cultivars:

'Bressingham Flair' is about 2' tall and does not require as much support as the species. The flowers are a little less intense and with a hint of pink in the magenta.

### Related Hybrids:

'Ann Folkard' is a natural hybrid which occurred in 1973 between *G. procurrens*, a trailing ground cover species, and *G. psilostemon*. This is a stunning plant, which American gardeners are just starting to discover. It is outstanding when scrambling over shrubs and bushes, and its "climbing" tendencies are unique in such a vigorous geranium. The leaves are always light green, sometimes appearing chlorotic, and require a second look to appreciate. The rich magenta flowers have a black center and contrast brightly with the leaves. This has to be a winner on the west coast and probably will do well in zones 5–7 east of the Rockies. We owe this plant to an amateur gardener, Rev. O.G. Folkard, from Lincolnshire, England, who set out to collect and hybridize geraniums which appealed to him, one of which he named for his daughter Ann. Such plants are powerful testimonials to the ability of amateur gardeners to have a significant impact on horticulture.

| *-sanguineum* (sang-guin' ee-um) | Bloody Cranesbill | 9–12"/12" |
|---|---|---|
| Spring      Magenta | Europe, Asia | Zones 3–8 |

Of the cultivated geraniums, this is probably the most common garden species in the United States. Plants are adaptable, able to tolerate heat and cold better than other species, and are free flowering. They generally grow in mounds, consisting of thick shallowly-divided basal leaves and thinner, deeply-divided stem leaves. The foliage also provides a touch of fall color, turning crimson-red. The 1–1½" diameter flowers are a rich magenta, often too fierce for the tastes of many gardeners. This genus has more than its share of that often intolerable magenta color. However, not everything can be pleasing to the eye. The flowers are solitary and the petals are unnotched.

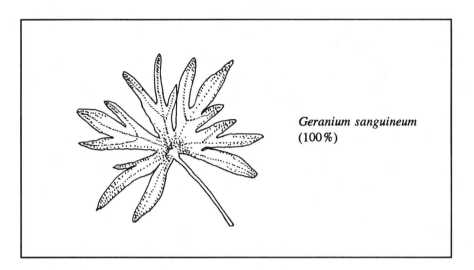

*Geranium sanguineum*
(100%)

Plants should be placed in full sun or partial shade in the front of the garden. In shade they are less compact, less floriferous, and taller than in the sun. This is the most trouble-free species for southern gardeners as the thick root stalk ferrets out moisture in times of drought, and the waxy basal leaves tolerate hot weather. Many cultivars have been introduced, but differences between some of them are minimal at best.

Propagate by division every 3-4 years or from seed.

### Cultivars:

'Alan Bloom' is a short-growing plant with relatively large magenta flowers.

'Album' has clear white flowers and grows 10-18″ tall. It is an excellent cultivar; far easier on the eyes than the species.

'Alpenglow' grows about 8″ tall with vivid rose-red flowers.

'Cedric Morris' has large rosy-magenta flowers over vigorous 1-1½′ tall plants. Plants flower earlier in the spring and occasionally throughout the season.

'Elsbeth', a fine English name, has some of the largest flowers of the species. She is bright purple and grows only about 9″ tall.

'Glenluce' has 1½-2″ diameter, clear pink flowers on compact plants.

'Holden' is a spreading plant, with small leaves and rosy-pink flowers. Named for Holden Clough Nursery in Lancashire, England in the early 1970's.

'John Elsley', named for the fine horticulturist at Wayside Gardens, South Carolina, was selected by Blooms of Bressingham at the same time they selected the cultivar 'Alan Bloom' (above). Little differences can be seen between them, although 'John Elsley' may be a little taller.

'Jubilee Pink' has magenta-pink flowers over compact foliage.

'Max Frei' produces purple-pink, saucer-shaped flowers over compact plants.

'Minutum' grows only a few inches tall and bears deep rose flowers less than 1″ wide.

'Shepherd's Warning' is an outstanding compact form with deep rose-pink flowers. Raised by the nurseryman Jack Drake, in Aviemore, Scotland, along with 'Jubilee Pink'. Plants are excellent as rock garden or wall plants.

Var. *striatum* is the best of the lot, and is often sold under the name 'Lancastriense' or 'Prostratum'. It is only 6–8″ tall, and although flower color is somewhat variable, the best forms have light pink flowers with crimson veins.

### Related Species:

*G. wallichianum*, Wallich geranium, is a prostrate species with 2′ long trailing stems, making this an excellent geranium for growing over stone walls or in patio pots. The late-summer flowers are purple and not outstanding. However, the cultivar 'Buxton's Variety' has small white marbled foliage and saucer-shaped campanula blue flowers with a distinct white center. A planting laden with flowers romping over rocks and walls is a magnificent sight. Plants commemorate E.C. Buxton, in whose garden it appeared around 1920. It may be raised from root cuttings, and comes true from seed.

| | | | |
|---|---|---|---|
| *-sylvaticum* (sil-va′ ti-kum) | | Wood Cranesbill | 30–36″/30″ |
| Spring | Purple-Violet | Europe | Zones 5–8 |

One of the earliest flowering geraniums, flowers appear as early as late April in the South and May further north. The 6–7″ wide roundish leaves are deeply cut into 7–9 divisions. The 1″ wide purplish violet flowers have a white base and are like tiny chalices open to the sky, being borne neither horizontal nor nodding. The seed capsules are thrust into the air like athletes showing the crowd they are number one. The flowers are usually violet-blue with a white center, but may be pink or white. The species is not as garden worthy as some of the cultivars. Plants are best placed in partial shade and a moisture-retentive soil.

Propagate by division every 2–3 years or by seed.

### Cultivars:

'Album' is a white flowered cultivar with light green leaves. It comes true from seed. Quite tolerant of shade.

'Mayflower', introduced around 1972, is the best of the group, bearing rich violet-blue flowers with a white base.

### Related Species:

*G. orientalitibeticum* is not closely related botanically to *G. sanguineum*, but the flowers are similar in color and form. The foliage of the former is deeply divided almost to the base, and marbled with yellow throughout. Plants are aggressive ground covers which require cool nights and excellent drainage to do well.

Quick Key to Geranium Species

    A. Plants very low growing, less than 8″ tall
      B. Plants with runners, acting
         as a ground cover . . . . . . . . . . . . . . . . . *G. procurrens*
      BB. Plants not growing as ground covers,
         no runners produced
         C. Peduncles usually 2-flowered, flowers
            erect or upwardly inclined . . . . . . . . . . . . *G. cinereum*
         CC. Peduncles usually 3-flowered,
            flowers horizontal or nodding . . . . . . . . *G. dalmaticum*
  AA. Plants usually 9″ or taller,
      may be erect or sprawling
      B. Flowers sterile, no seed produced
         C. Foliage aromatic, calyx inflated . . . . *G.* × *cantabrigiense*
         CC. Foliage not obviously aromatic,
            calyx not inflated . . . . . . . . . . . . . . *G.* × *magnificum*
      BB. Flowers not sterile, seed produced
         C. Flowers erect or upwardly inclined
            D. Peduncles 1-flowered . . . . . . . . . . . . *G. sanguineum*
           DD. Peduncles 2 to many flowered
              E. Flowers red to magenta
                with black central disc . . . . . . . . . . *G. psilostemon*
             EE. Flowers white, purple, blue, or pink
                F. Immature fruit erect,
                   flower usually violet-blue . . . . . . . . *G. sylvaticum*
                FF. Immature fruit nodding,
                   flowers white, purple, or pink
                   G. Flowers white or purple . . . . . . . . . *G. clarkei*
                   GG. Flowers usually pink . . . . . . . . . . *G. endressii*
         CC. Flowers not erect, directed horizontally
           or nodding
            D. Leaves not deeply divided, divisions
              cut only about ½ way down leaf,
              calyx not inflated . . . . . . . . . . . . . . *G. platypetalum*
           DD. Leaves divided so incisions reach
              more than ⅔ way down leaf, calyx
              may or may not be inflated
              E. Plant usually taller than 24″
                F. Flowers conspicuously nodding and
                   reflexed, dark maroon to almost black . . *G. phaeum*
                FF. Flowers slightly nodding, not
                   reflexed, blue to violet-blue . . . . . . . . *G. pratense*

EE. Plant usually less than 24″ tall
    F. Plants with thickened woody base,
       flowers purple to magenta, foliage
       strongly aromatic when crushed  . . *G. macrorrhizum*
    FF. Plants without thickened woody
       base, flowers lilac to blue, foliage
       not aromatic when crushed  . . . . . . *G. himalayense*

**Additional Reading:**

*Books:*

Yeo, Peter F. 1985. *Hardy Geraniums*. Timber Press, Portland, OR: 192 pages. It is impossible to deal with all the potential gems in this genus, but for geranium addicts like myself, I highly recommend this book. Dr. Yeo is one of the foremost geranium experts in the world and provides great detail concerning botanical and taxonomic differences between hundreds of species. Although not for the beginner, it is an excellent reference.

*Manuscripts:*

Bacon, L. 1993. Geraniums for the rock garden. *Quarterly Bulletin of the Alpine Garden Society* 61(2):171–190.
Bush, A. 1993. On the fast track with hardy geraniums. *Perennial Plants* 1(3):5–7.
Faustgen, J. 1993. Perennial portraits: Hardy geraniums. *Minnesota Horticulture* 121(9):2.
Forty, Joy. 1980. A survey of hardy geraniums in cultivation. *The Plantsman* 2(2):67–78. This treatise was further clarified in the form of a "Letter to the Editor" by Joy Forty, 1981. *The Plantsman* 3(2):127–128.
Harper, Pamela. 1976. True geraniums. *Horticulture* 54(4):56–57.
Hensel, Margaret. 1985. Hardy geraniums. *Horticulture* 63(7):20–23.
Leslie, A.C. 1993. *Geranium macrorrhizum*. *The Garden* 118(8):340–342.
Nelson, C. E. 1991. *Geranium cataractarum*. *The Kew Magazine* 8(2):51–53.
Parer, Robin. 1993. Hardy geraniums. *Fine Gardening* 29: 32–35.
Thompson, D. 1984. Hardy geraniums. *Pacific Horticulture* 45(3):17–21.
Wright, J.B. 1994. Hardy geraniums. *Horticulture* 72(1):32–36.
Yeo, P.F. 1984. *Geranium candicans* and *G. yunnanense* of gardens. *The Garden* 109(1):36–37.

## *Geum* (jee′ um)           Avens            Rosaceae

Over 50 species are included in this genus known for its bright, showy, 5-petaled flowers and dark green leaves. The compound foliage is cut in various ways, depending on the species, but the terminal lobe is always the largest. In some species, their charm is extended by the production of fluffy

467

seed heads, similar those of *Pulsatilla*. Species such as *G. reptans* are small enough to be included in the rockery, while taller ones, such as *G. montanum*, are sufficiently large for inclusion in the border. All require good drainage, ample moisture, and some protection from full afternoon sun. Most geums are easily grown in the northern part of the country, but struggle in the South.

Propagate by division in spring or fall, or from fresh seed. Multiplication of cultivars should be accomplished vegetatively. Unfortunately, natural hybridization takes place readily between species, and the resulting seedlings are often inferior.

Quick Reference to Geum Species

| | Height (in.) | Flower color | Seed head fluffy |
|---|---|---|---|
| *G.* × *borisii* | 9–12 | Orange | Yes |
| *G. chiloense* | 20–24 | Yellow, red | Yes |
| *G.* × *heldreichii* | 12–24 | Redish orange | No |
| *G. montanum* | 9–12 | Yellow orange | Yes |
| *G. reptans* | 6–8 | Yellow | Yes |
| *G. rivale* | 8–12 | Red, pink | No |
| *G. triflorum* | 9–12 | Mauve | No |

| -× *borisii* (bo-ris′ ee-eye) | Boris Avens | 9–12″/12″ |
|---|---|---|
| Spring    Orange-Scarlet | Hybrid | Zones 3–7 |

This hybrid arose as a result of a cross between *G. bulgaricum*, a 2′ tall species with nodding yellow flowers, and *G. reptans*, a 6–8″ yellow stoloniferous species. The trifoliate leaves have rounded lobes and the terminal lobe is twice as large as the laterals. Properly labelled plants form large clumps with 1–2″ wide, bright yellow, nodding flowers held well above the foliage on branching stems. Heavy flowering takes place for about 4 weeks in late spring and early summer and intermittently until fall. Plants are not often found in commerce. Plant in partial shade and keep uniformly moist.

**Cultivars:**

'Baby Tangerine' may be a hybrid of many other species but it is similar in habit to *G.* × *borisii*. With a long flowering period, bearing bright orange blooms and standing only about 6″ tall, it is best described as a miniature *borisii*. An excellent vigorous plant, useful for the rock garden or front of the border.

'Feuermeer' ('Sea of Fire') grows about 12″ tall and produces fire engine red flowers.

'Werner Arends' carries many semi-double orange flowers tinted red. This cultivar has often inadvertently been listed as *G. borisii* or *G. coccineum* 'Borisii'.

| | | | |
|---|---|---|---|
| ***-chiloense*** (chill-o′ en-se) | | Chilean Avens | 20–24″/18″ |
| Spring | Scarlet | Chile | Zones 4–7 |

(Syn. *G. quellyon*)

This species is the most common of garden avens but, in my opinion, is overrated. The 6–12″ long hairy leaves are pinnately divided into 5–7 lobes; the terminal being about twice as large as the other leaflets. The 1–1½″ wide scarlet flowers may be single or double. The species doesn't tolerate the excesses of the American climate, struggling a great deal in the summer and often dying out in the winter. Plants are short-lived even under the best of conditions. To be fair, some cultivars can look stunning when grown in a well-drained area out of the hot afternoon sun and kept consistently moist.

The botanical name of this and similar species continues to flip flop all over the place. From *G. chiloense* to *G. quellyon* and back again, and with cultivars which may be placed with this species or with *G. coccineum* or may be hybrids between them, the taxonomy continues to perplex.

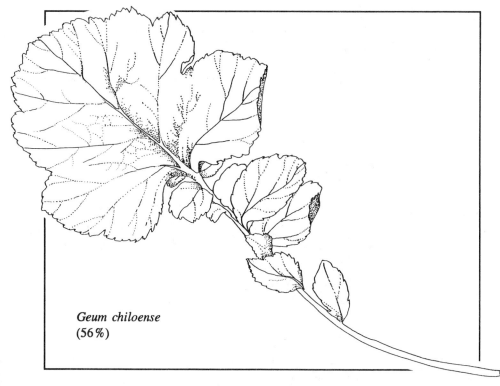

*Geum chiloense*
(56%)

## Cultivars:

Cultivars have superseded the species, many of which are hybrids between *G. chiloense* and *G. coccineum*, a shorter brick red species. Most cultivars are short-lived, perhaps performing well for a couple of years, then declining. According to some old-time gardeners, there appears to be a progressive loss of vigor of the hybrids compared to twenty years ago.

'Bernstein' carries light golden flowers on 18″ plants.
'Coppertone' is less than 1′ tall, bearing early wide open apricot flowers.
'Dolly North' has golden orange, semi-double flowers.
'Fire Opal' produces many intense orange-scarlet, semi-double flowers.
'Lady Stratheden' ('Goldball') has deep buttercup-yellow semi-double flowers.
'Mrs. Bradshaw' bears scarlet, semi-double flowers. The last two cultivars
    can be raised from seed. While both have their admirers, they produce
    too few flowers for the amount of leaf area.
'Prince of Orange' has many deep orange flowers.
'Princess Juliana', raised in 1923, bears soft yellow semi-double flowers
    that open about one week later than the others.
'Red Wings' is similar to 'Fire Opal', but has more orange in the flower.

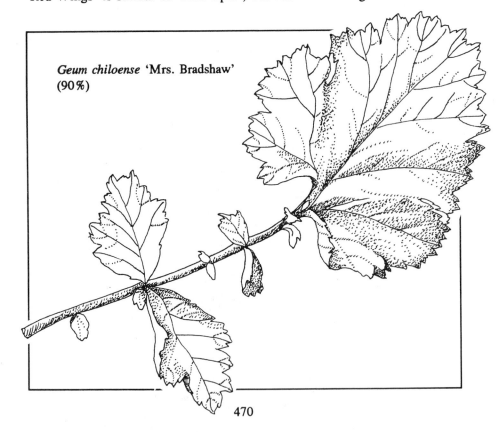

*Geum chiloense* 'Mrs. Bradshaw'
(90%)

'Rijnstroom' has copper colored single flowers on 18–20″ stems.
'Rubin' bears semi-double crimson flowers, about 12–15″ tall.

| -× *heldreichii* (hel-dritch-ee′ eye) | | | 1–2′/2′ |
|---|---|---|---|
| Summer | Orange-Red | Hybrid | Zones 4–7 |

A hybrid of confused lineage, but thought to be a hybrid between *G. montanum* and *G. coccineum*. Plants are taller than *G. montanum* and the 1–2″ diameter, reddish orange flowers are borne in twos and threes. It is not terribly well adapted to heat and persisted for about two years in north Georgia gardens.

Propagate by division in the spring.

**Cultivars:**
'Georgenberg' is a hybrid with soft, pale yellow flowers arising from nodding buds. Often listed as a cultivar of *G. chiloense*.
'Magnificum' bears semi-double orange flowers.
'Bank Jewel' ('Uferschmuck') has orange-red flowers.

| -*montanum* (mon-tah′ num) | | Mountain Avens | 6–9″/12″ |
|---|---|---|---|
| Spring | Golden Yellow | Southern Europe | Zones 3–7 |

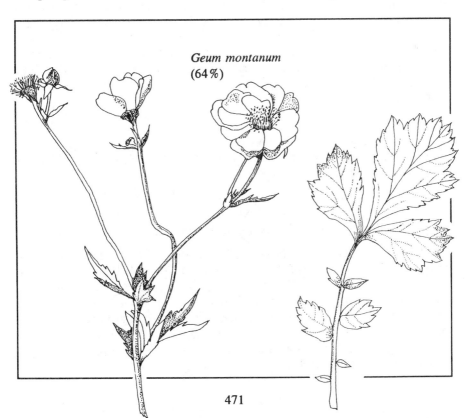

*Geum montanum*
(64%)

471

The foliage of the species is among the prettiest and longest lasting of the genus. The leaves are about 4″ long and densely pubescent; the terminal leaflet is about 2″ long. Leaves remain fresh well into the summer, unlike many species whose leaves deteriorate soon after flowering. The 1″ wide flowers are held in a 1–3 flowered inflorescence well above the foliage and are a lovely golden yellow. The seed heads are feathery and as pretty as the flowers.

Plants are native to sub-alpine areas around 6000′ elevation and do best in areas of cool summers, or at least cool summer nights.

### Related Species:

*G. rossii* grows 9–12″ tall and produces relatively large (1–1½″ wide) yellow flowers. The plants form a coarse mat made up of deeply divided leaves. They are stoloniferous and spread rapidly.

| | | | |
|---|---|---|---|
| *-reptans* (rep′ tanz) | | Creeping Avens | 6–8″/8″ |
| Spring | Yellow | European Alps | Zones 3–7 |

If full morning sun, good drainage, and somewhat basic soil are provided, this little plant can be a definite asset to the garden. However, if not given these conditions, it will throw its runners in the air, give up and die. The leaflets are deeply toothed, and unlike many others, the terminal leaflet is about the same size as the laterals. As a ground cover, plants multiply by rooting along the nodes of non-flowering runners. Many solitary, 1–1½″ diameter, pale yellow flowers are borne in early summer.

Propagate by cutting the rooted runners and replanting in the final location. Seed germinates within 2–3 weeks under warm (70–75° F), humid conditions.

### Related Hybrids:

*G.* × *rhaeticum*, a hybrid between *G. montanum* and *G. reptans*, has foliar characteristics intermediate between the two. One inch diameter golden-yellow flowers cover 6–8″ tall plants.

| | | |
|---|---|---|
| *-rivale* (ree-vah′ lee) | Water Avens, Indian Chocolate | 8–12″/10″ |
| Spring  Red-Orange | Eurasia, North America | Zones 3–7 |

While most species bear upright yellowish flowers and require consistent moisture and sharp drainage, this species has nodding, bell-shaped, reddish purple flowers and is, for all intents and purposes, a bog plant. The foliage consists of 7–13 leaflets, the terminal twice as large as the lateral ones. The leaflets are hairy and noticeably serrated. This is a good ground cover plant for cool, wet areas where little else does well. However, it is also useable in non-boggy areas, but constant moisture must be available. It performs poorly in areas of hot, humid weather.

The rootstock is thick and brown and if boiled in water, the resultant liquid tastes faintly like chocolate, a tale I have fortunately not had the pleasure of verifying.

Propagate by seed or division.

**Cultivars:**

'Album' bears nodding white flowers with rosy calyces (sepals) in early summer.

'Leonard's Variety' ('Leonardii') has drooping mahogany-red, bell-shaped flowers and deeply-cut green foliage. Very floriferous. Plants show hybrid vigor and may be a hybrid, possibly with *G. coccineum*.

'Leonard's Double' is similar to the above but carries double flowers.

'Lionel Cox' is about 12″ tall and has nodding primrose flowers with light green leaves.

**Related Hybrids:**

*G. × intermedium* is a hybrid between *G. rivale* and *G. urbanum* and forms aggressive ground covering clumps about 18″ tall. Plants bear pale yellow flowers enhanced by reddish brown sepals. Happy in wet areas.

*G. × tirolense* is a hybrid between *G. rivale* and *G. montanum*. 'Lemon Drops' has nodding wide-open yellow flowers with purplish centers.

| *-triflorum* (try-flor′ um) | | Prairie Smoke | 9–12″/12″ |
|---|---|---|---|
| Summer | Mauve | Central United States | Zones 1–7 |

These distinctive plants are native from the high Plains to rocky slopes through the Cascade Mountains to the Sierra Nevadas, Colorado and Nebraska. The drooping purplish red nodding flowers are campanulate to cup-shaped. Flowers occur in one or more flowered inflorescences, but often in threes. The flowers give rise to feathery silver and pink cottony fruit, which persist for many weeks after flowering. The leaves are quite different from other species in that there are about 30 leaflets on each 6″ long leaf. The entire plant is softly hairy.

Interesting for well-drained areas in full sun, winter hardy as the snow.

Quick Key to Geum Species

    A. Flowers upright, petals much longer than sepals
      B. Plants upright, do not produce runners
        C. Plants usually taller than 18″ . . . . . . . . . . *G. chiloense*
      CC. Plants usually less than 18″ tall
          D. Flowers usually solitary on flower stem . . *G. montanum*
          DD. Flowers not solitary . . . . . . . . . . . . . . *G. × borisii*
      BB. Plants prostrate, produce many runners . . . . . . . . *G. reptans*
    AA. Flowers nodding, petals barely longer than sepals
      B. Leaflets 7–13 . . . . . . . . . . . . . . . . . . . . . . . . *G. rivale*
      BB. Leaflets often to 30 . . . . . . . . . . . . . . . . . . . *G. triflorum*

**Additional Reading:**
Burrell, C. Colston. 1992. Prairie smoke. *Horticulture* 70(5):96.

## *Gillenia* (gil-ee′ nee-a)  Physic, Ipecac  Rosaceae
(Syn. *Porteranthus*)

Still an overlooked genus, *Gillenia* contains 2 species native to the United States which are wonderfully ornamental. Moist areas and partial afternoon shade are requirements for best performance. Propagate by division in the spring or by seed. The syrup, Ipecac, comes from a Brazilian shrub (*Psychotria ipecacuanha*), although American Ipecac has similar, although less effective, properties.

**-trifoliata** (tri-fo-lee-ah′ ta)  Bowman's Root, Indian Physic  2–4′/3′
Summer  White  Central, Southern United States  Zones 4–7

I was first "turned on" to this species in Aas, Norway, where it shimmered in the late afternoon sun. I was embarrassed to learn that it was native from New York to Georgia, but noticed that it was seldom available to gardeners in America. The 3-foliate leaves are borne on short leaf stalks, and each 2–3″ long ovate leaflet is serrated and pointed. Small insignificant stipules (leaf-like structures) are found at the base of the petiole on the upper nodes.

In the summer, plants bear such masses of 1″ wide, white, star-shaped flowers that they look like clouds of butterflies. The 5 white petals emerge from small, tubular, wine-colored sepals which persist long after the petals have fallen. The flowers are held above the foliage on wiry stems terminating in paniculate corymbs. Place in partial shade and moist areas or plants will languish. Unfortunately, support is usually required, particularly in the southern zones. A plant or two is well worth trying if you have the space.

**Related Species:**

*G. stipulata*, American Ipecac, is similar but does not have the persistent red sepals. The leaflets are narrower and the stipules are larger and more leaf-like than those of the previous species. Plants are native from New York to Georgia and Louisiana, and is easier to establish in the South than the previous species. Fortunately, it is becoming easier to find.

## *Gladiolus* (glad-ee′ o-lus)  Gladiolus  Iridaceae

The many species and their hybridization can be discussed only superficially in this book. Although there are over 250 species, it is difficult for the home gardener to find anything but the large-flowered hybrids. Recently, a number of miniature-flowered hybrids have become available, but one must search to find any of the actual species. Arguably, in point of beauty, the natural species seldom compare with today's fine garden hybrids. The modern hybrids evolved from *G.* × *gandavensis*, × *childsi*, × *nanceianus*, and × *lemoinei*, all of which are of little garden interest today. There has been so much additional hybridization that it is almost impossible to know what parents produced what cultivars. All modern hybrids have been lumped together under *G.* × *hortulanus*.

Named varieties abound and are usually classified as: large-flowered, which have flowers 4–5″ across; butterfly flowers, which are half the size as the large-flowered types and have striking throat markings or blotches; miniatures, which evolved from *G. primulinus* and have 1–3″ wide flowers borne on shorter stems; and open face types, whose flowers are wide open and point more upright than those in the other classes. For those interested in the history of gladioli and the cultivars available, a number of good books on bulb species and bulb catalogs are available.

Although hybrids abound, there are still a few species available. These cannot compete with the colors and flower size of the hybrids, but they add a touch of class and dignity to the garden.

| *-byzantinus* (bi-zan-teen′ us) | Byzantine Gladiolus | 2–3′/2′ |
|---|---|---|
| Summer          Maroon | Mediterranean | Zones 7–10 |

The leaves are narrower than the hybrid gladioli, and the 1–3″ long flowers are loosely arranged on the 6–12 flowered raceme. Plants grow with enthusiasm in the garden of Mrs. Robert Segrest, my gardening mentor in Athens, Georgia, but she "hates the color." On the other hand, many love the color and vigor of the plants. They are mostly maroon, but are sometimes red or copper colored and are borne on one side of the spike only. Corms are hardy in southern areas of the country, but must be dug in the North. They are lovely plants, provide long-lasting cut flowers, and give the serious gardener a glimpse into the genus before the hybridizers "improved" it.

Plant in a shady area in moist soils. Similar to all gladioli, thrips can be a terrible nuisance.

| *-callianthus* (cal′lee-an′ thus) | Abyssinian Gladiolus | 2–3′/1′ |
|---|---|---|
| Late Summer-Fall   White with purple throat | Ethiopia | Zones 7–10 |

(Syn. *Acidanthera bicolor*)

The proper name for this plant keeps flip-flopping from the old name, *Acidanthera*, to its new home, *Gladiolus*. It looks like, behaves like, and even smells like a gladiolus, so that is where it has been placed. This is one the loveliest of the summer-flowering bulbs (actually a corm) and it is unfortunate that the species has such a limited range and color. Although perennial in Athens, it must be lifted in the fall north of zone 7. The corms should be treated like those of other gladioli and dug in the fall after flowering but before the first severe frost, and dried in a warm room.

Remove cormels, dead roots, and stems, and store corms and cormels in a dry warm place (60–70° F) until spring. One of my gardening friends, Sharon Illingsworth, lives about 30 miles south of Thunder Bay, Ontario, Canada, and starts them inside in early May and sets them out at the end of the month. This way she is able to enjoy the late flowers before frost cuts them down. Those who live in areas where it is perennial must be patient in the spring as it is slow to emerge. It is a good species to combine with some of the spring-flowering plants which go dormant in the summer, such as *Mertensia* and *Doronicum*. Abyssinian gladioli has barely emerged when these species are at their peak. As they decline, it fills in those areas vacated due to summer dormancy. Unfortunately, flowering declines if corms are not lifted and divided every year. Even in Athens, I consider them annuals because flowering the second year is reduced and the third year is almost non-existent. The sword-like, mid-green leaves are topped with long, tubed, star-shaped, fragrant, 2″ diameter, white flowers with purple throats. Each flowering stem consists of 4–6 flowers arranged in a loose spike. The species is often grown for cut flowers and, when placed in a commercially available floral preservative, display excellent vase life.

### Cultivars:
'Muralis' is similar to the species but more vigorous, growing to 3½′ tall.

### Additional Reading:
Anon. 1993. Practical, romantic gladiolus. *Southern Living* 28(5):69.
Jarrett A. 1993. Saving dahlias and gladiolas. *Garden West* 7(7):34–35.
Peace, T. 1993. Annual style in the warm-weather garden. *Plants and Gardens* 48(4):38–43.


## *Glaucidium* (glow-sid-ee′ um)                                    Paeoniaceae

Consisting of a single species, *G. palmatum*, the genus is native to mountainous woods of Japan. Plants are highly sought after because of the large-lobed leaves (much like those of May-apple) and handsome peony-like flowers in the spring. The leaves are palmately lobed and the solitary, terminal, mauve to lilac flowers are about 3″ across.

They are difficult to establish in many areas because of their inability to perform well in warm climates, and need to be protected from desiccating winds in the winter. If planted in a protected area away from such drying winds, and planted in moist but not wet soils, they can be outstanding. Can do well in zones 4–6 and on the west coast. A white form, 'Album', occurs but is rare.

Propagate from seed or careful division in the spring.

## *Glaucium* (glow-kee′ um)    Horned Poppy    Papaveraceae

Approximately 25 species occur, many of them are annual or biennial, with a few true perennials. The genus comes from the greek *glaukos*, meaning gray-green, referring to the foliage color. In fact for most gardeners, the color of the foliage is the most handsome part of many of the species. The sap is yellow and the roots are poisonous. The striking horn-like seed pods have given rise to the common name.

The yellow horned poppy, *G. flavum*, is most common and bears 2″ wide golden-yellow flowers over pinnately divided gray-green foliage. They are native to coasts of the British Isles, the Mediterranean, and north Africa. The plants grow 2–3′ tall and become very lanky in areas of warm temperatures, although the foliage remains subtly colorful in the summer if soils are well-drained. Drainage is very important, and plants generally are terrific on the west coast, in the northeast, and in low rainfall climates such as Denver.

Occasionally the biennial *G. corniculatum*, red horned poppy, is grown. Plants bear red, orange or yellow flowers, often with orange or red spots at the base. The gray-green leaves are similar to the previous species. Beautiful foliage, handsome flowers, yet marginal performance unless cool and dry.

Easily propagated from seed at 65–70° F in humid conditions. No cold treatment is necessary.

## *Globularia* (glob-ew-lah′ ree-a)    Globe Daisy    Globulariaceae

About 20 species of this relatively unknown group of plants occur, many of them on the line between herbaceous perennial and small shrub. Those which are useful are generally found in the rock garden where their evergreen foliage and low growing habit are best taken advantage of. *G. cordifolia*, heart-leaved globe daisy, bears many 1″ diameter lavender-blue flower heads over flat mats of shiny, leathery foliage on creeping woody stems. A white-flowered form, 'Alba', and a rose-pink form, 'Rosea', also occur. *G. repens* is similar, but shorter and smaller. A more vigorous form occasionally seen is *G. tricosantha*, with long creeping stolons and stems which rise 5–7″ above the mats of evergreen foliage. The flower heads are larger but otherwise similar.

All species require full sun and excellent, well-drained soil. Success is more likely in a gritty area such as a rock garden than in the regular garden. Performance range is about zone 5–7 and zone 8 in the west. Propagate from seed, division, or softwood cutting.

## *Goodyera* (gud-yer′ a)    Rattlesnake-Plantain    Orchidaceae

Neither resembling a rattlesnake nor a plantain, this group of terrestrial orchids is nevertheless a favorite for native plant lovers. Of the approximately

30 species known, 3 or 4 are native to the United States and occasionally offered for sale through mail order sources. The common name is related to the network of white veins common to many species, thought to resemble the skin of rattlesnakes, and as useful remedies for snakebites. The botanical name comes from the 17th century English botanist, John Goodyer. The flowers are held in a slender spike and are relatively small compared to other members of the orchid family.

*G. pubescens*, downy rattlesnake-plantain, extends from Newfoundland and Quebec, west to Minnesota, and south to Arkansas and Georgia. The 3″ long leaves are produced in circles at the base of the stems and have an obvious white midrib with a network of white veins throughout the leaf blades. Between 50 and 80 small white flowers (about ⅓″ long) form a dense cylindrical spike from late spring to late summer, depending on locale. The hairy plants grow about 12–18″ tall. *G. oblongifolia* is native to Oregon and bears smaller, but equally handsome, mottled leaves and spikes with up to 30 greenish white flowers.

*G. repens*, creeping rattlesnake-plantain, produces slender runners (thus its name), and small (about 2″ long) leaves often marked with dark, rather than white, veins, although white-netted forms are common in North America (var. *ophiodes*). The greenish white flowers are about ⅛″ long and grow on one side of the flower stem only. Plants prefer cool damp woods are more successful further north than the previous species.

### Quick Key to Goodyera Species

    A. Inflorescence loosely-flowered, one-sided . . . . . . . . *G. repens*
    AA. Inflorescence dense, not one-sided . . . . . . . . . . *G. pubescens*

## *Grindelia* (grin-del′ ee-a)      Gum Plant      Asteraceae

A group of plants largely ignored by American gardeners, even though most of the 20 or so species are native to the western United States. The fact that they are native does not mean that they are wonderful garden specimens; and try as I may, I cannot find a listing of these plants anywhere in this country. Of course, it may be that nursery people have decided that a plant with flowers that look like dandelions may not enjoy a particularly robust market. The plants of all species are rather lax and unkempt, and the daisies are always in various tones of yellow.

While at first glance the flowers look like dandelions, simply touching the buds or beneath the flower will quickly reveal the origin of the common name. They secrete a glutinous substance which is unmistakenly sticky. They are native to open ground, along roadsides, and dry, rocky places. Therefore, decent drainage and full sun are required for some success. In their native habitats, plants grow on very poor soils. If heavily fertilized, they explode.

All species are similar, but *G. integrifolia* is a good vigorous native to start with. Some of the brightest flowers may be found in the non-native *G. chiloense*. Both probably hardy in zones 5–8.

Propagate from seed or cuttings after flowering.

## *Gunnera* (gun-e′ ra)          Gunnera          Gunneraceae

The inclusion of *Gunnera* in a book meant for American gardeners is pushing credibility a little; next thing you know, I'll be telling you how wonderful *Meconopsis* is in American gardens. However, although grown successfully only in the most forgiving climates, adventurous gardeners may be able to push back the climatic envelope a little. Plants are offered for sale by West Coast growers in Oregon, and L.H. Bailey in his *Standard Cyclopedia of Horticulture* states that "with protection, . . . may be grown in some of our northern states." He was likely referring to parts of northern California, coastal Oregon, or Washington. Accounts of winter survival to around 15° F have been penned, therefore there may be some hope yet. Mind you, once you see some of these monsters, you might want to flee on winged sandals. The big species are huge, the smaller ones are relatively normal, but spread without conscience.

While all this talk of winter survival is interesting, the necessity for cool summer climates, particularly in the evening, and wet roots are even more important and sometimes more difficult to provide. All species grow on stream banks, bogs, and even in shallow water. If they are allowed to dry out, the leaves decline into crispy candy. The smaller species, such as *G. magellanica*, require even more consistent moisture than the larger ones, such as *G. manicata* and *G. tinctoria*.

*G. manicata* is the most common and most highly prized member of the genus. The stems are thick and short, and the colossal orbicular leaves arise from the basal crown. The prickly petioles are as tall as your father and the leaves may be 8–10′ across with great striking channelled veins. The small flowers are packed together in a large corn-on-the-cob-like spike at the crown in early summer. Altogether impressive, but perhaps not for the back yard. Protect in winter with the fallen foliage and any other mulch available.

Plants of *Gunnera* may be raised from seed or divided with a newly sharpened chainsaw.

### Related species:

*G. hamiltonii* is a slow growing, compact, mat-forming species. The slate-green, triangular leaves are evergreen. Native to Stewart Island off the coast of New Zealand where it is an endangered species.

*G. magellanica* has small (2″ across), dark green, kidney-shaped leaves and is my favorite swampy ground cover. Plants are stoloniferous, taking over moist areas in no time. However, they are likely a little less hardy than *G. manicata*, not that thousands of gardeners in the United States are in deep debate as to which species of *Gunnera* they should use in their midwest garden.

*G. tinctoria* is similar, but a little smaller and more compact than *G. manicata* with reddish flowers.

## *Gymnocarpium* (gim-no-kar′ pee-um)      Oak Fern      Polypodiaceae

A small group of North American ferns which include the popular oak fern, *G. dryopteris*, and the lesser known Robert's fern, *G. robertianum*. Both are relatively small, less than 2′ tall, and bear similar sterile and fertile fronds. The fronds are in the shape of a triangle, the base of the frond of the oak fern being much wider than that of Robert's fern. They are both useful for shady moist areas, although Robert's fern is more at home in limestone areas. They add a layered carpet effect to the shady garden and are a handsome deep green color. Oak fern is a terrific deciduous plant with small, fist-like fiddleheads emerging all summer.

Oak fern is native as far north as Greenland, and winter hardiness is not a concern to gardeners. However, heat tolerance is marginal south of zone 5, perhaps to zone 6, when conditions are shady and moist.

## *Gypsophila* (gyp-soff′ ill-a)      Baby's Breath      Caryophyllaceae

This genus contains plants that are almost indispensable to the florist as fillers for arrangements. If one thinks of the many bouquets sold each day across the country, the economic importance is quickly realized. Although the commercial production of baby's breath, *G. paniculata*, is big business in many countries, it is also a lovely garden plant. The name *gypsophila* comes from the Greek word *gypos*, meaning gypsum, and *philos*, meaning friendship. This refers to its love of soils with a high pH, a soil condition which must be present if plants are to thrive. *G. elegans* is an excellent, easy to grow annual species for those wishing white or pink baby's breath flowers on much smaller plants.

Propagation of perennial species may be accomplished by seed or terminal cuttings taken immediately after flowering, or by divisions.

Quick Reference to Gypsophila Species

|  | Height (in.) | Flower color |
| --- | --- | --- |
| *G. paniculata* | 24–36 | White, pink |
| *G. repens* | 4–8 | White, pink |

*-paniculata* (pa nik-ew-lay′ ta)     Baby's Breath             2–3′/3′
   Summer         White          Europe, Northern Asia    Zones 3–7

Common baby's breath is a graceful plant covered with wisp-like blooms in mid-summer. The narrow, 4″ long, gray-green leaves are opposite and provide a lovely contrast for the myriad branches of 1/16″ wide tiny white flowers. Over one thousand flowers may be produced in a single panicle. The more flowers that are picked, the more that will be produced. If the first flowers are cut back immediately upon fading, a second bloom occurs in the fall. Although they are most valued for cutting, the plants make excellent fillers to cover barren areas left by oriental poppies, common bleeding hearts, or other plants which go dormant early. They should be grown in basic soil, full sun, and in areas of good drainage. In areas of Florida (zone 9, 10), it is treated as an annual and replanted from November to January every year.

*Gypsophila* is a long-day plant, and flowers faster when daylength is greater than 14 hours long—information useful in year-round forcing of baby's breath for cut flowers. It is also interesting to note that when the leaves of *G. paniculata* are analyzed for various nutrients, the level of calcium is about five times higher than most other garden genera. Magnesium level is also very high. This means that soils high in calcium and magnesium, or additional applications of these elements, are very helpful to optimize growth. This is true for most species of *Gypsophila*, the exception being the pink-flowered *G. pacifica*, which appears to be the most tolerant of acid soils.

Many of the double-flowered cultivars have been grafted to single-flowered forms. Plants should be planted below the graft union to encourage rooting from the stem of the cultivar. Another means of propagation is by terminal cuttings. In the garden, plants develop large fleshy roots and should be left undisturbed. Tissue culture is becoming the most common means of commercial propagation of large numbers of clonal material.

## Cultivars:

'Bristol Fairy' is the traditional double white-flowered baby's breath and grows 2–3′ tall. It is one of the best for cut flowers.

'Compacta Plena' is a smaller (18″) form of 'Bristol Fairy', but not as floriferous or as double.

'Festival' is a seed-propagated series consisting of 'Festival Pink' and 'Festival White'. Both are relatively short (12–18″ tall) and bear both single and double flowers.

'Flamingo' has double pink flowers and is vigorous, attaining heights of 3–4 feet.

'Perfecta' has larger white double flowers and is more robust than 'Bristol Fairy'.

'Pink Fairy' is a pink version of 'Bristol Fairy' about 18″ tall.

'Pink Star' has bright pink flowers on 18″ tall, compact plants.

'Red Sea' bears double rose-pink flowers on 3–4' tall stems.

'Rosy Veil' is a paler form of 'Pink Star'.

'Single White' is as the name implies. About 3' tall.

'Snowflake' ('Schneeflocke') consists of pure white double flowers. Also sold as 'Double Snowflake'.

'Viette's Dwarf', from the excellent Viette's Nursery in Virginia, is a dwarf form (about 12–18″ tall) with pinkish double flowers. Terrific for the small garden.

'Virgo' stands 3–4' tall and carries mostly double white flowers.

### Related Hybrids:

'Rosy Veil' ('Rosenschleier'), a hybrid between *G. paniculata* and *G. repens*, grows 12–18″ tall and bears handsome pale pink flowers.

| | | | |
|---|---|---|---|
| *-repens* (ree' penz) | | Creeping Baby's Breath | 4–8″/12″ |
| Summer | White | Europe | Zones 3–7 |
| (Syn. *G. dubia*) | | | |

This is a wonderful little plant for edging or the front of the border, and easy to grow. It tolerates heat but not wet feet. The ½–1″ long leaves are grayer than those of *G. paniculata*, and form a large mat in less than 2 years. The white to lilac flowers are not as delicate as those of its larger cousin, but still cover the foliage with hundreds of blooms during the summer.

This species is not as fussy about pH as *G. paniculata*, and plants do reasonably well in acid soils. Provided with good drainage and sunshine, they perform well as far south as zone 7b. Plants are excellent rock wall plants and cascade with abandon. This overlooked species should be used much more in American gardens.

Propagate by division in the summer or by seed. Seed is very small and should not be covered. Germination occurs in 3–4 weeks under warm (70–75° F), humid conditions.

### Cultivars:

'Alba' has clear white flowers.

'Bodgeri' produces sprays of double light pink flowers.

'Dorothy Teacher' bears blue-green leaves and soft pink flowers.

'Dubia' is compact with dark green leaves and red stems. The white flowers are flushed pink.

'Fratensis' has rich pink flowers.

'Rosea' has pale pink flowers, but is not as compact as 'Fratensis'.

**Related Species:**

*G. aretoides* forms dense cushions consisting of small, smooth, fleshy leaves over which are produced single- or few-flowered inflorescences of small white flowers. 'Caucasica' is even more dense with handsome blue-green foliage.

*G. cerastoides* has the general appearance of *Cerastium*, snow-in-summer, with blue-green hairy foliage. The flowers have 2 styles rather than the 5 in *Cerastium*, and are white to lilac with pink veins.

## Quick Key to Gypsophila Species

    A. Plants creeping, flowers usually single . . . . . . . . . . *G. repens*
    AA. Plants upright, flowers single or double . . . . . . . *G. paniculata*

**Additional Reading:**

Lawrence, G.H.M. 1953. The cultivated species of *Gypsophila*. *Baileya* 1:16–18.

# H

*Hakonechloa* (ho-kon-ee-klo′ a)        Hakone Grass        Poaceae

A terrific grass for its lime-green or yellow-green foliage, adding beauty when planted at the front of the garden. Native to Japan, plants have been grown there for years but have only recently made inroads in the American garden. They are only about 1′ tall with layers of 4–6″ long leaves, each about ½″ wide. The cascading foliage makes them wonderful candidates for hillsides or overflowing from containers. The only species, *H. macra*, spreads by stolons but is not invasive. The flowers occur in late summer, but plants are essentially grown for the foliage and not the flowers.

Other than the obvious ornamental value, particularly of the cultivars, there are two attributes I find most appealing. The first is its tolerance for shade. In areas of partial shade growing alongside hostas, plants are at their best. Full sun burns them up, but heavy shade causes the variegated forms to fade. The other characteristic is the handsome fall and winter color of the foliage, turning pinkish red in the fall and bronze in the winter.

Unfortunately, plants are only winter hardy to about zone 7, perhaps zone 6 with protection, which limits their northern use. They may be propagated by division, but they are slow growers and need not be divided for many years.

**Cultivars:**

'Albo-aurea' has longitudinal stripes of cream and yellow along with narrow bands of green. They are less vibrant than 'Aureola' but rather elegant.
'Albo-striata' differs by having white margins on the green leaves.
'Aureola' is the most available and the brightest of the listed cultivars. Known as golden variegated hakone, the leaves are golden yellow with thin stripes of green running the length of the leaf. They glow from a distance and draw viewers like a magnet. If variegated or golden plants

are to your liking, this a no-brainer. However, if variegated plants cause slight nausea, best to enjoy this in someone else's garden. They are less vigorous and slower growing than the species.

## *Hedychium* (he-dee' chee-um)   Ginger Lily   Zingiberaceae

The ginger lilies are probably the most popular garden ginger, consisting of about 40 species, mostly native to the tropics. A few species suitable for the garden are perennial south of zone 6, many south of zone 7, but all may be used as annuals or dug like dahlias in areas of warm summers and cold winters. In the southern states, the two common perennial species are the orange-flowered *H. coccineum* and the white-flowered *H. coronarium*. Both are strong, coarse plants with numerous reed-like stems which can grow 4–8' tall. The leaves of *H. coccineum* are long and narrow, sessile, and often with a well-defined white midrib. The many orange or scarlet (occasionally red) flowers with their long projecting red stamens are held at the top of the stem in dense spikes. Plants of *H. coronarium* have broader leaves with wonderful white, butterfly-like flowers. A common form is var. *chrysoleucum* with the same white flowers but with yellow centers. Not only are the flowers exquisite, they are also sweetly fragrant. They are less winter hardy and more difficult to locate, but very special. I can never seem to find *H. gardnerianum*, the kahili ginger, offered, but when I do I look forward to the very fragrant, clear yellow flowers with projecting red stamens in the Armitage garden. Plants are winter hardy only in the deep South, but can be planted in areas where summers are warm and dug if necessary.

Although the above have been around for a few years, a number of other species and hybrids are making their appearance. *H. densiflorum* bears spikes of small, yellow-orange flowers on 6' tall plants. For a short choice, *H. longicornutum* only grows about 2' tall, yet still produces bright red and orange flowers. *H. kewense* produces myriads of small, salmon-peach flowers with an orange throat. Plants grow up to 8' tall. All species perform better in moist soils with partial shade to full sun. In the Armitage garden my plants are in far too much shade, and I must support them because of their tendency to stretch. In more sun, they are self-supporting. A good place to see a good collection of *Hedychium* is Mercer Botanical Garden, a little-known gem just 30 minutes from the Houston Intercontinental Airport.

Propagate by division.

**Hybrids:**
'Assam Orange', a form of *H. densiflorum*, grows about 5' tall and bears spikes of orange flowers.
'Gold Flame' bears white flowers with golden yellow centers on 5' tall plants. The flowers are late, not appearing until the fall.

485

'Light Yellow' has pale yellow flowers on 6' tall plants.

'Short White' is not exactly short, attaining heights of 5-6'. The fragrant flowers are white with a yellow throat.

'Stephen' bears spikes of bright yellow flowers.

**Additional Reading:**

Chapman, Timothy. 1995. *Ornamental Gingers*. A terrific little book about all the ornamental garden-worthy gingers. Published by the author and available by writing him at: 6920 Bayou Paul Road, St. Gabriel, LA 70776.

## *Hedysarum* (he-dis' a-rum)    French Honeysuckle    Fabaceae

Plants are closely related to *Vicia*, vetch, and *Lespedeza*, but one or two species are far more colorful and a little better behaved. Although plants are almost impossible to locate except through highly specialized nurseries, the brilliantly red-flowered *H. coronarium*, french honeysuckle, may be worth trying. The bluish green leaves are pinnately compound and the flowers are held above them. Plants grow 3-4' tall, and while they are self-supporting in full sun and cool areas, they are flippy-floppy in climates with hot summers. They can be cut back after flowering to keep in bounds, and in general will be ugly if not trimmed up. The blood-red flowers are fragrant and when in bloom, are impossible to walk by. A white-flowered form, 'Alba', is also quite handsome, if not as brilliant.

*H. multijugum* is larger in every aspect, and is essentially a shrub. The flowers occur on new wood and plants can be cut back hard in the spring like butterfly bush, *Buddleia*. The purple flowers occur in the axils of the leaves as they develop.

Plants are best suited to the West Coast or the northern part of the country. Winter hardiness is not a problem, although where summers are warm, they are untidy and require significant maintenance. Full sun and good drainage are necessary for best performance.

## *Helenium* (hel-ee' ne-um)    Sneezeweed    Asteraceae

Of the 35-40 species, most are native to the United States, which makes it difficult to understand why the genus is said to be named for Helen of Troy. That fine lady notwithstanding, the ornamental value of the genus is enjoyed worldwide. They are characterized by broad, fan-shaped rays with 3 or more lobes at the end. Flowers are usually orange to yellow, often directed downward, at least in the species, and sport a rather conspicuous dome of disc flowers. They are particularly useful for their extended blooming time. Most flower in mid- to late-summer and combine well with summer flowering species lilies and obedient plant. They also flower naturally at about the same time as ragweed, thus being falsely accused of making one sneeze. They are adaptable to many climates and tolerate cold temperatures and moist conditions; dry soils result in unsightly plants. Most gardeners, especially those in the South, should be ruthless with these plants, cutting them back hard in mid-July. This encourages branched plants, healthy foliage, and many flowers. In general, sneezeweeds are large plants and require support to look their best. The leaves are alternate, often sessile, and have few or no serrations. They resemble *Helianthus*, sunflower, but differ by having a naked receptacle (the base of the flower) instead of pale bracts, long fruit rather than 4-angled fruit, and alternate basal leaves rather than opposite as in *Helianthus*.

Propagation is by division or seed.

<u>Quick Reference to Helenium Species</u>

|               | Height (ft.) | Flower color              |
|---------------|--------------|---------------------------|
| *H. autumnale* | 3–5          | Yellow, orange, mahogany  |
| *H. hoopesii*  | 2–4          | Yellow                    |

*-autumnale* (ow-tum-nah' lee)    Common Sneezeweed    3–5'/3'
   Late Summer   Yellow, Mahogany    Eastern North America   Zones 3–8

These large plants are best used at the back of the garden or in the center of island beds. The 4–6" long serrated leaves are lance-shaped, and the base of each leaf runs down the winged stem (decurrent). The 2–3" wide yellow flowers usually have brown to black centers and are borne in many flowered corymbs. Flowering starts in summer and continues for 8–10 weeks. Plants should be fertilized sparingly or tall spindly growth results.

Heleniums do well in gardens from zones 3–7, but as night temperatures rise plants require additional support and flowers become smaller. Thus, while some cultivars make excellent displays in the South, they soon become weedy and take over large portions of the garden. Cut plants back hard in early- to mid-July for best flowering in warmer climes and to encourage better flowering in late summer. Regardless of location, the dense foliage should be partially cut back after flowering to keep disease and insect pressure minimized. Plant in full sun and keep well watered.

Propagate by division every 2–3 years or by seed. The seed may be cooled for 3–4 weeks, but this is not always necessary. Germination is not particularly uniform, but should occur within 4 weeks after cooling.

**Cultivars:**

The many cultivars, each claiming to be bigger and better than the others, are probably hybrids between *H. autumnale*, *H. bigelovii*, and *H. hoopesii*.

What today's gardeners need, however, are smaller—not larger—cultivars. Only 'Crimson Beauty' and 'Wyndley' are sufficiently short and sturdy for today's smaller gardens. *Helenium* is another example of where our native species have been "Eurodized"; in this case, the Germans were particularly busy, but the British were no slouches either.

'Brilliant' is covered with hundreds of bronze flowers in late summer.

'Bruno' bears bronze-red flowers on 3–4' tall stems in late summer.

'Butterpat' is still one of the best of the yellow heleniums. It stands 4–5' tall and the horizontal petals are attached about ⅔ the way down the central disc.

'Coppelia' flowers earlier than many of the fall forms and bears large coppery-orange flowers on sturdy 3' tall stems.

'Crimson Beauty' grows only 2–3' tall and bears mahogany-brown ray flowers with a dull brownish center.

'Dunkle Pracht' defies pronunciation, but is a brilliant red cultivar growing up to 6' tall. The centers are delineated by a whitish circle formed by white markings at the base of each ray flower.

'Gartensonne' grows up to 6' tall and bears primrose yellow flowers with reddish brown centers.

'Kugelsonne' ('Sun Sphere') is 3–4' tall and bears many butter-yellow flowers.

'Moerheim Beauty' bears brownish red petals around a black disk on 3–4' high stems.

'Pumilum Magnificum' is similar to 'Butterpat', but has softer yellow flowers. The name 'Pumilum' means dwarf, but this cultivar reaches heights of 5'.

'Riverton Beauty' has golden yellow ray flowers around bronze centers. Plants are 3½–4' tall.

'Rubrum' produces beautiful 2–3" wide mahogany flowers on 6' tall plants.

'Waltraut' has golden brown flowers on 3' tall plants.

'Wyndley' produces 2–3" diameter, handsome, coppery-brown flowers and is only 2–3' tall.

'Zimbelstern' has yellow ray flowers surrounding a red and yellow bi-color disk.

### Related Species:

*H. bigelovii*, bigelow sneezeweed, is native to the Pacific Northwest and bears solitary 2" wide yellow daisies, composed mainly of the wide yellow-brown centers. Plants are 2–4' tall. 'The Bishop' has clean yellow flowers on 2–2½' tall stems. It is one of the more dwarf forms available.

| | | | |
|---|---|---|---|
| *-hoopesii* (hoop-ess' ee-eye) | | Western Sneezeweed | 2–4'/2' |
| Early Summer | Yellow | Rocky Mountains | Zones 3–7 |

The 2" diameter yellow-orange flowers are held in a 5–20 flowered corymb and are similar to those of the previous species. The basal gray-green leaves are up to 1' long and entire (no teeth). The stem leaves are smaller and sessile and are not decurrent like those of *H. autumnale*. The wingless stems are fuzzy (tomentose) when young but, become smooth later. The ray flowers are more strap-like and occur earlier than *H. autumnale*. Although this is a shorter species, support is often required. Plant in full sun and provide sufficient water to keep roots consistently moist. It is not as tolerant of hot summers as the previous species and does not do as well in the South. Both this and *H. autumnale* make excellent cut flowers. Plants grow on meadows and moist slopes and along streams throughout the southern half of the Sierra Nevada, and east to New Mexico and Wyoming. Plants have been known to cause poisoning in grazing sheep.

Propagate similar to *H. autumnale*.

### Quick Key to Helenium Species

A. Stems and branches winged, leaves decurrent
   at base, stems not fuzzy when young . . . . . . . . *H. autumnale*
AA. Stems and branches not winged, leaves
   not decurrent, stems fuzzy when young . . . . . . . *H. hoopesii*

*Helianthemum* (hee-lee-an' the-mum)        Sun-Rose        Cistaceae

Of the approximately 120 species, one of them, *H. nummularium*, is finally being widely recognized as a useful plant in the United States. The sun-roses are actually evergreen shrubs with woody stems and persistent foliage. Five-petaled, 1–2″ diameter, single, rose-like flowers are produced in numerous colors over green to gray-green foliage. Plants are particularly useful as edgings in gardens or along walkways. They are not winter hardy north of zone 5, nor warm hardy south of zone 7. The most important factor in successful culture is to provide rocky, sandy, or any well-drained soil. Otherwise, they will rot before you can say *Helianthemum nummularium*.

*-nummularium* (num-ew-lah' ree-um) Common Sun-Rose        1–2'/2'
   Summer        Various        Mediterranean        Zones 5–7
(Syn. *H. chamaecistus*)

When I travel in the Northeast or overseas and see these plants tumbling over rocks and walls and alight in pastel pinks or yellows, I want to go home and build a three acre rock garden to accommodate them. However, as rock gardens are not particularly popular in Georgia and my garden is of postage stamp proportions, I accept the fact that I can struggle with but a few. This low-growing subshrub with opposite, 1–2″ long, evergreen, gray-green leaves is the finest of the genus. The mature plant is usually wider than tall, and bears many 1–2″ wide flowers in loose 4–12 flowered, 1-sided, terminal corymbs. Where well-sited, the flowers cover the plants and totally obscure the foliage.

Plant in full sun in the North and partial shade in the South. They have few soil requirements other than excellent drainage. After flowering, shear plants back to encourage new growth.

I grew several in my heavy red clay soil, even though it was amended with compost. They were spectacular in the spring and early summer, but our rain and humidity during the summer killed the plants. However, on moving to sharper ground, I enjoyed moderate success with the cultivar 'Mutabile' for about 3 years. While the South may not be rock rose country, there are no excuses for not trying these further north and west. There is little doubt that most cultivars do better in cool summers and mild winters.

Propagate by division every 4–5 years or from 1–2″ long softwood cuttings taken in the spring.

### Cultivars:

Most of the plants available are hybrids of *H. nummularium*, *H. appeninum*, and others. Well over 100 hybrids have been named, but usually fewer than a dozen are available through American nurseries.

'Annabel' bears double pink flowers with deep green foliage.
'Ben Heckla', one of approximately 17 cultivars which start with "Ben," bears orange flowers with a red eye.
'Ben Nevis' has terrific tawny-gold flowers borne over green foliage.
'Broughton' ('Broughton Double Primrose') produces dozens of primrose yellow, double flowers. Outstanding.
'Buttercup' is 6–10″ tall and bears clear, clean yellow flowers.
'Cerise Queen' produces double red blooms. Although the double flowers detract from the charm of the singles, the flowers are more persistent.
'Fireball' has deep red double flowers.
'Fire Dragon' bears coppery-red flowers over gray-green foliage in early summer.
'Henfield Brilliant' has green foliage covered up with terracotta flowers.
'Jubilee' has double yellow flowers.
'Mutabile' is an interesting cultivar whose flowers open light pink then change to lilac, and finally to white. This variety is difficult to place in a specific color scheme, but has proven somewhat heat tolerant.
'Orange Sunrise' has golden orange flowers with a dark orange central ring.
'Raspberry Ripple' has gray-green foliage and raspberry-red and white flowers. Plants are less than 12″ tall.
'Red Orient' ('Supreme') produces single deep red flowers.
'Rice Creek Rose', named by Betty Ann Addison of Rice Creek Nursery in Blaine, MN, is about 10″ tall with pink flowers. A good rebloomer.

'Rose Queen' bears double rose-pink flowers. This and 'Cerise Queen' seem to retain their color in the heat.

'Snowball' bears double white flowers on 3-6″ tall plants.

'Spotlight' bears gray foliage and bright cherry-coral flowers. Well named.

'St. Mary's' has large white flowers over green leaves.

'Sudbury Gem' produces handsome rose-pink flowers over green foliage.

'Wisley Pink', a lovely muted pink flowering plant with gray-green leaves, is one of my favorites. Anyone who has visited Edinburgh Botanical Garden in June will remember this plant draped over rocks at the top of the rock garden like pink icing on a resplendent cake.

'Wisley Primrose' is a light yellow-flowered form similar in habit to 'Wisley Pink'.

'Wisley White' is the white-flowered sister.

**Related Species:**

*H. appeninum*, apennine sun-rose, is closely related but not as winter hardy (to zone 6 with protection). It is taller (18″) than *H. nummularium* and has long, arching branches bearing clusters of 1-2″ diameter white flowers with a yellow blotch at the base of the petals. Cultural requirements are similar to the previous species. Var. *roseum* has clear pink flowers.

*H. croceum* (syn. *H. glacum*) is a compact shrub growing about 12″ tall with many yellow to apricot flowers borne in early summer. Native to southern Europe and north Africa, plants are only cold hardy to about zone 7.

*Helianthus* (hee-lee-an′ thus)          Sunflower          Asteraceae

Not only do ornamental plants occur within the 150 species, but also commercially important food and oil crops. The annual sunflower, *H. annuus*, yields seeds with high oil content, and the tuberous roots of *H. tuberosum*, Jerusalem artichoke, are a valuable food crop in many areas of the world. However, the commercial world seems to have gone mad over the ornamental value of sunflowers. Sunflowers have recently become the Michael Jordan of the flower world with t-shirts, aprons, hats, cooking ware, place settings, and anything else that can be sold sporting brightly adorned portraits of the sunflower. Perhaps it is its ten minutes of fame, or as Kansans have long known, it is a wonderful plant deserving its place as that state's flower.

In the garden, the perennial species are easy to grow in full sun and tolerate a wide range of soil types. All species are tall and require considerable room. The flowers are always yellow and the leaves are usually rough and coarse. Most flower in late summer and fall.

Propagate by division after flowering, or by seed.

### Quick Reference to Helianthus Species

|  | Height (ft.) | Color of disc flowers | Flower time |
|---|---|---|---|
| H. angustifolius | 5–7 | Brown, purple | Fall |
| H. giganteus | 7–10 | Yellow | Fall |
| H. × multiflorus | 3–5 | Yellowish | Late summer |

| -angustifolius (an-gus-ti-fo' lee-us) | Swamp Sunflower | 5-7'/4' |
|---|---|---|
| Fall          Yellow | Eastern United States | Zones 6–9 |

(Syn. *H. simulans*)

This is one of the finest fall-flowering plants for the South, but unfortunately it is not terribly hardy in the North. The 5–7" long, narrow, entire leaves are mostly alternate, although opposite at the base of the unbranched stem. Leaves are stiffly hairy but not as coarse as those of other species. In the fall, the plants are smothered with 2–2½" wide, bright yellow flowers which light up the garden at a time when other plants are going downhill. Each flower has 10–18 narrow petals surrounding a dark brownish to purplish center. When placed in full sun, the plants are strong and self supporting; however, in partial shade, they are more open, less floriferous, and taller. In my partially shaded garden, they grow over 10' tall and stems break in high winds. The same plants in the sunny Horticulture Gardens grow no more than 6' tall and require no support. If they must be planted in partial shade, pinch plants once or twice in early summer to encourage branching. They are heavy feeders, require abundant moisture, and should be well fertilized if grown in full sun.

Propagate by divisions, cuttings, or seeds. Plants are aggressive and dozens of plantlets are produced around the base of the plants. If not removed, the garden will consist of little else within 2–3 years.

### Related Species:

*H. salicifolius*, willowleaf sunflower, has narrower leaves and smoother stems than *H. angustifolius*, but is otherwise similar in habit and flower color. They are more drought tolerant than swamp sunflower. It is winter hardy to zone 5. 'Lemon Queen' has numerous 2–2½" wide pale yellow flowers.

*H. resinosus* (syn. *H. tomentosus*), hairy sunflower, native throughout the southeastern United States, grows 6–8' tall with densely hairy stems. The leaves are dotted as if with resin, and sessile. Flowers with yellow central disks and golden yellow ray flowers are produced in August and September.

*Helianthus salicifolius*
(56%)

*-giganteus* (gi-gan-tee′ us)          Giant Sunflower          7–10′/4′
  Fall            Yellow          North America          Zones 5–9

I received a plant of unknown identity from Kim Hawks of Niche Gardens in Chapel Hill, NC, and was chased down and run down for its proper name by anyone who saw it in flower. The species is big, growing at least 6′ tall in full sun, with alternate, shallowly toothed, slightly hairy leaves. The many yellow flowers are 1–2″ across, borne in a panicle-like inflorescence, and appear in late summer to fall.

It is a good plant to hide or soften obstacles or corners. Our plant in the Horticulture Gardens effectively softens the end of our 5′ fence. Only one is needed.

## Cultivars:

'Sheila's Sunshine' became the name of the aforementioned plant sent to us by Kim. The flowers are a soft pastel yellow and is much easier on the eyes than the species itself. Named after Sheila Goff, an herb grower and gardening friend of Ms. Hawks.

493

**Related Species:**

*H. maximilianii*, Maximilian Sunflower, differs by having spike-like inflorescences rather than the paniculate inflorescence of *H. giganteus*. The leaves are generally folded lengthwise and usually entire. Also big and tall.

*H. schweinitzii* is a terrific plant, but unfortunately only available in local areas. The narrow lanceolate leaves grow on 5′ tall stems, and 1–2″ wide yellow flowers are borne in late summer. The best part of this species is its non-aggressive nature, and plants simply get better, not weedy. Native from Georgia to Alabama and North Carolina.

-× *multiflorus* (mul-tee-flo′ rus)   Many-Flowered Sunflower   3–5′/3′
Late Summer      Yellow      Hybrid             Zones 4–8

A hybrid resulting from *H. annuus*, annual sunflower, and *H. decapetalus*, thinleaf sunflower. Plants have hairy, coarse leaves up to 10″ long, 4–6″ wide, and oval to heart shaped. They are usually 4–5′ tall, but may reach heights of 7′ or more. The 3–5″ diameter flowers may be single or double and are usually yellow or yellow-orange. Flowers persist for 4–6 weeks and continue well into the fall. Leaves degenerate after flowering, and plants should be cut back soon thereafter. Place in full sun and provide copious water and fertilizer.

Propagate by division or cuttings similar to *H. angustifolius*.

**Cultivars:**

'Capenoch Star' has single lemon-yellow flowers that are a little cooler to the eye than the others.

'Corona Dorica' produces 3–4″ diameter double yellow flowers subtended by heart-shaped leaves on 5′ stems.

'Flore-pleno' is a 5′ plant with fully double (little or no center) bright yellow flowers.

'Loddon Gold' bears fully double, 3–5″ diameter, bright yellow flowers and grows 4½–6′ tall.

'Maximus' has large golden flowers, 'Maximus Flore Pleno' is similar but with double flowers.

'Meteor' grows about 5′ tall with deep gold semi-double flowers.

'Morning Sun' has lovely single yellow flowers with large yellowish brown centers and grows 5′ tall.

'Soleil D'or' ('Golden Sun') was selected in 1889 and has semi-double flowers with thin quill-like ray flowers. Still a winner.

'Triomphe de Gand' and 'Triomphe von Gant' are 5′ tall with semi-double gold flowers.

**Related Species:**

*H. decapetalus*, thinleaf sunflower, has rough, sharply serrated, thin leaves, above which are borne 3″ diameter, single, light yellow flowers. The 4–6′ tall

*Helianthus* × *multiflorus* 'Morning Sun'
(72%)

plants are covered with flowers in late summer and always make a handsome display. They are an important parent of *H.* × *multiflorus*, but not as showy.

*H. atrorubens*, Darkeye Sunflower, grows 2–5' tall with thin, opposite leaves and branched stems. Two inch wide flowers consist of deep yellow rays surrounding a dark red disc. A good southern wild flower in well-drained areas.

### Quick Key to Helianthus Species

A. Disk flowers pale to bright yellow
  B. Leaves ovate, base rounded,
    flowers single or double . . . . . . . . . . . . *H.* × *multiflorus*
  BB. Leaves lanceolate, much longer
    than wide, flowers single . . . . . . . . . . . . . . *H. giganteus*
AA. Disc flowers not yellow, brown or purplish . . . *H. angustifolius*

## *Helictotrichon* (he-lik-toe-tri′ kon)    Oat Grass    Poaceae

Grown primarily for the blueness of the foliage, *H. sempervirens*, blue oat grass, is one of about 100 species in this genus of handsome grasses. Plants are tufted with lightly rolled leaves, which are 6–18″ long and no more than ⅛″ even when flattened. The tufts are overtopped with showy, arching, one-sided panicles, consisting of ½″ long spikelets. The flower heads, held about a foot above the tufts, are brownish and dry to a golden wheat color in the fall.

Plants look good grouped together but occasionally a single plant may make a handsome specimen. They are also effective in areas where gray to blue foliage is needed to calm the garden down. They perform best in full sun with good air circulation and fertile, well-drained soil, in zones 4–7, and also in zone 8 on the west coast. Plants don't do as well in gardens where hot, humid summers are the norm. North of zone 5, some mulching is recommended.

### Cultivars:

'Pendula' has more nodding panicles and tends to look more pendulous than the species.
'Saphire' ('Saphirsprundel') produces leaves even bluer than the species and is more weather tolerant. A good choice.

## *Heliopsis* (hee-lee-op′ sis)    Heliopsis    Asteraceae

This genus closely resembles the true sunflower, *Helianthus*, and the literal translation of the name is "sun-like." It has a much smaller habit, however, and flowers in midsummer. There are about 12 species, many of which are rather weedy and few are used in gardens. The leaves are simple, rough and opposite. Plants should be grown in full sun and fertilized sparingly.

**-helianthoides** (hee-lee-anth-oi′ deez)   Sunflower Heliopsis   3–6′/4′
   Summer     Yellow, Orange     North America     Zones 3–9

This short-lived perennial has smooth, occasionally hairy above, 4–5″ long, serrated leaves and grows 4–5′ tall. The 2–3″ diameter, daisy-like flowers consist of pale yellow ray flowers surrounding brownish yellow central discs. The species itself is weedy, too tall, and is not floriferous enough to be a good garden plant. However, many cultivars which have ssp. *scabra*, often referred to as *H. scabra*, in the parentage, are much better and more popular in today's gardens. They all flower in shades of yellow, and it is rather absurd to believe that there are a whole lot of differences among them. Plants flower in late summer to early fall.

Plant in full sun in well-drained soil. Support is necessary, particularly if plants are shaded. Division is required every 2–3 years.

All cultivars should be divided every 2–3 years. The species and some cultivars come true from seed and are easily germinated in a warm (70–75° F), humid area.

**Cultivars:**
'Ballerina' ('Ballet Dancer') is about 2′ tall with bright yellow ray flowers surrounding a brown center.

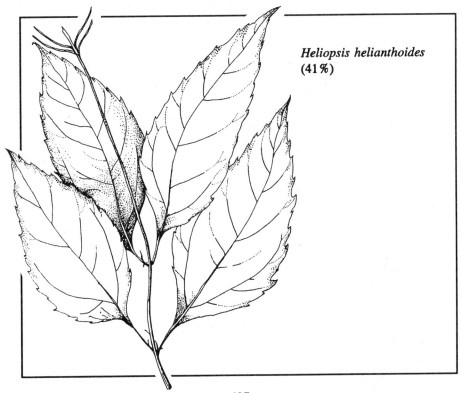

*Heliopsis helianthoides*
(41%)

'Golden Plume' ('Goldgefinger') is a floriferous, double-flowered, 3–3½' tall cultivar. This is the best of the double-flowered heliopsis.

'Goldgreenheart' ('Goldgrunherz') has interesting, if somewhat gaudy, chrome-yellow double flowers surrounding a slightly green center.

'Goldspitze' produces 2–3″ diameter, gold-yellow flowers on 3' tall plants.

'Hohlspiegel' ('Concave Mirror') has dark orange, concave, semi-double flower heads.

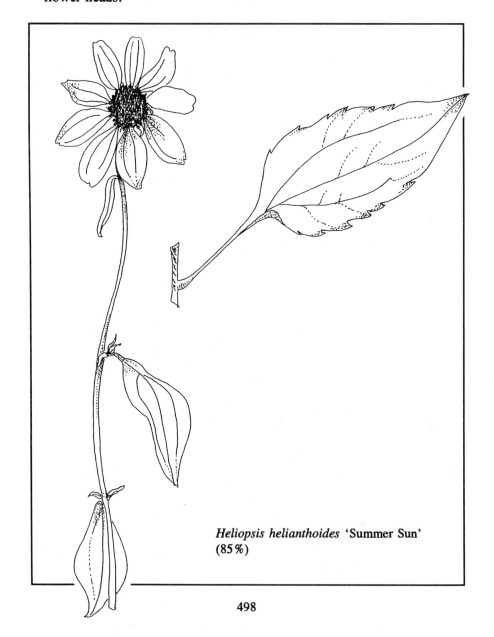

*Heliopsis helianthoides* 'Summer Sun' (85%)

'Incomparabilis' bears 3″ wide, semi-double flowers with warm orange overlapping petals.

'Karat' is about 3′ tall with bright yellow flowers.

'Light of Loddon' is similar to 'Karat' but grows 4′ tall. Both may need support, particularly in the South.

'Patula' is 2½–3′ tall with golden orange, semi-double flowers.

'Summer Sun' ('Sommesonne') is a delightful 2–3′ tall plant with 3″ diameter bright yellow flowers. This is the best cultivar for the South as it tolerates heat well and does not get too leggy. It flowers for 10–12 weeks and comes fairly true from seed.

'Spitzentanzerin' ('Toe Dancer') bears semi-double, golden yellow flowers on 4′ tall stems.

**Related Species:**

Ssp. *scabra* (syn. *H. scabra*) is characterized by sandpapery (scabrous) stems and leaves. Plants grow 2–4′ tall and 2–3′ wide. The upper leaves are often entire while the basal leaves may be toothed. The ray flowers are orange-yellow and the center varies from greenish yellow to brown. Leaves should be cut back in the South after flowering. A parent of a number of cultivars.

## *Helleborus* (hell-e-bor′ us)    Hellebore    Ranunculaceae

No garden should be without helleborus to herald the dawn of a new season. Walking by a clump on the edge of a path or on a hillside where the nodding flowers greet me, tells me spring has sprung and all is right with the world. The hellebores consist of about 15 species, all with some ornamental value. In addition, hybrids have been raised which combine the better characteristics of the parents. We have come a long way lately and American gardeners are using more hellebores than ever before. Many of the better garden centers and mail order nurseries now offer 4 or 5 different species, although only 2 are widely grown to any extent. All prefer moist soils and shaded conditions.

Most species have evergreen, much divided, compound or palmate leathery leaves. The margins are coarsely serrated or even spiny, depending on species. The nodding flowers are white, rose, green, or purple. The sepals are the showy part of the flower; the petals reduced to inconspicuous nectaries. Part of their charm is the early flowering time resulting in such common names as Christmas Rose and Lenten Rose. Because they flower when the weather is cool, they have an exceptionally long bloom time, often flowering from February to May. Fruit consists of 3–10 sessile follicles containing numerous seeds. Seed may be collected when follicles are papery and dry.

Garden species may be divided into two categories. The first group includes those with a leafy stem and flowers that are carried at the ends of the stems such as *H. argutifolius* (syn. *H. corsicus*), Corsican hellebore, and *H. foetidus*, bearsfoot hellebore. In the second group are those whose leaves and flowers rise directly from the rootstock, i.e., stemless. This includes *H. niger*, Christmas rose, and *H. orientalis*, Lenten rose.

Propagation from seed is difficult and exacting. Sow seeds in a well-drained medium and place at 75–80° F for 7 weeks. Move tray to approximately 32° F for 8 weeks and then raise temperature slowly to 40° F. Germination should commence at that temperature after which soil temperature may be elevated to 50–55° F until germination is complete. This technique is used for many members of the Ranunculaceae such as *Cimicifuga* and *Clematis*. Mother Nature, however, has no such difficulties and is much more efficient than gardeners. Seedlings of most species may be found under the plant litter at the base of 2–3 year old plants. Gentle removal and subsequent transplanting provides abundant plants for the spring garden. If necessary, roots of mature plants may also be divided in the spring, but large showy clumps will only result if plants remain undisturbed.

## Quick Reference to Helleborus Species

|  | Height (in.) | Flower color | Number of leaflets |
|---|---|---|---|
| *H. argutifolius* | 18–24 | Light green | 3 |
| *H. foetidus* | 18–24 | Light green | 7–10 |
| *H. niger* | 12–18 | White | 7–9 |
| *H. orientalis* | 15–18 | White, plum | 7–9 |

| **-argutifolius** (ar-gew-ti-fo′ lee-us) | Corsican Hellebore | 18–24″/18″ |
|---|---|---|
| Early Spring    Greenish | Corsica, Sardinia | Zones 6–8 |

(Syn. *H. corsicus*, *H. lividus* ssp. *corsicus*)

This stemmed species bears green flowers, but should be grown as much for the foliage as for the flowers. The rough foliage is unique in that it is gray-green, 3-parted, and the individual leaflets are thick and bear rather sharp teeth. The many green, cupped flowers have a tinge of white and are held well enough above the foliage so as not to be lost, but they are not as decorative as those of *H. niger* or *H. orientalis*. It is a stout, bushy plant with thick stems, which if well-grown falls over itself and forms almost hedge-like colonies. Plants should be given winter protection as far south as zone 8. Plants tolerate more sun than others, but not areas of high humidity. *H. foetidus*, *H. orientalis*, and *H. niger* are easier to establish in such areas. Without doubt the coarsest of the species, but this in no way diminishes its appeal.

Many seeds are produced, and if a mulch is placed at the base of the plant, seedlings will arise. Division may be accomplished in spring or fall.

**Related Species:**

*H. lividus* has similar flowers, but is only 12–18″ tall and has smooth-edged, dark green leaves with obvious pale netted white veins and often having entire margins. It is less winter hardy than *H. argutifolius* and difficult to grow in most areas of the country. All leaves arise from the flowering stem and plants often die after fruiting.

*H. × sternii* is a handsome hybrid between *H. argutifolius* and *H. lividus*. The foliage is more gray-green than other species, with obscure silver-white veins. The margins are usually rather spiny, however they are occasionally entire. The flowers are lime-green to green with purplish flush. Plants combine the greater size of *H. argutifolius* with the color of *H. lividus*. Truly handsome where well grown. Upon returning from a visit to Blackthorn Nursery in Kilmeston, Hampshire, England, I am convinced that there are fewer more handsome hellebores than those being propagated by the owner, Mr. Robbie White and his wife Susan. Blackthorn hybrids have gray-green foliage and are also more compact than the original hybrid. Their work with *H. orientalis* and *H. niger* (which see) is even more extraordinary. 'Broughton Beauty' has a compact habit, with flowers suffused rose and the foliage tainted a rosy purple. A wonderful handsome selection. Unfortunately, none of the hybrids of *H. × sternii* are easy to find in the trade. Plants are hardy from zone 6 to 8.

| | | |
|---|---|---|
| *-foetidus* (fe-ti' dus) | Bearsfoot Hellebore | 18–24"/18" |
| Early Spring   Light Green | Western, Southern Europe | Zones 5–9 |

The evergreen foliage is deeply divided into 4–9 narrow, dark green leaflets. In the first year, stems and leaves are produced. In the second year, several branched stems bear many cup-shaped, light green, nodding flowers, often rimmed with purple. The specific name, *foetidus*, means fetid or bad smelling, and refers to the flowers, although one must stick their nose in the flowers to get a good whiff. However, it is not a flower one brings in the kitchen to brighten the day. The plant does best in zones 6–7, and struggles with the heat in areas further south. Partial shade and well-drained soils are the only requirements for establishment. It develops quickly and can be as ornamental as any hellebore. I visited the lovely garden of Mrs. Wheezie Smith in Birmingham, Alabama (zone 7b), in late February. Dozens of plants of *H. foetidus* shone beneath her shade trees, *H. niger* was flourishing, and *H. orientalis* welcomed me at every corner. Who says February has no charm? Plants are not as persistent as the easier *H. orientalis*, sometimes succumbing to fungal problems (leaf spot, *Coniothyrium hellebori*) after about 3 years, especially in humid climates.

Plants self seed readily and may be left in place or moved carefully. If plants are many years old they may be divided, but that is a tricky operation at best. Plants resent being disturbed and if lifted for division, the parent plants may take considerable time to re-establish.

*Helleborus foetidus*
(41%)

## Cultivars:

'Wesker Flisk' has long narrow leaflets with stems, petioles, and inflorescence branches tinted red. The yellow-green flowers have a slight maroon tinge.

## Related Species:

*H. torquatus* produces dark flowers on the ends of leafy stems. The plants are deciduous, disappearing totally over the winter. Seldom used in America, it is a useful parent in the breeding of dark-flowered hybrids. 'Dido' is a double lime-green form. 'Wolverton Strain' is remarkable for its many pastel colors.

*H. viridis*, green hellebore, is an overlooked species of delicate beauty. It is only 15–18″ tall, has 7–11 very narrow light green leaflets and about 1″ wide, drooping green flowers. Much more subtle than most other hellebores, and well worth trying. Ssp. *occidentalis* has wider, coarser margins with more obvious serrations. Not as good as the species.

*-niger* (nigh' ger)  Christmas Rose  12–18″/12″
Winter, Early Spring  White  Europe, West Asia  Zones 3–8

The saucer-shaped, 2½″ wide flowers bear yellow stamens which contrast well with the clear white, petal-like sepals. Flowers are held on red-spotted peduncles. The flowers are usually solitary, but I have seen many plants with 2–3 flowers per flower stem. Tremendous variation in flower color, size, and earliness to flower occurs, particularly because most of the commercially available plants are seed propagated. Although flowering may occur at Christmas in sheltered locations, this seldom happens and plants are usually at their best in early spring. The dark green leaves are divided into 7–9 leaf segments, the margins toothed only towards the apex of each segment. Plants are more difficult to establish than *H. foetidus* or *H. orientalis*, being less tolerant of extremes of climate, including heat, cold, drought and wet feet. In one garden, plants may die at every corner, yet down the road, the microclimate may be to the plants' liking. It is not the species one should choose if success is important, but, my, they can be beautiful. Consistent moisture, shade and slightly basic soils are best.

**Cultivars:**

'Altiflorus' has longer-stalked, larger and more distinctly toothed leaves than the species. The petioles, peduncles (flower stalks) and the 2–3″ wide flowers are tinged with red spots.

'Blackthorn Strain' arose from the efforts of a single individual, Mr. Robbie White, at Blackthorn Nursery in Hampshire, England. When I escorted 25 keen gardeners to his nursery in March, no one could refrain from marveling at the beauty of the hybrid. Each plant results from a controlled cross (that is, the pollen of one parent is introduced by hand to the flowers of the maternal parent) and every plant is grown from the resulting seed. This $F_1$ hybrid has large white flowers suffused with pink, with each flower on stout stems close to the foliage. Absolutely breathtaking; the best part is knowing that each plant results from a controlled cross, and is not going to be a hit and miss seedling. Unfortunately, obtaining such plants in this country is next to impossible, but that does not mean they do not exist.

'Louis Cobbett' has a strong pink suffusion on the flowers.

Ssp. *macranthus* has small spiny leaves and white flowers tinged with rose held well above the foliage. The peduncle is not purple spotted as in *H. niger*.

'Potter's Wheel' is vegetatively propagated and has been selected for its large rounded white flowers with a distinct green eye. Few nurserymen try to vegetatively maintain clones because they are slow to increase by division.

'White Magic' has clean white flowers and a compact habit.

## Related Species:

*H.* × *nigercors* is a cross between *H. argutifolius* and *H. niger*. The flowers of the later have been combined with the profusion of the former to produce large white flowers with a hint of green. Plants are sterile and each one must be pollinated by hand. Plants bear coarse, jagged-edge foliage and "Christmas rose" type flowers at the end of short stems. 'Alabaster' is a cultivar similar to the above description which resulted from a cross between *H. argutifolius* and *H. niger* 'Potter's Wheel' by Elizabeth Strangman of Washfield Nursery, England.

## Related Hybrids:

*H. niger* has been crossed with *H. lividus*; the offspring bear large flat, white flowers suffused pink-brown which turn dull purple as they age. 'December Dawn' has 2″ wide flowers.

*H.* × *nigristern* is a cross between *H. niger* and *H.* × *sternii*; the offspring are variable, but bear large white flowers which are tinged pink-brown or green on the outside. The foliage is often marbled and the stems are purplish.

| | | | |
|---|---|---|---|
| *-orientalis* (o-ree-en-tah′ lis) | Lenten Rose | 15–18″/15″ |
| Early Spring   White, Purple | Greece, Asia Minor | Zones 4–9 |
| (Syn. *H.* × *hybridus*) | | |

One of the finest low-growing, early-flowering plants in cultivation, so easy that no garden should be without several clumps. The 12–16″ wide, leathery, dark green leaves are divided into 7–9 serrated segments and remain attractive all year, particularly in areas of mild winters. The nodding, 3–4″ wide flowers last for 8–10 weeks, and vary from white to plum-colored and are often spotted inside. As with *H. niger*, there is a great deal of variation in color and size of flowers.

Without doubt, like a chicken struggling to break out of the egg, the patience of breeders and growers will soon be paying dividends to gardeners. New cultivars of hellebores have teased gardeners for years; we have seen marvelous pictures in color books, occasionally seen some new colors in gardens, but we have never had the opportunity to purchase many new cultivars of hellebores. Ballard, Smith and Strangman are English breeders who have raised handsome cultivars, the pictures of yellow, black, red and double flowered-forms, like Pavlov's dogs, have long resulted in intense salivation for avid helleborists. It is easy enough to find a better hellebore, either with improved habit or different flower color or size, but the difficulty has always been the ability to propagate enough plants of the clone to offer. Full scale vegetative propagation is difficult; therefore, most of the plants offered are seedlings. However, if the parents are isolated, sufficient uniformity of the offspring results in new varieties. A number of people are trying very hard to obtain enough plants of new cultivars, and hopefully these will be available within the next few years. John Elsley of South Carolina has some exceptional hybrids now being offered commercially ('Royal Heritage'), Don Jacobs of Eco Gardens offers new cultivars he has worked on, and others in the country are doing the same. If patience is a virtue, gardeners looking for new hellebore cultivars must indeed be righteous.

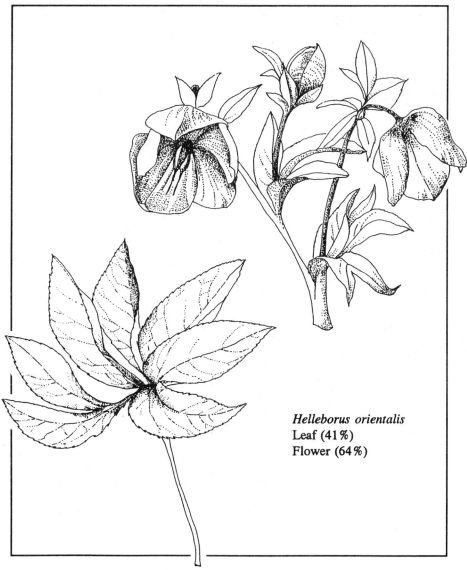

*Helleborus orientalis*
Leaf (41%)
Flower (64%)

505

The color for which breeders should be looking is towards primrose or yellow strains. The flowers stand out in the woodland garden from a distance and one's eyes are unfailingly drawn towards them. If a dozen different colors are blooming, the primrose/yellow strains of these "55-mile an hour" plants will dominate.

In almost all parts of the country Lenten rose is the easiest species to grow, requiring only shade and occasional water. Fertilizing in early spring as the new leaves emerge results in rapid growth of the clump. Clumps establish quickly and plants can be increased rapidly from the numerous seedlings produced in any rich soil. If the old leaves are damaged from winter winds or snow, cut them back. This procedure will also allow better view of the emerging flowers. The new leaves will also quickly fill in.

### Cultivars:

As stated above, numerous crosses and selections have been made, and may appear as this strain or that, but few $F_1$ hybrids or clones are yet available on a commercial scale. However, look at the articles and books in the additional reading section for a good tease. By the next edition of this book, I expect numerous clones available from which to choose.

'Cosmos' has white flowers with heavy spotting of pink on the sepals.
'Dusk' produces dull charcoal-purple flowers.
Ssp. *guttatus* is similar in habit and has white to cream colored flowers with red-purple spots inside the flowers.
'Party Dress' hybrids resulted from the breeding work of Mr. White at Blackthorn Nursery and flowers are consistently double. The nectaries of the normal flower have been transformed into a pinwheel appearance so the resulting flowers look more like a semi-double than the convoluted appearance of a double mum or daffodil. Because the seed set is poor, numbers are difficult to build up. The flowers are generally pink to purple, but occasionally a few creams and primroses result.
'Phillip Ballard' was raised in 1986 by Mrs. Ballard of Malvern, England, and is characterized by the charcoal-gray flowers with yellow stamens.
'Pluto' produces some of the darkest purple flowers of the group. Raised by Eric Smith, with *H. torquatus* as a parent.

### Related Species:

*H. atrorubens* (sometimes listed as var. *atrorubens*) is much darker than the type and usually bears 9 leaf segments. The rich plum-purple flowers are one of the first to open (early January in my garden). It is winter hardy only to zone 5 or 6.

*H. odoratus* is only about 1' tall with 3-5 lobed basal leaves with coarsely serrated margins. Three to five saucer-shaped, greenish flowers are produced in early spring.

*H. olympicus* (sometimes listed as var. *orientalis*) has 5–7 leaflets and many spreading white flowers with a green tinge.

## Quick Key to Helleborus Species

A. Flowers arising at apex of leafy stem
  B. Leaves divided into 3 leaflets, leaflets spiny . . *H. argutifolius*
  BB. Leaves divided into 7–10 leaflets, not spiny . . . . *H. foetidus*
AA. Leaves and flowers arising from
    rootstalk, plants stemless
  B. Flowers usually solitary or in 2's, peduncles
    red spotted, flowers usually white . . . . . . . . . . . *H. niger*
  BB. Flowers in 3's or more, peduncles not usually
    red spotted, flower green to dark purple . . . . . *H. orientalis*

**Additional Reading:**

Dillon, H. 1992. Heavenly hellebores. *Horticulture* 70(10):26–32.
Matthew, Brian. 1981. A survey of hellebores. *The Plantsman* 3(1):1–10.
Jones, S. 1987. *Helleborus orientalis. American Nurseryman* 165(3):166.
Mathew, B. 1994. *Helleborus* × *nigercors* 'Alabaster'. *Kew Magazine* 4(4):154–157.
Rackemann, Adelaide C. 1985. Green hellebore. *Horticulture* 63(10):64–66.
Rice, G. and E. Strangman. 1993. *The Gardener's Guide to Growing Hellebores*. Timber Press, Portland, OR.
Winterrowd, W. 1995. Hellebores. *Fine Gardening* 21:56–59.

## *Helonias* (hel-own-ee′ as)  Swamp-Pink  Liliaceae

An evergreen plant growing in swamps and bogs (*helos* translates to swamp), *H. bullata* is the only species in the monotypic genus. The basal leaves are about 1′ long and grow in a leathery tuft. Dense racemes consisting of many pink flowers with blue stamens occur in the spring. The strong flower stem is hollow and 2–3′ tall. In the garden, plants require copious moisture to succeed otherwise they languish and never rise to their full potential. I have seen plants flourishing in gardens in North Carolina and as far north as the Botanical Gardens in Montreal, Quebec.

This is a wonderful plant for the same boggy areas needed for many *Primula*, *Ligularia* and *Petasites*. If you have a wet area, beautify it by finding some seed of *Helonias* or visit a native plant center.

## *Hemerocallis* (hem-er-o-kal′ lis)  Daylily  Liliaceae

Daylilies have well-known culinary and medical properties. From treating abscesses of the breast, dropsy, bowel disorders, and as an anti-arsenic

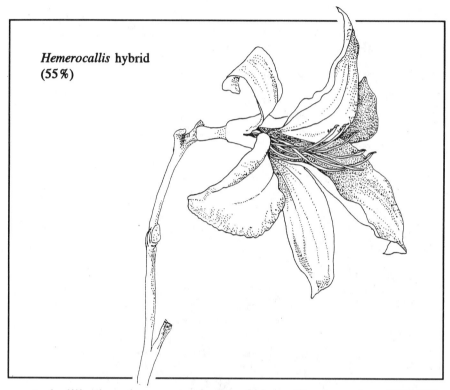

*Hemerocallis* hybrid
(55%)

agent, daylilies have been recognized in Chinese literature since 1000 BC. In Japan, the buds and flowers were long eaten in salads, and many people find the tight buds "crunchy to the teeth and nutty to the taste."

The modern daylily has undergone such a tremendous facelift in recent years that it is now one of the backbones of many perennial plantings. This is particularly true of commercial installations designed for public buildings, parks, or entrances to malls and condominiums where toughness and long-lasting color are so important. In few other genera has hybridization proceeded at such a rapid pace. American daylily breeders have done a magnificent job in bringing outstanding cultivars to the American gardener. Pauline Henry (eyes), Robert Grisbach (tetraploids), and Brother Charles (ruffles) are but three names to whom gardeners should give thanks.

The clamor for larger and more flowers, more colors, and greater vigor has resulted in the introduction of dozens of cultivars every year. Daylilies hybridize readily, and approximately 20,000 are now registered with the International Registration Authority and this figure seems to increase by about 500 named cultivars a year.

To try to bring some organization of the chaos of cultivars, a number of categories of daylilies have been artificially constructed by the International and the American Hemerocallis Society. Plants are classified into Evergreen,

Semi-Evergreen and Dormant. They are also arranged according to height of flower into: dwarf, below 6″ ('Buffy's Doll', 'Eenie Weenie'); low, 1–2′ ('Catherine Woodbury', 'Joan Senior', 'Stella d'Oro'); medium, 2–3′; tall, over 3′ ('Marion Vaughan', 'Whichford'). Flower diameter, flower color and pattern, and flowering season are also convenient categories for the hybrids. The wave of new cultivars is certainly not all bad and the popularity of the hybrids speak for themselves. The greater use of *H. minor* and *H. nana* to instill genetic dwarfness in hybrids has also opened up a new era of daylily use which has only recently being explored. There is little doubt that the breeders have done a tremendous service to horticulture by transforming some of the rather bland species into the wonderful flower colors and excellent garden performers found in today's hybrids.

Unfortunately, in our pursuit of hybrid grandeur, the old folks got left behind. The parents of the hybrids, i.e., the species, have been forgotten. In looking through garden catalogs, there are pages and pages of descriptions and lovely pictures of daylily hybrids, each seemingly better than the last. It is, in fact, uncommon to see anything but hybrids being offered. The dark brown buds of *H. dumortieri*, the fragrant, dense cluster of *H. middendorffii* flowers, and the fragrant old-fashioned lemon-lily, *H. lilio-asphodelus*, are becoming more difficult to locate. Some species, like *H. citrina* with their lemon colored fragrant flowers arising from long pointed buds, provide nocturnal flowers which open in late afternoon and remain abloom all night. It is still nice to see the common orange daylily, *H. fulva*, having escaped from old gardens, shining alongside roadways and in wild meadows. Perhaps the relative disdain of the species is a small price to pay for today's garden plants which are tough, reliable, and in colors and sizes enough to suit every taste. However, a few of the better species are included here for those still interested in old fashioned charm for the garden. It is impossible to list even a hundredth of the available hybrids, but consulting a plant catalog will yield some excellent choices.

All daylilies thrive in full sun, but tolerate partial shade as well. Mites and aphids are troublesome, and thrips can be damaging if allowed to proliferate. Diseases are few and far between, particularly if soil is relatively well drained. Propagate by dividing into plantlets with a single fan of leaves in early spring of fall.

## Quick Reference to Hemerocallis Species

| | Height (in.) | Leaves longer than flower stalk | Flower color | Flower stalk branched |
|---|---|---|---|---|
| *H. dumortieri* | 18–24 | Yes | Yellow | No |
| *H. lilio-asphodelus* | 30–36 | No | Yellow | Yes |
| *H. middendorffii* | 24–30 | No | Yellow | No |

**-dumortieri** (dew-mor-tee-ew' ree)  Early Daylily  18–24"/18"
  Spring  Yellow  Siberia, Japan  Zones 2–9

The leaves of this light yellow-flowered daylily are about ½" wide and 1½" long. The flower stalks (scapes) are a little shorter than the leaves, and thus the flowers are not held high above the foliage as in the hybrids. The scapes are unbranched and carry 2–4 sessile (no pedicel) flowers per stem. The flower buds are tinged brown outside, and the 2–3" long flowers are funnel-shaped and fragrant. It is a charming small daylily and the earliest to flower.

**-lilio-asphodelus** (lil-ee' o ass-fo-del' us)  Lemon-Lily  30–36"/30"
  Late Spring  Lemon  Siberia, Japan, China  Zones 3–9
  (Syn. *H. flava*)

The foliage is 18–24" long and about ¾" wide. The arching scape is branched and bears 5–9 lemon-yellow, 4" long flowers per stem. The flowers are sweetly fragrant and held well above the foliage. Plants are vigorous and spread rapidly. The dried flower buds were a famous aphrodisiac known as gum-jum, and were imported from China and Japan. There are few cultivars available, but the species provides a pleasing color, lovely fragrance, and strong and sturdy growth. This plant was popular, but has since been superseded by the newer hybrids.

**-middendorffii** (mid-an-dorf' ee-eye)  Middendorf Daylily  24–30"/24"
  Early Summer  Yellow  Siberia, Japan  Zones 3–9

Plants are similar in habit to *H. dumortieri*, and the flowers are also sessile on the scapes. The flower scapes, however, are longer than the 2' long, 1" wide leaves, resulting in the flowers being held above the foliage. The tightly clustered, 2–3" long flowers open after *H. dumortieri* but before *H. lilio-asphodelus*. They are fragrant and cup-shaped, and the petals are not as reflexed as those of the hybrids. Beneath each group of 2–4 flowers are conspicuous bracts. Plants are quite tolerant of shade and moisture.

Quick Key to Hemerocallis Species

  A. Flowers sessile or nearly so, 2–4 per unbranched scape
    B. Scapes shorter than leaves, leaves narrow
      (about ½" wide), flower buds tinged brown . . . *H. dumortieri*
    BB. Scapes longer than leaves, leaves about 1"
      wide, flower buds not obviously tinged . . . . *H. middendorffii*
  AA. Flowers on 1–2" long pedicels,
    5–9 flowers on branched scapes . . . . . . . . *H. lilio-asphodelus*

**Additional Reading:**

Baumgardt, John. 1978. The delirious daylily. *Horticulture* 56(5):41–47.

Eddison, Sydney. 1987. Small-flowered daylilies. *Horticulture* 65(5):56–59.

Kitchingman, R.M. 1985. Some species and cultivars of *Hemerocallis*. *The Plantsman* 7(2):68–89.

Kitchingman, R.M. 1987. A new meal every day eating *Hemerocallis*. *The Plantsman* 9(4):252–255.

**Associations:**

American Hemerocallis Society, Rte. 2, Box 360, DeQueen, AR 71832. Publication: *The Hemerocallis Journal*.


## *Hepatica* (he-pa-ti′ ca)　　　　Liverleaf　　　　Ranunculaceae

The early spring wardrobe needs no help in making the garden hormones flow in most of us. With early daffodils, forsythias, redbuds and bluebells, spring can more than hold its own. But as if that weren't enough, early spring, like a gardening bully, hordes more and more wonderful plants that tease and tantalize gardeners with their ephemeral beauty and demanding conditions. As if trilliums, trout lilies and primroses weren't sufficient, the hepaticas are additional icing on the early spring cake. In fact, their earliness calls to itself the undivided attention of every awakening gardener.

The shape of the leaves suggested the shape of the liver to early botanists, and so the genus is derived from the latin *hepar*, liver. In the 16th century, according to the Doctrine of Signatures, the likeness to the liver led to its adoption as a cure for liver ailments by herbalists and physicians (see *Pulmonaria* for additional details).

About 10 species of hepaticas are known, and some hybridization and selection has resulted in flowers of various colors, double flowers and intermediate forms. As I stumble upon more and more species and variants of this fine genus, I tend to agree with Lincoln Foster's suggestion that "it is possible that all hepaticas are but variants of a single circumpolar species with local variations in leaf pattern." They may be distinguished from similar genera such as *Anemone* by having 3 involucre bracts which are found just below the colored sepals. The flowers of *Hepatica* have no petals (apetalous) and the showy parts are sepals and stamens. The leathery leaves are always basal, usually 3–5-lobed, and long-petiolate. Often the leaves are suffused with purple, particularly those which persist from the previous year.

All require shade, moisture, lots of compost, and are said to do better where competition from other plants is minimal. In the Armitage garden, they compete with oak trees, squirrels, and any number of spring flowering plants. By mid-summer I can hardly find them in the forest of foliage of other plants and should probably get rid of the intruders, but they are doing just fine.

Propagation is best by division, although it is a slow process. Seeds are shed when they are green and may be gathered by placing a small bag over the senescing flowers. However, seed germination is more successful in nature than it is by gardeners, no matter how many times seeds are stratified, scarified or prayed over. Similar to *Helleborus*, nature does it better.

Quick Reference to Hepatica Species

|  | Flower color | Leaf lobes |
|---|---|---|
| *H. acutiloba* | Blue, white | Pointed |
| *H. americana* | Blue, white, pink | Rounded |

| *-acutiloba* (a-cute-i-lobe′ a) | | Hepatica | 3–9″/6″ |
|---|---|---|---|
| Early Spring | Lavender, White | Eastern United States | Zones 3–7 |

The leaves are 4–6″ across and each of the 3 lobes are, in their extreme form, pointed at the tips. There is some variation in the species and subdivisions

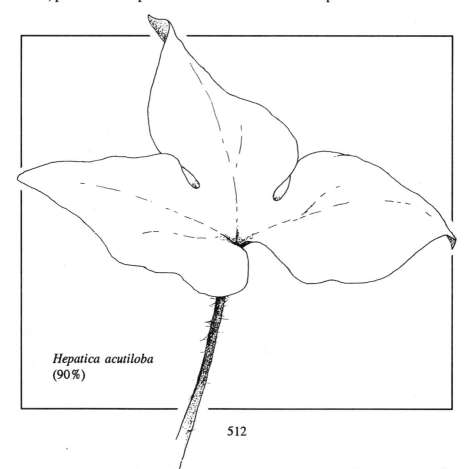

*Hepatica acutiloba*
(90%)

in the 3 lobes are not all that uncommon. Hybridization occurs between this and *H. americana*; therefore, not all plants in a colony exhibit this sharply lobed characteristic. The lavender flowers are about 1″ across and open before the new leaves appear in the spring. The first time the plants flower in the spring makes one wonder what all the fuss is about as they can look quite bedraggled, particularly if the old leaves have been beaten up by the winter. The contrast between the fresh lavender flowers and the dark bruised foliage is unavoidable; however, within a few days you will be in love with them.

The new foliage emerges while some flowers are still opening and continue to increase in size over a period of many weeks. Plants provide fresh early flowers, leathery handsome foliage all season, and an absolute lack of maintenance. The only thing not available is a consistent source of plants for gardeners unwilling to accept plants ripped from the wild. As the demand for hepaticas and other native species increases along with the awareness of their provenance, nursery-propagated plants will be the norm rather than the exception.

## Cultivars:

'Millstream Pink' was built up slowly by H. Lincoln Foster in his garden, Millstream, in Connecticut. These vigorous plants have large blossoms of vivid deep pink. To have 'Millstream Pink' is to have a legacy of one of the great American gardeners.

| *-americana* (a-me-ri-kah′ na) | Round-Lobed Liverleaf | 3–8″/6″ |
|---|---|---|
| Early Spring  Lavender, White | Eastern United States | Zones 3–7 |
| (Syn. *H. triloba*) | | |

Other than the morphological contrasts between them, few differences in garden worthiness, location or garden performance occur between this and the previous species. The leaf lobes of *H. americana* are decidedly more rounded, leaves are a little more hairy, plants are a little smaller, and flowers are a little bigger, but it is the similarities rather the differences that impress people. Intermediates occur when populations are grown near each other.

Both species are best planted in groups so that eventually sizable colonies can be enjoyed. Try your hand at seed propagation, it may be the only way to obtain sufficient plants. Both species occur as far west as Missouri and Manitoba, although they are more numerous east of the Mississippi.

## Cultivars:

I have seen plants in English gardens labelled as *H. triloba* 'Rosea' and 'Rose Form', but have not seen them offered in the United States. They produce many small pink and rosy-red flowers, respectively.

## Related Species:

*H. nobilis* is one of the two European species that sometimes are available through specialty nurseries. Native throughout temperate European woods and into Asia, the plant is hardly distinguishable from the American species, being somewhat intermediate between them. Flowers are generally more blue (less lavender) and a little larger than the American species. Numerous color forms have been propagated and may be found in European gardens. I have seen and fallen for 'Rosea' with rosy pink flowers, and 'Caerula' with sky blue blossoms. Other forms which lucky gardeners might find are 'Ada Scott' with double purple flowers, 'Alba' with white flowers, and 'Marmorata' whose blue flowers are spotted with white. Double flower forms such as 'Plena', 'Rubra Plena', and 'Little Abington' are listed, but not to be found without considerable searching.

*H. transsilvanica* is native to Romania and is distinguishable by the shallow broad lobes, each of which are notched at the tips. The flowers are large (up to 2″ across) and usually deep blue. My colleague, Mike Dirr, and I stumbled across these at the Wisley garden, England in March, and between clicking cameras and sore knees, we were suitably impressed. Crosses between *H. transsilvanica* and *H. nobilis* are intermediate and known as *H. × media*. 'Ballard's Variety' ('Ballardii') is vigorous and bears large sky blue flowers.

**Additional Reading:**

Myers, M. 1994. *Hepatica*, the forgotten genus. *The Garden* 119(2):82–85.

## *Heracleum* (hay-ra-clee′ um)　　　　Hogweed　　　　Apiaceae

Approximately 60 species occur, although only one, *H. mantegazzianum* (man-tee-gazz-ee-ah′ num), giant hogweed, is occasionally found in American gardens. Where seen, however, it is rarely forgotten. Rising from the thick roots in the spring, giant hogweed grows like Jack's beanstalk, producing large Queen Ann's Lace-like flowers 10–15′ above the ground. It must have also impressed early botanists, as the genus name comes from the Greek name for Hercules, *Herakleon*.

It is hard to believe that such biological production can occur at such an incredible rate. If we were able to make fuel from such a plant, any worries about foreign oil would dissipate. Plants are biennial, or occasionally perennial, and the statuesque plants bear ternately (in threes) or pinnately divided foliage. Long sheathed petioles arise from the hollow, ridged stems which are often reddish or purplish. Plants are covered with conspicuous white hairs and have a strong resinous smell. The massive umbels of white or slightly pinkish flowers occur in spring and may be enjoyed on the plant, or cut for drying.

While this plant is unforgettable, and while some people embrace it as a garden plant, it is a dangerous noxious weed. The dangerous part are the furocoumins in the sap, which cause a light sensitive reaction with the skin. Exposure to strong sunlight causes reddening, stinging and irritation of areas of the skin which have come into contact with the plant. The response generally occurs within 24 hours and painful fluid-filled blisters occur, which may end up in scarring. This is not a plant to have around children, and if plants are to be handled, protective clothing should be worn. Plants love moist areas and can reseed themselves with abandon. In England where it was introduced as a garden plant, it has been declared a noxious weed and may not be planted.

Seed propagation is best left to nature, and while plants are not nearly as aggressive in most American sites as it is in Britain, the dermatological problems are the same. My friend and garden writer, Rob Proctor of Denver, has giant hogweed all over his garden and loves it.

**Related Species:**

*H. sphondylium*, hogweed, is smaller (2-4' tall) with pale green-yellow flowers and entire to palmately divided foliage. Skin irritation is also a problem, but not nearly as severe.

**Additional Reading:**

Anonymous. 1995. Giant Hogweed. *Kew Information* Sheet T4.


*Hermodactylus* (her-mo-dak' ti-lus)    Snake's-Head Iris    Iridaceae

Named after Hermes, the greek name for the god Mercury, the genus is represented by its only member, *H. tuberosa*. The tubers are finger-like (thus the rest of the genus name *dactylos*) and plants are short-lived perennials. Plants are native to southern Europe and not great performers in much of the United States. Where they do well, they bear fragrant flowers in the winter and early spring, and are best suited to limey soils.

The square leaves are gray-green and about 12–15″ long. The solitary flowers bear green and black falls and standards. The flowers are relatively small, about 2–3″ wide, and more interesting than they are eye-catching. Part of their charm is their earliness to flower and their unusual tint. Hardy to about 5° F, plants are not often seen because of their relative obscurity and unavailability in the trade. A great fun plant.


*Hesperis* (hes' per-is)          Rocket          Brassicaceae

As many as 60 species of biennial or perennial plants have been described, all of which are characterized by white or purple 4-petalled flowers on long terminal racemes. Fifty-nine of them are never offered for sale and are not likely to be seen except in synoptic beds at good botanical gardens or as specimens on herbarium sheets. The favorite by far is the old-fashioned biennial, *H. matronalis*, dame's rocket, which pops up everywhere from the mid-west to the northeast and down to the southeast.

*-matronalis* (mah-tro-nah′ lis)   Dame's Rocket, Sweet Rocket      2-3′/3′
Late Spring   White, Purple   Central Europe, Southern Asia   Zones 3-8

Although not a true perennial, plants reappear every year from self-sown seed. Native to Europe and parts of Asia, plants have become naturalized all over Europe, as far north as Iceland, and throughout North America. The ½-¾″ wide, 4-petalled flowers open in late April and early May until late June and are wonderfully fragrant, particularly in the evening. The name *Hesperis* is derived from the greek *hespera* (the evening) referring to the evening fragrance. The 2-4″ long, alternate, hairy, sharp pointed leaves are sessile or borne on short petioles. Wherever I travel in the spring, from Georgia to Philadelphia to Boston, Dame's rocket pops up everywhere, providing lovely vigorous showpieces of white and purple that glow in the late afternoon sun. It has become so successful that people begin to think of it as a weed, but we should have more weeds like this!

The white-flowered form stands out in the shady garden more than the purple and should be selected whenever possible. The old seed heads can be cut back to the basal foliage by June if seedlings are not wanted. Plants require a consistent water supply to continue flowering and prefer partial shade, particularly at the southern end of their range. Plants become woody at the base and may persist for a number of years, but should be considered a biennial. Annuals may be planted around Dame's rocket because large gaps in the garden occur after plants disappear. Although they often disappear after flowering, seeds emerge quite readily and plants persist in the garden for years. Plants are nectar sources and usually attract an array of colorful moths and butterflies.

I teach this plant every year to my students who initially confuse the flowers with those of *Lunaria*, money plant. In general, flowers of *Hesperis* are later, leaves are longer and narrower, and the fruit is long and skinny when compared to the rounded fruit in money plant. And why, they ask, is this plant saddled with the name, Dame's Rocket? The specific epithet, *matronalis*, of matrons, is derived from the old name, Mother of the Evening, again referring to the evening fragrance. Wouldn't Mother's Violet be a more respectable name?

Plants are not easily found in catalogs, but seeds are available through any seed house. *Hesperis* is handsome in an informal area or in the border itself. It is a charming plant whose ease of cultivation makes it well worth growing.

### Cultivars:

'Alba' is the white-flowered form and is particularly outstanding.

'Alba-plena' is one of a number of double-flowered forms. It has white double flowers and is also fragrant.

'Lilacina Flore Plena' is a unusual lilac double form and 'Purpurea Plena' bears double purple flowers. The double forms must be propagated by division or basal cuttings.

*Hesperis matronalis*
(25 %)

**Related Species:**

*H. bicuspidata* (syn. *H. violacea*) is only 8–12″ tall with wavy to entire basal leaves and sessile lanceolate (lance-like) stem leaves. The flowers are reddish with violet veins. A true perennial, but short-lived. Winter hardy to about zone 5.

## *Heterotheca* (het-er-o′ theek-a)        Golden Aster        Asteraceae

As gardeners, we are on the leash of taxonomists or growers who provide up-to-date nomenclature for the plants we grow. In some cases, such as the wholesale emptying of the *Chrysanthemum* bin, we are slammed from wall to wall, while at other times name changes occur all around us but with little impact. A whole group of yellow aster-like plants are so closely related, that even with a microscope, differences are difficult to find. Such is the case with the two golden asters, *Chrysopsis* and *Heterotheca*, whose members play musical genus every few years. The main differences between them appear to be the following:

|  | *Heterotheca* | *Chrysopsis* |
|---|---|---|
| Ray Flowers | Bisexual | Female |
| Disk Flowers | Bisexual | Bisexual |
| Fruit | Angled | Ovoid (like an egg, but broadest below the middle) |
| Basal Leaves | Alternate | Rosette |
| Stem Leaves | Alternate | Alternate |

After all is said and done, however, some taxonomists put them together, others split them up, and gardeners generally don't give a flip.

The main species is *H. villosa*, hairy golden aster, whose 1–2″ long gray-green leaves are narrow and quite pubescent. The stems and leaf bases are bristly-hairy. The 1–1½″ diameter golden-yellow daisy flowers occur on short flower stems in multibranched corymbs. I have seen 4′ specimens in Georgia gardens absolutely covered with blooms from late summer until frost. When not in flower it is a large, rather mundane green thing and when frost occurs, plants blacken like burnt toast and should be cut back severely. Place in full sun and provide plenty of room. Plants are very adaptable and are particularly drought tolerant. I recall visiting the garden of a friend who had moved 2 or 3 months before. We were in the midst of a drought, not uncommon that summer, and the garden had not been watered. Disaster greeted me; many plants had succumbed, but the 5′ tall, 4′ wide golden aster was radiant with golden flowers. Plants are native to western and south-central United States and hardy in zones 5–8. 'Golden Sunshine' is 3–4′ tall, and produces 2″ wide yellow flowers a little later than the type.

Propagate by divisions after 2–3 years, or by seed harvested from the plants in the fall.

*Heuchera* (hew' ker-a)     Alumroot     Saxifragaceae

Fifty to seventy species are native to North America, and tremendous interest has recently been focused on this group of plants. A few short years ago, only *H. sanguinea*, coral bells, and hybrids, had gained significant popularity in North American gardens. While many improvements have been made in *H. sanguinea* and *H. × brizoides* by Alan Bloom and other European nurserymen, other lovely species had been ignored. Today, with the work of American plantsmen like Dick Lighty from Mt. Cuba Gardens, DE, Dale Hendricks of North Creek Nursery in Landsberg, PA, Dan Jacobs from Eco Gardens, GA, Dan Hinkley from Heronswood Nursery, Kingston, WA, and Dan Heims from Terra Nova Co., Tigard, WA, catalogs list numerous species with handsome foliage alongside those with colorful flowers. With the tremendous influx of European literature, it is easy to think that all plantspeople are English, German or Dutch. Not even close!

The mostly evergreen leaves are usually basal and long petioled, and the margins are lobed, wavy, or entire. The foliage is particularly ornamental in some species. Petals are small or absent and the sepals usually provide the showy part of the bloom. Some species have showy flowers, but many others are grown for their ornamental foliage alone. A number of species native to the mountains of New Mexico, Utah and California, such as *H. rubescens* and *H. versicolor*, provide low growing, compact alpine selections.

Many of the improved cultivars are hybrids between *H. sanguinea, H. americana*, and *H. micrantha*. Most species are readily raised from seed, but the hybrids must be vegetatively propagated. *Heuchera* does best in rich, moist, well-drained soil in partial shade. They are better adapted to cooler climates and some of the flowering forms don't do well in the South. Species grown for their foliage, such as *H. americana* and bronze leaf hybrids, look better in cooler times of the year and can appear rather washed out in the heat of the summer, regardless of locale. The improved foliage forms are much better in the heat than the older ones.

Plants in the genus *Heuchera* are fairly similar to plants of another American genus, *Tiarella*, and I am often asked "what makes them different?" This is especially vexing when plants are not in flower and even more so when people go on and on about the result of the cross between the two genera, X *Heucherella*. "How can I know *Heucherella* when I can't even tell the difference between *Heuchera* and *Tiarella*?" Here are a few hints.

|  | Leaves | Stamens in flowers | Conspicuous part |
|---|---|---|---|
| *Heuchera* | Obviously lobed | 5 | Usually sepals |
| *Tiarella* | Lobed or heart-shaped | 10 | Petals, stamens |

The leaves are tough, but with a little eyeballing, the flowers can be identified. In case all else fails, count the stamens. It is not as hard as it sounds.

Quick Reference to Heuchera Species

|  | Height (in.) | Flower color | Leaves obviously ornamental |
|---|---|---|---|
| *H. americana* | 18–36 | Greenish white | Yes |
| *H. micrantha* | 12–24 | Yellowish white | Yes |
| *H. rubescens* | 4–12 | Pink | No |
| *H. sanguinea* | 12–18 | Reddish, white | No |
| *H. villosa* | 12–36 | Pinkish | No |

| *-americana* (a-mer-cah′ na) | American Alumroot | 18–36″/18″ |
|---|---|---|
| Early Summer   Greenish White | Eastern North America | Zones 4–9 |

This often overlooked species has always been a tough, reliable performer grown for the handsome evergreen foliage rather than the flowers. The 4–6″ long leaves are rounded to heart shaped with 5–7 lobes. Its charm comes from

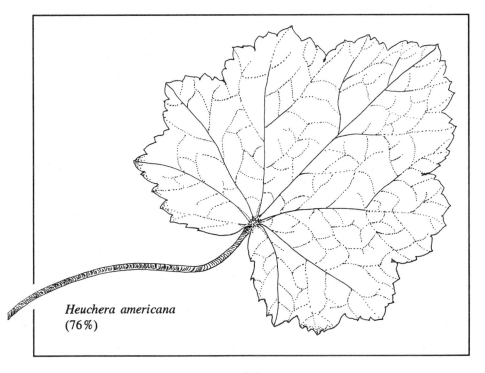

*Heuchera americana*
(76%)

the mottled purple color of the young foliage, which later subsides as the leaves mature. If proper cultural conditions are provided, new leaves are produced all season. The small, ⅛" wide flowers are borne in 15–24" long airy, unbranched panicles. Although not particularly ornamental, I enjoy them poking through the foliage and swaying in the afternoon breeze. It is one of the best *Heuchera* for the South and is most attractive in spring and late fall. The dark, healthy, purplish foliage stands out in November, December and January while everything else has succumbed to frost or fatigue.

Plants should be grown in shade and are not tolerant of full sun, particularly if moisture is lacking. It is important that the soil remain consistently moist if foliage is to be produced throughout the season.

Alumroot can be propagated easily by division in spring or early fall. The species can also be raised from seed. Cover the small seeds thinly and place seed tray at 68–70° F with high humidity. Grow on at 60° F. Numerous cultivars have been raised recently.

### Cultivars and Hybrids (*for leaf color*):

A large number of purple-leaf hybrids have arisen which are similar in habit and garden use to 'Palace Purple', but with deeper, more stable foliage color. This section could have been placed under *H. micrantha* as well as under *H. americana*. As wonderful as many of these selections are, the differences between them are minor. So many good forms have been raised recently that it is almost impossible to choose. As Dan Hinkley of Heronswood Gardens in Kingston, WA, so eloquently states, "try a dart."

'Amethyst Myst' from Terra Nova Nursery has amethyst foliage and is a vigorous grower, quickly filling in pockets in the garden.

'Bartram' was raised from the garden of the great American plant explorer, John Bartram, near Philadelphia, PA. To have a 'Bartram' is to embrace a bit of horticulture Americana. The dark green foliage with dark red veins and silver blotching at maturity isn't bad either.

'Bressingham Bronze', selected from 'Palace Purple', has deep purple, somewhat crinkled leaves. Good stable purple foliage.

'Burgundy Frost' has purple-lavender foliage with silver patterns between the veins.

'Can-can' demonstrates that so many heucheras have been offered that names are scraping the barrel bottom. Ruffled foliage with silver venation.

'Cappuccino' is said to be more sun tolerant than other cultivars. The color of the foliage is light bronze (like cappuccino?).

'Carousel' bears silver tinted, rounded, deep green leaves. The rosy red flowers are small but bright.

'Cascade Dawn' has purple-silver foliage with dark venation.

'Cathedral Windows' has dark leaves with dark gray veins. A great name, a good plant.

'Checkers' bears large white flowers over thick green leaves.

'Chocolate Ruffles' has intense purple leaves which are deeply cut and ruffled. The flower stems are also purple.

'Dale's Selection' is named for the nurseryman, Dale Hendricks, and produces purplish foliage handsomely mottled with white, red, and silver veins.

'Eco-magnififolia' came from Don Jacobs of Eco Gardens in Decatur, GA, and the silver-hued foliage has green veins and a green edge. Quite vigorous and unique. 'Eco-improved' is similar but with more silvering on larger leaves.

'Garnet', from Mt. Cuba Gardens, Delaware, has a purple (garnet) center in purplish leaves. Looks good throughout the season, although they tend to fade slightly in the heat.

'Mint Julep' has mid-green foliage overlaid with bright silver veins. From Terra Nova.

'Molly Bush' is a darker selection of 'Palace Purple' made by Alan Bush of the late Holbrook Farms, North Carolina. In the last edition of this book (1989), I mentioned that Mr. Bush was selecting consistency from 'Palace Purple' and this plant, named for his daughter, is the result. Grown from cuttings for best color.

'Montrose Ruby' arose from a cross between 'Palace Purple' and 'Dale's Selection' and named for the wonderful and sadly absent Montrose Nursery. Difficult to locate but an excellent plant, with a deep ruby color and large smooth leaves. The two previous cultivars are more stable in hot weather than 'Palace Purple'. They are also less subtle.

'Palace Passion' may be a winner as more plants become available. Plants have deep purple foliage with silver markings and coral pink flowers.

'Palace Purple' has been one of the finest introductions in recent years. The ivy-shaped foliage is deep purple, but the color is deeper in the spring and fall, fading to bronze-green under hot summer conditions. The flowers are of small consequence and add little to the plant. There is a good deal of variation in depth of color, and those with the darkest reds should be propagated vegetatively. Due to the demand for this plant and to the great detriment of the cultivar, a good many were sold as seed-propagated plants. The result was that green-leaf, purple-leaf, and all hues in-between were thrust at the gardening public. Today, the 'Palace Purple' name designates a plant which may be a superior garden plant or merely a mediocre one. If purchasing, demand vegetatively-propagated plants. Opinions differ as to its origin and taxonomic niche. It was originally selected by Brian Halliwell, curator of the herbaceous and alpine collections at Kew gardens, England. It has been listed under *H. micrantha* var. *versicolor*, *H. m.* var. *diversifolia*, *H. micrantha*, and *H. americana*. Regardless of its birthplace or pedigree, it can be an eye-catching plant worth trying at the front of the shady garden. Perennial Plant of the Year, 1991.

'Persian Carpet' produces handsome mounds of silver foliage with greenish purple venation. A knockout.

'Pewter Moon' has pewter veins on the silver-green leaves. The backsides of the foliage are purple. Flowers are light pink.

'Plum Puddin' was introduced by Terra Nova in 1996. The shiny leaves are deep burgundy and plants appear more compact than many others.

'Purple Petticoats' bears dark, compact, ruffled foliage, purple on the top and burgundy beneath.

'Purple Ruffles' is one of the fine Hinkley introductions, with purple ruffled foliage and small white flowers.

'Purple Sails' is a cross between *H. americana* and *H. micrantha*. Dark purple, undulating, maple-like leaves distinguish it from other purple-leaved forms.

'Regal Robe' looks terrific in the Armitage garden. The silver-purple marbled leaves are about 8″ across on low growing plants.

'Ring of Fire' resulted from a seedling of 'Eco-magnififolia'. Plants bear silver leaves with deep purple venation flowing into the center of the leaf.

'Ruby Ruffles' has ruby-red, ruffled foliage with a little contrast of silver. A cross between *H.* 'Ruffles' and *H.* 'Pewter Veil'.

'Ruffles', introduced by Dan Hinkley of Heronswood, produces mounds of green ruffled foliage with small white flowers.

'Silver Shadows' has to be one of the best silver-leaved forms. The leaves are thick and the plants are nicely compact. One of the finest I have tested.

'Sterling Silver', from Hal Bosger of Ohio, has silvery leaves suffused with blue and purple veining, particularly evident in the spring.

'Stormy Seas' produces dark heavily ruffled incised foliage. Another introduction from Dan Heims. An Armitage favorite.

'Veil' is attached to the name of many excellent new cultivars raised through tissue culture by Dan Heims. All are 15–20″ tall. 'Chocolate Veil' bears purple leaves with light silvering between the veins. 'Emerald Veil' has silvery foliage with a green edge and green veins. The veins are more purple than green in cool weather. 'Pewter Veil', a cross between 'Montrose Ruby' and 'Dale's Selection', is probably the most popular of the Veils. The silver netting between the pewter purple foliage remains handsome all year. 'Ruby Veil' has ruby purple leaves with a silvery gray venation pattern. 'Silver Veil' is also silver netted with cerise-rose flowers.

'Velvet Night' is probably the darkest heuchera, having plum-black leaves with metallic silver venation.

'Violet Knight' has silvery leaves with deep purple venation.

'Whirlwind' produces fluted, crested foliage quite different than most other bronze-green forms. Flowers are white.

**-micrantha** (mik-ran' tha)      Small-Flowered Alumroot  12–24"/12"
  Late Spring   Yellowish White   Western North America    Zones 4–7

The 2–4" long foliage is gray-green and heart-shaped with rounded, shallow lobes. In late spring, loose, airy spires of ⅛" wide yellowish white flowers appear. The petals are twice as long as the sepals (in most species, the petals are shorter or the same size). If well grown, which I have yet to see east of the Rockies, sufficient inflorescences are produced to put on a show. However, they are usually in the same class as those of *H. americana*. Place in partial shade, provide adequate moisture, and mulch well in the winter north of zone 5. A West Coast native, it does not do well under conditions of fluctuating temperatures common to the rest of the country. It is however a parent of several excellent garden hybrids.

The species may be raised from seed similar to *H. americana*; the cultivars are best raised from divisions.

### Related Species:

*H. cylindrica* is native to the West Coast and produces many ¼" wide green and cream-colored flowers on 2' long spike-like racemes (flowers

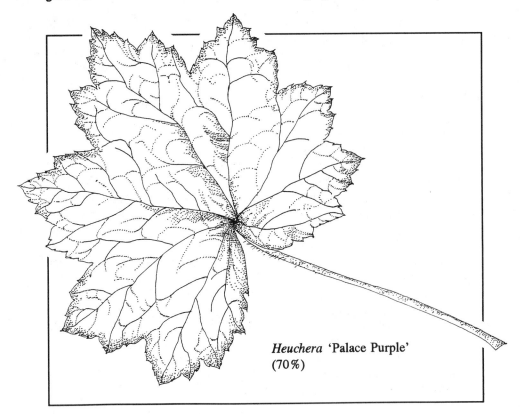

*Heuchera* 'Palace Purple'
(70%)

almost sessile on the flower stalk). The light green marbled foliage makes a good ground cover as plants spread out more than many other forms of *Heuchera*. They require the same conditions as *H. micrantha*.

Var. *glabella* is similar to the species, but the lower part of the stem and leaves are smooth, not hairy. A dwarf form is also available. 'Greenfinch' is a handsome 2–2½' tall form with greenish white flowers. 'Green Ivory', a selection of 'Greenfinch', is 2½–3' tall and bears many white flowers with green bases. 'Green Marble' has similar flowers, but also bears marbled light green leaves. 'Hyperion' is unusual for this species, bearing pink flowers with only a hint of green. All were raised by Alan Bloom of Bloom's Nursery, England.

| *-rubescens* (rew' bes-enz) | Alpine Heuchera | 4–6"/6" |
|---|---|---|
| Spring    Pink | California, Arizona | Zones 3–7 |

Plants form short, compact tufts of small leaves about 1" across. The leaves, which are deeply lobed and sharply toothed, are held on short stalks. The pink flowers occur in spring, and while they cannot compete with those of *H. sanguinea* or hybrids, their understated beauty enhances the garden. Place in a very well-drained location; they naturally grow on rocky slopes and in full sun in the north. They are more at home in Northern than Southern gardens, due to their intolerance of heat and humidity. Plants are difficult to find in the nursery trade, but specialist perennial or alpine nurseries may carry them.

Propagate by seed or division in the spring.

### Cultivars:

'Troy Boy' grows only 1–2" tall, bearing tiny, shiny green leaves and pink flowers.

### Related Species:

*H. versicolor* grows in southern Utah and is also more suitable for alpine conditions. Plants are a little taller than *H. rubescens* but are compact relative to the more common species. Pink buds give rise to pink flowers in the spring.

### Other miniatures:

*H. rubescens* and *H. versicolor* are but two of the miniature forms being more closely examined by breeders and gardeners. A few hybrids of mixed origin may be found here and there; all require excellent drainage and relatively cool temperatures. 'Constance' has handsome coral-pink flowers on 8" tall plants. The foliage is only about 2" tall when not in flower. 'Mayfair' bears pink flowers on 6" tall flower stems.

*-sanguinea* (sang-guin′ ee-a)    Coral Bells          12–18″/12″
    Late Spring        Red        New Mexico, Arizona    Zones 3–8

This species has undergone intensive breeding and selection and is a common denizen of American gardens. A relatively small garden *Heuchera*, it is at home as an edging, tucked away in a shady corner or at the front of the border. Although the plant is small, the ½″ long, campanulate, red flowers are much larger and showier than other species. They are held in 10–20″ long, loosely branched panicles and persist for 4–8 weeks. Removing spent flower stalks results in extended flowering time. The basal foliage is heart shaped or roundish with 5–7 slightly toothed lobes.

Coral bells require excellent drainage and full sun in the North, but partial shade in the South. They perform poorly in heavy clay and acid soils; therefore, coarse sand, manure and dolomitic lime must be added where necessary. Considerable hybridization and selection has been accomplished in the last 50 years, and Alan Bloom of Blooms of Bressingham in Diss, England, has been responsible for much of it.

The species and some cultivars may be raised from seed, but division every 2–4 years is the most successful means of propagation.

### Cultivars:

Most cultivars of *H. sanguinea* average 14–20″ tall. Hybridization (see *H. × brizoides*) has resulted in improved forms, but the parentage of many cultivars is confused. I have listed all the colorful hybrids separately, although they may be *H. sanguinea* or *H. × brizoides*. The following are cultivars of *H. sanguinea*.

'Alba' has 20″ tall stems of creamy white flowers.
'Maxima' bears burgundy-red flowers.
'Splendens' is the best known cultivar producing rich red flowers.

### Related Species:

*H. × brizoides*, so named because the smaller flowers and thin stems resembled quaking grass (*Briza maxima*), was a hybrid originally designated for crosses between *H. sanguinea* and *H. americana*; however, today these hybrids claim input from other species, including *H. micrantha*. There are profuse numbers of small (⅛″ wide) flowers and rounded, lobed foliage. Plants are generally taller than *H. sanguinea* cultivars, averaging 24–30″. The insertion of genes of *H. americana* has resulted in significant improvement in garden performance in eastern gardens, particularly in the Southeast.

Propagate all cultivars by division.

### Hybrids (*for flower color*):

More than likely, some of the following are listed as cultivars of *H. sanguinea*, others as cultivars of *H. × brizoides*. It is doubtful that mixed parentage does not occur in almost all coral bells grown for colorful flowers. There are so many similarities in the cultivars offered that it is impossible to distinguish significant differences between them. Pick a number.

'Apple Blossom' bears white flowers rimmed with red. Different and fun.

'Brandon Pink' has bright coral-red flowers.

'Bressingham Hybrids' are a popular seed-propagated group with coral, red, and pink flowers. Probably the best mixed strain available.

'Bressingham Blaze' has intense salmon-scarlet blooms.

'Canyon Delight', with rose-red flowers on 15–18″ plants, was selected by Canyon Creek Nursery in Oroville, CA.

'Canyon Pink' bears deep pink sprays of flowers from compact 3–5″ tall mounds.

'Carmen' has intense deep pink flowers over dark green foliage. Plants are about 2′ tall.

'Chartreuse' is not the most colorful, bearing light green flowers on 20″ tall plants. However, the flowers and plants complement each other well and are novel.

'Chatterbox' is a popular cultivar with large pink flowers. Raised by Bristol Nurseries, Bristol, CT.

'Cherry Splash' is so named because of the white splashes on the green foliage, over which are borne cherry-red flowers on 18–20″ tall stems.

'Coltus Bay Beauty' is a cross between *H.* 'Eco-magnififolia' and *H. sanguinea* which resulted in a plant with pink flowers over purple-veined foliage. Raised by Mary Fisher of Coltus Bay Nursery.

'Constance' is one of the few bicolored flowering cultivars I have seen. Pink and white flowers are carried on 8″ tall flowering stems. The small plants are better for the rock or alpine garden than for the main garden.

'Coral Cloud' produces dense sprays of coral-red flowers.

'Crimson Cloud' combines green foliage with silvering between the veins and crimson flowers in the spring.

'Edgehall' is an old cultivar with dull pink flowers, whose blood is found in many of today's hybrids. Still found occasionally today and of historical interest.

'Fairy Cups' is interesting at best. Plants have cupped leaves and cherry red flowers.

'Firebird' is 1–2′ tall with bright scarlet flowers on a compact habit.

'Firefly' has dark wine-red flowers.

'Fire Sprite' grows 18–20″ tall with rose-red flowers.

'Freedom' has marbled foliage, above which are held spikes of soft pink flowers.

'Frosty' is one of the numerous variegated heucheras, having white splashed foliage and dark red flowers on 15–18″ stems.

'Gaiety' bears many flower stems of pink flowers. Persistent bloomer and a good hummingbird plant.

'Huntsman' produces many rosy-pink flowers. An old but excellent cultivar.

'Jack Frost' has rose flowers and highly silvered foliage.

'June Bride' bears white flowers with a hint of pink.

'Leuchtkafer' has dark scarlet flowers on 2′ tall plants.

'Matin Bells' has flowers of coral-red.

'Mt. St. Helens' is an excellent garden performer with brick-red flowers. Originated from Sunny Borders Nursery.

'Oakington Jewel' is one of Blooms early introductions into the heuchera market and named after the original nursery. Some nurseries have rediscovered this bit of heuchera history. Plants bear red-crimson flowers on 2′ tall plants.

'Pearl Drops' produces many handsome creamy white flowers (pearl colored) over green foliage. Plants are about 2′ tall.

'Pink Cloud', one of the series of "clouds" has good pink flowers on 12–15″ plants.

'Pluie de Feu' ('Rain of Fire', 'Feuerregen') has cherry-red blooms.

'Pretty Polly' bears pale pink flowers on dwarf 10–12″ tall plants.

'Pruhoniciana' produces red and white bicolor flowers on 18–20″ tall plants.

'Queen of Hearts' has bright red flowers over 18–20″ tall plants.

'Rakete' bears dark green foliage and bright wine-red flowers.

'Raspberry Regal' is one of the finest heucheras available to the American gardener. This hybrid was reintroduced by Busse Gardens of Cokato, MN, and bears raspberry-red flowers on tall naked flower stems. The foliage is not particularly exciting, but the plant adds a robust dimension to the many cultivars. Terrific for cut flowers as well. I enjoy them with *Stylophorum diphyllum*, the native wood poppy.

'Red Spangles' produces bright scarlet flowers on 1–2′ tall plants.

'Scintillation' is up to 2½′ tall with pink-rimmed red bell flowers.

'Silver Rain' ('Silberregen') bears dozens of pure white flowers.

'Silver Veil' bears cerise-rose flowers above handsome silver-netted foliage.

'Sioux Falls' is 24–30″ tall with bright red bell flowers over green foliage.

'Snow Angel' has green and creamy white mottled foliage with spikes of pink flowers. Originated from Bluebird Nursery, Clarkson, NE.

*Heuchera* 'Raspberry Regal'
(40%)

'Snowflake' grows 2′ tall and bears clean white flowers.

'Snowstorm' is one of the older variegated heuchera, with white margined leaves and cherry flowers. Not terribly vigorous, plants have had problems becoming established in southern and southeastern gardens.

'Splendour' produces salmon-scarlet flowers.

'Splish Splash' has interesting leaves which have white centers and green margins, over which are produced pink flowers. Not exactly variegated, but certainly different.

'Strawberry Swirl' bears 30″ tall coral-pink flowers over ruffled green foliage with silvery patterns. This cultivar and 'Torch' are closest things to 'Raspberry Regal' for those looking for tall flower stalks.

'Tattletale' is a lovely clear pink.

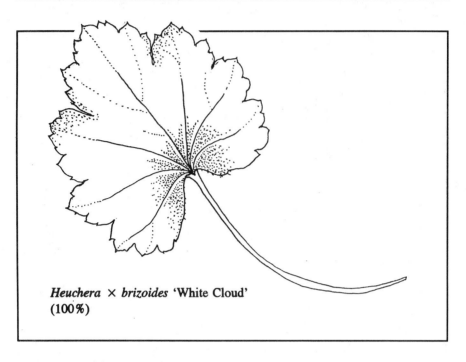

*Heuchera* × *brizoides* 'White Cloud'
(100%)

'Torch' is taller than many, growing 24–30″ tall with scarlet bell-like flowers. Used successfully as a cut flower.

'White Cloud' produces dozens of flower stalks upon which hundreds of small white flowers are carried. This is an excellent cultivar and is truly a "white cloud."

'White Marble' may be a cultivar of *H. pubescens*, a species with soft hairy leaves native from Pennsylvania to Virginia. Plants have marbled white foliage and semi-double white flowers.

'White Spires' has light green foliage and produce copious numbers of snow white flowers.

'Widar' likely belongs to the *H.* × *brizoides* group and originated in Denmark. The green foliage is set off by dark red flowers which are some of the most persistent in the trade. Named for Widar Weibull, a Swedish seedsman.

| | | | |
|---|---|---|---|
| *-villosa* (vil-lo′ sa) | | Hairy Alumroot | 1–3′/18″ |
| Summer | White | Southeastern United States | Zones 6–9 |

The rounded to heart-shaped leaf blades are deeply 5–7 lobed, each lobe somewhat triangular. The leaves and flower stem are hairy and the ¼″ wide, small, whitish pink flowers occur in open, airy panicles up to

3' long. This species is the latest to flower and among the tallest in the genus. Native to the Southeast, they are more at home in the heat and although not as showy as *H. sanguinea*. Plants are more reliable in the hot, wet summers and make a enjoyable, if not exceptional, border plant. Good for moist shade.

**Cultivars:**

'Autumn Bride' was found by Richard Simon at Bluemont Nursery in Maryland. It appears to be a form of var. *macrorrhiza* (which see), with smoother and somewhat deeper green leaves. Creamy white flowers appear in the fall and continue until frost. Terrific plant.

Var. *macrorrhiza* bears large pale green leaves which stand out in the garden. The small flowers are creamy white and perhaps not as exciting as the colored forms listed above, but handsome in their own right.

'Purpurea' is an excellent purple-leaved form of heuchera. The leaves are hairier and deeper purple than 'Palace Purple'.

Quick Key to Heuchera Species

    A. Petals twice as long as sepals
      B. Lobes of leaves triangular, very deeply cut . . . . . . *H. villosa*
      BB. Lobes of leaves rounded, not deeply cut  . . . . . *H. micrantha*
    AA. Petals shorter than sepals or only slightly longer
      B. Flowers ½–¾" long, petals red
         (white and pink in cultivars),
         stamens much shorter than sepals . . . . . . . . . *H. sanguinea*
      BB. Flowers less than ½" long
         C. Stamens exserted . . . . . . . . . . . . . . . . . *H. americana*
         CC. Stamens about same size as petals . . . . . . . . *H. rubescens*

**Additional Reading:**

Bloom, Alan. 1992. Classic Coralbells. *Horticulture* 70(5):66–69.

## X *Heucherella* (hew' ker-ell-a)      Foamy Bells      Saxifragaceae

Many examples of hybrids between species within a genus occur, but there are few between genera. X *Heucherella* was produced in 1912 at Nancy, France between a heuchera hybrid and *Tiarella cordifolia*. The most popular species (X *H. alba*) was produced in the 1950s by Alan Bloom of Blooms Nursery.

Plants are easily propagated by division, but do not set seed.

| -*alba* (al' ba) | | White Foamy Bells | 15–20"/12" |
|---|---|---|---|
| Spring | Pink, White | Hybrid | Zones 3–7 |

The leaves of this hybrid are longer than broad, and the white coral bell-like flowers are produced for many weeks in early- to mid-spring. Plants fill in due to their stoloniferous nature. The original hybrid was raised at Blooms Nursery between *Tiarella cordifolia* var. *collina* (*T. wherryi*) and a heuchera hybrid. Because of the bi-generic cross, plants have a "I must have one" aura about them and have become quite popular. They perform well in the northeast and northwest, reasonably well in the midwest, and struggle to persist for more than a year or two in the South.

## Cultivars:

'Bridget Bloom', raised by Bloom, has lovely shell-pink flowers, mounded habit, and blooms for at least 8 weeks. Plants often take a year or two to become established. I have seen some impressive plantings in the northeast and midwest, but in warm, humid summers it is marginal. Compared with the ease of its parents, it is a more difficult plant to recommend.

'Crimson Clouds' has deeper green, almost purple coloration on the leaves and dark pink flowers. Raised by Heims from tissue culture.

'Pink Frost', raised by Charles and Martha Oliver, bears pink starry flowers over silver-green foliage.

'Rosalie', another Oliver introduction, produces dark green leaves with purple centers. The flowers are deep pink.

'Snow White' probably produces the whitest flowers in this intergeneric cross.

'White Frost', also from the Olivers', has white flowers with a touch of pink.

| -*tiarelloides* (tee-a-rel-loi' deez) | | Foamy Bells | 15–24"/15" |
|---|---|---|---|
| Spring | Pink | Hybrid | Zones 3–7 |

The 3–4" long foliage combines the heart shape of *Tiarella cordifolia*, which is mottled when young and has 7 shallow lobes, with the flowering habit of *Heuchera* × *brizoides*. The plant is tufted at the base, stoloniferous, evergreen, and makes a wonderful ground cover. The small flowers bear a marked similarity to *Heuchera* and the tall, airy spires of pinkish flowers which open in late spring often rebloom in the fall.

Plant in a shaded area in the garden where moisture is available. It will not tolerate full sun, particularly in the South.

## *Hibiscus* (hi-bis' cus)      Hibiscus      Malvaceae

Hibiscus contains over 200 species, mainly from tropical and sub-tropical areas of the world. The diversity of the genus is easily seen when one passes a large shrub or small tree of Rose of Sharon, *H. syriacus*, admires the huge flowers of the hardy hibiscus, *H. moscheutos*, observes the handsome flowers of the greenhouse grown *H. rosa-sinensis*, and marvels at the reseeding tendencies of the annual Flower-of-the-hour, *H. trionum*. Many of the more choice species are native to southern United States and gardeners in those areas may expect additional cultivars in the near future.

Annuals have been used in the flower trade for some time and include the aforementioned white-flowered *H. trionum*, the red-leaved Red Shield, *H. acetosella*, the seed-propagated $F_1$ hybrids known as 'Southern Belle' or 'Disco Belle', and the marginally hardy shrubby Confederate Rose, *H. mutabilis*. Depending on severity of the winter and amount of mulching, some of these annuals may return as far north as zone 6, but from the gardening point of view, they should be treated as annuals; anything that returns is a bonus. Few species are cold hardy north of zone 5, but flowers are so bold and useful, they are worth trying even as annuals.

<u>Quick Reference to Hibiscus Species</u>

|                 | Height (ft.) | Flower color |
|-----------------|--------------|--------------|
| *H. coccineus*  | 5–7          | Scarlet, red |
| *H. moscheutos* | 2–3          | Various      |
| *H. mutabilis*  | 8–10         | Pink         |

| -*coccineus* (cock-sin-e′ us) | Swamp Hibiscus | 5–7′/3′ |
|---|---|---|
| Summer          Red | Georgia, Florida | Zones 7–9 |

Plants are some of the showiest in June and July in the southern states, producing many solitary, 3–5″ wide, red flowers in the upper leaf axils of the tall plant. The stamens are extended from the flower making them as handsome from close up as from a distance. The leaves are palmately compound and either look like those of Japanese maple or marijuana, whichever you happen to be most familiar with. Tony Avent of Plant Delights Nursery calls it a "see through" plant because of its tall, skinny stature. However, this plant will stop traffic and result in more questions from your visitors than any other plant in flower at that time. The plants become woody at the base and the stems and ornamental seed pods can also be enjoyed over the winter.

One of the bonuses of planting this species is that plants are not attacked by Japanese beetles, whereas its more common cousin, *H. moscheutos*, generally looks like a shotgun exploded through the leaves when the beetles arrive.

Plant in full sun in groups of 3–5 for best effect. They don't require a lot of room, so this is easier than it sounds. They are called swamp hibiscus for

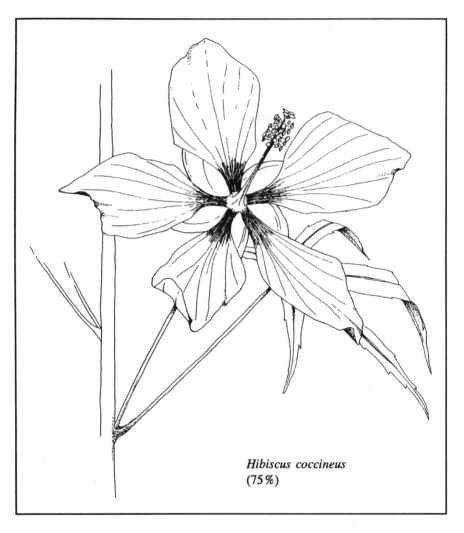

*Hibiscus coccineus*
(75%)

good reason—they love wet areas and require a sufficient supply of water, especially as they begin to flower, to be at their best. Shade results in even taller plants with a paucity of flowers. Plants are late to arise in the spring; don't give up too quickly.

### Related Species:

*H. grandiflorus*, velvet mallow, is 6–7′ tall with 12″ long, 3–5 lobed, velvety gray leaves. The 5–6″ wide flowers are usually pink to purple-rose, often with a crimson spot at the base. White-flowered forms are also known. Hardy in zones 7 to 9, possibly into zone 6 with sufficient winter mulching. Native to the coastal areas of the southeastern United States.

| *-moscheutos* (mos-kew' tas) | | Common Mallow | 3–4'/3' |
|---|---|---|---|
| Summer | Various | Eastern United States | Zone 5–9 |

Vigorous and robust, these large-leaved and large-flowered plants grace gardens south to Miami and as far north as Indianapolis. Once established, many stems emerge late in the spring and flower from early- to mid-summer. The unlobed ovate to lance-shaped leaves range from 4–10" in length and the 4–5" wide flowers are white, rose or pink and borne in the axils of the many stems.

Plants require full sun and good air circulation for disease suppression. Consistent soil moisture is also important but they need not be planted in swampy areas. The biggest problem is the scorge of Japanese beetles, which are attracted to this and other members of the Malvaceae family, such as hollyhocks.

The cultivars which are available may be selections of this species, but are likely hybrids with other vigorous members of the genus. Richard Hawke of the Chicago Botanic Garden continues to do an excellent job of evaluating various genera. For an excellent evaluation over 25 taxa of *H. moscheutos*, see his paper in the Additional Reading section.

## Cultivars:

'Anne Arundel' is a pink-flowered hybrid which grows 4–5' tall. The foliage is more deeply cut than most of the other cultivars. Very handsome.

'Blue River II' bears clear white flowers with no eye, up to 10" across. The deep green foliage bears a hint of blue. An excellent long flowering selection.

'Crimson Wonder' bears rich red ruffled flowers up to 10" across.

'Disco Belle', 'Disco Rosy Red' and 'Disco White' are all $F_1$ seed-propagated strains which are popular because of their compact habits and large flowers. Excellent plants for the smaller garden, but unfortunately, Japanese beetles can be devastating.

'Fleming Hybrids' are the result of the excellent work of the Fleming Brothers of Lincoln, NE. They all bear huge 8–10" wide flowers, often pink but many with picotee edges and centered with a red eye. Great plants, great work.

'George Riegel', introduced by Carroll Gardens in Maryland, bears fine light pink flowers with a dark red eye. About 4' tall in full sun.

'Giant Maroon' is self explanatory.

'Lady Baltimore' is probably the best known hybrid, producing 6–9" wide, deep pink, slightly ruffled flowers with red centers. Plants generally grow 4–6' tall.

'Lester Riegel' bears pink flowers with a red eye and deeper pink veins.

'Lord Baltimore' has large, crimson-red, ruffled flowers and deeply lobed leaves. Profuse bloomer.

'Southern Belle' is a mixed strain of red, white, pink, and bi-color flowers. They are larger than the other Belles such as 'Disco Belle'.

'Strawberry Swirl' has light pink flowers with clean white veins. Plants grow to about 4' tall.

'Sweet Caroline' bears large dark-veined light pink 6–8" wide flowers slightly ruffled at the edges. Plants grow quite large, sometimes attaining a height of 5'.

### Related Species:

*H. aculeatus*, pineland hibiscus, has wonderful yellow flowers on 2–3' tall plants. Likely hardy in zone 7 and south.

*H. lasiocarpos*, wooly mallow, has 4–6" long, hairy leaves with 4–5" wide pink or white flowers with red centers. Plants are about 4' tall. A handsome, relatively unknown species native from southern Illinois to Florida. Likely hardy in zones 5 to 9.

| *-mutabilis* (mew-tah' bi-lis) | | Confederate Rose | 8–10'/5' |
|---|---|---|---|
| Late Summer, Fall | Pink | China | Zones 7–10 |

The common name, Confederate Rose, makes one think that this species is native to the South. However, plants are from China and were given the common name when introduced to Florida. This is a large (up to 10' tall) shrubby plant with broad, fuzzy, palmately-lobed leaves and large pink flowers. The stems become woody by the end of the season and new growth in the spring is slow to emerge. The limits to cold tolerance are probably zone 7, perhaps zone 6b with sufficient mulching. Even as annuals, however, plants are worth a try.

The term "mutabilis" means "changing," referring to the change of flower color. In the species, flowers open white or pink, but change to deep red in the evening. I think the form with pink flowers that do not change color are even more handsome. Plants require full sun for best performance and consistent moisture. Less susceptible to Japanese beetles than *H. moscheutos*, but more tasty than *H. coccineus*.

### Cultivars:

'Flore-plena' is the most common form, bearing fully double pink blossoms which resemble large camellia flowers.

'Raspberry Rose' bears raspberry-red, single flowers.

'Rubrus' has more oval leaves and large scarlet, single flowers.

### Related Species:

*H. palustris* has attractive large pink flowers, although they sometimes are white or purple. Plants grow up to 8' tall with flowers up to 6" across. Native from Massachusetts to North Carolina and to Ontario and Illinois.

Quick Key to Hibiscus Species

   A. Entire stem woody, height of mature
      plant greater than 7' . . . . . . . . . . . . . . . . . . . *H. mutabilis*
  AA. Upper ⅔ of stem herbaceous, height of
      mature plant less than 7'
     B. Foliage not hairy, divided
       into narrow segments . . . . . . . . . . . . . . . . . *H. coccineus*
    BB. Foliage pubescent, at least underneath,
       foliage not lobed or divided . . . . . . . . . . . *H. moscheutos*

**Additional Reading:**

Hawke, R. 1993. Plant evaluation notes: *Hibiscus moscheutos. Chicago Botanic Garden* 4: 4 pp.

*Hosta* (hos' ta)      Plantain Lily, Funkia, Hosta      Liliaceae

Daylilies may be kings of the sun, but unquestionably hostas are the emperors of the shade. I remember walking down my grandmother's path in Montreal as a child, where variegated hostas had long ago been planted on either side. It was a dim, dark pathway but the light airy foliage always lit the way. Nothing else would grow there and that path was a living testament to the toughness of these lovely plants. They also made my grandmother seem like a horticultural genius.

Hostas have been around for centuries but were "rediscovered" in the last 20 years, and an incredible array of cultivars and interspecific hybrids have emerged. The nomenclature is in a constant state of flux and the parentage of plants is not always absolutely certain. Many times hostas are sold with a cultivar name only (i.e., no specific epithet), because there have been so many different species in the pedigree that it is far easier just to call it by a single name.

Although the flowers are handsome, hostas are usually grown for their foliage. Leaf texture may be shiny, smooth or puckered, various shades of green, blue-green, white, or edged with gold, yellow or white. They may be narrow, broad and wavy, entire, or even twisted. When not in flower, plants can range from 6" to 3' in height. In some taxa, magnificent 3' spires (racemes) of lilac, purple, or white flowers rise above the foliage in summer and in mature plantings are as ornamental as bright spring tulips. Where old large green-leaved hosta clumps occur, they are usually *H. fortunei* or *H. ventricosa*, whose lavender and violet flowers, respectively, overwhelm the landscape around them. I am reminded of the great old flowering clumps at Chesterwood in western Massachusetts, the Minnesota Arboretum in Chashassen, the Botanical Garden in Cleveland, and many other old garden plantings. Fragrance has become an important element in the garden, and hostas are not without their scented members. Using the white flowers of *H. plantaginea* as a building block, numerous plants are touted for their aromatic blossoms. These include the cultivars of *H. plantaginea* ('Honeybells', 'Grandiflora') and those with names like 'Fragrant Bouquet', 'Summer Fragrance' and 'Fragrant Blue'. However, if fragrance is very important, others such as *H.* 'Heaven Scent', 'Invincible', 'So Sweet' and 'Sugar and Cream' are also nicely scented. A highly-touted breakthrough in breeding recently resulted in the double white flowers of 'Aphrodite', which some gardeners have fainted over, especially after they received the bill. While the flowers of hosta are in themselves handsome, they have had little to do with the increased popularity of this genus. In fact, flowers are best removed from many plants less they detract from the foliage.

The diversity of leaf color and plant habit, not flowers, keep the hosta desire fueled. The huge number of taxa has resulted in horticulture classifications based on height and garden use to simplify their garden selection. Dwarf species and cultivars (less than 10″ tall) include species such as *H. pulchella*, *H. gracillima*, and *H. venusta*. They are suitable for the rock garden, edging, or small containers on the patio. Many fine dwarf cultivars encompassing all leaf colors and patterns have also become available. Small hostas (10–15″ tall) include *H. lancifolia*, *H. sieboldii*, *H. undulata*, and many hybrids. They are terrific for edging purposes and can grow together as ground covers or as background plants in the garden. Medium size taxa (15–22″ tall) can also be used for edging, but are generally planted as ground covers, background, or even as single specimens. Species include *H. crispula*, *H. decorata*, *H. fortunei*, *H. tardiflora*, and numerous selections. Large taxa (over 22″ tall) are for those who prefer a more grandiose scale and may be found in *H. montana*, *H. sieboldiana*, *H. tokudama*, *H. ventricosa*, and many others. They may grow 2–3′ tall and up to 4′ wide when properly grown.

There are literally hundreds of hybrids, cultivars, and species from which to choose, and more become available every year. Perhaps it is time to slow down lest there develop as many cultivars of hosta as there are of petunia. There are so many hostas now that the professional breeder must make serious financial decisions concerning the payback of new cultivars and hybrids which are only marginally different from those already on the market. The amateur breeder will continue to enjoy the results of his hobby, naming clones regardless of existing similarities.

Hostas grow best in rich, well-drained soil with constant moisture and light shade. They tolerate moderately heavy shade and grow well in areas where grass dies and ferns and mosses delight. The tolerance of sun for some taxa is constantly debated, and if moisture is plentiful and constant, many can tolerate the sun. This is especially true in the Northeast and Northwest where ample moisture is available. However, lots of plants do well in full sun, so beautify some of those shaded areas with hostas. Without doubt, these plants do not tolerate full sun in the South. Allowing hostas to dry out is the quickest way to ruin the planting. Under dry conditions, leaves are smaller, turn light brown and papery around the edges, and never reach their full growth potential.

The amount of puckering on the leaves dictates usefulness under trees. Those heavily puckered catch the drippings from tree leaves complete with gums, saps and other materials. Said drippings cause the hostas to look particularly wretched. Glossy or smooth-leaved plants are less prone to tree droppings.

Hostas are fabulous plants for the low maintenance garden, but are in no way problem free. Nothing is more frustrating than to discover plants ravaged by deer. Usually, the deer wait long enough to let you think that they may not be interested this year, then some silent dinner bell bongs inside the entire herds' heads, and yet another year is down the tubes. I am not sure what can be done, other than building a deer fence or spraying some disgusting smelling concoction on the plants every week. I live in the woods, and I know frustration. But I still love my hostas and refuse to give in to the teasing varmints.

Then there are slugs. Slugs and snails devour the newly emerging foliage with gusto. Hostas are to slugs what filet mignon is to people. Early and frequent application of slug pellets is essential to keep them at bay. Beer may also be used but why waste good beer? Without doubt, the gardener can reduce slug problems by good maintenance of the plants. Removing old leaves, weeding around the plants, and using an open mulch help to keep the plants growing vigorously. I have seen enough plantings of hostas in various parts of the country to realize that the love affair with these fine plants will abruptly end if the slug/snail problem is not treated seriously by the breeders. We have enough blues, yellows and variegated forms, what we don't have is enough slug resistant ones. I have seen partial lists of more "slug resistant" cultivars in various catalogs, but that list needs to be seriously tested in a proper program, expanded, and used as stock blocks for the program. I hope the breeders can tackle this problem or hostas may go the way of redtips.

Then there are voles. These little suckers burrow underground and bump into the roots of your prize hostas only. Not being happy with the interruption of their journey, they simply eat the obstruction. One day the plant is fine, the next day it is leaning to portside and can easily be lifted since almost all the roots have been devoured. If you don't rescue the plants at that stage, they may simply disappear down the vole hole, as if a fisherman from hell was slowly reeling it in. Gardeners claim that castor beans planted near the hostas help, others dilute castor oil with water and dump it in the holes, while those more frustrated don't even dilute it, trying to castor oil them to oblivion.

Black vine weevils have destroyed leaves of my plantings before I even knew they were there. They are about ½–1″ long, black and incredibly hungry. They appear in north Georgia around mid June and stay about 2–3 weeks. With heavy infestations, they cover the plants and ravage the leaves. Sevin dust is an effective control.

Most hostas do not need dividing for many years and are, in fact, quite slow growing. It often takes 4–5 years before hostas reach maturity of form and color and should not be judged too harshly if they are not "catalog-perfect" before then. Established clumps (greater than 5 years old) bear little resemblance to the majority of immature hostas grown in the average garden. Plants may be divided after 4–5 years, but only if necessary. Take a wedge-like slice when dividing and the division will not be missed. Divide early in the spring when the tightly curled leaves emerge. The number of crowns are easily visible at that time and damage is minimized. The price of a hosta varies with its availability and ease of propagation. Breakthroughs in tissue culture have occurred in recent years and many hostas offered today had their humble beginnings in a test tube.

Commercial production of hostas takes place throughout the country, generally in containers under shade. One of the problems with the production of any crop is that rapid turnover is correlated with relatively high fertility regimes. In areas of high temperatures, the use of nitrogen fertilizers results in loss of variegation in many cultivars. This is a lesson for both gardeners and producers; that is, hostas do not require large amounts of nitrogen fertility in the summer. They should be fertilized with a slow release fertilizer early in the spring as the leaf spears just begin to emerge.

Attempts have been made to key hostas into species, but with so many common cultivars and hybrids, the exercise is difficult and easily defeats all but the most patient plantspeople. There are, however, a number of characteristics which the observant plantsperson can use to detect differences between species and hybrids. These include foliage color, leaf texture (amount of puckering), margin, as well as the number of pairs of veins on either side of the leaf midrib. Floral characteristics include the denseness of the inflorescence, flower color, and even the color of the anthers.

### Quick Reference to Foliage Color and Flowering Season in Hosta

Since the first thing everyone looks at is the foliage, I have classified a few of the popular forms according to foliage color. Further description of size, use and flowering time are included in a few of the species and hybrids which follow. A great deal more information on cultivars and their performance may be obtained from growers, state and national organizations.

**Size Description:** Dwarf (less than 10″), small (10–15″), medium (15–22″), large (over 22″).

**Uses:** Use hostas any way you wish, stick them under the porch or grow them on the roof to cool the house. However, growers and writers have categorized cultivars into a few suggested uses.

*Edger:* Plants used for edging, mainly for small and medium hostas.

*Ground cover:* Plants are usually quick growers, often stoloniferous and can be planted in large groups.

*Background:* Plants are larger, mainly planted in clumps of 3–5.

*Specimen:* Plants may be any size, but are unique for fragrance, texture, color pattern, etc. They are among the most eye-catching. Often, one plant is sufficient to make a display.

## Leaves entirely green, including yellowish green

Do not underestimate the beauty of green in its many shades and hues. These taxa provide the garden with understated grace in various shapes, sizes and flower colors.

| Species | Size | Use | Flowering season |
|---|---|---|---|
| H. 'Andy Taylor' | Small | Edger | L. Summer |
| H. 'Aoki' | Medium | Background | Summer |
| H. 'Barney Fife' | Small | Edger | L. Summer |
| H. 'Big Boy' | Large | Specimen | Summer |
| H. 'Birchwood Parky' | Medium | Background | Summer |
| H. 'Black Hills' | Large | Specimen | E. Summer |
| H. 'Bubba' | Small | Edger | L. Summer |
| H. clausa | Medium | Ground cover | Summer |
| H. elata | Large | Background | E. Summer |
| H. 'Emerald Skies' | Small | Edger | Summer |
| H. 'Fall Bouquet' | Small | Ground cover | L. Summer |
| H. 'Flower Power' | Large | Background | Summer |
| H. fortunei | Large | Ground cover | Summer |
| H. f. 'Obscura' | Large | Background | Summer |
| H. 'Freisling' | Large | Background | Summer |
| H. gracillima | Medium | Edger | Summer |
| H. 'Green Piecrust' | Large | Background | E. Summer |
| H. 'Heartleaf' | Medium | Background | E. Summer |
| H. 'Hirao Supreme' | Large | Specimen | E. Summer |
| H. 'Honeybells' | Large | Background | E. Summer |
| H. 'Invincible' | Small | Ground cover | Summer |
| H. 'Jade Cascade' | Medium | Ground cover | E. Summer |
| H. kikutti | Medium | Edger | Summer |

| Species | Size | Use | Flowering season |
|---------|------|-----|------------------|
| *H. lancifolia* | Medium | Edger | L. Summer |
| *H.* 'Leather Sheen' | Small | Edger | E. Summer |
| *H. longissima* | Small | Edger | L. Summer |
| *H.* 'Maekawa' | Medium | Ground cover | Summer |
| *H. montana* | Large | Background | Summer |
| *H.* 'Montreal' | Medium | Ground cover | Summer |
| *H. nigrescens* 'Elatior' | Large | Specimen | E. Summer |
| *H.* 'Otome No Ka' | Dwarf | Small | E. Summer |
| *H.* 'Pearl Lake' | Medium | Background | Summer |
| *H. plantaginea* | Large | Background | L. Summer |
| *H. p.* 'Aphrodite' | Medium | Specimen | Summer |
| *H. p.* var. *grandiflora* | Large | Background | L. Summer |
| *H. rectifolia* | Medium | Ground cover | Summer |
| *H. r.* 'Tall Boy' | Medium | Background | Summer |
| *H.* 'Red Neck Heaven' | Small | Edger | E. Summer |
| *H.* 'Royal Standard' | Large | Background | L. Summer |
| *H.* 'Scooter' | Dwarf | Edger | Summer |
| *H. sieboldii* 'Alba' | Small | Edger | Summer |
| *H.* 'Sea Drift' | Large | Ground cover | Summer |
| *H.* 'Sea Lotus Leaf' | Medium | Ground cover | E. Summer |
| *H.* 'Sea Octopus' | Small | Edger | Summer |
| *H.* 'Snowden' | Medium | Ground cover | L. Summer |
| *H.* 'Snow Flakes' | Small | Edger | L. Summer |
| *H.* 'Snow Mound' | Medium | Ground cover | Summer |
| *H.* 'Snowstorm' | Small | Edger | Summer |
| *H.* 'Sweet Susan' | Medium | Ground cover | E. Summer |
| *H. tardiflora* | Small | Edger | Fall |
| *H.* 'Tiny Tears' | Dwarf | Edger | E. Summer |
| *H. undulata* var. *erromena* | Medium | Ground cover | Summer |
| *H.* 'Valentine Lace' | Small | Edger | Summer |
| *H.* 'Valerie's Vanity' | Small | Edger | E. Summer |
| *H. ventricosa* | Medium | Ground cover | L. Summer |
| *H. venusta* | Dwarf | Edger | Summer |
| *H.* 'Waving Wuffles' | Small | Edger | L. Summer |
| *H.* 'Weihenstephan' | Small | Ground cover | Summer |
| *H.* 'Wrinkles and Crinkles' | Medium | Ground cover | Summer |

## Leaves blue-green

Some of the finest hostas may be found here, providing contrast and calmness to the garden. The foliage may have an unmistakably blue hue, while others simply provide a hint of blue.

| Species | Size | Use | Flowering season |
|---------|------|-----|------------------|
| H. 'Abiqua Drinking Gourd' | Medium | Background | Summer |
| H. 'Big Daddy' | Large | Background | Summer |
| H. 'Big Mama' | Large | Specimen | Summer |
| H. 'Blue Angel' | Large | Specimen | Summer |
| H. 'Blue Blush' | Dwarf | Edger | E. Summer |
| H. 'Blue Boy' | Medium | Ground cover | Summer |
| H. 'Blue Cadet' | Small | Edger | L. Summer |
| H. 'Blue Diamond' | Medium | Edger | Summer |
| H. 'Blue Dimples' | Large | Background | E. Summer |
| H. 'Blue Skies' | Small | Edger | L. Summer |
| H. 'Blue Max' | Large | Background | Summer |
| H. 'Blue Moon' | Dwarf | Small | Summer |
| H. 'Blue Umbrellas' | Large | Background | Summer |
| H. 'Blue Vision' | Medium | Ground cover | Summer |
| H. 'Blue Wedgewood' | Medium | Edger | Summer |
| H. 'Bold Ruffles' | Large | Background | Summer |
| H. 'Bressingham Blue' | Medium | Background | Summer |
| H. 'Dorset Blue' | Dwarf | Small | E. Summer |
| H. 'Elvis Lives' | Medium | Ground cover | E. Summer |
| H. fortunei var. hyacinthina | Medium | Ground cover | Summer |
| H. 'Fragrant Blue' | Small | Edger | Summer |
| H. 'Hadspen Blue' | Small | Ground cover | L. Summer |
| H. 'Hadspen Heron' | Small | Edger | L. Summer |
| H. 'Happy Hearts' | Medium | Ground cover | Summer |
| H. 'Harmony' | Dwarf | Edger | E. Summer |
| H. 'Krossa Regal' | Large | Background | L. Summer |
| H. 'Lakeport Blue' | Large | Specimen | E. Summer |
| H. 'Love Pat' | Medium | Specimen | L. Summer |
| H. nigrescens | Medium | Background | L. Summer |
| H. 'Ryan's Big One' | Large | Specimen | Summer |
| H. 'Sea Monster' | Medium | Background | E. Summer |
| H. 'Sea Yellow Sunrise' | Dwarf | Edger | L. Summer |

| Species | Size | Use | Flowering season |
|---------|------|-----|------------------|
| *H. sieboldiana* | Large | Background | Summer |
| *H. s.* 'Elegans' | Large | Background | Summer |
| *H. s.* 'Helen Doriot' | Large | Specimen | Summer |
| *H.* × *tardiana* 'Halycon' | Medium | Background | L. Summer |
| *H. tokudama* | Medium | Ground cover | Summer |
| *H.* 'True Blue' | Medium | Ground cover | E. Summer |
| *H.* 'Winfield Blue' | Small | Ground cover | Summer |

## Yellow leaf blades

Among the most sought after of the hosta groups, the yellow foliage is an outstanding bright foil for other green-leaved plants. The dominant color in this group is yellow, gold or chartreuse.

| Species | Size | Use | Flowering season |
|---------|------|-----|------------------|
| *H.* 'Aspen Gold' | Large | Background | E. Summer |
| *H.* 'August Moon' | Large | Specimen | Summer |
| *H.* 'Birchwood Parky's Gold' | Medium | Background | Summer |
| *H.* 'Blonde Elf' | Dwarf | Edger | E. Summer |
| *H.* 'Bright Glow' | Small | Edger | Summer |
| *H.* 'Chartreuse Wiggles' | Dwarf | Edger | L. Summer |
| *H.* 'Feather Boa' | Small | Edger | E. Summer |
| *H. fortunei* 'Albo picta' | Medium | Background | Summer |
| *H. f.* 'Aurea' | Medium | Background | Summer |
| *H.* 'Fresh' | Dwarf | Edger | L. Summer |
| *H.* 'Gold Bullion' | Small | Ground cover | Summer |
| *H.* 'Gold Drop' | Small | Edger | Summer |
| *H.* 'Gold Edger' | Small | Edger | L. Summer |
| *H.* 'Gold Regal' | Large | Specimen | E. Summer |
| *H.* 'Golden Medallion' | Medium | Background | Summer |
| *H.* 'Golden Prayers' | Small | Edger | L. Summer |
| *H.* 'Golden Scepter' | Small | Edger | Summer |
| *H.* 'Golden Sculpture' | Large | Background | Summer |
| *H.* 'Golden Tiara' | Small | Edger | L. Summer |
| *H.* 'Great Expectations' | Large | Specimen | E. Summer |
| *H.* 'Harvest Glow' | Medium | Background | Summer |
| *H.* 'High Noon' | Large | Specimen | Summer |

| Species | Size | Use | Flowering season |
|---|---|---|---|
| H. 'Lemon Lime' | Small | Edger | Summer |
| H. 'Little Aurora' | Dwarf | Edger | Summer |
| H. 'Marilyn' | Small | Edger | E. Summer |
| H. 'Midas Touch' | Medium | Background | Summer |
| H. 'Moonglow' | Medium | Background | Summer |
| H. 'Moonlight' | Medium | Specimen | L. Summer |
| H. 'On Stage' | Medium | Background | Summer |
| H. 'Piedmont Gold' | Medium | Background | L. Summer |
| H. 'Platinum Tiara' | Small | Edger | Summer |
| H. 'Sea Fire' | Medium | Background | Summer |
| H. 'Sea Gold Star' | Medium | Edger | Summer |
| H. 'Shade Master' | Medium | Background | E. Summer |
| H. sieboldiana 'Golden Sunburst' | Large | Background | Summer |
| H. 'Solar Flair' | Large | Specimen | Summer |
| H. 'Sum and Substance' | Large | Specimen | Summer |
| H. 'Sun Power' | Large | Background | L. Summer |
| H. 'Super Bowl' | Medium | Background | E. Summer |
| H. 'Wogon Gold' | Medium | Ground cover | Summer |
| H. 'Zounds' | Medium | Background | E. Summer |

## White-edged leaves

Probably the most popular color combination in the genus, the white margins brighten up the garden while combining well with most other plants in the area. The margins may vary from pencil-thin to large areas taking up a significant part of the leaf. In general, this group has green leaf blades. One or two, such as *H. fluctuans* 'Variegata', may have bluish blades.

| Species | Size | Use | Flowering season |
|---|---|---|---|
| H. 'Allen P. McConnell' | Small | Edger | Summer |
| H. 'Antioch' | Large | Background | Summer |
| H. 'Arctic Circle' | Medium | Background | Summer |
| H. 'Bold Ribbons' | Small | Edger | E. Summer |
| H. 'Brim Cup' | Small | Background | E. Summer |
| H. 'Carol' | Medium | Background | Summer |
| H. 'Christmas Tree' | Medium | Background | Summer |
| H. 'Crested Surf' | Dwarf | Edger | Summer |

| Species | Size | Use | Flowering season |
|---------|------|-----|------------------|
| *H. crispula* | Small | Ground cover | E. Summer |
| *H.* 'Crowned Imperial' | Medium | Background | Summer |
| *H. decorata* | Small | Ground cover | E. Summer |
| *H.* 'Dew Drop' | Dwarf | Edger | E. Summer |
| *H.* 'Diamond Tiara' | Medium | Ground cover | E. Summer |
| *H. fluctuans* 'Variegata' | Large | Specimen | Summer |
| *H. fortunei* 'Marginato-alba | Medium | Ground cover | Summer |
| *H.* 'Francee' | Medium | Background | Summer |
| *H.* 'Fringe Benefit' | Large | Background | E. Summer |
| *H.* 'Ginko Craig' | Small | Edger | Summer |
| *H. gracillima* 'Variegata' | Small | Edger | Summer |
| *H.* 'Ground Master' | Medium | Ground cover | Summer |
| *H.* 'Honeysong' | Medium | Ground cover | Summer |
| *H.* 'Krossa Cream Edge' | Small | Edger | L. Summer |
| *H.* 'Lunar Eclipse' | Large | Specimen | E. Summer |
| *H. montana* 'Mountain Snow' | Medium | Background | E. Summer |
| *H.* 'North Hills' | Medium | Ground cover | Summer |
| *H.* 'Patriot' | Medium | Specimen | E. Summer |
| *H.* 'Pizzazz' | Large | Specimen | L. Summer |
| *H.* 'Resonance' | Large | Specimen | Summer |
| *H.* 'Shogun' | Large | Background | Summer |
| *H.* 'So Sweet' | Medium | Specimen | L. Summer |
| *H.* 'Shade Fanfare' | Medium | Background | Summer |
| *H. sieboldiana* 'Northern Halo' | Large | Specimen | Summer |
| *H. s.* 'May T. Watts' | Large | Specimen | Summer |
| *H. sieboldii* | Small | Edger | Summer |
| *H. s.* 'Louisa' | Small | Edger | Summer |
| *H.* 'Snow Cap' | Large | Specimen | Summer |
| *H.* 'Stilleto' | Dwarf | Edger | E. Summer |
| *H.* 'Sugar and Cream' | Large | Specimen | L. Summer |
| *H.* 'Summer Fragrance' | Large | Specimen | L. Summer |
| *H.* 'Thomas Hogg' | Small | Ground cover | E. Summer |
| *H. undulata* 'Albomarginata' | Medium | Ground cover | Summer |
| *H.* 'Vera Verde' | Dwarf | Edger | L. Summer |
| *H.* 'Wide Brim' | Large | Specimen | Summer |
| *H.* 'Yellow Splash' | Medium | Ground cover | Summer |
| *H.* 'Zager White Edge' | Medium | Specimen | E. Summer |

## Yellow- or gold-edged leaves

Many very popular plants are found in this color group because of the handsome contrast between the margins and the interior of the leaf blades. The margins always start out yellow or golden in the spring, but may turn more towards white in the heat of the summer.

| Species | Size | Use | Flowering season |
|---|---|---|---|
| H. 'Abba Dabba Do' | Medium | Background | Summer |
| H. 'Abiqua Moonbeam' | Medium | Background | Summer |
| H. 'Alvatine Taylor' | Medium | Background | Summer |
| H. 'Aurora Borealis' | Large | Specimen | Summer |
| H. 'El Capitan' | Medium | Ground cover | E. Summer |
| H. 'Ellerbroek' | Medium | Background | Summer |
| H. fortunei 'Aureomarginata' | Medium | Ground cover | Summer |
| H. 'Fragrant Bouquet' | Medium | Ground cover | E. Summer |
| H. 'Golden Tiara' | Small | Edger | Summer |
| H. 'Grand Tiara' | Medium | Specimen | Summer |
| H. 'Heaven Scent' | Medium | Specimen | E. Summer |
| H. 'Knockout' | Medium | Background | Summer |
| H. 'Mildred Seaver' | Medium | Background | E. Summer |
| H. montana 'Aureomarginata' | Large | Specimen | Fall |
| H. 'Northern Exposure' | Medium | Ground cover | E. Summer |
| H. 'Patrician' | Small | Edger | L. Summer |
| H. 'Regal Splendor' | Large | Specimen | E. Summer |
| H. 'Robert Frost' | Medium | Specimen | E. Summer |
| H. 'Samurai' | Large | Specimen | Summer |
| H. 'Sea Sprite' | Small | Edger | Summer |
| H. sieboldiana 'Frances Williams' | Medium | Specimen | Summer |
| H. s. 'Maple Leaf' | Large | Specimen | L. Summer |
| H. 'Shade Fanfare' | Medium | Ground cover | Summer |
| H. 'Sundance' | Medium | Background | Summer |
| H. tokudama 'Flavo-circinalis' | Medium | Ground cover | E. Summer |
| H. ventricosa 'Aureomarginata' | Medium | Ground cover | L. Summer |
| H. 'Winning Edge' | Medium | Ground cover | E. Summer |
| H. 'Yellow River' | Medium | Background | L. Summer |

## White leaf blades, usually with green margins or blotches

A difficult color combination to describe because the center of the leaf is mainly white, while the outside of the leaf is a different color, generally green. They are excellent for brightening up the shady areas of the garden.

| Species | Size | Use | Flowering season |
|---|---|---|---|
| H. 'Celebration' | Medium | Ground cover | L. Summer |
| H. 'Gene's Joy' | Dwarf | Small | L. Summer |
| H. undulata 'Medio-picta' | Medium | Edger | Summer |
| H. u. var. univittata | Medium | Edger | Summer |
| H. venusta 'Variegata' | Dwarf | Small | E. Summer |
| H. 'White Colossus' | Large | Specimen | Summer |
| H. 'White Magic' | Large | Specimen | Summer |

## Yellow leaf blades, with green or white margins

Some of the most eye-catching cultivars may be found here. The yellow-chartreuse leaves with green margins or blotches provide a colorful contrast.

| Species | Size | Use | Flowering season |
|---|---|---|---|
| H. 'Bright Lights' | Medium | Edger | E. Summer |
| H. 'Color Glory' | Large | Specimen | Summer |
| H. 'Emerald Tiara' | Small | Specimen | E. Summer |
| H. 'Excitation' | Dwarf | Edger | Summer |
| H. fortunei 'Viridis-marginata' | Medium | Specimen | Summer |
| H. 'Gold Standard' | Medium | Ground cover | Summer |
| H. 'Guacamole' | Small | Ground cover | Summer |
| H. 'Hallucination' | Medium | Background | Summer |
| H. 'Inniswood' | Medium | Background | E. Summer |
| H. 'Janet' | Medium | Ground cover | L. Summer |
| H. 'Just So' | Dwarf | Edger | Summer |
| H. 'Peedee Gold Flash' | Small | Edger | E. Summer |
| H. 'Pooh Bear' | Dwarf | Edger | E. Summer |
| H. 'Radiant Edger' | Small | Edger | Summer |
| H. 'Rascal' | Medium | Ground cover | Summer |
| H. 'September Sun' | Medium | Ground cover | E. Summer |
| H. sieboldii 'Kabitan' | Dwarf | Edger | Summer |
| H. 'Spritzer' | Medium | Specimen | L. Summer |
| H. 'Twist of Lime' | Small | Edger | E. Summer |

| *-crispula* (krisp' ew-la) | | Curled Leaf Hosta | 2-3'/2' |
|---|---|---|---|
| Early Summer | Lilac | Japan | Zones 3-8 |

A vigorous species, which when protected from wind and sun, is as lovely as any offered today. The 4-5″ wide, dark green leaves are up to 8″ long and have wavy, irregular white margins. They are glossy on the undersides, bear 7-9 pairs of lateral veins, and have long-pointed pendent tips. The 2″ long lilac flowers are held loosely on a many-flowered 2-3' tall raceme. This is one of the earliest white-margined hostas to flower. Grow in shade to partial sun.

| *-decorata* (de-ko-rah' ta) | | Blunt Hosta | 18-24″/2' |
|---|---|---|---|
| Summer | Violet | Japan | Zones 3-8 |

Similar to *H. sieboldii* in habit and coloration, the leaves are wider and more blunt on the apex. They are broadly oval, 3-8″ long and have 4-5 pairs of lateral veins. Slightly wavy, silvery-white margins surround the matte green leaves. The 2″ long, dark violet flowers are carried on leafless flower stems 1½-2' above the foliage.

**Related Species:**

*H.* 'Thomas Hogg' is synonymous with *H. decorata*, at least in this country, but may be a slightly different plant in Europe. In Europe, plants under this name may be hybrids of *H. sieboldii* and *H. decorata*.

| *-fortunei* (for-tewn' ee-eye) | | Fortune's Hosta | 15-24″/24″ |
|---|---|---|---|
| Summer | Lilac | Japan | Zones 3-8 |

Plants form extensive clumps of somewhat heart-shaped green to gray-green leaves after a few years. Leaves are 9″ long, 4″ wide, and have 9-11 veins on either side of the midrib. Each leaf is attached to the stem by a deeply furrowed petiole with distinct wings. The flower stem rises well above the foliage and usually has one to several bracts beneath the 1½″ long pale lilac flowers. This species provides excellent low maintenance plants for the shade garden.

**Cultivars:**

'Albopicta' is a popular cultivar with wavy yellow leaf blades ringed with pale green margins. Although the yellow tends to fade in the summer, this outstanding eye-catching plant is one of my favorites.

'Albopicta Aurea' has leaves which are almost totally white, but have a thin green central midrib.

'Aoki' is 1½-2' tall and is neat in appearance. It is early flowering with gray-green foliage and lavender-purple flowers.

'Aurea' offers shimmering pale yellow leaves in the spring with wavy margins, but is less vigorous than many other cultivars. Plants fade badly in full sun.

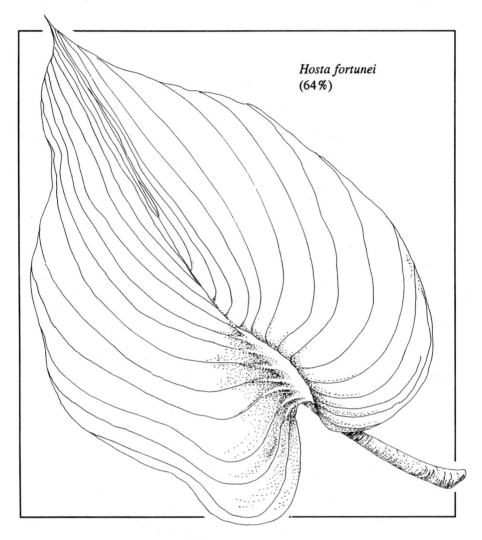

*Hosta fortunei*
(64%)

'Aureo-marginata' (syn. 'Obscura Marginata') has a narrow yellow margin, changing to yellowish green, and then to dark green toward the center. The flowers are light violet.

'Gold Standard' was found as a chance seedling in 1976. It offers vigorous growth, light gold leaves edged with green, and lavender flowers. It may be a hybrid with *H. fortunei* as one of the parents.

'Hyacinthina' is more vigorous, later flowering, and has large, gray-green leaves with a pencil thin white line at the edge.

'Marginato-alba' (syn. 'Albo-marginata') has a yellow margin in the spring that changes to white in the summer and remains until frost. The margin varies in width. The flowers are pale lavender.

*-lancifolia* (lan-si-fo' lee-a)  Lance Leaf Hosta  1½–2'/18"
Late Summer  Lilac  Japan  Zones 3–8

This is reported to be the oldest known hosta in cultivation, drawings of which date to 1690. A parent of many modern hybrids, it embodies numerous fine garden attributes. The 4–7" long, pointed foliage is pure green, glossy on both sides, and only about 1" wide. Each leaf has 3–5 pairs of lateral veins. The flower scape is 12–18" long and carries 1–1½" long deep lilac flowers in late summer persisting into autumn. Perhaps not one of the most decorative hostas, the glossy leaves are pleasant, and plants perform well and tolerate drier and sunnier conditions better than many other species and hybrids.

**Cultivars:**
Var. *viridis marginata* is a smaller plant (12–15" tall) with long-lasting yellow leaf blades edged with a narrow green band.

*-plantaginea* (plan-tage' i-nee-a)  Fragrant Hosta  24–30"/2'
Late Summer  White  China  Zones 3–9

This species and related hybrids are some of the most popular hostas. The large, arching, heart-shaped leaves are bright yellowish green with short pointed tips. They are up to 10" long with 7–9 veins on each side of the midrib. Although flowers of most hostas are of little interest and are often removed before opening, the flowers on this species are most handsome. The fragrant, 4–5" long, lovely white flowers are held well above the foliage almost at right angles to the stem instead of drooping as in many other species. They are densely arranged near the top of the raceme and the base of each is surrounded by a broad bract.

**Cultivars:**
'Grandiflora' has longer, narrower foliage and tends to make a looser clump. The large narrow flowers are 6" long.

**Related Species:**
Several excellent hybrids, of which *H. plantaginea* is one of the parents, are available. They differ from *H. plantaginea* by being taller, and having slightly longer and more yellow leaf blades. *H. plantaginea* and the hybrids tolerate more sun and heat than many others and do poorly in deep shade. They are well suited to southern climes.

'August Moon' has large crinkled yellow blades and white flowers.
'Honeybells' (*H. plantaginea* × *H. lancifolia*) has gorgeous yellow-green wavy leaves, above which rise the pale lilac, fragrant flowers in late summer.
'Piedmont Gold' is an excellent yellow-leaved hybrid which makes a beautiful 18–24" tall clump with numerous white flowers in the summer.

*Hosta plantaginea*
(60%)

'Royal Standard' was introduced to the United States by Wayside Gardens, Hodges, SC, and has green-yellow foliage that is slightly puckered and deeply veined. Leaves are 8" long, 5" wide, and rather thin. It is taller than *H. plantaginea*, growing to 3'. Foliage is not as yellow as 'Honey-bells', but the numerous white flowers have a pleasing fragrance.

'Sweet Susan' is a hybrid between *H. plantaginea* and *H. sieboldii*, and has glossy green leaves and large fragrant lilac flowers.

| *-sieboldiana* (see-bold-ee-ah' na) | Siebold Hosta | 2½–3'/4' |
|---|---|---|
| Summer          Lilac, White | Japan | Zones 3–8 |

Some of the finest garden plants are found in this species. The thick bluish green leaves are heart shaped to almost rounded and have 12–14 pairs of lateral veins. Leaves average 15" long and 12" wide. The light lilac flowers seldom rise above the foliage and are often hidden by the leaves.

In general, leaves decline by late August in the South and about a month later in the North. Plants may be cut back at that time if foliage becomes too unsightly. The flowers and bracts are densely clustered, and when in bud look like an artichoke. I think they detract from the magnificence of the plant and should be removed prior to opening.

## Cultivars:

'Aurora Borealis', a recent sport of 'Frances Williams', is 4–5' in diameter, taller, more vigorous and has more gold markings on the blue-green leaves. The white flowers rise just above the foliage.

'Elegans' was first offered around 1905 by Georg Arends Nursery (see *Astilbe*) in Germany. It has large leaves of conspicuous steel blue and flowers of light lilac to white. A mature plant grows 3' tall, 4–5' wide and is guaranteed to attract attention.

'Frances Williams' is named after Mrs. Frances Williams, an American horticulturist and hosta collector. She spotted a seedling of *H. sieboldiana* var. *elegans* with gold variegated margins in 1936 growing at Bristol Nurseries, Connecticut. Plants have blue-green leaf blades rimmed with golden bands. It is sometimes listed as 'Gold Edge' (distinct from 'Gold Edger', which see) or 'Golden Circles'. This is one of the finest hostas in cultivation today and is always found in the American Hosta Society's poll as one of the most popular hostas in American gardens.

'Golden Sunburst' consists of 2' tall clumps of golden yellow foliage prior to flowering. Creamy white flowers are borne in early summer.

'Helen Doriot' has intense blue puckered leaves with white flowers.

'May T. Watts' has heavily puckered leaves with gold centers surrounded by white margins. Introduced by the Planters Palette, Winfield, IL.

'Northern Halo' is a recent introduction from Walter's Gardens, Michigan, with creamy white margins surrounding blue-green centers.

'Robusta' bears leaves that are not as blue-green as those of 'Elegans' but equally broad. Although sometimes listed as *H. fortunei* 'Robusta', the flower is similar to that of *H. sieboldiana* and it fruits heavily, unlike *H. fortunei*. Lovely specimens can be found at Longwood Gardens.

## Related Species:

*H. × tardiana* has been applied to a series of plants resulting from the cross of *H. tardiflora*, a small dark green species, with *H. sieboldiana* var. *elegans*. These were raised in the late 1960's by Eric Smith, an outstanding hosta breeder in England. Plants are usually less than 18″ tall with blue-green leaves. Cultivars include 'Blue Dimples' with thick blue leaves with pale lavender flowers, and 'Blue Skies' with small, steely blue, heart-shaped leaves. These two cultivars are 15–18″ tall and bear many lavender flowers. 'Hadspen Blue' grows 12″ tall and has distinctive, 4″ wide, 5″ long, blue lanceolate leaves with slight undulations. 'Halcyon' has blue leaves with intense blue-lilac flowers rising slightly above them.

*H. tokudama* is closely related to *H. sieboldiana* and may in fact be a variety of *H. sieboldiana*. It is a pretty, diminutive species with deep blue-green, crinkled leaves. Plants are only about 18″ tall, rather slow growing, and produce lilac-white flowers similar to *H. sieboldiana*. Cultivars include 'Aurea-nebulosa', which has leaves with a chartreuse interior surrounded by a glaucous blue margin, and grows to 24″ tall, and 'Buckshaw Blue', which has bluer, more cup-shaped leaves than the species. The mauve flowers open just above the foliage.

**Other Related Hybrids:**

Many other hybrids with glaucous blue foliage have resulted from crosses between cultivars of *H. sieboldiana, H. tokudama, H. fortunei,* and others.

'Blue Cadet' is a dwarf form with lavender flowers in late summer. Plants are suitable for the small garden.

'Blue Umbrellas' is 2–4′ tall with blue-green textured foliage. Many white edged lavender flowers are produced in summer. A good specimen plant.

'Love Pat' has wide, puckered, gray-green leaves and creamy white flowers tucked into the foliage. Plants are about 2′ tall with lavender flowers in early summer.

'Krossa Regal', a distinctly vase-shaped form, ranges from 3–5′ tall when not in flower. The foliage is silvery-blue, leathery, and long-pointed. The lavender flowers, produced in late summer, extend another 2′ above the foliage.

'Snowden', a cross between *H. fortunei* 'Aurea' and *H. sieboldiana* 'Elegans', has long-pointed gray-green leaves in symmetrical 3′ tall mounds. The flowers are pure white with occasional green tinges.

| | | |
|---|---|---|
| *-sieboldii* (see-bold′ee-eye) | Seersucker Hosta | 12–20″/20″ |
| Summer        Purple | Japan | Zones 3–8 |
| (Syn. *H. albomarginata*) | | |

Known and grown as *H. albomarginata*, it is correctly *H. sieboldii*, named after Philipp Franz von Siebold, in whose Dutch nursery it appeared in the early 1800's. This is one of the smaller hostas, but one which quickly fills in due to its creeping rootstock. The 2–2½″ wide lance-shaped foliage has thin pure white margins and 3–4 pairs of lateral veins. Each leaf has a matte-like finish on the upperside but is glossy below. The inflorescence rises well above the foliage and bears a few blunt leaves along its length beneath the flowers. Flowers are 2–2½″ long, the outer segments strongly recurved and violet, while the inside is marked with violet stripes. Up to 30 flowers are carried on the raceme; they are neither particularly exciting nor do they detract from the foliage. This small, late-flowering hosta is most useful for edging and filling in small shady corners of the garden.

## Cultivars:

'Alba' has pure white flowers with plain green leaves.

'Louisa' combines the wide, white-margined foliage with small (1–2″ long) white flowers. It is an excellent small white-margined hosta, but is a slower grower than the species. Selected in 1965 by Mrs. Williams and named for her daughter.

'Kabitan' has greenish yellow leaf blades rimmed with a narrow band of green. The margins of the foliage are quite wavy and the light violet flowers appear earlier than other cultivars in the species. It is often incorrectly listed as a cultivar of *H. lancifolia*.

| *-undulata* (un-dew-lah′ ta) | | Wavy Hosta | 12–18″/18″ |
|---|---|---|---|
| Summer | Lilac | Japan | Zones 3–8 |

This is the common hosta offered by many mail order catalogs as the "variegated hosta." Plant are often listed as 'Variegata' or 'Medio-picta'. The 6″ long leaves are undulated (wavy), thus its specific epithet, and have 8–10 pairs of lateral veins. Leaves typically have green margins and clear white interiors and are often spirally twisted. The winged, red-dotted petiole is deeply furrowed. The 2″ long flowers are light lilac and carried on 2–3′ long flower stems bearing numerous well developed bracts.

## Cultivars:

'Albo-marginata' has thin creamy white margins surrounding the green center of the leaf blades (i.e., reverse of the species). Plants are 12″ tall and 14–18″ wide.

Var. *erromena* is a green leaf form with leaves up to 7–9″ long and 4–6″ wide. The 18″ long petioles are channeled with purple dots at the base. Flower stems average 3′ long. This variety probably resulted from a green sport of var. *univittata*.

Var. *univittata* is more vigorous than the species, growing 2–3′ tall. The foliage has much wider green margins than the species, reducing the white coloration to a narrow strip along the midrib.

| *-ventricosa* (ven-tri-ko′ sa) | | Blue Hosta | 2–3′/3′ |
|---|---|---|---|
| Late Summer | Violet | Eastern Asia | Zones 3–9 |

(Syn. *H. caerulea*)

Broad glossy leaves (up to 7″ wide) carried on a short, wide, shallowly furrowed petiole are characteristic of the species. The dark green, 7–9″ long foliage bears 7–9 pairs of lateral veins and unusually distinct cross veins, resulting in a net-like appearance. The flower stem is bractless and carries 20–30 bell-shaped flowers about 3′ above the foliage. The flowers, which are dark purple with darker stripes within, are borne horizontally but become pendent. The petals widen abruptly into campanula-like flowers.

**Cultivars:**

'Aureo-maculata' ('Variegata') has leaf blades of yellowish green surrounded by green margins, although the leaves become mostly green by flowering time.

'Aureo-marginata' is the reverse of the previous cultivar, having yellow margins that turn white and green leaf blades. This relatively new introduction was discovered in a bed of seedlings of *H. ventricosa* by Alan Bloom in 1968. Terrific plant.

| | | | |
|---|---|---|---|
| *-venusta* (ven-ews′ ta) | | Dwarf Hosta | 3–4″/8″ |
| Summer | Lilac | Korea | Zones 3–9 |

This is one of the dwarfest of hostas, although other hybrids are appearing which are scaled down versions of their predecessors. The green leaf blades are only about 1″ long by ¾″ wide, with 3–4 pairs of lateral veins. The flower stem rises 8–12″ above the foliage and carries 4–8 lilac flowers about 1½″ long. Plants are stoloniferous and spread well. Group 6–8 plants in a shady nook or cranny for best effect.

**Cultivars:**

'Variegated' has foliage with creamy white centers and green margins.

**Other Worthy Hybrids:**

Under the various species, I have mentioned a few of the older "tried and true" cultivars and hybrids. It must be obvious from the list of hybrids provided initially that there is a battalion of others I have not described in any detail. Numerous nurseries carry new selections every year and they work very hard to provide descriptions of their offerings. Find a few good nurseries and a few good books, and soon you head will be spinning with names and colors like the rest of us. Happy hunting.

Quick Key to Hosta Species

Far superior minds than mine have attempted scientific keys to the genus. All are useful to the hostaphile. It should be plain by now that a large number of hostas are hybrids or cultivars, and that a key to species has limited usefulness. However, in fairness to this great genus, the following key provides horticultural and botanical characteristics of some of the species and a few of the hybrids and cultivars. For a more complete key to the species, read the excellent book by George Schmid (see Additional Reading).

A. Plant less than 6″ tall, leaves green, not
    exceeding 4″ in length, including petiole,
    3–4 pairs of side veins . . . . . . . . . . . . . . . . . . . *H. venusta*
AA. Plant taller, leaves larger
    B. Leaf blade yellowish green, glossy on both
        sides, flowers fragrant, white, usually
        opening in evening . . . . . . . . . . . . . . . . . . *H. plantaginea*
    BB. Leaf blade green, bluish, or variegated, flowers not
        fragrant, usually purple to lilac, open during day
        C. Leaf blade with white, yellow, or gold margin
            D. Leaf blade with gold or yellow margin
                E. Leaf blades distinctly puckered on
                    underside, or on both sides
                    F. Leaves puckered on both sides,
                        very broad, flower stem barely
                        rising above foliage, flowers
                        pale violet to white . . . . . . . . . . *H. sieboldiana*
                  FF. Leaves puckered on underside    'Frances Williams'
                      less broad, flower stem well
                      above foliage, flowers dark violet . . . . *H. fortunei*
                EE. Leaf blade not puckered, flower    'Aureomarginata'
                  stem well above foliage . . . . . . . . . . *H. ventricosa*
            DD. Leaf blade with white margin    'Aureomarginata'
                E. Leaf margin undulated
                  F. Leaves broad (4–5″ across),
                      long-pointed flower stem with only
                      one bract-like leaf, broad border . . . . . *H. crispula*
                  FF. Leaves less broad (2–4″ across), long-
                      pointed flower stem bearing 3–4
                      prominent long petioled leaves . . . . . . *H. undulata*
                EE. Leaf margin not conspicuously    'Albomarginata'
                  undulated
                  F. Leaves not puckered on either side
                      less than 2′ tall when not in flower
                      G. Leaves narrow, elliptical,
                        short pointed . . . . . . . . . . . . . . *H. sieboldii*
                      GG. Leaves broader, ovate,
                        ends blunt . . . . . . . . . . . . . . . . *H. decorata*
                  FF. Leaves puckered on underside,
                      more than 2′ long . . . *H. fortunei* 'Marginato-alba'
        CC. Leaf blades without white, yellow, or gold margins
            D. Leaf blades entirely green or blue-green
                E. Leaf blades blue-green or gray-green

F. Flower stems barely rising above foliage,
   flowers pale lilac to white
   G. Plant less than 2′ tall,
      leaves 3–4″ wide . . . . . . . . . . *H. tokudama*
   GG. Plant more than 2′ tall,
      leaves up to 1′ wide . . . . . . . *H. sieboldiana*
FF. Flower stem rising well above
   foliage, flowers dark purple . . . . . . . . *H. fortunei*
EE. Leaf blades entirely green
   F. Plants 2–2½′ tall when not in flower
      G. Tube of flower abruptly widening
         into bell-shaped part of flower,
         dark violet . . . . . . . . . . . . . . *H. ventricosa*
      GG. Tube of flower expanding
         gradually, flower lilac . . . . . . . . *H. undulata*
   FF. Plants less than 2′ tall                      var. *erromena*
      when not in flower
      G. Flower mauve to lilac
         H. Leaves lance shaped, glossy on
            both sides, about 12–15″ tall,
            summer flowering . . . . . . . . *H. lancifolia*
         HH. Leaves ovate, less shiny,
            8–12″ tall, fall flowering . . . . *H. tardiflora*
      GG. Flowers white . . . . . . . . *H. sieboldii* 'Alba'
DD. Leaves not entirely green or blue-green, leaf blades
   white or yellow sometimes with a green margin
   E. Interior of leaf blades white
      F. Margin very wide, white reduced to
         broad stripe along midrib, leaf not
         conspicuously undulated . . . . . . . . . *H. undulata*
      FF. White and green both heavily          var. *univittata*
         splashed on leaf blade, leaf
         conspicuously undulated . . . . . . . . . *H. undulata*
   EE. Interior of leaf blade yellowish
      F. Leaves all the same color
         G. Flowers white,
            height 12–18″ . . . . . . . . *H.* 'Piedmont Gold'
         GG. Flowers lilac, height 10–12″ . . *H. fortunei* 'Aurea'
      FF. Leaves with greenish margin
         G. Height 10–12″,
            leaves ovate . . . . . . . . *H. fortunei* 'Albopicta'
         GG. Height 8–12″, leaves
            lance-shaped . . . . . . . . *H. sieboldii* 'Kabitan'

*Achillea* ×
'Anthea'

*Adiantum pedatum*

*Agapanthus*
'Loch Hope'

*Agastache rupestris*

*Alchemilla mollis*

*Allium schubertii*

*Allium*
'Globemaster'

*Anemonella thalictroides*

*Anthemis tinctoria*
'Grallagh Gold'

*Aquilegia chrysantha*

*Aquilegia canadensis*

*Arisaema sikokianum*

*Arisaema ringens*

*Artemisia*
'Huntington Gardens'

*Asarum shuttleworthii*
'Callaway'

*Asclepias incarnata*
'Ice Ballet'

*Astilbe × arendsii*
'Cattleya'

*Belamcanda flabellata*
'Hello Yellow'

*Campanula carpatica*
var. *turbinata*

*Campanula lactiflora*

*Carex buchananii*

*Catananche caeruleum*

*Cephalaria gigantea*

*Chrysanthemum coccineum* 'E.M. Robinson'

*Clematis integrifolia*

*Coreopsis verticillata*
'Moonbeam' & *Salvia farinacea* 'Victoria'

*Corydalis flexuosa*
'Blue Panda'

*Crocosmia*
'Lucifer'

*Delosperma cooperi*

*Dicentra spectabilis*

*Dictamnus albus*

*Disporum flavum*

*Doronicum carpetanum*

*Echinacea purpurea*
'White Swan'

*Echinacea purpurea*
'Bravado' & *Lilium*
'Yellow Star'

*Echinops ritro*

*Eryngium* × *oliverianum*

*Erysimum linifolium*
'Bowles Mauve'

*Erythronium tuolumnense*

*Euphorbia* × *martinii*

*Filipendula purpurea*

*Galanthus nivalis*

*Gaura lindheimeri*

*Geranium cinereum*
'Ballerina'

*Germanium sanguineum*
'Striatum'

*Gillenia trifoliata*

*Gladiolus byzantinus*

*Gypsophila repens*
'Rosea'

*Helenium*
'Wyndley'

*Helianthemum
nummularium*
'Wisely Pink'

*Helianthus angustifolius*

*Heliopsis helianthoides*
'Gold Greenheart'

*Hemerocallis*
'Mary Todd'

*Hosta*
'Bright Lights'

*Kalimeris pinnatifida*
& *Verbena*
'Taylortown Red'

*Kniphofia*
'Sunningdale Yellow'

*Lewisia cotyledon*

*Lupinus* Russell Hybrids

*Lycoris radiata*

*Lysimachia nummularia*
'Aurea'

*Lysimachia clethroides*

*Miscanthus sinensis*
'Silberspinne'

*Monarda citriodora*

*Muscari latifolium*

*Ophiopogon jaburan*

*Oxalis regnellii*
'Purpurea'

*Paeonia suffruticosa*
'Arcadia'

*Phlox paniculata*
'David'

*Phlox divaricata*
'Dirigo Ice'

*Phlox paniculata*
'Robert Poore'

*Polystichum setiferum*

*Primula vialii*

*Pulmonaria saccharata*
'British Sterling'

*Pulsatilla vulgaris*

*Ranunculus ficaria*
'Brazen Hussy'

*Ranunculus repens*
'Joe's Golden'

*Rudbeckia triloba*

*Santolina virens*

*Saponaria ocymoides*

*Saxifraga stolonifera*

*Scabiosa caucasica*
'Butterfly Blue'

*Silene polypetala*

*Sisyrinchium striatum*
'Variegatum'

*Sisyrinchium idahoense*
'California Skies'

*Stachys byzantina*
'Primrose Heron'

*Stachys macrantha*
'Robusta'

*Stokesia laevis*
'Klaus Jelitto'

*Stylophorum diphyllum*

*Thalictrum
rochebrunianum*

*Tovara virginianum*

*Tradescantia virginiana*
'Joy'

*Tricyrtis formosana*
(White form)

*Trillium cuneatum*

*Trollius ledebourii*

*Verbena*
'Homestead Purple'

*Viola pedata*

**Additional Reading:**

Books:

Aden, Paul. 1988. *The Hosta Book*. Timber Press, OR. 133 p. Now in its second edition.

Schmid, W. G. 1991. *The Genus Hosta*. Timber Press, OR. 428 p. Easily the most comprehensive and valuable book on the genus written in the last 50 years. Mr. Schmid is not only an expert in nomenclature and history of the genus, but an avid gardener as well. His garden, Hosta Hill, is the source of many of the photographs in the book. A must book for the library.

Manuscripts:

Aden, Paul. 1986. The cultivation of hostas. *The Garden* 111(5):222-225.

Greenfell, Diana. 1981. A survey of the genus Hosta and its availability in commerce. *The Plantsman* 3(1):20-44.

Hansen, Karel, J.W. 1985. A study of the taxonomy of cultivated hostas. *The Plantsman* 7(1):1-35.

Ingram, John. 1967. Notes on the cultivated liliaceae. 5. *Hosta sieboldii* and *H. sieboldiana*. *Baileya* 15:27-32.

Jones, S and Jones, C. 1990. In hosta heaven. *American Nurseryman* 172(7):44-53.

Lacy, Allen. 1986. Hosta revival. *Horticulture* 64(1):28-34.

Maekawa, F. 1940. The genus Hosta. *Journal of the Faculty of Agriculture of Tokyo University*, Sect. 3 (Botany) 5:317-425. Reprinted in *Am. Hosta Soc. Bull.* 1972 v4:12-64 and 1973 v5:12-59.

Pellett, D.J. 1993. Hosta. *American Nurseryman* 177(6):53-61.

Associations:

American Hosta Society, 3103 Heather Hill, S.E., Huntsville, AL 35802. Publication: *American Hosta Society Bulletin*.

## *Houttuynia* (hoo-tie' nee-a)       Chameleon Plant       Sauraceae

The genus contains several species but only one, *H. cordata*, has gained favor in recent years with the many-colored ground cover form, 'Chameleon'. The green alternate leaves of the 9–15″ tall species are approximately 2–3″ long, heart shaped, and distinctly "fragrant" when crushed. Hardy in zones 3–8, it has amazing adaptability. I have seen many plantings in this country and don't yet understand why people get excited about it. Plants require abundant moisture and are, in fact, classified as water plants. The foliage can be extremely colorful, with bright splotches of purple, pink and red. In the cooler times of the season, the leaves look like an elf has spilled paint all over them. However, there is a catch or two and one should be careful about embracing this plant too quickly. In fact, one should not

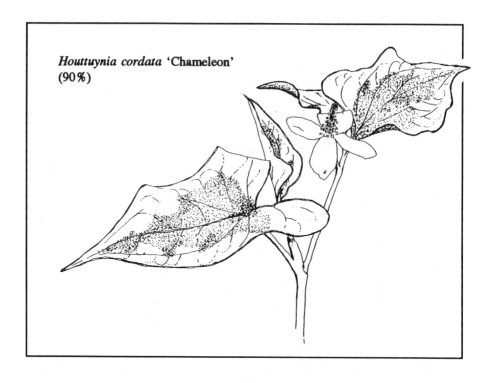

*Houttuynia cordata* 'Chameleon'
(90%)

embrace this plant at all. Although I have seen references to the lemony fragrance of the foliage, I use this plant to introduce my students to how bad plants can really smell. After tearing off a leaf and taking a whiff, at least two thirds of them make a face and say something unprintable about my teaching methods. Another problem is that once introduced to the garden, they want to take over. Plants remind me of mint in the way in which they invade, defying eradication and reveling in their obnoxious behavior. Lastly, the beauty of the variegated foliage often reverts to the plain green of the species. I can occasionally handle smelly, invasive plants if they provide sufficient beauty, but this plant is history when it reneges on its promise of colorful foliage. Gardeners in the South find more reversion than those in the North, likely the result of warmer temperatures. To each his own.

To be fair, I was also most pleasantly surprised when a planting at the University filled in to make an outstanding ground cover. The plants did all they were expected to do, making a dense carpet with excellent flower power. Of course, the planting was surrounded on all four sides with concrete, plants reverted to green and within a year appeared in the cracks of the sidewalk. But for that difficult area, *Houttuynia* was a great choice. This plant best illustrates the Armitage axiom "there is no such thing as a bad plant, only a bad use for a good plant."

Propagate by division to multiply as needed, or root 2–3" long terminal cuttings in spring and summer.

**Cultivars:**

'Chameleon' ('Tricolor', 'Variegata') has leaves splashed with white, pink and red. The ½" long, white flowers are secondary in interest and appear on 1–2" spikes in May and June. This is the only form of the species sold today. Comments as to its performance have been mentioned above.

'Plena' bears purple tinged green leaves and double white flowers.

## *Hyacinthoides* (high-a-sin′ thoid-eez)          Bluebell          Liliaceae

This genus includes 10 bulbous species native to western Europe and includes the English and Spanish bluebells. In John Gerard's famous Herbal, or *Generall Historie of Plantes* (1597), he enlightened his readers with such little-known facts as "the roots being beaten and applied with white wine, hinder or keep back the growth of hairs." At that time, the bulbs were also called sea onions and eaten by sailors (under duress, I'm sure).

Bluebells prefer moist, shady areas and are quite at home near coniferous woodlands where soils are somewhat acid. They should be planted in groups of at least 50 where their strap-like leaves will provide greenery before and after the bell-shaped, blue purple flowers have opened.

Taxonomically, storm clouds had been brewing for a long time. People finally accepted the movement of certain species from *Scilla* and their subsequent placement in *Endymion* and were beginning to understand the botanical differences which exist between the two genera. However, the correct name for *Endymion* on the grounds of priority is now *Hyacinthoides*, a name change which has become "official." These names are certainly confusing but let's bite the bullet and accept this new one.

*Hyacinthoides* was removed from *Scilla* because of botanical differences in bulb habit and flower morphology. The following table illustrates a few of the subtle differences.

|  | *Hyacinthoides* | *Scilla* |
|---|---|---|
| *Bulb morphology* | totally renewed each year, covered with tubular scales | not renewed each year, thin membranous cover |
| *Flower morphology* | bracts and bracteoles | bracts only |
| *Height* | usually more than 12" tall | usually less than 12" tall |

The two common species, *H. hispanica*, Spanish bluebell, and *H. nonscripta*, English bluebell, readily hybridize when planted near each other and many intermediate forms exist.

Propagate by lifting established clumps in the fall and dividing the bulbs for planting. There will be many more bulblets around the mother bulb than can be lifted. Bluebells reseed prolifically and seed can be sown in containers in the fall. Seeds germinate readily but plants require approximately one year before they form bulbs and are ready for planting. Flowering occurs about 18 months later.

*-hispanica* (his-pah' ni-ka)     Spanish Bluebell     12–15"/12"
    Spring          Blue          Europe, North Africa          Zones 4–7
(Syn. *Scilla campanulata, S. hispanica, Endymion hispanicus*)

By far the more robust of the common species, the foliage consists of 5–6 shiny green linear leaves, approximately 1" wide and convex on the back sides. Twelve or more 1" diameter, bell-shaped, nodding flowers are borne on each flower stem. They are held in an upright raceme and the petals are slightly flared at the base of the flower.

Plant the bulbs about 2–4" deep in a well-drained area in the fall. Plants tolerate considerable shade and the colors and fragrance brighten a woodland garden. Unfortunately, the leaves become weather beaten and shabby before they disappear. These plants are tough enough, however, that if the leaves are an eyesore, the foliage can be removed before it turns yellow and the sticky mess cleaned up. Bulbs should be planted in parts of the garden where leaf unsightliness will not be a problem. A number of cultivars and hybrids are readily available.

**Cultivars:**
Var. *alba* has creamy white flowers but can vary from clear white to soft pink.
'Blue Giant' has deep blue flowers on 18" tall stems.
'Blue Queen' bears bell-shaped flowers of porcelain blue.
'Dainty Maid' produces rosy pink flowers.
'Danube' ('Donau') bears dense racemes of dark blue flowers.
'Excelsior' has 1–2" diameter flowers of deep purple-blue.
'Queen of the Pinks' has long elegant spikes of soft clear pink.
Var. *rosea* has rose-pink flowers which can be quite variable in color and habit.
'Rosabella' bears soft pink flowers.
'White City' produces clean white flowers.
'White Triumphator' is a beautiful clear white-flowered selection with dark
    stems. This is one of the best whites.

*-non-scripta* (non-skrip' ta)     English Bluebell     12–15"/12"
    Spring          Blue          Western Europe          Zones 5–8
(Syn. *Scilla non-scripta, S. nutans, S. festalis, Endymion non-scriptus*)

In England in late May or early June, the oak and beech woodlands and fields are alive with nodding bluebells. Although not so prolific in the

United States, large clumps can be established quickly. The several strap-shaped leaves are up to 1¼" long and ½" wide. The 6–12 bell-shaped fragrant flowers appear on an arching terminal raceme. The petals are flared and reflex back more than those of the previous species. Plant the bulbs 4–5" deep and by the hundreds if possible, preferably on a wooded hillside or along the edge of a placid pond.

They are not plants for the herbaceous border, but are magnificent specimens for the woodland garden. Bulbs are inexpensive and will not need division for years.

The stems and bulbs exude a "slimy, glewish juyce" which were used "to set feathers upon arrows instead of glew, or to paste books with" (Gerard). If removing the flowers, it is important to snap or cut the stems near the base. Do not pull them from the bulb or significant damage and loss of plant vigor will occur.

**Cultivars:**
'Alba' is a white-flowered form.
'Rosea' bears pink flowers.

Quick Key to Hyacinthoides Species

A. Flowers 6–12, petals strongly reflexed, pedicels
(stems of individual flowers) not over ½" long  . *H. non-scripta*
AA. Flowers usually 12 or more, petals flared but
not reflexed, flower pedicels to 1½" long . . . . . . *H. hispanica*

## *Hyacinthus* (hy-a sin' thus)         Hyacinth         Liliaceae

If one was to read only major bulb catalogs, one would surely believe the definition of floral perfection was the florist's hyacinth, *H. orientalis*. There is a love-hate relationship between people and hyacinths. As a forced flower, its sweet scent and bright colors elicit responses of beauty, fragrance, and love. On the other hand, some bulb connoisseurs such as Louise Beebe Wilder in her delightful book *Adventures with Hardy Bulbs* look at them as "obese, fat-stalked, overstuffed, overscented Levantines." The sentiments of most people fall somewhere in between. The name *Hyacinthus* was given by Homer, the flowers said to have sprung from the blood of the dead Hyakinthos.

They are plants which prefer cool climates (to zone 3), performing poorly south of zone 6 where they can be used effectively only as annuals. Where they are effective as perennials, they may be left in the ground for many years, but are slow to multiply. Best results occur if replaced every 2 years, regardless of location. Bulbs are expensive and some industrious gardeners lift and dry them every spring and replant in the fall. Although I realize this results in better longevity of the bulbs, I have never felt that

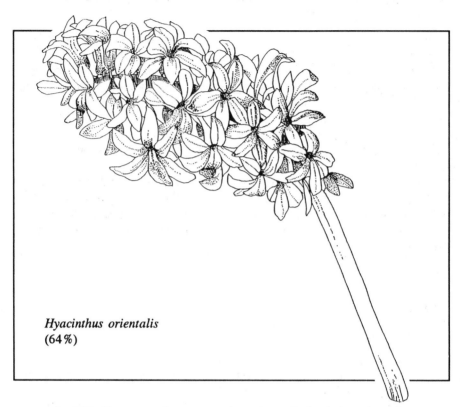

*Hyacinthus orientalis*
(64%)

energetic. If bulbs are to be removed, wait until the leaves have begun to turn yellow. Wash off the soil and store in perforated sacs at about 40° F in a well-ventilated area. Onion bags and unheated garages work well.

It is not necessary to plant great drifts, regardless of the advertisements, as 6–12 plants nestled in a protected area or beside a pond can make a very effective display. Plant sufficient numbers, however, to be able to bring some inside to savor the fragrance. Plant bulbs about 6″ deep in the fall and bulb-to-bulb for best display.

Unfortunately, some people are quite allergic to the papery exterior of the bulbs and severe dermatitis can result. This is not a common occurrence and usually only occurs with people who handle the bulbs every day. However, if skin irritation occurs, gloves should be used whenever bulbs are handled.

For forcing indoors, plant 3 bulbs in a 6″ wide pot and water well. Place the pots in the refrigerator (or anywhere where temperatures can be held between 30° and 40° F) for about 12 weeks. Once they are removed from the cool area, approximately 3 weeks are needed for full flowering if placed in a sunny spot at about 70° F. Therefore, if they are to be forced for a holiday such as Valentine's Day or Mothers Day or a birthday, place in the cool area about 15 weeks ahead of time.

Dozens of cultivars are available and it is a wonderful exercise in indecision to look through the gorgeous photos in the catalogs. There is nothing better than browsing through those catalogs to bring a little spring into long winter months.

**Related Genera:**

All previously recognized species of *Hyacinthus*, except *H. orientalis*, have been shuffled off to other genera. *H. amethystinus*, Spanish hyacinth, has become *Brimeura amethystinus*; *H. azureus*, azure hyacinth, has been relegated to *Muscari azureum*; and *H. candicans*, summer hyacinth, is now *Galtonia candicans*.

*Muscari azureum* (*H. azureus*) is a scaled-down version of the common grape hyacinth, *Muscari armeniacum*, but is easily distinguished by its open flowers compared with the closed mouths of the latter *Muscari*. Plants are 4–6" tall and flowers appear in late winter. Full sun and good drainage are required.

## *Hydrastis* (hid-ras′ tis)      Golden-Seal      Ranunculaceae

Oh, to be able to go to the woods and find some golden-seal! Unfortunately, it is more and more difficult to enjoy this plant because of unscrupulous digging and reduction of habitat from construction. Plants are slow enough to establish without having to go through the trauma of home gardeners digging for their own abode. Root and rhizomes have been used as a diuretic, a treatment for mouth ulcers and other ailments, perhaps explaining the relative rarity of plants today.

Plants grow 10–15" tall, arising from the gnarly yellow rhizome from which it gets its common name. Plants generally produce a single long-petioled, 5–8" wide, palmately-lobed, basal leaf. The lobes of the leaf are sharply pointed and unequally toothed. The stems which arise bear 2 leaves near the top, similar in shape but smaller than the basal leaf. The greenish white, ½" wide flower occurs at the top of the stem and is rather ephemeral. In fact, the 3 sepals fall off as the flowers open and there are no petals anyway. The ornamental value of the flowers is based on the many stamens which extend from their centers. The fruits ripen into scarlet berries about ⅔" long.

Plants are native in moist or low woodlands from Connecticut to Minnesota, Ontario, west to Kansas and Missouri and south to Georgia. Some nurseries are selling plants propagated from seed or are establishing their own stock plants.

## *Hydrophyllum* (hi-dro-fil′ um)      Waterleaf      Hydrophllaceae

About 4 species of this native genus are occasionally available to the American gardener. The name "waterleaf" does not mean that plants are happy in wet areas or swamps, but that watery or juicy leaves are found in some species. My favorite species is *H. canadense*, native from Quebec to northern Georgia and west to Missouri. The foliage is palmately lobed, often with creamy "watermarks" on the tops (another explanation for the common name). The plants bear white to lavender flowers on short stalks, seldom rising above the foliage. The flowers, whose stamens project from the petals, are 5-lobed and held in 3- to 5-flowered clusters (cymes) which start coiled up and straighten out once the flowers open. It is essentially hairless and that characteristic along with the fact that the flowers are borne within the canopy make this species different from the hairy biennial *H. appendiculatum*. Plants tolerate moderate shade and prefer moist, rich soils. I made the mistake of placing mine in deep fern-shade and they performed poorly.

Two other eastern species with pinnately divided leaves and more visible flowers are also handsome. Hardy from zone 4 to 7. In *H. virginianum*, John's cabbage, leaves consist of 3–7 segments and grows to 2½' tall. The white to lilac flowers are held above the foliage. Plants are cold hardy to at least zone 3 and south to zone 6. *H. macrophyllum* has 7–9 leaf segments, each being coarsely toothed. The white flowers are held well above the foliage and the entire plant is "watermarked" and hairy. Plants likely have the same hardiness limits as *H. canadense*.

A western native, *H. capitatum*, cat's breeches, is sometimes seen in catalogs but is relatively rare. The 4–5" long leaves are pinnately divided with each segment lobed at the ends. The white or lavender blue flowers are usually held in headlike ("capitate") inflorescences on short flower stalks. Plants are about 9–15" tall.

## *Hypericum* (hy-per' i-cum)        St. John's-Wort        Hypericaceae

With the hue and cry for low maintenance and the rush to ground covers, *Hypericum* is being used more and more in this country. The genus contains over 400 species of shrubs, sub-shrubs (partly woody) and herbaceous perennials, many of them ornamental. With so many species, the diversity of habit and flowering is difficult to generalize. However, in general, flowers are bright yellow, vary from ⅓" to 3" in diameter and may be solitary or clustered. They have 5 petals, 5 sepals, and many stamens that form a bushy center. Some species, such as *H.* × *inodorum* and *H. androsaemum*, produce ornamental fruit (capsules) used in bouquets and arrangements. Leaves of St. John's-wort are opposite or whorled and most species do best in partially shaded locations and moisture retentive soil.

The most common species are less than 2' tall and are suited for low borders or as ground covers, such as *H. calycinum* which spreads rapidly by underground stems. However, a number are shrubby and relatively large. They include the shrub-like *H. hookerianum*, which may bear 2" wide, somewhat pendent flowers which light up the 4–5' plant, *H. frondosum* 'Sunburst' with its large yellow flowers on a shrubby body, and *H. densiflorum*, whose flowers may be small but which makes a terrific shrubby plant tolerant of extreme heat and humidity.

The hardiness of St. John's-wort depends on the origin of the species or hybrid. With such a large genus, adaptability is extremely variable. In general, the species discussed here are cold tolerant to about zone 4 or 5, and heat tolerant only to the northern limits of zone 7. Most will survive in hot, humid climates but disease and die back limit their effectiveness. Those native to Europe, such as *H. calycinum,* have the most difficult time looking their best while Chinese and Japanese species have a wider climatic range. Species native to the eastern United States such as *H. densiflorum* (New Jersey to Georgia) do well throughout their range. While most are hardy perennials, a few such as the bog hypericum, *H. anagalloides*, is an annual except in the coastal areas of the United States.

The healing powers of St. John's-wort were (and are) renowned. Plants of St. John's-wort (probably *H. perforatum*) were used in combination with "white wine two pintes, oile olive foure pounds, oile of turpentine two pounds . . ., set in the Sun eight or ten daies . . ." to heal wounds, particularly those "made with a venomed weapon" (Gerard). Both the genus and common names likely arose from the belief in the magical healing powers of the plants. *Hypericum* comes from the greek words, *hyper* (over) and *eikon* (picture), because it was hung above pictures to ward off evil spirits. The common name was based on the belief that the potency of its healing powers was increased by smoking it in fires kindled on the eve of St. John's Day, June 24, in rites that go back to antiquity.

Quick Guide to Hypericum Species

|  | Height (in.) | Flower dia. (in.) | Use | Flowering wood |
|---|---|---|---|---|
| *H. androsaemum* | 24–36 | ¾–1 | Tall sub-shrub | New |
| *H. buckleyi* | 9–12 | ¾–1 | Small sub-shrub | Old |
| *H. calycinum* | 15–18 | 2½–3 | Ground cover | Old |
| *H. olympicum* | 9–12 | 1½–2 | Ground cover | New |
| *H. patulum* | 18–36 | 1½–2 | Medium sub-shrub | New |

| *-androsaemum* (an-dros-aye' mum) | Tutsan | 2–3'/2' |
|---|---|---|
| Summer | Yellow | Europe, North Africa | Zones 5–7 |

Plants are grown more for their habit and fruit than for the flowers. Although the bright yellow flowers are only about 1″ wide and cannot compete with those of many other species, they are not to be ignored. The entire, sessile leaves are

3-4″ long and do not have the black glands seen in many species. Tutsan, which probably comes from the french *toute saine* (heal all), in reference to its healing powers, produces colorful fruits which change from yellowish to deep red and finally to dark brown. Plants are grown commercially for the fruits which find their way to upscale bouquets and arrangements.

The species is hardy only as far north as zone 5 (try mulching heavily in zone 4), its southern limit is probably zone 7a. Plants are not as tolerant of heat as *H. calycinum* and parts of the plants tend to melt out every year in the Armitage garden (zone 7b), regardless of planting site.

Propagate by seed or terminal cuttings.

### Cultivars:

'Albury Purple' is certainly the most handsome cultivar available. Plants differ from the species by having foliage with a burgundy hue which contrasts well with the yellow flowers. Cut back the old wood hard as the best leaf color is on the new growth.

'Excellent Flair', is propagated from seed and is more compact than the species. Plants performed well in the Horticulture Gardens at Georgia for a year, then pooped out and died.

| *-buckleyi* (buk-lee′ eye) | Blue Ridge St. John's-Wort | 9–12″/24″ |
|---|---|---|
| Summer    Yellow | North Carolina to Georgia | Zones 5–8 |

This little-known species should be used more often, particularly in southern gardens. The plant forms rounded low-growing mats which make an effective ground cover. The stems do not root readily and therefore plants do not spread rapidly. Some fall color is also provided as the ¾″ long, blunt, gray-green leaves turn a lovely red in September and October. The 1–1½″ diameter flowers have 3 styles, distinct exserted stamens and occur in groups of three at the end of the stems.

Although not as flamboyant as *H. calycinum*, it is more adaptable to conditions in the eastern and southeastern states and may be counted on to grow and flower in those areas. This species is native to the Appalachian Mountains and is not commonly cultivated.

Propagate by seed or from soft basal cuttings in the summer.

| *-calycinum* (kal-i-sigh′ num) | Aaron's Beard | 15–18″/24″ |
|---|---|---|
| Summer    Yellow | Southeast Europe, Turkey | Zones 5–7 |

This is the main species offered in American horticulture, and its presence has diminished the importance and availability of others. The many protruding stamens suggest the name Aaron's beard and when in flower, this is one of the finest ground covers available. I have seen it cover areas under trees, crawl over hillocks and berms, and change barren hillsides into seas of green and yellow. One of the finest plantings may be seen at Butchard Gardens on Vancouver Island, Canada. The leaves are 3–4″ long, blue green and conspicuously fine netted beneath.

The 2–3″ wide flowers are usually solitary, consisting of hundreds of stamens with reddish anthers, and five styles. The many stamens are in 5 bundles giving the flower a rose-like appearance. The 4-angled stems grow upright as well as along the ground.

Plants perform better in the northern end of their hardiness zone than in the southern end. In the South, they grow well and are evergreen under normal winters but flower sporadically. In the heat of summer, leaves can dry out, turn black and fall off. In cold winters, the leaves may fall off or turn brown from desiccating winds, particularly when followed by bright sun. It is a vigorous grower and can be invasive if placed in a small garden area. Plants should be sheared back every few years to keep them in bounds.

Propagate by cuttings, division or seed. Cuttings should be taken from vegetative shoots in late spring or early summer. A rooting hormone is useful but not essential. Seeds germinate readily but not uniformly.

### Related Species:

*H. cerastoides* is also a short ground cover, growing 9–12″ tall. The star-shaped light yellow to deep yellow flowers are larger than the leaves and when they appear in late spring to summer, they cover the plant. Native to eastern Europe, likely hardy from zones 4–7.

*H.* × 'Hidcote' originated in Hidcote Gardens in England. It's parentage is in question but likely arose from *H. cyathiflorum* 'Gold Cup' × *H. calycinum.* Plants grow 18″–3′ tall with 2–3″ diameter sterile yellow flowers. The numerous stamens, which occur in 5 bundles, are shorter than the petals. The sterility of the flowers results in persistent flowering of the hybrid, a trait which has made it one of the most popular hypericums in Europe. It is not as adaptable to vagaries of climate found in North America, however. In the colder climes of its range, it will die down in winter to reemerge next spring. In warmer areas, leaves remain evergreen and plants reach heights of 3′. It is particularly susceptible to root rot and wilt and severe losses occur in warm, humid climates.

*H. wilsonii* is very similar to *H. calycinum* but smaller. The bright golden yellow flowers are about 2″ wide and borne on terminal stems.

| *-olympicum* (o-lim′ pi-kum) | Olympic St. John's-Wort | 9–12″/12″ |
| Late Spring    Yellow | Southeast Europe, Asia Minor | Zones 6–8 |

With delicate ½–1″ long sessile, pointed, grayish green leaves attached to trailing stems, plants are useful at the front of the garden, tucked in and around rocks and as a ground cover. The 1½–2″ wide flowers are large relative to the size of the plants and occur in 2–5-flowered cymes at the end of the stems. The many stamens are arranged in three bundles and the sepals are rigidly pointed, almost sharp. Flowers are produced mid-May to early June in zone 7. The species tolerates partial shade but also grows well in full sun.

Propagate by fresh seed or by soft basal cuttings in early summer or terminal cuttings in fall.

### Cultivars:

Var. *citrinum* bears handsome pale yellow flowers, but is otherwise similar to the species.

### Related Species:

*H. polyphyllum* differs by having grayer leaves, less pointed sepals often speckled with a few black dots, and the absence of a woody base. The golden yellow flowers are 1½–2″ across and occur in 4–10 flowered clusters at the end of the stems. It is likely that plants sold under this name are *H. olympicum*. 'Lemon Butterfly' ('Zitronenfalter') is 6–8″ tall with large bright yellow flowers. 'Sulfur Pearl' ('Schweflperle') is only 4″ tall and produces large bright yellow flowers. 'Sulphureum' has sulphur yellow flowers, as does 'Citrinum', which is probably the same thing.

*H. reptans* is only 6–9″ tall with narrow leaves which form dense tufts. Plants are heat tolerant to zone 8 and bear 1″ wide yellow flowers.

| *-patulum* (pat-ew′ lum) | Golden Cup St. John's-Wort | 18–36″/24″ |
|---|---|---|
| Summer    Yellow | China, Japan | Zones 5–7 |

This evergreen shrub bears shoots which are somewhat purplish, spreading, and drooping. The 1½–2½″ long leaves are gray-green beneath. The flowers are held in clusters of 2–4 and bloom profusely in June and July and sporadically until frost. The rounded petals overlap on the ½–2″ diameter flowers.

Only the species can be propagated from fresh seed but all cultivars may be propagated by taking 4–5″ long cuttings of non-flowering shoots, preferably with a piece from the parent plant in the summer. Insert the cuttings in a well-drained medium, keep moist and warm and rooting should take place in 3–4 weeks.

### Cultivars:

All varieties and cultivars of *H. patulum* flower on new wood; therefore, plants which don't die to the ground in winter should have the previous years' stems cut to a few buds of old wood in the spring.

'Sungold' is a pretty, arching 18–24″ tall sub-shrub with slightly larger flowers and greater cold hardiness than 'Hidcote'.

'Henryi' has flowers up to 3″ across and 2–3″ long leaves. It is vigorous and well worth searching out. Recently, this was placed in its own species, *H. henryi*, by some authorities.

**Related Species:**

*H. × moserianum* (*H. calycinum* × *H. patulum*) is 2–3′ tall with the 3″ wide flowers of *H. calycinum* and the overlapping petals of *H. patulum*. Flowers appear over several months and plants have reportedly performed well in zone 6. 'Tricolor', the most common cultivar, bears green, cream and pink leaves and red stems. Interesting but hardly ornamental. Even to my poorly-honed senses, it appears gaudy.

Quick Key to Hypericum Species

    A. Plants greater than 2′ tall, shrubby
      B. Styles 5, fruit inconspicuous . . . . . . . . . . . . . *H. patulum*
    BB. Styles 3, fruit a black berry . . . . . . . . . . . *H. androsaemum*
    AA. Plants less than 2′ tall, sub-shrubs
       or herbaceous perennials
      B. Styles 5, flowers 2–3″ across, stoloniferous . . . . . *H. calycinum*
    BB. Styles 3, flowers 1–2″ across,
       plants not stoloniferous
        C. No part of plant woody, sepals
          often with black dots . . . . . . . . . . . . . . *H. polyphyllum*
       CC. Base of plant woody, sepals without dots
         D. Leaves pointed at end, conspicuously
          gray-green, stamens in 3 bundles . . . . . . *H. olympicum*
        DD. Leaves blunt at end, mostly green,
          stamens not arranged in bundles . . . . . . . . *H. buckleyi*

*Hypoxis* (hi-poks′ is)        Star-Grass        Hypoxidaceae

Gardeners who grow this little bulbous plant in their garden are surprised to learn that the genus consists of approximately 150 species. Most of the grassy species with small yellow star-shape flowers are unknown and rather inconspicuous. However, *H. hirsuta*, yellow star-grass, native from Maine to Florida and west to Texas, is offered by many bulb specialists. Plants bear hairy, grass-like, 12″ long, 2–4″ wide leaves. The small 1″ yellow flowers are held in a 3–7 flowered inflorescence in late spring and summer. They will self-seed where they are comfortable, and unless planted in groups of a dozen or so, will likely go unnoticed in the garden. Plant about 2–4″ deep and 6–8″ apart in well-drained or raised beds. They are small, won't light up the front of the garden or rock garden, but interesting and well worth trying. Likely hardy in zones 4 to 8.

# I

*Iberis* (eye-beer' is)   Candytuft   Brassicaceae

Many gardens sport this popular genus in the form of *I. sempervirens*, the perennial matted candytuft. Approximately 40 annual or perennial species are known, many of which were discovered in Spain (originally known as Iberia). Although they have been superseded by more colorful bedding plants, a number of annual species exist such as the delightful *I. amara*, rocket or hyacinth-flowered candytuft. Only one perennial species, *I. sempervirens*, is grown to any extent although others are occasionally offered. The perennial species are actually sub-shrubs whose stems are woody at the base. The leaves are alternate and usually entire, while the 4-petaled flowers are often white or pink. Plants are tufted and well adapted to the front of the garden or cascading over rock walls. Full sun and well-drained soils are a necessity. All perennial forms should be cut back heavily after flowering at least once every 2 years to reduce fruit set and maintain quality foliage.

Quick Key to Iberis Species

|                   | Height (in.) | Flower color              |
|-------------------|--------------|---------------------------|
| *I. gibraltarica* | 9–12         | Outer pink, inner white   |
| *I. saxatilis*    | 3–6          | White, tinged purple      |
| *I. sempervirens* | 9–12         | White                     |

-*gibraltarica* (ji-brawl-tah' ri-ca)   Gibraltar Candytuft   9–12″/12″
    Spring   Pink and White   Gibraltar   Zones 7–9

Because of limited hardiness in most of the country, this is seldom seen in American gardens. The 1″ long evergreen leaves are toothed, particularly near the ends, and produced in basal rosettes. The flowers are arranged in 1½–2" long, flattened, umbel-like inflorescences. The outside flowers are pink to red, while those inside the inflorescence are white or slightly tinged pink. They are worth trying as a self-sowing annual north of zone 7. Seeds germinate readily and softwood cuttings of non-flowering shoots root within 14–21 days.

| *-saxatilis* (saks-ah' ti-lis) | | Rock Candytuft | 3–6"/6" |
|---|---|---|---|
| Spring | White | Southern Europe | Zones 2–7 |

The word *saxatilis* means "growing on rocks" and this compact plant is perfect in and around rocks. The evergreen, entire leaves are only about ⅛" wide and ¾" long. Flowering and non-flowering stems occur. At the tips of the former appear umbel-like inflorescences of ½" long white flowers often tinged with purple, especially as they fade. Plants are very cold hardy, unusual for a species native to Southern Europe.

Propagate similar to *I. gibraltarica*.

### Related Species:
*I. sayana* is a tough miniature candytuft for alpine gardens or trough gardens, requiring excellent drainage for best success. Plants grow 1–2" tall and spread to about 9" in width. The white flowers cover the plant in early spring. Hardy to zone 3, south to zone 6.

| *-sempervirens* (sem-per-vi' renz) | | Evergreen Candytuft | 9–12"/18" |
|---|---|---|---|
| Spring | White | Southern Europe | Zones 3–8 |

This is certainly the most popular of the candytufts. It has been used for centuries as an edging plant to bridge lawns with taller plantings in the garden. The evergreen foliage consists of numerous ¾" wide and 1–1½" long, entire leaves. Plants are woody at the base and can be cut back severely at least every other year to insure they do not get leggy. The flowers are invariably white, although there may be some variation in seed propagated material in clearness of color. Cool nights and days also result in more pinking of the flowers. The 1½–2" wide inflorescence is borne in the lateral axils rather than terminal as in *I. saxatilis*. Flowers open in early March in zone 7 gardens, April further north, and persist for 10 weeks.

All cultivars may be propagated by cuttings while the species is readily raised from seed.

### Cultivars:
The numerous selections offer improvements in flower color and habit, but there is little real difference between many of them. For best uniformity in the garden, select those which have been propagated vegetatively.

'Alexander's White' is 10–12" tall and very floriferous. An excellent cultivar for much of the country.

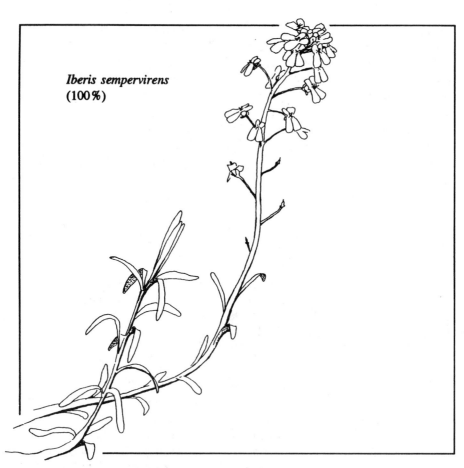

*Iberis sempervirens*
(100%)

'Autumn Beauty' is about 10″ tall with white flowers in the spring and re-blooming in the fall. The fall rebloomers are becoming more sought after; however, the jury is still out on their performance. Flowering in the fall is never as profuse as in the spring, although that is not uncommon for rebloomers of any genus. The problem occurs with summer maintenance. If summers are particularly hot and dry, plants are too exhausted to put on much of a fall effect. They do not tolerate being ignored as well as the non-rebloomers.

'Autumn Snow' is 8–10″ tall and has clear white flowers larger than those of the type. It blooms profusely in the spring and again in the fall. Probably the best of the fall rebloomers.

'Little Gem' is only 5–8″ tall and has small, clear white flowers. One of the best dwarf forms.

'October Glory' is about 8″ tall and reblooms well in the fall. See comments about 'Autumn Beauty'.

'Purity' is another white-flowered form and has lustrous, deep green leaves and an abundance of flowers. It is slightly taller than 'Little Gem' and smaller than 'Snowflake'.

'Pygmaea' is a prostrate form which hugs the ground and sends up small white blossoms in early spring. The most compact cultivar available.

'Snowflake' is 8–10" tall and bears 2–3" wide inflorescences of pure white flowers which shine on sunny spring days.

'Snowmantle' is more compact than 'Snowflake'.

## Quick Key to Iberis Species

A. Plants less than 6" tall, prostrate habit . . . . . . . . . . *I. saxatilis*
AA. Plants more than 6" tall, flower stems ascending
  B. Flowers conspicuously pink to red, at least
  outer flowers of inflorescence, leaves
  toothed near apex . . . . . . . . . . . . . . . . . *I. gibraltarica*
  BB. Flowers white, leaves entire . . . . . . . . . . . *I. sempervirens*

## *Imperata* (im-per-ah′ ta)    Blood Grass    Poaceae

The only ornamental useful form of this genus is *I. cylindica* 'Red Baron', a slow growing wine-red tipped grass. However, the non-red colored species itself is an aggressive weed. 'Red Baron' occasionally transforms to its green-leaved parent and those shoots should be eliminated aggressively.

I have seen some handsome plantings of Japanese blood grass, particularly in the northeast and midwest, where the red leaves become even redder as the season progresses, providing some excellent red fall color. They are very slow growing but add a nice touch of red to the perennial garden. The clumps are usually about 12" tall, 18" when grown well. While I have seen some handsome clumps, I have seen far more spotty and sparse plantings which do nothing for the garden and look weedy. Plants are better adapted to tubs and containers with other companion plants. They are listed hardy from zones 6 to 9, but the further south this grass is planted, the less the red color is seen. Oversold and overhyped for most gardens.

## *Incarvillea* (in-car-vill′ ea)    Hardy Gloxinia    Bignoniaceae

Long before President Nixon and the ping-pong team "opened" China to the West, hardy folk like the French Jesuits were active throughout the country in the 16th to 19th centuries. In fact, not only did they dispense spiritual learning but some also became fine plantsmen. Jean D'Incarville was a French Jesuit who became a botanical correspondent to the botanist Bernard de Jussieu. In his lifetime (1506–1557), he became an avid collector and botanist and this genus honors his name. The genus is not commonly grown in the United

States, perhaps because of the variability of performance in different areas of the country. Plants grow from a long taproot, and are usually available through bulb supply catalogs. It is not hardy in many areas of the country but when grown in the right location, the plants are magnificent. The flowers resemble gloxinia and the leaves are similar to Jacob's Ladder (*Polemonium*). Of the 6 species, only *I. delavayi* is readily available in the United States.

| -*delavayi* (del-a-vay' eye) | Delavay Incarvillea | 18-24"/18" |
|---|---|---|
| Spring | Rose-Purple | China | Zones 5-7 |

The specific epithet (*delavayi*) is also found with *Osmanthus delavayi*, and was found by Jean David Delavay, a French missionary and explorer in Yunnan, China. Between 1881 and 1888, he sent back more than 200,000 specimens, 4000 different species of which 1500 were new to botany.

The 12" long basal leaves consist of 6-11 pairs of pinnately compound leaflets (each 4-5" long) which form a handsome mound of foliage. Five to twelve flowers are carried on a raceme 1-2' above the foliage. The trumpet-shaped rose-purple flowers are 2-3" long and wide and have yellow throats. Remove blossoms after flowering to extend bloom time.

Although often listed as being hardy in zones 4-7, I have had little success in over-summering plants in zone 7. They are inhabitants of rocky, mountainous areas and do well where soils are well drained and nights are cool. Certainly, gardeners on the West Coast (zones 7-8) do much better than east and southern zones 7-8. Well-drained, sandy soils and partial shade are recommended. In zones 5 and 6, mulching the plants in the fall is good practice.

Plants have a long taproot, which make them difficult to divide. Division should be accomplished in spring immediately after flowering. Seed propagation is the easiest means to increase the various species. Fresh seed sown and placed under heat and high humidity result in seedlings in 10-20 days.

### Related Species:

*I. compacta* is 8-12" tall and more compact than the previous species. Most of the height of the species is due to the flower stem which carry 3-7 red-purple flowers. There is little or no plant stem.

*I. olgae* grows up to 3' tall with only 3-4 pairs of leaflets. The rosy-red flowers are borne in a branched inflorescence (racemose panicle).

*I. mairei* (syn. *I. grandiflora* var. *brevipes*) has 2-3 flowers, but each may be up to 3" across, often yellow inside.

## *Indigofera* (in-di-gof' er-a)          Indigo          Fabaceae

You would think with over 700 species of *Indigofera*, that a few of them would be commonly grown in the United States. However, try to find some plants from mail order or garden centers and frustration will quickly develop.

They are almost unknown in North American nurseries, so obtaining any of these plants will require some sleuthing. Of course, since I happen to live in the Valley of Nurseries in North Georgia, I am able to find an *Indigofera* just down the road. However since nurseries have not embraced them, this tells us that these plants are either difficult to establish and not sufficiently garden-flashy to propagate, or grow in big numbers. They are common in Europe and without doubt will become better known over here, given a little more time. They are essentially sub-shrubs which may die back or be cut back to the ground each year. Sometimes nurseries offer plants in the shrub sections, rather than the perennial area.

The indigo dye extracted from the leaves and young stems of some species, mainly *I. tinctoria*, has been traced on Egyptian mummy cloth from 2300 BC. Although plants are native to southeast Asia, indigo plantations were established by the English in India, Sumatra, and most notably, the West Indies during the colonial period and through the 19th century. The plants were also introduced to South Carolina in 1742 and grown extensively until the Civil War, and the importance of cotton resulted in its decline. Plants escaped from cultivation and may still be found in coastal areas of South Carolina and Georgia, south to Florida and west to Louisiana. When plants of *Indigofera* were in short supply, other "false indigos" were used (see section on *Baptisia*). The introduction of a synthetic dye by Baeyer in 1878 resulted in the decline of the plantations.

From the garden standpoint, plants are shrubby and bear pea-like flowers and pinnately compound leaves. Most commonly cultivated is *I. heterantha* (syn. *I. gerardiana*) which generally grows about 4' tall and has small (¼" long) pale pink to rosy-purple flowers held in 4–6" long terminal racemes. The 3–4" long leaves consist of 13–21 odd-pinnate leaflets.

*I. kirilowii* may be the most ornamental species available. Plants grow 2–4' tall and bear densely packed axillary racemes of rose-pink flowers. The inflorescences may be up to 5" long. The leaves, which are usually shorter than the inflorescences, consist of 7–11 leaflets. Another species sometimes found is *I. potaninii*, which is a little shorter than *I. heterantha* but is distinguished by having lilac-pink flowers in axillary racemes and leaves of only 5–11 leaflets.

The plant which has found a home in North Georgia is *I. decora*. I must say that the more I see of this plant, the more I enjoy it. *I. decora* is only about 12–18" tall with 9–11 leaflets. The base is woody and plants die to the ground in the winter. In the spring (mid to late May), the axillary pale pink racemes, which are almost as long as the 4–5" leaves, nod alongside the plant. Be warned, however, that it can be terribly invasive, colonizing by stolons and almost impossible to pull out.

Cut all plants back hard in late winter or early spring. *I. kirilowii* appears to be hardy to zone 6, the others to zone 7.

## *Inula* (in' yew-la)　　　　　　Inula　　　　　　Asteraceae

Although consisting of about 60 species, only one or two have outstanding ornamental properties not found in other yellow daisy flowers abundant in the summer garden. Most species are hairy and coarse, and bear alternate leaves. Plants range from 18″ tall to over 7′ and the flowers are equally varied in size. All flowers are orange-yellow and may be borne solitary or in few-flowered inflorescences. The foliage of some species, such as *I. candida*, is very hairy and silver-green. The leaves are particularly handsome but good drainage is essential. In general, *Inula* is easily grown when placed in full sun and moist, well-drained soil, although most tolerate somewhat boggy conditions. The tall species may be impressive in spring and summer, but after they flower, they generally decline rapidly.

*I. ensifolia* and *I. royleana* are the primary species for the formal garden, while *I. helenium* and *I. magnifica* are bigger, coarser and more suitable for larger, less formal areas. It is frustrating looking at some of the members of Asteraceae and scratching your head trying to figure out the genus, let alone the species. The genus is similar to *Arnica*, *Doronicum* and *Senecio* except for minor differences in flower and foliage. In the following table, some of the minor differences are noted. This stuff looks complicated and boring (and it is) but for those who must know more, here is more. The involucre bracts are the papery structures at the base of the flower head, and there may be one to many rows (series) of them. The term "clasping" means that the petiole clasps the stem like baby's fingers around a baseball bat. Other differences also occur in fruit but that is best left to reference books of a drier plane.

|  | Leaf arrangement | Involucre bracts | Stem leaves |
|---|---|---|---|
| *Arnica* | Opposite | Equal, not overlapping, 2–3 series | Not clasping |
| *Inula* | Alternate | Unequal, overlapping in many series | Not clasping |
| *Doronicum* | Alternate | Equal, not overlapping, 1–3 series | Clasping |
| *Senecio* | Alternate | Equal, in one series | Not clasping |

All species of *Inula* may be propagated by seed or division.

Quick Key to Inula Species

|  | Height (in.) | Flowers solitary | Leaves very hairy |
|---|---|---|---|
| *I. ensifolia* | 12–24 | Yes | No |
| *I. helenium* | 48–72 | No | Yes |
| *I. royleana* | 18–24 | Yes | Yes |

*-ensifolia* (en-si-fo' lee-a)       Swordleaf Inula       1–2'/2'
   Late Spring       Yellow       Europe, Asia       Zones 3–7

This is one of the best of the small inulas as it is self branching, compact, and produces many long-petalled, bright yellow to orange daisy-like flowers. The 1–2″ wide flowers are borne singly at the end of the stems and persist for about 6 weeks. The sessile leaves are less than 1″ wide and 3–4″ long. They are further distinguished from other low growing inulas by having 3–7 parallel veins. The species name means "sword-like" and refers to the shape of the leaves.

Plants are heat tolerant to zone 7 and are a good alternative to *Doronicum caucasicum*, another small yellow daisy. But unlike *Doronicum* they do not go dormant in the summer. Plants are short lived in the Southeast, persisting for 2–3 years.

Propagate by seed or division in the fall.

*Inula ensifolia*
(64%)

### Cultivars:

'Compacta' is more compact and grows 8–12″ tall.
'Gold Star' forms 10–15″ tall bushes covered with yellow daisies.

### Related Species:

*I. candida* is a handsome 9–12″ plant with white hairy foliage and solitary yellow flowers. They are native to Greece and require excellent drainage as found in rock gardens, containers or raised beds. Full sun is needed. Perhaps hardy in zones 5–7.

*I. salicina* is similar to *I. ensifolia* in that it grows about 2′ tall and bears many flowers with yellow rays and orange centers. A little more weather tolerant than *I. ensifolia*. Hardy in zones 4–7.

| | | | |
|---|---|---|---|
| *-helenium* (he-len′ ee-um) | Elecampane | | 4–6′/4′ |
| Summer | Yellow | Europe, Northern Asia | Zones 3–8 |

Although native elsewhere, plants have been naturalized in eastern North America. Dried roots yield a white, starchy powder called inuline which has long been valued for medicinal uses. In fact, elecampane is a living drugstore, also yielding a volatile oil, a resin, and a bitter extract, all of which were employed by apothecaries of old. If you grow this plant and don't like it, grind it up and try it on your sick cat. It enjoys full sun but will tolerate limited shade. The basal leaves can be as long as 3′ (1–2′ is a bit more common) and are held on petioles up to 1′ long. They become much reduced in size and sessile as they ascend the brownish furrowed stem. They are velvety beneath but rough-hairy above. The 2–3″ wide flowers usually occur in groups of 2 or 3, but are occasionally solitary.

Plant in well-drained moist soil in full sun. They are coarsely magnificent in flower but fade quickly after flowering, particularly if abundant water cannot be supplied. Plants require a lot of room to grow well and should be spaced at least 3′ from other specimens.

Propagate by seed or divide in the fall or early spring.

### Related Species:

*I. magnifica* is also a big course plant, growing at least 6′ tall. It differs from *I. helenium* in that the flowers are nearly 6″ across and arranged in a many-flowered inflorescence (corymb). The center of each flower (disk flowers) is deep yellow with orange tips, while the narrow well-spaced ray flowers are golden yellow and 2–3″ long. The stem often has purple striations. Better garden plants than *I. helenium*; hardy in zones 3–7.

*-royleana* (royl-ee-ah′ na)  Himalayan Elecampane  1½–2′/3′
Late Summer  Orange  Himalayas  Zones 3–7

The flowers are handsome but the unbranched habit does not make it an especially good garden plant. The 6–10″ long leaves are oval, slightly toothed, and densely fuzzy underneath (tomentose). The upper leaves are clasping; the lower are 3–4″ wide on long winged petioles. The solitary orange-yellow flowers are 3–4″ across and emerge from black buds in late summer and fall. With narrow ray flowers, the daisies look like big orange spiders.

This is a better plant for northern climates than southern. It tolerates moist conditions and needs cool nights for best performance.

Propagate from divisions in early spring or from seed.

### Related Species:

*I. orientalis* grows 2–2½′ tall and bears 4–6″ long entire leaves with marginal glands. The orange-yellow solitary flowers are up to 3″ wide. 'Grandiflora' was selected for even larger flowers. Native to the Caucasus, plants are cold tolerant to zone 3. A good garden plant where space is limited.

Quick Key to Inula Species

    A. Plants over 6′ tall in flower, flowers
       usually in 3's, disk flower yellow . . . . . . . . . . . . *I. helenium*
    AA. Plants less than 3′ tall
       B. Stems unbranched, leaves tomentose,
          oval with netted veins, buds black . . . . . . . . . . *I. royleana*
       BB. Stems branched, leaves not tomentose or hairy,
          linear with parallel veins, buds not black . . . . . . . *I. ensifolia*

## *Ipheion* (if′ ee-on)  Starflower  Alliaceae

The genus contains about 10 species but only *I. uniflorum*, spring starflower, is cultivated to any extent. It is a species that no genus seems to want. At one time or another, *I. uniflorum* has been classified under *Brodiaea* (where it is still often called *B. uniflora*), *Milla*, *Triteleia*, or *Tristagma*. Pertinent differences between common species of three closely related genera are given below.

|  | *Brodiaea* | *Ipheion* | *Triteleia* |
|---|---|---|---|
| Origin | North America | South America | North America |
| Root | Corm | Bulb | Corm |
| Leaves | Rounded | Flat | Keeled beneath |
| Fertile Stamens | 3 | 6 | 6 |
| Inflorescence | Umbel | 1–2 flowered | Umbel |

581

**-uniflorum** (ew-ni-flo' rum)  Spring Starflower  4–6"/8"
Early Spring  White, Pale Blue  Argentina, Uruguay  Zones 5–9

One of my favorite spring bulbs, I pack them in like peas whenever space becomes available in the Armitage garden. They are lovely along paths, at the front of borders, or in rockeries where they should be planted in generous drifts. The pale green, nearly flat leaves are ¼–⅜" wide, 6–9" long, and smell like garlic when crushed, although not as pungent. This garlic-like smell seems to turn some people off, so if it bothers you, don't crush them. The leaves come up in the fall and can in themselves add some winter interest to the garden if not covered with 4' of snow. The flowering stem rises about 6" above the foliage and usually bears one but sometimes two pleasantly fragrant blossoms. The 1" wide star-shaped flowers are about 1" long and have a lovely whitish, porcelain blue hue. Plants enjoy well-drained soils in full sun where colonies increase rapidly. In some gardens, particularly in the South, plants can become invasive. Plants have escaped from gardens throughout the country. I see them in old homesteads throughout Aiken, SC, to the fine gardens of Willamsburg, VA, where this pedestrian plant grows like the ubiquitous dandelion. However, unlike the dandelion, plants go dormant and disappear from mind and eye in late spring.

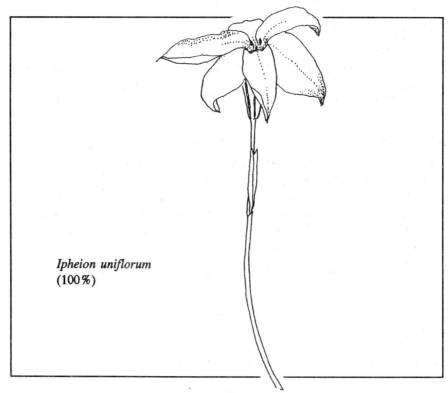

*Ipheion uniflorum*
(100%)

They also can be forced in containers. Plant about 7-10 bulbs in a 4 or 6″ pot, place the pot in the refrigerator or a cooler where temperatures are around 40° F, leave for 8-10 weeks, then bring out to flower. They cannot compete with tulips but their delicacy and scent are worth the effort. Don't crush the leaves!

Offsets are readily produced and if new colonies are wanted, simply lift existing plantings after flowering, separate bulbs and offsets, and replant immediately where desired. Plants should be divided every 2-4 years to maintain vigor.

**Cultivars:**

'Album' is a terrific large white-flowered form. The main vein of the clean white flowers is purple, making a handsome contrast.

'Alberto Castello' is similar to 'Album' but has larger flowers.

'Froyle Mill' has dark violet flowers.

'Rolf Fiedler' is outstanding. He has shorter, wider leaves than the species and handsome clear blue flowers on short flower stems.

'Wisley Blue' is most popular and has larger (up to 2″ wide) flowers of lavender blue.

## *Iris* (eye' ris)                Iris                Iridaceae

The age-old misconception that iris is a summer flowering plant should at once be dispelled. Few other genera provide flowers as long and as often as the iris. With reasonable selection and care, it is possible to have one kind of iris or another in flower for 7 or 8 months of the year. The genus took its name from the Greek goddess Iris, who was the messenger of Juno, the goddess of marriage. Iris walked between heaven and earth over a bridge made by the rainbow. Legend says that wherever she walked on earth, her footprints bore flowers with as many colors as the rainbow.

The iris was said to have first been adopted as an emblem in the 6th century by King Clovis of the Franks, after a clump of yellow flag iris had shown him where he could ford a stream and escape a superior force of Goths. It was revived as an emblem, the Fleur-de-Louis, in 1147 when Louis VII of France set off on the ill-fated second crusade. The emblem has been used since 1180 as a badge of the kings of France, and although referred to as the "Lily of France," was probably *I. pseudacorus*. The iris has been adopted by many kings since and has represented the birth of Christ in many classical paintings. Not to be outdone, even the Canadian Province of Quebec uses the Fleur-de-lis on her provincial flag. Countries of the world seem unabashedly attached to the beauty of the iris and in any one garden, English, Spanish, Dutch, Persian, German, Californian, Japanese, Louisiana, Pacific Coast, and Siberian irises may be found.

Plants range from the tiny *I. danfordiae*, Danford iris, to large water irises such as *I. pseudacorus*, yellow flag iris. Many species such as *I. sibirica* are easily grown, while others such as the exotic *I. susiana*, *I. haynei* and *I. samariae* require truly religious experiences to insure continued success. Bearded irises are the most common and so many cultivars have been produced that they have been divided into miniature dwarf, standard dwarf, intermediate, miniature tall, border, and standard tall bearded groupings. The standard tall bearded irises are the most common but many cultivars are available in all the bearded groups. Plenty of species, however, exist for hard-core taxonomic gardeners.

It would take many years to visit enough gardens around the world to see all the species and much longer to collect them for your own garden. Although interesting to see obscure species in botanical gardens, less than 20 are readily available commercially. However, there is enough choice of color, habit, and environmental needs within that group to satisfy all but the greediest of iris lovers.

The floral parts are in sets of 3. Flowers consist of 6 segments: 3 inner (standards) which generally are upright and 3 outer (falls) which are reflexed and are often bearded at the base. The standards are large and showy in most species but are reduced in *I. ensata*, Japanese iris, and nothing but short bristles in *I. setosa*, bristly iris. Three style branches arch over the anthers and the stigma is found on the underside of the branches near the end. This combination of style, anther, and stigma lies on the inner part of the fall and essentially makes a tunnel through which insects must enter to feed on the nectar, insuring that said insect collects lots of pollen to further impregnate other unsuspecting flowers.

Some species require constantly moist soil and perform best along sides of ponds or pools, thus the ability to maintain soil moisture is an important consideration in selecting iris species. Probably only *I. laevigata*, rabbit ear iris, has an absolute requirement for water, looking particularly shabby if planted in "normal" soils. *I. pseudacorus*, the Louisiana irises and most of the Japanese irises will succeed wonderfully well in damp soils. Many others, such as the bearded types, will be equally at home under "normal" conditions, that is, rich well-drained soils and full sun to partial shade. Although some species are bulbous (all of these are unbearded), most iris have underground rhizomes, a horizontally creeping stem, and may or may not be crested or bearded.

Due to the size of the genus, it continues to be stretched like cotton candy or squeezed like orange juice by taxonomists as more and more in-depth studies are conducted. For example, the further understanding of chromosomal differences has resulted in name or changes in relationships between taxa. Hybridization, both natural and formal, has also lead to much head scratching about where to place the resultant progeny. Recent classifications date from 1930 (Dikes-Diels), to Lawrence's in 1953 and to the work of Rodionenko in 1961. According to the various systems, the genus is divided into sub-genera which subdivide into sections, sub-sections, and groups or series. Each series may have 5–25 species and each species may be subdivided into numerous cultivars. The most recent work of Rodionenko also removed the bulbous iris from genus *Iris* to their own genera (*Xiphium, Iridodictyum,* and *Juno*). In this book, the genus remains intact but I note changes where appropriate. Gardeners need not lament the changes in academia, but rejoice in this great group of plants, no matter what names they are called.

Propagation of all the rhizomatous iris can be accomplished by dividing with a sharp spade or by pulling apart tangled rhizomes with garden forks. Although the latter takes more time and effort, healthier and faster flowering plants result.

The flowering times listed below illustrate the long seasonal interest (adapted from "The World of Iris," AIS, 1978). Not all species included in this list are described. The American Iris Society is a must for enthusiasts (see associations after Iris).

*Abbreviations*
E = early, M = mid, L = late
Dw = dwarf, Min = miniature, Int = intermediate, St = standard

| Mid to Southern States | Mid to Northern States | Group | Includes |
|---|---|---|---|
| L.Nov–L.Jan | Nov–Mar | Unguicularis | *I. unguicularis* |
| M.Feb–M.Mar | M.Mar–M.Apr | Reticulatas | *I. bakerana* |
| | | | *I. danfordiae* |
| | | | *I. histrio* |
| | | | *I. histriodes* |
| | | | *I. reticulata* |
| L.Feb–E.Apr | E.Apr–E.May | Min. Dw. Bearded | *I. chamaeiris* *I. pumila* |
| M.Mar–M.May | L.Apr–L.May | Medians | St. Dw. Bearded |
| | | | Int. Bearded |
| | | | Border Bearded |
| | | | Min. Tall Bearded |
| M.Mar–M.Apr | L.Apr–M.May | Junos | *I. bucharica* |
| | | | *I. willmottiana* |
| E.Apr–E.May | L.Apr–E.Jun | Arils | *I. hoogiana* |
| | | | *I. korolkowii* |
| | | | *I. hookeriana* |
| | | | *I. susiana* |
| E.Apr–L.May | L.Apr–M.Jun | Xiphiums | *I. xiphium* |
| | | | *I. xiphoides* |
| | | | Dutch hybrids |
| L.Apr–E.May | E.May–L.Jun | Vernae | *I. verna* |

| | | | |
|---|---|---|---|
| L.Apr–L.May | E.May–E.Jun | Evansias | *I. cristata* |
| | | | *I. tectorum* |
| L.Apr–L.May | M.May–M.Jun | Tall Bearded | *I. pallida* |
| E.May–E.Jun | M.May–L.Jun | Louisianas | *I. fulva* |
| | | | *I. hexagona* |
| | | | *I. nelsonii* |
| M.May–M.Jun | E.Jun–L.Jun | Siberians | *I. sibirica* |
| | | | *I. sanguinea* |
| M.May–M.Jun | M.Jun–M.Jul | Spurias | *I. graminea* |
| | | | *I. spuria* |
| E.Jun–L.Jun | L.Jun–L.Jul | Apogon | *I. ensata* |
| | | | *I. laevigata* |
| | | | *I. pseudacorus* |
| | | | *I. setosa* |
| | | | *I. versicolor* |
| M.Sep—M.Nov | E.Sep–E.Oct | Rebloomers | Many species |

When I teach this genus to my students, I find it easier to break them down into bulbous and non-bulbous species, then take the great group of non-bulbous taxa and divide them into those with a beard (Pogon or bearded iris), those with a crest (Lophiris or crested iris) and those with no beard or crest (Apogon iris). Peggy Martin, one of my former students, who, with her classmates, was struggling to learn the myriad of botanical terms and species in my Perennials class, simply called the apogon types the "nothing" iris. Hard to argue with Peggy's common sense.

Quick Reference to Iris Species

| | Height (in.) | Color of flowers | Bearded, crested or apogon | Bulbous or rhizome |
|---|---|---|---|---|
| *I.* 'Bearded hybrids' | 8–36 | Various | Bearded | Rhizome |
| *I. cristata* | 6–8 | Lavender | Crested | Rhizome |
| *I. danfordiae* | 2–4 | Yellow | Apogon | Bulbous |
| *I. ensata* | 24–30 | Various | Apogon | Rhizome |
| *I. foetidissima* | 18–24 | Lilac | Apogon | Rhizome |
| *I.* 'Louisiana Iris' | 36–48 | Various | Apogon | Rhizome |
| *I. pallida* | 24–36 | Violet | Bearded | Rhizome |
| *I. pseudacorus* | 24–36 | Yellow | Apogon | Rhizome |
| *I. reticulata* | 2–4 | Violet | Apogon | Bulbous |
| *I. sibirica* | 24–36 | Blue | Apogon | Rhizome |
| *I. tectorum* | 12–18 | Lilac | Crested | Rhizome |
| *I. unguicularis* | 9–12 | Lilac | Apogon | Rhizome |
| *I. verna* | 4–6 | Blue | Apogon | Rhizome |
| *I.* 'Xiphium hybrids' | 12–18 | Various | Apogon | Bulbous |

**-'Bearded hybrids'**                    Bearded Iris      8–36″/10–24″
    Early Summer        Various       Hybrid             Zones 3–10
(Syn. *I. barbata*)

The majority of people who first use iris in the garden try one of the bearded hybrids. When I wrote the first edition of this book in 1985, it was estimated that well over 90% of all iris used in this country were in this group and that 90% of those were the tall bearded types. Today, they are still wildly popular, but the acceptance of the siberians and Japanese have reduced the dependency somewhat. Market research, however, has not determined whether there was such a high demand because breeders turned out so many hybrids and cultivars, or there were so many available that it became difficult to buy anything else. Regardless of the reasons for their popularity, new cultivars continue to be produced and the demand continues.

Bearded iris are "bearded" because of the beard of hairs are easily visible in the middle of the falls. They may be classified into dwarf (less than 15″), intermediate (15–28″), and tall bearded (28″ or taller) iris. The American Iris Society has further divided the dwarfs into miniature (4–10″) and standard (10–15″) categories and the intermediates were split into intermediate, table and border iris groups.

### Dwarf Bearded (4–10″):

This group of bearded iris is often sold under *I. pumila*, dwarf iris, and although the species is sometimes available, its main contribution to gardening is the dominant parent of the miniature dwarf hybrids. *I. chamaeiris*, Crimean iris, has also been used in this group. Both are native to Southern Europe and exist in many colors. *I. pumila* differs from *I. chamaeiris* by having a shorter stem and longer flower. Other parents of lesser importance include *I. attica*, *I. griffithii*, and *I. flavescens*. The miniature dwarf forms (4–10″ tall) are the earliest to flower and stems are usually unbranched, bearing a few 2–3″ wide flowers with spotted falls. All irises in this class require fine drainage and are often grown in rockeries or on stone walls where drainage is not an issue.

### Cultivars of Miniature Dwarf Bearded Iris:

| | |
|---|---|
| 'Already' | Wine red flowers |
| 'Angel Eyes' | White with blue spots on falls |
| 'Banberry Ruffles' | Purple flowers |
| 'Blue Frost' | Light blue flowers |
| 'Butterfly' | Light blue splotched with purple |
| 'Cherry Spot' | White with cherry red falls |
| 'Commencement' | White, spotted yellow on falls |
| 'Curtsy' | White with lavender falls |
| 'Elfin Queen' | White with bits of yellow on the falls |

| | |
|---|---|
| 'Fashion Lady' | Orange yellow flowers |
| 'Golden Eyelet' | Golden orange with white beard |
| 'Grandma's Hat' | Blue standards with purple falls |
| 'Ink Spot' | Purple standards and falls with orange beard |
| 'Lena' | Red flowers |
| 'Little Sapphire' | Light blue flowers |
| 'Navy Doll' | Light yellow with purple splotch |
| 'Pixie Princess' | Blue flowers |
| 'Red Gem' | Deep red flowers |
| 'Ritz' | Yellow standards with a hint of blue |
| 'Sky Baby' | Ruffled blue flowers |
| 'Verona' | Blue to purple flowers with light yellow beard |
| 'Watercolor' | Light yellow with brown spot on falls |
| 'Wee Lad' | Mahogany red standards and purple falls |

### Standard Dwarf Bearded (10–15″):

Sometimes called Lilliputs, they are often more robust than the miniatures. They arose from crossing *I. pumila* with standard tall species and hybrids. The 3–4″ wide flowers open about a week later than the miniatures. Good drainage is beneficial although not as absolute a requirement as with the miniatures. The Lilliputs are quite at home in a small grouping at the front of a sunny border.

### Cultivars of Standard Dwarf Bearded Iris:

| | |
|---|---|
| 'Baby Blessed' | Lime yellow flowers |
| 'Baby Snowflake' | White flowers |
| 'Bingo' | Deep velvet purple flowers |
| 'Blue Denim' | Light blue flowers |
| 'Carrot Curls' | Orange flowers with crinkled edges |
| 'Cherry Garden' | Reddish purple standards with bluish beard |
| 'Dark Fairy' | Purple flowers |
| 'Early Sunshine' | Yellow flowers |
| 'Eyebright' | Deep yellow with brown venation |
| 'Elfin Queen' | White with a bit of yellow on falls |
| 'Jewel Baby' | Rich purple with a violet beard |
| 'Knotty Pine' | Tan-yellow with an orange beard |
| 'Lemon Flare' | Creamy white flowers |
| 'Little Rosy Wings' | Pale rose-pink flowers |
| 'Meadow Court' | Pale yellow with purple falls |
| 'Pippi Longstockings' | Bright yellow with purple spots |
| 'Rain Dance' | Clear blue flowers |
| 'Red Dandy' | Wine red flowers |
| 'Small Sky' | Light blue flowers |
| 'Snow Maiden' | White flowers with chartreuse veining |

| 'Sunlit Trail' | Yellow flowers |
| 'Tarheel Elf' | Deep purple to almost black |
| 'Wilma' | Light yellow flowers |

## Intermediate Bearded (15-28"):

In general, the flowering time falls between the dwarf and the tall bearded iris as plants resulted from crosses between the two. Other species which fit into this class or have been used in hybridization are *I. pumila, I. chamaeiris, I. melitta*, and *I. balkana*. They are handsome garden plants and attain respectable height and flower size without staking. The main difference between intermediate, table, and border bearded iris is their parentage and flowering time.

## Cultivars of Intermediate Bearded Iris:

| 'Blue Fragrance' | Blue flowers |
| 'Butterbit' | Yellow flowers |
| 'Brown Lasso' | Yellow golden standards and orchid falls |
| 'Lemonade' | Yellow with white falls |
| 'Little Angel' | White flowers |
| 'Pink Bubbles' | Flared, ruffled pink flowers and deep pink beard |
| 'Sweet Allegro' | Pink flowers |

## Tall Bearded (over 28"):

The tall bearded iris are still the most popular iris in gardens today. Many have escaped from cultivation and "blue flags" can be found around old farmsteads and meadows. Plants enjoy soil with a basic pH (as do the other bearded types) and full sun. The dazzling array of colors is the result of their complex parentage. The first tall bearded irises introduced commercially were selections from natural hybrids of *I. variegata* and *I. pallida*. Many selections were made between 1822 and the 1880's by French, Dutch and English hybridizers, but few breakthroughs occurred until the large-flowered species, *I. trojana, I. cypriana*, and *I. mesopatamica*, were discovered and introduced from the Near East. They resulted in "magical" crosses, for unbeknownst to the hybridizers, these species had twice the number of chromosomes (i.e., tetraploid) as those used previously. In the crosses that followed, fertile tetraploids with larger flowers and much improved vigor occasionally appeared and were used in further breeding. From this point on, hybridization knew no bounds and the thousands of cultivars available today do not even closely resemble the parents from which they sprang.

Tall bearded irises have been further classified into flower colors and shapes, but these are of interest only to those afflicted with irisitis, an incurable compulsion to grow every different tall bearded iris ever developed. Those so affected have been known to babble incomprehensibly about amoenas, plicatas and selfs, but they can be safely approached.

Several pests plague bearded iris and are particularly troublesome in heavy, poorly drained soils. Soft rot turns healthy rhizomes into mush. As leaves begin to yellow and die, they should be removed without delay or the fungus will infect the rhizome. Various leaf spots can be disfiguring as is the ailment known as scorch. Leaves turn red to brown all at once, resulting in death of the plant. The cause and cure are unknown. The iris borer is the most serious insect and is best controlled by removing dead debris in which they overwinter, particularly the spent iris leaves themselves.

There are simply too many cultivars of tall bearded iris to produce a useful list. Consult growers or specialists to keep abreast of the current cultivars. A number of awards are presented to new cultivars of iris, the most prestigious being the Dykes Medal. Consult the American Iris Society for recent winners and lists of popular cultivars. They can be helpful in choosing the best cultivars for different areas of the country.

*-cristata* (kris-tah′ ta)         Crested Iris              3–9″/15″
   Spring     Pale Blue, Yellow Crest    Eastern North America   Zones 3–8

Many irises are native to the United States but this is one of the finest available. The woody, spindle-shaped, shallow rhizomes creep along the surface resulting in rapid multiplication of the clump. The leaves are 4–6″ long and arise from the rhizome. One to two flowers are produced on each 2–3″ tall stem; the standards are shorter and narrower than the falls and the crest is a lovely deep yellow. Plants tolerate partial to heavy shade (although they flourish in morning sun) and look magnificent in great drifts in the woodland garden. The woodland floor awash in pale blue is a sight to savor. Plants combine well with Canadian columbine, *Aquilegia canadensis*, wood poppy, *Stylophorum diphyllum*, and all sorts of other woodsy plants.

**Cultivars:**
'Alba' (var. *alba*) is a white-flowered variety not as common or as vigorous as the type. Yellow crests contrast with the handsome flowers which contrast far more with the woodland floor than the type. I received a very vigorous form from one of our fine Southern gardeners and writers, Barrie Crawford. It grows significantly faster than the other white clumps in the Armitage garden demonstrating the diversity even in the forms of this species.
'Caerulea' (var. *caerulea*) has darker blue flowers than the species.

**Related Species:**
*I. lacustris*, dwarf lake iris, is similar but only about 3″ tall, and has narrower leaves and a more slender rhizome. The flowers are slate blue with a whitish patch and yellow crest on the falls. It is native to the

shores of the Great Lakes. Unless you are fortunate to live near those wonderful lakes, *I. cristata* is probably a better garden plant and far more available.

**-danfordiae** (dan-ford' ee-eye)       Danford Iris              4–6"/6"
   Early Spring       Bright Yellow     Eastern Turkey         Zones 5–9
(Syn. *Iridodictyum danfordia*)

The bulbs have a netted or reticulated cover with brownish fibers, thus belonging to the group known as reticulated iris. Brilliant yellow flowers with brown spots on the falls open in early spring or late winter depending on soil temperature.

Plants are short and should be planted where they can be enjoyed close up. The leaves are square, hollow, and barely developed at time of flowering, although they grow 12" long after flowering. The standards are less than ¾" long and the falls have small brown or black spots. These bulblets require 2–3 more years to flower. I love these plants when they flower in the spring but then I tend to forget about them. Plants like hot, dry conditions during their long summer dormancy and invariably they break into masses of small bulbs, resulting in more leaves but few flowers the next year. They should be treated as annuals or biennials and replaced every other year.

**Related Species:**

*I. winogradowii* (syn. *Iridodictyum winogradowii*) has to be one of the most beautiful of the dwarf iris. Although that statement is based on my limited experience, plants took my breath away when I saw them in the rock garden at Wisley, UK. The lemon-yellow flowers have an orange stripe in the center of the falls. They are larger than the Danford iris but likely the bulbs will behave the same, requiring replacement every other year. Difficult to find, and expensive.

**-ensata** (en' sata)                   Japanese Iris            24–30"/24"
   Summer       Various          Northern China, Japan      Zones 4–9
(Syn. *I. kaempferi*)

Occurring in east Asia to Siberia, *I. ensata* is by nature a meadow rather than a marshland plant. However, plants adapt well to afternoon shade and moist soils. The leaves are bright green and have a prominent center rib (unlike *I. laevigata*) and are 1–1½" wide. In its native form, plants are rather unimpressive, with ordinary red-purple flowers, small standards and floppy falls. However, over the centuries the Japanese have developed large-flowered plants characterized by the virtual elimination of the standards and subsequent increase in size of the falls. The flowers may be up to 10″ across and due to lack of standards, the overall appearance is that of a flattened flower head. Cultivars include singles (with 3 broad, overlapping falls), doubles (with 6 falls that are actually standards and falls lying together), and peony-style flowers with up to 12 flower parts. They look particularly good if placed at the base of stairs so that as you descend, the tops of the flowers are in view.

Plants perform well in any organic-rich soil where moisture can be consistently provided; they do not need to be planted in a bog. Fertilize plants in early spring and summer. Acidic conditions are necessary and lime must not be added to the soil. A number of lime tolerant cultivars were bred by the late German hybridizer Max Steiger and released in Europe in the late 1950's and early 1960's. Few are easily available in this country but may be found through specialty iris growers. Plant in full sun or afternoon shade.

The name *I. kaempferi* is commonly used for this species; however, upon study, it was found that plants were called *I. ensata* by the Swedish taxonomist, Thunberg, in 1794, whereas the name *I. kaempferi* was not provided by Franz von Siebold of Holland until 1858. So, *I. ensata* it is. Actually, it is one of the few times I am pleased with a name change; I never could spell *I. kaempferi* correctly.

Plants may be divided in spring and fall.

### Cultivars:

Cultivars which have been developed are truly magnificent and are becoming less expensive and more available every year. The flowers are so large that some gardeners remove them as soon as they fade. As with other popular species of iris, catalogs provide the most vivid descriptions of cultivars. The pictures are also prettier.

'Activity' is about 3′ tall and bears soft blue flowers with purple veins.
'Aichi' has pink flowers with darker pink veining.
'Aka-fukurin' has white flowers with red trim.
'Anna' bears lavender-blue flowers, fading to a dull white.
'Blue Beauty' bears sky blue flowers with a yellow blotch on the falls.
'Calico Maid' has double white flowers marbled in purple.
'Cry of Rejoice' produces purple flowers with yellow centers.
'Emotion' is about 3′ tall with double white flowers with a blue edge.
'Favorite' has clear blue flowers, 3′ tall.
'Gekkeikan' bears white flowers with a purple edge.
'Henry's White' produces clean white flowers with a slight yellow stripe on the falls.
'Higo' strain from Japan consists of 24–30″ tall cultivars with 6–9″ wide, heavily veined blooms. An important parent of many of the modern hybrids.
'Ise' has pale blue to almost white, single flowers.

'Jodelsong' bears purple-red flowers with bright yellow on the falls.

'Kagari Bi' is a handsome purple-flowered form with silvery veins on the falls.

'Light in Opal' is almost iridescent when the light lavender flowers open.

'Loyalty' has violet-blue double flowers with yellow striping on the falls.

'Nara' bears double violet flowers which bloom about 1 week later than the other cultivars.

'Nikiyama' has dark violet flowers with white veins.

'Nikko' is 18–24″ tall and produces single pale blue flowers with deep purple veining. These last three cultivars are part of the Higo strain.

'Oriental Fantasy' is about 30″ tall with white flowers bearing pink centers.

'Over the Waves' bears pure white highly ruffled flowers with a light purple border.

'Pink Lady' has large, single, light pink flowers.

'Pink Frost' has double, 8″ wide pink flowers which are lighter and more ruffled than those of 'Pink Lady'.

'Purple and Gold' has a name totally lacking in imagination but the single purple flowers with golden stripes on the falls have been lovely in the Georgia gardens for many years.

'Rikkipikki' was picked as the best pure white form by Rick Berry of Goodness Grows, Lexington, GA. Terrific plant.

'Royal Banner' has purple-red flowers with a yellow blotch.

'Sapphire Star' is an early flowering form with light lavender flowers and a faint white venation. Handsome.

'Strut and Flourish' bears double violet flowers which fade to lighter shades towards the end of the petals. A big plant, almost 4′ tall but most eye-catching.

'Summer Storm' has black buds, opening to deep purple with yellow markings.

'Variegata' has white-edged leaves which hold their variegation throughout the season. The flowers are dark purple. The foliage is much better than the flowers. Sometimes sold as 'Silver Band'.

'White Ladies' have white flowers with an obvious yellow striping on the falls.

**Related Species:**

*I. laevigata*, rabbit ear iris, is a most magnificent iris. The 2–3″ wide flowers are flattened and lavender blue. The blue-green leaves have visible black "watermarks" along the veins. Plants are easily distinguishable from *I. ensata* because of the smooth leaves compared to the raised central midrib of *I. ensata*. They are also more lime tolerant than *I. ensata*. *I. laevigata* is difficult to find in this country because of the narrow limits of adaptability. Roots must be constantly moist and it is best grown on streambanks, bogs, or other areas high in moist organic matter. The finest examples I have seen are at Longstock Water Gardens near Longstock, England. Some cultivars have been selected. 'Alba' bears pure white flowers which make it even prettier than the species; 'Rose Queen' has attractive pink flowers;

'Snowdrift' produces creamy white flowers with a hint of purple; and 'Variegata' has sharp white leaf variegations which contrast well with the blue flowers. Probably the best variegated form to hold its variegations throughout the season.

*I. spuria*, seashore iris, requires plenty of water in spring and fall but prefers to be hot and dry during the summer. The best thing about the spurias is that they remain as a clump, not opening in the middle like Louisiana or Bearded types do. It is a complex group due to its vast range, from North Africa to Denmark. Few sources can be found for this species, but countless cultivars have been bred in Europe. They are less tolerant of our harsher climate than that found in the British Isles or southern Germany, where they flourish. Hybrid forms grow to 4' in height and almost as wide. Flowers consist of long narrow falls, usually wider at the ends, particularly in the cultivars, and narrow upright often frilly standards in an assortment of colors. Flowers open in June and July. Some of my favorite hybrids are 'Cambridge Blue' with lavender and yellow flowers, 'Shelford Giant' with handsome creamy white and yellow flowers and 'Orange Maid', whose bright orange-yellow flowers can be seen from "miles away." Plants resent disturbance and should not be moved unless necessary.

| *-foetidissima* (foy-ti-dis′ i-ma) | | Stinking Gladwin | 18–24″/18″ |
|---|---|---|---|
| Summer | Lilac | Europe | Zones 6–9 |

This unusual species is the only iris grown for the fruit rather than (or instead of) the flowers. The leaves are evergreen, about 18″ long, and are characterized by their somewhat foul odor when broken or crushed. Another common name is roast beef plant, which may give an indication of its fragrance. With all this attention to its malodorous properties, I must say that the Armitage nose has not recoiled at the smell. That I have hay fever when I smell it may help. The purplish gray flowers are 2–2½″ across and rather insignificant. Not until autumn is the beauty of this plant appreciated. Then, the seed pods split open and reveal rows of scarlet seeds, which provide yet another common name, Coral iris. The seeds remain attached throughout the winter if not snatched by birds or squirrels. The fruiting stem may be hung upside down to dry and used for indoor decoration.

Plants do well in partial shade and are among the most shade tolerant of iris species. Due to their evergreen nature, the foliage can look cruddy in the spring. Taking old leaves off at that time does not hurt the plant and gets rid of many potential disease organisms. Two to three years are necessary to establish a clump of stinking gladwin. The first year in the Horticulture gardens yielded few seed capsules but 6–8 appeared the following year.

Propagate by seed, or lift and divide in the fall.

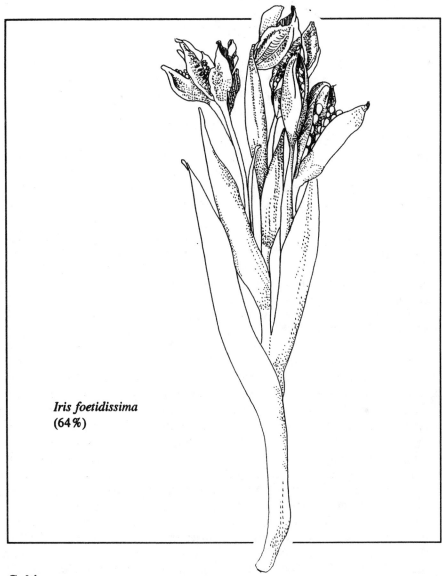

*Iris foetidissima*
(64%)

## Cultivars:

'Citrina' (var. *citrina*) bears flowers of pale yellow and mauve. A mixed up color scheme but not entirely without beauty.

'Fructo-alba' translates to white fruit and occurs very rarely. Difficult to find and not nearly as bright as the regular form anyway.

'Lutea' (var. *lutescens*) has handsome light yellow flowers.

'Variegata' has variegated leaves which add foliar appeal to an otherwise drab flowered plant. A slow grower.

-**'Louisiana Iris'**      Louisiana Iris      3–4'/3'
  Summer      Various      Southern United States      Zones 4–9

Louisiana irises constitute a unique group in the iris family, providing the color red to the iris spectrum. They consist of 5 species indigenous to a limited area of south central Louisiana and the Gulf Coast marsh areas of Texas to Florida. The 5 species normally thought of as Louisiana iris are *I. brevicaulis, I. fulva, I. giganticaerulea, I. hexagona* and *I. nelsonii,* although plant breeders have provided gardeners with many hybrids which are now more common than the species. They are a non-bearded, non-crested iris and generally have narrow falls and drooping standards. All of the species are handsome in their own right, but their hybridization, natural or otherwise, has resulted in numerous wonderful named hybrids. Guidelines for garden use include sun and lots of water. They do not require bogs but do better where copious water can be provided.

*I. brevicaulis*, Lamance iris, is the shortest species in the Louisiana complex, growing about 12–14″ tall with thick, short, often zig-zag stalks. The flowers are lilac-blue to deep blue and occur within the leaves. In the Armitage garden, plants become very leafy and after flowering, must be divided before they eat more space.

*I. fulva* has 4″ flowers in brick-red or copper-red as well as rare yellow flowers. This is one of the few red colored iris and does well in the sunny garden. *I. giganticaerulea* is very similar to, and may be a variety of, *I. hexagona*. Flowers are larger (4–6″ across) and occur only in Louisiana coastal areas. Plants thrive in flooded areas and may tolerate brackish water. *I. hexagona* is the most easterly native, occurring in Florida, South Carolina and Georgia. Long narrow light green leaves and lilac flowers with yellow markings on the falls. Plants move about the garden freely but can not be termed as aggressive. *I. nelsonii* has 4–5″ wide bright red to purple flowers, but generally more intense than the color of *I. fulva*. They are shorter than *I. fulva* and found only in Louisiana in a limited location south of the town of Abbeville. Not discovered until 1938, they became known as "Abbeville Irises", "Abbeville Reds", or because of their similarity to *I. fulva*, "Super-Fulvas".

The hybrids that have been developed have increased the range of color and usefulness of these plants. Early hybridization of *I. fulva* × *I. brevicaulis* by the famous iris pioneer, W.B. Dykes, resulted in 'Fulvula' in 1910. Through the 1920's and 1930's, dozens of hybrids were registered with the American Iris Society. Many crosses between *I. fulva* and *I. hexagona* became popular in the 1930's. The discovery of *I. nelsonii* in 1966 opened up the hybridization process to include red and terra cotta colors. Joseph Mertzweiller produced some of the first tetraploid cultivars in 1973 and tetraploids continue to evolve, although at a much slower rate than the diploids.

The northern limits of Louisiana iris continue to be expanded. Plants have been successful in Sioux Falls, ND, and have been described in many Plains states, the midwest and California. Plants tolerate full sun to a little afternoon shade in the South, consistent watering, and fertility and soil improved with organic matter.

One of the more knowledgeable gardeners about this fine group of hybrids is Josephine Shanks of Houston, TX. She is the Louisianas best friend, imploring us to give the group a try, and her enthusiasm and knowledge has helped many a gardener improve their garden.

**Cultivars:**

Numerous cultivars have been bred and are available in white ('Clara Goula', 'Rokki') to lavender ('Ione', 'Ashley Michelle'), red ('Sun Chaser', 'Parade Music'), yellow ('President Hedley', 'Professor Barbara'), and bicolors ('Colorific', 'Bold Pretender'). The Louisiana Iris Society of America provides cultivars and useful gardening information.

| *-pallida* (pa' li-da) | | Sweet Iris | 24–36"/24" |
|---|---|---|---|
| Summer | Lavender-blue | Northern Italy | Zones 4–9 |

This species is an important building block in the development of the bearded iris, yet it has some lovely attributes of its own. Although the flowers are fragrant, they are an unremarkable bearded lavender-blue, and much more statuesque flowers may be found in any number of bearded hybrids. Some say the flowers smell like grape juice. My sense of smell must not be that well-developed. The foliage, however, is an excellent soft gray-green color which is retained throughout the year and is a good foil for dark green plants in the garden.

Like other bearded species, *I. pallida* grows best in well-drained soils and is not particularly tolerant of wet feet. Full sun is preferred but partial shade is tolerated.

**Cultivars:**

'Argentea-variegata' has flattened leaves of silvery white and green stripes. The lilac-blue flowers complement the foliage.

'Variegata' ('Zebra') has white and cream streaking on blue-green leaves. An exceptional garden plant with all-season appeal.

Var. *dalmatica* is the best of the glaucous foliage plants with larger leaves and handsome foliage.

| *-pseudacorus* (sood-a' ko-rus) | | Yellow Flag Iris | 24–42"/24" |
|---|---|---|---|
| Early Summer | Yellow | Europe | Zones 5–9 |

Yellow flag iris has been grown for centuries and all parts of the plant have been found useful, in one way or another, over the years. The rhizome acts as a powerful cathartic; the powdered roots were used as snuff and contain antidotal properties for poisons. The seeds were roasted for a coffee-like beverage while the flowers produced a yellow dye.

This is a most adaptable species. To be sure, plants are at their best where the roots are submerged in water or at least constantly moist. Heights of 3–4' are not uncommon in such situations. However, they also grow well in drier areas as long as irrigation is provided when Mother Nature falls behind with rain. *I. pseudacorus* has grown well in my shaded garden, tucked away in a corner (as well as one can tuck a plant of this size), through two major droughts. When grown under less than ideal conditions, plants are shorter and less vigorous. This is not usually a problem as plants grown in streams and ponds are often too big for most gardens.

The 12–15" long leaves are sword shaped, bright green and rather coarse. The 2" long yellow flowers are not particularly big and often have brown veins with a brown blotch on the falls. The fruit capsules of all varieties are large and sought after for dried arrangements. I grow this species through plants of *Sedum* × 'Autumn Joy'. The sedum grows around the foliage throughout the summer and the sword-like leaves of the iris provide additional architectural interest.

I always include this plant as one of my "no-brainers" for beginning gardeners. However, I was taken to task at one lecture for even suggesting this as a garden plant when it is so inclined to naturalize in waterways. Like *Lythrum* in the north, *I. pseudacorus* can indeed escape and cause problems in steams and wetlands. It has a long way to go before it becomes the nuisance of lythrum, however, be forewarned. This plant likes it here!

Propagate by division of the rhizome every 2–4 years or raise from seeds. Seed propagated plants are variable and take 2 years to flower.

**Cultivars:**

'Bastardii' (var. *bastardii*) bears pale primrose flowers without the markings on the falls.

'Flore-pleno' is an ugly double-flowered form. Curious is a kind way of describing the flowers.

'Golden Queen' (var. *superba*) produces bright yellow flowers without the usual brown markings.

'Rising Sun' bears lovely yellow flowers, grows 3–4' tall and is likely a hybrid with *I. ensata*.

'Variegata' has yellow stripes on the leaves and is the finest of all the water irises for spring foliage effect. The flowers are lost in the variegated effect but the leaves are so outstanding that the flowers are not missed. Unfortunately, the variegation disappears as the summer warms up and reverts to common green. Next spring, however, leaves reappear variegated. Plants are not as tolerant of shade as the species.

**Related Species:**

*I. mandschurica* resembles the yellow flag iris but is considerably more difficult to find and to grow. Plants don't grow quite as tall and are at home in shallow water.

*I. versicolor*, blueflag iris, native to North America, is similar to *I. pseudacorus* in size, habit, and tolerance to moisture. This is the common blue flag iris found in moist soils from eastern Canada to Pennsylvania. The flowers occur in shades of reddish or bluish purple. It is adaptable to most moist climates but not common in the trade.

| *-reticulata* (re-tik-ew′ lah-ta) | | Reticulated Iris | 2–4″/6″ |
|---|---|---|---|
| Winter, Early Spring | Violet | Turkey | Zones 5–8 |
| (Syn. *Iridodictyum reticulata*) | | | |

The little bulbs are the earliest to emerge in the spring or even in late winter. In the Armitage garden, flowers appear by February 15 and persist until the first week in March, depending on the weather. Few plants surpass the richness of the purple and gold flowers which also possess the delightful fragrance of violets. Bulbs have netted veins similar to *I. danfordiae* and should be planted 2–3″ deep. The pointed leaves are acutely 4-angled and 1–3″ tall at flowering time, then elongate to 12–18″ tall after the flowers have finished. Because of their diminutive size at flowering time, bulbs must be planted in large numbers to make any

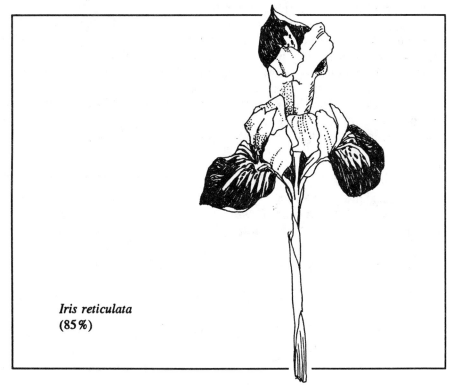

*Iris reticulata*
(85%)

kind of show. Leaves disappear by late spring or early summer and annuals may be used to fill in the gaps. All species in the reticulated iris group require dry summers for the bulbs to ripen and set buds for the next year. In areas with heavy summer rains, plantings decline in the first 3 years but those that adapt continue to flower in larger clumps each year. Many of my original bulbs have disappeared but those remaining are magnificent because 6–7 flowers open on each clump.

The offsets may be divided immediately after flowering.

**Cultivars:**

Many are hybrids with other bulbous iris, but are listed under *I. reticulata*.

'Cantab' has pale blue flowers with violet on the falls and shows up well in the spring.

'Clairette' is sky-blue whose blue to violet falls also have a white patch.

'Edward' bears dark blue flowers with orange on the falls.

'Gordon' is about 6″ tall with blue-violet flowers.

'Harmony' has royal blue flowers with a yellow and white blotch on the falls. This is the most common cultivar, and used in large numbers by the greenhouse industry for pot plant forcing. Place as many bulbs as possible in a pot, put in a cool place (35–40° F) for about 10 weeks, then bring out to room temperatures.

'Hercules' produces deep purple flowers with an orange blotch on the falls.

'Ida' bears blue flowers with a yellow blotch.

'Joyce' has handsome sky blue blossoms with white blotches on the falls.

'J.S. Dijt' has purplish red flowers with a little white and yellow on the falls.

'Natascha' bears creamy ivory flowers with a gold-yellow blotch.

'Pauline' produces purple to violet flowers with a white blotch on the falls.

'Purple Gem' has deep purple flowers.

'Spring Time' bears light blue and dark blue bicolored flowers.

**Related Species:**

*I. histrio* (syn. *Iridodictyum histrio*), Syrian iris, is distinctly bluer than *I. reticulata* and has a hint of red in its makeup. Flowers earlier than *I. reticulata*.

*I. histriodes* (syn. *Iridodictyum histriodes*), harput iris, is larger (6–9″) and flowers 1–2 weeks later than *I. histrio*. Both have a creamy white area on the falls, flower earlier and produce many smaller offsets than *I. reticulata*.

| *-sibirica* (si-bi′ ri-ka) | Siberian Iris | 24–36″/24″ |
|---|---|---|
| Spring       Blue | Central Europe, Russia | Zones 3–9 |

Native to moist meadows, Siberian iris does well in a moist or bog garden. However, they perform admirably in normal garden situations as long as moisture can be delivered throughout the season, although they are smaller than when grown in their favorite bog. This dwarfing response to lack of water also occurs with *I. sanguinea*, an unexciting blue-flowered species, *I. pseudacorus* and *I. versicolor*.

Siberian iris has 2–5 blue-purple flowers per stem, but may occasionally be lavender or white. The 1–2″ wide flowers are held well above the narrow lance-like foliage. Many cultivars are available, including vigorous tetraploids (twice as many chromosomes as usual), which make the species pale in comparison. One of my favorite plantings, however, is the 6–8 plants of the species which line a sunny path in my garden. The many flowers (each plant produces 12–20 flowers) unfurl in mid May and provide that certain touch of class that is the hallmark of the Siberian iris. I prefer them to tall bearded types not only because of their smaller, more delicate flowers, but because they are less prone to soft rot or iris borer.

*Iris sibirica*
(81%)

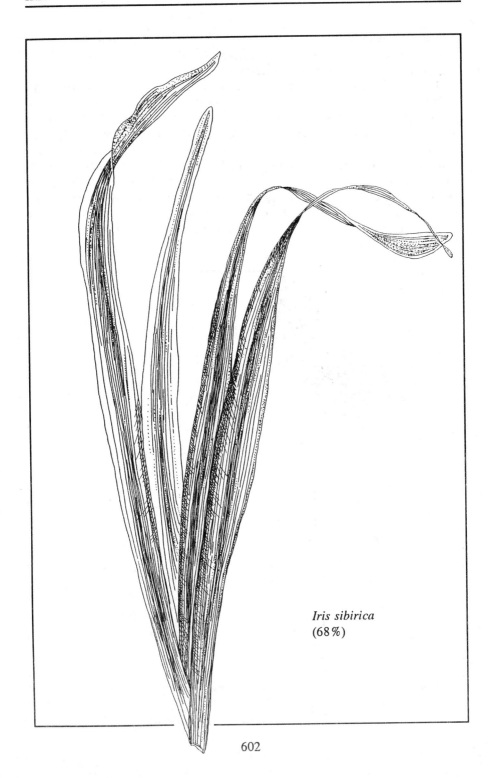

*Iris sibirica*
(68%)

Unlike the bearded iris, they should not be disturbed until the clump is obviously producing fewer flowers than normal. Use two spading forks to divide and do not allow the divisions to dry. They resent being disturbed and may take a year or so to look their best.

## Cultivars:

Many fine cultivars of Siberian iris are available and I must give way to those ubiquitous iris catalogs for a proper overview of available colors and range of vigor. Busse Gardens of Cokato, MN, for example, lists over 80 cultivars. Here are a few I think are outstanding.

'Ann Dasch' bears violet blue flowers mottled all over with very pale blue.
'Blue Brilliant' has proven to well adapted to many locales and bears clear blue standards and lighter blue falls. It flowers on 2–3' stems.
'Butter and Sugar' has large flowers on upright 2' tall stems. The blossoms consist of bright butter yellow falls between clean white standards.
'Caesar's Brother' is about 3' tall with very dark velvety violet flowers. A classic in the siberian iris world.
'Chartreuse Beauty' produces large very light blue flowers. Beautiful.
'Fourfold White' has clear white flowers with yellow at the base of the falls. This tetraploid is particularly vigorous.
'Heavenly Blue' produces light lavender flowers with a little white on the falls.
'Lavender Bounty' has falls of lavender and even lighter standards. Plants flower early and grow about 3' tall.
'Limeheart' bears creamy white to light yellow flowers.
'Llewllyn' produces dozens of beautiful soft lilac flowers.
'Mildred Peck' has lovely lavender-pink flowers borne on 3' tall stems.
'Pansy Purple' produces beautiful soft velvet violet flowers.
'Perry's Blue' has handsome sky blue flowers.
'Persimmon' is 3' tall with rich blue flowers.
'Sally Kerlin' bears deep violet flowers with rounded falls and white blotches.
'Soft Blue' has beautiful light blue flowers with a hint of lavender.
'Super Ego' is the gift to give to the person who thinks they know everything. The bicolor flowers are light blue and lavender.
'Swank' has large deep purple flowers with a yellow blotch on the falls. Compact and floriferous.
'Tycoon' has large violet-blue flowers with long drooping falls.
'White Swirl' produces clear white flowers which carry a touch of yellow. This superb iris was an important parent of numerous cultivars.

## Related Species:

*I. chrysographes*, goldvein iris, has dark maroon flowers with gold markings on the falls. An outstanding but little known species. Consistently moist soil is required. Numerous forms exist, the most sought after is probably 'Nigra' or

'Black Form' which is so dark purple as to appear black. Plants have been hybridized with other related forms such as *I. forrestii.*

*I. sanguinea* is native to Siberia as well as Japan, Korea and China. Plants are generally shorter than *I. sibirica* and the unbranched flower stems usually bear only 2 purple terminal flowers. 'Snow Queen' (often offered under *I. sibirica*) is about 2½' tall with milky white flowers. *I. sanguinea* used to be called *I. orientalis,* which is a distinct species, resulting in all sorts of confusion.

| *-tectorum* (tek-tor' um) | | Roof Iris | 12–18″/18″ |
|---|---|---|---|
| Summer | Lilac | China, Japan | Zones 4–8 |

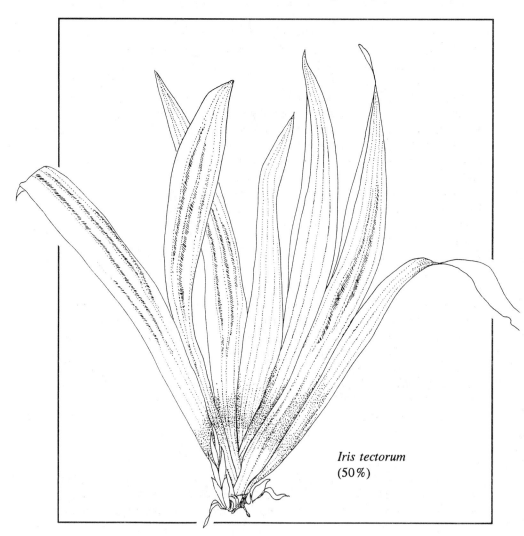

*Iris tectorum*
(50%)

Because of the interesting shape of the flowers, the evergreen foliage and the increased availability, this species has gained popularity every year. Its specific name, *tectorum*, means "growing on roofs" from the custom of being grown on the edges of thatched roofs in Japan. The powdered roots were also used by women in China for whitening their skin.

The large 6″ wide lilac flowers are mottled with dark blue to black blotches. Plants belong to the crested iris group (as does *I. cristata*), because of the conspicuous whitish brown jagged crest (rather than a beard) on the flowers. The standards lie almost level with the falls, resulting in an open, wide flower. Each flower stem usually bears 2 flowers and the evergreen leaves are 6–8″ wide, yellow-green and somewhat floppy.

Partial shade is tolerated but roof iris prefers full sun and well-drained soils. A number of reports on culture, particularly from England, suggest that plants are heavy feeders and must be moved from site to site every other year. The reports state that without heavy fertilization, the plant quickly depletes the soil and flowering is sparse. I have not found this to be necessary in the States. Plants should be fed by applying 1–2 tablespoons of a complete fertilizer such as 8-8-8 around the soil at the base of the plant (take care not to allow the granules to touch the leaves or the crown) in the spring as the plant becomes active.

Propagate by division of the rhizomes immediately after flowering, just as the last flower has faded. Plants can be moved at any time of year, providing they are irrigated well.

**Cultivars:**

Var. *alba* is harder to find and more expensive but is no longer rare. The flowers are white with a yellow crest on the falls.

'Variegata' has lavender-blue flowers and variegated foliage.

**Related Species:**

*I. gracilipes*, slender iris, is another graceful species of the Crested Iris group. It is shade tolerant, 8–10″ tall, and bears beautiful lilac-pink flowers with an orange crest over narrow, arching foliage.

| | | | |
|---|---|---|---|
| *-unguicularis* (un-gwik-ew-lah′ ris) | | Algerian Iris | 9–12″/12″ |
| Winter, Spring | Lavender | Algeria, Greece | Zones 7–9 |

This is a useful and easily identified iris. Useful for its late winter bloom time and easily identified by the almost total absence of a stem. The 18–20″ long and ½–1″ wide evergreen leaves are produced in a tuft and the flowers are cradled in the leafy center. The solitary blossoms are nicely fragrant and are usually lilac-blue to white. A wonderful plant for mild climates but it also can be disappointing when frosts knock back the leaves and flowering is sparse. Tolerates partial shade but prefers full sun. In the Armitage garden, I have had flowers on Christmas Day as well as on Valentine's Day. On other years, the frosts have beaten plants up to the point where no flowering has occurred at all. Terrific in the Pacific Northwest and the Gulf States.

**Cultivars:**

'Alba' bears white flowers; the falls have a central green-yellow line.

'Abington Purple' produces purple-blue flowers with a yellow stripe down the falls.

'Mary Barnard' has darker violet-blue flowers.

'Oxford Dwarf' produces deep blue flowers with white, blue-veined falls.

'Speciosa' has deep violet flowers with a central yellow stripe. The leaves are shorter and more narrow than the species.

'Walter Butt' bears large pale silver-lilac flowers. Quite handsome.

| *-verna* (ver′ na) | | Vernal Iris | 4–6″/12″ |
|---|---|---|---|
| Spring | Blue | Eastern United States | Zones 6–10 |

This dwarf native plant has a creeping rootstock similar to *I. cristata*. The 1½″ long flowers are dark blue with a large orange blotch on the falls. They are similar in habit to the dwarf bearded irises, but much smaller. This species is taxonomically very close to the bearded irises and some people refer to the flower as semi-bearded. Upon inspection, the pubescence on the falls is noticeable. The shortened stems are no longer than 6″ long. The narrow foliage is approximately 6″ long during flowering but elongates to 9–12″ after flowering.

Plants prefer shady, dry areas but do not grow as well as crested iris, particularly in woodland settings. They are most at home in a raised bed where good drainage can be provided. Garden-in-the-Woods in Framingham, MA, has some wonderful plantings.

Propagate by division of the rhizome after flowering.

| -'Xiphium hybrids' (zi′ fee-um) | English, Spanish, Dutch Iris | 12–18″/12″ |
|---|---|---|
| Spring Various | Southern Europe, Northern Africa | Zones 6–9 |

These bulbous iris are mainly seen in florists shops as cut flowers and few are sufficiently weather tolerant to be used in all but southerly gardens. As a group, they have been reclassified to the genus *Xiphium* and include English, *X. latifolium* (syn. *I. xiphoides*), Spanish, *X. vulgare* (syn. *I. xiphium*), and hybrid Dutch iris. In American gardens, the Dutch irises are the most hardy and popular of the group. They are more tolerant of inclement weather than the others and are widely available in many colors. All irises from this group now offered by bulb houses, however, are hybrids.

The English irises are the last of the group to flower and do so in June–July. They are predominantly *X. latifolium* (syn. *I. xiphoides*) but other species have undoubtedly played a role in their development. Growing 1–2' tall, they have the largest flowers (up to 4" across) of the group. Although no yellow flowers are available, white, blue, pink, or purple occur and all have a gold blotch on the falls. They are native to the French and Spanish Pyrenees, but are called English iris because they reached the Low Countries from England, most probably without notice of their true habitat. They grow well in English gardens but are difficult in America because of the requirement for constantly moist soil. Copious amounts of water and rich soils are necessary.

Spanish iris is smaller in all respects than the English iris. While *X. vulgare* (syn. *I. xiphium*) is an important species, it is likely a hybrid of *X. vulgare, X. tangitanum* (syn. *I. tangitana*), and others. Plants are 12–18" tall with 3–4" diameter flowers in a wide range of colors. Bright sunshine and warm, dry exposures are preferred. Seldom grown or seen in American gardens.

The Dutch iris was produced by the Tubergen Nurseries in Haarlem, Holland and are best described as a large and earlier-flowering strain of Spanish iris. They are the first to flower, starting in mid-May and continuing through June. In zone 7 and south, the foliage appears in the winter and although the leaves may be killed back by frosts, little damage to the flower bud occurs (unless the petal color is visible at time of frost). They are hardier than the others and may be occasionally overwintered to zone 6, but cold winters every few years will likely get them. Plants are 15–24" in height and flowers are 4–5" in diameter. They are particularly popular as cut flowers and may be forced in greenhouses year round. When planted in groups of a dozen or so, they make lovely garden plants requiring little room, and can be enjoyed inside and out. There are dozens of cultivars in a varied range of colors from bright yellow to the darkest blue.

In general, bulbs should be planted about 6" deep and once planted, need not be disturbed. However, all species and hybrids in the Xiphium group can be split into bulblets after the foliage has died down. Many naturally split into 2 larger bulbs as well as many smaller offsets. The larger bulbs may be replanted and will flower the following year, the smaller ones should be set aside and allowed to mature in a propagation bed until large enough to flower.

### Related Species:

*I. bucharica* (syn. *Juno bucharica*), Bokhara iris, bears fragrant creamy standards and yellow on the falls on 12–18" tall stems in April. This is a terrific plant for late spring flowering but unfortunately, at least in the Armitage garden, does not return in subsequent years. The leaves are 8–12" long, 2½" wide, glossy above, whitish underneath, and arranged like a ladder up the short stem. Very uniris-like. Foliage disappears by mid summer.

## Quick Key to Iris Species

A. Rootstock bulbous
  B. Standards minute, spreading,
    flowers yellow, stemless . . . . . . . . . . . . . . *I. danfordiae*
  BB. Standards conspicuous, erect, flowers
    variously colored, may be stemless
    C. Plants stemless or nearly so, less than
      1′ tall, flowers purple, leaves 4-sided . . . . . . *I. reticulata*
    CC. Plants with stems more than 1′ tall,
      flowers variously colored, leaves
      linear and furrowed . . . . . . . . . . *I.* 'Xiphium hybrids'
AA. Rootstock a rhizome
  B. Falls with a crest or beard
    C. Falls with fringed crest on lower part of fall
      D. Stem none or very short, leaves less
        than 6″ long, sword-shaped . . . . . . . . . . . *I. cristata*
      DD. Stem 1–2′, leaves more than
        1′ long, arching, broad . . . . . . . . . . . . *I. tectorum*
    CC. Falls with colored hairs (beard) along midrib
      D. Height 2–3′, flowers violet, bracts surrounding
        buds quite dry when flowers open,
        silvery-white, leaves blue-green . . . . . . . . *I. pallida*
      DD. Height 8–36″, flowers variously colored,
        bracts surrounding bud often flushed
        purple, usually dry when flowers open,
        leaves green to gray-green . . . . . . *I.* 'Bearded hybrids'
  BB. Falls without conspicuous crest or beard
    C. Plants more than 18″ tall
      D. Leaves linear, usually less than ½″ wide . . . *I. sibirica*
      DD. Leaves sword-like, usually more than ½″ wide
        E. Flowers yellow . . . . . . . . . . . . . . *I. pseudacorus*
        EE. Flowers not yellow
          F. Flowers not showy, foliage emitting
            disagreeable odor when crushed, seeds
            scarlet and persistent in capsule . . . *I. foetidissima*
          FF. Flowers large and showy, foliage
            odor not disagreeable, seeds not
            scarlet or persistent . . . . . . . . . . . . . . *I. ensata*
    CC. Plants less than 12″ tall
      D. Leaves about 6″ long, stems
        short but obvious . . . . . . . . . . . . . . . . . . *I. verna*
      DD. Leaves 18–20″ long, plants
        nearly stemless . . . . . . . . . . . . . . . . *I. unguicularis*

**Additional Reading:**

The scope of this book does not lend itself to a thorough enough discussion for the serious iris enthusiast. Some of the better publications include:

Books:

American Iris Society. 1978. *The World of Irises*. B. Warburton (ed).

Cassidy, G.E. and S. Linnegar. 1982. *Growing Irises*. Timber Press, Portland, OR. 160 p.

Caillet, M. and J.K. Mertzweiller. 1988. *The Louisiana Iris, the history and culture of five native American species and their hybrids*. Texas Gardener Press, Waco, TX. 225 p. A must for Louisiana iris gardeners.

Dykes, W.R. 1912. *Irises*. Present Day Gardening Series. (out of print) 110 p.

Dykes, W.R. 1913. *The Genus Iris*. Dover Books (1975, reduced facsimile from 1913 publication). A classic.

Kohlein, F. 1987. *Iris*. Timber Press, Portland, OR. 370 p. This was originally published in Germany in 1981, translated and released in America in 1987. The best of the modern treatises on the genus.

Manuscripts:

Brearley, Christopher. 1985. The crested irises of North America. *The Plantsman* 7(2):114-115.

Hermes, A.R. 1993. Crested iris. *Horticulture* 71(2):80.

Hewitt, J. 1996. *Iris sibirica*. *The Garden* 121(6):340-344.

Hoog, M.H. 1980. Bulbous irises. *The Plantsman* 2(3):141-164.

Hudak, Joseph. 1976. The iris of May. *Horticulture* 54(5):37-39.

Ingram, John and William J. Dress. 1968. The Louisiana irises and Hortus Third. *Baileya* 16(2):92-97.

Lamb, J. 1992. An eye for Iris. *Horticulture* 70(5):42-47.

Leslie, A. 1992. *Iris pseudacorus*. *The Garden* 117(5):204-206.

Lloyd, Christopher. 1986. A pride of Iris. *Horticulture* 64(12):21-25.

Mackintosh, Esther. 1983. The americanization of Japanese iris. *Horticulture* 61(2):23-25.

Mathew, B. 1993. *Iris chrysographes*. *The Plantsman* 14(4):193-196.

Mathew, B. 1993. The spuria irises. *The Plantsman* 15(1):14-25.

Mathew, B. 1993. The cheerful Algerian. *The Garden* 118(11):513-515.

Miller, A.M. 1993. Siberian iris. *Fine Gardening* 33:46-48.

Service, N. 1988. Bearded irises: comments on the species in section iris. *The Plantsman* 10(1):6-26.

Service, N. 1990. Winter flowering irises, series Unguiculares. *The Plantsman* 12(1):1-9.

Weiler, John. 1986. The saga of remontant SDB. *The Garden* 111(10):475-477.

Weiler, J. 1993. Reblooming irises. *Fine Gardening* 30:44-46.

White, Ann Blanco. 1984. Trial of *Iris spuria* cultivars 1984. *The Garden* 109(12):519-521.

White, Anne Blanco. 1985. An iris for all seasons. *The Garden* 110(12): 573–576.

Associations:

Society for Siberian Irises, 631 G24 Highway, Norwalk, IA 50211.
The American Iris Society, 6518 Beachy Ave, Wichita, KS 67206.
  Publication: *Bulletin of the American Iris Society*.

## *Ixia* (iks-ee′ a)  Wand Flower, Corn Lily  Iridaceae

The corn lilies are native to the Cape Province of South Africa and are rather uncommon in American gardens. Flowers arise from corms planted 2–3″ deep after the last frost. Plants can survive a winter temperature in the upper 20's but really should be thought of as frost-free plants. They are winter hardy only from zone 9 south but with winter protection, may survive in zone 8. Soils with a basic pH are preferable and lime should be incorporated in acid soils prior to planting. The common name, wand flower, refers to the thin, wiry stems which wave in the wind while the other common name, corn lily, is in reference to the plants appearing in grassy fields.

About 45 species are known, but the corms offered in catalogs are hybrids developed by Dutch nurserymen. The plants have 8–12″ high wiry stems and narrow, grass-like leaves. The cup-shaped flowers are composed of 6 brightly-colored segments, and a spike of 9–12 blooms is produced from each corm. The colors are bold and brilliant, ranging from white with a blue, red, or purple center to yellow and red forms usually with an eye of a different color.

Corms are inexpensive and the resulting flowers are gorgeous. They are worth trying, even as annuals, to add brightness to the late spring and early summer garden. They are excellent container plants, and container and all can be moved to a protected site during the winter, if necessary. Alternatively, they may be treated as gladioli and removed in fall, stored in a cool place and replanted in the spring. At this time, the small cormels may be removed.

These are fun plants, to be placed where they can be admired, costing little and returning lots.

**Cultivars:**

'Afterglow' has orange flowers with dark red centers.
'Bluebird' produces white flowers with deep blue centers.
'Bridesmaid' bears white flowers with a red eye.
'Hogarth' has creamy yellow flowers with a purple eye.
'Marquette' consists of deep yellow flowers with purple tips.
'Rose Emperor' bears rose-pink flowers with a deeper colored eye.
'Uranus' makes dark yellow flowers with red centers.

'Venus' consists of magenta flowers with a darker center.
'Wonder' produces pink double flowers.

**Related Species:**

*I. maculata* has yellow flowers with black spots on the throat.

*I. paniculata* bears 6-12 large (1-1½" wide) creamy white to yellow flowers.

*I. viridiflora*, green ixia, is one of the more interesting species. Plants have 1-2" wide flowers consisting of extraordinary blue-green petals with a purple-black eye.

## *Ixiolirion* (iks-io-lir' ee-on)     Siberian Lily     Amaryllidaceae

This small group of bulbous plants occurs in fields and rocky hillsides in western and central Asia at altitudes up to 8000 ft. Some authorities recognize four species while others believe that all plants are variants of *I. tataricum*.

| *-tataricum* (tar-tar' i-kum) | Siberian Lily | 12-20"/18" |
|---|---|---|
| Spring     Blue | Central Asia | Zones 7-9 |

(Syn. *I. montanum*)

The 3-8 linear leaves give rise to a spreading inflorescence (umbel) of 4-6 sky blue, lily-like blossoms on slender, rounded stems. The flowers bear segments with 3-5 dark lilac ribs. They should be lifted (like gladioli) when planted north of zone 7. They are hardy to 5° F but require sunny, well-drained sheltered positions. In the South, winter drainage is most important as bulbs rot if soil does not drain rapidly.

Similar to other half-hardy minor bulbs, *Ixiolirion* is inexpensive and can be used even as an annual. Many of the minor bulbs are hidden treasures which will be discovered only with a little plant exploration of our own.

# J

*Jeffersonia* (jef-er-son′ ee-a)        Twinleaf        Berberidaceae

"Though an old man, I am but a young gardener" summarizes the thoughts of many of us who find that the more we learn, the more we understand how little we know. The above quote is attributed to Thomas Jefferson, one of America's best known naturalists and gardeners who also just happened to be the third President of the United States. Twinleaf, *J. diphylla*, commemorates Mr. Jefferson, and refers to the way in which each leaf is deeply cleft into two leaf "twins." The 1″ wide white flowers grow singly on leafless stems, changing into a small pear-shaped pod which comes off like a lid. The leaves are small at flowering time and reach full size when the fruits mature.

Plants are native from New York and southern Ontario to Wisconsin, Iowa and south to Alabama. They naturally flower in April and May and in the garden should be placed in partial shade and moist soils. They grow best in limestone soils and benefit from the addition of lime in the spring. My friends, Norm and Doris Giles, who garden in the acid soils of north Georgia, place a few marble chips around the plants, which provide some alkalinity consistently over time. Their plants look a great deal better than mine. Don't even think about digging these from the wild, or the President will come back to get you. Good native nurseries are producing plants from seed and they are becoming more available as demand rises.

### Related Species:

*J. dubia* flowers in late spring or early summer and is native to northeast Asia. The 2-lobed leaves are rounded to kidney-shaped with lavender flowers. They are handsome and appear to be more acid-tolerant than our native species.

*Juncus* (yung' kus)                    Rush                    Jungaceae

The rushes are not in every gardeners vocabulary. In fact, most people see them as some sort of aquatic weed, if they see them at all, or as Moses' hide-out. The flowers are small and consist of 3 petals and sepals (like lilies) and the leaves are usually cylindrical and often hollow. All of the approximately 225 species thrive in moist or wet locales and most belong in the wild, not in the garden. They are useful around semi-natural ponds where they aid in providing stability to the soil. They are also useful as bird cover in aquatic areas. Recently, 2 or 3 rushes have found their way into various catalogs and nurseries and are being touted as reasonable garden plants for the boggy or pond area. They still look like aquatic weeds to me. Regardless, they require sun to partial shade and should not be immersed in water more than 3″ deep.

*J. effusus*, common rush, is probably the best known species and tolerates conditions from zones 4–9. Plants are stemless, all the leaves being basal, and they grow 18–30″ tall. They become yellowish in the fall, turn brown and then disappear. The species has some ornamental value but one selection seems to have caught on. 'Spiralis' is known as corkscrew rush because each leaf looks like a green corkscrew. Although they will survive dry conditions, continuous moisture is much preferred. They are best planted in containers that can be constantly wet or on the edges of ponds. The growth habit is essentially prostrate and resembles a squirming octopus in need of euthanasia. Children are said to like this plant, but they also like pulling wings off of butterflies. Who can trust them? Curious is an apt word, interesting and unusual also fit. Perhaps that is enough. Hardy in zones 7–9.

'Carmen's Grey', blue rush, sends up bluish stems which grow about 12″ long. Plants provide yellow fall and evergreen winter garden interest and appear to be more tolerant of drier soils, although moist conditions are still appreciated. 'Carmen's Japanese' may be the same thing but the stems don't appear as bluish grey. Both (or the one) come from Ed Carmen of Carmen's Nursery in Los Gatos, California.

# K

*Kaempferia* (kem-fer-ee′ a)     Peacock Ginger     Zingerberidaceae

A genus of plants especially designed for the hot, humid areas of zones 8–10, absolutely unknown elsewhere in the country. They are one of the most attractive genera in the ginger family, and are known as peacock gingers due to their patterned leaves. A few have no pattern, but some are strikingly similar to the houseplant known as Prayer Plant, *Maranta*. Although the leaves are attractive, the small purple or purple and white flowers, which bloom spring through summer, are also appealing. The majority are less than 12″ tall and are highly desirable ground covers for deep shade.

I was shown the fine collection of *Kaempferi* at Mercer Botanical Garden near Houston, TX by their fine horticulturist, Linda Gay. Since I was an obvious neophyte to the genus, she took pity on me and showed me some of the better forms. I thought the green-leaved, non-patterned form, *K. pulchra* var. *mansonii*, was terrific, covering lots of ground and bearing clean, deep green leaves and lots of lavender flowers. But many fine patterns occur in this low grower, including 'Bronze Peacock', with bronze-patterned foliage, and 'Roscoe', whose large leaves and white patterns were most handsome. *K. gilbertii* has narrow, white-marginate leaves and purple and white flowers, while *K. atro-virens* has striking silver patterns on the bronze. 'Brownie' bears chocolate-brown leaves with a small amount of silver. Both have small purple and white flowers.

If I lived in the Southwest or in Florida, I definitely would learn all I could about the genus. With moisture and shade, they are equal to any ground covers found elsewhere.

**Additional Reading:**

Chapman, Timothy. 1994. *Ornamental gingers*. A small but wonderful book on the many of the most ornamental gingers, including *Kaempferia*. Published by the author and available through him at 6920 Bayou Park Road, St. Gabriel, LA 70776.

## *Kalimeris* (kal-i-mer′ is)                Kalimeris                Asteraceae

This group of about 10 species is from eastern Asia and consists of alternate leaves and white to lavender flowers. Few differences occur between *Kalimeris*, *Boltonia* and *Aster*, and all can be fine flowering plants. I was asked to identify some plants which could have been any of the 3 genera and found that only by looking closely at the structures of the flower through a 10X scope, could I even make an intelligent guess. It seemed to be that there must be characteristics relatively easy to distinguish, otherwise why not stick them all in a single genus. None of the distinguishing details were easy to evaluate, but with the help of the scope, the bracts around the flowers (involucre bracts) and the little hairs attached to them (pappus bristles) could be seen. The term *scarious* means thin, dry and often translucent. For what it is worth, here are some of the differences.

| | |
|---|---|
| *Aster* | margins not scarious, unequal, overlapping in 2, usually many series, pappus bristles uniform |
| *Boltonia* | margins scarious, equal, overlapping in 1–3 series, pappus bristles non-uniform |
| *Kalimeris* | margins scarious, equal, overlapping in 2, usually many series, pappus bristles uniform |

Only two species of *Kalimeris* are found in cultivation.

**-*pinnatifida*** (pin-a-tif′ i-da)          Japanese Aster          1–2′/2′
    Summer                    White          Japan                    Zones 4–8
(Syn. *Asteromoea mongolica*)

In talks I present or lists of plants I make, this plant goes near the top of "no-brainers": one which can be planted without fear of failure. I have seen this double white-flowered sun-loving plant from Vermont to south Georgia, Washington to California, and have seldom been disappointed. Most of the leaves are pinnately lobed (pinnatifid) although upon examination, some of the leaves are entire. The double white flowers with their yellow stamens

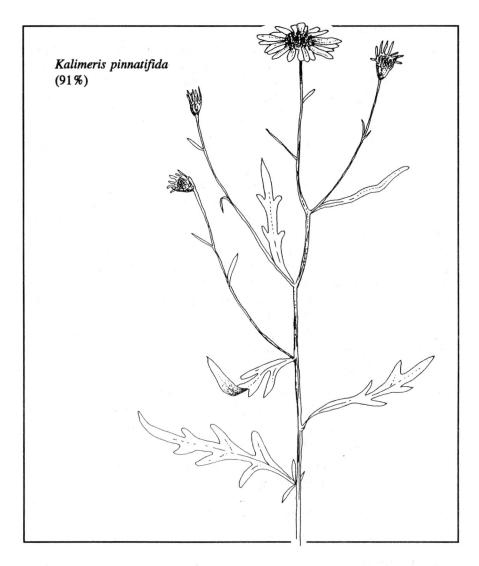

*Kalimeris pinnatifida*
(91%)

sometimes start out single but as plants mature throughout the season, flowers are double.

Other than its remarkable adaptability, there is nothing particularly spectacular about the plants. It is their ability to be totally ignored and abused that endears them to gardeners. If gardeners are confused about what plant to begin with, I recommend this one.

They are best suited to sunny conditions but also do well in partial shade. Even in the shaded Armitage garden, plants are always one of the best performers.

**Related Species:**

*K. incisa* has single starry lavender flowers with yellow centers and oblong-lanceolate leaves. Plants grow about 2' tall and are also excellent garden performers. Hardy in zones 4–8.

## *Kirengeshoma* (ki-reng-ge-show' ma)   Yellow Waxbells   Hydrangeaceae

Only one or two species have been described in this genus and only *K. palmata*, yellow waxbells, has been introduced to gardeners in America. Reports on garden performance have been mixed, and those who do well with it extoll its virtues. However, many gardeners have struggled. It is definitely a plant which should not be given up after a single failure.

| *-palmata* (pahl-may' ta) | | Yellow Waxbells | 3–4'/4' |
|---|---|---|---|
| Summer | Yellow | Japan | Zone 5–7 |

The opposite, 7–10 palmately lobed foliage is hairy and toothed around the margins and is possibly the best part of this plant. The basal leaves are 6–7" wide, while those near the top are smaller and sessile. The leaves are carried on thinly branched stems, the tops of which often have a purplish cast when sunlight falls upon them. The 1½" long, waxy, bell-shaped flowers may be found nodding from the axils of the topmost leaves in late summer and fall. Unfortunately, individual flowers start to turn brown at the edges in a matter of days. There are usually 3 flowers in each inflorescence (cyme) and the weight of the flowers and subsequent fruit causes stems to bow to the ground. Waxbells produce the "Stephen King" of fruit. Three long pointed horns protrude from a brownish green swollen capsule; the effect is enough to cause a nightmare.

Plants are cold hardy to zone 5 but have not been grown enough in the South to determine heat tolerance. I have tried it and it quickly surrendered to the elements. Native to cool woodland areas, its performance is dubious further south than zone 7. Great care must be taken in choosing a site. One in semi-shade, sheltered from strong winds, in a constantly moist but not boggy area, with an abundant source of organic matter and an absence of lime should be chosen.

*Kirengeshoma* has been called a "rarity for the connoisseur." This is a plant for those interested in experimentation, and with a willingness to fail several times before being successful. An unusual plant from its bowed gracefulness to its horned fruit, it adds a touch of grace to the shade garden.

Propagate by division after 3–5 years only if necessary. Allow plants to remain undisturbed for as long as possible.

**Related Species:**

*K. koreana,* native to Korea, may grow to 6' tall. The narrow petals of the soft yellow flowers turn upward at the tips.

**Additional Reading:**

Chatto, Beth. 1986. Kirengeshoma. *Horticulture* 64(9):34–35.

## *Knautia* (not-ee' a)          Knautia          Dipsacaceae

Well known to Europeans as a hedgerow or meadow plant, the pale purple-blue flower heads of field scabious (*K. arvensis*) attracts little interest in gardening circles. However, one of its relatives in this genus of 60 or so members has attracted a considerable following as a short-lived but colorful garden plant. The flower heads of *K. macedonica* resemble pincushion flower (*Scabiosa*) but they are deep purple, rather than lavender or pale yellow. The old name for the plant (*Scabiosa rumelica*) is still used in catalogs and gardens. The leaves are entire at the base of the plant but pinnately lobed as they ascend the stem.

Plants work well in the Northeast and coastal Northwest, but they not terribly tolerant of warm nights. Plants start out neat and tidy in the spring, growing to a height of about 2–3', but as hot days of July unfold, they can become stretched, flobbing miserably by mid summer. This in no way precludes plants from the garden, and where appropriate, a single cut back in mid spring helps plants retain a little dignity later on. Leave 12–15" of growth behind. I have had no success keeping plants more than 2 years, 3 years may be pushing it even in cool climates. Hardiness is from zone 4–7.

Plants can be propagated from seed if placed in moist containers at 70–72° F.

## *Kniphofia* (nee-fof' ee-a)     Red Hot Poker, Torchlily     Liliaceae
(Syn. *Tritoma*)

The 60–70 species are characterized by basal tufts of long, coarse, V-shaped, sword-like leaves and spike-like inflorescences of bright, shortly stalked flowers. Although best known for orange-red flowers, species and cultivars occur with green, coral, yellow, red, scarlet, and bicolor blooms. Torchlilies may be as small as 18" (*K. macowanii,* Macawon torchlily), to the 8' giant hybrids. Many of the plants in today's gardens are *K. uvaria,* common torchlily, whose red flowers become yellowish green as they mature. Flowers on the upper half of the spike are still opening and bright red, while the lower ones are finished and yellow green and the spike is often described as two-tone. Many cultivars have been raised from seed, resulting in a much variation. New Zealand is one of the finest areas in the world to see torch lilies. Numerous fine cultivars are grown there such as 'Apricot Torch', 'Winter Gold' and 'Winter Torch'. The bold magnificent deep orange spires of *K. uvaria* and *K. praecox* dominate roadsides and gardens in June and July.

| *-uvaria* (oo-vah' ree-a) | | Common Torchlily | 3–5'/4' |
|---|---|---|---|
| Late Spring | Red | South Africa | Zones 5–8 |

The gray-green evergreen foliage is 18–36" long and sharply pointed. After the flowers senesce, the leaves decline and plants can be an eyesore. Cut the foliage about halfway back to improve appearance without injury. The flower stems must be removed after flowering to insure continued bloom, to say nothing of the dead flowers detracting from those newly emerged. In the Horticulture Gardens at the University of Georgia, 20 flower stems, which emerge from our original clump of 3 seed propagated plants, dominate the late spring garden. Flowers open as early as May 10 in the garden, but late May and early June are more common in zone 7. Plants require full sun, and do not tolerate wet feet. In zones 5 and 6, the foliage can be tied over the crown of the plant in the fall to exclude water, which may subsequently freeze and kill the plant.

Seed of *K. uvaria* should be placed at 40° F temperatures for at about 6 weeks. Germination will be erratic but seedlings should begin to emerge within 3 weeks. Keep soil moist and out of direct sunlight. Retain the seed tray for 3 months before discarding.  Plants flower the second year. Cultivars and hybrids may also be divided in the fall.

### Cultivars:

Occasionally a few other species are offered, but some fine hybrids are presently available to extend the choice of flowering season, height, and color. The parentage is confused but *K. uvaria, K. galpinii, K. praecox* and *K. macowanii* appear to have taken some liberties with each other. Most flower in late spring and early summer.

'Ada' has 3–4' tall upright deep orange-yellow spikes.

'Alcazar' bears bright red flowers with a hint of salmon in early summer on 3–4' tall stems.

'Border Ballet' is a 2' tall mixture of plants bearing flowers of red, pink, yellow and creamy white.

'Bressingham Comet' has flowers of yellow and bright red on 2' tall plants.

'Bressingham Sunbeam' bears soft yellow candles, the plants growing only 2' tall.

'Candlemass' produces rush-like foliage with yellow-orange flowers. About 3' tall.

'Cobra' grows about 3' tall with dark bronze flower buds which give way coppery yellow flowers. From Bressingham Gardens.

'Corallina' bears coral-red flowers in late summer and fall on 2' tall stems.

'Earliest of All' blooms in early summer with orange-red and yellow flowers. Plants grow 18–24" tall.

'Fairyland Hybrids' are a group of seed-propagated plants with orange flowers in late spring. About 2–3' tall.

'Glow' ('Coral Sea') blooms with pastel coral-red flowers on 2–3' tall plants in late summer.

'Gold Mine' is about 3' tall and bears golden amber yellow flowers.

'Ice Queen' is an excellent foil to stronger colors in the garden, as are all the white-flowered forms. The heads are creamy white to pastel yellow, growing about 5' tall.

'Innocence' blends copper-orange flowers which turn pastel yellow and finally to creamy yellow on narrow inflorescences. Two to three feet tall.

'Little Maid' was bred by Beth Chatto of Essex, England and opens yellow, fading to creamy white. Growing only 18–24" tall, it looks terrific in containers as well as the garden.

'Maid of Orleans' has ivory flowers on 2' tall stems. Against a dark background, it stands out without being as garish as some of the screaming scarlet flowered forms.

'Paramentier' is a 3–4' tall plant with dozens of reddish orange to salmon flower stalks.

'Pfitzeri' ('Wayside Flame') has flaming orange-red flowers up the stem in late summer and fall.

'Primrose Beauty' grows 3' tall with primrose yellow flowers. A stunning plant.

'Primrose Mascot' bears primrose yellow flowers in mid summer on 2–3' tall plants.

'Rosea Superba' has rose-red flowers on 2½–3' tall plants.

'Royal Castle' grows 2–3' tall with vibrant yellow-orange flowers.

'Royal Standard' bears scarlet buds which open to bright yellow flowers.

'Samuel's Sensation' produces scarlet flower heads on tall 5' plants.

'Shenandoah' is one of the more cold-hardy cultivars, blooming with an orange top and yellow base in early summer.

'Shining Scepter', a Bloom cultivar, grows about 3' tall with golden tangerine flowers in mid summer.

'Springtime' has upper flowers of coral red tipped yellow and muted yellow basal flowers. 'Royal Standard' and 'Springtime' are 3–4' tall.

'Sunningdale Yellow' is outstanding, bearing wide candles of deep yellow. Plants grow about 3' tall.

'Underway' produces apricot-orange flowers in midsummer.

'Vanilla' has grassy foliage with creamy white flowers in summer on 2–3' tall plants.

'White Fairy' produces large creamy white flowers on robust 3' tall plants.

**Additional Reading:**

Taylor, Jane. 1985. Kniphofia, a survey. *The Plantsman* 7(3):129–160.

Redgrove, H. 1987. Winter flowering kniphofias in New Zealand. *The Plantsman* (Letters to the Editor) 9(3):190–191.

## *Kosteletzkya* (kos-tel-lets-kee' a)    Virginia Mallow    Malvaceae

A relative newcomer which native plant enthusiasts gush over, *K. virginica* resembles *Hibiscus* but with small pink flowers. Plants are native from Florida to Texas and north to southern New York. *K. virginica* is the best known of the 30 or so species and its common name, seashore mallow, reflects its common habitat.

Plants grow 3–4' tall with hairy foliage and bear solitary pink flowers from mid summer through fall. Although tolerant of marshy conditions, plants also grow well in common garden soils.

Full sun is necessary. Propagate by seed or division.

# L

*Lamiastrum* see *Lamium galeobdolon*

*Lamium* (lay-mee' um)  Dead Nettle  Lamiaceae

Most of the approximately 50 species are considered weeds. Related to stinging nettle, *Urtica dioica*, but lacking the stinging hairs, they are known as dead nettles. The stems are often stoloniferous and creeping at the base, while the leaves are generally ovate to kidney-shaped. The most popular species is *L. maculatum*, an excellent ground cover for semi-shaded locations.

*Lamium* is easily propagated by cuttings throughout the season. Division may be accomplished at any time as long as adequate moisture is provided to the plantlets.

*-galeobdolon* (ga-lee-ob' do-lon)  Yellow Archangel  9–15"/18"
  Spring  Yellow  Europe, Western Asia  Zones 4–8
(Syn. *Lamiastrum galeobdolon, Galeobdolon luteum*)

Plants spread by short underground stolons and are best used where allowed to roam freely as they are difficult to keep under control. The 1–3" long leaves are oval, slender-pointed, and serrated. During late spring, spikes with whorls of 5–6 yellow flowers, each about ¾" long, arise from the leaf axils. Heavy to partial shade is best in the southern end of its range, but some direct sun is tolerated further north. Plants are useful for filling in heavily shaded areas where little else grows. If plants become leggy, just cut it back.

The "proper" botanical name keeps changing for this poor fellow. From *Lamium* to *Lamiastrum* to *Galeobdolon* and back to *Lamium*, no genus seems to want this plant. Regardless of its name, it is a hard working blue collar type which seems not to care where the eggheads put it.

Propagate by divisions or terminal cuttings.

*Lamium galeobdolon*
(56%)

## Cultivars:

'Compactum' is much more compact than the species, not growing as rapidly, and is useful for small areas.

'Confold Wood' produces golden yellow foliage in the spring and fades to green over the summer.

'Florentinum' is similar to 'Variegatum' and equally aggressive. The veins of the leaves turn red in the cool weather of fall and spring.

'Herman's Pride' was found by Herman Dykhousen of Holland while travelling in Yugoslavia. Plants are not nearly as spreading as 'Variegatum' and grow in upright clumps. Plants have smaller flowers and leaves and are less aggressive than the species. The foliage has beautiful silver markings between the green veins and is most striking. This is an excellent cultivar, particularly in the spring while the plants are still compact. As the summer progresses, plants become a little leggy but not nearly as much as the cultivars of *L. maculatum*.

'Silver Carpet' ('Silberteppich') has smaller, more silvery leaves than 'Variegatum' and is much less aggressive.

'Silver Spangled' has long running stems with silver splashed on the green leaves. Plants are intermediate in size between 'Herman's Pride' and the species.

'Variegatum' is the most common form with silver variegation running through the leaf blade while the midrib and margins remain green. It is a terrific plant suitable for the darkest areas of the garden.

## Related Species:

*L. orvala* is a clumping species, similar in habit though not as handsome as 'Herman's Pride'. Plants grow in 18″ clumps and bear red to purple axillary flowers. 'Album' produces large white flowers.

| *-maculatum* (mak-ew-lah′ tum) | | Spotted Nettle | 8–12″/18″ |
|---|---|---|---|
| Spring | Red to Purple | Europe, West Asia | Zones 3–8 |

The oppositely arranged, 1–2″ long leaves usually have white stripes or blotches beside the midrib. The purplish red flowers bloom at the end of the stem all summer and are partially lost in the leaves. Although some cultivars grow well as far south as zone 8, the species performs best in areas of cooler nights which keep growth more compact. In the summer in zones 7–9, plants become straggly and must be cut back to maintain some semblance of order. Provide an evenly moist, well-drained soil in partial shade. If plants repeatedly dry out, bare patches appear.

## Cultivars:

The species is seldom used in the United States, having been replaced by a number of selections with superior foliage.

'Album' has white flowers and a silver stripe in the middle of the green leaves.

'Aureum' has the same white midvein area as the species, but the rest of the leaf is a soft yellow. The flowers are light pink. It is not as aggressive and will not do well in full sun, particularly south of zone 7.

'Beacon Silver' ('Silbergroshen'), one of the most popular cultivars, has silver leaves surrounded by green margins. The foliage stands out well and catches the eye even in a shaded area. Flowers are pinkish purple. Occasionally the leaves are flecked with tiny purple dots, the result of a foliar disease. The stippling does little damage. Rather boring but an excellent performer.

'Beedham's White' has chartreuse foliage with handsome contrasting white flowers.

'Chequers' has a wide silver stripe in the middle of each leaf and deep pink flowers. It is similar to 'Beacon Silver' but with broader green margins. Plants are 9–12″ tall when in flower.

'Pink Pewter' bears soft pink flowers and silvery foliage with narrow green margins.

'Roseum' is similar to 'Chequers' but the leaves are wider and the flowers are paler pink.

'Shell Pink' has leaves with white blotches and large light pink flowers.

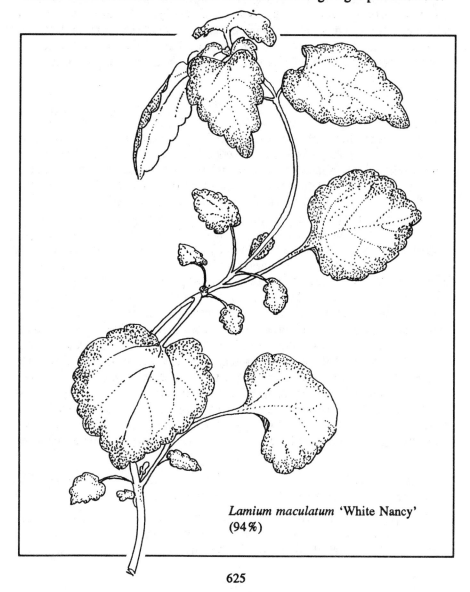

*Lamium maculatum* 'White Nancy' (94%)

'White Nancy' is 6–8″ tall and fills in rapidly. It has often been described as a white-flowering 'Beacon Silver'. The additional white of the flowers in the summer is particularly appealing. I thought this was one of the better forms but it loses vigor in areas of hot summers and has not lived up to expectations.

**Related Species:**

*L. album*, white dead nettle, has a more upright growth than *L. maculatum*. Some botanists lump the species together while others split them off because the leaves are more pointed and sharply toothed. The green foliage contrasts well with the white flowers. Not as aggressive as *L. maculatum* but worth trying. 'Goldflake' has leaves with golden stripes, 'Pale Peril' produces golden shoots in the spring, then fades to lime green as the summer progresses.

| *Lathyrus* (lath′ I-rus) | Sweet Pea | Fabaceae |
|---|---|---|

The genus consists of over 100 members, but unless one searches for seeds from specialists, it is almost impossible to find plants of more than one or two species for the garden. The annual sweet pea, *L. odoratus*, is best known as a colorful vigorous climbing vine whose tendrils provide support, allowing plants to grow up 10′ tall. A number of perennial species also occur. *L. grandiflorus*, two-flowered sweet pea, has spectacular 1½″ long rose-red flowers, and *L. latifolius*, everlasting sweet pea, bears flowers in many colors. It is native to Europe but has escaped and may sometimes be found growing wild in eastern United States. Many species are native to North America including the climbing purple-blue marsh pea, *L. palustris*, and *L. venosus*, showy wild pea, whose purple and white flowers are borne on stems up to 6′ long. Although known by botanists from Saskatchewan, south to Texas and east to Georgia, these plants are unfamiliar to gardeners. Not all members of the genus are climbers and a few non-viney participants are also known. *L. gmelinii* (syn. *L. luteus*) is a wonderful bushy plant, growing 12–18″ tall. The yellow to orange flowers are held in 4- to 12-flowered inflorescences (racemes) above the compound leaves. The most common and available species seems to be *L. vernus*, which bears the wretched common name of spring vetchling.

Most species tolerate winter temperatures to about 5° F; the most cold hardy to about −5° F, occasionally lower with good snow cover or mulch. Heat is a nemesis, and all species look best in early spring in most areas of the country.

| *-vernus* (ver′ nus) | | Spring Vetchling | 9–12″/18″ |
|---|---|---|---|
| Spring | Red to Violet | Europe | Zones 5–7 |

Two to three pairs of 1½–3″ long light green leaflets per leaf are produced on sparsely branched stems. In early spring, five to eight ¾″ long, reddish violet flowers are borne on short axillary racemes. The racemes are shorter than the leaves and may be lost in the foliage without a thorough search. Plants are deep rooted and thus able to tolerate drought. It is not a rapid spreader and the foliage dies down after flowering.

Although cold tolerant to zone 5, zone 4 with mulch, plants are not particularly heat tolerant. They have not performed well in zone 7b, and struggle to survive in hot summers everywhere in the country. In partial shade, plants did little more than survive, and in full sun, death was swift. The application of lime around the base of the plants or in the planting hole helps their performance.

To propagate, carefully divide the rootstock about 2 weeks after flowering. Use a sharp knife and allow at least one eye to remain on each piece of separated root. Seeds should be soaked in warm water overnight prior to sowing. Transplant when seedlings reach the 3–5 leaf stage. If seeds are sown in the spring, flowering occurs 1 year later.

### Cultivars:
'Albiflorus' has creamy white flowers with a hint of blue.

'Albo-roseus' bears rose and white flowers. This may occasionally be listed as 'Variegatus'.

'Cearulea' ('Cyanus') bears light blue flowers.

'Rose Fairy' has crimson-magenta flowers on 12–15′ tall plants. The shiny green foliage contrasts well with the flowers.

'Roseus' produces pink blossoms.

### Related Species:
*L. gmelinii* var. *aureus*, golden yellow vetchling, grows 18″ tall and bears light green leaves topped with erect heads of fawn or yellowish brown flowers. It was absolutely stunning in Edinburgh Botanic Garden. The quality of the foliage declines later in the season in all but the coolest areas of the United States.

### Additional Reading:
Norton, S. 1994. Survey of the genus *Lathyrus*, annual and perennial. *The Garden* 119(5):216–221.

## *Lavandula* (lav-an' dew-lah)          Lavender          Lamiaceae

Lavender is an indispensable herb and a surprisingly useful ornamental plant. All parts of common or English lavender, *L. angustifolia*, are fragrant and provide oils for the perfume industry. The genus name comes from the latin *lavo*, "I wash," referring to lavender water, long used as a fragrant wash. Lavender was also early recognized as a useful herb by Gerard who explained that flowers when "mixed with Cinnamon, Nutmegs, and Cloves, made into pouder, and given to drinke in the distilled water thereof, doth helpe the panting and passion of the heart, prevaileth against giddinesse, turning, or swimming of the braine, and members subject to the palsie." (*Gerard's Herbal*). Lavender farms still operate in England, France, and New Zealand for perfumes and potpourri.

The flowers are held in a terminal long stalked spike, usually blue or purple, sometimes white or pink. In general, the native habitat is on poor soils in dry and hilly areas, thus the need for excellent drainage is pre-ordained. Most are frost tender, although a few can be expected to be perennial if cold weather does not persist below 5° F. Winter protection should be provided in their northern limits.

**-angustifolia** (an-gust-i-fo′ lee-a)    Common Lavender          2–3′/3′
   Summer          Blue          Mediterranean Region          Zones 6–9
(Syn. *L. spica*, *L. officinalis*)

Two and one-half inch long, ¼″ wide opposite gray-green evergreen leaves occur on square stems. The 3–4″ long terminal flower spikes consist of 6–8 whorls of lavender flowers subtended by gray-green bracts. The fragrant flowers are often dried and used in potpourri. The plants are pretty enough to be included in the mainstream garden and need not be shunted off to languish in obscurity, visited only when flowers are to be sacrificed. They are superb for edgings, and the gray-green foliage calms even the harshest of leaf and flower colors.

Plants require full sun and well-drained soil. If soils are poorly drained, plants rot quickly. High humidity and lots of rain can also result in similar chaos, particularly in areas of hot summers. Pruning to 6–8″ in the spring results in vigorous new growth. For drying, pick flowers when showing color but before fully open. Hang them in a cool, dry spot.

Propagate by taking 3–4″ long cuttings of non-flowering shoots with a heel of older wood in the fall or early spring. Roots will appear in 14 days if placed in sand and mist. Remove cuttings from mist as soon as roots appear. Seed sown and placed in 70–75° F and humid conditions will germinate rapidly, although erratically. More uniformity will result by cooling the seed flat at 40° F for 2–4 weeks prior to placement in warm temperatures. I have lost enough plants to the vagaries of weather, both summer and winter, to propagate my favorite cultivars every year.

### Cultivars:
Selections have been based on improvements in flower color and habit. Some may be selections of lavandin, *L.* × *intermedia*, a hybrid between *L. angustifolia* and *L. latifolia*.

'Alba' produces creamy white flowers.
'Baby White' is one of the more handsome white-flowered forms. The plants are about 15″ tall, compact and free-flowering.
'Blue Cushion' has lavender-blue flowers on mounded plants which grow about 15″ tall.
'Fred Boutin' grows 15–18″ tall with violet-purple flowers over silvery foliage.
'Grappenhall' has long lavender-blue flowers on 2–3′ tall plants.
'Grey Lady' produces lavender-blue flowers and handsome silver-gray foliage.
'Grosso' bears large fat lavender flower spikes over 2–3′ tall mounded plants.

'Hidcote Blue' grows about 18″ tall and has deep purple flowers.

'Hidcote Giant' is similar to 'Hidcote Blue' but grows up to 4′ tall.

'Hidcote Pink' bears very light pink, almost white flowers. The whitish buds open to show the pink flowers.

'Irene Doyle' is sometimes called two seasons lavender because of its propensity to rebloom in the fall. This will happen if summer conditions do not stress it out too badly.

'Jean Davis' has pinkish white flowers, blue-green foliage, and is 10-15″ tall.

'Lavender Lady' is an excellent seed-propagated cultivar which flowers the first year from seed. The lavender-blue flowers are held over compact green foliage.

'Loddon Pink' is about 15-18″ tall with soft pink flowers.

'Mitcham's Grey' has dark violet flowers and gray foliage.

'Munstead Dwarf', which bears early lavender flowers, grows only 12″ tall.

'Provence' has lavender-blue flowers, and is a cultivar of *L.* × *intermedia*.

'Rosea' is a light pink flowered form, often used as an ingredient of Eau de Cologne. Cultivars sold as 'Hidcote Pink', 'Jean Davis', 'Loddon Pink' and 'Rosea' are difficult to tell apart.

'Royal Purple' bears long spikes of lavender flowers.

'Seal' can grow up to 4′ tall and bears long stems of pale lavender flowers.

'Sidonie' is a natural hybrid (parentage unclear) which occurred in a Sydney, Australia garden. It is unlike any other lavender, with fern-like foliage and long flower stems (2-3′) topped with rich blue flowers. Outstanding.

'Twickle Purple' has such a great name it should be fun to try. The flowers are light purple and the bushy plants grow 15-18″ tall.

'Woodbridge White' was recently released in New Zealand and bears an interesting mix of bicolor (lavender and white) flowers. Plants are also compact and do well in containers. Quite handsome. 'Woodbridge Snow' has a similar habit but flowers are white.

### Related Species:

*L. latifolia*, spike lavender, is similar to common lavender but has silver green foliage. Plants are fuller and grow 1-1½′ tall. Cold hardy to zone 6 or 7.

*L. stoechas*, French lavender, has purple flowers crowned with a cluster of ¾-1″ long, petal-like veined bracts. Well grown, these are among the most beautiful of the lavenders. In ssp. *pedunculata*, the flower stems (peduncles) are longer than the spikes and have rosy red bracts. The long bracts are the chief attraction of this unique flower. A white form, 'Alba', is also available. 'Swan River Pink' is a true pink from Swan Valley, Western Australia. Cold hardy to zone 7.

### Additional Reading:

DeWolf, Gordon P. 1955. Notes on cultivated Labiates. 5. *Lavandula*. *Baileya* 3:47-57.

Tucker, Arthur O. 1981. The correct name of lavandin and its cultivars (Labiatae). *Baileya* 21:131–133.

Tucker, Arthur O. and Karel J.W. Hensen. 1985. The cultivars of lavender and lavandin (Labiatae). *Baileya* 22(4):168–177.

*Lavatera* (lah-va-te' ra)  Tree Mallow  Malvaceae

The tree mallows are much more popular in Europe than in America, essentially telling us that the climate in much of this country is not to its liking. About 25 species of annuals, biennials and perennials are known, most native to the Mediterranean, Europe and California. The popular annual *L. trimestris* is popular in northern and western states, but the perennial forms have not really been embraced by American gardeners. The flowers of lavatera are similar to other members of the mallow family, and the differences between *Lavatera, Alcea* (hollyhock), *Malva* and *Sidalcea* can be found under *Alcea*.

The only lavatera I had grown prior to a few years ago was the annual, and while it was beautiful as could be, every insect and disease organism for miles around found it equally appealing. In more forgiving climates such as Gilroy, CA, I saw this same plant beautiful and only slightly ruffled. The perennial forms are not terribly perennial, stem hardy to zone 7, perhaps root hardy to zone 6 (5 with mulch and prayers), and are actually small to mid-size woody shrubs. In colder areas, they may die to the ground in the winter but new growth returns in the spring. Almost all the perennial forms offered are cultivars or hybrids of *L. thuringiaca*, the tree lavatera.

*-thuringiaca* (thur-inge-ee' a-ca)  Tree Mallow  5–7'/5'
  Spring  Pink  Southeastern Europe  Zones 6–9

A big plant for a big area, not to be shoehorned into a tiny space. The 3- to 5-lobed, heart-shaped to orbicular leaves are slightly hairy and 3–4" long. The stems become quite woody with age and the flowers are usually borne solitary in the upper part of the plant. Not at all difficult to grow, the plant is undemanding as to soil and rainfall, but requires full sun and a moderately well-drained location. Japanese beetles and mealy bugs can cause havoc, but they are far less disfigured than their annual cousin. The species is seldom grown, having been replaced by a number of cultivars.

### Cultivars:

Most authorities believe that the following are probably hybrids of *L. thuringiaca* and a similar species, *L. olbia*. All flower in late spring to early summer.

'Barnsley' is one of the more recent cultivars and probably the best one. Plants were introduced by Rosemary Verey of Barnsley Gardens, England, in 1986. They are 6–8' tall multistemmed shrubs with beautiful fringed flowers. The 2" wide flowers open white and fade to pink, each with a contrasting red eye. Sometimes flowers will revert to rose-red after a few years. If only a few stems revert, simply cut them off.

'Bredon Springs' has rich pink flowers with white centers borne on long spikes. Plants grow 5–6' tall and bear softly hairy leaves.

'Burgundy Wine' is shorter (about 3–5') and more sprawling in habit than 'Barnsley'. The flowers are vivid rose-purple to pink-purple.

'Candy Floss' has gray-green foliage and bright pink flowers on 3–4' tall plants. The flowers have a whitish center due to the white stamens.

'Ice Cool' ('Peppermint Ice') has handsome white flowers, occasionally fading to pink. The 3–5' tall shrubs bear light to gray-green foliage.

'Kew Rose', introduced in 1989, bears deep pink flowers with purplish stems. Plants can get big, up to 10' in height.

'Lisanne' was recently raised by Orchard Nurseries in Lincolnshire, UK from a cross between 'Ice Cool' and 'Barnsley'. White flowers with a pink eye are produced on 4' tall, well-branched plants.

'Shorty' is a terrific descriptive name for the plant habit, being much shorter than other cultivars. Plants grow 18–24" mounds consisting of many stems, with many light pink flowers.

'Wembdon Variegated' has marbled yellow and white leaves with dark pink flowers. Plants are about 6' tall.

**Related Species:**

*L. oblongifolia* is a dry-loving, gray-leaved plant native to southern Spain. Plants may grow for 2–3 years before the pink flowers occur, and even then do not flower until late summer or fall. The flowers arise in the axils, and the petals are deeper pink in the center than on the outside. Probably hardy to about zone 7.

*L. olbia*, also known as tree mallow, differs from *L. thuringiaca* mainly by having most flowers in long leafless racemes. They are native to the Mediterranean, therefore benefitting from low humidity and well-drained soils. The summer and fall flowers are normally deep red-purple, but a little lighter rose form, 'Rosea', is sometimes offered. Plants are 4–5' tall.

## *Leontopodium* (lee-on-toe-pod' ee-um)    Edelweiss    Asteraceae

After being weaned on Julie Andrews and the Von Trapp Family's stirring rendition of "Edelweiss" in the movie "The Sound of Music," I was ready to be stunned by the beauty of that mystical plant. After all, a plant which stirs the hearts of the Swiss and left the world with such passionate feelings should be at least as pretty as, say, a dandelion. I suppose in its mountainous habitat, edelweiss (*L. alpinum*) has its moments, but bringing it down to lowland gardens has done nothing for its mystique.

The silvery white woolly flowers are held within the silvery green downy leaves, which surround the flowers in the shape of a 3″ star. If plants are provided with alpine conditions, cool temperatures, sunny area and rocky soils, they will be all they can be. Many gardeners have such conditions, but for the rest of us, enjoy the movie and let well enough alone.

## *Lespedeza* (les-pe-dee′ za)     Bush Clover     Fabaceae

While technically shrubs, this group of plants behaves so much like an herbaceous perennial that it may be included with clear conscience. Approximately 40 species occur, all with alternate trifoliate leaves and pea-like flowers usually arranged in loose racemes. The plants used in American gardens have long pendant branches and are terrific growing on a bank, allowing the flowering stems to be better seen. Their late summer and fall flowering habit is also a bonus for tired gardens.

Propagate by divisions of the clump or from seed.

### *-thunbergii* (thun-berg′ ee-eye)     Thunberg Bush Clover     3–5′/5′
Pink, White     Fall     Japan, China     Zones 4–7

This is the real treasure of the group, having long (4–5′) pendant wiry stems which bear dozens of 6–8″ long racemes of rose-purple pea flowers. In the fall, when they are at their peak, the stems are so laden with flowers that they almost lie on the ground. In warm climates some summer flowering may occur, but the best is saved for the end. I have seen this plant in more and more gardens from Swarthmore, PA to lower Georgia. In the gardens of my Charlotte friend, Ann Armstrong, and my colleague in Athens, Mike Dirr, the plants have always been outstanding. While in flower they are spectacular, but they need room and can take over a substantial area in a heartbeat. A serious drawback is their tendency to reseed themselves and occasionally root at stem nodes which lie on the ground. They also can be rather messy looking when not in flower. The good news is that they can be whacked down to the ground in early spring, prior to new growth. Flowers occur on new wood and the plants are better for the punishment.

### Cultivars:
'Alba' ('Albaflora') bears good white flowers but the stems are not as arching as the species. More upright, less architectural.
'Gibralter' has long (4–5′) arching stems with vivid rosy pink flowers in terminal clusters.

### Related Species:
*L. bicolor*, differs by having smaller, less showy flowers earlier in the season, usually mid to late summer into early fall. All in all, useful but not outstanding. A white form, 'Alba', is also available.

## *Leucanthemum* see *Chrysanthemum* × *superbum*

## *Leucojum* (lew-ko' jum)　　　　Snowflake　　　　Amaryllidaceae

The snowflakes consist of 9–10 low-growing bulbous species with nodding white flowers. The predominately white flowers are responsible for the common name. They are divided into two distinct groups based on the appearance of the leaves. The hardy, robust and larger-flowered species have shiny strap-like leaves and include the popular spring and summer snowflakes, *L. vernum* and *L. aestivum*, respectively. The second group was a separate genus, *Acis*, but now shares the same roof. This group has thread-like leaves and is more difficult to establish. The only thread-leaf species cultivated to any extent is the autumn snowflake, *L. autumnale*. The autumn snowflake tolerates drier soils than the other species.

The flowers of all species consist of 6 segments, 3 outer and 3 inner of approximately equal size. They are white and tipped with green, yellow, or a tinge of red. Bulbs should be planted in the fall in large drifts, 3–5″ deep. Flowering begins the next spring, immediately after the snowdrops (*Galanthus*) and continues into early summer.

*Leucojum* is often confused with *Galanthus*, but a number of recognizable differences separate the genera.

|  | *Leucojum* | *Galanthus* |
| --- | --- | --- |
| Flower stalk | Hollow | Solid |
| Number of leaves | Numerous | 2–3 |
| Number of flowers | 2–5 | 1 |
| Flower segments | 2 equal groups | 2 unequal groups |

Snowflakes are better plants for the South than snowdrops. They tolerate partial shade but prefer a sunny location with adequate moisture. The bulbs should be left undisturbed for at least 3 years while they slowly increase. They can easilly be moved when overcrowded. Plants propagated from seed take 3–4 years to attain flowering size. The bulbs are inexpensive enough that seed propagation can be left to the breeders.

<u>Quick Reference to Leucojum Species</u>

|  | Number of flowers per flower stem | Flowering time |
| --- | --- | --- |
| *L. aestivum* | 2–8 | Mid Spring |
| *L. autumnale* | 1–3 | Late Summer |
| *L. vernum* | 1–2 | Early Spring |

**-aestivum** (ies' ti-vum)          Summer Snowflake          12–18"/10"
   Mid Spring          White          Central, Southern Europe          Zones 4–8

The name summer snowflake is a misnomer, for the species flowers only several weeks after *L. vernum*, spring snowflake. Three to five flowers usually occur on the hollow scape, each about 1" across, bell-shaped and drooping. The pure white segments are tipped inside and out with jade green. The dark green leaves are about ½" wide and 1–1½' long.

### Cultivars:

'Gravetye Giant' is a large-flowered cultivar useful when planting only a few bulbs in a small corner. It produces 1–1½" long flowers on taller stems and is worth the extra expense.

Var. *pulchellum* blooms earlier and has smaller flowers than the species, but otherwise is almost identical.

### Related Species:

*L. nicaeense*, also spelled *L. nicaense*, (syn. *L. hiemale*), Mentone snowflake, named after the town in France to where it is native, has 1–2 drooping rosy-white bells per stem appearing in April in the South. The stems are solid, unlike the hollow stems of *L. vernum* and *L. aestivum*. They are not hardy north of zone 7, and even there require protection.

**-autumnale** (ow-tum-nah' lee)          Autumn Snowflake          4–6"/6"
   Late Summer          White          Southern Europe, Mediterranean          Zones 5–8

Autumn snowflake does not have a large following because it is not as easily established as other species, not as easily found in garden catalogs, and more expensive. On the other hand, the flowers, described as "delicately flushed lilies-of-the-valley," open when small bulbs are most welcome. Other characteristics separate the species from the common snowflakes. The nodding ½–¾" long flowers are tinged with red and open in late summer in the South or early fall in the North. The thread-like leaves appear after the flowers and remain evergreen. The foliage dies away in early summer, and bulbs may be divided and moved. Bulbs are planted in the spring or early summer and are not usually available for fall planting.

Some gardeners throw their hands up in frustration when trying to establish this bulb, while others would not have a garden without it. Plants are native to dry, sandy soils and excellent drainage is a must. Size precludes it from areas other than the rock garden or small containers where it can be enjoyed on the patio or deck.

### Related Species:

*L. roseum* is 4–6" tall and bears pale pink to rose colored flowers in the fall. It is further distinguished by having a shorter flower stem and usually has only one flower per stem, compared to the 2–4 flowers commonly found on the stem of *L. autumnale*. The above two species are in the "I love a challenge" class. I am confident there are many gardeners who welcome such plants.

*-vernum* (ver' num)          Spring Snowflake          10–12"/10"
   Early Spring          White          Central Europe          Zones 3–9

This most accommodating snowflake seems to thrive in virtually all conditions. It overlaps the flowering time of snowdrops (*Galanthus*) in the

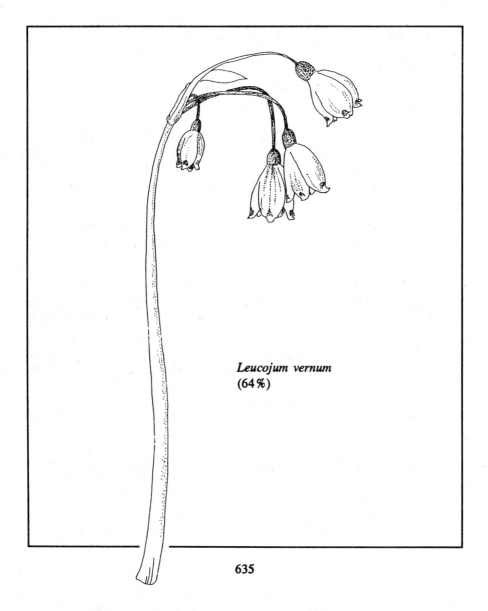

*Leucojum vernum*
(64%)

South and flowers about 2 weeks later in the North. The plant is not as tall but the leaves are a little broader (up to ¾" wide) than those of the summer snowflake. The flowers are white, drooping, and usually borne 1–2 per flower stalk. The white segments are tipped with green similar to *L. aestivum*.

Unfortunately in the past, there have been a number of instances where plants ordered as *L. vernum* turned out to be *L. aestivum*. There seems to be enough stock of both species and there need be no problem when dealing with an established bulb supplier.

### Cultivars:
Var. *carpathicum* usually bears 2 flowers per stem. Each flower is tipped with yellow rather than green. Most handsome.

Quick Key to Leucojum Species

    A. Leaves strap-like, flower in spring
      B. Flowers 2–8 (usually 2–5), open late
           spring, tipped green . . . . . . . . . . . . . . . . . *L. aestivum*
      BB. Flowers 1–2, bloom early spring, tipped green or yellow
         C. Flowers tipped green . . . . . . . . . . . . . . . . *L. vernum*
        CC. Flowers tipped yellow . . . . . . *L. vernum* var. *carpathicum*
    AA. Leaves thread-like, flower in late summer or fall . . . *L. autumnale*

### Additional Reading:
Elliott, J. 1992. *Leucojum*—the snowflakes. *The Plantsman* 14:70–79.
Mathew, B. 1992. *Leucojum tingitanum. Kew Magazine* 9(4):156–160.

## *Lewisia* (loo-is' ee-a)            Lewisia            Portulacaceae

It is fitting that this beautiful native western genus commemorates the great explorer, Captain Merriwether Lewis, who with his friend, William Clark, explored the Rockies and beyond in the early 1800s. The genus consists of approximately 20 species, and a few specialist nurseries, mainly in the Northwest, offer a fine selection to gardeners. However only one species, *L. cotyledon*, is commonly offered in the garden trade, the others being relegated to collectors' gardens.

Plants form tight symmetrical rosettes of spatulate (like a spatula), deep green, thick fleshy leaves. The showy flowers are usually pink-purple with dark stripes, although colors vary in any one population. Hybrids have been developed by breeders and hobbyists, and gardeners can enjoy yellow, red, orange, salmon, cream or white flowers. Dozens of flowers are produced, each consisting of 7–10 petals and many stamens, which are held in racemes or panicles.

Lewisias are almost unknown by gardeners in the East, and when they see them, they gasp in admiration, then assume something so beautiful would be impossible to grow. The fact is that lewisia is much tougher than it first appears, but not without problems. Plants don't have a prayer of survival in "normal" garden soils, no matter how well drained you think they may be. While lewisias are cold tolerant to about zone 6, they are susceptible to crown rot when moisture accumulates around the plant. A rock garden or addition of gravel to the soil or growing in gravel is one key to success in areas of summer rain and humidity. Full sun is also beneficial. Plants succeed well in stone walls, where light and drainage are optimized. My friend, John Elsley of Greenwood, SC, was successful with lewisia in the gravel path by his house. In Garden-in-the-Woods in Framingham, MA, plants look wonderful in their scree garden.

*L. cotyledon* is an evergreen species, as are *L. cantelovii* and *L. columbiana*, other species sometimes offered in the trade. However, a number are deciduous, such as *L. brachycalyx* and *L. oppositifolia*, which if available, are worth trying because they are dormant during wet winters.

**Cultivars and Hybrids:**
'Ashwood' strain is a mix of plants with red, apricot or yellow flowers.
'Edithae' is 3–4″ tall and has pink flowers with darker veins.
'George Henley', a hybrid between *L. columbiana* and *L. cotyledon*, bears dozens of wonderful brick red flowers.
'Kathy Kline' bears white flowers, but a mix with her name (Kathy Kline hybrids) consists of numerous colors.
'Norma Jean' produces pink flowers on 8–10″ tall plants.
'Paula' has lavender to pale purple flowers.
'Pinkie' (*L. cotyledon* × *L. longipetala*) has flowers in various shades of pink on relatively dwarf plants.
'Rose Splendour' has pale pink to rosy flowers.
'Trevosia' resulted from crosses between *L. columbiana* and *L. cotyledon* var. *howellii*. The handsome salmon-pink flowers are produced over fleshy dark green leaves.

## *Liatris* (lie′ a-tris)　　　　　Blazing Star　　　　　Asteraceae

Liatris sends up tall stems, at the end of each is an inflorescence of 15–45 oblong, usually purple flowers. Although belonging to the daisy family, the flowers consist of disc flowers only, and are very undaisy-like. Flowers provide architectural as well as botanical interest. They are one of the few cultivated flowers with the unusual habit of opening from the top of the inflorescence to the base (basipetally). The straight, strong stems carry narrow, entire, alternate foliage.

With the exception of *L. spicata*, species are often found on dry stony ground or on the edge of woods. Many are tolerant of poor, dry soils but are quite happy on fertile, well-drained soils; *L. spicata* requires more moisture than others.

*Liatris* experienced a meteoric rise as a cut flower in the 1980's and are still popular today. Few florists do not include gayfeather in bouquets and arrangements today, yet 10 years ago, this was not the case. Dutch flower exporters included it in the "Dutch Mix" sent to American florists and liatris soon became popular as a "Dutch" flower. The irony is that *Liatris* is native to North America, and in fact is a wild flower in much of this country! Growers in the United States are paying more attention to this plant as a viable crop for cut flower production.

The tuberous roots should be planted 4–6″ deep in well-drained soil in full sun. Plants associate well with *Rudbeckia, Monarda*, and *Echinacea*. All species are easily raised from seed which flower the following year. The tuberous roots may be lifted, cut with a sharp knife allowing at least one eye to remain, and replanted. Dust the cut ends with a fungicidal powder.

## Quick Reference to Liatris Species

|                  | Height (ft.) | Flower color |
|------------------|--------------|--------------|
| *L. pycnostachya* | 3–5          | Mauve        |
| *L. spicata*      | 2–3          | Mauve        |

*-pycnostachya* (pik-no-stak′ ee-a)    Kansas Gayfeather    3–5′/2′
  Summer    Mauve    Wisconsin to Louisiana and Texas    Zones 3–9

Largest of the cultivated species, this is arguably the least useful for the garden. The 10–15″ long lower leaves are lance-like and about ½″ wide and become reduced in size as they ascend the stem. The flower spike is 15–18″ long and consists of numerous ½–¾″ wide flowers along the length. Leafy bracts, often longer than the individual flowers, are produced under the flowers.

*L. pycnostachya* is too tall for most gardens and the spikes become so heavy they fall over, resulting in the growing end of the spike twisting upwards. Support is necessary, particularly in the second year. Plants should be treated as biennials, at least in the South. Experiments in Georgia indicate that 2 years of good performance was the norm, 3 years if conditions were perfect. Although problems exist, it flowers heavily and 12 flower stems per plant are not uncommon in the second year. The species is found in moist soils of the Great Plains but does not tolerate wet feet in winter. A well-drained, moisture retentive soil in full sun is necessary for best results.

**Cultivars:**
Var. *alba* has creamy white flowers.

**Related Species:**
  *L. aspera*, rough gayfeather, grows 3–4′ tall and bears 15–40 one inch wide rounded lavender flowers, each spaced well apart. The flowers occur

later than other species and is terrific cut fresh or dried. A favorite for many birds. It occurs from North Dakota to Ontario and Ohio in the north to Texas and Florida in the south.

*L. scariosa*, tall gayfeather, is similar with dense flower spikes. The leaves are quite smooth and the basal ones up to 2″ wide. The individual flower heads are distinctly stalked. Much of the material sold as *L. scariosa* is probably *L. aspera*. 'September Glory' bears purple flowers which open almost simultaneously. 'White Spire' is similar to 'September Glory' but has white flowers. Both are better garden plants than *L. pycnostachya*.

| *-spicata* (spi-kah′ ta) | Spike Gayfeather | 3–4′/2′ |
|---|---|---|
| Summer Mauve | Maine to Florida and Louisiana | Zone 3–9 |
| (Syn. *L. callilepis*) | | |

This is the best species for the garden, particularly some of the cultivars. The basal leaves are usually 10–12″ long and ½″ wide, progressively reduced in size up the stem. The inflorescence is 6–15″ long and individual mauve flower heads are sessile. The flowers are

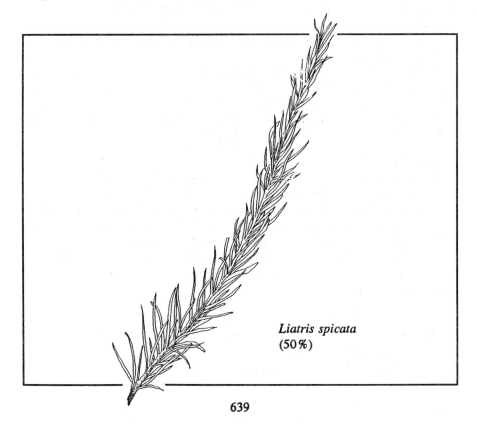

*Liatris spicata*
(50%)

excellent in the garden and even better if brought in as a cut flower. *Liatris* should be thought of in the same way gardeners think of gladioli. That is, the plants look fine until flowers are finished, then the plants begin to look shabby. It is not you, that's the way it is with liatris. Plants are sometimes found under the name of *L. callilepis*, which most authorities treat as a synonym of *L. spicata*, although some European taxonomists still treat it as a separate species.

Plants were trialed in the cut flower program at the University of Georgia. In the first year, plants were the same size as 'Kobold' and no support was necessary. The flowers were darker purple, and growth and yield were excellent. In the second year, however, plants grew 3–4' tall and required support to maintain straight spikes. Yield and quality of flowers were still excellent. It is a fine cut flower and should be produced by more commercial growers in this country.

## Cultivars:

'August Glory' has purple-blue flowers on 3–4' tall plants.

'Floristan White' is 3' tall and bears many creamy flowers. It performed well and showed no signs of decline after 4 years in Georgia tests.

'Floristan Violet' bears darker purple flowers than the species.

'Kobold' ('Gnome') is one of the finest selections for the garden. Plants are seldom taller than 2½' and multiple spikes of lilac-mauve flowers are produced in early summer.

'Silvertips', introduced by Carroll Gardens, has lavender blooms with a silver sheen. Plants are 3–4' tall.

Var. *montana*, native to the mountains of Virginia and North Carolina, is only 10–20" tall and bears ¾ " wide flowers on compact spikes. It can be found through wild flower specialists.

## Related Species:

*L. microcephela* performs well in dry soils and full sun. Plants grow up to 2' tall, although ours are around 18". The flowers are normal rose-purple, but the leaves are narrow and grass-like. Usually multi-stemmed and ornamental. A terrific plant for those who find *L. spicata* too tall. Native to the southern Appalachian Mountains, hardy in zones 6–9.

*L. mucronatum*, native to central and south Texas, bears 3–5' tall stems with lilac-mauve flowers. Superb specimens may be seen at the San Antonio Botanical Garden.

## Additional Reading:

Dress, William J. 1959. Notes on the cultivated Compositae. 3. *Liatris*. *Baileya* 7:23–32.

Gaiser, L.O. 1946. The genus *Liatris*. *Rhodora* 48:163–183, 216–263, 273–326, 331–362, 393–412.

*Libertia* (lee-bert' ee-a)           Libertia                    Iridaceae

*Libertia* have short creeping rhizomes (similar to *Iris*), long fibrous roots and evergreen foliage. Unfortunately, it is difficult to locate these plants, perhaps because they are so tender, being cold hardy only to zone 7b or 8. The flower consists of 6 segments, the 3 outer ones usually shorter, firmer and less showy than the inner ones. Of the eight species, *L. formosa* is most easily obtained, although occasionally a couple of others will surface. The subject of liverworts is not normally discussed in mixed company; however, a Belgian woman, Marie A. Libert, did some of the best work on these non-descript flowerless plants in the early 1800's. Ironically, she is now remembered for this genus with outstanding flowers.

*Libertia* is closely related to *Sisyrinchium* and *Diplarrhena*, but the segments of the former are all equal in size while in the latter, the inner segments are shorter than the outer.

*-formosa* (for-mo' sa)          Showy Libertia              15–20"/12"
   Spring           White          Chile                       Zones 7–9

The ¾" long white flowers are held in tapering 1' long inflorescences and remain effective for 3–4 weeks. The flowers are densely clustered, unlike other species whose flowers are loosely arranged. The 6–12" long sword-like leaves are about ½" wide and produced in a fan-like arrangement similar to leaves of *Iris*. Plants should be placed in full sun or partial shade in groups of at least a half dozen. I have admired this species in Europe but have not been successful with it in North Georgia, nor have I seen outstanding clumps anywhere but in the Northwest. Plants simply do not tolerate the heat and humidity during the summer, and the lack of summer vigor inhibits subsequent flowering the next spring.

Division of the rhizome is the easiest method of propagation, but seed may also be used. Plants require 2 years to flower from seed.

**Related Species:**

'Grandiflora' has flowers significantly larger than those of the species. The plant is also more robust, resulting in a better garden plant.

**Related Species:**

*L. ixioides* is native to New Zealand and bears three to eight 1" wide white flowers, often tinged green on the outside. The flowers are less densely arranged and have longer pedicels than *L. formosa*. It is difficult to establish in United States but is probably the loveliest species.

*L. pulchella* has white flowers similar to *L. formosa* but the foliage is much narrower, almost grassy. Hardy to zone 7 or 8.

*Ligularia* (lig-yew-layer' ee-a)          Ligularia          Asteraceae

These large plants may be 6' tall in flower and equally broad. Some, such as *L. dentata*, bigleaf ligularia, are grown for their attractive foliage, while *L. stenocephala*, narrow-spiked ligularia, also has attractive flowers. All species and cultivars must be grown in moist, cool areas. I have seldom seen well-grown plants south of zone 6; in fact, except for parts of New England, I have seldom seen plants of this genus look good for longer than a month anywhere east of the Rocky Mountains. In Michigan, if plants survived the cold winters, the hot summers were not to their liking. In North Georgia, plants look lovely in the spring but wilt every day during the summer and beg to be put out of their misery. To be fair, I have seen spectacular ligularia in proper sites, but those sites are not easy for the average gardener to provide. Around ponds, along stream banks, or wherever their roots can stay constantly moist and afternoon shade can be provided are potential locations.

Only a small number of the approximately 80 species are garden worthy. All have bright yellow daisy flowers held in a raceme or in a branched inflorescence just above the long-petioled leaves. Large alternately arranged leaves arise from the base and ascend the stem.

The petioles of the basal leaves completely encircle the stem with a short sheath. This encircling sheath separates *Ligularia* from the closely related genus *Senecio*. Propagation is primarily by division although seed may be sown when fresh.

Quick Key to Ligularia Species

|  | Height (ft.) | Leaf shape | Inflorescence shape |
|---|---|---|---|
| *L. dentata* | 3–4 | Kidney | Branches |
| *L. przewalskii* | 5–6 | Triangular | Raceme |
| *L. stenocephala* | 3–4 | Triangular | Raceme |
| *L. wilsoniana* | 4–6 | Kidney | Raceme |

*-dentata* (den-tah' ta)                    Bigleaf Ligularia          3–4'/4'
     Summer          Bright Orange          China                    Zones 5–8
(Syn. *L. clivorum*)

The long-stalked leaves are the best part of the plant. They are disk-shaped to kidney-shaped, up to 20" wide, and coarsely toothed. Large clumps of established plants are particularly impressive. The 2–5" diameter, bright orange flowers are held in branched corymbs. The 10–14 ray flowers are long and strap-like but always appear to be wilting even in moist growing areas. Personally, I think the flowers detract from the plant. Allow flowers to develop the first year to become familiar with the bloom, then remove the developing flower stalks in subsequent years. However, if you are lazy like me, the flowers come and go without great fanfare.

Grow plants in cool, moist conditions or not at all. Although plants recover from constant wilting, too many other lovely plants are available to allow these to tie up garden space unless the correct site is available.

## Cultivars:

'Dark Beauty' has very dark leaves with bright orange flowers.

'Desdemona' is one of the most popular cultivars, bearing large deep purple foliage. Leaves are beet red upon emergence in the spring, become green on top but remain purple on the undersides as they mature. They are more compact than the species.

'Golden Queen' is similar but with bright orange flowers.

'Gregynog Gold' (*L. dentata* × *L. veitchiana*) has bright orange flowers held on an upright, conical inflorescence over richly veined heart-shaped serrated leaves. Plants can reach 6' tall. Developed in Wales, it is seldom seen in commercial catalogs in this country.

'Moorblut' ('Moor's Blood') bears deep purple foliage and orange flowers.

'Orange Princess' has green leaves and light orange blooms.

'Othello' is similar to 'Desdemona' but not as compact and with smaller flowers. There is not, however, a great deal of difference between them.

'Sommergold' has deep orange flowers.

## Related Species:

*L. hodgsonii*, Hodgson's ligularia, is similar to *L. dentata* but grows only 2–3' tall. Leaves are tinged purple on the undersides and green and hairy on top.

*L.* × *palmatifolia* is a hybrid between *L. dentata* and *L. japonica*, a species with palmately divided leaves. The hybrid is intermediate with lobed rounded foliage. They are about 5' tall and have golden yellow flowers in late summer. Hardy to about zone 6.

| *-stenocephala* (sten-o-seph' a-la) | Narrow-Spiked Ligularia | 3–4'/5' |
|---|---|---|
| Summer          Yellow | Japan, North China | Zones 5–8 |

Unlike *L. dentata*, this species is better known for flowers than foliage. The purplish flower stems end in spike-like 12–18" long racemes bearing many 1–1½" wide bright yellow flowers. The light green leaves are triangular to heart-shaped with coarse triangular teeth around the margin. The large leaves (up to 1' long and as wide) lose abundant amounts of water on warm days resulting in wilted foliage. It is one of the earliest flowering ligularia.

This is a popular form of ligularia and is a classic garden plant where moist conditions can be maintained. That it wilts during hot days is simply something to accept, the rewards of contented plants more than makes up for it. However, seldom are plants content south of zone 6. Regardless of zip code, moist soil conditions, cool nights and afternoon shade are necessary. They do not require dividing but if additional plant material is needed, division should be accomplished in early spring or middle fall. Copious amounts of water must be provided for plantlets to become established.

**Cultivars:**
'The Rocket' is more compact, and has 18–24" long upright racemes of
  smaller lemon yellow flowers. The long spikes are useful design compo-
  nents in the garden. It may also be listed as a cultivar of *L. przewalskii*.
'Weihenstephan' is similar to 'The Rocket' but has larger gold flowers.

**Related Species:**
  *L. przewalskii* (sha-val' skee-eye), Shavalski's ligularia, is named after the Russian explorer, Nicolai Przewalski. Plants are similar and the two species are often confused. Both are native to northern China, bear spike-like yellow flowers and dark flower stems. However, the stems of *L. przewalskii* are blacker and the leaves are palmately cut, not heart shaped. The plant is taller and usually has five ray florets in each flower compared with three in *L. steno-cephala*. Plants are used like 'The Rocket' and equally effective.
  *L. macrophylla* has large, wide, sword-like leaves like no other. The bluish leaves are attached to the stem by obvious winged petioles. The many yellow flowers are about 1" wide and held in dense crowded panicles. Growing 4–5' tall, these are handsome, impressive plants.

| | | | |
|---|---|---|---|
| *-wilsoniana* (wil-son-ee-ah' na) | | Giant Groundsel | 4–6'/4' |
| Summer | Yellow | China | Zones 5–8 |

One of the many species named for "Chinese Wilson," Ernest Henry Wilson, this plant bears dark green kidney-shaped basal leaves with sharp serrations. The yellow daisy flowers are held in a long raceme in July to August. It can be distinguished from other raceme-bearing plants by having circular hollow petioles.
  Like other ligularias, cool weather and moist conditions are beneficial, but this little known species deserves more use.

**Related Species:**
  *L. tussilaginea*, green leopard plant, is totally unpronounceable but fortu-nately the pundits have declared the more precise name, *Farfugium japonicum*, to be correct. The rounded glossy green leaves are usually left alone by insects and diseases, but that is about the best that I can say about it. While there is nothing particularly wrong with the plant, it is just kind of a "green thing." Plants tolerate drier conditions than most other species, although moisture is

still preferred. The better known cultivar, 'Aureo-maculata', leopard plant, is splashed with yellow dots and looks like a "green thing" with ugly yellow spots. Yellow daisies top the plants in mid to late fall. Hardy in zones 7-9.

*L. siberica*, as the name implies, is cold hardy to around zone 3. The numerous daisy-like yellow flowers are 1-2" wide over rounded green leaves with handsome silver-white backs. Moisture is necessary.

<u>Quick Key to Ligularia Species</u>

A. Inflorescence cylindrical and spike-like
    B. Leaves palmately cut, stems black . . . . . . . . *L. przewalskii*
    BB. Leaves not palmately cut, stems purple
        C. Petioles not hollow . . . . . . . . . . . . . *L. stenocephala*
        CC. Petioles hollow . . . . . . . . . . . . . . . . . *L. wilsoniana*
AA. Inflorescence branched, not spike-like . . . . . . . . . *L. dentata*

**Additional Reading:**

Dress, W.J. 1962. Notes on cultivated Compositae. 7. *Ligularia. Baileya* 10:63-87.
Loewer, Peter. 1983. The late blooming ligularia. *Horticulture* 61:12-13.

## *Lilium* (lil' ee-um)           Lily               Liliaceae

Few gardeners can scour garden catalogs and then show sufficient self-discipline to refrain from ordering at least a dozen lily bulbs for the garden. They grow from 1-7' in height, flowers cover the entire spectrum of the rainbow (except blue), bloom from early summer to late fall, are exceptionally hardy and long lived, and are relatively inexpensive. Many of the 80-90 species are still available to the gardener, but with the recent interest in commercial hybridization, the hybrids are often touted with more fanfare than the species. Magnificent additions within the genus have occurred with the work of American and European plant breeders, and gardeners are the ultimate winners.

There are so many hybrids out there, it has become very confusing for the gardener to choose. While there are numerous classifications (8 or 9 at last count), I teach my students the big three: Asiatics, Orientals, and Martagons or Turk's Caps, along with a few species. Asiatic hybrids are earliest to flower, have smaller leaves than the Orientals, generally, but not always, have upward facing flowers and range from 1-3' in height. The Asiatics, however, provide the most variability, with outward and, my favorites, downward facing flowers in a tremendous color range. Asiatics are least fussy about the soil and fertility requirements, adapting to almost any well-drained soil and an occasional feeding. Some of the better known hybrids include the Pixies, a terrific breakthrough in robust, dwarf lilies, 'Connecticut King', 'Enchantment' and many newer hybrids. Orientals are distinguishable from Asiatics by usually being taller, having larger flowers (often outward facing or nodding), and with much wider, more succulent leaves along the stem. The flowers are generally more fragrant than those of Asiatics. I find the leaves the easiest method of distinguishing them. Some hybrids include 'Casablanca', 'La Reve', 'Stargazer', Imperial Strain, and my two favorites, 'Olivia' and the dwarf 'Trance', a breeding breakthrough in Orientals. Many, many more are available through specialists. The Martagons include martagon, superbum and numerous other species and hybrids with pendulous flowers whose petals are rolled back (reflexed). The Martagon forms have whorled leaves and usually only grow to about 3' tall. Paisley and Backhouse hybrids would be included with this group. They do better in alkaline soils (pH 6.5 to 7.5), struggling a little in acid soils. Other groups are also important (the fragrant Trumpet and Aurelian classes are fun to grow), but there is only so much lily nomenclature I can hammer into their heads. Of course, none of this identification nonsense is at all necessary to enjoy the plants. Stick them in and get out of the way.

Lilies are native to three main areas of the world, and their provenance somewhat determines their position in the garden. European species (*L. bulbiferum, L. candidum, L. martagon, L. pyrenaicum, L. monadelphum*) and their hybrids require rich soils well amended with organic matter. Many Asiatic species (*L. auratum, L. leichtlinii, L. henryi, L. regale, L. rubellum, L. speciosum, L. tigrinum*) and their hybrids produce roots not only at the base of the bulb but also at the stem just above the bulb. These should be planted 8–10" deep to allow for stem-rooting. North American species (*L. canadense, L. pardalinum, L. philadelphicum, L. superbum*) and their hybrids are not stem rooted but often have stoloniferous or rhizomatous bulbs. Well-drained soils amended with leaf mold and peat moss provide the greatest success.

General statements about the ease of lily culture in this country are impossible due to the diversity of climate. While it is enjoyable to read about the ease of growing lilies in England (or elsewhere), the cultural information must be applied to American gardens most cautiously. However, a broad rule, provided by Alan and Ester Macneil in *Garden Lilies*, (see Additional Reading), states that most Asiatic types do well in areas east of the Rocky Mountains, while those native to the Pacific coast (*L. pardalinum, L. parryi, L. washingtonianum*) and to Europe often struggle there. European species do well on the west coast, and western American species do better on the other side of the ocean than on the other side of the mountains.

Lilies usually arrive packed in moist peat moss and should not be removed until planting time. They dry out quickly if exposed to the air because they have no natural protection around the bulb to prevent desiccation. Planting depth varies with species but in general they should be planted 2–3 times deeper than their diameter. However, *L. davidii* should be planted 8" deep while *L. candidum* requires shallow planting. All lilies look better when planted 12–18" apart in groups of 3–5. Organic matter should be spread around the emerging stems in early spring, especially those which are stem rooters. The taller lilies, particularly those with large trumpet flowers, should be staked. Insert bamboo stakes close to the stems (without piercing the bulbs) when they are about 1' tall and tie securely as they grow.

Remove flowers when they fade to reduce seed set. If flowers are to be brought inside, cut as little stem as possible. The leaves and stem manufacture food for next year's flowers and if too much is removed, performance declines in subsequent years. The stems can be removed in the fall after they have died back, although I like to leave some of the stem around all winter so bulbs can be located in spring. Most are sun-loving plants but many tolerate partial shade. The most important cultural requirement is good drainage; although abundant water is required in the summer, bulbs abhor poorly drained soils in the winter.

A number of diseases have plagued lilies from the beginning of their cultivation and still persist today. Botrytis, a fungal disease, is known as gray mold because of the grayish residue that occurs on leaves and stem particularly after prolonged rain. Bottom leaves usually fall off and although plants are disfigured, little permanent damage occurs. Basal rot is caused by *Fusarium oxysporum* and occurs on infected bulbs. Symptoms are yellow foliage and total disintegration of the bulb. It occurs more often in warm climates than in areas with cooler summer conditions. Most lily propagators dip their bulbs in fungicide after harvesting from the field, and basal rot is not as serious today as in the past. However, it will not go away. The most serious disease is lily mosaic virus which is carried from plant to plant by aphids. Symptoms vary, but in general, irregular yellow streaks or mottling appear on the leaves and many become twisted and distorted. The most susceptible species are *L. formosanum* and *L. auratum*, although *L. canadense*, *L. japonicum* and *L. superbum* are often infected and act as carriers. It is advisable to plant these some distance from other lily species. The virus can also be spread from tulips, particularly Rembrandt types, and planting tulips and lilies side by side is not recommended.

While diseases of the lily are frustrating to the gardener, the bulbs were used for many medicinal purposes in Medieval times. When pounded with honey, ulcers and scurvy were diminished, and when mixed with barley and baked, it was said to cure dropsy. Even corns were soothed with an ointment made from boiling the bulbs. Modern medicine has failed to confirm these uses, but studies are alive and well.

Lilies are propagated vegetatively or sexually. Vegetative propagules include scales, stem bulbils, or division. The advantage of vegetative propagation is to multiply hybrids or cultivars which will not come true from seed. The biggest disadvantage is the transmittance of viral or fungal pathogens from mother to daughter plant. Scale propagation may be done on most species in June and July in the United States. Discard the outer scales and peel the inner scales of the bulb. Dip the cut end in a fungicide (available at a garden center) and place into clean coarse vermiculite or a mixture of sand and peat moss. Tie a polyethylene bag over the container and place in a warm area. Small scales such as those of *L. superbum* or *L. pumilum* should be almost covered while bigger ones, such as those of *L. henryi*, may be left protruding above the surface. Bulbils will form on the scales in 4–10 weeks and some top growth will occur. At that time place the container in a cooler for at least 6 weeks of cold temperatures (less than 40° F). Pot up in the spring and allow for additional growth or place in the garden at this time.

Stem bulbils occur on *L. henryi*, *L. tigrinum*, many of the Backhouse hybrids, and occasionally on *L. bulbiferum*. Simply remove these bulbils when ripe (usually in midsummer) and plant them in peat medium in a propagation frame. Overwinter to provide the necessary chilling and place container and plantlet in the garden the next spring. For those so inclined, breaking off the top of the plant just when flower buds are visible will force many plants to form adventitious stem bulbils. Species such as *L. speciosum* have rhizomatous bulbs and careful removal of the daughter bulbils is a useful method of propagation. Reproduction by seed is time consuming for some species but surprisingly fast for others. The main advantage of seed propagation is freedom from disease. Many species germinate rapidly and top growth occurs in 2–3 weeks. Others form a bulbil prior to top growth development, and in these species, it appears as if nothing is happening and seeds are often discarded too soon. Germination responses of some of the species are shown below. Some such as *L. candidum*, *L. henryi*, and *L. philadelphicum* are variable in their response and could be placed in either category. Those in the slow germination category may be accelerated by providing 40° F for 6 weeks.

| Fast germinators | Slow germinators |
| --- | --- |
| *L. amabile* | *L. auratum* |
| *L. candidum* | *L. bulbiferum* |
| *L. formosanum* | *L. canadense* |
| *L. longiflorum* | *L. henryi* |
| *L. philadelphicum* | *L. martagon* |
| *L. pumilum* | *L. pardalinum* |
| *L. regale* | *L. speciosum* |
| *L. tigrinum* | *L. superbum* |

Most lilies require a minimum 6 weeks of cold to develop good flowering stems. Lilies raised from seed may take 4 years to flower. Others, such as *L. formosanum*, Formosa lily, flower the first year after the cold treatment.

**Hybrids:**

Hybrids can be found under names such as Mid-Century and Preston hybrids and numerous cultivars may occur within each hybrid group. They have been placed in 8 divisions by the North American Lily Society and the Royal Horticultural Society for ease of classification. The divisions are based on the parentage of the hybrids, the position (nodding, upright), and shape of the flower (trumpet, star, bowl).

## Quick Guide to the Hybrids—A Tiny Sampling Only

| | Flower color (inside/outside) | Height (ft.) | Flower shape | Flower time* |
|---|---|---|---|---|
| African Queen Strain | Gold apricot | 5–6 | Trumpet | J, A |
| Aladdin Hybrids | Mix | 2–3 | Erect | J, J |
| Aurelian Hybrids | Mix | 4–6 | Trumpet | J, A |
| Backhouse Hybrids | Orange to yellow | 5–6 | Nodding | J, J |
| –Mrs R.O. Backhouse | Yellow, purple spots | 5–6 | Nodding | July |
| –Sutton House | Yellow/purple spots | 5–6 | Nodding | July |
| Bellingham Hybrid | Mix | 4–7 | Nodding | J, J |
| –Shuksan | Yellow-orange, red dots | 4–5 | Nodding | July |
| Black Dragon Strain | White/purple-brown | 5–8 | Trumpet | J, A |
| Byam's Ruby | Ruby red | 1–2 | Erect | June |
| Bright Star | Orange/ivory | 3–4 | Trumpet | J, J |
| Connecticut Yankee | Apricot-orange | 3–4 | Outward | J, J |
| Copper King Strain | Deep apricot/maroon red | 4–6 | Trumpet | J, A |
| Corsage | Ivory-pink | 2–3 | Outward | J, J |
| Crystal Palace Strain | Greenish white | 5–6 | Trumpet | J, J |
| Fiesta Hybrids | Mix | 3–5 | Nodding | J, J |
| –Burgundy Strain | Cherry red | 3–5 | Nodding | J, J |
| –Citronella Strain | Golden yellow | 3–4 | Nodding | J, J |
| Golden Speldor Strain | Deep yellow/maroon stripe | 3–6 | Trumpet | J, A |
| Golden Sunburst Strain | Clear yellow | 5–7 | Nodding | J, A |
| Green Mt. Hybrids | White/green throat | 5–7 | Trumpet | J, A |
| Harlequin Hybrids | Pink to tangerine | 4–5 | Nodding | J, J |
| –Minuet | Soft yellow | 4–5 | Nodding | July |
| Imperial Strain | Crimson, gold, pink | 5–6 | Outward | J, A |
| Mid Century Hybrid | Mix | 3–5 | Erect, Outward | J, J |
| –Bounty | Yellow | 3–5 | Outward | July |
| –Cinnabar | Maroon red | 2–3 | Erect | July |
| –Enchantment | Nasturtium red | 2–3 | Erect | July |
| –Prosperity | Lemon yellow | 3–4 | Outward | July |
| –Tabasco | Dark red, black spots | 3–4 | Outward | July |
| Moonlight Strain | Chartreuse yellow | 5–6 | Trumpet | July |
| Olympic Hybrids | Ivory to sulphur/purple | 5–6 | Trumpet | July |
| Paisley Strain | Ivory to mahogany | 4–5 | Nodding | June |
| Pink Perfection Hybrids | Orchid purple | 4–6 | Trumpet | J, A |
| Pixie Strain | Pink, orange, white | 2–3 | Erect | J, J |
| Preston Hybrids | Mix | 2–5 | Erect, Outward | J, J |
| –Brenda Watts | Deep red, purple dots | 3–4 | Outward | June |
| –Spitfire | Deep apricot, brown spots | 2–5 | Erect | July |
| Thunderbolt | Tangerine orange | 6–7 | Trumpet | J, A |

649

Specialists list many more hybrids, all of which have unique characteristics slightly different from others.

*In zone 4–5:  J, J = June, July    J, A = July, August
  In zone 6–7:  Those listed J, J would flower in May and June,
          those listed J, A would flower in June and July.

**Species:**

The proliferation of hybrids has left some of the species out in the cold from the viewpoint of garden appeal. The species, however, possess a charm of their own and although some are uncommon, others such as tiger lily and regal lily will always occupy a space in the summer garden.

Quick Guide to Lily Species

|  | Ease of growth | Flower color | Height (ft.) | Flower shape | Flower time |
|---|---|---|---|---|---|
| *L. amabile* | MD | Red, black spots | 2–3 | Nodding | J, J |
| *L. auratum* | ME | White, yellow band | 2–4 | Bowl | A, S |
| *L. bulbiferum* | MD | Red-orange | 3–4 | Cup | J, J |
| *L. canadense* | D | Golden yellow | 2–4 | Nodding | June |
| *L. candidum* | E | White | 2–4 | Trumpet | June |
| *L. formosanum* | ME | White | 4–6 | Trumpet | Aug. |
| *L. henryi* | E | Light orange | 4–6 | Nodding | J, A |
| *L. maculatum* | ME | Orange | 2–3 | Upward | M, J |
| *L. martagon* | MD | Purple-red | 3–4 | Nodding | J, J |
| *L. monadelphum* | D | Yellow, lilac spots | 4–5 | Nodding | J, J |
| *L. philadelphicum* | D | Orange-red | 2–4 | Erect | J, J |
| *L. pumilum* | E | Coral-red | 1–2 | Nodding | J, J |
| *L. regale* | E | White | 4–6 | Trumpet | J, A |
| *L. speciosum* | E | White, red spots | 4–5 | Nodding | J, A |
| *L. superbum* | E | Orange | 4–7 | Nodding | J, A |
| *L. tigrinum* | E | Orange, spotted | 4–5 | Nodding | A, S |

*Ease of growth:*  E = easy, ME = moderately easy, MD = moderately difficult, D = difficult (for gardens east of Rocky Mountains).

*Flower time:*   In zones 4, 5:  A, S = August, September
          J, A = July, August
          J, J = June, July

        In zones 6, 7:  A, S would flower in July and August
          J, A in June and July
          J, J in May and June

| *-auratum* (ow-rah' tum) | | Goldband Lily | 2–4'/1½' |
|---|---|---|---|
| Summer | White | Japan | Zones 4–9 |

*L. auratum* has often been described as "the queen of the lilies" and is well deserving of the name. The large flowers have prominent gold bands down the center of each white petal and are heavily spotted with gold and crimson. The wonderfully fragrant blooms are borne horizontally and each of the 5–15 blossoms is 6–10" in diameter. The flowers are funnel shaped, the petals are slightly reflexed, but no long flower tube is produced as in the trumpet lilies. The red anthers contrast prominently with the white petals.

The introduction of *L. auratum* bulbs to England and North America in 1862 created a ground swell of interest in this and other lilies. Unfortunately, the wholesale propagation of bulbs in Japan was handled poorly and basal rot and lily mosaic decimated plantings. Few old established plantings remain. This species and *L. formosanum*, Formosa lily, are the two most susceptible to lily mosaic and complete destruction of the entire plant, including the bulb, can occur within 1 year. Propagation and cultural techniques have greatly improved and although there is far less incidence of disease, the reputation still lingers.

This species is more frost tender than many others and should be mulched well in zones 4 and 5. Bulbs require a well-drained soil and do not tolerate lime. They are also particularly sensitive to winter moisture. Bulbs grow on volcanic ash and lava debris in Japan, indicating their dislike of moisture around the bulbs. The bulbs are not stem rooters and should be planted about 6" deep. In the Armitage garden, flowers opened during the first 2 weeks of June for about 3 years, until other woody plants took over the area. Although not a long-lived species, often disappearing in a 2–3 years, it is lovely enough that frequent renewal is justified.

**Cultivars:**

'Earth Angel' bears white flowers with a particularly visible yellow band. Plants are only about 2' tall. This is also used in greenhouse production for potted plants.

'Opala' is a handsome large-flowered white form.

Var. *platyphyllum* is better than the type with larger less heavily spotted flowers. It is a vigorous grower and can reach heights 6–8'.

Var. *rubro-vittatum* has a crimson rather than a yellow band through the petals. 'Crimson Beauty' and 'Red Band' are names given to selections of this variety.

Var. *virginale* is an albino form of the species, with pale yellow banding and few or no spots.

**Hybrids:**

*L. × parkmanii*, raised in Boston in 1869 by Francis Parkman, an amateur gardener, is a cross between *L. auratum* and *L. speciosum*. The segments are crimson inside with white margins and the flat flowers are up to 12″ across. The original hybrids were lost but subsequent crosses have been made. This is considered to be one of the finest hybrids ever produced.

'Empress of China' (*L*. 'Jilian Wallace' × *L. auratum* 'Crimson Queen') has a pale green stripe in the center of the petals, and maroon spots.

'Empress of Japan' (*L. auratum* × *L. speciosum*) bears white flowers with a golden band and purple spotting on the petals. The 'Empress' forms were raised at the Oregon Bulb Farm.

'Excelsior' (*L. auratum* var. *platyphyllum* × *L*. 'Jilian Wallace') has rose petals with narrow white margins.

Imperial Strain, Potomac hybrids, and Jamboree Strain also are hybrids between *L. auratum* and *L. speciosum*.

| | | | |
|---|---|---|---|
| *-bulbiferum* (bul-bi′ fe-rum) | Fire Lily | | 3–4′/1½′ |
| Summer | Orange-Red | Eastern and Central Europe | Zones 2–8 |

The species is occasionally offered but is often outclassed by many of the hybrids. It is, however, hardy, vigorous, and one of the easiest lilies to grow. The orange red, cup-shaped flowers are erect or outward facing and have yellow blotching at the base. If the flowers are disbudded or if the stem is damaged, many bulbils appear in the axils of the leaves. For large scale production, plants are topped to induce bulbil formation from the leaf axils.

Bulbs should be planted 6–8″ deep and are not particular as to soil type. They are tolerant of shade and should be placed where they remain undisturbed.

**Cultivars:**

Var. *chaixii* is a dwarf plant seldom over 2′ tall with orange flowers.

Var. *croceum* has brilliant, deep orange flowers. In Northern Ireland, it is the symbol of the Order of the Ulster Orangemen, who celebrate the victory of William of Orange in 1691. This variety is also one of the parents of the hybrid 'Redbird', a purple-stemmed plant bearing red flowers with mahogany spots.

**Hybrids:**

*L. bulbiferum* has been used extensively in hybridization resulting in erect-flowered hybrids known as *L*. × *hollandicum* or *L*. × *maculatum*.

| | | | |
|---|---|---|---|
| *-candidum* (kan′ di-dum) | Madonna Lily | | 2–4′/1½′ |
| Summer | White | Eastern Mediterranean | Zones 4–9 |

This may be the earliest lily in cultivation, grown circa 1500 BC in Crete. The Madonna lily has always represented the good and beautiful to artists and poets. The Madonna flower is depicted in paintings and frescoes by Botticelli and Titian and is still considered by many to be the "lily of the valleys" mentioned in Song of Solomon 2:1–2. The 10–20 funnel-shaped flowers are pure white (the name *candidum* means not just white but "of dazzling white"), 3–4″ long and equally wide. They are delicately fragrant and each waxy flower faces outward to allow full view of the lovely yellow stamens.

This is one of the few bulbs which must be planted near the surface; only 1″ of soil should cover the bulb. Basal evergreen leaves form soon after bulbs are planted in the fall. It is best placed in the company of other low-growing plants which shade the bulb but not the stem leaves. For this reason, Madonna lily does well in the mixed border where it persists for many years.

**Hybrids:**

*L.* × *testaceum* (*L. candidum* × *L. chalcedonicum*) bears pendent fragrant ivory flowers flushed with pink and scarlet anthers. One of the oldest hybrids (early 1800's), plants are known as the Nanking lily, even though the original hybrids probably arose in Holland or Germany. Difficult to establish but worth an expensive bulb or two.

'Apollo' (*L.* × *testaceum* × *L. chalcedonicum* var. *maculatum*) has tan flowers with apricot shading.
'Zeus' (*L.* × *testaceum* × *L. chalcedonicum*) has deep red flowers.

All hybrids bear pendulous flowers.

**Related Species:**

*L. longiflorum*, Easter lily, is a beautiful garden plant. If potted lilies are received as gifts, plant immediately after flowering, or as soon as weather allows. The pure white flowers are 4–7″ long and 1–1½″ broad. Unfortunately, bulbs are only winter hardy to zone 8 (zone 7 if well mulched). The good news is that numerous crosses with the easter lily are now available, expanding the color selection and the climatic adaptability. 'Aladdin' hybrids are multicolored hybrids between *L. longiflorum* and various Asiatic hybrids. About 2′ tall, with upward facing, slightly fragrant flowers. 'Aladdin's Dream' is a pink-flowered form which was selected from the hybrids above. 'Longidragon' (*L. longiflorum* × 'Black Dragon') has trumpets of white flowers with chartreuse throats, but the back of the tepals are purple-black.

| *-formosanum* (for-mo-say′ num) | Formosa Lily | 5–6′/1½′ |
|---|---|---|
| Late Summer          White | Taiwan | Zones 5–8 |

The outward-facing flowers are funnel-shaped with reflexed petals. The 2–4″ long off-white blooms often have purplish brown markings on the outside to match the purplish hue of the stem. Five to six fragrant flowers are borne in the stem axils in late summer in the South and autumn in the North. The late flowering characteristic is sufficient to recommend the species, but in the North, insufficient time may be available for the bulb to ripen after flowering and bulbs may only persist a year or two. In the South, this is not a problem. One of the drawbacks to the species is the height, up to 4–6′ tall, requiring some support in windy areas. On the other hand, the seed capsules are among some of the most handsome in the genus and add interest to the fall garden.

Unfortunately, bulbs are susceptible to virus diseases, particularly lily mosaic. The virus causes rapid decline of the bulb and increases the potential of infection to other bulb species in the garden. To avoid infection, it is not advisable to plant Formosa lilies among other lilies. (See also *L. auratum*).

**Cultivars:**

Var. *pricei* is only 18–24″ tall and a definite improvement on the species. Plants are suitable for the front of the garden and should be planted like *L. candidum*, using other plants to provide shade for the base. Flowers open earlier, and bulbs are more cold hardy than the species. This is one of the fastest species to flower from seed, flowering the first year. Germination occurs in 3–4 weeks in warm (70–75° F), humid areas. Var. *pricei* also comes true from seed.

| | | | |
|---|---|---|---|
| *-henryi* (hen′ ree-eye) | | Henry Lily | 4–6′/2′ |
| Late Summer | Orange | Central China | Zones 4–7 |

One of the building blocks of the hybridizer, it has been a parent of many a grateful hybrid as well as an excellent long-lived species, flowering prolifically in mid to late summer. This lily was found by Augustine Henry (1857–1930), a plant explorer from Ireland who explored in China, and named *L. henryi* by E.H. Wilson. The bulbs are exceptionally large (8–10″ in diameter), and relatively resistant to fungi and virus. The length and width of the leaves vary considerably, but become smaller near the top of the stem. The stem itself varies from green to dark purple. The 2″ wide nodding, light orange flowers have strongly reflexed petals and the centers have numerous raised projections called papillae.

This stem-rooting species should be planted 6–8″ deep. The major disadvantage is the inherent inability of the stems to stand upright. They start to bend long before the flower buds have reached appreciable size and touch the ground as the flowers open. Support early in the growing season or allow to grow through shrubs in the mixed border. It is native to limestone cliff faces in China and is therefore tolerant of high pH soils.

Under favorable conditions, large amounts of seed form and seedlings reach flowering size in about 3 years. Multitudes of small bulbs forming at the base of the stem may also be detached and grown on.

**Hybrids:**

The Aurelian hybrids (*L.* × *aurelianense*) are the most important hybrids associated with *L. henryi*. They arose from crosses with *L. sargentiae*,

Sargent's lily, a trumpet lily with white, brown-tinted flowers. The resulting crosses produced hybrids whose flowers vary in shape from trumpet, bowl-shaped, pendant to sunburst types.

**Cultivars:**

Many clones from various strains of the Aurelian hybrids have occurred over the years, all benefited from the added vigor and stronger garden constitution of their parents.

'Black Beauty' is a vigorous hybrid resulting from the cross between *L. henryi* and *L. speciosum*. Flowers are deep crimson with recurved petals. These normally incompatible species resulted from embryo culture, a powerful technique for the development of future hybrids.

'Bright Star' is a sunburst-type lily (star-shaped flowers which open flat) with white flowers and an orange-gold center.

'Eureka', a bowl-shaped, outward facing, pale orange lily also resulted through embryo culture (*L. henryi* × 'Wiltig', an asiatic hybrid).

'First Love' has 6–8″ wide gold flowers with pink edges. The flowers are clearly bowl shaped and outward facing.

Golden Clarion Strain consists of trumpet-shaped flowers ranging from yellow to gold, usually with maroon or deep crimson on the outside.

Golden Shower hybrids bear long pendant-type flowers on long pedicels. They are bright yellow with maroon tinges on the outside.

'Heart's Desire' has bowl-shaped flowers in shades of white, cream, yellow, or orange.

'Honeydew', a trumpet form, has long, pendulous, greenish yellow flowers outside, deep yellow inside.

'Limelight' bears funnel-shaped trumpets of chartreuse yellow. Unfortunately, it appears rather sensitive to virus.

'Pink Perfection' has 6–8″ long, deep pink, trumpet flowers. Plants grow 8′ high in the Armitage garden.

'Thunderbolt' bears deep apricot starburst flowers with tinges of green and purple on the outside of the petals.

| *-martagon* (mar′ ta-gon) | Martagon Lily, Turk's-Cap | 3–4′/1½′ |
|---|---|---|
| Summer  Purple-Red | Europe, Asia | Zones 3–7 |

This lily has an extremely wide distribution, ranging from Portugal to northern Mongolia, and from Britain to Siberia. As would be expected, it is variable in habit and adaptable to a wide range of climates and garden environments. Plants tolerate heavy shade as well as full sun, a plus for many gardens.

The word "martagon" may be derived from a Turkish word denoting a special form of turban used by sultans. This rather loose translation has evolved into the common name of this plant, the Turk's-cap lily. Many other species with the same nodding flower orientation are referred to as turk's-cap flowers. Alchemists in the 15th century held the martagon in high regard for its ability to change metals into gold, perhaps because of the golden roots.

Plants are distinguished by 3–4 whorls of leaves consisting of 6–9 leaves per node. The nodding flowers are dull purplish red and spotted dark purple throughout. The petals are strongly recurved and each stem bears 20–30 small flowers. The 1–2″ wide flowers are fragrant, but the fragrance is in the nose of the smeller; I find the odor rather unpleasant. There are even those who claim it "stinks."

### Cultivars:

'Album' is an albino form with creamy white, unspotted flowers and pale green leaves. It is particularly outstanding in front of a solid green background in the garden and, unlike other albino forms, grows vigorously.

Var. *cattaniae* is similar to the species but has dark maroon, unspotted flowers and hairy buds and stems. I find the unspotted nature of the flowers more pleasant than the type. Crosses made in Scotland between these two varieties yielded cherry-colored flowers sold as 'Gleam' and 'Glisten', but I am not aware of a commercial source in the United States.

### Hybrids:

Backhouse hybrids resulted from *L. martagon* and its varieties, particularly var. *cattaniae* and *L. hansonii*, a nodding orange-yellow species. They were developed at the end of the last century and are still widely grown. Named clones include 'Mrs. R.O. Backhouse', with orange-yellow flowers flushed with pink, and 'Brocade' with pale buff-yellow recurved flowers. They are vigorous, excellent garden plants. These hybrids look terrific at Winterthur Gardens in Delaware.

Paisley hybrids (*L. martagon* 'Album' × *L. hansonii*) contain nodding flowers of clear white, orange and mahogany. The hybrids are occasionally listed as *L.* × *martha*. No named cultivars have yet been developed.

---

*-philadelphicum* (fil-a-delf′ I-cum)     Wood Lily     2–4′/1½′
    Summer     Orange-Red     Eastern North America     Zones 4–7

This North American native ranges from Nova Scotia to Ontario and from southern Quebec as far south as North Carolina. Fiery orange-red erect flowers with dark maroon spots contrast with the dark green whorled leaves. Open wooded areas and areas with partial afternoon shade are common locales to find this native. The flowers are sufficiently showy that mass plantings are not necessary, and if provided ample space, are visible from one end of the garden to the other.

Unfortunately, this is not one of the easier lilies to establish and only a small percentage persists more than 2 years. However, those that do become established are long lived. The rock garden serves the needs of this diminutive lily better than the mixed border, particularly when the soil is sandy and highly acidic. Given the wide distribution, it is surprising that establishment is so difficult. Sowing seed in the cold frame in fall, with subsequent planting of the seedlings next spring, reduces root disturbance and helps establish the plants.

*-pumilum* (pew mi-lum)·          Coral Lily                        1–2'/1½'
   Summer          Coral-Red          Eastern China, Siberia          Zones 3–7
(Syn. *L. tenuifolium*)

The exceptionally waxy, coral-red, nodding flowers are unlike any others. The petals are highly reflexed and practically unspotted. Each stem may bear up to twenty, 2″ wide flowers in early summer, although 10 is more common. The numerous leaves are narrow and grass-like. As coral lily is a stem-rooting species, bulbs should be planted about 4–5″ deep.

Plants are not long-lived and accepting this fact makes them much less frustrating to grow. They persist 2–4 years in full sun. Prolific amounts of seed are produced which provide new seedlings to perpetuate the species for many years. Three years is about the maximum length of time bulbs persist, although removing spent flowers keeps plants in place a little longer but eliminates the source of fresh seed for new plantings.

## Cultivars:
'Golden Gleam' is a golden form of the species.
'Red Star' bears star-shaped scarlet flowers about a week later than the type.
'Yellow Bunting' is a pure yellow form which comes true from seed.

*-regale* (re-gah' lee)                    Regal Lily                        4–6'/2'
   Summer          White          China                              Zones 3–8

The regal lily was discovered by the great plant explorer E.H. Wilson in western Szechwan in 1903. Imagine his thrill of gazing upon drifts of pure white lilies "not in twos and threes but in hundreds, in thousands, aye, in tens of thousands. The air in the cool of the morning and in the evening is laden with delicious purfume exhaled from each bloom." (*The Lilies of Eastern Asia*, 1925, E.H. Wilson). While we cannot duplicate this sight, a half dozen bulbs can provide almost as much pleasure. The trumpet-shaped flowers are white with a canary yellow inner funnel and usually wine colored on the outside. The stigmas are green and the anthers golden yellow. There may be up to 20 flowers per stem, 5″ wide and 6″ long, although 8–10 is more common. An evening walk in the garden while the regal lilies are in flower provides a heavy, unparalleled fragrance, never to be forgotten. When in flower, this is the dominant plant in the garden. Other plants should be chosen to complement and not compete.

Bulbs are planted 6″ deep in well-drained soil in partial shade or full sun. One problem with regal lilies is that they appear in early spring and may be nipped by late spring frosts. Planting through low growing plants such as *Campanula carpatica* protects the new shoots while providing color at the base. Bulbs are long-lived and multiply rapidly; however, once planted, they resent disturbance.

Seeds are produced prolifically and flowering plants can be produced in as little as 2 years.

| *-speciosum* (spece-ee-o′ sum) | | Speciosum Lily | 4–5′/2′ |
|---|---|---|---|
| Summer | White with Red | Japan | Zones 4–8 |

Once grown in large numbers for the cut flower trade, the species has been superseded by the hybrids. It is still, however, a popular late-flowering lily for gardens with full sun and lime-free soil. The 6″ wide, white, fragrant flowers have reflexed petals flushed with pink and heavily spotted with pink or crimson. They have red fleshy bumps (papillae) in the center of the blossom, similar to *L. henryi*. A well grown plant may have as many as 30 blossoms per stem although 15–20 is far more realistic. Plant bulbs about 6″ deep. Due to their susceptibility to virus and disease, keep them away from *L. auratum* and *L. formosanum*.

### Cultivars:

'Album' (var. *album novum*) has white flowers with a pale green band radiating from the center. Purple spots also occur on the tepals.

'Roseum' bears 8″ wide soft pinkish red flowers with a white margin around the petals.

'Rubrum' produces large, 8″ wide ruby-red flowers with a broad white margin. These are commonly known as rubrum lilies.

'Uchida' may be a cultivar of var. *rubrum* or a hybrid with *L. auratum*. Nevertheless, the vigorous plants perform well and bear rich carmine-pink, spotted flowers. 'Uchida' is more virus resistant than the species.

### Hybrids:

'Allegra' ([*L. auratum* × *L. speciosum* 'Rubrum'] × *L. speciosum* 'Album') has beautiful white recurved flowers with a central green star.

Other hybrids such as *L.* × *parkmanii* have been listed under *L. auratum*.

| *-superbum* (soo-perb′ um) | | American Turk's Cap Lily | 4–7′/2′ |
|---|---|---|---|
| Late Summer | Orange | Eastern United States | Zones 4–8 |

The variable American turk's cap lily used to be far more abundant in eastern United States than it is today. Peter Hanson of Brooklyn, after whom *L. hansonii* was named, "once found a spot in New Jersey where there were at least 5000 plants of this noble lily in flower at once, ranging up to 2m high and bearing as many as 30 flowers to a stem, but out of the whole number it was difficult to find three exactly alike." (*Monograph of the Genus Lilium*, 1877–1880, by H.J. Elwes). *L. superbum* is a martagon-type lily (see *L. martagon*), with orange-red, heavily spotted, reflexed flowers often with a green center at the base. The stems are usually flushed with dark purple and may bear up to 40 flowers, although 20 is more common. Plants prefer damp conditions and perform better if they do not dry out during the summer. They can be found in many wet areas in the Arnold Arboretum, although bulbs are more tolerant of being dried out than many other species. The leaves are whorled like *L. martagon* and the bulbs are rhizomatous resulting in the establishment of large colonies. Seed sown in the fall will reach flowering size in 2 years.

### Cultivars:

A number of cultivars were raised by Mrs. J.N. Henry, an amateur lily enthusiast from Gladwyne, PA. She also discovered *L. iridollae*.

'Norman Henry' has fine, unspotted, butter-yellow flowers.
'Port Henry' bears clear pale orange flowers with only faint spotting. Other cultivars were also selected which bear the Henry name, but unfortunately are difficult to locate.

### Related Species:

*L. canadense*, Canada lily, is a beautiful plant with whorled leaves and butter yellow flowers. It has a similar growth habit to *L. superbum*, but it is distinguished by dark-spotted yellowish flowers rather than orange, by less reflexed petals, and by the absence of a green spot at the base of the flower.

*L. iridollae*, pot of gold lily, was found by Mrs. J.N. Henry (see cultivars above) in southern Alabama. Native to Alabama and Florida, it bears nodding pure yellow flowers on 3' tall stems. Unfortunately, this little gem is difficult to find but if a source is discovered, it should definitely be used in southern gardens.

*L. michauxii*, is a similar but more southerly species of *L. superbum* and was thought to be a variety (*L. superbum* var. *carolinianum*). Native to the southeastern United States, plants are tolerant of summer heat and humidity. It is not as floriferous as *L. superbum* but bears 3–5 fragrant, nodding, light orange or crimson turk's-cap flowers. The species is well worth growing in zones 7–10.

---

*-tigrinum* (ti-gri' num)    Tiger Lily    4–5'/2'
 Summer, Fall  Orange, Spotted    China, Korea, Japan    Zones 3–9
(Syn. *L. lancifolium*)

The few demands as to soil type, sun or shade, or irrigation make the tiger lily one of the easiest to grow. The 2–4″ long flowers have strongly recurved petals and may be up to 9″ wide. Each stem bears 8–20 deep orange flowers with purplish black spots. Bulbs are stem rooters and should be planted 6″ deep and mulched around the base to allow full development of stem roots. The purplish green stem has white cobweb-like hairs and numerous black bulbils which are formed in the leaf axils.

*L. tigrinum* was used as a food plant for more than a thousand years by the Chinese, the bulbs being quite edible and said to taste like artichoke. It is interesting that *L. candidum*, Madonna lily, has been grown for an equal length of time for beauty, not the food value. Debates still rage in lily circles as to which species was first cultivated.

Unfortunately, *L. tigrinum* has a history of being infected with lily mosaic virus. In this species, however, the symptoms are almost entirely masked. Aphids spread it to other species quite readily and thus the tiger lily is seldom found in the gardens of lily enthusiasts. Established plants, however, live for years and multiply rapidly. Vigorous efforts have been made to raise virus-free stock and it is better to pay the extra price for this material than to infect the rest of the garden.

Plants multiply readily from bulbils formed at the base of the bulbs. Abundant seed is also produced which is scattered randomly by birds and plants germinate along roadsides and streams. Plants are regular citizens of roadsides throughout the Northeast and the Eastern Townships in Quebec, Canada.

## Cultivars:

Many seed propagated cultivars are available as White, Yellow, Pink, Red, Cream, Orange, and Gold Tiger Lilies. All are variable and flowers are heavily sprinkled with black dots.

Var. *fortunei* has bright salmon-orange flowers and is distinguished by the dense woolly hairs which coat the stem. It is later flowering than the species and is particularly useful in the South where frost doesn't occur until November or December.

Var. *splendens* has larger, brighter reddish orange flowers than the type and is one of the best varieties for the late garden.

Var. *flaviflorum* has yellow flowers but is particularly susceptible to virus and has not proven to be a good selection.

Var. *flore-plena* has double flowers but, in my opinion, is rather coarse. The style and grace of a lily flower lies in its clean lines and simple architecture. Double-flowered lilies destroy such grace.

## Hybrids:

'Cardinal' (*L. tigrinum* × *L. amabile*) has nodding, orange-red flowers which bloom late in the season.

Mid-Century hybrids include some of the best known lilies. They resulted from crosses between *L. tigrinum* and *L. × hollandicum*. 'Enchantment' bears bright orange, outward facing flowers on 2' tall stems. An excellent cut flower species. 'Cinnabar' is only 1½–2' tall and bears bright maroon-red, erect flowers.

**Related Species:**

*L. pardalinum*, leopard lily, has 9–20 whorled leaves and 2–4" wide nodding flowers. They are yellow at the base, orange-scarlet above and spotted maroon. Native to California, they are magnificent for western gardens but perform poorly in the East.

<u>Quick Key to Lilium Species</u>

The majority of lilies encountered will be hybrids and this key may be of little use. However, for gardeners with a fascination for species, it may be of value.

A. Flowers erect or nearly so
   B. Leaves whorled about stem, stem smooth . . *L. philadelphicum*
   BB. Leaves scattered about stem, top
      part of stem somewhat hairy . . . . . . . . . . . . *L. bulbiferum*
AA. Flowers horizontal or pendulous
   B. Flowers trumpet shaped with distinct tube, ends
      of petals may be spreading but not reflexed
      C. Tube hardly widening from base of
         tube to middle, petals tinged purple
         on outside, flowers 5–6" long . . . . . . . . *L. formosanum*
      CC. Tube widening from its base upward,
         flowers 2–7" long
         D. Flowers 2–3" long, petals pure white . . . . *L. candidum*
        DD. Flowers 4–7" long, petals white with purple
           tinge on outside or inside of flower . . . . . . . *L. regale*
   BB. Flowers not trumpet shaped, petals strongly recurved
      near tips, flowers horizontal or pendulous
      C. Flowers horizontal, bowl shaped, white
         with yellow band on petals . . . . . . . . . . . . *L. auratum*
      CC. Flowers pendulous
         D. Leaves arranged in whorls
           E. Color of flowers white to rose to purple . . *L. martagon*
           EE. Color of flowers yellow to orange-red . . . . *L. superbum*
         DD. Leaves scattered, not in whorls
           E. Flower color white, or rose
              with red or rose spots . . . . . . . . . . . *L. speciosum*
           EE. Flower color scarlet to orange or yellow
              F. Plants usually less than
                 2' tall, leaf veins 1 . . . . . . . . . . . . *L. pumilum*

FF. Plants usually 3-7' tall,
leaf veins more than 1
   G. Leaves with 5-7 veins, upper
      leaf axils with bulbils . . . . . . . . . *L. tigrinum*
   GG. Leaves many-veined, few if
      any bulbils in upper axils . . . . . . . . *L. henryi*

## Additional Reading:

Books:

Anonymous. Yearly. *The North American Lily Society Yearbooks*. These are excellent sources of information written by amateur and professional plantsmen.

Elwes, H.J. 1880. *A Monograph of the Genus Lilium*. This was the most ambitious work on lilies ever undertaken. Information was compiled on species and hybrids known at the time and excellent botanical drawings were included. Unfortunately, the work was well beyond the reach of almost all who wished to own it or even refer to it (see Synge, Patrick).

Macneil, Alan and Esther Macneil. 1946. *Garden Lilies*. Oxford University Press. The Macneils provide good listings of the species and although not particularly useful for the hybrids, the book is well written and informative.

Slate, George, L. 1939. *Lilies for the American Garden*. A source of good information on lilies for the United States.

Synge, Patrick M. 1980. *Lilies*. Batsford Ltd., London. This recent revision of Elwes monograph and its supplements make that fine work available to gardeners. Although most suitable for British readers, the information on species and hybrids is superior to any other I have found. A must for lily enthusiasts.

Manuscripts:

Baxter, Felicity. 1986. Lilium albanicum. *The Garden* 111(7):324-326.

Blake, Felice. 1987. The loveliest species of all, *L. mackliniae*. *Bulletin of the North American Lily Society* 41(2):19-20.

Gibson, R. J. 1986. The aurelians of Leslie Woodriff. *Bulletin of the North American Lily Society* 40(3):2-3.

Hermes, Alfred R. 1986. Lilies that last. *Horticulture* 64(6):26-31.

Ingram, John. 1967. Notes on the cultivated Liliaceae. 6. *Lilium pensylvanicum* Ker (L. dauricum Ker). *Baileya* 15:109-111.

Synge, Patrick M. 1980. Some newer hybrid lilies. *The Plantsman* 1:250-252.

Associations:

North American Lily Society, Box 476, Waukee, IA 50263.
   Publication: *North American Lily Society Quarterly Bulletin*.

*Limonium* (li-mon′ ee-um)    Statice, Sea-Lavender    Plumbaginaceae

Well over 150 species of statice have been characterized and a number have become well established in the garden and florist trade. The common annual statice, *L. sinuatum*, is available in many colors from seed. Another annual grown by commercial plantsmen for cut flowers is rat-tail statice, *L. suworowii* (soo-vo-roo′ wee-eye) (syn. *Psylliostachys suworowii*), with its unique spiked inflorescence of small dark purple flowers. For statice enthusiasts, many species are available as cut flowers. Most prefer well-drained, slightly acidic soils, and full sun. Some of the better ones include *L. sinense*, an annual with small yellow flowers; *L. perezii*, Perez statice, a 3-4′ tall stout plant with 12-15″ wide flat dark blue flowers with white centers; *L. roseum* (syn. *L. perigrinum*), rosy statice, a tender perennial with fleshy leaves and unique rose flowers. The best forms are available from tissue culture only. Other statice bred for cut flowers are *L.* × 'Misty Blue', *L.* × 'Misty Pink', and *L.* × *caesium*. Unfortunately, they are seldom available to the gardener. Common perennials such as *L. latifolium* and *L. tataricum* bear large airy heads of tiny flowers in shades of lavender and blue and are useful fresh or dried. The flowers are composed of outer sepals (calyx) and inner petals (corolla) and may be different colors. In some species, the corolla falls early, leaving the calyx in full color.

Statice prefers partial shade in the southern part of the range (zones 7, 8) but tolerates full sun further north. Good drainage is essential as they are susceptible to various fungal diseases prevalent in moist soils. This is particularly true of *L. sinuatum*.

To dry the cut flowers, harvest before they fully open. Tie the stems in bundles and hang upside down in a shady, dry, airy shed.

Propagate by root cuttings (see *Anemone*) and division in early spring or by seed. Seeds are small and should be barely covered. Germination occurs in 2-3 weeks under warm (70-75° F), humid conditions.

Quick Reference to Limonium Species

|  | Height (in.) | Hairy leaves | Color of corolla |
|---|---|---|---|
| *L. latifolium* | 24-30 | Yes | Blue |
| *L. tataricum* | 10-15 | No | Ruby-red |

*-latifolium* (lah-tee-fo′ lee-um)    Sea Lavender    24-30″/30″
    Summer    Lavender-Blue    Bulgaria, Southern Russia    Zones 3-8

Plants may reach 3′ tall and 3′ wide with over a dozen flowering stems when well established. The flower stalk is slender and multi-branched, creating a flower head 18-24″ across. The 6-10″ long leaves are produced in rosettes and are often just as wide (*latifolium* means wide leaf). Small branched hairs cover the leaves which taper at the base into petioles nearly as long as the blades. Plants are susceptible to crown and root rot and should be spaced 18″ or more, otherwise air circulation is restricted and disease increases.

Propagate from seed in late fall or from division. Seed is the easiest and least disruptive form of propagation. The roots are long and division is difficult. Established clumps should not be disturbed.

**Cultivars:**
'Blue Cloud' has lighter blue flowers than the type.
'Violetta' bears dark violet flowers and is an outstanding garden plant.

**Related Species:**
*L. bellidifolium* is only 4–10″ tall at flowering, and bears sprays of lilac flowers over handsome lanceolate foliage (*bellidifolium* means beautiful-leafed).

*L. gmelinii*, Siberian statice, produces 2–3′ tall spires of smoky lilac flowers in late summer. This is an extremely vigorous grower, particularly when provided with deep, rich soil and plenty of moisture.

| | | |
|---|---|---|
| *-tataricum* (ta-tah′ ri-kum) | German Statice | 10–15″/15″ |
| Summer      Red/White | Southeastern Europe | Zones 4–8 |

(Syn. *Goniolimon tataricum*)

Similar to *L. latifolium*, the habit and flowers are smaller. The flowers appear whitish to light blue but upon close inspection, ruby-red inner petals are evident. The rosette leaves are smooth and about 4–6″ long. This species is grown commercially as a dried cut flower but the flower stalks are stiffer than common sea lavender.

The genus of this species is in doubt and has been split off to *Goniolimon* by some taxonomists. *Goniolimon* differs from *Limonium* by having hairy styles and capitate stigmas (compact cluster of stigmas). Give us a break, get a life!

Propagate by seed, root cuttings or division.

**Cultivars:**
Var. *angustifolium* (syn. *L. dumosum*) has narrow silver-gray lance-like leaves.
Var. *nanum* is only about 9″ tall and bears pinkish flowers.

Quick Key to Limonium Species

    A. Plant 10–15″ tall, corolla reddish, leaves
       smooth, not hairy, 4–6″ long . . . . . . . . . . . . . . . *L. tataricum*
   AA. Plant 24–30″ tall, corolla lavender,
       leaves hairy, 6–10″ long . . . . . . . . . . . . . . . . . *L. latifolium*

**Additional Reading:**
Armitage, A.M. 1993. *Specialty Cut Flowers*. Timber Press, Portland, OR.
    A book about commercial production of cut flowers, including statice.
    Much more detail about cut flower species than in most gardening books.

## *Linaria* (lyne-ah′ ree-a)    Toadflax    Scrophulariaceae

Sometimes, one needs a plant roadmap to determine whether some plants are annuals, perennials or "perennial-annuals," those which readily self-sow, and are therefore always there. *Linaria* is such a genus with about 100 species, one of which is the common toadflax, *L. vulgaris*, a well-known, relatively handsome perennial weed along northern roadsides. Another good-looking weed, *L. genistifolia* var. *dalmatica,* is listed as a noxious weed in the state of Washington and should be treated with caution, particularly in the West. Some of these "old-fashioned" species are being rediscovered and may be considered as perennials to zone 5, but are not happy with high temperatures, making them spring annuals (like pansies) in the southern parts of the country.

*L. purpurea*, purple toadflax, is native to central and south Italy and Sicily but has been naturalized in the British Isles and occasionally in the United States as well. They are closely related to snapdragons and have long, narrow racemes of small flowers, each with a single spur (like a columbine) at the base. Plants grow 2–3′ tall and flower all summer long in moderate climates. The narrow leaves are whorled at the bottom part of the stem but may be alternate at the top.

The flowers are usually purple but the most popular form is 'J. Canon Went', a pink-flowered form which comes true from seed. 'Springside White' has white flowers and gray-green leaves. 'Antique Silver', a 4–6″ tall plant with pinkish silver flowers and 'Natalie', with blue flowers and gray-green foliage on 15–18″ plants are hybrids increasing the toadflax palette. Cut back plants if they get weedy. Plants are winter hardy to about 10° F and will be perennial with a little mulch; however, self-seeding also helps to keep plants all over the garden. South of zone 6, it should be treated as a fall planted annual, although if plants make it through the summer, they should return. Good drainage is a must.

*L. alpina*, alpine toadflax, is hardy to zone 4 or 5, and bears small violet/yellow or sometimes entirely yellow flowers. Plants grow only 4–8″ tall and are best in rock gardens with good drainage and cool summers.

Occasionally *L. triornithophora* is offered as a perennial but is only hardy to about 23° F (zone 8, maybe), and will self-sow in temperate climates. It is an eye-catching ornamental plant with large flowers, resembling birds on the fly. Its wonderful common name is Three Birds Flying.

## *Linum* (ly′ num)    Flax    Linaceae

Flax has been grown for centuries for oil, fiber and ornament. The perennial *L. perenne* and the annual *L. usitatissimum*, common flax, were grown for fiber to make linen, cordage and rope. During Tudor times in England, when linen tableclothes adorned the tables of abbots and kings, a royal proclamation was issued that a better source of cordage was necessary to properly equip the newly established Royal Navy. *Linum* was replaced by

*Cannabis sativa* as the source of royal rope. Little did they know about the other mind-bending properties of this now infamous plant! Linseed oil is produced from the seeds of *L. usitatissimum*. Flax is still farmed aggressively in Europe and few travellers seeing rolling fields of blue flax flowers are unimpressed with the beauty. Beats the heck out of corn and soybeans.

Three or four species out of the approximately 150 are used for ornamental purposes. The red-flowered *L. grandiflorum*, red-flowering flax, is an excellent annual but most others are perennial. In general, they are short-lived plants but reseed prolifically. Named cultivars may be propagated vegetatively. The flowers are 5-petaled and are colored blue, white, yellow, or occasionally red. Although the individual flowers last only a day, so many flowers are produced that the plant is in flower over a 4–6 week period. The leaves are alternate, narrow, and usually entire. *Linum* is easily grown in a light, well-drained soil in full sun.

Propagate by divisions or stem cuttings, or from seed sown in a cool area where soil temperature is 50–60° F.

Quick Reference to Linum Species

|  | Height (in.) | Flower color |
| --- | --- | --- |
| *L. flavum* | 15–18 | Yellow |
| *L. narbonense* | 18–24 | Blue |
| *L. perenne* | 12–18 | Blue |

| -*flavum* (flay' vum) | | Golden Flax | 15–18'/12" |
| --- | --- | --- | --- |
| Summer | Yellow | Europe | Zones 5–7 |

The fact that this species is not offered by more nurserymen is a shame, especially as some cultivars and varieties are of exceptional garden merit. The 1″ diameter golden yellow flowers consist of petals much larger than the sepals. Up to 50 flowers may be carried in a single inflorescence (cyme). The base of the stems are somewhat woody, and the narrow, lanceolate leaves have 3–5 veins and there are small glands on each side of the leaf base. Plants benefit from a loose mulch of pine straw, leaves, or wheat straw over the winter.

**Cultivars:**

'Compactum' is superior to the type, stands 6–9″ tall, and is covered with yellow flowers.

**Related Species:**

*L. capitatum*, purging flax, is similar to golden flax but the leaves are in basal rosettes and the flowers occur in a dense inflorescence. Flower heads of *L. flavum* are much looser.

*L.* × 'Gemmel's Hybrid' is a hybrid between *L. campanulatum*, with yellow flowers and orange veins, and *L. elegans*, a 6″ plant with yellow flowers. I saw this plant when wandering through Harlow Car Gardens near Harrogate, England in 1990. A compact plant (only 9–12″ tall), it was smothered in exceptionally bright golden flowers. Perhaps it will be offered in the United States in the near future.

| *-narbonense* (nar-bon-en' see) | | Narbonne Flax | 18–24″/18″ |
|---|---|---|---|
| Summer | Blue | Southern Europe | Zones 5–8 |

This long-lived blue-flowered species is one of the best for the garden. Winter protection must be provided in zone 5 and further north. The 2″ wide funnel-shaped flowers are blue with a clear white center. The stamens are also white contributing to the bicolor effect. The ¾″ long, narrow leaves have 3 veins. After flowering, cut back stems to 8″. Similar to the other *Linum* species, well-drained soils are necessary, and plants flower well in full sun or partial shade.

### Cultivars:
'Heavenly Blue' has ultramarine flowers on 12–18″ tall stems. More compact than the species, it does not fall over with rain and wind. Greater compactness, however, is still required and would be most welcome.
'Six Hills' bears brighter blue flowers.

### Related Species:
*L. suffruticosum*, thistle flax, has 1″ diameter white flowers with purple veins and needle-like leaves. Plants are more useful for gardens west of the Rocky Mountains. Native to southern Europe.
Var. *nanum* is only 2–4″ tall and prostrate. It is excellent where low growing white-flowered plants are needed.
Var. *salsoloides* (syn. *L. salsoloides*) has narrower leaves and less purple tint to the flowers.

| *-perenne* (pe-ren' ee) | | Perennial Flax | 12–18″/12″ |
|---|---|---|---|
| Spring | Blue | Europe | Zones 4–8 |

The flowers are more open than those of *L. narbonense*, smaller, and without a white eye. The ¾″ wide, azure blue flowers open for up to 12 weeks when planted in partial shade. In the garden of my good friend, Laura Ann Segrest, the first flowers open in early April and continue into late June. Further north, plants continue to flower even longer. Plants are easy to distinguish from similar species by the wiry stems (try to break

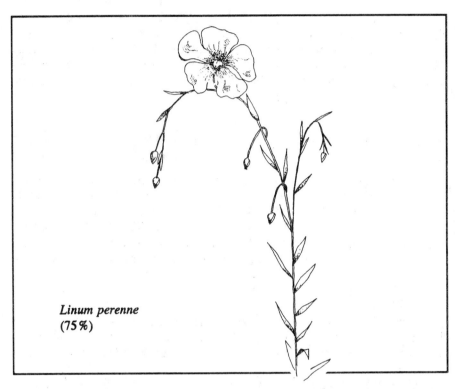

*Linum perenne*
(75%)

them) and the many nodding flower buds. The narrow 1″ long leaves transpire little water and tolerate the heat of southern summers. As with other flax species, it abhors wet feet and will not return next spring if winter drainage is poor. When planted in a group of 6 or more, the plants provide a lovely display. The stems become long and leggy in the heat of the summer and require pruning after flowering.

Seed-grown plants often flower the first year. Divide in spring or early fall.

### Cultivars:
'Alba' is widely available with white flowers on upright stems. It is not a clear white, however, and appears washed out in full sun.

'Alpinum' (ssp. *alpinum*), alpine flax, grows 8–12″ tall with slender, wiry stems which carry ¾″ wide, clear blue flowers. It is not as floriferous as the species, but if given well-drained soil in full sun, lovely drifts of blue result.

'Caerulea' has clear, sky-blue flowers.

'Diamant White' grows about 15″ tall with white flowers.

'Saphyr' has blue flowers and is more compact than the species. It is an excellent garden plant.

## Quick Key to Linum Species

A. Flowers yellow . . . . . . . . . . . . . . . . . . . . . . . *L. flavum*
AA. Flowers blue or white, not yellow
    B. Flowers blue with white eye, funnel
       shaped, 1½–2" in diameter . . . . . . . . . . . *L. narbonense*
    BB. Flowers blue without eye, saucer
       shaped, 1" or less in diameter . . . . . . . . . . . . *L. perenne*

*Liriope* (lear'ree-ope, le-rye'o-pee)      Lily-Turf      Liliaceae

In the *Standard Cyclopedia of Horticuture* by L.H. Bailey (written 1900, revised until 1943), *Liriope* received a minimum of space because it was "little cultivated." Today, it is one the premier and dominant landscape ground cover plants in the South. Of the five species, *L. muscari* is most commonly cultivated.

*-muscari* (mus-cah' ree)         Blue Lily-Turf      12–18"/12"
    Late Summer      Lilac      Eastern Asia      Zones 6–9

A healthy disregard for heat, humidity, and drought, and a built-in resistance to insects and diseases make this an excellent ground cover. The strap-like, dark green, 1–1½" wide evergreen leaves emerge from the crown of the plant. The lilac-purple flowers are borne on dense spike-like flower stalks in August. Dark black berries ripen in the fall and persist into the winter. Plants are not particular concerning soils if drainage is adequate. Large clumps are formed by means of the short, thickened stoloniferous roots. When planted 8–12" apart, *Liriope* provides an effective ground cover which can be used as a substitute for grass. Plants tolerate heavy shade although they will take longer to spread and the flower stems will be more elongated compared with plants grown in full sun. In late winter, plantings may be mowed to the ground to eliminate old foliage and allow a new flush of growth in the spring. I suppose the true pinnacle of success of a plant is when it does so well as to be taken for granted. This is true for this plant in the South.

*Liriope* is closely related to *Ophiopogon*, mondo grass, but is hardier, has broader leaves, and flowers above the foliage while the flowers of mondo grass often flower deep within the foliage.

Propagation by division results in many plantlets which can be replanted or handed over the fence to a new neighbor. The seed coat is hard and soaking seeds in warm water before sowing results in more uniform and faster germination. Tissue culture has also been successfully used to multiply slower cultivars.

*Liriope muscari*
(64%)

## Cultivars:

*Green-leaved forms:*

'Big Blue' bears wide dark green leaves and lavender flowers. One of the most popular forms.

'Christmas Tree' (Munroe #2) has unique lilac flowers on spikes much wider at the base which taper towards the tip resembling a Christmas tree.

'Lilac Beauty' bears showy, stiff, lilac flower clusters held well above the foliage.

'Majestic' has larger, deep lilac flowers. This form is similar to 'Big Blue' but grows slightly more upright.

'Munroe's White' (Munroe #1) is the best white-flowered cultivar but is slower growing than the lilac types. The flowers stand out and add an additional dimension to the species.

'Royal Purple' has deeper purple flowers than other selections.

*Variegated forms:*

The variegation pattern does not stand out as well in heavy shade as in full sun.

'Gold Banded' has wide arching leaves with a narrow gold band down the middle and bears lavender flowers.

'John Burch' produces attractive variegated foliage and cockscomb-shaped lilac flower spikes.

'Silvery Midget' grows about 8″ tall, and bears short green leaves with narrow white bands.

'Silvery Sunproof' has almost white leaves in full sun but more green or yellow-green in partial shade. Flowers are lavender.

'Variegata', the prettiest and most common of all the lily-turfs, bears creamy margins which brighten up any landscape. Seeds yield about 65% variegated plants. Flowers appear about 2 weeks later than the species. This variety does not spread as rapidly as the type so it is more expensive to purchase.

**Related Species:**

*L. spicata*, creeping liriope, is cold hardy to zone 4 and used as a rapidly spreading ground cover. It is only 12–18″ tall and has narrower leaves (only about ¼″ wide) than *L. muscari*. Plants, in effect, resemble unmowed feathery grass. Foliage tends to be more yellow-green during the winter than *L. muscari*. The pale lavender flowers are not as showy as those of *L. muscari*.

**Additional Reading:**

Fagan, Ann E., M.A. Dirr, and F.A. Pokorny. 1981. Effects of depulping, stratification, and growth regulators on seed germination of *Liriope muscari*. *HortScience* 16(2):208–209.

Hume, Harold H. 1961. The Ophiopogon-Liriope Complex. *Baileya* 9: 135–158.

Rackeman, Adelaide. 1987. Lilyturf. *Horticulture* 65(8):42–43.

Smith, Gerald and Henry Clay. 1982. Liriope culture in Georgia. Co-operative Extension Service, University of Georgia, Bulletin 755, 10 pp.

*Lithodora* (lith-o-door′ a)          Lithodora          Boraginaceae

*Lithodora* is fairly common in European gardens and is greatly admired for the lovely blue flowers and creeping habit. However, there are also mentions of lithodora in the dozen or so American garden catalogs I have piled around me. Of the approximately seven species, *L. diffusa* is the best garden species. Although best suited to the climate of the Pacific Northwest, with adequate protection and a proper site, it can also be a valuable plant in parts of the Northeast as well.

Over the years, *Lithodora* has been both included and separated from a closely related genus, *Lithospermum*. The two genera are now considered separate and while botanical differences are subtle, the easiest way to distinguish the two is through the flower color. In general, flowers of *Lithodora* are blue or purple, while those of *Lithospermum* are mostly yellow to orange or white. As simple as that seems, one or two cultivars and variants of *Lithodora* may have white flowers as well. The habits of both may be upright or sprawling.

| | | |
|---|---|---|
| *-diffusa* (di-few′ sa) | Acidsoil Lithodora | 8–12″/12″ |
| Summer        Blue | Southern Europe | Zones 5–7 |
| (Syn. *Lithospermum diffusum*) | | |

This low growing plant has ¼–1″ long, alternate, narrow, sessile leaves, hairy on both surfaces. The foliage is evergreen in mild climates. The ½″ long flowers occur at the end of lateral stems which emerge from every leaf axil. They are deep blue with reddish violet stripes and appear from midsummer to fall. Plants are not tolerant of weather extremes and suffer in the South, particularly if placed in full sun or allowed to dry out. In the partially shaded raised garden of my friends, Elizabeth and John Barton, in Athens, plants performed relatively well for a couple of years. However, they never flourished. Cold temperatures of about 5° F are tolerated and mulching is beneficial in zones 5 and 6. Trim plants back if they become weedy to maintain some semblance of compactness. Sharp drainage is a must, particularly as stress from hot summers or cold winters increases. Planting on a slope or in raised beds greatly increases the chance of success. *Lithodora* is one plant that knocks your socks off when it is well-grown, but due to temperature extremes, is a difficult plant to grow well in much of the country. The common name results from the intolerance to lime, and like *Iris ensata*, Japanese iris, requires acid soils for optimum performance. This is not true of other species of *Lithodora* or *Lithospermum*.

If propagated by soft stem cuttings in humid, warm conditions, rooting will take place in 14–21 days. Seeds may also be used but the seed coat is hard and germination takes a long time unless seeds are soaked in warm water for at least 2 days, or the seed coat is scarified with light sandpaper or other abrasive material.

**Cultivars:**

Var. *alba* has white flowers but is not as showy as the species or the following cultivars. Who wants a white lithodora?

'Cambridge Blue' bears beautiful porcelain-blue flowers.

'Grace Ward' consists of silvery green mats with intense blue flowers.

'Heavenly Blue' is one of the lower growing (3″) cultivars and an excellent plant with numerous clear blue flowers.

**Related Species:**

*L. oleifolia*, olive lithodora, forms mounds consisting of ascending stems loaded with pink flower buds which open to lavender blue flowers. Not as cold hardy, probably only to about zone 7.

## *Lithospermum* (lith-o-sperm' um)   Puccoon   Boraginaceae

Although little used, a number of handsome plants native to the United States are occasionally offered. Flowers are usually orange-yellow but white is not uncommon. Much more adaptable to temperature extremes than *Lithodora* and easier to grow. Nevertheless, many species are native to sandy soils and drainage is still important.

*L. canescens*, puccoon, is also known as red-root and Indian paint because the red juice in the roots was used as a dye or for facial paint by native Americans in Ontario to Alabama and west to Arizona. The 9–12" tall mounded plants bear small yellow-orange flowers in early spring. The flowers are sessile or almost so along the terminal one third of the flowering stems. *L. incisum* (syn. *L. angustifolium*) is quite showy with large handsome bright yellow flowers. The lobes of the flowers are fringed, making it easily distinguishable from other species. Native to the Midwest and west to British Columbia, south to Texas. This genus performs well as far south as zone 7, and north to zone 5, 4 with protection.

## *Lobelia* (lo-bee' lia)   Lobelia   Campanulaceae

*Lobelia* consists of over 250 species of annual and perennial herbaceous plants. One of the most popular bedding plants is the blue-flowered annual lobelia, *L. erinus*, used for edging or in hanging baskets. The perennial species, however, provide a brilliant splash of summer color and range from the deepest scarlet to the darkest blue. All have alternate leaves and tubular or star-shaped flowers on racemose inflorescences held well above the leaves.

The perennial lobelias are somewhat short-lived and must be replaced or divided at least every 3 years. Many are native to stream banks and other areas of moist soil and prefer a rich, moist, but well-drained location in the shaded garden. In the Northeast and Northwest, plants tolerate full sun or partial shade, but in the Midwest and South, some shade is essential. Regardless of where they are grown, a light (½–1" deep) winter mulch is beneficial. If mulched heavily, plants die. Remove mulch early in the spring.

Lobelias are native in many parts of the world but the American species are most numerous and colorful. The cardinal flower, *L. cardinalis*, is everyone's favorite and has been used as a parent in many outstanding hybrids. However, dozens of others, while perhaps not as eye-catching, are potential gems in the garden. *L. glandulosa*, with light blue flowers, and

*L. elongata*, with deeper blue flowers, have 3–4′ tall spires and, although difficult to locate, make fine garden plants.

Considerable breeding has produced hybrid strains with dark stems and brilliant scarlet or purple flowers. They are excellent additions to the lobelias and without doubt, will be offered more by perennial specialists.

The species may be propagated from seed or division; the hybrids and named cultivars should only be divided. Seed is tiny and should be lightly covered to insure it does not dry out. Sow under warm (70–75° F), moist conditions.

Quick Reference to Lobelia Species

|  | Height (ft.) | Flower color |
|---|---|---|
| *L. cardinalis* | 2–4 | Red |
| *L.* × *gerardii* | 3–5 | Purple |
| *L. siphilitica* | 2–3 | Blue |
| *L.* × *speciosa* | 3–5 | Red, pink |

| *-cardinalis* (kar-di-nah′ lis) | | Cardinal Flower | 2–4′/2′ |
|---|---|---|---|
| Summer | Red | North America | Zones 2–9 |

This species has an extensive natural range, occurring as far north as New Brunswick, south to Florida, and west to Texas. The plant is usually unbranched with 3–4″ long, dark green, irregularly toothed leaves attached either directly to the stem or by a very short petiole. Each 1½″ long flower is brilliant cardinal and the lower lip, consisting of 3 distinct lobes, is bent downwards. Up to 50 flowers may be produced on a single 2′ long inflorescence. One forgets the morphology, taxonomy and everything else, however, when the hummingbirds arrive. Then, they are hummingbird flowers, and the few dollars spent for plants produces dividends unparalleled in the New York Stock Exchange. In the Armitage garden, flowering begins in early August and continues for about 3 weeks. Flowers open from the base to the apex (acropetally) but by the end of 3 weeks, the inflorescence looks "tired."

Soil amended with copious amounts of aged manure or peat moss, and one which will retain moisture during dry weather is essential for garden performance and longevity. Growth and flowering occur in dry areas but flowers are not as persistent or dramatic. In most parts of the country, shade should be provided for part of the day, and certainly during late afternoon. Abundant seed is produced which may be sown in a greenhouse, cold frame, or allowed to self-sow.

**Cultivars:**

'Alba' has white flowers.
'Rosea' bears rose-pink flowers.

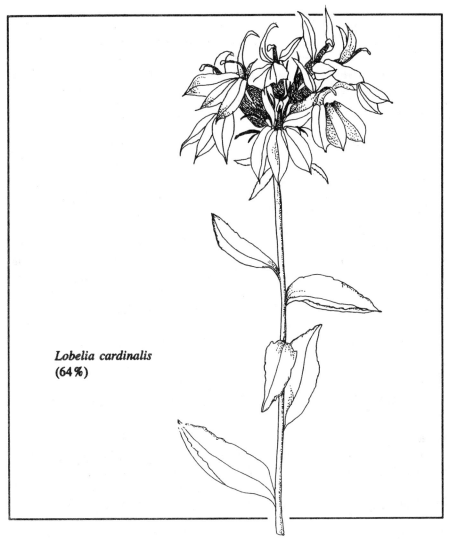

*Lobelia cardinalis*
(64%)

**Related Species:**

   *L. bridgesii*, Bridges lobelia, is similar but has soft pink rather then red flowers. Recently reintroduced into cultivation but almost impossible to find.

   *L. splendens* (syn. *L. fulgens*), Mexican lobelia, is closely related to *L. cardinalis*. Plants have larger bracts beneath the flowers, are more pubescent, and usually have bronze stems and leaves. Bronze-leaf cardinal flowers, particularly if grown from seed, are very likely *L. splendens*. Although spectacular in flower, they are much less cold hardy (to zone 7 or 8), shorter lived, and not as tolerant of dry soils as *L. cardinalis*. 'Illumination' bears large spikes of deep scarlet flowers over bronze foliage.

*L. tupa*, blood lobelia, has unique wrinkled, gray-green, soft downy leaves. Plants are more branched and usually not as tall as *L. cardinalis*. The 2–4″ long tubular scarlet red flowers are held in terminal racemes, and while not as spectacular as cardinal flower, provide a lovely display in late summer and early fall. Plants are native to Chile and cold hardy only to zone 7. They do moderately well in the South.

| -× *gerardii* (ger-ard-ee′ eye) | | Hybrid Purple Lobelia | 3–5′/2′ |
|---|---|---|---|
| Summer | Purple | Hybrid | Zones 5–7 |

Plants are the result of a cross between either *L. cardinalis* or *L. × speciosa* 'Queen Victoria', and *L. siphilitica*. To add to the confusion, they are sometimes mistakenly included under *L. × hybrida*. The habit of the plant is similar to *L. cardinalis*, with unbranched stems bearing many star-shaped purple flowers, with a pink tinge, on spike-like racemes. The 4–6″ long clasping leaves are dark green and elliptical. Stems are strong and seldom need staking. This hybrid appears longer-lived than the species. Moist soil, partial shade and a light winter mulch are recommended. They grow and perform well in the Montreal Botanical Gardens.

Terminal cuttings or division are the common methods of propagation but *L. × gerardii* comes fairly true from seed.

### Cultivars:

'Rosenkavalier' has pink flowers.
'Vedariensis' (still listed as *L. × vedariensis*) has green foliage with a red tinge and dark violet flowers.

### Related Species:

*L. sessilifolia* is native to Korea, Taiwan and Japan and winter hardy to zone 5, zone 4 with protection. The violet-blue flowers are held in dense terminal spikes. The upper leaves are sessile (thus the name) and the plants grow 3–5′ tall. Plants appear to be more adaptable to drier soils than other species.

| -*siphilitica* (si-fi-li′ ti-ka) | | Big Blue Lobelia | 2–3′/1½′ |
|---|---|---|---|
| Late Summer | Blue | Eastern United States | Zones 4–8 |

The specific name arose from the supposed medicinal properties but it is now grown for ornamental value only. The 1″ long blue flowers are surrounded by leafy bracts and tend to look weedy. The flowers, which tend to fade into the bracts, are held in dense terminal racemes above the unbranched plants. They appear later than cardinal flower and persist for about 4 weeks. The 3–5″ long leaves are narrowed at both ends and attached directly to the flower stem (the bottom leaves have short petioles). Constant moisture and partial shade are necessary for optimum performance and, unfortunately, plants are short lived and should be divided and moved every 2-3 years. With all the name changes to our favorite plants, such as *Chrysanthemums* and *Iris*, why don't the taxonomists get to work at changing this one?

Propagate the species by seed and cultivars by division.

**Cultivars:**
'Alba' is a white-flowered form of the species.
'Blue Peter', developed by Blooms Nursery in England, has light blue flowers on a 3' plant and may prove more perennial than others.

**Related Species:**
*L. elongata* has long, narrow leaves and bears light blue flowers on one side of the flower stem. Grows 3-4' tall and performs well in zones 7-9.

| -× *speciosa* (spe-cee-o' sa) | Hybrid Lobelia | 3-5'/3' |
|---|---|---|
| Summer          Red, Pink | Garden Hybrid | Zones 5-8 |
| (Syn. *L.* × *hybrida*) | | |

*L.* × *speciosa* is a catch-all name for the numerous hybrids developed from *L. splendens*, *L. cardinalis*, and *L. siphilitica*. The addition of the other two species to *L. splendens* results in hybrids which are longer lived and more tolerant of soil types and moisture. If a perennial bronze-foliaged cardinal flower is desirable, it will be well to stay away from *L. splendens* and consider the hybrids. Unfortunately, they don't have the winter hardiness of *L. cardinalis* or *L. siphilitica*; however, some of these are most glorious plants and worth a try even if they only bring but a single year of glory.

Propagate hybrids from offshoots in late summer and fall and from stem cuttings in midsummer for cultivars. Seed is available for some hybrids.

**Cultivars:**
'Bees' Flame' bears vermillion-red flowers and beet-red foliage and can reach heights of 5'. This is an absolutely magnificent plant in moist, partially shaded conditions.
'Compliment' series is available from seed and is a midsize group with flowers of red, pink, purple or scarlet. Not as spectacular as some of the others, but hardy, persistent and colorful.
'Elm Fire' ('Elmfeuer') is a recent introduction with deep maroon leaves and scarlet flowers.
'Dark Crusader' provides dark purple foliage in combination with blood red flowers.
'Pink Flamingo' is one of many hybrids developed by the North Carolina plantsman, Thurman Maness. Crossing *L. cardinalis* and *L. siphilitica* provided numerous selections. 'Pink Flamingo' has leaves similar to *L. siphilitica* and rich rosy-pink flowers in late summer.
'Queen Victoria' is the most popular cardinal flower with brilliant red flowers over bronze foliage. In flower, plants grow 3-5' tall. Hardy in zones 6-8.

'Rose Beacon' grows 2–3' tall and bright rosy pink flowers. Another Maness hybrid.

'Royal Robe' may be a cultivar of *L. cardinalis* but more likely a hybrid of *L. × speciosa*. Plants bear deep red flowers with maroon leaves.

'Ruby Slippers', developed by Maness, bears bright garnet red flowers on robust plants.

'Russian Princess' has bright reddish purple flowers with purple foliage.

'Sparkle Divine', a hybrid developed by Maness, bears purple-fuchsia flowers on long inflorescences on 3' tall plants.

'Tania' is a recent Royal Horticultural Society award winner, with rosy lavender flowers over silvery green foliage in late summer. Plants grow about 3' tall.

'Wildwood Splendor', also developed by Maness, produces large lavender flowers in late summer.

A number of tetraploids (double the usual number of chromosomes, see *Hemerocallis*) were developed by Wray Bowden at Ottawa, Canada. Parents include *L. siphilitica*, *L. cardinalis*, 'Queen Victoria' and 'Illumination'. The plants have large flowers, thick, stiffly erect stems, thick leaf blades, and well developed fibrous roots. The stems usually have a bronze cast and although still somewhat short lived, are winter hardy to zone 3 and appear to be excellent garden plants. Numerous cultivars have been developed but six of the best are listed.

'Brightness' is 3–4' tall with bright cherry red flowers atop dark bronze foliage.

'Hamilton Dwarf' is only 2' tall with 6" long blood red racemes maturing to crimson.

'Oakes Ames' bears deep scarlet flowers and bronze stems and leaves.

'Robert Landon' produces large cherry red flowers and has proven exceptional in tests in Ottawa.

'Simcoe' also has scarlet flowers on 2' long racemes.

'Wisley' has lighter red flowers and stem color than 'Oakes Ames'.

Quick Key to Lobelia Species

    A. Flowers red to scarlet
      B. Stems green, or mostly so,
        flowers obviously lipped . . . . . . . . . . . . . . *L. cardinalis*
      BB. Stems bronze or tinged red,
        flowers star shaped or lipped . . . . . . . . . . *L. × speciosa*
    AA. Flowers blue to purple
      B. Flowers clear blue, obviously lipped, hairy . . . *L. siphilitica*
      BB. Flowers purple, star shaped, not hairy . . . . . . *L. × gerardii*

**Additional Reading:**

Bowden, Wray. 1984. Perennial tetraploid lobelia hybrids. *The Garden* 109(2):55–57.

Higgenbottom, J. 1992. What's new in '92. *American Nurseryman* 175(4):52.
Hugo, Nancy Ross. 1990. Cardinal flower. *Horticulture* 68(9):64.
Lammers, T.G. 1993. *Lobelia bridgesii*. *Kew Magazine* 10(2):70–75.

*Lunaria* (loon-air′ ee-a)        Honesty, Money Plant        Brassicaceae

Honesty has been a popular garden plant since Victorian times when it was grown for the round papery-thin fruit (silicles). The most common species is the biennial dollar plant, *L. annua*, and the only one listed in the majority of garden catalogs. However, *L. rediviva*, perennial honesty, is more persistent where conditions are suitable.

*Lunaria* is not difficult to grow and does well in almost any garden soil if some afternoon shade is provided. The leaves are opposite, toothed and heart shaped. The purple or white flowers are held above the foliage and fruit is present while the uppermost flowers are still opening.

Quick Reference to Lunaria Species

|  | Height (ft.) | Flower color | Fruit shape |
| --- | --- | --- | --- |
| *L. annua* | 2–3 | Purple, white | Round |
| *L. rediviva* | 3–4 | Purple | Oblong |

*-annua* (an-ew′ a)        Honesty, Money Plant        2–3′/2′
    Spring        Purple        Europe        Zones 4–8
(Syn. *L. biennis*)

While technically a biennial species, it self sows so readily that it is always somewhere in the garden, although probably not where originally planted. A visit to my friend Mrs. Laura Ann Segrest is always a delight in April when money plant is in flower and the fruit all over her garden. There is a great deal of variation in the species and the heart-shaped leaves may be opposite or alternate. They are coarsely toothed and the upper leaves are sessile. The flowers of the species are purple but the var. *alba*, with white flowers, is just as common. In the Armitage garden, I try to segregate the purple flowering plants to where the yellow daffodils flower. The late daffodils and the early lunarias make a wonderful combination. I leave the white-flowered ones in the shaded garden where they brighten up the place. When seed or plants are purchased, there is a good chance that both colors will be present. The fruit is the most ornamental part of the plant and is 2″ wide, round, and papery thin. If brought inside, the stems must be cut just as the green color disappears from the fruit. Hang upside down in a cool, well ventilated place for 3–5 weeks. They dry exceptionally well and make wonderful additions to winter bouquets. The down side of this species is that they seed everywhere so you better not get tired of them because

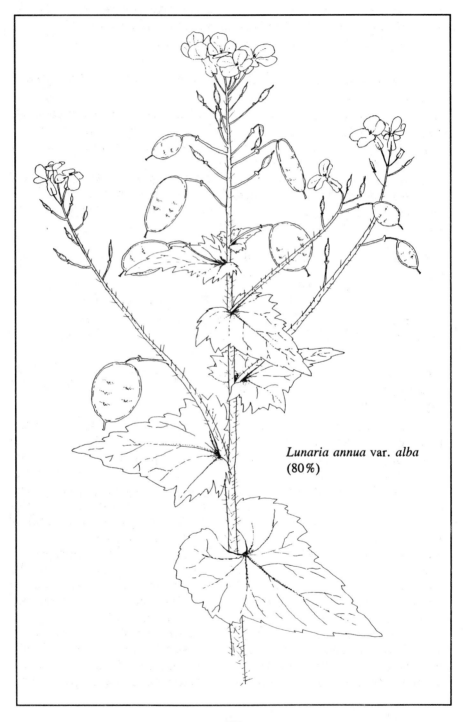

*Lunaria annua* var. *alba*
(80%)

they will be your partners for a long time. Susan is brutally honest in her evaluation of the plants, wondering why I have left so many weeds around. In the spring, when hundreds of seedlings are present, I ask the same question.

Plants should be placed in full sun in the North and away from afternoon sun in the South. The white-flowered forms are handsome in the spring shade garden as light reflects off the flowers and brightens the surrounding greenery. Flowering occurs in late April in north Georgia (zone 7), and mid May in Iowa (zone 5).

The species and varieties can be raised from seed (although var. *variegata* yields variegated and green leaf forms). Seed germinates irregularly over time; placing seed at 35–40° F for 4 weeks enhances uniformity.

**Cultivars:**

Var. *alba* has white flowers (see text).

Var. *atrococcinea* has deep red flowers.

'Munstead Purple' has flowers of rich purple.

Var. *variegata* bears leaves with irregular white margins resulting in a plant with interesting foliage, good-looking flowers and desirable fruit. This cannot be said of many other plants.

| | | | |
|---|---|---|---|
| *-rediviva* (re-di-veev' a) | | Perennial Honesty | 3–4'/2½' |
| Spring | White | Europe | Zones 4–8 |

This plant's existence has been a well-kept secret. In the first edition of this book (1989), I could find no offering of perennial honesty in the United States. At this writing, however, a number of nurseries are now listing it. Plants are larger than *L. annua*, have finely toothed, petioled leaves and smaller, lighter purple, more fragrant flowers. Other than overall size, the main difference is the 2–3" long, 1" broad elliptical fruit compared to the round fruit of *L. annua*. They may be dried similarly. Although not as well known as money plant, this species is worth seeking. Well-drained soil in partial shade provides optimum growing conditions; however, the soil should not be allowed to dry out.

Propagate from division in spring or by seed. Seed must be kept warm and moist for the first 2 weeks, then placed at freezing or just above for 4–6 weeks. Finally expose seeds to 70–75° F until germination occurs. This system of germination is best accomplished by sowing seed in the fall and burying the seed trays in soil for the winter. In the spring, seed will germinate.

Quick Key to Lunaria Species

   A. Upper leaves sessile, silicles round . . . . . . . . . . . . *L. annua*
   AA. Upper leaves with long petioles, silicles elliptical . . . *L. rediviva*

**Additional Reading:**

Brandies, Monica. 1986. Lunaria. *Horticulture* 64(8):26–27.

*Lupinus* (loo-py′ nus)　　　　　　　Lupine　　　　　　　Fabaceae

Flowers more perfect than those of the lupine hybrids are difficult to imagine. One of my most vivid memories is the Lupine Garden at Chatsworth House, England. Great drifts of orange, blue, white and purple assailed my senses as I neared the walled garden. As each flower took shape, nowhere could I look without sucking in my breath in utter delight. The scene was simply too perfect to be true. However, not to be outdone, the western states threw down the "sucking breath" gauntlet and held me affixed with fields of blue lupines in Texas, Colorado and California. This utter delight stuff was killing me.

Well over 70 species are found in the central mountain and plains states; Texas claims a few dozen, the northwest has their fair share and just when I thought I could recognize a lupine, I was introduced to the unifoliate lupines of the southeastern sandhills. It is a given that lupines are beautiful, so why aren't nurseries making lots of money by selling them to us? Unfortunately, many are difficult to propagate and/or produce in containers and lack garden persistence when grown away from the native habitat. A few nurseries offer *L. perennis*, a species with blue flowers native from Maine to Minnesota and south from Louisiana to Florida, and the small blue flowers of *L. sulphureus* can be found within a few catalogs. The northwestern species, *L. polyphyllus*, from which the hybrids obtain so much of their beauty and vigor can also be occasionally found. Unlike other west coast natives, plants are tolerant of cold, heat and humidity (zones 3–6). Leaves consist of 10–16 finger-like leaflets and flowers are normally deep blue, although var. *albus* has white flowers and var. *roseus* has rose blooms. Another lovely perennial species is *L. arboreus*, the tree lupine, native to California and growing well only on the West Coast. This sub-shrub bears many stems with lemon-yellow flowers although occasionally violet or white are seen.

Numerous handsome annuals such as *L. hartwegii*, Hartweg lupine, a 2–3′ tall plant with blue and rose spikes, occur. As much as I enjoy the garden hybrids, nothing comes close to the natural beauty of the native species in their native habitat. May we be smart enough to protect them!

As beautiful as the native species are, they are not well known among gardeners. Without doubt, the most popular of the perennial species are the various hybrids, including the most famous of them all, the Russell hybrids (probably because they are the only ones easily available). Few flowers withstand close scrutiny as well as the lupine; they look even more perfect from 3 inches than from 3 feet. The multicolored spires add an aristocratic aura to the garden available from few other species. They should be placed in the fall garden in zones 5 and south in October and success is more likely if transplanted to the garden from at least one gallon containers. The smaller the transplant, the more time that is necessary to establish the plants before the onset of cold weather. Since few of us live in England, let's set the record straight. Lupines, at the best of times, are short lived perennials and for gardeners who live in areas of hot summers, they are best grown as annuals. They look terrific in March and April if planted in October. Even in the Northeast, lupines tend to be short-lived and should routinely be replaced. Plant in full sun in the fall in well-drained, acidic soil. They are relatively easy to grow if soils are rich and conditions are cool and flowers persist for weeks in the spring garden. Often self-sown seedlings emerge, and although the progeny will not be the same colors as the parents, half the fun is guessing just what is coming next.

Propagate species and hybrids from seed. Some of the species are difficult to germinate and should be soaked in warm water overnight or placed in containers and provided with 4–6 weeks of cold, moist stratification between 30° and 40° F. Seeds of the hybrids are available as complete mixes or as single colors.

**Hybrids:**

James Kelway of Langport, England crossed *L. polyphyllus* with *L. arboreus* in the late 1890's and other English pioneers such as Downer and Harkness continued the early development of lupines by developing hybrids with many different flower colors. One of the first breakthroughs was the red 'Downer's Delight' raised about 1917 and honored by the Royal Horticultural Society in 1918. In 1911, the flowers of the various cultivars, forms and hybrids of *L. polyphyllus* caught the attention of a hobby gardener from Yorkshire, England by the name of George Russell. Continuing Kelway's work, he included other species such as *L. mutabilis* (a 5' plant with white and blue flowers) from South America, and *L. nanus* (a lovely 1' tall annual with blue flowers) from California. By 1937, Russell had perfected flowers of blue, purple, yellow, intense reds, deep pinks, and numerous combinations of bicolors. Many of these original breakthroughs are still available today as Russell hybrids. Some of the new hybrids from Russell's work are offered as 'Russell Hybrid Improved'. Continued development of the herbaceous lupines has continued since Russell's time and new cultivars appear every year. Some of the following cultivars are listed as Russell hybrid cultivars, others as *L. polyphyllus* hybrids, or on their own. Hybridization has merged the various germplasm and little "purity" of hybrids has been maintained.

**Cultivars:**

'Carmine' bears tall carmine flowers.

'Chandelier' has yellow flowers on 3' tall plants.

'Delicate Pink' bears soft pink flowers.

'Gallery Hybrids' are 15–18″ tall and occur in shades of blue, pink, red and white.

'Garden Gnome' is a dwarf (18–24″) form in many colors.

'Ivory' is a handsome form with creamy white flowers.
'Little Lulu' is available in many colors on 18–24″ tall plants.
'Minarette' consists of dwarf (18–20″) plants in mixed colors.
'My Castle' is 2–3′ tall with brick-red flowers.
'Noble Maiden' bears white flowers atop 2′ tall plants.
'Popsicle' is a series of colors ranging from blue, pink, red, white and yellow. A popular compact series.
'Red Flame' has bright red blooms.
'The Chantelaine' produces pink and white bicolor flowers.
'The Governor' produces perfect blue and purple flowers on 2–3′ stems.
'The Pages' bears tall racemes of carmine flowers.

**Additional Reading:**

Foster, Catherine Osgood. 1984. Lupines. *Horticulture* 62(5):32–35.

## *Lychnis* (lick′ nis)       Campion       Caryophyllaceae

Lychnis comes from the Greek *lychnos*, meaning lamp, and provides an apt description of the flame-colored flowers of certain species. The name *campion* is believed to be derived from champion because some species were used to make garlands for victors in public games or tournaments. Much of the older literature still refers to plants in the genus as champions. About 20 species are included, although the number changes constantly. Flowers have 5 petals, plants have opposite leaves and swollen nodes, similar to other members of the family. There was so much variation in species originally placed in the genus, that many have been transferred to other genera such as *Silene* and *Agrostemma*. Such is the imperfection of plant classification. For the garden taxonomists (people who derive special pleasures from tearing apart flowers), a few of the differences between the three genera are presented below.

Some differences between *Agrostemma, Lychnis,* and *Silene*

    A. Number of styles (female part of the flower), 3 . . . . . . . *Silene*
    AA. Number of styles, 4 or 5
       B. Styles opposite the petals . . . . . . . . . . . . . . . *Agrostemma*
       BB. Styles alternate with the petals . . . . . . . . . . . . . . *Lychnis*

To add to the confusion, a carmine-red flowered intergeneric hybrid arose between *Lychnis* and *Silene*: X *Lychsilene grandiflora.*

Of the 20 species, many are brilliantly colored but short lived garden plants. Most have simple, opposite leaves and bright orange, rose, or red flowers produced singly, in twos or in many-flowered clusters. In many areas of the South, they are like shooting stars, brilliant during their time but quickly disappearing. Further north, they persist longer but still must be replaced every few years.

All species are easily propagated from seed which may be sown directly in the garden or in containers for subsequent transplanting.

Quick Reference to Lychnis Species

| | Height (in.) | Flower color | Inflorescence few- or many-flowered |
|---|---|---|---|
| L. × arkwrightii | 18–24 | Orange-scarlet | Few |
| L. chalcedonica | 24–36 | Scarlet | Many |
| L. coronaria | 24–36 | Rose | Few |
| L. flos-cuculi | 12–24 | Deep rose | Few |
| L. × haageana | 10–18 | Orange-scarlet | Few |
| L. viscaria | 12–18 | Red | Many |

-× *arkwrightii* (ark-right' ee-eye)      Arkwright's Campion    18–24"/12"
  Early Summer      Orange-Scarlet      Hybrid Origin              Zones 6–8

This hybrid between *L. chalcedonica*, Maltese cross and *L.* × *haageana*, Haage campion, is gaining popularity due to the brilliant orange-scarlet flowers. The 1½" wide flowers are carried in a 3–10 flowered cyme and contrast well with the dark bronze foliage. They have notched petals and are often borne singly the first year. Garden longevity is a little better than *L.* × *haageana* but not as permanent as *L. chalcedonica*. In the South, longevity is 2–3 years; in the North, an additional season may be possible. Plants should be pinched early in the season to force additional shoots and reduce the potential legginess. In their first year in the Horticulture Gardens at Georgia, plants flowered from April 27–June 25. After flowering, the swollen seed pods turned from green to brown providing additional interest in the season. Shade should be provided in zones 7 and 8 but full sun is acceptable further north.

Propagate by division or stem cuttings. Little variation occurs with seed grown plants, which flower the first year.

### Cultivars:

'Vesuvius' is similar but has vermillion flowers, a color one either loves or hates. Very popular, best treated as an annual or a two year plant.

-*chalcedonica* (chal-ce-don' i-ka)      Maltese Cross          24–36"/18"
  Summer            Scarlet            Eastern Russia          Zones 3–7

Maltese cross was a favorite in every grandmother's garden (it was in mine) and is indeed an old-fashioned flower. Evidence suggests that the plant was introduced to Europe at the time of the Crusades. It was believed to have been brought back to France by Louis IX from the Holy Land and is also known as Jerusalem Cross. That it had travelled from Russia and was cultivated in Constantinople (*chalcedonica* means of the Chalcedon district, near Constantinople) at that time further suggests that it was an early introduction indeed. Ease of cultivation and rich flower color keep this species popular today. The ¾–1″ wide flowers are deep scarlet and held in dense rounded clusters of 20–50. The individual flowers are shaped like a cross, partly accounting for some of the common name. The opposite, 2–4″ long dark green leaves often clasp the stem. This is the most persistent species of the genus. Plants perform best in well-drained soil with consistent moisture and full sun.

They are easily raised from seed and divisions.

**Cultivars:**

'Alba' has white flowers.

'Carnea' produces carmine-red flowers.

'Rosea' bears rose colored flowers.

Var. *rubra-plena* (*flore-plena*), a double red form, is even more brilliantly colored than the type. Plants are difficult to produce commercially, thus difficult to locate. White, salmon, and rose forms are available but none is equal to the scarlet.

**Related Species:**

*L. alpina* is related only in that it is as cold hardy as *L. chalcedonica*. Lavender flowers cover the 5–9″ mat-forming plants in late spring. Best for the rock garden.

| *-coronaria* (ko-ro-nah′ ree-a) | Rose Campion | 24–36″/18″ |
|---|---|---|
| Spring | Rose | Southern Europe | Zones 4–7 |

Rose campion is probably the showiest species when well grown. The woolly, 2–4″ oblong leaves are grayish green and contrast with the 1–2″ wide, single, rose to red flowers profusely produced during the summer. This species was the first of the genus to receive the name lamp-flower, not for the glory of the flowers, but because its leaves were downy and soft "fit to make candle-wicks." "Wanting cotton, they used the downy Substance which covers its leaves for the Wicks of Lamps." The flowers almost do glow, making them difficult to coordinate with other plants. There are, however, other problems associated with this species. It is not a true perennial, and although plants may survive a number of seasons, they should be treated as biennials or annuals. In the South, flowering is magnificent and flowers decline rapidly. In almost all areas, second year plants are often better than first year and may bloom profusely on 3′ high and wide bushy gray-green specimens. The heat and summer rains of the second season result in loss of much of the foliage and plants that return to life the next spring are tired from their struggle to survive. However, they seed themselves prolifically and never disappear. In the North, flower colors are brighter due to cooler night temperatures in the summer. The plants are also short-lived there. For best results, place in full sun, or provide shade from afternoon sun, in well-drained soil. To overwinter plants in areas of little snow cover, plant in raised beds or place a liberal addition of gravel around the roots.

Propagation of all species can be accomplished from seed or basal cuttings taken in the spring.

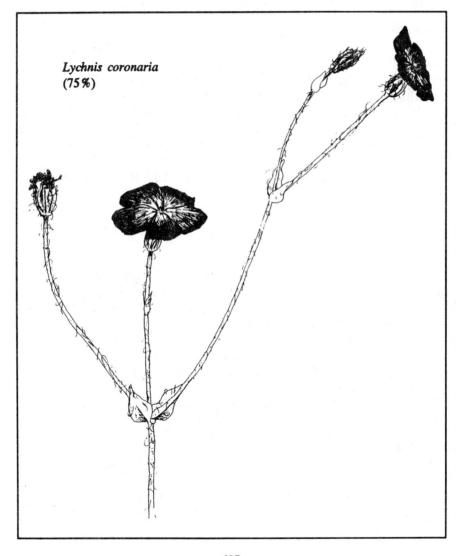

*Lychnis coronaria*
(75%)

**Cultivars:**

'Alba' has white flowers.

'Angel Blush' have white flowers with a pink blush throughout.

'Atrosanguinea' bears carmine-red flowers.

'Blood Red' has flowers which are more red than magenta.

'Dancing Ladies' is a mixture of white and carmine, usually with a dark eye.

'Flore-plena' has double flowers.

'Oculata' is very similar to 'Angel Blush' and differs by having a pink eye rather than being flushed with pink.

**Related Species:**

*L. flos-jovis*, Flower-of-Jove (Jupiter) is similar, also bearing white-woolly foliage. The plants are only 1–2' tall with muted scarlet flowers about ¾" wide. The lobed flowers are carried in a loose inflorescence somewhat similar to the flower head of primrose. Plants are longer lived than those of rose campion and should be used more in this country. 'Hort's Variety' bears clear rose-pink flowers on 10" tall plants.

*L.* × *walkeri*, a hybrid between *L. coronaria* and *L. flos-jovis*, has carmine-red flowers on short flower stems. 'Abbotswood Rose' is a compact, floriferous plant covered with bright pink to cerise flowers in late spring.

| | | | |
|---|---|---|---|
| *-flos-cuculi* (flos-kew-kew' lee) | Ragged Robin | 12–24"/12" |
| Summer | Deep Rose | Europe | Zones 3–7 |

From the rosette of narrow, grass-like, gray-green leaves emerges many stems bearing 1–3 rose to red flowers. The petals are deeply cut into four segments thus resembling a "ragged robin." Flowering persists for 6–8 weeks. Plants are adapted to sunny, moist areas and do well in the garden only if sufficient moisture can be provided. I saw a magnificent display of this plant in 1992 at the European Floriade in Holland where they were combined with field orchids and native European grasses. Beautiful in their simplicity.

Seed is the best means of propagation. Seed placed in warm (70–75° F), humid conditions germinates within 21 days.

**Cultivars:**

'Alba' has clear white flowers but is otherwise similar to the species.

'Alba Plena' bears double white flowers.

'Rosea Plena' ('Pleniflora') is an excellent selection, bearing double flowers of pink to deep rose. This double campion was known as bachelor's buttons during Elizabethan times.

-× *haageana* (hah'gee -ah' na)   Haage Campion   10–18″/12″
Summer   Orange-Scarlet   Hybrid Origin   Zones 5–7

It is interesting that this plant, which became popular when first introduced is a hybrid between two species seldom used as ornamental plants. The cross occurred between *L. fulgens*, brilliant campion, a 2–3′ tall plant with bright scarlet flowers and *L. coronata* var. *sieboldii*, crown campion, a 10–12″ tall plant with white, slightly notched petals. The result is a good garden plant with large, 2″ wide, orange-scarlet flowers. The flowers are distinctive, having petals with 2 lobes, each having small teeth on the margin.

Full sun and consistent moisture are keys to growing this hybrid, but partial shade is beneficial in the South. Although often placed at the front of the garden because of size, the bright flowers are noticeable even in the shadow of taller neighbors. Plants may go dormant in late summer in the southern half of the country but reappear the following spring. As with other species of *Lychnis*, 2–3 years is the normal life span, after which replacement is necessary. Slugs enjoy dining on this delicacy and suitable slug deterrents should be used in early spring. The popularity has declined due to the various problems with the hybrid.

Plants come fairly true from seed.

-*viscaria* (vis-cah' ree-a)   German Catchfly   12–18″/10″
Early Summer   Magenta   Europe   Zones 3–7
(Syn. *Viscaria vulgaris*)

This plant is sometimes included in a separate genus, *Viscaria*, however, similarities with other *Lychnis* species indicate it should be included here. The foliage is grass-like and grows in tufts. The 1″ wide magenta flowers appear in early summer and are sometimes difficult to weave into the overall color scheme. The flower stalk is sticky (viscous) just below the 3–5 flowered panicle, as are the internodes, thus accounting for the specific and common name.

Plants tolerate full sun in the North but partial shade is required in the South. They are more tolerant of dry conditions than many other members of the genus.

Propagate by seed or division.

**Cultivars:**
'Alba' ('Albiflora') bears white flowers.
'Splendens Plena' ('Flore-plena') has double rose-pink flowers and is the best form of the species.

**Related Species:**
*L. yunnanensis*, Yunnan campion, is 10–12″ tall with white to pink flowers. The flower stems are sticky, similar to *L. viscaria*.

## Quick Key to Lychnis Species

A. Foliage gray-white, woolly throughout
  B. Flowers borne singly or in 2-3's,
    magenta, plants 2-3' tall . . . . . . . . . . . . . . *L. coronaria*
  BB. Flowers borne in clusters, pink,
    plants 1-2' tall . . . . . . . . . . . . . . . . . . . . . . *L. flos-jovis*
AA. Foliage predominantly green or bronze,
  but may be hairy
  B. Inflorescence a dense head, terminal
    C. Flowers orange-scarlet, 5-15
      flowers in head, foliage bronze,
      plants 18-24" tall . . . . . . . . . . . . . . . . *L.* × *arkwrightii*
    CC. Flowers red-scarlet, 20-40
      flowers in head, foliage green,
      plants 24-36" tall . . . . . . . . . . . . . . . . *L. chalcedonica*
  BB. Inflorescence open, panicle, raceme or cyme
    C. Petals deeply 4-lobed . . . . . . . . . . . . . . *L. flos-cuculi*
    CC. Petals notched, toothed, or entire
      D. Petals slightly notched,
        flower stalks sticky . . . . . . . . . . . . . . . . *L. viscaria*
      DD. Petals toothed,
        flower stalks not sticky . . . . . . . . . . *L.* × *haageana*

**Additional Reading:**

Lawrence, G.H.M. 1953. The cultivated species of *Lychnis*. *Baileya* 1:105-114.
Leslie, Alan. 1992. *Lychnis flos-cuculi. The Garden* 117(12):558.

*Lycoris* (lie' core-is)       Resurrection Flower       Amaryllidaceae

This bulbous genus consists of about eleven species with wonderful eye-catching flowers. The leaves arise in fall, winter or early spring and persist until late spring or early summer, then disappear. The unwary gardener might believe that the bulbs have died and should be removed. In late summer and fall, however, smooth straight flower stalks arise from seemingly barren ground (thus its common name) to produce umbels of small trumpet-like flowers of pink, red, yellow or white. The flowers and plant habit are remarkably similar to *Nerine sarniensis*, an excellent cut flower species native to south Africa also exhibiting summer dormancy. In some species, the stamens are extended far beyond the petals, resulting in another common name, spider flower. Bulbs should be planted about 6" deep in the fall in full sun or partial shade and overplanted with annuals or low-growing perennials.

*L. squamigera*, autumn lycoris, is the most reliably cold hardy. All species spread by bulb offsets and some do a good deal of travelling by seed. Divide and replant after flowering. Offsets flower in 1-2 years.

## Quick Reference to Lycoris Species

|  | Height (in.) | Flower color | Flowering time |
|---|---|---|---|
| *L. aurea* | 12-24 | Yellow | Summer |
| *L. radiata* | 12-18 | Red | Fall |
| *L. squamigera* | 18-24 | Pink | Late summer |

| *-aurea* (ore-ee′ a) | | Golden Lycoris | 1-2′/2′ |
|---|---|---|---|
| Summer | Yellow, Gold | China | Zones 7-10 |

(Syn. *L. africana*)

In the fall, bulbs produce ¾″ wide, glaucous, sword-shaped foliage, which dies back in late spring. The 3″ long funnel-shaped golden-yellow flowers appear on 18″ long scapes in summer. The stamens and style protrude slightly from the flower (exserted). Bulbs should be planted so the neck is just below the soil surface. Since flower buds are formed during winter and spring, beds must be well drained during those seasons or flowers will not develop.

**Related Species:**

*L. straminea* produces straw-colored flowers in late summer to early fall. Plants are about 2′ tall.

| *-radiata* (raid-ee-ah′ ta) | Short Tube Lycoris, Spider Lily | 12-18″/12″ |
|---|---|---|
| Fall     Red | China, Japan | Zones 7-10 |

*L. radiata* has the shortest flower tube, thus the common name, and the smallest flower among the common garden species. The 1½-2″ long flowers, however, provide brilliant splashes of deep red in September and October. The long stamens look like spider legs and spider lily is an apt common name. A good deal of variability in flowering time occurs, including some early forms which flower as early as August. The leaves, which emerge in fall and persist through the winter, are only 4-6″ long and ¼″ wide making them much less of a nuisance than those of the other species. Unfortunately, flowers persist for less than 2 weeks. In the Armitage garden, like dandelions, groups of blood red flowers appear everywhere in the fall. We should all have such dandelions. Plant in full sun—fewer flowers occur in partial shade.

691

*Lycoris radiata*
(64%)

**Cultivars:**
Var. *alba* has white flowers with yellow tinges at the base of the segments.
It is pretty but cannot compare to the species.
Var. *pumila* is a dwarf form of the species, growing only 6–9″ tall.

**Related Species:**
*L. albiflora* is similar to the species but bears smaller white flowers and narrower leaves. Bulbs are marginally hardy in zone 7.

*L. sanguinea*, red heart lycoris, bears four to six 2″ long dull red flowers in August and September. The stamens are not as exserted as *L. radiata*. Plants are 12–20″ tall.

***-squamigera*** (skwah-mi' ge-ra)  Autumn Lycoris  18–24"/24"
  Late Summer  Rose-Pink  Japan  Zones 5–9

Autumn lycoris is the most common because of its greater growing range. Cold hardy to zone 5, the lovely rose-pink flowers may be enjoyed by more gardeners. Approximately four to seven, 3" long fragrant flowers appear on 2' tall scapes in mid to late summer. Although the flowers are wonderful, the spring foliage is messy as it dies down. The 9–12" long and 1–2" wide leaves are fresh in early spring, but look terrible in late spring and summer. The size and density of the foliage make it difficult to interplant annuals. Bulbs spread rapidly and make wonderful gifts to neighbors. Divide every 4–5 years.

### Cultivars:
Var. *purpurea* bears lilac to purple flowers.

### Related Species:
*L. sprengeri* is similar to the above species except that the plants are not as tall. The rosy pink flowers appear in late summer. Not as cold tolerant as *L. squamigera*.

Quick Key to Lycoris Species

> A. Flowers pink or red, not yellow
> > B. Flowers rose-pink, up to 3" long,
> > > foliage greater than ¾" wide . . . . . . . . . . *L. squamigera*
> > BB. Flowers red, about 1½" long,
> > > foliage about ¼" wide . . . . . . . . . . . . . . . . *L. radiata*
> AA. Flowers gold to yellow . . . . . . . . . . . . . . . . . . . . *L. aurea*

## *Lygodium* (lie-goad-e' um)  Climbing Fern  Schizaeaceae

To people new to gardening, a climbing fern seems to be an oxymoron. People normally think of ferns as green blobs which just sit there, not as vigorous clematis-like plants. Although not well known, there are about 40 species of this genus around the world, most of which are native to the tropics. Only one or two are sufficiently hardy to be grown outdoors, one being our native Hartford fern, *L. palmatum*. As I see these plants in the gardens of my friends, I marvel at the light green airy appearance and the lushness of the rampant growth. Why is it then, that I can hardly get these plants to grow at all? I can't even get them to grow through a 2' tall azalea. I will keep trying.

*L. palmatum*, Hartford fern, has been reported from southern New Hampshire to eastern New York, Ohio, Kentucky and south to Florida. Two types of leaves (fronds) occur on well-grown plants. The sterile fronds are palm-shaped, deeply lobed into 5–7 blunt segments. The fertile fronds are found only on the top of the branched vine, similar in shape but much smaller and more constricted. Most of the vine is evergreen, however, the

693

fertile fronds are deciduous. Plants, which multiply by the running rootstalk, are vigorous in zones 7–10 and growth can be rampant. Place in moist, partially shaded areas and acidic soil. They do not do well in basic soils or those where high levels of lime occur.

The only other species occasionally found in American gardens is the Japanese climbing fern, *L. japonicum*. The native habitat is immense, extending to Japan, India, China, Indonesia, Malaysia, New Guinea and Australia. Plants introduced to this country have escaped and are fairly common in southern and west coast gardens. The differences between the two species are fairly easy to distinguish; the airy sterile fronds of this species are pinnately lobed or compound, rather than palmate. Vigorous, handsome and equally aggressive (at least for others).

Propagate by division and place daughter plants in different areas in the garden.

## *Lysichiton* (lie-si' ki-ton)   Skunk Cabbage   Araceae

Do plants really smell like skunks? Do they look like cabbages? If you are able to visit a colony of these plants on a still day, your nose would start twitching and your eyes would dance about looking for white-striped creatures. The smell is not oppressive but it is there, particularly if you were told the common name ahead of time. Healthy plants don't look like Iceburg lettuce but the large leaves could be construed as cabbage, I guess.

Only two species occur, both being aquatic plants living in shallow water only in moderate climates. *L. americanum* (*L. americanus*) is native to the northwest while the other species, *L. camtschatcense* (*L. camtschatcensis*), grows in northeast Asia. Both are stemless, have upright, bold light green leaves about 2–4' long and 1–2' wide. The margins of the leaves are usually wavy and they smell musky particularly if bruised. After flowering, leaves remain upright but ultimately appear wilted during the summer. In the spring, the flowers emerge from the base surrounded by a cloak (spathe) of yellow or white. Neither are particularly well-known in gardens because they are aquatic, have a limited growing range. However, if happy, they colonize readily.

*L. americanum* is native from San Francisco to Santa Cruz mountains, north to Alaska and east to Montana in boggy areas. Plants are also quite at home in the Midwest and even the Northeast, assuming that they are in a wet area. The flowers consist of a greenish spadix surrounded by a bright yellow spathe which emerge before the leaves. The spathe color is the most easily distinguishable difference between the two species. *L. camtschatcense* bears flowers with a white spathe which are actually rather sweetly scented. Plants are also more compact in all parts than *L. americanum*. Regardless of the species, the cold hardiness range is about zone 5, warm to about zone 7, as long as consistent moisture is maintained. Slugs can certainly be a problem.

## *Lysimachia* (lie-sim-ak′ ia)        Loosestrife        Primulaceae

*Lysimachia* was named in honor of King Lysimachus of Thrace. It was believed that the plant was used to pacify angry oxen by "appeasing the strife and unrulinesse which falleth out among oxen at the plough, if it be put about their yokes." (*Gerard's Herbal*). The origin of the legend began with King Lysimachus who, as a last resort, waved a plant of *Lysimachia* before a pursuing, maddened beast, thus tranquilizing it. Loosestrife is a literal translation of the Greek word *Lysimachia*.

Approximately 150 species occur with opposite or whorled leaves and small rounded or bell-shaped flowers borne either singly or in narrow racemes. In general, plants establish easily in rich, moist soil and some species travel through the garden at the speed of light. Most loosestrifes thrive in the northern part of the United States and Canada but a few make good garden plants for the South.

*Steironema* is (was) a genus very closely related to *Lysimachia* and has been shuttled into and out of the loosestrifes. Presently, it has all but disappeared as a listed genus; the five or so species formally included having been transferred to *Lysimachia*. For those curious about such things, differences do occur. Botanically, they differ in that *Steironema* has 5 undeveloped stamens (stamenoidia) along with the 5 normal stamens, whereas *Lysimachia* has only the 5 normal stamens. Also the bases of the stamens are joined in *Lysimachia*, but separate in *Steironema*. Since no plant sources I can find list *Steironema* any longer, I will toss everything into *Lysimachia*.

### Quick Reference to Lysimachia Species

|  | Height (in.) | Flower color | Habit |
| --- | --- | --- | --- |
| *L. ciliata* | 24–36 | Yellow | Upright |
| *L. clethroides* | 24–36 | White | Upright |
| *L. nummularia* | 4–8 | Yellow | Creeping |
| *L. punctata* | 12–24 | Yellow | Upright |

-*ciliata* (cil-ee-ah′ ta)        Hairy Loosestrife        2–3′/2′
   Summer        Yellow        North America        Zones 5–8
(Syn. *Steironema cilaitum*)

One of the few native loosestrifes useful for the garden, plants bear shiny green leaves about 4″ long and 2″ wide. The smooth leaves are usually opposite but sometimes occur in whorls of 4, and are distinctive by their hairy margins (ciliate). The yellow flowers sometimes have a blotch of red at their base and are borne singly or in twos in the upper portion of the plant in summer. They grow best in moist conditions but tolerate drought better than most other species. They have a running root system and plants can appear out of nowhere, multiplying quickly to become a nuisance. Plants do well in full sun but tolerate partial shade. More flowers are formed in the sun, more foliage in the shade.

Propagate by division any time.

### Cultivars:

'Purpurea' is usually the only form found for sale. The foliage emerges deep purple and holds the color well, except in the hottest months, when it fades to muted green. The yellow flowers contrast well with the foliage. Equally aggressive as the species.

### Related Species:

*L. fraseri*, a stoloniferous native to eastern North America, also produces yellow flowers in the axils of the 2' tall plants. Plants have square stems and opposite leaves. Also known as *L. lanceolata* and *Steironema lanceolatum*. Try in zones 5 to 8.

| | | | |
|---|---|---|---|
| *-clethroides* (kleth-roi' deez) | Gooseneck Loosestrife | 2–3'/3' |
| Late Summer | White | China, Japan | Zones 3–8 |

This was one of my favorite plants when I lived in Montreal. The fine foliage and the handsome white, arching flower spikes were not only appreciated in the garden but could also be enjoyed inside as a cut flower. Growth was vigorous but its wandering nature was not difficult to control. In Michigan, although plants were still enjoyable, I found myself wondering how plants appeared in areas where I knew they had not been planted. In Georgia, this beautiful northern plant liked it so much that it began to explore every square inch of my garden and was seriously thinking about trying out the neighbor's. Unfortunately, the flower heads were smaller and the plants rather weedy, and it was relegated to a local plant sale. I now enjoy it in other people's gardens. This may well become the next kudzu of the South.

Numerous ½" wide white flowers are held in a 12–18" long, narrow, curved raceme which resembles a goose's neck, thus the common name. The inflorescence straightens as the fruits mature. The slightly pubescent, 3–6" long leaves are opposite and narrowed at each end. Moist, but not waterlogged soils, and full sun result in optimum growth. Due to its rambling nature, sufficient room must be provided. A garage on one side and pavement all around just might help. Gooseneck loosestrife is grown commercially as a cut flower in northern Europe and the United States and is finding its way into florist bouquets throughout the country. Given a little floral preservative, cut flowers persist for nearly a week.

Propagation is not difficult by division or seed.

### Related Species:

*L. ephemerum* produces narrow, branching 12–15″ long spires of starry white flowers over several weeks. The opposite foliage is gray green, sessile, and joined at the base around the stem. The most important characteristic is the lack of invasiveness. This is a decent plant and deserves to be planted much more widely. Unfortunately for me, it does not do well in southern gardens. I had high hopes for it in the Armitage garden and the Georgia gardens, but heat and humidity don't seem to agree with it. Fair in Michigan, okay in New York, terrific in the Northwest. Hardy to zone 6 (perhaps 5), and well worth trying in the Northeast as well.

| *-nummularia* (num-ew-lah′ ree-a) | Creeping Jenny | 4–8″/24″ |
|---|---|---|
| Early Summer Yellow | Europe | Zones 3–9 |

This European native has become naturalized in the eastern United States and is often found at the edge of wooded areas. The fragrant 1″ diameter, bright yellow flowers are borne singly in the axils of the opposite, rounded 1″ long leaves. Plants are prostrate and each long stem produces roots along the length resulting in rapid multiplication. Large patches of creeping Jenny quickly appear in shady areas where soil is moist. Plants are used as ground covers by streams, pools, or other wet areas.

Propagate by division in spring or fall.

### Cultivars:

'Aurea' is popular and with good reason. The lime green to yellowish leaves brighten up any shady area in which it is planted. The vigor declines in the heat but plants return in the fall. The yellow flowers are not as noticeable.

### Related Species:

*L. congestiflora*, dense-flowered loosestrife, forms dense mats of dark green stems and terminal ½–¾″ wide yellow flowers. Native to China, it is cold hardy to about zone 7a if winter mulch is provided. Introduced by Dr. Don Jacobs of Eco Gardens in Georgia, plants are presently being offered by Southern nurseries. 'Eco Dark Satin' bears yellow flowers with a red throat.

*L. japonica* is about 12″ tall with small yellow flowers and opposite foliage. The most interesting cultivar is the carpet-forming 'Minuitissima'. Only 1–2″ tall, it is terrific between flagstones in walkways where it acts like grass and may be abused with abandon. The starry yellow flowers open in June and July. I saw some fantastic carpets in the garden of Margaret

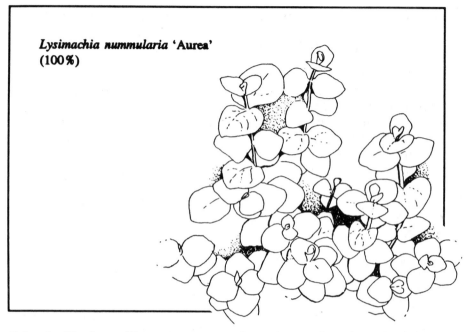

*Lysimachia nummularia* 'Aurea'
(100%)

Grigg in Charlotte. Plants were everywhere, but unobtrusive when not in flower. Hardy in zones 5 to 8.

| *-punctata* (punk-tah′ ta) | | Yellow Loosestrife | 1–3′/1′ |
|---|---|---|---|
| Summer | Yellow | Europe, Western Asia | Zones 4–8 |

This species has also found the United States to its liking and is found growing in moist areas throughout the country. Particularly fond of moist, shady areas, the plant is often known as the "ditch-witch" of the countryside. The 1–3″ long whorled leaves occur in groups of 3's or 4's. The ¾–1″ wide flowers are also whorled and borne in the upper leaf axils from May to September. They are lemon-yellow with a small brownish circle in the throat. Plants are much better for zones 4 and 5 than for 7 and 8 where they become more weedy and the flowers lose their sparkle.

Propagate by cuttings or seed.

**Related Species:**

*L. vulgaris*, also known as yellow loosestrife, has similar growth habit and leave arrangement, as well as flowers of the same color. The main difference is that most of the flowers of this species are borne at the end of the stem (terminal) whereas those of *L. punctata* are produced in the axils of the leaves along the stem. Both species are aggressive and love moist conditions.

## Quick Key to Lysimachia Species

A. Leaves whorled, flowers whorled . . . . . . . . . . . *L. punctata*
AA. Leaves opposite (occasionally whorled)
    B. Flowers white, arching, terminal
      racemes, plants upright . . . . . . . . . . . . . . *L. clethroides*
  BB. Flowers yellow, borne singly
    in leaf axils
    C. Leaf margins hairy, plants upright . . . . . . . . . *L. ciliata*
  CC. Leaf margins not hairy, plant prostrate . . . *L. nummularia*

**Additional Reading:**

Chatto, Beth. 1986. *Lysimachia. Horticulture* 64(7):22–23.
Ingram, John. 1960. Notes on the cultivated Primulaceae 1. *Lysimachia. Baileya* 8:85–97.

## *Lythrum* (li′ thrum)      Lythrum, Purple Loosestrife      Lythraceae

*Lythrum* is one of those plants whose beauty enthralls those who don't know it well, but is an aggressive overbearing weed to those who do. Although native to Europe and Asia, plants have become naturalized in North America and can be seen along highways and byways in the northern United States and Canada during the summer. Southern Ontario, upper New York state and the northeast, among other places, are ablaze with this "weed" in July through September. They have been listed as noxious weeds in many states, and I expect that they will be so listed in many more states before long. Some excellent breeding has resulted in sterile cultivars, which seemed to be the answer to the wetland problem, allowing gardeners to plant loosestrife without guilt. If only the sterile cultivars are used, and they are nowhere near fertile plants, then few seedlings will occur. However, recent research has shown that sterility only occurs when no plants of the wild species are in the neighborhood. When plants of 'Morden Pink' or 'Morden Gleam', two sterile cultivars, were planted near *L. salicaria*, the seed of the resulting hybrids was over 80% viable and germinated, thus contributing to the spread of this purple lava flow.

Regardless of the problems, there is no denying their effectiveness in the garden. Excellent breeding work has produced some fine garden cultivars. The entire leaves are opposite and bear small pink or purple flowers on leafy spike-like racemes along the length of the 4-angled flower stem. In general, moist soils are preferred but plants grow well in well-drained garden soils if not allowed to dry out. All forms should be cut back after flowering to keep seeding down to a minimum. Plants look terrible after flowering, so cutting them back improves the place anyway. Of the 25 or 30 species, only 2 or 3 closely related ones are cultivated.

Quick Reference to Lythrum Species

|  | Height (ft.) | Flowers distinctly stalked |
|---|---|---|
| *L. salicaria* | 3-5 | No |
| *L. virgatum* | 2-3 | Yes |

| -*salicaria* (sal-i-kah′ ree-a) | | Purple Lythrum | 3-5′/2′ |
|---|---|---|---|
| Summer | Purple-Rose | Europe, Australia | Zones 3-9 |

This species has naturalized in cooler areas of the United States and Canada and is particularly abundant in marshes and wet meadows, often crowding out native wetland species. Plants are tolerant of heat and humidity and do well in southern gardens as long as adequate moisture is supplied. Full sun and moist well-drained soils insure vigorous growth and abundant flowers. The willowy, lanceolate, 4-6″ long leaves are slightly hairy, heart shaped at the base and often clasp the stem. The ¾″ wide flowers, borne in almost sessile whorls in dense terminal leafy racemes, persist from early summer to early fall. Japanese beetles have a particular fondness for purple lythrum.

The species may be propagated by seed, and self seeds prolifically. Every spring, dozens of seedlings are culled from the Horticulture Gardens. Cultivars must be multiplied by division or stem cuttings in the spring.

**Cultivars:**

'Atropurpureum' has dark purple flowers.

'Brightness' produces rosy pink flowers on 3′ tall plants.

'Firecandle' ('Feuerkerze') bears intense rose-red pointed racemes.

'Flash Fire' ('Stitchflamme') is a hot pink form standing about 3′ tall. Probably a hybrid.

'Happy' is a handsome dwarf cultivar which produces many lavender-pink flowers on 15-18″ tall plants. Not as eye-catching as the taller forms, but effective.

'Pink Spires' bears deep pink sterile flowers and stands about 3′ tall.

'Purple Spires' is similar but with purple flowers.

'Robert' has deep pink flowers, is only 2′ tall and has excellent fall color.

'Roseum Superbum' bears rosy-purple flowers up to 1″ wide and is very vigorous.

'Rosy Spires' has sterile deep rose flowers.

'The Beacon' has bright rose-red spires borne on 3½′ tall plants. The brightness of the flowers act as a "beacon" in the garden. An excellent cultivar.

'Zigeunerblut' ('Gypsy Blood'), likely a hybrid with other species, bears blood red flowers.

*Lythrum salicaria*
(100%)

| *-virgatum* (vir-gah' tum) | | Purple Loosestrife | 2–3'/2' |
|---|---|---|---|
| Summer | Purple | Europe, Asia | Zones 3–9 |

There is little difference between this and the previous species. The base of the leaf is narrower and seldom clasps the stem. Each ½" wide flower is borne on a small flower stalk (pedicel) while those of *L. salicaria* are nearly sessile. The stems are more twiggy but this characteristic is not easy to discern. It is an excellent plant for the garden and responds well to moisture and full sun.

The species self sows prolifically. Seeds of cultivars do not come true. Propagate similar to *L. salicaria*.

**Cultivars:**

'Dropmore Purple' is a cross between *L. salicaria* × *L. virgatum* and has become one of the best cultivars. It has rosy-purple flowers on 2½' tall stems.

'Morden's Gleam' (*L. alatum* × *L. virgatum*) has rose flowers on 2–3' tall stems.

'Morden's Pink' bears bright pink flowers. Both are more compact than the type and sterile. The Morden series emerged from the excellent breeding program at Morden, Manitoba, Canada and are cold hardy to zone 2.

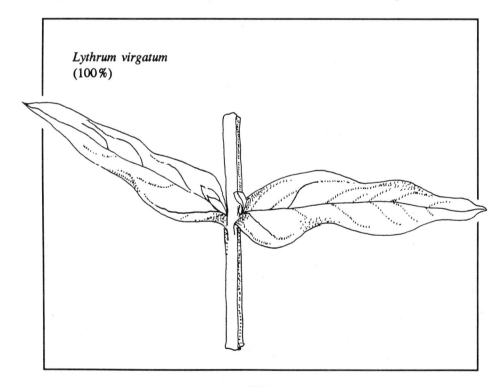

*Lythrum virgatum*
(100%)

'Morden Rose' is more compact than the others in the series and bears rose-red flowers.

'Rose Queen' is only 18″ tall and has light pink flowers.

'The Rocket' has deeper pink flowers and stands around 2½′ tall.

## Quick Key to Lythrum Species

A. Flowers sessile or almost so, leaves rounded
or heart shaped at base . . . . . . . . . . . . . . . . . . *L. salicaria*

AA. Flowers borne on distinct pedicels, leaves
narrowed at base . . . . . . . . . . . . . . . . . . . . . *L. virgatum*

## Additional Reading:

Anderson, N.O and P.D. Ascher. 1993. Male and female fertility of loosestrife (*Lythrum*) cultivars. *J. Amer. Soc. Hort. Sci.*

Lindgren, C.J. and R.T. Clay. 1993. Fertility of 'Morden Pink' *Lythrum virgatum* L. transplanted into wild stands of *L. salicaria* L. in Manitoba. *HortScience* 28(9):954.

# M

*Macleaya* (ma-klay′ ya)  **Plume Poppy**  Papaveraceae

The genus consists of three species, although hybridization has resulted in at least one intermediate form. Few people looking at the 6–10′ tall plants would guess they are part of the poppy family. Stay away from these plants unless you have a large area ready for poppy colonization. The main species in American gardens is *M. cordata*, long known as *Bocconia cordata*.

*-cordata* (kor-dah′ ta)  **Plume Poppy**  6–10′/6′
    Summer        Cream  China, Japan  Zones 3–8
(Syn. *Bocconia cordata*)

This most impressive towering plant is topped by 10–12″ long plumes (panicles) of numerous cream-colored flowers. Each flower is apetalous (no petals) and has only 2 sepals, but bears 25–30 ornamental stamens. The 8″ wide heart-shaped leaves are pubescent beneath and consist of about 7 lobes. As in many members of the poppy family, *Macleaya* bleeds yellow sap. Its stature relegates it to the back of the border or the middle of the island bed, but it is also most impressive as a specimen plant where nothing detracts from the pleasant foliage. The backs of the leaves are gray-blue and some of the few good times with this plant is when the young leaves are fluttering in the wind. A terrific cut foliage and flower choice for bold arrangements. Neither the flowers nor the foliage is particularly persistent in the vase, but they are impressive for short term celebrations.

Seldom is sufficient room provided and plants often outgrow their welcome. They spread aggressively which detracts from, rather than adds to, the beauty of the garden. Some gardeners claim with a straight face that one plant will cover 1 acre. Not quite, but many people who have planted this poppy are constantly trying to find unwary people to take divisions.

However, to be fair, they are terrific plants if room is available or in large containers. If a girdle is required, truss them up in 3–5 gallon containers and place them where the foliage can be enjoyed.

Propagate by divisions in the spring or from seed. The small seed should be barely covered and placed in a warm (70–75° F), moist environment. Germination occurs within 2 weeks but is not particularly uniform.

**Cultivars:**

'Alba' has whiter flowers than the species.

'Flamingo' produces gray-green stems and small pink flowers.

**Related Species:**

*M.* × *kewensis* is a hybrid between *M. cordata* and *M. microcarpa*. The terminal inflorescence has many lateral branches and consists of creamy white to buff-colored flowers.

*M. microcarpa*, small fruited plume poppy, is similar in habit to *M. cordata* but bears bronze flowers consisting of 8–12 stamens. The non-descript flowers open in early summer and the fruit contains a single seed compared with the 4–6 seeded capsule of *M. cordata*. The roots are even more rhizomatous.

## *Macrothelypteris* (ma-kroh-the-lip′ ter-is)   Mairiana      Thelypteridaceae
Maiden Fern

(Syn. *Thelypteris torresiana*)

*M. torresiana* is the only one of about 9 species of these terrestrial ferns which are sufficiently hardy to be included. Plants used to be part of the large genus known as *Thelypteris*, which has been reduced to about 2 species. The *macro* part of the name refers to its size and this plant will grow 3–4′ tall and equally wide under suitable conditions. Plants grow from creeping rhizomes which allow it to naturalize freely. The large pale green fronds are triply lobed or cut (tripinnatifid) and make a large airy display. They do have a rather musky, acrid odor when you get your nose up too close.

Ferns are hardy from zone 7 (7b) and south, enjoying bright light but requiring some afternoon shade and sufficient moisture to allow rootstalk to run. They are, however, one of the more sun tolerant ferns. Mulch well in the winter in zone 7.

Propagate by division in the spring as new growth appears.

## *Maianthemum* (may-anth′ e-mum)   May Lily, Mayflower   Liliaceae

The genus name comes from *maios*, the month of May, and *anthemon*, blossom, referring to its timely spring flowering. About three species of these carpet-like ground covers occur, one of which, *M. canadense*, Canada mayflower, is found all over the woodlands of northern North America. Plants are native as far west as British Columbia, east to Delaware and south to the Appalachian mountains of north Georgia.

In general, *M. canadense* stands 3–6″ tall and produces a creeping rhizome which can cloth a shady woodland area in masses of handsome foliage and fruit. A single leaf is produced from the underground stem which essentially disappears as the flowering stem appears. The flowering stem bears 2 lily-of-the-valley-like leaves, each about 3″ long. The small white flowers, consisting of 2 sepals and 2 petals, are produced on short racemes in the spring. The flowers give way to reddish berries with darker speckles. On one of our student field trips to Cape Cod, we came across what seemed like acres of maylilies in the Heritage Plantation in MA. Such a small plant, such a marvelous sight! The further north, the better the plants perform and multiply. They do poorly in the South; save your money.

Purchase plants by the dozens when available as one plant does little. Moist shade in coniferous woods is excellent; deciduous woods also work but the large leaves of some oaks and maples may smother the plants. They are easily propagated by division in the spring.

## *Malva* (mal′ va)                    Mallow                    Malvaceae

Closely related to *Hibiscus*, plants are equally beautiful in flower, but subject to attack by a host of insects and diseases. The leaves are usually lobed or dissected and the flowers, with 5 notched petals, are carried singly or in clusters. Many similarities occur between various genera in the family, a useful key to their differences may be found under *Alcea*, the hollyhocks. Approximately 30 species of annual, biennial and perennial species occur and all of them are relatively easy to grow, insects and other assorted bugs not withstanding. Two or three are particularly useful for the garden.

*-alcea* (al-see′ a)                 Hollyhock Mallow            2–3′/18″
Summer          Rose, White          Europe                    Zones 4–7

The deeply 5-parted, light green stem leaves contrast with the 2″ wide deep rose to white flowers that appear in the axils. Flowering begins in early summer and continues for 6–8 weeks. The flowers are produced singly in the leaf axils near the top of the plants. The small, triangular sepals are beneath pale red to whitish petals. All mallows enjoy full sun, well-drained soils and moderate to high pH. Garden performance is superior in the North compared to the South where spider mites, thrips, Japanese beetles, and a potpourri of foliar diseases find the plants particularly appealing.

Propagate by seed, terminal cutting in spring, or division. Seeds should be placed at 40° F in moist medium for 6 weeks. Germination is non-uniform and seedlings emerge over a 2–3 month period.

**Cultivars:**

'Fastigiata' has essentially superseded the species and is offered by most
perennial specialists. Plants are more upright, well branched and carry
2″ diameter pink to rose-pink flowers.

**Related Species:**

*M. moschata*, musk mallow, grows to 3′ tall and is naturalized in the
northeastern United States. The leaves differ from the former species by
being 5-parted with each part additionally 1–2 parted. Although the showy
rose-colored flowers are up to 2½″ wide, garden performance is fair at best
in the South, much better in zones 3–5. Plants are summer hardy to zone 8
but perform consistently well only in zones 3–5. 'Alba' has deeply cut
leaves and white flowers. 'Rosea' bears pink flowers.

| | | | |
|---|---|---|---|
| *-sylvestris* (sil-ves′ tris) | | Tree Mallow | 1–3′/2′ |
| Late Spring | Mauve | Europe, North Africa | Zones 4–8 |

This short-lived plant (sometimes grown as a biennial) resembles other
species but has shallowly 5–7 lobed, rough, hairy leaves. The petals of the
large mauve flowers are three times the length of the sepals. The flowers
of some forms often have dark stripes resulting in bicolors. They occur
singly or in 2–5 flowered clusters in the upper leaf axils.

Plants perform well in full sun or partial shade and well-drained soils.

**Cultivars:**

'Alba' grows about 2′ tall with clean white flowers.

'Brave Heart' bears large pale rose-pink flowers with a distinctive dark
purple eye on upright 3′ tall plants.

'Cottenham Blue' flowers earlier than others, with pale blue flowers and
darker veins on 2–3′ tall upright plants.

'Mauritiana' is taller, smoother and has more obtuse lobes. The dark rosy
red flowers have dark purple stripes.

'Primley Blue' is the best known blue-flowered cultivar. Plants are much
more prostrate, usually growing only about 18–24″ tall. The flowers are
a soft blue with darker veins.

'Zebrina', also known as *Alcea zebrina* and *M. zebrina*, is 2–3′ tall with
white to very pale pink flowers striped with raspberry-red veins. The
flowers look like pinwheels all summer.

Quick Key to Malva Species

    A. Leaves deeply lobed
        B. Stem leaves 5-lobed and each lobe 1–2 parted  . .  *M. moschata*
        BB. Stem leaves only once 5-lobed  . . . . . . . . . . . . .  *M. alcea*
    AA. Leaves shallowly 5-lobed or parted  . . . . . . . . .  *M. sylvestris*

## *Malvaviscus* (mal-va-vis' kus)    Sleeping Hibiscus    Malvaceae

Fascinating shrubby plants from Mexico and South America, they draw crowds because of their swirling 1–2″ vibrant scarlet flowers which never fully open (thus the common name). The petals twist about the extended stamens, appearing to squeeze them tighter and tighter. The plants grow 3–5′ tall bearing hairy unlobed or somewhat 3-lobed leaves. The only species which is sufficiently cold hardy to be called a perennial is *M. arboreus*, also known as wax mallow and turk's cap. They seem to be hardy to zone 7b, perhaps all of zone 7, and are certainly worth a try, even if they only grow as an annual.

The variety most offered is var. *drummondii* (also known as *M. drummondii*), with leaves almost as long as they are broad and bearing prominent hairs on the top surface of the leaves. The flowers are similar to the species. This is a plant for the more daring gardeners who want to try something "other worldly." Plant in well-drained soil in protected areas. Flowers occur on new wood, therefore cut back or shape in early spring when signs of life reappear. Plants are prone to spider mites and Japanese beetles.

Propagate by softwood cuttings or seed.

### Cultivars:
'Pink' is a little seen variant of *M. arboreus*. Equally handsome.

## *Matteuccia* (ma-too' see-a)    Ostrich Fern    Dryopteridaceae

Although about four species occur, *M. struthiopteris* (syn. *M. pennsylvanica*), the ostrich fern, is one of the best, biggest and most popular terrestrial ferns used today. The tall, erect, gracefully arching plant grows in tufts of ostrich-plume-shaped, dark green fronds. Both vegetative and fertile fronds occur; the vegetative ones emerging from the base and spreading out at the tip, like a big shuttlecock. The fronds can be up to 4′ long and 12″ wide, each one cut into 40 or so pairs of leaflets. Each leaflet is cut into about 30 pairs of subleaflets or lobes. The stiff fertile leaves arise from the base, consist of small leaflets divided to the midrib, and grow about 2′ tall. They begin green after the first flush of vegetative fronds, then turn brown with the many spore cases. The vegetative fronds wither with the first frost but the fertile ones remain "everbrown" throughout the winter. By the end of the season, the fronds become a little ragged and can be trimmed back. Plants spread by underground rhizomes rapidly forming colonies in damp areas. They can become invasive.

Simply one of the most classic of the ferns and excellent where a bold grouping is needed. Moisture is essential, and plants tolerate a good deal of sun. Plants do well in the North, but in the heat and humidity of the South (zone 7 and south) they are marginal, never quite attaining the majesty of growth where summers are cool.

708

Some taxonomists still treat *M. struthiopteris* and *M. pennsylvanica* as separate species, the former being the European ostrich fern, the latter known as the American ostrich fern. The differences, other than native habitat, are that the fronds of the European form are lighter green and a little smaller. Today, the two forms are lumped together by most gardeners.

## *Mazus* (may' zus)                    Mazus                    Scrophulariaceae

For some reason, this charming ground cover is not at all well known. About 30 species have been described, each with creeping stems, and producing many white to purple-blue flowers in the spring. The basal leaves are rosette or opposite, the stem leaves are alternate, toothed or incised. The most cold hardy and highly useful species is *M. reptans*, native to the Himalayas. Hardy to zone 6 (perhaps 5), plants are terrific for planting among flagstones and in rockgardens or pathways. The small 2-lipped flowers occur in late spring and are held in few-flowered racemes. Generally, flowers are lavender-blue, but 'Alba' is probably more available and the flowers stand out well on the 2–4″ tall plants. 'Purperblau' is a handsome lavender form. I like these plants growing in and around my flagstone walk in the garden. Not quite as tough as turf, but a whole lot more pleasant.

Some plantspeople are starting to offer *M. japonicus* from eastern Asia, in particular the white form 'Albiflorus'. Plants are also about 2–4″ tall, and covered with white flowers. I have a difficult time seeing much difference between the two species.

Plants tolerate full sun or partial shade; in the South, some afternoon shade is appreciated. Consistent moisture is necessary but wet feet are a no-no. Easy to propagate by division any time in the season. Cuttings may also be used.

## *Meconopsis* (me-ko-nop' sis)    Himalayan Blue Poppy    Papaveraceae

More than any other plant mentioned among gardeners or shown in slides on someone's talk, the Himalayan blue poppy elicits classic garden emotions of beauty, grandeur, awe and most of all, frustration and failure. The first encounter with the blue poppies, usually somewhere in the British Isles, leaves people breathless, and always asking, "where do I get them?" They seem so easy and carefree in such gardens, reseeding and hybridizing everywhere that we all feel that they must do well in our own gardens. But this is not the case, except for small pockets of meconopsis-climates on the West Coast, protected areas along the St. Lawrence river in Quebec, and here and there where summers are cool, winters are mild or the ground is consistently insulated with snow. For North American gardeners who do well with this genus, congratulations, I'll be over soon. However, . . .

I don't mean to rain on anyone's parade but let's get real concerning some of the promotions of these plants. They die, usually within one year but maybe

709

they struggle through a couple of years. They won't look like the photo, which is probably why you bought the plants in the first place. There are many plants like this in garden catalogs, but promoting *Meconopsis* as a "new crop for everyone" really gets my goat, as it is simply not true. A few years ago, a respectable mail order nursery used a photo of blue poppies on their cover! They sold a lot of poppies but disappointed a lot of people. Regardless of what I say, people want to know about these plants and a number of beautiful species and hybrids do exist. The best known are the blue forms, such as *M. betonicifolia* and *M.* × *sheldonii*, however red (*M. napaulensis*), yellow (*M. paniculata, M. regia*) or white species and forms also exist. *M. dhwojii* has interesting blue-green, mostly basal, pinnately compound leaves. The flowers on this plump 2' tall plant are light yellow, after which they die. All species are native to the Himalayas except the papier-mâché Welsh poppy, *M. cambrica*.

The Welsh poppy is native to western Europe, including the British Isles, and produces yellow to orange flowers which look at first glance very much like California or Iceland poppies. They reseed everywhere in their native habits, springing up in sunny fields or at the base of shady walls. They are common in the Northwest, where deadheading is recommended to reduce their reseeding tendencies. The bright green hairy foliage contrasts well with the 2" wide whimsical flowers. Double forms ('Floro-pleno'), deep orange ('Aurantiaca') and named cultivars such as 'Frances Perry' with scarlet flowers, may occasionally be found. This is the one species of *Meconopsis* that we should be experimenting with a great deal more. In the Southeast, it might be able to be planted with the fall pansies, in the north, as a summer annual. *M. villosa*, native to Nepal, has a similar habit and flower.

The best known blue form is the common Himalayan blue poppy, *M. betonicifolia*, which naturally grows in alpine meadows at altitudes of 9000–12,000 ft. Plants are short-lived and occasionally monocarpic, meaning that they produce their 4–6 flowers in summer, then produce seed and die. *M. grandis* is similar but differs in the shape of the bottom leaves, being tapered into a narrow stalk at the base compared with the cordate bases of the lower leaves of *M. betonicifolia*. They are generally longer-lived. The hybrid between these two species, *M.* × *sheldonii*, was raised in 1937 in Oxford, England and is sterile. A number of named cultivars have since been developed. I think of many fine United Kingdom gardens when I think about the blue poppies, but some of the finest blue-poppy-scenes are found in Mt. Stewart in Northern Ireland and Branklyn Gardens in Scotland. The cultivar 'Branklyn' was raised there and has a hint of mauve in the flowers. 'Slieve Donard', raised by the famous Northern Irish nursery of the same name, has longer, more pointed petals than the original cross.

After all is said and done, it would be a shame never to see such marvelous plants. Since visiting European gardens is not a realistic choice for many of us, visit a few Northwestern gardens or go to a garden talk where the speaker tells you how easy these plants are to grow. One of the characteristics of gardeners is to never say never. Purchase some seeds or a few plants for the challenge, the worst that will happen is they won't live and who knows, they may surprise us all.

## *Melianthus* (me-lee-anth' us)    Honey Flower    Melianthaceae

A group of about 6 species of shrubs from South Africa, from the lowlands to the higher elevations of the Transvaal. Judging from their native habitat, it can be assumed that most species are not particularly winter hardy, and zone 7 is about the furthest north one can go without serious protection. The best known is honey flower, *M. major*, which looks like a large blue-green fern when young. The alternate leaves are about 1' long, divided into 9-11 toothed leaflets. Soft to the feel and a terrific hue, these leaves are highly sought after by the discerning gardener. By the way, this handsome foliage also smells. Rubbing part of a leaf under your nose evokes fragrances of peanut butter or as my Jewish friends, Avis and Gerson Aronivitz exclaimed, "it smells just like Hava." My confreres, Wayne Winterroud and Joe Eck at North Hills, VT, used it to perfection in containers and throughout their garden, knowing full well it would not overwinter. I have viewed these plants often in my travels and generally they looked good when they were about 2' tall. However, where they perennialize, they can get quite lanky. I have also seen these as 6-8' tall woody monsters, whose charm and usefulness disappeared at foot 3.

Unfortunately, it is one of the least cold hardy members of the genus, not tolerating most winter climates well at all. In the Armitage garden, plants stayed about 2' tall, struggled in the wet summer and perked up in the fall and winter. I lost it during the late winter, as much due to the moisture as the temperature. The foliage is so handsome that I ordered it again and with better drainage it looked good. Then it died the next year. I think I have emerged from my Melianthus-stage of life, but I still enjoy it where it does well. The reddish brown flowers occur in axillary and terminal racemes and aren't terribly memorable.

A couple of other species are occasionally offered, both from higher altitudes and perhaps more cold hardy. *M. cosmosus* has dark green foliage which is much more dissected than *M. major*. Shorter and less robust is *M. pectinatus*, also with finely cut green foliage. This genus is certainly worth trying to push the garden envelope a little further. Full sun to partial shade and a location with well-drained soils protected from drying winds would be nice.

## *Mertensia* (mer-ten' see-a)    Bluebells    Boraginaceae

Plants from this genus include those from high elevations as well as those from lowland areas. Many of the 40-45 species are native, including the outstanding blue-clustered flowers of Rocky Mountain bluebells, *M. alpina*, the western *M. lanceolata*, better known as languid ladies, the tall northern *M. paniculata* and the well-known eastern member, Virginia bluebells, *M. virginica*. Other less well known and occasionally available members are native to Asia such as *M. sibirica* and the magnificent blue-leaved *M. asiatica*. All have alternate leaves with blue to pink flowers which unfold in a one-sided raceme or cyme.

Few plants are easier and less pretentious for most gardeners than *M. virginica*, which provides so much pleasure that it should be part of every spring garden. I look forward with anticipation to its appearance in my garden every March and April.

| | | | |
|---|---|---|---|
| *-asiatica* (ayes-ee-at' i-ca) | | Asian Bluebells | 6–12"/15" |
| Spring | Blue | Japan | Zones 4–7 |
| (Syn. *M. simplicissima*) | | | |

A plant with a number of fine qualities and one serious flaw for most American gardens. It is unique in that a tight rosette of blue leaves forms which is unlike any other bluebell normally seen. The flowering stems extend from the rosette but plants remain prostrate, bearing blue flowers from spring to early summer in the axils. The flowers are not as visible against the leaves as in other species, so the foliage has to look good for the plant to look good. Therein lies the flaw; this is a difficult plant to gush over when half the leaves are turning yellow and the flowers are fair at best. I love the foliage of this plant in early spring, but I have not seen too many outstanding specimens as the season wears on. Certainly worth a try for the interest aspect.

Needs excellent drainage; a rocky area is best and plants should be protected from desiccating winds.

### Related Species:

*M. maritima*, oyster plant, is somewhat similar in that foliage is blue-green. I would like to see this native plant (Montana to northern California) offered as a possible replacement for the above species. Plants are more upright and if it could be propagated could be quite useful. Not in commerce now. Likely hardy to zone 4 or 5.

| | | | |
|---|---|---|---|
| *-virginica* (vir-jin' i-ka) | | Virginia Bluebells | 1–2'/1' |
| Spring | Lavender-Blue | Eastern United States | Zones 3–8 |

From the moment the blue green mouse-ear shaped leaves break the soil in the spring until they disappear in summer, these plants provide immense pleasure. The 4" long, 3–4" wide alternate leaves are smooth with prominent veins. Clusters of 5–20 one inch long tubular flowers are borne in nodding racemes at the end of the stems. The buds and young flowers are pink, but turn

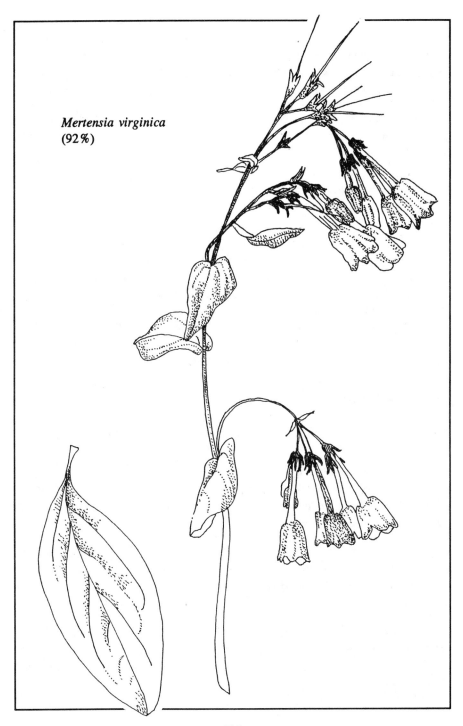

*Mertensia virginica*
(92%)

a lavender-blue as they mature. The leaves yellow as summer progresses and completely disappear by midsummer in most parts of the country. This creates a problem if planted in large numbers or in a prominent place; however, annuals may be used to advantage to cover the empty spaces or they may be planted in shady areas where their absence will be less conspicuous. Moist areas and partial shade are necessary for Virginia bluebells, particularly in zones 6–8. Plantings should not be disturbed and given time, will slowly colonize the area.

Propagate by fresh seed, or by spring division when colonies are sufficiently large.

### Cultivars:
'Alba' has white flowers but is not as vigorous as the species.
'Rubra' has pink flowers but is no great improvement on the species.

### Related Species:
*M. paniculata* is native from central and western Canada to central Idaho and western Montana. The plants are 2–4' tall but bear flowers similar to Virginia bluebells. They do not go dormant unless under heavy stress.

*M. sibirica*, Siberian bluebells, is also a lovely garden plant. Plants grow to 18" tall and are fuller and less coarse in appearance than *M. virginica*. The foliage does not go dormant in the summer. Why it is so difficult to find remains a mystery. More plants need to be grown in the United States to provide additional information on garden tolerances.

### Additional Reading:
Hipps, Carol. 1990. Virginia bluebells. *Horticulture* 68(3):88.

## *Miscanthus* (mis-kanth′ us)  Eulalia Grass, Miscanthus Grass  Poaceae

Of all the changes which have occurred in American gardening in the last 20 years, the embracing of ornamental grasses has to be one of the most significant. Who would have thought that the stuff around which the lawn-mower and chemical industries have been built would become such a garden passion. Many people saw the beauty of native grasses, but like goldenrod, these pioneers could never get past the bias in people's minds. The acceptance of native and "wild" landscapes in gardening brought many grasses into the mainstream of the gardening public, and their low maintenance and classic forms found many converts. But it was the efforts of Wolfgang Oehme, James van Sweeden and Kurt Blumel who introduced many American gardeners to the beauty of ornamental grasses, particularly *Miscanthus*.

The group of Chinese and Japanese plants include species and cultivars ranging from 3 to 12' tall. They are grown for their low maintenance, handsome and sometimes quite colorful foliage, and their late summer and fall flowers which provide additional architectural interest throughout the winter. Their winter beauty is equal to their summer charm. About three species are offered in American nurseries but by far, the most popular is the many selections of common eulalia grass, *M. sinensis*. New cultivars continue to be added to enhance the habit, provide more colorful foliage and to create even better flowers.

## Quick Guide to Miscanthus Species

|  | Height (ft.) | Evergreen |
|---|---|---|
| *M. floridulus* | 10–12 | No |
| *M. sinensis* | 3–8 | No |
| *M. transmorrissonensis* | 3–4 | Yes |

| *-floridulus* (flor-id-ewe' lus) | Giant Eulalia Grass | 10–12'/4' |
|---|---|---|
| Fall          Silver | Asia | Zones 5–9 |

(Syn. *M. giganteus*)

The plants are similar to *M. sinensis*, however, their mature size of 10–14' and tall silvery plumes provide additional garden uses. These are robust plants, each can measure up to 2–3" in diameter. They are big enough to be used as hedging or screen, strong enough to be a good windbreak and tolerant of salt spray. If it is so good, why don't we see more of it? Plants are generally too tall for most gardens and the green foliage, although dramatic, is not as sexy as newer cultivars of *M. sinensis*. The bottom leaves also have a tendency to fall off by late summer, leaving a rather bare bottom.

In August and September, the flowers start out as reddish tan buds which give way to the big silvery plumes well above the foliage. Fall also results in a reddish hue to the clumps. They must be planted in fertile, moist soil in full sun. Some morning shade is fine, however the more shade, the more chance of toppling.

Propagate by seed or by chainsaw. This is not a plant which one divides with a shovel.

| *-sinensis* (si-nen' sis) | Common Eulalia Grass | 3–7'/3' |
|---|---|---|
| Fall          Silvery | Asia | Zones 6–9 |

The explosion in the use of ornamental grasses can be directly traced to the use of this grass by forward-looking architects and landscape planners, followed by the introduction of a continuous stream of new varieties. The attributes of eulalia grass are obvious in the sunny landscape; they may be used as specimen plantings and provide colorful foliage in the spring and summer. However, probably the most valuable feature is their winter habit; the clumps remain "evertan" and the flowers stay fresh-looking all winter, providing something other than snow and slush to look at during the cold season.

All plants require plenty of space to be at their best and sun is necessary, although they tolerate more shade than most people admit. Rust on the leaves can be a problem, particularly in densely planted situations. They tolerate drought but irrigation is useful for best growth. Although the main selling point is the foliage, the flowers are also terrific in arrangements and are particularly pretty with cone flowers and fall salvias. The species and a few cultivars ('Gracillimus', 'Variegatus', 'Zebrinus') have been available for many years, but many selections which improve the habit or flowering have recently been introduced.

## Cultivars:

### Habit (Green foliage):

'Adagio' is a terrific plant because of its compact habit (only about 2' tall) with narrow leaves and pinkish plumes which later turn white.

'Arabesque' also has narrow foliage and is a good choice for smaller gardens. Plants are 2–3' tall with salmon-white flowers.

'Goliath' wears its name well. A vigorous grower, up to 9' in height, with early, very large flowers. Big and robust for the full-figured garden.

'Gracillimus' is one of the older selections, with narrow green foliage and silvery flowers. The leaves of mature specimens are less than ½" across. A terrific specimen plant, however, they tend to be floppy after a few years in the garden. Many of the newer "gracillimus-type" selections ('Arabesque', 'Morning Light') are improvements.

'Silver Spider' ('Silberspinne') is an elegant plant with narrow leaves and wide-open flower heads. I first saw this in its full glory at Bluemont Nursery in Maryland, and I had to have some. They grace the Armitage garden and the University Horticulture Garden with equal aplomb.

'Strictus' has been the "zebrinus-type" choice in recent years because the stripes are more visual and the plants are more upright with little tendency to fall over. The smaller and more compact habit have made it highly sought after in smaller gardens.

'Yaku Jima' is a handsome, compact, fine-textured form of miscanthus. Plants grow 3–4' tall and while they are not small, they are useful for smaller gardens. Older and only slightly different than 'Nippon'.

### Variegated or Striped Foliage:

'Cabaret' is fast becoming one of the more popular selections, although it has been difficult to find in the past. The wide green leaves bear a clean white band down the middle and is an excellent non-floppy variegated form. The flowers are similar to the species.

'Cosmopolitan' is another wide-leaved, wide white-banded selection similar in habit to 'Cabaret'. A sport with silver bands rather than white has been called 'Cosmo Revert' by Heronswood Gardens in Kingston, WA.

'Goldfeder' ('Golden Feather') has green leaves with gold margins. Slow growing and 3–5' tall.

'Morning Light' is a variegated variety of *M. sinensis* 'Gracillimus' and is botanically known as 'Gracillimus Variegatus'. The much improved horticulture name 'Morning Light' was penned by Kurt Bluemel. Vertical bands of white run along the narrow leaf margins, making them look even more narrow. This compact grower (4–5' tall) has handsome flowers which emerge reddish, then age to a soft tan color. Poised to emerge from the pack as one of the most popular cultivars.

'Rigoletto' is a dwarf form of variegated miscanthus grass. Shorter and more upright than 'Variegatus'. Arose from Bluemel Nursery in Maryland.

'Sarabande' is becoming the narrow leaf grass of choice in many landscapes. The fine texture, the silver plumes and the upright, non-floppy habit is a great improvement.

'Silver Arrow' ('Silberfeil') is a variegated type with more upright growth and a pink tint to the plumes.

'Variegatus' is one of the grandaddies of the group, with wonderful variegated foliage. Its drawback is that it is big and tends to flop over later in the season. Plants are being replaced by more narrow-leaved variegated forms like 'Rigoletto' and 'Morning Light'. In the Armitage garden, it is colorful and shade tolerant.

*Leaves Banded:*

'Puenktchen' ('Little Dot') is a "zebrinus-type" of grass but more compact and low growing (3' tall) with gold bands across each leaf.

'Strictus' (see description under *Habit*).

'Tiger Cub' is another more recent, small, compact "zebrinus-type" which is giving 'Strictus' a run for the money. The stripes show up early in the growing season and remain until frost.

'Zebrinus' is another of the founders of the miscanthus club. The horizontal yellow to golden leaf stripes (like a zebra) made it a favorite but it is big and floppy, giving way to the many new "zebrinus-type" selections.

*Flowers:*

'Condensatus' has much denser, larger flowers than the type and broader foliage. Flowers have a purplish tint.

'Malepartus' differs by having more bronze-green foliage and large feathery pink-purple plumes when they first appear, turning silver at maturity. Plants are 6–7' tall.

'November Sunset' is a robust late-flowering form with large silver plumes. Plants are 6–8' tall with copper-tan color in the winter.

'Rotsilber' ('Red-silver') bears almost red flowers in the fall over silvery green foliage. The flowers fade to the normal silver-tan as winter sets in.

'Silver Feather' ('Silberfeder') is a selection with a relatively wide separation between the foliage and the flowers. Numerous, very large silvery flowers separate it from the species.

*Fall Color:*

'Autumn Fire' ('Herbstfeuer') is at least 4' tall in most climates. The foliage turns reddish in the fall and the flowers are creamy white.

'Autumn Light' is hardy to zone 5 and produces silver plumes in early to mid September.

'Blondo' is 5–7' tall whose claim to fame appears to be additional cold hardiness.

'Graziella' is also a "gracillimus-type" with narrow foliage but with large silvery plumes held well above the leaves. The foliage turns burgundy to bronze in the fall.

'Purpurescens' is one of the more colorful selections. The foliage starts to turn red in the summer, changing to deep purple-red as the weather gets colder. My kind of grass, colorful foliage, good flowers and compact grower.

'Nippon' is a relatively recent selection with compact (3–4' tall) narrow leaves and good red-bronze fall and winter color.

| *-transmorrissonensis* (tranz-mor-ih-son-en' sis) | | |
|---|---|---|
| | Evergreen Miscanthus | 3–4'/4' |
| Fall          Tan | Taiwan | Zones 6–10 |

A relatively new species to the landscape trade, this 3–4' plant forms dense clumps of glossy green, narrow leaves. The airy flowers are 6–8" long and appear like long horses' tails. There are a number of selections of *M. sinensis* with similar traits, however, the evergreen foliage (at least in the North) sets this species apart. A handsome plant for full sun and moist conditions. All the miscanthus grasses are useful for winter interest, but this provides some greenery as well.

Quick Key to Miscanthus Species

    A. Mature height over 10' tall . . . . . . . . . . . . . . *M. floridulus*
   AA. Mature height less than 10' tall
      B. Foliage tan and straw-like in winter . . . . . . . . *M. sinensis*
     BB. Foliage essentially green in the winter . . . *M. transmorrissonensis*

**Additional Reading:**

Numerous articles about the wonders of grass gardening have appeared as well as a few good books. A couple of good books which describe most of the grasses and their relatives are listed below. Greenlee's is outstanding.

Greenlee, J. 1992. *The Encyclopedia of Ornamental Grasses*. Rodale Gardening Press, Emmaus, PA.

Grounds, R. 1989. *Ornamental Grasses*. Christopher Helm Press, London, UK.

## *Mitchella* (mi-chel′ la)      Partridge Berry      Rubiaceae

Only two species are found in the genus, and one, *M. repens*, is a handsome plant native from Newfoundland to Minnesota and south to Florida and Texas. The genus commemorates the work of Dr. John Mitchell (1676–1768), a botanist in Virginia who corresponded with Linnaeus about many American native genera. They are native to the ground flora of rich woods, usually acidic in nature and often found under conifers like hemlock and larch. Plants are evergreen and the creeping stems are covered with small shiny, rounded opposite leaves. Plants are not going to cause a collective intake of breath but they are handsome ground covers on well-drained soils. The deliciously fragrant, small off-white flowers are borne in pairs in spring, and each pair gives rise to a single bright scarlet-red berry in the summer and fall which often persists right through the winter. The fruits are the most colorful part of the plant and under suitable conditions, plants are heavily berried. They are edible, but hardly flavorful, unless you are a partridge.

The leaves are among the most handsome of evergreen ground covers, and plants multiply by rooting at the nodes when they touch the ground. I love it around water, such as by a small pond in the garden.

Propagate by taking pieces of the stem and pinning down the nodes into moist soil. Cuttings may be excised and easily rooted or seeds may be cleaned from the berries and sown in moist soils. Seeds may require up to 2 years to germinate.

## *Mitella* (my-tel′ la)      Bishop's-Cap, Mitrewort      Saxifragaceae

About 20 species of modest plants with heart-shaped leaves and small whitish flowers are known. Most are native to the western United States where they flourish in moist, shady woodlands. However, the only species which is easily obtainable is two-leaved bishop's-cap, *M. diphylla*, native from Quebec to Minnesota and south to Missouri and South Carolina. Plants grow about 12″ tall and produce a pair of sessile or very short-stalked leaves about half way up the flowering stems. The basal leaves are 3–5 lobed, roughly hairy on both sides, and 1–2″ long. The leaves provide much of the plant's charm. Many white, fringed flowers, each about ⅛″ wide, are held in a long 8–10″ raceme in spring. While not terribly colorful, a close look provides exquisite flowers that look like a bit of lace. After flowering, black shiny fruit occur. Plants do well in zones 3–7.

I often get plants of this genus confused with those of *Tiarella* and *Heuchera*, and I have been seen scratching my head many times while looking at such plants. To those who are smarter than me, ignore my frustrations; to those who are similarly confused, here are a few hints to help us out. The foliage is similar in all species, but first look for leaves on the flower stem, then look closely at the flowers, in particular, the petals and the stamens. Once you look at enough of these, the foliage will call out their names and even without flowers, you will have no problems.

| | Leaves on flower stems | Petals on flowers | Number of stamens |
|---|---|---|---|
| *Heuchera* | No | Entire | 5 |
| *Mitella* | Yes (2) | 3-cleft | 10 |
| *Tiarella* | No | Entire | 10 |

Use plants as ground covers in partially shaded areas where soils are consistently moist and friable. Propagate by seed or division.

### Related Species:

*M. breweri* occurs in the Rocky Mountains of British Columbia, the Sierra Nevadas and the Olympic Range in Oregon. It is more compact and mounded than *M. diphylla* with small white flowers. Probably hardy in zones 4–7.

## *Molinia* (mo-lean' ee-a)          Moor Grass          Poaceae

A small number of European grasses with showy flowers and good fall color to the foliage. The plants are entirely deciduous, disappearing in the winter, and provide no winter interest. However, the stiff see-through flower stems stand well above the foliage and are handsome in summer. The best known of the moor grasses is purple moor grass, *M. caerulea*, available from most nurseries that handle ornamental grasses. The arching leaves are about ½" wide and 12–18" long and plants form thick tussocks which grow about 2' tall. The flowers are yellowish to dark or light purple, thus the common name, and appear in late June to mid July about 2' above the tufted foliage.

Handsome leaves, airy flowers, easy culture and good fall color make it a terrific plant for massing together in the landscape. Their only drawback is their relatively slow growth rate; small divisions require 2–3 years before they flower. Buy bigger divisions or don't complain. Plant in full sun and acid soils in zones 4–9. Afternoon shade is tolerated in the South.

Propagate by division in early fall or spring.

### Cultivars:

'Moorflamme' ('Moor Flame') is a compact cultivar with scarlet fall color.
'Variegata' is the most popular cultivar of moor grass, each leaf colored with yellow-white stripes along the 15" length. The plants are a great improvement on the species, if more colorful grasses are desired.
'Skyracer' is a cultivar of ssp. *arundinacea*, tall moor grass, and is more robust and much taller than purple moor grass. Plants are 7–8' tall when in flower and the stiff stems dance on the slightest wind. Terrific yellow-orange fall color.

## *Monarda* (mo-nard' a)     Bee-Balm     Lamiaceae

Monarda is one of the plants that many people cannot do without in their summer garden, and is also one of those plants that many people cannot do with, because of the well-deserved reputation of being so mildew susceptible. I have seen great swaths of scarlet bee-balm in the Smokey Mountain National Park in North Carolina, growing in semi-shaded locations, with nary a spore of mildew. How can such beautiful plants become such an eyesore when they are brought into a more pampered garden setting? Certainly one of the answers to that question resides in the fact that whenever a species which has evolved to a climate over many years is taken from that climate, bad things usually happen. The other problem has been caused by breeders concentrating on flower color while ignoring disease tolerance. Lastly, the community of American plant breeders is woefully small and most breeding and evaluation has taken place in Europe, where disease pressure is far different than that found in most American regions.

About 16 species are known but two are fairly common. The leaves are toothed, aromatic, and usually opposite. The flowers are terminal, obviously 2-lipped and often surrounded by brightly colored bracts. The most common species and the one in which significant breeding has occurred is common bee-balm, *M. didyma*. Other good but not as ornamental plants include wild bergamot, *M. fistulosa*, and the annual *M. citriodora*.

*Monarda* is named for Nicholas Monardes, a Spanish botanist who authored the first book on medicinal flora of North America in 1571. His book, published when he was 78 years old, was translated to English as *Joyfull Newes* in 1578.

### Quick Guide to Monarda Species

|  | Height (ft.) | Flower color |
|---|---|---|
| *M. didyma* | 2–4 | Red |
| *M. fistulosa* | 2–5 | Rose, purple |

| *-didyma* (di' di-ma) | | Bee-Balm, Oswego Tea | 2–4'/3' |
|---|---|---|---|
| Summer | Red | Eastern North America | Zones 3–7 |

John Bartram, the American botanist, first collected bee-balm near Oswego, NY on Lake Ontario. The leaves were used to make tea and plants were routinely included in kitchen gardens for their herbal properties. Plants are also well-known for the high yields of nectar for bee production. Growing naturally along stream banks with overhanging trees suggests its rightful place in the garden is an area where moisture can be freely provided.

The four-sided stems bear 4–6″ long, thin, scented, pointed leaves. The bright scarlet flowers are surrounded with red tinged bracts and carried in globular terminal, whorled clusters. Removing the faded flower heads results in 8 weeks or more of flowering. If grown well and properly cared for, a planting of bee-balm is a magnificent sight. Unfortunately, this is seldom the case. If plants dry out, the stress results in greater susceptibility to foliar diseases such as powdery mildew. While powdery mildew can be present even in native plantings, it can be much worse in the garden, particularly if plants are crowded, or the soil is not consistently moist. Spray with a fungicide starting in early June through frost. This "mildew-thing" may be overblown for gardeners who grow bee-balm without a problem. However if mildew is a problem, try some of the cultivars which are listed as more resistant.

Bee-balm multiplies by underground stems or self sows and can be extremely invasive, taking over large areas of the garden. Clumps tend to die out in the center and must be divided every 2–3 years for aesthetic purposes. Provide full sun or afternoon shade.

As garden plants, they are lovely in the North; but in the South, they are more trouble than they are worth. However, if placed in a rather wild, moist area where large clumps can form and some mildew is not as objectionable, they make wonderful plants attractive to bees, butterflies, and hummingbirds.

**Cultivars:** A good number of cultivars have been raised and all are superior to the type for garden culture. Many catalogs list mildew resistance for cultivars they offer. Breeding for mildew resistance has become more important with today's breeders, yet all such claims should be taken with a grain of salt. To paraphrase a well-known saying, "the proof is in the garden." Many are hybrids between this and *M. fistulosa*, wild bergamot.

'Alba' is the white form of the species and is often seen in interspersed in the red wild populations in native habitats. Other cultivated white forms bear larger flowers.

'Adam' bears cerise flowers, is more compact, and withstands dry conditions better than other cultivars.

'Aquarius' produces light pink flowers on 2–3′ tall plants.

'Beauty of Cobham' stands about 3′ tall with pale pink flowers.

'Blue Stocking' ('Blaustrunpf') carries violet-blue blossoms. One of my favorite blues, appears to be robust and more heat and drought tolerant than many others. Self-sows with abandon.

'Cambridge Scarlet' is one of the most enduring cultivars, having been introduced in the early 1900's. The 3′ stems bear flaming scarlet flowers over vigorous plants. Still popular but being superseded by more mildew resistant selections.

'Cherokee' is one of a number of new hybrids bred by Piet Oudolf of the Netherlands. Selections were based on disease resistance as well as colorful flowers. Most bear Indian names. 'Cherokee' has rose-pink flowers on 3' tall stems.

'Commanche' bears darker pink flowers with tan centers.

'Croftway Pink' was introduced in 1932 and is still among the more popular cultivars. Plants bear rosy pink flowers which blend quietly into the garden. Not mildew resistant.

'Donnerwolke', introduced in 1973, produces dozens of lilac flowers on 3' plants. It was spectacular when I saw it at the Montreal Botanical Garden.

'Gardenview Scarlet' is a new introduction from Henry Ross at Gardenview Park outside Cleveland, OH. Introduced as a scarlet, mildew resistant clone, it has, for the most part, lived up to its highly mildew resistant reputation. However, monarda is monarda . . .

'Kardinal' has deep red flowers on 3' tall stems.

'Jacob Cline', from the well respected plantsman Don Cline, is grown by a number of nurseries who feel it is one of the most mildew resistant of any of the available cultivars. The flowers are deep red.

'Loddon Crown' produces mahogany to purple-red flowers and purple-tinged foliage. About 3' tall.

'Mahogany' has some of the darkest wine-red flowers of any cultivar and grows 3' tall.

'Marshall's Delight' is named for former Agriculture Canada breeder, Henry M. Marshall. It was developed in Morden, Manitoba from a cross between 'Cambridge Scarlet' and *M. fistulosa* var. *menthaefolia*. Plants bear rich pink flowers on relatively mildew-free plants.

'Melissa' is a pink-flowered selection about 3–4' tall.

'Panorama' is a seed-propagated strain of 3' tall plants of mixed colors.

'Pisces' is another Oudolf selection, this one with pale rosy pink flowers.

'Prairie Fire' has lilac-red flowers.

'Prairie Night' is a handsome old (1955) cultivar with rosy red blooms.

'Raspberry Wine' bears clear wine red flowers over dark green foliage. Introduced by White Flower Farm in Litchfield, CT.

'Scorpio' is claimed by some nursery people as being the most mildew resistant one of the bunch. Needs far more testing to substantiate the claim. Flowers are purple and plants are about 3' tall.

'Scorpion' bears red flowers over green sepals in early summer.

'Sioux' is one of the few white-flowered forms available. The flowers are slightly tinged with pink.

'Squaw' is relatively mildew resistant with deep red flowers.

'Snow Maiden' ('Snow White') provides creamy white flowers on 3' high stems. Plants were introduced in 1955 but is still relatively popular.

'Sunset' bears purple-red flowers on 3' tall plants. Fairly mildew resistant.

'Twins' produces dark pink flowers.

'Vintage Wine' erupts with many red-purple flowers in mid summer.

'Violet Queen' has deep purple flowers. I have some trouble seeing significant
differences between flowers described as violet-blue ('Blue Stocking'),
lilac-blue ('Prairie Night'), or purple ('Violet Queen'). Probably just me.

| *-fistulosa* (fist-ew-low' sa) | Wild Bergamot | 2–5'/3' |
|---|---|---|
| Late Summer   Rose, Purple | North America | Zones 3–7 |

The stem is less noticeably 4-angled than *M. didyma* and the 4″ long
leaves are slightly more hairy and less toothed. The flowers are also borne

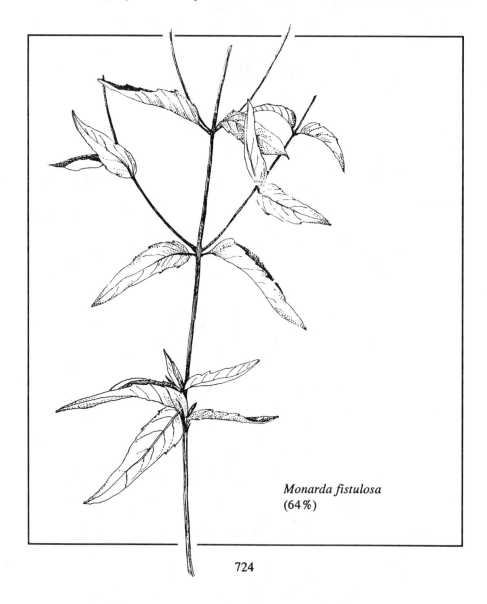

*Monarda fistulosa*
(64%)

in tight whorls surrounded by bracts and range from light lavender to whitish pink. The throat of the sepals on each flower is densely hairy, a totally useless piece of information for gardeners; however, this characteristic helps distinguish this species from the previous. The stems grow out of the previous flower head, creating a candelabra effect. Heights of 5' are not uncommon. Because the flowers are not as brilliantly colored as common bee-balm, little interest has been shown in developing this as a garden plant. However, their greater tolerance to dry conditions and resistance to mildew have made them important in the breeding of the hybrids discussed above. Plants are better suited to a wild area rather than the cultivated garden. Plants were, and still are, used in the treatment of headaches and fevers.

Division every 2–3 years will maintain plant vigor. Seed is also available. Germination takes place in 2–3 weeks if seed is lightly covered and placed in a warm (70–75° F), moist environment.

**Related Species:**

*M. punctata*, spotted bee-balm, bears lovely whorled yellow to cream colored flowers with purple spots (*punctata*). The bracts beneath the flowers range from pink to lavender. Plants are tolerant of dry soils, relatively tolerant to mildew and perform well in zones 4–8.

Quick Key to Monarda Species

    A. Stems acutely 4-sided, sepal throat
        slightly hairy, flowers bright red . . . . . . . . . . . . . *M. didyma*
    AA. Stems bluntly 4-sided, sepal throat
        densely hairy, flowers lavender to pale pink . . . . . *M. fistulosa*

**Additional Reading:**

Bakalar, E. 1991. Bee balm. *Horticulture* 69(5):104.
Collicutt, L.M. 1989. 'Marshall's Delight' monarda. *HortScience* 24(3):525.
Hayward, Gordon. 1983. Bee Balm. *Horticulture* 61(7):16–19.

*Morina* (mo-reen′ a)        Whorlflower        Morinaceae

That this group of plants is seldom seen in American gardens amply demonstrates the good sense of American gardeners. Only one species, *M. longifolia*, is sufficiently ornamental to think about using; however, the lovely whorled shell pink flowers belie the spiny prickly nature of the entire plant. This is definitely a plant not to let the fingers do the walking, as the rosette of leaves and the bracts subtending the flowers can draw blood. *Morina* is found only in gardens where the gardener does all the work because the plant, when not in flower, essentially looks like a wicked thistle needing removal. The closest garden plants I can think of are the prickly bear's breeches, *Acanthus spinosus* var. *spinosissimus* and "ornamental" members of the plume thistles, *Cirsium*.

Without the flowers, they are about 9–12" tall, about 2' in flower. In their defense, I must concede that the flowers are colorful, starting out white, turning to shell pink and occasionally to bright crimson. Full sun and excellent drainage are necessary. Plants are native to the Himalayas and hardy in zones 6 and 7, zone 8 on the west coast. Heat and humidity are not appreciated.

## *Muhlenbergia* (myoo-len-ber' jee-a)    Muhly Grass    Poaceae

A poorly known group of ornamental grasses, the muhlys are, however, beginning to gather a close following. The genus contains more than 150 species from open grasslands, mostly from Mexico and southern United States, although a few are native to Asia. They are grown for the thread-like leaves and the thin stems which together create a bewitching weeping effect. Some of the more useful species are grown for their clumping bamboo look (*M. dumosa*), while others such as *M. filipes* and *M. capillaris* produce flowers like purple baby's breath. The limitation with all the muhly grasses is their relative lack of cold tolerance, most being winter hardy no further north than zone 7, some like bamboo muhly, *M. dumosa*, probably zones 7–8, *M. pubescens* to zone 9. They all tolerate full sun to some afternoon shade and are best planted in small clumps.

Bamboo muhly looks like clumping bamboo in every way from its graceful hanging habit to the light airiness of the thin foliage. The small purplish flowers are insignificant compared to the evergreen foliage. Plants have done well in Raleigh, NC, a solid zone 7, so maybe they have more cold hardiness than at first believed. Plants grow 4–6' in a single season, so plants are also useful if they don't survive the winter. They are also terrific in large containers, which may be brought into a protected area during the winter.

To me, the neatest species is *M. filipes*, purple muhly, whose light airy panicles of purple flowers dominate the fall garden. They emerge in mid to late fall and as they mature, they slowly turn to a tan color. Good drainage is needed, but plants are drought and wind tolerant.

A favorite of those who enjoy blue foliage is *M. lindheimeri*, lindheimer's or blue muhly. Drought and heat tolerant, this 2' tall Texas native sports thin soft blue leaves about 15" long. The flowers are grayish to purple providing this species with the best combination of foliage and flowers in the genus. Hardy to zone 7.

All the muhlys can be seed propagated, however, some of the better selections are unstable from seed and vegetative propagation such as division ensures continuation of the good stuff.

*Muscari* (mus-car' ree)          Grape Hyacinth          Liliaceae

Grape hyacinths have graced gardens for centuries and are well known for the bright many-flowered cone of urn-shaped blue flowers in the spring. However, flowers are also shades of pink, white and yellow. The musky odor of yellow brown-flowered *M. racemosum*, musk hyacinth, is responsible for the name *Muscari*. It is interesting that this species, after which the genus was named, has now been placed in a totally different genus (*Muscarimia moschatum*) by some authorities. Nothing is sacred.

All species are sun lovers and need little more than well-drained soil to look their best. They are excellent plants for the rock garden, especially in large bold groupings. In Minau, an exquisite island garden in southern Germany, grape hyacinths depicted the Sea of Constance (in which the garden resided) in a portrayal of the Island's location using tulips, hyacinths and grape hyacinths. The "river" of Muscari at Keukenhof Graden in Holland is much more famous. I guess you had to be there. . .

The flowers are tightly held in a dense raceme and often consist of upper sterile flowers and lower fertile ones. Usually, but not always, the mouth of the flowers is constricted. The two most common in the garden are *M. armeniacum* and *M. botryoides* and differences are difficult for anyone but the taxonomist to unravel. Fortunately, there are no differences in garden requirements. Regardless of the name on the package, enjoy their beauty. Other species provide equal enjoyment, one of my favorites being one-leaf grape hyacinth, *M. latifolium*.

Quick Reference to the Muscari Species

|  | Height (in.) | Flower color | Flower shape |
|---|---|---|---|
| *M. armeniacum* | 6–8 | Pale blue | Cone |
| *M. botryoides* | 6–8 | Pale blue | Cone |
| *M. comosum* | 6–12 | Mauve | Plume |
| *M. latifolium* | 6–8 | Bicolor | Cone |

*-armeniacum* (ar-men-ee-ah' cum)     Armenian Grape Hyacinth     6–8"/6"
Spring          Pale Blue          Turkey          Zones 4–8

Depending on the source of bulbs, this or *M. botryoides* is the most common grape hyacinth. The 6–8 leaves are about ¼" wide and appear in the fall. In areas without significant snowfall, they are rather messy throughout the winter and early spring but do serve a useful function. Edith Edelman, the curator of the perennial border at the North Carolina State University Arboretum, suggests using *Muscari* as a marker for other

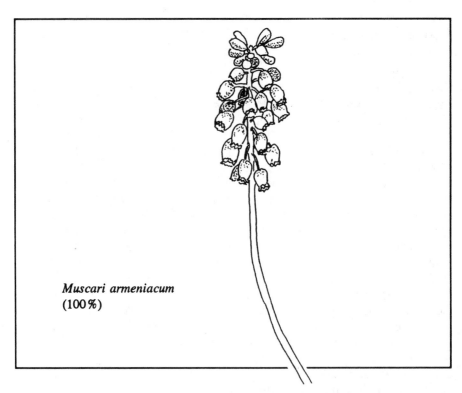

*Muscari armeniacum*
(100%)

spring-flowering bulbs whose leaves have not emerged at time of spring cleaning. Having a bulb or two of grape hyacinths reminds you that other bulbs are still sleeping and to keep the trowel away. The leaves soon fade into the background as the blue conical flower spikes begin their annual emergence. Each mature bulb will send up 1-3 flower spikes with 20-40 densely packed, ¼" long, pale blue urn-shaped flowers.

All cultivars may be propagated by bulbils. Separate and replant in the fall. Seed is produced but offspring may not be the same as the parent.

### Cultivars:

'Blue Spike' is one of the fullest of the grape hyacinths due to the double, soft blue flowers.

'Cantab' bears flowers of soft blue on 6" stems.

'Christmas Pearl' is an early violet-flowering selection, about 8" tall.

'Early Giant' has cobalt blue flowers with a white rim at the mouth of each flower.

'Fantasy Creation' bears double blue flowers on compact flower stems. A terrific cultivar.

'Heavenly Blue' bears gentian blue flowers and multiplies rapidly.

'Saphir' has dark blue flowers with a white rim.

**Related Species:**

*M. aucheri* usually has two thin leaves and bright azure flowers. It is best known for the variety 'Tubergenianum', Tubergen's grape hyacinth, which bears many densely arranged deep blue and pale blue flowers on the same spike. Plants grow 4–8″ tall. 'Dark Eyes' has dark blue flowers with a white edge, while 'Sky Blue' has soft blue flowers.

| *-botryoides* (bot-ree-oi′ deez) | | Common Grape Hyacinth | 6–8″/6″ |
|---|---|---|---|
| Early Spring | Blue | Italy, France | Zones 2–8 |

The common name for the genus was based on this species because the flowers looked like a miniature bunch of blue grapes. Bulbs are common in the garden trade not only because of the lovely blue flowers but because of the white and pink varieties available. The 2–4 leaves are usually shorter than the inflorescence and about ⅛″ wide. *M. botryoides* is more cold hardy than *M. armeniacum* and flowers earlier. Otherwise, there is hardly any difference.

Propagate by bulbils although the species will self sow.

**Cultivars:**

Var. *album* bears clean white flowers. This makes a good garden plant and is the white grape hyacinth of catalogs.

Var. *carneum*, a pink-flowered form, fades quickly to flesh-colored flowers and is not particularly attractive.

**Related Species:**

*M. azureum*, azure grape hyacinth, has 2–3 thin leaves and blue flowers with a darker stripe on the lobes. The flowers are earlier and campanulate, not constricted as with the other species. Also more tolerant of shade than the other species. Hardy to zone 5. 'Album' is a white form, 'Amphibolis' has pale blue larger flowers.

| *-comosum* (ko-mow′ sum) | | Tassel Grape Hyacinth | 6–12″/6″ |
|---|---|---|---|
| Spring | Mauve | Western Asia, North Africa | Zones 4–8 |

(Syn. *Leopoldia comosa*)

This species and common variety *monstrosum* have the dubious distinction of being "conversation-piece" plants. In describing this plant, Louise Wilder (*Adventures with Hardy Bulbs*) states that "the fact that the uppermost flowers . . . are gathered into a bunch, and stand wildly on end on long pedicels, while the lower flowers, that are cylindrical, droop dismally, does give the plant a somewhat distraught appearance." Louise was looking at the sterile upper flowers which have been modified into thin filaments, resulting in the interesting appearance. The 3–4 thick leaves are up to 1½′ long. The species is different enough to have been renamed *Leopoldia comosa* by some authorities although I have not seen it listed as such in any trade catalogs.

Propagate by bulbils.

### Cultivars:

Var. *monstrosum* (syn. *plumosum*) is even more atypical for a grape hyacinth and well described by its varietal name. All the flowers of the inflorescence are sterile and look like slender filaments. This altogether curious plant is most attractive under sunny, pleasant skies but after a rain, looks like a half-drowned puppy dog in need of a home. It is the kind of plant one orders in a weak moment, based on the glowing commentary of a bulb catalog. It is seldom ordered again.

*-latifolium* (lah-tee-fo' lee-um)   One-Leaved Grape Hyacinth   9-12"/5"
Late Spring      Violet/Blue      Turkey                    Zones 3-8

One of my favorites, because of the lack of messy foliage (only one leaf produced) and the neat racemes of two tone flowers. The uppermost sterile flowers are a good blue, the bottom fertile ones are violet. I have had these in the Armitage garden for 4 years now and they are as reliable as any other grape hyacinth I've planted. They are later than others, not in full flower until mid to late April. They spread themselves around where they are happy. One such place is Denver, where they flower with abandon through grass, through snow and wherever the seed happens to fall.

Quick Key to Muscari Species

```
    A. Flowers in cone-like inflorescence
      B. Plant bears solitary leaf . . . . . . . . . . . . . . . M. latifolium
      BB. Plant bears more than 1 leaf
          C. Leaves 4-8, equal or longer than scape  . . M. armeniacum
          CC. Leaves 2-3, usually shorter than scape . . . . . M. botryoides
    AA. Flowers in tassel- or plume-like inflorescence
      B. Top of inflorescence only bears slender sterile
          flowers inflorescence tassel-like . . . . . . . . . . M. comosum
      BB. All flowers slender, sterile,
          inflorescence plume-like  . . . . M. comosum var. monstrosum
```

## *Myosotis* (my-o-so' tis)        Forget-Me-Not        Boraginaceae

The forget-me-nots have always had a special appeal to gardeners of all ages. There are many stories as to the derivation of the common name but most agree that the tale of the young man collecting these flowers for his lady standing on the riverbank sounds the best. He slipped and fell into the fast-moving stream and as he was being swept away, he clenched the flowers in his hand and cried "Forget me not!" to his lover on the shore.

None of the 40–50 species is particularly long lived but most are self-sowers and appear to be perennial. They grow less than 1' tall and produce inflorescences coiled like the tail of a scorpion (scorpioid cymes). The leaves are alternate and usually hairy. All species do well in partial shade but full sun may be tolerated in the North if ample moisture is available.

Quick Reference to Myosotis Species

|  | Height (in.) | Habit |
|---|---|---|
| *M. scorpioides* | 6–8 | Prostrate |
| *M. sylvatica* | 6–8 | Upright |

| *-scorpioides* (skor-pee-oi' deez) | | True Forget-Me-Not | 6–8"/8" |
|---|---|---|---|
| Spring | Blue | Europe, Asia | Zones 3–8 |

Also referred to as the water forget-me-not because it grows naturally in water; constant moisture is required if plants are to perform well in a "normal" garden. Because of the stoloniferous nature and prostrate growth habit, stems may grow to 18" long. The lovely ¼" wide flowers are bright blue with a small yellow eye. Plants look particularly beautiful in a partially shaded woodland growing on the banks of a stream. They also may be grown in shallow water in a garden pond.

Propagate by divisions in spring or fall and by seed.

**Cultivars:**
'Sapphire' has bright sapphire blue flowers.
'Semperflorens' is much more compact than the type and more floriferous.
'Thuringen' bears sky blue flowers.

| *-sylvatica* (sil-va' ti-ka) | | Woodland Forget-Me-Not | 6–8"/6" |
|---|---|---|---|
| Spring | Blue | Europe | Zones 3–7 |

This is the common forget-me-not of the "normal" garden, where moisture may be inconsistent. Plants are usually biennial, but their reseeding nature should make them appear to be perennial, even if they move about a little. Dense cymes of fragrant, ⅜" wide azure-blue flowers with distinctive yellow eyes are produced in April and May. The 2–3" long hairy leaves are lance shaped, somewhat pointed and have 3 faint veins. In the North, flowers are produced prolifically in late spring and sporadically

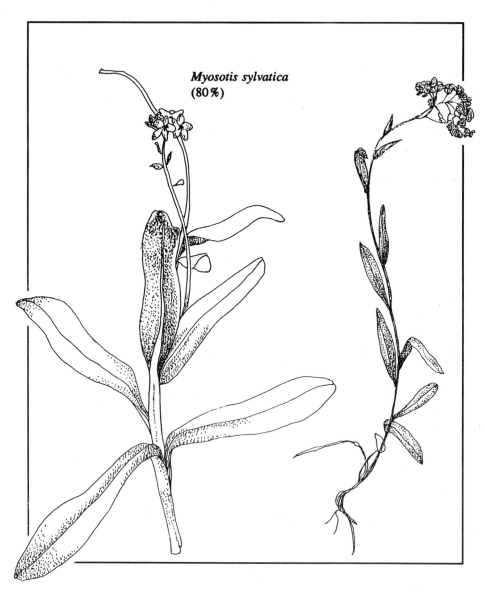

*Myosotis sylvatica*
(80%)

through the late summer. In the South, the dense leaves must be thinned in
June to reduce the incidence of leaf rot which occurs due to afternoon
thunderstorms and hot humid weather. If not thinned, the hairy leaves hold
water, creating perfect conditions for diseases. Plants seldom last more than
2 years in the South or 3 in the North. However, they self sow abundantly
and many additional plantlets emerge in the spring.

Propagate by seed or by division in the spring or fall.

**Cultivars:**

'Alba' has white flowers but why anyone would want to grow a white forget-me-not is beyond me.

'Blue Ball' bears indigo blue flowers over compact, ball-shaped plants.

'Royal Blue' is taller than the species and produces dark blue flowers.

'Victoria Blue' is an early flowering cultivar with gentian blue flowers.

'Victoria Rose' also flowers earlier than the type and bears pink blossoms with a yellow eye. Surprisingly pretty.

**Related Species:**

*M. alpestris* is similar to *M. sylvatica*. The differences are in the length of the pedicel relative to the calyx (much longer in *M. sylvatica*, about equal in *M. alpestris*). Most plants sold as *M. alpestris* are probably *M. sylvatica*. Both are fine species and the only importance to the gardener in distinguishing between the two is the satisfaction of knowing what one is growing.

Quick Key to Myosotis Species

    A. Plant stoloniferous, prostrate habit . . . . . . . . . *M. scorpioides*
    AA. Plant not stoloniferous, upright . . . . . . . . . . . . *M. sylvatica*

**Additional Reading:**

Charest, A. 1993. Forgiving forget-me-nots. *Fine Gardening* 34(Nov/Dec): 62–63.

*Myrrhis* (mi′ ris)            Sweet Cicily            Apiaceae

Consisting of one species of aromatic perennial herb, *M. odorata*, the 3–4′ plants are useful for multiple applications in the garden. For herb fanciers, the herb can be used for whatever herb fanciers use it for. For the rest of us, sweet cicily bears umbels of clean white flowers in early summer and its fresh green foliage makes a bracing contrast to other plants in the garden. The parsley-like foliage can be cut back periodically so the freshness can be maintained. Hardy to zone 7 (zone 6 with some protection).

Propagate by seed.

# N

*Narcissus* (nar-sis′ us)        Jonquil, Daffodil        Amaryllidaceae

Their bright yellow, white and orange flowers splash across the dreary early spring landscape to bring the world to life. Such is the role of Narcissus, the first of the major bulbs to welcome spring. The attributes of the daffodil have been praised for centuries. Homer spoke of "The Narcissus wonderously glittering, a noble sight for all, whether immortal gods or mortal men . . ." Centuries before Homer, the flowers were used by the Egyptians in funeral wreaths and have been found in crypts and tombs, preserved after 3000 years.

The origin of the word *Narcissus* has two main schools of thought. It was believed to have been named for the golden-haired youth, Narcissus, who was changed by the gods into a flower after he gazed so longingly at his own image in a stream, believing the image was that of his long-lost sister. Others believe that Narcissus was derived from the Greek *narcoun*, to be numb. The narcotic, Narce, was thought to be present in the flower's scent. Accounts of the dulling properties of Narcissus flowers stemmed from the time of Sophocles. Few people in those days brought cut narcissus in the home because they believed that the scent of Narcissus was most harmful. This belief persisted at least until the 19th century. Personally, I much prefer the first explanation.

All daffodils and jonquils belong to the genus *Narcissus*. The common name, jonquil, popular in the Southern United States and in England, comes from the Latin word *juncus* meaning rush, and refers to the round leaves on *N. juncifolius*, rush-leaf daffodil. The term has since been accepted to describe dwarf, small-cupped daffodils with rush-like leaves. In some people's minds, the common name, daffodil, is used only for the large trumpet flowered forms like 'King Alfred', but for most gardeners is used to describe just about all species and varieties. Although the large-flowered hybrid daffodils are best known, there are many smaller species which are greatly overlooked. Some of the species flower as early as January in Southern areas and as late as June in Northern gardens. For instance, *N. minimus* (syn. *N. asturiensis*), least daffodil, is a terrific early bloomer, flowering in late February in Bronxville, New York, in early February in Tidewater, Virginia, and as early the first day of the new year in Charlotte, North Carolina. Vast beauty and charm reside in these relatively undiscovered species, although finding them can be an altogether frustrating experience. However, half the fun of gardening is the hunt for something different and the discovery of something new. A well-drained soil, deeply worked and containing humus is ideal for narcissus. Bulbs prefer neutral to slightly acid soil and lime should be incorporated to highly acid soils. Bulbs flower abundantly in woodland soils with natural leaf mold, but should be planted away from hungry tree roots. Narcissus can be naturalized wherever bulbs may be left undisturbed, however if naturalizing in lawns, the grass cannot be cut until the narcissi leaves have yellowed. Removal of leaves too early results in poor performance in subsequent years. Many times I am asked about how much cold daffodils require to flower. The simple answer is as much as possible; the longer the cold, the stouter and taller the flower stem. (Also see tulips). However, if they were not planted in the fall, put them in the refrigerator until early spring. Don't give up, get them in the ground as soon as possible and be patient; some leaves will appear the first spring, they will likely flower the following spring.

About 60 species of narcissus are known, many available to gardeners, although the greatest breakthroughs in garden daffodils have resulted from interspecific hybridization. Some marvelous breeding has created today's large-flowered hybrids, often resulting from an embarrassing number of parents. There has been so much breeding work in Narcissus that twelve categories, based on flower morphology, have been developed to classify the species and hybrids. In the daffodil flower, the cup is known as the corona and the outer flared segments are collectively called the perianth. Following is a table of classification and a few cultivars of each type. This is but a smattering of what is out there.

I. TRUMPET NARCISSUS: One flower to a stem, corona as long as, or longer than perianth segments.

    a. *Yellow:* Perianth colored, corona colored, not paler than the perianth.

    **Cultivars:** 'Arctic Gold', 'Bestseller', 'Dutch Master', 'Explorer', 'Golden Harvest', 'Golden Spur', 'King Alfred type', 'Kassells Gold', 'Lemon Glow', 'Little Gem', 'Marieke', 'Modoc', 'President Carter', 'Primeur', 'Rathowen Gold', 'Rembrandt', 'Rijnveld's Early Sensation', 'Royal Gold', 'Standard Value', 'Unsurpassable', 'Yellow Triumphator'.

b. *Bicolor:* Perianth white, corona colored.

**Cultivars:** 'Bravoure', 'Foresight', 'Holland's Sensation', 'Karelia', 'Las Vegas', 'Little Beauty', 'Magnet', 'Monticello', 'Mrs. E.K. Krelage', 'Preamble', 'Topolino', 'Trousseau', 'World's Favorite'.

c. *White:* Perianth white, corona white, not paler than the perianth.

**Cultivars:** 'Beersheba', 'Cantatrice', 'Empress of Ireland', 'Matterhorn', 'Mount Hood', 'Rhine Wine', 'White Ideal', 'W.P. Milner'.

d. *Other combinations:*

**Cultivars:** 'Apricot Surprise' (apricot perianth, orange corona), 'Glenfarclas' (yellow/red), 'Honeybird' (yellow/white), 'Lunar Sea' (soft yellow/white), 'Red Curtain' (yellow/red), 'Spellbinder' (perianth sulphur yellow, corona sulphur yellow outside, white inside), 'Rushlight' (lemon yellow perianth, white corona edged in yellow).

II. LARGE-CUPPED NARCISSUS: One flower to a stem, corona more than one-third, but not equal to the length of the perianth segments.

a. *Yellow:* As in Ia.

**Cultivars:** 'Autumn Gold', 'Bermuda', 'Berlin', 'Biscayne', 'Brackenhurst', 'Carbineer', 'Carlton', 'Caruso', 'Cheddar', 'Curly', 'Daydream', 'Fortissimo', 'Fortune', 'Galway', 'Gigantic Star', 'Modern Art', 'Monal', 'Nimrod', 'Rustom Pasha', 'Scarlet Elegance', 'St. Keverne', 'St. Patrick's Day', 'Yellow Sun'.

b. *Bicolor:* As in Ib.

**Cultivars:** 'Accent', 'Beau Monde', 'Big Gun', 'Cool Flame', 'Duke of Windsor', 'Easter Bonnet', 'Flower Record', 'Fragrant Breeze', 'Ice Follies', 'Joanne Strauss', 'Kilworth', 'Mrs. R.O. Backhouse', 'Mysterious', 'Passionale', 'Peaches and Cream', 'Pink Beauty', 'Pink Pride', 'Professor Einstein', 'Roseworthy', 'Romance', 'Roulette', 'Salome', 'Salmon Trout', 'Satin Pink', 'Silver Standard', 'Sweet Charity'.

c. *White:* As in Ic.

**Cultivars:** 'Dr. Alex Fleming', 'Filly', 'Milk and Cream', 'Misty Glen', 'Orange Bride', 'Tutankhamun', 'Stainless', 'White Plume', 'Williamsburg', 'Zapollo'.

d. *Other combinations:* As in Id.

**Cultivars:** 'Ambergate' (copper orange/red), 'Bantam' (yellow/red), 'Binkie' (perianth sulphur yellow, corona sulphur yellow turning to white), 'Ceylon' (yellow/red), 'Charter' (perianth primrose yellow with white base, corona cream tinged yellow), 'Cloud Nine' (lemon yellow/white), 'Daydream' (perianth yellow, corona white), 'Fortissimo' (yellow/red), 'Handcross' (perianth dresden yellow, corona

736

*Narcissus* 'Ice Follies'
(50%)

pale yellow), 'Kissproof' (apricot/red), 'Pinza' (yellow/red), 'Scarlet O'Hara' (yellow/red), 'Scarlet Royal' (soft yellow/red).

III. SMALL-CUPPED NARCISSUS: One flower to a stem, corona not more than one-third the length of the perianth segments.

 a. *Yellow:* As in Ia.
    **Cultivars:** 'Apricot Distinction', 'Dinkie', 'Jezabel', 'Lemonade', 'Perimeter'.

 b. *Bicolor:* As in Ib.
    **Cultivars:** 'Amor', 'Audubon', 'Barrett Browning', 'Blarney', 'Cherry Spot', 'Dreamlight', 'Hawkeye', 'Limerick', 'Merlin', 'Rim Ride', 'Queen of the North', 'Sinopel', 'White Lady'.

 c. *White:* As in Ic.
    **Cultivars:** 'Angel', 'Chinese White', 'Dallas', 'Foggy Dew', 'Frigid', 'Veronica'.

d. *Other combinations:*
Cultivars: 'Birma' (deep yellow petals, small orange-red trumpet), 'Hollywood' (yellow/gold), 'Sabine Hay' (orange/red).

IV. DOUBLE NARCISSUS: Flowers double.
Cultivars: 'Acropolis' (white), 'Anne Frank' (white/orange), 'Apotheose' (yellow/orange), 'Bridal Gown' (creamy white), 'Cheerfulness' (white), 'Cheerfulness Primrose' (primrose yellow), 'Erlicheer' (white), 'Flower Drift' (white/yellow), 'Golden Ducat' (yellow), 'Mary Copeland' (white with orange-red cup), 'Petit-Four' (white/rose), 'Pink Pageant' (pink/white), 'Queen Anne's', 'Sir Winston Churchill' (white/orange), 'Replete' (white/red), 'Rip van Winkle' (yellow), 'Tahiti' (yellow interspersed with segments of Saturn-red), 'Texas' (yellow interspersed with yellow and red), 'Unique' (lemon yellow), 'White Lion' (white with straw yellow segments), 'White Marvel' (white), 'Yellow Cheerfulness' (yellow).

V. TRIANDUS NARCISSUS: Obvious characteristics of *N. triandus*, the dominant parent of the hybrids: Slender round leaves, drooping white flowers borne in clusters, perianth segments bent back to reveal a globular corona, like teardrops. Often called the angel's tears daffodil. Usually 9–12″ tall. Also available as var. *alba*. Hardy in zones 4–9.

a. *Large corona:* Corona not less than ⅔ the length of perianth segments.
Cultivars: 'Hawara' (soft yellow), 'Honey Guide' (soft lemon yellow), 'Ice Wings' (white), 'Lapwing' (white/yellow), 'Liberty Bells' (yellow), 'Thalia' (white), 'Tradition' (yellow), 'Tresamble' (white), 'Tuesday's Child' (white/yellow).

b. *Small corona:* Corona less than ⅔ the length of the perianth segments.
Cultivars: 'April Tears' (yellow), 'Arish Mell' (white), 'Hawera' (yellow), 'Lemon Heart' (pale yellow), 'Petrel' (white), 'Rippling Waters' (creamy white), 'Silver Chimes' (white).

VI. CYCLAMINEUS NARCISSUS: Obvious characteristics of *N. cyclamineus*, the dominant parent. Perianth segments turned back, long cylindrical corona, serrated at the edge, early blooming, usually 6–10″ tall. Hardy in zones 6–9.
Cultivars: 'Bartley' (yellow), 'Beryl' (straw), 'February Gold' (yellow), 'February Silver' (white with yellow cup), 'Charity May' (yellow), 'Dove Wings' (white/pale yellow), 'Foundling' (white/rose-pink), 'Garden Princess' (yellow), 'Itzim' (yellow), 'Jack Snipe' (white with yellow cup), 'Jenny' (white), 'Jetfire' (yellow/red),

'Larkwhistle' (gold), 'Lilac Charm' (white/pink), 'Little Witch' (deep yellow), 'March Sunshine' (yellow), 'Mite' (yellow), 'Peeping Tom' (golden yellow), 'Rapture' (lemon yellow), 'Rival' (lemon yellow), 'Surfside' (white/yellow), 'Tracy' (white), 'Trena' (white/yellow).

VII. JONQUILLA NARCISSUS: Obvious characteristics of *N. jonquilla*, the dominant parent. Rush-like channelled leaves, fragrant golden-yellow flowers borne in clusters of 3–6, with a cup-shaped corona. Usually 6–12″ tall. Hardy in zones 4–9.

**Cultivars:** 'Baby Moon' (pale yellow), 'Bellsong' (lemon yellow), 'Bunting' (yellow/orange), 'Canary' (white/yellow), 'Dickcissel' (yellow/white), 'Golden Perfection' (yellow), 'Intrigue' (yellow/white), 'Lintie' (yellow with orange cup, 6″), 'Pipit' (soft lemon), 'Quail' (golden yellow), 'Sailboat' (white), 'Step Forward' (yellow/cream), 'Sugarbush' (white with chartreuse cup), 'Sundial' (sulphur yellow), 'Suzy' (yellow with dark orange cup), 'Tittle Tattle' (yellow), 'Trevithian' (lemon yellow), 'Verdin' (pale yellow/white), 'Waterperry' (ivory/apricot).

VIII. TAZETTA NARCISSUS: Obvious characteristics of *N. tazetta*, the dominant parent of the hybrids. Four to six narrow leaves, flowers almost flat with a shallow corona, very fragrant. Flowers borne 4–8 to a 12″ tall stem, often referred to as paperwhites or bunch-flowered narcissus. Usually 12–15″ tall. Some are hardy in zones 5–9, others, such as paperwhites, are only hardy to zone 7.

**Cultivars:**

*Those hardy in zones 5 to 9*: 'Avalanche' (white/yellow), 'Canary-bird' (yellow/orange), 'Cragford' (white with orange-red cup), 'Falconet' (yellow/red), 'Geranium' (white with orange cup), 'Golden Dawn' (gold), 'Laurens Koster' (white/yellow), 'Scarlet Gem' (white with orange-red cup), 'Silver Chimes' (white).

*Those tender (zones 7 to 9)*: 'Chinese Sacred Lily' (white/yellow), 'Galilee' (white), 'Grand Soleil' (yellow/orange), 'Minnow' (white/yellow), 'Nazareth' (pale yellow with lemon-yellow cup), 'Ziva' (white).

IX. POETICUS NARCISSUS: Obvious characteristics of *N. poeticus*, the dominant parent. Narrow blue-green leaves. Flowers are solitary, white with small saucer-shaped corona of pale yellow, edged red and often referred to as Pheasant-Eyes. Sweetly fragrant and late flowering. Hardy in zones 4–9.

**Cultivars:** 'Actaea' (white with yellow cup edged red), 'Cantabile' (white with green cup edged red), 'Felindre' (white with green and yellow cup), 'Milan' (white with yellow and red cup).

## X. Species Other Than Those Previously Listed:

**-*bulbocodium*** (bul-bow-ko' dee-um)  Hoop Petticoat Daffodil  8–12"/6"
Early Spring    Yellow    Southern France, Morocco    Zones 6–8

Another stunning but frustrating "I have to have" species. Although plants are small, they are beautiful when flowering in large masses or where they are naturalized. The petticoat daffodils always elicit interest and conversation because of their unique flower shape. Three to four rush-like leaves, up to 15" long, emerge early in the spring. Unique solitary bright yellow flowers on 8" stems arise through the foliage. The perianth is made up of narrow segments but the cup is widely expanded to resemble a petticoat. Excellent drainage is necessary to overwinter the bulbs. Plant in containers or protected areas because inclement weather in January and February can spoil emerging blossoms. Don't expect much success as a perennial in the Southeast or Northeast. The Pacific Northwest is the best area to see the species in the garden.

### Cultivars:
Var. *citrinis* has lemon yellow blossoms.
Var. *conspicuous* is the latest to bloom and produces deep golden yellow flowers.
'Primrose' describes the color of this beautiful flower.
'Tenuifolius' bears a 6-lobed wide yellow corona above thin thread-like leaves.

### Related Species:
*N. cantabricus*, Cantabrian daffodil, bears fragrant white "petticoat" flowers in early spring. Only one leaf is formed and flowering occurs as early as January or February in North Carolina. This is sometimes offered as *N. bulbocodium* var. *monophyllus*. Likely cold hardy to zone 7.

*N.* × *romieuxii* is a tetraploid, probably the result of *N. bulbocodium* × *N. cantabricus*. The sulphur yellow "petticoat" flowers are the first yellow daffodils to emerge in the spring. Hardy to zone 7.


**-*canaliculatus*** (kan-al-ick' u-lah' tus)    Chinese Lily Narcissus    6–9"/6"
Spring    White with Yellow Cup    Southern France    Zones 7–9
(Syn. *N. tazetta* 'Canaliculaus')

This has been reclassified as a subspecies of the paperwhite group of narcissus, *N. tazetta*, of which it is essentially a dwarf form. Bulbs must be well established before sufficient flowers are produced; plants are best in their second or third year. Four to six flowers are produced per stem.

### Related Species:
*N. nanus*, dwarf daffodil, (sometimes sold as *N. lobularius*) is 6–8" tall and bears small, fragrant white flowers with a rich yellow cup.

*N. obvallaris*, tenby daffodil, has 12″ long stems topped with golden yellow flowers with a long yellow, green tinged cup.

| *-cyclamineus* (cyk-la-min′ ee-us) | Cyclamen Daffodil | 4–6″/6″ |
|---|---|---|
| Spring          Yellow | Spain, Portugal | Zones 5–7 |

These are neat flowers. E.A. Bowles described them "like the ears laid back of a kicking horse." I first came across these beautiful cyclamen-like flowers on a spring trip to Wisley Gardens in England where they are naturalized along with other small bulbs in a meadow. Even my good friend, Michael Dirr, who is always looking up at this tree or that one, found himself on his hands and knees admiring without apology. Dirr and Armitage in a meadow, sounds like the beginning of a bad poem.

Unfortunately, they are more difficult to naturalize in the United States for the same reasons that many southern European species are difficult. Our temperature extremes, hard unforgiving storms, heaving due to snow and ice, etc., aren't conditions that allow the species to take over. However, even a dozen bulbs, enjoyed for a couple of years, will make your spring an unforgettable one. Put them where drainage is excellent such as a raised bed or a rock garden and in full sun. If you have trouble with the species, select some of the cultivars with *N. cyclamineus* as the dominant parent (Group VI).

XI. SPLIT CORONA NARCISSUS: Distinguished by the corona (cup) being split for at least one-third its length. Very showy, and also referred to as collar and papillion daffodils.

a. *Collars:* Corona split for at least a third of its length.

**Cultivars:** 'Cassata' (white with gold collar), 'Changing Colors' (white with multicolored collar), 'Flyer' (all yellow), 'Floralie' (white with soft yellow), 'Orangery' (creamy white with orange collar), 'Mol's Hobby', 'Palmares' (white with salmon-pink collar), 'Pearlax' (white/rose corona), 'Pink Supreme', 'Sovereign' (white with orange collar), 'Tricollet' (white with orange corona).

b. *Papillons (Butterflys):* Distinguished by the sunburst of color from the center of the corona (cup).

**Cultivars:** 'Anna Floor' (white with green and orange corona), 'Broadway Star' (white with orange-white corona), 'Burning Heart' (yellow with dark orange corona), 'Dolly Mollinger' (white with orange and white corona), 'Firestreak' (white with cream and red corona), 'Papillion Blanc' (white with green and yellow corona), 'Space Shuttle' (white with yellow-orange corona), 'Spring Diamond' (white with orange and white corona).

XII. MISCELLANEOUS NARCISSUS: All daffodils not falling into any of the above categories. Most of these are miniatures falling into various divisions. I'm not sure why cultivars fall into this division and not remain in standard divisions, but I assume a catch-all division is required.

**Cultivars:** 'Tete-a-tete' (yellow), 'Jumblie' (yellow/orange-red cup), 'Kenelis' (white with pale yellow cup), 'Quince' (soft yellow), 'W.P. Milner' (trumpet with corkscrew petals and frilled cup).

## Additional Reading:

*Books:* There are many sources of information concerning daffodils. Any book on flowering bulbs is sure to have a section on the genus. The better catalogs attempt to properly classify the species and hybrids.

Gray, Alec. 1955. *Miniature Daffodils*. Transatlantic Arts, New York.
Jefferson-Brown, Michael. 1991. Narcissus. Timber Press, Portland, OR. A good recent treatise of the genus.
Lawrence, Elizabeth. 1957. *The Little Bulbs, A Tale of Two Gardens*. Criterion Books. In this most charming book, she discusses experiences with the small bulbs in her gardens in Raleigh and Charlotte, NC, and those of her friend Mr. Krippendorf in his garden in Ohio. This was recently reprinted by Duke University Press in 1986.
Wilder, Louise Beebe. 1936. *Experiences with Hardy Bulbs*. Macmillan Co., New York. I highly recommend this book for information about many garden bulbs.
Wister, J.C. 1930. *Bulbs for American Gardens*. The Stratford Co., Boston.

*Manuscripts:*

Davis, Rosalie. 1986. Planting daffodils. *Horticulture* 64(10):54–55.
Donald, Kate. 1984. Narcissus cyclamineus. *The Garden* 109(7):285–287.
Skelmersdale, C. 1993. Little charmers. *The Garden* 118(9):406–410.
Willis, David. 1981. The origins of pink daffodil cultivars. *The Plantsman* 3(1):51–59.

*Associations:*

American Daffodil Society, Tyner, NC 27980. <u>Publication:</u> *Daffodil Journal*.

## *Nectaroscordum* (nek-ta-ro-skor' dum)   Sicilian Honey Garlic   Liliaceae (Syn. *Allium siculum*)

The botanical name comes from *nektar* from Greek mythology ("the drink of the Gods") and *scordium* ("plant smelling of garlic"). The genus, which consists of about three species, is closely related to *Allium*, which is redolently obvious when the leaves are crushed. The plants may smell like onions, but they do not look like any other onion I know. Botanically, they differ from *Allium* by having outer petals with 3–5 veins, while those of *Allium* have only one.

A truly interesting and fascinating bulb; plants grow to 4' tall and bear 20–30 pendulous, bell-shaped green flowers tinged with white and purple margins. They are held in a loose umbel from the top of the stem, opening in early summer. The fascination of the plants accounts for their beauty because they are surely not subtle or diminutive. The strap-shaped leaves emerge early in the spring, mature by flowering time, then disappear once flowering is complete. Plants are invasive where they are comfortable and can become a nuisance, but few places in the United States afford such comfort. *Nectaroscordum siculum* is native to France and Italy and high humidity or severe winters are not well tolerated. Plants are hardy from zones 7 to 8.

Bulbs should be set 2" deep and about 18" apart. Leave bulbs undisturbed once established.

### Cultivars:

'Bulgaricum' (ssp. *bulgaricum*) is similar but has white to yellow flowers which are tinged pale pink and green above, edged white and flushed green below. They are native to eastern and central Europe and a little more cold hardy (perhaps to zone 6).

## *Nepeta* (nep' e-ta)          Nepeta          Lamiaceae

One of the better known representatives of this genus is the old-fashioned, light blue-flowered plant, *N. cataria* or catnip. There is nothing particularly special except in its perverse ability to make cats crazier than they already are. The famous French botanist and plant explorer, J.P. de Tournefort wrote in the early 1700's about the effect of this magical plant on the feline race. ". . . when a Cat has smelt it (even before she has well seen it) hugg'd it and kiss'd it, wantonly running upon it and scouring away from it by turns, and has rub'd herself against it very much and long, using strange Postures and playing with it, she at last eats it up and devours it entirely." This is not a pretty picture! It is also said that catnip repels rats, whether because of the oils in the plant or the fact that a cat may jump on the plants at any moment. Apparently cats don't bother young plants as much as mature plants.

The genus, however, is much more than common catnip, and consists of over 250 species. *Nepeta* has square stems, opposite leaves and white to blue flowers, although a little-known ornamental species, *N. govaniana*, Kashmir nepeta, has yellow flowers. Many of the commonly offered species, particularly *N.* × *faassenii* and 'Six Hills Giant' are best grown as edging plants but tend to cascade over the area they are designed to edge, either a charming sight or a terrible nuisance depending on one's degree of patience. The gray-green leaves help blend other plants together when used in the garden. They perform best in full sun and well-drained soil and tolerate partial shade in zones 5 and 7. Afternoon shade is necessary further south. Plants prefer full sun in northern areas. The more common species such as *N.* × *faassenii* and *N. racemosa* (syn. *N. mussinii*) are low growing edgers, but some excellent taller more upright species are starting to be more recognized. These include *N. grandiflora, N. nuda* and *N. sibirica*.

There is confusion as to the identity of species sold under the name *Nepeta*. It is easy to know *Nepeta* by its unique fragrance and the grayish leaves and lavender flowers, however, the species are so closely related, it is difficult to tell them apart without a label. The most popular one is the hybrid Faassen's catnip, *N.* × *faassenii*, with numerous cultivars, however, they are very similar to *N. racemosa*; so similar that the some taxonomists have folded it into *N.* × *faassenii*. Other species mainly differ in their habit and vigor.

I used to think that *Nepeta* was easy to distinguish from other genera; plants were usually shorter, more floppy and always easy to tell apart by the difference in foliage smell. However, with the increased popularity of the taller, less fragrant forms (such as *N. sibirica*), I needed a way to distinguish *Nepeta* from blue-flowered tall *Salvia*. To do so, tear apart a flower and find the stamens. If the plant is a *Salvia*, there will 4 stamens, but 2 will be long and 2 will be short or rudimentary. If the plant is a *Nepeta*, the 4 stamens will be the same size.

Quick Reference to Nepeta Species

|  | Height | Flowers | Flower color | Leaf length |
|---|---|---|---|---|
| *N.* × *faassenii* | Up to 2' | Sterile | Lavender | 1–2" |
| *N. govaniana* | 2–3' | Fertile | Yellow | 3–4" |
| *N. nervosa* | Up to 2' | Fertile | Lavender | 3–4" |
| *N. sibirica* | 3–4' | Fertile | Lavender | 2–4" |

| -× *faassenii* (fah-sen' ee-eye) | Faassen Nepeta | 18–24"/18" |
|---|---|---|
| Early Summer    Lavender-Violet | Hybrid | Zones 4–7 |

Plants were named for J.H. Faassen, a Dutch nurseryman, in whose nursery the hybrid first appeared. Originally, the parents were listed as *N. mussinii* and the rather nondescript white-flowered *N. nepetella*, however, since the former's name has now been changed to *N. racemosa*, plants are officially listed as *N. racemosa* × *N. nepetella*. Generally growing 1–2' tall, the bushy plants consist of upright and prostrate flowering stems. The small (1–2" long) scalloped, gray-green leaves have short petioles and are straight across at the base (truncate). The many flowers are lavender to violet-blue and occur in elongated racemes almost always in the leaf axils. If flowers are closely studied, one can see that the sepals (calyx) is almost as long as the petals (corolla). Since plants are sterile, no seed is formed, therefore plants raised from seed cannot be *N.* × *faassenii*. Flowers appear about a week later than those of *N. racemosa* but are more persistent. This hybrid is a better garden plant, although not as cold hardy as many other species.

Propagate by spring division or by terminal cuttings. Take 3″ long cuttings in summer and root in sand or peat-perlite mix. Rooting occurs within 2 weeks.

### Cultivars:

All cultivars should be sheared to 12–15″ after flowering for repeat blooms.

'Blue Dwarf' ('Blauknirps') produces many pale blue flowers on compact plants.

'Blue Ice' produces interesting icy blue flowers which fade to creamy white on maturity.

'Blue Wonder' is 12–15″ tall, compact, and bears dark blue flowers on 6″ tall spikes. Cut back after flowering for repeat bloom in the fall.

'Dropmore' has larger leaves and flowers and is more upright than the hybrid. Bigger and more noticeable; can grow up to 2' tall.

'Little Titch' is only 9–12″ tall.

'Pool Bank' produces purple-blue to blue flowers on 3' tall plants.

'Porcelain' ('Porzellan') bears porcelain soft blue flowers with blue-gray foliage. Very handsome.

'Six Hills Giant' is the best known catnip and taller and sufficiently different to be classified under a horticultural (rather than taxonomic) species called *N. gigantea.* One of the finest plants I have seen, it is used extensively in the British Isles for edging pathways and for mass plantings. The 9–12″ tall racemes consist of dark violet flowers borne in axils and terminals atop 3' tall erect plants. Plants are greener and flower later than the species. To discriminate from other catnips, I pick a flowering stem and expect it to stretch from wrist to elbow. A quick and dirty test like that often helps me out, it may do the same for you.

'Snowflake' bears creamy white flowers.

'Souvenir d'Andre Chaudron' ('Blue Beauty') is another orphan whose parentage is being questioned. It is often listed as a cultivar of *N. sibirica,* borne out by being more cold hardy, at least to zone 3, and with little nepeta odor. Compact plants produce many lavender-blue flowers on 2–3' tall upright plants. Plants can flop over in late summer and may also become invasive.

'White Wonder' is a white flowering form of 'Blue Wonder'.

### Related Species:

*N. racemosa* (syn. *N. mussinii*) produces gray, hairy, heart-shaped leaves with a rounded apex are about 1″ long and highly scented. Plants are similar but are more prostrate and shorter than *N.* × *faassenii*. The pale blue flowers consist of numerous ½″ long, lipped flowers held in loose terminal racemes. They make a pleasant, if not outstanding plant for the garden. The species and cultivars set seed profusely. In the Armitage garden, plants did well but the flowers faded in the sun and never attained the sparkle I have seen overseas. Plants persisted for about 3 years before succumbing to heat, cats, dogs, and children.

*-govaniana* (go-van-ee' a-na)          Yellow Catnip          2–4'/2'
　　Summer                Yellow          Himalayas          Zones 4–7

A most un-nepeta-like nepeta. The yellow flowers and the mild catnip odor belie its roots. The flowers are held differently than other catnips as well, being borne in long, lax 2–3-flowered racemes rather than the many densely flowered racemes seen in other species. Flowers occur in mid to late summer in the axils of the large serrated oblong-elliptical leaves.

Little seen in America, more curious than useful.

### Related Species:
*N. grandiflora* is also a tallish catnip, growing 30–36" on sturdy stems. The relatively large lavender-blue flowers are held in spikes (flowers with no flower stems) and bloom for many weeks. A good plant for zones 5–7, zone 8 in the West.

*-nervosa* (ner-vo' sa)          Veined Nepeta          1–2'/2'
　　Early Summer          Lavender-Blue          Iran          Zones 5–7

The term *nervosa* refers to the nerves or veins on the foliage and the most obvious characteristic is the strong veins on the entire or slightly toothed 3–4" long leaves. The lower leaves have short petioles while the upper ones are sessile. The lavender-blue flowers are held in a dense cylindrical raceme in which the sepals of each flower are about half the length of the petals.

Plants, which are useful for edging, fall over the edges of beds. They form spreading mats and flower for a long time in early and mid summer. Some shade should be provided in the afternoon, particularly in the South, and plants may be sited on poor soils. Fertilize sparingly or plants will get stringy. This is as heat tolerant a catnip as is available. Similar to other species and cultivars, they should be cut back hard when the plants look like string beans.

Propagate by cuttings or division.

### Cultivars:
'Blue Carpet' is about 1' tall and produces violet-blue flowers.

*-sibirica* (si-bi' ri-ca)          Sibirian Catnip          24–36"/24"
　　Summer                Lavender          Sibirica          Zones 3–7

A number of characteristics distinguish this catnip from others. It is probably the most cold hardy, taller than most and more invasive. The 2–4" long lanceolate leaves have broad, almost rounded teeth and are slightly gray on the topsides. The rich blue flowers are held in many whorls in a long raceme.

Similar but not nearly as strong in fragrance as other nepetas, they are nonetheless one of the most handsome plants, particularly when provided with a little afternoon shade. Overly rich moist soils result in rampant plants. Plants may require support but if they get too flippy-floppy, give them a haircut early in May or after they flower.

**Related Species:**

*N. nuda* is little known in the American garden trade but a most impressive plant, if well grown. The well-branched plants are at least 3' tall (I have seen them almost 5' tall) and leaves up to 3" long. The lavender-blue flowers have purplish spots and are carried in axils and terminals. Likely cold hardy to about zone 6.

Quick Key to Nepeta Species

  A. Flowers yellow . . . . . . . . . . . . . . . . . . . . . . . *N. govaniana*
AA. Flowers blue
    B. Mature leaves generally less than 2" long  . . . *N. × faassenii*
  BB. Mature leaves generally greater than 2" long
      C. Leaves strongly veined,
        plants usually 2–3' tall . . . . . . . . . . . . . . . . *N. nervosa*
     CC. Leaves not strongly veined,
        plants usually 3' or taller . . . . . . . . . . . . . . *N. sibirica*

**Additional Reading:**

DeWolf Jr., Gordon. 1955. Notes on Cultivated Labiates. 6. *Nepeta. Baileya* 3:98–107.
Haywood, G. 1988. The attraction of catmints. *Horticulture* 66(8):22–25.
Sheldon, E. 1993. The catmint muddle. *American Horticulturist* 72(8):34–38.

*Nerine* (ner' ene)          Nerine          Amaryllidaceae

A group of bulbs native to South Africa which resemble *Lycoris* and *Amaryllis*. *Nerine* consists of about 20 autumn flowering species, but seldom are any of them seen in North American gardens, except in some West Coast areas. The strong 2' stems of *N. bowdenii* and *N. sarniensis* terminate in 10–15 tubular crimson to rosy pink flowers and have been used for many years as a commercial cut flower. All species are native to South Africa, and only *N. bowdenii* is marginally hardy in zones 7–9, others can be used in containers to be removed like a gladiolus. The large umbels of rosy pink flowers emerge on leafless stems in late summer or fall, then go dormant during the summer. In mild climates, the strap-like leaves are evergreen. A number of gardeners in the Southeast have been pleasantly surprised with the performance of *N. bowdenii* as a perennial in their gardens. The summer is the dormant period and in their native habitats, they prefer to be dry.

I was fortunate to live in New Zealand for a short period of time and with a fine scientist, Dr. Ian Warrington, was able to study and appreciate the beauty of *N. sarniensis*, the Guernsey lily. The flowers of the species are crimson and almost iridescent. Their importance as a cut flower in that country and in the Channel Islands have resulted in greenhouse forcing protocol as well as an aggressive breeding program. Although not quite as hardy as *N. bowdenii*, if you are successful with the latter, try the Guernsey lily.

In containers, mix in a significant amount of organic matter and plant with the necks of the bulbs slightly above the surface of the soil. Withhold water until the flower scapes appear.

Numerous hybrids such as 'Salmon Supreme' and 'Mother of Pearl', among others, have been bred and are outstanding. All you have to do is find them!

**Additional Reading:**

Smithers, P. 1993. Nerine sarniensis. *The Garden* 118(5):190–193.

Warrington, I.J., Seager, N.G. and Armitage, A.M. 1989. Environmental requirements for flowering and bulb growth in *Nerine sarniensis*. *Herbertia* 45:74–80.

# O

*Oenanthe* (o-nanth′ ee)        Flamingo Plant        Apiaceae

I first saw this plant when a member of a garden audience asked me "Do you know what this is?" as a stump-the-professor type of question. The audience sat on the edge of their seats as I, in my usual professorial manner, tugged at my chin, scratched my head and mumbled something inaudible. My best guess was a poor looking container of Bishop's Weed, *Aegopodium podagraria*, but alas and alak, I was stumped once again. I remember seeing a plant similar to this one at Wisley Gardens in England but could not put a name to it. Without doubt, senility was setting in quickly.

The plant was, and is, *Oenanthe javanica* 'Flamingo', a bishop's weed look-alike with tricolor foliage. Its claim to fame is the pink hues on the leaves, particularly when young. The white umbels are produced in mid summer. Plants grow well from zones 6–8, but are not as aggressive as its look-alike. They require full sun to partial afternoon shade and prefer moist soils. In their native habitats, they are generally found in marshlands, moist meadows, and other damp habitats. Plants may be planted in "normal" garden soils, but growth will be slower. Plants are not common but have become easier to find in the last 2–3 years.

Propagate by seed, divisions, stem cuttings or layering.


*Oenothera* (ee-no-the′ ra)    Evening Primrose, Sundrop    Onagraceae

Of the 125 or so species of annuals, biennials, and perennials, about a half dozen are well-known garden plants. Many are native to the United States and Canada and have become well established in gardens. The leaves are alternate, and stems are often woody at the base. The 4-petalled flowers are usually yellow, although white and rose flowers occur on a number of lesser-known species. Height ranges from 4–6″ for the diminutive *O. acaulis*, dandelion sundrop, to the 4′ tall common evening primrose.

749

A number of species have vespertine flowers, which means they open in the evening, and accounts for one of their common names. For example, the flowering habit of the common evening primrose, *O. biennis*, now more of a roadside weed than a garden plant, fascinated the English poet Keats who was "startled by the leap of buds into ripe flowers" and for "shutting again with a loud popping noise about sunrise." However, many species do not exhibit this nocturnal manner and are referred to as sundrops. Japanese beetles find *O. biennis* particularly tasty and Harry Phillips (*Growing and Propagating Wild Flowers*) reports that their presence spares neighboring plants from attack. I want to be the neighbor.

One of the neatest plants around has to be the large-flowered evening primrose, known as Lamarck's sundrop, twirling primrose, or my favorite, magic primrose (*O. glazioviana*, syn. *O. lamarkiana*). This biennial has the Tinkerbell habit of spinning open its flowers in the evening, changing from being ignored during the day to being the center of attention in the evening. Like a tailgate party on a Saturday afternoon's football game, the anticipation of the flowers unfolding is an excuse for picnics and wine. Tina James of Reistertown, MD was responsible for getting the plants back into the garden trade, and seeds are often sold as the Tina James evening primrose. Plants of 'Tina James' are used to perfection at the marvelous children's garden at Michigan State University, created by Jane Taylor. A sign tells everyone the exact time when the flowers will open each evening, and people literally line up to see the wonderful event. Jane's garden is an enchanted place, dusk with Tina James is magical.

Flowers of most species persist only for a day or so, but many buds are produced, resulting in long flowering garden plants. As with other genera, differences of opinion as to what plants belong in what species continually occur. There are many similarities between species and it is inevitable that shunting back and forth occurs. Changes in *O. lamarkiana* and *O. missouriensis* have occurred, and *O. tetragona* has also "officially" disappeared. As gardeners, we should select the cultivar we like, and not worry too much if the nursery has it filed under the correct name. However, we might as well keep up with this nomenclature stuff if at all possible.

This genus, along with *Epilobium*, *Fuschia* and *Gaura*, belongs to the evening primrose family, Onagraceae, one of the easiest families to recognize. In general, recognizing family characteristics is difficult for most students of perennial plants and of little interest to others. Plants of this family bear flowers with 4 or 8 petals and 4 sepals, an uncommon number. However, the telltale sign is to look at the base of the open flowers. There, the 4 translucent sepals are reflexed behind the flower like pennants in the wind, and are very persistent. They also look like old bud scales and once recognized in one member of the family, are easily recognized in others.

Quick Reference to Oenothera Species

| | Height (in.) | Flower color | Flowers nocturnal |
|---|---|---|---|
| *O. caespitosa* | 4–8 | White, pink | Yes |
| *O. fruticosa* | 18–24 | Yellow | No |
| *O. missouriensis* | 6–12 | Yellow | No |
| *O. odorata* | 18–24 | Yellow | Yes |
| *O. perennis* | 12–24 | Yellow | No |
| *O. speciosa* | 12–24 | White | No |

| | | |
|---|---|---|
| *-caespitosa* (say-spi-to′ sa) | Tufted Evening Primrose | 4–8″/12″ |
| Early Summer    White, Pink | Western North America | Zones 4–7 |

This prostrate species is native from northern Mexico and northwards to Washington and east to the Sierras. Plants naturally grow in scrubby soils in very dry areas, at altitudes of 3000 to 8000 feet. If they are to be grown, they are most suitable for the front of the border or in the rock garden. Plants are stemless and the 4″ long narrow, hairy leaves are clustered together in a rosette. Erect flower buds give way to 2–3″ wide fragrant flowers which open at night, almost covering the plant. They open white and fade to pink with contrasting yellow stamens. Flowering persists for 4–6 weeks but one must be present in late afternoon and evening to enjoy them as they seldom open at midday. Beautiful plants for dry, sheltered, sunny locations, but lousy elsewhere. Forget them in the South. They require excellent drainage and do poorly in hot, humid climates.

Propagate by seed or division in the spring. Seeds should be lightly covered and sown in a well-drained medium. Place seed tray in warm (70–75° F), humid conditions.

**Cultivars:**

Var. *eximea* is similar in flower habit but has stems, resulting in a somewhat taller plant (8–12″).

**Related Species:**

*O. acaulis* has 2–3″ wide white flowers which fade to rose and open in the evening. Plants have dandelion-like leaves and grow 6–9″ tall. In fact, the leaves are so similar to dandelions they are often mistaken for weeds and pulled out in spring. Full sun and well-drained soils are needed. Probably not winter hardy north of zone 5.

*-fruticosa* (froo-ti-ko′ sa)　　　Common Sundrops　　　18-24″/2′
　　Summer　　　Yellow　　　Eastern North America　　　Zones 4-8
(Syn. *O. tetragona*)

The reddish, slender, hairy stems bear 1-3″ long, hairy, entire, lance-shaped sessile leaves. The basal leaves are 2-4″ and a little over 1″ wide. Erect flower buds open to a terminal cluster of 1-2″ wide, bright yellow flowers making this one of the prettiest species of the genus. The seed capsule is one way of distinguishing this species from other yellow-flowered forms. It is shaped like a club, tapering to a slender stalk (clavate). Full sun is necessary for best performance. Dry soils are tolerated. One of the mainstays of the evening primrose group was *O. tetragona,* however, it has now been classified as *O. fruticosa* ssp. *glauca.* Many of the better garden cultivars belong to this subspecies.

Propagate by seed or division in summer.

## Cultivars:

'Erica Robin' produces bright yellow flowers on willowy stems. The leaves emerge yellow with red spots.

'Fireworks' ('Fyrverkeri') grows about 18″ tall with red stems and buds which open to 2-3″ wide bright yellow flowers. In the trials at the University of Georgia, flowering occurred from May 20 to mid June.

Ssp. *glauca* (*O. tetragona, O. youngii*) differs by having broader, grayer leaves and is relatively smooth compared to the hairy leaves of the species.

'Golden Sunray' sounds like a coreopsis, but is a tall (2′) plant with coreopsis-yellow flowers and dark green leaves.

'Highlights' ('Hohes Licht') grows 12″ tall with 2″ wide yellow flowers.

'Illumination' has thicker, more bronzy leaves with large yellow flowers.

'Lady Brookborough' bears dozens of bright yellow flowers.

'Summer Solstice' ('Sonnenwende') is about 18-24″ tall with yellow flowers in June and July.

'Yellow River' is about 18″ tall and has 2-3″ wide deep yellow flowers. The foliage turns mahogany brown in the fall.

## Related Species:

*O.* 'Cold Crick' was recently found by Polly Rowley of Cold Crick Nursery near Middleburg, Virginia. It is only 8-12″ tall but is covered with bright yellow flowers in spring and early summer. I think this has great potential for American gardens.

*-missouriensis* (mi-sur-ree-en′ sis)　　　Ozark Sundrops　　　6-12″/12″
　　Summer　　　Yellow　　　Southcentral United States　　　Zones 4-7

When plants are well grown, their beauty is unrivaled. Although they are small in stature, the paper thin flowers may be up to 5″ across. Solitary, bright to lemon-yellow, funnel-shaped flowers persist for many days. The sepals are often spotted red in the bud stage and remain so even while the flowers are open. The fruit capsule is ellipsoid and winged, a rather curious sight indeed. The spreading plants are deeply rooted and bear short reddish stems with upright growing tips (decumbent). The 1–4" long leaves are petioled and entire. Plants are native to Missouri and Kansas and south to Texas.

Plants struggle in the summer heat in the South, while in the North the addition of a winter mulch is beneficial. Plant in full sun to partial shade and allow soil to occasionally dry out. Good drainage is a must. Apparently, our old friend has been given a new name and soon the name *O. macrocarpa* may replace *O. missouriensis*. Stay tuned.

Propagate by seed as soon as ripe or by division after flowering.

### Cultivars:
'Greencourt Lemon', found in the garden of Countess von Stein Zepplin in Germany, has gray-green leaves and pale yellow 3" wide flowers. Grown only vegetatively.

### Related Species:
*O. drummondii*, beach evening primrose, is native to areas on the Atlantic and Pacific coasts, down to Baja California. The spreading plants are covered with sharp, stiff hairs throughout and bear gray-green leaves and pale yellow 2–3" wide flowers. Terrific salt-tolerant plants for sandy soils, heavy soils should be avoided. Probably hardy in zones 8–10, maybe into zone 7.

| *-odorata* (o-do-rah' ta) | | Twisted Evening Primrose | 18–24"/2' |
|---|---|---|---|
| Early Summer | Yellow | Southern South America | Zones 4–8 |

The fragrant, solitary yellow flowers have a red tinge, are 2–3" wide, and open in late afternoon. The base of the plant is somewhat woody and the sessile, 4–6" long stem leaves have conspicuous wavy edges.

This is a fair garden performer at best but other yellow-flowered species are available which are hardier, more floriferous, and provide open flowers during the day and evening.

Propagate by seed or division.

| *-perennis* (pe-ren' is) | | Nodding Sundrops | 12–24"/18" |
|---|---|---|---|
| Summer | Yellow | Eastern North America | Zones 3–8 |

(Syn. *O. pumila*)

This common sundrop occurs over much of eastern North America and may be treated as a biennial or perennial. The 1–2" long leaves are lance-like, slightly hairy, and entire. The plant often begins to flower when 5–9" tall but the flower stalk continues to expand to 1½–2' in height. The

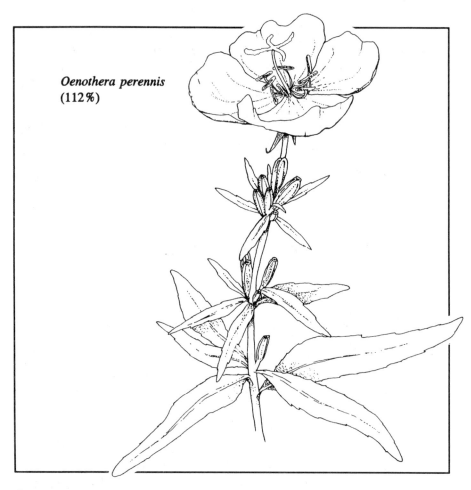

*Oenothera perennis*
(112%)

flower buds are nodding, thus the common name, and reveal handsome 1″ wide yellow flowers. The leafy flower stalk is often branched, and diurnal flowers (open during the day, closed at night) are carried in loose panicles or racemes. This species is commonly offered by nurserymen but is not as showy as *O. fruticosa*. Perhaps it is so popular because people look at the botanical name and believe they are purchasing a long-lasting perennial plant.

Grow in full sun with decent drainage. Cut back hard after flowering when plants look bedraggled. New rosettes will form soon after.

Propagate by seed any time or by division in the spring or fall.

### Related Species:

*O. biennis*, common evening primrose, is a most variable species, but in general has leafy, erect branched stems and large yellow flowers which open in the evening. Plants can reach 8′ in height, but generally flower when 5–6' tall. They should be treated as annuals or biennials, but often reseed themselves. Plants are native to eastern North America but have naturalized in Europe, earning the common name German Rampion.

| *-speciosa* (spee-see-o' sa) | Showy Evening Primrose | 12–24"/18" |
|---|---|---|
| Summer        White, Rose | Southcentral United States | Zones 5–8 |

Due to the stoloniferous rootstock, plants tends to spread much more rapidly than many other species. The 1–3" long linear leaves are pinnately lobed and bear a soft pubescence. The 1–2" diameter diurnal flowers, which appear in the axils of the upper leaves, are white then mature to a pink-rose color. If grown in full sun and moderately good soil, handsome, compact plants result. However, in rich soils or when heavily fertilized, plants become a rampant nuisance. Plants are naturalized along roadsides in north Georgia and may be found in dry places, fields, and prairies. High humidity is tolerated but plants do better in the plains states and western part of the country than in the East and South. However, they have done well enough in Georgia, becoming an aggressive weed, albeit beautiful, and I will not plant it again. (See *Chasmanthium*)

Propagate from seed or division.

### Cultivars:

'Alba' is a strong growing white-flowered form. Almomst as invasive.

'Ballerina Hot Pink' is an outstanding deep pink (even in the heat). Bred by Ian Collins and Dan McDonald of Sydney, Aus. Much better than the species.

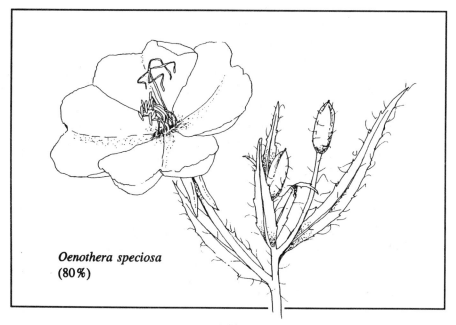

*Oenothera speciosa*
(80%)

**Related Species:**

*O. berlandieri*, Mexican evening primrose, is a bit of a mystery plant. It has arisen in catalogs in recent years and some of the most handsome cultivars have been paired with it. However, it is hardly ever listed in a reputable reference volume and when referenced is usually shuttled to another species. It has been listed as *O. speciosa* var. *childsii* or simply *O. speciosa*. Nevertheless, plants appear to be less invasive and much neater than those of *O. speciosa*. Plants bear slender prostrate branches about 6-12″ tall, upon which are produced 1″ diameter rose-colored flowers. They are excellent for container culture. 'Siskiyou', from the terrific nursery of the same name, bears 2″ wide pink saucer-shaped flowers over 8″ plants. 'Woodside White' is about 15″ tall producing large white flowers with a chartreuse eye. Performance has been excellent in zones 6-8.

*O. rosea*, rosy evening primrose, has rose-colored flowers but the buds are erect, not nodding. The flowers open pale pink and mature to rich rose. This species is becoming less difficult to locate and sometimes seed can be found from rare plant specialists.

## Quick Key to Oenothera Species

    A. Flowers yellow
      B. Plants more than 1′ tall
        C. Flowers open in late afternoon and
          evening, not on bright days . . . . . . . . . . . . *O. odorata*
        CC. Flowers open on bright days
          D. Buds and tip of flower
            head nodding . . . . . . . . . . . . . . . . . . . . *O. perennis*
          DD. Buds and tip of flower head erect . . . . . . . *O. fruticosa*
      BB. Plants less than 1′ tall . . . . . . . . . . . . . . *O. missouriensis*
    AA. Flowers rose, pink, or white
      B. Flowers open in late afternoon and evening,
        not on bright days, plants less than 1′ tall . . . . *O. caespitosa*
      BB. Flowers open during day, open white,
        age to rose, plants more than 1′ tall . . . . . . . . *O. speciosa*

**Additional Reading:**

Bishop Hipps, C. 1990. Evening primrose. *Horticulture* 68(8):64.

James, Tina. 1996. *A light in the night.* This delightful little book is a story of children, old men, and the enchanting magic primrose, *O. glazioviana*. Published by the author and available by writing her at 12812 Bridlepath Road, Reisterstown, MD 21136.

*Omphalodes* (om-fa-lod' eez)        Navel-Seed        Boraginaceae

A number of species of *Omphalodes* are occasionally grown in the United States, and like most members of the Boraginaceae, have blue flowers, alternate leaves and bear hard fruits (nutlets). The common name, navel-seed, comes from the deep groove in the nutlet, a characteristic which separates *Omphalodes* from the other members of the family. It is sometimes confused with *Myosotis* and *Cynoglossum* because of their similar size, foliage, and blue flowers. Some of the more visible differences include:

|  | *Omphalodes* | *Cynoglossum* | *Myosotis* |
|---|---|---|---|
| Habit | Creeping(*) | Upright | Upright |
| Leaves | Petioled | Petioled | Sessile |
| Pubescence | Sparsely | Stiff | Slightly |
| Flowers | Blue | Dark blue | Blue with eye |
| Nutlet | Slightly hairy | Prickly | Smooth, shiny |

(*) *O. verna*, the most common in cultivation.

An annual species, *O. linifolia*, flaxleaf navel-seed, about 1' tall with fresh white flowers, is occasionally grown, but the two perennials offered are *O. verna*, blue-eyed Mary, and *O. cappadocica*.

Quick Reference to Omphalodes Species

|  | Height (in.) | Stoloniferous |
|---|---|---|
| *O. cappadocica* | 8–12 | No |
| *O. verna* | 4–8 | Yes |

-*cappadocica* (kap-a-doe' si-ca)        Navel-Seed        8–12"/10"
    Blue        Spring        Asia Minor        Zones 6–8

Plants are not as vigorous or as "cute" as the better known *O. verna*, but as plants become more available, they are starting to be appreciated a little more. The 3–4" long basal leaves are quite hairy and have prominent lateral veins. The basal leaves have long petioles but the smaller stem leaves are almost sessile as they ascend the stem. The ½" wide flowers are bright blue and held on long flower stems (pedicels) forming elongated racemes near the top of the plants. Occasionally clones will appear with white centers to the blue flowers.

A cool, shady well-drained site works best. Excellent drainage is a must. They are not particularly tolerant of high heat and humidity and are better plants for the west coast zone 8 than the southern zone 8.

Seed is the method of choice for these plants. Although division may be used, they do not recover well when the roots are disturbed.

**Cultivars:**
'Starry Eyes' bears flowers with the margin of each purple petal outlined in pinkish white, resulting in a eye catching starry effect. Quite handsome.

| *-verna* (ver' na) | | Blue-Eyed Mary | 2–8"/12" |
|---|---|---|---|
| Spring | Blue | Southern Europe | Zones 6–9 |

*O. verna* is well established in European gardens but only beginning to be appreciated in the United States. Spreading rapidly by underground stems, it makes a useful ground cover for partially shaded locations. The 1–3" long oval leaves are long petioled, and have a short, abrupt point at the end. They are entire, conspicuously veined and remain evergreen in the South. The long flower stems bear 2–4 deep blue, ½" wide flowers with white throats which cover the foliage in spring and early summer. The blue-eyed flowers were a favorite of Queen Marie Antoinette, thus accounting for the popular name.

Although tolerant of poor soils and dry shade, garden performance is enhanced in moist areas and partial shade, as long as soils are well-drained. Full sun results in stunted plants which never attain the graceful habit seen in partial shade. Slugs tend to dine on it, as they do on many other stoloniferous species, and slug repellent should be applied in early spring.

Propagate from seed or division in spring immediately after flowering.

**Cultivars:**
Var. *alba* is similar, but has white flowers.

Quick Key to Omphalodes Species

    A. Plants stoloniferous, obviously creeping . . . . . . . . . . *O. verna*
    AA. Plants not stoloniferous, not spreading
        by underground root . . . . . . . . . . . . . . . . . *O. cappadocica*

*Onoclea* (o-no' clay-a)       Sensitive Fern       Dryopteridaceae

The genus consists of but one species, *O. sensibilis*, the sensitive fern, but what a wonderful bachelor it is. The common name was apparently given by early North American settlers who noted that plants were highly sensitive to early frosts, and one of the first ferns to collapse in the fall.

This is a unfern-like fern, consisting of broad smooth pinnatifid leaflets. Pinnatifid means that the leaflets don't quite terminate at the stem, but are winged. Plants consist of two types of leaflets; the sterile green forms which are easily recognized, and the fertile brown 12" tall stalks. The fertile stalks consist of small, hardened, bead-like divisions of fertile leaflets, which turn dark brown with age. Ferns are also known as Bead Fern because of the appearance of the fertile stalks. The fiddle heads are pale red in the spring.

They tolerate little sun if grown in dry conditions, but have no problem with high light in wet soils. Plants multiply through their creeping rootstalk, forming extensive colonies over time. One of our favorite native ferns, easily grown from southern Canada to Florida.

The only other fern which resembles sensitive fern is the native Netted Chain Fern, *Woodwardia areolata*. *Woodwardia* is smaller and the fertile fronds are not beaded, but form puckered, narrow leaflets. The sori (spore cases) are carried in broken chain-like rows on these fertile fronds.

## *Onopordum* (o-no-por' dum)        Scotch Thistle        Asteraceae

If one found themselves staring down the massive spiny stem of this plant in Scotland or in some other northwestern European land, the last thing one would suggest is that it would actually be sold as a garden plant. Gardens have come a long way, baby! James V of England chose this plant as the Scottish emblem and is known as the scotch thistle, Cotton thistle, Queen Mary's thistle or the silver thistle. The first time I saw a Scotch thistle (*O. acanthium*) was on a tea-towel that somebody gave my mother upon returning from a trip to Scotland. To me, it represented nothing more than additional dishes to dry. However, as I have matured as a gardener, I have had to open my mind to the creativity of designers and the need for something impressive, regardless of garden size. Thus, I have had to accept Scottish weeds in the garden.

While they are deadly, I grudgingly admit that the large gray leaves with their deep sinusus and spiny fingers on the 6-8' tall plants do add an exclamation mark to the garden. The leaves generally run down the side of the stems resulting in winged stems where the leaves attach. They are biennial and produce a handsome silver rosette the first year before extending to their full height the second year. The branched silvery stems are particularly handsome set off against a background of dark shrubbery. The thistle flowers are usually purple but occasionally white flowered forms occur. Landscapers should love this stuff. Plants may seed wildly; be careful, one plant is about all a garden can handle.

Plants differ from Cardoon, *Cynara cardunculus*, by being taller and having winged stems. Leaves are more hairy in cardoon than in Scotch thistle.

Propagate from seed sown in summer, planted out to form a rosette prior to hard frosts.

### Related Species:

*O. acaulon* forms handsome white-pubescent rosettes in the summer and fall and then sends up white flowers on short flower stems in late spring or summer. Since plants are essentially stemless, they are only about 12" tall. Hardy to zone 7.

*O. bracteatum* is only about 4′ tall and bears white pubescent leaves often tipped with yellowish spines. The large 6″ diameter purple flower heads are produced in late spring and summer. A little easier for mid-size gardens although hardy only to about zone 7.

## *Ophiopogon* (o-fee-o-po′ gon)    Mondo Grass    Liliaceae

The 5–10 species of edging and ground cover plants are often confused with *Liriope muscari*, common lily-turf. Both genera are tufted, have basal leaves, and bear bluish purple flowers in summer. However, the leaves of mondo grass are more narrow than those of common lily-turf, the smaller flowers are hidden by the leaves, the fruits are metallic blue compared to the lustrous black fruits of *Liriope*, and the species are less cold hardy. These differences, however, do not make mondo grass any less useful or ornamental.

*Ophiopogon* is an excellent edging plant and ground cover which tolerates full sun but prefers areas of moist soils and partial shade. The most common species is *O. japonicus*, dwarf mondo grass.

| *-japonicus* (ja-pon′ i-kus) | Dwarf Mondo Grass | 8–15″/12″ |
|---|---|---|
| Summer    Lilac | Japan, Korea | Zones 6–9 |

The numerous dark green grass-like leaves are 15″ long and ¼″ wide. Light lilac flowers are held in short terminal racemes, almost hidden by the foliage. The long underground stolons and tuberous roots result in spreading, drought tolerant airy plants useful as edging or ground covers.

The most common method of propagation is by division, although seeds germinate in 6 weeks if the berries are soaked for 24 hours to facilitate removal of the pulp.

### Cultivars:

'Nippon' is even smaller (2–4″ tall) and has whitish flowers in the summer. This is similar and may be the same thing as 'Nana'.

'Gyoko-ryu', introduced by Dr. John Creech, is even shorter and more compact than 'Nippon'.

'Variegatus' has white-margined foliage with negligible blooms. Known as Silver Mist plant.

### Related Species:

*O. jaburan* is coarser than *O. japonicus*, with light purple to white flowers. Plants grow 15–18″ tall but are not as good a ground cover as the previous species. Cold hardy to zone 9.

'Aurea bears yellow-striped leaves which provides additional foliar interest. 'Variegatus' has white-striped leaves and is also more effective than the species. Both look particularly good in groups of 12 or more.

*O. planiscapus* 'Nigrescens', black mondo grass, is an interesting introduction from England. The dark purple leaves appear almost black and plants are about 6″ tall. The flowers are light lilac to pink and followed by black berries in the fall. Growth is slow, but the foliage provides a wonderful contrast to light colored foliage such as the light green species of hosta, or in concert with creeping Jenny (*Lysimachia congestiflora* 'Aurea'). It is listed as being cold hardy as far north as zone 5, but zone 6 is more realistic. Partial shade in the South is recommended, full sun is best in the North. I have seen listed a black form called 'Ebony Knight', but it does not significantly differ from 'Nigrescens'.

**Additional Reading:**

Hume, H. Harold. 1961. The Ophiopogon-Liriope complex. *Baileya* 9: 134–158.
Rackemann, Adelaide. 1987. Lilyturf. *Horticulture* 65:42–43.

## *Origanum* (o-ree-gah′ num)         Oregano         Lamiaceae

About 20 species occur which are better known for the herbs oregano and marjorum than for their ornamental value. Although sweet marjorum, *O. majorana*, is solely used as a culinary herb, oregano has made breakthroughs into the ornamental arena. Common oregano, *O. vulgare*, is used as a bright underplanting while a number of cultivars of this and a closely related species, *O. laevigatum*, are enjoyed as a garden plant and a long lasting cut flower.

The opposite leaves of all species are aromatic and the flowers are whorled like a salvia. The majority of them require alkaline soils and in fact turn over and die in acid soils or in poorly drained soils. They are native to the Mediterranean and therefore do not appreciate high heat when combined with high humidity.

*-vulgare* (vul-gah′ ree)    Oregano, Pot Marjoram, Wild Marjoram   1–3′/2′
Summer        Violet        Europe        Zones 3–7

This rhizomatous plant is seldom used but a number of cultivars selected for leaf color are coming out of the closet. The leaves are 1–2″ long, usually entire but sometimes slightly toothed. Each leaf has many glands which when broken result in the familiar fragrance of this herb. The violet to purple flowers are held in a loose panicle occurring in early to late summer. The bracts which surround the flowers actually provide the ornamental value, although flowers are more useful in the related species than this one.

Place in well-drained soils and provide some afternoon shade for golden forms. Propagate by cuttings or division.

**Cultivars:**

'Album' has bushy, light green leaves with white flowers. Plants are about 15" tall.

'Aureum' is a popular form with golden foliage and purple flowers. Used as a spreading 4–6" tall ground cover.

'Compactum Aureum' is even shorter and more compact than 'Aureum'. Particularly useful for growing between rocks on a pathway or a patio.

'Dark Leaf' has dark bronze foliage with strong fragrance and flavor. The foliage tends to fade in the heat.

'Variegata' bears golden-green variegated foliage.

**Related Species:**

*O. laevigatum* is becoming more and more popular as more nurseries offer this fine species. Unfortunately, it is cold hardy only to about zone 7, maybe zone 6. Flowering occurs in late summer to fall in most areas and is a terrific butterfly plant. Plants are subshrubs, being woody at the base but dying to the ground in the fall. Growing 18–24" tall, they are used as striking garden plants and cut flowers. They do best in gravelly soil and are highly drought tolerant. 'Herrenhausen' has reddish purple foliage, deepening even more in the fall. The flowers are pale lilac to purple, depending on temperature. Plants grow upright but can sprawl. 'Hopley's' is better known as a cut flower than as a garden plant, but will be tried in gardens as more material becomes available. Plants can grow over 2' tall and produce strong pink to mauve flowers with large bracts. A knockout!

## *Ornithogalum* (or-nith-og' al-um)     Ornithogalum     Liliaceae

Over 150 species are found in this bulbous genus and many are useful for border plants or as cut flowers. The most common species, *O. umbellatum*, star-of-Bethlehem, has been grown for centuries and is such a vigorous colonizer that many gardeners consider it a weed. Others such as *O. thyrsoides*, chincherinchee, and *O. arabicum*, Arabian star flower, are better behaved and produced throughout the world for cut flowers, becoming more common in American florist shops and flower markets. With the exception of some South African species (e.g., *O. dubium*), all produce white flowers with green stripes on the petals. Those from South Africa are generally in orange-yellow-red tones and are insufficiently hardy to be considered perennial except in the most frost-free areas of the country. Hybrids are vigorously being produced for commercial cut flower production although gardeners will likely not benefit. In fact, few species perform well except in mild moderate climates on the west coast, although few situations exist that deter *O. umbellatum* from colonizing the world. As a general rule of thumb, they are best treated similar to *Gladiolus*.

In general, plant most species 2–3″ deep and in bold clumps. Allow 10–12″ between larger species, about 6″ between the smaller ones. Plants go dormant soon after flowering.

Quick Reference to Ornithogalum Species

|  | Height (in.) | Flower color | Flower number |
|---|---|---|---|
| *O. arabicum* | 18–24 | White, black center | 6–12 |
| *O. nutans* | 12–15 | Greenish white | 3–12 |
| *O. thyrsoides* | 12–15 | White | 12–30 |
| *O. umbellatum* | 6–9 | White | 10–20 |

| *-arabicum* (a-ra′ bi-kum) | | Arabian Star Flower | 18–24″/18″ |
|---|---|---|---|
| Summer | White | Mediterranean | Zones 8–10 |

Due to lack of winter hardiness in most parts of the country, this species is not as popular as other members of the genus. The 12–18″ long leaves emerge early and generally lie on the ground. In North Georgia, leaves emerge in December and are invariably damaged by frosts. The clusters of fragrant white flowers rise 1–2′ high in early summer and have conspicuous yellow anthers and a jet black ovary. Flowers do not open all at once, but there are always enough to provide a nice show. They tend to close just before nightfall when they appear like "immense pearls clustered in some sumptuous ornament" (Wilder, *Adventures with Hardy Bulbs*). The flower heads are also popular as a cut flower because of their excellent shelf life. If the stems are waxed, the flowers will last for several months.

Plant bulbs about 6″ deep in a well-drained area of the garden in full sun. Lift again in the fall prior to the first hard frost. Store the bulbs in peat moss in a cool, dry place and replant after the last frost date in the spring. In zones 8–10, they can remain in the ground and flowers appear in late spring to early summer, although the flower heads require staking to prevent twisting of the flower stem. They are best suited to west coast gardens of California and the Pacific Northwest.

Propagate by removing offsets when the bulbs are lifted. The offsets usually require 2–3 years before flowering. Bulbs raised from seed will be of plantable size in 18–24 months.

| *-nutans* (new-tanz) | | Drooping Star-of-Bethlehem | 12–15″/12″ |
|---|---|---|---|
| Early Summer | Greenish White | Southern Europe | Zones 5–9 |

This species has naturalized in the Northeast but is not a particularly well-known plant in America. The narrow ⅜″ wide leaves are about 12–18″

long, and often have a white line running lengthwise down their middle. The 2″ wide greenish white flowers are star shaped, somewhat drooping, and have lovely white margins in front and green midribs in the rear. They are loosely borne on a 12–15″ tall stem in late spring and early summer, and shortly after flowering the plant withers away. Where bulbs are comfortable, they can become quite a nuisance. I have known many a good gardener to toss bulbs over their shoulder as they weed their garden. *O. nutans* can tolerate partial shade and is often planted on the edge of woodlots or in partially shaded areas. It also may be naturalized through grass, and because the leaves disappear quickly, the grass may be cut before it gets knee high, a common problem when naturalizing other bulbs such as daffodils in grassy areas.

Propagate similar to *O. arabicum.*

**Cultivars:**

Var. *boucheanum* has larger, whiter flowers than the type but is difficult to locate.

| *-thyrsoides* (thur-soi′ deez) | | Chincherinchee | 12–15″/12″ |
|---|---|---|---|
| Summer | White | South Africa | Zones 8–10 |

Like *O. arabicum*, chincherinchee is known mainly as a cut flower in the florist shop. In most areas of the country it is not cold hardy, however, bulbs are inexpensive and can economically be treated as annuals. Alternatively, bulbs may be lifted, similar to gladiolus and tuberous begonias. Bulbs produce 5–6 broad leaves above which emerge 12–30 pure white, ¾″ long flowers with brown centers on 12″ tall flower stems in early summer. Similar to *O. arabicum*, plants are best adapted to west coast gardens.

The common name, chincherinchee, is an onomatopoeic word used to describe the sound of the south winds as they blew through the stalks and flowers in the hedgerows in Cape Province of South Africa. In the United States, the species is still referred to as star-of-Bethlehem, particularly by users of cut flowers, perhaps because chincherinchee is so difficult to get your tongue around. Star-of-Bethlehem should be reserved for *O. umbellatum.*

The shelf life of the flowers is legendary and they will last for months in water or on the plant. If you can't grow them in the garden, pick some up at the florist and enjoy them at home. Plants are poisonous and should not be included in your salad. In South Africa, incidents of cattle poisoning occurred when plant parts were accidently included in the forage. Even cows are smart enough to avoid them in fields.

Propagate similarly to *O. arabicum.*

**Cultivars:**

Var. *album* has dark-centered pure white flowers that are more densely arranged on the stem.

Var. *aureum* bears golden yellow flowers.

'Mount Blanc' and 'Mount Everest' are white double-flowered forms developed specifically for the cut flower trade.

**Related Species:**

*O. saundersiae* is known as giant chincherinchee because of its imposing size. The clean white flowers have a large green-black eye and are borne at the top of the 3' tall plants. It is used as cut flower but can be used effectively if planted in groups of at least three. Plants must be lifted and stored over winter.

| *-umbellatum* (um-bel-ah' tum) | | Star-of-Bethlehem | 6–9"/6" |
|---|---|---|---|
| Late Spring | White | Mediterranean | Zones 4–9 |

*Ornithogalum umbellatum*
(80%)

This is the best known species due to its ability to survive where most others can not. Although native to the Mediterranean, it has become naturalized in many areas of the northeastern United States and as far south as Mississippi. Plants have been grown and enjoyed for hundreds of years; Linnaeus believed that this plant was the "Dove's dung" mentioned in the Bible (2 Kings 6:25) and eaten by the Samarians during the great famine. Other accounts of the edibility of these bulbs abound through folk literature, however, in *Plants of the Bible*, H. and A. Moldenke showed the bulbs to be poisonous unless cooked. Regardless of culinary properties, this species has been and will continue to be around for quite some time.

Bulbs produce a mound of narrow, smooth leaves, each about 12" in length, followed by a flower stem carrying 10–20, star-shaped white flowers. Each flower is about 1–2" across and striped green on the outside of the 3 outer segments. The flowers are also remarkable for their consistency in opening just before noon and closing again before sunset. It is so punctual that plants are known as the eleven o'clock lady in English, French, and Italian languages. Other common names include six o'clock flower, wake-at-noon and sleepy Dick.

This species is not fastidious as to planting site. Deep shade should be avoided but partial shade to full sun is acceptable. Once established, bulbs are drought tolerant.

Bulbs multiply rapidly by bulbils and should be planted where they may be allowed to roam. They are aggressive thugs at times; in the Armitage garden they have mounted a quiet but sustained attack over the years. If additional plants are required, dig the bulbs after flowering, remove the offsets, and replant them in a suitable location.

### Quick Key to Ornithogalum Species

A. Plant more than 1' tall
  B. Flowers white with black
     center, stamens yellow . . . . . . . . . . . . . . . . *O. arabicum*
  BB. Flowers white or greenish white,
      center not black, stamens not yellow
     C. Blossoms nodding, usually fewer
        than 12 flowers per stem . . . . . . . . . . . . . . *O. nutans*
     CC. Blossoms erect, usually more
         than 12 flowers per stem . . . . . . . . . . . . . *O. thyrsoides*
AA. Plant less than 1' tall . . . . . . . . . . . . . . . . . . *O. umbellatum*

## *Orontium* (o-ron' tee-um)          Golden Club          Araceae

Useful for ponds, pools or swampy area, golden club is a handsome aquatic plant where controlled. The thick rhizomes of *O. aquaticum* give rise to leathery basal leaves which are elevated or float, depending on the depth of water. Plants can be potted up and placed in water no deeper than about one inch. Many yellow flowers are held on each long narrow spadix but the small green spadix drops off before the flowers appear. Flowers occur in spring.

Plants will spread in the margins of ponds and wet areas by self seeding in the wet environment. The seeds are shed from the green berries that form after flowering. This is the only species in the genus and is native from Massachusetts to Kentucky and south to Florida. Plants may be considered hardy to about 0–5° F.

## *Osmunda* (os-mun' da)      Flowering Fern      Osmundaceae

Named for Osmunder, the Saxon god of war, some of the most vigorous garden ferns may be found in the 12 species of the genus. They are probably the largest and coarsest of our native ferns with massive rootstocks which in mature clumps can be seen up to 1' above the soil line, like short tree trunks. The roots themselves are black and wiry and were aggressively harvested for osmunda fibre, widely used as a growing medium for orchids.

They differ from other genera of ferns by having large, globular spore cases (sporangia) with a short, stout stalk. The species within the genus may be distinguished by where the sporangia are found. They are held in separate areas on the leaf stem (interrupted fern), at the top of the rachis, (royal fern), or on separate fertile structures, (cinnamon fern).

Plants are quite happy in moist areas and if properly irrigated should do well in most garden soils. All are temperate ferns and while they are warm hardy to zone 7b, they are more vigorous when grown in cooler areas.

Quick Reference to Osmunda Species

| | Fronds | Fertile sporangia |
|---|---|---|
| *O. cinnamomea* | Pinnate | Separate stems |
| *O. claytonia* | Pinnate | Share rachis with pinna |
| *O. regalis* | Twice-pinnate | Top of rachis |

| | | |
|---|---|---|
| *-cinnamomea* (sin-a mo' mee-a) | Cinnamon Fern | 3–5'/3' |
| | Eastern United States | Zones 3–7 |

One of the classic woodland ferns, the cinnamon fern is a popular, easy to grow showy plant. In early spring, the fertile leaves are first to appear, arising bright green then turning cinnamon-brown as the spores mature. They are stiff and erect and consist of pairs of spore cases which look like stunted leaflets.

767

They decline in late spring to mid summer. After the fertile leaves have formed, the handsome fiddle heads, which are originally covered with silver-white hairs, unfurl from the clumps of above ground roots to form the arching sterile fronds so well known in eastern woodlots. The base of each frond bears scattered tufts of cinnamon colored wooly fibers, thus accounting for its common name. In the fall, the fronds turn a handsome golden color, then bronze before succumbing to frost. In North America, cinnamon fern is native from Labrador to Florida and west to Illinois and Minnesota. Plants are also occur naturally in Central and South America, West Indies and eastern Asia.

One of the more heat tolerant ferns, they do relatively well as far south as zone 7b, assuming sufficient and consistent moisture is available. Otherwise, they are stunted compared with their northern siblings. Shade, moisture and humus-rich soils are essential.

Spores must be sown immediately upon maturity as they do not remain viable for very long once they have been shed.

| | | | |
|---|---|---|---|
| *-claytonia* (klay-ton-ee' a) | Interrupted Fern | 3–4'/3' |
| | Eastern North America | Zones 3–6 |

Another fern which can eat up significant acreage where it is well established. I find this a fern which evokes more comments about its curiosity than about its beauty. The sterile fronds are wider at the middle than at either end and always arch outward. When they arise in the spring, they are often covered with woolly pinkish hairs which soon disappear. The fertile stems grow upward. It is the curious arrangement of leaflets (pinna) and spore cases (sporangia) on the same stem which makes this fern unique. Usually 3–8 fronds occur in which the leaflets are interrupted by 4 or more pairs of dark brown sporangia. Once the spores have been shed, the sporangia fall off leaving the stems bare in the center for the rest of the season. The leaflets below the spore cases are smaller and more widely spaced than leaflets on the rest of the plant. The species was named for John Clayton, also well remembered for the wonderful spring wild flower, *Claytonia*.

Similar to other members of the genus, shade and rich moist soils are needed for best performance. They perform poorly in hot summers and although occasionally enjoyed as far south as zone 7, they are not nearly as striking as further north.

Propagate similar to cinnamon fern.

| | | | |
|---|---|---|---|
| *-regalis* (ray-gah' lis) | Royal Fern | 4–6'/4' |
| | Almost Everywhere | Zones 4–7 |

The closer you get to this plant, the less it looks like a fern and more it looks like a plant in the legume family, like locust, or indigofera or even sweet peas. The leaves are twice-pinnate, meaning that the leaflets (pinna) are divided once again into pinnate leaflets. Where they are happy, they are some of the biggest, most robust plants around, not just in the fern family, but in all herbaceous plants. Of course, in the Armitage garden, they look like the dog uses them for his bed. I was ready to dismiss this fern as another one that I would have to get on a airplane to admire, until I visited my friends, Donna and Ed Lambert, in Athens, GA. Donna's love of ferns has made her woodland garden a mecca for fern lovers everywhere. She has transported incalculable loads of leaf litter to enrich her soils (something I have been lazy to do, thus the difference in our gardens) and her ferns, including the royals, have responded in glorious fashion. However, unless you have Donna, they prefer to be planted in areas with less heat and humidity.

The smooth fiddle heads arise in early spring from the massive wiry root tussocks of the established clump. The roots of this species were the main source of osmunda fiber mentioned previously, although the other species are also used. The foliage is a translucent green, which if the light behind it is just right, appear to be almost fluorescent. The light brown sporangia are formed on the top of the sterile leaves, thus accounting for its other common name, flowering fern.

Plants can handle more direct sun than the other members of the genus and can tolerate full sun in the north if immersed in moisture throughout the season. Its natural habitat is in wetlands, along streams, bogs and low spots in pastures and meadows. It will tolerate water up to its "knees," but is equally happy at the edge of streams or in boggy settings.

Propagate similar to cinnamon fern.

### Quick Key to Osmunda Species

  A. Sporangia borne on separate stems
    than the fertile fronds . . . . . . . . . . . . . . . . *O. cinnamomea*
  AA. Sporangia and leaflets share same stems
    B. Sporangis at top of the frond . . . . . . . . . . . . . *O. regalis*
    BB. Sporangia formed in the middle
    of the frond . . . . . . . . . . . . . . . . . . . . . . . . *O. claytonia*

## *Oxalis* (oks-ah' lis)    Wood Sorrel    Oxalidaceae

To talk about the beauty of wood sorrel to many gardeners elicits chuckles or outright rebuke, depending on the manners of the listener. However, with well over 800 species, it makes little sense to dismiss the whole genus because of a few bad experiences with a weed or two. Most are low growers and many arise from tubers and are usually found in the bulbous section of the catalog. They are cosmopolitan, but centers of diversity exist in North America, South America and South Africa. Most species have three palmate leaflets, which usually fold down at night. The flowers occur as singles or in small inflorescences and often close in the evening. Flower color ranges from yellow, to white and pink. They often produce copious amounts of seed which are ejected forcibly when the seed is ripe causing the weedy species to appear everywhere, although the seed of the sought after ones never seem to germinate. There are some really obnoxious members, in particular the yellow flowered greenhouse/house-plant weed, *O. repens,* which puts roots down to China and chuckles over attempts to remove it. I'm not sure *O. corniculata* is a great deal better. Although numerous species have been recently introduced to American garden-ers, only 3 or 4 enjoy much popularity and none are seen on a regular basis.

The term *Oxalis* comes from the Greek word for sharp, referring to the sharp taste of the leaves which results from the presence of oxalic acid. Too many leaves of *Oxalis* can cause severe discomfort, even death; however, the leaves of one of the European species, *O. acetosella* has long been harvested for soups and salads.

Some of the more weedy species arise from long fibrous roots, while the more ornamental forms tend to come from small tubers. Propagate the former from seed, the latter from division of the clump.

<u>Quick Reference to Oxalis Species</u>

|  | Number of leaflets | Flower color | Number of flowers |
|---|---|---|---|
| *O. adenophylla* | 9–22 | Pink | 1 |
| *O. deppei* | 4 | Red to pink | 5–12 |
| *O. regnellii* | 3 | Pale pink to white | 2–4 |
| *O. violacea* | 3 | Pink to white | 2–8 |

| *-adenophylla* (a-den-o-fil′ la) | | Sauer Klee | 2–4″/6″ |
|---|---|---|---|
| Late Spring | Pink | Chile, Argentina | Zones 6–8 |

In my opinion, this is the most beautiful member of the genus. The plants are grown from a brown ragged looking tuber covered with a mass of fibers. One of the best characteristics of the plants are the smooth silver-gray leaves consisting of around 12, but up to 22 leaflets. If conditions are to their liking, the plants form compact mounds, slowly spreading over time. The leaves are handsome enough but the flowers add yet another dimension. The are generally formed singly but may be as many as three in one inflorescence. They are about 1″ across with a white center in the pale pink to lilac-pink petals.

One of my friends, Linda Copeland, who is a fine gardener in Atlanta, did an experiment to force flowers on potted tubers in the greenhouse. She found that if tubers were potted and placed in a cold (40° F) area for about 10 weeks, they would flower after another 4–5 weeks. They made knockout plants which were either given as gifts or planted in the spring garden.

Tubers are highly susceptible to wet feet and are best planted in a rock garden or where drainage is excellent.

They naturally occur in full sun above the tree line in the Andes Mountains so cold weather should not deter them, however, wet feet is sure death, particularly in the winter. I have had little success in perennializing them in the Athens area but my heavy clay soils are more suitable for pottery than for this oxalis.

This species is well worth trying, even if a few bite the dust.

**Related Species:**

*O. enneaphylla*, scurvy grass, is a smaller version of *O. adenophylla*. The leaves consist of 9–20 blue-green leaflets, and large white flowers with lavender veins occur in late spring and summer.

Cold hardy to zone 8, zone 7 with protection.

| *-regnellii* (reg-nel-lee′ eye) | Purple Oxalis | 4–8″/12″ |
|---|---|---|
| Summer        Pink | South America | Zones 6–8 |

One of the most popular and tougher species in the genus. The leaves consist of 3 triangular leaflets, purple to purple-green on the top side and deep purple beneath. As the plants mature the tubers multiply and significant clumps form. The pink, sometimes white, flowers are about 1″ across and contrast well with the foliage. The centers of the leaves often have triangular markings and are occasionally sold as *O. triangularis*.

Normally a good deal of shade is recommended, but I was very surprised when we had to put some mature plants in full sun in the Horticulture Gardens at The University of Georgia. Within 3 days, the plants looked like they had been burnt up and totally disappeared. However, within 2 weeks, the leaves re-emerged and plants thrived in that hot, sunny environment. Place in the front of the garden in decently drained soils.

Tubers are cheap, give them a go.

**Related Species:**

*O. deppei* (*O. tetraphylla*) usually has 4 leaflets and is known as the lucky clover, good luck clover or good luck plant. This is the clover we all want to look over. Plants arise from true bulbs and give rise to green leaves often with a V-shaped purple band. The red to lilac-pink flowers have yellow throats are produced in 5–10 flowered umbels in late spring and summer. 'Iron Cross' has deep purple V-shaped banding which form a "iron cross."

| *-violacea* (vie-o-lac-ee′ a) | Violet Wood Sorrel | 6–8″/12″ |
|---|---|---|
| Spring, Summer    Pink, White | North America | Zones 6–8 |

Native from Florida to Massachusetts and west to Minnesota and Colorado, this little gem can provide all sorts of color in partially shaded areas. The 3 leaflets are purple-bronze underneath and green above. Many

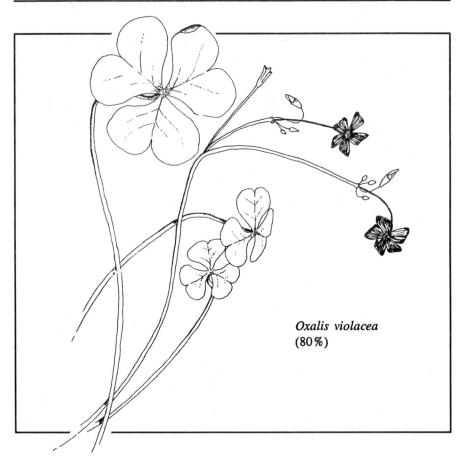

Oxalis violacea
(80%)

pink to white flowers per flowering stem occur which can smother the plants from late spring all the way through summer.

No doubt, this sorrel can look weedy, particularly when they get overgrown or flag in hot, dry weather. They may be easily cut back and always pick up when watered or when cooler weather prevails. Allow them to naturalize and they will soon become established in areas where they will be maintenance free. Plants tolerate heavy shade, but fewer flowers are formed, but they perform well in full sun if watered well.

Quick Key to Oxalis Species
    A. Leaflets greater than 10 . . . . . . . . . . . . . . . . *O. adenophylla*
   AA. Leaflets less than 10
      B. Leaflets usually 4 (occasionally 3), flowers red . . . *O. deppei*
     BB. Leaflets usually 3
        C. Leaflets tinged purple (at least underneath) . . . *O. regnellii*
       CC. Leaflets green throughout . . . . . . . . . . . . . *O. violacea*

772

# P

*Pachysandra* (pa-kis-an' dra)          Spurge          Buxaceae

Although only about 5 species occur, the genus includes one of the most cultivated species in the landscape today, Japanese spurge, *P. terminalis*. The spurges' main function in life is as a ground cover, particularly under trees where they compete well for the limited sun, nutrients and water associated with wooded areas.

Plants multiply by rhizomes and have alternate leaves, usually grouped in whorls at the end of the stems. While the plants are grown mainly for the foliage, the flowers provide interest as well. They are unisexual and may be white or pinkish, and the long stamens of the male flowers give rise to the generic name. Pachysandra comes from *pachys*, thick, and *andros*, man, in reference to the thick stamens. Fruit is formed on female plants, however most forms in cultivation are male.

The spurges are easily propagated by division, or by rooting softwood terminal cuttings in the summer.

Quick Reference to Pachysandra Species

|  | Height (in.) | Leaf length (in.) | Inflorescence length (in.) |
|---|---|---|---|
| *P. procumbens* | 9–12 | 3–5 | 4–5 |
| *P. terminalis* | 9–12 | 1–3 | 1–2 |

-*procumbens* (pro-kum' benz)   Allegheny Spurge          9–12"/12"
   Spring      Pinkish White   Southeastern United States   Zones 5–9

Although native from West Virginia, south to Florida and west to Louisiana it is seen far too seldom in Southern gardens and almost never in the North.

Plants are evergreen in the South, although in the Armitage garden (zone 7b), the leaves can look terrible by March and I remove the worst of them. New leaves emerge from the ground on long petioles and may be up to 4″ long. The leaves are mottled purple and coarsely toothed towards the apex, but entire near the tapered base. Flowers are white but have a pink tinge, particularly if the weather is cool. The flowers are borne at ground level in the axils of the leaves and not terminal as in *P. terminalis*. Leaf litter or other mulch around the plants may have to be removed to find the flowers. It is not nearly as vigorous a ground cover as Japanese spurge but individual clumps are far more handsome. This is a much overlooked plant and a good substitute for *P. terminalis* where only a small planting is needed.

I was walking around Mt. Cuba estate in Delaware with the curator, Richard Lighty, who has forgotten about 10 times more about native

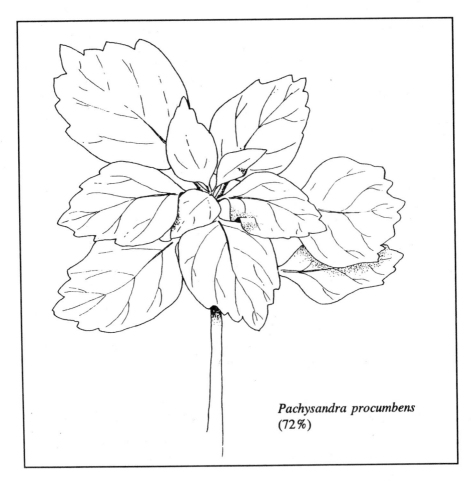

*Pachysandra procumbens*
(72%)

Piedmont plants than I ever knew. He pointed out that there may be at least two strains of the species. He showed me a miniature form found in Holden Arboretum and a larger form, sometimes referred to as 'Penn State Strain'. Hopefully, someone will work with this species and provide more vigor so more people can take advantage of it.

**Related Species:**

*P. axillaris* is a Chinese species similar to *P. procumbens*. Plants are more woody and a little taller and the white flowers are borne in the axils of the leaves. The foliage is slow but not mottled like our American native. Probably similar in hardiness.

| | | | |
|---|---|---|---|
| *-terminalis* (ter-mi-nah' lis) | | Japanese Spurge | 9–12″/18″ |
| Late Spring | White | Japan | Zones 4–9 |

This is certainly one of the most functional plants used in today's landscapes. It is interesting that this visitor from Japan has found conditions

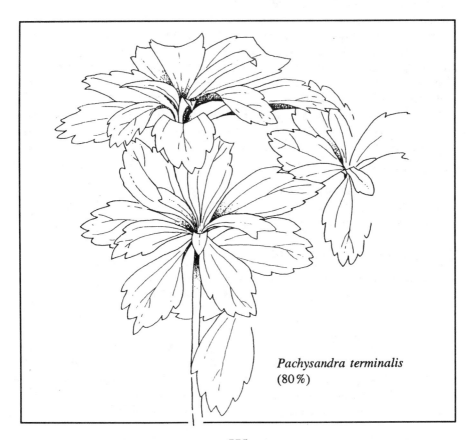

*Pachysandra terminalis*
(80%)

in America more to its liking than its American cousin, Allegheny spurge. Because of the rhizomatous nature, plants colonize an area aggressively, thus making a useful and rapid growing ground cover. The dark evergreen leaves are alternate but are grouped in whorls at the top of the stems. They are toothed towards the apex, 1–3″ long and about half as wide. The creamy white flowers are borne at the top of the stems (*terminalis* is derived from the position of the flowers).

A number of diseases such as Rhizoctonia root rot, Fusarium leaf blight, and leaf blight canker are becoming more prevalent. Euonymus scale also results in significant damage to overgrown clumps. Thinning and grooming the plantings as well as application of fungicides should be practiced regularly. While it may be overused, a carpet of shining Japanese spurge under mature trees is a beautiful sight. The plantings under the copper beaches at Longwood Gardens are particularly remarkable.

## Cultivars:

'Green Carpet' provides a 6–8″ tall carpet. It has darker green leaves and is more compact than the species.

'Green Sheen' has polished green leaves that are almost like a mirror. An introduction from the late Dr. J.C. Raulston of the North Carolina Botanical Garden, Raleigh, NC.

'Silveredge' has thin silver-white margins and is similar to 'Variegata'.

'Variegata' bears irregularly white variegated leaves. Plants are not as vigorous as the species but the leaves are more interesting.

'Variegata' and 'Silveredge' should be located in partial shade because leaves scorch in full sun. Although minor differences may be seen, the two cultivars are essentially the same.

## Related Species:

*P. stylosa* is seldom seen and even less available. This Japanese native bears light green foliage and spreads slowly. The whitish pink flowers are produced in late winter to early spring.

Quick Key to Pachysandra Species

    A. Leaves 1–3″ long, shiny, flowers terminal  . . . . .  *P. terminalis*
    AA. Leaves 3–5″ long, dull, flowers borne at base  . .  *P. procumbens*

## *Paeonia* (pay-on′ ee-a)              Peony              Ranunculaceae

The peony's great popularity rests upon hardiness, ease of culture, and freedom of bloom in many areas of North America. Add to that the tremendous number of flower colors, forms and plant habits and it is not surprising that the peony has attracted the interest of amateur and professional breeders, botanists, taxonomists and horticulturists, all of whom have become enamored by the genus. The common garden peonies are classified into herbaceous species, most of which have arisen from the Chinese peony, *P. lactiflora*, and the common peony, *P. officinalis*, and woody species, mainly selections of *P. suffruticosa*. The herbaceous species have received the most attention and are far more important garden plants than the tree forms. This is not surprising considering the array of flower shapes and colors, to say nothing of the handsome red follicles formed after the flowers have disappeared.

The classification of the herbaceous species has been tackled by a number of wise and learned men, one of the most recent being F.J. Stern, who in 1946 divided the genus into 3 sections, 4 subsections, 16 groups, 33 species, and 12 botanical varieties. All but five of the species and varieties have synonyms, twenty-six have from 1 to 10 synonyms each, seven have from 10 to 20, and one has 34. This not only shows the magnitude of the work of the botanists of the past but also that much confusion exists as to what constitutes a species, subspecies, etc. A more useful horticultural classification based on flowering time divides the genus into three divisions, early-, mid- and late-flowering species and is a useful guide for those wishing to select garden species. The following list of species and their flowering times is based on John C. Wister's book, *The Peonies*, 1962.

**Division I.** Mostly early May blooming (late March to April in the South)
Very early blooming: *P. wittmanniana, P. w.* var. *macrophylla, P. mlokosewitschii, P. daurica, P. tenuifolia*
Later flowering: *P. anomala, P. veitchii*
Latest: *P. coriacea, P. arienina, P. bakeri, P. obovata*

**Division II.** Mid-May Blooming
*P. officinalis, P. humilis, P. mollis, P. peregrina*

**Division III.** Late-May Blooming
*P. lactiflora*

Unfortunately, most of the true species are very difficult to find in commerce, and when you find an enterprising nursery who is propagating them, give them a try. The emerging buds and new leaves of some of the species are incredibly handsome. That they are not easily found is a testament to their relative difficulty compared with the ease of common peonies. With the exception of *P. veitchii, P. tenuifolia, P. mlokosewitschii* (mlo-ko-sa-vich' ee-eye), *P. maifleuri, P. emodi* and the double forms of *P. officinalis*, most are not terribly good garden plants anyway. The truly good herbaceous peonies are selections of only 2 or 3 species and the gardener need not be confused with classification to enjoy their beauty.

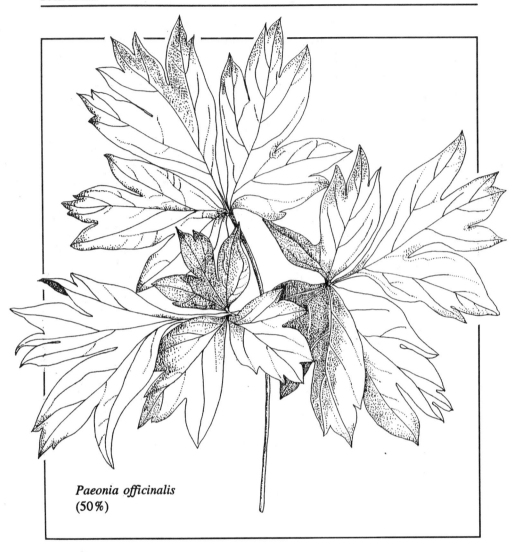

*Paeonia officinalis*
(50%)

The American Peony Society divides the flowers of herbaceous peonies into four different forms:

*Single:* Five or more petals are arranged around a center made up of stamens with pollen-bearing anthers.

*Japanese:* This is really a double form but is characterized by 5 or more petals around a center made up of stamens with non-pollen bearing anthers (stamenoides). The absence of pollen distinguishes this form from the single flower form. The term "anemone flowered" is used when the stamens in the center have been transformed into narrow petal-like structures called petaloids.

778

*Semi-double:* Five or more outer petals are arranged around the center consisting of broad petals and stamens with pollen-bearing anthers. There may be a distinct center of stamens or they may be in rings intermixed among the petals, however, the stamens are always clearly visible and prominent.

*Double:* There are 5 or more outer petals but the stamens have been completely transformed into petals, making up the bulk of the flower. Often there is no trace of the stamens although in some cultivars they may be present or partially petaloids. In double types, however, stamens are not a prominent part of the flower.

**Flowering Times:**

Peony cultivars are classified not only by flower type but also by relative flowering time. Early-flowering cultivars may flower as early as late March in the South or mid-April further north while the late-flowering types may be in bloom 4–6 weeks later. Those which flower in the middle are referred to as mid-season cultivars.

**Peonies in the South:**

Peonies love cold weather; the colder the winter, the better they grow. They go dormant in the fall and require a certain number of chilling hours (hours below 40° F) to break dormancy, grow and flower the next year. Therefore, it is unreasonable to expect peonies to do well in Sarasota, Florida or McAllen, Texas. However, many cultivars do well as far south as zone 7b. Many people leave the chilly climates of the Midwest or Northeast to live in the South and are convinced that peonies cannot be grown in the Atlanta area. While not all peony cultivars do as well in the South as the North, there is no excuse for transplanted northerners to pine over the absence of their beloved plants. A fair number of cultivars (although only a small fraction of the total available) have been tested at the University of Georgia gardens and a few general statements may be made concerning selection of peony cultivars for southern areas.

1. Select early to mid-season cultivars. The later the flowering time, the warmer the weather and the weaker the stem strength. There is also more chance for disease as the weather becomes warm and humid. Also, with warmer weather, doubles may not fully open.

2. Select single or Japanese flower forms. In general, semi-double or doubles should be used cautiously, particularly if they flower late. The more petals on the flower, the more rain will be trapped in the flower and disease, especially botrytis, will disfigure the blooms. This still leaves a vast selection of lovely cultivars from which to choose. For those who wish to have semi-doubles or doubles in the southern garden, select only early flowering cultivars.

Many books specifically dealing with peonies are available (see end of peony section) which go into great detail concerning their cultural requirements. In general, they prefer full sun, well-drained soil and abundant water, particularly when they are vigorously growing in the spring. Plants may be fertilized with a low nitrogen fertilizer such as 8-8-8 but overfertilization can result in reduced flowering. Attention should be paid to planting depth when putting the crowns in the ground. The buds (eyes) on the rootstock should be approximately 2″ below the soil; if they are planted too deep, poor flowering will result. Work in Israel by Dr. Abe Halevy suggests that deep planting inhibits flowering due to the absence of light on the crowns. As the soil layer increases, no light reaches the developing flowering buds and flower initiation does not take place. The relationship of crown depth to flowering is fascinating and additional research is certainly needed.

**Failure to Flower:**

The American Peony Society has listed many reasons and possible solutions why peonies fail to flower well. They include:

A. *No buds appear:*

1. Plants too young and immature.    Allow them to mature.

2. Planted too deep or too shallow.    Examine and if eyes are more than 3″ below ground, lift and replant.

3. Clumps too large and too old.    Divide the clump if it stops flowering (after 3–10 years) leaving 3 eyes per division.

4. Too much nitrogen.    Cut down on frequency or concentration of fertilizer.

5. Moved and divided too often.    If the clump is flowering well, it should not be moved. Clumps can remain in place well over 10 years.

6. Too much shade.    Move to sunny location.

B. *Buds appear but flowers do not develop:*

1. Buds killed by late frost.    Better luck next year.

2. Buds killed by disease. They usually turn black and die.    Plant earlier cultivars. Spray fungicide as directed for botrytis.

3. Buds attacked by thrips. They open partially, turn brown and fall.    Spray as directed.

4. Buds waterlogged due to excessive rain.    Plant singles or Japanese forms. Bagging buds will help.

5. Plants undernourished.    Fertilize with 8-8-8 and bonemeal.

6. Excessively hot weather.    Plant early flowering cultivars.

Hybridization and selection of peonies has continued unabated and it is impossible to recommend cultivars. There are still many hybrids available today from the work of Professor A.P. Saunders, who created more hybrid races and varieties than all other breeders, past and present, combined. He was responsible for the breakthroughs that allowed coral to be introduced. His selections 'Coral Charm' and 'Coral Sunset' are part of many of today's fine cultivars. Growing some of his hybrids is like owning a piece of peony history. Cultivars and hybrids of many other fine breeders such as Auten, Nicholls, Kreckler, Klehm, Franklin, Lemoine, Sass, and Crosse are also available. Every year new hybrids and selections appear and it is more difficult to keep up with them all. Numerous catalogs glowingly describe hybrids and cultivars and usually provide more than adequate information. The American Peony Society also publishes a list of best cultivars.

### Tree Peonies:

Tree peonies are not trees at all, but have woody stems which do not die down to the ground in the winter. In the U.S., they are more accurately called shrub peonies as they seldom attain a height of more than 4', although I have dropped my jaw on seeing the 7-8' forms in Wales and Scotland. The most common tree peonies were derived over 1400 years ago from garden forms of the Chinese moutan peony, *P. suffruticosa*. The herbaceous peonies were valued by the Chinese for the medicinal value of their roots while the "improved" or moutan peony was treasured for its ornamental value. By the year 750, lists of over thirty named varieties, including some yellow-flowered types, had been registered in China, although it was not until the late 1700's that plants found their way to Europe. Until 1846, although hundreds of so-called distinct varieties were imported, they were the same 5 or 6 varieties brought back by the original European explorers. At that time, Robert Fortune, a plant explorer for the Royal Horticultural Society, returned to England with 25 of the finest selections from China, from which today's garden forms have arisen. The yellow tree peony, *P. lutea*, and the maroon tree peony, *P. delavayi*, were not discovered until 1883 and 1884, respectively, and have since been used to create additional hybrids. In America, the first tree peonies were imported from England in the early 1800's and numerous references to the "almost unknown" plant which are "... adorned by gorgeous blossoms" continued to appear in the American gardening magazines as late as 1928.

The culture and care of tree peonies are shrouded in mystery but once established, they are as long lasting as many of the herbaceous types. John C. Wister in *Peonies, The Manual of the American Peony Society*, provides a list of cultural notes. I have interspersed a few of my own comments.

1. Tree peonies are native to mountainous areas and are used to cold and snow in the winter, and heat in the summer. In the Pacific

Northwest, adequate summer heat is often lacking and a sufficiently long enough cold period is not available in the extreme southern states, while some protection may be needed in the Northeast. The southern limit of tree peonies has not been defined and in Atlanta, Georgia, gardeners have had some success while others cannot produce plants with more than one flower per year.

2.  A slightly basic soil is preferable; good drainage is essential.

3.  Plant in the fall. Plant grafted plants 6–12" below the graft union to encourage formation of roots on scion wood.

4.  Plant in partial shade. This is particularly true south of zone 6.

5.  Winter protection by covering or wrapping with straw or other material is desirable north of New York City.

6.  Pruning should be accomplished occasionally if needed. There is seldom a good reason to cut plants back hard, however, this can be done if necessary. Cutting back to 8–12" high may be beneficial at times to encourage the formation of new shoots. All pruning, trimming and cutting should be accomplished in early fall.

7.  Remove all suckers originating from the rootstock. Production of suckers is greatest the first 2 years after planting.

Commercial propagation of tree peonies has been accomplished for over 900 years by grafting the desired cultivar on an herbaceous peony root stock, and is still practiced today. Research has been conducted on grafting to stocks of *P. suffruticosa* but suckering is too heavy. In all grafted plants, regardless of rootstock, the plants should be set deep enough to encourage the scion to form its own roots. Cuttings of *P. suffruticosa*, if taken in September, root at about a 40% rate, which may be practical for the amateur but not the commercial propagator. Little success has been reported with softwood cuttings taken in April. They may also be propagated by layering, that is, pegging some of the branches in March to root into the ground. At least 2 years is needed for sufficient root production.

Many fine cultivars of tree peonies are available and a list of the best is difficult to put together. If I had to have but one cultivar, I would select 'Joesph Rock', one of the finest forms to be introduced. Not only that, but it commemorates one of the great American plant explorers, who was commissioned by David Fairchild of the U.S. Department of Agriculture to explore areas of India, Burma and Indo-China in the 1920's and then by Charles Sprague Sargent of the Arnold Arboretum in 1922 to investigate the Yunnan area of China. He remained in China for 27 years, collecting over 80,000 plant specimens. Not only is 'Joseph Rock' beautiful, but adds to the excitement few people associate with gardening.

Many hybrids with *P. suffruticosa* and *P. lutea* are also being introduced. Terrific plantings may be seen around the country, and should be visited to be appreciated. Consult the American Peony Society, a specialist peony producer, or your favorite nurseryman.

**Additional Reading:**

*Books:*

Boyd, James (ed.). 1928. *Peonies—The Manual of the American Peony Society.* American Peony Society.

Harding, A. 1917. *The peony.* Reissued 1993, Sagapress Timber Press, Portland, OR.

Wister, John C. (ed.). 1962. *The peonies.* American Horticultural Society.

These fine reference books cover the two main classes and provide outstanding lists of peonies with proven garden performance, along with some enjoyable reading.

*Manuscripts:*

Davis, Rosalie. 1986. Dividing peonies. *Horticulture* 64(11):58–59.

Haw, Stephen. 1986. A problem with peonies. *The Garden* 111(7):326–328.

*Associations:*

American Peony Society, 250 Interlachen Road, Hopkins, MN 55343.
    Publication: *American Peony Society Bulletin.*

## *Panax* (pan' ax)                    Ginseng                    Araliaceae

There are only two reasons to grow *Panax.* One is that you have discovered how much money this crummy little plant is worth and you have decided to be a ginseng entrepreneur. Good luck! The other is that you discovered, once you went broke trying to sell ginseng, that this tough plant tolerates, even prefers, deep shade.

The only garden species available is *P. quinquefolius,* American ginseng, a poor substitute for the real thing, *P. ginseng,* from Korea and northeast China. The leaves are formed in a single whorl of 3 leaves, each leaf divided into 3–7 leaflets. The greenish white flowers are formed in a small umbel in late spring or summer which give way to bright red fruit. They are good plants for heavy shade and rich, moisture retentive soils. Plants can be said to be moderately ornamental at best but most certainly are excellent objects of conversation.

Propagate by division.

## *Panicum* (pah' ni-cum)                    Switch Grass                    Poaceae

Although long ignored as an ornamental grass, switch grass has always been a constant in the American landscape, an early colonizer that was part of the immense tallgrass prairie which was such a familiar feature of the interior United States. The movement to ornamental grasses has stimulated interest in *Panicum* as well as other native species and numerous selections of *P. virgatum* have been developed.

The ½–¾″ wide, flat-bladed upright leaves are green to gray-green in the species and form relatively tight clumps when in full sun. The panicles of airy flowers emerge in the early fall and are useful as cut flowers both for fresh and dried arrangements. Plants persist through the winter and some selections provide stunning fall color, turning a muted beige during the winter.

They are best planted in clumps of at least three, thereby allowing them to present their foliage and flowers en masse. On the campus of the University of Georgia, they are used in large numbers to provide low maintenance islands of color and form. They are easy to grow, needing nothing more than sun and a little water.

Propagate by division after 3–4 years. Seedlings can be a nuisance and if the area is well suited to switch grass, they become a nightmare. Cultivars are only propagated by division and should be selected whenever possible.

### Cultivars:

'Haense Herms' is similar to the species but is a little more compact and has a red-orange tint in the fall. The whitish flowers and red foliage in the fall is a marvelous combination.

'Heavy Metal', from Kurt Bluemel of Baldwin, MD, has metallic blue leaves on upright compact plants. The foliage turns an amber yellow in the fall, turning to beige in the winter. Outstanding!

'Rehbraun' was a favorite of mine before the advent of better, newer selections. The plants are about 3–4′ tall and are a lovely reddish brown color in the fall.

'Rotstrahlbusch' is about 3′ tall without flowers, up to 4′ when the airy amber flowers emerge in summer. The foliage turns a handsome red in the fall.

'Squaw' is 3–4′ tall with good red fall color.

'Strictum' is one of the older cultivars, producing narrow upright clumps of bluish green foliage. Its main attribute is its usefulness in smaller gardens.

'Warrior' is particular vigorous and striking, growing 4–5′ tall with excellent red fall color.

### Additional Reading:

Cramer, H.L. 1994. Graceful grasses for small places. *Fine Gardening* 40: 64–69.

## *Papaver* (pa-pah′ ver)          Poppy          Papaveraceae

The poppies are usually represented in American gardens by the Oriental poppy, *P. orientale*. However, about 40 species of poppies are known and

I would be hard pressed to find an ugly one among them, except when they are dying in my garden. There are some terrific plants in this genus, unfortunately, few are commonly available. One of the most northerly species in the plant kingdom, *P. radicatum*, is found on the north coast of Greenland.

The most famous species is the annual red poppy, *P. rhoeas*, immortalized by the Canadian poet, John McCrae, in the hauntingly beautiful poem "In Flanders Field." I bore my students to death with the story of the red poppy partly because it is an interesting part of horticultural sociology and also because I feel very close to the two main figures in the story. John McCrae lived in the small college town of Guelph, Ontario where I went to school and his small house on Water Street is marked with a small inscription. The person who made the red poppy famous, however, was the "poppy lady," Moina Michael, an unassuming teacher who lived in the countryside around Athens, GA. She was so inspired by John McCrae's poem that with nothing but determination and spirit, she single-handedly made the poppy into the Veterans Day flower. They have been sold to raise money in the United States, England and Canada on every Veterans Day since 1925. This is also the same species which was selected and reselected by the Reverend W. Wilks of Shirley, England and is popularly known as the Shirley poppy. Other annuals or biennials include mission poppy, *P. californicum*, tulip poppy, *P. glaucum*, *P. commutatum*, the stunning but infamous opium poppy, *P. somniferum*, and the subtly beautiful biennial, *P. triniifolium*. For garden purposes, few poppies are long-lived and Oriental poppy and *P. bracteatum*, great scarlet poppy, are the only true perennials available through most nurseries. Iceland poppy and alpine poppy may persist for 2–3 years. Many self sow prolifically and new plants can be counted on year after year.

Poppies are characterized by nodding flower buds, solitary flowers on long flower stalks, milky juice, and leaves that are lobed or dissected. The seed capsule is hard, oval, and decorative.

Quick Reference to Papaver Species

|  | Height (in.) | Flower diameter (in.) | Plants go dormant |
|---|---|---|---|
| *P. alpinum* | 8–10 | 1–2 | No |
| *P. nudicaule* | 12–18 | 3–6 | No |
| *P. orientale* | 18–36 | 5–7 | Yes |
| *P. somniferum* | 24–36 | 3–4 | No |

| *-alpinum* (al-pine' um) | | Alpine Poppy | 8–10"/8" |
|---|---|---|---|
| Summer | Multicolored | European Alps | Zones 4–6 |

A dwarf species, it is most suited for the rock garden or front of the border. Plants are not heat tolerant and seldom survive the summer south of zone 6. Regardless of geographic location, well-drained soil is absolutely essential. Plants are tufted (i.e., all leaves emerging from same place) with 2-6" long gray-green leaves. The 1" wide silky flowers are held on bristly-hairy 4-10" long flower stalks. Although not particularly long lived, plants self sow prolifically.

Seed sown in January will be ready for planting in March. Plants flower the first year from seed.

**Cultivars:**

Var. *burseri* bears white flowers. Some authorities believe *P. burseri* is the correct name for plants grown as *P. alpinum.*

**Related Species:**

*P. kerneri* has ½" wide yellow flowers and is closely related to *P. alpinum.*

*P. pyrenaicum,* Pyrenees poppy, has green rather than gray-green leaves. The plants are 4-6" tall and the 1" wide flowers are yellow to orange.

| *-nudicaule* (new di-kaw' lee) | | Iceland Poppy | 12-18"/12" |
|---|---|---|---|
| Spring | Multicolored | Subarctic Regions | Zones 2-7 |

This northern species is becoming more and more popular in, of all places, the South. Although not perennial, fall plantings produce spectacular drifts of vibrant flowers in the spring. Plants are becoming more visible in public and private gardens every year. Although unable to survive the hot summer in the South, Iceland poppies are perennial in the North, living a couple of years and flowering from early spring to early summer. Plants are rosetted, stemless, and produce 4-6" long, gray-green pinnately lobed leaves. The silky flowers are up to 6" wide and are borne on 12" high leafless flower stems. Most are seed propagated and mixtures are the norm. The selections from the species also make a wonderful potted plant for indoor use and more plants will be seen in florists displays and mass market outlets. It is also the only species suitable for cut flowers.

Seed propagated plants flower the first year. Seeds collected from $F_1$ hybrids, however, result in plants dissimilar from the parent plant. In areas where they are perennial, division may be accomplished after a few years, but the need for division is highly unlikely.

**Cultivars:**

A number of cultivated forms offer specific colors and heights. It seems each new cultivar claims larger and more vibrant flowers than the previous. The majority are propagated from seed and some variation inevitably results.

'Champagne Bubbles' is an $F_1$ hybrid with 3" diameter flowers in mixed colors.
'Coonara Pink' has 2" wide flowers in pastel pink shades.
'Kelmscott Strain' is 12-18" tall and consists of mostly pastel colors.

'Monarch Mix' bears flowers up to 2" wide in many bright colors.

'Popsicle' has 3–4" wide flowers in an assortment of colors.

'Summer Promise' contains both solid and bicolor 2–3" diameter flowers on 2' tall stems.

'Wonderland Mix' is more compact than the type and bears 2–3" diameter flowers. Bright orange 3" wide flowers are available as 'Wonderland Orange'. This is the best selection for windy areas and has proven resilient even in the wind swept beds of Auckland Botanical Gardens.

### Related Species:

*P. atlanticum* has gray-green foliage and peach to pale pink flowers on 12–18" tall plants in late spring or early summer. Quite handsome.

*P. pilosum* is reputed to grow up to 3' tall, but I have not seen it much taller than about 18". Flowers are orange-yellow with whitish spots at the base of the petals. Likely hardy to about zone 6.

| *-orientale* (o-ree-en-tah' lee) | | Oriental Poppy | 18–36"/24" |
|---|---|---|---|
| Early Summer | Scarlet | Southwest Asia | Zones 2–7 |

This is certainly the most conspicuous and popular poppy in North America. There are few sights more arresting than the vibrant orange-red flowers of 2 or 3 plants massed in the garden. The leaves are pinnately lobed and sharply toothed although they appear sharper and more bristly than they feel. The flowers of the species are 3½–4" across and scarlet with a black blotch on the base of each petal forming a black eye. The plants, however, have the unfortunate habit of disappearing by mid to late summer. Plants such as *Mertensia virginica*, Virginia bluebells, which also do this can easily be replaced by a few annuals, but with large plants such as Oriental poppies, more planning is necessary. Large filler plants such as *Gypsophila*, *Perovskia*, and *Boltonia* will cover much of the space vacated by the poppies and flower later.

In the South (south of zone 7a), Oriental poppies perform poorly and are seldom used. The only success I have had is with seed grown plants planted in the fall. Dormant plants ordered from catalogs invariably break dormancy within 2–3 weeks of fall planting and are killed or badly damaged by winter weather. Some mail order firms will ship in the spring and if the plants can be obtained early enough, they do much better in zones 7 and 8 than those fall shipped. Nevertheless, Oriental poppies are cold climate plants and nothing can be done to change that fact.

Oriental poppies are propagated by root cuttings and division. Root cuttings are taken in the spring by dividing the roots into 3–4" lengths, inserting upright in sandy soil, and barely covering. If the root sections are harvested early in the spring or immediately after flowering, the plant may be replaced without damage. Division may be necessary every 3–5 years and should be done after flowering when dormant. This allows root recovery and growth in the fall so plants may flower the next year. Dividing in spring results in poor flowering that year.

### Cultivars:

Many cultivars are available, some are hybrids with other species, particularly *P. bracteatum*, great scarlet poppy, a species similar to *P. orientale*. New cultivars are being bred, mainly in Germany, and seem to double every 3 years.

*Bi-colored:*

'Carousel' has lovely white flowers with orange margins.

'China Boy' has ruffled orange flowers with a creamy white center.

'Maiden's Blush' produces large ruffled white flowers with a soft pink edge. About 2-3' tall.

'Picotee' was an early picotee (bicolor) form with white flowers and deep salmon edges.

'Pinnacle' bears bicolored flowers of white and red. Subtle but handsome.

'Showgirl' has ruffled pink flowers with white centers.

*Lavender:*

'Lavender Glory' is about 30″ tall with lavender flowers.

*Orange:*

'Beauty Queen' has light bronze apricot flowers, about 3-4' tall.

'Dubloon' flowers earlier than most cultivars and bears orange, fully double blossoms.

'Fireball' produces double orange flowers on 2' tall plants.

'Harvest Moon' bears marvelous large double golden yellow flowers.

'Prince of Orange' does as its name suggests, princely not withstanding.

'Salmon Glow' bears double flowers of salmon-orange.

*Pink, Salmon:*

'Betty Ann' is about 30″ tall with handsome pink petals with crinkled margins.

'Cedar Hill' produces light rose flowers on 3' tall plants.

'Cedric Morris' bears large pink flowers with frilled petals and a black center.

'Degas' is only about 2' tall and bears salmon flowers with dark spots. Plants bloom later than most others.

'Glowing Rose' has watermelon pink flowers on stout 2-3' tall plants.

'Helen Elizabeth' bears salmon-pink flowers without the blotching found in 'Barr's White'. This is a classic.

'Julianna' has no basal blotches but is a brilliant pink throughout.

'Karine' is relatively short with clear pink flowers and small red spots at the base.

'Lighthouse' bears large light pink flowers with a wide dark center. Stunningly handsome.

'Mrs. Perry' has pale salmon-pink flowers with black blotches over 3' tall plants. This cultivar and 'Marcus Perry' were raised at the famous Enfield Nursery in England, owned by Mr. Amos Perry.

'Prinzessin (Princess) Victoria Louise' produces flowers of light pink with prominent black spots.

'Queen Alexander' is a common salmon pink-flowered form with a black center.

'Raspberry Queen' is large, vigorous and sports dark rose-pink flowers.

'Watermelon' is aptly named, producing watermelon-pink flowers.

*Red:*

'Allegro' is an excellent dwarf form, growing less than 20" tall with large scarlet flowers.

'Avebury Crimson' has single brilliant red flowers on 3' tall plants.

'Beauty of Livermere' is one of the finest reds I have seen.

'Big Jim' is big, up to 3' tall, and bearing deep red flowers with crinkled margins.

'Bonfire' has fire red flowers.

'Brilliant' also produces fiery red flowers.

'Carmen' bears deep red flowers on strong 2–3' tall plants.

'Claret' bears burgundy red flowers.

'Curlilocks' produces deeply serrated red-orange flower with black center spots. This can be an absolute knockout.

'G.I. Joe', originally included at the request of my then 8 year old son, has deep red flowers and is quite lovely despite the name. It was nice to show him that not all G.I. Joes throw grenades and major in hand-to-hand combat.

'Glowing Embers' bears ruffled scarlet flowers on 2' plants.

'Goliath' grows nearly 4' tall with orange-red flowers and a black eye.

'Ladybird' produces dozens and dozens of small deep red flowers with black spots. I first saw these at Falkland Garden in Scotland and they were some of the smallest poppies I had seen but also some of the most floriferous.

'Marcus Perry' has brilliant scarlet-red flowers.

'Surprise' bears dozens of vermillion red flowers with black spots on 3–4' tall plants.

'Turkinlouis' ('Turkish Delight') is one of the mainstays of the showstopper crowd. Beautiful scarlet flowers with dark centers.

'Warlord' has large deep red flowers.

*White:*

'Arwide' bears 3" wide white flowers with orange venation and black centers.

'Barr's White' has pure white flowers and blackish spots at the base of the petals.

'Black and White' is, as the name suggests, white with black spots at the base of the petals.

'Fatima' is a compact plant with white flowers and pink margins.

'Perry's White' is not new but still is a beautiful cultivar. Off white flowers with a black eye make the flowers appealing.

'Snow Queen' produces large white flowers with black basal spots.

'Springtime' is another white-flowered form with pink margins.

'White King' has large white flowers with black spots at the base.

### Related Species:

*P. bracteatum*, great scarlet poppy, grows 2–2½' tall and bears large blood-red flowers. It differs from *P. orientale* in having 2 large leafy bracts at the base of the flowers and lacks the black blotch at their base.

| -*somniferum* (som-ni' fe-rum) | Opium Poppy | 2–3'/3' |
| --- | --- | --- |
| Late Spring    Multicolored | Greece, Orient | Zones 8–10 |

In northern areas of the country, this species should be treated as an annual, but it self sows prolifically in zones 6–7, and often overwinters with protection in more southerly regions. It is the oldest poppy in cultivation and has been used not only for narcotics, but for the edible seeds, often sold as birdseed under the name of "mawseed." The narcotic properties of the species have long been recognized, in fact, poppy juice was mixed with baby food to make babies sleep. Opium is made from the sap of the green seed capsules and was known by the Greeks and Egyptians several centuries before the birth of Christ. The plants are tall and the lack of branching further accentuates the height. The gray-green leaves are unequally toothed at the base and clasp the stem. The plants are not particularly attractive but the flowers more than compensate. They are 4–5" across and range from white through pink, red to purple, although no yellow or blue flowers yet exist. In most flowers, showy black blotches are found at the base of the petals, providing additional beauty. Unfortunately the flowers drop their petals quickly and make poor cut flowers. There are two common flower forms found in gardens today: the carnation-flowered and the peony-flowered strains. The former has fringed petals, the latter does not. The peony-flowered strain is sometimes listed as *P. paeoniae-florum* and the flowers resemble those of double peonies.

*P. somniferum* is a short-lived plant but the seed is viable, particularly after being chilled in the winter. Every spring, southern gardens are alive with seedlings of opium poppies, many in different places than the year before. Those allowed to remain flower profusely. Each spring, I take my students to the beautiful garden of Mrs. Laura Ann Segrest in Athens, Georgia. We stand in awe of the symphony of color provided by this magnificent plant now better known for its ability to cause pain rather than its potential for beauty.

Laws are changing in the U.S. about growing this plant. Many field grown cut flower growers have been producing opium poppy for the decorative pods, which are a common item in floral shops and in dried arrangements.

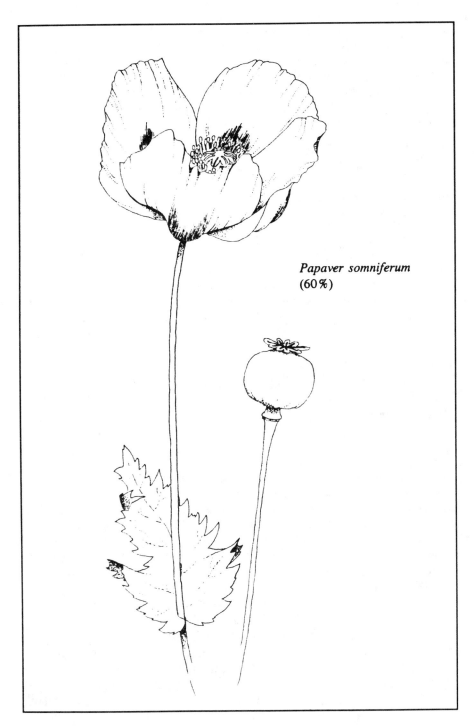

*Papaver somniferum*
(60%)

There is as much chance of getting high on these things as seeing the man on the moon. However, many states aggressively prohibit the growing of plants, period. Most states do not, and as garden plants, who cares. However, if you are a serious athlete, one thing is well known: the ingestion of poppy seeds which come from this plant, such as found on poppy seed buns, will appear in drug tests. Since most of us need not worry about random drug tests, let's enjoy them for their beauty and be done with all this legal mumbo-jumbo.

### Cultivars:
Var. *album* has white flowers and whitish seeds.

Quick Key to Papaver Species

    A. Plants less than 12″ tall . . . . . . . . . . . . . . . . . . *P. alpinum*
    AA. Plants greater than 12″ tall
        B. Stem leaves with broad, clasping base . . . . . . *P. somniferum*
        BB. Stem leaves not clasping
            C. Flowers borne on leafless stems, stem leaves
               gray green, shallowly pinnately lobed . . . . . *P. nudicaule*
            CC. Flower stems with some leaves, stem leaves
               green, deeply pinnately divided . . . . . . . . . . *P. orientale*

### Additional Reading:
Christopher, Thomas. 1981. Poppies. *Horticulture* 59:24–29.
Cullen, James. 1968. The genus Papaver in cultivation. 1. The wild species. *Baileya* 16(3):73–90.


## *Paradisea* (pa-ra-dees′ ee-a)          St. Bruno's Lily          Liliaceae

A genus consisting of only two species, both of which resemble a cross between a tuberose and *Anthericum*, the St. Bernard lily. They are grown from tubers, from which emerge 6–8 basal leaves about 1″ across. The white, almost transparent flowers are held in a 15–20 flowered spike well above the foliage. The flowers are held on one side of the raceme, rather than all around it. The characteristic of holding the flowers so high above the foliage along with their one-sided position are some of the main differences between this and *Anthericum*, whose flowers barely emerge above the leaves. The most common species is *P. liliastrum*, which when in flower, are about 2′ tall. The flowers are subtly fragrant and the tips of the petals are often tinged with green. The other species occasionally offered is *P. lusitanica*. It differs by being more vigorous, taller (up to 5′ tall) and bearing flowers on two sides of the raceme.

This species is seldom grown in American gardens mainly because of difficulty with availability. Hardiness is not well established but plants tolerate sustained temperatures of at least 5° F, probably lower. Heat tolerance is unknown, but since plants are native to alpine meadows of southern Europe, I don't hold out much hope for success in southern gardens.

Propagate by removal of small tubers in the spring. Seed is also viable.

*Paris* (par' is)                    Paris                    Liliaceae

An almost unknown genus closely related to *Trillium*, these interesting plants will probably remain no more than that because of difficulties of propagation. However, as I leaf through my catalogs, I occasionally come across a member or two. Not until I saw a clump of *P. tetraphylla* in Sissinghurst and then in Scotland did I begin to appreciate why they are so sought after. Plants are native to Japan and should be reasonably hardy in zones 5–8.

In *P. tetraphylla*, the foliage is in 2–3 whorls of 4 sessile leaflets, each whorl about 8″ above the one below it. The single flower sits atop the terminal whorl and consists of 4–6 greenish sepals. Blue-black poisonous berries may occur in late fall. Three other species are known but are even more unavailable than the one described. The name *Paris* has nothing to do with the city, but comes from the latin *par*, meaning equal, and refers to the regularity of the leaves and flowers.

If you can find any species, give them a try. Plant them in a rich soil in dappled shade.

**Additional Reading:**
Mitchell, B. 1989. Paris, part I. *The Plantsman* 9(2):81–89.

*Patrinia* (pa-trin' ee-a)            Patrinia              Valerianaceae

*Patrinia* consists of about 15 species and has enjoyed a meteoric rise in popularity. One of the reasons to explain this rise is that they look good with many other garden plants and are excellent companions for almost everything. When I first saw some of the yellow-flowering species, I thought they just looked like overgrown mustard plants, and wondered what all the fuss was. The leaves are opposite, often pinnately cut or lobed, and provide a coarse presence in the garden. The small individual flowers are usually yellow, sometimes white, and are held in airy corymbose panicles well above the foliage. The flowers are persistent, lasting well into the fall in most gardens.

Quick Reference to Patrinia Species

|  | Height (in.) | Flower color |
|---|---|---|
| *P. gibbosa* | 12–18 | Yellow |
| *P. scabiosifolia* | 36–60 | Yellow |
| *P. villosa* | 24–30 | White |

**-gibbosa** (jib-bos' a)                                                     12–18"/18"
   Summer           Yellow           Japan           Zones 5–8

A small version of the more common forms sold, *P. gibbosa* is handsome if not particularly showy. The 4–6" long leaves, which are pinnately cut and coarsely serrated, appear to be blistered. The soft yellow flowers are held in a 4" wide loose inflorescence (cyme) in early summer and persist for at least 6 weeks. Plants are effective in the front to mid position in the garden. They need full sun, although some afternoon shade in the South does not hurt, and decent drainage.

Propagate by seed.

**-scabiosifolia** (skab-ee-o' si-fo-lee-a)   Scabious Patrinia    3–6'/2'
   Summer           Yellow           Japan, Korea      Zones 5–8

The leaves at first glance look like those of the common scabious plant, *Scabiosa*. The oblong to ovate basal leaves are hairy and deeply toothed and the pinnately cleft, coarsely toothed stem leaves are borne on short-petioles or almost sessile. The yellow flowers are produced the second year and are held in many inflorescences well above the foliage. They may be cut and brought inside for persistent color in arrangements.

For many years, there was confusion when plants were placed in the garden; some were 5–6' tall while others were only about 3' tall. Apparently two forms exist in the horticulture trade, the tall one referred to the Korean form, the smaller referred to the Japanese or compact form. Both are heat tolerant and excellent plants for hot, humid summers.

Propagate by seed.

**Cultivars:**

'Nagoya' is the name under which the shorter "Japanese" form is marketed. Plants are more suited to the smaller garden, but at 3' in height, this is not a tiny plant. They have done very well in the heat and humidity including gardens in Tallahassee, FL and in the University of Georgia gardens.

**Related Species:**

*P. triloba* is a stoloniferous slow-growing 12" tall ground cover with small sulphur-yellow flowers, each with a small spur at the base. They are produced in late spring and early summer on short flat inflorescences. The red stems bear palmately parted and irregularly serrated leaves. Excellent for rock gardens where it flowers later than many other rock plants. Prefers a lightly shaded area in consistently moist soil. Best in zones 5–7.

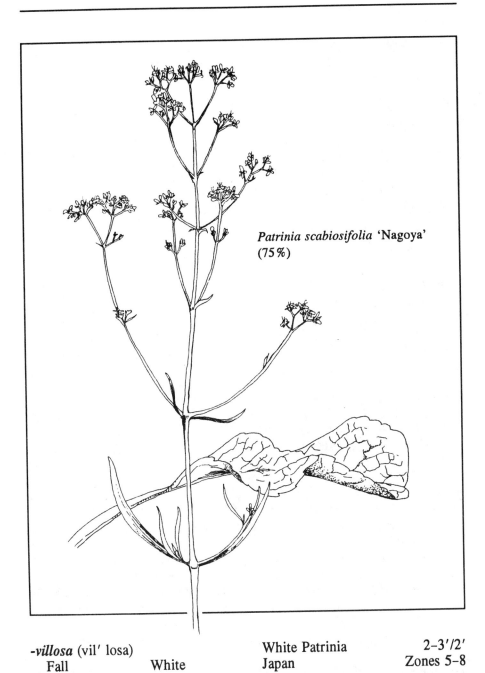

*Patrinia scabiosifolia* 'Nagoya'
(75%)

-*villosa* (vil' losa)            White Patrinia        2–3'/2'
  Fall           White        Japan        Zones 5–8

The 2–3' tall plants are somewhat stoloniferous and make useful clumps
in the late summer and fall garden. The off-white flowers are held in flat
heads just above the foliage, which resembles the leaves in the other

species. The white flowers blend with and accentuate other plants in the fall. Introduced by Dan Hinkley of Herronswood Nursery, Kingston, WA. Propagate by seed.

Quick Key to Patrinia Species

A. Plant with yellow flowers
   B. Plants usually less than 18" tall,
      stem leaves with long petioles . . . . . . . . . . . . . *P. gibbosa*
   BB. Plants usually more than 2' tall, stem
      leaves with short petioles or sessile . . . . . . . *P. scabiosifolia*
AA. Plants with white flowers . . . . . . . . . . . . . . . . . *P. villosa*

**Additional Reading:**

Cohen, S. 1994. Perennials for a brilliant fall finale. *Fine Gardening* 40:30–33.

## *Peltoboykinia* (pel-to-boy' kin-ee-a)                                   Saxigragaceae

Taxonomic confusion reigns in the Saxifrage family, but probably no more than in the group of water loving plants found within. The genus *Boykinia* is found in the southeastern United States (*B. aconitifolia*) and the west (*B. rotundifolia, B. jamesii*) but are seldom seen in gardens. A Japanese member, *B. tellimoides*, is more common, although still relatively unknown, in public and collectors' gardens. The leaves are rounded to peltate (meaning that the petiole attaches near the middle of the leaf, rather than the base), and was recently changed to *Peltoboykinia*. Plants are about 2' tall and have rounded deeply 7–9 lobed leaves. Plants prefer moist soils but do not require wet feet to do well. The thick creeping rhizomes will spread, and although invasive, it is less so than other similar plants used around water, such as *Darmera*. The flowers appear in terminal inflorescences (cymes) and are rather non-descript greenish yellow. This is a fine foliage plant for the moist area near water. If provided with moist conditions, plants perform in zones 6–7 in the East, to zone 8 in the West. They do far better in cool summers than hot ones. Plants may be divided at any time. Use a hefty shovel.

I find that many people, including myself, get confused with all these big, leafy water lovers, so I have outlined some of the main differences among them. Because *Petasites* belongs to the family Asteraceae, the flower structure is totally different (like an aster) and is easy to distinguish when in flower.

|  | Family | Flowering time | Flower color | Number stamens |
|---|---|---|---|---|
| *Boykinia* | Saxifragaceae | With lvs | White | 5–10 |
| *Darmera* | Saxifragaceae | With emerging lvs | Pink | 10 |
| *Peltoboykinia* | Saxifragaceae | With lvs | Greenish yellow | 10 |
| *Petasites* | Asteraceae | With emerging lvs | Pink, white | Many |

*Peltoboykinia* is much smaller, and better behaved, than *Darmera* or *Petasites* and will not eat your house.

**Related Species:**

*P. watanabei*, also from Japan, is similar in habit and culture as the above. Leaves are more deeply divided and plants are shorter.

## *Pennisetum* (pen-i-say′ tum)      Fountain Grass      Poaceae

A genus of about 80 species of annual and perennial grasses, 2 or 3 of which have gained in popularity. They are loosely tufted plants with flat leaf blades and dense, plumose spike-like panicles of flowers. The many plumose (meaning feathery) inflorescences make these plants different from most other species. Upon examining the spikes, you may see that the upper flowers are perfect (male and female parts together) while the lower ones are male or sterile. This arrangement of flowers helps to distinguish *Pennisetum* from other genera. But who wants to look at individual flowers when the feathery spikes are so beautiful. Some of the most handsome species are annuals including *P. setaceum*, particularly the purple-leaved cultivars, *P.* 'Burgandy Giant' with its wide purple leaves and purple-red flowers and *P. villosum*, called feathertop because of the feathery plumes covering the plants. The most common perennial form is *P. alopecuroides* whose many cultivars have become mainstream plants throughout the country.

### -*alopecuroides* (a-lo-pek-ew-roi′ deez) Perennial Fountain Grass   24–30″/24″
     Late Summer      Silver-Bronze      East Asia, West Australia   Zones 5–9

The leaves are about ½″ wide and 20–24″ long. The leaves turn yellowish to brown in the fall and persist in the winter. The feathery bottle brush flowers arise in late summer to fall and range from coppery bronze to deep purple. Plants grow well on almost any site, and require full sun to be at their best. The species may self-sow and become a nuisance, however, most of the named cultivars are easily propagated by division. A species, *P. caudatum*, with silvery early flowers, are sometimes offered but are so similar to *P. alopecuroides* that they have now been clumped together.

**Cultivars:**

'Cassian' has golden tinged foliage with excellent color in the fall. The creamy inflorescences are held well above the foliage and tipped with silver. Plants grow about 30″ tall. A little less cold hardy than most others, supposedly only hardy to zone 6.

'Hameln' is the most popular cultivar due to the compact 24–30″ tall growth. Essentially it is similar to the species, but more compact and better behaved. The flowers are silvery white in late summer and fall.

'Little Bunny' is the most dwarf of the available cultivars. It is great for small gardens, growing less than 12" tall, with the silvery plumes just peeking above the foliage. Useful for the smallest gardens or the rock garden.

'Moudry' is probably the most handsome form, often referred to as black fountain grass. Plants grow to about 30" with deep green leaves and long black plumes of flowers in the fall. Can reseed vigorously. This is sometimes referred to as 'Viridescens'.

'Weserbergland' is similar to 'Hameln' but taller and more spreading in habit.

**Related Species:**

*P. orientale*, oriental fountain grass, is occasionally offered and differs by having foliage which is more blue-green, and silvery pink flowers on 2–3' tall plants. The plants are not as covered with flowers as other species but it is one of the most persistent flowering grasses, blooming from May to September. Plants are hardy from zones 7–9 (zone 6 with protection) and should be used more often in southern climates.

*Penstemon* (pen-stay' mon)　　　Bearded Tongue　　　Scrophulariaceae

Penstemon seems to have sufficient members for almost everybody's garden, but their popularity over here has not mirrored its popularity overseas. Of the 250 species, many are native to western North America and Mexico and require rather stringent environmental conditions to do well. Originally, the eastern United States was fertile ground for early plant explorers and *P. hirsutus*, native from Quebec to Kentucky, and *P. laevigatus*, from Pennsylvania to Florida, went to England to become gentrified. It was not until the 1800s that David Douglas ventured west and discovered 18 new species of western penstemons including *P. ovatus*, *P. heterophyllus* and *P. venustus*.

Numerous hybrids have been introduced from Europe, some the result of the early species found in this country, and their popularity is on the rise. All species are relatively drought tolerant and in fact, the biggest limitation to many of the hybrids doing well in the United States is the amount of winter moisture in many regions. Except for a few of the Eastern U.S. species, plants demand sunny, dry locations.

All have opposite leaves, and showy flowers with long corolla tubes which open to 5 petals. Most species have red, pink, or lavender flowers, although *P. confertus* bears many whorls of sulphur yellow blooms. Flowers have 5 stamens, the characteristic upon which the genus name is based, but one of them is sterile (stamenoid) and lacks a well-developed anther.

Height ranges from 6" up to 3'. A number of low-growing species such as *P. caespitosa*, mat penstemon, *P. pinifolius*, pine leaf penstemon, with its needle-like leaves, *P. crandallii*, Crandall's penstemon, and large-flowered species such as the pink-flowered *P. davidsonii* and *P. newberryi* occur. One or two of the eastern plants have also been introduced into cultivation. The

798

pink-purple flowered *P. smallii* is one of the finest wild flowers I have grown and *P. laevigatus*, smooth bearded tongue, and *P. australis*, southern penstemmon, are being slowly adopted by gardeners. The latest Eastern species to enjoy a meteoric rise is *P. digitalis* and its red-leaved cultivar 'Husker Red'.

The lack of consistent winter hardiness and the aversion to wet feet have created problems in cultivating many of the showier hybrids. They are marginally hardy in the northern states and in the South, significant improvements in soil and drainage are required to provide longevity. Where rainfall is low, drainage is excellent, and sun is available, you have many beautiful forms from which to choose.

Some of the hardiest garden species are:

| | |
|---|---|
| *P. angustifolius* | *P. glaber* |
| *P. barbatus* | *P. hirsutus* |
| *P. confertus* | *P. laevigatus* |
| *P. diffusus* | *P. ovatus* |

To be on the safe side, cuttings should be taken in the fall or seed started in winter. All others, such as the showy *P.* × *gloxinoides*, should be well mulched after cuttings have been taken.

Quick Reference to Penstemon Species

| | Height (in.) | Flower color |
|---|---|---|
| *P. barbatus* | 18–36 | Pink, rose |
| *P. campanulatus* | 18–24 | Various |
| *P. digitalis* | 24–36 | White |
| *P.* × *gloxinoides* | 18–24 | Red, scarlet |
| *P. pinifolius* | 10–20 | Scarlet |
| *P. smallii* | 18–24 | Lavender, purple |

*-barbatus* (bar-bah' tus)     Common Bearded Tongue     18–36″/18″
    Spring    Pink, Rose    Southwestern United States, Mexico    Zones 2–8

The tubular flowers are borne in thin spires and consist of lip-like flowers similar to *Salvia*. The lower lip has short bristly hairs which extend into the throat, thus providing the common name, bearded tongue. The leaves and stems are glaucous (covered with a whitish substance, epicuticular wax, that rubs off), and the leaves are lance-shaped to linear. The flowers are 1–2″ long and usually occur in long narrow, 2–3-flowered racemes which open from the bottom (acropetally) and persist 2–3 weeks. Each flower is strongly 2-lipped and varies from light pink to carmine. Plants are quite winter hardy and also tolerate the heat of the South. In the University of Georgia Horticulture

Gardens, flowers opened from early May to mid June. Plants persisted for about 3 years before division became necessary.

Plants are presently available in a mixture of colors only. Propagation of the named cultivars is by terminal cuttings taken in early to late summer. Some of the named series such as 'Hyacinth Mix' and 'Twilight' can be propagated by seed as can the species and var. *torreyi*.

## Cultivars:

'Albus' is the white version of the species. A good choice for a tough white penstemon.

'Bashful' is a relative newcomer with orange flowers on 12–14″ tall plants.

'Coccineus' grows 15–18″ tall with scarlet flowers and 'Crystal' is similar to 'Bashful' but bears white flowers.

'Hyacinth Mix' is a popular seed-propagated series which bears mixed colors of red, pink, and scarlet.

'Praecox' flowers earlier than the species; 'Praecox Nana' is earlier and shorter.

'Skylight Mix' is another excellent seed-propagated selection. The large tubular flowers are violet to cherry red and often, although not always, white inside the tube. Short-lived but beautiful.

Var. *torreyi* is a scarlet form of the species with little or no beard on the lower lip. It is often sold as 'Torre'.

'Twilight' is a seed-propagated cultivar bearing 2–3″ long flowers.

*-campanulatus* (kam-pahn′ ew-lay-tus)  Harebell Penstemon  18–24″/24″
Summer          Various          Mexico, Guatemala    Zones 7–8

This species is not often seen in gardens but appears to be the dominant parent of a number of hybrid strains making their way into this country. Hardiness in American gardens is marginal, as the hybrids are not tolerant of winter temperatures below 25° F or hot summer temperatures of the South. *P. campanulatus* has narrow, lance-shaped, sharply toothed leaves and 3″ long tubular flowers. The stamenoide (see introduction) if one takes the time to look, is bearded and a good identifying characteristic for the species. The flowers are pink, dark purple, or violet and borne in a long, narrow inflorescence in mid-summer.

## Cultivars:

'Pulchellus' has violet to lilac colored flowers.

'Purpureus' bears purple flowers.

*-digitalis* (di-gi-tah′ lis)      Smooth White Penstemon      2–3′/18″
Summer      White      Eastern United States      Zones 4–8

This fine native plant can't compete with the color of some of the hybrids, however the 4–5″ long oblong-lanceolate leaves are dark green throughout the summer. The white flowers, which are occasionally flushed with light pink, are held in a panicle well above the leaves in early to mid summer. This is one of the finest species for hot summers and has thrived in the Armitage garden for years. Plants are native from Maine, west to South Dakota and south to Texas.

## Cultivars:

'Husker Red', developed at the University of Nebraska, has the same white flowers but the leaves are a deep maroon color. The foliage remains colorful throughout the summer except in southern climates. Plants need full sun to maintain their color. In the shaded Armitage garden, it reverts close to the species once the heat hits. The 1996 Perennial Plant of the Year designated by the Perennial Plant Association.

'Woodville White' has cleaner white flowers than the species.

| -× *gloxinoides* (gloks-in-oi' deez) | Gloxinia Penstemon | 18–24"/20" |
|---|---|---|
| Summer | Various | Hybrid | Zones 5–7 |

The specific epithet has no official botanical standing but refers to hybrids between *P. hartwegii* and *P. cobaea*. *P. hartwegii* has drooping scarlet or blood-red flowers and entire leaves while *P. cobaea* has large reddish purple to whitish flowers and sharply toothed leaves. The hybrids have inherited the large flowers from *P. cobaea* and are often referred to as gloxinia penstemons. The flowers are about 2″ wide, equally long and borne on tall, open racemes.

None of the hybrids is particularly hardy except on the west coast and all should be well mulched regardless of location.

## Cultivars:

'Midnight' has dark green leaves, stands about 18″ tall and bears deep purple bell flowers. Performs well in hot, humid climates.

## Hybrid Cultivars:

Many of the more commonly offered cultivars are hybrids with mixed parentage, but certainly include *P. barbatus*, *P. campanulatus* and *P. × gloxinoides*, among others. I tried to figure out which cultivars belonged to which species, but it is better to lump them all together. The main thing to remember is that this is not England and they will not, in general, be long-lived. Provide full sun and good drainage and don't get carried away.

'Alice Hindley' is a hybrid of *P. campanulatus* and bears large (2½–3″ long) pale mauve wide-mouthed tubular flowers with white interiors. Plants are about 2′ tall and late flowering. This is a magnificent plant when well grown.

'Apple Blossom' bears white flowers with a pink blush.

'Blackbird' has relatively small but deep purple flowers.

'Blue Robin has handsome azure blue flowers on the outside and pink centers.

'Catherine de la Mare' has bluish flowers which fade to purple. Plants are about 18" tall.

'Charles Rudd' bears large tubular cherry-red flowers with a white interior.

'Chester Scarlet' is about as scarlet as I have seen. Growing a little over 2' tall, plants are showstoppers.

'Edithae' is a low grower with large pink-purple flowers.

'Elfin Pink' is about 12" tall with clear pink tubular flowers. Probably a *P. barbatus* hybrid.

'Evelyn' is about 18" tall with many 1" long flowers of pale pink borne over very bushy plants. It is hardier than most of the penstemons, probably having *P. barbatus* in its parentage.

'Firebird' is one of the best known selections due to the exceptionally deep red flowers.

'Garnet' has dozens of large, 1½–2" long wine-colored flowers which open in late summer and fall. The thin, lanceolate leaves are bright green but this hybrid is only moderately hardy in the United States, likely having *P. hartwegii* or *P. campanulatus* in its parentage. Originally introduced as 'Andenken an Friedrich Hahn'.

'Hewell's Pink' bears large tubular flowers of pink with a white spotted interior.

'Hidcote Pink' is a light pink form with many nodding flowers on 3–4' tall stems.

'Hopley's Variegated' is an interesting variegated penstemon with lavender flowers. Grows about 2' tall and hardy to zone 6.

'Mother of Pearl' bears many pearl white (white with shades of pink) flowers in mid summer.

'Papal Purple' is only 12–15" tall with pale purple tubular flowers. From Washfield Nursery in Kent, England.

'Pink Endurance' bears tubular flowers which are cherry pink on the outside and white inside.

'Port Wine' really does have flowers of a port wine color. Plants grow about 18" tall.

'Prairie Dawn', bred by Glenn Viehmeyer at the University of Nebraska, produces pale pink flowers.

'Prairie Dusk' provides clear purple flowers.

'Prairie Fire', part of the wonderful Prairie series, bears lilac-red flowers, mottled with white inside. All of the Prairie series are evergreen in southern climates.

'Purple Bedder' consists of 2' tall plants with deep purple flowers.

'Radjah' produces bright scarlet red flowers on 2–3' tall plants.

'Rose Elf' is a prolific flowering plant with shell-pink flowers. A *P. barbatus* hybrid.

'Rubicundus' has wide tubular scarlet flowers with white centers.

'Ruby' is similar to 'Firebird' with 2½" long intense rich ruby red flowers on 3' tall plants.

'Schooley's Yellow', bred by Dale Lingren at the University of Nebraska, has bright yellow flowers on 2' tall plants. A good deal of *P. barbatus* appears to be in this hybrid.

'Sissinghurst Pink' bears light pink flowers.

'Snowstorm' is one of the better white-flowered forms I have seen. Large white flowers with purple stamens are produced are on 2–3' tall plants.

'Southgate Gem' produces many large deep scarlet red flowers.

'Sour Grapes' was raised by Margery Fish of England and the flowers are bunched together as the name suggests. The indigo-blue buds swell to form flowers in shades of amethyst and blue. This beautiful plant is likely a hybrid with *P. hirsutus*, hairy penstemon, native to the northeastern states.

'Stapleford Gem' is confused with 'Sour Grapes' but is distinct because of its lighter color and taller and more robust habit.

'White Bedder' is a dwarf (12–15") form with tubular white flowers.

'Windsor Red' has deep red flowers.

| *-pinifolius* (pie-ni-fo' lee-us) | | Pine-Leaf Penstemon | 10–20"/15" |
|---|---|---|---|
| Summer | Scarlet | Southwest United States | Zones 7–8 |

The woody base and the needle-like leaves, many crowded at the top of the stem, provide the unique characteristics of this native penstemon. The tubular flowers are scarlet to coral-red and cover the plant in the summer. Plants require excellent drainage and are terrific in hot, dry rocky areas or rock gardens where they perform well.

### Cultivars:

'Magdalina Sunshine', from the Magdalina Mountains of New Mexico, is a recent selection with bright yellow flowers. It is said to be more compact and an improvement on other yellow forms, but it is a little too early to tell. Found by Jay and Ann Lund of Portland, OR.

'Mersea Yellow' is about 12" tall with bright yellow flowers.

| *-smallii* (small-ee' eye) | | Small's Penstemon | 18–24"/2' |
|---|---|---|---|
| Late Spring | Lavender | Eastern United States | Zones 6–8 |

The flowers of this wonderful native plant are pink-purple on the outside and stripped with white inside. The 4–6" long leaves are smooth on the bottom and sometimes slightly pubescent above. The plants tolerate shade but do better in at least 6 hours of full sun.

A good plant for eastern and southern gardeners who love penstemon but have trouble with the fancier kinds.

## Quick Key to Penstemon Species

A. Leaves needle-like . . . . . . . . . . . . . . . . . . . . . *P. pinifolius*
AA. Leaves not needle-like
    B. Flower less than 1″ wide (usually ½–¾″ wide)
        C. Flowers white, never purple or violet . . . . . . *P. digitalis*
        CC. Flowers rose to violet . . . . . . . . . . . . *P. campanulatus*
    BB. Flower more than 1″ wide
        C. Margins of leaves entire . . . . . . . . . . . . . . *P. barbatus*
        CC. Margins of leaves serrated
            D. Leaves ovate, flowers about 1″ long . . . . . . *P. smallii*
        DD. Leaves not ovate, flowers at
            least 2″ long . . . . . . . . . . . . . . . . *P.* × *gloxinoides*

**Additional Reading:**

Chatto, Beth. 1986. Penstemons. *Horticulture* 64(8):10–11.
Lord, Tony. 1984. Peerless penstemons. *The Garden* 119 (7):304–309.

*Associations:*

American Penstemon Society, Box 450, Briarcliff Manor, NY 10510.
    Publication: *American Penstemon Bulletin.*

## *Perovskia* (pe-rof′ skee-a)         Perovskia         Lamiaceae

Although approximately 7 species occur, only *P. atriplicifolia* is used to any extent. The stems are square in cross section and the flowers are borne in terminal racemes or panicles.

| | | | |
|---|---|---|---|
| *-atriplicifolia* (a-tri-pli-ki-fo′ lee-a) | Russian Sage | | 4–5′/4′ |
| Summer | Light Blue | Afghanistan to Tibet | Zone 5–9 |

As a garden plant, *Perovskia* provides beauty and fragrance. The plant has pungent foliage ("like the feet of Russian soldiers"—not really, it was actually named for the Russian general, V.A. Perovsky, 1794–c1857), but only when bruised or crushed. The tubular light blue flowers are two-lipped and arranged in whorls along many-branched 12–15″ tall panicles. The coarsely toothed gray-green leaves are 1–2½″ long and 1″ wide. The loose flowers and small foliage provide a feeling of lightness and airiness to the garden. The flowers appear in mid to late summer and are particularly stunning when combined with a white-flowered plant such as *Boltonia*. Flowers persist for up to 15 weeks; lasting from early July to mid September in my Georgia garden. Plants lean toward the light and tend to flop over as they mature.

    Full sun and adequate drainage must be provided to survive wet winters. Late frosts will knock plants back badly, but in most cases they recover and

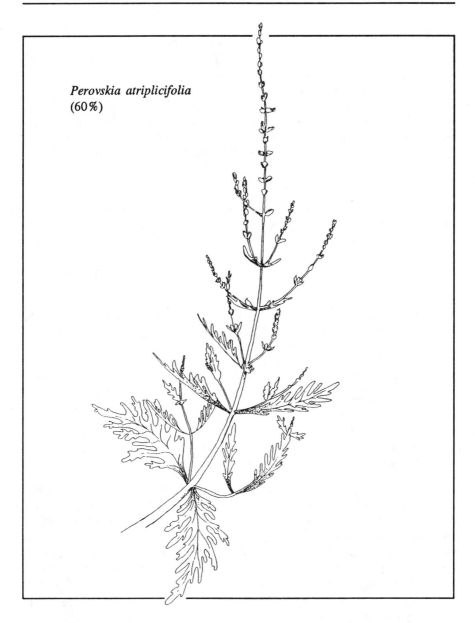

*Perovskia atriplicifolia*
(60%)

grow rapidly. Cut back to 12–18″ after the first hard frost in the fall. Leave some of the stem buds as these provide next year's growing points.

Two problems plague this plant. The first is its tendency to flop even in the brightest sun. It is simply difficult to make this plant sit up straight. The other is that it is only a mediocre plant in areas of high heat and humidity. The flopiness combined with the poor color in hot summers does little to

805

enamour it to many gardeners in such areas. However, it is inspirational enough in other parts of the country, being voted the Perennial Plant of the Year by the Perennial Plant Association in 1995.

Propagate by offshoots which occasionally arise after 2–3 years or take softwood cuttings in the summer. Take a 3″ long shoot, including stem and leaves, dip in root hormone, place in sand, and cover to maintain humidity. Use of plastic to maintain humidity is better than a mist system, as excessive moisture in the rooting bench results in loss of cuttings. Roots appear in 14–21 days.

### Cultivars:

'Blue Mist' flowers earlier and has lighter flowers than the species.

'Blue Spire' has deep violet flowers and deeply cut foliage.

'Filagran' has filigreed foliage with light blue flowers. More delicate appearing than the species.

'Longin' is probably the same as 'Blue Spire' but is a more popular name.

### Related Species:

*P. abrotanoides*, Caspian perovskia, is more branched, taller, and bears darker blue flowers than *P. atriplicifolia*. The gray-green linear-oblong leaves are 1–2″ long and deeply cut. Plants are less compact than Russian sage and are inferior garden plants.

*P.* × *hybrida* is the name given to the hybrid between *P. abrotanoides* and *P. atriplicifolia*. The foliage is gray-green and the inflorescence is longer than either.

## *Petrorhagia* (pet-ro-rah′ gee-a)    Tunic Flower    Caryophyllaceae
(Syn. *Tunica*)

The genus was recently known as *Tunica* but neither name is well-known beyond the rock garden crowd. Although 25–30 species occur, only *P. saxifraga* appears to have any significant following. The plants resemble creeping baby's breath (*Gypsophila repens*) and are used to clamber over rocks or onto pathways. They are native to high elevations and rocky or sandy soils, therefore telling us that drainage is most important to success. It is undemanding in its cultural needs, as long as it hangs from walls or in raised beds. Heat results in long internodes and plants should be cut back hard in early to mid summer in the South.

The flowers are pale pink, often with darker veins, and the combination of small leaves and tiny flowers provide a delicate picture. Numerous cultivars have been selected. Double forms such as 'Alba Plena' and 'Pleniflora Rosea' are covered with white and rosy flowers respectively. 'Lady Mary' also has double soft pink flowers and 'Rosette' is a compact form with double pink blooms.

Plants are hardy from zone 5–7, although they also do well in zone 8 on the West Coast. In the South, the foliage is wonderfully evergreen and will do well in hot weather if drainage is good and plants are trimmed occasionally. I have been pleasantly surprised and can now recommend this plant to growers and gardeners alike.

## *Phalaris* (fa-lah′ ris)         Canary Grass, Ribbon Grass         Poaceae

Approximately 20 species with many narrow flat blades and narrow spiky panicles, only a few of which are ornamental. They grow in normal garden soils in full sun or partial shade. The only selection readily available is *P. arundinacea* 'Picta', known as Gardeners garters, which is grown for the white-striped variegated foliage. From early herbals, it was one of the first variegated grasses to be brought into gardens. Their stoloniferous nature make plants effective as a ground cover but they can become invasive. The plants grow about 18–24″ tall but flops over with time. While it is a useful ground cover, it never seems to cover the ground particularly well, leaving patches here and there. Plants are evergreen in mild climates, but should not be thought of as an ornamental winter grass. All selections of ribbon grass grow well in boggy soils and can also be submerged a few inches in a garden pond or pool.

A number of improved taxa have been selected, each with a better habit or cleaner variegation, and usually less invasive. 'Dwarf Garters' is a dwarf form of 'Picta', growing only 10–15″ tall and spreading more slowly. The variegation is similar to 'Picta', but it is better as a garden plant than as a ground cover. 'Feesey's Form' is much improved over 'Picta', having much less green and more white on each leaf. The leaves are tinged pink in spring. It is about the same size as 'Picta' but spreads slowly. Plants were originally distributed by Mervyn Feesey of England. Both 'Dwarf Garters' and 'Feesey's Form' are excellent plants when used with bedding plants or to soften harsh colors. The golden variegated form, 'Luteo-picta' which bears gold and green variegated foliage is similar to 'Picta' in that it spreads rapidly. The variegation is beautiful in early spring but tends to fade in the heat of the summer.

Propagate all selections by division only.

## *Phlomis* (flo′ mis)         Phlomis         Lamiaceae

This genus of garden plants is finally finding homes in this country and more species are being offered by nurserymen. Given the proper conditions of soil, sun, and moisture, they can be outstanding, but I have not seen enough outstanding plants in my travels through the United States. Often with gray-green foliage and flowers of yellow or lavender, these coarse plants look good in flower bud, and in flower when well grown.

807

Quick Reference to Phlomis Species

|  | Leaf color | Leaf shape | Flower color |
|---|---|---|---|
| *P. fruticosa* | Gray-green | Elliptical to lanceolate | Deep yellow |
| *P. italica* | Gray-green | Oblong to lanceolate | Pink-mauve |
| *P. russelliana* | Green | Ovate | Sulphur yellow |

| *-fruticosa* (froo-ti-ko′ sa) | | Jerusalem Sage | 2–4′/3′ |
|---|---|---|---|
| Spring | Yellow | Mediterranean | Zones 4–8 |

This shrubby plant is the best of the genus for American gardens because of the late summer flowers and gray-green foliage. The 2–4″ long leaves are coarse, wrinkled and white-woolly beneath. The stems have woolly hairs, and are slightly yellowish. The leaves are evergreen in milder climates and the gray color is retained all winter. The most arresting features (as well as the prettiest) are the flower buds, tightly whorled in the axils of the uppermost leaves. Twenty to thirty tightly closed flower buds occur in tiered whorls, so the flower stems are like light green candelabras. The butter yellow flowers open in late spring and provide a pleasing contrast to the gray-green foliage. Plants flower in the summer in the North, but during the winter in southern California.

Full sun is required in the North and partial shade in the South. They are fairly drought resistant and salt tolerant. In the South, leaves remain evergreen in the winter but plants die to the ground north of zone 7.

Propagate by division in the fall or spring, or sow seed. Shoot cuttings, taken in the fall, may also be used. Treat with rooting hormone, place in a loose medium, and cover with clear plastic to maintain humidity. Rooting occurs in 7–14 days.

**Related Species:**

*P. chrysophylla*, goldleaf Jerusalem sage, is 24–30″ tall with whorls of golden-yellow flowers. It is a low growing evergreen subshrub (woody stems) whose leaves are more heart-shaped than those of *P. fruticosa*. It has not been available long enough to know the hardiness constraints.

*P. longifolia* has long (4–6″) leaves and whorls consisting of 12–20 butter yellow flowers. The leaves are green on the upperside and gray-green below. One of the most handsome of the yellow phlomis. 'Bailanica' simply differs in the leaf shape, having ovate leaves rather than lanceolate leaves.

| *-italica* (ee-tal′ i-ca) | | Italian Sage | 1–2′/2′ |
|---|---|---|---|
| Summer | Pink-Mauve | Baleric Islands | Zones 6–8 |

Having been under the false impression that all plants of the genus had yellowish flowers, I soon learned once again how little I knew. Happens all the time. This is one of the many species with pink to mauve flowers which are a well kept secret in this country. Plants cannot be called tidy, producing branched shrub-like growth. The green leaves are covered in whitish felt, particularly on the underside and soften the plant considerably. The flowers are held in distant whorls, each consisting of 5–6 flowers.

Plants do well in dry areas, disliking the combination of high humidity and heat. Place in full sun and well-drained soil.

**Related Species:**

*P. cashmeriana*, Kashmir sage, is more robust, growing to 3' in height and bears many more pale lilac flowers than *P. italica*. A better plant if a pink-flowered phlomis is wanted.

*P. samia* has gone through some confusing times lately. The flowers are pink to purple and the plant bears oval to lance-shaped leaves which end in a tapered point (acuminate). The confusing part is that it has sometimes been offered with yellow flowers, but that is either a misprint or a misunderstanding of the catalog maker. Grows up to 3' tall and hardy in zones 7–9.

| | | | |
|---|---|---|---|
| *-russelliana* (ru-sel-ee' ane-a) | Jerusalem Sage | 3–4'/3' |
| Summer  Sulphur Yellow | Syria | Zones 5–8 |

Plants are bigger, coarser and greener than *P. fruticosa* and require more room in the garden. The ovate (like an egg) dull green leaves are 4–6" across and 6–7" long and the 3–5 whorls of flowers are a soft yellow. Not as hardy as *P. fruticosa* or as easy to establish.

**Related Species:**

'E.A. Bowles' ('Edward Bowles') is a terrific robust plant which is probably a hybrid between *P. fruticosa* and *P. russelliana*. The size and color of the leaves are intermediate between the two. The pale yellow flowers are less butter yellow than *P. russelliana* but not as soft as *P. fruticosa*. My first choice if I can ever find it.

Quick Key to Phlomis Species

   A. Flowers yellow
      B. Leaves gray-green, 1–3" wide . . . . . . . . . . . . . *P. fruticosa*
      BB. Leaves green, 4–6" wide . . . . . . . . . . . . . . *P. russelliana*
   AA. Flowers pink or purple . . . . . . . . . . . . . . . . . . . *P. italica*

## *Phlox* (floks)  Phlox  Polemoniaceae

Phlox has enough marvelous members that at least one plant should reside in everyone's garden. Although the best known species is *P. paniculata*, garden phlox, many occur which are more disease resistant, lower growing, and easier to cultivate. If fact, the genus is represented by species ranging from 6" to 5' in height. The annual phlox, *P. drummondii*, has undergone significant improvements through breeding and is easily grown from seed. The most common perennial phlox is moss phlox, *P. subulata*, whose magnificent mantles of fluorescent pink, white and blue radiate from hills, roadsides, and gardens everywhere in this country. The first specimen of this plant was sent to England by John Bartram in 1745 and was termed a "fine creeping Spring Lychnis." In 1919, the intrepid plant explorer, Reginald Farrer, enthusiastically wrote that "the day that saw the introduction, more than a century since, of *P. subulata*, ought indeed to be kept as a horticultural festival."

All species are native to North America and have opposite leaves. In general, low-growing phlox tolerate a little shade whereas taller species do best in full sun. Phlox require well-drained soils to remain in the garden for any length of time yet are often the first plants to show signs of drought. Fall planting is best although early spring planting is almost as safe. One of the finest breeders of phlox, particularly the low-growing forms, was H. Lincoln Foster, whose Connecticut garden was called Millstream House. Many of our finest cultivars and hybrids bear the Millstream name and attest to his foresight. His recent passing has left a major void in horticulture.

Two major pests of phlox result in serious damage. Spider mites attack all species with equal fervor and are particularly damaging in hot, dry weather. Miticides, not insecticides, should be used at the first sign of infestation. If the weather stays particularly warm and dry, continue application every week. Powdery mildew is a fungal disease characterized by white, felt-like growth on the leaves and stems in midsummer. It is particularly offensive on garden phlox, *P. paniculata*. Some cultivars are so susceptible to mildew that they are impossible to grow without application of fungicides, however, many new cultivars have been bred for mildew resistance. If necessary, fungicides may be sprayed around June 15 and applied 10–14 days thereafter. *P. maculata*, spotted phlox, has become more popular in recent years because of the relative disdain to mildew. However, relative is the operative word.

Most low-growing phlox are propagated by seed or terminal cuttings. Root cuttings may be used with all species and is commonly practiced on *P. paniculata* cultivars and other upright species. Two inch long pieces of larger diameter roots are cut and placed upright, with the base end down, and covered with 1″ of sand or peat-perlite mix. The mix must be kept moist and the environment humid.

Quick Reference to Phlox Species

|  | Height (in.) | Flower color | Petals notched |
|---|---|---|---|
| *P. divaricata* | 12–15 | Blue | Slightly |
| *P. maculata* | 24–36 | Various | Slightly |
| *P. paniculata* | 36–48 | Mauve | Slightly |
| *P. stolonifera* | 6–12 | Lavender | No |
| *P. subulata* | 6–9 | Various | Slightly |

***-divaricata*** (di-vah-ri-kah′ ta)     Woodland Phlox          12–15″/12″
    Spring        Blue           Eastern North America    Zones 3–8

This is one of the most useful and still overlooked phlox for today's gardens. The leaves are dark green, oblong, and 1½–2″ long. Plants spread slowly by creeping rhizomes above which 12–15″ tall flower stems ascend in the spring. Shoots which do not bear flowers (sterile) don't ascend, but root at the nodes. The somewhat fragrant 1½″ wide flowers are usually light blue but vary to lighter or darker shades. The ends of the petals are slightly lobed and the flowers are loosely held in panicles. This species makes a wonderful edging plant for partially shaded, moist well-drained areas. Most of the cultivars and species can be trimmed or cut back after flowering to encourage additional growth.

Woodland phlox may be propagated from seed. The cultivars and hybrids are best multiplied from terminal shoot cuttings or root cuttings.

### Cultivars:

'Blue Dreams' is an excellent selection with blue-lilac flowers on 8–10″ long stems. Plants are also more robust than the species.

'Clouds of Perfume' (what a great name) has pale blue flowers with narrow petals. They have more fragrance than normally associated with other selections.

'Dirigo Ice' is 8–12″ tall and bears icy blue flowers with slightly notched petals. This is a mainstay in the Armitage garden and always draws second looks.

'Fuller's White' is more dwarf (8–12″) and is so completely covered with clear, white flowers in the spring that it looks like a snowbank. The leaves are slightly smaller than those of the species and the flowers are definitely notched at the end of the petals. It is also more sun tolerant than the species. Although the species is an excellent garden plant, it cannot hold a candle to this cultivar. Bred in the early 1970's by Henry Fuller of Sherwood Farm in Connecticut. Henry wanted it to be named Sally for his wife, Sally wanted it to be called Sherwood for the garden. Linc Foster settled the issue by naming it 'Fuller's White'. A great name, a great plant. Flowering starts in early April and persists for 4–5 weeks in my garden, flowers in May in the Northeast.

Var. *laphamii* is native to the western United States and bears dark blue flowers with entire petals on 18″ stems. Cut back hard after flowering.

'London Grove Blue' has deep blue fragrant flowers on compact plants.

'Louisiana' bears purple-blue flowers with a magenta eye.

'May Breeze' is similar to 'Dirigo Ice' but with a little more pink.

'Opelousas' bears violet-red flowers on 12–15″ stalks.

'Twilight' is most unusual, producing many light lavender star-shaped flowers. The petals are much more narrow than those of other selections.

### Related Species:

*P.* × *arendsii*, Arend's phlox, is the result of crosses between *P. divaricata* and *P. paniculata*, garden phlox, and arose in Arends nursery in

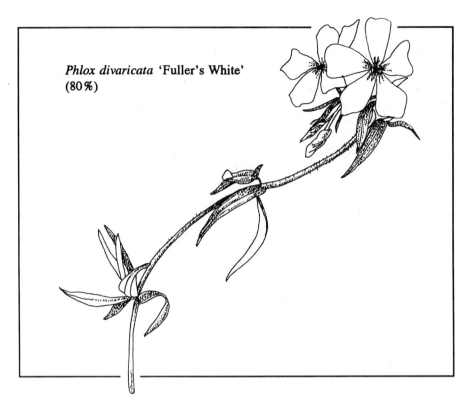

*Phlox divaricata* 'Fuller's White'
(80%)

Germany in 1912. It is intermediate in height and quite floriferous. 'Anja' bears reddish purple flowers, 'Hilda' produces mauve blossoms and 'Susanne' has white flowers with a red eye. They are finally being offered in the States and are worth a try. None are mildew resistant.

*P. bifida*, sand phlox, is a low-growing plant with short linear leaves and deeply notched violet-purple to white petals which appear in early spring. It is tough and views poor soils and drought with contempt. 'Colvin's White' is a pure white form bearing deeply cut flowers in spring. The species has been used in creating *P.* × *lilacina* hybrids (see *P. subulata*) and is hardy from zones 4–8.

*P.* × *chattahoochee*, Chattahoochee phlox, often mistakenly offered as a cultivar, is a cross between *P. divaricata* var. *laphamii* and the pale purple-flowered downy phlox, *P. pilosa*. The flowers have entire petals with a striking purple eye and the foliage consists of longer, wider, dark green leaves. It is short-lived, flowering itself to oblivion as well as being mildew and fungal susceptible. But when it is alive, it is outstanding. Flowering occurs from early April to early June.

*P. pilosa* tolerates full sun and flowers between *P. divaricata* and *P. paniculata*. Plants grow 1–1½' tall and are covered with short hairs. Plants are stoloniferous and multiply rapidly. They perform well in the South. Two

Phlox × chattahoochee
(85%)

good selections are available. 'Eco Happy Traveler', from Don Jacobs at Eco Gardens, bears fragrant deep rose flowers and 'Ozarkiana', which has light pink blooms with white centers. All are wonderfully fragrant.

**-maculata** (mak-ew-lah' ta)   Wild Sweet William, Spotted Phlox   24–36″/24″
   Early Summer   Mauve-Pink   Eastern North America   Zones 3–8

This species is coming into its own now that additional cultivars have entered the market. The mauve-pink flower color did little to inspire excitement and the species labored in relative obscurity. The leaves are 2–4″ long, linear to lance-like and arranged up the stem like the steps of a ladder. They are also thick, glossy dark green and slightly pointed. The stems are hairy and usually, but not always, mottled red. The main differences between this species and *P. paniculata* are earlier flowering, darker green leaves, spotted stems, and better mildew resistance.

813

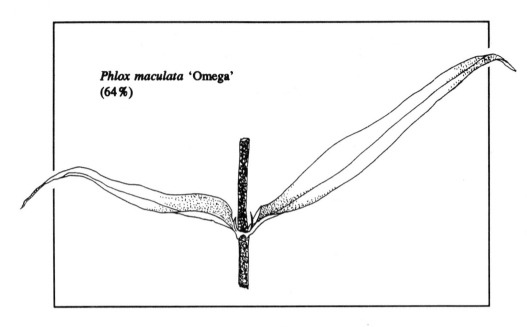

*Phlox maculata* 'Omega'
(64%)

Propagate by division of offshoots, from root cuttings, and occasionally from terminal cuttings.

## Cultivars:

'Alpha' bears rose-pink flowers with a hint of a darker eye.

'Delta' has long panicles of white flowers with rose colored eyes.

'Magnificence' is likely a hybrid or cultivar of *P. carolina*. The 3' tall plants are relatively mildew resistant and bear rosy pink flowers.

'Miss Lingard' brought the species out of obscurity. It is an excellent pure white cultivar which flowers earlier and is a little more mildew resistant than the popular summer phlox. (The parentage of 'Miss Lingard' is confusing. She has also been attributed to *P. carolina*, Carolina phlox, and may well be a hybrid between the two species).

'Natascha' has pink and white flowers and grows about 2' tall.

'Omega' produces white blossoms with a small lilac eye and is more floriferous than 'Miss Lingard'.

'Rosalinde' has dark pink flowers.

*-paniculata* (pa-nic-ew-lah' ta)   Garden Phlox   3–4'/2'
    Summer   Magenta   Eastern North America   Zones 4–8

This species is surely the most magnificent of upright phlox and more cultivars and colors have been advertised in catalogs than all others put together. This has resulted in a most popular plant, which if placed in the right location will flower spectacularly. Sites in full sun with good ventilation are necessary for best performance. Some cultivars perform better in the North than in the South as they are not particularly heat tolerant. Under hot summer conditions, plant vigor diminishes and susceptibility to root rot organisms increases.

Unfortunately, some cultivars are very susceptible to powdery mildew, particularly in the North. To reduce the incidence of disease, thin clumps to 4 or 5 strong shoots in the spring, and always apply water to the base of

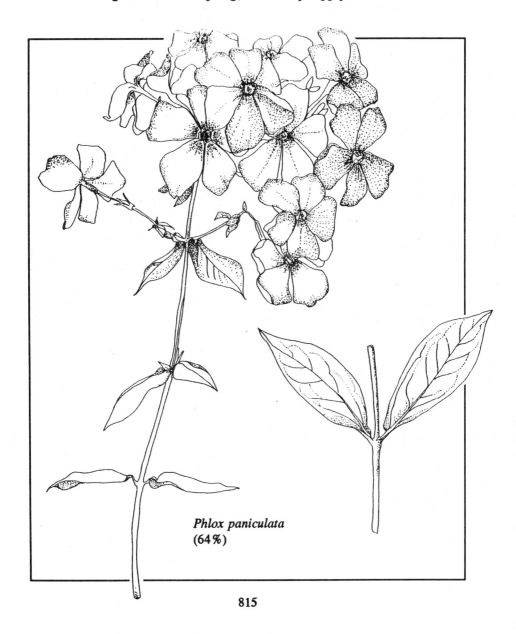

*Phlox paniculata*
(64%)

the plant and not the foliage. If overhead watering is necessary, water in the morning to allow the leaves to dry during the day. Watering at night results in rapid mildew infestation, a reason why plants struggle where late afternoon and evening summer thundershowers are common. Mildew is less of a problem in dry seasons and windy locations. Fungicides are available and application should begin in most areas by early June and continue every 10 days to 2 weeks. If you think this is more trouble than these plants are worth, you may be right. Take advantage of less mildew susceptible species such as *P. maculata*.

The leaves are 2–5″ long, and have slender points at the end but are not as thick as those of *P. maculata* or *P. carolina*. The flowers are held in a large, dense pyramidal panicle, up to 8″ across, each tubular flower averages 1″ across, often in shades of pink or lilac. The stamens and styles are often equal to or longer than the corolla tube.

Most garden phlox cultivars are propagated from root cuttings (see *Papaver* for details). Offshoots, which often arise at a considerable distance from the parent plant, may be divided in the spring.

### Cultivars:

The species itself is seldom seen in gardens and has been replaced by selections with greater vigor, floriferousness, and attractiveness. Tremendous numbers of cultivars are offered and the best way to choose is to consult one of the many garden catalogs. One of the concerns of the gardener is susceptibility to mildew and only by trying different cultivars and visiting gardens where many are planted will a good evaluation be made. Some of the newer cultivars are definitely more resistant than older ones. Have fun!

*Orange:* There are no true oranges, but the breeders are closing in.

'Orange Perfection' is a vigorous selection with salmon-orange flowers with a small red eye early in the summer.

*Pink/Salmon:*

'Aquarelle' has rose-pink flowers with a darker eye.

'Bidermeier' bears very pale pink flowers with a rose-red eye.

'Bright Eyes' has pale pink blossoms with a crimson eye. One of the best performers and surely one of the most popular.

'Dodo Hanbury Forbes' has pink to rosy flowers borne in large trusses.

'Dorffreude' bears deep pink flowers with a red eye on 3′ tall plants.

'Dresden China' produces pastel pink flowers with a deeper rose-pink eye.

'Elizabeth Arden' is a beautiful pink-flowered selection with a red eye.

'Eva Cullum' has large heads of clear pink flowers with a dark red eye. Plants are 2–2½′ tall and do not require staking. Eva Cullum, the lady, was in charge of the retail department of Bloom's Nursery in the 1970's and was honored with the introduction of this plant by Alan Bloom.

'Evangeline' has pink-salmon flowers with a hint of white in the center.

'Fairest One' has salmon pink blooms with a dark red eye.

'Fesselballon' is about 2' tall and produces pink flowers with a dark eye. Nice fragrance.

'Sir John Falstaff' bears large flowers of salmon pink on 2-3' tall plants.

'Fairy's Petticoat' has large heads of pale pink with darker eyes.

'Flamingo' is about 2' tall with flaming pink flowers and a white eye.

'H.B. May' produces large bright pink flower heads on 3-4' tall plants.

'Juliet' has pale pink flowers with a white eye on 2' plants.

'Otley Choice' was bred in the 1940's but is still available today. The flowers are similar to 'Bright Eyes'.

'Pinafore Pink' bears flowers similar to 'Bright Eyes' but occur on dwarf 12-15" tall plants.

'Pink Gown' is compact, only 24-30" tall, with rosy pink flowers in late summer.

'Salmon Beauty' is an early flowering form with salmon-pink flowers with a white eye.

*Purple, Lavender:*

'Amythest' has deep lilac flowers.

'Ann' is a late bloomer with large lavender flower heads.

'Blue Boy' bears lavender blue flowers on 3' tall plants. Plants flower in late summer.

'Bouvardier' has violet-red flowers with a very light pink eye.

'Caroline van den Berg' bears flowers of imperial purple.

'Franz Schubert' has lilac blooms with a star-shaped darker eye. In recognition of the great composer, the plant was raised and named by Blooms of Bressingham.

'Katherine' has lavender flowers on 2-3' tall plants. So far, mildew resistance looks good.

'Lavender' is, for all intents and purposes, the species. It is tough, vigorous, absolutely fool-proof and mildew resistant. It's only drawback is the lack of sexy flowers.

'Lilac Time' produces large heads of lilac blue flowers.

'Progress' has pale violet blossoms with a darker eye.

'Robert Poore', introduced by Kim Hawkes of Niche Nursery in Chapel Hill, NC is outstanding. Similar in habit to 'Lavender', but the color is a much more vibrant purple. No mildew.

'Russian Violet' bears purple-violet flowers in large trusses. Plants are 3-4' tall.

'Starlight' produces deep violet flowers.

'Sternhimmel' has light lavender flowers on 2-3' tall plants.

'The King' bears purple-lavender flowers on 2-3' tall plants.

*Scarlet, Red:*

'Barnwell' bears rose-red flowers with a deeper red eye.

'Charles H. Curtis' is one of the prettiest sunset red flowering selections. Large flowers and a vigorous habit have made the plant popular.

'Leo Schlageter' has bright red to scarlet flowers on 30″ plants. An old cultivar from Arends nursery in Germany which continues to stay around.

'Mrs. R.P. Struthers' has deeper green leaves than many selections, almost bronze in the spring. The flowers are scarlet red.

'Newbird' bears plum red flowers on medium size trusses.

'Othello' sports deep red flowers with 6–7 week long blooming period.

'Sandra' produces bright scarlet flowers on 2′ tall plants.

'Spitfire' is an old cultivar from Germany, introduced in the 1930s as 'Frau Alfred von Malthner', but is still an excellent salmon-red form.

'Starfire' has striking cherry red flowers which immediately catch the eye, even from a distance. Probably the truest red.

'Tenor' is an early bloomer, bearing rosy scarlet flowers on 2′ tall plants.

'Windsor' bears pale rose flowers with a salmon eye.

*Variegated Leaves:*

'Harlequin' was produced by Alan Bloom of England and has variegated foliage with violet blue flowers. Plants appear to have lost vigor as they are difficult to produce.

'Norah Leigh' bears creamy white leaves with a center line of green. The foliage is far more remarkable than the rather common pink-lavender flowers. It makes a wonderful accent for the front or middle of the garden. Afternoon shade is required.

*White:*

'Blue Ice' bears white flowers with a pinkish-blue eye.

'David' is probably the best white today. Plants are as mildew resident as any paniculata selection in cultivation. The original plant was first spotted in the Conservancy Garden at the Brandywine Museum by Richard Simon of Bluemount Nursery. Excited as only Richard could be, he rushed in to see the director, Mrs. F.M. Moobury, who really hadn't noticed this diamond in the rough. Hardly able to contain himself, Richard politely asked for a few cuttings to propagate in his nursery, and to his and everyone else's great delight, the plants were even better in cultivation than in the wild garden from whence they originated. The plants were named for David, Mrs. Moobury's late husband.

'Mia Ruys' is a compact plant, growing less than 2′ tall.

'Mt. Fuji' ('Mt. Fujiyama') was the most popular white for years but newer and better selections are superseding it, such as 'David' above. Plants are still very nice, bearing very dense 12–15″ long flower heads. It shines from a distance.

'Prime Minister' is white with a hint of pink and a red eye.

'White Admiral' has clear white large flower heads. Plants bloom 1–2 weeks later than 'Mt. Fuji'.

'World Peace' blooms late in the season with pure white flowers over handsome glossy green leaves.

***-stolonifera*** (sto-lo-ni′ fe-ra)     Creeping Phlox          6–12″/12″
   Spring     Violet, Lavender    Eastern North America    Zones 2–8

This species is possibly the most shade tolerant of the phlox and forms a dense cover under quite shady conditions. Creeping phlox is low growing and, similar to woodland phlox, produces both flowering and sterile shoots. The leaves on the sterile shoots are 1–3″ long and narrowed at the base while those on the flowering shoots are oval, no more than 1″ long, and not as narrow at the base. The petals are usually unnotched, and the lavender ¾″ wide flowers are held 2–3 in a cyme. Plants spread by stolons and by rooting at the nodes of the sterile stems. An excellent species, it is not as brilliant or as vigorous a garden performer as other low growing species but its classiness and subtlety make it a long time favorite. It is so good that it was denoted as the 1990 Perennial Plant of the Year by the Perennial Plant Association. Plants tolerate partial shade and consistent moisture.

Propagate by division any time of year. Terminal cuttings of sterile shoots may also be used.

### Cultivars:
'Ariane' bears loose heads of white flowers with a yellow eye.
'Blue Ridge' has blue-lilac flowers. Good performer, very popular.
'Bruce's White' is characterized by white flowers with a yellow eye.
'Fran's Purple' has starry lilac and purple flowers over it 8–10″ stems.
'Homefires' bears showy rich pink flowers.
'Irridescens' produces somewhat iridescent blue-mauve flowers.
'Melrose' has large pink flowers.
'Pink Ridge' forms 6″ tall mats with dark mauve pink flowers.
'Sherwood Purple' bears purple-blue, highly fragrant flowers over 6″ stems
   and is the most popular cultivar.

### Related Species:
*P. × procumbens* is a cross between *P. stolonifera* and *P. subulata*. It combines some of the vigor of *P. subulata* with the larger flowers of *P. stolonifera*. The plants grow 1′ tall and bear ¾″ wide purple flowers. Numerous cultivars have been bred. 'Millstream Variety' is a trailing form with rose-pink flowers spoked with darker stripes. Flowering plants are 9–12″ tall. 'Variegata' is one of the finest varieties I have seen and has dark green leaves edged in white. They produce mauve-pink flowers. The foliage is better than the flowers.

*P. × 'Spring Delight'* is reported to be a cross between *P. paniculata* and *P. stolonifera*. It grows 15–20″ tall and produces dozens of rose-pink flowers. An outstanding performer, an Armitage favorite.

***-subulata*** (sub-ew′ lah-ta)     Moss Phlox          6–9″/12″
   Early Spring    Various    Eastern North America    Zones 2–8

It is difficult to drive or walk any distance in the spring and not see this species carpeting a bank and providing spring color to an otherwise drab and dreary residential landscape. Plants may be found in blue, white, and purple, but the overwhelming majority in landscapes are pink with a darker eye, thus accounting for one of its common names, mosspink. Plants make few demands, but full sun and well-drained soils result in best performance. They are so abundant and so successful that they have to put up with names like "gas station plant" and "trailer park plant." Success is measured in many ways.

The narrow linear leaves are only about ½″ long, close together, and quite stiff almost to the point of being prickly. Three to five flowers are borne in a loose panicle just above the matted foliage. The petals are slightly notched to entire and open flat. The stamens protrude from the flower and the style is up to ½″ long. Differences between *P. subulata* and *P. nivalis* (the two are often confused) can be found under *P. nivalis*.

All taxa require relatively well-drained soils and full hot sun for best flowering.

Propagate by division or layering. To layer, place a section of non-flowering shoot on the ground and cover lightly with soil. Keep the area moist and the stem will root into the soil. Cuttings may also be taken, preferably in late fall for best rooting.

### Cultivars:

There is little difference among selections within any color and the same plant may be masquerading under two or three different names. Some of these definitely are sections or hybrids with other low growers such as *P. ovata*, *P. bifida*, *P. douglasii* and *P. nivalis*. They may also be listed under *P.* × *frondosa* (*P. subulata* × *P. nivalis*) and *P. lilacina* (*P. subulata* × *P. bifida*).

*Blue, Purple:*

'Atropurpurea' bears wine-red flowers.
'Blue Hills' has notched flowers of deep blue.
'Blue Emerald' has medium blue flowers.
'Emerald Cushion Blue' produces many blue flowers on vigorous plants.
'Hillview Pink' discovered at the fine Washington nursery, Hillview Gardens, bears dozens of rosy pink flowers.
'Millstream Jupiter' is an outstanding selection from Lincoln Foster of Millstream Garden. The flowers are deep blue with a yellow eye.

*Pink:*

'Apple Blossom' has pale pink lilac flowers with a darker eye.
'Emerald Cushion Pink' produces light pink flowers on a plant of mounding habit.
'Encore' has light pink flowers and will rebloom if cut back hard after flowering.
'Maiden's Blush' produces pink flowers with a red eye.
'Millstream Daphne' has deep pink flowers with a dark eye. Compact and vigorous.

'Millstream Laura' bears pastel pink flowers on compact plants.
'Morning Star' produces flowers of pale pink.
'Perfection' has pinkish flowers.
'Sunrise' produces peach-pink flowers on compact plants.
'Venus' bears pink flowers.
'Vivid' has strong red-pink blossoms.

*Red:*

'Beauty of Ronsdorf' is probably a selection of *P. douglasii* and bears bright rosy red flowers on mounded compact plants.
'Crackerjack' is a showstopper with brilliant crimson red flowers on compact plants.
'Crimson Beauty' produces rose-red flowers.
'Fort Hill' bears fragrant rosy pink flowers which are deeply cut on the petals.
'Mars' has very intense red blooms.
'Red Wings' grows vigorously and bears rose-red flowers all spring.
'Scarlet Flame' is a deep scarlet red with an even darker eye.

*White:*

'Candy Stripe' was originally introduced as 'Tamanonagalei' so it is no surprise that the name was changed. The white flowers are striped with pink. Eye catching.
'Coral Eye' is another Foster creation and bears beautiful pink-white flowers with a deep coral eye.
'Schneewittchen' ('Snow White') has small white flowers on miniature plants.
'Snowflake' is the showiest white I have seen. Incredibly compact and absolutely covered with starry clean white flowers in the spring; it is a mound of snow.
'White Delight' is more open than the above but bears good white flowers.

### Related Species:

*P. glaberimma*, smooth phlox, is an excellent stoloniferous species with baby bottom smooth stems. Plants bear rosy pink flowers similar to *P. carolina* and grow 2–3' tall. 'Interior' has been selected with deeper purple-red flowers. The best form is 'Triflorum' which only grows 8–12" tall and produces many pink flowers in groups of three ("triflorum"). Eats up heat and humidity.

*P. nivalis* is similar in habit, appearance, and flowering time to *P. subulata*, and has been overlooked by breeders and gardeners alike. All make excellent plants for the rock garden or front of the border. The 1" wide flowers are usually entire but may be slightly notched and range from purple to pink or white. Plants differ from moss phlox in that the petals are normally entire (notched in *P. subulata*), and the stamens and style are much shorter (up to ½" long in *P. subulata*, less than ⅛" long in *P. nivalis*). Full sun and well-drained soils are necessary for success. 'Camia' is a lovely pink form with flowers a little larger than the species. Other hybrids with *P. nivalis* include 'Eco Brilliant' and 'Eco Flirtie Eyes' ('Brilliant' × a white form of *P. subulata*) have mauve and white-eyed flowers, respectively. Both were selected by Dr. Don Jacobs at Eco Gardens in Decatur, Georgia.

## Quick Key to Phlox Species

A. Plants prostrate or matted, usually less than 12″ tall
　　B. Leaves narrow-linear, ⅛″ or less wide . . . . . . . *P. subulata*
　　BB. Leaves not narrow-linear, usually at least ½″ wide
　　　　C. Style and stamens much shorter than
　　　　　　corolla tube, plant not stoloniferous . . . . . *P. divaricata*
　　　　CC. Style and stamens about as long as
　　　　　　corolla tube, plant stoloniferous . . . . . . . . *P. stolonifera*
AA. Plants erect, usually more than 12″ tall
　　B. Inflorescence narrowly cylindrical to cone-shaped,
　　　　leaves thick, stem usually purple spotted . . . . . . *P. maculata*
　　BB. Inflorescence broadly pyramidal, leaves
　　　　thin, leaf margins with bristly hairs,
　　　　stem not purple spotted . . . . . . . . . . . . . . . *P. paniculata*

**Additional Reading:**

*Books:*

Wherry, E.T. *The Genus Phlox.* Wickersham Printing Co., 1955.

*Manuscripts:*

DeWolf, G. 1991. Garden phlox. *Horticulture* 69(2):96.
Locklear, J.H. 1994. On fire for phlox. *American Horticulture* 73(6):38–42.
Thomas, Christopher. 1986. The phlox that bloom in the spring. *Horticulture* 64(6):44–50.

## *Phormium* (for-mee′ um)　　　　　Flax Lily　　　　Agavaceae

I include this genus at the request of my West Coast friends, particularly Stephanie Shelton, who has been such a help in preparing this book. The West Coast is about the only area in the country where the genus thrives, although more and more designers and gardeners are using them in large containers as annuals. The two species of large leafy plants, both native to New Zealand, are *P. colensoi* (syn. *P. cookianum*) and the more popular *P. tenax*. Both are winter hardy to zone 8 or 9. The leaves, which are all basal, yield an incredibly tough fiber, thus the common name. When we lived in New Zealand, we marvelled at the colors, forms and toughness of these plants, used equally in succinct highway medians to brilliant town squares. In America, we should use more of these dramatic plants in landscape beds and containers. The lack of available plants makes the exercise more difficult, but still worth trying.

The best form for smaller plants is *P. colensoi* which generally grow 3' tall and bear pendulous flowers, a distinguishing feature from the erect flowers of *P. tenax*. Numerous cultivars have been developed, some of which are hybrids. 'Bronze Elf' has bronze foliage; 'Cream Delight' has soft creamy variegation, growing about 3' tall; 'Jack Spratt' is a dwarf, upright form with pale bronze leaves; 'Maori Chief' and others in the Maori series have bronze leaves striped with pink and red in various patterns; 'Thumbelina', only about 12" tall, provides bronzy purple leaves; 'Yellow Wave' growing up to 4' in height, has leaves strongly variegated with yellow.

*P. tenax* is the best known, due to its magnificent habit and large erect flowers. The leaves often attain lengths of 6-9' and are 2-5" wide. The flowers may then grow up to 15' above the basal foliage. They are usually dull red but may vary to almost pure yellow. Cultivars have been developed to show off leaf color and flowers, and more dwarf forms have also been selected. 'Aurora' produces leaves striped in red, salmon pink and yellow; 'Burgundy' bears deep clret leaves; 'Goldspike' grows about 5' tall and bears yellow striped leaves; 'Guardsman' is erect, grows 5' tall and has bronze leaves striped with red and deep pink; 'Williamsii' has wide green leaves heavily veined in yellow. The tips of the leaves droop slightly.

Plants may be divided (with saw or very strong shovel) or raised from seed.

## *Phuopsis* (foo-op' sis)          Phuopsis          Rubiaceae
(Syn. *Crucinella*)

Only one species, *P. stylosa*, occurs in the genus and is one of those plants you can pass by without seeing, but once having stopped to view it, is not easily forgotten. It is a mat former with long stems of tiny sticky whorled leaves and produces many small pink flowers at the tips. It must be grown in excellently drained soils and is best for rock gardens or hanging off walls.

The flowers and foliage have a peculiar smell, some people find it pleasant, others recoil in horror. Once flowering has occurred in the spring, cut the plants back hard to reduce weediness. I like this plant very much but it is best grown in cooler summer climates and needs to be maintained to ensure flowering. Plants melt out in high humidity, high heat summers. It is short-lived regardless but may reseed vigorously if conditions are to its liking. Cutting back reduces both problems. Plants are perennial to about zone 6 (with protection) but may reseed anywhere.

Propagate from seed, division or cuttings.

## *Phygelius* (fie-geal-ee' us)          Phygelius          Scrophulariaceae

Phygelius is seldom grown as a perennial in American gardens except on the West Coast. These native South African plants are sufficiently cold hardy to about zone 7, but they grow and flower poorly in the heat and humidity of southern gardens. Therefore, the renewed interest in the genus is as a summer annual in areas when cold is too severe but the summers are more to the plants' liking. I love the plants when I see them well grown but my experiences in North America have ended in disappointing long, leggy weedy things. In the Armitage garden, perhaps too much shade was the problem, so I should not be so negative.

Plants are generally semi-evergreen sub-shrubs with a woody base. The lower leaves are opposite but often alternate as they ascend the stem. The tubular flowers are usually one-sided and pendulous, with 5 lobes and pink to orange in color. In mild winters, plants are evergreen to semi-evergreen but in cold winters, they may be killed all the way back to the soil line. Cut back any old growth in the spring just above ground level anyway to induce new vigorous growth. Suckering occurs so plants may spread rather quickly in good sites. All should be planted in full sun and in a well-drained area. Using the lee of a wall is common practice to provide a little more protection from wind and cold. Protective siting and winter mulching may allow plants to survive into zone 6.

Only two species are found; *P. aequalis* with 2–3' tall plants bearing dusty pink flowers and *P. capensis* with 4–6' tall shrubby growth and red and yellow flowers. The hybrid between them (*P. × rectus*), which originally produced pale red pendulous flowers, has been selected to yield some excellent cultivars. Plants flower in summer and can persist into the fall.

Propagate by the suckers or by stem cuttings.

### Cultivars:

'African Queen' has scarlet flowers which are a lighter tone inside.

'Coccineus' is a cultivar of *P. capensis* with long narrow scarlet-red flowers.

'Devil's Tears' bears beautifully vivid scarlet flowers.

'Moonraker' is a popular plant with soft pastel yellow flowers. It is a cross between 'Yellow Trumpet' and 'Winchester Fanfare' and the flower color is similar to the former. The flowers are borne all around the stem rather than on one side as in 'Yellow Trumpet'.

'Pink Elf' is probably the most distinct form of this group. Plants are more compact than most others and bears rosy pink flowers all around the flowering stem.

'Pink Trumpet' produces salmon-pink flowers on 3' tall plants.

'Salmon Leap' has bright rosy salmon flowers.

'Winchester Fanfare' produces one-sided inflorescences of dull red flowers, similar but not as pendulous as 'African Queen'.

'Yellow Trumpet' is a cultivar of *P. aequalis* and has pale yellow flowers with deeper yellow lobes. The plants are compact and vigorous. It has also been offered as 'Cream' and 'Cream Delight'.

**Additional Reading:**

Coombs, A.F. 1988. *Phygelius* in the wild and in cultivation. *The Plantsman* 9(4):233–246.
Lancaster, R. 1993. The dream makers. *The Garden* 118(12):557–559.

*Physalis* (fi-sal-is)               Chinese Lantern               Solanaceae

Of the 80–100 species, only the common Chinese lantern, *P. alkekengi*, is found in American gardens. The name comes from the Greek *physa* meaning bladder and it is mainly grown for its decorative orange fruit which resembles a bladder. It was believed that all members of this genus were edible and of great medicinal value. Sufferers of gout were said to have relieved the disorder by "... taking eight of these berries at each change of the moon." (Miller, P., *The Gardener's Dictionary*, 1805). It became discredited as a medicinal plant by the end of the eighteenth century and all that can now be said is that if some person "... foolishly be invited to taste of the fruit, they will not surely die; for if not their medical virtues, their innocency has been abundantly proved." (Thornton, R.J., *A Family Herbal*, 1814). The annual *P. ixocarpa*, however, is quite edible. It is native to Mexico and the southern United States, and has wonderful names such as jamberberry, tomatillo, and tomatillo ground cherry.

*-alkekengi* (al-ke-ken' jee)          Chinese Lantern          18–24"/24"
    Summer           White          Japan                    Zones 3–9
(Syn. *P. franchetii*)

This species spreads by underground stems and, where it does well, can become a nuisance, creating a definite glut of Chinese lanterns in the neighborhood. The opposite leaves are deltoid-ovate (shaped like a fat arrowhead) and up to 5" long. One inch wide white flowers with yellow stamens are carried singly in the upper leaf axils. The actual fruit is small and cherry-like but is surrounded by the dark orange-red inflated husk, which arises from the mature calyx. Fruit is 2–3" long and up to 6" in circumference. Harvest by late summer because if left on the plant, fruits become skeletonized.

Plant in full sun and provide constant moisture, particularly when the lanterns are developing. Allowing plants to dry out results in weedy looking specimens with small fruit. Fertilize in the spring with side dressing of complete fertilizer but excessive applications may result in luxurious foliar growth with little fruit production.

Seeds should be chilled for 4–6 weeks at 40° F. Germination is very slow and may require 6–8 months. Division in early spring or fall is possible.

**Cultivars:**
'Gigantea' has larger flowers and fruit (up to 8" wide) than the type.
'Pygmaea' grows only 12–15" tall.

*Physostegia* (fie-so' stee-gee-a)          Obedient Plant          Lamiaceae

Twelve species are known; all tall and erect with square stems, and lance-like opposite leaves. The only species cultivated to any extent is *P. virginiana*, known as obedient plant or false dragonhead.

| *-virginiana* (vir-jin-ee-ah' na) | Obedient Plant | 3–4'/3' |
|---|---|---|
| Late Summer          Pink | Eastern United States | Zones 2–9 |

This species grew for many years in our cut flower trials at the University of Georgia because of its straight stems, classic spike-like flower heads, and outstanding flowering. Large clumps are formed which spread vigorously in good soil. Plants not supported flop over, especially in rich soils. This is not a plant for the "nice-guy" gardener, as merciless roguing is needed to keep plants contained. Obedient it is not. The 1" long flowers are normally pinkish and sessile on 12–18" tall spikes. *P. virginiana* is a long day plant and begins to flower in August and continues until late September.

Plants are not fussy as to soil but perform better in acid pH. They are heavy feeders but if too much fertilizer is applied, growth is even more rampant than normal. Plant in well-drained soils in full sun.

**Cultivars:**

'Alba' has white flowers and blooms earlier than the species or cultivars; about 3 weeks earlier than 'Pink Bouquet'. Plants are shorter than the species.

'Grandiflora' has larger flowers and is taller than the species.

'Nana' is only 12–18" tall. 'Alba Nana' is a similar sized white form.

'Pink Bouquet' is a bright pink cultivar which grows 3–4' tall. Plants are beautiful but not self supporting.

'Red Beauty' is not red, but deep pink, at best. However, the plants are vigorous and a little closer to the elusive true red cultivar, which will likely occur some day.

'Summer Snow' has clean white flowers and is a little less invasive than the species.

'Variegata' is a pleasing variegated form in which the leaves are edged white. It reminds me of *Phlox paniculata* 'Norah Leigh' in that the foliage is more outstanding than the flowers.

'Vivid' is 2–3' tall with vibrant pink flowers. It is the most compact and upright of any form.

**Additional Reading:**

Cantino, Philip D. 1980. The systematics and evolution of the genus Physostegia (Labiatae). Ph.D. thesis. Harvard University, 454 p.

Cantino, Philip D. 1982. A monograph of the genus Physostegia (Labiatae). Contributions from the Gray herbarium. 211:1–105.

Scott, B. 1988. Obedient plant. *Horticulture* 66(12):80.

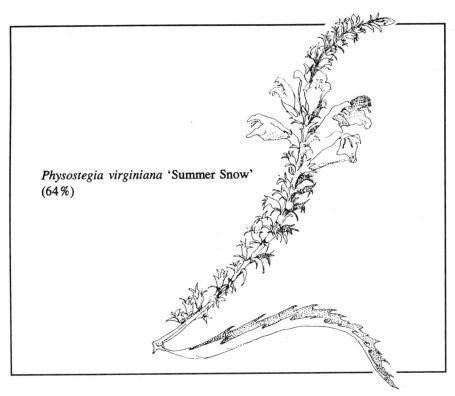

*Physostegia virginiana* 'Summer Snow'
(64%)

*Phyteuma* (fie-tew' ma)          Rampion          Campanulaceae

Not many people know about this diverse genus, consisting of approximately 40 species with violet to blue flowers. They are not exactly commonly available, however, recently some of the more adventurous nurseries, and not just those on the West Coast, have begun to offer them. The leaves are alternate, but often arranged so closely together as to resemble a mound. The flowers are generally arranged in a dense head-like inflorescence (like clustered bellflower, *Campanula glomerata*) and sit just above the foliage. All species prefer full sun and do not like wet feet. The species I prefer is *P. scheuchzeri* sometimes called the weakstem rampion, due to its almost total lack of stem and tufted growth. The clustered blue-mauve flowers are about 6–12″ above the leaves. Plants do better on limed soils and need to have decent drainage, particularly in the winter. Hardy in zones 6 (5 with protection) to 8.

A few other species may also be offered. The spiked rampion, *P. spicata*, is a 2–3′ tall plant with heart shaped basal leaves and large creamy white flower heads. The variety *coeruleum* has blue flowers. *P. orbiculare*, round-headed rampion, grows 1–2′ with rounded violet-blue flower heads in the summer. All are worth trying in zones 5–8.

## *Phytolacca* (fi-to-la′ ca)    Pokeweed    Phytolaccaceae

To recommend pokeweed as a garden plant invites laughter and derision from almost all gardeners, particularly those in the South who curse its very existence. Poke salad, which includes the young leaves of pokeweed, has historically been used as a southern green. However, regardless of your taste, it is not often included in the garden boundaries. The enemy among us is our native American pokeweed, *P. americana*, and not even I will try to talk anyone into its ornamental value.

However, the genus consists of over 30 species and a few of them, believe it or not, are quite handsome. Unfortunately, some of the more civilized species like Indian Poke, *P. acinosa*, are marginally hardy in zone 8, but its tall racemes of creamy flowers with a white margin are intriguing. The species with the most potential however is Chinese Poke, *P. clavigera*, which makes dense plantings of ovate green leaves with white midribs, over which arise cylindrical racemes of pink flowers. They are leafy, to be sure, but they are not as untidy or invasive as our native. Plants have not been tested extensively but should be hardy to about zone 6 or 7. All species produce fleshy purple berries, which can make one seriously ill. Keep little kids away.

The leaves are just as tasty to slugs and other critters as our native species. I planted *P. acinosa* in the Armitage garden and while it was neater and more decorative than the native, it was chewed badly by caterpillars. It also reseeded at the base but was easy to remove.

## *Pimpinella* (pim-pen-el′ la)    Pimpenella    Apiaceae

A relative of the ubiquitous Queen Ann's lace, *Pimpinella* has not caught on in the hearts and dirt of American gardeners. Two species were grown for medicinal purposes, *P. major* and *P. saxifraga*, and one *P. anisum*, aniseseed, is used for cooking. The only one used ornamentally is *P. major* and it is generally only seen as part of the "wild" border. The leaves are pinnately compound with 3–9 segments and each segment is toothed. The finely cut leaves provide a lacy look to the border. The flowers consist of flattened compound umbels and are generally white and look like big obedient roadside weeds.

Plants are native to the British Isles, and south to Portugal in open meadows and hedges. Provide full sun and place in an area where they will not detract from the garden when they decline after flowering. They perform well on the West Coast and are hardy in zones 5–7 elsewhere.

**Cultivars:**

'Rosea' is the best cultivar and the only one worth spending money on. The soft pink flowers rise well above the finely divided foliage.

## *Pinellia* (pie-nel-lee-a)  Pinellia  Araceae

The genus is related to Jack-in-the-pulpit and calla lily but is must less familiar. The woodland plants are natives to China and Japan and grow from a small tuber. Some species have simple heart-shaped leaves, others bear compound leaves, which are generally divided into 3–7 segments and attached to the stems by long petioles. The flowers consist of a rolled up spathe and a long narrow spadix, often with a long "tail." They are not as interesting or spectacular as the Jacks, but they are great fun for the woodland gardener.

A number of useful species are occasionally offered. The most common is *P. pedatisecta*, green dragon, with its compound leaves and long green tail wiggling out of the spathe. Plants reseed where they are growing well. Such places include partially shaded woodland areas in which adequate water is available, I have them planted under oak trees but sometimes insufficient water is available and they do not take off as I had hoped they would. However, if you are a lover of aroids like I am, we just keep trying. Plants are hardy in zones 6–8.

Other good species include *P. tripartita*, which has broad trifoliate (in three parts) leaves and narrow creamy spathes outside and purple inside. The spadix is inside the spathe, and doesn't wiggle out like the previous species.

Propagate by breaking up the tubers or grow from seed.

## *Plantago* (plan-tag' o)  Plantain  Plantaginaceae

Two hundred plus species exist in this genus and at least 190 of them are in my lawn. They are tough, impossible to eradicate, and obnoxious weeds. So why are they in this book about ornamental plants? One man's ceiling is another man's floor, or one person's weed is another person's treasure. Between pulling plantain and cultivating it, life is confusing. The common weed, and its ornamental cousins, is *P. major*, with its wide basal leaves and slender spikes of forgotten flowers.

We have used 'Rubrifolia' effectively for the last few years by combining it with light green foliage or white-flowered short stature plants like *Campanula carpatica* 'White Clips'. As the name suggests, the leaves are purplish and the flower stems are also dark. They are something I would not want too many of, but they make an effective purple spot of color. The foliage does not fade significantly in the heat of the summer. 'Atropurpurea' is more greenish purple than 'Rubrifolia' but they are sold interchangeably. A singularly monstrous form is 'Rosularis' in which a bundle of tangled globular green leaves replace the flower on the scape. A curiosity at best, and sure to spark heated debate on the meaning of ornamental plant. A variegated form ('Variegata') with cream and green leaves is also cultivated. This is sometimes listed as *P. asiatica* 'Variegata'. All cultivars are hardy in zones 4–9.

*Platycodon* (pla-tee-ko' don)    Balloonflower    Campanulaceae

The genus is related to *Campanula, Adenophora,* and *Codonopsis* but is characterized by the inflated flower bud which looks like it will burst as it matures. The only available species, *P. grandiflorus,* is one of the best plants for a child's garden as kids like me are truly fascinated by the size of the buds. The flowers are also distinguished by opening at the top rather than on the sides or at the base.

| *-grandiflorus* (grand-i-flor' us) | Balloonflower | 2½–3'/2' |
|---|---|---|
| Summer | Blue | China, Japan | Zones 3–7 |

The leaves, unequally spaced on the upper part of the stem and often whorled at the base, are sharply serrated, ovate and about 1–3" long. The flowers are usually solitary, 2–3" across and bluish purple. When the "balloon finally pops," it reveals a 5-lobed blossom with rich purple veins and yellow-white stamens. Flowers look particularly good with Coronation Gold yarrow or some of the yellow lysimachias. Platycodon is one of the latest perennials to emerge in spring so care must be taken not to plant over or dig it out accidently during spring cleaning. Full sun is necessary in the North but plants appreciate some protection from the afternoon sun

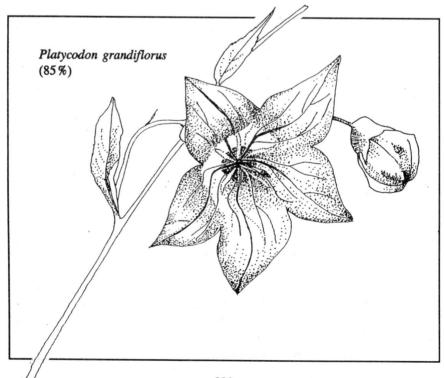

*Platycodon grandiflorus*
(85%)

(i.e., partial shade) in the South. They are long lived and ten-year-old plants are not uncommon. They seldom need dividing, and have few insect or disease pests, making this a truly low maintenance species. However, plants of the species, particularly in the South, are too tall and flop over if support is not provided. This is alleviated by proper cultivar selection.

Seed germinates readily with warm temperature and moisture. Some literature states that Platycodon does not divide well. I have divided and moved clumps in the spring when shoots were 2–4″ tall without damage.

## Cultivars:

'Albus' has white flowers with yellow or bluish veins.

'Apoyama' produces violet flowers on 10–15″ tall plants. An excellent dwarf upright form.

'Apoyama Fairy Snow' is a dwarf white-flowered form.

'Astra' is a seed-propagated dwarf strain (size of Sentimentals) in blue, white and pink. What I have seen is excellent.

'Hakone Double Blue' bears double bright blue flowers on 15–24″ tall plants. The flowers are fuller than those of var. *plenus.*

'Freckles' has white flowers spotted with blue. An introduction from Hillview Gardens in Washington. I have not seen this but hopefully it is not the same as the next item.

'Florovariegata' has white flowers streaked with blue. I received this from an excellent nursery lady, Laurie Crane of Mountainside Nursery in Boonsboro, MD. Unfortunately, the variegation was not stable and after about 3 years, all had reverted to a milky white. Plants were rather tall and weak as well.

'Fuji' series, a seed strain from Japan, with blossoms of pink, white and blue grow 2–3′ tall. They are most suitable for cut flowers.

'Komachi' is 12–24″ tall with clear blue flowers. The bud swells to about 2″ in diameter but never opens. Interesting but frustrating if you are expecting to see them pop.

'Mariesii' is dwarfer (1–2′ tall) and more compact than the species with 2″ diameter flowers. This has always been a reasonably good cultivar but with the advent of more dwarf selections, others have superseded 'Mariesii'.

'Misato Purple' grows 15–18″ tall and bears violet-purple flowers.

'Plenus', a double-flowering form, is interesting but not particularly handsome.

'Sentimental Blue' is an outstanding dwarf selection with large 2″ diameter flowers on 6–9″ tall plants. 'Sentimental White' can sometimes be found but seed availability has been a problem. Other colors, including pink, are being worked on. Flowers from seed the first year.

'Shell Pink' is a seed propagated selection with 2″ wide pink flowers on 18–24″ tall stems.

## Additional Reading:

*Books:*

Bailey, L.H. 1953. *The Book of Bellflowers*. Macmillan Co. (See *Campanula*).

*Manuscripts:*

Dirr, Michael A. 1986. *Platycodon grandiflorus. American Nurseryman* 164(5):202.

Hanes-Fox, R. Plant of the month: Platycodon. *Canadian Gardener* 4(2):9.

## *Podophyllum* (pod-o-fil-um)　　　　May Apple　　　　Berberidaceae

Everyone who has ventured into an Eastern woodlot in the spring has been impressed with the clumps of big shiny green umbrella-like leaves. The trend to more natural gardens and the maturity of our urban woodlots have shot up the popularity of many shady native members and may apple is surely one of them. There are fewer more delightful sights than new leaves of our native *P. peltatum* freshly emerged from the soil, still pulled tight around the stem like a closed parasol. They open slowly to form dark green, palmately lobed umbrellas (peltate), sometimes in patches so thick that the ground beneath them must be experiencing a drought even during torrential rain. The white nodding flowers are formed only on the axil where the leaves form a "V" and can be seen through rather than from above the plants. Plants with only a single leaf will not flower. The fruit start off green and ripen to yellow.

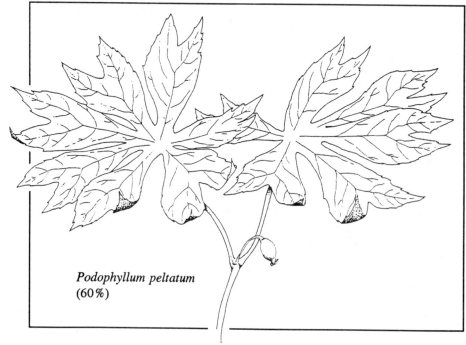

*Podophyllum peltatum*
(60%)

May apple has provided useful medicines for some time. Doses of tea made from the roots eased liver ailments, rheumatism, arthritis and acted as an antidote for poisons and snakebites. It was also used by North American indians to treat tumors and growths of various sorts while resin from the plant was used in the removal of benign warts and skin growths. Reports also showed that the addition of Jacob's ladder, *Polemonium reptans*, to the tea increased its potency.

When teaching these plants to my students we eventually understand terms like "peltate," "axillary" or "palmately compound." These plants illustrate those terms so well that anybody could explain them, however, it all falls apart when someone asks how can this plant be in the same family as Barberry, Mahonia and Nandina. They don't remotely resemble each other. I am left muttering about single ovaries with numerous ovules on a thickened placenta and fruit a berry. Then I remember that other native woodlanders such as twinleaf, blue cohosh and epimedium are also in this family. It is good to know that the taxonomists are as confused as we are. Enjoy the plants, ignore the family.

Our native does not have a lock on the genus, however, as the Chinese species, particularly *P. hexandrum* (syn. *P. emodi*), have gained a significant following. The 3–5 lobed leaves are about 10″ across, each lobe is 3-lobed again at the tip. The rosy white upward-facing flower appears before the leaves emerge or just as they are emerging. The large red fruit occurs in mid summer. Hardy in zone 6–8. Another handsome species is *P. versipelle* with its huge 15″ wide peltate leaves deeply divided into 5–8 lobes. The flowers are borne in umbels, approximately 6–10 per inflorescence, and are usually concealed by the tallest leaf. The flowers are crimson red and unfortunately smell pretty bad. The leaves, however, are wonderful and make the trouble of finding these plants well worthwhile. Hardy to about zone 6.

## *Polemonium* (po-lee-mo′ nee-um)  Jacob's Ladder  Polemoniaceae

Many of the 20–30 species are similar in habit and appearance, and are excellent garden plants. The alternate leaflets are arranged ladder-like along the long leaves. The flowers are usually a shade of blue, but pink, white, and yellow blossoms also occur. Plants range in height from about 3′ (*P. foliosissimum*) to about 8″ (*P. viscosum*). Many are native to Europe and the western United States and are not particularly long-lived in the eastern half of the country (*P. reptans* is an exception). The foliage is very handsome on most species and plants are ornamental, even when not in flower. In general, I have seen little success with the genus south of zone 7a, particularly *P. caeruleum* and *P. foliosissimum*. They are good plants in cooler climates and require full sun to partial shade, and well-drained soil.

Quick Reference to Polemonium Species

| | Height (in.) | Flower color |
|---|---|---|
| *P. caeruleum* | 18–24 | Blue |
| *P. carneum* | 18–24 | Pink |
| *P. pulcherrimum* | 8–12 | Blue, yellow throat |
| *P. reptans* | 8–12 | Light blue |

| | | | |
|---|---|---|---|
| **-*caeruleum*** (se-ru′ lee-um) | | Jacob's Ladder | 18–24″/18″ |
| Summer | Blue | Europe | Zones 2–7 |

The leaves bear up to 20 leaflets which supposedly represent the ladder of which Jacob dreamed and the rest of us climbed. The 3–5″ long basal leaves form dense tufts and are attached to the base of the stem by 4–6″ long petioles. The stem leaves are much smaller and the petiole diminishes until the leaves are sessile at the top of the stem. The leaflets are mostly entire and taper to a long point. The 1″ wide light to deep blue flowers sport yellow stamens and occur in drooping terminal cymes.

Plant in full sun to partial shade in well-drained soils. In general, this species is not tolerant of hot, humid conditions and does not do well south of zone 7, although it will produce many evergreen leaves for a few years. Further north and west, it is a much better plant where flowers will be produced for weeks. Plants have tons of cold hardiness and perform well over a wide geographic range. I have seen excellent stands in zone 6 and in southern Ontario, zone 4.

Propagate by seed or division. Sow seed in a humid, 70–75° F environment. Germination occurs in 2–3 weeks. Remove seedlings from warm, humid environment as soon as first true leaves are visible.

### Cultivars:

'Album' has white flowers which are a pleasant contrast with the dark green leaves.

'Apricot Delight' is a selection from Mileager's Garden in Racine, WI. With apricot-lilac flowers, it is the oddball of the group.

'Brize D'Anjou' is a recent introduction from Blooms of Bressingham and has clean variegated leaves of green and white. They are unique and not easy to overlook. Blue flowers occur in summer.

'Dawn Light' bears clean white flowers on 18″ plants.

'Golden Showers' is a seed-propagated form released recently by Ray Brown of Plant World Botanic Gardens in Devon, UK. According to Ray's description, the foliage ranges from green to fully variegated with freckled and frosted forms between. Normal blue flowers.

'Himalayanum' has larger (up to 1½″ across), deeper blue flowers than the species. This variety was considered to be a separate species (*P. himalayanum*) and may still be offered as such.

'Primadonna' produces light blue flowers on 12–15" plants.

**Related Species:**

*P. boreale*, arctic polemonium, grows 9" tall with ½" diameter blue-purple flowers and 13–23 leaflets per leaf. This species was extolled for years by L.H. Bailey and admired by the English plantsman Graham Stuart Thomas. Its nomenclature is in great need of study. It has been described as a hybrid with *P. reptans*, or as a variety of *P. caeruleum*. Regardless of the location in the taxonomic cupboard, it should be sought out and tried in North American gardens. Hardy at least to zone 3.

*P. foliosissimum*, leafy polemonium, is the best of the upright blue species, if properly grown. It is stouter, stronger, and has larger flowers than *P. caeruleum*. The flowers have bright yellow stamens and plants are exceptionally vigorous. It is longer lived than *P. caeruleum* and produces little seed. The species does not tolerate heat and high humidity. Unfortunately, although native to western United States, it is seldom offered in the United States.

| | | | |
|---|---|---|---|
| *-carneum* (kar-nee' um) | Salmon Polemonium | 18–24"/18" |
| Summer  Pink to Salmon | Western United States | Zones 6–8 |

The reason I include this species is purely selfish. It is a lovely plant but, unfortunately, not as easy to grow as it is beautiful. Generally, the 3–8" long leaf consists of 12–21 leaflets. The 1½" long, pink flowers fade to purplish and are held in lax, few-flowered cymes. Rather fussy about the environment, it does not tolerate heat or full sun and is less cold hardy than other species. Even moisture is required but plants decline rapidly if drainage is poor. However, when sited properly, it is a wonderful plant and if you find a nursery carrying the plant, don't hesitate to try it.

| | | | |
|---|---|---|---|
| *-pulcherrimum* (pul-cher' i-mum) | Skunkleaf Polemonium | 8–12"/12" |
| Summer  Blue, Yellow Throat | Western United States | Zones 3–7 |

This low growing species is particularly suited to a dry stone wall in full sun or partial shade. The leaves are 4–6" long and consist of up to 30 leaflets, although usually fewer than 25. Small (¼" long) flowers are held in dense cymes and are usually blue with a yellow throat but vary to violet on the petals with white interiors.

Propagate by seed or division.

**Related Species:**

*P. pauciflorum* is sometimes called yellow jacob's ladder due to the pale yellow tubular flowers hanging near the ends of the 18" tall stems. Flowers have a bluish to reddish blush and appear during the summer. Likely hardy to zone 7, maybe 6.

| *-reptans* (rep' tanz) | Creeping Polemonium | 8–18"/12' |
|---|---|---|
| Spring    Light Blue | Eastern North America | Zones 2–7 |

This is one of the few eastern species and it is a wild flower through much of the eastern woodlands and the midwest plains. They are excellent foliage plants and provide fresh greenery all season. Plants are seldom over 1' high. The common name is a misnomer as the plant has a shallow rhizome and is not stoloniferous. The stems are weak and diffuse, but the plant doesn't really creep anywhere. The 7–15 leaflets are about 1" long and topped by light blue, ½" long flowers borne in loose drooping clusters (corymbs). If placed in partial shade and kept moist, plants are easy to grow.

**Cultivars:**

'Alba' bears white flowers.

'Blue Pearl' grows 8–10" tall with bright blue flowers.

**Related Species:**

*P.* × *richardsonii* is the name given to hybrids between *P. caeruleum* and *P. reptans*. Plants are about 10–12" tall and are intermediate in their habit. The 1" wide flowers are sky blue and massed at the end of the stems. Flowers appear in early summer but plants are good rebloomers. 'Album' has white flowers.

Quick Key to Polemonium Species

> A. Plants usually less than 18" tall
> > B. Flowers have a yellow or white throat . . . . . *P. pulcherrimum*
> > BB. Flowers same color throughout . . . . . . . . . . . . *P. reptans*
> AA. Plants usually more than 18" tall
> > B. Flowers pink . . . . . . . . . . . . . . . . . . . . . . . . *P. carneum*
> > BB. Flowers blue . . . . . . . . . . . . . . . . . . . . . . . . *P. caeruleum*

**Additional Reading:**

Davidson, J.F. 1950. The genus *Polemonium*. Univ. California Publ. Bot. 23:209–282.

Pritchett, D. 1993. A biosystematic study of California alpine polemoniums. *Fremontia* 21(2):24–26.

*Polianthes* (po-lee' anth-eez)          Tuberose          Agavaceae

This genus consists of over 10 species, however only *P. tuberosa*, the highly fragrant tuberose, is available to American gardeners. The name *Polianthes* may have been derived from *poly*, many, and *anthos*, flower, referring to the many-flowered stalks. Others have suggested that it was derived from *polios*, shining, white, and *anthos*, flower, referring to the shiny flowers. Only Linnaeus knows for sure.

In the early 1900's, North Carolina was one of the major producers of tuberose tubers for export, producing over six million tubers within a 25 mile radius of Magnolia, NC. Today there is little tuber production in this country, most of it having moved to countries where labor is less expensive. Cut flower production, however, is still alive and well in the southern United States and California.

| *-tuberosa* (tew-ber-o' sa) | | Tuberose | 3–4'/3' |
|---|---|---|---|
| Late Summer, Fall | White | Mexico | Zones 7–10 |

Best known for its fragrance and glistening white blossoms, tuberose bears the flowers that look like they have just been waxed. The fragrance is delicious to some and overbearing to others. Flowers are still used for weddings and 1 or 2 stems is all that is needed to scent an entire room. The plant is derived from a tuberous rootstock, thus the name "tuberose." The leaves are linear, channeled, and spotted with brown on the underside. The 2–2½" long white, funnel-shaped flowers appear on a 2–3' raceme between August and October.

Since tuberose is a heat-loving species, tubers must be started in the house or greenhouse in the spring before soils are warm. Alternatively, plant in the ground after the threat of frost. After the first fall frost, lift the tubers and hang them in a warm (45–50° F), dry place. In the Carolinas, Georgia, parts of Tennessee, Florida, the Gulf Coast states and much of California, plants are perennial under most winters if mulch is provided. The best mulch is the layer of dead leaves which carpets the ground after the first hard frost.

Tuberose may be propagated from offshoots removed in the fall when tubers are dug and replanted the following spring.

## Cultivars:
'Gracilis' has narrower leaves and flowers with longer tubes.

'Marginata' is a variegated form of tuberose, with white margins on the narrow leaves. Only growing 8–12" tall, this miniature is more of a collectors item than a plant grown for the fragrant flowers. If it is a collectors item, you know it will be difficult to locate.

'Mexican Single' is a better cultivar with flowers more closely spaced on the stalk.

'The Pearl', a double-flowered form, has been around for ages and is the best cultivar for the garden. This is one of the unusual instances where doubling the flower petals is a definite improvement. However, it is not as good a cut flower as the single forms because the extra petals decline and turn brown more rapidly.

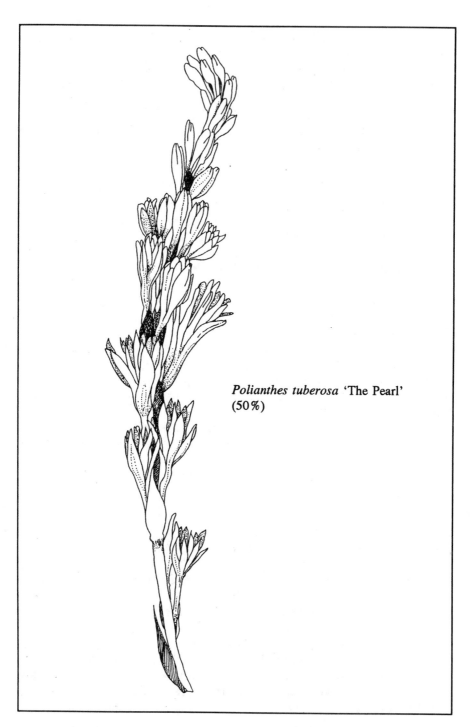

*Polianthes tuberosa* 'The Pearl'
(50%)

***Polygonatum*** (po-lig-o-nay' tum)     Solomon's Seal     Liliaceae

Of the approximately 60 species, a number have left the realm of wild flowers and joined the mainstream of garden plants. The botanical name comes from *poly*, many, and *gonu*, knee joints, referring to the many jointed rhizome from which the leaves rise. The common name Solomon's seal may have been derived from the circular sunken scars that remain on the rootstock after the leaf stalks die and fall off; the scar somewhat resembles a seal impressed on wax on official documents or letters in former times. Gerard, the English plantsman, believed the powdered roots were an excellent remedy for broken bones. He wrote in the late 1590's that roots pulverized and drunk in ale, "soddereth and gleweth together the bones in a very short space ..." He believed that this property of sealing wounds was why the plant received the name Solomon's seal.

Most species are comprised of long, graceful, unbranched shoots bearing alternate leaves and whitish, pendulous flowers hanging from the leaf nodes. They range in height from the 6″ tall *P. humile*, dwarf Solomon's seal, to great Solomon's seal, *P. commutatum*, whose stems may grow 7′ long. The main reason for including these plants in the garden is their architectural qualities. The leaf orientation is delightful and the variegated forms are particularly showy. Leaves persist until frost and turn a lovely brownish yellow in the fall. The 1–3″ diameter blue-black fruit is interesting if not spectacular and adds to the charm. Placed in the company of red-flowered plants, red colors are redder and bright colors brighter. An indispensable genus for the landscape architect.

Plants tolerate heavy shade and grow well in shady, moist areas. All are readily propagated in the fall by division of the rootstock. It is necessary to leave at least one bud on the divisions. Seed should be stratified at 40° F for 6 weeks before sowing.

Quick Reference to Polygonatum Species

| | Height (in.) | Flower color | Flowers per axil |
|---|---|---|---|
| *P. biflorum* | 12–36 | White | 1–3 |
| *P. commutatum* | 36–72 | White | 3–8 |
| *P. humile* | 6–9 | White | 1–2 |
| *P. odoratum* | 18–24 | White | 1–2 |

***-biflorum*** (bi-flo' rum)     Small Solomon's Seal     1–3′/2′
    Spring     White-Green     Eastern North America     Zones 3–8

This North American species extends as far north as New Brunswick, south to Florida, and west to the Mississippi Valley in shady, cool, woodland areas. The 4–4½″ long, alternate leaves are nearly sessile, and have 2–5 main nerves running down the leaves, although only the midrib is prominent toward the leaf tip. The ½–¾″ flowers are greenish white and occur in pairs beneath the arching stems. There is significant variation in the species and flowers may be bunched in 3's and 4's, although 2 flowers per node is the most common.

Plants require shade and moisture and are easily propagated by division of the rhizome.

*-commutatum* (kom-mew-tah′ tum)   Great Solomon's Seal   3–7′/4′
Late Spring   White-Green   United States to Mexico   Zones 3–7
(Syn. *P. giganteum*, *P. canaliculatum*)

A plant which truly needs space, it will gobble up all available acreage as its wings expand. Plants have been known to reach 7′ in height (although 5′ is more reasonable) and may form colonies equally wide, so it is not a good subject for the average suburban garden. However, there are few plants more outstanding on the edge of moist woodland areas where the 3–7″ long leaves can be displayed to advantage. Approximately 10 prominent nerves extend the full length of the leaves. The ¾″ long yellowish green to whitish green flowers are held in a 3–8-flowered umbel in the leaf axils. At one time, this species was lumped in with *P. biflorum* causing considerable confusion.

*-humile* (hum-e′ lee)   Dwarf Solomon's Seal   5–9″/3″
Spring   White-Green   China, Japan, Korea   Zones 5–8

After seeing many of the pendulous species of Solomon's seal rising to 3–4′ in height, the appearance of this little guy is surprising, but equally delightful. Early in the spring, they pop out of the ground, flowers already formed, and rise straight up, to the imposing 5–9″ height. Generally one, sometimes two, whitish flowers are formed at the axil but many of the new stems may have none at all. Plants spread nicely, forming a decent clump in 2–3 years. I received some plants from the fine plantsman, Charles Cresson of Swarthmore, PA, and they have thrived in the Armitage garden under conditions of moderate shade. A great plant.

There are at least three names being given to the dwarf forms, some which are out and out wrong and others which may represent other dwarf forms. Plants have been listed as *P. falcatum*, which normally grows at least 18″ tall, usually 2–3′. The dwarf form of *P. falcatum* ('Pumilum') is still 15″ tall. *P. hookeri* is only 3–5″ tall but bears lilac to purplish flowers. *P. hirtum* is also relatively small but usually bears 3–5 flowers at each axil. Therefore, my money stays on *P. humile* until the next revision.

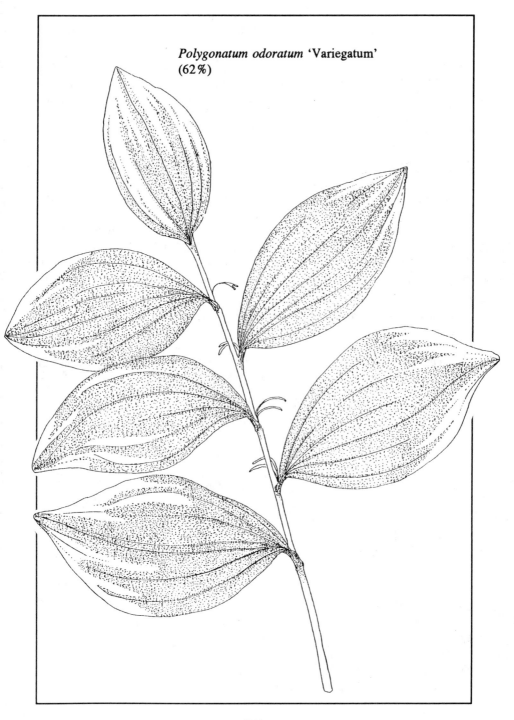

*Polygonatum odoratum* 'Variegatum'
(62%)

*-odoratum* (o-do-rah' tum)     Fragrant Solomon's Seal     18–24″/2′
   Spring      White-Green     Europe, Asia     Zones 3–8
(Syn. *P. officinale*)

The 1″ long white flowers are constricted at the base and wear a skirt of yellow green. They usually occur in pairs, occasionally singly, dangling from the leaf axils underneath the leaves. On quiet spring evenings, the flowers exude a subtle lily-like fragrance. The stems are somewhat angular and carry 8–12 lance-like leaves along their 18″ length.

### Cultivars:
'Thunbergii' is bigger and stouter in every way than the species. Shoots grow 3′ tall, leaves are up to 6″ long and flowers are 1–1½″ long.
'Variegatum', with its soft green leaves edged in a broad strip of creamy white, is the best form of this species. The variegation makes the plant jump out, and is a bright addition to dull shade. Flowers appear in mid April in the South, a few weeks later to the North, and persist for 2–3 weeks. They make excellent cut stems whose clean lines add beauty to any arrangement.

### Related Species:
*P.* × *hybridum* is a hybrid between *P. multiflorum*, Eurasian Solomon's seal, and *P. odoratum* and is intermediate between the parents. 'Flore-pleno', has double, more persistent flowers. 'Striatum' has leaves which are striped creamy white, and not just on the edges as in *P. odoratum* 'Variegata'. The differences between the two variegated forms are minor and plants are probably mixed up in the trade.

### Quick Key to Polygonatum Species
   A. Plant usually less than 3′ tall, 1 or 2 flowers per axil
     B. Plants less than 10″ tall . . . . . . . . . . . . . . . . . *P. humile*
    BB. Plants more than 10″ tall
       C. Major veins 1–5, leaves slightly hairy
         beneath, usually 2 flowers per axil with
         little or no fragrance . . . . . . . . . . . . . . . . *P. biflorum*
      CC. Major veins more than 5, leaves not
        hairy underneath, 1–2 flowers per axil
        with obvious fragrance . . . . . . . . . . . . . *P. odoratum*
  AA. Plant more than 3′ tall, usually 4–5′,
     3–8 flowers per axil . . . . . . . . . . . . . . . . . *P. commutatum*

### Additional Reading:
Martin, C. 1993. Herbalist's notebook. *Mother Earth* 136:52–53, 82.
Ownby, R.P. 1944. The liliaceous genus *Polygonatum* in North America. *Ann. Missouri Bot. Garden* 31:373–413.
Stroombeek, C. 1993. The ONA's plant selection committee's 1992 recommendations. *Perennial Plant* 1(2):31–33.

***Polygonum*** (po-lig′ o-num)    Smartweed, Knotweed    Polygonaceae
(Syn. *Persicaria*)

Let's dispense with the name thing immediately. Many taxonomists have sliced up the entire genus and placed nearly all of it into *Persicaria*, and a few into *Fallopia*. However, many other taxonomists disagree and have retained *Polygonum* pretty much intact. Rather than change something which may be changed right back again, I have retained everything in *Polygonum*. The plants can't read, so lets not fret about what name is correct.

Although most of the approximately 150 species are not ornamental, a few make welcome additions to the garden palette. In this country, polygonums have been colored with a "weedy" crayon, due to the persistence of such unwelcome guests as *P. aviculare*, the common knotgrass of lawns and patios, *P. pensylvanicum*, Pennsylvania smartweed, and the most common of all our weeds, *P. persicaria*, lady's thumb. Unfortunately, these intruders have blinded gardeners and nurserymen alike to the beauty of some of the cultivated species. Indeed, it is a determined gardener who grows the better species as they are almost impossible to find in catalogs or nurseries. I find it difficult to understand why so few nurserymen are offering the garden worthy selections that abound throughout England and the rest of Europe.

All species have alternate leaves and many have somewhat swollen leaf nodes. Its name has the same roots as that of *Polygonatum* (which see), but *gonu* refers to the jointed stems rather than jointed rhizomes in this genus. Several climbing species occur such as the handsome silver fleece-vine, *P. aubertii*, and annual black bindweed, *P. convolvulus*, which can be an incredibly tiresome pest. Other species may attain heights of 5–7′ and require ample space. The big, stoloniferous forms have received a lot of unfair press about their aggressive nature, however, our ignorance about where to site it or how to take advantage of its obvious attributes, should reflect on the gardener, not the plant. Obviously, they need a lot of room. So be it, give them room and enjoy them or leave them be.

*P. amplexicaule*, mountain fleeceflower, can be a noble, beautiful plant and magnificent cultivars such as the blood red 'Atrosanguineum' are even better. *P. molle*, *P. rude*, and *P. sachalinense* are handsome and look wonderful in a large shady setting where space is not a concern. Otherwise they should be left to others. On the other hand, the leaves of *P. vaccinifolium* are less than 1″ long and plants are less than 1′ tall. Long pink flower spikes rise above the spreading plants. People tend to run from many of the more vigorous forms not because they aren't ornamental (in some cases, showstoppers), but because of their tendency to colonize huge areas. Once established, they do not go gently into that good night; small land mines are needed to eradicate them. However, with the selection of clumping forms of the taller species, they are beginning to creep into commerce once again.

Plants known as magic carpet, *P. capitatum*, must be mentioned here although it is an annual in most of the country. Some references list it as cold hardy to zone 6 but it dies in zone 7. However, plants often reseed themselves and this low-growing specimen with gorgeous foliage and pretty pink, dense, globular flowers is well worth planting in shady or sunny locations.

Most species are comfortable in semi-shade with constant moisture. While they are not bog plants, dry soil inhibits establishment. Unfortunately, the more ornamental species are not particularly heat tolerant and perform poorly south of zone 7. However, heat tolerance is improved if consistent moisture is available.

All species are easily propagated from division and most may be raised from seed.

### Quick Reference to Polygonum Species

|                  | Height (in.) | Flower color |
|------------------|--------------|--------------|
| *P. affine*      | 6–9          | Rose-red     |
| *P. amplexicaule*| 36–60        | Red          |
| *P. bistorta*    | 18–30        | Pink         |
| *P. vaccinifolium*| 6–12        | Rose-pink    |

**-affine** (a-fee′ nee)   Himalayan Fleeceflower   6–9″/12″
  Summer, Fall   Rose-Red   Himalayas   Zone 3–7
(Syn. *Persicaria affinis*)

Whenever I think of this species, I think of the stairs descending towards the water garden at Wakehurst Place in Ardingly, England. The bank along the stairs and the area leading to the small stream are covered with the small rosy-red spikes of *P. affine*. Although there are far grander plants and displays at Wakehurst, I always look forward to that bank of polygonum when I return.

Plants are most effective as front of the border subjects or ground covers, bearing erect, mostly basal leaves (2½–4″ long) which taper to the petiole. The deep green 4″ long leaves turn bronze in fall. Numerous deep rose-red flowers are arranged in dense 2–3″ long terminal spikes and turn whitish as they mature. Plants are most effective in cool, moist areas and provide stability and beauty to a troublesome bank, or carpet stones in a rock garden. It is not as invasive as many of the other species and may be controlled with selective pruning. Some shade is tolerated but full sun and moisture are necessary for dense plantings.

The easiest method of propagation is division in the spring or fall. Terminal cuttings (3–4″ long) and seed propagation are also effective. Seeds require stratification (place in moist sand or peat moss at 40° F for 6–8 weeks).

**Cultivars:**
'Border Jewel' bears dark red flowers over deep green foliage which turns
    red in the fall. About 8-12" tall.
'Darjeeling Red' has deep pink flowers and is a vigorous selection.
'Dimity' is smaller and more refined (if a polygonum can be called refined)
    than other selections. Pink upright flowers on 4-6" tall plants.
'Donald Lowndes' is about 8-10" tall and carries double salmon-pink
    flowers. An excellent selection for American gardens.
'Superbum' is more vigorous than other cultivars and the pink flowers turn
    crimson as they mature.

**Related Species:**
*P. milettii* (syn. *P. sphaerostachyum*), Millet's knotweed grows 18-24"
tall and is similar to *P. affine* in that most of the leaves arise from the base
of the plant and narrow, dense spikes of flowers. The flowers are a magnificent deep crimson and are held on long flower stalks extending well above
the foliage. Copious moisture and partial shade are necessary for suitable
growth. Hardy in zones 4-7.

| *-amplexicaule* (am-pleks-i-kaw' lee) | Mountain Fleeceflower | 4-6'/3' |
|---|---|---|
| Summer          Red | Himilayas, China | Zones 4-7 |

(Syn. *Persicaria amplexicaulis*)

A plant which, regardless of what the catalogs say, requires significant
space in the garden. It is a stout, clumping species which can flower from
summer until the first frost. The alternate leaves are longer than wide and
somewhat pointed at the tips. A characteristic to this species is the obvious
manner in which the leaves clasp the stem (*amplexicaulis* means leaves
clasping stems). The flowers, which may be pink, red or white, arise in
short spikes at the ends of the stems in summer and fall. I have seen some
marvelous plantings of polygonum in the equally marvelous gardens at
Wave Hill on the Hudson River in New York.
    The plants do not spread as rapidly as some of the other stoloniferous
forms but they still form dense large clumps which get denser and larger
with time. Pickaxe or backhoe is needed if removal becomes necessary. Full
sun and consistently moist soils are needed for best performance.
    Propagate by division of the clump; be careful of your back.

**Cultivars:**
'Atrosanguineum' is as big as the species but bears deep crimson-red flowers.
'Firetail' is the best cultivar in this group of big clumpers. Plants grow about
    4' tall with large heart-shaped clasping leaves and crimson flower spikes
    which, if grown well, can be 6" long. Known as 'Speciosum' in Europe.
'Inverleith' bears dark crimson flowers on short spikes on 3-4' tall plants.

**Related Species:**

*P. campanulatum*, lesser knotweed, is a creeping, stoloniferous species which grows 3-5' tall, and bears white or pink-red flowers in dense panicles. The narrow leaves generally have purple midribs. Look out!

*P. japonica* (syn. *P. cuspidatum, Fallopia japonica, Reynoutria japonica*), Japanese knotweed, is a creeping, clumping form which can also get out of hand. Plants grow about 6' tall and bear creamy white flowers. Avoid the species; 'Compactum' is only about 18" tall and bears pink flowers in the summer. 'Spectabilis ('Variegata') is big but at least it has unique leaves splashed with white, yellow and pink. I didn't say it was pretty, only unique. It will also colonize your neighbor's place.

| | | | |
|---|---|---|---|
| *-bistorta* (bis-tor' ta) | | Snakeweed | 18-30"/30" |
| Early Summer | Pink | Europe, Asia | Zones 3-7 |

(Syn. *Persicaria bistorta, P. regelianum*)

This clump-forming plant has 4-6" long, wavy, medium green leaves with a striking white midrib. Most leaves arise from the base of the plant and form handsome clumps even when not in flower. The flowers, however, are held well above the foliage and are made up of 4-5" long dense spikes of soft pink. The stamens of the individual flowers protrude resulting in a bottle brush appearance. The flowers are long lasting and are used as a cut flower in the florist trade. They look terrific in Chicago Botanical Garden and throughout the Midwest and North.

Propagate similar to *P. affine*.

**Cultivars:**

'Carneum' has cherry red flowers with contrasting white stamens. Plants are actually a subspecies (ssp. *carneum*) but may also be incorrectly labeled as a species (*P. carneum*).

'Superbum' is larger with bigger flowers than the species and is superior to the species. This cultivar is easier to find than other polygonums mentioned here.

| | | | |
|---|---|---|---|
| *-vaccinifolium* (va-seen-i-fo' lee-um) | Vaccinium Fleece Flower | 6-12"/18" |
| Late Spring | Rose-Pink | Himalayas | Zones 5-7 |

The antithesis of the large bullying polygonums must be this rock covering, ground hugging species. The elliptical leaves are ½-¾" long, smooth, entire and acute at both ends (somewhat like a cranberry, *Vaccinium*). The long woody stems may be up to 3' long and the 2" long spikes of rosy pink flowers arise from the dense foliage in late spring and early summer.

I first saw this plant in Christchurch Botanic Garden in Christchurch, New Zealand. It took on the shape of the large rock beneath it and was absolutely covered with flowers, to the point that leaves were not visible.

Terrific for cooler summers and well-drained soils. An excellent rock garden plant.

## Quick Key to Polygonum Species

A. Plants taller than 18″
  B. Plants taller than 3′ . . . . . . . . . . . . . . . *P. amplexicaule*
BB. Plants less than 3′ . . . . . . . . . . . . . . . . . . . . . *P. bistorta*
AA. Plant less than 18″ tall
  B. Length of leaves greater than 2″ long,
    plants taller than 12″ . . . . . . . . . . . . . . . . . . . . *P. affine*
BB. Length of leaves less than 1″, plants
    usually less than 12″ tall . . . . . . . . . . . . *P. vaccinifolium*

**Additional Reading:**

Anon. Japanese knotweed. Kew Information Sheet T5, Royal Botanic Gardens, Kew, England.
Goode, Jeanne. 1983. Smartweeds. *Horticulture* 61(8):26–29.

## *Polystichum* (po-lis′ ti-kum)      Holly Fern      Polypodiaceae

Over 200 species belong to this large genus of ferns, some native to wide areas of North America, others to Europe and the Far East. Most are course, rigid ferns and most are evergreen. They are small to medium size terrestrial ferns, a few of which are very popular in American gardens. The stalk and rachis (the main axis of the leaf) are highly scaled and the spores are contained in rows of round indusia (spore cases) on the underside of the fronds. They do not occur on separate stems (like cinnamon fern). Partial shade and moist soils are necessary for best performance.

## Quick Key to Polystichum Species

|  | ×-pinnate | Color of stripe |
|---|---|---|
| *P. acrostichoides* | 1 | Rusty |
| *P. polyblepharum* | 1 | Rusty |
| *P. setiferum* | 2 | Rusty |
| *P. tsus-sinense* | 2 | Black |

*-acrostichoides* (a-kro-sti-koi′ deez)     Christmas Fern     12–18″/12″
                                 North America     Zones 4–8

A very common woods fern, particularly in the East, and the easiest species to establish. The common name came from the fact that the fern is green at

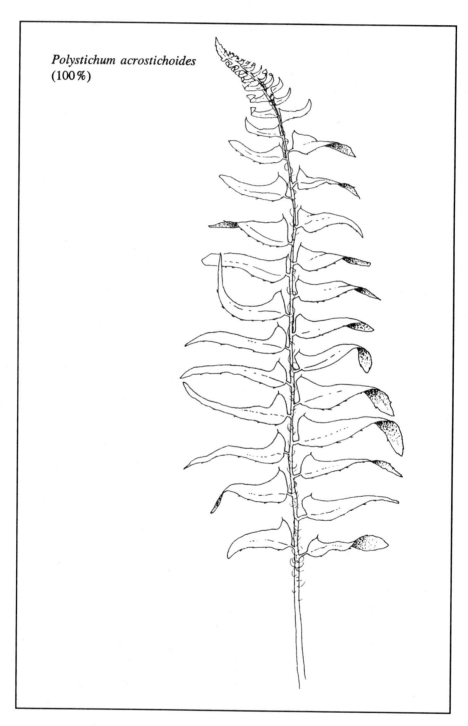

*Polystichum acrostichoides*
(100%)

Christmas although it is mainly the sterile fronds which remain green, the fertile ones tend to wither. The spores are borne on sharply reduced pinna (leaflets) on the top one third of the fertile fronds. The fronds are wider in the middle than at either end and each pinna has an "ear" on the one side. The other characteristic that occurs is that the bottom two pinna are usually pointed down.

Describing fern morphology is boring and does not begin to describe reasons for including it in the garden. Christmas fern has a classic fern shape and its ease of growth and evergreen nature are wonderfully rewarding. It does not compete with other larger, more colorful ferns, but it is tough and undemanding. In the Armitage garden, ferns cohabitat with hostas and wildflowers and make the shade that much more pleasant.

**Related Species:**

*P. braunii*, Braun's holly fern, is more common in the northern states than in the South. The leaflets (pinna) are cut into about a dozen subleaflets, giving this semi-evergreen plant a much finer feel than Christmas fern. New fronds have a silvery flush to them and as they mature, turn glossy green. Easily grown.

*P. munitum* is the Western equivalent to the Christmas fern. It differs by having more pointed and longer fronds. Evergreen, smaller and hardy to zone 5.

| | | |
|---|---|---|
| *-polyblepharum* (pol-lee-bleph-a' rum) | Tassel Fern | 15–24"/20" |
| | Japan, Korea | Zones 6–8 |

The evergreen glossy green fronds make this one of the most handsome ferns available. The base of the stipes are heavily tufted with membranous brown scales and bear fronds 12–20" long and about 10" wide.

Not as easy to establish as Christmas fern, nor as vigorous, but well grown specimens are unbeatable, shimmering in the shaded garden unlike any other.

| | | |
|---|---|---|
| *-setiferum* (say-ti' fe-rum) | Soft Shield Fern | 1–2'/18" |
| | Europe | Zones 5–7 |

These ferns are not seen as much as other species probably because American gardens tend to be hotter and more humid than their native habitat. The other reason it is not seen as much is simply that it is seldom offered, certainly relative to more popular cinnamon and Christmas ferns. Plants form a rosette which are handsomely dissected and usually soft to the touch. The light green fronds unfurl over a long period of time and look like a tight knot at the top of each one. The knot is often a softer, more cinnamon color than the fronds. Soft shield fern is immensely popular in Europe and the West Coast and over 300 cultivars have been selected.

**Cultivars:**

'Acutilobum' has sharply pointed leaflets (pinnae) on the narrow fronds.

'Congestum' is shorter and more compact than the species and carries dense fronds with overlapping leaflets.

'Cristatum' has the ends of the fronds crested. Awful thing.

'Divisilobum' has arching greatly dissected fronds.

'Herrenhausen' has finely divided fronds on a 10–12″ plant.

'Proliferum' is known as Alaska fern and is more cold hardy than the other selections. Fronds are finely divided and plants are 12–18″ tall.

'Rotundatum' produces almost round leaflets (pinnae) on the upright fronds. There is also a crested form ('Rotundatum Cristatum').

| *-tsus-sinense* (tsoo-see-men′ see) | Korean Rock Fern | 1–2′/2′ |
|---|---|---|
| | Japan | Zones 6–8 |

Handsome ferns for well-drained location, they are characterized by the contrast of the black stems with the green fronds. They are not dwarf but they seldom grow more than a foot tall. Well-grown plants may attain 2′ in diameter.

In the Armitage garden, plants do not thrive, but nor do they badly struggle. They grow very slowly and one has to look hard to be overwhelmed. However, in small groups or set against a natural rock background, they are impressive.

<u>Quick Key to Polystichum Species</u>

    A. Fronds simple, only 1-pinnate
        B. Lower pair of pinna pointing downwards,
            fronds green but not glossy . . . . . . . . . . *P. acrostichoides*
        BB. Lower pair of pinna not pointing downward,
            fronds glossy green . . . . . . . . . . . . . . *P. polyblepharum*
    AA. Fronds 2-pinnate
        B. Rachis green, fronds soft to the touch . . . . . . . . *P. setiferum*
        BB. Rachis black, fronds not particularly
            soft to the touch . . . . . . . . . . . . . . . . . *P. tsus-sinense*

## *Potentilla* (po-ten-till′ a)   Cinquefoil   Rosaceae

Most of the 500 species of cinquefoil are herbaceous, although the best known and probably the most useful species in North American gardens is the woody bush cinquefoil, *P. fruticosa*. Cinquefoils prefer cool soils and cool nights to look their best but there are few areas where plants are as pretty as the catalog photo. I am not familiar with any species doing well south of zone 7a, although not all species and cultivars have been tested.

Many herbaceous species are offered in the trade (more than this genus warrants); some are seed propagated resulting in significant variation.

The name comes from *potens*, meaning powerful, in reference to the supposed usefulness of the genus in medicine and magic. In particular, common cinquefoil, *P. reptans*, was considered most effective against ague (chills, fever). The number of leaves needed was immaterial as long as "Jupiter is in the ascendant and the Moon applying to him" (Culpepper, 1649). Rudimentary dentists also provided their unsuspecting patients with a root concoction because "the decoction of the roots held in the mouth doth mitigate the paine of the teeth." (Gerard, 1597).

Most cinquefoils have palmate leaves, which people may mistake for strawberries, and are seldom more than 2' tall. The 5-petaled flowers may be yellow, red, rose, or white. Many species, useful for the rock garden, form lovely mats of 4–12" tall foliage.

Quick Reference to Potentilla Species

|                    | Height (in.) | Flower color | Leaves in 3's or 5's |
|--------------------|--------------|--------------|----------------------|
| *P. atrosanguinea* | 18–30        | Red          | 3                    |
| *P. nepalensis*    | 12–24        | Purple       | 5                    |
| *P. recta*         | 12–30        | Yellow       | 5                    |
| *P. tabernaemontani* | 6–9        | Yellow       | 5                    |
| *P. tridentata*    | 6–12         | White        | 3                    |

| *-atrosanguinea* (at-ro-sang-guin' ee-a) | Himalayan Cinquefoil | 18–30"/24" |
|---|---|---|
| Summer | Red | Himalayas | Zones 5–7 |

Having seen this in numerous places around the world, I can confidently state that its main contribution to gardening is as a parent for a number of named hybrids, and not for its own beauty and performance. The silky-hairy leaves are three-parted with toothed margins. The 5–8" long petioles make the plant look stretched by early summer. The 1" wide flowers are deep red but plants are not particularly floriferous. Full sun, cool nights and good drainage are prerequisites for good performance.

Propagate the species by seed and the hybrids by division.

**Related Species:**
Var. *argyrophylla*, undersnow cinquefoil, is similar to Himalayan cinquefoil except that the flowers are yellow rather than red. Formally known as *P. argyrophylla*.

*P.* × *bicolor* (syn. *P.* × *menziesii*) resulted from crosses between *P. atrosanguinea* var. *argryophylla* and *P. atrosanguinea*. The silvery-gray foliage is often as decorative as the flowers. Many of today's garden hybrids have been selected from this hybrid.

**Hybrids:**

'Firedance' only grows 12″ tall, is more compact and produces deep coral flowers.

'Flamenco' has blood red flowers with a dark eye. They can stretch to 2′ tall.

'Gibson's Scarlet' was highly touted as a tough, brilliantly colored plant but has not lived up to expectations in the United States. The flowers are deep scarlet and plants are more compact than *P. atrosanguinea*.

'Gold Kugel' is an orange-golden-flowered selection which tends to get a little weedy.

'Glory of Nancy' ('Gloire de Nancy') is an old hybrid with large, 2″ wide double flowers of red and gold. It also has lovely gray-green leaves and is one of the better hybrids.

'Hamlet' is a scarlet double flowered form.

'Monsieur Rouillard' bears double orange-red flowers.

'Reyneur' also has scarlet semi-double flowers with a very small black center.

'Vulcan' has deep red double flowers, growing only about 12″ tall.

'William Rollinson' has semi-double vermillion flowers with yellow reverse. Plants grow about 15″ tall.

'Yellow Queen' has bright yellow single flowers over silvery foliage and attains but 12″ in height.

| *-nepalensis* (ne-pa-len′ sis) | | Nepal Cinquefoil | 12–24″/20″ |
|---|---|---|---|
| Summer | Crimson | Nepal | Zones 4–7 |

This single-flowered species produces many strawberry-like purple to crimson flowers in early summer and continues to flower sporadically throughout the summer. Although flowering continues for a relatively long time, plants only persist for 2–3 years in most settings. The basal leaves are long stalked, up to 1′ long, and the 2″ long leaflets are coarsely toothed. The 1″ wide flowers are rose-red and held in loose, branching panicles. The plant is compact until the long leafy stems rise up to 2′ or more in the summer, at which time severe pruning is necessary.

The species and cultivars arise fairly true from seed.

**Cultivars:**

'Miss Wilmott' (var. *willmottiae*) is 10–12″ tall and produces carmine flowers with a darker base. It is a better choice than the species.

'Melten Fire' has strawberry red flowers with a flush of lemon yellow and purple centers.

'Roxana' bears orange-scarlet flowers on 18″ stems.

**Related Species:**

*P.* × *hopwoodiana*, a cross between *P. nepalensis* and *P. recta*, the weedlike sulphur cinquefoil, is about 18″ tall with pink flowers, rosy red at the base and edged white on the margins.

*P. thurberi*, thurber cinquefoil, is native to New Mexico and California. It is shorter than *P. nepalensis* and commonly has 7 leaflets rather than 5. The flowers are a rich dark brown to purple and are held in an open inflorescence. In *P. nepalensis*, the petals are nearly twice as long as the sepals but are about the same size in *P. thurberi*. From the garden viewpoint, there is little difference between them, although *P. thurberi* may be longer lived and more heat tolerant.

*P. × tonguei*, a cross between *P. anglica* and *P. nepalensis*, is offered by many nurserymen. It has lovely salmon, single flowers with a pinkish center. Plants are only 3–8″ tall and make a pretty ground cover for sunny area. Cold hardy to zone 5, it has problems with heat above zone 7.

| *-recta* (rek′ ta) | | Sulphur Cinquefoil | 12–30″/15″ |
|---|---|---|---|
| Summer | Yellow | Southern Europe | Zones 3–7 |

Introduced from Europe, this species can be a troublesome weed, particularly in the limestone areas of the Midwest and Northeast. Plants are tufted with leaves consisting of 5–9 toothed, densely-hairy leaflets each about 2–3″ long. Three-quarter inch diameter yellow flowers are carried on terminal compact corymbs.

All are easily seed propagated under warm (70–75° F) moist conditions. Plants may also be divided after 2–3 years.

### Cultivars:

Var. *sulphurea* is similar to the species but has sulphur-yellow flowers.
'Macrantha' (var. *warrenii*) has 1″ diameter bright yellow flowers in loose terminal clusters. It is not as weedy as the species and flowers for a longer time. This is the best form of the species for the garden.

### Related Species:

*P. megalantha* (syn. *P. fragiformis*), native to Japan, has a fuzzy cuddly rosette of leaves consisting of 3 leaflets. The plants are 6–8″ tall and bear solitary 1–2″ wide bright yellow flowers in the spring.

| *-tabernaemontani* (ta-ber-nay-mon-tah′ nee) | Spring Cinquefoil | 6–9″/12″ |
|---|---|---|
| Spring          Yellow | Western Europe | Zones 4–7 |

(Syn. *P. neumanniana*)

The name keeps changing on this dwarf plant, darting in and out of *P. tabernaemontani*, *P. verna* and now *P. neumanniana*. However, they work well in well drained sunny areas regardless of the name. The mat-producing species has numerous decumbent 2–5″ long rooting stems. The long-petioled leaves are 5–7 palmate, wedge-shaped and serrated near the apex. The ½″ wide golden yellow flowers are held in 3–5-flowered cymes at the end of 6–8″ long ascending stems.

**Cultivars:**

'Nana' is only about 4″ tall and covered with golden yellow flowers almost the same size as the species. The best of the species.

**Related Species:**

*P. aurea*, golden cinquefoil, is also a low growing potentilla (8–10″) with yellow flowers. *P. aurea* has fewer stems and smaller flowers than spring cinquefoil. The stems of *P. tabernaemontani* root much like runners and thus the plant becomes a mat whereas those of *P. aurea* ascend resulting in clumps. Plant offered in the trade as *P. aurea* var. *verna* ('Verna') look like the cultivar 'Nana' described above. It is a useful, colorful ground cover for full sun.

| *-tridentata* (tri-den′ ta-tah) | Three-Toothed Cinquefoil | 4–10″/12″ |
|---|---|---|
| Summer          White | Northeastern North America | Zones 2–8 |

The species, native from Greenland to North Georgia, is included because of its tenacious growing habit. It grows on rock outcroppings and fills in areas thought to be unfillable, and is particularly useful for acid soils. The basal leaves consist of 3 leaflets with 3 prominent teeth at the apex (thus the common name). The stem leaves, however, are often entire. The small, ¼″ wide white flowers cover the plants in early summer and although many plants are more ornamental, they can be lovely when properly sited and are particularly useful on dry banks and rocky areas.

Propagate by seed or division of the runners.

**Cultivars:**

'Minima' is a dwarf more compact form of the species.

**Related Species:**

*P. alba*, white cinquefoil, is a handsome 3–5″ tall ground cover well suited for the rock garden or other sunny well drained area. Plants have glossy leaves with 5 palmate leaflets and pure white flowers in early spring.

Quick Key to Potentilla Species

    A. Basal leaves in 3's
       B. Flowers white, about ¼″ across . . . . . . . . . . *P. tridentata*
      BB. Flowers red to dark purple, about 1″ across . . *P. atrosanguinea*
   AA. Basal leaves 5–7
       B. Flowers rose to purple . . . . . . . . . . . . . . . *P. nepalensis*
      BB. Flowers yellow
         C. Stems upright, flowers about 1″ across . . . . . . . *P. recta*
        CC. Stems trailing like runners,
           flowers less than ½″ across . . . . . . . *P. tabernaemontani*

**Additional Reading:**

Brearley, Christopher. 1991. Herbaceous potentillas. 13(1):42–53.
Mitchell, Irene. 1984. Cinderella cinquefoil. *Horticulture* 62(12):22–24.

*Primula* (prim' eu-la)               Primrose               Primulaceae

Primroses are nature's way of welcoming spring, and their absence from the garden is excusable only if climate does not allow successful culture. Many species are not long lived but their beauty makes them well worth growing, even as annuals. There are over 400 species, many of which are more at home in the moist climate of the British Isles, New Zealand, and the Pacific Coast than in areas of the United States where summer droughts and temperature extremes are common. However, many primroses are perfectly cold hardy to zone 3 and nearly all are cold hardy to zone 5. A few species do well in the South (as far south as zone 8), although it is often assumed, incorrectly in many cases, that they will not survive hot, dry summers. One should never assume anything without testing, and within this genus, numerous highly adaptable species exist. However, having said that, almost without exception, primroses demand relatively cool summers, adequate levels of moisture and well-drained soils that allow moisture to drain freely away from roots in the winter, to perform their best. While one can see many species growing in full sun in England, etc., the great majority of this country is not even close to the English climate. Shade is necessary for most available primroses, however the water lovers tolerate more sun as long as their love is fulfilled.

The majority of primulas are native to north temperate zones and species occur in bogs, meadows, woodsides, and rockeries. They range in size from the tiny 1″ tall *P. minima*, least primrose, to tall, stately candelabra primroses such as *P. japonica*. The unique *P. vialii* has violet-blue flowers held in a short, dense spike, completely atypical of primrose. Many of the common garden primroses are hybrids of *P. veris*, common cowslip, *P. vulgaris*, English primrose, and *P. juliae*, Julia primrose, and are known as polyantha primroses or "polys" for short. Breeders have increased the size of the flowers while making the plants more compact. They are popular as potted plants in Europe and are gaining momentum as bedding and potted plants in this country. *P. malacoides*, another pot plant species is used extensively in winter gardens of Australia and New Zealand. Great drifts of white, pink, and burgundy brighten the winter landscape at every corner.

The meadowland species of Europe such as *P. veris*, *P. elatior* and *P. vulgaris* are most common in the United States, but species from China (*P. pulverulenta*), Japan (*P. japonica*, *P. sieboldii*), the Himalayas (*P. denticulata*, *P. florindae*), and mountainous regions of Europe (*P. auricula*, *P. allionii*) are also increasing in popularity. All require consistently moist soil and partial shade. Winters seldom result in plant losses, but fluctuations of soil moisture during the hot summer months can be devastating.

There are so many species that one can become as much a primula collector (or at least an admirer) as a hosta or daylily collector. In my case, since north Georgia is not the most amenable area for primrose culture, I must use my camera and eyes more than my soil and trowel. A number of primula I have admired won't make it into the headings of this book, due to lack of space and availability, however I love *P. burmanica*, with its stout flower stems rising 2' in the air and covered with purple-red flowers, *P. capitata* with its rich blue-violet button-like heads of flowers, and *P. glomerata*, whose flowers remind me of *Scabiosa*. If you can find some of these, have fun and send me a few.

The taxonomy of this diverse genus has long occupied the minds of botanists and is presently divided into thirty sections. The most valuable sections horticulturally are Auricula, which contains *P. auricula* and other low-growing species for cool climates and the cool greenhouse; Candelabra, containing a vast array of species with whorls of flowers in tiers on long flower stems; Denticulata, the home of the drumstick primrose, *P. denticulata*; and Vernales, where the ever-popular cowslips, oxslips, and polyanthas reside.

Quick Reference to Primula Species

| | Height (in.) | Type of inflorescence | Need for moisture |
|---|---|---|---|
| *P. auricula* | 2–8 | Umbel | Moderate |
| *P. denticulata* | 8–10 | Globe | Moderate |
| *P. florindae* | 24–30 | Umbel | Critical |
| *P. japonica* | 12–24 | Umbels in tiers | Critical |
| *P.* × *polyantha* | 8–12 | Umbel | Low |
| *P. sieboldii* | 4–8 | Umbel | Moderate |
| *P. vialii* | 12–15 | Spike | Moderate |
| *P. vulgaris* | 6–9 | Solitary | Low |

**-auricula** (ow-rik' ew-la)              Auricula Primrose          2–8"/8"
   Spring            Yellow          European Alps          Zones 3–7

Although the flower color of the ancient species is bright yellow, many color forms are still common in cultivation. The 1" wide flowers are bell shaped and usually fragrant. The thick leaves are 2–3" long and equally wide. Two main forms of *P. auricula* occur, those with flowers and stems densely coated with a white mealy substance (farina) and those which are smooth and not powdery. Both types contain flowers of a single color (i.e., no eye) and those with a white or yellow eye. Plants are shallow rooted and should have winter protection to reduce heaving from alternate freezing and thawing. The species is not difficult to grow, but unfortunately, is difficult to locate. Although some of the cultivars are beautiful, there is something wonderful about growing the species that gardeners have been trying to "improve" for over 350 years.

Auricula enthusiasts have developed dozens of cultivars which are often found in the homes and gardens of collectors, much like African violets. They are classified as show, alpine, double and border auriculas, and remind me of delicate Hubbard figurines. I bought a couple of plants of Barnhaven hybrids recently but they succumbed within a year to the tough southeastern climate. Beautiful but not particularly rugged.

The species and some named cultivars are best propagated from seed. Divisions or 1–2″ long stem cuttings may be taken from established plants after flowering or in the fall. Root in a moist mixture of clean peat and sand. When plants are large enough, they can be placed in the garden.

### Cultivars:

Dozens have been developed, here are but a few.

'Barnhaven hybrids' have large vibrant flowers borne on diminutive foliage. One of the finest hybrids developed.

'Dale's Red' bears brick red flowers with yellow center—one of the most popular auriculas.

'Gold of Ophir' has bright yellow flowers.

'Red Dusty Miller' is a farinaceous cultivar with rose-red flowers.

'The Mikado' is dark red and vigorous.

'Yellow Dusty Miller' is farinaceous and bears yellow flowers.

### Related Species:

*P. × pubescens*, a cross between *P. auricula* and *P. rubra*, bears rose-purple flowers with a white eye. Probably the oldest hybrid primrose in cultivation, it is represented by many forms and cultivars. 'Beverley White' has creamy white flowers on 6–8″ long flower stems. 'Mrs. J.H. Wilson' bears 1–2″ diameter rose-purple flowers with white eyes.

*P. latifolia*, sticky primrose, has sticky foliage and ½″ wide rose-red flowers arranged in 10–25 flowered umbels. Plants require limey soils to perform well. They are sometimes listed as *P. viscosa*.

| *-denticulata* (den-tik-ew-lah′ ta) | Drumstick Primrose | 8–10″/12″ |
|---|---|---|
| Spring   Lilac, White | Himalayas | Zones 4–7 |

The globular flower heads atop thin stems make this species easy to recognize. The leaves are spatulate (look like spatulas), and sharply toothed. They are 4–6″ long at flowering time, and later expand to a foot after flowering. Flowers appear when leaves are just emerging, and both leaves and flower stems expand at the same time. Drumstick primroses are some of the earliest to flower, opening in March and April.

In North Georgia, my plants were wonderfully green all winter until temperatures of 10° F settled in for several nights. Without snow cover, those temperatures were particularly devastating and plants were badly damaged. Many plants recovered and flowered well but flower stems were thin and weak. The use of winter mulch in all climes where snow cover is minimal is highly recommended. Evergreen boughs or loose pine straw should be placed over the plants during the winter. Leaves or other materials that layer and become heavy and smother the plants should be avoided. If plants are grown in a warm greenhouse during the winter and planted in the spring, they may not receive sufficient cold to flower. Fall planting is best because plants receive natural cold treatment in the fall and winter and flowering is improved. Moist, partially shaded areas are necessary for best garden performance.

All are best propagated by seed. Sow seed in May to June for fall planting or September to October for spring planting. Division is also a useful method of propagation.

**Cultivars:**

'Alba' is a popular white flowered form.

'Cashmeriana' is a large purple flowered form with yellow powdery farina beneath the foliage.

'Cashmeriana Rubin' ('Rubins') has carmine-red flowers.

'Karryann' has creamy yellow variegation on the leaf margins. Flowers are light mauve.

'Ronsdorf Strain' is a seed-propagated mixture of white, purple, bluish, or rose flowers held about a foot above the foliage.

| *-florindae* (flo-rin' day) | | Florinda Primrose | 2–3'/2' |
|---|---|---|---|
| Late Spring, Summer | Yellow | Tibet | Zones 6–8 |

If you have read anything about the early plant explorers who suffered immense hardships and adventures in China, you will want to obtain some of these plants, found by Frank Kingdom-Ward and named for his wife, Florinda. If you enjoy high escapade combined with plant lore and horticulture history, you will enjoy the tales.

Plants enjoy damp locations and look their best in a moist soils beside a stream or pond. The broad glossy leaves are ovate and have a heart-shaped base and are attached to the stem by reddish winged petioles. At the top of the strong stems are borne up to 40 pendulous, yellow, farinose flowers. The term "farinose" means having a mealy, granular texture, which often can be rubbed off. There may be up to 40 such flowers, each about 1" across and with a strong fragrance. I haven't seen many good plantings in the United States of this species, but a sunny area with rich, consistently moist soils will please both the gardener and the plant.

Propagate by seed or division.

**Cultivars:**

'Keilour Hybrids' have flowers in shades of yellow.

**Related Species:**

*P. sikkimensis*, Sikkim primula, is similar to the former species, but is usually shorter. The glossy, wrinkled leaves are oblong and the flowers are yellow or creamy white. It also needs consistent moisture.

| *-japonica* (ja-pon' i-ka) | | Japanese Primrose | 12–24"/24" |
|---|---|---|---|
| Late Spring | Various | Japan | Zones 5–7 |

This and many related species have been placed in the division Candelabra due to the many whorls of flowers superimposed on the flower stem. *P. japonica*, which is probably the least temperamental of the candelabra types, bears 2–6 whorls of purple flowers; each whorl consists of 8–12 flowers nearly 1" across and held at right angles to the stem on ¾" long pedicels. To round a corner and see a display of these plants in full bloom is a marvelous sight. The leaves are 6–12" long, 2–4" wide and have irregular sharp dentations on the margins. As with all the candelabra types, conditions for success are critical. Moist soil and a boggy area which does not dry out in the summer are ideal. Place where there is some water movement as plants languish under stagnant conditions. Roots require cool, moist conditions and the tops should be in a shady area. One of the finest displays I have seen in this country is at Winterthur Gardens, Delaware (zone 6), although lovely plantings also occur at Sky Hook in Vermont (zone 4). One of the grandest planting must be at Longstock Water Gardens in England where hundreds of stately candelabras vie for attention with the gunneras, *Iris laevigata*, hosta, mimulas, ferns and other moisture loving species. A trip in early summer to any of these gardens is worth the effort.

Significant natural hybridization occurs among cultivars and species in the Candelabra group and it is best to locate taxa some distance from each other. Self-sown seedlings develop into lovely, but differently colored plants than the parents.

Most candelabra primroses can be raised from seed. Sow seed as soon as ripe or as soon as received. Seeds sown in June or July may be large enough to plant out the same year. If sowing is delayed until the fall, plants will not be large enough to transplant until the following spring. *P. japonica* and *P. pulverulenta* are effectively propagated by division but others of the candelabra group may also be carefully divided.

**Cultivars:**

'Album' produces white flowers.

'Jim Saunders' arose from Longstock Water Garden and is named after one of their former head gardeners. The flowers are a rich cherry red.

'Miller's Crimson' has bright red flowers.

'Postford White' is one of the finest cultivars to date. It has large white flowers, each with a yellow eye. Better than 'Album'.

'Rosea' has pink to rose blooms. 'Miller's Crimson' and 'Rosea' come true from seed.

'Redfield Hybrids' arose from seedlings in the Redfield garden in Hampton, CT.

'Rowallane Hybrids' arose from Rowallane Garden in Northern Ireland. Vigorous and beautiful.

**Related Species:**

*P. × bullesiana* is a cross between *P. bulleyana* and *P. beesiana*, a species with fragrant rose flowers with yellow eyes named for Bee's Nursery in Chester, UK. Flowers occur in rich shades of violet, wine, and yellow.

*P. bulleyana*, named for A.K. Bulley, the founder of the aforementioned Bee's Nursery, has flowers of deep reddish orange and has been hybridized with a number of other candelabra species to produce an array of interesting flower shades.

*P. chungensis* bears whorls of fragrant red tubular flowers with orange petals.

*P. heladoxa* has large, golden yellow flowers with deeply notched petals. Six, 12–20 flowered whorls may occur on 24″ tall plants. Plants are particularly showy in moist, open places.

*P. pulverulenta* has deep red flowers with a deeper red or purple eye. The scape is mealy and carries many whorls of flowers. The best cultivar is 'Bartley's Strain', with lovely soft pink flowers. *P. pulverulenta* is an important parent in many hybrid candelabra primroses.

| | | | |
|---|---|---|---|
| -× *polyantha* (pah-lee-anth′ a) | | Polyantha Primrose | 8–12″/9″ |
| Spring | Various | Hybrid | Zone 3–8 |

This is the most common and popular group of primroses in American gardens. It is a mixture of *P. veris*, the fragrant, deep yellow cowslip primrose, *P. vulgaris*, the sulphur yellow English primrose, and probably *P. juliae*, the bright purple-flowered Julian primrose. The parents themselves are lovely species, and some such as *P. juliae* have also been hybridized to yield such excellent cultivars as 'Wanda', a dark purple red flower, and the most interesting 'Garryarde Guinevere', with purple-tinted foliage and shell pink flowers.

The many years of hybridizing *P. × polyantha* have resulted in a glorious array of flower colors, some with large eyes and others clear faced. The small leaves are dark green and heavily veined. The flowers

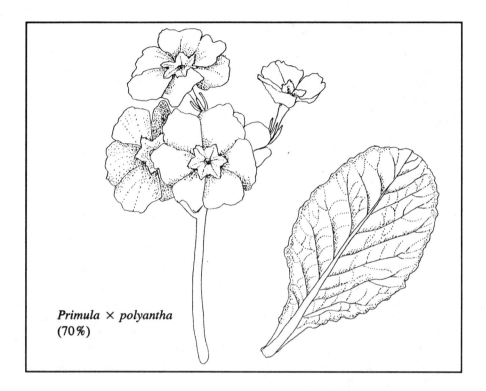

*Primula* × *polyantha*
(70%)

may be up to 1½" across in single or bicolor shades and arranged in umbels on 4–6" tall stems. The polys belong to the Vernales group and although members do not appreciate dry soils, the requirement for constant moisture is not as critical as for other groups of primrose. Natural fertilizer, such as composted cow manure, applied generously once a year is most helpful. Polys associate well with bleeding hearts, dwarf hostas, forget-me-nots, and hellebores.

The polyantha hybrids have received tremendous attention from plant breeders, particularly those in the greenhouse trade. The florist primrose has long been a staple in the pot plant market in Europe and Japan and is quickly catching up in this country. If a potted primrose is purchased as a gift, enjoy it indoors and then plant outside when weather permits. Primroses are also the leading bedding plant in the Northwest where conditions are ideal. Slugs and spider mites are the principal pests of polys. We have trialed many cultivars of polys as fall planted landscape plants at the Horticulture Gardens but they can't yet compete with pansies. The cold weather and lack of snow cover results in a good deal of leaf disfiguration and death and plants struggle. However, we keep looking for more uses in the East for these beautiful hybrids.

Propagate by division or fresh seed.

**Cultivars:**

Many strains and hybrids are available from nurseries, additional colors and names are being developed by American, European, and Japanese breeders every year.

'Danova' series is a mix of colors and has been the best performer in all our trials.

'Pacific Giant' is a seed mixture of large-flowered plants in shades of blue, yellow, red, pink, or white.

'Monarch' strain has 2″ diameter flowers of mixed colors but is also available in single colors.

'Giant Bouquet' is similar to 'Monarch' and bears 2–2½″ diameter flowers.

| -*sieboldii* (see-bold′ ee-eye) | | Siebold Primrose | 4–8″/8″ |
|---|---|---|---|
| Late Spring | Various | Japan | Zones 4–8 |

Plants are pubescent everywhere but the flower. The 2–4″ long ovate leaves are heart-shaped at the base and have scalloped margins. The petioles are often longer than the leaf blades. The 1–1½″ wide flowers are held well above the foliage in 6–10 flowered umbels. They are usually purple with a white eye but may be white or rose. It is a wonderfully showy species and needs to be tried more often. In North American gardens, the foliage often goes dormant in late summer.

The species is somewhere between *P. japonica* and *P. × polyantha* in its requirement for moisture. Plants must not be allowed to dry out repeatedly but do not have to be planted in a bog-like setting. They have been used successfully in moist woodland plantings.

Propagation by seed but cuttings may be taken similar to *P. auricula*.

**Cultivars:**

'Akatonbo' has dark rose, lacy flowers.

'Isotaka' bears 8–10 flowered umbels of beautiful white blooms backed in purple-pink hues.

Var. *purpurea* bears masses of purple red flowers.

'Snowflake' produces large white flowers.

'Sumina' produces large blooms of wisteria blue.

**Related Species:**

*P. kisoana* is one of the best primroses for gardeners who don't have primrose-friendly garden spots. Heat tolerant and with a low degree of difficulty in normal soils. The rounded leaves are wrinkled and the stoloniferous nature allows colonies to increase. The pink flowers are only 4–6″ tall but they make a pleasant mat in the spring. A white form also may be found but it is not as vigorous as the pink.

| *-vialii* (vee-ahl' ee-eye) | | Vial's Primrose | 12–15″/12″ |
|---|---|---|---|
| Spring | Violet-Purple | China | Zones 5–7 |

The first time people see a well-grown clump of this plant, they guess that it is anything but a primrose. The leafless flower stems emerge from the large rosette and bear spikes of violet-purple flowers. The flowers are red in bud, then turn their violet color and fade to pink. They are plants to be enjoyed on the West Coast or in overseas travels; I have seen few successful plantings in the East, and none in the South. Of course, half the fun is trying. Provide moisture retentive alkaline soils and partial shade.

Propagate from seed or division.

| *-vulgaris* (vul-gah' ris) | | English Primrose | 6–9″/9″ |
|---|---|---|---|
| Spring | Yellow | Europe | Zones 5–8 |
| (Syn. *P. acaulis*) | | | |

This is one of the easier primroses to grow, tolerating drier soil conditions and more heat than many others. The leaves are tufted, often wrinkled, and downy beneath resulting in a soft pubescent feel. They are about 2–3″ long at flowering time but, like *P. denticulata*, continue to expand and within a month of flowering, double in size. The tubular, 1″ wide flowers are sulphur yellow, often with a dark yellow blotch near the eye, and are borne singly. The flowers do not have the "take-your-breath-away" quality of other primroses but a group of a dozen in full spring finery helps provide that elusive, relaxing feel of the English garden. This species and *P. kisoana* are the most rewarding for Southern gardeners.

This species has also been an important parent of the *P.* × *polyantha* hybrids and so many crosses, self-crosses, and back crosses have occurred that the Vernales group is becoming a taxonomic free-for-all.

Propagate by seed or division.

### Cultivars:

'Jack-in-the-Green' is an old cultivar whose curious charm has stayed the test of time. The flowers are pale yellow and are surrounded by large greenish sepals which looks like a loose fitting collar.

'Quaker's Bonnet' is only one of numerous double forms of *P. vulgaris*. Double deep rose flowers occur in spring.

'Rubra' has rose colored flowers.

Ssp. *sibthorpii* has early-emerging pink flowers, although some may be nearly white. Doubles and hose-in-hose variants sometimes occur. The earliest of the early primroses. Undemanding and handsome, highly recommended.

## Quick Key to Primula Species

A. Flowers held in whorled umbels
borne in tiers along scape . . . . . . . . . . . . . . . . *P. japonica*
AA. Flowers not in tiers, borne in single
umbels, spikes or solitary
  B. Flowers sessile
    C. Flowers in rounded heads . . . . . . . . . . . *P. denticulata*
    CC. Flowers in cylindrical spikes . . . . . . . . . . . . . *P. vialii*
  BB. Flowers on pedicels
    C. Flowers borne singly, tubular . . . . . . . . . . *P. vulgaris*
    CC. Flowers 5–20, not tubular
      D. Base of leaves heart-shaped or rounded
        E. Base of leaves heart-shaped
          F. Flowers yellow, farinose . . . . . . . . . *P. florindae*
        FF. Flowers seldom yellow,
            not farinose . . . . . . . . . . . . . . . . . *P. sieboldii*
      DD. Base of leaves tapers to winged petiole . . . *P. auricula*

**Additional Reading:**

Lovejoy, Ann. 1993. The primrose path. *Horticulture* 71(5):38–42.
Martin, Tovah. 1985. A primrose palette. *Horticulture* 63(3):45–53.
Richards, John. 1986. Petiolarid primulas in cultivation. *The Plantsman*
7(4):217–232.

*Associations:*

American Primrose Society, 2568 Jackson Highway, Chenalis, WA 98532.
  Publication: *American Primrose Society Quarterly.*

## *Prunella* (pru-nell′ a)         Self-Heal         Lamiaceae

The genus is still occasionally listed as *Brunella*, from the German Die Braune, a disease of the throat called quinsy, which these plants were supposed to heal. Of the approximately 12 species, the most common is *P. vulgaris*, the common self-heal which invades lawns. All species have opposite leaves, terminal spikes of whorled flowers and self-sow vigorously. The only species of any use in the garden, and its usefulness is debatable, is *P. grandiflora*, which is often offered as *P.* × *webbiana*.

| *-grandiflora* (grand-i-flor′ a) | Self-Heal | 9–12″/12″ |
|---|---|---|
| Summer         Purple | Europe | Zone 5–7 |

The opposite leaves are 3–4″ long and 1–2″ wide, usually with entire margins and dark green color. The purple flowers are held on short compact inflorescences, each flower is subtended by a small bract. Consistently moist soil and full sun to partial shade are preferable. In areas of cool summers, they should not be planted where they can escape and roam freely throughout the border. Plants which are allowed to dry out quickly die. Growth is better in zone 5 than in zone 7.

**Cultivars:**

'Alba' has pale pink to white flowers.

'Little Red Riding Hood' has crimson red spikes and is about 6″ tall.

'Loveliness' has pale lavender flowers.

'Pink Loveliness' bears pink flowers. I was pleasantly surprised with the performance of this cultivar in the Georgia gardens, but their longevity under warm humid environments is marginal at best.

'Red Cap' has rosy red flowers.

'White Loveliness' produces large white flowers and is the best white form.

**Related Species:**

*P.* × *webbiana* likely resulted from the crossing of *P. grandiflora* and *P. g.* var. *pyrenaica* (syn. *P. hastaefolia*) and are often simply listed as *P. grandiflora*. The only differences between *P. grandiflora* and *P.* × *webbiana* are that *P.* × *webbiana* has shorter blunter leaves, more compact flower spikes, and is shorter. Both have dark purple flowers and similar growth habits.

*Pteridium* (ter-id-ee′ um)　　　　Bracken Fern　　　　Polypodiaceae

A fern which one either loves or hates, depending on its ability to colonize the entire homestead. *P. aquilinum* is the dandelion of roadsides on the West Coast, and anyone who has traveled in northern Europe cannot help but comment on these aggressive but useful weeds along the roadways. The ferns are 2–3 pinnate, one of the compound terrestrial ferns in the group. The fronds look like big wings, and the genus name comes from the Greek word *pteron*, meaning wing.

Plants are large, 2–4′, and aggressive in well-drained soils. They are northern ferns and do poorly in areas of high heat and humidity. Interestingly, although ferns can be incredibly aggressive, this is a difficult fern to transplant, especially if given a piece from your neighbor. The best bet is to gather the rhizome with a newly developing frond, transplant to rich soil, then once established, plant it out. A few ornamental cultivars have been selected, including 'Cristatum' with crested fronds. 'Grandiceps' is much less aggressive and is a curious plant with reduced fronds.

Bracken ferns are beautiful to those who can't grow them, they are miserable for those who can't get rid of it. Perhaps I can trade with someone for a few pieces of kudzu?

## *Pulmonaria* (pul-mon-air′ ee-a)     Lungwort     Boraginaceae

This is one of the "hottest" genera in the perennial stables these days, due to some excellent breeding work and the realization that plants perform well throughout much of the country. Of the 12–14 species, 4 are particularly attractive for the shade garden. All produce blue or pink flowers in the spring, generally opening one color, usually pink, then turning blue before falling. This charming habit has given rise to the common name of Soldiers and Sailors. Flowers open before the foliage emerges or at the same time, often as early as early March in the South and a few weeks later in the North. The alternate stem leaves are often spotted and sometimes provide better identification characteristics than the basal leaves.

The breeding efforts of Dan Heims of Terra Nova Nursery have repainted the palette of pulmonarias. On the one hand, we have much more choice, on the other hand, it is difficult to tell one from the other or to know if all cultivars perform equally well. I think this is one of the best genera for partially shaded gardens and will only receive more attention in the future.

In the 16th and 17th centuries, Jerusalem cowslip, *P. officinalis*, became an example of the "Doctrine of Signatures," practiced by herbalists of that time. This doctrine, based on a treatise by Theoprastus Bombast von Hohenheim (1493–1541), better known as Paracelsus, suggested that the outward appearance of plants dictated their virtues. Thus the perforated leaves of common St. John's-wort indicated that it was useful remedy for cuts and wounds; the convoluted shell of the walnut was specific for troubles of the brain; and the spotted leaf of *Pulmonaria*, which so resembled a diseased lung, was an obvious cure for ailments of that organ. The ancient study of herbalism had fallen to some of its lowest depths of irrationality during those times but is finally recovering. Today, the practice of herbalism flourishes and counts many gardeners and non-gardeners alike among the converts. Fortunately, those who appreciate the curative properties found in so many of our garden plants also understand that they don't need an outward appearance for inward contentment.

All the lungworts should be planted in partial shade and provided with adequate moisture. However, one of the quickest ways to lose them is to have wet soils, particularly in the winter. I am an expert in killing these plants, although I am getting the hang of this drainage thing. They spread by creeping rootstocks, but not to the point of being invasive. They can look lousy in the summer if allowed to dry out or if drowned. If leaf margins look tattered, they may be cut back in the summer, fertilized lightly, and will return fresh.

A drawback to the genus is its susceptibility to powdery mildew. I have seen plants turn white with the fungus, particularly if air circulation is poor, the air is wet, and temperatures remain cool. We are presently testing about 30 cultivars for their susceptibility, and hopefully will find some better than others. A fungal spray (mildicide) may be applied in early spring. If planted in morning sun, mildew is much less of a problem. Cutting back and discarding infected leaves also helps reduce the incidence.

Presence or absence of obvious leaf spotting is a fairly easy beginning point to separate species from each other. Cultivars of *P. officinalis*, *P. longifolia* and *P. saccharata* are almost always spotted, *P. angustifolia* and *P. rubra* seldom are. This is how I begin teaching students the difference between them, however, I expect as breeders do more hybridization, this distinction may blur.

### Quick Reference to Pulmonaria Species

|                   | Height (in.) | Spotted leaves | Flower color |
|-------------------|--------------|----------------|--------------|
| *P. angustifolia* | 9–12         | No             | Bright blue  |
| *P. longifolia*   | 9–12         | Yes            | Purple blue  |
| *P. rubra*        | 12–24        | No             | Coral red    |
| *P. saccharata*   | 9–18         | Yes            | Blue         |

| *-angustifolia* (ang-gus-ti-fo' lee-a) | Blue Lungwort | 9–12"/24" |
|---|---|---|
| Spring        Bright Blue | Central Europe | Zones 2–7 |

Unspotted, bristly, lanceolate leaves emerge with the first flowers. Tight pink buds open into deep blue, drooping, funnel-shaped flowers. The flowers are among the bluest and most ornamental in the genus. It makes an excellent ground cover under shrubs and competes well with many trees for water and nutrients. It performs better in the North than in the South (below zone 6) because the foliage tends to wilt under the warmer temperatures. Spring flowering is not affected but the foliage declines more rapidly in the South. The leaves are sort of "just there" and these plants should be placed where the flowers can be enjoyed, then allow them to be overgrown with more colorful partners.

Propagate by division after flowering.

### Cultivars:
'Azurea' sports lovely gentian blue flowers, tinted red in bud.
'Blaues Meer' has larger brighter blue flowers than the species.
'Johnson's Blue' is a smaller form (only about 8–10" tall and wide) with narrower leaves.
'Mawson's Variety' bears some of the brightest, largest blue flowers. Bigger than the species in all aspects.
'Munstead Blue' has rich blue flowers and is similar to the previous cultivar.
'Rubra' bears light red flowers. As far as I know, this is the only pinkish open flower in the species.

*-longifolia* (long-gi-fo' lee-a)     Long-Leafed Lungwort     9–12"/24"
    Spring     Purple-Blue     Western Europe     Zones 3–8

The name *longifolia* describes the long, narrow foliage (at least 6 times as long as wide). The dark green leaves are gray spotted and pointed, becoming narrower and smaller up the stem. Crowded terminal racemes of purple-blue flowers vie for attention in the spring, a little later than other species. It is a good plant for use as a ground cover or in the front of the border and is even more adaptable to southern conditions than other species.

Propagate by division after flowering.

### Cultivars:

'Bertram Anderson' has violet-blue flowers and dark green leaves spotted with silvery green.

'Cevennensis' is a naturally occurring variety from the Cevennes in France. Plants have long (up to 2' long) narrow silver-spotted leaves with dark violet-blue flowers. Stunning in containers and the garden. A drawback is the brownish flower buds. Looks like they are already finished blooming.

'Little Blue' is almost identical to the previous cultivar.

*-rubra* (rew' bra)     Red Lungwort     12–24"/30"
    Early Spring     Bright Red     Southeastern Europe     Zones 4–7
    (Syn. *P. montana*)

This species recently appeared in catalogs and gardens and is unique in a number of ways. Specifically, the flowers open early in the spring, one of the earliest of the lungworts to flower, and the coral red blooms are a marked departure from the usual blue hues. In fact, this color is not at all common in plants of Boraginaceae. The light green foliage is evergreen in milder climates and has soft hairs that produce a velvety texture. The oblong leaves narrow abruptly into the stem and are virtually sessile. It is a pretty plant which makes an interesting splash in spring and then disappears into the summer landscape. Plants do better in the North than the South and are outstanding on the West Coast.

### Cultivars:

'Albocorollata' has handsome white flowers that open later than the species.

'Barfield Pink' has soft unspotted foliage and red flowers with white margins.

'Bowle's Red' has deeper red flowers and lime-green slightly spotted leaves.

'Redstart' has dark red flowers and is more compact than the species.

'Salmon Glow' has showy salmon flowers.

*-saccharata* (sa-ka-rah' ta)     Bethlehem Sage     9–18"/24"
    Spring     Blue     Italy, France     Zones 3–7

This has become the most popular species of pulmonaria because of the availability of good cultivars and the highly prized spotted foliage. Leaves

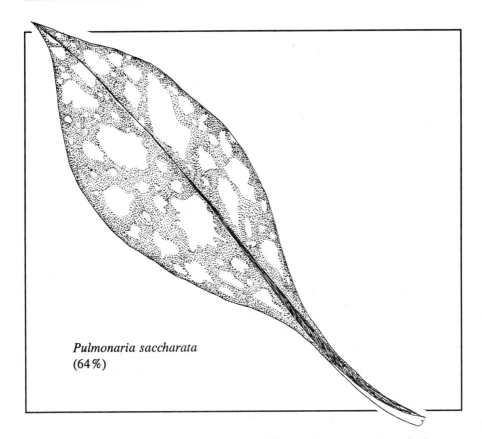

*Pulmonaria saccharata*
(64%)

are green and more spotted than *P. longifolia,* and appear to have had sugar dusted over them, thus the specific name. Leaves are about 3 times as long as broad and the white blotches tend to coalesce. The pink flower buds open into funnel-shaped flowers which turn blue with age. It is a useful addition as a foliage accent, even if plants did not flower.

Plants require sufficient moisture if leaves are to remain ornamental throughout the season. The spotted leaves show up well in the garden but few things look worse than wilted, ratty, spotted leaves. Although not as water loving as *Ligularia* or *Primula japonica,* in well-drained soils adequate moisture must be provided during the warm days and nights of summer.

Propagate from division after flowering.

### Cultivars:

Many of the following are hybrids with *P. saccharata, P. angustifolia,* and occasionally *P. longifolia.* Trying to discriminate one from the other requires faith and guesswork. However, the explosion of hybrids is the gardeners gain. While I describe the flowers, it is the foliage which makes these plants special.

'Alba' has white flowers and can be raised from seed.

'Apple Frost' is a compact grower with silver spotting over apple green leaves.

'Argentea' bears white flowers and almost solid silver leaves.

'Benediction', named for the Seattle gardener, Loie Benedict, bears deep blue flowers in early March and large silver-spotted leaves. Beautiful.

'Berries and Cream', from Collectors Nursery in Battle Ground, WA, has silvery leaves and rosy pink flowers. It is unique.

'Blue Ensign' has wide unspotted dark green leaves, likely from *P. angustifolia*, and large blue flowers. Excellent selection.

'Blue Mist' has small leaves with many small white spots and flowers of the lightest blue.

'Boughton Blue' has silvery gray blotches randomly throughout the long, narrow leaves. The flowers are clear blue.

'British Sterling' used to be one of my favorites, but it is not as vigorous as I would like it to be. Magenta flower buds open to blue flowers over shiny leaves with silvery white spots which coalesce nicely. Most of the green is around the margin. Sounds awful, but quite beautiful.

'David Ward' will take the gardening world by storm now that it is introduced. The leaves are essentially variegated, with thin white margins around dull green blades. I first saw this plant at Butterstream Gardens outside Dublin, Ireland. Everyone there did a double take.

'Dora Bielefeld' has lighter green foliage than many other cultivars. Plants have moderate silver spotting and persistent pink flowers.

'Excalibur' is quickly becoming popular due to the leaves being almost totally silvery white with a green margin and midrib. Absolutely brightens up the shade. Rosy flowers are secondary. Another terrific selection from Dan Heims.

'Glacier' has rounded green leaves with a good deal of silver spotting. The round leaves are different from most of the others. Flowers are almost white in early spring.

'Highdown' is taller than the species. Dangling rich blue flowers are produced earlier.

'Janet Fisk' is an excellennt taxa, with heavily marbled foliage and pink flowers which fade to lavender. Vigorous and heat tolerant, but has not proven to be reliably persistent.

'Kingswood' has a random pattern of white throughout the dark green leaves. Blue flowers.

'Leopard' bears green foliage marked with silver blotches, and red-purple flowers.

'Lewis Palmer' has long, narrow silver-spotted foliage, the spots sometimes running together. Flowers open deep blue and fade to pink.

'Little Star' from Dan Heims, has narrow leaves, with silver spots. Deep blue flowers emerge early in the spring. Compact and neat.

'Margery Fish', named after the noted English horticulturist, is more vigorous than the species and a favorite in Europe. She varies from heavy spots to almost entirely silver. Still a popular and pleasing plant, but being superseded by others on this list.

'Merlin' comes from Europe and has both pink and blue flowers on the same plant in the spring. The leaves are short and moderately spotted,

'Milky Way' rapidly makes large clumps due its vigor. The heavily spotted leaves are long and narrow (like 'Roy Davidson') with deep blue flowers.

'Mrs. Kittle' has clean white spots on dark green foliage. Not a big plant, but she looks good in the Armitage meleage. Light rosy flowers.

'Mrs. Moon' is an old favorite with large silver-spotted leaves and pink flower buds which turn light blue. She is probably a hybrid with *P. officinalis.*

'Nuernberg', from Germany, has pink and blue flowers together and leaves heavily spotted with silver.

'Pierre's Pure Pink' is named for Pierre Bennerup of Sunny Border Nursery, one of our more colorful confreres. The pink salmon flowers remain that color without fading, and the leaves are moderately spotted.

'Pink Dawn' has striking spotted leaves with sprays of pink flowers.

'Roy Davidson' is a hybrid with *P. longifolia* and *P. saccharata.* The spotted leaves are longer than they are wide, but not to the extent of *P. longifolia.* They are heat tolerant and do well in the South. The flowers are pale blue, similar to 'Mrs. Moon'.

'Regal Ruffles' is quite different in flower than most other lungworts. The flowers are ruffled and tucked in the rosette of leaves.

'Silver Streamers', also from Collectors Nursery, has ruffled almost pure silver foliage.

'Sissinghurst White' has large white flowers and silver-white spotted leaves. The flowers are most handsome but the foliage is not as striking as the species.

'Spangled Gentian' from Don Jacob's of Eco Gardens, has long narrow leaves and gentian blue flowers.

'Smokey Blue' produces silvery spotted foliage and pink flowers which turn blue over time.

'Spilled Milk', again from the indomitable Mr. Heims, has broad foliage which is mostly silver, although spots of green are found here and there.

### Related Species:

*P. officinalis,* Jerusalem cowslip, has rough, heart-shaped leaves usually spotted with white. They are not particularly showy, but the early blue and pink flowers are cheerful in the late winter and early spring. Flowers differ from *P. saccharata* by being smaller, while the leaves are more elliptical, sharp-pointed and rougher to the touch. 'Cambridge Blue' has darker blue flowers and 'White Wings' bears clean white blooms. A good selection.

## Quick Key to Pulmonaria Species

A. Leaves usually unspotted, or slightly so
    B. Flowers remain coral to red, do not turn blue . . . . . *P. rubra*
    BB. Flowers open pink, turn blue as they age . . . . *P. angustifolia*
AA. Leaves definitely spotted
    B. Leaves much longer than wide, white spotted . . *P. longifolia*
    BB. Leaves ovate, rounded at both ends,
        white blotched . . . . . . . . . . . . . . . . . . . . . . *P. saccharata*

**Additional Reading:**

Lovejoy, Ann. 1993. Pulmonarias. *Horticulture* 71(3):54–58.
Mathew, Brian. 1982. Pulmonaria in gardens. *The Plantsman* 4(2):100–111.

## *Pulsatilla* (pul-sa-til′ a)　　　Pasque Flower　　　Ranunculaceae

About a dozen species are known, all of which used to be included with *Anemone*. Although some taxonomists still retain this marriage, the presence of feathery elongated styles on the fruit resulted in the separate genus. The fruits, which are as ornamental as the flowers, double the garden value. Flowers are apetalous (no petals) and wrapped in furry, pointed involucral leaves that unfurl as the satiny flowers open. Flower colors include the darkest violet (*P. pratensis*), forget-me-not blue (*P. halleri* 'Budapest'), yellow (*P. sylvestris*), and white, the North American *P. occidentalis*. Blossoms are borne singly in the axils of feathery, tufted foliage. The foliage dies back in mid to late summer.

In my first edition (1989), the only listing of *Pulsatilla* I found in a collection of nursery catalogs was *P. vulgaris*, common pasque flower. As I sit at my desk today and pour over even more catalogs, I find but one additional species in but one nursery listing. Maybe more people would get excited if they visit the Denver Botanic Gardens in early spring and see the various forms and species of pasque flower spilling over everywhere in their rock garden. They reseed themselves, flower through the snow and act like a wonderful weed.

While the common pasque flower is certainly worth growing, so is *P. alpina*, alpine pasque flower, with its much divided foliage, white flowers (yellow in var. *sulphurea*) and huge feathery seed heads. Seldom do we see the considerable charm of *P. nuttalliana*, lion's beard, native of the western United States whose large blossoms appear even before the leaves unfurl. Perhaps the loveliest of dwarf pasque flowers is *P. vernalis*, vernal pasque flower, whose light purple campanulate flowers open even before the snow disappears. But then again, I believe *P. halleri*, either with its pinkish flowers (ssp. *slavica*) or darker flowers (ssp. *styricha*) may be my favorite today. Tomorrow is yet another day. A rock garden enthusiast or a local specialty grower can assist in locating some of the difficult to obtain species. I surely hope to see more diversity listed by the time the third edition appears.

*Pulsatilla* should be planted in full sun in the North and full sun to partial shade in the South. Many species are excellent rock garden plants and all require excellent drainage. They are not long-lived at the best of times but if drainage is poor, plants seldom survive the season. All pasque flowers are better suited to climates with moderate summer temperatures and low humidity.

| *-vulgaris* (vul-gah′ ris) | | Common Pasque Flower | 9–12″/12″ |
|---|---|---|---|
| Early Spring | Purple | Europe | Zones 5–7 |

The emergence of the plants is a good enough reason to grow therm. The silky hairy leaves pushing out of the ground in late winter or early spring are themselves exceptionally ornamental. The wine purple, urn-shaped flowers appear before the foliage has fully emerged and consist of 6 pointed sepals which encircle egg yolk yellow stamens. Soon after the flower has closed for the last time, the feathery seed head rises 12–15″ above the foliage. The basal leaves are 4–6″ long, pinnately dissected, and silky hairy when young.

Propagate by fresh seed because seeds go dormant soon after maturity (see *Actaea*). Plants may be carefully divided after they have been well established but, in general, do not transplant well.

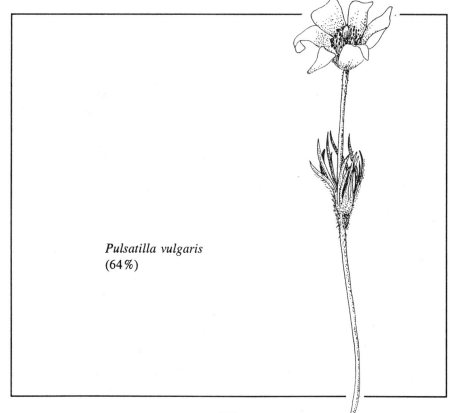

*Pulsatilla vulgaris*
(64%)

**Cultivars:**

'Alba' has pretty, creamy white flowers which offer better contrast to the leaves than the purple flowers of the species. Plants flower in early April in north Georgia and persist 2 weeks, but the silky flower heads last well into May.

'Grandis' is the same as the species but is more vigorous, bigger and more suitable for the border.

'Rubra' has flowers which some call red but are really more of an intense purple.

**Additional Reading:**

Haw, Stephen. 1986. Pasque flowers. *The Garden* 3(4):165–168.

*Puschkinia* (push-kin' ee-a)          Striped Squill          Liliaceae

This small genus is closely related to *Scilla* and *Chionodoxa* and differs botanically in minor ways. They are less ornamental than those two genera but sufficiently pleasing if planted where they can be admired "up close and personal." Only one species is common in cultivation, *P. scilloides*.

| *-scilloides* (skil-loi' deez) | | Striped Squill | 4–6"/6" |
|---|---|---|---|
| Early Spring | Pale Blue | Orient | Zones 4–8 |

This is similar to *Scilla*, thus the specific name *scilloides*, meaning "like Scilla." Two to four linear leaves arise in the spring, followed by a leafless flower stalk with 2–6 nodding pale blue, bell-shaped flowers. The petals of each flower have a deep blue stripe running down their center. This stripe plus the paleness of the flowers are good identification features. Plant in hundreds or at least a dozen where they may be admired close up, otherwise they are easily overlooked. Not the least of its charms is the pleasant fragrance, which smells like a spice cabinet whose contents were removed so just a faint reminder remains.

*Puschkinia* tolerates full sun or partial shade. Plant bulbs about 4" deep in mid- to late September. Flowering occurs as early as mid-February in the South and a month or so later in the North. They seldom need division but if flowering is sporadic, the offsets may be removed and replanted.

**Cultivars:**

'Compacta' has flowers closer together on the scape, and more flowers than the species. It is not easy to locate.

'Libanotica' has smaller flowers of purple-blue.

*Pycnanthemum* (pink-nan-the' mum)          Mountain Mint          Lamiaceae

The mountain mints consist of about 21 species with highly aromatic foliage. They are not particularly showy but the strong minty fragrance of the leaves, particularly when crushed, may be reason enough to include a plant or two in the garden. The flowers, which are white or purplish, distinctly two-lipped and mixed with conspicuous bracts, are produced at the tips and often in the axils as well. The common name is a bit of a misnomer, as most of the species are more common in lowlands than in the mountains. I have had the common mountain mint, *P. incanum*, in my garden for years and every spring, as it emerges and grows into a tight little ball, I sniff a few leaves. It leaves me alone and vice versa. Being in an area which gets shadier every year, plants get leggy and topple over by mid summer, creating a green hair ball of absolutely no value. Therefore I find myself cutting it back hard in late spring and again in the summer, if I remember. The flowers are nothing to write home about, so why do I allow it to take up space where other more reasonable plants could grow? I have no idea, and when next spring comes, it is history! I will go to the north Georgia mountains and see it there. This species is much happier in full sun and cool nights than in my garden.

However, a number of other species are slowly being introduced including the 3' tall *P. muticum,* with ovate leaves and silvery green flowers and bracts. The best ones, however, are probably those with narrow more refined foliage. *P. tenuifolium* grows in a compact clump consisting of leaves at least 4 times longer than wide. The flowers are a decent white on the ends of the stems. *P. virginianum,* native to moist meadows of the Southeast, grows 2-3' tall with white flowers and small bracts in the summer. Glossy narrow leaves make it a useful addition.

All mountain mints are better behaved in full sun and moist but not wet soils. An early haircut does wonders for their disposition; cut back in late spring. Most grow well from zone 3-7.

# R

*Ranunculus* (rah-nun' kew-lus)    Buttercup    Ranunculaceae

The genus is somewhat similar to *Anemone* in its diversity. Species with tuberous roots (classed as bulb species in the commercial trade) and with fibrous roots are grown. About 250 species occur, but only a few are worthy of inclusion in the garden. The tuberous-rooted species, *R. asiaticus*, was a popular florist plant and cut flower early in this century and is undergoing a renaissance as new cultivars are developed. It can be grown as a garden plant, but tubers must be lifted in the fall in most parts of the country. The small yellow buttercup that children put under their chins to see their skin turn yellow is *R. acris*, tall buttercup, and double forms of this diminutive wild flower have been developed for the garden. One species that has received much attention is an indestructible ground cover. The lesser celandine, *R. ficaria*, has bright yellow flowers and forms tight mats of round, crisp leaves which advance though the neighborhood like lava from Mt. St. Helen. This tuberous-rooted species is about 2–3″ tall but its "pleasant face" so impressed William Wordsworth that it became the subject of his long poem "To the Lesser Celandine" and two more "To the Same Flower." Appreciate it where useful, but keep it out of your garden. Several other species should be treated the same way. *R. repens*, creeping buttercup, jogs more than creeps and, as pretty as the flower is, particularly the less invasive double form, 'Flore-pleno', it can take over an area within a couple of years. Plants may be admired along the Riverwalk in San Antonio where they smother banks with glossy green leaves and double yellow flowers. I like this plant more in my neighbor's garden than in mine.

The flowers of buttercups are usually yellow, but *R. aconitifolius* has white flowers and those of *R. asiaticus* are offered in a rainbow of colors. The leaves are often basal and then alternate up the stem. Leaf shape ranges from compound to lobed to scalloped and are even grass-like in *R. gramineus*. The flowers generally have 5 petals and sepals in single-flowered species. I was asked how to tell "yellow buttercups" from the marsh marigold, *Cathra palustris*. Numerous differences occur, but *Cathra* has no petals compared to the 5 in *Ranunculus*. The petals have a small nectary at their base, a good identification characteristic which serves to separate this genus from *Adonis*, another closely related genus. A few species such as *R. ficaria* and its selections go summer dormant. Others, like the European water butter-cup, *R. aquatilus*, and the native swamp buttercup, *R. septentrionalis*, thrive in wet places, thus the name *Ranunculus*, derived from *rana*, a frog.

## Quick Reference to Ranunculus Species

|  | Height (in.) | Flower color | Root type |
|---|---|---|---|
| *R. aconitifolius* | 24–36 | White | Fibrous |
| *R. acris* | 24–36 | Yellow | Fibrous |
| *R. asiaticus* | 12–30 | Various | Tuberous |
| *R. montanus* | 3–6 | Yellow | Creeping |

| *-aconitifolius* (a-kon-ee-ti-fo′ lee-us) | Aconite Buttercup | 24–36″/30″ |
|---|---|---|
| Spring          White | France | Zones 5–8 |

The name *aconitifolius* refers to the similarity of the foliage to that of species of *Aconitum*. The glossy green leaves are palmately parted into 3–5 sections. The similarities end there as the flower of this plant is single, about 1″ across, and white. The upper leaves are sessile and flowers are held many to a stem, producing loose sprays in late spring and early summer. The species itself is seldom seen except in botanical gardens and available only from specialty seedsmen. The species and its varieties are best planted in full sun to partial shade and benefit from consistently moist soil. The garden form is the double selection, 'Flore-pleno'.

Propagate from seed or division in fall or early spring.

**Cultivars:**

'Flore-pleno', with double white flowers, was introduced to Britain by Huguenot refugees and became known as Fair Maids of France. It is also known as white bachelors' button being "very suggestive of buttons, but only remotely so of bachelors" (Sutherland, W., *Handbook of Hardy and Herbaceous Plants*, 1871). It is a better garden plant than the species and does not spread as rapidly as other members of this genus.

'Grandiflorus' (var. *platanafolius*) has larger flowers than the species and if the single form is to be grown, this is the variety of choice.

'Luteus-plenus' is an obscure double, yellow-flowered form seldom seen and even more difficult to locate. The flowers are similar to those of the double meadow buttercup, *R. acris*, but the plant is not hairy.

877

| *-acris* (ah' kris) | | Meadow Buttercup | 18–36"/30" |
|---|---|---|---|
| Spring | Yellow | Europe | Zones 3–7 |

Although native to Europe, the species has found conditions in Canada, the Atlantic states and as far south as Virginia to its liking, and has naturalized in these areas. The golden yellow flowers are about 1" across, have spreading sepals and are hairy beneath. The flower buds are also hairy. Leaves are palmately divided into 3–7 sections, 5 being most common, and often are marked with black spots. The plant is highly branched and bears many flowers. It is a wonderful weed, with fleshy roots, and, fortunately, two controllable forms also occur.

All forms may be propagated by division or seed.

### Cultivars:

'Flore-pleno', yellow bachelor's button, is sold under names such as 'Plenus', 'Plena', and 'Multiplex' but all have the same double yellow button-like flowers. Plants are handsome, but if moisture is available and soil is rich, they may spread rather quickly. Plants combine well with *Crocus tommasinianus* or other lavender hue.

'Hedgehog' has dark brown markings on the leaves and pale yellow flowers.

Var. *stevenii* is much less invasive and has single and semi-double flowers. Heights of 3' are not uncommon, however, and plants are more prone to topple than the lower growing forms.

### Related Species:

*R. bulbosus* is one of the many yellow-flowered species which all kind of look the same. The plants arise from bulb-like roots and bear 3-lobed leaves and single yellow flowers. The most common form is 'Flore-pleno'. These plants can gallop around the garden; full sun and moist soils equals an invasion. I have a good deal of trouble telling all these buttercups apart, and pulling up the plants to check for swollen roots is hardly good etiquette, particularly at someone else's garden. I have put a little table after *R. repens* for those who can't stand not knowing what it is. For the remaining smart people, a yellow buttercup is a yellow buttercup.

*R. ficaria*, lesser celandine, has a rosette of dark green, heart-shaped or scalloped basal leaves which often have brown or silver markings. Native to Europe, they have become naturalized in the United States and can become very invasive. It is everywhere in the fine arboretum at Planting Fields in Long Island, NY. I was asked to lecture there, and had prepared to talk about some of the cultivars listed below, but as Vinnie Simeone, the acting assistant director, led me through colony after colony of lesser celandine on the property, I realized I might be shouted out of the place. Fortunately, the audience was polite and I survived the suggestion that some of the cultivars are much less invasive than their parent. However, a number of forms are worth a go in the garden. 'Aurantiaca' has brown (sometimes a little silver) mottled leaves and shiny orange-yellow flowers. It is also aggressive. One of my favorite little plants in the Armitage garden is 'Brazen Hussy', given to me by Pam Harper, one of this country's treasured writers and gardeners in Virginia. The 6″ tall plants have bright yellow flowers over chocolate brown leaves. They are in flower before most everything but the earliest daffodils. Great fun plant with a wonderful name; multiplies slowly by root bulblets. Both selections go summer dormant. 'Double Mud' produces double burnt yellow flowers, the outside row of petals has muddy purpling. 'Green Petal' is a particularly gruesome double-flowered plant with green petals bearing a hint of yellow.

*R. repens*, creeping buttercup, differs from *R. acris* in a number of subtle ways. Creeping buttercup is shorter and can be equally invasive. It creeps

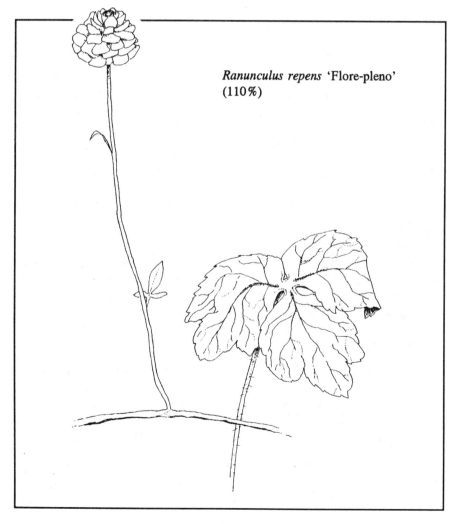

*Ranunculus repens* 'Flore-pleno'
(110%)

faster but nobody accused *R. acris* of being a homebody. The basal leaves of *R. repens* are divided into 3 leaflets and the flowers are usually borne singly while the leaves of *R. acris* are not divided, but are 3-7-lobed and the flowers are generally borne several together in an inflorescence (cyme). The most common form is the double 'Flore-pleno', but the most handsome form of creeping buttercup, without any doubt, is 'Susan's Song'. The leaves are chartreuse with margins of dark green. Terrific in foliage, the flowers are a normal yellow. My friend Ann Armstrong from Charlotte, NC, introduced me to this plant where she had it growing in combination with burgundy-leaved *Ajuga*. Stunning, but rampageous.

The differences between a number of these look-alike yellow buttercups may be useful. The following table may help.

Quick Guide to a Yellow Buttercup

| | Leaves | Root | Flowers born | Height (in.) |
|---|---|---|---|---|
| *R. acris* | 3-7 (usually 5) deeply lobed | Fibrous | Several | 24-36 |
| *R. bulbosus* | 3 leaflets, each segment deeply divided | Bulb-like corm | Several | 12-24 |
| *R. ficaria* | Entire, heart-shaped | Tuberous | Singly | 9-24 |
| *R. repens* | 3 leaflets, each segment shallowly divided | Stoloniferous | Singly | 10-24 |

| *-asiaticus* (ah-see-ah' ti-kus) | Persian Buttercup | 12-30"/24" |
|---|---|---|
| Spring | Various | Asia, Crete | Zones 8-10 |

This is a magnificent plant when grown well. In California, I have seen great rows of ranunculus cultivars in pastel shades, each flower fully double and seemingly perfect. I had to remind myself that I was in the rarified growing area of the Salinas Valley and would not have the same success on the East Coast. The history of this species is like a roller coaster. Few flowers have risen so high, to fall so low. In 1665, there were 20 types listed in the catalog of the Royal Gardens of Paris, but by 1775, a nurseryman named James Maddock listed nearly 800 kinds and fifty thousand seedlings were raised annually in his nursery alone. By 1820, the number listed by nurserymen had dropped to 400 and in 1898, Shirley Hibberd wrote in her book, *Familiar Garden Flowers*, that the named varieties were reduced to "a few dozen only, or perhaps less than a score." Today it is difficult to find more than "mixed colors." One of the main reasons for the decline is the difficulty of cultivation. Tubers do not tolerate frost and must be lifted after the leaves have turned yellow, and cool spring temperatures are necessary for best quality flowers. They also must have excellent drainage, and successful gardeners use raised beds. For most gardeners, it is a difficult plant to grow well, although if tubers are planted in early spring and mulched, those plants which do flower are worth the extra effort. Seed-propagated plants should be transplanted early in spring after danger of frost.

The leaves are 2- or 3-parted and the plant is erect. The flowers are about 3″ across and almost always double. Flower color is quite variable but tubers may be ordered in separate shades of red, yellow, etc.

Tubers can be divided after digging in the fall. Seed of newer hybrid forms may be sown approximately 5 months prior to planting out. Seeds should be sown at 60–62° F but no chilling requirement is needed. Germination occurs over 6–8 weeks.

**Cultivars:**

A number of horticultural divisions of this species have resulted from the many years of breeding and selection. The florists' section, called Persian Ranunculi, are variable in form and color and the most highly cultivated members of the genus. The gardeners' section, called Turban Ranunculi, thought to be var. *africanus*, have larger, broader leaves which are less cut than those of the species. The petals are curved inward forming a spherical flower very much like a double peony.

'Bloomingdale Strain' was the first hybrid from seed and this low-growing strain has become popular with greenhouse growers as a pot plant. It is more heat tolerant and flowers earlier than previous selections. The large flowers occur in vibrant mixed colors and are enjoyable as an indoor plant or as a garden specimen.

'Color Carnival' is a mixed bag of colorful 18–24″ tall plants, usually available only from seed. The double flowers are camellia-shaped.

'Superbissima' is a vigorous tall form with large semi-double flowers, available in mixed colors from red to white.

'Tecolote Strain' ('Tecolote Giants') are taller than the previous strain and better for cutting. This strain has been around for a long time and is available in separate shades. New cultivars are being introduced, primarily by Japanese breeders, and ones such as 'Early Dwarf Strain' are exciting and appear easier to grow than many of the previous types.

| *-montanus* (mon-tah′ nus) | Mountain Buttercup | 3–6″/12″ |
|---|---|---|
| Late Spring      Yellow | Europe | Zones 5–8 |

(Syn. *R. geranifolius*)

The leaves are 3–5-lobed and the flowers are borne singly. The leaves, which emerge from the base, are petioled but those on the stems are sessile. The yellow flowers possess the classic buttercup shape and color and are borne singly or up to 3 per inflorescence. The creeping rootstock results in rapid spread in good soils, making it a good ground cover, but not as invasive as *R. ficaria* or *R. repens*.

Propagate from division or seed.

### Cultivars:

'Molten Gold' is similar to the species but has larger, golden yellow flowers. It does well in well-drained soils and full sun to partial shade.

### Related Species:

*R. yakuschimanus* is only 2–3″ tall and bears ½″ wide waxy yellow flowers over yellow-veined leaves. It is a wonderful undiscovered little ground cover gem.

### Quick Key to Ranunculus Species

A. Flower usually white, single . . . . . . . . . . . . . *R. aconitifolius*
AA. Flower not usually white, single or double
    B. Plant 3–6″ tall, flower yellow . . . . . . . . . . . *R. montanus*
   BB. Plant 9–24″ tall, flowers various
       C. Rootstock tuberous, flowers various,
         petals reflexed and usually double . . . . . . . . *R. asiaticus*
      CC. Rootstock not tuberous, flowers yellow,
         petals curled up but not reflexed,
         double in 'Flore-plena' . . . . . . . . . . . . . . . . *R. acris*

### Additional Reading:

Carlson, M. 1993. Jeepers, creepers. *Gardens West* 75(5):55–56.

## *Ratibida* (rah-ti-bid′ a)    Ratibida, Mexican Hat Plant    Asteraceae

One of our native prairie coneflowers, ratibida is distinguished from other coneflowers mostly by the tan brown to black cylindrical receptacle (disk) and pinnately divided leaves. A couple of taxa of *Rudbeckia* are quite similar, such as *R. laciniata* and *R. nitida* (which see) but in those the disks are greenish and the leaves are simple (not divided or deeply lobed). General differences between coneflowers are discussed under *Rudbeckia*.

Two species are occasionally offered to gardeners, differing in rather subtle characteristics. The most distinctive feature of *R. columnifera* is the long, narrow cone (2″ long), at the base of which are attached 3–7 dropping, yellow ray flowers. Plants grow 2–3′ tall. While handsome in its own right, two cultivars are making forays into American gardens. 'Buttons and Bows' has double the number of ray flowers, each rust colored and attached to the elongated cone. A particularly handsome form is var. *pulcherrima*, with mahogany red flowers dropping from the tawny brown cone. Plants perform in full sun and any reasonable soil. Cool climes are more to their liking than warm ones, and if comfortable will flower 4–6 weeks. They grow well in zones 3–7.

*R. pinnata* is the classic prairie plant, with drooping yellow ray flowers and a prominent cone. It differs mainly in having leaves with 3–7 narrow segments and ray flowers longer than the raised disk. Plants generally grow 3–5' tall. Hardy in zones 3–7.

Propagate from seed.

**Additional Reading:**

Sabuco, J.J. 1993. Ratibida. *The Plantsmans Journal*. 2(1):20–21, 23.

## *Rehmannia* (ray-mahn' ee-a)     Chinese Foxglove     Gesneriaceae

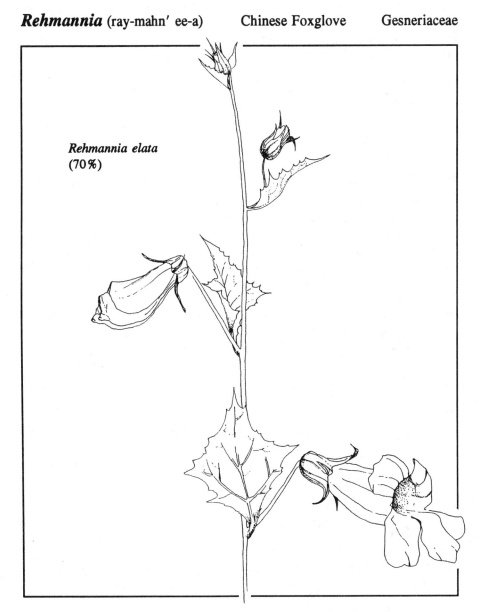

*Rehmannia elata*
(70%)

I have been impressed with the persistence and flowering of *R. elata*, Chinese foxglove, in the sunny garden at the Georgia gardens. The alternate leaves are up to 10″ long and have 3-6 lobes. The entire plant is hairy, similar to other members of this family (African violet). The flowering stems arise all season, although late spring is the most floriferous time. The large bright rose flowers have a yellow throat and are obviously 2-lipped. They resemble *Mimulus* or foxgloves. Plants reseed freely and a few small plants quickly become a large colony. The main limitation is its cold hardiness. Zone 7 is not a problem, and, since our plants have been totally evergreen down to 0° F and I suspect they may do fine to about zone 6.

Other species which may be found are *R. glutinosa*, with reddish brown to yellow flowers and *R. angualata*, similar to the above but with sessile leaves.

Propagation is easy from fresh seed or divisions from the colony.

## *Rhazya* see *Amsonia*.

## *Rheum* (ray′ um)　　　　　Rhubarb　　　　　Polygonaceae

Telling non-gardeners that rhubarb can be used as an ornamental plant is like telling them to grow goldenrod as a cut flower. In both cases, however, it is simply a matter of selecting the right form and not closing your mind before opening your eyes. The fresh tall panicles of edible rhubarb, *R. rhabarbarum* (*R.* × *cultorum*), always added a dimension of height in the spring in the Armitage garden. Other rhubarbs may have more pizzazz, but good old rhubarb adds leaf texture, decent flowers and a tasty petiole to boot. Of course, if the petioles are eaten, there is little left of the plant to consider anyway. However, a number of species are truly ornamental and commercially available in the United States. They taste terrible, but are magnificent garden specimens.

| *-compactum* (com-pak′ tum) | Dwarf Rhubarb | 2–3′/3′ |
|---|---|---|
| Summer　　　White | China | Zone 5–7 |

One of the smaller ornamental rhubarbs, it does not require an area all its own, like the bigger specimens. The glossy, heart-shaped leaves are 12–18″ wide with wavy margins, and in the summer creamy white flowers give rise to a wide panicle with many drooping branches. A handsome plant for flower and foliage.

Full sun and well-drained soils work well.

### Related Species:

*R. kialense* is a difficult to locate but a charming find. Plants are stoloniferous and can create a dense ground cover. The pleated leaves are reddish green and the greenish red flowers are held in open panicles. Useful in zones 5–7.

*-palmatum* (pahl-mah′ tum)          Ornamental Rhubarb          5–7′/6′
Summer          Red, White          China          Zone 5–7

This most imposing specimen makes one forget that rhubarb is a vegetable. A constant supply of moisture, well-drained soils, partial shade, copious fertilizer in the spring and lots of room are prerequisites. The dark green, 2–3′ wide basal leaves are deeply and sharply palmately lobed (thus the species name). Deep red 2′ long panicles reach to the sky. In combination with red peonies or variegated Solomon's seal, the plant is unforgettable. Unfortunately, plants are not as easy to grow as garden rhubarb and are more sensitive to drought and heat; they succumbed after a couple of lean years in my garden, and are best for cooler climates. However, if constant moisture is maintained, success is more likely. Fall planting is best. Once established, plants persist for many years.

Propagation of cultivars is best accomplished by division, being sure that each division has a dormant crown bud. The species and varieties may also be raised from seed.

**Cultivars:**
'Atrosanguineum' is the best form. Leaves emerge in the spring with a dark purple hue that persists, at least on the reverse, into summer. The flowers are deep cherry red followed by attractive fruit.
'Bowles' Variety' is similar to the previous cultivar but has rose-red flowers.
Var. *tanguticum* bears dark purple leaves which are less deeply cut than the species. The flowers appear on erect side shoots rather than terminal as in the previous forms and may be white, pink, or red. Often raised from seed, considerable variation occurs.

**Related Species:**
*R. alexandrae* is 3–4′ tall and bears undivided foliage that resembles overgrown plantain leaves. The pale greenish yellow flowers are borne in a narrow panicle in spring.

*Rhodohypoxis* (ro-do-hi-poks′ is)          Red Star          Hypoxidaceae

Including this bulbous plant may be pushing the perennial envelope a little far, as plants are native to South Africa. However, they naturally occur at 7000–8000′ elevations in the Drackensburg Mountains, providing winter hardiness to around 25–28° F. They are so beautiful, with 6 tepals (petals and sepals) colored in various shades of pure white to pale pinks to deep reds, that they are well worth trying, if only for a season. The flowering plants are 3–6″ tall and are perfectly suited to nooks and crannies of the rock garden. They enjoy plenty of moisture in the spring and early summer but abhor wetness in the winter, a problem in all but the best well-drained, water-retentive soils (there is an oxymoron, for sure).

The only species available is *R. baurii*, which produces keeled narrow leaves and flowers in ones or twos on 5–6″ tall scapes. In the wild, three distinct forms are found: *R. baurii* var. *baurii*, with deep pink to red flowers, var. *platypetala* with white flowers and var. *confecta*, with bicolored flowers. Hybridization and selection has occurred and named cultivars have arisen but today most catalogs offer a mixture of white, pink and red-flowered forms. They are sometimes found in flower in florist shops, having been produced as a pot plant for sale on Valentine's or Mother's Day. One of the ways to enjoy them more than 1 year is to grow the bulbs in pots and plunge them in the garden in the early spring. Bring them out before winter sets in and store them cool but not freezing. Gardeners on the Pacific coast and those with protected locations might be pleasantly surprised by leaving them in the garden over the winter. Nothing ventured, nothing gained!

## Cultivars:
'Albrighton' has deep red flowers.
'Dawn' opens pale pink and fades to white.
'Eva Kate' is a vigorous selection with deep pink flowers.
'Fred Broome' consists of light pink and rosy pink flowers.
'Harlequin' has flowers which change from pink to white.
'Helen' bears white flowers with smudges of pink on the edges of the tepals.
'Pictus' is a vigorous white, with pink blushing on the tepals.
'Ruth' provides clean white flowers.
'Tetra Red' has intense red blossoms.

## Related Species:
*R. milliodes* is more vigorous and has flowers in which the tepals are in two layers of three, separated by a noticeable gap. No such gap occurs in *R. baurii*. They are also more tolerant of wet feet and drainage is less of a problem. Several colors exist, although 'Claret' with deep red flowers is beautiful.

## Additional Reading:
Robinson, Allan. 1996. *Rhodohypoxis. The Garden* 121(6):345–347.

## *Rodgersia* (ro-jerz′ ee-a)          Rodgersia          Saxifragaceae

Rodgersia contains about five wonderfully ornamental species, native to China and Japan. The genus commemorates the American navy commander, Admiral John Rodgers, who was in charge of the expedition during which *R. podophylla* was discovered. It is ironic that, although discovered by an American, so few are grown in America. However, more nurseries are now offering Rodgersia so perhaps this will change.

They survive in ordinary soil but perform best in rich, moist soils and partial shade. The flowers are borne in large panicles (like those of *Astilbe*) on tall stems and may be white, yellow, or shades of red. All species are apetalous (no petals) and color is provided by the sepals and stamens. Leaves of most species are compound, basal and dark green. Plants spread to 5' and sufficient room is needed to look their best. One or two plants is all that is required to provide unique architectural detail along a stream, lake, or water feature. They are best naturalized along a waterside or large pond.

Quick Reference to Rodgersia Species

|  | Height (ft.) | Flower color | Leaf arrangement |
| --- | --- | --- | --- |
| *R. aesculifolia* | 3–6 | White | Palmate |
| *R. pinnata* | 3–4 | Rose-red | Pinnate |

| *-aesculifolia* (ees-skew-li-fo' lee-a) | Fingerleaf Rodgersia | 3–6'/6' |
| --- | --- | --- |
| Late Spring        White | China | Zones 5–6 |

The large basal leaves are usually composed of seven, 4–10″ long leaflets which are coarsely toothed and narrowed at the base. They are palmately compound and resemble the leaves of the horse-chestnut, *Aesculus*. The 1½–2' long panicle consists of flat clusters of creamy white flowers which open later than the other species. One of the characteristics of this species is the shaggy brown hair which covers the petioles, flower stalks and principal leaf veins. Flowers are not as spectacular as other species but plants are beautiful when sited properly.

Propagate by division or seed. Sow the tiny seeds on the surface and subirrigate so seeds and seedlings are not washed away. Germinate at 70–75° F; after seedlings have emerged, place at 50–60° F.

**Related Species:**

*R. henrici* is so similar to the above that some authorities consider them the same. The difference is that the leaflets are more sharply pointed (acuminate) and the flowers are red-purple.

*R. podophylla*, bronzeleaf rodgersia, is similar to the above species but the leaves consist of 5 glossy green leaflets, each with 3–5 shallow lobes towards the tips. The foliage turns bronze in the summer. The yellowish white flowers are held in 1' long dense attractively nodding panicles. The flowers differ from *R. aesculifolia* by having pointed sepals and shorter panicles.

| *-pinnata* (pi-nah' ta) | Featherleaf Rodgersia | 3–4'/4' |
| --- | --- | --- |
| Late Spring        Rose-Red | China | Zones 5–7 |

The foliage is often bronzed, particularly in the spring when temperatures are still cool. The leaves are pinnately compound but on some plants the leaflets are so closely attached that the leaves look palmate. It is necessary to closely inspect a number of leaves to be sure. The term for this confusing arrangement is pseudo-pinnate, which has a certain romantic ring to it. In fact, hybrids between *R. aesculifolia*, *R. pinnata* and others have resulted in the blurring of leaf arrangement among species. I was pleasantly surprised to see this plant in the fine gardens at Michigan State University. They leaves were a little crispy by the beginning of August but were doing relatively well.

Usually, there are five to nine 6–8″ long leaflets, widest in the middle and narrowed at both ends. The rose-red flowers are borne in branched panicles but considerable variation in flower color occurs. The branching habit of the inflorescence results in a terrific show of flowers.

Propagate similarly to *R. aesculifolia*.

**Cultivars:**

Var. *alba* has a long, loose inflorescence composed of creamy white flowers. In some cases the flowers are almost yellow. A beautiful form.

Var. *elegans* bears rose-pink flowers.

Var. *rosea* has rose flowers.

Var. *rubra* has dark red flowers.

Var. *superba* has bronze-purple leaves not as coarse as the type and a longer inflorescence of persistent rose-red flowers. This is the best garden specimen.

**Related Species:**

*R. sambucifolia*, elderberry rodgersia, is so named because of the obvious resemblance of the leaves to those of *Sambucus*, elderberry. Plants are about 3′ tall, with 7–11 pinnately arranged leaves. The flat-topped panicles consist of many densely held white or pink flowers. 'Rothaut' ('Red Skin') has bronze leaves.

Quick Key to Rodgersia Species

    A. Leaves palmately compound, shaggy
       hair on flower stalk and petiole . . . . . . . . . . . *R. aesculifolia*
  AA. Leaves resemble or are pinnately
       compound, not obviously hairy . . . . . . . . . . . . . *R. pinnata*

*Rohdea* (row-dee′ a)          Sacred Lily          Liliaceae

I first saw some plants (*R. japonica*) about 10 years ago but only because someone pointed them out to me. I have since seen them offered by many nurseries as an "evergreen addition to the winter garden," or as "tough complement to more colorful plants" or even as "glossy green specimen plants." I keep looking at these things and obviously, I am missing something. To me, they just look like upright green foliage plants, like an old *Aspidistra*, which should be in the home, not in the garden. The leaves are often dried out at the tips and look tattered and torn. They are tough, but so is a rock. They must be darlings of the landscape set where everything is homogenous and low maintenance, but it is a waste of good space in a garden. To be fair, they do well under difficult circumstances like dry shade.

The thick green basal leaves are about 15" long and 2–3" wide and in the summer, a short spike of inconspicuous yellow-green flowers are produced, themselves giving way to red berries. A couple of cultivars are occasionally seen; the leaves of 'Aureo-striata' and 'Striata' are striped with yellow and white respectively and 'Marginata' has white margins. A slight improvement but still nothing to spend a lot of money on. Gardeners in zones 5–9 can ignore me and spend their money.

**Additional Reading:**
Hattori, K. 1994. Plant of good fortune. *The Garden* 119(7):316–318.

## *Romneya* (rom-knee′ ya)  Matilja Poppy,   Papaveraceae
California Tree Poppy

Barely cold hardy in most of the country, this impressive plant is nevertheless a fine perennial where it survives. The impressive part comes from the large stature (plants grow 8′ tall) but plants are best known for the 4–5" wide fragrant silky white flowers and smooth blue-green foliage. The leaves are about 6" long, consisting of 3–4 spreading lobes, one always terminal. Flowers consist of 3 sepals, 6 petals (in 2 whorls of 3) and many yellow stamens. They open in late summer and fall.

Only one species occurs (*R. coulteri*) but var. *trichocalyx* has more finely divided leaves and is a little slower growing. Native to southwest California, they tolerate temperatures to about 15° F if grown in soils with excellent drainage and planted in protected areas. The stems become woody at the base but the entire plant generally dies down to the roots in the winter. Plants may be pinched back in the spring or early summer to allow branching and maintain a bit more dwarfness. They spread by underground rhizomes and can be invasive. Flowering occurs on the current seasons growth. This is a beautiful plant where it is hardy and certainly useful, if at times a little too rambunctious, on the West Coast.

The suckers which are often sent up from the roots may be separated and used for propagation or use root cuttings or seed. Germinate seed at 65–70° F.

## *Roscoea* (ros-ko′ ee-a)  Roscoea   Zingiberaceae

*Roscoea* probably should be placed in the almost-impossible-to-grow-but-I-must-have-one group of plants, such as *Meconopsis*. Gardeners come back from European travels with tales of beauty and a need to try such plants. Roscoea belongs to the ginger family, which is a pretty good hint that it won't be happy in Peoria. The only member of that family any of us can grow reasonably easily is the ginger lily, *Hedychium*, and its range doesn't extend terribly far. However, in the spirit of adventuresome gardening, *Roscoea* is certainly worth a try, if you can locate some.

The main species is *R. cautleoides*, whose leaves and flowers resemble the cautleya orchid. The leaves are about 6″ long and 1″ wide, although not always fully expanded at flowering. The 6–7 pale yellow flowers are carried well above the upright foliage and look like a cross between an iris and an orchid. 'Kew Beauty' has pale yellow, larger more orchid-like flowers. Plants may be more winter hardy than most think, perhaps to zone 6, however heat and humidity are not at all to their liking. If Roscoeas are your thing, try the fabulously pink to purple flowers in *R. alpina*, *R. humeana* and *R. purpurea*. All of the species are outstanding, but if they were as good here as in European gardens, we would see them offered by many more nurseries. Maintain even soil moisture in partial shade.

Propagate from divisions or seed.

## *Rosmarinus* (rose-ma-reen′ us)       Rosemary       Lamiaceae

*R. officinalis* is the penultimate herb/ornamental providing beauty, fragrance and persistence. Rosemary is familiar to everyone because of the aromatic leaves used for potpourri, perfumes and seasoning. These gray-green Mediterranean plants are woody shrubs, and can easily grow 4–6′ tall over time. The flowers are usually light blue to white and occur in late winter to early spring and attract bees from miles away. Numerous cultivars have arisen with different habits and leaf and flower colors. They are grown by herb specialists as culinary companions to thyme, oregano and lavender or as ornamental standards (small potted trees). Plants are hardy to zone 7 (to zone 6, with protection). The roots are more cold tolerant than the tops and so winters may cause top death, however, new growth will occur in the spring. The biggest threat to winter persistence is poorly drained soils.

Place in full sun, and if a sheltered dry area is available, rosemary can even be pruned and groomed as a hedge. Both acid and basic soils are appropriate.

### Cultivars:
'Albus' has white flowers.

'Arp' has light blue flowers and is quite cold hardy.

'Athens Blue Spires' is an upright vigorous hardy form whose light blue flowers absolutely cover the erect branches in late winter or early spring. Probably one zone more cold hardy than others. From the New Crop Program at the University of Georgia.

'Aureus' bears leaves speckled with yellow.

'Beneton' is an excellent stiff upright form. Holds its upright shape well.

'Blue Boy' is a dwarf form with small leaves.

'Golden Rain' has yellow variegated foliage.

'Lockwood de Forest' is a procumbent form, otherwise very similar to 'Tuscan Blue'.

'Majorca Pink' bears pink flowers.

'Prostratus' is a common low growing prostrate form.

'Tuscan Blue' has dark blue flowers and narrow leaves.

'Silver Spires' may be the same silvered plant grown in 1654 in Europe and then lost to cultivation. This upright sport was recently found in Mayfields Nursery in Surrey, UK by Ms. Christine Wolters. The plant has pale green leaves with white margins and, in full sun, can almost appear white.

**Additional Reading:**

Moore, S. 1994. Growing: pray, love, remember: From Aphrodite to Ophelia. *Garden Design* 13(5):35–36.

Hildebrand, I. 1993. Herbs as bonzi. *Prairie Gardener* 54:31–33.

Ocone, L. 1993. Robust and rugged rosemary. *Sunset magazine* 54:60–62.

## *Rubus* (rub′ us)  Brambles  Rosaceae

*Rubus* is best known for the tasty blackberries and raspberries or for the pain inflicted by the prickles and thorns that attack when we try to get rid of them. Of the 250 species, a number are quite ornamental, however, finding them in American catalogs is a challenge. One of my more memorable encounters with the genus was with a group of friends wandering around the grounds of Chesterwood, the former home of Chester French, in western Massachusetts. In the wooded area, we reveled in the colonies of interrupted ferns intermingled with thimbleberry, *R. odoratus*. I have also cursed the ragged canes of brambles which are everywhere in my garden. Some of these brambles, however, can be incredibly ornamental, such as those of *R. thibeticus* 'Silver Fern' whose cultivar description is right on.

Most of the species are shrubs and extremely variable, and it is difficult to tell one from another in many cases. If plants are successful, they can become invasive, requiring far more time to remove than to plant.

Quick Reference to Rubus Species

|  | Spines | Flower | Habit |
|---|---|---|---|
| *R. calycinoides* | Sparsely | White | Prostrate |
| *R. odoratus* | None | Pink-Purple | Arching |

| *-calycinoides* (kal-e-si-noid-eez) | Ornamental Raspberry | 6–12″/2′ |
|---|---|---|
| Summer  White | Taiwan | Zones 6–8 |
| (Syn. *R. pentalobus*) | | |

The brown hairy stems have small prickles on the woody procumbent stems which roots as it creeps along. The wrinkled simple leaves are ovate to almost rounded. Each leaf has 3–5 lobes with sharp serrations and the insignificant white flowers are borne singly, but plants should not be grown for the flowers. This is an excellent ground cover plant for partially shaded situations and will not take over the entire garden.

Propagate by cutting away the rooted stems.

### Related Species:

*R. microphylla* also has rounded, shallowly 3-lobed leaves but many more white flowers with maroon sepals. Small red fruit is formed in the summer. 'Varieagtus' has marbled pink and white foliage. Hardy to zone 7b.

| | | |
|---|---|---|
| *-odoratus* (o-do-rah' tus) | Thimbleberry | 2–3'/3' |
| Summer   Pink-Purple | Eastern North America | Zones 3–7 |

The most common and easiest to grow ornamental bramble, this vigorous deciduous shrub inhabits shady woodlands throughout the Northeast. The simple leaves are 5-lobed, serrated and pubescent beneath. The stems are light brown, peeling and hairy, and grow up and out, arching over and over. The best news about the stems is that they have no spines. The term *odoratus* means fragrant, and the pink-purple 2″ wide flowers have a pleasant, if not overbearing fragrance. About 7–10 five-petaled flowers are held in each inflorescence above the leaves in June to August. The fruits are red to orange and produced in late summer and fall.

Plants are aggressive ground covers in moist, shady areas and should not be planted in a small area. They are terrific for shaded woodlands and the combination of bright flowers, deep green leaves and the lack of spines make them useful. However, many a gardener has become frustrated with the aggressiveness nature and vows "never again."

### Cultivars:

'Albus' is similar to the species but has lighter green leaves and white flowers.

### Related Species:

*R. tricolor* is a prostrate grower with 4-sided stems and deep glossy green leaves which are white-tomentose beneath. The stems are not spiny, but bristly. The 1″ wide white flowers are produced singly or as a few flowers together. Hardy in zones 7 (perhaps 6) to 8.

Quick Key to Rubus Species

    A. Stems arching, no spines, flowers pink-purple . . . . *R. odoratus*
    AA. Stems prostrate, sparsely spiny, flowers white . . *R. calycinoides*

### Additional Reading:

Hinkley, D.J. 1994. Brambles for borders. *Horticulture* 72(3):34–38.

## *Rudbeckia* (rud-bek' ee-a)　　　　Coneflower　　　　Asteraceae

If one had been tramping about Sweden in the early 1700's, one may have met a physician with a keen botanical interest. His name was Olaus Olai Rudbeck and the genus which bears his name is one of the best known throughout the world. That all species of *Rudbeckia* are native to North America didn't stop Linnaeus from commemorating his former teacher in 1753.

*Rudbeckia* consists of about 30 species of annuals, biennials, and perennials. Some of the best known wild flowers, such as the annual black-eyed Susan, *R. hirta*, are found in the genus. In the Armitage garden, *R. hirta* reseeds prolifically most years and flowers for 2–3 months beginning the first week of June. This just happens to be my wife Susan's favorite flower. One of our favorite trips is to the Smokey Mountains in North Carolina where the wild black-eyed Susans compete with mountain mints, lobelias and monardas in openings alongside hiking trails in the summer and early fall. Life is good.

Hybridization and selection have yielded magnificent cultivars such as 'Marmalade', 'Rustic Colors', 'Golden Flame' and the outstanding 'Indian Summer'; however, regardless of claims to the contrary, they should be treated as annuals.

Several genera are buried under the name coneflower, including purple coneflower, *Echinacea*, and *Ratibida* (*Lepachys*), prairie coneflower. Numerous specific morphological differences occur which are the final word in separating some of the genera (such as disc scales being persistent on *Rudbeckia*, deciduous in *Ratibida*). However a few horticultural clues may be useful.

|  | *Coreposis* | *Echinacea* | *Ratibida* | *Rudbeckia* |
|---|---|---|---|---|
| Leaf arrangement | Opposite | Alternate | Alternate | Alternate |
| Ray flowers | Yellow | Purple(1) | Yellow | Yellow |
| Shape of disc | Flattened | Raised | Columnar | Raised(2) |

(1): cream colored in *E. pallida*
(2): columnar in *R. laciniata*

In the perennial *Rudbeckia* species, all have yellow to gold ray flowers and brown to black centers. The size and shape of the center (cone) and the height of the plant are distinctive. Of the useful coneflowers, *R.* 'Goldsturm' is about 2' tall while selections of *R. laciniata* and *R. maxima* can reach 7–10'. The foliage may be entire or deeply cut and is almost always alternate. Growing coneflowers is not at all difficult, thriving in full sun to partial shade in ordinary garden soil. Some species, such as *R. laciniata*, benefit from moist soils, while *R. hirta* tolerates dry conditions. Once coneflowers start flowering, color is provided until frost. *R. triloba* starts flowering in the Armitage garden in early to mid June, *R. laciniata* in mid June, and *R. fulgida* and *R. maxima* in late July.

Quick Reference to Rudbeckia Species

|  | Height (in.) | Color of disc |
|---|---|---|
| R. fulgida | 18–30 | Brown-purple |
| R. laciniata | 30–72 | Greenish |
| R. maxima | 48–72 | Black |
| R. nitida | 36–48 | Greenish |
| R. triloba | 24–36 | Black |

| *-fulgida* (ful-gi' da) | Orange Coneflower | 18–30"/24" |
|---|---|---|
| Summer      Yellow | Southeastern United States | Zones 3–8 |

This species has entire, slightly hairy foliage. The 3-veined basal leaves are twice as long as broad (oblong to lanceolate) and carried on much-branched stems. The 2–2½" wide flowers consist of up of 12–14 yellow ray flowers surrounding a brownish purple disc. Plants are rhizomatous and form large clumps after 2–3 years. Although not invasive, colonies form rapidly in rich loose soil. The species is seldom seen but several varieties and cultivars are popular.

Propagate by seed, division or terminal cuttings.

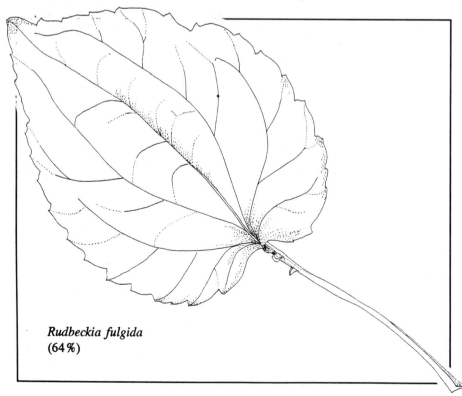

*Rudbeckia fulgida*
(64%)

## Cultivars:

The varieties and cultivars may be separated by shape and size of foliage. Differences are slight but all are improvements on the species.

Var. *deamii* grows about 2′ tall, has larger basal leaves and is more floriferous than the species. The basal leaves are not as wide as the species (⅜ to ½ as broad as long), while the upper stem leaves are about as large as the basal leaves and have small, well-spaced teeth. Stems are not as branched. Plants are slightly better than the species.

*Rudbeckia* 'Goldsturm' (64%)

Var. *speciosa* (*R. newmanii*, *R. speciosa*) has basal leaves which are entire or shallowly lobed. The stem leaves are coarsely toothed. Plants are about 24–30″ tall and the flowers are 2–3″ across and have deep orange ray petals.

Var. *sullivantii* is much like var. *deamii* but the stem leaves are successively reduced in size until the uppermost are merely large bracts. In 1937, a free flowering and more compact plant was selected in Foerster's Nursery in Germany. This clone was called 'Goldsturm' and became one of the most pervasive plants in the perennial trade, with good reason. The dark green foliage contrasts beautifully with the 3–4″ wide deep yellow flowers. The center consists of a nearly black cone. Full sun and moist soils are necessary for best performance. Plants are magnificent from late July well into September. The popularity of 'Goldsturm' has resulted in demands which could not be met by vegetatively propagated means. In response to the demand, growers resorted to seed-propagation and today I doubt there are many true 'Goldsturm' out there. From seed, most plants are var. *sullivantii* which, fortunately, is almost as good. This messing up of vegetative clones has also occurred in Coronation Gold yarrow, *Heuchera* 'Palace Purple' and *Sedum* 'Autumn Joy' with far worse results.

| *-laciniata* (la-sin-ee-ah′ ta) | Cutleaf Coneflower | 30–36″/4′ |
| Summer          Yellow | North America | Zones 3–9 |

Plants are native from Quebec west to Montana and south to Florida, Texas and Arizona, growing in moist fields and grassy roadsides. The dull green lower leaves are deeply 3–7 lobed while the upper leaves are sessile and less deeply cut into 3 lobes. The stems, which branch only near the top, have short stiff hairs which feel like sandpaper when handled. The 2–3½″ wide blooms are made up of drooping yellow ray flowers surrounding a green cylindrical disc. Plants do best in moist soils but drier soils may be tolerated as long as irrigation is provided during drought. Place in full sun to partial shade. Plants are long lived and 10 years of good garden performance is not uncommon. Cutting spent flowers after the first flush results in additional flowering in the fall.

Propagate the species from seed, division, or terminal cutting. Cultivars must be propagated vegetatively by division or cuttings.

### Cultivars:

'Golden Glow' propelled this species from an overlooked wild flower to a garden staple. Introduced to the garden trade in 1894 as var. *hortensia*, it has been popular ever since. Unlike most others in this species, they can be quite invasive. Plants grow 3–5′ tall and are covered with large, fully double lemon yellow flowers. Unfortunately, they are also often covered with aphids, to which this cultivar is most prone. 'Golden Glow' has been replaced by newer cultivars which are shorter and a little less attractive to aphids.

'Goldquelle' ('Gold Fountain', 'Gold Drop') bears double yellow flowers and is clump-former, growing 2½–4' tall. In full sun, stems are sufficiently strong to support the heavy flowers; in shady areas, they fall like cooked spaghetti. Likely a hybrid with *R. nitida*.

'Herbstsonne' ('Autumn Sun') grows up to 7' tall and is one of the finest coneflowers in cultivation. Arguably, the plant is not a cultivar of *R. laciniata* but probably a hybrid between it and *R. nitida*. Most catalogs list it as *R. nitida*. Dozens of long, drooping sulphur yellow petals surround a green cylindrical disc producing a glorious scene in late August through October. Towering over red dahlias, blue asters and purple coneflowers, it is the king of the sunny fall garden. In the North, the stems usually don't require staking, however, they may need some support in the South. Cold hardy to about zone 5.

'Soleil D'or' ('Golden Sun') bears single flowers consisting of wide golden ray flowers.

**Related Species:**

*R. nitida* is similar to *R. laciniata* in that the yellow ray flowers droop and the disc is greenish and quite columnar. However, plants are shorter with rounded, sparsely toothed, almost entire leaves. They are native to the South and winter hardy to zone 6 or 7. Various cultivars have been assigned to the species over the years, the most well-known being 'Herbstsonne' (see above). Plants can't read, so sleep should not be lost as to where they belong.

| *-maxima* (max-i' ma) | Giant Coneflower | 5–8'/3' |
|---|---|---|
| Summer　　　Yellow | United States | Zones 5–9 |

The common name is particularly fitting as these plants look down on most others in the garden. The bold 2' long and 8–10" wide basal leaves are blue-green and clasp the stem as they ascend. The distinctive leaves, along with the handsome yellow flowers, have made this plant a favorite of garden designers. As a contrast to fine textured species or simply to raise the ceiling of the garden room, these have become more and more common since their introduction to commercial production in this country in the late 1980's. The leaves tend to be more evergreen the further south one travels. The yellow drooping ray flowers are attached to a black cylindrical cones and although the flowers may be 3½" in diameter, they always look small because of the immense size of the plant. In full sun, plants are upright and do not need support. Don't put in shade.

Propagate by root cuttings (see *Anemone*).

| *-triloba* (tri-lo' ba) | Three-Lobed Coneflower | 24–36"/18" |
|---|---|---|
| Summer　　　Yellow | United States | Zones 3–10 |

The much branched plants carry many small (1½" across) yellow flowers with purplish black, raised central discs. Flowers appear about the same time as 'Goldsturm' and last nearly as long. The basal leaves are obviously

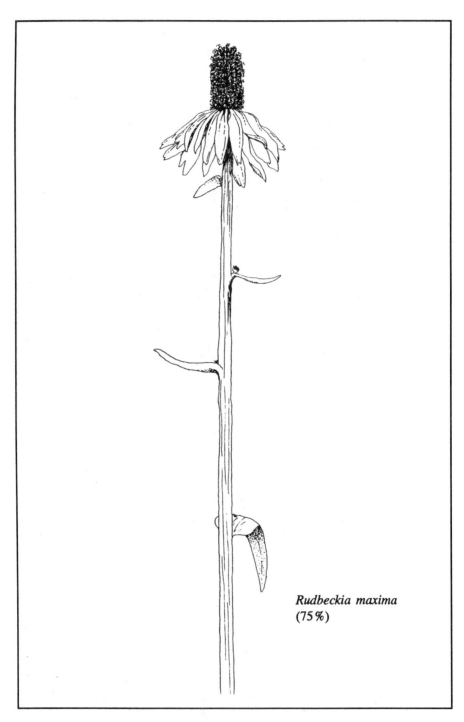

*Rudbeckia maxima*
(75%)

three-lobed but the stem leaves less so. Plants are seldom listed in perennial catalogs, perhaps because *R. triloba* is technically a biennial (although that does not stop the common foxglove from being listed everywhere). This is unfortunate because it is more persistent than many biennials. Some years it returns in the same spot, others it does not. Plants perform well in open areas but also tolerate partial shade. Support may be necessary to keep plants upright if shade is present. However, even without support, the attractive flowers turn up to the sun to blanket the ground. This overlooked native plant should be included in more gardens. This is such a good plant that it was designated a Georgia Gold Medal Winner in 1996 and actively promoted to gardeners throughout the Southeastern United States.

Propagate the species by division, seed, or cuttings; var. *nana* is best propagated by division. Plants propagated from seed in the spring flower the first year.

**Related Species:**

*R. subtomentosa*, sweet coneflower, grows about 4' tall and differs from *R. triloba* in having all the leaves with obvious petioles and a dull purple-brown disc rather than the black seen in the former species. The stems are also covered with soft down. Smell the flowers and you may pick up the scent of anise, accounting for its common name. Although plants sometimes open up in the middle, particularly after a hard rain, they are useful and showy for areas of full sun. Hardy to zone 5 (4 with a little protection).

Quick Key to Rudbeckia Species

    A. Leaves (at least lower ones) obviously lobed
      B. Leaves 3–7 deeply cut lobes, cone cylindrical,
        greenish, mature plants at least 4' tall . . . . . . . . *R. laciniata*
      BB. Basal leaves 3 lobed, cone raised, brown to
        dark purple, mature plants less than 3' tall . . . . . . *R. triloba*
    AA. Leaves not obviously lobed
      B. Leaves blue-green, entire, mature
        plants at least 6' tall . . . . . . . . . . . . . . . . . . . *R. maxima*
      BB. Leaves not blue-green
        C. Cone cylindrical, greenish, plants
          usually more than 4' tall . . . . . . . . . . . . . . . *R. nitida*
        CC. Cone not cylindrical, black, plants
          usually less than 4' tall . . . . . . . . . . . . . . . *R. fulgida*

**Additional Reading:**

Darke, R. 1993. Rudbeckias. *Fine Gardening* 33:38–41.

Iannarelli, P.G. 1990. Rudbeckia rising. *Horticulture* 68(8):36–38.

Krizek, L. 1992. Black-eyed Susan. *The Plantsmans Journal* 2(1):12–14, 23.

Nicholson, M.E. and R.G. Hawke. 1995. Rudbeckia for cultivated landscapes. Plant Evaluation notes, Chicago Botanic Garden 8:4 pp.

*Rudbeckia triloba*
(80%)

## *Ruta* (roo' ta)   Rue   Rutaceae

Many herbs are considered highly decorative and rue surely belongs in that category. A number of plants travel under the common name rue, including rue anemone (*Anemonella thalictroides*), goat's rue (*Galega officinalis*), wall rue (*Asplenium ruta-muraria*), and the various species of *Thalictrum* which make up the meadow rues. The alternate, pinnately compound leaves of rue are particularly pungent and dotted with purple glands. The yellow flowers, consisting of 4 sepals and 4 petals (occasionally 5 of each) and 8–10 stamens, are usually borne in flattened corymbs. Plants may be propagated by seed or cuttings. Of the 40 species, only *R. graveolens* is used to any extent outside the herb garden.

| *-graveolens* (gra-vee' o-lenz) | | Rue, Herb of Grace | 12–36"/30" |
|---|---|---|---|
| Summer | Pale Yellow | Southern Europe | Zones 4–8 |

This species was well established in European monastery gardens in the 1100's because its aromatic odor suggested medicinal value. If one could swallow the concoction of leaves and stems without gagging, it was supposed to help one stay young. In fact, the original Greek name was Rute, from *ruomai*, to preserve, a reference to the plant's effect on longevity. It is a sub-shrub, meaning that the base of the plant becomes woody but dies back to the ground in the winter. The ¾" diameter flowers are rather dull yellow. The flowers are all right, but compared to the blue foliage of some of the cultivars, they take a back seat. The reason for its popularity as an ornamental plant is because of the lovely glaucous blue, delicately cut foliage, particularly on some cultivars. It should also be mentioned that handling of the foliage can cause dermatitis (like poison ivy) in susceptible individuals when the skin is exposed to sunlight. This happens more in nurseries handling large quantities of material but can occur with gardeners as well. Plant in full sun and well-drained soil. Wet feet result in doomed plants.

Propagate the cultivars from terminal cuttings in late summer and early fall.

### Cultivars:

'Blue Beauty', a mounding 18" tall plant, bears excellent blue-green foliage and is an asset to the front of the border. It is so similar to 'Blue Mound' that I can see no difference.

'Curly Girl' has curly lacy blue foliage which is bushy and compact.

'Jackman's Blue' is more popular in Europe than here and is about 30" tall. The foliage is glaucous blue and topped by the same pale yellow flowers found in the species. The cultivars help soften some of the screaming reds and yellows in the summer and fall garden.

'Variegata' has dissected leaves edged with creamy white.

# S

## *Sagina* (sa-geen' a)          Pearlwort          Caryophyllaceae

Who could believe that this tiny plant is related to such flowering favorites as carnations and Maltese cross? Yet a quick study of the small white flowers shows the similarities. They consist of 5 petals and sepals and are usually borne singly on short stalks in the spring. The mat forming, ground hugging plants are becoming more popular in patio containers, around flagstones, or as ground covers in the rock garden. The main species offered is *S. subulata*, pearlwort, whose tight compact growth habit makes it the best one for sculpting. The bright green narrow leaves are about ½″ long and form a tight mossy carpet when planted in partial sun and gritty well-drained soils. Abundant summer rain is a problem, because water droplets become trapped in the leaves, resulting in rotting and melting out of various parts of the mat. Division and an occasional shearing help alleviate the problem. High humidity is not much to its liking, particularly if grown on heavy soils. Plants are winter hardy to about 0° F, maybe to zone 6.

The best use for pearlwort is in containers where watering and drainage can be better controlled. They are neat plants when the green mats ooze over the sides of containers, they are sad when they melt out in the garden. Propagate from division or seed, the cultivar from division only.

### Cultivars:

'Aurea' is a golden yellow leaved form. Not as common, but handsome.
   Requires more shade than the species.

## *Salvia* (sal' vee-a)          Sage          Lamiaceae

One of my fondest memories as a young boy was drinking the nectar from the red salvia flowers that my friend's dad planted in his garden every summer. Plucking out the center of the flower (I had no idea it was called the corolla) and squeezing out the "honey" was a favorite summer pastime. It is an activity I have not yet outgrown. Those who know *Salvia* only as an annual bedding plant are surprised to learn that this is a vast genus, consisting of over 700 species. Salvia is collectors' dream! And collectors there are. I think most plantspeople go through a "Salvia stage of life" sometime in their garden careers, collecting dozens of sages with unpronounceable names, falling in love with all of them, and then like a teenager, coming around to the real world. Been there, done that. Unfortunately, nurseries feed this habit by introducing new ones every year, most of which are admired briefly before they die. To collect them all is impossible, but the trying is not. There are sufficient ornamental species available today that the collector can enjoy this hobby for a lifetime. In this respect, *Salvia* is much like *Campanula*, and zealots of both will constantly drag you over to see their newest find. But with so many sages from which to choose, it should not be surprising that a few new ones do "hit the ground running." Since the last edition, salvia fever has peaked, and now we can concentrate on those which have stood at least a short test of time.

In general, members have 4-sided stems, opposite leaves and whorled flowers. The tubular 2-lipped flowers are produced in terminal and axillary whorls. Blue and red are the predominant flower colors but those with red flowers are almost always annuals or short-lived perennials. Yellow is also available in the handsome *S. koyamae*. Plants range in height from the grey-leaved, 1' tall *S. chamaedryoides* to immense 4' hulks such as *S. involucrata*, both native to Mexico. Many have interesting scented foliage when bruised, and it is always fun to play the game of "What is this smell?" with your friends. *S. rutilans* smells of pineapple, *S. microphylla* (syn. *S. grahamii*) resembles currants, and *S. officinalis* smells of sage. The scents seem obvious but 9 times out of 10, another person will smell something totally different. My wife, Susan, is convinced that pineapple sage should be changed to carrot cake sage. Still others are heaped in tradition and folklore and possible new medicinal uses. *S. officinalis* comes complete with culinary and medicinal histories, as does the relatively recently discovered *S. divinorum*, of the Sierra Mazateca region of Mexico, where it is held in high esteem by the native peoples of the area.

Many species are native to Mexico, the southwestern United States or Central America, and winter hardiness in much of the country is a problem. Many of our more common species were sent to England in the late 1700's and early 1800's. John Ruskin wrote in *Proserpina* in 1879 that "the exotic sages have no moderation in their hues" and was particularly unhappy with the brilliant blue of *S. patens*, stating that "there's no color that gives me such an idea of violence—a sort of rough, angry scream—as that shade of blue, ungradated." Regardless of Ruskin's hysteria, some of these "exotic" sages are available in various catalogs and nurseries. As gardeners, we have our own homeboys who continue to introduce and popularize this genus. Mr. Salvia, John Dufresne of Greensboro, North Carolina, has provided outstanding information and hybrids, and John Fairey and Carl Schoenfeld of Yucca Do in Waller, Texas, have explored Mexico and the Southwest to add to and feed our *Salvia* habit. Plant collecting and hybridization are alive and well in the United States, you simply have to know where to look.

Many of the species we read about are annuals or half hardy perennials which overwinter north of zone 8 only during exceptionally mild winters. I have had my "salvia binge" as I have grown or studied most of those on the following list. That I survived says something of the toughness of a gardener.

A relative hardiness guide to several salvias is provided below. Few of the "hardy" salvias survive north of zone 4 and those designated as "half hardy" overwinter in zones 8–10, occasionally zone 7. Annuals and biennials will die after flowering regardless of location, although they may reseed readily. Of course, even the most tender half hardy may overwinter for a few years proving the age old truism that plants can't read. The hardiness zones are guidelines at best.

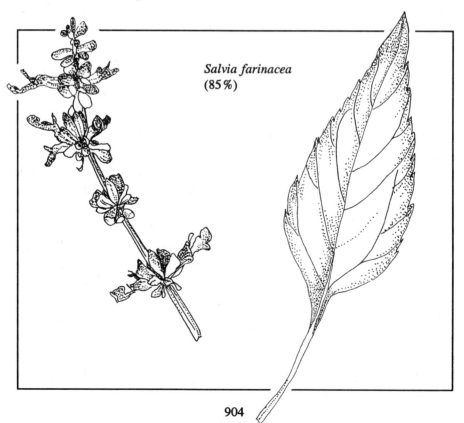

*Salvia farinacea*
(85%)

| Species | Hardy, half hardy, annual, biennial | Flower color | Hardiness zones |
|---|---|---|---|
| S. aethiopis | Biennial | Dull white | 7–9 |
| S. apiana | Half hardy | White | 8–10 |
| S. argentea | Biennial | Whitish, yellow | 6–8 |
| S. arizonica | Half hardy | Sky blue | 7–10 |
| S. azurea | Hardy | Azure blue | 5–9 |
| S. blepharophylla | Half hardy | Scarlet red | 8–10 |
| S. bulleyana | Hardy | Pale yellow, black | 7–9 |
| S. cacaliifolia | Half hardy | Dark blue | 8–10 |
| S. candelabrum | Half hardy | Violet blue | 8–10 |
| S. chamaedryoides | Hardy | Blue | 7–10 |
| S. clevelandii | Half hardy | Blue | 8–10 |
| S. coccinea | Annual | Bright red | 9–10 |
| S. confertifolia | Half hardy | Red | 8–10 |
| S. darcyi | Half hardy | Bright red | 7–10 |
| S. discolor | Half hardy | Blue-black | 9–10 |
| S. farinacea | Half hardy | Light blue | 8–10 |
| S. forskaohlei | Hardy | Violet blue | 5–8 |
| S. glechomifolia | Half hardy | Blue | 7b–10 |
| S. greggii | Half hardy | Red | 7–10 |
| S. guaranitica | Half hardy | Violet blue | 7–10 |
| S. haematodes | Half hardy | Bluish violet | 7–10 |
| S. hians | Hardy | Bluish | 6–9 |
| S. horminum | Annual | Lilac | 9–10 |
| S. indica | Annual | Lavender | 9–10 |
| S. 'Indigo Spires' | Half hardy | Blue | 7–10 |
| S. interrurpta | Half hardy | Blue | 8–10 |
| S. involucrata | Half hardy | Pink | 8–10 |
| S. jurisicii | Hardy | Deep blue | 4–7 |
| S. koyamae | Hardy | Yellow | 6–8 |
| S. lavandulifolia | Hardy | Violet blue | 5–10 |
| S. leucantha | Half hardy | Blue and white | 7b–10 |
| S. lyrata | Hardy | Lavender | 6–9 |
| S. madrensis | Half hardy | Yellow | 7–10 |
| S. microphylla | Half hardy | Red | 8–10 |
| S. miniata | Half hardy | Red | 8–10 |
| S. nipponica | Hardy | Yellow | 6–9 |
| S. officinalis | Hardy | Purple | 4–7 |
| S. patens | Half hardy | Gentian blue | 8–10 |
| S. penstemoides | Hardy | Red | 6–8 |
| S. pratensis | Hardy | Blue | 3–7 |

| Species | Hardy, half hardy, annual, biennial | Flower color | Hardiness zones |
|---|---|---|---|
| S. prunelloides | Annual | Blue | 9–10 |
| S. puberula | Half hardy | Pink | 7–10 |
| S. regla | Half hardy | Orange-scarlet | 8–10 |
| S. rutilans | Half hardy | Bright red | 8–10 |
| S. sclarea | Biennial | Whitish blue | 5–9 |
| S. sinaloaensis | Half hardy | Deep blue | 8–10 |
| S. splendens | Annual | Red | 9–10 |
| S. × superba | Hardy | Purple | 5–9 |
| S. transsylvanica | Hardy | Dark blue | 4–7 |
| S. uliginosa | Hardy | Sky blue | 6–10 |
| S. van houttei | Half hardy | Wine red | 8–10 |
| S. verticillata | Hardy | Lilac blue | 5–8 |

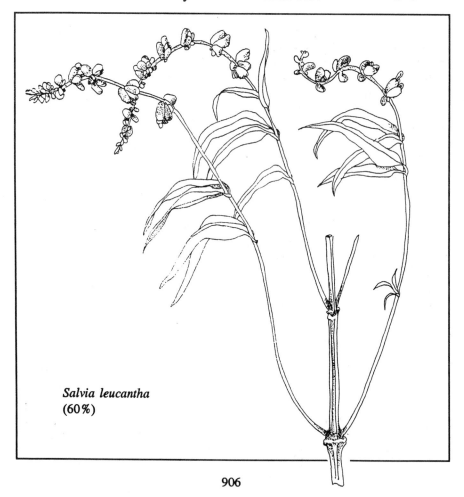

Salvia leucantha
(60%)

Looking at the above list, depending on where you live, the choice of perennial ornamental sages may be somewhat limited. However, incorporating several half hardy species such as pineapple sage, *S. rutilans* (usually sold as *S. elegans*, the foliage really does smell of pineapple) or *S. guaranitica*, with violet blue flowers and mild currant scent to the leaves, is well worth the effort. Numerous half hardy hybrids are also available and attractive, such as 'Marashino' and 'Cherry Queen'.

A potential drawback to some of the sages is that they are fall-flowerers only. But if you condemn a plant because of that you might as well condemn plants that enjoy the shade. Fall-flowering salvias can rejuvenate a tired garden and add an entire new dimension. Some of these include velvet sage, Hildago sage and wine sage. Many of half hardy sages grow so rapidly that it really doesn't matter if they return or not. Take a few cuttings in over the winter or buy new ones in the spring. For example, *S. leucantha*, velvet sage, grows to 3–4' tall producing dozens of magnificent lavender-blue flowers with white corollas which cover the plant from late summer through frost. The leaves are velvety, fragrant and unappetizing to insects or diseases. The form 'Blue on Blue' is entirely blue and equally excellent. *S. van houttei*, wine sage, is 3' tall with claret red flowers which start blooming in mid-summer and continue until frost. Probably the most wonderful flower color is found with the orange-scarlet Hildago sage, *S. regla*, which stops people in their tracks. Unfortunately, it does not flower until late October, already too late for many northern gardens. They should all be raised from cuttings which root easily throughout the growing season.

## Quick Reference to Salvia Species

|  | Height (in.) | Flower color |
|---|---|---|
| *S. argentea* | 24–48 | White with yellow |
| *S. azurea* | 36–48 | Azure blue |
| *S. greggii* | 20–30 | Red |
| *S. guaranitica* | 36–40 | Deep blue |
| *S. jurisicii* | 12–18 | Deep lilac |
| *S. koyamae* | 20–30 | Yellow |
| *S. officinalis* | 12–20 | Purple |
| *S. pratensis* | 12–36 | Bright blue |
| *S. sclarea* | 30–48 | White/lilac |
| *S.* × *sylvestris* | 18–48 | Blue violet |

| *-argentea* (ar-gen-tee′ a) | Silver Sage | 24–48″/3′ |
|---|---|---|
| Summer　　　　Whitish | Southern Europe | Zones 6–8 |

Grown for the large white-woolly foliage, plants make a wonderful contrast to other green leaved plants in the garden. The wedge-shaped, wrinkled, and irregularly toothed stem leaves are sessile and about 6–8″ long. The flowers appear the second year on seed-propagated plants but are not particularly exceptional. They appear in a slightly branched large panicle, each whorl consisting of 6–10 whitish yellow flowers. The inside part of the flower, the corolla, is about 3 times longer than the calyx. Having given the details of this flower's structure, I now recommend their removal as soon as possible. This allows the foliage to remain the dominant feature of the plant and insures the plant produces leaves rather than marginally attractive flowers.

In late summer plants often look the worse for wear, particularly if the summer has been hot and rainy. Hairy leaved plants such as this and *Stachys* tend to retain moisture, allowing leaf diseases to become established. This is a terrific plant for containers and requires well-drained gritty soils to do well. In the North, plants do well down to zone 5, in the South, they perform well north to zone 7a, struggle in 7b, and quickly melt out further south.

Propagate by seed or self-rooting lateral offshoots which may be detached in the spring and replanted.

### Related Species:

*S. aethiopis*, African sage, is also a biennial with basal rosettes of large toothed leaves. The leaves are dull green but have long white hairs (tomenta) in the center in the winter and early spring. The flowers are dull white.

| *-azurea* (a-zew′ ree-a) | Azure Sage | 3–4′/4′ |
|---|---|---|
| Fall    Azure Blue | Southeastern United States | Zones 5–9 |

This large plant attains 3–4′ in height when the long slender spikes of azure-blue flowers appear. The lance-shaped basal foliage is about 3″ long but the leaves become smaller and narrower as they ascend the stem. Flowers are borne in the upper leaf axils in spike-like whorled inflorescences. The pedicels (the individual flower stalks) are short, resulting in flowers densely arranged on the stalk. A native of the Southeast, it is much more tolerant of heat and humidity than many other species. Two or three plants placed about the garden dominant the fall scene. Some of the finest specimens I have encountered were in the Horticulture Gardens at Massey University in Palmerston North, New Zealand.

Propagate from seed, division, or terminal cuttings.

### Cultivars:

Var. *grandiflora* (syn. ssp. *pitcheri*, *S. pitcheri*) has paler green, more hairy leaves and larger, paler blue flowers than the species. It is more available but no better than the type.

**Related Species:**

*S. uliginosa*, native to southern Brazil and Uruguay, grows 4–5' tall and bears cambridge flowers with small white throats in late summer and fall. However, in the trial gardens at the University of Georgia, they also bloom in early June, slump in the summer and perk up again in the fall. The flowers are densely arranged in 7–20 flowered whorls and occur until frost in the North and through October in the South. Hardy from zones 6 (occasionally 5) to 9. They can be beautiful but also very invasive, particularly in heavy soils. Plants may need support in areas of hot summers.

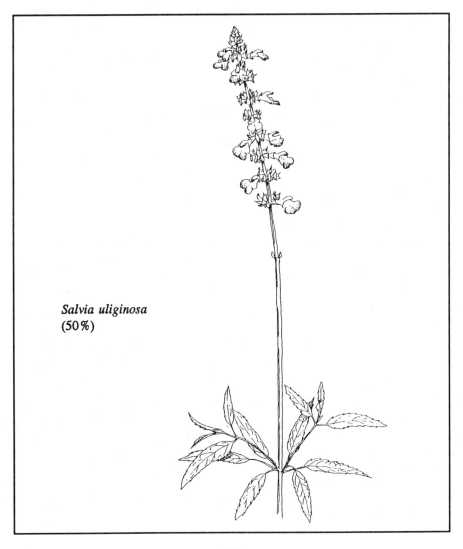

*Salvia uliginosa*
(50%)

**-greggii** (greg-ee' eye)      Texas Sage      2–3'/3'
Summer      Red      Texas, Mexico      Zones 7–10

This fine Texas native has found its way into mainstream perennial gardens, and provides more winter hardiness than most other red forms. The 1–2″ long ovate leaves have entire margins and produce a heavy sage fragrance when rubbed. The typical form has scarlet flowers and was found near Saltillo, Mexico by a Mexican trader, Josiah Gregg in 1870. The 2-lipped flowers, which may be red, pink, violet or white, are held in whorls of twos or threes and have a wide lower lip and smaller upper lip. Flowers occur in mid- to late summer and flower well into the fall. The plants are a bit unruly and get rather messy as the season progresses. Cutting back after a month in the garden helps keep it more compact. Texas sage has become popular because of its heat, humidity and drought tolerance, characteristics which also occur in some of the more handsome hybrids produced using the species.

**Cultivars:**
'Alba' has white flowers with a green calyx. Also sold as 'White'.
'Desert Blaze' has variegated leaves with narrow white edges. Plants are only about 18″ tall and bear red flowers in spring and fall.
'Cienego D'oro' has pale yellow flowers, growing 15–18″ tall.
'Furman's Red' grows much more upright than the former cultivars, stretching up to 3' in height. The bright red flowers occur throughout the season, but are heavier in late spring and fall. Hardy to zone 6b.
'Keter's Red' has an orange-red flower.

**Related Species and Hybrids:**
*S. darcyi*, brought to the United States from Mexico by Yucca Do Nursery, grows 3–4' tall with orangy red flowers and light green heart-shaped foliage. Plants are likely hardy from zones 7–10.

*S.* × *jamensis* is the name given by James Compton for the naturally occurring yellow-flowered hybrid between *S. greggii* and *S. microphylla* found at an elevation around 2000–3000' in a Mexican mountain pass in 1991. Other colors also occurred and names have been published. 'La Luna' has creamy yellow flowers, and 'El Doranzo' bears peach colored flowers. I have yet to see plants available in the United States but they will emerge. Likely hardy in zones 7–10.

'Cherry Queen' is one of the many hybrids produced by Richard Dufresne (as are many others listed here). This hybrid is the result of crossing *S. greggii* and *S. blepharophylla*, eyelash sage. We have had this sage in the Horticulture Gardens at Georgia for 5 years and every year it starts flowering in May and continues until frost. An absolutely outstanding plant for southern gardens.

'Marashino', a hybrid with *S. greggii* and *S. microphylla*, is an excellent marashino-cherry-red sage.

'Red Velvet' (*S. greggii* × *S. microphylla*) is about 3' tall and has velvet red flowers.

'Raspberry Royale' (*S. greggii* × *S. microphylla*) bears magenta flowers in late summer and fall. Similar to the latter hybrid. All of the above hybrids are alive with hummingbirds and butterflies.

| | | |
|---|---|---|
| ***-guaranitica*** (gar-an-it' I-ca) | Blue Anise Sage | 4–6'/4' |
| Summer　　Deep Blue | Brazil, Argentina | Zones 7–10 |
| (Syn. *S. ambigens*) | | |

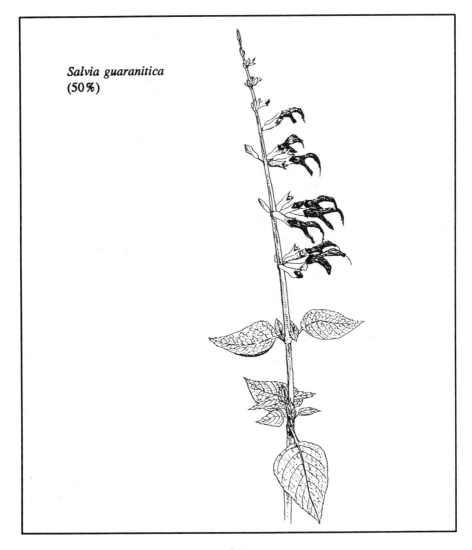

*Salvia guaranitica*
(50%)

This outstanding sage, with long deep blue flowers, begins to flower in early to mid-summer and continues all season. The dark green leaves are 4–6″ long, and sparsely hairy. They don't have much smell when crushed and do not smell like anise. Flowers are held in whorls of 3–8, the corolla (the petals) can be up to 3″ long, and the calyx (sepals) may be a different color. The lower lip is shorter than the upper one.

This is a full sun plant, growing in partial shade simply makes the plants taller and in need of support. Plants may be cut back early in the season to promote more compactness and to control height. Good drainage helps a good deal, particularly in the winter. Divide or take cuttings every third year to maintain vigor.

In Georgia, we think so highly of this species that we awarded it the prestigious Georgia Gold Award for herbaceous plants in 1995.

### Cultivars:

'Argentina Skies' was shared with me many years ago by Charles Cresson of Swarthmore, PA. The flowers are pastel blue and a much more muted color than that of the species. Beautiful, although not as floriferous.

'Blue Ensign' has large Cambridge blue petals with green sepals.

'Black and Blue' is a huge subshrub with hairy leaves and large dark blue flowers with almost black sepals. Plants often reach 5–6′ in height.

'Costa Rica Blue' may be the same as 'Black and Blue' which may be the same as 'Late Blooming Giant'. They are all big, flower later than the species and have darker calyces than the corollas.

'Purple Splendour' is smaller than the former but also has dark violet blue sepals, however, the leaves are smooth.

### Related Hybrids and Species:

*S.* × 'Indigo Spires' is also a tall growing blue-flowering sage. It is one of the most vigorous and floriferous hybrids (*S. farinacea* × *S. longispicata*) I have seen. In flower, plants easily grow 3–4′ tall and bloom for many months. As fall settles in, the flower color becomes more intense and the spires live up to their name. Unfortunately for Northern gardeners, it is hardy only to about zone 7b, but for those who grow it, the best advice is to plant and get out of the way. Cut the flowers back occasionally for repeat bloom.

'Purple Majesty' is a hybrid between *S. guaranitica* and *S. gesneraeflora*, a Mexican red-flowered species. The resultant hybrid is at least 5′ tall and 3′ wide with deep purple flowers. Hardy to zone 7b.

| | | | |
|---|---|---|---|
| *-jurisicii* (jur-i-sic′ ee-eye) | Jurisici's Sage | 12–18″/12″ |
| Early Summer | Lilac | Yugoslavia | Zones 4–8 |

This species has labored in obscurity for many years but has some excellent attributes. Plants are relatively small and in some cases less than

1' tall, eliminating the problem of staking—a major headache with other species, particularly in zones 6 and south. Thus it may be grown either as a rock garden plant or placed in the front of the border. Stems have long spreading white hairs but the foliage is smooth except around the margins. The branched flower spikes of deep lilac are 8" long and consist of 3–7 whorls of upside down flowers. This curious habit of inverted flowers combined with the fact that most of the foliage is deeply lobed into pinnate sections (pinnatisect) make this species unique among the garden sages.

Plants tolerate a wide range of soils, accept a lack of rainfall, and, given a sunny location, generally behave.

Propagate from division or seed.

**Related Species:**

*S. chamaedryoides*, blue oak sage, is also a terrific low form, growing 12–18" tall and 15" wide. The silvery gray-green foliage is topped with racemes of sky blue flowers. A nice change from the 3–4' tall salvias available. Cut plants back in early to mid-summer if necessary to maintain compactness. They are intolerant of poorly drained soils and do best in raised beds or containers.

*S. forskaohlei* (for-ska' oh-lie) is about as tough a salvia as I have tried to kill. In the Armitage garden, it sits in a shaded corner, becomes crowded out by its neighbors, yet its bold green leaves and violet-blue flowers still try to look good. People should have such an attitude! In more sun, this is a fine plant.

| | | | |
|---|---|---|---|
| *-koyamae* (ko-yam' aye) | | Yellow Sage | 20–30"/18" |
| Late Summer, Fall | Yellow | Japan | Zones 6–8 |

Few of the yellow-flowered sages have become popular, mainly because of lack of hardiness or simply for not being as good as they sound. This species is hardier than most and if properly sited, is an attractive, if not a knee-jerker plant. The foliage is as handsome as the flowers, and the hairy large green leaves along with plants that multiply rapidly result in a ground cover effect. In late summer and fall, the pale yellow flowers occur on 20–30" tall flowering stems. Worth trying in a partially shaded environment, but I have yet to be impressed. Full sun and dry soils should be avoided.

**Related Species:**

*S. bulleyana*, native to China, bears branched stems with yellow flowers, often with a purple-black lower lip. Plants grow 2–3' tall and may be hardy in zones 7–9. Very unusual and fascinating.

| | | | |
|---|---|---|---|
| *-officinalis* (o-fish-i-nah' lis) | | Common Sage | 12–20"/15" |
| Summer | Purple | Mediterranean | Zones 4–7 |

Parsley, sage, rosemary and thyme is more than a recipe for flavor or a song title. Culinary sage, *S. officinalis*, has been used to flavor food throughout history, often masking the smell and taste of the food itself. However, recently the species has undergone promotion as an ornamental garden plant, doing more than providing fragrance, but also handsome foliage and flowers. One of the best treatments I have seen is the incredible rose garden at Motisfont Abbey in England where Graham Stuart Thomas interplanted many colorful perennials with the roses, including the various cultivars of culinary sage. Surprisingly effective and an outstanding combination.

Plants require full sun and excellent drainage; they will not do well in heavy, poorly drained soils. Excellent for containers or raised beds where soils and drainage can be controlled. In areas of high humidity and lots of summer rain, they can look pretty sad and ragged.

### Cultivars:

'Albiflora' has long narrow leaves and white flowers.

'Aurea' is grown for its golden yellow foliage.

'Berggarten' is the best blue-flowered form, with wide handsome gray-green leaves and deep blue flowers over compact plants.

'Icterina' is sometimes sold as 'Tricolor' but differs in having light green leaves with wavy yellow margins, not the many colors of 'Tricolor'.

'Purpurescens' has purplish leaves and holds the color well in the summer. Looks terrific with lime green to yellow-foliaged material, such as *Acorus* 'Ogon' or yellow hostas.

'Rubrifolia' has long narrow leaves and purple-red flowers.

'Salicifolia' has even more narrow leaves than others. The leaves are generally 6–7 times longer than wide.

'Tricolor' bears leaves flecked and streaked with purple, yellow, pink, violet and white. Looks almost as odious as it sounds.

| | | |
|---|---|---|
| *-pratensis* (prah-ten' sis) | Meadow Sage | 12–36"/36" |
| Summer        Lavender-Blue | Europe | Zones 3–7 |

(Syn. *S. haematodes*)

The few stem leaves are small and sessile, but the 3–6" long basal leaves are oblong, have wavy margins and long petioles. The many flowering stems rise from the basal leaves and normally bear lavender-blue flowers. Variability in flower color and size is evident in seed grown plants. If spent blooms are removed, another flush usually results. Plants tolerate a wide range of garden soils but the leaves deteriorate if plants dry out too many times.

Considerable debate rages whether *S. pratensis* is a separate species from *S. haematodes* or if they are minor variations of each other. Seldom are both species offered from the same nursery, although it is possible to find them listed in separate catalogs. Because *S. pratensis* is such a variable species, I decided to list them together although it is probably safe to say that plants listed as *S. haematodes* are more floriferous, form larger panicles and have slightly larger flowers than those sold as *S. pratensis*. Taxonomic foofaraw aside, a number of good selections exist.

The species and varieties may be propagated from cuttings, division or seed but cultivars should be propagated from division or terminal cuttings only. The rootstock is quite woody and care must be taken during division to avoid damage. Cuttings are more reliable than division.

### Cultivars:

'Alba' is a white-flowered form.

'Atroviolacea' has dark violet flowers.

'Baumgartenii' is similar to 'Atroviolacea' but bears lighter violet flowers.

'Haematodes' is what the true *S. haematodes* has been reduced to by some
taxonomists. Plants are floriferous with lilac-blue flowers. If you buy *S. haematodes*, this is what you should obtain.

'Lupinoides' produces bluish white flowers.

'Rosea' has rose-purple flowers.

'Rubicundra' bears rose-red blossoms.

'Tenorii' is probably the best of the plants listed under this species and has
lovely, very deep blue flowers.

'Variegata' produces handsome light blue flowers streaked with white.

### Related Species:

*S. patens*, gentian sage, bears 1½–2" long gentian blue (dare I say violent blue) flowers borne sparsely in 2–3-flowered whorls. The 30" tall plants arise from tubers. They are half hardy and should be treated as annuals in most of the country. Although the flowers are some of the largest in the genus, the lack of floriferousness makes the plants rather unexciting. 'Alba' has white flowers, 'Cambridge Blue' bears light blue flowers.

*S. verticillata* came on strong recently, particularly the dwarf selection 'Purple Rain'. I was most impressed with its performance in the gardens at Michigan State University. However, it seems to be an on-again, off-again plant in most places and somewhat disappointing. Although when growing well, it does have many branched inflorescences of dark purple flowers over coarse arrow-shaped leaves. It is also relatively short and compact, growing about 2' tall. I saw a white form 'Alba' in the Oxford Botanical Garden but I have not yet seen it in this country. Plants perform well in zones 5–7.

| *-sclarea* (sklah' ree-a) | | Clary Sage | 30–48"/3' |
|---|---|---|---|
| Summer | White, Lilac | Southern Europe | Zones 4–7 |

A short-lived perennial or more often than not, a biennial, which is used for its coarse look, large stature when in flower and good foliage. Plants produce a large basal rosette consisting of many 8–10" long broad, wrinkled leaves which are rough to the touch and hairy. The many-branched flowering stems, which emerge the second year, are 4-sided, rough and sticky. They bear small white to lilac flowers but it is the pink, lilac or white bracts that surround the flowers that provide the ornamental value. They are particularly pretty in bud when the bracts are tight around the emerging inflorescences. They soon explode into hundreds of flowers (and bracts) in late spring, filling the garden with bees and butterflies. I have seen wonderful plantings in Long Island where they were combined with purple Japanese iris and red valerian (*Centranthus*). This is an interesting plant but not one to become too enamoured with. Its history of curing ailments of the eyes is fascinating (the seeds and leaves were used for eye lotions) and the bracts are numerous, however, it is short-lived, messy after flowering and smelly. Being a subjective sense, the smell of the leaves and stems varies from musky (it is sometimes called muscatel sage) to disgusting. Generally, the smell is not too apparent unless you rub the stems, but on a warm, still day, you know the clary is in flower. Plants produce huge numbers of seeds which can be a problem if they decide to self sow.

Excellent drainage is necessary and they may need the support of other large plants around them or staking. They are better where humidity is not too high, in the Southeast the explosion of growth is even quicker, and the mess that follows even worse.

Propagate from seeds.

### Cultivars:

'Turkestanica' is more robust, grows taller and has prettier pink to lilac flowers. Recommended over the species if available. Where nights are hot, the bracts fade to whitish.

-× *sylvestris* (sil-ves' tris)         Hybrid Sage         18–48"/36"
   Summer         Violet Blue         Hybrid         Zones 4–7
(Syn. *S. nemerosa, S.* × *superba, S. sylvestris* var. *superba*)

A quick glance at the list of synonyms shows that most people, myself included, are confused as to the parentage of the numerous selections which attach themselves to the name *nemerosa, superba* or *sylvestris*. There is sufficient difference in foliage and flower, I believe, to separate cultivars such as 'East Friesland' and 'Lubecca' from ones like 'Blue Queen' and 'Rose Queen'. The former should be listed under *S.* × *sylvestris* (*S. pratensis* × *S. nemerosa*) and the latter under *S. nemerosa*. The former are sterile and set little seed whereas the latter are mostly seed-propagated. Seems a pretty obvious difference to me. However, I am going to lump them all together and let the taxonomists fight it out. Without doubt, not only do differences in habit and color exist between cultivars, so does their performance.

Given cool nights and good moisture, the cultivars can be truly spectacular. Numerous dense flower spikes ranging from lavender to deep rich violet-blue rise from basal leaves in May and June to make a wonderful show. Unfortunately, I have been disappointed with the hybrids in zone 7; while they survive and flower adequately, they lose their upright habit, flop over, and fade rapidly. They certainly do well, however, north of zone 7. If grown in the South, a low-growing cultivar is much preferred. They are drought tolerant and survive during droughts where many plants succumb.

### Cultivars:

'Blue Hill' ('Blauhuegal') has true blue flowers with a long season of bloom.

'Blue Queen' ('Blaukoenigin') has violet-blue flowers on 18–24″ tall stems with good heat and drought tolerance. Raised from seed and often forced in modern greenhouses, plants are becoming more and more available. Parentage close to *S. nemerosa*.

'East Friesland' ('Ostfriesland') has deep purple flowers and is only 18″ tall. It is better than the type where summers are hot, as it does not require support. Sterile, raised vegetatively.

'Lubecca' is similar to 'East Friesland' but is about 30″ tall. Both have violet-blue flowers.

'May Night' ('Mainacht') has larger deep indigo flowers which are larger than 'Lubecca'. Plants grow approximately 18″ high. The latter three cultivars are quite similar and are outstanding when grown in full sun, cool nights and well-drained soil. Perennial Plant of the Year, 1997. All are hybrids and should not be raised from seed. Terminal cuttings or division should be used to multiply or rejuvenate named cultivars.

'Montrose Best' came from the fine nursery of Nancy Goodwin in Hillsborough, North Carolina. It was a chance seedling with deep blue-purple corollas and reddish calyces. Occasionally offered by mail order nurseries.

'Rose Queen' ('Rosakoenigin') is the rose-flowered counterpoint to 'Blue Queen'. Floriferous and handsome.

'Rose Wine' has rosy red flowers on 2′ tall plants.

'Viola Klose' has dark blue flowers.

'Wesuwe' is about 18″ tall with red-purple flowers.

### Related Species:

*S. discolor* is a good garden plant, but hardiness north of zone 8 is questionable. The 2′ tall plants have many deep blue flowers with black calyces over 2″ long green leaves with grayish backs. The flower stems are obviously sticky.

*S. transsylvanica* is similar to *S. pratensis* and *S.* × *sylvestris* in that the plants can grow to 3′ tall. They carry large masses of lavender-blue flowers on branched flowering stems held well above the dull green leaves. They were particularly handsome in August at the University of Minnesota Botanic Garden when they had a carpet of white zinnias at their feet.

## Quick Key to Salvia Species

A. Flowers (of species) blue, violet or lavender
  B. Leaves a rosette, silvery and white woolly . . . . . *S. argentea*
  BB. Leaves not a rosette, green
    C. Plants herbaceous, not woody at base
      D. Leaves pinnately lobed . . . . . . . . . . . . . *S. jurisicii*
      DD. Leaves not pinnately lobed
        E. Corolla (petals) less than ½" long . . . *S.* × *sylvestris*
        EE. Corolla more than ½" long . . . . . . . . *S. pratensis*
    CC. Plants a subshrub, woody at base
      D. Corolla less than 1" long
        E. Foliage gray pubescent, plants
          less than 3' tall . . . . . . . . . . . . . . . *S. officinalis*
        EE. Foliage not pubescent, plants
          taller than 3' . . . . . . . . . . . . . . . . . . . *S. azurea*
      DD. Corolla greater than 1" long . . . . . . . . *S. guaranitica*
AA. Flowers not blue, violet or lavender
  B. Flowers red or yellow
    C. Flowers red (in species) . . . . . . . . . . . . . . . *S. greggii*
    CC. Flowers yellow . . . . . . . . . . . . . . . . . . . *S. koyamae*
  BB. Flowers not red or yellow,
    bracts highly ornamental . . . . . . . . . . . . . . . . *S. sclarea*

**Additional Reading:**

Bloom, Alan. 1980. Salvias. *The Garden* 105(7):290–291.

Caye, D. 1994. Clary sage. Simple, beautiful. *Flower and Garden* 38(3):64.

Compton, James. 1985. Some worthwhile Mexican salvias. *The Garden* 110(3):122–124.

Compton, James. 1987. Salvia guaranitica. *The Plantsman* 9(1):38.

Compton, James. 1993. Salvias from the high Sierras. *The Garden* 118(11): 499–501.

Compton, James. 1993. Mexican salvias in cultivation. *The Plantsman* 15(4):193–215.

Lacy, Allen. 1990. Late-season salvias. *Horticulture* 68(10):36–39.

Martin, Tovah. 1984. Salvia savvy. *Horticulture* 62(7):12–20.

Ogden, Scott. 1993. Tender and hardy salvias. *Fine Gardening* 33:62–67.

## *Sanguinaria* (san-gwi-nah' ree-a)      Bloodroot      Papaveraceae

Plants of this monotypic genus are becoming more popular each year, and with good reason. Bloodroot is a good example of the continued blurring of the distinction between wild flowers and garden plants. Although best used in shady woodland settings, it is adaptable to more formal shade gardens as well. The common name is most appropriate, as it has a yellowish red sap which becomes obvious upon division of the rootstock. The sap was used by the Indians as a dye for coloring and paint. This is a terrific plant for demonstrating that color is not only on the outside.

**-canadensis** (kan-a-den' sis)   Bloodroot, Puckoon      3–6″/8″
  Early Spring      White      Eastern North America    Zones 3–8

Walking down a meandering woodland path through a drift of these clean white flowers reaffirms one's faith in this crazy world. The solitary, 2″ wide flowers appear on 6″ long flower stalks before the blue-green leaves have fully matured. The individual flowers, which remain closed on cloudy days, abscise in a few days but additional flowers arise over a 2–4 week period. The ephemeral bloom of bloodroot was bemoaned even by Thomas Jefferson, who wrote in 1776 that on "April 6, Narcissus and Puckoon open; April 13, Puckoon flowers fallen" (Lawrence, 1987).

In north Georgia, the bloodroots are at their peak in mid-March through early April. In the North, they may flower as late as early May. The wavy,

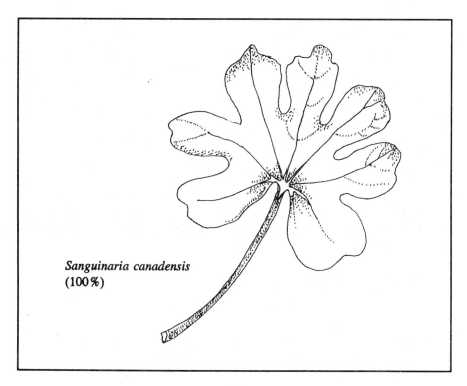

*Sanguinaria canadensis*
(100%)

lobed, kidney-shaped leaves continue to expand once the flowers have finished and are almost as pretty as the flowers. The foliage persists until mid- to late summer before disappearing. Lack of rain results in more rapid disappearance. They combine well with early spring flowers such as *Mertensia virginica* (Virginia bluebells), *Chrysogonum virginianum* (green and gold), and *Aquilegia canadensis* (Canadian columbine).

Propagate the species from seed, but it is easier to divide the clumps of plants immediately after flowering. Seed must be sown in moist peat moss, warmed to 68° F for 2–4 weeks, cooled 4–6 weeks at 40° F and then slowly raised to 50–55° F. 'Multiplex' should be vegetatively propagated by division.

### Cultivars:

'Multiplex' is a wonderful cultivar for the garden. The sterile, clean, white, double flowers consist of approximately 50 petals. Flowers persist twice as long as the single flowered species. More expensive, harder to find.

### Additional Reading:

Haywood, Gordon. 1982. Bloodroot lines. *Horticulture* 60(2):50–53.

## *Sanguisorba* (san-gwi-sor′ ba)          Burnet          Rosaceae

The genus contains about 30 species but few nurseries offer them to the public. While it does not offer the splashy color of salvia or black-eyed Susan, there are, nevertheless, some reasonable species. Plants have handsome pinnate leaves, similar to those of *Melianthus*, another little known garden plant, and bottle brush flowers in summer. In some species, separate male and female flowers occur on the same plant, and in others the flowers are perfect (both male and female parts are present in the same flower). All flowers are apetalous and consist of small sepals and long stamens. They look good with fall-flowering plants like monkshood and *Sedum* × 'Autumn Joy'. In general, plants prefer a cool, damp soil but tolerate dry conditions if irrigation is provided.

The name *Sanguisorba* comes from *sanguis*, blood, and *sorbere*, soaking up, in reference to its reputed ability to stop bleeding. The young leaves of *S. officinalis* were, and still are, occasionally used to flavor salads, soups and drinks.

Quick Reference to Sanguisorba Species

|  | Height (ft.) | Flower color |
|---|---|---|
| *S. canadensis* | 4–5 | White |
| *S. obtusa* | 3–4 | Reddish pink |

*-canadensis* (kan-a-den' sis)     Canadian Burnet     4–5'/4'
    Summer     White     Eastern North America     Zones 3–7
(Syn. *Poterium canadense*)

The 12" long pinnately compound leaves consist of 7–15, oblong, sharply toothed leaflets. Two- to six-inch long rounded spikes of whitish, perfect flowers appear at the end of each stem. The stamens are exserted and give the flowers a bottle brush appearance. The individual flowers are up to 1½" wide and the inflorescence extends 6–8" long. Flowering begins in early summer and lasts well into mid-summer, particularly if flowers are removed as they fade. Planted in combination with the orange spikes of *Kniphofia*, the whites of burnet seem whiter and the oranges of the torch lily brighter.

Plant in full sun in the North, but partial shade and a cooling soil mulch are useful in the South. Plants are vigorous and adequate room for expansion must be provided. They enjoy boggy soil, however, and if planted by the waterside, may become a pest.

Propagate by seed (similar to *Sanguinaria*) or division in the spring.

### Related Species:

*S. officinalis*, great burnet, is also a large plant, with erect, often reddish stems. The basal leaves consist of 13–25 leaflets while the stem leaves are small and sessile. The dark purple flowers are held in short inflorescences during the late summer and are much shorter than either *S. canadensis* or *S. obtusa*. 'Lemon Splash' bears leaves splashed with yellow. Hardy in zones 4–7.

*-obtusa* (ob-tew' sa)     Japanese Burnet     3–4'/3'
    Summer     Pink, Red     Japan     Zones 4–7

This is the most ornamental burnet as it combines gray-green leaves with reddish pink flowers. The 18" long pinnate leaves consist of 13–17 leaflets with a gray-green underside. The flowers have long stamens, at least 4 times as long as the sepals, resulting in an airy, 4' long inflorescence. Conditions necessary for optimal growth are similar to the previous species, however, because plants are not as leafy or vigorous they are more appropriate for the border than *S. canadensis*. They are later than *S. canadensis* and fare well with late-flowering plants.

Propagate by seed or division in the spring similar to *S. canadensis*.

### Cultivars:

'Alba' is similar but has white flowers.

#### Quick Key to Sanguisorba Species

    A. Flower spikes 2–6" long, flowers white . . . . . . . *S. canadensis*
    AA. Flower spikes 2–4" long, flowers pink to red . . . . . *S. obtusa*

*Santolina* (san-to-leen' a)     Lavender Cotton     Asteraceae

Mainly used as low border or edging plants, their gray-green to bright green color shows off the foliage and flowers of plants associated with them. They consist of aromatic, alternate finely divided leaves. Of the 8 species, only a couple of species are grown to any extent. Regardless of species, exceptionally good drainage is recommended.

*-chamaecyparissus* (ka-mie-sip-pa-ris' is)     Lavender Cotton     1–2'/2'
   Summer                    Yellow             Mediterranean     Zones 6–8
(Syn. *S. incana*)

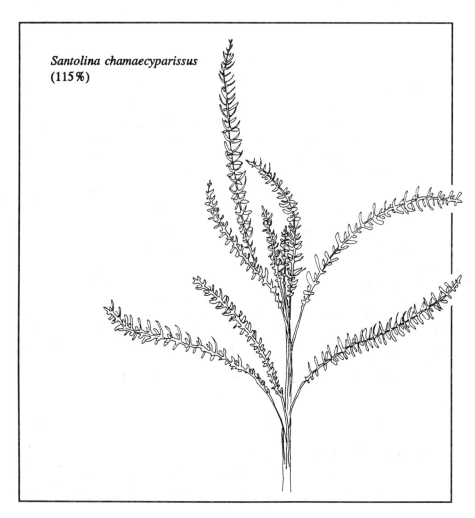

Santolina chamaecyparissus
(115%)

Plants are often used as an edging plant because of the evergreen, aromatic, gray-green leaves, which in sandy soils and bright light develop a white sheen. The 1½" long alternate leaves are crowded on the stem and white woolly underneath. The flowers are comprised of disc flowers only, resulting in a globular head of marginal attractiveness. Although some people feel the flowers look like "bright yellow lollipops in midsummer" I feel they detract from the foliage and serve no useful function. The shrubby plants become rather woody at the base and require a hard pruning immediately after flowering to keep tidy. However, they may be trimmed at any time and are used as small hedging and in knot gardens in warm, dry parts of the country. The gray leaves combine particularly well with low-growing red flowering plants such as *Dianthus deltoides*.

Plants are tolerant of a wide range of summer temperatures, but not summer humidity. Hot wet summers cause fungal problems and plants which open up in the middle. Drier climates are more to their liking. Winter hardiness north of zone 6 and summer hardiness south of zone 7, except in the Northwest, is marginal. The aromatic nature of the plant caught the attention of herbalists many years ago and was an antidote against the bites of "all serpents and venomous beasts" (*Gerard's Herbal*).

Propagate any time from terminal cuttings. Seed germination is irregular but placing sown seed at 40° F for 2–4 weeks may enhance uniformity.

### Cultivars:

'Lambrook Silver', from Lambrook Nursery, has more silvery leaves than the species.

'Lemon Queen' is dwarf and mound-forming.

'Nana' is a name given to dwarf variants in general, which may include 'Weston' and 'Little Ness'.

'Pretty Carroll' originated from Carroll Gardens in Westminster, MD, and is a hybrid between the species and *S. chamaecyparissus* 'Nana'. Plants are intermediate between the two and an improvement on the species.

'Plumosus' bears finely cut lacy, silver tinted foliage.

### Related Species:

*S. pinnata* has narrow pinnate leaves and off-white flowers. Plants make large mounds of gray-green. Also Mediterranean, hardy in zones 6–8. 'Edward Bowles' has gray-green highly dissected leaves and pretty sulphur yellow flowers.

| | | | |
|---|---|---|---|
| *-virens* (vi' rens) | Green Lavender Cotton | 1–2'/3' |
| Summer  Yellow | Italy, France | Zones 7–8 |
| (Syn. *S. rosmarinifolia*) | | |

Green lavender cotton, long known as *S. virens*, is also known as rosemary lavender cotton, and now named *S. rosmarinifolia*. The leaves have

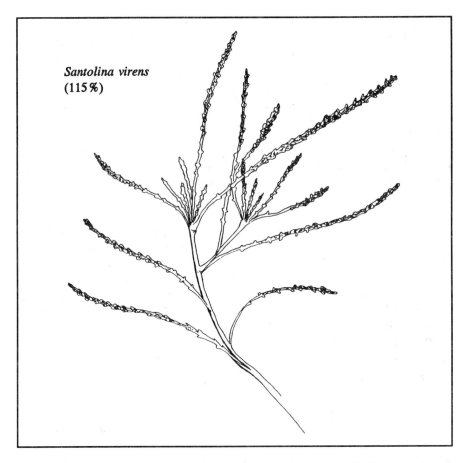

*Santolina virens*
(115%)

the look of rosemary but not the fragrance. They do smell like a sanitized santolina, the fragrance is there but not nearly as obvious as the common species. Plants have narrow bright green leaves and solitary bright yellow flowers on 2' tall stems. They are wonderful plants and while they are much brighter in leaf than *S. chamaecyparissus*, they do not blend and unite other plants as well. Native to the Mediterranean area, plants are only winter hardy to zone 7 (6 with luck).

**Cultivars:**
'Primrose Gem' has thread-like leaves and pale yellow flowers.

**Additional Reading:**
Anon. 1993. Readers' ℞ for deer. *Flowers and Garden* 37(6):95.
Anon. 1993. A subtly different santolina. *Sunset Magazine* (Southern California edition) 191(4):52.
Kourik, R. 1992. Santolina. *Fine Gardening*: May/June:55–57.

*Saponaria* (sa-po-nah′ ree-a)       Soapwort       Caryophyllaceae

A number of common annual and perennial species, suitable for the low border or rockery, are found in the genus. The midwest roadside weed, bouncing bet, *S. officinalis*, is responsible for the common name. In *Gerard's Herbal*, 1597, the author points out that the leaves "yeelde out of themselves a certain juice when they are bruised, which scoureth almost as well as soap." Actually, the "soap" is rather gooey and is a poor substitute for 'Tide'. The leaves are opposite and entire and the flowers usually have 5 petals. In general, plants tolerate full sun but appreciate well-drained soil.

Quick Reference to Saponaria Species

|                | Height (in.) | Habit        | Flower color |
|----------------|--------------|--------------|--------------|
| *S. lutea*     | 3–6          | Mat forming  | Yellow       |
| *S. ocymoides* | 6–9          | Trailing     | Pink         |
| *S. officinalis* | 12–30      | Upright      | Pink         |

*-lutea* (lew-tee′ a)                Yellow Soapwort            3–6″/6″
  Summer          Yellow          Western Alps               Zones 5–7

Although different from the common soapworts and more challenging to grow, this species makes a lovely rock garden plant. The ½″ wide leaves are pale green and form a mat which seldom grows taller than 4″. Clusters of small yellow flowers with violet stamens rise from the mat in early summer and continue for 3–4 weeks. It is not as cold tolerant as other soapworts and requires mulch north of zone 5. Unfortunately it is similar to other species in its intolerance to heat and poor drainage.

*-ocymoides* (o-kim-oi′ dees)            Rock Soapwort            6–9″/9″
  Early Summer          Pink          European Alps            Zones 2–7

Ease of growth and fresh pink flowers in May and June make the species the most popular garden plant of the genus. The flowers are held in loose sprays (cymes) at the ends of the many branches. It climbs and clambers over rocks and is a particularly valuable trailing plant for walls or raised stonework. The 1″ long leaves are flat and olive green. The lower ones have a short petiole while the uppermost are sessile. Plants should be pruned hard after flowering to force new shoots and restrain growth. Once established, they also reseed themselves with abandon, providing a most soapworted garden. Plants are highly tolerant of cold temperatures, but not at all happy in hot summers or in soils that are poorly drained. Although a zone 8 summer rating is often recommended, I would not grow plants above zone 7a as they tend to die out due to winter rains and summer humidity.

The species and most of the varieties may be propagated from seed. Germination is more rapid and uniform if the seed is stratified for 4–6 weeks at around 40° F. Plants may be divided and terminal cuttings may also be taken any time of year.

**Cultivars:**

'Alba' ('Albiflora') is a difficult to locate white-flowered form of the species. The flowers are pure white and is a good plant where a white trailer is needed.

'Carnea' has flesh pink flowers but is otherwise similar to the species.

'Floribunda' is more floriferous than other selections. The flowers are soft pink and similar to the species.

'Rubra compacta' is a non-trailing compact form of the species with crimson flowers. It is a terrific little plant for the front of the border.

'Splendens' has large intense rose flowers and is the best garden selection.

'Splendissima' apparently has larger flowers than 'Splendens' but I have not seen much difference between them.

'Versicolor' is interesting but rather ugly. The flowers open white, then turn rose. To each his (or her) own. This is likely a cross between 'Alba' and 'Splendens'.

**Related Species:**

*S. caespitosa* is a densely tufted hairy plant with short linear leaves, growing 4–8″ tall. The light pink flowers are about 1″ across and held on short stems over the lime green foliage in mid- to late summer.

*S.* × *lempergii* is a hybrid between two obscure species (*S. cypria* × *S. haussknechtii*) originated by Dr. Fritz Lemberg in Styria, Austria. The only cultivar available is 'Max Frei' with soft hairy leaves and many large 1″ pink flowers. They are not as tolerant of heat or poorly drained soils as other species. These are best grown in a rock garden situation, or in a raised bed where water can be quickly drained away. We have killed a good number of these hybrids in our trials at the University of Georgia. Hardy in zones 3–7a.

| | | | |
|---|---|---|---|
| *-officinalis* (o-fish-i-nah' lis) | Bouncing Bet | 12–30″/18″ | |
| Summer | Pink | Southern Europe | Zones 2–8 |

Naturalized in much of the eastern and midwestern parts of the country, it gets little respect and is often considered little more than a pretty weed. Bouncing bet has thrown off the comfort and safety of the garden to become an inhabitant of the open road. She is known as lady-by-the-gate and few old gardens exist where her name is not appropriate. Bouncing bet is also the origin of the soap making story, although some people who used the soap also came down with dermatitis.

Plants are more upright than other species although they sprawl when planted in rich soil. The leaves are 2–4″ long, about 2″ wide, and somewhat elliptical. They are also conspicuously 3-nerved and usually dark green. The individual flowers are 1–1½″ across, have 5 notched petals and are held in terminal and axillary cymes. Full sun is necessary; if too much shade is provided, plants become leggy and tall and flowers fade to almost white. Pinching in late spring helps to clean up this coarse and untidy plant as well as force additional flower formation. Plants are far more heat/humidity tolerant than other species. They bloom throughout the summer and spread by underground stolons, thus a few plants can result in a significant colony in a few years. It is interesting that bouncing bet, particularly the double forms, is now being grown commercially as a cut flower for some of the "uptown" modern florists. There is hope that this Rodney Dangerfield of the plant kingdom can be associated with more than the "characteristic odour of American sidewalk ends, where the pavement peters out and the shacks and junked cars begin" (Peattie, D.C., *Flowering Earth*). The double forms are far more common than the single-flowered species.

Stolons are easily divided at any time. Cuttings and seed may also be used. Seed should be stratified as mentioned under the previous species. Not all seed propagated plants of the double varieties will be double, in some cases up to 40% of the offspring may be single.

**Cultivars:**

'Alba-plena' bears white double flowers. All double forms produce 1–1½″ diameter double flowers which resemble shaggy carnations.

'Rosea-plena' has double flowers in shades of rose to pink. This is the most common form in cultivation.

'Rubra-plena' produces red double blooms.

'Variegata' ('Dazzler') has pink single flowers and green and creamy white variegated leaves. The variegation is stronger in cool weather and fades in the heat.

Quick Key to Saponaria Species

    A. Plants upright, usually taller than 24″ . . . . . . . *S. officinalis*
    AA. Plants trailing or mat forming, usually less than 12″ tall
        B. Plants mat forming, flowers yellow . . . . . . . . . . *S. lutea*
        BB. Plants trailing, flowers pink . . . . . . . . . . . . *S. ocymoides*

**Additional Reading:**

Anon. 1993. Grow your own soap. *The Historical Gardener* 2(2):2, 12.

## *Sasa* (sa′sa)        Dwarf Bamboo        Poaceae

This Japanese dwarf bamboo genus has about 150 species, and one or two are becoming more common. They are shorter than many bamboos, usually growing about 3–4' tall and rapidly multiplying by underground rhizomes. They are being pushed as understudy plants to choke out weeds, however, the problem is that they soon become as weedy as the ones they choke out, and a lot more difficult to eradicate. They are best in a woodland area where they can ramble undisturbed and unmolested. A couple of species are offered. *S. palmata* grows 3–5' tall with wide evergreen leaves which cluster at the tips of the stems (thus the term "palmata"). The leaves are bright green with rough margins which may be brown and dry in the autumn. The other species offered is *S. veitchii* which is equally invasive. The leaves are held along the stem and not clustered at the ends. The whitish dry margins are even more conspicuous and as hard as I try, I find nothing ornamental about this tendency to look half dried out. People write about the beauty of the papery tanned margins, but I don't buy it.

However, both species can fill in difficult areas of dry shade and are slightly better than looking at bare weedy ground. However, the fact that they are a bamboo should be warning enough that they should be used close enough to walk to but far enough away that you get tired getting there. Hardy in zones 6–8.

## *Sauromatum* (sough-o-ma' tum)        Voodoo Lily        Araceae

Another unique member of the aroid family which brings us the spathe and spadix arrangement of flowers revered in calla lilies and demanded by gardeners on the edge. It is closely related to *Amorphophallus* and *Dracontium* and I outlined their differences under the former. The only species generally available is *S. venosum* (formerly *S. guttatum*). The large corms can sometimes be purchased as indoor forcing plants, to be placed on a saucer where flowers and stems will emerge without soil or water. For gardeners living north of zone 7, this can be done or the corms can be held dry in the dark over winter until they can be replanted.

When flowers develop, the spathe is long and pointed, finally unpeeling like a banana into a flattened organ. The 3' long spadix is purple and skinny and sticks straight up from the laid back spathe. Similar to other genera mentioned in this group, the flowers are malodorous, particularly when the sun hits them. The spadix has an internal mechanism for self-heating in order to disperse the pungent compounds more efficiently to attract bugs and such. If you can get near enough, feel the spadix once the spathe has peeled back, it will be significantly warmer than the air or the rest of the plant. It is also interesting that in heat releasing plants like *Arum* and *Sauromatum*, salicylic acid levels (the active ingredient in aspirin) in the spadix are also elevated. That the raised acid causes production of the heat or vice versa is not yet understood, but to think we understand much about plants is being optimistic indeed. After flowering, the spotted stems and the single

928

sickle-shaped leaf emerge. If conditions are right (partial shade, well-drained soils), seedheads may arise from the spent flowers. They will also multiply fairly rapidly, forming a colony in a few years.

Winter hardiness has always been in question. With a little winter protection, they should make it to zone 7 (perhaps even 6b), although many texts call them zone 8-10 plants. Who cares, try a plant or two, you may be happily offended.

### Additional Reading:

Anon. Voodoo lily. Kew information sheet T6. Royal Botanic Gardens, Kew, England.

Gurr, S.J and P. Gurr. 1993. Take an aspirin. *The Garden* 118(5):206-207.

## *Saururus* (sough' rur-us)　　　　Lizard's Tail　　　　Saururaceae

Although I do love this plant, I must be looking at the wrong lizards. The name comes from *saura*, lizard, and *oura*, tail, but to my poorly trained eye, the flowers look more like fishhooks or swan's necks than lizards tails. The only species in this country is *S. cernuus*, the specific name meaning nodding. The 12" long inflorescences are interesting to look at in bloom as the white flower is comprised of the white stalks of the stamens; the flowers being totally bereft of petals or sepals. Plants thrive in a rich wet lowland area, and look dreadful under dry land conditions. The heart-shaped leaves alternate their way up the erect stem and flowers occur in early summer in the South, late summer in the North. One of the best plantings I have seen occurs in the quarry garden at the Atlanta History Center, where the moist, shady conditions allow the creeping stems to fill in, resulting in hundreds of lizard tails all wagging at once. This is one of the country's best native plant gardens and if you find yourselves in Atlanta, the complex is well worth a visit.

Plants are native to shallow water and swamps from New England and southwestern Quebec to Minnesota and south to Florida. Hardy in zones 5-9.

## *Saxifraga* (saks-if' rag-a)　　　　Saxifrage　　　　Saxifragaceae

Exceptionally large and enormously diverse, this genus contains more than 300 species and 200 additional natural hybrids and varieties. The name is derived from the Latin *saxum*, rock, and *frangere*, to break, in reference to the fact that the dust-like seeds find their way into minute crevices to germinate. Along with other plants which were swept into the *Doctrine of Signatures* (see *Pulmonaria*), saxifraga's supposed ability to break rocks elevated it to the medicinal purpose of shattering kidney stones. Some species such as *S. granulata*, meadow saxifrage, are well established in song and verse. The double form of this European meadow saxifrage is known as Pretty Maids, and a row of them grew in Mary, Mary, quite Contrary's garden.

The genus consists of small plants, most dwarf and none more than moderate size, best suited for the rock garden. An exception is our native *S. pennsylvanica*, Pennsylvania saxifrage, which grows to 3' tall. Species are predominantly perennial although a few such as *S. sibthorpii*, Sibthorp's saxifrage, are annuals. Many form rosettes of leaves in cushions which may be hard and encrusted, in others moss-like. Most of the species are evergreen, especially the rosette formers, however, a few have alternate, deciduous leaves. The flowers are arranged singly or more often in floriferous panicles and racemes. Flower color is predominantly white but yellow, pink or red are also found. Flowers consist of 5 petals and sepals, and 10 stamens.

They are mainly alpine plants and, in their native habitats, extremely resistant to adverse weather. They rejoice in sharp drainage and cool climes. Hot summers are not to their liking and, in general, the further north one gardens, the more chances of success. Few species tolerate full sun and moderate shade is recommended for all locales in the United States. Excellent drainage is essential.

Botanists have classified *Saxifraga* into 15 sections, each clearly distinguished by visible characteristics. However, even within a section, there are numerous morphological differences between species. Although a great number of saxifrages are garden worthy, only a few sections contain species that are of special value to the garden. The mossy saxifrages (Dactyloides) form cushions of soft-leaved evergreen rosettes. This includes species such as *S. caespitosa*, tufted saxifrage, the magnificent white-flowered *S. trifurcata*, threefork saxifage, and the popular *S. × arendsii* hybrids. A popular section is the encrusted saxifrages (Euaizoonia). Species in this group have rosettes with stiff, spade-shaped lime encrusted leaves which provide a silvery effect. The rosettes die after flowering but underground runners give rise to new ones in the fall. They superficially resemble hens and chicks until their open sprays of summer flowers give them away. This section includes the variable *S. paniculata*, aizoon saxifrage, with many varieties and cultivars. Another section of importance is the Kabschia saxifages (Porophyllum), characterized by firm dense green cushions of evergreen rosettes. The leaves are small, stiff, and often needle sharp. The section Robertsoniana contains species which form dense, dark green cushions of evergreen rosettes. It is represented in the garden by the ever-present London pride, *S. × urbium*, found in garden centers throughout Europe and now in the United States. For the southern gardener, the section Diptera contains the useful and popular strawberry geranium, *S. stolonifera*. It is hardy in zones 7–10 but can be enjoyed as a houseplant further north. Intersectional hybridization has occurred and a number of useful hybrids such as *S. × andrewsii*, Andrew's saxifrage, have arisen. Much of the interest and breeding of the genus has occurred in Germany, Czechoslovakia and other European countries. However, let us not forget the tremendous efforts of Lincoln Foster from Connecticut who hybridized a whole group of saxifrages under the catch-all series of Millstream

Hybrids. Look for constellation names, mythological figures ('Aladdin', 'Demeter', 'Midas'), figures from Shakespeare ('Falstaff', 'Prince Hal'), friends and family members ('Timmy Foster', 'Wendy') and of course those with the famous garden prefix ('Millstream Cream').

Saxifrages are little used and poorly understood in the United States. Although our climate is not as forgiving as that of England, Germany and the Netherlands, they are plants which, once established, provide years of graceful, maintenance-free beauty. A frequent problem is that the early spring flowering of some hybrids and species get damaged by late spring frosts.

Propagation is usually by seed, but division, cuttings, and rooted offsets are also used to multiply hybrids and cultivars. The fine seed needs exposure to low temperatures to germinate. Placing the seed flat at 32–40° F for 6 weeks results in more uniform germination. Seedlings are very slow to develop and it may take 2–3 years before plants reach flowering size. For best results, seedlings should not be exposed to temperatures greater than 60° F.

The following is but a handful of the saxifrages that may be found through specialist nurseries. The list includes the more available and easy to grow species.

Quick Reference to Saxifraga Species

|  | Height (in.) | Flowering season | Flower color | Section |
|---|---|---|---|---|
| S. × arendsii | 6–9 | Spring | Various | Dactyloides |
| S. cochlearis | 6–12 | Spring | White | Euaizoonia |
| S. cotyledon | 18–24 | Summer | White | Euaizoonia |
| S. paniculata | 6–24 | Summer | Yellow | Euaizoonia |
| S. stolonifera | 3–8 | Summer | White | Diptera |
| S. trifurcata | 6–12 | Spring | White | Dactyloides |
| S. × urbium | 9–12 | Spring | White | Robertsoniana |

| -× *arendsii* (ah-rendz' ee-i) | Arend's Saxifrage | 6–9"/12" |
|---|---|---|
| Spring          Various | Hybrid | Zones 5–7 |

Developed by the Arends nursery in Ronsdorf, Germany (as were many of the hybrid *Astilbe*), the hybrid is a relatively recent addition to the saxifrage family. Plants are mossy-leaved carpet formers and, if proper conditions are provided, will cover a large area in a season. The rosettes remain evergreen and attractive throughout the year. Dozens of thin flower stalks rise over this mossy covering, each bearing a single 5-petaled flower in white, rose, pink or red shades. Semi-shaded conditions and moist soil are preferred. The sunnier the site, the more moisture retentive must be the soil. A problem in growing the mossy saxifrages in warm areas is that they often "melt out," that is, the centers of the plants rot and disappear. This is a particularly severe problem in areas of high humidity. Adding some fine soil or sand to the center of the plant helps reduce the loss.

### Cultivars:

'Blood Carpet' ('Blutenteppich') is one of the many cultivars in the Carpet series of hybrid saxifrages, most of which are available from seed. It is 4–8″ tall with dark carmine-red flowers. There is very little, if any, difference between this and 'Scarlet Carpet'.

'Flower Carpet' is similar to 'Blood Carpet' but the flowers are pinker. It is a reliable, free flowering cultivar that can be raised from seed.

'Flowers of Sulphur' stands about 4″ tall and has pale sulphur yellow flowers. It is vigorous with firm tight cushions of foliage.

'Gaiety' is an early flowering hybrid with deep pink flowers on 4–6″ long scapes. One of the best hybrids with pink flowers.

'Purple Carpet' ('Purpurteppich') is 3–4″ tall with deep purple flowers.

'Rosea' has rose-pink flowers on 6″ tall plants. They have done surprisingly well in the heat of a Georgia summer, however, they were on raised beds with excellent drainage.

'Snow Carpet' has masses of relatively large, clear white flowers, and is about 5–7″ tall. It is an old standard cultivar but still one of the best for white flowers.

'Triumph' is one of the best hybrids. The firm lacy green 6–8″ long cushions are handsome and the dark red flowers are brilliant. Remove the flower stems after fading. Self-sown plants are interesting but flower colors and habits are not true. Divide pieces of carpet after flowering but prior to the heat of summer.

| | | | |
|---|---|---|---|
| *-cochlearis* (kok-lee-ah′ ris) | | Snail Saxifrage | 6–12″/10″ |
| Spring | White | Alps | Zones 5–7 |

Numerous small hemispherical rosettes, comprised of many spoon-shaped entire leaves thickly encrusted with lime (leaves exude $CaCO_3$), characterize the species. Rosettes are 1–2″ across, but so closely packed they form small mounds from which 10–12″ tall reddish scapes arise. The ¾″ diameter star-shaped white flowers are held in loose one-sided panicles. Some direct sun is tolerated but partial shade is preferable. Lime should be added regularly for best performance, particularly in areas of acid soils.

Seedlings require 2–3 years to reach flowering size; vegetative propagation is faster and more reliable. Division of the rosettes in early spring or late fall is possible. Propagate in spring by lifting the mother plant and gently tearing down on the outer rosettes. Pieces of root must be removed with the offset which can be immediately planted.

**Cultivars:**

Var. *major* has rosettes 1½ times larger than the species. The flowers are
a little larger but not significantly so.

Var. *minor* has smaller flowers on 4″ long scapes and grows 6″ wide.

*-cotyledon* (kot-i-lee′ don)　　Jungfrau Saxifrage　　　18–24″/10″
Summer　　　White　　　Pyrenees, Alps to Greenland　　　Zones 3–7

Masses of flat rosettes are produced, each 5–6″ in diameter. The 3″ long
leaves are strap shaped, finely toothed and broader towards the apex. Although
the flowering rosettes die after flowering, the central crown sends out new ones
so that the plant forms a small colony. The branched scapes rise 18–24″ and
bear ¾″ wide white flowers with red veins or red dots on the petals. This is
one of the encrusted saxifrages that is not obviously encrusted with lime. In
fact, this species should be grown in lime-free soils in partial shade.

Propagation is similar to *S. cochlearis*.

**Cultivars:**

Var. *caterhamensis* is one of the prettiest because of the conspicuous red
spotting on the petals. It also is more vigorous than the species.

Var. *icelandica* has large rosettes of iron-gray leaves with 4′ tall flower stems.

Var. *minor* is a dwarf version of the species and smaller in every way,
bearing flowers on 6″ tall inflorescences.

*-paniculata* (pa-nik-ew-lah′ ta)　　Aizoon Saxifrage　　　6–24″/15″
Summer　　　Yellowish White　　　Europe, North America　　　Zone 2–6
(Syn. *S. aizoon*)

This species occurs in most of the alpine and boreal parts of Europe and
Asia, in North America from Greenland and Labrador to Saskatchewan,
south to Nova Scotia, New Brunswick, the mountains of Vermont and Lake
Superior. With such an extensive range, it is not surprising there are many
forms and subspecies. Plants form cushions and mats of small rosettes, 3″
in diameter or less, consisting of spatulate leaves with forward-pointing
teeth and silvery encrustations on the margins. The flowers vary tremen-
dously but are borne in a loose 6–18″ tall panicle. The ½″ diameter flowers
are yellowish white to white, often spotted purple.

Although tolerant of lime-free situations, lime should be added to the
garden site for best performance. Areas of rocky outcrops and partial shade
are preferred.

Propagate similar to *S. cochlearis*.

**Cultivars:**

Var. *baldensis* has small rosettes (approximately 2″ across) with reddish
flower scapes.

Var. *globrata* has very short flower stalks.

Var. *lutea* has pale yellow flowers and is 6–10″ tall in flower.

Var. *major* is the largest form of the species and sends up 15–18″ high inflorescences. The scapes are reddish and the large leaves (1–2″ long) have a reddish tinge, which deepens in winter.

Var. *rosea* has pale pink flowers with yellowish green rosettes.

| -*stolonifera* (sto-loni′ fer-a) | Strawberry Begonia | 4–6″/12″ |
|---|---|---|
| Summer          White | Eastern Asia | Zones 7–9 |

(Syn. *S. sarmentosa*)

Also known as strawberry geranium and mother-of-thousands, plants colonize an area with threadlike runners, called stolons, similar to strawberries. The rounded leaves are silver veined above and reddish beneath. The flowering stems branch into 15–18″ tall loose racemes of many 1″ wide white flowers whose two lower petals are 3–4 times longer than the other three. Plants are useful as shade tolerant ground covers, particularly in the South, quickly making large colonies after a few years. They are also used in hanging baskets for patio and deck. Plants are cold hardy to zone 7.

### Cultivars:

'Harvest Moon' originated from Terra Nova nursery and offers conspicuous chartreuse leaves. They form a handsome clump before the runners start foraging for new ground. Best with some afternoon shade.

'Maroon Beauty' have similar rounded leaves and silvery veins. The leaves have reddish tones and red pubescent on the stems.

'Tricolor' has variegated leaves of green white and pink, also known as 'Variegata'.

### Related Species:

*S. fortunei* is clump forming with large glossy green leaves. The white flowers rise about 18″ above the leaves in late summer or early fall. 'Rubrifolia' has rosy red flowers. 'Wada's Variety' is particularly good with sprays of white flowers. Better for cooler climates, but tolerate heat if given some shade.

*S. cuscutiformis* has a habit very similar to *S. stolonifera*, but is more eye-catching. Red stolons crawl out from under the clumping rounded multicolored leaves. In the fall, white flowers, spotted yellow and red, are held 4–5″ above the foliage in a loose raceme.

*S. veitchiana,* also in the Diptera group, is a useful ground cover with leaves somewhat similar to 'Maroon Beauty' and bearing white flowers. They are slower growing than *S. stolonifera* but is a good saxifrage for cold and heat, being useful in zones 6–8.

**-trifurcata** (tri-fur-cah' ta)          Threefork Saxifrage          6–12"/36"
    Spring          White          Spain, Austria          Zones 5–7

This is one of the prettiest plants in this group. A massive mat in flower, with clouds of clear white flowers flowing through and clambering over rocks, is a magnificent sight. The stems are somewhat woody and the leathery, gray-green leaves are 3 lobed and divided into numerous triangular sections. The branched, reddish racemes are held 6–12" above the mossy foliage and flower for 3–4 weeks in spring.

One of the most sun tolerant saxifrages, it can be planted in full sun if sufficient moisture is provided. However, afternoon shade is beneficial.

Propagate by division similar to *S. × arendsii*.

**-× urbium** (ur-bee' um)          London Pride Saxifrage          9–12"/20"
    Spring          White, Pink          Hybrid          Zones 5–7

Although often sold as *S. umbrosa*, that species is seldom found in gardens today. *S. × urbium* is a hybrid between *S. spathularis*, a white-flowered species from Portugal and northwest Spain, and *S. umbrosa*, native to the Pyrenees Mountains. Plants bear loose evergreen rosettes that form dense dark green carpets from which arise the 1' high, wiry, sticky scapes. The longer flower stems is one of the main characteristics which distinguishes *S. × urbium* from *S. umbrosa*. The ¼" wide white flowers are starry with a red tinge in the middle. The stamens are longer than the petals and provide an airy look to the sea of bloom. Soil pH is not as critical and it will grow in acid or alkaline soils as long as moisture can be provided. Shady, moist areas are preferred and plants are particularly appealing among ferns.

Easily propagated by division of the mat at any time, but preferably after flowering or in early spring prior to the formation of flower buds.

### Cultivars:

The following may be selections of *S. umbrosa* or *S. × urbium*, depending on who you believe. If you believe me, I'm not sure anybody really knows.

'Aureopunctata' ('Variegata') has golden variegated leaves and provides a lovely splash of color even when not in bloom. It is more sun tolerant than the other forms of the species.

'Chambers Pink Pride' is similar to the type but has soft pink flowers on 9" tall scapes. One of my favorites.

'Clarence Elliott' ('Elliott's Variety') bears compact foliage with tiny rose flowers on red 6" tall scapes.

'Walter Ingwersen' ('Ingwersen's Variety') bears bronze foliage and deep red flowers on 4" tall scapes.

'Primuloides' is short with small primrose-like leaves and bright pink flowers. 'Clarence Elliott' and 'Walter Ingwersen' were derived from this selection.

### Quick Key to Saxifrage Species

A. Petals unequal, 2 or 3 of them 4 times longer than
 the others, plants extensively stoloniferous . . . . . *S. stolonifera*
AA. Petals not unequal, not stoloniferous
 B. Cushions or mounds of rosettes,
  rosettes do not die after flowering
  C. More or less dense cushions of variously notched
   or forked leaves, soft-leaved rosettes
   D. Leaves in 3 prongs, similar to
    stag horns, flowers white . . . . . . . . . . . *S. trifurcata*
   DD. Leaves notched, flowers usually
    rose, pink, purple, or white . . . . . . . . *S.* × *arendsii*
  CC. Leaf margins more or less toothed, leaves
   usually spoon shaped and leathery . . . . . . . *S.* × *urbium*
 BB. Rosettes made up of stiff tongue- or spade-
  shaped leaves, usually lime-encrusted,
  flowering rosettes die after flowering
  C. Leaves entire or nearly so, spoon-shaped . . . *S. cochlearis*
  CC. Leaves distinctly toothed
   D. Flower stem branched from base . . . . . . . *S. cotyledon*
   DD. Flower stem branched in upper part . . . . *S. paniculata*

**Additional Reading:**

Kelly, John. 1993. Saxifrages. *The Garden* 118(5): 214–219.
Kohlein, Fritz. 1980. *Saxifrages and Related Genera*. B.T. Batsford Ltd., London, England. Translated from German in 1984, this book provides excellent descriptions of the many species and hybrids of the genus.

*Scabiosa* (skab-ee-o' sa)   Pincushion Flower   Dipsacaceae

The pincushion plant was named for the dark purple flower heads of the annual *S. atropurpurea* whose tufted appearance resembles a velvet pincushion. The dark color of that flower also signified death and accounted for one of its other common names, mournful widow (the dark-purple *Geranium phaeum* is known as mourning widow, also in reference to the color). Many of the 60 species are perennial but only 2 or 3 are used to any extent in gardens today. *S. atropurpurea* and the perennial *S. caucasica* are popular cut flowers, and *S. graminifolia* and *S. lucida* are smaller and more suited to the front of the border. Other scabiosa-looking species may be found in the genera *Knautia* and *Cephalaria*.

Quick Reference to Scabiosa Species

|  | Height (in.) | Flower color |
|---|---|---|
| *S. caucasica* | 18–24 | Bluish |
| *S. graminifolia* | 10–18 | Pink |
| *S. ochroleuca* | 24–36 | Yellow |

| *-caucasica* (kaw-ka′ si-ca) | | Scabious | 18–24″/18″ |
|---|---|---|---|
| Summer | Bluish | Caucasus Mountains | Zones 3–7 |

Up until the early 1990's, this was by far the most popular of the perennial scabiosa providing warm blue shades in late summer to complement the yellow daisies flowering at that time. At that time, two cultivars of *S. columbaria* (see related species) emerged to great promotion and fanfare and have proven to be equally popular. The basal leaves are lanceolate, entire and covered with a whitish bloom giving the leaves a gray-green appearance. The stem leaves are pinnately lobed and opposite. The 3–4″ wide inflorescences are flat, and the petals shallowly 3–5 lobed. The petals are pale blue and surround a white to pale yellow center.

Plant in full sun in the North and South, in enriched loamy soil. They should be planted in groups of 3 or more near the front of the garden for best effect. This species does well in cool climates, especially the Northwest, but is not as vigorous during hot summers. It is not a highly recommended garden plant for the Southeast and even in the Northeast, plants grow rather slowly, but are popular nevertheless. They can be divided every 3–4 years.

The species has emerged as an important cut flower, acres being grown in California, the midwest and the South. Flowers persist for about a week after cutting.

Seed sown in warm conditions (70–75° F) and high humidity should emerge in 2 weeks. Transplant to containers and grow until planting size. Two inch long basal cuttings may be taken in spring, rooted and grown on during the summer, and planted in the garden in the fall. Plants may also be divided every 3–4 years.

### Cultivars:

'Alba' is a white flowered form which comes true from seed but is otherwise similar to the species. 'Perfecta Alba' has larger cream-white flowers with fringed petals.

'Blue Perfection' ('Perfecta Blue') has fringed, lavender-blue flowers and stands 2′ tall. It was selected from var. *perfecta* which has large fringed flowers in shades of blue.

'Bressingham White' has 3″ diameter flowers of clear white on 3′ tall stems and has effectively replaced an older white cultivar, 'Miss Willmott'.

'Denise' bears large lavender flowers on 2' tall plants.

'Compliment' ('Kompliment') is 20–24″ tall with dark lavender flowers.

'Fama' has large dark, lavender-blue flowers with a silver center on 18″ tall stems. The flower color and plant habit are excellent. Popular as a cut flower.

'House Hybrids' ('Issac House Hybrids') are a mixture of blue and white shades. They arose from selections from Issac House in Bristol, England and have been a parent in many of the more recent selections.

'Loddon White' bears large creamy white flowers not too unlike 'Bressingham White'.

'Moerheim Blue' has larger, darker blue flowers than the species.

'Moonstone' has lighter almost pastel blue flowers.

'Rumor' has lavender-blue flowers on 18–24″ tall stems.

### Related Species:

*S. columbaria* differs from the above species by being hairier and having oblanceolate basal leaves rather than lanceolate basal leaves in *S. caucasica*. Differences may also be seen in flower structure if placed under magnification. However, from the gardening standpoint, the main differences are its being more compact and shorter, as well as producing more flowers over a longer period of time. 'Butterfly Blue' and 'Pink Mist', with lavender-blue and lavender-pink flowers, respectively, are terrific garden plants.

*S. lucida* is only 1–2' tall and is an excellent choice for the front of the garden. The leaves and stems are smoother than the other species. The 1–1½″ wide flowers are rosy lilac and appear in late spring and flower for 6–8 weeks.

| *-graminifolia* (grah-mi-ni-fo′ lee-a) | Grassleaf Scabious | 10–18″/18″ |
|---|---|---|
| Summer | Pink to Lilac | Southern Europe | Zones 5–7 |

One of the smaller scabious, plants are best suited to the front of the garden. It has a woody rootstock and entire, grasslike leaves which form loose mats of ascending stems. The foliage, silvery white due to a whitish pubescence on the leaves, forms a pleasant backdrop for the 1½–2″ wide pale pink flower heads which bloom for about 6 weeks in mid-summer. Plants struggle in hot humid summers but are more heat tolerant than the previous species. A sunny well-drained location is best.

Propagation is easiest by division but seed sown in December will provide sufficiently large plants for the garden by May.

### Related Species:

*S. japonica* var. *alpina* is about 9–12″ tall with finely cut, leathery, somewhat hairy foliage. The lavender-blue 2″ wide flowers appear most of the summer. Herronswood Nursery in Washington selected a pink-flowered form called 'Pink Select'.

**-ochroleuca** (ok-ro-loo' ka)          Cream Scabious          24–36"/24"
   Summer      Cream to Yellow      Southeastern Europe      Zones 5–7

This short lived species has branched pubescent stems with a whitish pubescence on both sides of the leaves. The bottom leaves are slightly lobed and
taper down to form a petiole while the stem leaves are pinnately dissected into
11–13 linear lobes. The flowers are formed at the end of long scapes resulting
in a wiry mass of stems. The 1–2" wide primrose yellow flowers are more
globular than the previous species. This is an outstanding plant when grown in
full sun and well-drained soil. It seeds itself prolifically and makes an excellent
colony. Plants closely resemble *Cephalaria gigantea* in flower and *S. columbaria* in habit (it is also called *S. columbaria* var. *ochroleuca*).

I have problems telling this species apart from *Cephalaria gigantea*. You
would think that if plants are in a different genus, they should be easy to
tell apart. Not for me. Obviously, plants of *Cephalaria* are taller, but
depending on height alone to discriminate differences is always a crapshoot.
If you see them side by side, the differences are obvious, however, seeing

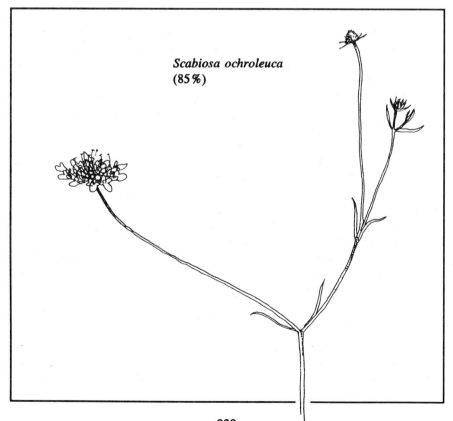

*Scabiosa ochroleuca*
(85%)

them one at a time can leave you guessing. The stems of *Cephalaria* are erect, robust and strongly ridged, those of *Scabiosa* are more branched, less erect and ridges in the stem are much less obvious. The leaf segments are much narrower in *Scabiosa* than in *Cephalaria*. For the small to medium-size garden, *Scabiosa* is much easier to use than the giant *Cephalaria*.

## Cultivars:

Var. *webbiana* is a dwarf variant which does not exceed 12″ in height. It has round-toothed wrinkled leaves and flower heads that are creamier white than the species. Propagate by seed, division, or basal cutting similar to *S. caucasica*. Outstanding.

### Quick Key to Scabiosa Species

    A. Leaves all linear and entire . . . . . . . . . . . . *S. graminifolia*
    AA. Leaves not linear, some lobed or cut
      B. Flowers yellowish white . . . . . . . . . . . . . . *S. ochroleuca*
      BB. Flowers lilac or blue . . . . . . . . . . . . . . . . *S. caucasica*

## *Schizostylis* (shy-zo-stii′ lus)        Kaffir Lily        Iridaceae

The common name hints at the fact that the genus, and its only species, *S. coccineus*, is native to South Africa, which in turn suggests cold hardiness to about zone 7b or 8. The have similar leaves and swollen rhizomes as siberian iris. The scarlet flowers, whose flower spike resembles a miniature gladiolus, are about 2½″ wide and occur on one side of the flower stem only. It may reach about 20″ in length and bear four to ten, 6-petaled flattened flowers in late summer and fall.

Plants are a little finickity due to their lack of cold tolerance, their dislike for high heat and humidity and their need for consistent drink. Sounds like my wonderful mother. Moisture is necessary, and if provided, plants perform reasonably well in full sun or partial shade. I have yet to see a "write-home-to mother" planting east of the Rockies, although the Mercer Botanical Garden in Houston, TX, has some showy specimens. As a plant, they are fair even at their best, being better as cut flowers than garden plants anyway, regardless of their location. They share this characteristic with many plants, gladioli being the best example. Plant in groups of at least three in the garden or put in containers that can be protected during the winter.

Propagate by lifting and dividing after at least 3 years of growth. Dividing too early can result in significant loss of plants.

## Cultivars:

'Alba' has white flowers.
'Major' is larger in every way than the species, also having larger more plentiful scarlet flowers.

'Mrs. Hegarty' is a fall flowerer, with clear pink flowers.
'November Cheer' has late clear pink flowers. They don't open until the fall.
'Oregon Sunset' bear coral flowers.
'Salmon Charm' has rose-salmon flowers.
'Sunrise' has large deep pink flowers.
'Viscountess Bing' is very late to flower, not opening until September or
    October. The starry flowers are shell pink.

## *Scilla* (skil′ la)                    Squill                    Liliaceae

*Scilla* is a large genus, consisting of 80–100 bulbous species native to
Europe, Asia and Africa. A thin covering (tunic) envelops the bulbs, from
which arise strap-like leaves and bell-shaped flowers. The garden species
are generally less than 12″ tall, however, species such as *S. natalensis*,
Natal squill, and *S. hyacinthoides*, hyacinth squill, have blue flowers on
18–36″ tall racemes. Several species have been taxonomically rearranged.
The taller woodland plants, *S. hispanica*, Spanish bluebell, and *S. non-
scripta*, English bluebell, are found under *Endymion*. A number of
differences exist among *Scilla*, *Puschkinia*, and *Chionodoxa*, which are
similar. See *Chionodoxa* for botanical differences.

The garden squills should be planted in the fall in full sun or partial shade
in any well-drained soil. Most flower early in the spring or late winter starting
with *S. mischtschenkoana*, followed closely by *S. bifolia*, *S. sibirica*, and finally
*S. peruviana* in late spring or early summer. Bulbs combine well with other
early spring flowerers such as daffodils, chionodoxas, winter aconites, and
grape hyacinths. They are inexpensive, long lasting, and should to planted in
large drifts, preferably 50 or more. Several late summer and fall flowering
squills, such as *S. hyacinthoides* and *S. autumnale* either lack hardiness or are
not sufficiently showy to be worth the time or expense.

All the squills may be lifted and divided every 4–5 years. Separate the bulbs
and bulblets by size, replant the largest, and grow on the smaller sizes in a
nursery bed for another year before placing them in their final location. Four
to five years are required for squills to reach flowering size from seed. Seeds
should be shallowly sown and placed at 60–65° F under humid conditions.

Quick Reference to Scilla Species

|  | Height (in.) | Flower color | Number of flowers/stem |
|---|---|---|---|
| *S. bifolia* | 4–6 | Mauve | 3–12 |
| *S. mischtschenkoana* | 4–6 | Pale blue | 2–4 |
| *S. peruviana* | 8–12 | Lilac | 20–50 |
| *S. sibirica* | 3–6 | Dark blue | 1–3 |

---

***-bifolia*** (bi-fo' lee-a)    Two-Leaved Squill        3–6"/3"
  Spring    Mauve-Blue    Southern Europe to Asia Minor    Zones 4–8

This early spring bulb is excellent for naturalizing as it multiplies rapidly by offsets. The deep mauve-blue flowers are almost as rich as those of *S. sibirica*, although a great deal of variability occurs. The foliage usually consists of 2 narrow (⅛–½" wide), bronze green, channelled leaves about 6" long, although up to 4 leaves may be present. Plants bear 6–8 star-like flowers, each about ¾" in diameter on a 4–6" high raceme. They flower early (in February and March) or as soon as the snow melts, and are held on long thin pedicels and dance in the spring breeze. Plants reseed all over the place where comfortable.

**Cultivars:**

Var. *alba* has creamy white flowers.

Var. *praecox* flowers about a week earlier than the other varieties and is more robust. It has more flowers than the species.

Var. *rosea* has blooms of soft shell pink.

Var. *rubra* bears rosy salmon flowers.

Var. *taurica* has 3–5 leaves and bears deep blue flowers on long pedicels. It is an excellent plant but difficult to locate. In the trade, it is confused with *S. sibirica* var. *taurica* which has lighter blue flowers.

**Related Genera:**

*S. bifolia* has been crossed with *Chionodoxa luciliae* and the resulting progeny are known as X *Chionoscilla* (which see).

---

***-mischtschenkoana*** (mist-cheng-ko-ah' na)  Tubergen Squill    4–6"/6"
  Late Winter, Early Spring    Pale Blue    Iran, Afghanistan    Zones 4–7

The species was long known as *S. tubergeniana*, from the van Tubergen nursery in Holland from which it was introduced, and unfortunately this small little plant has one of the longest tongue-tying names among garden plants. Plants are similar to *S. sibirica* var. *taurica* in habit and leaf color but 3–4 basal leaves are up to 1" wide and the yellow bulb is about twice as large. They are also the earliest flowering of any of the squills. The flower spikes appear in early February in the Armitage garden and about 3 weeks later further north. Flowers break through the ground before the leaves and each spike bears 3–4 light blue flowers with a stripe down the middle of the segments. The flower color is similar to that of the later flowering *Puschkinia*. This is a great plant, and should be more common.

**Cultivars:**

'Alba' is white with a hint of lilac.

'Zwanenburg' is even better than the species. It has larger flowers and darker stripes on the petals. It is better because the species can get lost in old leaves or garden debris in late winter and early spring; this is showier.

*-peruviana* (pe-roo-vee-ah′ na)      Cuban Lily                      6–10″/6″
   Late Spring            Lilac          Mediterranean Area       Zones 6–9

The Cuban lily is a misnomer as it has nothing to do with Cuba or Peru but is native to Southern Europe and North African regions around the Mediterranean Sea. The name is thought to have come from the ship, Peru, which brought the bulbs to England.

Unlike other species, plants bear 6–9 leaves in a dense basal rosette and a 6–10″ long raceme with bright blue, star-like flowers. The strap-like light green leaves are 6–12″ long and 1–1½″ across with sparsely bristly margins. They are evergreen, at least in zones 7 and 8. This is a later flowering species than most of the common squills, opening in mid- to late spring in the South, late spring to early summer in the North. When the flowers begin to open, they appear to rest on the leaves but as flowering continues, the scape elongates. The compact raceme is about 6″ across when it begins to open and consists of 50–100 blue flowers with a hint of lilac. As the flowers open up the flower stem, the pedicels (individual flower stems) elongate resulting in an rounded ball of flowers.

Bulbs are quite large and should be planted so the neck is at soil level, or with the base about 4″ deep. Although bulbs are not common in the trade, they should be tried more frequently as they become available. It is the showiest of the squills and does well if placed in raised beds in a warm, sunny location. Plants in the Armitage garden flowered well even after 0° F for a couple of nights. They are not as cold hardy as some of the smaller squills, but they're not the wimps that some writers claim them to be.

### Cultivars:
Var. *alba* has white flowers.
Var. *elegans* bears rosy red flowers.
Var. *glabra* has lilac flowers but the leaves are not hairy. This is a common form and often sold as the species.

### Related Species:
*S. scilloides* differ from most of the squills in that they flower in the fall. A good deal of diversity occurs in the species; some with bright pink, mauve-pink or pale blue flowers. Three to seven grass-like leaves give rise to a dense raceme of flowers. Hard to locate, but a gem. Hardy in zones 6–8.

*-sibirica* (si-bi′ ri-ka)      Siberian Squill                    3–6″/4″
   Spring            Deep Blue      Eastern Russia, Siberia       Zones 2–7

This most popular species has many attributes. It is exceedingly tough and cold hardy, revelling in arctic chills, and has the most penetrating blue color of any species, heightened even more by the blueness of the anthers. Although only 1–3 nodding flowers appear on the reddish scape, there are often 3–4 scapes on mature bulbs which more than make up for the paucity of flowers per stem. The individual ¼" wide flowers, which often point in one direction, usually have a darker blue stripe on the on the tepals. Bulblets are produced readily and self-sown seedlings are abundant. A small planting spreads rapidly.

Three to four strap-like leaves, 6" long and about ½" wide, are produced in early spring. The flowers and the foliage appear a little later than snowdrops (*Galanthus*) to continue nature's gift of spring cheer. As with most small bulbs, planting 3 or 4 is disappointing. Plant at least 25 or preferably hundreds. The few dollars paid for 100 bulbs will be enjoyed much longer and with far less indigestion than the same amount paid for dinner at the local Burger Doodle. They may be planted under trees in a woodland or as a spring wake-up in the front of the borders. However, plant them where they are allowed to ramble. They are among the most cold hardy of spring bulbs, but do not appreciate heat and humidity. Even though they go dormant in the spring, soil temperatures stay too warm in the South to allow for catching its breath, and they don't do particularly well south of zone 7a.

### Cultivars:

'Alba' makes a pretty show in the woodland setting with its white flowers against the backdrop of green.

'Azurea' has flowers of light blue.

'Spring Beauty' (syn. var. *atrocoerulea*) is a popular form of the species and has large flowers in a lovely shade of deep blue with bright blue anthers. It is robust but produces a minimum of seed. This results in the longer lasting flowers but clumps do not multiply as rapidly as the species.

'Taurica' produces light blue flowers with a dark blue stripe in the center of each segment. They are usually earlier than the species.

### Related Species:

*S. litardieri* (syn. *S. pratensis*) bears 3-6 leaves and narrow racemes of lilac blue flowers. About 10 campanula-like flowers are produced in early spring.

### Quick Key to Scilla Species

A. Flowers in a dense inflorescence
   having over 20 flowers . . . . . . . . . . . . . . . . . *S. peruviana*
AA. Flowers in a lax inflorescence,
   usually less than 10 flowers
   B. Flowers appearing just before
      the foliage . . . . . . . . . . . . . . . . . . . *S. mischtschenkoana*
   BB. Flowers appearing after foliage has emerged
      C. Usually 2 leaves per bulb, up to 4,
         3-8 flowers per scape, scape solitary . . . . . . . . . *S. bifolia*
      CC. Usually 3-4 leaves per bulb, 1-3
         flowers per scape, scapes 1-6 . . . . . . . . . . . *S. sibirica*

## *Scrophularia* (skro-few-lah' ree-a)      Figwort      Scrophulariaceae

A widely distributed, highly variable genus of about 200 species, one or two of which ever finds their way into American gardens. The roots from plants of this genus were said to heal swelling of the lymph glands in the neck, the disease known as scrofula. The only plant I have seen in gardens is one which I wish was more available, *S. aquatica* 'Variegata', now properly known as *S. auriculata* 'Variegata'. This has some of the finest foliage, boldly marked with dark green and cream. It reminds me of some of the sharply variegated forms of *Brunnera* and *Symphytum*, all equally difficult to find because of their difficulty in propagation.

The specific epithet helps to site the proper place in the garden for the plant, however while consistency of moisture is most helpful, it does not want to be immersed in water. I grew this plant for a couple of years in the Armitage garden until it became overgrown with more vigorous plants. It is native to western Europe suggesting that heat and humidity are not particularly to its liking, however, it is cold hardy to about zone 5 or 6.

The leaves are about 8″ long, opposite and borne on stems that reach 2–3′ in height. The small reddish brown flowers are inconsequential and are interesting if not ornamental. I highly recommend the plant for its leaf variegation, but do not expect it to be long-lived. In the South, it may get a little leggy, in the North, they maintain a reasonable habit.

Propagate from division, although an occasional terminal cutting might be successful. Often, cuttings either fail to root or revert back to the all green form.

## *Scuttelaria* (sku-te-lah' ree-a)      Skullcap      Lamiaceae

Another large genus with few species ever offered to the gardener. While it sounds like nursery people have been a little neglect in their responsibility to offer good plants of this or other genera, the fact is that if there were good garden plants within a given genus, they would be offered. Many times, species are only short-lived or have very tight regional preferences or are difficult to propagate, thus few are offered. In the case of *Scuttelaria*, little attention has been paid to it, thus it has been ignored. That is beginning to change with the availability of a number of good plants, particularly *S. altissima* and *S. supina*.

Plants resemble *Salvia*, having square stems and alternate leaves, particularly if comparing some of the red or rose-flowered forms. They do not have the obvious smell of sage, but the smell of all salvias is not necessary pungent. The easiest way to discern *Scuttelaria* from *Salvia* is to open the flower and examine the stamens. In *Scuttelaria*, there are 4 similar stamens; in *Salvia*, only two are fertile and normal size, the other two are rudimentary (no anthers). Have fun ripping away.

Many of the skullcaps are low-growing spreading plants and often quite woody at the base. One or two, such as *S. altissima*, are upright. Grow in well-drained soils and provide some afternoon shade in the South, full sun in the North. One of the finest scutellarias is alpine skullcap, *S. alpina*, native to mountainous area of southern Europe, Russia and Turkestan. These low growers have many stems with small (1–1½" long) leaves and purple flowers crowded together in a short terminal raceme. The flowers have two lips, the bottom one is sometimes yellow. The bracts beneath the flowers are larger than the 6–8" long flowers themselves. They are handsome rock garden type plants whose native habitat is on rocky limey soil. The addition of lime to acid soils often promotes growth and flowering. Plants are weather hardy from zones 4–7. In the South, the stems can become leggy, and benefit from cutting back either in the spring or immediately after flowering. 'Alba' has white flowers, 'Bicolor' bears purple and white blooms and 'Greencourt' produces fresh green leaves and mauve flowers over 10" tall plants. One of the better selections goes under about three different names. *S. alpina* var. *lupulina*, *S. alpina* ssp. *supina* and *S. supina* are probably all the same thing, bearing handsome light yellow flowers, usually a few weeks earlier than the *S. alpina*.

A popular upright forms is *S. altissima* which grows 2–3' tall with one sided open racemes of creamy yellow, blue blushed tubular flowers. Plants are native to southeastern Europe and the Caucasus. Full sun and excellent drainage are needed.

## *Sedum* (sed' um)            Stonecrop            Crassulaceae

Curiously, few species of this large and diverse genus are seen in American gardens. Although many species are not particularly decorative, there is a wealth of plants usable in the border and rock garden. That *Sedum* is not used more often may be because many of them are rock garden plants and rock gardens have not been in vogue for many years in America. The other sad truth is that they "all sort of look alike," at least within the rock garden or border species.

Finding the correct name for a stonecrop is an adventure in frustration, for even the great plant hunters came back from expeditions with bags of rare plants suitably given their botanical names and "some kind of stonecrop." Several species are native to North America such as *S. nevii*, a lovely white-flowered, low-growing rosette former and *S. ternatum*, whose star-like white flowers are effective in the spring garden. As other wimpy plants expire and leave barren ground as their tombstone, the sedums continue to provide color and vigor.

The basic botanical definition of *Sedum* is a flowering plant with 5 petals, 5 sepals and 10 stamens. The petals are seldom attached to each other and the sepals are often fleshy and leaf like. Leaves are also fleshy and usually alternate or whorled. There is, however, so much confusion in taxonomic circles as to what does or does not constitute a species of *Sedum* that the number has risen from 29 during Linnaeus's time, 88 in 1828, 228 in 1885, 470 by the botanist Berger in 1930, but only 350 by Froderstrom in the same year, and 340 species listed by Jacobson in 1960. Since then, approximately 160 new names have been published in *Index Kewensis* placing the number between 500 and 650. However, just to keep us honest, recent changes in nomenclature have taken many of our common upright forms such as *S. alboroseum*, *S. spectabile* and *S. telephium* and assigned them to the genus *Hylotelephium*, reducing the number once again. Do not lament if unsure of the botanical name of a stonecrop in the garden, you are in good company.

In general, plants prefer well-drained soils and full sun. In the South, a number of rock garden species are at their finest during the cool fall, winter, and spring months and barely hang on during the summer. Partial shade is beneficial south of zone 6. All tolerate drought and require little maintenance.

The majority of stonecrops are easily propagated by 1–3″ long terminal cuttings taken in spring through summer. They generally root within 2 weeks. Too much water in the propagation phase results in root rots and severe decline. Seed may also be sown and plants will reach flowering size in 2 years. For many rock garden species, division is easy and the method of choice.

## Quick Reference to Sedum Species

| | Height (in.) | Flower color | Flowering time |
|---|---|---|---|
| *S. acre* | 2–3 | Yellow | Late Spring |
| *S. aizoon* | 12–15 | Yellow | Summer |
| *S.* × 'Autumn Joy' | 12–24 | Pink | Late Summer |
| *S. kamtschaticum* | 4–9 | Yellow | Summer |
| *S. spurium* | 2–6 | Rose | Late Summer |
| *S. ternatum* | 2–6 | White | Late Spring |

| | | |
|---|---|---|
| **-acre** (a′ ker) | Goldmoss Stonecrop | 2–3″/18″ |
| Spring    Yellow | Europe, North Africa, West Asia | Zones 3–8 |

The small stature and minute leaves of this common mat-former make it excellent for planting between stepping stones, on walls and ledges, or as a filler in areas where few plants grow. The stems are decumbent (grow along the ground with their tips sticking up) and bear crowded alternate leaves. Each light green, pointed, ¼″ long leaf overlaps the one above it like shingles on a roof so that the stems appear scaly. The golden yellow ½″ wide flowers are produced in terminal cymes. Flowering commences in late spring and continues well into summer. In North Georgia (zone 7b), it is at its best in late May, in upper New York (zone 5), mid-June.

Vigorous growers, plants obediently fill in any miserable area in the garden. They can grow so fast as to become weedy, but if provided full sun, reasonable soil, and a little moisture, the flowers can be very showy. Plants should be thinned every 2–4 years to keep them in check, otherwise little maintenance is required.

Division may be accomplished any time of year, and even pieces of plant accidently broken will root where they fall. Seed should be covered lightly and watered gently or from the bottom so it is not washed away. Provide consistent moisture and place the seed flat at 70–75° F. Two years are necessary to reach flowering size.

## Cultivars:

'Aureum' is a lovely plant with young leaves and shoot tips edged with a golden tint in the spring. Unfortunately, the tint is lost in the summer. The flowers are lighter yellow than the species.

'Elegans' is similar to 'Aureum' but the leaves and shoot tips are silvery. It does not lose the tint as rapidly but is not as showy as 'Aureum'. Neither of these cultivars is as vigorous as the species.

Var. *majus* is larger than the species and has paler green leaves with flowers up to ¾" across. The stems are not as densely packed as the species and are more prone to breakage in winter.

Var. *minus* is the opposite of *majus* and seldom grows over 1" tall. All parts are smaller than the species, making a compact, neat carpet.

## Related Species:

*S. album* forms evergreen mats of green to bronze leaves, and produces dense inflorescences of small whitish flowers. 'Murale' has bronze foliage to complement the white flowers.

*S. reflexum*, stone orpine, has bright yellow flowers over a loose mat of creeping, rooting stems. The linear, bluish green leaves are rounded in cross section (terete) and densely arranged on the stems. Plants flower in midsummer and grow 6–10" tall. Good plants for the South. 'Blue Spruce' is a wonderful blue needle-leaf selection which fills in rapidly. Yellow flowers appear in summer. 'Cristata' is a curious little anomaly with fasciated (flattened, looking like crests) leaves and all in all resembling a cockscomb. The young leaves have been used in salads and soups. Some people think the term curious is far too kind, but what the heck, gardening is supposed to be fun.

| | | | |
|---|---|---|---|
| *-aizoon* (aye' zoon) | | Aizoon Stonecrop | 12–15"/18" |
| Summer | Yellow | Siberia, China, Japan | Zones 4–8 |

The leaves are alternate and sessile, scattered along the unbranched stem and bent somewhat backwards (reflexed). The flat leaves are about 2" long and ½" wide, the margins sharply and irregularly toothed. The terminal yellow flowers are held on a short scape and literally sit on top of the plant. The individual flowers are about ½" across and the flat inflorescence (cyme) is 3-4" wide. Unlike the previous species, plants die to the ground in late fall.

Although not the most ornamental sedum, the flowers are showy for a few weeks in midsummer. It is tall enough to compete with *S. spectabile* cultivars (e.g., 'Meteor') but too tall to be used for the carpeting effect provided by *S. acre*.

Propagate by division after flowering.

### Cultivars:

Var. *aurantiacum* is showier than the species due to its red stems, dark green leaves, deep orange to yellow flowers and red fruit. Plants grow 10-18" tall.

'Euphorboides' is more compact than the species and has larger (up to 4" across) deep yellow flower heads.

### Related Species:

*S. alboroseum* (syn. *Hylotelephium erythrostictum*) grows about 2' tall and has opposite fleshy leaves and greenish white flowers in dense inflorescences (cymes). The species is seldom grown but 'Medio-variegatum' is quite popular. The leaves are patterned with a broad green margins around the central creamy white interiors.

There is confusion as to the status of *S. maximowiczii* (macks-i-mo-wick' zee-eye) Some authors consider it synonymous with *S. aizoon*, others feel that the red, taller stems, and broader leaves make it a subspecies of *S. aizoon*, while others consider it a separate species. Regardless, plants with a *maximowiczii* label are often more showy in leaf and flower than *S. aizoon* and more useful for the garden.

| -× 'Autumn Joy' | | Autumn Joy Sedum | 12–24"/24" |
|---|---|---|---|
| Late Summer, Fall | Pink | China | Zones 3–8 |

This has been one of the most popular garden plants in the last decade. The 2-3" long fleshy leaves are sessile, sharply and irregularly toothed. When my kids were young, they liked to gently part the upper and lower base of a leaf and blow it up like a balloon. To do this, one must have great patience and a plant tough enough to survive the rigors of being unclothed by hordes of little children. The upper leaves are smaller with more rounded bases than the lower leaves and all have a prominent midrib. In the winter, green shoots are always just below the surface and by early March, mounds of light green foliage freshen the garden. By midsummer, the flower buds have initiated and start to appear. Plants require full sun, otherwise stems are weak and the heavy flowers cause the stems to topple. Because my plants are in partial shade, I cut them back to 12" in late June. Flowers are smaller and more numerous but plants are

**Sedum** × 'Autumn Joy'
(70%)

more attractive than if they are spread-eagled across the ground. Alternatively, the plants may be supported and larger flowers will result. I also grow 'Autumn Joy' through a large clump of *Iris pseudacorus* which provides natural support. Support in shaded gardens is especially useful in the South where plants often grow over 2' tall. North of zone 7, cutting back the plants is not necessary unless they are over fertilized. The flower buds appear whitish, slowly turn shell-pink, and age to a deep bronze red. Many flowers are supported by the flat-topped 6" diameter corymbs. They bloom well into the fall and dry on the stem. To some gardeners, these dried flowers are picturesque and provide lovely decoration to the winter garden. To me, however, they simply look like dead flowers and I remove them after they turn brown.

Authorities list the plant as a cultivar of *S. spectabile, S. telephium* or *S. purpureum* (a synonym of *S. telephium*) but was raised by Arends nursery in 1955 from a cross between *S. telephium* and *S. spectabile*. It is commonly listed as a cultivar of *S. spectabile* but that species has opposite, scattered leaves and 'Autumn Joy' has alternate leaves. One of the major problems which occurs with very popular plants like this one is that demand outstrips supply. This results in a scramble for plants, and before too long, instead of propagating by the relatively slow method of cuttings, propagators grow the plants from seed. In a hybrid like 'Autumn Joy', the resulting plants are simply not 'Autumn Joy', they are one of the parents or a different hybrid, but they aren't what the label says. More and more people notice that the plants of 'Autumn Joy' do not flower in the autumn, but much earlier in the summer. This is usually the result of seed-propagated plants but, because they look so similar, are difficult to avoid.

Divide in early spring or fall. Terminal cuttings root in 7–10 days.

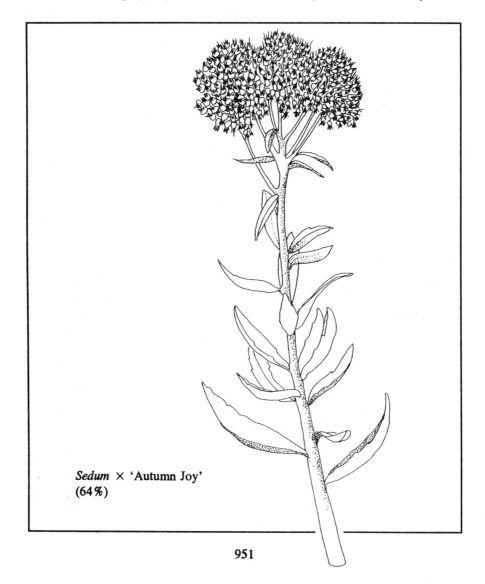

*Sedum* × 'Autumn Joy'
(64%)

**Related Species:**

*S.* × 'Arthur Branch' is an improved form of 'Atropurpureum' and much better than 'Mohrchen', because of better upright stems and consistently purple foliage.

'Atropurpureum' is a hybrid between *S. caucasicum* and *S. telephium*. It has been, and arguably still is, the best purple form with dark bronze foliage and rose-red flowers.

*S. caucasicum* (syn. *Hylotelephium caucasicum*), great stonecrop, is 2' tall with opposite succulent leaves and flat flower heads of greenish yellow stars. Plants hybridize readily, often with *S. telephium* (syn. *Hylotelephium telephium*).

*S.* × 'Frosty Morn', from Barry Yinger, sports a white border around the leaves and flowers with light pink flowers in late summer and fall.

*S.* × 'Mohrchen' is a dark leaved introduction from Germany which I find is highly overrated. Plants look a lot better in Germany than they do in most of this country. The stems are floppy and plants resent heat and humidity. Other than that, they are fine. Red flowers appear in late summer.

'Munstead Red' is a hybrid with the same parentage as 'Atropurpureum' but with deeper redder flowers.

*S. spectabile* (syn. *Hylotelephium spectabile*), showy stonecrop, is up to 2' tall and bears 3" long opposite or whorled leaves. Cultivars are similar to but not as compact as *S.* × 'Autumn Joy'. Some of the better ones follow: 'Brilliant' has deep pink flowers. 'Carmen' is the best cultivar and bears many carmine-pink flowers on 18–24" stems. 'Iceburg' is a cousin of 'Autumn Joy' with white flower heads in the fall. 'Meteor' is indistinguishable from × 'Autumn Joy'. According to Evans (see references), plants are not as compact and flowering is not as long lasting. I can see no difference. 'Indian Chief' has reddish flowers which fade to rosy pink. An excellent selection. 'Stardust' has silvery pink flowers on 18" tall stems.

*S.* × 'Sunset Cloud' ('Atropurpureum' × 'Ruby Glow') bears blue-green leaves and wine-colored flowers. The leaves are an excellent addition to the garden.

*S.* × 'Vera Jameson' is short (9–12" tall) with bronze leaves and 2–4" wide flower heads of ½" wide pink flowers. An excellent selection for the sunny garden. Vera Jameson was an avid gardener who lived in Gloucestershire, England. She discovered a chance seedling she believed to be a chance cross between 'Atropurpureum' and 'Ruby Glow', and gave it to nurseryman Joe Elliott (*Campanula glomerata* 'Joan Elliott'), the son-in-law of Norah Leigh (*Phlox* 'Norah Leigh'). Mrs. Jameson was the penultimate gardener, pulling weeds until she died in 1989 at the age of 90. The best specimen I have seen was in one of the finest gardens I been fortunate to visit. Vera literally shimmered in the fabulous garden of Wayne Winteroud and Joe Eck, called North Hill, in southern Vermont.

*-kamtschaticum* (kamt-sha' ti-cum)    Kamschatka Stonecrop      4–9″/15″
Summer              Yellow          Kamchatka, Korea, Japan  Zones 3–8

The normally unbranched pale green stems give rise to flat, terminal inflorescences of 6–10 yellow flowers. The leaves are alternate, about 1½″ long and ½″ wide, and sharply toothed above the middle but entire near the base. The ½″ wide flowers are showy, but seldom is the plant a mat of yellow as in *S. acre*, then are followed by red seed pods. There is a good deal of variability in the species and plants which were originally given species or subspecies status (*S. ellacombianum*) are sufficiently similar to be lumped together under *S. kamtschaticum*. Plants spread well if provided good drainage and full sun, and although too tall and open for a ground cover, are excellent for hillsides and banks. A tangled mass of stems occurs in the summer, and after flowering, which occurs sporadically throughout the year, small rosettes of leaves appear at the base of the plant which are next year's leaves. Most of the rest of the plant dies away by late fall.

## Cultivars:

'Diffusum' bears dozens of yellow flowers which arise from dark purple buds.
'Takahira Dake' is more compact and erect than the species with reddish
    stems and more flowering branches. The flowers are similar to the type.
'Variegatum' has a broad white band on the leaf margins, and flowers
    oranger than the species. It is not as vigorous and remains more
    compact. The leaves revert to green readily and any such growth should
    be removed to the base.
'Weihenstephaner Gold' is a terrible name for a wonderful plant. Dozens
    of golden yellow flowers cover this ground hugging plant. Highly
    recommended. Plants are sometimes listed under *S. floriferum*.

## Related Species:

*S. ellacombianum* is sometimes classified as a subspecies of *S. kamtschaticum* but the stems are not branched, the leaves are opposite and have scalloped rather than toothed margins. It is shorter (4–6″) and more compact. Beautiful star-shaped flowers on lime-green foliage can be seen in the spring and summer. However, after all is said and done, there is little difference from the garden point of view.

*S. floriferum* is, as the name suggests, a floriferous species. It produces numerous flowering shoots along the whole length of the stem. Very similar to *S. kamtschaticum*, it is often listed as a variety (*S. kamtschaticum* var. *floriferum*). The flowers are smaller and paler yellow, but overall, plants put on a better show than the kamschatka form.

*S. middendorffianum*, Middendorf stonecrop, has unbranched stems and narrower leaves (about ¹⁄₁₀″ wide). Plants are more upright than Kamschatka sedum. The leaves also have a sunken median groove making them somewhat V-shaped. The flowers of all three species are similar.

*-spurium* (spur' ee-um)          Two Row Stonecrop          2-6"/18"
  Summer          White to Rose          Caucasus          Zones 3-7

One of the tougher and showier stonecrops for a ground cover or rock garden. Many evergreen shoots arise from branches which root at the nodes, making a vigorous and rapidly spreading plant. The leaves are opposite, about 1" long with shallow teeth or scallops on the upper parts of the leaves. In leaf, it is straggly, coarse, uninteresting and invasive. Ronald Evans, *Handbook of Cultivated Sedums*, in describing *S. spurium*, states that "no plant should be called completely useless, however, and from its vegetative aspect, it could be recommended for quickly covering a heap of rubble." In spite of Mr. Evans's opinion, plants have become popular because of the showy flowers. The flowering stems are about 4" long and give rise to terminal 4-branched inflorescences consisting of many ¾" diameter flowers. The anthers are orange-red, the petals rosy red and flowers persist for 3-4 weeks. A large planting of *S. spurium* can be a brilliant blaze of color. The opposite leaves are bright green with a reddish margin and the leaves near the end of the stems turn redder in the fall and remain evergreen. Plants are not as vigorous in the South as in the North and as with most sedums, look terrible in midsummer.

Although native to moist alpine meadows, it is not tolerant of wet feet and should be grown where drainage is excellent.

All forms of this species may be divided any time during the season.

**Cultivars:**

Many of the cultivars have been selected for the bronze-purple foliage. In general, the color is better in the spring and fall and in many cases, leaves fade badly in areas of high heat and humidity.

'Album' is a white-flowered form of 'Dragon's Blood'.

'Atropurpureum' has burgundy leaves and rose-red flowers.

'Bronze Carpet' has a distinct bronzing of the leaves and is similar to 'Dragon's Blood'. The leaves are less permanently bronzed than 'Dragon's Blood' and some reversion to green stems occurs.

'Coccineum' is similar to the species but has scarlet flowers.

'Dragon's Blood' is the most popular cultivar with foliage strongly and permanently suffused with purplish bronze. During the spring and summer, plants are covered with dark red starry flowers. It is not as vigorous as the species. In the South, plants often melt out in the summer, particularly if drainage is not improved.

'Erdblut' ('Blood of the Earth') is about 4" tall with blood red flowers.

'Fuldaglut' has maroon leaves all season and burgundy flowers. A very striking mat of color. Similar to 'Ruby Mantle' and often interchanged.

'Green Mantle' produces fresh green leaves but no flowers are produced.

'Purple Carpet' ('Purpurteppich') is a compact growers with dark purple leaves.
'Red Carpet' has red flowers over bronze foliage and grows 3-4″ tall.
Similar to 'Bronze Carpet'.
'Ruby Mantle' have deep pink to red flowers over consistently dark
burgundy leaves.
'Tricolor' produces stripes of pink, white and green on the leaves.
'Variegatum' has green leaves surrounded by creamy pink margins. Some
leaves are entirely pinkish red but reversion to green shoots is not
uncommon.

### Related Species:

*S.* × 'John Creech' is a wonderful plant for a place where the 2-3″ tall
plant can be viewed. It is vigorous and grows well, given sharp drainage
and sun. Pink flowers occur in late May and June.

*S.* × 'Ruby Glow' (*S. cauticolum* × *S. telephium*) is about 12″ tall and
bears iridescent dark ruby flowers. It is an excellent front of the border
plant and is particularly colorful in late summer and fall. It is now listed as
*Hylotelephium* × 'Ruby Glow'.

*S. spathulifolium* is native to the West Coast and bears ¾″ wide yellow
flowers and short trailing stems of blue-green spatulate leaves. 'Atropurpureum' has dark purple leaves. 'Cape Blanco' has silvery leaves with a
purplish red margin and dozens of yellow flowers. Handsome in the North
and West, does poorly in hot, humid summers.

| | | |
|---|---|---|
| *-ternatum* (ter-na′ tum) | Whorled Stonecrop | 2-6″/18″ |
| Late Spring          White | Eastern United States | Zones 4-8 |

The common name comes from the arrangement of leaves in whorls of
three. The rounded pale green stems root from the nodes. After flowering,
stems die in the fall but offshoots remain, resulting in evergreen plants. The
¾″ long, roundish leaves are borne in rosettes crowded at the ends while
the lower stem is barren. The pure white star-like flowers are effective for
2-4 weeks in April and May. Plants tolerate shady moist conditions better
than most other species. For rocky slopes, few species are better. Unfortunately, *Botrytis* infections can be serious and plants are lost in mild, wet
winters in areas of little or no snow.

Reproduce vegetatively from stems which root and break away from the
mother plant. These remain small during the winter and begin to grow the
next spring. Plants may also be divided in early spring or fall.

### Cultivars:

'Minus' is similar but smaller in all parts with a mature height of 2-3″, and
bears leaves only at the end of the stems. The flower is smaller but
otherwise similar to the type.

'Shale Barrens' is covered with fine white flowers. Leaves are larger and growth is more compact than the species.

**Related Species:**

*S. dasyphyllum* is a ground hugging plant with gray-green foliage. Starry white flowers emerge in June and July. Best to provide afternoon shade. Hardy in zones 4–7.

*S. nevii* is an Eastern native species and badly ignored. Its tufted growth is only about 3–4″ tall but consists of blue-green foliage, and reminds some people of hens and chicks (*Sempervivum*). The white flowers have dark purple anthers and are quite handsome. A terrific plant for partial shade.

Quick Key to Sedum Species

    A. Plants creeping (growing along the ground) or
        decumbent (lying on ground with ends ascending)
        B. Flowers yellow . . . . . . . . . . . . . . . . . . . . . . . . *S. acre*
      BB. Flowers white or rose
            C. Flowers white . . . . . . . . . . . . . . . . . . . *S. ternatum*
           CC. Flowers rose . . . . . . . . . . . . . . . . . . . . . . . *S. spurium*
   AA. Plants upright
        B. Flowers yellow
            C. Height 12–15″, leaves broadest at or
               below middle, teeth begin below middle
               of leaf, many flowers (16–200) . . . . . . . . . . . *S. aizoon*
           CC. Height 4–9″, leaves broadest above
              middle, teeth begin above middle of
              leaf, few flowers (8–65) . . . . . . . . . . . *S. kamtschaticum*
      BB. Flowers pink . . . . . . . . . . . . . . . . . . *S.* × 'Autumn Joy'

**Additional Reading:**

*Books:*

Clausen, R.T. 1975. *Sedum of North America North of the Mexican Plateau.* Cornell University Press.

Evans, Ronald L. 1984. *Handbook of Cultivated Sedums.* Science Reviews Ltd., Middlesex, England. This excellent well-written text covers most of the species found in gardens today. The best book on Sedum I have found.

*Manuscripts:*

Bloom, Alan. 1978. Herbaceous sedums. *The Garden* 103(9):372–373.

Foster, Catherine O. 1982. Sedums reconsidered. *Horticulture* 60(6):38–49.

Hansen, Karel and Nynke Groendijk-Wilders. 1986. An account of some sedums cultivated in Europe. *The Plantsman* 8(1):1–20.

Lovejoy, Ann. 1991. *Sedum spathulifolium. Horticulture* 69(1):80.

McCauley, S. 1993. Sedums for all seasons. *Carolina Gardener* 6(2):29–30.

## *Selaginella* (sel-ag-in′ ell-a)  Club Moss  Selaginellaceae

*Selaginella* is grown for their interesting and often beautiful scale-like foliage. They occur in a range of vibrant greens, golden or variegated leaves, and some with the most iridescent blue leaves such as *S. uncinata*, peacock-moss, and the climbing *S. willdenovi*. Most prefer acid soils, some shade and consistently moist conditions.

Over 700 species are known but I am only familiar with a few of them. Peacock moss is a strutting miniature peacock in filtered sunlight due to the evergreen metallic blue-green foliage. Plants mine the soil and rapidly form a ground cover 2–4″ tall, but I have never seen them invasive. Too much shade mutes the color, but does not bother the vigor. It is a second-looker type of plant, one you can walk on and by, but once you see it, you will want some. Probably cold hardy to zone 6, warm to 9 or 10. *S. pallescens*, moss fern, is an erect plant with branching stems of bright green foliage, growing 8–12″ tall. This is a common plant for greenhouse forcing and for containers. Unfortunately, only hardy to zone 9. A golden-leaved form, 'Aurea', can occasionally be found. *S. involens*, Irish moss, is similar and cold hardy to about zone 6. The branching 8–12″ tall stems carry densely crowded bright green leaves. 'Aurea' is golden yellow in the spring, green-yellow as plants mature.

## *Selinum* (se-leen′ um)  Selinum  Apiaceae

Another difficult to distinguish member of the carrot family, whose flowers look like so many of those wonderful roadside Queen Ann's Lace-type weeds. The six species are native to the Himalayas and seldom have they found their way to American gardens. However, *S. tenuifolium* is really quite wonderful with her white flowers on top of bronze flower stems, although it is the feathery fresh green asparagus-like foliage that makes the plant special. It provides height, color and texture to the garden. It is a little wild looking, but a little wilderness among formality is not so bad.

Probably hardy in zones 4–7. Propagate by collecting and sowing the seeds.

## *Semiaquilegia* (sem-ee′ a-kwi-lee′ gee-a)  Semiaquilegia  Ranunculaceae

When I first read about this plant, I thought the name was a joke. Once convinced that the name was authentic, I thought of ways a plant could be half a columbine—half as tall, half as pretty, half as colorful; it was definitely a slow day. When I saw the plant, I realized that it was just as tall, just as pretty and just as colorful as many columbines, but its name was so intriguing that I had to grow it. In the Armitage garden, to everyone else, it was just a spurless columbine, but to me it was a special plant with a story.

The main difference between this and most columbines is the lack of spurs and that the sepals are spread apart, almost star-like. Flowers are always pale rose to wine red. They differ from the spurless forms of *A. vulgaris* in color and the spreading of the sepals.

Regardless of taxonomic differences, they are handsome 1–2' tall plants which flower prolifically and fit in well wherever columbines would be grown. The main species available is *S. ecalcarata,* whose wine red flowers were extraordinary for the 3 years it graced my place. The other species sometimes sold is *S. adoxoides* which is similar but with pale rose colored flowers.

They persist like other columbines, lasting 2–3 years and prefer partial shade and moist soils. Hardy in zones 4–7.

## *Sempervivum* (sem-per-veev' um)     Hens and Chicks,     Crassulaceae
Houseleek

If there was but a single plant my grandparents remembered, it would be hens and chicks. Used everywhere from small side gardens to plantings on grave sites, few gardens were complete without *Sempervivum.* One of the reasons for its popularity was the ease of growth and adaptability to any and all conditions. The name comes from the latin *semper*, always, and *vivo*, live, and live forever it does. Hens and chicks belong to the same family as *Sedum* but differs in the floral parts; in multiples of 6 or more while those of *Sedum* are in fives. All of the approximately 25 species appear similar and all are known as hens and chicks.

All species have thick, fleshy, alternate leaves and flowers which rise from the rosettes in coarse cymes. The flowers are often rosy red but may be white, green, yellow, or purple. Young plants are formed around the base of the plant and after flowering, the flowering rosettes—"hens"—often die leaving the "chicks" to carry on for another year.

Removing the offsets and planting elsewhere is the easiest method of propagation. Seed may also be obtained but 3 years are necessary before plants flower.

Several species are offered by specialists including the cobwebbed houseleek, *S. arachnoideum,* which weaves gray threads from leaf to leaf and forms dense webbing, particularly in full sun. Rose-red flowers appear in midsummer on stout flower stems. *S. soboliferum* produces dense mats of small green rosettes. The many offsets are attached to the mother plant by thin weak stolons and detach easily. Due to the ease with which offsets were formed and allowed to leave home, this species was the original hens and chicks. Pale yellow flowers are formed. Hillview Garden Products of Kenniwick, WA, listed two dozen selections of hens and chicks in their 1995 catalog, Sunny Border Nursery in Kensington, CT sells over 50 taxa and Blue Meadow Farm in Montague Center, MA carried over 30 types at their nursery, and there are dozens more. Differences in foliage color, foliage shape and flowers distinguish one from the other. For most of us, the common houseleek, *S. tectorum,* is all we ever see. Get hold of a good catalog and give a few others a try.

**-*tectorum*** (tek-to' rum)  Common Houseleek  8–12"/9"
  Summer  Purple-Red  Pyrenees, Alps, Apennines  Zones 3–7

The 3–4" diameter rosettes consist of 50–60 leaves, often tinged purple on the margins. The plant is stoloniferous and the new offsets are densely crowded around the parent. The leaves are flat on the face, rounded on the back and often reddened at the base. The hairy 12" long flower stem is clothed with hairy lance-like leaves. The flowers are 12-parted, purple-red, and about 1" across. The offsets are strong and produced on thick stolons. It is evergreen in all parts of the country. In the South, drainage is more critical than in the North.

### Cultivars:

Var. *calcareum* has smooth leaves with brown-purple tips.
Var. *cupreum* has larger rosettes which are rosy in cool seasons.

### Related Species:

*S. tectorum* has hybridized with many species, in nature as well as in gardens, producing numerous named forms and hybrids. *S.* × *pomellii*, Pomel's houseleek, and *S.* × *thompsonii*, Thompson's houseleek, are hybrids between *S. arachnoideum* and *S. tectorum* while *S.* × *schottii*, Schott's houseleek, is the union of *S. montanum* and *S. tectorum*.

### Additional Reading:

Praeger, L. 1932. Sempervivums. *Bulletin of the Royal Horticultural Society*: 1–23.

## *Senecio* (se-ne' see-o)  Senecio  Asteraceae

This is an enormous genus, containing about 1000 species from the tropics of Africa and Madagascar, New Zealand, North and South America, Japan and China. Many are annuals, including one of most useful gray-leaved plants, dusty miller, *S. cineraria*, and an even more beautiful relative, *S. viraviva*. Some are vines (*S. confusus*) and many are awful weeds like common groundsel, *S. vulgaris*. In general, the daisy-like flowers are yellow to orange but a number like the handsome *S. smithii* also have white flowers. When I take gardeners to Europe, we come across what has to be one of the toughest, most salt-tolerant plants ever, the shrubby *S. grayii*, with its white-margined leaves and abundant yellow daisies. In the American garden, however, most senecios are best suited to the wild area and often look particularly wretched after flowering.

Only a few perennial forms are ever offered to gardeners, with good reason. I have found a couple of native species and one from western Asia to be reasonable plants for the marginal tracts of the garden, but with the diversity of forms, habitats and adaptability in the genus, there are likely some hidden gems just waiting to be discovered.

Quick Reference to Senecio Species

|  | Height (in.) | Flower color | Flowering season |
|---|---|---|---|
| *S. aureus* | 6–12 | Yellow | Spring |
| *S. doria* | 3–5 | Yellow | Summer |
| *S. tomentosus* | 2–3 | Yellow | Summer |

| *-aureus* (ore-e′ us) | | Squaw-Weed | 6–12″/12″ |
|---|---|---|---|
| Spring | Yellow | Eastern, Central United States | Zones 3–8 |

I love this little plant because it does its thing with no fuss or mess. Its thing is to emerge early in the spring and send up purple flower buds which open to starry yellow flowers a few weeks later. The heart-shaped, blunt-toothed, basal leaves form rosettes and the stem leaves are finely and pinnately divided. The 1″ wide flowers persist for about 4 weeks in the landscape. They self seed and one year-there may be only a small group and the next year there may be a whole carpet.

In the Armitage garden, they come and go along a shaded path, welcome in the spring, forgotten in the summer.

**Related Species:**

*S. tomentosus* is a much bigger plant, growing to 2–2½′ tall. The young leaves, which are long and slender, are covered with a whitish woolly substance. The yellow flowers with orange centers are borne on long flower stems, also with the same woolliness. Full sun is necessary.

| *-doria* (dor-i′ a) | | Senecio | 3–5′/3′ |
|---|---|---|---|
| Summer | Yellow | Western Asia | Zones 4–7 |

Plants have bright green ovate to linear leaves which may be 12″ long and 4″ wide. The yellow flowers are only about 1″ wide but dozens of them occur at the tops of the stems. This is a heat tolerant senecio which enjoys poor soils and hot sun. Flowering late in the summer, it makes a useful companion to late blues and purples at that time. Cut back after flowering as it can look particularly bad late in the year.

Quick Key to Senecio Species

    A. Height less than 18″ . . . . . . . . . . . . . . . . . . . . . *S. aureus*
  AA. Height more than 18″
      B. Leaves (at least when young) covered
        with white tomentose . . . . . . . . . . . . . . . . . *S. tomentosus*
    BB. Leaves without tomentose . . . . . . . . . . . . . . . . . *S. doria*

## *Shortia* (short′ ee-a)          Oconee Bells          Diapensiaceae

Two species from Japan and one from North America make up this slow growing woodland genus. The genus, named after Dr. Charles Short, a Kentucky botanist, was the subject of a plant-hunt equal to any manhunt seen on "America's Most Wanted." The plant hunter, Micheaux, originally discovered the plant in 1788 in the mountains of South Carolina, but the specimen was in fruit rather than flower, thus was not described in his *Flora Boreali-Americana*. Asa Gray, the great American botanist, re-examined the specimen, preserved with many of Micheaux's collections in Paris, and named the plant *Shortia* in 1842. However, no other living plants could be found and great hunts and searches were all for naught until it was finally rediscovered in 1877. Found in Oconee County, South Carolina, thus the common name. The leaves resembled those of the closely related genus, *Galax*, thus its specific epithet, *galacifolia*.

The basal, evergreen, rounded, deep green leaves have shallow almost wavy margins and are borne on long petioles, plants are 4–8″ tall when in flower. The white flowers are borne singly and slightly nod down. The plant is considered rare, but it is less rare than local. To grow *Shortia* in the garden is a challenge, but the addition humus and leaf mold appear to be essential. Thus planting in an area naturally rich in such materials, or the ability to add them consistently, is best. To place these plants in ordinary garden soil is like planting water lilies in a rock garden. Partial shade is also necessary. Plants are hardy in zones 6–8.

### Related Species:

*S.* × *interdexta* is the name given to the intergeneric hybrid between *S. galacifolia* × *S. uniflora*, originally described in 1951. Plants are seldom seen except in botanical gardens and they are a little more vigorous but significantly different from either parent. Plants go under the name 'Wimborne'.

*S. solanelloides*, fringed galax, are native to Japan, and have coarsely toothed leaves and up to 6 flowers in a loose raceme. They are deep rose at the center fading to white as they age.

*S. uniflora*, Nippon bells, is more similar to *S. galacifolia*, and differs by having heart-shaped leaves with more deeply toothed leaves. Also native to Japan.

### Additional Reading:

Doonan, S. 1993. The Diapensia family. *Bull. of the American Rock Garden Society* 51(2):97–106.

## *Sidalcea* (see-dal′ see-a)          Checker-Mallow          Malvaceae

*Sidalcea* is related closely to the genus *Sida*, a little-known group of plants native to North America, and to *Alcea*, the hollyhock. It bears mallow-like flowers but is not as tall as hollyhock. In recent years, improvements have occurred in flower and habit. About 20 species, all native to western North America, are known ranging in natural habitat from open forest glades

(*S. malviflora*) to mountainside streams (*S. candida*). Most have rose to pink flowers but one species, *S. candida*, has small white flowers with bluish anthers. Most of the improvements in the genus have occurred with *S. malviflora*, checkerbloom. Plants thrive in climates with relatively cool summers and mild winters, warm, humid summers stress plants resulting in higher susceptibility to diseases and insects. Cut back after flowering for additional blooms.

*Sidalcea* is often confused with other members of Malvaceae such as hollyhocks (*Alcea*), mallows (*Malva*) and *Lavatera*; see *Alcea* for ways of telling them apart.

| *-malviflora* (mal-vi-flo' ra) | Checkerbloom | 2–5'/3' |
| Summer    Rose, Pink, Purple | California | Zones 5–7 |

The 2" wide lilac flowers are borne in terminal racemes. The basal leaves are rounded and lobed while the stem leaves are deeply cut into 5–7 smooth segments. *Sidalcea* thrives in cool, dry climates and performs poorly in the heat and humidity of the midwestern and eastern states. Misery was its middle name in the Armitage garden. Plant in full sun to partial shade in well-drained soil.

Seldom is the species seen in cultivation as it is too variable and tall to be of ornamental value. Improvements in flower color and plant habit resulted from crosses between *S. candida*, white checker-mallow, and *S. malviflora*.

Propagate by lifting the clump in the fall, using vigorous sections from the outside of the plant and discarding the center. Divide every 3–4 years. The species and a number of named forms (e.g., 'Stark's Hybrids') may be raised from seed in April and planted in the fall.

**Cultivars:**
'Brilliant' is 2–2½' tall and carries carmine-red flowers.
'Elsie Heugh' is offered by most nurserymen and bears lovely pale pink, fringed flowers on a 2–3' tall plant.
'Loveliness' is a recent introduction and is characterized by the shell pink flowers and compact habit. Plants stand 2½' tall and seldom need support.
'Mr. Lindbergh' has rosy red flowers and grows 2' tall.
'Mrs. Alderson' is 3–4' tall and bears spikes of large rose-pink flowers. This was the parent from which the dwarf cultivars, 'Oberon' and 'Puck', arose.
'Oberon' has deep rose-pink flowers and is 2–2½' tall.
'Party Girl' is more compact, growing 2–3' tall, and bearing shell pink flowers in late summer.
'Puck' is the dwarfest of the cultivars and attains a height of 2' and bears clear pink flowers. This cultivar and 'Oberon' are worth trying where other cultivars grow too tall, particularly in the South. These excellent cultivars were bred by Bloom's Nursery in England.
'Rosanna' is about 3' tall with rose red flowers.
'Rose Queen' has rose-pink flowers on 3–4' tall stems. One of the oldest cultivars, it is becoming more difficult to find.

'Stark's Hybrids' is a seed-propagated mix bearing pale pink to deep rose flowers that range in height from 2–3'.

'Sussex Beauty' grows 3–4' tall and has bright, satiny pink flowers.

'William Smith' has salmon-rose flowers and grows to 3' tall.

**Related Species:**

*S. candida*, white prairie-mallow, is native to Wyoming, Colorado, Washington and Oregon. The white or cream flowers are held on dense terminal racemes on top of 2–3' tall plants. 'Bianca' is 3' tall with clean single blooms.

## *Silene* (si-lee' nee)　　　　Campion　　　　Caryophyllaceae

Of the approximately 300 species, a few have found their way into widespread cultivation, particularly those suitable for the front of the garden or for the rock garden. The leaves are entire and the flowers are borne solitary or on 1-sided spikes. The tips of the petals may be entire (*S. caroliniana*) but more often are notched (*S. virginica*) or fringed (*S. polypetala*). The calyx (the group of sepals) is often inflated giving the flowers a bladder-like appearance.

Silene is closely related to *Lychnis* and *Viscaria*, and the genera are often used interchangeably. Differences between *Silene* and *Lychnis* were discussed under *Lychnis* and are based on the number of styles. The differences among *Silene* and *Viscaria* are less obvious, as seen in the following table.

|  | Number of styles | Number of cells in seed capsule | Number of stamens | Number of species |
|---|---|---|---|---|
| *Lychnis* | 5 | 1 | 10 | 10 |
| *Silene* | 3 | 3 | 10 | 300 |
| *Viscaria* | 5 | 5 | 10 | 4 |

Another genus, *Melandrium*, comes and goes in and out of *Silene*, depending on who is tweaking the genus. It supposedly differs from *Silene* by having one cell in the seed capsule rather than the three found in *Silene*. However, enough authorities keep the genus together that I am happy to do the same. *Viscaria vulgaris*, catchfly, is an interesting plant whose common name comes from the fact that flies stick to its sticky stem.

A number of striking species are grown for the rock garden such as *S. acaulis*, moss campion, *S. hookeri*, Hooker's campion, and *S. argaea*, but these can be difficult and disappointing for many gardeners. These species need cool climates and exceptional drainage. One of the native flowers to the British Isles, *S. dioica*, red campion, is on every roadside over there and is occasionally grown on the West Coast. 'Clifford Moor', from Yorkstock Nursery in England, has golden variegated foliage and pink (male only) flowers. 'Graham's Delight' also has variegated foliage and deep pink flowers. Two species which are also useful and much less demanding for the front of border or in the rock garden are *S. polypetala*, fringed campion, and *S. schafta*, schafta campion.

Quick Reference to Silene Species

|  | Height (in.) | Flower color | Petal tips |
|---|---|---|---|
| S. acaulis | 2–4 | Pink | Shallow notch |
| S. caroliniana | 4–8 | Pink | Entire |
| S. polypetala | 4–6 | Pink | Fringed |
| S. schafta | 3–6 | Magenta-pink | Entire |
| S. virginica | 10–20 | Scarlet | Deep notch |

| -acaulis (a-kaw' lis) | | Moss Campion | 2–4"/6" |
|---|---|---|---|
| Spring | Pink, Lavender | Europe | Zones 2–6 |

The plant is one referred to as "circumpolar," inhabiting high northern and southern areas around the world. The term "acaulis" mean stemless and these tiny plants form cushions of densely packed narrow leaves less than ½" long. The solitary pinkish to red, sometimes lavender, flowers have shallowly notched petals and sit on top of the matted growth. Unfortunately, many plants tend to be shy flowerers.

Plants are exceptionally pretty with their smooth matted plant habit, but only if grown in cool climates. They prefer mountain ranges but if your garden is not on top of a mountain, fret not. Be sure, however, that plants are essentially grown on rocks so that drainage is exceptional.

**Cultivars:**
'Cenisia' has double flowers.
'Floribunda' is a good selection which flowers more prolifically than others.
'Frances' has golden yellow leaves.
'Mt. Snowden' is very compact and bears white flowers.

**Related Species:**
S. alpestris, alpine campion, is another rock gardenish plant, needing excellent drainage and morning sun. White flowers with fringed petals are carried over 4–8" tall plants in late spring and early summer. The narrow, glossy leaves are evergreen in zones 5–7.

S. uniflora (syn. S. maritima) is similar in that it is also one of the smooth leaved species in the genus and is also alpine, happy to zone 3 at least. The flowering stems rise 6–8" tall and bear 1–4 white split (bifid) flowers with an inflated calyx in summer. 'Robin Whitebreast' is a common name for the double form, whose large flowers resemble a carnation. At the Georgia trial gardens, we have thoroughly enjoyed 'Swan Lake' with milky white double carnation flowers. They are also good for dripping out of containers.

**-caroliniana** (car-o-lin-ee-aye′ na)    Carolina Campion    4–8″/6″
  Spring            Pink            Southeastern United States    Zones 5–8

One of our lesser know native campions, these plants make ideal rock garden specimens with a range of variants and colors. The linear leaves are linearly bunched at the base with a central darker green midrib. The flowers are arranged in a corymb and consist of 5 petals usually unnotched or just slightly notched. The tubular calyces are not inflated. Colors range from a creamy white through pale pink to carmine.

Plants require full sun to afternoon shade and excellent drainage. In their native habitat, plants are often found on limey soils, but drainage is much more important than soil pH. Plants are short-lived in general, but particularly tricky in poor conditions. Propagate by seeds or root division.

### Cultivars:

'Millstream Select' was found by H. Lincoln Foster in a group of seedlings. Deep colors of pink and carmine from seeds collected in his garden, Millstream, and are still occasionally found in alpine seed lists.

**-polypetala** (pah-lee′ pet-a-la)    Fringed Campion    4–6″/18″
  Late Spring        Pink            Southeastern United States    Zones 6–8

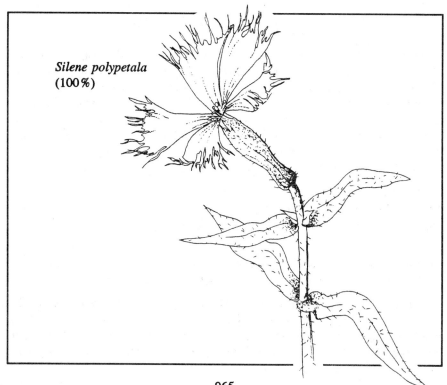

Silene polypetala
(100%)

This wild flower is on the endangered species list for the State of Georgia. However, collections reside happily in botanical gardens in the Southeast and tissue culture techniques have increased numbers substantially. The evergreen foliage is dark green and contrasts well with the light lavender-pink, fringed petals which emerge in late spring. The flowers are 1¼" in diameter and produced for 3–4 weeks. If placed in full sun, the foliage yellows and becomes sparse, therefore, partial to heavy shade is recommended. Plants require well-drained moist soil. If planted in the front of the border, be sure soil is porous enough to reduce water retention around the crown.

Division may be accomplished in spring or fall. Seed may also be used but plants will not flower without a cold period. Tissue culture techniques were fine tuned by Dr. Michael Dirr and Mildred Pinnell at the University of Georgia.

### Related Species:
'Longwood' is a hybrid between *S. virginica* and *S. polypetala*. This work was started by Dr. Jim Ault while working at the University of Georgia in 1985. He went to Longwood Gardens in Pennsylvania. His new hybrid has beautiful deep pink, fringed petals, earlier than *S. polypetala*, but is short-lived, at least where I have tried it.

| *-schafta* (shaf' ta) | | Schafta Campion | 3–6"/12" |
|---|---|---|---|
| Summer | Magenta-Pink | Caucasus | Zones 4–8 |

Many unbranched stems ascend laterally from a woody rootstock to form tufted mats of light green foliage. One or two pinwheel-shaped flowers (¾" diameter) are produced at the end of each stem during midsummer to late summer and continue for 3–4 weeks. The 1" long calyx is not inflated and is light green with 10 veins. The magenta-pink petals are notched. Full sun and coarse, gritty soil are preferable. Plants are valuable not only because of their colorful blooms but also because of late flowering.

Propagate by seed, division, or terminal cutting.

### Cultivars:
'Shelly Pink' has pale pink flowers.
'Splendens' has rose-colored flowers on 8–10" tall plants.

| *-virginica* (vir-gin'-I-ca) | | Fire Pink | 10–20"/12" |
|---|---|---|---|
| Spring | Scarlet | Southeastern United States | Zones 4–7 |

I love seeing this plant glowing like embers when I travel through the mountains of Georgia and North Carolina, however they are native from western New York to southern Ontario and Minnesota and south to Georgia and Oklahoma. About 2–4 smooth leaves are produced which are opposite, up to 1' long and wider in the middle than at either end. The flowers are "55-mph" flowers, particularly if you come across a colony. They thin petals are deep red and cleft at the tips and the sepals are sticky.

As beautiful as they are in their native habitat, they are best left there. Plants don't do nearly as well in the lowlands as they do at home. They are short-lived, although they may self-sow if placed in a well-drained sunny area where night temperatures fall in the 60's in the summer. They are seed-propagated by many nurseries and are available without guilt.

**Related Species:**

*S. regia*, wild pink, is even more eye-catching than *S. virginica*. Plants are taller (up to 4') and bear 10–20 pairs of downy (finely hairy) leaves and stunning scarlet flowers. Native west to Missouri and Ohio and south to Georgia. I was fortunate to see some wonderful plantings in the Holden Arboretum in Ohio. I don't see these commonly offered as I do *S. virginica* but they are available from seed.

Quick Key to Silene Species

    A. Petals entire or very shallowly notched
        B. Flowers solitary or few-flowered, mat-former . . . . *S. schafta*
      BB. Flowers many in inflorescence, loosely tufted . . *S. caroliniana*
    AA. Petals obviously notched or fringed
        B. Plants mossy, flowers solitary,
           height less than 6" . . . . . . . . . . . . . . . . . . . . . *S. acaulis*
      BB. Plants not mossy, flowers not solitary,
          plants taller than 6"
          C. Petals scarlet, with an obvious center notch . . . *S. virginica*
        CC. Petals pink, fringed at tips . . . . . . . . . . . *S. polypetala*

**Additional Reading:**

Hugo, Nancy Ross. 1992. Fire Pink. *Horticulture* 70(4):104.
Swezey, L.B. 1993. Low ground cover for rock gardens. *Sunset Magazine* (Central West) 191(3):42.

*Silphium* (sil-fee' um)        Rosin-Weed        Asteraceae

These coarse tall-growing relatives of the sunflower are native to the Prairies, Midwest, east to Georgia and south to Florida. In the flower heads of *Silphium*, only the ray flowers are fertile, forming the seeds around the disc, which, unlike the sunflower, yields no fruit. Generally, the flowers are yellow with black centers and the leaves are opposite (sometimes alternate). Plants yielded a great deal of resin ("rosin") and thus their common name. They are tough plants, putting up with winds, cold winters and hot summers without complaint. They are not used more often in gardens mainly because they are so big (some growing 7–8' tall) and rather weedy-looking. They look much better with a prairie sky in the background than a bungalow.

However, what is big and tall to one person is bold and impressive to some gardeners and is always a structural specimen to the designer. Of the twenty or so species, two are fairly available and provide fun and entertainment as well as long-lived beauty. *S. laciniatum* is called compass-plant because the coarse leaves align themselves in a North-South direction to minimize exposure to the midday sun. It is the leaves which make this plant interesting, not only because of their peek-a-boo habits with the sun but also because they are deeply cut (pinnatifid) like a pin oak, and may expand to 15" in length. The yellow flowers open in the summer on plants 5–8' tall. *S. perfoliatum* also has interesting foliage, the older leaves being connate-perfoliate (the opposite leaves are joined together around the stem) resulting in a cup-like attachment. Its common name is cup-plant and was used to collect rain water by the prairie Indians. It may be put to better use as a living bird water basin. The 3–5' tall plants have 4-angled stems with light yellow flowers consisting of 20–30 ray flowers in July to August.

Other species which need little more than full sun are *S. dentatum*, with narrow light yellow petals and *S. compositum*, made up exclusively of small ray flowers. Both are native to the Southeastern United States and both are tall; the former about 6', the latter up to 10' in height. Pinch out the terminal bud in late spring to force branching and more compact growth.

Both species benefit from full sun, poor soil and being ignored. Too much TLC, such as adding nitrogen fertilizers, results in lanky weak plants. Put them in the back forty and enjoy them on their terms, not yours, and you will be most pleased. Hardy in zones 3–7.

## *Silybum* (si' lee-bum)                    Silybum                    Asteraceae

The genus is represented in gardens by only one species, *S. marianum*, known as holy thistle, blessed thistle or St. Mary's thistle. It is quite a stretch to include this genus in a book about perennials, because at best it is a biennial, and in some cases an annual. However, it is cold hardy to about zone 7 or 7b and quite useful in Californian or Northwestern gardens. Therefore, they can be treated like digitalis or dame's rocket in climates where they overwinter. In cooler climates, plants can be treated as an annual.

The reason that it is worth a try, even though it is so short-lived, is because of the handsome, white marbled, thistle-like, basal leaves. They are 1–2' long and 8–12" wide and has wavy or deep cut margins and vicious spines. The foliage is much more pleasant to look at than to work with. The flowers are held in rosy purple heads and are surrounded by spiny bracts.

They rise 3–4′ above the rosettes in early summer and although they are slightly fragrant, they are secondary to the foliage.

Plants are native to the Mediterranean area, therefore excellent drainage and full sun is required. In the South, grow in raised beds. Plants are hardy to about 5° F. Propagate by seeds.

## *Sisyrinchium* (si-see-ring′ kee-um)　　　Blue-Eyed Grass　　　Iridaceae

Although many of the 90 species are native to North America, few have found their way into our gardens. The common name came from *S. angustifolium*, with grass-like leaves and starry blue flowers, native from Southern Canada into much of the eastern United States. In general, plants have linear to sword-shaped leaves in the form of a fan. The stems are flattened or winged and usually bear a 2–8 flowered cluster of small flowers, enclosed in a pair of bract-like structures called a spathe (similar to jack-in-the-pulpit). These spathes are really rather useless unless you want to know what makes one seemingly identical species different than another. The similarity and size of the individual spathes are some of the characteristics which help to distinguish species within the genus. It is a complex genus and species are difficult to tell apart and are often sold under the wrong name. But we gardeners are used to that.

Some of the more handsome plants are *S. bellum*, similar to *S. angustifolium*, but having blue flowers with yellow throats and unequal spathes. One of the finest species is *S. douglasii*, properly called *Olsynium douglasii*, western grass-widow, which bears large satiny purple, nodding flowers among rush-like foliage. Some of the blue-eyed grasses, however, bear yellow flowers, such as the 4–6″ tall *S. brachypus*, or white flowers (*S. arenarium*). One of the bigger forms and most ornamental is *S. striatum,* Argentine blue-eyed grass. Since the last edition, blue-eyed grasses have found favor among growers and gardeners and the number of species and hybrids available has increased. They are not yet heucheras but it is nice to see a few more being offered.

| *-angustifolium* (ang-gus-ti-fo′ lee-um) | Narrow-Leaf Blue-Eyed Grass | 10–14″/12″ |
|---|---|---|
| Spring　　　　Blue | Eastern United States | Zones 3–8 |

The narrow foliage and the branching stems are characteristic of the species. The stems are broadly winged and the leaves are usually shorter than the flower stems. Two to three clusters of blue flowers, usually with yellow eyes and about ¾–1″ wide, are produced in the spring.

They are terrific little plants which require no care and just blend in with the rest of the garden. Obviously, they cannot be buried in the back of the garden, but by a path or in the partial shade of high pines, they do just fine. Plants tolerate full sun and good drainage certainly helps.

**Related Species:**

*S. atlanticum* is also native to the eastern United States and Canada, from Nova Scotia south to Florida and west to Missouri. They may grow up to 2′ tall, with 1″ wide violet flowers and narrow leaves.

*S. bellum* is the western equivalent to *S. angustifolium*, being native to California. The stems are more narrowly winged and the flower clusters are enveloped with shorter spathes. Flowers are similar to *S. angustifolium*, but plants are not as cold or heat tolerant. They are sometimes placed with *S. idahoense*, which shows the extent of taxonomic confusion. 'Album' has milky white flowers. 'Wayne's Dwarf' is a dwarf plant (3–5″ tall) with blue flowers.

*S. bermudianum*, native to you know where, bears surprisingly large violet blue flowers with yellow centers. Plants are about 1′ tall and persist as far north as zone 7.

*S. idahoense* is very confused. I have seen plants labeled as such with small *S. angustifolia*-like flowers and also with large magnificent blue flowers. Some authorities place *S. idahoense* separately from other species, others throw in *S. maconii* and *S. bellum* as part of *S. idahoense*. Plants sold as *S. idahoense* should provide 1″ wide beautifully lavender-blue flowers with a dark violet throat. 'California Skies' is particularly wonderful. 'Album' is a white form with yellow stamens. Excellent drainage, low humidity and cool nights are beneficial.

| | | | |
|---|---|---|---|
| *-striatum* (streye-a′ tum) | | Argentine Blue-Eyed Grass | 12–24″/18″ |
| Early Summer | Cream | Argentina, Chile | Zones 4–8 |
| (Syn. *S. demissum*) | | | |

This lovely plant bears 9–12 creamy yellow flowers on an upright spike, similar to a gladiolus. The ¾–1″ wide flowers are darker in the center and striped with purple on their backsides, thus the name "striatum". The foliage is wider than most species (up to 1″ across) and can be mistaken for *Iris* when not in flower. Plants have creeping rootstocks and form large clumps but are not at all invasive. After flowering, plants become messy and should be fertilized to reduce the number of leaves which naturally turn yellow, or cut back to 6″ of the ground. Full sun and well-drained but moist soils are ideal. It is not as floriferous in the South as further north but worth trying regardless of locale.

Propagate by division or seed. Plants should be divided at least every 2–3 years. The small seeds should be barely covered and placed at 70–75° F and high humidity. Germination is erratic but seedlings should emerge within 3–4 weeks.

**Cultivars:**

'Aunt May' ('Variegatum') is particularly attractive with creamy white margins of the gray foliage providing additional interest after flowering. This is by far the most impressive yellow blue-eyed grass in the garden, if grown well. However, leaves can look tired under hot/humid conditions.

**Related Species:**

*S. brachypus* is aligned closely with *S. californicum* and may be the same thing. Native to the western United States, plants grow 8–12" tall and produce relatively wide (¼" wide) gray-green leaves. Star-shaped yellow flowers are produced in summer. Hardy in zones 8 (maybe 7) to 9.

*S. macrocephalum* produces many branched flower stems with butter yellow flowers, each with brown venation on the undersides. Plants grow over 2' tall. Native to South America, likely hardy only to zone 7b.

*S. convolutum* is native to Central America and appears to be hardy to about zone 7b. The yellow flowers have brown veins and the leaves are sickle-shaped (falcate) and appear convoluted. The starry flowers are held well above the grassy foliage in late spring and summer. Plants spread out, and grow 8–12' tall.

**Hybrids:**

A number of hybrids have been selected, parentage poorly known. The lack of parental guidance is unfortunate as one is always taking a chance in the East with species native to the far West and vice-versa. Regardless, there are some interesting plants out there.

'Biscutellum' has grassy leaves, grows about 12–15" tall and produces yellowish flowers with a hint of purple.

'Devon Skies' appears to have *S. angustifolia* in it and differs by having pale sky blue flowers.

'E.K. Balls' ('Ball's Mauve') is about 8" tall with mauve flowers and fan-shaped gray-green foliage. Plants require sharp drainage.

'Mrs. Spivey' bears lots of small star-shaped white flowers over grassy leaves in the spring and early summer. She is only about 6" tall. One of my favorites.

'Pole Star' ('North Star') also has white flowers which are a little less numerous but bigger than those of 'Mrs. Spivey'.

'Quaint and Queer' has probably been sold more because of the name than the plant itself. It is certainly more queer than quaint. The flowers on this 8–12" tall plant are said to be yellow and dull purple, but they are really kind of brownish. To each his own.

## *Smilacina* (smy-lass-ee' na)  False Solomon's-Seal  Liliaceae

Approximately 25 species of this native wild flower are known and all are found in moist shady areas. It is similar to Solomon's seal, *Polygonatum biflorum*, with alternate leaves on arching stems, berries in the fall, and golden fall color. Plants of both genera may be found side by side at the edge of humus-rich woods. There, the similarities end. The small flowers are borne in dense terminal inflorescences in *Smilacina*, whereas those of

971

*Polygonatum* are less conspicuous and bell shaped, borne in the leaf axils beneath the arching stems. Fruit is red in *Smilacina* and blue black in *Polygonatum*. False Solomon's seal is best used for naturalizing in a wild flower garden or near wood's edge.

| *-racemosa* (ra-say-mo' sa) | | False Solomon's-Seal | 2–3'/4' |
|---|---|---|---|
| Spring | Cream | North America | Zones 3–7 |

This wild flower is native from Quebec, south to Tennessee, east to Virginia and west to Arizona. One of my favorite plantings, however, is at Wakehurst Place, Ardingly, England, where huge, shining panicles drew me like a moth to light. What a difference a mild winter and cool summer can make, even with some of our natives. However, regardless where plants are grown, if happy, the flowering panicles can be seen 50 yards away. The arching stems bear 10–15 slender-pointed lanceolate leaves, each about 5–9" long. The rootstock is long and thick and over the years produces an ever widening clump. Hundreds of flowers are borne in a somewhat pyramidal panicle at the end of each stem. The individual flowers are small (1/8" wide), fragrant, and composed of 6 spreading, equal segments. After flowering, numerous red berries with small purple spots develop. They are a favorite food for many small animals and seldom persist.

Plants thrive in shaded, moist areas such as the edge of a wooded area or near a pond or stream. The soil should be lime free, rich in humus and deep enough to allow easy penetration of the rootstock. They should not be disturbed for at least 3 years to allow establishment of the spreading root system. It is not tolerant of hot weather and does much better in cool climates. Although plants grow and survive south of zone 7, they are not particularly ornamental unless copious amounts of water are supplied.

Seed must be stratified and germination can take up to a year. Careful division of mature plants in the spring or fall is the most common method of propagation.

### Cultivars:
Var. *cylindrica* has shorter leaves and is smaller than the type. The panicle is more cylindrical than pyramidal but there are few obvious differences between this variety and the species. Its native range extends south to Georgia, therefore is a little more heat tolerant.

### Related Species:
*S. stellata*, starry Solomon's-seal, is also known as star-flowered lily-of-the-valley because of the similarity of the leaves to those of *Convallaria*. It is 1–2' tall, has light green linear leaves and starry white flowers in an open raceme. Although the flowers are a little larger, the inflorescence is much smaller than *S. racemosa* and not as ornamental.

**Additional Reading:**

Martin, C. 1993. Herbalist's notebook: Solomon seal and wintergreen. *Mother Earth* 136:52–53, 82.

## *Solanum* (so-lah′ num)          Potato Vine          Solanaceae

Over 1400 species of plants occur in this mainly tropical genus, and none of the ornamental forms are hardy north of zone 7. Of course, the genus is probably known by anyone who has ever eaten a potato, *S. tuberosum*, or egg-plant, *S. melongena*, but except for the advertisements on TV, they can hardly be called ornamental. Gardeners in the East also know the prickly horse-nettles, mainly *S. carolinense*, which can be found from New England to Florida, while those in the West have come to recognize buffalo-bur, *S. rostratum*. Without doubt, with so many species out there, there are probably some cold hardy extraordinary taxa just waiting to become the next 'Autumn Joy' sedum. However, until that time, I include only the potato vine, *S. jasminoides*.

The vine grows about 6–8′ tall with many 3–5-parted leaves on many branched stems. The flowers are held in short racemes of white flowers, tinged with blue. They are stellate (star-like) and the yellow stamens stick out from the centers. The cultivar 'Album' is better known and has darker green leaves and pure white flowers. Hardiness appears to be zone 7b to 10.

Another vine, *S. crispum*, is better known by well-traveled gardens as it is all over gardens in Europe such as Sissinghurst and Glasnevin. The lilac blue flowers are clustered on the woody 6–20′ tall vines but the cultivar 'Glasnevin' has larger clusters of darker blue flowers and golden yellow stamens. More cold hardiness has been attributed to 'Glasnevin' than to *S. jasminoides*, but I have not noticed it. And my eyes cloud over when I see a well grown vine of *S. wendlandii*, with its 2–2½″ wide lilac-blue flowers. Native to Costa Rica. All species are terrific if they can be protected from winter winds and desiccation. Full sun is necessary.

**Additional Reading:**

Askey, L. 1993. Twine a new vine. *Southern Living* 28(12):4.

## *Solidago* (so-li-dah′ go)          Goldenrod          Asteraceae

Considered a nuisance weed by some, or a handsome wild flower by others, the genus has been all but ignored as a garden flower in the United States. Perhaps because goldenrods have been unfairly accused of causing hay fever (ragweed is the bad guy), or because they are common roadside fixtures, few find their way into cultivation. This is not the case in Europe where garden hybrids have been developed and used for late summer flowering. Hybridization of some of their finest cultivars has relied heavily on our native goldenrod, *S. canadensis*, as one of the parents. Once again, the Europeans introduce new and attractive garden forms from plants that are common in our own back yard.

*S. virgaurea*, European goldenrod, was highly valued for healing wounds, either externally or internally applied. However, even in England, where everything seems to grow so well, our native *S. canadensis* was not particularly popular. William Robinson wrote in 1883 that these "North American Composites in borders exterminate valuable plants, and give a coarse, ragged aspect to the garden." Of course, they still do. However, today's compact and colorful hybrids would make even Mr. Robinson sit up and look twice. The taller hybrids resulted from *S. canadensis* and *S. virgaurea* while the shorter ones originated from X *Solidaster luteus* (an intergeneric cross thought to be descended from *S. missouriensis* and *Aster ptarmicoides*) and *S. brachystachys*, a 6-9" miniature goldenrod. Only the smaller forms can be recommended as they do not dominate the garden or require support. Except for a few cultivars, I have trouble finding them attractive. I prefer the taller goldenrods by the roadside rather than in my garden. All do best in humusy soils and full sun.

The biggest problems with goldenrod, other than their poor reputation, are their height (which may be overcome with shorter, stronger hybrids) and their susceptibility to rust, a fungal disease. Rust is characterized by bronze pustules on the stems and lower sides of the leaves, and can be reduced by good air movement, bright light and well-drained soils.

Divide or use stem cuttings for the hybrids while the species may be raised from seed. The seeds germinate readily if placed under warm, humid conditions.

### Hybrid Cultivars:

'Baby Gold' stands 2-2½' tall with large racemes of bright yellow flowers.

'Cloth of Gold' is a dwarf but vigorous grower with dense, deep yellow flowers and grows 18-24" tall.

'Crown of Rays' ('Strahlenkrone') has to be one of the best goldenrods I trailed. I received this many years ago as a cultivar for use as a cut flower. The plants grow 2-3' tall without falling over, and are covered with bright yellow plumes of flowers in mid- to late summer.

'Golden Baby' grows 2' tall with golden yellow plumes.

'Goldengate' has bright lemon-yellow flowers atop 2' tall compact plants.

'Goldenmosa' has yellow-green foliage and bears yellow flowers in early August on 2½' tall stems.

'Golden Wings' is 5-6' tall, too tall for most gardens. Although a lovely deep yellow, it is too close in habit to *S. canadensis* to be of value.

'Golden Thumb' ('Tom Thumb', 'Queenie') grows about 1' tall with yellow flowers and yellowish green foliage. My choice as the most ornamental and useful dwarf form.

'Lemore' is 2½-3' tall with large inflorescences of primrose-yellow flowers. The flowers fade to white as they mature. Not as good a garden selection as 'Golden Thumb'.

'Leraft' has large panicles of bright yellow flowers, growing only 18–20" tall.
'Lightening Rod' originated at Collectors Nursery in Battle Ground, WA, and appears to be a variegated form of *S. canadensis*. The green leaves are streaked with gold. Interesting.
'Peter Pan' ('Goldstrahl') has canary yellow flowers and stands 2–3' tall. Plants associate well with red flowers of *Lobelia cardinalis* and *Crocosmia* hybrids. Flowering continues through early September and October.
'Super' bears wonderful sulphur-yellow flowers in mid-summer.

## Related Species:

Although the hybrids are best for garden, those who would like to incorporate wild flowers in a meadow or in a sunny wild area might consider other useful North American species.

*S. caesia*, wreath goldenrod, has distinctive wavy, yellow flower spikes and bluish purple, wiry stems. Flowers form along the whole length of the arching stems, not just at the top. Plants grow 2–3' tall and flower in late August and September. This is one of the more unusual goldenrods and an excellent cut stem.

*S. odora*, sweet goldenrod, is an excellent plant for the fragrant garden. The narrow leaves smell like anise when crushed. It stands 3–4' tall and bears yellow flowers on small, spreading, one-sided panicles. Hardy from zones 3–9.

*S. rugosa*, rough stemmed goldenrod, is 4–5' tall and has conspicuous hairy stems. The arching stems form a large panicle of golden yellow flowers in late September and October. Not as stoloniferous as some other native goldenrods, it can be used without fear of invasion. Ken Moore of the North Carolina Botanical Garden, introduced 'Fireworks', a popular shorter, more compact plant. Plants look particularly good in combination with fruit of *Callicarpa americana*, our native beautyberry.

*S. sempervirens*, seaside goldenrod, is 4–6' tall and flowers on one side only, forming a dense one-sided raceme in September and October. A useful plant for saline and sandy areas, the roots also retard sand erosion.

*S. sphacelata*, 'Golden Fleece', was introduced by Dick Lighty of Mt. Cuba Gardens in Delaware and has become a hot item for the late summer and fall garden. The rounded leaves give rise to many sprays of golden yellow flowers. Quite different from others and well worth a try.

## Additional Reading:

Bubel, Nancy. 1985. Goldenrods for the Garden? *Horticulture* 63(5):20–23.
Cohen, S. 1993. Select natives for the perennial border. *Native Notes* 5(3): 12–13.
Jepson, J. 1993. Goldenrod: a paradoxical native weed with a colorful story. *The Herb Companion* 5(6):44–48.
Lovejoy, A. 1994. Prospecting for goldenrods. *Horticulture* 72(8):46–48, 50–51, 74.

## X *Solidaster* (so-li-das' ter)     Golden Aster     Asteraceae

The interspecific hybrid (X *S. luteus*) is intermediate between the parents (probably *S. missouriensis* and *Aster ptarmicoides*) and arose as a natural hybrid in the nurseries of Leonard Lille, in Lyons, France. The flowers are much flatter than those of goldenrod and the plants make exceptionally good cut flowers. They are, in general, shorter than goldenrod and flower much earlier.

Grow in full sun, in areas of good air movement to reduce rust and in well-drained soils.

### Cultivars:

'Lemore' is the original hybrid with yellow flowers on 2–2½' tall plants.
'Yellow Submarine' bears wonderful deep yellow flowers massed together in summer. Some catalogs list it as a cultivar of *Solidago*, but it appears much more like a golden aster than a goldenrod to me. Regardless, it is terrific.

## *Sorghastrum* (sore-gas' trum)     Indian Grass     Poaceae

Of the 15 species, only *S. nutans*, Indian grass, is in cultivation. This native prairie grass may be found from Canada to Mexico, from Maine to Florida and throughout the Prairie states. It is a clump former, therefore will not root around everywhere. The blue-green leaves are about ½" wide, 8–12" long, and plants grow 2–3' tall. The narrow, feathery 8–12' long panicles of tan-yellow flowers are held well above the foliage in late summer, resulting in plants 5–6' tall. As fall approaches, the flowers become more bronze and then turn an attractive burnt orange. They are excellent for fresh or dried cut flowers.

Plants are sufficiently large to be used as a specimen in the border, but if room allows, they are even more attractive as mass plantings. Provide full sun, moisture retentive soils for best performance. They will reseed. Plants are hardy in zones 4–9.

Propagate from seed, move seedlings or divide immediately after flowering or in the spring.

### Cultivars:

'Sioux Blue' has wonderful blue-gray foliage and is much more in demand than the species. Selected by Longwood gardens, Kennett Square, PA.

## *Sparaxis* (spa-raks' is)     Wandflower     Iridaceae

This colorful bulbous genus is winter hardy only in the warmest parts of the country but may be grown for late spring color and handled in the same manner as *Gladiolus* and *Ixia*. Of the four species, the most colorful is *S. tricolor*.

976

| *-tricolor* (tri' ko-lor) | | Wandflower | 9–12"/12" |
|---|---|---|---|
| Spring | Orange-Red | South Africa | Zones 9–11 |

The lance-shaped leaves arise early in the spring and give rise to short spikes bearing 3–6 flowers of intense orange-red with yellow throats. The 1½–2" diameter flowers have 6 equal and flared segments but due to the great variability in the species, flowers range from pure white to yellow or red. However, the yellow throat is consistent in all flowers.

Bulbs should be planted as soon as the threat of frost has passed, and lifted and separated in the fall. They are best placed in containers in the fall in a cold frame and planted out, pot and all, in the spring. Fortunately, the corms are inexpensive and mistakes in culture are affordable. This species is too lovely not to try at least once. I grew it in Georgia but corms lasted only one year.

Plants do well in California where the warm days, cool nights, and dry summers resemble its native habitat, however, they do equally well in Houston and Minneapolis. Although single colors have been named, wandflower is generally available only as a mix of colors. But my, what a brilliant mix it is.

## *Spartina* (spar-tee' na)  Prairie Cord Grass  Poaceae

A grass native to the Prairies, whose toughness has allowed it to be used for planting on hills and banks for soil erosion. It seldom grows more than 2' tall and is an aggressive, rhizomatous spreader. The flowers are not particularly showy but the ½" wide glossy green leaves are wonderful planted en masse. Do be careful, the leaves are rather sharp-sided and can be lethal. They turn a golden yellow in the fall, providing a nice autumn tint. The grass can be very invasive, and should be planted with caution. Plants may be grown in zones 4–9.

'Aureomarginata' is better as an ornamental grass because of the thin gold margin on the leaves. Propagate the species by seed or division, the cultivar by division only.

## *Spigelia* (spy-geel' ee-a)  Spigelia  Loganiaceae

Thirty species are native from the southeastern United States to South America. Plants bear opposite, entire leaves and tubular upright flowers. They are wonderful woodland plants along paths in shaded, moist areas.

| *-marilandica* (mar-I-land-I' ca) | | Indian Pink, Pinkroot | 1–2'/2' |
|---|---|---|---|
| Early Summer | Red | Southeastern United States | Zones 6–9 |

In late spring and early summer, the most wonderful red flowers with yellow throats are produced from rather non-descript plants. The upright tubular flowers, which are 2" long, 1" wide and sharply lobed, stop people

977

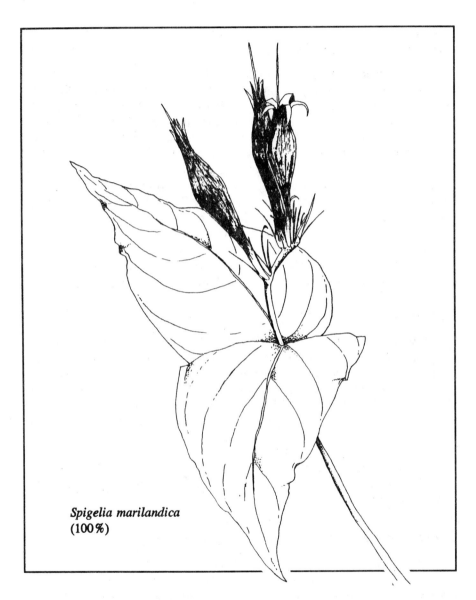

*Spigelia marilandica*
(100%)

dead in their tracks. They are borne on a one-sided cyme above the 4–7 pairs of 4″ long ovate sessile dark green leaves. Unfortunately, plants are not easy to locate and they are relatively expensive. However, if you can find a reliable nursery who propagates them from seed, and doesn't dig from the wild, then the price is well worth it. Place in the front of the garden or in wild flower areas in partial shade and moist soils. En masse, they are a striking, beautiful addition to any garden.

**Related Species:**

*S. gentianoides* is a rare species which occurs in a small area of Alabama and Florida only. Dr. Jim Affolter at the State Botanical Garden of Georgia is studying propagation techniques and means of fostering its survival. The tubular pink flowers are exquisite, although only those south of zone 7 will ever enjoy them as a perennial.

## *Spiranthes* (spy-rant' eez)        Ladies'-Tresses        Orchidaceae

This large group of plants range throughout all the continents, except Africa, and many are native to the United States. That they are seldom offered for sale may be due to their difficulty of propagation, the lack of large flowers or the lack of demand. In general, the flowers are relatively small (usually less than ½" long) and often spiral around the flower stem (thus the genus name). Some of the most intriguing natives are *S. gracilis*, slender ladies'-tresses, and *S. grayii*, little pearl-twist, both with obvious spirals of white flowers on 2' tall plants. One of the more common species is *S. cernua*, nodding ladies'-tresses, with slightly nodding white flowers in a spiral spike.

The only one I ever see for sale is another native, *S. odorata*, with bigger flowers and not as obviously spiraled. The fragrant flowers are held in two rows forming a rather dense spike, white and often marked with green. Plants grow about 2' tall and are best planted in moist soils in sunny to partially shaded conditions. 'Chadds Ford' is taller with larger flowers than the species.

Plants perform in zones 5–8 if proper conditions can be provided.

## *Stachys* (sta' kis)        Betony        Lamiaceae

Over 300 species occur and a handful are used as ornamental plants. Leaves are opposite and flowers are generally blue to purple, although some species bear white, yellow, or red flowers. It is represented in American gardens by the ubiquitous lamb's ears, *S. byzantina*, and we have been lamb-eared to death. The flowers are not particularly handsome and in one case, plant breeders produced a non-flowering garden cultivar. Most species do well in well-drained garden soils in partial shade to full sun. Good drainage is necessary.

Quick Reference to Stachys Species

|                | Height (in.) | Foliage color | Flower color |
| -------------- | ------------ | ------------- | ------------ |
| *S. byzantina* | 12–15        | Gray          | Purple       |
| *S. macrantha* | 12–24        | Green         | Purple       |
| *S. officinalis* | 18–24      | Green         | Red-purple   |

**-byzantina** (bi-zan-teen' a)    Lamb's-Ears    12–15"/12"
  Spring        Purple    Caucasus to Iran    Zones 4–7
(Syn. *S. lanata*, *S. olympica*)

Mats of velvety white, woolly leaves have made this a much used species for edging and design work. The foliage provides an excellent demonstration of the term tomentose—a covering of dense matted, short, woolly hairs. Plants look best in spring when the foliage is fresh but tend to decline by mid-August, particularly in humid, wet summers. The hairy foliage traps moisture and dew, and if summers are hot, particularly at night, significant leaf disease occurs resulting in dead patches. In the Armitage garden, it looks fresh in the spring but usually melts out in the summer. I can't begin to tell you how many of these I have killed. Zone 7b seems to be the marginal zone of performance, doing fine in many gardens, dying in many more. If the decaying foliage is cut back in late summer, plants may recover in the fall.

The purple flowers are held in whorls on a 4–6" densely hairy spike. The corolla tube is less than ½" long and barely protrudes from the calyx. In most perennials, the onset of flowering is anticipated, but in this case the flowers detract from the foliage. Not only do they take the eye from the handsome foliage to the mundane flower, but look worse once they have faded. Flowers should be removed as they develop.

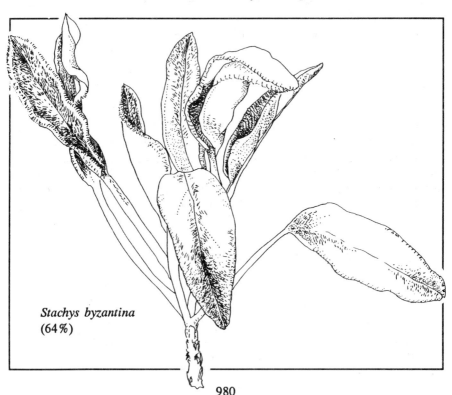

*Stachys byzantina*
(64%)

980

Moist but well-drained soils are ideal. In the North, full sun is tolerated, in the South, some afternoon shade is definitely appreciated. Too much shade should be avoided because leaves don't dry off. Subirrigation is better than overhead watering and all irrigation should be accomplished in the morning to allow the foliage to dry out.

Cultivars are propagated by division and the species may be raised from seed. Germination is erratic, but not difficult, at warm temperatures (70–72° F) and humid conditions.

### Cultivars:

'Cotton Boll' certainly has an interesting flower spike. The spikes appear normally but the flowers have been modified into fuzzy clusters of woolliness. Worth keeping on the plant for the double takes.

'Countess Helene von Stein' ('Big Ears') was named for the Countess von Zeppelin of Germany and is characterized by having leaves twice the size of the species. Plants appear to be more heat and humidity tolerant than others, but it has yet to take the Armitage garden test. Very shy to flower.

'Primrose Heron' is a recently introduced cultivar with primrose-yellow foliage in the spring that reverts to gray-green as summer progresses. I think this is the best of all the lamb's ears, even though I can't seem to keep it alive any better than the others.

'Sheila McQueen' is about 1' tall and is more compact than the type. The leaves are slightly larger and less woolly.

'Silver Carpet' is the best cultivar for low maintenance gardening. No flowers are produced and carpets of silvery foliage spread rapidly.

### Related Species:

*S. germanica*, downy woundwort, also bears gray, very tomentose leaves. The basal leaves have long petioles, the stem leaves are nearly sessile. The flowers are rosy pink to purple and densely hairy.

| | | | |
|---|---|---|---|
| -*macrantha* (ma-kranth' a) | | Big Betony | 12–24"/12" |
| Late Spring | Purple | Caucasus | Zones 2–8 |

(Syn. *S. grandiflora, Betonica macrantha*)

While the flowers of the previous species are not particularly revered, a flowering mass of this species makes a magnificent sight. The broadly ovate, dark green leaves are wrinkled and roughly hairy (scabrous). All leaves have scalloped edges but the uppermost leaves are much smaller than those toward the base. Plants spread rapidly to form mats in rich moist soils. The violet flowers are held in 2–3 distinct whorls of 10–20 flowers each about 8" above the foliage. The corolla tube is about 1" long and 3–4 times longer than the calyx. They can be seen from a football field away, particularly if paired with a chartreuse plant like *Alchemilla*.

On first seeing these plants, they are often mistaken for blur salvias, however, they don't have the herbal smell of *Salvia* and the flowers have 4 stamens, whereas *Salvia* has only two normal ones.

Plants are seen everywhere in European gardens, but their relative absence in this country suggests their dislike of summer heat and humidity found in so many American states. When people accompanying us to the British Isles see these plants, everyone west of the Pacific Northwest wants to know what it is and why they can't find it. Plants don't look like the woolly stuff they know as *Stachys*. Full sun and well-drained soils are preferable in the North but partial shade is necessary in the South. More flowers are produced in cooler areas of the country but if moisture is applied consistently, plants tolerate heat. In the Armitage garden, plants performed well in the spring but few flowers were produced and they keeled over the second year. I will try again.

Although many forms come true from seed, division is the fastest and best means of propagation.

### Cultivars:
'Robusta' ('Superba') is the most common form, grows 24″ tall and bears spikes of 4–5 whorls of rosy-pink flowers. This is the best form for the garden.
'Rosea' is similar to the species but produces rose-red flowers.
'Violacea' has deep violet flowers.

### Related Species:
*S. monieri* (syn. *S. densiflora*) is a little-known attractive stoloniferous plant with pink to rosy densely clustered flowers. Plants are about 2′ tall and form good size clumps with ovate-oblong leaves. Native to the Alps and Pyrenees in southern Europe. Useful in zones 5–8.

| *-officinalis* (o-fi-shi-nah′ lis) | | Wood Betony | 18–24″/24″ |
|---|---|---|---|
| Late Spring | Violet-Pink | Europe | Zones 4–8 |
| (Syn. *S. betonica*) | | | |

Few differences exist between this and the previous species. The 4–5″ long, ovate lower leaves have long petioles and scalloped margins while the upper leaves are lanceolate and sessile. About 15–20 half inch flowers are held in a dense spike. They are usually violet-pink, occasionally pink or white. Cultural requirements are similar to *S. macrantha* but it will not tolerate as much shade.

Propagate similar to *S. macrantha*.

### Cultivars:
'Alba' has creamy white flowers.
'Grandiflora' produces larger flowers than the species and are soft pink.
'Rosea Superba' bears rose-pink flowers and corrugated leaves.

Quick Key to Stachys Species

    A. Leaves densely whitish woolly, corolla short
       and barely exerted from the calyx . . . . . . . . . . . *S. byzantina*
   AA. Leaves green, corolla much longer than calyx
      B. Upper stem leaves ovate, corolla
        3–4 times longer than calyx . . . . . . . . . . . . *S. macrantha*
     BB. Upper stem leaves lanceolate,
        corolla twice as long as calyx . . . . . . . . . . . *S. officinalis*

**Additional Reading:**

Leslie, A.C. 1993. *Stachys byzantina. The Garden* 118(6):240–242.
Parke, M. 1989. The versatile lamb's ears. *Horticulture* 67(2):44–45.

*Stenanthium* (sten-an-the′ um)      Stenanthium      Liliaceae

    Unknown, unused, and unloved, yet an interesting group of bulbous plants native to the United States. The botanical name comes from *stenos*, narrow, and *anthos*, flower, describing the narrow flower segments. The best species for eastern gardeners is *S. gramineum*, with 2′ long broad grass-like leaves and a tall panicle of small white, greenish or purple flowers. Plants are native from Pennsylvania to Missouri, south to Florida and west to Texas. Flowers occur in mid- to late summer, followed by drooping fruit in the fall. The best form of this species is var. *robusta*, whose flowers are more numerous and held much more densely on the panicle resulting in a more ornamental display. In the West, gardeners might want to try *S. occidentale*, native the coast ranges in northern California through the Cascades to Canada. Plants are 1–2′ tall with basal, grassy leaves and drooping greenish to white flowers with reflexed petals. The flowers are larger but not as numerous as *S. gramineum*.
    Place in full sun in a sheltered location. Hardiness is confused but probably hardy to zone 6. Plants are difficult to find, but worth a try. Propagated by seed or division.

*Stipa* (stee′ pa)      Needle Grass, Feather Grass      Poaceae

    Approximately 150 species of this temperate grass occur, with twisted leaf blades and narrow panicles of flowers. The flowers are characterized by long needle-like awns (leaf-like structures at the base of each flower) which catch the light and sway lithely in the breeze. In full bloom, they provide a richness of movement and color that can only be found in nature. Although they are handsome, many are short-lived, going dormant after flowering and looking pretty grisly, susceptible to fire, and making great homes for natures little critters.

Two species are more popular than others, and are used throughout the country. *S. gigantea*, giant feather grass, is one of the showiest of the species. They are hardly gigantic when not in flower, the rolled leaves are 1½–2' long and plants are only about 2' tall. Flowering stems arise in late spring or early summer and top out at 5–6'. Combined with gold stamens, the 4–5" long golden awns make a wonderful display in any bit of breeze. Plants are native to southern Europe and perform well in zones 7–10.

Another species with terrific ornamental value is *S. tenuissima*, Mexican feather grass. In this species, the bright green leaves are very thin and flexible and eddy with the wind. They are about 2' tall, not a lot taller even when flowering. The flowers are tan to yellowish green in early summer and although the awns are only a couple of inches long, they are handsome, particularly if they catch the late afternoon sun. To me, they are the most engaging of any species in the genus. Plants are native to Mexico and the Southwest and hardy in zones 7–9. Plants can self seed readily.

All feather grasses require well-drained soils and full sun for best performance.

## *Stokesia* (stoks' ee-a)         Stokes' Aster         Asteraceae

The only species, *S. laevis*, occurs from South Carolina to Florida and Louisiana. This wild flower has undergone a series of breeding "operations" resulting in larger and more colorful flowers than the species. It has adapted itself so well to formal gardens that it is seldom thought of as a wild flower anymore. Plants are a major cut flower crop, persisting for a week after cutting.

| *-laevis* (lay' vis) | | Stokes' Aster | 12–24"/18" |
|---|---|---|---|
| Summer | Blue | Southeastern United States | Zones 5–9 |
| (Syn. *S. cyanea*) | | | |

The dark evergreen entire leaves, which often have a pronounced white midrib, are 6–8" long, alternate and provide pleasant greenery in the winter when not covered by snow. Leaves at the base have a long petiole but become sessile toward the top of the plant. Soft spiny projections can be observed at the base of the leaves and also subtending the flower buds. Two to four flowers are borne on a single stalk but open one or two at a time. Many flower stalks are present and flowering continues for about 4 weeks. The individual flowers are 4" across and consist of two series of ray flowers. The outer are much larger than the inner set and have 4–5 deeply cut lobes. Plants are best placed at the front of the border in filtered sunlight and well-drained soil as they do not tolerate wet feet in the winter. If planted in zone 5, a winter mulch is recommended.

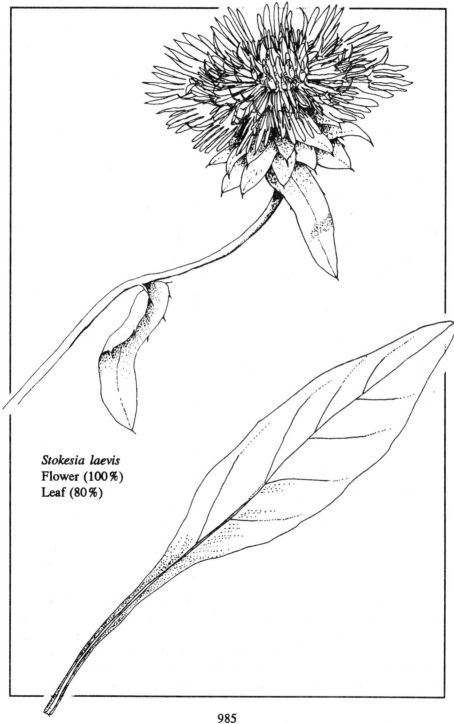

*Stokesia laevis*
Flower (100%)
Leaf (80%)

Propagate by divisions in the spring. The species may also be raised from seed. Germination is irregular; seeds should be placed at 40° F for 6 weeks prior to sowing at 70° F.

**Cultivars:**

'Alba' has white flowers and, although not as floriferous as the blue cultivars, the flowers contrast well against the foliage.

'Blue Moon' has dark blue flowers on 2' tall plants.

'Blue Danube' produces lavender-blue flowers up to 4" in diameter. The most popular of the named forms.

'Blue Star' has a little less lavender in the flowers and is almost a spode blue.

'Klaus Jelitto', named for the great German seedsman, bears lavender flowers which are a little larger than the species.

'Mary Gregory' was introduced by Niche gardens in Chapel Hill, NC. The flowers are yellow rather than lavender and persist for a long time. A big change!

'Omega Skyrocket' was discovered by Ron and Susan Dieterman of the Atlanta Botanical Garden and introduced by Sauls Nursery in Atlanta. It is unique in that plants grow 3–4' tall and bear white to pale blue flowers. It is the most robust stokesia I have seen. Plants do not require support and are more easily used as long stemmed cut flowers than others.

'Silver Moon' bears creamy white flowers. They are larger than those of 'Alba' and equally handsome.

'Wyoming' bears many flowers of rich deep blue.

## *Stylophorum* (sty-lah' for-um)    Celandine Poppy    Papaveraceae

This genus consists of 3 species but only the native species, *S. diphyllum*, is common in American gardens. An outstanding plant for no maintenance gardeners, who will rejoice in the reseeding habit and color of the plants in early spring.

| *-diphyllum* (di-fil' lum) | Celandine Poppy | 12–18"/12" |
|---|---|---|
| Spring    Yellow | Eastern North America | Zones 4–8 |

This species is native to woodsides from Pennsylvania to Tennessee, and from Wisconsin to Missouri. Cut stems exude a yellow sap once used by American Indians for dye. Since they cohabit with bloodroot, you can have a veritable finger painting time, painting all sorts of unsuspecting faces. Plants emerge early in the spring and produce 8–12 basal light green leaves, 10–15" long and deeply cut into 5–7 lobed

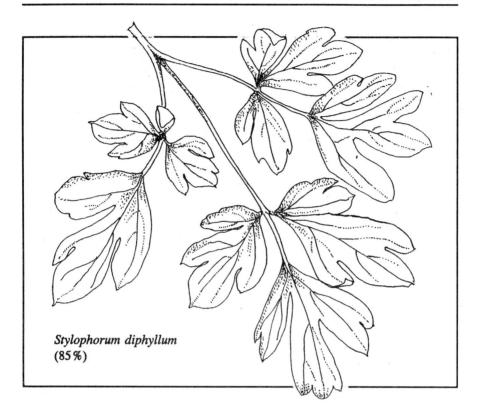

*Stylophorum diphyllum*
(85%)

divisions. The 1½–2″ bright yellow flowers consist of 4 petals and many stamens and open in March and April. Three to five flowers open in each terminal inflorescence.

A beautiful plant for the shaded, moist wild flower garden, which in the Armitage garden reseeds itself everywhere. It is wonderful growing with Labrador violets, where the purple leaves and violet flowers seem tailor-made for the yellow flowers of the celandines. I received my first few plants from my friends, Ed and Donna Lambert, whose woodland garden is a gardener's mecca. In their garden, the celandines are everywhere, and in the spring cover the ground with sunshine. If left undisturbed, plants colonize large areas. Foliage disappears by late June in dry garden conditions, however, if grown in consistently moist soils, foliage persists into fall. People are inevitably drawn towards the plants regardless of other plants in flower at the time. One of the finest wild flowers for bright, effective spring color.

Seed is not difficult to germinate if sown in a moist medium at 68–72° F. Since they reseed prolifically, sit back and let nature do it. Plants should be left undisturbed but may be divided successfully if care is taken not to damage the long thick roots. Divide in early spring or fall.

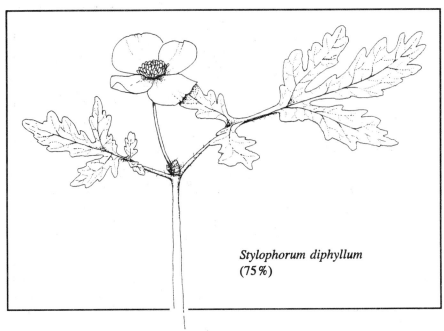

*Stylophorum diphyllum*
(75%)

### Related Species:

*S. lasiocarpum* is native to central and eastern China but is being seen more and more in the United States. They have flowers similar to *S. diphyllum* but the leaves are bigger and with more deeply cut margins. The sap is red, rather than yellow.

*Symphytum* (sim' fi-tum)  Comfrey  Boraginaceae

I was never a big fan of these plants and had to be talked into their virtues. However, a few of the 35 species are enjoyable additions to the flower garden. *S. officinale* was used in Europe in monastery gardens in the 12th century and is still found in herbal gardens. It was used as a poultice to help the healing of broken bones and became known as boneset. A number of species were introduced as forage and make excellent plants for the production of compost. Some gardeners grow *S. officinale* or *S. asperum*, a 5–6' tall species, in a shaded wild flower area.

Most species are upright and 2–4' tall although *S. grandiflorum*, a rapidly spreading ground cover with yellow-white flowers, and *S. × rubrum*, a red-flowered form, are less than 18". Some of the clearest and prettiest blue flowers in the plant kingdom occur in this genus. The tubular flowers are often blue or purple and held in scorpioid cymes, similar to those of forget-me-nots and Virginia bluebells. The leaves are alternate and often hispid (raspy, like sandpaper). All species are most suitable for moist areas in sun or dappled shade.

Divide the fleshy roots in the spring and replant immediately.

Quick Reference to Symphytum Species

|  | Height (in.) | Flower color |
|---|---|---|
| *S. caucasicum* | 18–24 | Blue |
| *S. grandiflorum* | 12–15 | Yellow |
| *S. officinale* | 36–48 | Purple |
| *S.* × *rubrum* | 15–18 | Red |
| *S.* × *uplandicum* | 36–48 | Blue |

| *-caucasicum* (kaw-ka' si-cum) | Caucasian Comfrey | 18–24"/24" |
|---|---|---|
| Spring          Blue | Caucasus | Zones 3–7 |

The softly hairy foliage consists of 8" long basal leaves and 6" long upper leaves. The base of the leaves runs along the stem for a short distance (decurrent). The drooping, ¾" long, bell-shaped flowers open pink, then turn azure-blue with maturity. The corolla (petals) is 2–3 times longer than the calyx (sepals) and flowers are borne in terminal, paired, scorpioid cymes. The flowers start red-purple then change to blue (essentially going through pink as well). Partial shade and moist soils are necessary for best performance. The coarse textured plants are excellent subjects for the wild flower area but are also useful in the border or as short specimen plants in the garden.

| *-grandiflorum* (grand-i-flo' rum) | Large-Flowered Comfrey 12–15"/18" |
|---|---|
| Spring    Pale Yellow, Cream    Caucasus | Zones 3–8 |

(Syn. *S. ibericum*)

Rhizomes give rise to many unbranched stems resulting in rapidly spreading colonies. The stem is roughly hairy (scabrous) and bears shiny, ovate leaves of different sizes. Those on flowering stems are only about 1½" long while those on non-flowering (sterile) stems are up to 7". The sterile stems lie on the ground with the ends pointing up (decumbent) and are characteristic of the species. Tubular, creamy yellow, almost white, ¾" long flowers are produced in many terminal few-flowered cymes for about 3–4 weeks. A vigorous grower that competes well against weeds, it is shade and drought tolerant. Although tolerant of dry conditions, growth is superior in moist soils.

## Cultivars:

'Variegatum' is an outstanding cultivar bearing creamy white margins around the light green leaves. The plant is much brighter than the species, particularly when planted in shady corner of the garden.

| | | | |
|---|---|---|---|
| *-officinale* (o-fish' i-nal) | | Common Comfrey | 3–4'/4' |
| Spring | Purple | Europe | Zones 4–7 |

The largest of the bonesets and reasonably handsome when in flower. The large leaves are ovate to lanceolate (wider in middle than at either end) and densely pubescent. The upper and middle leaves are obviously decurrent (the leaves run down the stem) and sessile. The strong stems are winged erect and heavily branched.

The inflorescences are many flowered and are white, pink or purple-violet. Plants are big and require "fencing in" or they fall over in rains and winds and forlornly lay on the ground. Full sun helps the strength, partial shade is tolerated.

**Related Species:**

*S. asperum*, prickly comfrey, has dark green prickly-hairy leaves on plants which grow 3–4' tall. The flowers are at first reddish, then fade to blue. Also big, coarse and raspy.

| | | | |
|---|---|---|---|
| *-× rubrum* (ru' brum) | | Red Flowered Comfrey | 15–18"/18" |
| Early Summer | Red | Hybrid | Zone 3–7 |

This may be used as a ground cover because of its tendency to spread, although not as rapidly as one of its parents, *S. grandiflorum*. The foliage is dark green and not as hairy as many of the other species. Dark red, tubular flowers bequeathed by *S. officinale* 'Coccineum' occur in terminal cymes. The drooping red flowers, however, do not contrast well with the hairy dark leaves. Full sun may be provided in the North but partial shade is best in the South. Provide even moisture in times of dry weather.

| | | | |
|---|---|---|---|
| *-× uplandicum* (up-land' i-kum) | | Russian Comfrey | 36–48"/36" |
| Late Spring | Blue | Hybrid | Zones 4–7 |
| (Syn. *S. peregrinum*) | | | |

This upright plant is the result of a cross between *S. asperum*, a 4' tall bristly plant, and *S. officinale*. The stems are highly branched and bear 8–10" long basal leaves and 2–3" long upper leaves. The basal leaves are decurrent (see *S. caucasicum*), and all foliage is softly hairy. The 1" long, tubular flowers appear in various shades of purple and blue in forked cymes in the upper axils of the plant.

**Cultivars:**

'Variegatum' has leaves with broad creamy white margins and lilac blue flowers. This is a fabulous plant but can only be propagated by division or root cuttings, therefore it is difficult to build up any numbers, thus will always have greater demand than supply.

**Other Hybrids:**

A few named hybrids are out there, but it is almost impossible to tell what name belongs to what species, and are most likely all hybrids.

'Gold in Spring' is from Herronswood Nursery and produces early pink and white flowers and yellow foliage as it emerges.

'Goldsmith' is about 1' tall and bears green leaves edged and splashed with gold and cream. Flowers are pink to blue in spring.

'Hidcote Blue' is a vigorous spreader with soft blue and white flowers on 1–2' tall plants.

'Hidcote Pink' is similar but with pink and white flowers.

'Langthorn's Pink' grows up to 3' tall with pink flowers in early summer.

'Pink Robins' is about 2' tall with dark green leaves and deep pink narrow flowers.

Quick Reference to Symphytum Species

    A. Flowers purple, blue, or lilac
      B. Plants usually less than 2', flowers bell
        shaped, calyx not divided to middle . . . . . . . *S. caucasicum*
      BB. Plants usually taller than 2', flowers
        tubular, calyx divided to the middle . . . . . *S.* × *uplandicum*
    AA. Flowers white, yellow, or red
      B. Flowers creamy yellow or white
        C. Plants usually less than 2' tall . . . . . . . . *S. grandiflorum*
        CC. Plants usually taller than 2' tall . . . . . . . . . *S. officinale*
      BB. Flowers red . . . . . . . . . . . . . . . . . . . . . *S.* × *rubrum*

*Symplocarpos* (sim-plo-kar' pus)     Skunk Cabbage    Araceae

Like many members of the Araceae family, plants can raise the temperature of the flowers, which are formed in the fall to arise in late winter or earliest spring, thus ensuring that no damage occurs from freezing weather. It is usually the earliest plant to flower in its native habitat. The only species, *S. foetidus*, is native to swampy areas in Quebec to Manitoba, south to Georgia, Tennessee, Illinois and Iowa. The mottled brown spathe is strongly incurved and bloated and totally surrounds the narrow spadix. The cabbage-like leaves arise after flowering and although the common name suggests a rugged smell, an unpleasant odor only occurs if leaves are crushed or plants are disturbed. Its sister with the same common name, *Lysichiton*, is smellier.

Plants will only proliferate in bogs, swamps or in stagnant water. Where they are happy, there they shall stay, produce offspring, and multiply rapidly. More of a curiosity than a great ornamental beauty.

*Synthyris* (sin-theye' rus)         Synthyris         Scropulariaceae

Native to the Plains states and west to California, these small blue-flowered plants are slowly becoming better known. The best performer is probably *S. missurica*, native to southeastern Washington and Idaho to northeastern California. The plants are about 2' tall, and consist of 2-3" wide rounded basal leaves which are coarsely toothed and held on long petioles. The small individual blue flowers, which consist of a four-lobed corolla (petals), 4 distinct sepals and only 2 stamens, are held in a narrow raceme.

I have this plant in the Armitage garden and it has performed surprisingly well, neither capturing one's fancy with its flavor nor disappointing people with its demise. It flowers for me in April, 2-3 weeks later in the North. Light afternoon shade and well-drained soils are all that is necessary. Plants are tough, being winter hardy to zone 3 and tolerating zone 7 summers.

### Cultivars:
'Major' is bigger in every way.

### Related Species:
*S. pinnatifida* has deeply cleft basal leaves and grows only about 8" tall. Native in Montana and Utah.

# T

*Tanacetum* (tan-a-see' tum)  Tansy  Asteraceae

This genus is one which was filled by changes to the genus *Chrysanthemum*, a number of which are well-known garden plants, such as pyrethrums (*C. coccineum*, *T. coccineum*) and feverfew (*C. parthenium*, *T. parthenium*). The problem with all these name changes is more than simply confusion, all the parentheses make for boring reading. For the species just mentioned, please refer to *Chrysanthemum*, however, old-fashioned *Tanacetum* is listed in many catalogs with a few fine species. One of the few linkages among species is that they all have scented foliage, sometimes, like tansy, highly aromatic. They also all have alternate leaves and single or double daisy flowers.

Some handsome species are low growing mound-formers with attractive, white, hairy, finely divided leaves, such as *T. densum* and *T. haradjanii*, which require full sun and exceptionally well-drained soils to be at their best. Lots of these small downy-leaved species (*T. compactum* and *T. nutallii* as well) are reasonably cold hardy, but cringe with the onset of wet winters and hot, humid summers. I love seeing the dwarf forms as well as the hefty species like *T. corymbosum*, whose white daisy flowers with yellow centers so handsomely combine with their coarse dark green foliage, and *T. macrophyllum* whose deeply cut large leaves set off the white yarrow-like flowers effectively. However, I seldom see any of these, short or hefty, perform well in the United States and seldom do I ever see them offered for sale to the gardening public. In the Pacific Northwest, more success occurs than in the rest of the country.

The species that seems to be most adaptable, although it still does miserably in the warm Armitage garden, is *T. vulgare*, common tansy or golden buttons. The fresh green, coarse leaves of tansy are highly aromatic to the touch and are often harvested, dried, and used as potpourri. The mainly basal leaves are cut into 7–10 pairs of narrow segments, each one pinnately lobed, resulting in the appearance of a cutleaf fern. Plants can get

993

to 4' tall but generally peak out about 2'. The button-like yellow flowers are formed in late summer. 'Crispum' is referred to as curly tansy, and while I find most of the *crispums* of the horticulture world ugly as sin, I like this one. The leaves are larger, appear lighter green, and are more deeply cut than the species, and flowering occurs sparsely if at all.

Plants are hardy in zones 5–7 and should be placed in full sun or afternoon shade.

### *Telekia* (tel-ee-kee- a)　　　　　　Telekia　　　　　　Asteraceae

Telekia is one of those coarse-leaved yellow summer daisies similar to sunflowers, *Inula* and *Buphthalmum*. In fact, they are so similar to *Buphthalmum*, the two species of *Telekia* were only recently removed from that genus. For those who are curious as to why such divorces take place, oftentimes the irreconcilable differences are indeed subtle, at least to the non-taxonomist. Some characteristics which separate this species from *Buphthalmum* are doubly serrated, highly aromatic leaves (entire margins to single serrate in *Buphthalmum*), flowers are held in racemes (usually solitary in *Buphthalmum*) and plants are much larger in *Telekia* than in *Buphthalmum*. The scent and large size are the most visible characteristics which differentiate them from each other.

The most common species is *T. speciosa* which bears large basal leaves (14″ long and 10″ wide) on 6–8″ petioles and sessile upper stem leaves, reduced in size and rounded at the base. The stems are branched near the top and can grow to 6' in height. The large leaves are pubescent, sessile, double toothed, and strongly aromatic. The species is seldom seen in gardens because of its coarse, gangling, large habit. It is a vigorous grower and spreads rapidly. The yellow flowers are about 2″ across, held in a loose raceme and bloom in mid- to late summer. For some gardeners and designers, they are excellent as accents or back of border plants and provide a pleasing effect for a few months; however, they decline rapidly after flowering and should be cut back before they turn crispy.

*T. speciossisma* is similar but only grows about 2' tall on unbranched stems. Flowers are smaller but similar to the previous species.

Plants are hardy from zones 2–7a, marginal at best in 7b, and do reasonably well in zones 7 and 8 on the West Coast.

### *Tellima* (te' li-ma)　　　　　　Fringe-Cup　　　　　　Saxifragaceae

The genus has been reduced to a single species, *T. grandiflora*, native to western North America. *T. odorata* and *T. breviflora* are considered synonyms of *T. grandiflora* and the pink-flowered *T. parviflora* has been placed in the genus *Lithophragma*.

*Tellima* is often confused with *Tiarella* and *Mitella* and, in fact, is an anagram of *Mitella*. *Tellima* differs from both genera in having an inflated calyx (similar, but not as obvious as that found in *Silene*). The fruit of all three is a capsule, but in *Tellima*, the capsule has 2 beak-like projections, whereas *Mitella* and *Tiarella* have none. All have similar shade and moisture requirements, however, if we put the confusion behind us and concentrate on garden performance, *Tiarella* is better than the other two.

The 3–4″ long leaves are heart shaped, slightly toothed and evergreen. They are mostly basal and have 5–7 lobes. The ½″ long flowers are greenish to creamy white and as many as 30 may occur on a single scape. As the flowers mature, they change to rose-red. The sepals are united into an inflated calyx tube and the petals are pinnately cut into long, thread-like segments resulting in a "fringed cup."

Plants should be grown in ample shade and moist soil rich in organic matter. Incorporate plenty of peat or other water-holding material to maintain moisture around the roots. After blooming, the flowers become messy and should be removed unless seeds are to be collected. Plants perform well in zones 4–7. They are native to cool, moist, coniferous woods, and are not particularly happy in hot climates. 'Odorata' has fragrant flowers. 'Purpurea' ('Rubra') is about 1–1½′ tall with redder stems and foliage and flowers tinged pink.

## *Teucrium* (tewk′ ree-um)          Germander          Lamiaceae

Members of this genus of herbs were used medicinally for hundreds of years. The name was derived from King Teucer, the first king of Troy, who used germander to relieve stomach pain and gout. The plants, somewhat woody at the base and technically subshrubs, are usually grown for their attractive, opposite leaves rather than the small purplish mint-like flowers. Of the 100 or so species, a handful are particularly decorative but even fewer are available, although additional species are finding their way out of obscurity. A tall form is our very own *T. canadense*, wild germander, which is native to southern Canada and the United States. Three feet tall in moist soil, it bears purple to cream-colored flowers in a loose unbranched spike. I truly love *T. fruticans* with its woody white tomentose stems, handsome foliage and large lavender flowers. Unfortunately, it is an annual in all but the mildest climates. In a bad mood? You will enjoy the sharp spiny foliage of *T. subspinosum*, fortunately another annual which will only inflict pain for a single season. A species commanding a loyal following in England is *T. scorodonia* 'Crispum', crispy wood germander. The wavy, crested, green leaves are tinged purple in winter and very decorative particularly in the cooler months. It is winter hardy to zone 6 with mulch. Another crinkled leaf species is *T. massilense*, scented germander, whose gray-green foliage is accentuated by rose-colored flowers on 18″ plants. The foliage is particularly aromatic. The most common germander is wall germander, *T. chamaedrys*. All species are aromatic and neighborhood cats will reward your plant selection with their never-ending presence.

***-chamaedrys*** (sha-mie′ dris)        Wall Germander      10–12″/12″
   Summer        Pink, Purple      Europe          Zones 4–9

This small evergreen subshrub is popular because of the compact habit and shiny green leaves. The scalloped, lustrous green, ovate leaves are about 1″ long and borne on branched ascending stems. Two to six rosy-purple flowers are produced in a single whorl in late summer and continue for approximately 3–4 weeks. Individual flowers are ½–¾″ long and the long lower lip is usually spotted white and red. Plants can be cut back hard almost to the ground in the fall or early spring.

Plants tolerate a particularly cruel form of abuse called "edge hedging" where they is sheared into formidable evergreen globs. When planted as a hedge, invariably some plants will be less vigorous than others, perhaps because of more shade or poorer soil. Doubtless a cat will love a portion of it to death, or a particularly cold winter will kill a few plants. The result is a spotty planting which pleases no one. When allowed to grow naturally, plants are far more decorative. Plants should be grown in full sun (although tolerant of partial shade) and not be allowed to dry out.

Propagate by seed or by 1–2″ terminal cuttings in May and root in a peat-perlite mixture. Excessive moisture in the rooting bench should be avoided. Rooting takes place in 3–4 weeks and plants may be grown on in pots and placed in the garden in the fall or subsequent spring. Divisions may be taken in the spring.

**Cultivars:**

'Prostratum' ('Nanum') is 6–10″ tall with rose-pink flowers in summer.
'Variegatum' has leaves with green and creamy variegation.

## *Thalictrum* (tha-lik′ trum)        Rue          Ranunculaceae

The wonderful variation in this genus is still waiting to be discovered. The meadow-rues consist of numerous excellent species for the garden and, although grown as ornamental plants for hundreds of years, they continue to be somewhat obscure. In Europe, leaves of *Thalictrum* were used as a cure for the plague and jaundice, but few recoveries were recorded. The Romans also believed that to lay a newborn baby on a pillow stuffed with thalictrum flowers was to ensure riches throughout life.

Many species have fern-like foliage and great puffs of airy flowers. The apetalous (no petals) flowers are ornamental because of the colored sepals and stamens. In some cases, male and female flowers occur on separate plants, such as the dainty early meadow-rue, *T. dioicum*, but others are bisexual. In general, they should be planted in partial shade with adequate moisture. Many are tall and most suited for the middle or back of the border, however, *T. alpinum*, alpine meadow-rue, *T. ichangense*, and *T. kiusianum*, Kyoshu meadow-rue, grow less than 9″ tall.

Some of the more ornamental species are native to Japan, Europe and China, but North America is no slouch either. *T. dasycarpum*, with its bright green leaves and flower heads of lavender and white, *T. dioicum*, early meadow-rue, with dull green leaves and small flowers, and *T. polygamum*, with creamy white panicles of flowers on 6–8′ tall plants, should all be used more.

Quick Reference to Thalictrum Species

|  | Height (ft.) | Flower color | Leaflet color |
|---|---|---|---|
| *T. aquilegifolium* | 2–3 | Lilac | Blue-green |
| *T. delavayi* | 2–4 | Lilac | Green |
| *T. flavum* | 3–5 | Yellow | Blue-green |
| *T. kiusianum* | 6–9″ | Lavender | Green |
| *T. minus* | 1–2 | Green | Green |
| *T. rochebrunianum* | 3–6 | Lavender | Green |

**-aquilegifolium** (a-kwi-leeg′ i-fo-lee-um) Columbine Meadow-Rue  2–3′/3′
   Late Spring       Lilac       Europe, Northern Asia       Zones 5–7

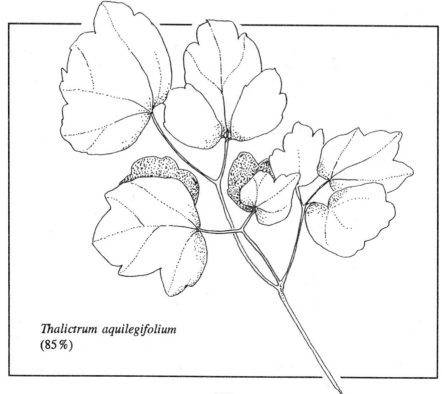

*Thalictrum aquilegifolium*
(85%)

This is one of the prettiest and showiest of the meadow-rues. The lovely blue-tinted leaves are similar to columbine, thus the specific name. There are many leaflets, each about 1½" wide and 3-5 lobed. The flowers are ornamental because of the conspicuous ½" long lilac stamens. The sepals are greenish or white and abscise rapidly. The lilac flowers are held in a 6-8" wide, many-flowered corymbose panicle, and look like a big purple powder puff. This is the earliest meadow-rue to flower and opens as early as April 25th in the Armitage garden. Unfortunately, flowers persist only for about 2 weeks. However, the drooping, somewhat inflated fruit (achenes) are interesting with their 3 small wings and persist throughout the growing season. Plants can grow up to 5' tall but generally top out at about 3' in most of the country.

Plants perform well in the South as well as the North. The leaves, flowers, and seeds are ornamental and the plant is heat tolerant. It should be planted in a rich moist soil in partial shade. Direct sun results in less vigorous plants and later flowering.

Seed germinates readily and is the best method of propagation for the species and varieties. Cultivars may be divided in early spring or early fall. Divisions are slow to recover and must be handled carefully. Although divisions may be used to increase stock, division of the clump is not necessary for at least 5 years.

### Cultivars:
'Album' has white flowers atop a 3-4' tall plant. The white flowers contrast well with the blue-green foliage. The plant is otherwise similar to the species.
'Atropurpureum' ('Purpureum') has dark purple stems and stamens. The variety listed as 'Purpureum' is likely the same, however, the stems are not as highly colored as 'Atropurpureum'. Apparently there is also a dwarf (2') form of the variety.
'Dwarf Purple' stands about 2½' tall, has lilac flowers and is otherwise similar to the species.
'Roseum' bears handsome light pink to pale rose flowers.
'Thundercloud' has deep purple flowers and larger flower heads than the type.
'White Cloud' is the best of the white-flowered forms with larger, whiter flowers than 'Album'.

-*delavayi* (de-la-vay' ee)         Yunnan Meadow-Rue         24-48"/36"
    Summer          Lilac          Western China          Zones 4-7

From the point of view of garden performance and show, it is a lovely plant. The foliage is divided in 2-3 sections, each with three, ½" wide leaflets. The foliage is more fern-like and graceful than that of *T. aquilegifolium*. Lilac sepals and creamy yellow stamens characterize flowers held in an airy, open, pyramidal panicle. The flowers are excellent for cutting but if the plants are grown too close together, the flowering stems get terribly tangled and are almost impossible to extract intact. Although often listed summer hardy to zone 8, plants survive there, but are not particularly effective south of zone 7a. Regardless of geographic location, plants require support to keep the slender stems erect when in flower. Similar to other meadow-rues, rich, moist soil and partial shade are beneficial.

Propagate the species from seed or division and the cultivars from division. 'Hewitt's Double' is commercially propagated by tissue culture.

### Cultivars:
'Album' has white sepals but is not as vigorous as the type.

'Hewitt's Double' has double lilac flowers which last longer than flowers of the type. The stamens are petal-like (petaloid) resulting in the fuller flowers. An excellent garden plant.

### Related Species:
*T. dipterocarpum* differs so little that, from the gardener's viewpoint, it is the same. Most plants sold under *T. dipterocarpum* are probably *T. delavayi*. The fruits are keys to separating the two species. The fruit of *T. delavayi* has 1 or 2 inconspicuous wings whereas those of *T. dipterocarpum* has 3 distinct wings. For gardeners with curiosity and patience, a 10X magnification lens is useful. Garden culture and performance are similar.

*-flavum* (flay' vum)       Yellow Meadow-Rue      3–5'/4'
Summer     Yellow      Southern Europe      Zones 5–8
(Syn. *T. rugosum, T. speciosissimum*)

One of the more vigorous species, plants burst through the ground in spring with stems as thick as the necks of football linemen. The species has large green 2–3 compound leaflets but the most common and more handsome form, 'Glaucum', has glaucous blue foliage. Good sized clumps form within 2–3 years as a result of the vigorous deep seated roots. The 1½" wide leaflets and leaves are useful in floral decorations and plants are worth growing for the foliage alone. The flowers are perfect (male and female parts on the same flower), consisting of pale yellow sepals and bright yellow, slender, protruding stamens, are held in an upright compact 2–4" wide pyramidal panicle, and have a faint but pleasant odor. Plants are often sold under the name of *T. glaucum* because of the foliage. The species is more heat tolerant than others and worth growing in the South. Plant in rich, moist soil in partial shade.

Divide the plant when needed or raise from seed.

### Related Species:
*T. speciosissimum*, yellow meadow-rue, has been blended into *T. flavum*, and has essentially disappeared. However, plants with more delicate bi- or tri-ternately compound leaves, consisting of smaller leaflets, are sometimes

found under the *T. speciosissimum* banner. The leaves are not at all glaucous. Plants bear similar yellow flowers.

**-kiusianum** (kee-oo-see-a' num)     Kyoshu Meadow-Rue     4–6"/12"
Summer          Lavender          Japan          Zones 6–8

Plants occupy the opposite end of the height spectrum from *T. rochebrunianum* but are equally handsome. This stoloniferous species produces mats of green foliage with a bronze tinge. They get lost in the border situation but are wonderful growing over rocks or hanging down walls. The flowers are lilac and are borne on 4–6" tall stems in summer.

**Related Species:**
*T. ichangense* (syn. *T. coreanum*) is also short, growing 6–9" tall when in flower. The biternate leaves consist of rounded leaflets, often peltate. The mauve to pink flowers are borne in late spring to summer. Full sun or partial shade. Hardy in zones 5–7.

**-minus** (my' nus)          Lesser Meadow-Rue          12–24"/24"
Summer          Yellow          Europe, Asia          Zones 3–7
(Syn. *T. adiantifolium*)

This species is particularly variable and consists of many races (a group of plants from the same species but with slightly different properties; a race comes true from seed) to which over 200 different specific names have been given. Names such as *T. babingtonii*, *T. foetidus*, *T. kochii*, *T. majus*, and most commonly, *T. adiantifolium*, have been applied to this species.

In general, the leaflets are 3-lobed and look like those of the maidenhair fern, *Adiantum pedatum*. The ½" wide perfect flowers are borne in a loose panicle with spreading branches. The greenish sepals abscise rapidly and the yellow color of the flower is the result of the slender stamens. The roots are stoloniferous but plants are not invasive. The plant is best grown for the elegant foliage and not the rather inconspicuous flowers.

Propagate good forms vegetatively by division. Seed propagated plants will vary.

**Cultivars:**
Var. *adiantifolium* is the best form. Because of the variability within the species, leaves can range from minute to the size of a half dollar. Plants of this description will at least have maidenhair-like foliage.

**-rochebrunianum** (rosh-broon-ee' aye-num)     Lavender Mist     4–5'/3'
Summer          Lavender          Japan          Zones 4–7

To me, the finest upright species in the genus, this Japanese native combines handsome foliage and wonderful lavender flowers in late spring and summer.

It is an excellent background plant, able to rise 5–6' tall, but its tall, skinny habit lends itself better in groups of three than as a single specimen. The leaves are 3–4 ternate (meaning leaves are 3–4 times divided into threes) providing an airy, delicate look. The pendulous flowers consist of small lavender sepals with thread-like stamens much shorter than the sepals. The purplish stems are thicker than *T. delavayi* and plants are self supporting.

The only downside I have found with this plant is its lack of longevity. Perhaps this occurs more in the South than in the North, but I have been mystified by the sudden death in summer or poor regrowth in the spring.

### Cultivars:

'Lavender Mist' is the common name of the species as well as the most common cultivar available to gardeners. The cultivar differs from seedlings by having more violet flowers with gold stamens. This is the most popular of the tall lavender-flowered species, as well it should be. Others like *T. delavayi* and *T. dipterocarpum* are not offered as often. Better than the species.

Quick Key to Thalictrum Species

    A. Plants less than 12" tall
        B. Flowers yellow . . . . . . . . . . . . . . . . . . . . . . . . . . *T. minus*
        BB. Flowers lilac to lavender . . . . . . . . . . . . . . . *T. kiusianum*
    AA. Plants taller than 12", flowers yellow or lilac
        B. Flowers lilac
            C. Foliage blue green, flowers held in a
                tight many-flowered fluffy panicle . . . . . *T. aquilegifolium*
            CC. Foliage green, flowers in a loose,
                airy pyramidal panicle
                D. Stems almost black, leaves
                    2–3 pinnate or ternate . . . . . . . . . . . . . *T. delavayi*
              DD. Stems with purple hue,
                leaves 3–4 ternate . . . . . . . . . . . *T. rochebrunianum*
        BB. Flowers yellow . . . . . . . . . . . . . . . . . . . . . . . *T. flavum*

### Additional Reading:

Dumaine, Susan. 1988. Meadow Rues. *Horticulture* 66(5):32–37.

*Thelypteris* (thel-ip-ter' is)   Beech Fern, Marsh Fern   Polypodiaceae

The genus has been sliced and divided by taxonomists and nobody seems to agree where the various species actually belong. Some attribute two species to the genus, others more than twenty. I include the beech ferns, marsh fern, New York fern and Massachusetts fern here. They are small and medium sized ferns and are always deciduous. They spread by creeping rootstalks and arise with slightly scaly, not chaffy, stems. The sterile and the fertile fronds are similar, unlike other ferns that have distinct fertile structures. The sori (spore cases) are generally found in wide-apart rows near the margins. They are mainly found in the North and in fact can be rather unruly, taking over large areas of the garden. Two main groups are grown, beech ferns and marsh/New York ferns.

The beech ferns include the narrow beech fern, *T. phegopteris* (syn. *Phegopteris connectilis*) and the broad beech fern, *T. hexagonoptera* (syn. *Phegopteris hexagonoptera*). They both have triangular-shaped fronds which droop about 45 degrees making urn-shaped plants. The favored habitats of the narrow beech fern are wet pockets near running water, in nature often under small waterfalls. In the garden, moisture is necessary for best performance. They are usually light green in color and are easily distinguished from the broad beech fern by the lowest pair of leaflets which droop downward and out-ward and are distinctly spaced from the next upper pair. The broad beech fern has much broader fronds and is larger and more erect than its cousin, the narrow one. This is normally found in open, rather sunny spots and does not perform well near running water. The beech ferns have sori which are uncovered (no indusia) which distinguish them from other members of *Thelypteris*. Both ferns are best in zones 3-6, will do all right in zone 7 but will not be as aggressive. They can be invasive where happy.

The marsh fern, *T. palustris*, has upright, narrow, oblong fronds in a twisted habit. The leaflets are opposite and almost perpendicular to the stem. They enjoy sunny moist areas where the delicate lacy fronds seem to dance in the breeze. Easily grown by streams, lakes and ponds. Hardy to about −20° F. The New York fern, *T. noveboracensis* (syn. *Parathelypteris novae-boracacensis*), also has oblong fronds which are much broader in the middle than at either end. Usually, plants have about 3 fronds, and the creeping rootstalks result in large clumps. The fronds are never opposite, always slightly alternate. Easy to grow in the North in moist but not wet areas. A little more difficult south of zone 6.

## *Thermopsis* (the-mop′ sis)     False Lupine     Fabaceae

The genus was well named, coming from *thermos*, lupin, and *opsis*, like. The flowers in all but one or two of the 23 species are yellow and similar in shape to the lupine. The compound leaves consist of 3 palmately arranged leaflets and 2 smaller leaf-like stipules. Occasionally they may be confused with the closely related *Baptisia*, however, they usually emerge and flower much sooner than *Baptisia*, the foliage of most *Baptisia* species is blue green and the seed pods are inflated. In *Thermopsis*, the foliage is green and the seed pods flat. While they are related and cosmetically resemble lupines and false indigos, they are ornamental plants on their own, providing early color on plants that are not bulbs. A number of species are native to the United States and may be used to provide lupin-like flowers where an upright, yellow, early flowering plant is desired.

Quick Reference to Thermopsis Species

|  | Height (in.) | Flower color |
|---|---|---|
| *T. caroliniana* | 30–48 | Yellow |
| *T. lupinoides* | 9–12 | Yellow |
| *T. montana* | 12–24 | Yellow |

*-caroliniana* (ka-ro-lin-ee ay′ na)    Southern Lupine    30–48″/48″
    Spring        Yellow        Eastern United States    Zones 3–9
(Syn. *T. villosa*)

This is surely an overlooked garden plants. The blue-green leaves are divided into 3 obovate leaflets, each 2–3″ long and finely hairy beneath. The bright yellow, pea-like flowers emerge in April in the South, 2–3 weeks later

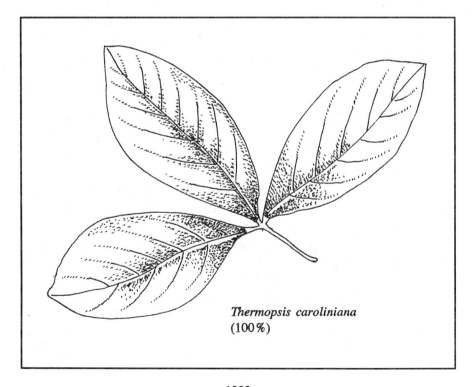

*Thermopsis caroliniana*
(100%)

in the North, and remain colorful for 3–4 weeks. They are held in compact, erect, 6–12″ long racemes. The undersides of the leaves are barely pubescent to almost glabrous, but the hollow stems are quite hairy and are responsible for the other botanical name, *T. villosa*, which is likely going to be accepted as the proper botanical name. The pods are also hairy. On a three-year-old clump at the University of Georgia, over 30 flower stems were produced.

Plant in partial shade to full sun in the South, full sun in the North. The flower stalks are a little longer under shade and plants may require support. The foliage should be cut back about a month after flowering as it declines rapidly, particularly in dry situations.

Seed propagation is the best means of increasing numbers and fresh seed germinates well. Older seed requires a scarification treatment for uniform germination. Treatment with sulfuric acid is effective but should only be undertaken by trained personnel (i.e., someone with experience in a seed laboratory). Division is more difficult as plantlets do not transplant well and require significant time to recover.

### Cultivars:
'Album' is a more compact (2½′ tall), beautiful, but rare cultivar with creamy white flowers.

### Related Species:
*T. fabacea* grows up to 3′ tall and also bears bright yellow flowers and rather large leaflets. The axils of the plant often have short spines and the erect flowers are also found in the axils. They spread more rapidly than *T. caroliniana*.

*T. montana*, mountain thermopsis, is the western cousin of *T. caroliniana*. It is 12–24″ tall, has a shorter (up to 8″ long), less dense raceme, and bears linear-lanceolate leaflets compared with the obovate leaflets of *T. caroliniana*. Very closely related; its main difference is its different provenance. Some authors claim it is invasive in rich soils, but I have not noticed a problem. Hardy in zones 3–8.

| | | | |
|---|---|---|---|
| *-lupinoides* (loo-peen-oi′ deez) | Lanceleaf Thermopsis | 9–12″/18″ |
| Spring Yellow | Alaska, Siberia | Zones 2–7 |
| (Syn. *T. lanceolata*) | | |

Small stature and sessile, silky hairy leaves differentiate this species from the previous. Plants form 1–2′ wide clumps but are not at all invasive. The bright yellow flowers appear whorled and are held in a terminal upright raceme well above the foliage. The strongly recurved pods are unique and provide one of the identifying characteristics of the species.

Place in full sun or partial shade, particularly if planted south of zone 6. Native to northern locales, it is not as tolerant of heat as the previous species. This is a good, if not spectacular, plant in the right climate.

Propagate by seed. Although division is possible, months are necessary for the plants to recover.

Quick Key to Thermopsis Species

    A. Plants less than 18″ tall, pods recurved . . . . . . *T. lupinoides*
  AA. Plants greater than 18″ tall, pods straight
      B. Leaflets ovate to obovate, raceme dense . . . . *T. caroliniana*
    BB. Leaflets linear to linear-lanceolate,
      racemes loose . . . . . . . . . . . . . . . . . . . . . . . *T. montana*

*Thymus* (time′ us)            Thyme           Lamiaceae

"I know a bank where the wild thyme grows" stated Oberon, king of the fairies, in Shakespeare's *A Midsummer Night's Dream* and "Where the heck is the thyme?" muttered my Mother when she was cooking, connects the past with the present when we think about this large genus of plants. Common thyme, *T. vulgaris*, grows on the hillsides throughout the Mediterranean and the British Isles and was long used for its fragrance, flavoring and its many curative properties. As early as 3000BC, thyme was used to prevent nightmares and even for help in the mummification process by the ancient Egyptians. Traditionally, thyme has been used to relieve spasms and coughing, and recent studies have borne out the benefit of the species as an antispasmodic and antitussive. A few of the approximately 350 species are used as ornamental plants, including cultivars of *T. serphyllum*, wild thyme, *T. × citriodorus*, lemon thyme, and *T. pseudolanuginosus*, woolly thyme. It would seem that all you have to do is smell the leaves of various thymes and separate them with your nose. No such luck! Caraway thyme, *T. herbabarona*, usually smells obviously of caraway, and is so tough that it is sometimes used as a "thyme" lawn. The cultivar 'Lemon-scented' smells like lemons. Even common thyme has a superficial lemon scent.

All prefer full sun and outstanding drainage; they rot quickly if grown in wet areas. Hot summers and high humidity result in "melt-down" in the deep South but if cut back, plants recover well. Thyme is better in the North than the South, but the lure of thyme in the garden has no boundaries. Rocky outcrops where drainage is sharp and soil is gritty are best. Although native to Europe, wild thyme has escaped in eastern United States and can be seen in meadows and hillsides in New England.

Leaves are opposite, usually less than ½″ long and oval to oblong. The stems tend to creep along the ground and become woody with age. The lavender to pink flowers are crowded together in dense terminal heads and sometimes arise from the leaf axils as well. They are extremely rich in nectar and bees are always hovering around flowering plants.

All plants, regardless of cultivar and species, should be cut back often to rejuvenate the plants and avoid rot. The further south, the more pruning is necessary.

Quick Reference to Thymus Species

|  | Fragrance | Habit |
|---|---|---|
| *T. × citriodorus* | Lemon | Upright |
| *T. pseudolanuginosus* | Slight thyme | Prostrate |
| *T. serphyllum* | Thyme | Prostrate |
| *T. vulgaris* | Thyme | Prostrate |

| -× *citriodorus* (cit-ree-o-dor' us) | Lemon Thyme | 9–12"/12" |
|---|---|---|
| Fall          Pale Lilac | Garden Hybrid | Zones 5–8 |

Lemon thyme is one of the more popular garden hybrids, having arisen from *T. pulegoides* and *T. vulgaris*. The fragrance from the ¼" wide oval to lanceolate leaves is remarkably lemon-like. The stems are erect and can grow up to 1' tall. The oblong inflorescence is usually consists of pale lilac to pink flowers. Many cultivars have been offered, some of which may be prostrate, many which have golden or variegated foliage.

**Cultivars:**
'Anderson's Gold' is a dwarf, carpeting form with golden foliage in the winter.
'Archer's Gold' is a compact upright form with golden leaves.
'Argenteus' bears silver-green leaves.
'Argenteus Variegatus' has silver variegated foliage.
'Aureus' is a popular small 6–9" tall bush, with green leaves dappled with yellow. Foliage tends to fade in the heat.
'Golden Queen' bears pale green leaves with light golden variegation.
'Silver Queen' has variegations of cream to dull silver on the green leaves.

| -*pseudolanuginosus* (soo-doe-lah-new-gi-no' sus) | Woolly Thyme | 3–4"/12" |
|---|---|---|
| Summer          Pink | Unknown | Zones 5–8 |

The common name comes from the long hairs on the prostrate stems, the hairs as long as the width of the stems. The stems are somewhat 4-sided with elliptical gray leaves. The plants are best known for the fuzziness and are terrific rock garden plants, used only where drainage is spectacular. In areas of copious rain and hot, humid weather, woolly thyme self destructs by mid-summer. The pale pink flowers are borne in mid-summer but plants are not as floriferous as other species.

**Cultivars:**
'Hall's Variety' ('Hall's Woolly') is 3–4" tall and bears lavender-pink flowers over soft woolly foliage.

*-serphyllum* (ser-pil' um)       Wild Thyme      4–6"/12"
Summer, Fall      Pink, Purple      Europe      Zones 5–8

The best known of the prostrate forms, which if given cool nights, full sun and good drainage will multiply rapidly. Plants have escaped throughout New England and cloth hillsides in the Berkshires in late summer and fall. The oval leaves are pubescent with short petioles to almost sessile. The pink to purple flowers are held in a dense rounded inflorescence, usually terminal but also axillary. Over 40 cultivars have been described and a few are available through herb nurseries and better retail centers, ranging from creeping to upright habits, with white, pink, red or purple flowers, and with foliage from deep green to gold and variegated forms.

### Cultivars:
'Annie Hall' has pale pink flowers on prostrate stems.
'Aureus' bears golden leaves with a creeping habit.
'Coccineus' has deep green leaves and dark red flowers. This is sometimes listed under *T. praecox.*
'Goldstream' produces lilac flowers on creeping stems with yellow and green variegated foliage.
'Pink Chintz' has woolly dark green leaves and salmon-pink flowers.
'Snowdrift' bears white flowers on creeping stems.

### Related Species:
*T. praecox,* creeping thyme, is a mat-forming, creeping species with 2–3" tall stems and mauve to purple flowers. The lanceolate leaves are slightly hairy. 'Albus' is an unusual white-flowered form, 'Dorothy Klaber' is a dense grower with dark pink flowers, 'Porlock' bears rounded leaves and pink flowers, and 'Reiter's Red' forms tight green mats with crimson flowers.

*T. vulgaris,* common thyme, is the culinary thyme most often used in cooking but ornamental cultivars are also available. Stems are about 12" tall often branching and with woody stems. The leaves are sessile and about ¼" long. 'Argenteus' has silver-edged leaves, 'Aureus' bears golden yellow leaves and rosy flowers, 'Compactus' is only 4" tall with pale gray-green leaves, and 'Silver Posie' has mauve flowers and silver-variegated foliage.

### Quick Key to Thymus Species

    A. Leaves sessile, margins rolled backwards . . . . . . . . *T. vulgaris*
   AA. Leaves with short petioles. margins not rolled back
      B. Plants prostrate, less than 6" tall
        C. Stems obviously hairy,
          leaves elliptical . . . . . . . . . . . . . *T. pseudolanuginosus*
       CC. Stems pubescent, but not obviously
          hairy, leaves oval . . . . . . . . . . . . . . . . . . *T. serphyllum*
     BB. Plants upright, obviously lemon-scented . . . *T.* × *citriodorus*

## *Tiarella* (tee-a-rel′ a)  Foamflower  Saxifragaceae

Approximately 5 species occur, 4 of which are native to North America and 1 to Asia. They all have basal leaves with long petioles and racemose white to pink flowers. There are generally 10 stamens, often alternately long and short, with 5 sepals and 5 petals. Foamflower is an ideal white flowering ground cover for the shaded garden and can be spectacular in mass plantings. They are excellent low maintenance plants and should be more widely planted. (Also see *Heuchera* and *Mitella*).

### Quick Reference to Tiarella Species

|  | Height (in.) | Leaf shape | Stoloniferous |
|---|---|---|---|
| *T. cordifolia* | 6–12 | Simple | Yes |
| *T. c.* var. *collina* | 6–12 | Simple | No |
| *T. trifoliata* | 9–20 | Trifoliate | No |

**-cordifolia** (kor-di-fo′ lee-a)  Allegheny Foamflower  6–12"/36"
  Spring  White  Eastern North America  Zones 3–8

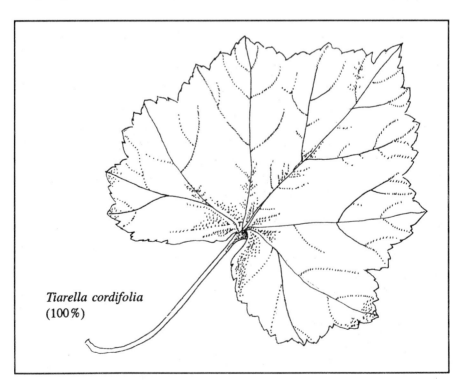

*Tiarella cordifolia*
(100%)

Plants are native from Nova Scotia to Michigan and south to Georgia and Alabama. Each 3–4″ wide, heart-shaped leaf consists of 3–5 lobes. The evergreen foliage has burgundy variegation along the veins most noticeable in the spring and fall and often turn completely bronze during the winter. Foliage is similar to *Heuchera americana*, American alumroot, in this respect although significant differences in flowers occur. Delicate pink-tinged flower buds gracefully evolve into starry creamy white flowers on 3–4″ long racemes. The ¼″ wide flowers consist of sepals about ½ as long as the petals, 10 stamens with brown anthers, and remain in flower for about 6 weeks. Plants are stoloniferous and rapidly form large masses. They are effective with other shade and moisture tolerant species such as trilliums, woodland phlox, false Solomon's seal, or Christmas fern.

*Tiarella* requires moisture retentive, highly organic soils in medium to heavy shade. They will romp about and make "ground covers" although they don't pretend to compete with *Vinca* or *Pachysandra*. Dry soils or exposure to full sun results in anemic, scrawny plants which never fill out. Soils may be enriched with organic matter such as well-rotted leaves. Wet feet, particularly in the winter, also result in significant losses.

Propagate from seed or division. Seed should be shallowly sown in early spring in a protected area such as a cold frame. Transplant seedlings to 3–4″ containers in 6–8 weeks.

### Cultivars:

Some terrific work by Sinclair Adams of Dunvegan Nursery in West Chester, PA has resulted in a sweeping improvement of the species. Nurserymen such as Don Jacobs and Dan Heims have also bred significant improvements.

'Brandywine' is a large-leaved form (3–4″ wide) with light green heart-shaped leaves, each one with bold red venation.

'Dark Eye' from Dan Heims, is a vigorous grower and fills in rapidly. The burgundy center of the heart shaped leaves accounts for its name.

'Eco Red Heart', from Don Jacobs, has deep red centers in the leaves and pink to white flowers.

'Freckles' is a medium sized foamflower with reddish spotting giving the leaves a freckled appearance. From Terra Nova and Dan Heims.

'Ink Blot' is a medium to small selection with dark green leaves and blotches of red, particularly near the center. Also from Dan Heims.

'Laird of Skye' has little marking on the dark green leaves but they are handsomely scalloped. The white flowers contrast well with the yellow stamens. From Dunvegan Nursery.

'Moorgrun' bears light green leaves and many white flowers in the spring.

'Pinwheel' appears to be vigorous and has starry white flowers with narrow petals. From Heims.

'Running Tapestry' has 2–3″ wide heart-shaped leaves with red venation, less obvious than the venation in 'Brandywine'. The white flowers appear above the 10–12″ flowering stems.

'Slick Rock' is a vigorous runnering plant with small 2″ wide leaves with 5 lobes, the uppermost leaf being longer than the others. Plants were originally found by Jim Plyer near Slickrock Creek, North Carolina.

'Tiger Stripe', from Dan Heims, has light green foliage with red veins. The flowers are white in early spring.

'Winterglow' has large leaves flecked with red throughout and white flowers. The fall color is golden yellow, better than most others at that time of year.

**Related Species:**

Var. *collina* (syn. *T. wherryi*), Wherry's foamflower, differs in subtle ways. The plant is taller and, unlike the stoloniferous *T. cordifolia*, is a clump-forming species. Upon close inspection, one notices that the anthers are yellowish orange rather than brown as in *T. cordifolia*. It is equally attractive and ornamental. Plants have performed well in zone 7b. 'Dunvegan' is a wonderful clump-former bearing dissected 5-lobed leaves and wonderful pinkish flowers. They have been the best of the foamflowers in the Armitage garden. 'Oakleaf' was the first of the cultivated forms easily available to the American gardener and one which spurred the interest in the genus. Somewhat resembling dark green oak leaves (fortunately, oak leaves are highly variable) with pink buds and pink flowers, later fading to white. Plants were originally developed at the Brandywine Conservancy, Chadds Ford, PA and introduced by Dunvegan Nursery.

**Related Species:**

*T. polyphylla* is native to China, Japan and the Himalayas and resembles *T. cordifolia*. The white flowers are more nodding than our native species and racemes are more branched. They are likely only cold hardy to zone 5 or 6, but insufficient data is available to be sure. In the Armitage garden, it was badly outcompeted and outperformed by *T. cordifolia* and its cultivars.

| *-trifoliata* (tri-fo′ lee-ah-ta) | Three Leaved Foamflower | 9–20″/24″ |
|---|---|---|
| Spring            White | Western North America | Zones 4–7 |

This species is almost unknown in gardens in the eastern United States, although native to the Pacific Coast. Instead of entire lobed leaves, the foliage consists of 3 leaflets (trifoliate). The middle one has 3 lobes and the laterals 2. The leaflets provide a more delicate appearance than the previous species, but the lovely bronze tint found in the others is not present in *T. trifoliata*. The flowers are minute, consisting of thread-like petals held in long, narrow panicles. Plants are less tolerant of heat and humidity than previous species and less suitable to gardens east of the Rockies.

Seed is the best means of propagation. Propagate similar to *T. wherryi*.

**Cultivars:**

'Filigree Lace' is a hybrid from Charles Oliver between *T. trifoliata* and *T. cordifolia*. Deeply lobed leaves compete with the racemes of white flowers. The habit is more clumping than running.

<u>Quick Key to Tiarella Species</u>

    A. Leaves simple
        B. Plants stoloniferous, form mats, anthers brown . . *T. cordifolia*
        BB. Plants not stoloniferous, form clumps,
            anthers yellowish orange . . . . . . . . *T. cordifolia* var. *collina*
    AA. Leaves trifoliate . . . . . . . . . . . . . . . . . . . . . . *T. trifoliata*

**Additional Reading:**

Adam, S. and S.L. Kitto. 1993. Tiarella 'Oakleaf'. *Perennial Plants*, the publication of the Perennial Plant Association 1(4):12–13.

## *Tigridia* (ti-gri' dee-a)        Tiger Flower        Iridaceae

The botanical name is derived from the Latin *tigris*, tiger, in reference to the South American "tiger," better known as the jaguar, thus the spots on the tiger. All 30 species of this colorful genus are native to South and Central America. However only the showiest species, *T. pavonia*, is commonly offered for sale. Bulbs are consistently winter hardy only south of zone 8, and must be treated similar to gladioli in the rest of the country. Plants are a fascinating addition to the garden and it always surprises me that so few people try them. Perhaps that individual flowers only remain open for a single day and that they clash with just about everything account for their absence. More than likely, gardeners are like me, they simply keep forgetting to order them.

Plants are 20–24″ tall with a fan of basal leaves and 2–3 stem leaves. Flowers are 4–6″ wide and their riot of color and shape is almost indescribable. They are red, orange, yellow, or white and variously blotched with red or yellow in the center. The flower, which opens in early July in the South and as late as early September in the North, consists of 3 large outer segments and 3 smaller inner segments surrounding the speckled cup-like center. The flowers persist but a day (another common name is one-day lily), but the succession of bloom lasts for 2–4 weeks.

Plant 3–4″ deep in rich well-drained soils in full sun. The best cultural method is to treat as annuals, replacing the bulbs each year. Although the foliage returns each year in zones 7 and 8, few flowers appear. Digging bulbs every fall and separating the bulbils is possible, but their relatively low cost justifies spring replacement.

**Cultivars:**

Generally they are only available as a mixture of colors, but a few varieties may be obtained from specialists.

Var. *alba immaculata* bears white flowers with centers free of spots. A number of cultivars are available without the spots in the center and all bear the "immaculata" name. This is such an exotic looking flower, growing an unspotted form is like raising a spotless leopard.

## *Tovara* (to-vah' ra)                 Tovara                 Polygonaceae

Named for the Spanish physician, Simon Tovar, plants are used as tall ground covers or edging. The plant continues to flip-flop between genera, originally starting out in the genus *Polygonum*, then being switched to *Tovara* because of obvious differences in habit and flower structure, now back to *Polygonum*. The genus consists of a single species with small, but not inconspicuous flowers, and may be listed under either genus.

*-virginianum* (vir-jin-ee-aye' num)   Virginia Tovara            2–4'/6'
      Summer      Brownish Green      Eastern North America   Zones 4–8
(Syn. *Polygonum virginianum*)

Like most members of the genus *Polygonum*, plants can become a nuisance within a few years of planting. The pure green-leaved species is seldom seen but the green and white variegated form, 'Variegata', is handsome. The elliptical 4–10″ long leaves are slow to emerge in the spring but clothe the plants in dense green and white by early summer. The tiny pink flowers, which are formed in late summer and fall, are held in slender terminal and axillary spikes. Seeds are viable and hundreds of little tovaras may appear in the summer and spring, quickly making you curse the person from whom you received such an innocent looking thing. My plant came from one of my favorite nursery people, Robyn Duback, Robyn's Nest Nursery, Vancouver, Washington. I think she delighted in sending me this obnoxious weed to pay back for bent shovel and pick (see *Aruncus*).

Plants should be protected from the wind as leaves are damaged easily. In most soils and surely rich, moist ones, and partial shade, tovara spreads rapidly and can become an awful nuisance if planted close to non-aggressive species.

Propagate by division in spring or fall.

**Cultivars:**

'Painter's Palette' is similar to 'Variegata' but has a V-shaped reddish pink blotch in the center of each leaf. The new leaves are creamy white and touched with light green and pink. A superior cultivar, but no less aggressive.

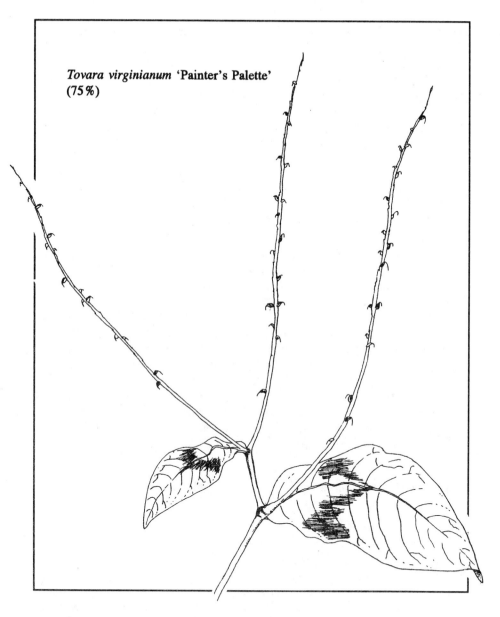

*Tovara virginianum* 'Painter's Palette'
(75%)

*Trachystemon* (tra-kee-stay' mon)    Trachystemon    Boraginaceae

Two species have been described but only *T. orientalis* is occasionally offered. It loves moist soils and spreads rapidly with wet feet and cool climes. There is little to recommend the species, except for its toughness. The roughly hairy 6–8″ long and 5–6″ wide leaves are ovate to cordate and look like small burdock foliage. I can grow burdock without having to buy it. Of course, I did buy it and placed in my shaded back section. I now have my own patch of $6.95 burdock.

The blue flowers, which resemble borage flowers are quite handsome and arise early in the spring prior to the foliage. This plant looks like an aggressive weed and in cooler, moister climates and/or a sunnier location than where it camps in the Armitage garden, it can become a nuisance.

Propagate by seed or division after flowering.

## *Tradescantia* (tra-des-kant' ee-a)  Spiderwort  Commelinaceae

Approximately 70 species of tender and hardy plants are named after John Tradescant, the English horticulturist and botanist. He received a plant from a friend in Virginia which was subsequently named *Tradescantia virginiana* by Linneaus. The genus commemorates both father and son. Tradescant the Elder became gardener to Charles I in 1629 and was followed by his son after his death in 1638. Tradescant the Younger traveled to Virginia in 1637 and brought back to England such staples as Virginia creeper and Michaelmas daisies. Some of the better-known species of *Tradescantia* are known as wandering jew, and are indoor plants only, or occasionally used in the South as an annual creeping ground cover.

Several ornamental species native to the United States occur. *T. hirsuticaulis* is a compact species (18–24" tall) with dark purple flowers somewhat hidden in the light green, strap-like foliage. *T. ohiensis*, has 3' tall stems which bear light blue flowers about 1" across. Although these species are occasionally seen in gardens, only hybrids of *T. virginiana*, often offered under the now invalid name of *T.* × *andersoniana*, are commonly available.

*-virginiana* (an-der-son-ee-aye' na)  Spiderwort  1–2'/3'
   Summer  Variable  Hybrid  Zones 4–9
(Syn. *T.* × *andersoniana*)

The hybrid name *T.* × *andersoniana* was proposed in 1935 by Anderson and Woodson, who were puzzled by the variation within the hardy species of the American genus. The name was proposed for the hypothetical cross between *T. ohiensis*, *T. subaspera*, and *T. virginiana*. Apparently, that name is invalid, due to a lack of description, and garden hybrids are best included as *virginiana* hybrids. The dense, linear dull green, linear foliage is 18" long and declines after flowering. Many flower buds are formed in terminal umbels and although each flower opens for one day, flowering continues for 6–8 weeks. The flower parts occur in threes; 3 sepals, 3 petals, and 6 stamens form the 1–3" diameter flower. They usually occur in blue to purple hues but pink, white, and red flowered cultivars are available.

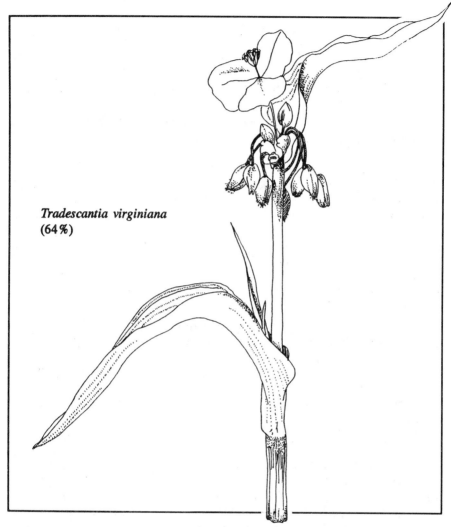

*Tradescantia virginiana*
(64%)

Plant in full sun in any well-drained garden soil. Plants grow well, but produce fewer flowers, in partial shade and wet soil. Divide to rejuvenate the clump every 2–3 years. When the foliage declines, cut back to 8–12″. New foliage reappears in the fall.

Propagate all cultivars by division in spring or fall.

## Hybrids:

*Blue and purple flowers:*

'Barbel' is about 2′ tall, with large 1–1½″ wide flowers in late summer.
'Bluestone' bears mid-blue flowers.
Var. *caerulea plena* has double dark blue flowers.

'Concord Grape' is a new hybrid from Dr. Kevin Vaughn and bears grape-colored flowers in mid- to late summer.

'Isis' has Oxford blue 3″ diameter flowers. This is one of the best of the blue cultivars.

'J.C. Weguelin' is an excellent, vigorous cultivar with 2½″ wide China blue flowers.

'Joy' is a relatively new cultivar with purple flowers held close to the large, dome-like plant. Plants grow about 2′ tall.

'Leonora' has violet-blue flowers on 18″ tall plants.

'Little Doll' is a compact plant with light blue flowers for 4–6 weeks.

'Pauline' bears lilac flowers about 2–2½″ wide.

'Purple Dome' stands about 2′ tall and is laden with flowers of rich purple.

'Purple Profusion' has more narrow foliage and purple flowers on a compact habit.

'Valor' is 18–24″ tall and bears crimson-purple flowers.

'Zwanenburg Blue' bears 3″ wide, deep blue flowers.

*Carmine and red flowers:*

'Carmine Glow' has deep carmine flowers.

'Hawaiian Punch' bears many pink to purple flowers (Hawaiian Punch?) and good green foliage. Competes well with 'Red Cloud'.

'Purewell Giant' bears flowers between deep rose and purple.

'Red Cloud' has rosy red blooms on 2′ tall plants. One of the best cultivars available.

'Rosi' produces lilac-rose flowers and grows about 20″ tall.

'Rubra' bears red flowers.

*White flowers:*

'Bilberry Ice' has white flowers with a blue tint on the margins and a dark purple stripe along the center of the petal.

'Innocence' has large creamy white flowers.

'Iris Pritchard' bears pure white flowers suffused with violet.

'Osprey' has large blue feathery stamens which contrast well with the large white flowers.

'Snowcap' is probably the purest white form with 2½–3″ wide flowers.

**Additional Species:**

*T. bracteata* is native to the Midwest and forms clumps with narrow foliage. The flowers are usually rose-colored but may be white or blue.

*T. hirsuticaulis* is only about 1′ tall with deep purple flowers and contrasting yellow stamens. A wonderful native form.

**Additional Reading:**

Miller, Heather. 1983. *Tradescantia. Horticulture* 61(6):20–21.

*Tricyrtis* (tri-ser' tis)                    Toad-Lily                    Liliaceae

The toad-lilies have a particular personality that is difficult to explain. Gardeners often grow them because they are unusual rather than showy, however, the flowers never fail to elicit conversation and their curious beauty should be admired close up. When pointing out a toad-lily, I can almost guarantee that you will be asked the origin of the common name. A name like toad-lily doesn't easily slip through the conversation unnoticed. The name probably came from their spotted flowers, however, with the discovery of *T. imeldae* (named after the former first lady of the Phillipines), on Mindanao in the Phillipines, a more descriptive account was provided. The area where this species was found is occupied by the Tasaday tribe, who rub the juice from the flowers and leaves on their hands before setting out to collect frogs; apparently it is considered attractive to frogs and makes them less slippery. Perhaps they should be called frog-lilies.

Several species form compact clumps, although others are stoloniferous and form large patches. They grow from 6" up to 3' tall usually with arching stems. The flowers, which are terminal or, more often, occur in the axils of the leaves, consist of 6 tepals (sepals and petals look alike) and 6 stamens. Most selections open in the fall and continue for at least 6 weeks, however, a few species such as the yellow-green-flowered *T. latifolia* bloom as early as June. Numerous hybrids have recently become available and the new diversity in toad-lilies is partially responsible for its upsurge in popularity. Flowers of most species are shades of purple, but yellow, tricolors and white can be found. To speak freely about toad-lilies, without guilt or shame, is the mark of a true gardener.

Quick Reference to Tricyrtis Species

|  | Height (ft.) | Roots stoloni- ferous | Base of leaves clasping the stems | Flower color |
| --- | --- | --- | --- | --- |
| *T. formosana* | 1–2 | Yes | No | Crimson spots |
| *T. hirta* | 2–3 | No | Yes | White, crimson spots |
| *T. macranthopsis* | 1–2 | Yes | Yes | Yellow |
| *T. macropoda* | 2–3 | Yes | No | White, purple spots |

*-formosana* (for-mo' sah-na)          Formosa Toad-Lily          1–2'/2'
   Late Summer          Lilac          Taiwan          Zones 4–9
(Syn. *T. stolonifera*)

This species is not as well known as the next but is becoming more popular with availability. Often listed as *T. stolonifera*, recent studies have shown that *T. formosana* and *T. stolonifera* are the same. The base of the leaves of the species narrow to a tubular sheath rather than being wrapped around the stem as in *T. hirta*. However, most plants grown as *T. formosana* have a semi-clasping leaf base indicating some degree of hybridization with *T. hirta*. The lower leaves are 4–5″ long and the upper are about 1″ wide with widely spaced internodes. The leaves are hairy on the undersides, particularly along the veins. The flowers are held in terminal cymes and open over a long period. Although borne in the terminals first, flowers subsequently appear in the top 4–6 leaf axils. They are funnel shaped, about 1″ long and ½″ wide. The background color is white to slightly pinkish and the interior is prominently spotted with crimson and has a small yellow eye in the center. The filaments and styles are spotted crimson. Overall, it is a most interesting flower. In north Georgia (zone 7b), flowers open the second week of September and persist until frost. The roots are stoloniferous and if grown in moist, semi-shady conditions, a large colony develops in 3–5 years. It is not, however, invasive. This is the best garden species because of the flower size, color, vigor and longevity.

Division is the propagation method of choice, accomplished in early spring. Seed may also be sown in a cold frame in the fall or early spring. Plants require about 6 months to reach transplantable size.

## Cultivars:

'Alba' has clean white flowers with crimson spots. Contrasts better with the foliage than the more common purple-pink flowers.

'Amethystina' has bluish purple flowers with a white throat spotted with red. It opens earlier than the species, flowering from late July until frost. Introduced by John Elsley of Wayside Gardens, it is becoming more common in cultivation. Plants do not seem to be as cold tolerant and are listed to zone 6, however, with additional testing in northern states, the variety may prove as cold hardy as the species.

Var. *stolonifera* is a hybrid between *T. formosana* and *T. hirta*. It is similar to the species but grows to 3½′ tall. It bears paler flowers with pink-lavender pots on the petals.

| *-hirta* (hir′ ta) | | Common Toad-Lily | 2–3′/2′ |
|---|---|---|---|
| Late Summer | Lilac | Japan | Zones 4–8 |

The common species has 2–3′ long gracefully arching stems. The stems carry many closely-set, clasping, soft-hairy pointed leaves about 3–6″ long and 1–2″ wide. In each leaf axil, one to three 1″ diameter flowers, which typically have a whitish or pale purple background covered with darker purple spots and blotches, are carried on short stalks (pedicels). Flowers also occur at the end of the stems.

*Tricyrtis hirta*
(64%)

Flowering begins in mid-September in the South, a week or two later in the North, but is not as persistent as *T. formosana*. In our gardens, flowering was completed by mid-October whereas the flowers of *T. formosana* continued for an additional 3 weeks. The roots are not stoloniferous and large clumps do not form, however, there has been some hybridization between this and *T. formosana*. Moist, fertile soil in partial shade is ideal.

Divide in the early spring while plants are still dormant. Seed propagation is similar to *T. formosana*. Seeds collected from garden plants may not be true if other species are grown nearby.

**Cultivars:**

'Alba' has greenish white flowers with pink stamens.

Var. *albescens* has cleaner white flowers than 'Alba'.

'Lilac Towers' bears flowers in the axils on long arching stems. The flowers have a white background with lilac spotting. 'Lilac Towers' and 'White Towers' may be hybrids between *T. hirta* and *T. affinis*, a short white-flowered species.

Var. *masamunei* has leaves without hairs but otherwise is similar to the species. It is seldom seen in gardens.

'Miyazaki' appears to be a hybrid between *T. hirta* and *T. formosana* with graceful arching stems and lovely pink to white axillary flowers with crimson spots which open in early fall. Introduced by Wayside Gardens.

'Miyazaki Gold' is similar to the above but with gold-edged leaves.

'Variegata' bears lavender flowers and gold-edged leaves.

'White Towers' has 3' long arching to almost horizontal stems with pure white flowers along the axils. More vigorous than the other white forms.

| *-macranthopsis* (ma-kranth-op' sis) | | Yellow Toad-Lily | 1–2'/2' |
|---|---|---|---|
| Late Summer | Yellow | Japan | Zones 6–8 |

This is a wonderful little known form which tolerates moderately heavy shade and bears 1–4 yellow flowers which hang from the axils of arching 1–3' long stems. I first saw this plant in the fine garden of Willis Hardin of Homeplace Nursery in Commerce, GA. He is one of the finest gardeners in the state and tries, usually successfully, plants that "should not grow." In his garden, *T. macranthopsis* was arching everywhere, obviously enjoying the pine shade, moist conditions and woodland soils. Leaves are 3–5" long and 1–2" wide and pointed at the apices. The base of each leaf tends to clasp the stem. The flowers are about 1½" long and have subtle brown spots within.

**Related Species:**

*T. latifolia* has terminal primrose-yellow flowers with brown spots within. The 3' tall plants flower as early as June, but usually in July to early August.

*T. macrantha* is similar in habit, flowering time and flower color to *T. macranthopsis* but the leaves do not clasp the stem. Both basal lobes are on the upper side of the stem. An equally good garden plant.

| *-macropoda* (ma-kro' po-da) | | Toad-Lily | 2–3'/2' |
|---|---|---|---|
| Late Summer | Lavender | China | Zones 5–8 |

The stems do not arch over but are upright, similar to the growth habit of *T. formosana*. The oblong to ovate leaves, which measure about 4" long and 2" wide, are sessile or with a very short stalk and do not clasp the stem. Flowers are mostly held terminally but some are also borne in the leaf axils. They are erect, lavender or white with small purple spots and the outer petals are reflexed.

**Hybrids:**

Hybrids which have arisen from Japan have become popular recently. However, little is known about the parentage nor have they been grown for sufficient lengths of time in this country to be sure of hardiness or performance in a given area. The tongue-twisting names, however, should be reason enough to try them.

'Golden Gleam' ('Golden Form') is as handsome in leaf as it is in flower. The leaves on the 18–20″ long stems are lime green, although they fade somewhat in hot summers, and the dark purple flowers occur in early fall.

'Jasmin' is a hybrid between *T. hirta* and *T. formosana* and the flowers (which are mainly axillary) are white with dark purple spots. Closer to the latter species than the former.

'Kohaku' is a hybrid of *T. macranthopsis* and *T. hirta*. Plants bear arching 18″ long stems and large cream-white flowers with brown spots along the axils. The arching stems result in a plant less than 12″ tall.

'Lemon Lime' has green-yellow foliage with light bands of green on 18″ stems. The flowers are lilac colored.

'Seiryu' is similar to *T. formosana* 'Amethystina' but is more stoloniferous and forms clumps within a couple of years. The flowers open in early fall.

'Shirohototgisu' has not been named to enhance its marketability. The plants are 2–3′ tall with white flowers in late summer and fall.

'Sinonome' produces white flowers with purple speckling. Plants multiply to produce a good sized clump by stolons.

'Togen' has large foliage (about 3 times larger than most others) on 2–3′ long stems. The lavender flowers are mostly terminal.

'White Flame' is a variegated form with white leaves bearing green variegations. The spotted lavender flowers are borne in late summer and fall. Plants grow 18–24″ tall.

<u>Quick Key to Tricyrtis Species</u>

A. Flowers yellow or yellow with spots . . . . . . . *T. macranthopsis*
AA. Flowers not yellow
   B. Flowers mainly in axils, plants not stoloniferous,
     lower leaf bases clasping stem . . . . . . . . . . . . . . . . *T. hirta*
   BB. Flowers mainly terminal, plants stoloniferous,
     lower leaf bases not clasping stem
     C. Style as long as stigmas . . . . . . . . . . . . . *T. formosana*
     CC. Style half as long as stigmas . . . . . . . . . . *T. macropoda*

**Additional Reading:**

Mathew, Brian. 1985. A review of the genus *Tricyrtis*. *The Plantsman* 6(4): 193–224.

*Trillium* (tril-lee′ um)                    Trillium                    Liliaceae

Although many trilliums also occur in Asia, trilliums are the epitome of the American wild flower. There are about 30 species and many are very similar, making accurate identification difficult. They are cherished in woodlands and gardens and people's passion for them has resulted in many trilliums being dug indiscriminately from the wild to end up dead in suburbia. The debate of digging wild flowers is no more visceral than when it comes to trilliums. Digging from a native stand when the plants are visible, that is, when they are in leaf or in flower, is not smart ecologically but even dumber horticulturally. It is difficult enough to justify one person digging 5 plants for their garden even though they probably are not going to have a major impact on the population; however, wholesale suppliers digging illegally can no longer be tolerated. Moreover, if trilliums and most other ephemeral wild flowers are dug in leaf and flower, they are doomed to die when placed in the garden and that is dumb. Many people contend that digging a few plants helps the population by spreading them around to other areas where they can multiply. This is a valid statement if plants are in danger from construction, flooding or other potential problems. I know many people who have saved many wild flowers from destruction and I know a few who use that reason to explain away their plants. Let's face it, people will dig some plants, and hopefully the hue and cry against digging is having an effect. Certainly, if plants must be dug, wait until they are dormant; otherwise, you are committing wild flower murder. Many nurseries are trying to propagate trilliums and other wild flowers and "nursery-grown" plants may be expensive but they have an excellent chance of survival and are not disrupting any stands. Enough said! I cannot imagine the Armitage garden without trilliums and numerous species vie for attention with epimediums and Virginia bluebells. The expense for the plants is negligible compared to the pleasure they bring me every spring.

All species bear single stems with 3 whorled leaves and a solitary flower, each flower with 3 leaf-like outer sepals and 3 petals and 6 stamens. The color and shape of the flower and amount of leaf mottling and leaf shape are distinguishing characteristics between species, but some species are very difficult to tell apart. The species are divided by the presence or absence of a flower stalk (pedicel). I enjoy both groups although the pedicelled types are more ornamental to most people.

As I read my comments of the first edition, in which I dismissed most of the non-pedicelled species as "unexceptional," it is obvious to me that I have become a born-again trillite.

## Quick Reference to Trillium Species

|  | Flowers with pedicel | Flower color |
|---|---|---|
| *T. catesbaei* | Yes | Pink |
| *T. cernuum* | Yes | White |
| *T. cuneatum* | No | Maroon, purple |
| *T. erectum* | Yes | Maroon |
| *T. flexipes* | Yes | White |
| *T. grandiflorum* | Yes | White |
| *T. luteum* | No | Yellow |
| *T. rugelii* | Yes | White |
| *T. sessile* | No | Maroon |
| *T. stamineum* | No | Maroon |

| | | |
|---|---|---|
| *-catesbaei* (kats-be' eye) | Rose Trillium | 10–12"/10" |
| Spring          White | Southeast United States | Zones 7–9 |

(Syn. *T. stylosum*)

The rose trillium is one of the more common Southern trilliums and is easily recognized by the wavy margins of the leaves that turn upward and the rose-colored flower beneath the canopy of leaves. The flower is declined, meaning that is seldom erect, and often hugs the plant stem beneath the leaves. The petals emerge white but later turn rose to pink. All parts of the flower (petals, sepals and mature stamens) are reflexed (turned up). A beautiful pedicelled trillium, but one which requires a lot of bending and reclining to appreciate.

Many similar forms or species also occur (*T. nervosum, T. peristans*, see Mitchell, 1992).

### Related Species:

*T. cernuum*, nodding trillium, is another plant whose flower is tucked beneath the leaves and seldom raises its head to be seen. The flowers are white with purple anthers and the leaves have short petioles. The petals flare back exposing the anthers like shooting arrows. Plants are native from Newfoundland across Canada, down through Illinois, Iowa and south to the mountains of Georgia.

*T. rugelii* is the Southern equivalent to *T. cernuum*. The plants and flowers are bigger, and flowering occurs earlier, at least in the Armitage garden. Occasionally, plants will bear flowers with red on the petals, but this is not common.

| | | |
|---|---|---|
| *-grandiflorum* (grand-i-flor' um) | Great White Trillium | 18–24"/2' |
| Spring          White, Pink | Eastern North America | Zones 4–7 |

Every time I read about the species, I find another common name listed. It is known as wake-robin, showy trillium, snow trillium, wood lily, great white trillium, and trinity flower. Plants occur as far northeast as Quebec, west to Minnesota, southwest to Missouri and south to northern Georgia.

The sessile leaves are often wavy and may be up to 6″ long, although 3–4″ is more common. The flowers consist of 3 large flaring petals with wavy edges subtended by 3 smaller greenish sepals. The 2–3″ wide flower usually opens white then fades to a soft pink. About 6–8 weeks after flowering, white berries are produced. Foliage persists only to late summer, particularly if plants are allowed to dry out regularly.

Rhizomes should be planted approximately 4″ deep in highly organic, moist, well-drained soils in partial to heavy shade. Soils should be neutral to slightly acidic. The addition of well rotted compost such as aged manure or rotted leaves results in more rapid growth and larger plants. Interplant with other species of trilliums or with hepaticas, wild gingers, bloodroot or native ferns. If plants are stressed due to poor soil or lack of shade, they will rapidly perish.

This is arguably the most ornamental trillium and the most abused flower of the woods. More plants have been dug from the woods, the majority dying, than all other wild flowers combined. This may have made some sense at one time when few nurseries propagated wild flowers but today this species is offered by many mail order and local nurseries for a reasonable price. Unfortunately a few disreputable nurseries still dig from the wild. Nature takes years to build up a colony but man requires only 5 minutes and a shovel to destroy it.

Propagation of the plant has been studied by Dr. Harry Phillips of the University of North Carolina. From his work, he demonstrates that propagation by seed is a long process, generally taking up to 8–12 months for germination and 2–3 years to produce a flowering plant. The seeds should be inspected as the berries ripen (about 5–6 weeks after flowers open). Seeds are mature when they are a dark or russet color and should be sown immediately. Sow in a moist medium and allow the seed flat to overwinter in a protected area. Germination occurs the next spring. If seeds are purchased they will be dormant and much slower to germinate. Eight years for germination have been reported. Removing the soil around the base of the plant and cutting a V-shape groove along the length of the rhizome causes the production of bulblets which may be removed 1 year later. The wound should be dusted with fungicide prior to replanting.

### Cultivars:

Var. *roseum* is a beautiful pink-flowered form which is absolutely magnificent. I remember first seeing in the garden of Mrs. Gertrude Wister in Swarthmore, PA, one of the finest shade gardens anywhere, here or abroad. Colonies of pink trilliums shone like rosy beacons from the beds of green throughout the garden. Some authorities feel this form is simply a variation of natural flower color and should not be treated as a separate variety.

'Flore-pleno', a double form, is beloved or disliked with equal fervor. Some find the flowers unobtrusive and charming while others feel the doubleness reduces the natural charm of the plant and replaces it with artificiality. I feel the latter, but a great plant.

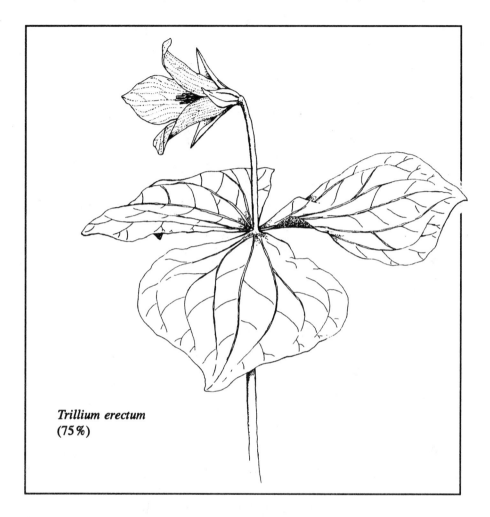

*Trillium erectum*
(75%)

## Related Species:

*T. erectum*, stinking Benjamin, bears more erect flowers and rhomboidal leaves (leaves wider in center, pointed at both ends) than *T. grandiflorum*. The flowers are usually maroon but white (f. *albiflorum*) and light yellow (f. *luteum*) forms also occur. The purple flowers are malodorous but the non-purple forms lack the disagreeable smell.

*T. flexipes* has pure white flowers on long pedicels, held horizontally or level with the leaves. The petals are spreading to give the flower a somewhat flattened appearance and occasionally is flushed with pink. The leaves are more ovate than rhomboid. The lack of a maroon center and the erect flower are the most obvious characteristics of the species. I think this is my favorite.

*Trillium flexipes*
(150%)

| *-sessile* (sess′ ile) | | Sessile Trillium, Toad Trillium | 6–12″/9″ |
|---|---|---|---|
| Spring | Maroon | Eastern, Central United States | Zones 4–7 |

One of the many sessile-flowered trilliums, the toad trillium is as much appreciated for the wonderfully mottled leaves as for the rather difficult-to-love maroon flowers squatting atop the leafy throne. I am the first to admit that trying to distinguish the numerous maroon sessile-flowered species and forms is almost impossible without a hand lens or microscope or better yet, a trained wildlife biologist whose expertise lies in the genus. I have learned that *T. sessile* has shorter petals, broader leaves and significantly less mottling (at least when in flower) than *T. cuneatum*. When the plants emerge from the ground, they are mottled but this disappears as they mature. The easiest way to recognize *T. recurvatum* is the recurved sepals which hug the stem and the tips of the petals which curve inward and often touch each other. I also discovered the unpleasant smell of *T. underwoodii* and the fruity odor of *T. cuneatum*. There appears to be more variability in the toad trillium, *T. cuneatum*, than in other species. Usually strongly mottled, the maroon to bronze flower petals may be 1–3″ long and leaves may be broadly to slightly ovate. *T. lancifolium* has leaves much more narrow than they are long and have long, narrow petals whereas *T. reliqueum* is about the most noble of the mottled, sessile trilliums. However, let's be honest, they all are quite similar in appearance and for me, I simply enjoy them and have long given up worrying about their identity. Few of these

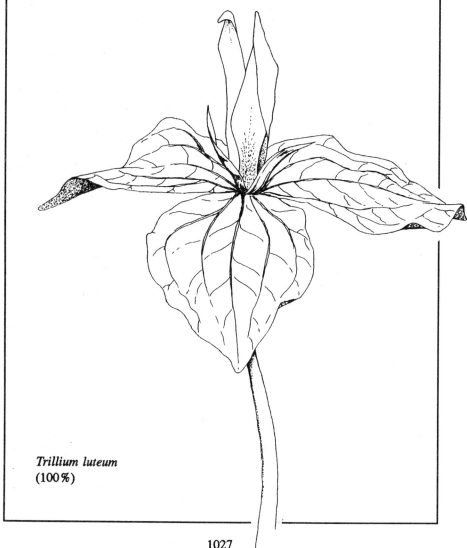

*Trillium luteum*
(100%)

species will be available as nursery grown plants and wandering with a guide through the woods on a Saturday morning may be the closest you will come to seeing more than a few of these plants at a time. If you can find nursery-grown plants, forget about their name (it will likely be incorrect anyway), plant them and enjoy them in your garden.

**Related Species:**

*T. luteum*, yellow trillium, has long narrow petals which are generally light yellow or bronze-green. The flowers are also sweetly scented. A beautiful plant.

*T. stamineum* is easy to distinguish by the twisted purple petals.

Quick Key to Trillium Species

    A. Flowers with pedicel
        B. Flowers nodding, under the leaves
            C. Flowers pink . . . . . . . . . . . . . . . . . . . . . . *T. catesbaei*
            CC. Flowers white . . . . . . . . . . . . . . . . . . . . *T. cernuum*
        BB. Flowers upright, above leaves
            C. Flowers normally white, not malodorous
                D. Petals with wavy margin, fading to pink . . *T. grandiflorum*
                DD. Petals with straight margin, not fading to pink . . *T. flexipes*
            CC. Flowers normally maroon, malodorous . . . . . . *T. erectum*
    AA. Flowers sessile
        B. Flowers yellow . . . . . . . . . . . . . . . . . . . . . . . *T. luteum*
        BB. Flowers not yellow
            C. Petals twisted . . . . . . . . . . . . . . . . . . . . . *T. stamineum*
            CC. Petals not twisted
                D. Petals 2X longer than stamens, flower fetid . . . *T. sessile*
                DD. Petals 3X longer or more than stamens,
                    flower fruity or musky-scented . . . . . . . . *T. cuneatum*

**Additional Reading:**

Bishop, M. 1996. Protean wood lilies. *The Garden* 121(6):353–355.

Mitchell, R.J. Trillium—the Asiatic species. 1989. *The Plantsman* 10(4): 216–231.

Mitchell, R.J. 1990. Trillium—the pedicellate species. *The Plantsman* 12(1): 44–60.

Mitchell, R.J. 1992. Trillium—the *Trillium catesbaei* complex. *The Plantsman* 13(4):219–225.

Phillips, Harry R. 1985. *Growing and Propagating Wild Flowers*. The University of North Carolina Press, Chapel Hill, NC, 331 pp. This excellent text deals with many aspects of American wild flowers and is a must for all gardeners interested in use and propagation of native plants. The section on Trillium is particularly informative.

## *Trollius* (tro′ lee-us)          Globeflower          Ranunculaceae

About 20 species are native to Europe, Asia, and North America and all are suited to moist, heavy soils. They are not tolerant of heat or drought and perform poorly south of zone 6. However, where cool, moist soils exist, *Trollius* is not difficult to grow in sun or partial shade. If this condition is fulfilled, plants may succeed as far south as zone 7. The dark green foliage is palmately divided or lobed and often declines by mid- to late summer. The foliage of most species should be pruned at that time. The orange to yellow solitary flowers consist of showy sepals. The small petals are found in the midst of the stamens and their size relative to the stamens is a useful identification characteristic.

Propagate by division in late fall or early spring. A year is necessary for plants to recover and flowering is reduced the first year after division. Fresh, ripe seed obtained from flowering plants requires approximately 3 weeks to germinate, although germination will probably be less than 40%. Purchased or old seeds require over a year to germinate, if they germinate at all, and 5% germination is not uncommon.

Quick Reference to Trollius Species

|  | Height (in.) | Flower color | Sepals |
|---|---|---|---|
| *T.* × *cultorum* | 24–36 | Orange, yellow | Rolled in |
| *T. europaeus* | 20—24 | Yellow | Rolled in |
| *T. ledebourii* | 24–36 | Orange | Spreading |
| *T. pumilus* | 9–12 | Yellow | Spreading |

| -× *cultorum* (kul-to′ rum) | | Hybrid Globeflower | 2–3′/3′ |
|---|---|---|---|
| Late Spring | Orange to Yellow | Hybrid Origin | Zones 3–6 |

Plants grown under this name are hybrids among *T. europaeus*, *T. asiaticus*, and *T. chinensis*. All cultivars have showy globular, buttercup-yellow flowers consisting of layers of incurved petal-like sepals which eventually open to expose the many stamens. The leaves consist of 5–6 deeply cut lobes and are also ornamental. Cut back foliage in mid- to late summer.

### Cultivars:
'Alabaster' is one of the more unusual globeflowers with cream-tinged flowers rather than the common yellow or orange. It is not as vigorous (2′ tall) and flowers tend to lose their globe shape early. However, it is well worth trying.

'Canary Bird' bears tight, globe-shaped, light yellow flowers with a tinge of green.

'Commander-in-Chief' has deep orange, 3″ wide flowers.

'Earliest of All' is one of the earliest of this group and flowers in early May. The flowers are pale orange-yellow.

'Etna' is vigorous, growing 3′ tall with dark orange flowers.

'Fire Globe' ('Feuertroll') bears some of the deepest orange flowers.

'Goldquelle' is one of the most popular cultivars and produces 2½" wide pure yellow flowers. The many blossoms are long lasting and useful for cut flowers.

'May Gold' stands about 2' tall with 2½" diameter lemon yellow flowers in early spring. This is one of the earliest cultivars to flower.

'Orange Globe' ('Orangekugel') bears golden orange flower globes in mid-summer.

'Orange Princess' is an excellent choice for cut flowers. It has 2½–3" wide, deep orange flowers and grows 2' tall.

'Pritchard's Giant' commonly reaches 3' in height. The medium yellow flowers are long lasting and retain their globe shape. This is also an excellent cut flower cultivar.

'Salamander' is similar to 'Fire Globe' with 2½" wide fiery orange flowers.

| *-europaeus* (u-ro' pay-us) | | Common Globeflower | 20–24"/24" |
|---|---|---|---|
| Early Spring | Yellow | Northern Europe | Zones 4–7 |

The 1–2" diameter lemon yellow globular flowers are usually borne singly or occasionally in 2s. Ten to fifteen sepals enclose the many stamens and the 5 small spatulate petals. The leaves are 5-parted and the leaflets are lobed and toothed. The lower leaves are petioled while those higher on the stem are sessile. This is a common garden plant in Europe and being planted more in the United States. Plants are more tolerant of dry soil than most others, although performance is still mediocre if soils dry out.

### Cultivars:

'Superbus' is similar to the species but flowers more prolifically. It is more difficult to find the species in commerce than this cultivar.

| *-ledebourii* (led-e-boor' ee-eye) | | Ledebour Globeflower | 2–3'/2½' |
|---|---|---|---|
| Spring | Orange | Siberia | Zones 3–6 |

Plants are vigorous and heights of 3' are not uncommon in well-grown specimens where soils are consistently moist. The leaves are deeply cut to the base and the leaflets lobed and toothed. The deep orange, cup-shaped flowers consist of 5 spreading sepals which readily display the many stamens and narrow, upright petals. The petals are more visible than those in the previous species and are about the same length as the stamens. It flowers approximately one week later than *T. europaeus*. These are magnificent plants for the shaded bog garden or other suitably moist area.

### Related Species:

*T. chinensis* is closely related to *T. ledebourii* but much later flowering. It grows up to 3' tall with 5-lobed basal and stem leaves and bowl-shaped

2–2½" wide golden yellow to orange flowers in summer. Native to China and Russia, hardy in zones 5(4)–7. 'Golden Queen' is about 2' tall.

| | | | |
|---|---|---|---|
| ***-pumilus*** (pew' mi-lus) | Dwarf Globeflower | 9–12"/12" |
| Spring | Yellow | Himalayas | Zones 4–6 |

This species is particularly suited to the rock garden or the front of the moist border. The stems are almost leafless and the 1–2" wide basal leaves are 5-parted. Each leaflet is 3-lobed and attached to the stem by a petiole. The 1" wide flowers consist of 5–6 notched stamens and 10–12 narrow petals about the same size as the stamens. Rich, moist well-drained soils and afternoon shade are ideal. A lovely plant for small niches in the garden.

**Related Species:**

*T. acaulis* is about 6" tall and is also known as dwarf globeflower. It differs from *T. pumilus* by having stem leaves as well as basal leaves. The solitary 1½–2" wide flowers are golden yellow and consist of 12–16 petals. Hardy in zones 5–7.

*T. laxus* is native from New Hampshire to British Columbia, and easier to establish in the shady, moist garden than many of the foreigners. Plants are approximately 9–12" tall and bear solitary 1–2" diameter yellow flowers (white to cream in var. *albiflorus*) in early spring. Excellent plantings may be found in The Garden in the Woods in Framingham, Massachusetts and the Denver Botanic Garden.

Quick Key to Trollius Species

    A. Flowers globe shaped, at least when they emerge
        B. Petals usually exceeding stamens,
           flowers yellow to orange . . . . . . . . . . . . . . *T.* × *cultorum*
        BB. Petals equal to or a little shorter
           than stamens, flowers orange . . . . . . . . . . . *T. europaeus*
    AA. Flowers spreading
        B. Petals much exceeding stamens,
           plant 2–3' tall . . . . . . . . . . . . . . . . . . . . . *T. ledebourii*
        BB. Petals about the same length or shorter
           than stamens, plant 9–12" tall . . . . . . . . . . . . . *T. pumilus*

## *Tulbaghia* (tul-baag-e' a)      Society Garlic      Amaryllidaceae

All of the twenty or so species are native to South Africa and can only be included as perennials in frost free areas. However, the main species, *T. violacea*, can tolerate temperatures as low as 20° F. *T. violacea* is grown from tuberous rootstocks and produces 5–9 strap-shaped basal leaves and umbels with up to 20 lilac-pink flowers in early summer. They are sometimes called pink agapanthus due to their lilac-pink flower color. The "garlic" in its common name comes from its garlicky fragrance. The flowers seem to evoke different senses from different names. To some, they are sweet; to others, they are sickly sweet.

Plants don't compete with many of the more colorful bulbous plants often offered, however, it is a charming plant in a container (to be brought in the winter) or as an annual for those who are better at replacing than redigging. Plants require consistent watering and full sun, and love heat.

### Cultivars:

'Silver Lace' has larger flowers than the species.

'Variegata' produces leaves with creamy stripes running down the leaves. Better than the species.

### Additional Reading:

Benham, Steve. 1993. *Tulbaghia*, a survey of the species in cultivation. *The Plantsman* 15(2):89–110.

## *Tulipa* (tew' li-pa)　　　　　　Tulip　　　　　　Liliaceae

Few plants herald spring like the tulip. Although gardeners are deluged with advertisements in newspapers and garden centers for hybrid tulips each fall, it is well worth remembering that over 100 species are known and many are excellent garden plants. Some of the easiest and most ornamental include *T. batalinii*, *T. clusiana* and *T. tarda*. Hybrid tulips range in height from the 6" tall Duc von Tol type to the stately 3' tall stems of the Darwins, and flower from late March to late May. The garden tulip was introduced to Europe in 1572 by Ogier Ghiselin de Busbecq, Ambassador of the Holy Roman Empire to Suleiman the Magnificent of Turkey. At that time, great numbers of tulips existed in Turkey and by 1715 a list of 1,323 varieties appeared in a paper by Sheik Mohammed Lalizare in the reign of Ahmed III. In 1948, *The Classified List of Tulip Names*, published by a joint committee of the Tulip Nomenclature Committee in England and the General Dutch Bulb-Growers' Society, included well over 4,300 names. There are many more today.

All hybrid tulips and most species should be treated as annuals, biennials or short-lived perennials in this country. While this is not a particularly popular opinion, it is nevertheless true. Most tulips perform poorly the second year, worse the next year, and seldom "strut their stuff" by the forth spring. Unfortunately, this is difficult for many gardeners to understand. Many of my friends consider a bulb a perennial, which once planted, should return year after year. In their zeal for tulip perenniality, they tell me that their tulips look as good the third year as the first. I know that the quality of the tulip has not gone up, rather their standards have gone down.

In the South, it is even more difficult to find tulips performing well for more than 2 years. Sufficient cold is not available to force the flower stalk to its potential height, high night temperatures reduce stored food in the bulb, and warm summer soils promote pests and diseases. The depth of planting should be 3 times the diameter of the bulb, except in heavy clay soils, where shallow planting is more beneficial. In general, the depth of planting for most cultivars in average soils is about 5″. Plant in full sun in mid-September in zones 2–4, as late as early November in zones 7–8. Don't line the bulbs up like tin soldiers all in a row. Plant in bunches of at least 25, no more than 6″ apart, preferably bulb to bulb.

If plants are left in the garden, the spent flowers must be removed before seed develops, and leaves allowed to yellow prior to removal, regardless of where one gardens. Since the leaves provide food to the developing bulb, it makes little sense to tie the leaves up in elastic bands or string to "get them out of the way." To propagate, bulbs should be removed, cleaned and graded by size. The largest bulbs may be replanted and bulblets placed in a propagation bed where they grow and mature. Three years are required to produce a mature bulb from a small bulblet. In my opinion, treat the tulips as 1 or 2 year plants, then consign them to the compost pile.

The most recent reorganization of the genus provides 23 different classes of tulips, many of minor importance in this country and some almost impossible to find. The following is a summary of some of the classifications used for garden tulips and a few corresponding cultivars. There are literally thousands of cultivars; those mentioned are typical of their classification. Flowering time will differ depending on the area of the country.

| Classification | Comments | Cultivars |
|---|---|---|
| Duc van Tol | Very early, rarely exceeding 6″. | — |
| Single Early | Derived from *T. gesneriana* and *T. suaveolens*, 12–14″ tall, usually fragrant, flower in April and early May. | 'Bellona' 'Diana' 'General de Wet' 'Princess Irene' |
| Double Early | 10–12″ tall, flower late April and early May. | 'Electra' 'Peach Blossom' |
| Mendel | Derived from Duc von Tol and Darwin tulips. Less than 18″ tall, bloom in mid-May. | 'Apricot Beauty' 'Olga' 'Pink Trophy' |
| Triumph | Derived from single early and Darwin tulips. About 2′ tall, bloom in mid-May. | 'First Lady' 'Merry Widow' 'Pink Glow' |
| Darwin | Short, rounded petals, flower almost rectangular in outline. Up to 3′ tall, flower mid- to late May. | 'Aristocrat' 'Golden Age' 'Mamasa' 'Pink Supreme' |

| Classification | Comments | Cultivars |
|---|---|---|
| Darwin Hybrids | Derived from Darwins and *T. fosteriana*. Grow less than 2' tall, have largest flowers of all classes, bloom late April to mid-May. | 'Apeldoorn' 'Big Chief' 'Golden Parade' 'Orange Sun' 'Parade' |
| Lily-Flowered | Derived from *T. retroflexa* and cottage tulips. Flowers have pointed, reflex petals. About 2' tall, May flowering. | 'Alladin' 'Red Shine' 'West Point' 'White Triumphator' |
| Cottage | Have egg-shaped blooms, grow 20–30" tall. Late, single tulips. | 'Halcro' 'Maureen' 'Mrs. J. Scheepers' |
| Rembrandt | Darwin tulips with streaks on petals. | 'American Flag' 'Union Jack' |
| Parrot | Have feather-like petals, usually in colorings of red, orange, blue, and green. Flower with Darwins. | 'Black Parrot' 'Blue Parrot' 'Fantasy' 'Flaming Parrot' |
| Double Late | Bear peony-like flowers in May. Grow 16–24" tall. Blooms are up to 4" across and long lasting. | 'Eros' 'Gold Medal' 'Orange Triumph' |
| Fosteriana hybrids | Derived mainly from *T. fosteriana*, has broad gray-green leaves and bears 4" wide flowers on 12" tall stems in April. | 'Candela' 'Canopus' 'Red Emperor' 'White Emperor' |
| Greigii hybrids | Leaves heavily mottled and striped with purple. Bears large flowers, with black base on 9" stems in May. Useful for foliage effect alone. | 'Plaisir' 'Prima Donna' 'Oriental Speldor' 'Red Riding Hood' |
| Kaufmanniana hybrids | Known as the water-lily tulip, one of the earliest to bloom. Short (4–8") stems useful for rockery or exposed positions. | 'Gaiety' 'Heart's Delight' 'Stressa' 'Tartini' |
| Bouquet | Multi-flowered tulips, each 2' stem bears 3–5 flowers. Derived mainly from *T. praestans*. | 'Georgette' 'Orange Bouquet' 'Toronto' |

**Other Species:**

| Classification | Comments | Cultivars |
|---|---|---|
| *T. acuminata* | Known as the horned tulip, has narrow pointed petals, May flowering. | 'Fireflame' |
| *T. batalinii* | As handsome a flower as found in any of the hybrids. Generally yellow flowers, often with red tinge. This is a "must-try" group. | 'Bright Gem' 'Bronze Charm' 'Red Jewel' 'Yellow Jewel' |
| *T. clusiana* | Known as Lady tulip, 9–12″ long. White flowers striped with red, April flowering. One of the most perennial species for Southern gardeners. | 'Candycane' |
| *T. praestans* | Multi-flowered, 12–18″ tall. Flowers in shades of red open in late April to early May. | 'Fusilier' 'Tubergen's Var.' 'Zwanenburg' |
| *T. tarda* | Flowers in March, 6–9″ tall. Bears up to 5 white flowers with yellow eye per stem. Rock garden. | — |

*Tunica* see *Petrorhagia*

*Tussilago* (tuss-I-lag′ o)          Coltsfoot          Asteraceae

The name comes from *tussis*, cough, referring to the medicinal use of the leaves. This must explain its occasional appearance in gardens here and there as it is a difficult plant to explain based on its ornamental properties. A number of species occur in the genus but only *T. farfara*, coltsfoot, is grown commercially, although I have not been able to find it offered in many nurseries around the country. This is probably good, as the flowers are almost identical to dandelions, not exactly high on the list of ways to spend money. The flowers emerge before the leaves and are borne on 4–6″ scapes with numerous purple scales. They open about the same time or a little earlier than dandelions. When the blooms begin to decline, the orbicular to heart-shaped leaves appear which become more angular as they mature. The leaves have a soft cottony matting early in the season, which diminishes with age.

Plants grow in moist areas and are hardy to zone 6. Why anyone would want to pay for this plant is somewhat beyond me, but then I've always contended that a field of dandelions can be beautiful, as long as it is not my field. A variegated form ('Variegata') also exists, which allows for a field of variegated dandelions.

# U

*Uniola* see *Chasmanthium*

*Urospermum* (your-o-sperm' um)          Urospermum          Asteraceae

Two species occur in this little found genus, both of which are native to the area around the Mediterranean. Only *U. dalechampii* seems to be grown, and generally only grown if seed is collected from the parent plant. The plants form 2–3' tall pubescent (softly hairy) stems and many gray-green hairy leaves. The bottom ones are about 6" long and 2" wide with winged petioles, the upper ones are thinner and the base of the leaves clasp the stem. The soft yellow daisy flowers occur in the summer.

We seldom see these plants in the United States and Canada and perhaps there is no overwhelming reason to rush out and try to find seed. However, the flower color is easy to work into the garden and plants are reasonably easy to grow. The drawbacks are that they are Mediterranean, therefore care little for heat and humidity. They act as biennials in most of the country but would likely be more perennial in West Coast gardens.

Propagate by seed or division.

*Uvularia* (oo-vew-lah' ree-a)          Bellwort, Merry Bells          Liliaceae

The botanical name comes from *uvula*, the soft palette of the mouth, and refers to the drooping flowers. All of the 5 species are native to the eastern United States and are graceful woodland plants which are showy only to those who love and appreciate subtle flowers and form. I started with a few plants of the sessile bellwort, *U. sessilifolia* and in three years, they have spread out and about beneath an old dogwood in the back garden. Lots of people pass them by without so much as a second glance, until I wrestle them down and make them tell me how much they enjoy their subtle beauty.

Plants are about 12–18″ tall with thin forked stems bearing light green leaves and bell-shaped, drooping yellow flowers. The flowers are twisted in bud and slightly so in flower. A little fertilizer in the spring does wonders for the plants, making them much more vigorous than seen in the woodlands. They spread by rhizomes in woodland soils, thriving in moist, shady areas. They do well under the shade of oaks and beeches and other deciduous trees. After flowering, a three-lobed fruit is formed, which rests on the leaves through the summer. For differences between this genus and the similar *Disporum* and *Polygonatum*, see *Disporum*.

Quick Reference for Uvularia Species

|  | Height (in.) | Leaves |
|---|---|---|
| *U. grandiflora* | 12–24 | Perfoliate |
| *U. perfoliata* | 12–18 | Perfoliate |
| *U. sessilifolia* | 12–18 | Sessile |

| *-grandiflora* (grand-flo′ ra) | Large-Flowered Bellwort | 12–18″/12″ |
|---|---|---|
| Spring      Yellow | East, Central North America | Zones 3–9 |

The leaves are perfoliate and are finely hairy beneath. The stems fork about 8″ above the soil with 1 or 2 leaves beneath the fork. The pale yellow flowers are a little larger than other species measuring about 1–1½″ long with the stamens exceeding the styles (female part of the flower). The fruit, which is a capsule, is three-sided and delicately handsome in its own right. Sounds terribly technical; grow them because you like them, it is doubtful you will impress anyone with them.

### Cultivars:
'Sunbonnet' is a vigorous form which I placed in the Armitage garden. Later, I bought some plants of the straight species and I am not convinced there is a great deal of difference.

### Related Species:
*U. perfoliata* is similar to the above but the pale yellow flowers are only about 1″ long and the stamens are shorter than the styles. The leaves are not hairy beneath. Equally terrific.

*U. sessilifolia* is less "bulky" than the others, with thinner stems and smaller lighter yellow flowers. The name refers to the sessile (no petiole) leaves on stems which terminate in small but handsome pale yellow flowers. *U. caroliniana* (syn. *U. pudica*) is very similar but has stems with minute coarse hairs. No difference from the garden point of view.

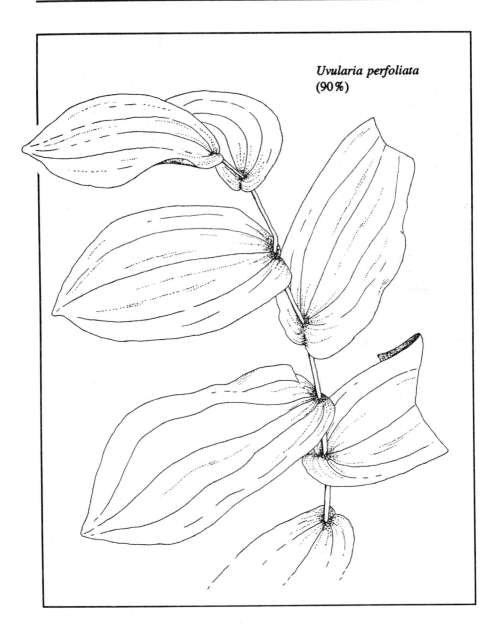

*Uvularia perfoliata*
(90%)

## Quick Key to Uvularia Species

    A. Leaves perfoliate
        B. Leaves hairy on undersides . . . . . . . . . . . . *U. grandiflora*
        BB. Leaves not hairy beneath . . . . . . . . . . . . . . *U. perfoliata*
    AA. Leaves sessile . . . . . . . . . . . . . . . . . . . . . . . *U. sessilifolia*

# V

*Valeriana* (va-le-ree-ah′ na)    Valerian, Garden Heliotrope    Apiaceae

Well over 200 species occur in the genus, but I wager that no one has become tired from seeing it all over the place. The botanical name was derived from *valeo*, strong, in reference to its supposed medicinal uses. Plants are characterized by thickened tap roots and being strongly scented throughout. The basal leaves are often rosetted and the stem leaves are usually pinnately compound. The flowers, which are generally white, are held in a terminal umbel or cyme. Both upright and low growing spreading species occur, but generally only 1 or 2 species will be available through mail order specialists.

The most familiar is common valerian, *V. officinalis*, native to Europe and Asia but widely naturalized elsewhere, including Canada and the United States. Although their preferred location is along streams and other wet areas, they tolerate the drier soils typical of most gardens. Plants grow 3–5′ tall, and with lots of sun, they stand without support. The stem leaves are odd-pinnate, usually with 15–21 segments (7–10 pairs plus the terminal). The flowers appear in early to mid summer and are sweetly fragrant. They are generally whitish, but light lavender or pink flowers may occur. The rhizomes bear short stolons, resulting in quick multiplication. This is one of the "old fashioned" garden plants, prized for that fragrance. Cultivars include 'Alba' with whiter flowers, 'Coccinea' with blood-red flowers, and 'Rubra' with bright red flowers.

*V. phu* is similar in habit but not as tall as common valerian and the stem leaves differ by being pinnately parted into 3–4 pairs of segments plus the terminal one. Flowers are pinkish white but not nearly as ornamental as *V. officinalis*. 'Aurea' is a handsome cultivar which emerges with yellow stems and leaves. They remain yellow until the heat of the summer makes them fade to light green.

## *Vancouveria* (vang-koo-ve′ ree-a)    Vancouveria    Berberidaceae

Three species of ground-hugging plants, *Vancouveria* are native to woodlands of the northwest United States. They are similar to *Epimedium* but have 6 stamens and petals rather than 4. If cool, moist conditions can be provided, they are useful ground covers for areas with light shade. The genus commemorates the great seafarer, Captain George Vancouver.

| *-hexandra* (heks-an′ dra) | | American Barrenwort | 10–12″/12″ |
|---|---|---|---|
| Early Summer | White | Washington to California | Zones 5–7 |

Each 2–3″ long leaf is 2 or 3 times ternately (in threes) compound resulting in carpets of fern-like foliage that die to the ground in the fall. The white, ½″ long flowers have reflexed sepals and petals and are held in 10–20-flowered panicles at the end of a leafless flower stem. Plants when well-grown remind me of a poorly-grown white barrenwort that I shouldn't have planted.

Plants spread by slender, underground rhizomes in cool, moist, acidic, organic soils. They are difficult to establish in areas of hot, dry summers. Although the flowers are showier, it is not as tough as *Epimedium*.

Propagate by dividing the rhizome in spring or fall.

### Related Species:

*V. chrysantha*, golden vancouveria, has ½″ long yellow flowers held in a few flowered panicle on 12″ tall plants. Native to southern Oregon and northern California.

*V. planipetala*, redwood ivy, has white flowers sometimes tinged lavender. This species and the previous are evergreen, prefer a pH around 5.0, and are more difficult to establish than *V. hexandra*.

## *Veratrum* (vay-rah′ trum)    False Hellebore    Liliaceae

This genus contains 18 species, and include some of my absolute favorite plants. How I wish more were available to the gardener, although only *V. viride* seams to be grown in the United States. Plants are not commonly offered by nurseries, thus *Veratrum* is not well known by the gardening public. The leaves, seeds and roots are poisonous (all contain veratrine) and this unfortunate character flaw has also limited popularity. The leaves are particularly showy in the spring and are followed by tall panicles in the summer. The most common species, *V. viride*, Indian poke, has yellowish green flowers, but *V. album*, white false hellebore, and *V. californicum* have whitish green flowers. *V. nigrum*, black false hellebore, produces dark purple flowers but is seldom available. The botanical name comes from *vere atrum*, truly black, in reference to the color of the roots; *veratrum* was the ancient name for hellebore, thus the common name.

*-viride* (vi' ri-dee)                Indian Poke                2–6'/2'
    Summer        Yellow-Green        North America        Zones 3–7

Native from New Brunswick to Georgia, and west to Oregon and Alaska, this wild flower is most impressive. The pleated, light green leaves are reminiscent of light green pleated hosta foliage as they emerge to form large arching mounds. The leaves are alternate and as the stem emerges, the distances between the leaves become more obvious. The oval lower leaves are about 12" long, 3" wide, and clasp the stem with a long narrow sheath while the upper stem leaves become progressively smaller. The 18–24" long flower stalks of broad, yellow-green flowers are somewhat reminiscent of a green *Verbascum*.

This species is both interesting and ornamental. It is best in the spring as the fresh foliage emerges, however, even though I have trouble getting excited about green flowers, the large skinny panicles certainly bring many comments. Each individual flower is bell-shaped with 6 nearly equal segments. Moist soils are necessary; if allowed to dry out, the edges of the foliage turn brown. Protection from afternoon sun is helpful to maintain freshness of the foliage. *Veratrum* does not perform particularly well under the stress of high heat and humidity and is more suited for zones 4–6 than zones 7 and 8. In the spring, slug pellets or other deterrents help keep the foliage fresh. Leaves of *Veratrum* and *Hosta* are gourmet treats for slugs. Partial shade is best, leaves scorch in full sun and windy conditions.

Seedlings require a year before they can be transplanted and reach flowering size in 3 years. Seeds must be subjected to a warm-cold-warm stratification period. Sow seed in the fall and allow it to remain under snow cover or mulch until spring. See seed treatment for *Actaea*. Division in the fall or early spring is a more effective and faster means of propagation.

**Related Species:**

*V. album* is similar, bearing flowers slightly tinted white outside and green inside. All the specimens I have seen have a lot more green than white. Plants are shorter, growing 2–3' tall.

*V. nigrum* has wide basal leaves although the upper stem leaves are more lanceolate. The flowers are earlier than *V. viride*, held in similar narrow panicles but are purple-black. Plants are 2–4' tall.

*Verbascum* (ver-bas' cum)                Mullein                Scrophulariaceae
(Syn. *Celsia*)

When mullein is mentioned, most people think of the large, hairy roadside weed with small yellow flowers, *V. thapsus*. This European species has become naturalized everywhere and was widely used for candles (stems), shoe lining (leaves), and narcotics (seeds) along with additional medicinal virtues. As interesting as the history is, it is not enough to invite the plants from the road to our gardens. Few realize that this genus contains wonderful, more civilized garden brethren. *Verbascum* contains about 300 species, many are biennial and hybridize readily. Species range in height from the 8" high *V. dumulosum*, a vivid yellow-flowering plant that cascades over rocks (as well as its hybrid with the dwarf *V. pestalozzae*) to the 6–8' tall Olympic mullein, *V. olympicum*, whose branched yellow racemes disdainfully look down upon the rest of the garden members. *V. thapsiforme* (syn. *V. densiflorum*) also has handsome large yellow flowers and highly variable in height, ranging from 2 to 4 feet. *V. bombyciferum* is a spectacular biennial species with rosettes of 12–18" long, downy, silvery-white leaves. With foliage like that, the rather ordinary yellow flowers are irrelevant. Hybridization has resulted in named selections, and availability of useful *Verbascum* hybrids is slowly increasing.

A few perennial species occur, all more or less tomentose (hairy), with soft alternate leaves on stems arising from a rosette of basal leaves. Flowers are generally yellow but occasionally purple or white-flowered species occur. *Verbascum* tolerates a wide range of soils and conditions. Most do best in full sun and in poor soils.

## Quick Reference to Verbascum Species

| | Height (in.) | Flower color | Leaves gray-green |
|---|---|---|---|
| *V. chaixii* | 2–3 | Gray-green | Yes |
| *V. olympicum* | 3–5 | Yellow | Yes |
| *V. phoenicium* | 2–4 | Purple | No |

| | | | |
|---|---|---|---|
| *-chaixii* (shay' zee-eye) | | Nettle-Leaved Mullein | 2–3'/3' |
| Late Spring | Yellow | Southern Europe | Zones 5–8 |

The stalked 3–6" long basal foliage is wedge shaped at the base with round-toothed (crenate) margins. The upper leaves are sessile with rounded bases. Leaves are green or slightly whitish green and hairy. The 1" diameter yellow flowers are held in tall racemes, each blossom bearing purple, woolly stamens. The inflorescences are unbranched initially but are many-branched as plants age.

Some authorities refer to this species as biennial, but it is perennial (although short lived) in most gardens. Well-drained soils in full sun are necessary for optimum performance. Spider mites find all verbascums particularly appealing and plants should be treated with miticides during the summer.

Seed germinates quickly under warm, moist conditions. Root cuttings may also be used for propagation. Take 3" long root cuttings in late winter or early spring and insert them upright in equal parts of moist sand and peat. Place them at 50–70° F and transplant when 3–4 leaves have developed.

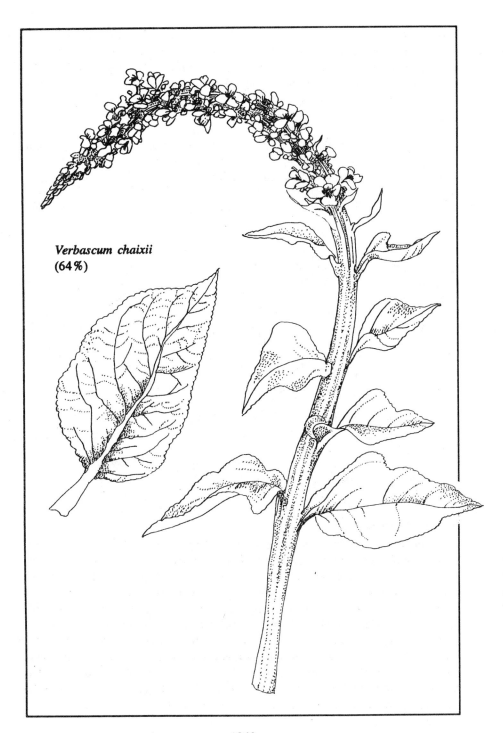

*Verbascum chaixii*
(64%)

## Cultivars:

Var. *album* has white flowers, but is otherwise similar to the species. The rose to purple stamens on the white backdrop of the petals give the flowers an attractive wine-pink hue. Flowers open about June 1 in zone 7 and remain for about 4 weeks.

## Related Species:

*V. nigrum*, dark mullein, has purple stamens, long pedicels and yellow flowers. The plants are barely pubescent. The flowers are only about ½" across and the inflorescence is unbranched. It is one of the parents (with *V. spinosum*, spiny mullein) of 'Golden Bush', an upright 2-3' tall, yellow-flowered mullein which sends up multitudes of stems and flowers for 4-6 weeks.

| *-olympicum* (o-lim' pi-cum) | | Olympic Mullein | 3-5'/4' |
|---|---|---|---|
| Summer | Yellow | Greece | Zones 6-8 |

This imposing, long-lived perennial requires good drainage, full sun and lots of space. Part of its appeal is the entire, white, woolly, 6-8" long leaves that are attractive even when the plant is not in flower. They are arranged in basal rosettes up to 3' across. The 1" diameter flowers are bright yellow with white-bearded stamens and held in branched 2-3' tall panicles. Plants remain in flower for 6-8 weeks and if spent inflorescences are removed, they can reflower in the fall.

The more I see this species, the more I appreciate it. It is too tall and gangly to be called beautiful but is more than just interesting. Plants are constantly changing and if provided with basic needs of moisture and sun, they will return for years and years. Fertilizer should be applied sparingly; plants grown in rich soils and treated too kindly reach heights of 7-8 feet.

Propagate by seed or root cuttings similar to *V. chaixii*.

## Related Species:

*V. bombyciferum* grows 5' tall, the entire plant being densely felted, especially the flowering spike. The sulphur yellow flowers are small (about 1" across) but numerous in a tall spike. 'Polar Summer' is commonly offered but is very similar to the species. Plants are biennial.

*V. leianthum* is a stately and incredibly impressive 6-8' tall plant with dozens of yellow flowers in summer. Probably hardy only to zone 7.

*V. widemannianum* grows to a flowering height of well over 4' but it is the wonderful white-hairy rosettes which give plants their beauty. The basal leaves are about 12" long and 4-5" wide. The stem leaves are less tomentose and smaller and bear branches of many 1-2" wide salmon to purplish flowers. A biennial, enjoy the explosion, then remove.

*-phoenicium* (foy-nee′ see-um)  Purple Mullein  2–4′/2′
   Spring    Purple, White    Southern Europe, Northern Asia  Zones 6–8

Dark green 18″ diameter rosettes of crinkled, shallowly lobed foliage give rise to 8–10 unbranched racemes, each bearing 1″ diameter rose-pink to purple flowers. Flowers are borne about 1 month earlier than those of *V. chaixii*. The leaves are smooth above and pubescent beneath. Plants can be quite variable and seedlings may yield flowers of purple, red, rose or white. Full sun and well-drained soils are best but plants tolerate afternoon shade, particularly south of zone 7. If over fertilized, it can grow to 5′.

This is a fair garden plant for the South but terribly susceptible to spider mites. Although tolerant of drought, it has never been outstanding in the Armitage garden for the 5 years I have grown it. Flowers are fleeting, blooming for about 2 weeks, and then disappear into anonymity.

Seed propagation is easy under moist, warm (70–75° F) conditions. Flower color will vary.

### Related Species:

*V.* × *hybridum* resulted from crosses between various vigorous species such as *V. pulverulentum*, *V. sinuatum*, *V. olympicum* and *V. phoenicium*. Many forms with large sterile flowers with slightly tomentose foliage have resulted. Flowers occur in late spring to early summer and cutting back the spent flowers results induces secondary inflorescences. Unfortunately, due to the biennial nature of many of the parents, they are short lived and only survive 2–3 years.

Propagate hybrids by root cuttings similar to *V. chaixii*.

### Hybrid Cultivars:

'Cotswold Gem' is 3–4′ tall and bears racemes of rosy flowers with purple centers. A number of other 'Cotswold' cultivars have appeared including 'Cotswold Beauty', dull yellow with lilac stamens, and 'Cotswold Queen' which produces terra-cotta flowers with maroon stamens.

'Domino' is a popular plant in the United States and produces 1–1½″ diameter rose-pink flowers on 3–3½′ long stalks.

'Gainsborough' has pale sulphur yellow flowers and gray-green leaves. It is about 3–4′ tall but can reach 5′ in rich soils.

'Golden Bush' grows about 2′ tall with pure yellow flowers on upright spikes.

'Hartleyi' sends up many shoots of large canary yellow flowers suffused with plum. A magnificent plant.

'Helen Johnson' bears dull green leaves and salmon-peach flowers with a darker eye, on 3–4′ tall stems. Lovely, but still too tall.

'Letitia' is only 1′ tall with abundant clear yellow flowers. Terrific for well-drained sunny locations, and exceptional for containers.

'Mt. Blanc' has foliage similar to 'Gainsborough' but bears white flowers.

'Royal Highland' has dense spikes of apricot-yellow flowers on 3′ tall stems.

'Silver Candleabra' bears 4–6' tall spikes of bright yellow flowers with silver woolly foliage.

Quick Key to Verbascum Species

>A. Flowers not yellow . . . . . . . . . . . . . . . . . . *V. phoenicium*
>AA. Flowers yellow or mainly yellow
>>B. Anthers purple, woolly, leaves with
>>rounded lobes, plant 2–3' tall . . . . . . . . . . . . . *V. chaixii*
>>BB. Anthers not purple, woolly,
>>leaves entire, plant 3–5' tall . . . . . . . . . . . . *V. olympicum*

**Additional Reading:**

Davis, Rosalie, H. 1986. Stalking the cultivated *Verbascum*. *Horticulture* 54(11):22–25.

*Verbena* (ver-been' a)          Vervain, Verbena          Verbenaceae

*Verbena* consists of approximately 250 species and 6 or 7 are in cultivation. The most common is the annual bedding plant, *V.* × *hybrida*, the result of hybridization of *V. peruviana*, *V. incisa*, *V. phlogifolia* and *V. platensis*. Demand for the annual is high and additional species are being incorporated into this stew every year. The annual hybrids so dominated the market that the perennial species were not as common as they should have been. However, a recent plethora of perennial hybrids has occurred and the verbena market is much stronger as a result of these improvements.

The perennial species are generally rose-purple, persistent bloomers, and hardy south of zone 6. Plants usually have opposite, dentate foliage, 4-sided stems and terminal flowers. They perform best in well-drained soils in full sun.

Verbena has numerous historical references, *V. officinalis* was the classical name for certain sacred branches and supposedly was used to staunch Christ's wounds on Calvary. Plants were also used medicinally, the term vervain is rooted in the celtic words *fer*, to remove, and *faen*, stone, referring to its use in treating bladder stones.

Quick Reference to Verbena Species

| | Height (in.) | Flower color | Upright or spreading |
|---|---|---|---|
| *V. bonariensis* | 36–48 | Violet | Upright |
| *V. canadensis* | 8–18 | Red, Pink | Spreading |
| *V. rigida* | 12–24 | Violet | Upright |
| *V. tenuisecta* | 8–12 | Purple | Spreading |

**-bonariensis** (bo-nah-ree-en' sis)   South American Verbena,   3–4'/3'
                                         Tall Verbena
Summer          Rose-Violet             South America              Zones 6–9

This is one of the taller verbenas and particularly effective in the middle of the border. It was named for the city of Buenos Aires, where first discovered. It has since become naturalized in the United States from South Carolina to Texas. The 4″ long elliptical leaves are sessile and clasp the stem. They are sharply serrated above the middle and entire towards the base. The wiry stems

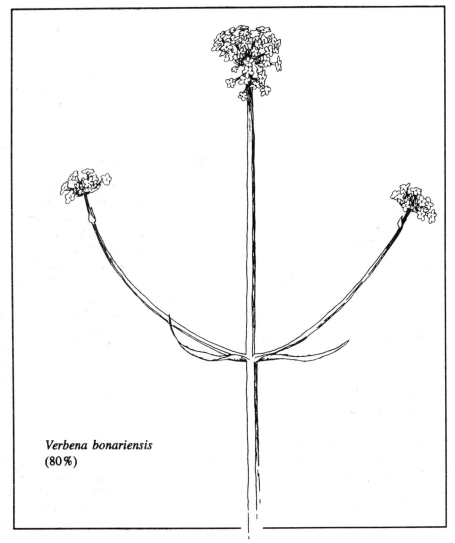

*Verbena bonariensis*
(80%)

are roughly hairy and conspicuously 4-angled. The flowers consist of 5 petals and a corolla tube nearly twice as long as the calyx. The individual flowers measure only about ¼" across but the entire panicle is 2–4" wide.

It is an excellent plant for many gardens but needs to be massed in groups. If grown in rich soil or over fertilized, it can easily reach 5' and require severe pruning. Cutting back the plant results in a many-branched specimen which takes on a shrub-like habit. Once in flower, it remains in bloom until frost. A drawback, however, is the susceptibility to powdery mildew, which should be treated with appropriate chemicals beginning in June. Personally, I prefer not to spray for mildew and although the white spots are unsightly, the disease does not appear to reduce vigor.

Propagate from root cuttings in the spring similarly to *Anemone* × *hybrida*. Seed sown in moist media should be placed at 40° F for 3–4 weeks, after which time the tray may be moved to 60–70° F temperatures. Germination is erratic and seedlings appear over a 3–5 week period. Two to three inch terminal cuttings of new spring growth may also be rooted and transplanted 3–5 weeks later.

-*canadensis* (kan-a-den' sis)    Clump Verbena, Rose Verbena    8–18"/36"
    Summer       Red, Pink       North America                  Zones 8–10

This species is usually treated as a annual in most of the country but is native from Virginia to Florida and west to Colorado and Mexico. The many-branched pubescent stems lie on the ground with the ends ascending (decumbent), and rooting may occur where the lower stems touch the soil. The deeply lobed ovate leaves are 1–3" long and about 1" wide with a triangular to wedge-shaped base. The rose-red to pink corolla tube is about twice as long as the calyx but each flower is only about ½" wide. Up to 20 flowers may be present on each of the stalked spikes.

This species has an excellent clumping habit and may be cut back severely if the stems lose leaves or become too long. A sunny place in the border with excellent drainage is necessary. If drainage is poor, plant vigor declines rapidly and no amount of corrective surgery will improve its demeanor. Like other members of the genus, susceptibility to mildew and spider mites are problems.

### Cultivars:

All of these are likely hybrids, with *V. canadensis* as an important parent.

*Lavender:*

'Abbeville' was found by Richard Berry of Goodness Grows Nursery, Lexington, GA near the town of Abbeville, SC. Flowers are a cool light lavender with a tiny hint of white. Vigorous.

'Lavender' bears lavender flowers with a trace of white and 'Rosea' has bright rose-red blooms. Both grow 8–12" tall.

'Lavender Lace', from Steve Woods of Woods Cottage Nursery in Perth, Australia, bears flowers with a subtle blend of lavender and white. Outstanding in the heat.

*Pink:*

'Appleblossom' has pale pink lightly fragrant flowers. More dwarf than most of the canadensis forms. Moderate vigor.

'Pink Parfait' bears handsome pink and white flowers. In our trials, plants weren't as vigorous as many other cultivars. However, it still enjoys many followers.

'Sarah Groves', named for the grand-dame of Southern gardening, Sarah Groves of Oxford, GA, bears clusters of soft pale pink flowers which change to a richer pink with age. Almost a bicolor.

'Silver Anne', from England, is one of the best warm pinks around. Vigorous and handsome without being gaudy. I have seen plants of this called 'Homestead Pink' but to my eye, they are identical to 'Silver Anne', and 'Silver Anne' they should be called. Let's not get carried away with this Homestead thing.

*Reds/Pinks:*

'Big Red' (formerly but no longer called 'Homestead Red') from Robbrick Nursery, FL also has good red flowers, a little smaller than the previous two. Between this and the other three red cultivars, there is a good choice for red-flowered verbenas.

'Evelyn Scott' is a good true red from Goodness Grows Nursery. Floriferous with moderate vigor.

'Gene Cline', named after plantsman Gene Cline of Canton, Georgia, is about 6–9″ tall and bears deep rose flowers. An excellent ground cover for sunny well-drained areas.

'Graystone Daphne' produces fragrant pink-lavender flowers on 8″ tall plants.

'Marie's Rose' bears red-purple flowers on vigorous 8–10″ plants.

'Pink Sunrise', introduced by Plants Delight Nursery, has coral-pink flowers on 6″ plants.

'Taylortown Red' is a fine form from McCorkles Nursery, GA and is similar to 'Evelyn Scott'. Good red color, perhaps a little more vigorous and more floriferous than Evelyn.

'Summer Blaze' (formerly 'Clear Red') supposedly has clear red flowers and good vigor. I have not yet trailed this so do not know if it differs from the next three.

*Purple/Magenta:*

'Batesville Rose', from Greg Grant, is packed with magenta-rose flowers. Very eye-catching.

'Homestead Purple' really kicked the verbena market in the backside, causing the interest in many other cultivars to be rekindled. The dark purple flowers are early and plants are vigorous, eating up all competition around them.

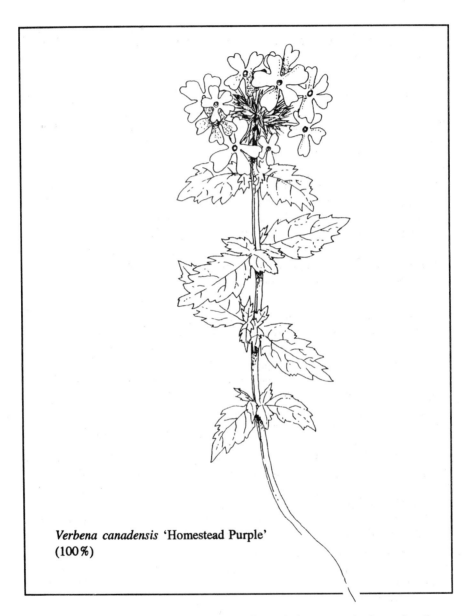

*Verbena canadensis* 'Homestead Purple'
(100%)

The name Homestead came from the Georgia homestead where the plants were found and does not designate a series of colors. Other cultivars with the Homestead name have nothing to do with 'Homestead Purple' in vigor, flower or form.

'Ultramarine' is equally vigorous to 'Homestead Purple' and has a slightly different shade of purple.

*White:*

'Snowflurry', from Garden Delights Nursery, Raleigh, NC is a semi-upright vigorous "virtual flowering machine." White flowers and true from seed.

*Two to Three tones:*

'Carrousel' is an older form with lavender and white flowers. Not as vigorous.

'Lulu Norris' from Ladyslipper Rare Plant Nursery in Woodstock, GA, selected this tricolor form with the top of the flowers purple-violet, the bottom light purple and set off with a clear white center.

'Fiesta' introduced by Greg Grant, has large bright pink flowers with flecks of purple that intensify with age.

'Texas Form' has flowers said to be a blend of medium red on the upper petals changing to a light pink on the lower petals.

**Related Species:**

*V. peruviana*, Peruvian verbena, hugs the ground and bears bright scarlet flowers. The leaves are not as incised or deeply cut as *V. canadensis*, nor are plants as tall or as winter hardy (zones 8–10).

| | | |
|---|---|---|
| *-rigida* (ri' gi-da) | Veined Verbena, Rigid Verbena | 12–24"/18" |
| Summer    Purple | Brazil, Argentina | Zones 7–10 |
| (Syn. *V. venosa*) | | |

This South American species has become naturalized from North Carolina to Florida, and gardeners are taking advantage of the heat and drought tolerance and persistent flowering, continuing through mid-October in milder gardens. Tuberous roots are formed, which if mulched heavily in the fall, survive as far north as zone 7. The 4-angled stems, similar to those of *V. bonariensis*, bear oblong, rigid, sessile leaves. Each 2–4" long leaf is roughly pubescent and has wide spreading teeth. The intense purple flowers are about ½" wide and consist of a ½" long corolla tube 2–3 times longer than the calyx. In general, this plant looks like a miniature *V. bonariensis* with similar cultural and propagation requirements. An excellent front of the border species, it requires no pruning to maintain vigor or habit.

Propagate similar to *V. bonariensis*.

**Cultivars:**

'Flame' stands only 6" tall and produces an abundance of scarlet flowers. It is more vigorous than the species and spreads more rapidly. It is likely a hybrid between *V. rigida* and another low-growing species such as *V. canadensis*.

'Lilacina' has purple-blue flowers.

'Polaris' bears lavender-blue flowers on compact 12–15" tall plants. They are very handsome but can reseed everywhere.

**-tenuisecta** (ten-you-I-sec' ta)   Moss Verbena        8–12″/Spreading
   Spring         Lavender      Southern South America    Zones 7–10
(Syn. *V. erinoides*)

Here is a plant which should be as common in the South as bedstraw is in
the North. Naturalized from southern Georgia to Louisiana and south to
Florida, it flourishes by roadsides and in fields. Many decumbent stems bear
triangular leaves about 1–1½″ long which are divided into linear segments. The
spikes are terminal, solitary and composed of 5–15 small (½″ wide) lavender
flowers. The flowers are about 1′ long and compactly arranged when they first
open but elongate to 1½″ or more as the flowers mature.

*Verbena tenuisecta*
(64%)

I first obtained 8 terminal cuttings from south Georgia and plants rooted in less than 2 weeks and carpeted 20–30 square feet in the first 6 weeks. It overwinters in zone 7b two years out of 5 and thus I take cuttings in the fall and overwinter them. Given sufficient protection, it is hardy in zone 8. If plants become leggy, they may be sheared with a lawnmower to 2″ tall and they return as fresh as ever. If sheared too close to the ground they will take a long time to fill in. For gardeners further north, it makes an excellent annual. Although not as colorful as the annual hybrids, it requires far less maintenance and provides better garden performance.

Propagation is easy from 2–3″ terminal cuttings taken any time in the season. Rooting occurs in 5–8 days if cuttings are placed in a moist, warm area.

**Cultivars:**

The cutleaf forms resulted from *V. tenuisecta, V. tenera* and hybrids between them. They are usually lower to the ground, have deeply cut almost lacy leaves and flower throughout the summer. Cold hardy to zone 7 at best.

*White:*

'Alba' is the white form sometimes available from seed. Altough not quite as floriferous or vigorous as the species itself, it provides a good low growing white.

*Pink:*

'Cotton Candy' ('Texas Cotton Candy') bears medium pink flowers with a white center. Slow growing, but handsome. Raised by Greg Grant.

'Edith' has lavender pink flowers over deeply cut foliage. Compact and floriferous, named for Edith Eddelman of the North Carolina Botanic Garden in Raleigh, NC.

'Flamingo Border Pink' from Edith Eddelman is a lacy foliaged plant with red violet flowers.

'Sissinghurst' is an excellent cultivar with coral pink flowers and lacy foliage. Likely a cultivar of *V. tenera*, but who cares. Has been sold as 'St. Paul', 'Rosea', and 'Tex Tuf Pink'.

'Tapien Pink' is a vigorous cut leaf form which appears to be less susceptible to mildew. Arose from Proven Winners breeders. The best pink verbena I have ever grown.

*Purple:*

'Imagination' from Benary Seed is the most well known and one of the few available from seed. Very similar to the wild *V. tenuisecta* of the Southeast.

'Maonettii' ('Aphrodite') has purple flowers with white edges. Low to the ground and not as rapid a grower as many others.

'Michelle' comes from Garden Delights in Raleigh, NC and produces vivid purple flowers on mats of foliage.

'Royalty' from Greg Grant, bears dense cutleaf foliage over which dark purple flowers abound. Very low growing, quite vigorous.

'Sterling Star' is a new cutleaf form with lighter lavender blue flowers than 'Imagination'. Also from seed.

'Tapien Blue' is a vigorous lavender-blue flowered form. Relatively resistant to mildew.

'Tex Tuf Purple' has small violet purple flowers over cut foliage. Also sold as 'Texas Peruviana'.

### Quick Key to Verbena Species

 A. Plant upright, flowers borne in panicles or cymes
  B. Plant 1–2' tall, corolla tube
   2–3 times longer than calyx . . . . . . . . . . . . . . . *V. rigida*
  BB. Plant 3–5' tall, corolla tube
   1½–2 times longer than calyx . . . . . . . . . . *V. bonariensis*
 AA. Plant spreading, flowers borne in spikes
  B. Flowers lavender, purple, foliage
   cut into linear divisions . . . . . . . . . . . . . . . *V. tenuisecta*
  BB. Flowers red, rose, foliage not
   cut into linear divisions . . . . . . . . . . . . . . . *V. canadensis*

**Additional Reading:**

Armitage, A.M. 1995. Verbena, what's going on out there. *Greenhouse Grower Magazine*. Sept. 87–89.

Armitage, A.M. 1996. Verbena revisited. *Greenhouse Grower Magazine*. Oct. 36–38.

## *Vernonia* (ver-non' ee-a)     Ironweed     Asteraceae

The ironweeds are native to the tropics and regions of North America. This is a huge genus, consisting of approximately 1000 species, although most have been left to their own devices in the wild, and only a handful have graced the garden. The plants are often large, being small trees, shrubs or robust perennials characterized by alternate, usually simple, leaves with clusters of rose or purple flowers in the fall. The flowers are all tubular, consisting of disk flowers only and surrounded by bracts. The flower color takes on rusty shades that account for its common name. The species I have tried are reasonably ornamental, very vigorous and provide some good fall color in a garden that is tired out from the summer. All require full sun; plants grow well in moist soils or in drought conditions.

The most popular species is *V. noveboriensis*, New York ironweed, which grows 3–7' tall. The plants have pointed lanceolate leaves which are entire or slightly toothed. Each flower head may be 6–8" across and consists of 30–50 flowers. *V. glauca* is similar but has a pale undersurface to the leaves. Both of these species make excellent backdrops in the garden and need not be relegated to the "wildflower" garden, whatever that means. If the mature height is too tall, use the Armitage technique for height control;

whack them back. Cut them back hard about a month after emergence. This results in shorter as well as better filled out plants.

A naturally shorter species is *V. fasciculata*, which grows about 3' tall, although 2' plants are touted but 6' specimens can also occur, particularly in shaded areas. Native to prairies and moist woodlands from North Dakota to Oklahoma, plants are resilient and long lived. The purple flower heads are smaller than the previous species and consist of about 30 small flowers per head. *V. altissima* (syn. *V. gigantea*) grows 4–6' tall in gardens and has finely toothed narrow leaves and small purple flower heads. These ironweeds are cold hardy to at least zone 5, many into zone 3 and south to zone 8.

## *Veronica* (ve-ron' i-ca)   Speedwell   Scrophulariaceae

There are about 250 species including a dozen herbaceous members suitable for the garden. The name "Veronica" is thought to have arisen because markings on the flowers of some species resemble the markings on the sacred handkerchief of St. Veronica. One species, *V. officinalis*, was substituted for tea in Europe until the 19th century. Most species have opposite leaves, and flowers are usually held in racemes. In general, *Veronica* has blue flowers but *V. peduncularis* is a wonderful 8–12" tall species with white flowers tinged with rose. A new cultivar of this species, 'Georgia Blue', has blue flowers on 12" tall mats.

Species vary from the prostrate *V. repens*, creeping speedwell, to the 4' tall *V. longifolia*, long leaf speedwell. Identification between some species is difficult and the length of the pedicel (individual flower stalk) in relation to the length of the sepals is a useful identification characteristic.

Full sun and well-drained soils are their only demands, otherwise they are relatively easy to grow. Significant variability occurs in some species, particularly *V. teucrium*, Hungarian speedwell (*V. austriaca* ssp. *teucrium*) and nursery catalogs may list the same cultivar under 2 or 3 different species. The genus is undergoing continued taxonomic scrutiny so names continue to change or to be swallowed up in other species.

Quick Reference to Veronica Species

|  | Height (in.) | Flower color | Inflorescence terminal or axillary |
|---|---|---|---|
| *V. alpina* | 4–8 | Blue | Terminal |
| *V. austriaca* ssp. *teucrium* | 6–20 | Deep blue | Axillary |
| *V. gentianoides* | 6–20 | Pale blue | Terminal |
| *V. incana* | 12–18 | Blue | Terminal |
| *V. longifolia* | 24–48 | Lilac | Terminal |
| *V. pectinata* | 3–6 | Deep blue | Axillary |
| *V. prostrata* | 3–8 | Blue | Axillary |
| *V. spicata* | 10–36 | Blue | Terminal |

| *-alpina* (al-pine′ a) | | Alpine Speedwell | 4–8″/12″ |
|---|---|---|---|
| Spring | Blue | Europe, Asia | Zones 3–8 |

This small, undemanding plant bears shiny green entire leaves about 1–1½″ long. The upper leaves are larger than the lower and all are elliptical to oblong. Plants spread by a creeping rootstock but are not rampant. The flowers are up to ¼″ across and held in a dense spike-like raceme. Each raceme persists for at least one week.

This plant performs almost as well in the heat of zone 8 as in the cool of zone 3. The flowers are borne in the spring and continue off and on again in September and October in the South. Plants are evergreen in the South but die back in the North. It is an excellent plant for the front of the border or for the rock garden.

Propagate by division in the spring or fall. Seed germinates quickly when sown in moist media and placed in warm humid conditions.

### Cultivars:

'Alba' is a white-flowered form which has essentially replaced the species in cultivation. It is vigorous and free flowering.

'Goodness Grows' is an outstanding long-flowering hybrid which likely arose from *V. alpina* 'Alba' and *V. spicata* at Goodness Grows Nursery in Lexington, Georgia. It has the low-growing habit (10–12″) of the former and the long blue racemes of the latter.

| *-austriaca* (ow-stree-ah′ ca) | | Austrian Speedwell | 2–3′/2′ |
|---|---|---|---|
| Summer | Blue | Mainland Europe | Zones 4–7 |

(Syn. *V. latifolia*)

Recent taxonomic reshuffling has forced me to include this species, although it is seldom, if ever, found in commerce. The stems are usually erect, although they may be somewhat drooping to procumbent (on ground). The lavender flowers always arise from the leaf axils and are never terminal.

The form found in catalogs and gardens is a subspecies, ssp. *teucrium* (syn. *V. teucrium*) and all the named cultivars are less than 2′ tall with blue flowers. This is such a variable group that some botanists divide it into 5 subgroups. For our purposes, it is a low-growing, prostrate plant with ascending sterile and flowering stems. The 1½″ long leaves are ovate to oblong and more or less toothed or sometimes slightly lobed. They resemble the leaves of germander, *Teucrium*, thus its specific epithet. The ½″ wide flowers arise in elongated axillary racemes from the upper 2–3 nodes. The lack of terminal flowers is a defining identification characteristic for this species. When in flower, plants are a sea of blue. In zone 7, flowers open in early May and persist for about 4 weeks. In Philadelphia (zone 6), flowering begins about 2 weeks later. In warm climates, cut back hard after flowering. It does best in full sun but will also tolerate some afternoon shade.

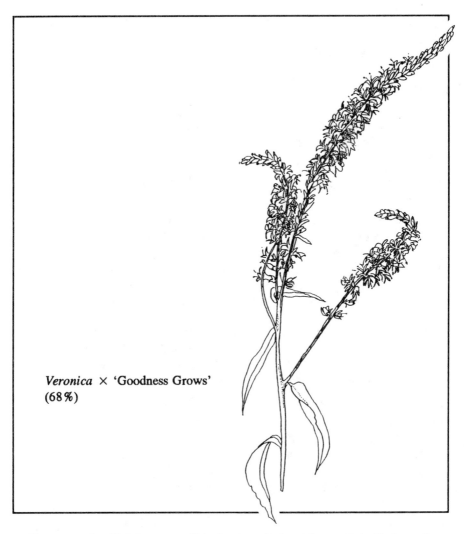

*Veronica* × 'Goodness Grows'
(68%)

Propagate by division as well as by terminal cuttings of sterile branches. Seed may be treated similar to *V. incana*.

**Cultivars of ssp. *teucrium*:**

'Blue Fountain' is more erect and one of the tallest selections of this species. It has dense bright blue racemes on 20-24″ tall plants.

'Crater Lake Blue' is an outstanding 12-15″ selection with short racemes of intense blue flowers. It is one of the best cultivars for filling in a sunny area in the front of the garden.

'Knallblau' produces dozens of rich blue-purple flowers on 6-9″ tall plants.

'Royal Blue' bears deep blue flowers on 12-18″ tall bushy plants.

'Shirley Blue' is only about 8″ tall with short, dense racemes of mid to dark blue flowers.

'True Blue' is an excellent 12″ tall, free-flowering cultivar with deep blue flowers.

### Related Species:

*V. repens*, creeping speedwell, is a prostrate species that loves to scramble over rocks or walls in full sun and well-drained conditions. The light blue to almost white flowers are held in terminal racemes and appear in late summer.

| *-gentianoides* (gen-tee-a-noi′ deez) | | Gentian Speedwell | 6–20″/18″ |
|---|---|---|---|
| Spring | Pale Blue | Caucasus | Zones 4–7 |

For reasons I do not comprehend, this species is seldom seen in American gardens. Flowering stems with small bract-like leaves rise above rosettes consisting of many entire 1–3″ long leaves. The ½″ wide, pale blue to almost white flowers (not at all gentian) are held in loose 10″ long racemes. It differs from most upright garden species in that the pedicel (the connecting stem between the flower and the raceme) is much longer than the sepals. Usually the pedicel is about the same size or shorter. When not in flower, the creeping root-stock forms dense mats of glossy foliage. This useful plant suits the front to mid-border and is useful for the rock garden because of its mat-forming tendencies.

Full sun and well-drained soil should be provided. It is more tolerant of moist soils than other species and should not be allowed to dry out.

Propagate similar to *V. alpina*.

### Cultivars:

'Variegata' has white margined foliage but flowers are similar to the species. Splashes of white appear on the basal leaves but are not particularly obvious. The variegation is most obvious on the small stem leaves where each margin is dressed in pure white. Much more interesting than the species.

| *-incana* (in-kah′ na) | | Woolly Speedwell | 12–18″/18″ |
|---|---|---|---|
| Summer | Blue | Russia | Zones 3–7 |

Without getting into the discussion, let it be known that many taxonomists and indeed growers, treat this as a subspecies of *V. spicata* (*V. spicata* ssp. *incana*). Therefore in trying to find some of the cultivars listed here, be sure to check under *V. spicata* as well. For me, there are enough garden differences that I have left well enough alone.

This is one of the few veronicas grown for the foliage as well as the flowers. The 1–3″ long toothed leaves are white-tomentose, resulting in an overall silvery-gray appearance. The lower leaves are matted and oblong while the uppermost are lanceolate; all are narrowed at the base. Small blue flowers (¼″

across) are borne on short pedicels in 3–6″ long terminal racemes and persist for about 4 weeks. This is a popular edging plant that provides good foliage contrast. Plants perform poorly in high heat and high rainfall areas because the hairy leaves trap moisture, resulting in foliar disease.

Provide full sun to partial shade in well-drained soils. Plants particularly dislike wet, cold soils.

Divide the plants in spring or take 2″ long terminal cuttings from the sterile basal branches during the summer. Sow the fine seed in a well-drained medium and barely cover. If seed is covered too deeply, germination is poor. After germination, reduce the temperature to approximately 60° F.

## Cultivars:
'Candidissima' has 6″ long leaves that are not as tomentose as the species. Otherwise, plants are similar.

'Glauca' bears more silvery foliage and deeper blue flowers than the species.

'Romilley Purple' bears deep violet-blue flowers on 2′ tall stems. Although popular in Europe, it is difficult to find in this country. Likely has some *V. spicata* in the parentage.

'Rosea' has a pink tinge to the flowers.

'Saraband' is about 18″ tall with compact gray-green leaves over which are produced dense racemes of violet-blue flowers. This is a hybrid with one of the forms of *V. spicata*.

'Silver Carpet' bear gray-green foliage and erect purple flowers. Plants are about 12″ tall.

'Silver Slippers' is an interesting if not colorful selection. The gray lance-like leaves form a dense low growing mat but few or no flowers are produced. Good for rock gardens where drainage is excellent.

'Wendy' is also a hybrid with *V. spicata* and bears grayish foliage and lavender-blue flowers. It grows to 2′ tall.

## Related Species:
*V. cinerea*, ashen speedwell, has mounds of thyme-like silvery leaves and pale blue flowers.

*V. bombycina*, cotton speedwell, native of Turkey to Lebanon, forms dense cushions of densely white-hairy leaves. Beautiful in leaf and even nicer when the silver-blue flowers appear. Better in cooler climate and low humidity.

| *-longifolia* (long-gi-fo′ lee-a) | | Long-Leaf Veronica | 2–4′/2′ |
| Summer | Lilac | Europe, Asia | Zones 4–8 |

Heights of 2½′ are average but 3½–4′ tall plants occur in rich soils and warm climates. The stem is hairless or nearly so and the 2½–4″ long leaves are sharply toothed and pointed. Leaves are oblong to lanceolate with slightly hairy undersides. The lower leaves are opposite but the uppermost are often arranged in whorls. The ¼" wide flowers are arranged in dense 12" long racemes. Flowering persists for 6-8 weeks. This tall lanky plant is most effective in groups of 3 or more. If placed in too much shade or fed too generously, staking is required. This is more of a problem in the South than in the North. The species is native to moist areas and does poorly if soil is allowed to dry out.

Propagate by division in the spring or sow seed similar to *V. incana*.

### Cultivars:

Var. *alba* is 1½' tall and bears white flowers.

'Blaureisen' is an excellent blue upright form which is especially suitable for cut flowers. Often sold as 'Foerster's Blue' but they are not the same.

'Blue Giant' is 3-3½' tall with lavender-blue flowers.

'Foerster's Blue' stands 1-2' tall and produces deep blue flowers for 8 weeks in the summer.

Var. *glauca* has deep purple flowers and blue-green foliage.

'Icicle' is a fine white flowered veronica and is probably a hybrid with *V. longifolia* var. *subsessilis* and *V. spicata*. It grows 18-24" tall and flowers from June to September.

'Rosea' is greatly branched and has rose-pink flowers. Plants can attain heights of 3'.

'Schneerriesen' bears good white flowers on 18-20" tall plants. Good cut flower form.

Var. *subsessilis* is one of the best, most popular forms. It is 2-3' tall, much more branched and compact with longer inflorescences and larger flowers than the type. Flowering occurs about 2 weeks later than the species.

### Related Species:

*V. exaltata* is closely related and considered a synonym by many taxonomists. It blooms in mid to late summer and bears light blue ¼" diameter flowers in dense terminal racemes. Plants grow 4' tall but little or no staking is required.

*V. spuria*, bastard speedwell, is similar to *V. longifolia* but is distinguished by the triangular leaf base (cuneate) and the loose arrangement of flowers on the raceme. Leaves are occasionally arranged in whorls. Var. *elegans* produces more stems and has downy leaves.

| *-pectinata* (pek-ti-nah' ta) | | Comb Speedwell | 3-6"/Spreading |
|---|---|---|---|
| Spring | Deep Blue | Asia Minor | Zones 2-7 |

This prostrate species is particularly useful for edging or for dry areas in the rock garden. The base of the plant is woody and the foliage forms a dense evergreen mat. The sessile, oval leaves are ½-¾" long and covered with long white hairs. They are bluntly toothed and somewhat resemble the teeth of a comb, thus earning the plant's common name. It spreads by rooting at the nodes of the prostrate stems. The axils of the ascending stems bear 3–5" long, many-flowered, elongated racemes consisting of ¼" diameter blue flowers with white centers.

Native to dry, shady areas, plants are more tolerant of drier conditions than other species. Good drainage and full sun to partial shade are ideal.

Propagate by division in early spring or treat seed similar to *V. incana*.

**Cultivars:**

Var. *rosea* has numerous racemes of rose-pink flowers. The racemes are a little shorter (2–4" long) than the type but otherwise few differences are obvious.

| | | |
|---|---|---|
| *-prostrata* (pros-trah' ta) | Harebell Speedwell | 3–8"/Spreading |
| Summer      Blue | Europe, Northern Asia | Zones 5–8 |
| (Syn. *V. rupestris*) | | |

Plants produce both sterile and flowering stems. The sterile stems remain prostrate and form mats of grayish green, slightly hairy foliage. The ascending flowering stems grow to 8" tall. Ovate to linear leaves are wedge shaped at the base and ½–1" long. They have a neat serration along the edges and are completely covered in flowers in the spring. Short dense racemes of pale to deep blue, ⅓" diameter starry flowers are formed in the axils of the ascending stems.

This is a fine plant for front of the garden, rockeries or edging. When the flowers cover the foliage, they provide brief (2–4 weeks) but brilliant spots of color throughout the garden. If the mats of foliage become too vigorous, they may be pruned to desirable proportions. Provide full sun and well-drained soil. These are tough plants, able to withstand the abuse of rock crawlers and dogs, and persist for many years if properly sited. It is brilliant at the Denver Botanic Garden, often blooming through late snowfalls.

Propagate by division or by seed similar to *V. incana*.

**Cultivars:**

'Alba' produces white flowers.
'Blue Sheen' has small racemes of wisteria-blue flowers on 2–3" tall plants.
'Heavenly Blue' has gained immense popularity. It bears sapphire blue flowers and creeps along at a height of about 2–4".
'Loddon Blue' has rich deep blue flowers and is about 4" tall.
'Mrs. Holt' has bright pink flowers in the summer and grows about 6" tall. It is not as vigorous as the type.
'Spode Blue' bears light blue flowers.
'Purpurea' produces deep violet flowers.
'Trehane' has bright yellow-green foliage from which arise short racemes of deep blue flowers. The plants are 6–8" tall.

| | | | |
|---|---|---|---|
| ***-spicata*** (spee-kah′ ta) | | Spiked Speedwell | 10–36″/24″ |
| Summer | Blue | Europe, Northern Asia | Zones 3–7 |

One of the most popular veronicas in North American gardens, it is also the parent of many hybrid cultivars. The 2″ long glossy leaves are lanceolate and toothed except at the base and tip. The blue flowers are only about ¼″ in diameter but have long purple stamens. They are held in dense 1–3′ long spike-like racemes. Flower color ranges from deep blue to white with an occasional light pink. Flowers are produced for 4–7 weeks and provide excellent color for the front and middle of the garden. Plants require sunny well-drained conditions. In the South, winter drainage is particularly important because plants succumb to many root rot organisms which proliferate in wet, cool soils.

Propagation of the species and varieties from seed is similar to *V. incana*. Terminal cuttings and divisions are the best means to propagate cultivars.

**Cultivars:**

'Alba' is similar to the species but with white flowers.

'Barcarolle' was raised at Bloom's Nursery in Diss, England and is one of a number of hybrids between *V. incana* and *V. spicata*. It has rose-pink flowers, stands 12–15″ tall and has leaves which are somewhat gray-green, due to the influence of *V. incana*.

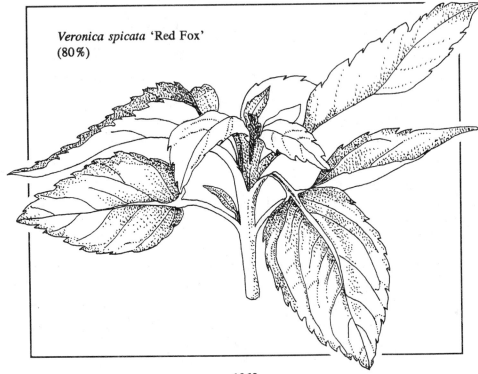

*Veronica spicata* 'Red Fox'
(80%)

'Blue Banquet' is a seed-propagated hybrid from Pan-American Seed Co. in West Chicago. Its deep blue flowers are not unique but the foliage is glossy green and less susceptible to foliar diseases.

'Blue Charm' is one of the taller members of the group. Plants grow nearly 3' tall and produce lavender-blue flowers in early to mid summer.

'Blue Fox' has bright lavender-blue flowers on 15-20" tall stems.

'Blue Peter' grows 24" tall and produces dark blue flowers on 12" spikes.

'Blue Spires' has glossy green leaves and many deep blue flower spikes on 12-18" tall plants. Plants flower for about 4 weeks in late June and July in the Georgia Horticulture Gardens.

'Heidekind' is 8-10" tall with compact rose pink spikes in late spring. It is not as cold hardy as the species and does poorly north of zone 5.

'Minuet' has a similar parentage to 'Barcarolle' and grows 12-18" tall. The foliage is grayer than that of 'Barcarolle'.

Var. *nana* is similar to the species but only about 8" tall.

'Noah Williams' is a variegated form with white margins and creamy white flowers.

'Red Fox' has deep rosy-red flowers and glossy leaves. It stands about 15" tall, is free flowering and blooms for over 5 weeks.

Var. *rosea* has pinker flowers than the above cultivar.

'Sightseeing Mix' is a seed-propagated mixture of blues, pinks and lavenders on 18" tall plants. Vigorous and a good performer.

'Snow White' has branching spikes of white flowers on 18" tall stems.

'Waterperry' is a wonderful 4-6" tall plant with dozens of light blue flowers in the spring or early summer. Great in open rocky areas where it can be allowed to spread.

**Related Species:**

*V. pinnata* is 8-12" tall with numerous finely divided 2½" long leaves. The flowers are dark blue on branched racemes. 'Blue Eyes' has lighter blue flowers than the species and is only about 10" tall.

'Sunny Border Blue' is 18-24" tall with violet-blue flowers in mid summer to fall. Introduced into the trade in 1946 by Robert Bennerup of Sunny Border Nurseries, Kensington, Connecticut. It is such a good plant that it was the Perennial Plant of the Year in 1993.

Quick Key to Veronica Species

    A. Inflorescence axillary
      B. Calyx (sepals) with 5 lobes
        C. Non-flowering stems ascending . . *V. austriaca* ssp. *teucrium*
        CC. Non-flowering stems prostrate . . . . . . . . . . *V. prostrata*
      BB. Calyx with 4 lobes . . . . . . . . . . . . . . . . . . . *V. pectinata*
    AA. Inflorescence terminal
      B. Plants 4-8" tall . . . . . . . . . . . . . . . . . . . . . . . *V. alpina*

BB. Plants greater than 8″ tall
    C. Leaves white woolly . . . . . . . . . . . . . . . . . . *V. incana*
    CC. Leaves not white woolly, but may be hairy
        D. Pedicels much longer than the sepals . . . *V. gentianoides*
        DD. Pedicels same size as or shorter than sepals
            E. Entire length of leaf sharply
              serrated, leaves often whorled . . . . . . *V. longifolia*
           EE. Leaves not toothed at base or tip,
              leaves opposite, not whorled . . . . . . . . . *V. spicata*

**Additional Reading:**

DeWolf, Gordon, P. Jr. 1956. Notes on cultivated Schrophulariaceae. 4. Veronica. *Baileya* 4:143–159.

Kelaidis, Panayoti. 1992. Veronicas, adaptable perennials bloom in vivid blues. *Fine Gardening* 25(May/June):34–38.

McClintock, David. 1989. A new—presumably hybrid—veronica. *The Plantsman* 10(4):214–215.

Ruffier-Lanche, R. 1958. Notes on some veronicas. *Baileya* 6:55–57.

## *Veronicastrum* (ve-ro-ni-kas′ trum)   Culver's Root   Scrophulariaceae

The are two species, the most commonly cultivated one being culver's root, *V. virginicum*, which has been tossed back and forth between this genus and *Veronica*, obviously indicative of the close taxonomic relationship.

| *-virginicum* (vir-jin′ i-cum) | Culver's Root | 4–6′/4′ |
|---|---|---|
| Late Summer   Pale Blue, White | Eastern United States | Zones 4–8 |

The lanceolate leaves are arranged in whorls of 3–6 around the un-branched stems. Each pointed leaf is 2–4″ long, sharply toothed, smooth above and somewhat pubescent below. The pinkish white to pale blue ¼″ long flowers are arranged in dense, terminal, erect 6–9″ long racemes. After flowering, lateral racemes take over resulting in a 4–6 week flowering period. Plants make excellent cut flowers and a good trick to obtain fuller stems is to remove the terminal flower bud as soon as it can be handled. This results in the lateral flowers opening together.

This is an imposing plant if grown in full sun, watered well and fertilized 2–3 times a year. If placed in partial shade, plants need support and are rather unattractive.

Propagate by seed similar to *Veronica incana*, but germination requires 4–6 weeks. Terminal cuttings (remove flowers) and divisions are also used.

**Cultivars:**

'Album' has pure white flowers more persistent than those of the species. Much more common than the blue forms and an exceptional garden plant.

'Roseum' bears pink flowers.

**Related Species:**

*V. sibiricum* is the Russian representative which is similar in habit and size. The flowers are blue. Perhaps more cold hardy (zone 3) than our native and useful for gardeners who can't overwinter *V. virginicum*.

## *Vinca* (ving- ka)                    Vinca, Periwinkle                    Apocynaceae

Of the 12 species, 2 are popular ground covers. In some parts of the country, small oceans of periwinkle may be found around every corner. All species have opposite leaves and solitary flowers borne in the leaf axils. The annual bedding plant, Madagascar periwinkle, formally called *Vinca rosea*, is correctly known as *Catharanthus roseus*.

---

*-major* (may' jor)           Large Periwinkle           12–18"/24"
   Spring           Blue           Europe           Zones 7–9

Due to the lack of winter hardiness, *V. major* is seldom used as an outdoor ground cover north of zone 6, and even there, some protection is necessary. The non-flowering stems are prostrate while the ascending flowering stems bear 2–3" long glossy, ovate, evergreen leaves with small hairs on the margins. The blue, funnel-shaped flowers are 1–2" in diameter with sepals almost as long as the corolla tube. They are borne in abundance in early spring and sporadically throughout the summer. Non-flowering stems root at the tips where they touch the ground. If provided with moist soils in partial shade, plants fill in vigorously. It is also an excellent plant for trailing over banks, or cascading from window boxes or planters. More variegated plants are probably sold for large wooden and clay pots than for ground covers in the North.

Propagate by terminal cuttings of non-flowering stems in late spring or divide throughout the season.

**Cultivars:**

'Alba' has white flowers.

'Aureomaculata' ('Maculata', 'Oxford') has leaves with dark green margins and lighter yellowish green centers. Arose from a sport of 'Variegata'.

'Aureomarginata' bears green leaves with bright yellow margins. The yellow color is deepest in the spring and tends to fade in the summer.

'Hirsuta' ('Pubescens') bears more pubescent leaves than the species and red-purple flowers with narrow petals. The petals of the purple flowers are narrower than the species. It is similar in flower to 'Oxyloba' but is more hairy on the petioles and the corolla tube.

'Oxyloba' produces leaves more lanceolate than the species. The deep purple flowers are much more narrow than the species and even more narrow than 'Hirsuta'.

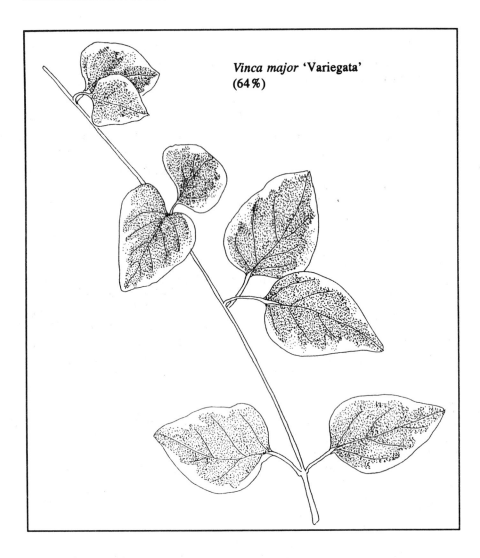

*Vinca major* 'Variegata'
(64%)

'Reticulata' has foliage netted with yellow lines.
'Variegata' ('Elegantissima') is popular in hanging baskets and window
   boxes. Plants have dark green leaves with irregular yellow-white
   margins, and blue flowers.

| | | | |
|---|---|---|---|
| ***-minor*** (mine' or) | | Common Periwinkle | 6–12″/Spreading |
| Spring | Blue | Europe | Zones 4–9 |

   That this species is so widely used in the United States testifies to its
toughness and ability to tolerate a wide range of climatic conditions. Such

a lovely plant has a rather gruesome history. In the Middle Ages, it adorned the heads of criminals on their way to execution and in Italy was called *Fiore di morte* because it was placed on the bodies of dead infants. However, not everyone shared such gloom and plants soon became known as Joy of the Ground, a name occasionally used today.

*V. minor* consists of non-flowering stems which root at all nodes, with elliptical 1½" long evergreen leaves with smooth, entire margins. The tubular bluish purple flowers are ¾–1" across and the sepals are about ⅓ as long as the corolla tube. Flowers open in the spring and, similar to *V. major*, appear sporadically all season. Plants are vigorous and prefer shade and moist areas. An excellent species for erosion control on banks.

Propagate by division throughout the season. Terminal cuttings of non-flowering stems may also be used.

**Cultivars:**
'Alba' has white flowers which make a nice contrast with the dark green foliage.
'Alboplena' bears white double flowers.
'Argenteovariegata' has white variegated foliage.
'Atropurpurea' produces dark purple flowers.
'Aureovariegata has leaves variegated with deep yellow. The variegation may be on the margins or the entire leaf may be yellow.
'Bowles Variety' (var. *bowlesii*) bears light blue 1–1¼" diameter flowers and is less vigorous than the species. This is also known as 'La Graveana' ('La Grave').
'Multiplex' has double, plum-purple flowers.
'Jekyll's White' has single pure white flowers and is more floriferous than 'Alba'.
'Sterling Silver' bears dark blue flowers and foliage with white margins.
'Variegata' produces yellow variegated leaves and pale blue flowers.


*Viola* (vie′ o-la)                    Violet                    Violaceae

Some of the oldest plants on record, violets have been cultivated commercially as early as 400BC by the Greeks for their medicinal properties. They were raised in monastery gardens in the Middle Ages and were important items in the cut flower markets of Europe in the 19th century and well into the 20th century. Over 500 species of violets are distributed in the north and south temperate zones. For garden purposes, violets may be divided into two large groups. The first is the true violets such as *V. cornuta*, tufted violet, and *V. odorata*, sweet violet, which are treated as perennials and flower in late fall and early spring. The second group is the true pansies such as *V. tricolor*, heartsease, *V. lutea* and *V. altaica*.

Hybridization of these species and others has given rise to the myriad of modern garden pansies, collectively known as *V.* × *wittrockiana*. Although perennial in most of the country, they are available as bedding plants and generally used as annuals for early spring flowering.

Two kinds of flowers are produced by most true violets. In the spring, the large, showy, infertile flowers consisting of 5 sepals, petals and stamens open. They consist of a flat lower petal (a landing strip for insects), two side petals or "wings" and two upper petals. The lower petal bears a spur, similar to *Aquilegia*. In the summer, flowers with rudimentary or no petals are formed at the base of the plant. These never open but self pollinate within the closed calyx and are known as cleistogamous flowers. Seed capsules are formed which spew out small seeds to distances of up to 9'. Many of the non-stoloniferous species appear like magic because of this quarterback-like property. The dried, open seed capsules can easily be seen if the leaves are pushed aside in late summer and fall.

The foliage of all cultivated violets is evergreen. Garden species of violets are low growing and suitable for the front of the border or for a wild flower garden. Most tolerate full sun but prefer shaded, moist conditions. A number of native wild flowers such as *V. papillionacea* (syn. *V. sororia*), confederate violet, *V. pedata*, bird's-foot violet, and *V. canadensis*, Canada violet, are ornamental but little selection or hybridization has been undertaken to introduce them as garden subjects. Their potential for improvement is great.

Species hybridize readily making identification difficult. In fact, L.H. Bailey stated in *The Standard Cyclopedia of Horticulture* (Vol III, 1943) that there were more natural hybrids than there were species. Taxonomic differences among species are subtle and for those inclined to use a 10X hand lens, one of the best structures to study is the shape of the style. It is one of the few morphological factors that distinguish violet species. See the section on Additional Reading at the end of the genus.

Quick Reference to Viola Species

|  | Height (in.) | Stems | Stoloniferous | Color of seeds |
|---|---|---|---|---|
| *V. cornuta* | 4–12 | Yes | No | Black |
| *V. cucullata* | 3–6 | No | No | Black |
| *V. labradorica* | 1–4 | Yes | No | Brown |
| *V. odorata* | 2–8 | No | Yes | Cream |
| *V. pedata* | 2–6 | No | No | Copper |
| *V. pubescens* | 8–12 | Yes | No | Brown |
| *V. rotundifolia* | 3–6 | No | No | White |

| -*cornuta* (kor-new' ta) | Horned Violet, Tufted Violet | 4–12"/12" |
|---|---|---|
| Spring        Violet | Pyrenees | Zones 6–9 |

The stems are more or less prostrate at the base before ascending and the whole plant appears tufted, thus accounting for its common name. A vigorous grower, it is often used as a ground cover and an accent plant. The evergreen leaves are ovate, 1–2″ long, less than 1″ wide and are hairy beneath. The nodes of the stem bear opposite leafy stipules about the same length as the petiole.

The 1–1½″ diameter flowers are borne on 2–4″ long peduncles which arise from the leaf axils. The petals are spread apart, resulting in star-like flowers on some varieties. They are slightly fragrant with a long slender spur, thus accounting for the other common name.

Flowers occur in spring and, if the plant is cut back in the summer, again in the fall. In the South, plants are heat tolerant and although some stress related damage may occur during July and August, they do not perish like annual pansies.

Propagate by division in the fall or early spring. Terminal cuttings, approximately 2″ long, taken in spring or summer will root in 10–15 days if placed under moist, warm conditions. Seed germinates quickly if lightly covered and placed at about 70° F under high humidity. After germination, move the seedlings to 55–60° F location.

## Cultivars:
'Alba' has clean, pure white flowers.

'Blaue Schonheit' ('Beautiful Blue') is just that.

'Blue Perfection' is 6–8″ tall and produces sky blue flowers in early spring and again in the fall.

'Broughton Blue' bears many attractive pale blue flowers with darker blue veins in the center.

'Chantreyland' is similar to the above cultivar but has apricot flowers.

'Jersey Gem' has broad petals of rich blue purple.

Var. *lilacina* is one of my favorite violas as it bears abundant pale lilac-blue flowers with spreading petals. It is relatively heat tolerant and is a good performer in much of the country.

'Lord Nelson' is one of the most durable selections of the species and produces small (¾″ across) violet flowers with a tiny yellow eye.

'Rosea' bears large rose-pink flowers.

'Scottish Yellow' has pure yellow 1–1½″ wide flowers.

'White Perfection' has clean white flowers on 6–8″ tall plants.


-*cucullata* (kuk-eh-lah′ ta)     Marsh Blue Violet     3–6″/12″
    Spring     Violet     Eastern North America     Zones 4–9
(Syn. *V. obliqua*)

The leaves and flower stems arise from the rootstock, making this a stemless species. The pale green foliage is broadly ovate to heart shaped, 3–4″ wide, and held on 3–5″ long petioles. The margins are somewhat wavy and the whole leaf is essentially hairless. The stipules are lanceolate

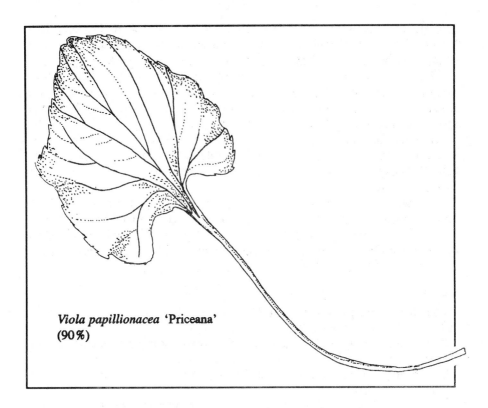

*Viola papillionacea* 'Priceana'
(90%)

and entire. Each ½–1″ diameter flower has purple veins on the lower petal while the lateral ones have dense beard-like hairs. Plants are distinguished from other native blue violets by the long flower stems which help to carry the flowers well above the foliage. Scaly rhizomes result in large clumps but plants are not stoloniferous, and they can throw seed everywhere.

Plants are particularly effective in moist shady places. The foliage is produced throughout the year resulting in an effective ground cover. It self sows everywhere, however, and can soon become an awful nuisance. I would not knowingly plant any of the native blue violets (see Related Species) in the garden due to their self seeding habit.

**Cultivars:**
'Freckles' produces a unique flower with a light blue background liberally sprinkled with purple flecks. It grows about 6″ tall.

'Red Giant' has rose-red flowers.

'Royal Robe' bears deep blue flowers on 4–6″ tall flower stems.

'White Czar' has lovely white flowers with a yellow center and dark netted markings in the throat. Plants grow vigorously and tolerate more sun than the species. It possibly is a hybrid with *V. odorata* 'Czar'.

**Related Species:**

*V. papillionacea* is perhaps the most common violet in the east. Heart-shaped leaves with blunt teeth and smooth stalks occur. The flowers vary from dark violet to blue, and occasionally white. Can be a tremendous weed. 'Priceana', the confederate violet, has white flowers, a large purple center and a small yellow eye.

*V. sororia*, woolly blue violet, is similar to the other species above but the petioles and lower leaf surfaces are quite hairy.

*-labradorica* (lab-ra-do' ri-ka)             Labrador Violet       1–4"/12"
    Spring       Violet       Northern United States, Greenland       Zones 3–8

One of the shortest garden violets, they are wonderful plants which if allowed to do their own thing, will make fine combinations with other early spring flowers. Plants are native to northeastern states, parts of Canada, and as far north as Greenland, but it is one of the best little plants in the

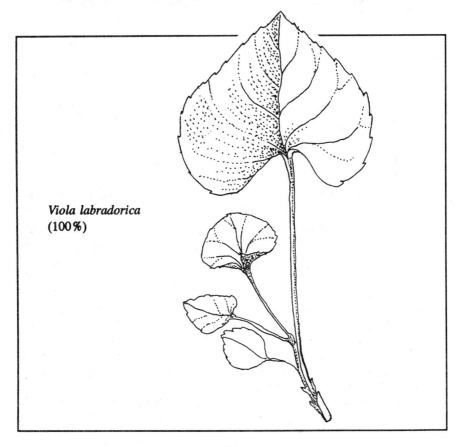

Viola labradorica
(100%)

Armitage garden (zone 7b). Plants were unknown for many years but they are now more available for gardeners throughout the country. The 1″ wide, broadly ovate foliage is shallowly toothed and arises from a short stem. The stipules are lanceolate with sparse teeth on the margins. The mauve ¾″ wide flowers, suffused with dark purple, appear in early spring and sporadically the rest of the season.

Spreading by slender creeping rhizomes, and throwing seed about, plants fill in areas rapidly. I have the purple-leaved variant, which is much better than the species. They are terrific companions with foamflowers, wood poppies and mayapples. Provide shade and moisture and sit back and enjoy.

Divide every 2–3 years if it starts to ramble too aggressively. Seed may be treated similar to *V. cornuta*.

## Cultivars:

Var. *purpurea* has leaves suffused with purple and appear dark green, particularly in the spring and fall. New spring and fall growth is dark purple which lightens somewhat during the summer. Flowers are similar to the type. True from seed.

| | | | |
|---|---|---|---|
| *-odorata* (o-do-rah′ ta) | | Sweet Violet | 2–8″/15″ |
| Spring | Violet | Europe, Asia | Zones 6–8 |

Whenever this species is planted in a garden, centuries of history are planted with it. Plants have been cultivated as long as there have been gardens, and is mentioned frequently in Greek and Latin classics. The flower market in Athens, Greece handled violets as early as 400BC and the sweet violet became the symbol of Athens. As F.E. Dillistone writes in *Violet Culture for Pleasure and Profit*, violets were "as proud a device of the Ionic Athenians as the rose of England or the lilies of France." It was also adopted as the symbol and password of Napoleon's supporters after he was exiled to Elba; he always presented sweet violets to Josephine on their wedding anniversary. The medicinal and chemical uses are also well documented but the fragrance distinguishes it from others. The substance that provides the fragrance is ionine, which is soporific, meaning that the nose perceives the odor but for a short time. Thus the scent of violets is sweet, but not long lasting. This property spawned huge acreage of violets for the perfume industry, particularly in France and also in England. The use of violets for perfume continued into the 1940s and 1950s until chemists found a way to manufacture ionine synthetically. Little natural "fragrance of violet" is found in today's perfumes. Sweet violets, however, are still sold as cut flowers in Europe but are only useful for local markets due to the transitory nature of the fragrance.

The tufted foliage is broadly ovate to kidney shaped and arises from the rootstock. Each finely pubescent leaf is 2–3″ wide and has blunt shallow serrations on the margin. The ¾" long flowers are usually violet, but rose and white forms also exist. Flowers occur in the fall and appear throughout the winter in mild climates and into the spring. Prostrate runners root at the tips and allow it to spread rapidly. Flowering occurs the second year from rooting. Large-flowered double types arose in the late 1800s and became known as Parma violets. They are fragrant but their ancestry is rather obscure, perhaps being derived from *V. suavis* rather than *V. odorata*.

Plants grow best in the cool times of the year (this is true for all violets), but are not winter hardy below zone 6 without protection. Full sun is tolerated as long as adequate soil moisture is provided, otherwise partial shade is necessary. Every gardener should have one or two plants if for no other reason than to occasionally feel like Josephine. I would not have a garden without them.

Division of the plantlets resulting from the stoloniferous runners is practiced in the fall. Seed of the species and varieties should be handled similar to *V. cornuta*.

**Cultivars:**
'Czar' was one of the earliest selections and bears single, deep violet flowers on narrow stems. 'White Czar' may also belong here. See *V. cornuta*.
'Deloris' has large purple blooms.
'Duchesse de Parme' bears double lavender-violet flowers, 'Lady Hume Campbell' has double lavender flowers, and 'Marie Louise' produces deep double violet-mauve flowers. These cultivars carry flowers on long stems which are suitable for cutting. These are but 3 of the group of plants referred to as Parma violets, an important cut flower crop in Europe in recent years. They are not particularly easy to find in this country.
'Fair Oaks' produces fragrant rosy lavender flowers.
'John Roddenbury' has light blue flowers with a wonderful sweet fleeting scent.
'L'Arne' bears purple flowers.
'Queen Charlotte' has dark blue to purple flowers on 6–8" tall stems.
'Rosina' has rose-pink flowers with a dark center.
'White Queen' has small white flowers on 6" tall plants.

| | | | |
|---|---|---|---|
| *-pedata* (pe-dah' ta) | | Bird's-Foot Violet | 2–6"/12" |
| Spring | Violet | Eastern North America | Zones 4–8 |

One of our prettiest native flowers, *V. pedata* is easy to identify because the leaves look like a bird's foot. This particular bird has feet palmately divided into 3–5 narrow segments. Plants are stemless and flowers are ¾–1½" across, borne on 2–6" long peduncles. The upper 2 petals are dark violet while the lower 3 are pale lilac with dark veins. Five orange stamens are clustered in the center. It is not the easiest violet to cultivate and demands especially good drainage and partial shade. Planting in soil over a layer of coarse gravel helps establishment. The rhizome must be kept free of standing water or rot will develop.

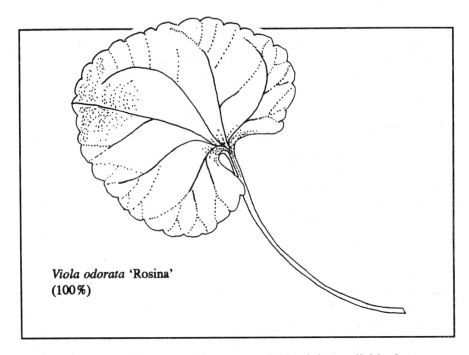

*Viola odorata* 'Rosina'
(100%)

There are enough commercial sources of this violet available that no one need remove them from the wild. Transplanting from the wild is likely to be unsuccessful.

Seed must be refrigerated for 5–6 weeks at 35–40° F to insure germination. If seed is sown directly in the garden, seedlings will appear the following spring. Leaf-bud cuttings (a leaf blade, petiole, with a piece of rhizome attached) may be placed in sand in late fall and winter. Rooting will occur in 4–7 weeks. Division of the rhizome may also be accomplished in late fall and winter.

### Cultivars:

Var. *alba* has white flowers that contrast well with the palmate foliage.

'Artist's Palette' is a handsome blue and white bicolor from Don Jacobs of Eco Gardens in Decateur, GA.

Var. *concolor* is a southern variant of the species and bears larger (1½") violet flowers with a white spot at the base of the lower petal. It is particularly suited to southern gardens.

### Related Species:

*V. dissecta*, cut leaf violet, is similar to bird's-foot violet in that the leaves are also divided. The leaves are divided into 3 segments, each segment being deeply divided. The white to pale rose flowers are about 1" across and are nicely fragrant. The foliage is the best part of the plant. This is an undiscovered gem.

**-pubescens** (pew' bes-cens)    Downy Yellow Violet    8-12"/12"
    Spring        Yellow        Eastern North America    Zones 3-7

The stem and triangular to kidney-shaped foliage is softly pubescent to the touch, thus the common name. The round, toothed leaves are 3-4" across and usually occur on short petioles at the top of the stem. The lower stem is often bare of leaves for 2-3" and the upper is often branched. The large stipules (about ½" wide) are lanceolate and entire. The bright yellow ½" wide flowers are borne in the leaf axils and consist of lower petals veined with purple, providing a nice contrast to the yellow.

Plants are native to dry, rich, shaded areas and should be placed in a well-drained shady area in the garden. They are not as heat tolerant as many violets and performs better in zones 4-6 than in zone 7.

Propagate from seed similar to *V. cornuta*. If seedlings fail to germinate within 6 weeks, place in refrigerator for 4-6 weeks and treat like *V. pedata*. Divide the short rhizome in late fall or early spring.

**Related Species:**

*V. nuttallii*, Nuttall violet, also has downy foliage (but only underneath) and yellow flowers. The leaves are present at the base of the plant (lacking in *V. pubescens*) and narrower. Native to the North American prairie states.


**-rotundifolia** (ro-tund-I-fo' lee-a)    Roundleaf Violet    3-6"/9"
    Spring        Yellow        Maine to North Georgia    Zones 3-7

This native species has oval to circular 2-4" wide foliage directly from the rootstock. Plants produce sprawling purplish stems after flowering which result in a matlike habit. The lower 3 petals of the 2" wide yellow flowers are brown veined and quite eye-catching. Flowers are borne on 2-4" long stalks in early spring. Plants perform particularly well in cool climates but simply open up and look sad where summers are hot.

Propagate by seed similar to *V. cornuta* or by division in spring or fall.

**Related Species:**

*V. striata*, cream violet, has creamy yellow flowers with black striations on the lower petal. Native from New York to Georgia, plants are easy to grow and self seed with abundance but are not obnoxious.

**Hybrid Violets:**

There are many fine violets in commerce today which don't fit any particular species, and are the result of some wonderful selection and hybridization. Here a few of my favorites.

'Fiona' bears beautiful light blue tinged flowers.

'Helen Mount' is an old fashioned "Johnny jump-up" but one of the best. She has purple upper petals and orange-yellow lower ones.

'Irish Molly' has flowers the size of garden violas and are bronze orange
with darker centers.
'Maggie Mott' has mauve flowers with a lovely silver tinge. The centers are
cream-colored.
'Molly Sanderson' bears small dark purple to black flowers with yellow centers.
'Thalia' is compact with lower petals cream and upper ones purple.

## Quick Key to Viola Species

    A. Plants stemless, leaves and flowers
       arising directly from rhizome
       B. Leaves palmately divided . . . . . . . . . . . . . . . . . *V. pedata*
    BB. Leaves not palmately divided
          C. Plant stoloniferous . . . . . . . . . . . . . . . . . . *V. odorata*
          CC. Plant not stoloniferous, grows in clumps
                D. Plant less than 8″ tall, foliage
                   round, dark green, flowers yellow . . . . *V. rotundifolia*
                DD. Plant more than 8″ tall, foliage
                    broadly ovate or kidney-shaped,
                    pale green, flowers violet . . . . . . . . . . . *V. cucullata*
    AA. Plants with stems
       B. Flowers 1″ or more across, violet,
          stipules deeply toothed . . . . . . . . . . . . . . . . . *V. cornuta*
    BB. Flowers less than 1″ across, yellow
        or violet, stipules not deeply toothed
          C. Flowers yellow, foliage very pubescent . . . . *V. pubescens*
          CC. Flowers violet, foliage bronze,
              not obviously pubescent . . . . . . . . . . . . *V. labradorica*

## Additional Reading:

*Books:*

Baird, Viola Brainard. 1942. *Wild Violets of North America*. A beautifully
illustrated and well documented text.

*Manuscripts:*

Coombs, Roy E. 1979. Parma violets. *The Plantsman* 1(3):167–176.
Coombs, Roy E. 1981. Cultivated violets, are they really scented? *The
Plantsman* 3(1):60–62.
Coombs, Roy E. 1982. The Parma Violet 'Marie Louise'. *The Plantsman*
4(2):112–115.

# W

*Waldsteinia* (wald-stein' ee-a)        Barren-Strawberry        Rosaceae

Approximately 5 species of this strawberry-like genus occur and 2 are
occasionally seen in American gardens. Both bear trifoliate leaves, yellow
flowers, and small inedible fruits. *Waldsteinia* is more ornamental than, but
not as vigorous as, another insidious relative known as mock strawberry,
*Duchesnea indica. Waldsteinia* differs by having short surface runners,
smaller fruit and 2–5 pistils (*Duchesnea* has 15 or more). *Waldsteinia* is a
favored guest; *Duchesnea* an uninvited party crasher.

*-fragarioides* (fra-gah-ree-oi' deez)    Barren-Strawberry        4–6"/24"
   Spring               Yellow        Eastern United States    Zones 4–7

The strawberry-like glossy, evergreen leaves are slightly hairy and are
divided into three 1–2" long wedge-shaped toothed leaflets. The yellow
flowers, about ½" across, are carried in 3–8 flowered racemes on 4" long
scapes. Full sun or partial shade is tolerated. Plants form a pretty mat
particularly useful for edging or filling in areas along a path. Unfortunately,
the flowers do not emerge through the mat but push out the sides so the
planting is never covered with blooms. Performance is poor in hot, wet
climates and although native as far south as North Georgia, it does not
thrive under cultivated conditions in zone 8.
   Propagate by division in spring or fall or sow seed in warm, moist conditions. It germinates erratically. After germination, place the plants at 60–65° F.

## Related Species:

*W. lobata* is native from North Carolina to Georgia and is the best plant
for warm southern climates. It differs from the previous by having lobed
rather than divided leaves. Performs well in zones 7–9.

*W. parviflora* has 3-lobed leaves and yellow flowers on longer scapes, each flower nodding and hairy. Native from Virginia to Georgia, also good for warm gardens. Useful in zones 6–8.

*W. ternata*, Siberian barren-strawberry, is native to Siberia and is a better ground cover than *W. fragarioides*. The leaves occur in rosettes and are borne on short petioles resulting in more compact plants. Cool climates are also necessary for best growth. A winner in the Pacific Northwest.

## *Woodsia* (woods-ee′a)  Woodsia Fern  Dryopteridaceae

Small ferns, native to temperate and tropical regions. Approximately 25 species occur, a few are evergreen, but many are deciduous, and seldom grow taller than 12″, in essence keeping them out of mainstream gardening. As a group, Woodsia can be distinguished from other genera by the star-shaped or fringed spore cases found on the underside of the fronds. Most of the woodsias are better plants for the North than the South.

*W. ilvensis*, rusty woodsia, is native to the northern United States and Asia and forms a small clump of fronds which are green above and silvery white beneath. They are similar to resurrection ferns in that they turn rusty brown in times of drought but become green again after rain. They are only about 6″ tall with about 12 opposite pairs of leaflets. The most common woodsia is *W. obtusa*, blunt-lobed woodsia, which can be up to 16″ tall and is often evergreen in northern climes. About 8 pairs of leaflets occur, the lowest pair have blunt lobes. The plants naturally grow in limestone areas and lime should be added in most garden situations. Full sun to partial shade is tolerated. The interloper to the native species is *W. polystichoides*, native to China, Japan and Korea. Cold hardy (zone 4), deciduous and forms clumps about 12″ tall. Attractive when planted among rocks. Prefers full sun or afternoon shade.

## *Woodwardia* (wood-ward-ee′ a)  Chain Fern  Blechnaceae

About ten species of chain fern occur, and two are fairly common garden plants. The chain ferns can be distinguished from other ferns by the way in which the spore cases are arranged on the fertile parts of the plant. They are in rows arranged parallel to the midrib like links of sausages. The veins closest to the midrib are obviously netted or chained. Both garden ferns are extensively creeping and forking, moving around the soil with ease. All are deciduous. Moisture and partial shade are needed.

| *-areolata* (ar-e′ o-lah′ta) | Netted Chain Fern | 18–24″/12″ |
| Summer | United States | Zones 4–8 |

The chain fern creeps and crawls throughout the Armitage garden, and is a welcome weed. They multiple by underground rhizomes and a sizable colony can occur within 3 years. The fertile fronds look much different from the sterile ones. The sterile fronds, which are beautifully bronzed when they emerge, are about 2′ tall and 6″ wide with about 10 pairs of nearly opposite leaflets. Usually, the third pair is the longest. The leaflets (pinnae) are slightly wavy and the veins are raised and netted. The fertile frond is similar in shape to the sterile one but all leaflets are greatly contracted and often recurved over the sausage-like fruitdots, which nearly occupy the entire width of the leaflet.

The foliage and habit are similar to the sensitive fern, *Onoclea sensibilis*, but plants are not as big and the sterile fronds are more glossy. Since I get them confused unless they are side by side, I thought some others might as well. The following table may help to keep them straight.

|  | *Woodwardia areolata* | *Onoclea sensibilis* |
|---|---|---|
| Fertile frond | Long, thin, contracted leaflets | Beaded structure, lacking long leaflets |
| Sterile frond | Nearly opposite leaflets | Opposite leaflets |
| Leaflets | Wavy margin | Margins indented |

**Related Species:**

*W. virginica*, Virginia chain fern, has a similar sausage-like arrangement of fruit dots but they are borne on the main fronds, not on separate sterile ones. It has a similar creeping rootstalk, resulting in good size colonies. The fronds are cut into about 15 pairs of almost opposite leaflets. When not fruiting, it can be confused with the cinnamon fern, *Osmunda cinnamomea*, but it does not have those cinnamon tufts of hair at the base of the stalks, and cinnamon fern grows in clumps rather than creeping.

# Y

*Yucca* (yu′ ka)                    Yucca                    Agavaceae

Most of the 40 species of yucca are native to southwestern United States, although a few are also found in the West Indies. They are evergreen and are grown mainly for their architectural form and dramatic flair in the landscape, at least where they are relatively novel. In the Southwest, they are put in new landscapes like junipers of the North, and even our subdivision in north Georgia has a couple of green yuccas standing guard, with dozens of white flowers on their heads and hundreds of weeds at their feet. They are tough, withstanding the abuse of anyone foolish enough to mess with them. The leaves of most species are sharp pointed, which, while somewhat dangerous, is not all bad. Around Palm Sunday, the landscapes may take on a special look as small children impregnate individual colored egg receptacles on the pointy tips, culminating in kaleidoscopic Easter egg trees. Who says creativity is a thing of the past?

The spiny leaves are well known and have resulted in common names like Adam's needle, dagger plant, Spanish bayonet, Spanish dagger and needle palm while the upright flower stems provide the popular name of Roman candle. A number of species can be grown as far north as zone 5 (even zone 4) and nearly all of the cultivated forms are cold hardy to zone 7. A number of variegated cultivars have been selected from a couple of species, such as *Y. filimentosa* and *Y. filifera*. The habit of yucca ranges from small trees like *Y. elata* (soap tree), *Y. schottii* (Schott's yucca) and *Y. thompsoniana* (Thompson's yucca) which grow 7–12′ tall to the stemless forms with their bold rosettes. A number of nurseries have discovered the appeal of these fine plants and species and cultivars are often available through mail order sources. The main species available is still *Y. filimentosa*, Adam's needle.

*-filimentosa* (fee-lah-men-to' sa)　　Adam's Needle　　　　　2–3'/5'
　　White　　　　　Summer　　　Eastern United States　　Zones 5–9

The rough, thick leaves are often concave or spoon-shaped and plants also go under the name of spoonleaf yucca. The margins of the leaves end in narrow thread-like filaments. The erect plants are almost stemless and form handsome clumps after a few years. The plants themselves grow 2–3 feet tall but the flower stems may rise 8–10' in height. The inflorescence consists of creamy white pendant flowers in the summer and persists for many weeks. The variegated forms are excellent plants for the garden, where their bright yellow or white banded leaves always draw the eye.

Full sun and good drainage are necessary. They are cold hardy to about zone 5, however, plants in protected areas have been successful as far north as zone 4.

**Cultivars:**
'Bright Edge' bears leaves with yellow margins.
'Elegantissima' has blue-green leaves with bright white flowers and stiffer
　　symmetry.
'Gold Heart' produces leaves with creamy yellow centers. Plants grow
　　about 30" tall.
'Golden Sword' has bright yellow centers particularly in the cool seasons.
　　Flower stems can rise to 6' in height.
'Polar Bear' ('Eisbar') has branched inflorescences which grow 4–5' tall.
　　Plants flower after about three years from seed, significantly earlier than
　　most cultivars.
'Rosenglocken' produces flowers with pink-tinged flowers but does not
　　appear to be as vigorous.
'Variegata' bears white-margined foliage.

**Related Species:**
*Y. filifera* (syn. *Y. flaccida*) is similar but has smaller more flexible leaves than *Y. filimentosa*. 'Garland Gold' has leaves with wide gold bands down the centers. 'Ivory' bears creamy white flowers which are held more horizontally than pendant. Equally cold hardy as *Y. filimentosa*.

*Y. rostrata*, blue yucca, comes from Mexico by way of Yucca-Do nursery and has bluish foliage throughout the year. Likely hardy in zones 7–10.

**Other Hybrids:**
A number of variegated forms are offered and their parentage has caused a good deal of head scratching. *Y. filimentosa*, *Y. filifera*, *Y. gloriosa* and *Y. aloifolia* are probably involved. Unless they are lined up one after another, it is tough to see a lot of differences between them.

'Bell Tree' ('Schellenbaum') is at least 6' tall with a large inflorescence of white flowers, usually brown tinged on the outside.

'Color Guard' is similar to 'Golden Sword' with gold centered leaves. Plants are about 4' tall when not in flower; 6' in flower. Probably cold hardy to about zone 6.

'Fountain' ('Fontane') is dwarf (3' tall) with creamy white flowers and wide leaves.

'Giant Bell' ('Glockenriese') is over 6' tall with stiff leaves and creamy white flowers, often slightly tinged brown on the outside.

'Gold Edge' is similar to 'Bright Edge' but has thinner leaves and clear yellow margins. Equally cold tolerant as 'Color Guard'.

'Snow Spruce' ('Schneefichte') and 'Snow Fir' ('Schneetanne') are both about 6' tall with starry white flowers and yellow-white flowers respectively. Selected by Foersters Nursery in Germany.

# Z

*Zantedeschia* (zan-te-desh' ee-a)            Calla Lily            Araceae

Approximately 8 species are native to South Africa and all have been promoted as commercial cut flower crops, and a few cultivars are offered as garden plants. The well-known flowers consist of the large ornamental spathe enclosing the erect spadix. Plants must be dug and stored through the winter (similar to a gladiolus) in all but the warmest areas of the country. The flowers are used by florists in arrangements, particularly the white calla, *Z. aethiopica*, and unfortunately have been associated with funerals, making some people hesitant to use them as garden plants. Placed in containers or in the garden, they provide a classical air to the patio, porch, or garden. In the garden, they prefer partial shade but tolerate full sun. The flower stems are longer on plants grown in the shade. Callas are also excellent water plants and may be planted in a bog or beside a pond or pool. If planted below the water freezing line, plants may be over-wintered in situ.

Two problems can plague the genus. The first is an infectious bacteria, *Erwinia*, causing soft rot of the rhizomes. It occurs more in heavy soils, particularly if waterlogged for a significant period of time. The disease is easy to diagnose; the leaves begin to turn yellow, then black and the entire plant collapses in a matter of 7–10 days. Also the crown and roots smell awful. To avoid this problem, place in well-drained soils and take care if digging them in the fall to bring in or divide. Avoid cutting or injuring the rhizome and be sure they are sun-dried ("curing the rhizomes") well prior to storing. If the rhizomes are divided, be sure they are dusted with a fungicide and cured before placing back in the ground or storing. The other problem are those monsters, Japanese beetles. They love to descend to the depths of the flower and scratch and chew their way through it. Usually you find them on he day you wish to cut the flower and bring it in the house.

Quick Reference to Zantedeschia Species

|  | Height (in.) | Flower color | Leaf shape |
|---|---|---|---|
| *Z. aethiopica* | 24–30 | White | Arrow |
| *Z. albo-maculata* | 24–30 | Greenish-white | Arrow |
| *Z. rehmannii* | 9–15 | Pink | Lanceolate |

| | | | |
|---|---|---|---|
| *-aethiopica* (aye-thee-o' pi-ka) | | White Calla | 24–30″/24″ |
| Summer | White | South Africa | Zones 8–10 |

In my garden travels around the world, I cannot help but associate certain plants with certain countries. Calla lilies are to New Zealand as tulips are to Holland. Naturalized throughout the country in paddocks and low lying moist areas, they share space with hundreds of sheep and brighten up dark and dismal winter days. To see hundreds of white callas in drifts around a pond is indeed a magnificent sight. The plants are stemless; all parts arise from the broad rootstock. The dark green leaves are twice as long as broad, and carried on long petioles. The pure white spathe flares outward and is 6–10″ long. The spadix is prominent but only about ⅓ the length of the spathe.

Breeding has resulted in dwarf 1½–2′ tall compact forms as well as those with cream and green tints in the spathe. I love to see callas growing in the landscape, and special places like Sea Island, GA, use special plants like white calla at the base of trees or in container plantings. The cut flower industry in this country has planted thousands of callas, both white and colored forms, in California, Georgia and Florida. I have grown numerous callas in my zone 7b garden, but every third winter or so will wipe them out. Gardeners and cut flower growers, beware.

Propagate by cormels that readily form after the first year's growth. Lift the plants and separate from the main corm. Seed collected from plants may be sown in pots in the fall and will germinate within 1–3 months. Grow in pots until sufficiently established for placement in the final location.

**Cultivars:**

Var. *childsiana* ('Child's Perfection') is dwarfer, more compact and more floriferous than the type. They are particularly useful as potted plants for the greenhouse industry.

'Crowborough' was developed in Crowborough, England and is more winter hardy and sun tolerant than the species. Otherwise, few differences exist.

'Green Dragon' is a terrible looking thing. Torn by indecision to be green or white, the flowers are a feeble green/white blend. Plants are vigorous and grow 4–5′ tall.

'Little Gem' is 12–18″ tall and suitable for patio containers or indoors. It is more fragrant than the type.

**-albo-maculata** (al-bo-mak-ew-lah' ta)     Spotted Calla     24-30"/24"
Summer          Creamy White          South Africa          Zones 8-10

The leaf blades are 12-18" long, 3-4" wide and spotted with white. The creamy white spathe is trumpet shaped (not flaring as in the previous species), 4-5" long, and has a purple blotch at the base. The main value is increased cold tolerance over other species which permits overwintering in zone 7 with protection. It has been used extensively in hybridization to take advantage of cold hardiness genes.

Propagation is similar to *Z. aethiopica*.

**Related Species:**

*Z. elliotiana*, Elliot's calla, has silvery white spots on the foliage and produces 4-5" long bright yellow spathes in summer. Spathes do not have a purple blotch on the back. Plants are not as hardy as either of the above species.

**-rehmannii** (ray-mahn' ee-aye)     Pink Calla     9-15"/20"
Summer          Pink, Rose          South Africa          Zones 8-10

This dwarfer species has 7-15" long lanceolate leaves covered with small greenish or white spots. The 4" long spathe is trumpet shaped and varies from pink to rose to white with a pink tint. Its size makes it particularly suitable for pot culture.

Propagate similar to *Z. aethiopica*.

**Related Species:**

Many hybrids are available which are commercially used as cut flowers or pot plants. Some of the finest cultivars have emerged from nurseries in New Zealand and California. These plants sport red, pink, yellow, gold and green spathes mostly with spotted leaves. Many of the hybrids have the purple blotch in the bottom of the spathe associated with *Z. albo-maculata*. Cultivars include 'Black Magic', yellow with a prominent black blotch in the spathe, 'Galaxy', red and yellow flowers, 'Golden Sun', golden yellow flowers on compact plants, 'Majestic Red', rose-red flowers, and 'Pink Perfection', light pink spathe. 'Black Magic' is the best.

Quick Key to Zantedeschia Species

    A. Leaves lanceolate, flowers pink or rose  . . . . . . . *Z. rehmannii*
    AA. Leaves arrow shaped, flowers usually white or yellow
        B. Spathe white, flared at top,
           leaves not spotted white . . . . . . . . . . . . . . . *Z. aethiopica*
        BB. Spathe creamy white, not flared,
           leaves spotted white . . . . . . . . . . . . . . *Z. albo-maculata*

**Additional Reading:**
Traub, H.P. 1948. The genus *Zantedeschia*. *Plant Life* 4:8-32.

*Zauschneria* (zowsh-ner' ee-a)     California Fuchsia     Onagraceae

Approximately four species of this little-known genus occur, all are small sub-shrubs native to the western United States. Recent discussion in taxonomic circles have placed all the species under *Epilobium cana*, however, that change has not filtered down to producers and gardeners can still find these plants under *Zauschneria*. The most popular species in American gardens is *Z. californica*, although national popularity is used loosely; *Z. cana* is also becoming more available. The bright red-orange flowers are great hummingbird attractors and are well known as Hummingbird Trumpet.

Plants are better performers where drainage is excellent and are often used in xerophytic settings. I was so impressed with the garden of Panayoti Kelaidis and his wife, Gwen, in Denver where flaming red and handsome orange-flowering plants were blazing in the Colorado sunlight. They are exceptional plants people and King and Queen of the *Zauschneria* world.

| | | | |
|---|---|---|---|
| *-californica* (ka-li-forn' i-ca) | | California Fuchsia | 1–2'/18" |
| Late Summer | Scarlet | California | Zones 6–9 |

The linear to lanceolate, sessile, pubescent foliage are generally green, and not gray-green, as seen in *Z. cana*. The linear to linear-lanceolate leaves are white-woolly and velvety to the touch. The lower leaves are opposite while those toward the top are alternate. The 1–1½" long bright scarlet flowers are held in racemes and are fuchsia-like. Plants are tetraploid (having twice the number of chromosomes) resulting in increased vigor.

The showy flowers and low growing habit make plants suitable for the front of the border or the rock garden. It tolerates either full sun or partial shade but good drainage is essential, particularly in the Southeast, where winter rains are common. One of the drawbacks is the hairy, messy seeds which detract from the plants in the fall. Removal of the spent flowers reduces the problem. The hardiness ratings are difficult to make sense of, although most hardiness ratings are purely speculative anyway. Since humidity and afternoon rain are not preferred, they do better in zone 6 of Denver, CO than zone 7b of Athens, GA, and do much better in zone 8 of Portland, WA than zone 8 of southern Alabama. The soils also make a hugh difference. Sandy or gritty soils are much better than heavy clay soils.

Propagate by seed in a moist, warm (70–75° F) environment. Seed emerges within 3 weeks. Terminal cuttings may also be used in early summer. Cut 2–3" long terminals and place in sand or a peat-vermiculite mix. Maintain moisture and warmth until roots appear (usually within 2–3 weeks).

### Cultivars:
'Albiflora' is unusual in that the flowers are white.
'Dublin' ('Glasnevin') is smaller than the species, growing only 12–18" tall.
   From the Irish National Botanical Garden outside Dublin, Ireland.

'Sir Cedric Morris' has rosy red flowers on more compact plants. 'Solidarity Pink' bears pale pink flowers.

**Related Species:**

*Z. cana* is similar but has leaves which are more gray-green than the former species. That is likely too simple a difference, however, a good deal of variability and hybridization have taken place. The leaves are smaller (sometimes they go under the name of *Z. microphylla*).

*Zephyranthes* (ze-fi-ranth' eez)      Zephyr Lily      Amaryllidaceae

The zephyr lily takes its name from *zephyros*, west wind, a reference to the New World (being in the west), from where the genus arrived in Europe. Thus it also became known as the Flower of the West Wind. Individual species also have their common names. Flowers of *Z. grandiflora*, rosepink zephyr lily, open after every rain and are known as rain lilies. The most common member of the genus, native to the southern states, is the atamasco lily, *Z. atamasco*.

All have narrow leaves and funnel-shaped flowers borne singly on a hollow scape. In general, they prefer moist conditions in full sun and are rather tender, usually being winter hardy only to zone 8, zone 7 with protection. However, they make excellent potted plants for the deck or patio and 10–12 bulbs of *Z. grandiflora*, in a 6–8″ container makes a glorious display. If the bulbs are stored over winter, place in moist sand or peat moss in a cool (50° F) area. If pot grown, simply keep the soil moist, not wet, and store in the same area.

Most of the approximately 35 species are spring and summer flowering, however, *Z. candida* and *Z. rosea* flower in late summer and fall. There are few obvious differences among species based on botanical characteristics, and the easiest way to separate them is by flower color and season of bloom.

Quick Reference to Zephyranthes Species

|  | Height (in.) | Flower color | Bloom season |
|---|---|---|---|
| *Z. atamasco* | 18–36 | White | Spring |
| *Z. candida* | 9–15 | White | Fall |
| *Z. grandiflora* | 9–15 | Rose | Summer |
| *Z. rosea* | 9–15 | Rose | Fall |

*-atamasco* (a-ta-mas' ko)      Atamasco Lily      18–36″/18″
    Spring      White      Southeastern United States      Zones 7–10

The earliest flowering and most robust zephyr lily, it produces 4–6 bright green, channeled evergreen leaves about 18″ long and ¼″ wide. The pure white fragrant flowers emerge as pointed, pink striped buds and open flat and starlike. The perianth may be up to 4″ long. Flowers open in April and May

*Zephyranthes atamasco*
(70%)

and continue for 4–6 weeks. This species is native to damp, acid, meadowlands and dry conditions result in small, fleeting flowers. However, great populations can be found along roadsides in south Georgia and Alabama, attesting to its inherent toughness. If planted in protected areas and provided with mulch, bulbs may overwinter as far north as New York City. If bulbs are removed in the fall, dig before the first hard frost and store in peat moss in an area which does not freeze. Replant in the spring after the last frost.

Propagate by removal of the small bulblets in the fall or by seed. Seeds sown in a warm (70–75° F), moist area germinate within four weeks. Flowering occurs the second or third year.

**Related Species:**

*Z. candida* is known as La Plata lily because the abundance of these silvery flowers around an unnamed river in Argentina. The presence of such beauty led the discoverer, Diaz de Solis, to name it Rio de La Plata (River of Silver). Plants produce grassy leaves and silvery white crocus-like flowers with rich orange stamens which open in late May. A terrific plant. 'Ajax' is a hybrid between *Z. candida* and *Z. citrina*, a lemon colored

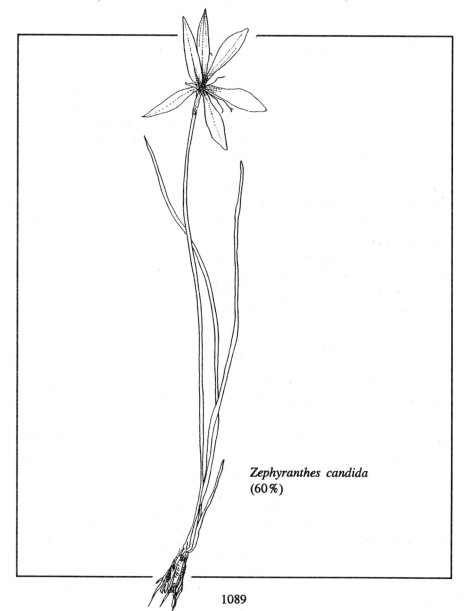

*Zephyranthes candida*
(60%)

crocus-like species. The leaf shape is similar to *Z. candida* and the pale primrose-yellow flowers resemble *Z. citrina*. Hardy to zone 8.

*Z. flava* (*Z. flavacens*, *Pyroliron*), yellow rain lily, is about 1' tall with golden yellow flowers.

*Z. treatiae* is native to Florida and blooms 2–4 weeks earlier than atamasco lily. The dull gray-green foliage is less than 1/10" wide and red flower buds open to blossoms of pure white. Hardy in zones 8b and 10.

| *-grandiflora* (grand-I-flo' ra) | Rosepink Zephyr Lily | 9–15"/18" |
|---|---|---|
| Summer      Rose | Guatemala | Zones 9–10 |

(Syn. *Z. carinata*)

The foliage is 10–15" long, narrowly strap-shaped and spreads out over the ground. The rose-red flowers are 3–4" long and emerge from a maroon-red flower bud atop a 7" tall scape. My great uncle Peter in Mansonville, Quebec, Canada beams over his pots of lilies that flower like magic on his porch after every summer rain. The same excitement and enthusiasm comes from Mark Krause, one of the outstanding horticulturists at Disney World in Orlando, Florida. It is little wonder that this is the most popular species of zephyr lily. Bulbs look wonderful in containers and bring rave reviews from guests.

Propagate similar to *Z. atamasco*.

**Related Species:**

*Z. rosea*, Cuban zephyr lily, has flowers of similar color to *Z. grandiflora* but less than half the size and appear 3–4 weeks later. Leaves are about 8" long and ¼" wide. It is also a good container plant but not as long lived in the ground as *Z. grandiflora*.

**Additional Reading:**

Herklots, G.A.C. 1980. Windflowers, Part I: *Zephyranthes*. *The Plantsman* 2:8–19.

Herklots, G.A.C. 1981. Windflowers, Part II: *Zephyranthes* subgenus *Cooperia*. *The Plantsman* 3:108–112.

## *Zigadenus* (zi-ga-day' nus)      Death Camas, Zygadene      Liliaceae

Most of these native North American bulb species are unknown to gardeners, however, a number of the 16 or so species are poisonous to livestock and well known to ranchers in the midwest and plains states. All species of *Zigadenus* (also spelled *Zygadenus*) contain a toxic alkaloid which can cause vomiting and result in comas in humans. The most poisonous and the species which accounts for the common name is *Z. nuttallii*, native from Tennessee and west to Texas and Kansas. *Z. venenosus* also goes by the same common name and is found on the west coast from California to British Columbia. Both have white flowers and arguably should not be used as garden plants. The later, in fact, is not particularly ornamental anyway. One of the taller species is *Z. glaberrimus*, which can grow to 3' tall with creamy white flowers.

The only species for gardens, and this can be debated, is the least toxic and probably the most ornamental of the group, *Z. elegans*. I saw this plant in all its glory at Smith College in western Massachusetts in August where it was blooming its head off in 90 degree heat. Plants are native to Colorado, Nevada, Oregon and north to Alaska, but has escaped into Arizona, Texas and parts of New Mexico. Plants grow about 12″ tall with grassy foliage that is 6–12″ long and about ½″ wide. The flowers, which consist of six teals, are greenish on the outside and creamy white on the inside and open wide in a saucer shape. They are attached to stiff 1″ long pedicel allowing the flowers to face upward. They also have an obvious gland at the base of the teals (the botanical name comes from *zygion*, yoke and *aden*, gland), a characteristic useful to distinguish it from *Tofieldia*, a genus with similar flowers. Not a bad little plant, just don't put it anywhere where kids or animals might want to chew on it.

Propagate by division.

## *Zizia* (ziz-e' a)  Golden Alexanders  Apiaceae

About four species occur, native to North America, and a couple of them are well-known plants in the Atlantic states and the Midwest. *Zizia* has yellow umbels of flowers over 2–2½' tall plants and differs from other yellow umbelliferous species in that the central flower has no pedicel (flower stalk) and the fruit is ribbed but not winged.

Two species are occasionally offered, neither are much to get excited about but both can be useful in the right spot (so can a billboard when you are looking for a hotel in the middle of the night). The basal and stem leaves of *Z. aurea*, golden alexanders, are biternate (divided into three and then redivided into three again) and sharply toothed. The umbel consists of up to 20 flowers on a pedicel of approximately the same length, except for the sessile center one. They flower in April to June and are fairly common in the Atlantic states. The other familiar species, mainly in the Midwest, is *Z. aptera*. This zizzy differs from the other by having entire basal leaves which are bluntly toothed on the margins. The inflorescences are similar, although they usually consist of fewer flowers.

Propagate by seed or division.

# Bibliography of Reference Books

*Additional manuscripts appear with appropriate genus*

Aden, Paul. 1988. *The Hosta Book*. Timber Publishing Co., Portland, OR.

Angier, Bradford. 1994. *Field guide to medicinal world plants*. Stackpole Books, Harrisburg, PA.

Armitage, A.M. 1993. *Specialty Cut Flowers*. Timber Press, Portland, OR.

Bailey Hortorium. 1976. *Hortus Third, a Consise Dictionary of Plants Cultivated in the United States and Canada*. Macmillan Publishing Co., New York, NY.

Bailey, L.H. 1944. *The Standard Cyclopedia of Horticulture*, 3 volumes. MacMillan Publishing Co., New York, NY.

Bailey, L.H. 1951. *Manual of Cultivated Plants*. Macmillan Publishing Co., New York, NY.

Bailey, L.H. 1953. *The Garden of Bellflowers*. MacMillan Publishing Co., New York, NY.

Beckett, Kenneth A. 1981. *Growing Hardy Perennials*. Croom Helm Ltd., London, England.

Bender, Steve and Felder Rushing. 1993. *Passalong Plants*. University of North Carolina Press, Chapel Hill, NC.

Bloom, Adrian. 1981. *Adrian Bloom's Guide to Garden Plants*. Book 3. *Perennials*, part 1. Jarrold and Sons Ltd., Norwich, England.

Bloom, Adrian. 1981. *Adrian Bloom's Guide to Garden Plants*, Book 4. *Perennials*, part 2. Jarrold and Sons Ltd., Norwich, England.

Bloom, Alan. 1965. *Hardy Plants of Distinction*. W.H. and L. Collingridge Ltd., London, England.

Bloom, Alan. 1968. *Alan Bloom's Selected Garden Plants*. Jarold and Sons Ltd., Norwich, England.

Bloom, Alan. 1975. *Making the Best of Alpines*. Jarold and Sons Ltd., Norwich, England.

Bloom, Alan and Adrian Bloom. 1992. *Blooms of Bressingham Garden Plants*. Harper Collins Publishing, London, England.

Boulos, Loutfy. 1983. *Medicinal Plants of North America*. Reference Publications, Algonac, MI.

Bown, Deni. 1988. *Aroids*. Timber Press, Portland, OR.

Boyd, James. 1928. *Peonies. The Manual of the American Peony Society*. J. Horace McFarland Co., Harrisburg, PA.

Brown, Emily. 1986. *Landscaping with Perennials*. Timber Press, Portland, OR.

Bryan, J.E. 1989. *Bulbs*, 2 vols. Timber Press, Portland, OR.

Caillet, Marie and Joseph K. Mertzweiller. 1988. *The Louisiana Iris*. Texas Gardener Press, Waco, TX.

Cassidy, G.E. and S. Linnegar. 1982. *Growing Irises*. Croom Helm Ltd., London, England.

Challis, Myles. 1992. *Large-leaved Perennials*. Wardlock Publishing Co., London, England.

Chatto, Beth. 1978. *The Dry Garden*. J.M. Dent and Sons Ltd., London, England.

Chatto, Beth. 1982. *The Damp Garden*. J.M. Dent and Sons Ltd., London, England.

Chittenden, Fred J. (ed.) 1974. *The Royal Horticultural Society Dictionary of Gardening*. 4 volumes and supplement. Clarendon Press, Oxford, England.

Coats, Alice M. 1956. *Flowers and Their Histories*. Adam and Charles Black, London, England.

Cook, J. Gordon. 1968. *ABC of Plant Terms*. Merrow Publishing, Waterford, England.

Coombes, Allen J. 1985. *Dictionary of Plant Names*. Timber Press, Portland, OR.

Coon, Nelson. 1963. *Using plants for healing*. Hearthside Press Inc., New York, NY.

Crawford, Barrie F. 1985. *For the Love of Wildflowers*. Buckeye Press, Columbus, GA.

Damp, Philip. 1981. *Growing Dahlias*. Croom Helm Ltd., London, England.

Davis, Dilys. 1992. *Alliums*. Timber Press, Portland, OR.

Doerflinger, Frederic. 1973. *The Bulb Book*. Charles and Davis Ltd., Devon, England.

Druse, Ken. 1996. *The Collector's Garden*. Clarkston Potter, New York, NY.

Duncan, Wilber H. and Leonard E. Foote. 1975. *Wildflowers of the Southeastern United States*. University of Georgia Press, Athens, GA.

Dykes, W. R. 1912. *Irises in Present-Day-Gardening Series*. Ballantyne, Hanson and Co., Edinburgh, Scotland.

Evans, Ronald L. 1984. *Handbook of Cultivated Sedums*. Science Reviews, Middlesex, England.

Everett, T.H. 1981, 1982. *The New York Botanical Garden Illustrated Encyclopedia of Horticulture*, 10 volumes. Garland Publishing Co., New York, NY.

Evison, Raymond J. 1991. *Making the Most of Clematis*, 2nd ed. Floraprint Ltd., Nottingham, England.

Fielder, Mildred. 1975. *Plant Medicine and Folklore*. Winchester Press, New York, NY.

Fish, Margery. 1970. *Ground Cover Plants*. David and Charles, Newport Abby, Devon, England.

Fisher, John. 1982. *The Origins of Garden Plants*. Constable and Company Ltd., London, England.

Foster, H. Lincoln. 1968. *Rock Gardening*. Houghton Mifflin Co., Boston, MA.

Foster, H. Lincoln and Laura Louise Foster. 1990. *Cuttings from a Rock Garden*. Atlantic Monthly Press, New York, NY.

Fox, Derek. 1985. *Lilies*. A Wisley handbook. Cassell Ltd., London, England.

Genders, Roy. 1960. *Bulbs all the Year Round*. Latimer Trend and Co., Whitstable, England.

Genders, Roy. 1973. *Bulbs. A Complete Handbook*. Robert Hale and Co., London, England.

Gerard, John. 1636. *Gerard's Herbal. The Essence Thereof Distilled by Marcus Woodward*. Cresent Books, New York, NY.

Giles, F.A., R. McIntosh Keith and D.C. Saupe. 1980. *Herbaceous Perennials*. Reston Publishing Co., Reston, VI.

Greenlee, John. 1992. *The Encyclopedia of Ornamental Grasses*. Rodale Press, Emmaus, PA.

Griffiths, M. 1994. *Index of Garden Plants*. Timber Press, Portland, OR.

Grigsen, G. 1974. *A Dictionary of English Plant Names*. Allen Lane, London, England.

Grounds, Roger. 1989. *Ornamental Grasses*. Christopher Helm Publishers, Bromley, Kent, England.

Halevy, A.H. (ed). 1985–1989. *CRC Handbook of Flowering*, 6 volumes. CRC Press, Bria Raton, FL.

Hansen, R. and F. Stahl. 1993. *Perennials and their Garden Habitats*. 4th ed. Timber Press, Portland, OR.

Harding, Alice. 1993. *The Peony*. Sagapress/Timber Press, Portland, OR.

Harper, Pamela and Fred McGourty. 1985. *Perennials. How to Select, Grow and Enjoy*. HP Books Inc., Tuscon, AZ.

Harris, James G. and Malinda Woolf Harris. 1994. *Plant Identification Terminology, an Illustrated Glossary*. Spring Hill Pub., Payson, UT.

Hay, Roy and Patrick Synge. 1975. *The Color Dictionary of Flowers and Plants for Home and Garden*. Crown Publishers Inc., New York, NY.

Heath, Brent and Becky Heath. 1995. *Daffodils for American Gardens*. Elliot and Clark Publishing, Washington, DC.

Hebb, Robert S. 1975. *Low Maintenance Perennials*. Arnold Arboretum of Harvard University, Jamaica Plain, MA.

Holmes, Roger. 1993. *Taylor's Guide to Natural Gardening*. Houghton Mifflin Co., Boston, MA.

Hopkinson, Patricia, Diane Miske, Jerry Parsons and Holly Shimizu. 1994. *Herb Gardening*. Knopf Publishing, New York, NY.

Hudak, Joseph. 1976. *Gardening with Perennials*. Timber Press, Portland, OR.

Huxley, Anthony (ed.) 1992. *The New Royal Horticultural Society Dictionary of Gardening*. 4 volumes. MacMillan Press Ltd., London, England.

Jefferson-Brown, Michael. 1991. *Narcissus*. Timber Press, Portland, OR.

Jelitto, L. and W. Schacht. 1990. *Hardy Herbaceous Perennials*, 2 vol. 3rd ed. Timber Press, Portland, OR.

Jones, David L. 1987. *Ferns*. Timber Press, Portland, OR.

Kelsey, H.R. and W.A. Dayton. 1942. *Standardized Plant Names*, 2nd ed. J. Horace McFarland Co., Harrisburg, PA.

Kohlein, Fritz. 1984. *Saxifrages and Related Genera*. B.T. Batsford Ltd., London, England.

Kohlein, Fritz. 1987. *Iris*. Timber Press, Portland, OR.

Kohlein, Fritz and Peter Menzel. 1994. *Color Encyclopedia of Garden Plants and Habitats*. Timber Press, Portland, OR.

Lacy, Allen. 1988. *The American Gardener*. Farrar Straus Giroux, New York, NY.

Lawrence, Elizabeth. 1986. *The Little Bulbs*. Duke University Press, Durham, NC.

Lewington, Anna. 1990. *Plants for People*. Oxford University Press, New York, NY.

Lloyd, Christopher. 1984. *The Adventurous Gardener*. Random House Inc., New York, NY.

Lynch, R. Irwin. 1904. *The Book of the Iris*. John Lane Publishing, London, England.

MacNeil, Ester and Alan MacNeil. 1946. *Garden Lilies*. Oxford University Press, New York, NY.

Mathew, Brian. 1973. *Dwarf Bulbs*. Arco Publishing Co., New York, NY.

Mathew, Brian. 1978. *The Large Bulbs*. B.T. Batsford Ltd., London, England.

Mathew, Brian. 1987. *Flowering Bulbs for the Garden. A Kew Gardening Guide*. Collingridge Books, Middlesex, England.

McGourty, Frederick. 1989. *The Perennial Gardener*. Houghton Mifflin, Boston, MA.

Mickel, John T. 1979. *How to Know the Ferns and Fern Allies*. William C. Brown Co., Dubuque, IA.

Morse, Harriet K. 1962. *Gardening in the Shade*. Charles Scribners and Sons, New York, NY (available through Timber Press, Portland, OR).

Nehrling, Arlo and Irene Nehrling. 1964. *The Picture Book of Perennials*. Hearthside Press Inc., New York, NY.

Oakes, A.J. 1990. *Ornamental Grasses and Grasslike Plants*. Van Nostrand Reinhold, New York, NY.

Oehme, Wolfgang and James van Sweden. 1990. *Bold Romantic Gardens*. Acropolis Books, Herndon, VA.

Pankhurst, Alex. 1992. *Who Does Your Garden Grow*. Earl's Eye Publishing, Colchester, England.

Parke, Margaret. 1993. *A Garden for Cutting*. Stewart, Tabori and Chang, Inc., New York, NY.

Patterson, Allen. 1981. *Plants for Shade*. J.M. Dent and Sons Ltd., London, England.

Perry, Frances. 1958. *Complete Guide to Hardy Perennials*. Charles T. Branford Co., Boston, MA.

Phillips, Harry R. 1985. *Growing and Propagating Wild Flowers*. University of North Carolina Press, Chapel Hill, NC.

Phillips, Roger and Martyn Rix. 1991. *Perennials*, 2 vols. Random House, New York, NY.

Pinnell, M.M., A.M. Armitage and D. Seaborn. 1985. *Germination Needs of Common Perennial Seed.* University of Georgia Research Bulletin 331. Athens, GA.

Reader's Digest Staff. 1978. *Reader's Digest Encyclopaedia of Garden Plants and Flowers.* 2nd ed. Reader's Digest Assoc., London, England.

Reader's Digest Staff. 1986. *Magic and Medicine of Plants,* Reader's Digest Assoc., Pleasantville, NY.

Rickett, H. William. 1967–1973. *Wild Flowers of the United States.* 6 vols. Publication of the New York Botanical Garden, McGraw Hill, New York, NY.

Schmid, W. George. 1991. *The Genus Hosta.* Timber Press, Portland, OR.

Snyder, Leon C. 1983. *Flowers for Northern Gardens.* University of Minnesota Press, Minneapolis, MN.

Still, Steven. 1987. *Manual of Herbaceous Ornamental Plants,* 3rd ed. Stipes Publishing Co., Champaign, IL.

Sudell, Richard. 1938. *Herbaceous Borders.* Charles Scribners and Sons. New York, NY.

Symons-Jeune, B.H.B. 1953. *Phlox.* Collins Press, London, England.

Synge, Patrick, M. 1980. *Lilies. A Revision of Elwes' Monograph of the Genus Lilium and its Supplements.* B.T. Batsford Ltd., London, England.

Thomas, Graham Stuart. 1970. *Plants for Ground-Cover.* J.M. Dent and Sons Ltd., London, England.

Thomas, Graham Stuart. 1982. *Perennial Garden Plants.* J.M. Dent and Sons Ltd., London, England.

Thomas, Graham Stuart. 1984. *The Art of Planting.* J.M. Dent and Sons Ltd., London, England.

Titmarsh, Alan. 1983. *The Rock Gardener's Handbook.* Croom Helm Ltd., London, England.

Trehane, Piers. 1989. *Index Hortensis.* Quarterjack Publishing, Wimborne, Dorset, England.

Usher, George. 1947. *A Dictionary of Plants Used by Man.* Hafner Press, New York, NY.

Van Pelt Wilson, Helen. 1976. *Successful Gardening with Perennials.* Doubleday and Company Inc., Garden City, NY.

Wasowski, Sally. 1994. *Gardening with Native Plants of the South.* Taylor Publishing Co., Dallas, TX.

Weathers, John. 1911. *The Bulb Book.* E.P. Dutton and Company, New York, NY.

Wherry, Edgar T. 1955. *The Genus Phlox.* Morris Arboretum Monograph III. Wickersham Publishing Co., Lancaster, PA.

Wilder, Louise Beebe. 1936. *Adventures with Hardy Bulbs.* MacMillan Publishing Co., New York, NY.

Wister, John (ed.). 1962. *The Peonies.* American Horticultural Society, Washington, DC.

Wyman, Donald. 1977. *Wyman's Gardening Encyclopedia.* Macmillan Publishing Co., New York, NY.

Yeo, Peter. 1985. *Hardy Geraniums.* Timber Press, Portland, OR.

Zakary, M. 1982. *Plants of the Bible.* Cambridge University Press, Cambridge, England.

# Glossary of Terms Employed in Text

**a-** prefix meaning not or without, e.g., apetalous, without petals.

**acuminate** usually referring to a leaf blade whose sides are somewhat concave and taper to a point.

**alternate** arrangement of leaves where one leaf occurs at each node.

**apex** the tip or terminal end.

**aromatic** obviously scented, at least if broken or crushed.

**ascending** gradually curving upward.

**basal** pertaining to leaves which arise from the base of the plant.

**bearded** having long hairs.

**biennial** of two season's growth, flowers and fruit are produced the second season from seed germination. Plants die after fruiting.

**biternate** twice divided into threes, e.g., leaves of *Aquilegia* whose primary divisions are again divided into three.

**bract** a much reduced leaf, usually scale-like and associated with flowering, e.g., flowers of *Eryngium* are subtended by bracts.

**bulb** a fleshy underground stem with a short, central axis surrounded by fleshy, scale-like leaves, e.g., *Lilium*.

**bulbil** small bulb arising around the parent bulb.

**bulblet** small bulb arising in the leaf axils.

**calyx** the sepals as a group, directly below petals.

**campanulate** bell-shaped, as flowers of *Campanula*.

**cespitose** growing in tufts or dense clumps.

**ciliate** having small hairs.

**clasping** leaf without petiole, with the base partly surrounding the stem.

**clustered** leaves tightly arranged, but not opposite or alternate. Also in reference to flowers.

**composite** a member of the *Asteraceae*.

**compound leaf** a leaf with two or more leaflets. Palmately compound when three or more leaflets arise from the same point, pinnately compound when the leaflets are arranged along a common axis, ternately compound when the leaflets are in 3's.

**connate-perfoliate** with the bases of opposite leaves fused around the stem.

**cordate** heart-shaped.

**corm** solid bulb-like underground stem, not differentiated into scales, e.g., *Crocus*.

**cormel** small corm arising from parent corm.

**corolla** the petals as a group.

**corona** an extrusion of tissue that stands between the corolla and the stamens or on the corolla, e.g., the cup of *Narcissus*.

**corymb** More or less flat-topped, indeterminate inflorescence, the outer flowers open first.

**crenate** rounded teeth on margin.

**crown** the central growing point beneath or near the surface of the ground.

**cyme** more or less flat-topped, determinate inflorescence, the outer flowers open last.

**decumbent** reclining or lying on the ground but with ends ascending.

**decurrent** extending down the stem, as the leaf of *Verbascum*.

**decussate** leaves arranged along the stem in pairs, with each pair at right angles to the pair above or below.

**deltoid** triangular.

**dentate** having teeth perpendicular to the margin, do not point forward.

**determinate** refers to an inflorescence whose center flower opens first and axis prolongation is thereby arrested.

**dibble** to insert a finger into a warm, moist medium.

**dioecious** male and female flowers on separate plants.

**disk flower** tubular flower at the center of composites, e.g., *Aster*.

**diurnal** flowers open only during the day.

**downy** having soft hairs.

**emarginate** with a shallow notch at the apex.

**ensiform** sword-shaped.

**exserted** projecting beyond, as in stamens beyond a corolla.

**farinaceous** having a powdery or mealy coating, as in some species of *Primula*.

**filament** the stalk of the stamen.

**flaccid** limp.

**foliage** leaves.

**gland** a general term for oil-secreting organs, sometimes a projection at the base of a structure.

**glaucous** covered with a waxy bloom or whitish substance that rubs off easily.

**globose** round or spherical shape.

**glossy** shining, lustrous.

**habit** the general outline or shape of a plant.

**hairy** pubescent with long hairs.

**hastate** in the shape of an arrowhead; the basal lobes are pointed and nearly at right angles.

**head** a short, dense inflorescence; the inflorescence of a composite consisting of ray and disc flowers.

**herbaceous** having no persistent, woody tissue above the ground.

**hispid** having stiff or bristly hairs.

**hybrid** plant resulting from a cross between two or more plants.

**imperfect flower** one which lacks either stamens or pistils.

**incised** sharp incisions, between toothed and lobed.

**incomplete flower** one which lacks either calyx, corolla, stamens or pistils.

**indeterminate** inflorescence whose center flowers open last; the growth and elongation of the main axis is not arrested with the opening of the first flowers.

**lateral** borne at or on the side, as in the flower bud borne in a leaf axil.

**linear** long and very narrow, as in leaves.

**lobe** usually a division of leaf, calyx, or petals cut to about the middle.

**mealy** a granular appearance.

**midrib** the main vein of a leaf or leaflet.

**native** inherent or original to an area.

**node** a joint on a stem from which leaves arise.

**oblong** longer than broad, the sides nearly parallel.

**obovate** broadest above the middle.

**opposite** two at a node, as arrangement of leaves.

**ovate** egg-shaped in outline, broadest below the middle.

**paired** occurring in two's.

**palmate** fan-like from a common point.

**panicle** an indeterminate inflorescence whose primary axis bears branches of pedicelled flowers.

**parallel** running side to side from base to tip, as in monocot leaves.

**parted** cut deeply but not quite to base.

**pedicel** the stalk of a flower or fruit.

**peduncle** the stalk of a flower cluster or of a single flower when flower is solitary.

**peltate** the petiole attached inside the margin, the leaves are typically shield-shaped.

**perfect flower** having both functional stamens and pistils.

**perfoliate** the leaf-blade surrounding the stem so that the stem appears to pass through the leaf.

**perianth** the calyx and corolla together. Often used when calyx and corolla are indistinguishable.

**petaloid** structure not a petal but resembles a petal.

**petiole** leaf stalk.

**plumose** feather-like.

**procumbent** lying flat but stems not rooting at the nodes or tips.

**prostrate** lying flat on the ground.

**pubescent** covered with short, soft hairs.

**punctate** with translucent or covered dots, depressions, or pits.

**raceme** a simple, indeterminate inflorescence with pedicelled flowers.

**racemose** having flowers in racemes.

**rachis** the axis bearing leaflets or the primary flowers of an inflorescence.

**reflexed** bent abruptly backward or downward.

**revolute** rolled toward the back, as in a revolute margin.

**rosette** a crown of leaves, at or close to the surface of the ground.

**rotate** wheel-shaped with inconspicuous corolla tube, usually refers to flowers.

**sarmentose** having long, flexuous runners.

**scape** a leafless peduncle arising from a basal rosette. Occasionally bract-like leaves may be present.

**sessile** without a petiole or stalk.

**simple** a leaf not compounded into leaflets, an unbranched inflorescence.

**spike** an unbranched, indeterminate inflorescence with sessile flowers.

**spikelet** a secondary spike.

**stalk** a supporting structure for a leaf, flower, or fruit.

**stellate** star-like.

**sterile** barren, not able to produce seed.

**stipule** one of a pair of leaf-like appendages found at the base of the petiole in some leaves.

**stolon** a horizontal stem that roots at the tip and gives rise to a new plant.

**stoloniferous** bearing slender stems, just on or under the ground, which root at the tips.

**tepal** a segment of perianth not differentiated into calyx and corolla, e.g., tulips.
**terminal** at the end.
**ternate** in threes.
**tomentose** densely woolly, hairs soft and matted.
**trailing** prostrate but not rooting.
**trifoliate** three-leaved, e.g., *Trillium*.
**tuber** a short, thickened organ, usually an underground stem.

**umbel** an indeterminate inflorescence, usually flat-topped with pedicels arising from a single point, like an umbrella.
**umbellate** having umbels.
**undulate** wavy, as a leaf margin.

**verticillate** arranged in whorls.
**viscid** sticky.

# Index to Scientific Names

# Index to Common Names